Lecture Notes in Computer Science 11728

Igor V. Tetko · Věra Kůrková ·
Pavel Karpov · Fabian Theis (Eds.)

Artificial Neural Networks and Machine Learning – ICANN 2019

Deep Learning

28th International Conference on Artificial Neural Networks
Munich, Germany, September 17–19, 2019
Proceedings, Part II

Editors
Igor V. Tetko
Helmholtz Zentrum München - Deutsches Forschungszentrum für Gesundheit und Umwelt (GmbH)
Neuherberg, Germany

Pavel Karpov
Helmholtz Zentrum München - Deutsches Forschungszentrum für Gesundheit und Umwelt (GmbH)
Neuherberg, Germany

Věra Kůrková
Institute of Computer Science
Czech Academy of Sciences
Prague 8, Czech Republic

Fabian Theis
Helmholtz Zentrum München - Deutsches Forschungszentrum für Gesundheit und Umwelt (GmbH)
Neuherberg, Germany

ISSN 0302-9743 ISSN 1611-3349 (electronic)
Lecture Notes in Computer Science
ISBN 978-3-030-30483-6 ISBN 978-3-030-30484-3 (eBook)
https://doi.org/10.1007/978-3-030-30484-3

LNCS Sublibrary: SL1 – Theoretical Computer Science and General Issues

This Springer imprint is published by the registered company Springer Nature Switzerland AG
The registered company address is: Gewerbestrasse 11, 6330 Cham, Switzerland

Preface

The fast development of machine learning methods is influencing all aspects of our life and reaching new horizons of what we have previously considered being Artificial Intelligence (AI). Examples include autonomous car driving, virtual assistants, automated customer support, clinical decision support, healthcare data analytics, financial forecast, and smart devices in the home, to name a few, which contribute to the dramatic improvement in the quality of our lives. These developments, however, also bring risks for significant hazards, which were not imaginable previously, e.g., falsification of voice, videos, or even manipulation of people's opinions during elections. Many such developments become possible due to the appearance of large volumes of data ("Big Data"). These proceedings include the theory and applications of algorithms behind these developments, many of which were inspired by the functioning of the brain.

The International Conference on Artificial Neural Networks (ICANN) is the annual flagship conference of the European Neural Network Society (ENNS). The 28th International Conference on Artificial Neural Networks (ICANN 2019) was co-organized with the final conference of the Marie Skłodowska-Curie Innovative Training Network European Industrial Doctorate "Big Data in Chemistry" (http://bigchem.eu) project coordinated by Helmholtz Zentrum München (GmbH) to promote the use of machine learning in Chemistry. The conference featured the main tracks "Brain-Inspired Computing" and "Machine Learning Research." Within the conference the First International Workshop on Reservoir Computing as well as five special sessions were organized, namely:

Artificial Intelligence in Medicine
Informed and Explainable Methods for Machine Learning
Deep Learning in Image Reconstruction
Machine Learning with Graphs: Algorithms and Applications
BIGCHEM: Big Data and AI in chemistry

A Challenge for Automatic Dog Age Estimation (DogAge) also took place as part of the conference. The conference covered all main research fields dealing with neural networks. ICANN 2019 was held during September 17–19, 2019, at Klinikum rechts der Isar der Technische Universität München, Munich, Germany.

Following a long-standing tradition, the proceedings of the conference were published as Springer volumes belonging to the *Lecture Notes in Computer Science* series. The conference had a historical record of 494 article submissions. The papers went through a two-step peer-review process by at least two and in majority of cases by three or four independent referees. In total, 503 Program Committee (PC) members and reviewers participated in this process. The majority of PC members had Doctoral degrees (88%) and 52% of them were also Professors. These reviewers were assigned 46 articles. The others were PhD students in the last years of their studies, who reviewed one to two articles each. In total, for the 323 accepted articles, 975 and 985 reports were submitted for the first and the second revision sessions. Thus, on average, each accepted article received 6.1 reports. A list of reviewers/PC Members, who agreed to publish their names, are included in these proceedings.

Based on the reviewers' comments, 202 articles were accepted and more than 100 articles were rejected after the first review. The remaining articles received an undecided status. The authors of the accepted articles as well as of those with undecided status were requested to address the reviewers' comments within two weeks. On the basis of second reviewers' feedback, another 121 articles were accepted and the authors were requested to include reviewers' remarks into the final upload. Based on these evaluations, diversity of topics, as well as recommendations of reviewers, special session organizers, and PC Chairs, 120 articles were selected for oral presentations. Out of the total number of 323 accepted articles (65% of initially submitted), 46 manuscripts were short articles with a length of five pages each, while the others were full articles with an average length of 13 pages.

The accepted papers of the 28th ICANN conference were published as five volumes:

Volume I Theoretical Neural Computation
Volume II Deep Learning
Volume III Image Processing
Volume IV Text and Time series analysis
Volume V Workshop and Special Sessions

The authors of accepted articles came from 50 different countries. While the majority of the articles were from academic researchers, the conference also attracted contributions from manifold industries including automobile (Volkswagen, BMW, Honda, Toyota), multinational conglomerates (Hitachi, Mitsubishi), electronics (Philips), electrical systems (Thales), mobile (Samsung, Huawei, Nokia, Orange), software (Microsoft), multinational (Amazon) and global travel technology (Expedia), information (IBM), large (AstraZeneca, Boehringer Ingelheim) and medium (Idorsia Pharmaceuticals Ltd.) pharma companies, fragrance and flavor (Firmenich), architectural (Shimizu), weather forecast (Beijing Giant Weather Co.), robotics (UBTECH Robotics Corp., SoftBank Robotics Group Corp.), contract research organization (Lead Discovery Center GmbH), private credit bureau (Schufa), as well as multiple startups. This wide involvement of companies reflects the increasing use of artificial neural networks by the industry. Five keynote speakers were invited to give lectures on the timely aspects of intelligent robot design (gentle robots), nonlinear dynamical analysis of brain activity, deep learning in biology and biomedicine, explainable AI, artificial curiosity, and meta-learning machines.

These proceedings provide a comprehensive and up-to-date coverage of the dynamically developing field of Artificial Neural Networks. They are of major interest both for theoreticians as well as for applied scientists who are looking for new innovative approaches to solve their practical problems. We sincerely thank the Program and Steering Committee and the reviewers for their invaluable work.

September 2019

Igor V. Tetko
Fabian Theis
Pavel Karpov
Věra Kůrková

Organization

General Chairs

Igor V. Tetko	Helmholtz Zentrum München (GmbH), Germany
Fabian Theis	Helmholtz Zentrum München (GmbH), Germany

Honorary Chair

Věra Kůrková (ENNS President)	Czech Academy of Sciences, Czech Republic

Publication Chair

Pavel Karpov	Helmholtz Zentrum München (GmbH), Germany

Local Organizing Committee Chairs

Monica Campillos	Helmholtz Zentrum München (GmbH), Germany
Alessandra Lintas	University of Lausanne, Switzerland

Communication Chair

Paolo Masulli	Technical University of Denmark, Denmark

Steering Committee

Erkki Oja	Aalto University, Finland
Wlodzislaw Duch	Nicolaus Copernicus University, Poland
Alessandro Villa	University of Lausanne, Switzerland
Cesare Alippi	Politecnico di Milano, Italy, and Università della Svizzera italiana, Switzerland
Jérémie Cabessa	Université Paris 2 Panthéon-Assas, France
Maxim Fedorov	Skoltech, Russia
Barbara Hammer	Bielefeld University, Germany
Lazaros Iliadis	Democritus University of Thrace, Greece
Petia Koprinkova-Hristova	Bulgarian Academy of Sciences, Bulgaria
Antonis Papaleonidas	Democritus University of Thrace, Greece
Jaakko Peltonen	University of Tampere, Finland
Antonio Javier Pons Rivero	Universitat Politècnica de Catalunya, Spain
Yifat Prut	The Hebrew University Jerusalem, Israel
Paul F. M. J. Verschure	Catalan Institute of Advanced Studies, Spain
Francisco Zamora-Martínez	Veridas Digital Authentication Solutions SL, Spain

Program Committee

Nesreen Ahmed	Intel Labs, USA
Narges Ahmidi	Helmholtz Zentrum München (GmbH), Germany
Tetiana Aksenova	Commissariat à l'énergie atomique et aux énergies alternatives, France
Elie Aljalbout	Technical University Munich, Germany
Piotr Antonik	CentraleSupélec, France
Juan Manuel Moreno-Arostegui	Universitat Politècnica de Catalunya, Spain
Michael Aupetit	Qatar Computing Research Institute, Qatar
Cristian Axenie	Huawei German Research Center Munich, Germany
Davide Bacciu	University of Pisa, Italy
Noa Barbiro	Booking.com, Israel
Igor Baskin	Moscow State University, Russia
Christian Bauckhage	Fraunhofer IAIS, Germany
Costas Bekas	IBM Research, Switzerland
Barry Bentley	The Open University, UK
Daniel Berrar	Tokyo Institute of Technology, Japan
Soma Bhattacharya	Expedia, USA
Monica Bianchini	Università degli Studi di Siena, Italy
François Blayo	NeoInstinct, Switzerland
Sander Bohte	Centrum Wiskunde & Informatica, The Netherlands
András P. Borosy	QualySense AG, Switzerland
Giosuè Lo Bosco	Universita' di Palermo, Italy
Farah Bouakrif	University of Jijel, Algeria
Larbi Boubchir	University Paris 8, France
Maria Paula Brito	University of Porto, Portugal
Evgeny Burnaev	Skoltech, Russia
Mikhail Burtsev	Moscow Institute of Physics and Technology, Russia
Jérémie Cabessa	Université Panthéon Assas (Paris II), France
Francisco de Assis Tenório de Carvalho	Universidade Federal de Pernambuco, Brazil
Wolfgang Graf zu Castell-Ruedenhausen	Helmholtz Zentrum München (GmbH), Germany
Stephan Chalup	University of Newcastle, Australia
Hongming Chen	AstraZeneca, Sweden
Artem Cherkasov	University of British Columbia, Canada
Sylvain Chevallier	Université de Versailles, France
Vladimir Chupakhin	Janssen Pharmaceutical Companies, USA
Djork-Arné Clevert	Bayer, Germany
Paulo Cortez	University of Minho, Portugal
Gennady Cymbalyuk	Georgia State University, USA
Maximilien Danisch	Pierre and Marie Curie University, France
Tirtharaj Dash	Birla Institute of Technology and Science Pilani, India
Tyler Derr	Michigan State University, USA

Sergey Dolenko	Moscow State University, Russia
Shirin Dora	University of Amsterdam, The Netherlands
Werner Dubitzky	Helmholtz Zentrum München (GmbH), Germany
Wlodzislaw Duch	Nicolaus Copernicus University, Poland
Ujjal Kr Dutta	Indian Institute of Technology Madras, India
Mohamed El-Sharkawy	Purdue School of Engineering and Technology, USA
Mohamed Elati	Université de Lille, France
Reda Elbasiony	Tanta University, Egypt
Mark Embrechts	Rensselaer Polytechnic Institute, USA
Sebastian Engelke	University of Geneva, Switzerland
Ola Engkvist	AstraZeneca, Sweden
Manfred Eppe	University of Hamburg, Germany
Peter Erdi	Kalamazoo College, USA
Peter Ertl	Novartis Institutes for BioMedical Research, Switzerland
Igor Farkaš	Comenius University in Bratislava, Slovakia
Maxim Fedorov	Skoltech, Russia
Maurizio Fiasché	F-engineering Consulting, Italy
Marco Frasca	University of Milan, Italy
Benoît Frénay	Université de Namur, Belgium
Claudio Gallicchio	Università di Pisa, Italy
Udayan Ganguly	Indian Institute of Technology at Bombay, India
Tiantian Gao	Stony Brook University, USA
Juantomás García	Sngular, Spain
José García-Rodríguez	University of Alicante, Spain
Erol Gelenbe	Institute of Theoretical and Applied Informatics, Poland
Petia Georgieva	University of Aveiro, Portugal
Sajjad Gharaghani	University of Tehran, Iran
Evgin Goceri	Akdeniz University, Turkey
Alexander Gorban	University of Leicester, UK
Marco Gori	Università degli Studi di Siena, Italy
Denise Gorse	University College London, UK
Lyudmila Grigoryeva	University of Konstanz, Germany
Xiaodong Gu	Fudan University, China
Michael Guckert	Technische Hochschule Mittelhessen, Germany
Benjamin Guedj	Inria, France, and UCL, UK
Tatiana Valentine Guy	Institute of Information Theory and Automation, Czech Republic
Fabian Hadiji	Goedle.io, Germany
Abir Hadriche	University of Sfax, Tunisia
Barbara Hammer	Bielefeld University, Germany
Stefan Haufe	ERC Research Group Leader at Charité, Germany
Dominik Heider	Philipps-University of Marburg, Germany
Matthias Heinig	Helmholtz Zentrum München (GmbH), Germany
Christoph Henkelmann	DIVISIO GmbH, Germany

Jean Benoit Héroux	IBM Research, Japan
Christian Hidber	bSquare AG, Switzerland
Martin Holeňa	Institute of Computer Science, Czech Republic
Adrian Horzyk	AGH University of Science and Technology, Poland
Jian Hou	Bohai University, China
Lynn Houthuys	Thomas More, Belgium
Brian Hyland	University of Otago, New Zealand
Nicolangelo Iannella	University of Oslo, Norway
Lazaros Iliadis	Democritus University of Thrace, Greece
Francesco Iorio	Wellcome Trust Sanger Institute, UK
Olexandr Isayev	University of North Carolina at Chapel Hill, USA
Keiichi Ito	Helmholtz Zentrum München (GmbH), Germany
Nils Jansen	Radboud University Nijmegen, The Netherlands
Noman Javed	Université d'Orléans, France
Wenbin Jiang	Huazhong University of Science and Technology, China
Jan Kalina	Institute of Computer Science, Czech Republic
Argyris Kalogeratos	Université Paris-Saclay, France
Michael Kamp	Fraunhofer IAIS, Germany
Dmitry Karlov	Skoltech, Russia
Pavel Karpov	Helmholtz Zentrum München (GmbH), Germany
John Kelleher	Technological University Dublin, Ireland
Adil Mehmood Khan	Innopolis, Russia
Rainer Kiko	GEOMAR Helmholtz-Zentrum für Ozeanforschung, Germany
Christina Klüver	Universität Duisburg-Essen, Germany
Taisuke Kobayashi	Nara Institute of Science and Technology, Japan
Ekaterina Komendantskaya	University of Dundee, UK
Petia Koprinkova-Hristova	Bulgarian Academy of Sciences, Bulgaria
Irena Koprinska	University of Sydney, Australia
Constantine Kotropoulos	Aristotle University of Thessaloniki, Greece
Ilias Kotsireas	Wilfrid Laurier University, Canada
Athanasios Koutras	University of Peloponnese, Greece
Piotr Kowalski	AGH University of Science and Technology, Poland
Valentin Kozlov	Karlsruher Institut für Technologie, Germany
Dean J. Krusienski	Virginia Commonwealth University, USA
Adam Krzyzak	Concordia University, Canada
Hanna Kujawska	University of Bergen, Norway
Věra Kůrková	Institute of Computer Science, Czech Republic
Sumit Kushwaha	Kamla Nehru Institute of Technology, India
Anna Ladi	Fraunhofer IAIS, Germany
Ward Van Laer	Ixor, Belgium
Oliver Lange	Google Inc., USA
Jiyi Li	University of Yamanashi, Japan
Lei Li	Beijing University of Posts and Telecommunications, China

Spiros Likothanassis	University of Patras, Greece
Christian Limberg	Universität Bielefeld, Germany
Alessandra Lintas	University of Lausanne, Switzerland
Viktor Liviniuk	MIT, USA, and Skoltech, Russia
Doina Logofatu	Frankfurt University of Applied Sciences, Germany
Vincenzo Lomonaco	Università di Bologna, Italy
Sock Ching Low	Institute for Bioengineering of Catalonia, Spain
Abhijit Mahalunkar	Technological University Dublin, Ireland
Mufti Mahmud	Nottingham Trent University, UK
Alexander Makarenko	National Technical University of Ukraine - Kiev Polytechnic Institute, Ukraine
Kleanthis Malialis	University of Cyprus, Cyprus
Fragkiskos Malliaros	University of Paris-Saclay, France
Gilles Marcou	University of Strasbourg, France
Urszula Markowska-Kaczmar	Wroclaw University of Technology, Poland
Carsten Marr	Helmholtz Zentrum München (GmbH), Germany
Giuseppe Marra	University of Firenze, Italy
Paolo Masulli	Technical University of Denmark, Denmark
Siamak Mehrkanoon	Maastricht University, The Netherlands
Stefano Melacci	Università degli Studi di Siena, Italy
Michael Menden	Helmholtz Zentrum München (GmbH), Germany
Sebastian Mika	Comtravo, Germany
Nikolaos Mitianoudis	Democritus University of Thrace, Greece
Valeri Mladenov	Technical University of Sofia, Bulgaria
Hebatallah Mohamed	Università degli Studi Roma, Italy
Figlu Mohanty	International Institute of Information Technology at Bhubaneswar, India
Francesco Carlo Morabito	University of Reggio Calabria, Italy
Jerzy Mościński	Silesian University of Technology, Poland
Henning Müller	University of Applied Sciences Western Switzerland, Switzerland
Maria-Viorela Muntean	University of Alba-Iulia, Romania
Phivos Mylonas	Ionian University, Greece
Shinichi Nakajima	Technische Universität Berlin, Germany
Kohei Nakajima	University of Tokyo, Japan
Chi Nhan Nguyen	Itemis, Germany
Florian Nigsch	Novartis Institutes for BioMedical Research, Switzerland
Giannis Nikolentzos	École Polytechnique, France
Ikuko Nishikawa	Ritsumeikan University, Japan
Harri Niska	University of Eastern Finland
Hasna Njah	ISIM-Sfax, Tunisia
Dimitri Nowicki	Institute of Cybernetics of NASU, Ukraine
Alessandro Di Nuovo	Sheffield Hallam University, UK
Stefan Oehmcke	University of Copenhagen, Denmark

Erkki Oja	Aalto University, Finland
Luca Oneto	Università di Pisa, Italy
Silvia Ortin	Institute of Neurosciences (IN) Alicante, Spain
Ivan Oseledets	Skoltech, Russia
Dmitry Osolodkin	Chumakov FSC R&D IBP RAS, Russia
Sebastian Otte	University of Tübingen, Germany
Latifa Oukhellou	The French Institute of Science and Technology for Transport, France
Vladimir Palyulin	Moscow State University, Russia
George Panagopoulos	École Polytechnique, France
Massimo Panella	Università degli Studi di Roma La Sapienza, Italy
Antonis Papaleonidas	Democritus University of Thrace, Greece
Evangelos Papalexakis	University of California Riverside, USA
Daniel Paurat	Fraunhofer IAIS, Germany
Jaakko Peltonen	Tampere University, Finland
Tingying Peng	Technische Universität München, Germany
Alberto Guillén Perales	Universidad de Granada, Spain
Carlos Garcia Perez	Helmholtz Zentrum München (GmbH), Germany
Isabelle Perseil	INSERM, France
Vincenzo Piuri	University of Milan, Italy
Kathrin Plankensteiner	Fachhochschule Vorarlberg, Austria
Isabella Pozzi	Centrum Wiskunde & Informatica, The Netherlands
Mike Preuss	Leiden University, The Netherlands
Yifat Prut	The Hebrew University of Jerusalem, Israel
Eugene Radchenko	Moscow State University, Russia
Rajkumar Ramamurthy	Fraunhofer IAIS, Germany
Srikanth Ramaswamy	Swiss Federal Institute of Technology (EPFL), Switzerland
Beatriz Remeseiro	Universidad de Oviedo, Spain
Xingzhang Ren	Alibaba Group, China
Jean-Louis Reymond	University of Bern, Switzerland
Cristian Rodriguez Rivero	University of California, USA
Antonio Javier Pons Rivero	Universitat Politècnica de Catalunya, Spain
Andrea Emilio Rizzoli	IDSIA, SUPSI, Switzerland
Florian Röhrbein	Technical University Munich, Germany
Ryan Rossi	PARC - a Xerox Company, USA
Manuel Roveri	Politecnico di Milano, Italy
Vladimir Rybakov	WaveAccess, Russia
Maryam Sabzevari	Aalto University School of Science and Technology, Finland
Julio Saez-Rodriguez	Medizinische Fakultät Heidelberg, Germany
Yulia Sandamirskaya	NEUROTECH: Neuromorphic Computer Technology, Switzerland
Carlo Sansone	University of Naples Federico II, Italy
Sreela Sasi	Gannon University, USA
Burak Satar	Uludag University, Turkey

Axel Sauer	Munich School of Robotics and Machine Intelligence, Germany
Konstantin Savenkov	Intento, Inc., USA
Hanno Scharr	Forschungszentrum Jülich, Germany
Tjeerd olde Scheper	Oxford Brookes University, UK
Rafal Scherer	Czestochowa University of Technology, Poland
Maria Secrier	University College London, UK
Thomas Seidl	Ludwig-Maximilians-Universität München, Germany
Rafet Sifa	Fraunhofer IAIS, Germany
Pekka Siirtola	University of Oulu, Finland
Prashant Singh	Uppsala University, Sweden
Patrick van der Smagt	Volkswagen AG, Germany
Maximilian Soelch	Volkswagen Machine Learning Research Lab, Germany
Miguel Cornelles Soriano	Campus Universitat de les Illes Balears, Spain
Miguel Angelo Abreu Sousa	Institute of Education Science and Technology, Brazil
Michael Stiber	University of Washington Bothell, USA
Alessandro Sperduti	Università degli Studi di Padova, Italy
Ruxandra Stoean	University of Craiova, Romania
Nicola Strisciuglio	University of Groningen, The Netherlands
Irene Sturm	Deutsche Bahn AG, Germany
Jérémie Sublime	ISEP, France
Martin Swain	Aberystwyth University, UK
Zoltan Szabo	Ecole Polytechnique, France
Kazuhiko Takahashi	Doshisha University, Japan
Fabian Theis	Helmholtz Zentrum München (GmbH), Germany
Philippe Thomas	Universite de Lorraine, France
Matteo Tiezzi	University of Siena, Italy
Ruben Tikidji-Hamburyan	Louisiana State University, USA
Yancho Todorov	VTT, Finland
Andrei Tolstikov	Merck Group, Germany
Matthias Treder	Cardiff University, UK
Anton Tsitsulin	Rheinische Friedrich-Wilhelms-Universität Bonn, Germany
Yury Tsoy	Solidware Co. Ltd., South Korea
Antoni Valencia	Independent Consultant, Spain
Carlos Magno Valle	Technical University Munich, Germany
Marley Vellasco	Pontifícia Universidade Católica do Rio de Janeiro, Brazil
Sagar Verma	Université Paris-Saclay, France
Paul Verschure	Institute for Bioengineering of Catalonia, Spain
Varvara Vetrova	University of Canterbury, New Zealand
Ricardo Vigário	University Nova's School of Science and Technology, Portugal
Alessandro Villa	University of Lausanne, Switzerland
Bruno Villoutreix	Molecular informatics for Health, France

Paolo Viviani	Università degli Studi di Torino, Italy
George Vouros	University of Piraeus, Greece
Christian Wallraven	Korea University, South Korea
Tinghuai Wang	Nokia, Finland
Yu Wang	Leibniz Supercomputing Centre (LRZ), Germany
Roseli S. Wedemann	Universidade do Estado do Rio de Janeiro, Brazil
Thomas Wennekers	University of Plymouth, UK
Stefan Wermter	University of Hamburg, Germany
Heiko Wersing	Honda Research Institute and Bielefeld University, Germany
Tadeusz Wieczorek	Silesian University of Technology, Poland
Christoph Windheuser	ThoughtWorks Inc., Germany
Borys Wróbel	Adam Mickiewicz University in Poznan, Poland
Jianhong Wu	York University, Canada
Xia Xiao	University of Connecticut, USA
Takaharu Yaguchi	Kobe University, Japan
Seul-Ki Yeom	Technische Universität Berlin, Germany
Hujun Yin	University of Manchester, UK
Junichiro Yoshimoto	Nara Institute of Science and Technology, Japan
Qiang Yu	Tianjin University, China
Shigang Yue	University of Lincoln, UK
Wlodek Zadrozny	University of North Carolina Charlotte, USA
Danuta Zakrzewska	Technical University of Lodz, Poland
Francisco Zamora-Martínez	Veridas Digital Authentication Solutions SL, Spain
Gerson Zaverucha	Federal University of Rio de Janeiro, Brazil
Junge Zhang	Institute of Automation, China
Zhongnan Zhang	Xiamen University, China
Pengsheng Zheng	Daimler AG, Germany
Samson Zhou	Indiana University, USA
Riccardo Zucca	Institute for Bioengineering of Catalonia, Spain
Dietlind Zühlke	Horn & Company Data Analytics GmbH, Germany

Exclusive Platinum Sponsor for the Automotive Branch

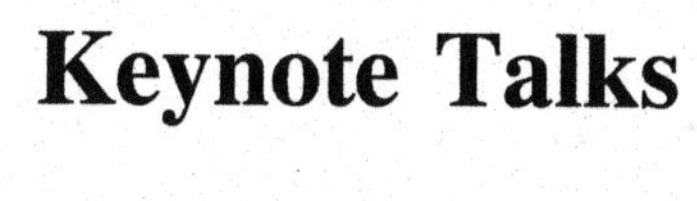
Keynote Talks

Recurrent Patterns of Brain Activity Associated with Cognitive Tasks and Attractor Dynamics (John Taylor Memorial Lecture)

Alessandro E. P. Villa

NeuroHeuristic Research Group, University of Lausanne,
Quartier UNIL-Chamberonne, 1015 Lausanne, Switzerland
alessandro.villa@unil.ch
http://www.neuroheuristic.org

The simultaneous recording of the time series formed by the sequences of neuronal discharges reveals important features of the dynamics of information processing in the brain. Experimental evidence of firing sequences with a precision of a few milliseconds have been observed in the brain of behaving animals. We review some critical findings showing that this activity is likely to be associated with higher order neural (mental) processes, such as predictive guesses of a coming stimulus in a complex sensorimotor discrimination task, in primates as well as in rats. We discuss some models of evolvable neural networks and their nonlinear deterministic dynamics and how such complex spatiotemporal patterns of firing may emerge. The attractors of such networks correspond precisely to the cycles in the graphs of their corresponding automata, and can thus be computed explicitly and exhaustively. We investigate further the effects of network topology on the dynamical activity of hierarchically organized networks of simulated spiking neurons. We describe how the activation and the biologically-inspired processes of plasticity on the network shape its topology using invariants based on algebro-topological constructions. General features of a brain theory based on these results is presented for discussion.

Unsupervised Learning: Passive and Active

Jürgen Schmidhuber

Co-founder and Chief Scientist, NNAISENSE, Scientific Director, Swiss AI Lab IDSIA and Professor of AI, USI & SUPSI, Lugano, Switzerland

I'll start with a concept of 1990 that has become popular: unsupervised learning without a teacher through two adversarial neural networks (NNs) that duel in a mini-max game, where one NN minimizes the objective function maximized by the other. The first NN generates data through its output actions while the second NN predicts the data. The second NN minimizes its error, thus becoming a better predictor. But it is a zero sum game: the first NN tries to find actions that maximize the error of the second NN. The system exhibits what I called "artificial curiosity" because the first NN is motivated to invent actions that yield data that the second NN still finds surprising, until the data becomes familiar and eventually boring. A similar adversarial zero sum game was used for another unsupervised method called "predictability minimization," where two NNs fight each other to discover a disentangled code of the incoming data (since 1991), remarkably similar to codes found in biological brains. I'll also discuss passive unsupervised learning through predictive coding of an agent's observation stream (since 1991) to overcome the fundamental deep learning problem through data compression. I'll offer thoughts as to why most current commercial applications don't use unsupervised learning, and whether that will change in the future.

Machine Learning and AI for the Sciences—Towards Understanding

Klaus-Robert Müller

Machine Learning Group, Technical University of Berlin, Germany

In recent years machine learning (ML) and Artificial Intelligence (AI) methods have begun to play a more and more enabling role in the sciences and in industry. In particular, the advent of large and/or complex data corpora has given rise to new technological challenges and possibilities.

The talk will connect two topics (1) explainable AI (XAI) and (2) ML applications in sciences (e.g. Medicine and Quantum Chemistry) for gaining new insight. Specifically I will first introduce XAI methods (such as LRP) that are now readily available and allow for an understanding of the inner workings of nonlinear ML methods ranging from kernel methods to deep learning methods including LSTMs. In particular XAI allows unmasking clever Hans predictors. Then, ML for Quantum Chemistry is discussed, showing that ML methods can lead to highly useful predictors of quantum mechanical properties of molecules (and materials) reaching quantum chemical accuracies both across chemical compound space and in molecular dynamics simulations. Notably, these ML models do not only speed up computation by several orders of magnitude but can give rise to novel chemical insight. Finally, I will analyze morphological and molecular data for cancer diagnosis, also here highly interesting novel insights can be obtained.

Note that while XAI is used for gaining a better understanding in the sciences, the introduced XAI techniques are readily useful in other application domains and industry as well.

Large-Scale Lineage and Latent-Space Learning in Single-Cell Genomic

Fabian Theis

Institute of Computational Biology, Helmholtz Zentrum München (GmbH), Germany
http://comp.bio

Accurately modeling single cell state changes e.g. during differentiation or in response to perturbations is a central goal of computational biology. Single-cell technologies now give us easy and large-scale access to state observations on the transcriptomic and more recently also epigenomic level, separately for each single cell. In particular they allow resolving potential heterogeneities due to asynchronicity of differentiating or responding cells, and profiles across multiple conditions such as time points and replicates are being generated.

Typical questions asked to such data are how cells develop over time and after perturbation such as disease. The statistical tools to address these questions are techniques from pseudo-temporal ordering and lineage estimation, or more broadly latent space learning. In this talk I will give a short review of such approaches, in particular focusing on recent extensions towards large-scale data integration using single-cell graph mapping or neural networks, and finish with a perspective towards learning perturbations using variational autoencoders.

The Gentle Robot

Sami Haddadin

Technical University of Munich, Germany

Enabling robots for interaction with humans and unknown environments has been one of the primary goals of robotics research over decades. I will outline how human-centered robot design, nonlinear soft-robotics control inspired by human neuromechanics and physics grounded learning algorithms will let robots become a commodity in our near-future society. In particular, compliant and energy-controlled ultra-lightweight systems capable of complex collision handling enable high-performance human assistance over a wide variety of application domains. Together with novel methods for dynamics and skill learning, flexible and easy-to-use robotic power tools and systems can be designed. Recently, our work has led to the first next generation robot Franka Emika that has recently become commercially available. The system is able to safely interact with humans, execute and even learn sensitive manipulation skills, is affordable and designed as a distributed interconnected system.

Contents – Part II

Weights Initialization

Parameters Optimisation

Pruning Networks

Domain Knowledge Incorporation

Domain Adaptation Approaches

Multiclass

Feature Selection

Adaptive Graph Fusion for Unsupervised Feature Selection

Sijia Niu, Pengfei Zhu(✉), Qinghua Hu, and Hong Shi

College of Intelligence and Computing, Tianjin University, Tianjin 300350, China
{narska_0919,zhupengfei,huqinghua,serena}@tju.edu.cn

Abstract. The massive high-dimensional data brings about great time complexity, high storage burden and poor generalization ability of learning models. Feature selection can alleviate curse of dimensionality by selecting a subset of features. Unsupervised feature selection is much challenging due to lack of label information. Most methods rely on spectral clustering to generate pseudo labels to guide feature selection in unsupervised setting. Graphs for spectral clustering can be constructed in different ways, e.g., kernel similarity, or self-representation. The construction of adjacency graphs could be affected by the parameters of kernel functions, the number of nearest neighbors or the size of the neighborhood. However, it is difficult to evaluate the effectiveness of different graphs in unsupervised feature selection. Most existing algorithms only select one graph by experience. In this paper, we propose a novel adaptive multi-graph fusion based unsupervised feature selection model (GFFS). The proposed model is free of graph selection and can combine the complementary information of different graphs. Experiments on benchmark datasets show that GFFS outperforms the state-of-the-art unsupervised feature selection algorithms.

Keywords: Graph fusion · Unsupervised feature selection · Self-representation

1 Introduction

The ubiquitous use of electronic sensors, digital imaging devices and social networks produce mountains of high-dimensional data, which terribly leads to the curse of dimensionality. In the high-dimensional feature space, the classification and clustering models, which are computationally controllable in low-dimensional space, could become absolutely intractable [3,4]. To alleviate the situation, feature selection is regarded as an indispensable step to search the most informative and discriminative features from the original data, which can effectively reduce the storage space and time complexity [7]. In the past, consistent efforts have been devoted to the development of new feature selection algorithms [3,8,15,20,28]. According to the availability of the label information, feature selection methods can be categorized into supervised [20], semi-supervised [1] and unsupervised [8] ones. For unsupervised learning, the class label information is unavailable to guide the selection of minimal feature subset.

Compared with supervised cases, unsupervised feature selection is more challenging due to the lack of label information [29]. Laplacian score reflects the locality preserving power of features [8]. And pseudo labels indicate the affiliation relations of samples, which can be generated by spectral clustering (SPEC [27], MCFS [3], NDFS [12]),

I. V. Tetko et al. (Eds.): ICANN 2019, LNCS 11728, pp. 3–15, 2019.
https://doi.org/10.1007/978-3-030-30484-3_1

matrix factorization (RUFS [22], EUFS [24]), linear predictors (UDFS [26], JELSR [10]), consensus clustering or dictionary learning [29]. Among them, spectral clustering is widely used in that it can effectively generate the pseudo labels from the graphs. Graphs can be constructed by kernel similarity [9] or self-representation [13,16]. For the traditional spectral clustering algorithm, the sample similarity matrix is firstly calculated, which can be measured by different kernel functions, e.g., Gaussian kernel, polynomial kernel, linear kernel, etc. The quality of constructed graphs could be affected by the parameters of kernel functions. The majority of unsupervised feature selection methods chose to calculate k-nearest neighbor graphs with Gaussian kernel function by experience. Unlike the traditional method, the self-representation based methods learn the affinity matrix automatically to get the graph structure and can uncover the latent subspace structure especially on high-dimensional data. Self-representation represents a sample by a linear combination of all samples and uses the representation coefficients to reflect the sample relationships [5,13,17]. For spectral clustering based unsupervised feature selection algorithms, it is difficult to evaluate the effectiveness of different graphs. No matter which method is used, most existing algorithms only select one graph by experience. However, the chosen graph maybe is not optimal for unsupervised feature selection. On the other hand, if we want to select graph based on their respective importance, we need to set a weight to each graph respectively with additional parameters, which is unsatisfactory especially in unsupervised learning task [19].

Therefore, the problems about choosing one of many methods to construct a perfect graph for unsupervised feature selection or defining the weight of each graph with diverse methods have not been fully explored. In this paper, we propose a novel adaptive multi-graph feature selection method to fuse graphs automatically to obtain more appropriate representation and perform feature selection simultaneously to select the discriminative features in unsupervised learning tasks. We construct graphs by several self-presentation based methods [6,13] and the representative kernel similarity based method [9]. Considering the importance of different graphs for given data, we apply the parameter-free auto-weighted multiple graph learning method to learning a set of weights of all graphs automatically without any additional parameter [21]. The proposed model is free of graph selection and can combine the complementary information of different graphs. The main contributions of our work are summarized as below.

- Multi-graph constructed by various methods are adaptively fused to get more appropriate graph structure for spectral clustering.
- A novel unsupervised feature selection algorithm is proposed by conducting graph fusion, generation of pseudo labels and feature selection simultaneously.
- Extensive experiments on benchmark datasets demonstrate the effectiveness of the proposed method.

2 Graph Constructed Methods

In our work, the fused graphs for spectral clustering mainly constructed by two types of methods which are sample similarity based and self-presentation based ones.

2.1 Kernel Function Based

For sample similarity based graphs, the sample relations are often measured by kernel functions. The kernel functions mainly include Gaussian kernel, Polynomial kernel, PolyPlus kernel, and Linear kernel etc. For sample similarity based methods, the factors that affect graph construction consist of the parameters of kernel functions, the number k of nearest neighbors or the size ϵ of the neighborhood [2], which are selected by experience in most cases.

Owing to the space limit, we show the detail of Gaussian kernel here. Given two samples $\mathbf{x}_i$ and $\mathbf{x}_j$, the sample similarity between them based on Gaussian kernel is defined as [9]:

$$S_{ij} = \begin{cases} exp(-\|\mathbf{x}_i - \mathbf{x}_j\|^2/\sigma^2), & \|\mathbf{x}_i - \mathbf{x}_j\| < \varepsilon, \varepsilon > 0 \\ 0, & otherwise \end{cases} \tag{1}$$

where ε is sufficiently small. From Sect. 1, we know the majority of representative unsupervised feature selection methods use Gaussian kernel for spectral clustering. In our experiments, we put Gaussian kernel based graphs with various k values to be fused.

2.2 Self-representation Based

Self-presentation based methods assume that a sample can be linearly reconstructed represented by a set of bases and are used to measure the sample relationships. The representative methods include sparse subspace clustering (SSC) [5], low-rank representation (LRR) [13], multi-subspace [18], and least squares representation (LSR) [16]. The main difference of these models lies in the self-representation loss and the regularization imposed on the representation coefficient matrix. For a given data matrix $\mathbf{X}$, the common formulation of learning self-representation matrix $\mathbf{Z}$ can be summarized as [17]: $\min_{\mathbf{Z}} L(\mathbf{X} - \mathbf{XZ}) + \lambda R(\mathbf{Z})$.

For SSC, $L(\mathbf{X} - \mathbf{XZ}) = \|\mathbf{X} - \mathbf{XZ}\|_F^2$ and $R(\mathbf{Z}) = \|\mathbf{Z}\|_1$, which is used to obtain a sparse solution tending to be block diagonal. For LRR, $L(\mathbf{X} - \mathbf{XZ}) = \|\mathbf{X} - \mathbf{XZ}\|_{2,1}$ and $R(\mathbf{Z}) = \|\mathbf{Z}\|_*$, which aims to find low-rank affinity matrix and uses the robust l_2, 1-norm to alleviate the noisy case. As for LSR, $L(\mathbf{X} - \mathbf{XZ}) = \|\mathbf{X} - \mathbf{XZ}\|_F^2$ and $R(\mathbf{Z}) = \|\mathbf{Z}\|_F^2$. After the sample relationship matrix $\mathbf{Z}$ was learned by self-representation, the affinity matrix can be obtained for spectral clustering. In our experiments, we put these three methods based graphs to be fused.

3 The Proposed Method

3.1 The Objective Function

We present the method of Auto-Weighted Multiple Graph Learning (AMGL) to fuse graphs and describe our objective function for feature selection in this subsection.

We denote $\mathbf{X} = [\mathbf{x}_1, \mathbf{x}_2, ..., \mathbf{x}_n] \in \mathbb{R}^{d\times n}$ as the data matrix, where d is the dimension of features and n is the number of samples. For a given $\mathbf{X}$, $\mathbf{U} = \{u_{ij}\} \in \mathbb{R}^{n\times n}$ ($\forall i, j \in 1, 2, ..., n$) is the affinity matrix and the corresponding degree matrix can be constructed to $\mathbf{D}$ with $D_{ii} = \sum_{j=1}^{n} u_{ij}$. And as a description of graph, Laplacian matrix $\mathbf{L}$ is calculate with $\mathbf{L} = \mathbf{D} - \mathbf{U}$. For multiple graphs, let m be the number of graphs and $\mathbf{L}_v$ means any matrix of the set of Laplacian matrices. We define the cluster indicator matrix, i.e., the pseudo class labels matrix $\mathbf{F} = [f_1, f_2, ..., f_n]^T \in \mathbb{R}^{n \times c}$, where c is the number of classes.

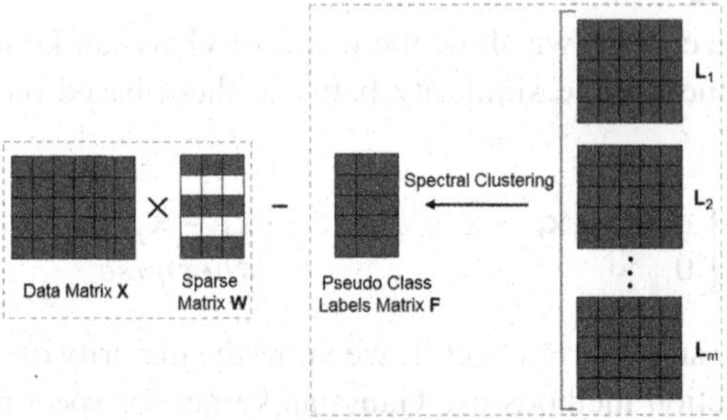

Fig. 1. The framework of the proposed adaptive graph fusion for unsupervised feature selection. $\mathbf{L}_1, \mathbf{L}_2, ..., \mathbf{L}_n$ can be calculated by kernel similarity based or self-representation based methods.

Therefore, from AMGL, the formulation of multiple graphs clustering is [21]:

$$\min_{\mathbf{F} \in \mathcal{C}} \sum_{v=1}^{m} \sqrt{Tr(\mathbf{F}^T \mathbf{L}_v \mathbf{F})}. \tag{2}$$

In spectral clustering, $\mathbf{F}$ is constrained with $\mathbf{F}^T\mathbf{F} = \mathbf{I}$. And according to the derivative of Eq. (2), the parameter-free auto-weight vector φ_v of multiple graphs can be calculated. The real problem we should solve is as follow:

$$\min_{\mathbf{F}^T\mathbf{F}=\mathbf{I}} \sum_{v=1}^{m} \varphi_v Tr(\mathbf{F}^T \mathbf{L}_v \mathbf{F}), \tag{3}$$

where $\varphi_v = \frac{1}{2\sqrt{Tr(\mathbf{F}^T \mathbf{L}_v \mathbf{F})}}$.

During feature selection with our method, the features which are most related to the pseudo class labels are selected. Except for the $\mathbf{F}$ mentioned above, we propose to learn the weight matrix $\mathbf{W} \in \mathbb{R}^{d \times c}$ for selection simultaneously. Based on Eq. (2) and the nonnegative constraint [12], we propose the objective function for feature selection:

$$\begin{aligned} &\min_{\mathbf{F},\mathbf{W}} \sum_{v=1}^{m} \sqrt{Tr(\mathbf{F}^T \mathbf{L}_v \mathbf{F})} + \alpha(\|\mathbf{X}^T\mathbf{W} - \mathbf{F}\|_F^2 + \beta\|\mathbf{W}\|_{2,1}) \\ &s.t. \quad \mathbf{F}^T\mathbf{F} = \mathbf{I}, \quad \mathbf{F} \geq 0, \end{aligned} \tag{4}$$

where α and β are positive constants. To sum up, in Eq. (4), the first term learns the pseudo class labels using AMGL with spectral clustering. The second term is the regression model while the third term is $l_{2,1}$-norm regularization. The group sparsity ensures

Algorithm 1. Graph Fusion Based Unsupervised Feature Selection (when $d > n$)

Input:

Data matrix $\mathbf{X} \in \mathbb{R}^{d \times n}$; Laplacian matrices set $\mathbf{L}$; Parameter α, β, μ, c, and m.

Set the iteration step t = 1;
Initialize $\mathbf{F^t} \in \mathbb{R}^{n \times c}$ and set $\mathbf{G^t} \in \mathbb{R}^{d \times n}$ as an identity matrix; Initialize the weight vector $\varphi_v{}^t = \frac{1}{m}$ for each graph.

repeat

$\mathbf{A}^t = \alpha(\mathbf{I} - \mathbf{X}^T\mathbf{G}^{t-1}\mathbf{X}(\mathbf{X}^T\mathbf{G}^{-1}\mathbf{X} + \beta\mathbf{I})^{-1})$;

$F_{ij}^{t+1} = F_{ij}^t \frac{(\mu\mathbf{F})_{ij}}{(\sum_{v=1}^{m} \varphi_v \mathbf{L}_v \mathbf{F^t} + \mathbf{A^t}\mathbf{F^t} + \mu\mathbf{F}\mathbf{F}^T\mathbf{F})_{ij}}$;

$\mathbf{W}^{t+1} = \mathbf{G}^{t-1}\mathbf{X}(\mathbf{X}^T\mathbf{G}^{t-1}\mathbf{X} + \beta\mathbf{I})^{-1}\mathbf{F}^{t+1}$;

Update the diagonal matrix

$$\mathbf{G}^{t+1} = \begin{bmatrix} \frac{1}{2\|\mathbf{w}_1\|_2} & & \\ & \cdots & \\ & & \frac{1}{2\|\mathbf{w}_d\|_2} \end{bmatrix};$$

$\varphi_v{}^{t+1} = \frac{1}{2\sqrt{Tr(\mathbf{F}^{t+1^T}\mathbf{L}_v\mathbf{F}^{t+1})}}$

$t = t + 1$;

until Converge.

Output:

The index by sorting all d features according $\|\mathbf{w}_i{}^t\|_2 (i = 1, ..., d)$ in descending order.

$\mathbf{W}$ sparse in row and enables $\mathbf{W}$ to evaluate the interrelation between cluster labels and features, which is beneficial for selecting discriminative features. The framework of the proposed adaptive graph fusion for unsupervised feature selection is shown in Fig. 1.

3.2 Optimization and Algorithm

In the subsection, we show an iterative algorithm to solve the graph fusion and the optimization problem of feature selection.

Laplacian Matrices Set. We have introduced several methods of constructing graph in the Sect. 2. In our method, we choose to calculate affinity matrices according to k-nearest neighbor method with a few k values and choose several self-representation based methods and then calculate graph structure matrix according to each affinity matrix. For self-representation based, due to the asymmetry of $\mathbf{Z}$, we use [16] $\mathbf{Z}^* = (|\mathbf{Z}| + |\mathbf{Z}^T|)/2$ to calculate the final affinity matrix $\mathbf{Z}^*$. Then we set these affinity matrices to the laplacian matrices set $\mathbf{L} = \{\mathbf{L}_1, \mathbf{L}_2, ..., \mathbf{L}_v\}$ as a input of Algorithm 1.

Unsupervised Feature Selection. Following [12], we introduce the optimization rules. The $l_{2,1}$-norm regularization is non-smooth and the objective function can not convex in $\mathbf{F}$ and $\mathbf{W}$ simultaneously. To reduce the complexity of the optimization process, we write the objective function as follow:

$$\min_{\mathbf{F},\mathbf{W}} \sum_{v=1}^{m} \sqrt{Tr(\mathbf{F}^T\mathbf{L}_v\mathbf{F})} + \alpha(\|\mathbf{X}^T\mathbf{W} - \mathbf{F}\|_F^2 + \beta\|\mathbf{W}\|_{2,1}) + \frac{\mu}{2}\|\mathbf{F}^T\mathbf{F} - \mathbf{I}\|_F^2 \quad (5)$$
$$s.t. \quad \mathbf{F} \geq 0,$$

where μ is a positive parameter to control the orthogonality. Then for the ease of representation, we define

$$\mathcal{L}(\mathbf{F},\mathbf{W}) = \sum_{v=1}^{m} \sqrt{Tr(\mathbf{F}^T\mathbf{L}_v\mathbf{F})} + \alpha(\|\mathbf{X}^T\mathbf{W}-\mathbf{F}\|_F^2 + \beta\|\mathbf{W}\|_{2,1}) + \frac{\mu}{2}\|\mathbf{F}^T\mathbf{F}-\mathbf{I}\|_F^2. \quad (6)$$

Let $\frac{\partial\mathcal{L}(\mathbf{F},\mathbf{W})}{\partial\mathbf{W}} = 0$, we get [12]

$$\frac{\partial\mathcal{L}(\mathbf{F},\mathbf{W})}{\partial\mathbf{W}} = 2\alpha(\mathbf{X}(\mathbf{X}^T\mathbf{W}-\mathbf{F}) + \beta\mathbf{G}\mathbf{W})^{-1}\mathbf{X}\mathbf{F} \Rightarrow \mathbf{W} = (\mathbf{X}\mathbf{X}^T + \beta\mathbf{G})^{-1}\mathbf{X}\mathbf{F}. \quad (7)$$

$\mathbf{G}$ is a diagonal matrix and is inferred during the process of derivation and $G_{ii} = \frac{1}{2\|\mathbf{w}_i\|_2}$, where $\mathbf{w_i}(i = 1, 2, ..., d)$ is the row vector of $\mathbf{W}$. Replace $\mathbf{W}$ of Eq. (5) with Eq. (7) and it can be rewritten as

$$\min_{\mathbf{F},\mathbf{W}} \sum_{v=1}^{m} \sqrt{Tr(\mathbf{F}^T\mathbf{L}_v\mathbf{F})} + Tr(\mathbf{F}^T\mathbf{A}\mathbf{F}) + \frac{\mu}{2}\|\mathbf{F}^T\mathbf{F}-\mathbf{I}\|_F^2 \quad s.t.\mathbf{F} \geq 0, \quad (8)$$

where

$$\mathbf{A} = \alpha(\mathbf{I} - \mathbf{X}^T(\mathbf{X}\mathbf{X}^T + \beta\mathbf{G})^{-1}\mathbf{X}) \quad (9)$$

and $\mathbf{I} \in \mathbb{R}^{n\times n}$ is a identify matrix.

To set auto-weight for each graph based on Eq. (3) and with the multiplicative updating rules [14], we let ϕ_{ij} be the Lagrange multiplier for the constraint of $\mathbf{F} \geq 0$ and $\Phi = [\phi_{ij}]$, the function is

$$\sum_{v=1}^{m} \varphi_v Tr(\mathbf{F}^T\mathbf{L}_v\mathbf{F}) + Tr(\mathbf{F}^T\mathbf{A}\mathbf{F}) + \frac{\mu}{2}\|\mathbf{F}^T\mathbf{F}-\mathbf{I}\|_F^2 + Tr(\Phi\mathbf{F}^T). \quad (10)$$

Setting its derivative w.r.t. $F_{ij} = 0$ and using KKT condition [11] $\phi_{ij}F_{ij} = 0$, the updating rules of $\mathbf{F}$ is

$$F_{ij} \leftarrow F_{ij} \frac{(\mu\mathbf{F})_{ij}}{(\sum_{v=1}^{m} \varphi_v\mathbf{L}_v\mathbf{F} + \mathbf{A}\mathbf{F} + \mu\mathbf{F}\mathbf{F}^T\mathbf{F})_{ij}}. \quad (11)$$

In Eqs. (7) and (9), we need to compute the inverse of $\mathbf{X}\mathbf{X}^T + \beta\mathbf{G}$. However, for most of high-dimensional data, the feature dimension is much larger than the number of samples [29], which leads to the complexity to compute $\mathbf{W}$ and $\mathbf{A}$ would be very large. According to the Woodbury matrix identity [29], we can get

$$\mathbf{W} = \mathbf{G}^{-1}\mathbf{X}(\mathbf{X}^T\mathbf{G}^{-1}\mathbf{X} + \beta\mathbf{I})^{-1}\mathbf{F}, \quad (12)$$

and

$$\mathbf{A} = \alpha(\mathbf{I} - \mathbf{X}^T\mathbf{G}^{-1}\mathbf{X}(\mathbf{X}^T\mathbf{G}^{-1}\mathbf{X} + \beta\mathbf{I})^{-1}). \quad (13)$$

When the feature dimension is higher than the number of samples, Eqs. (12) and (13) are used to update $\mathbf{W}$ and $\mathbf{A}$. Otherwise, Eqs. (7) and (9) are used.

Based on all the above analysis, the optimization algorithm, when $d > n$ is satisfied, is summarized in Algorithm 1. If $d > n$ is not satisfied, only replace the updating rules of $\mathbf{A}$ and $\mathbf{W}$ with $\mathbf{A}^{t+1} = \alpha(\mathbf{I} - \mathbf{X}^T(\mathbf{X}\mathbf{X}^T + \beta\mathbf{G}^t)^{-1}\mathbf{X})$ and $\mathbf{W}^{t+1} = (\mathbf{X}\mathbf{X}^T + \beta\mathbf{G})^{-1}\mathbf{X}\mathbf{F}^{t+1}$ in line 3 and line 5 of Algorithm 1, respectively.

3.3 Convergence Analysis

From the optimization process above, we update one of $\mathbf{W}$ and $\mathbf{F}$ while keeping the other one fixed. Then we prove the convergence with $\mathbf{W}$ or $\mathbf{F}$ fixed respectively. For convenience, we denote

$$f(\mathbf{F}) = \sum_{v=1}^{m} \sqrt{Tr(\mathbf{F}^T\mathbf{L}_v\mathbf{F})}, \quad g(\mathbf{F}) = Tr(\mathbf{F}^T\mathbf{A}\mathbf{F}) + \frac{\mu}{2}\|\mathbf{F}^T\mathbf{F} - \mathbf{I}\|_F^2. \tag{14}$$

With $\mathbf{W}^t$ fixed, there is $\mathcal{L}(\mathbf{F}^t, \mathbf{W}^t) = f(\mathbf{F}) + g(\mathbf{F})$. From [21] and [23], we have $f(\mathbf{F}^{t+1}) \leq f(\mathbf{F}^t)$ and $g(\mathbf{F}^{t+1}) \leq g(\mathbf{F}^t)$, respectively. Because $f(\mathbf{F})$ and $g(\mathbf{F})$ are continuous functions, it is easy to prove $f(\mathbf{F}^{t+1}) + g(\mathbf{F}^{t+1}) \leq f(\mathbf{F}^t) + g(\mathbf{F}^t)$, i.e., we have

$$\mathcal{L}(\mathbf{F}^{t+1}, \mathbf{W}^t) \leq \mathcal{L}(\mathbf{F}^t, \mathbf{W}^t). \tag{15}$$

For

$$\min_{\mathbf{W}} \|\mathbf{X}^T\mathbf{W} - \mathbf{F}\|_F^2 + \beta Tr(\mathbf{W}^T\mathbf{D}\mathbf{W}), \tag{16}$$

Eq. (7) is the solution to it [23].

According to Eq. (6) and the proof in [23], we have

$$\mathcal{L}(\mathbf{F}^{t+1}, \mathbf{W}^{t+1}) \leq \mathcal{L}(\mathbf{F}^{t+1}, \mathbf{W}^t) \leq \mathcal{L}(\mathbf{F}^t, \mathbf{W}^t). \tag{17}$$

Finally, we know that $\mathcal{L}(\mathbf{F}, \mathbf{W})$ will monotonously decrease in each iteration with the updating rules in Algorithm 1, i.e., $\mathbf{F}$ and $\mathbf{W}$ can converge to the local optimal value.

4 Discussion

In this paper, we used two categories of methods for graph construction, i.e., kernel similarity based and self-representation based ones, to construct graphs. But the proposed method is not limited to the above two graph construction methods. We can fuse as many kinds of graphs as want. In fact, our proposed method is not a simple extension of AMGL. Firstly, AGML is developed for clustering and semi-supervised classification while the proposed method is used for unsupervised feature selection. Second, the motivation of AMGL is adaptive fusion of multi-view graphs. However, our work aims to adaptively fuse graphs generated by different methods on single-view data.

5 Experiments

In this section, extensive experiments verify the effectiveness of the proposed method.

5.1 Datasets

In this paper, eight diverse publicly available datasets are selected for comparison, including four biological datasets (i.e., TOX-171[1], ALLAML (see Footnote 1), CLL-SUB-111 (see Footnote 1), SMK-CAN-187 (see Footnote 1), two handwritten digit

[1] http://featureselection.asu.edu/datasets.php.

datasets (i.e., USPSdata_20[2], binalpha[3]), one face image dataset (i.e., PalmData25 (see Footnote 3)) and one shape dataset (i.e., Mpeg7 (see Footnote 3)). Datasets descriptions is summarized in Table 1.

Table 1. Datasets descriptions.

Datasets	#Samples	#Features	#Classes	#Domains
TOX-171	171	5748	4	Biology
ALLAML	72	7129	2	Biology
CLL-SUB-111	111	11340	3	Biology
SMK-CAN-187	187	19993	2	Biology
USPS	1854	256	10	Digit
binalpha	1404	320	36	Digit
PalmData25	2000	256	100	Image
Mpeg7	1400	4000	2	Shape

5.2 Comparison Method

To validate the effective of our proposed GFFS for feature selection, we compare it with the following representative unsupervised feature selection methods:

- LS [8] selects features consistent with Gaussian Laplacian matrix according to the power of locality preserving.
- SPEC [27] is a filter method that use spectral clustering.
- MCFS [3] is a filter method that select features based on spectral analysis and sparse regression with l_1-norm regularization.
- UDFS [26] creates pseudo labels by a linear classifier and $l_{2,1}$-norm regularization.
- NDFS [12] is a filter method and perform spectral clustering to learn the cluster labels of the inputs, during which the feature selection is performed simultaneously.
- EUFS [24] directly embeds feature selection into a clustering algorithm via sparse learning without the transformation.

5.3 Evaluation Metrics

We apply three common evaluation metrics, i.e., classification accuracy (**ACC**), normalized mutual information , and clustering accuracy [17,25] to evaluate the performance. Due to the space limit, only the detailed definition of **NMI** are described as below.

[2] http://www-i6.informatik.rwth-aachen.de/.
[3] https://sites.google.com/site/feipingnie/.

Table 2. Classification accuracy (**ACC** %) of different feature selection methods. The top two results are highlighted in bold.

DATA	LS	SPEC	MCFS	UDFS	NDFS	EUFS	GFFS	GFFS(k1)	GFFS(k2)	GFFS(k3)
TOX-171	49.75	54.11	66.04	60.35	64.08	54.11	66.08	**66.10**	65.84	**66.74**
ALLAML	65.85	84.04	75.77	87.28	81.27	86.44	**89.25**	82.51	**88.10**	87.53
CLL-SUB-111	58.13	59.47	56.59	63.55	66.45	61.33	**68.88**	**66.97**	63.01	65.57
SMK-CAN-187	60.23	61.32	63.32	63.35	64.65	63.59	**68.21**	**67.35**	66.78	67.26
USPS	68.59	86.56	88.11	77.32	90.40	90.39	**91.39**	90.79	**91.19**	90.90
binalpha	24.03	34.73	54.89	50.54	58.48	49.30	**59.25**	58.86	58.22	**58.93**
PalmData25	96.92	95.04	98.90	98.88	98.90	98.16	**98.97**	98.93	**99.05**	98.96
Mpeg7	54.59	1.43	66.54	56.38	66.54	56.14	**68.48**	**66.62**	66.60	66.59

We denote $\mathbf{C}$ as the set of clusters learned from the ground truth and $\mathbf{C}'$ is Their mutual information metric $\mathbf{MI}(\mathbf{C}, \mathbf{C}')$ is defined as follows:

$$\mathbf{MI}(\mathbf{C}, \mathbf{C}') = \sum_{c_i \in \mathbf{C}, c_j \in \mathbf{C}'} p(c_i, c_j') log_2 \frac{p(c_i, c_j')}{p(c_i)p(c_j')}, \tag{18}$$

where $p(c_i)$ and $p(c_j')$ are the probabilities that a data point selected from the point belongs to clusters c_i and c_j' respectively. $p(c_i, c_j')$ is the joint probability that select data point belongs to the cluster c_i and c_j' simultaneously. The normalized mutual information (**NMI**) are defined as follows:

$$\mathbf{NMI}(\mathbf{C}, \mathbf{C}') = \frac{\mathbf{MI}(\mathbf{C}, \mathbf{C}')}{\max(\mathcal{H}(\mathbf{C}), \mathcal{H}(\mathbf{C}'))}, \tag{19}$$

where $\mathcal{H}(\mathbf{C})$ and $\mathcal{H}(\mathbf{C}')$ are the entropies of $\mathbf{C}$ and $\mathbf{C}'$ respectively. The range of $\mathbf{NMI}(\mathbf{C}, \mathbf{C}')$ is from 0 to 1. In detail, if the two sets of clusters are identical then $\mathbf{NMI} = 1$ while $\mathbf{NMI} = 0$ if the two sets are independent.

5.4 Parameter Setting

Following the experiment setting in [12,22,26], for all the comparison methods, the k value of k-means clustering method is set to 5 and we set the parameters of themselves as the best value. For UDFS, EUFS and the proposed method GFFS, we tune parameters α and β in the range of $\{10^{-6}, 10^{-4}, 10^{-2}, 1, 10^2, 10^4, 10^6\}$ by the grid search strategy. For the graphs are intended to fuse, we choose Gaussian kernel function and $(3, 5)$, $(3, 5, 7)$, $(3, 5, 7, 15)$ as the k value sets with reporting the average result named 'GFFS' and we set $(3, 5, 7, 9)$, $(3, 5, 7, 9, 13)$, $(3, 5, 7, 9, 13, 15)$ as other k sets by experience which are abbreviated to k1, k2 and k3 respectively to show the result in tables. We choose LSR, SSC and LRR as the alternative self-presentation based methods construct other graphs. Additionally, we used k-nearest neighbor classifier and k is set as 10 for

Table 3. Clustering performance (**NMI** %) of different feature selection methods. The top two results are highlighted in bold.

DATA	LS	SPEC	MCFS	UDFS	NDFS	EUFS	GFFS	GFFS(k1)	GFFS(k2)	GFFS(k3)
TOX-171	9.41	9.83	12.44	19.51	31.29	15.25	**33.37**	28.96	**31.71**	30.98
ALLAML	7.89	20.11	11.34	19.55	30.00	11.01	**33.79**	**30.20**	24.15	27.12
CLL-SUB-111	10.51	19.67	20.20	21.29	21.25	25.05	**26.17**	21.07	20.90	**25.10**
SMK-CAN-187	2.05	1.75	0.25	4.25	6.89	2.44	**10.13**	6.89	**9.38**	7.76
USPS	37.31	52.48	55.49	44.91	57.48	54.10	**58.63**	57.53	57.26	**57.93**
binalpha	36.83	36.93	52.64	53.39	53.38	46.08	**54.67**	**54.78**	54.20	54.18
PalmData25	85.42	83.88	89.33	88.69	89.19	87.74	**89.78**	89.24	**89.62**	89.37
Mpeg7	53.60	27.21	58.65	55.93	63.67	55.93	**64.78**	63.74	**63.89**	63.89

Table 4. Clustering accuracy (%) of different feature selection methods. The top two results are highlighted in bold.

DATA	LS	SPEC	MCFS	UDFS	NDFS	EUFS	GFFS	GFFS(k1)	GFFS(k2)	GFFS(k3)
TOX-171	38.18	38.83	40.90	45.11	51.30	43.15	**51.56**	49.50	**51.36**	50.17
ALLAML	66.29	75.29	68.22	68.40	73.41	68.38	**78.02**	70.85	74.49	**76.19**
CLL-SUB-111	46.52	50.55	50.07	51.97	53.11	**55.69**	**53.96**	52.43	52.22	52.71
SMK-CAN-187	53.48	56.48	51.80	61.84	64.06	58.90	**67.55**	64.36	**66.80**	64.90
USPS	45.62	55.00	59.17	49.43	61.68	59.17	62.61	**64.54**	**64.79**	64.03
binalpha	21.37	23.27	36.36	36.02	37.21	31.52	**38.56**	**39.05**	37.68	37.30
PalmData25	64.76	62.17	69.39	68.53	69.11	66.94	**70.64**	69.52	**69.88**	69.36
Mpeg7	30.95	7.35	37.46	33.74	42.50	33.68	**44.40**	**43.34**	42.49	42.57

all methods. For feature dimensions, the numbers of features are set as $\{10, 20, ..., 150\}$ and we show the average results of different feature dimensions.

5.5 Experiment Result

The results for different methods on eight datasets are listed in Tables 2, 3 and 4. On these datasets, the proposed method GFFS achieves the best performance in most cases. The reason is that GFFS fuses graphs meanwhile learns the pseudo class labels matrix and the feature selection matrix, which enable it select informative features. While both GFFS and NDFS utilize $l_{2,1}$-norm regularization term and the nonnegative constraint, we pay attention to fuse to better graph instead of using a single graph by experience, which can combine the complementary information of different graphs.

Due to the space limit, we only address the sensitiveness of parameters on the proposed method in terms of ACC and the curves of convergence on TOX-171, PalmData25, and Mpeg7 datasets in Figs. 2 and 3. From these figures, we see that our method is not sensitive to α and β and converges around 25 iterations.

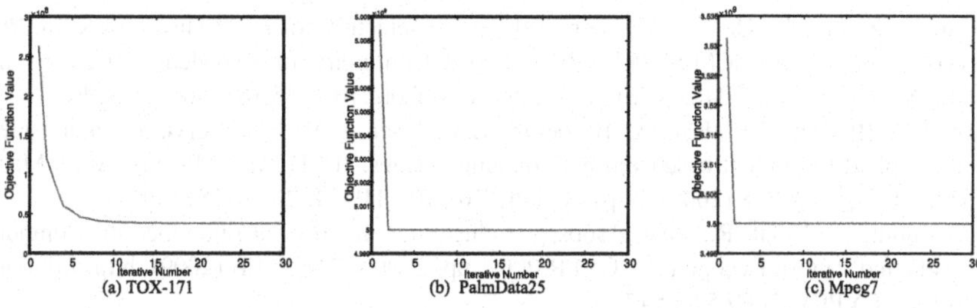

(a) TOX-171 (b) PalmData25 (c) Mpeg7

Fig. 2. The convergence curves of GFFS on TOX-171, PalmData25, and Mpeg7 datasets.

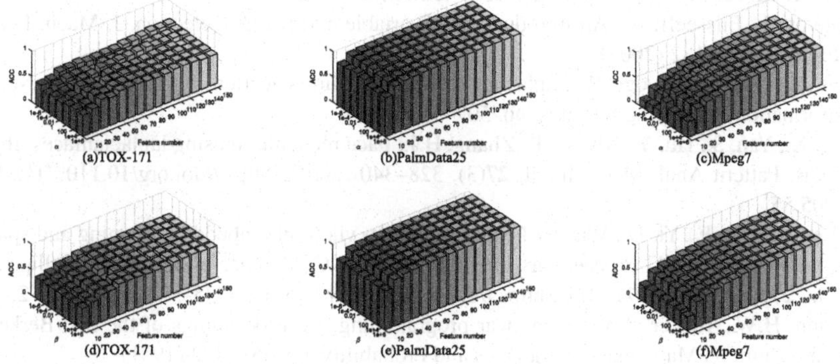

(a)TOX-171 (b)PalmData25 (c)Mpeg7
(d)TOX-171 (e)PalmData25 (f)Mpeg7

Fig. 3. Classification accuracy (**ACC**) with different α and β. (a), (b), (c): different β keeping $\alpha = 0.01$; (d), (e), (f): different α keeping $\beta = 0.01$.

6 Conclusion

In this paper, we proposed a novel adaptive graph fusion based unsupervised feature selection (GFFS) algorithm. Different from the existing models that use either kernel similarity or self-representation to generate the affinity matrix, GFFS avoids graph selection by automatically learning the weights of graphs and fusing them in a parameter-free way. Extensive experiments on benchmark datasets validate that the proposed model outperforms the state-of-the-art unsupervised feature selection methods. In the future work, we will extend the proposed model to semi-supervised feature selection tasks.

References

1. Benabdeslem, K., Hindawi, M.: Efficient semi-supervised feature selection: constraint, relevance, and redundancy. IEEE Trans. Knowl. Data Eng. **26**(5), 1131–1143 (2014). https://doi.org/10.1109/TKDE.2013.86
2. Cai, D., He, X., Han, J.: Document clustering using locality preserving indexing. IEEE Trans. Knowl. Data Eng. **17**(12), 1624–1637 (2005). https://doi.org/10.1109/TKDE.2005.198

3. Cai, D., Zhang, C., He, X.: Unsupervised feature selection for multi-cluster data. In: Proceedings of the 16th ACM SIGKDD International Conference on Knowledge Discovery and Data Mining, pp. 333–342. ACM (2010). https://doi.org/10.1145/1835804.1835848
4. Dy, J.G., Brodley, C.E., Kak, A., Broderick, L.S., Aisen, A.M.: Unsupervised feature selection applied to content-based retrieval of lung images. IEEE Trans. Pattern Anal. Mach. Intell. **25**(3), 373–378 (2003). https://doi.org/10.1109/TPAMI.2003.1182100
5. Elhamifar, E., Vidal, R.: Sparse subspace clustering. In: IEEE Conference on Computer Vision and Pattern Recognition, CVPR 2009, pp. 2790–2797. IEEE (2009). https://doi.org/10.1109/CVPRW.2009.5206547
6. Fang, Y., Wang, R., Dai, B.: Graph-oriented learning via automatic group sparsity for data analysis. In: 2012 IEEE 12th International Conference on Data Mining (ICDM), pp. 251–259. IEEE (2012). https://doi.org/10.1109/ICDM.2012.82
7. Guyon, I., Elisseeff, A.: An introduction to variable and feature selection. J. Mach. Learn. Res. **3**, 1157–1182 (2003)
8. He, X., Cai, D., Niyogi, P.: Laplacian score for feature selection. In: Advances in Neural Information Processing Systems, pp. 507–514 (2005)
9. He, X., Yan, S., Hu, Y., Niyogi, P., Zhang, H.J.: Face recognition using laplacianfaces. IEEE Trans. Pattern Anal. Mach. Intell. **27**(3), 328–340 (2005). https://doi.org/10.1109/TPAMI.2005.55
10. Hou, C., Nie, F., Yi, D., Wu, Y.: Feature selection via joint embedding learning and sparse regression. In: IJCAI Proceedings-International Joint Conference on Artificial Intelligence, vol. 22, pp. 1324–1329 (2011). https://doi.org/10.5591/978-1-57735-516-8/IJCAI11-224
11. Kuhn, H.W., Tucker, A.W.: Nonlinear programming. In: Proceedings of the 2nd Berkeley Symposium on Mathematical Statistics and Probability, pp. 481–492 (1951)
12. Li, Z., Yang, Y., Liu, J., Zhou, X., Lu, H., et al.: Unsupervised feature selection using nonnegative spectral analysis. In: AAAI, vol. 2, pp. 1026–1032 (2012)
13. Liu, G., Lin, Z., Yan, S., Sun, J., Yu, Y., Ma, Y.: Robust recovery of subspace structures by low-rank representation. IEEE Trans. Pattern Anal. Mach. Intell. **35**(1), 171–184 (2013). https://doi.org/10.1109/TPAMI.2012.88
14. Liu, Y., Jin, R., Yang, L.: Semi-supervised multi-label learning by constrained non-negative matrix factorization. In: AAAI, vol. 6, pp. 421–426 (2006)
15. Liu, Y., Zhang, C., Zhu, P., Hu, Q.: Generalized multi-view unsupervised feature selection. In: Kůrková, V., Manolopoulos, Y., Hammer, B., Iliadis, L., Maglogiannis, I. (eds.) ICANN 2018. LNCS, vol. 11140, pp. 469–478. Springer, Cham (2018). https://doi.org/10.1007/978-3-030-01421-6_45
16. Lu, C.-Y., Min, H., Zhao, Z.-Q., Zhu, L., Huang, D.-S., Yan, S.: Robust and efficient subspace segmentation via least squares regression. In: Fitzgibbon, A., Lazebnik, S., Perona, P., Sato, Y., Schmid, C. (eds.) ECCV 2012. LNCS, vol. 7578, pp. 347–360. Springer, Heidelberg (2012). https://doi.org/10.1007/978-3-642-33786-4_26
17. Lu, C., Tang, J., Lin, M., Lin, L., Yan, S., Lin, Z.: Correntropy induced L2 graph for robust subspace clustering. In: Proceedings of the IEEE International Conference on Computer Vision, pp. 1801–1808 (2013). https://doi.org/10.1109/ICCV.2013.226.
18. Luo, D., Nie, F., Ding, C., Huang, H.: Multi-subspace representation and discovery. In: Gunopulos, D., Hofmann, T., Malerba, D., Vazirgiannis, M. (eds.) ECML PKDD 2011. LNCS (LNAI), vol. 6912, pp. 405–420. Springer, Heidelberg (2011). https://doi.org/10.1007/978-3-642-23783-6_26
19. Nie, F., Cai, G., Li, X.: Multi-view clustering and semi-supervised classification with adaptive neighbours. In: Proceedings of the Thirty-First AAAI Conference on Artificial Intelligence, 4–9 February 2017, San Francisco, California, USA, pp. 2408–2414 (2017). http://aaai.org/ocs/index.php/AAAI/AAAI17/paper/view/14833

20. Nie, F., Huang, H., Cai, X., Ding, C.H.: Efficient and robust feature selection via joint l2, 1-norms minimization. In: Advances in Neural Information Processing Systems, pp. 1813–1821 (2010)
21. Nie, F., Li, J., Li, X., et al.: Parameter-free auto-weighted multiple graph learning: a framework for multiview clustering and semi-supervised classification. In: IJCAI, pp. 1881–1887 (2016)
22. Qian, M., Zhai, C.: Robust unsupervised feature selection. In: IJCAI, pp. 1621–1627 (2013)
23. Tang, J., Liu, H.: Unsupervised feature selection for linked social media data. In: Proceedings of the 18th ACM SIGKDD International Conference on Knowledge Discovery and Data Mining, pp. 904–912. ACM (2012). https://doi.org/10.1145/2339530.2339673
24. Wang, S., Tang, J., Liu, H.: Embedded unsupervised feature selection. In: AAAI, pp. 470–476 (2015)
25. Xu, W., Liu, X., Gong, Y.: Document clustering based on non-negative matrix factorization. In: Proceedings of the 26th annual international ACM SIGIR Conference on Research and Development in Informaion Retrieval, pp. 267–273. ACM (2003). https://doi.org/10.1145/860435.860485
26. Yang, Y., Shen, H.T., Ma, Z., Huang, Z., Zhou, X.: L2, 1-norm regularized discriminative feature selection for unsupervised learning. In: IJCAI Proceedings-International Joint Conference on Artificial Intelligence, vol. 22, p. 1589 (2011). https://doi.org/10.5591/978-1-57735-516-8/IJCAI11-267.
27. Zhao, Z., Liu, H.: Spectral feature selection for supervised and unsupervised learning. In: Proceedings of the 24th International Conference on Machine Learning, pp. 1151–1157. ACM (2007). https://doi.org/10.1145/1273496.1273641
28. Zhao, Z., Wang, L., Liu, H., et al.: Efficient spectral feature selection with minimum redundancy. In: AAAI, pp. 673–678 (2010)
29. Zhu, P., Hu, Q., Zhang, C., Zuo, W.: Coupled dictionary learning for unsupervised feature selection. In: AAAI, pp. 2422–2428 (2016)

Unsupervised Feature Selection via Local Total-Order Preservation

Rui Ma, Yijie Wang(✉), and Li Cheng

Science and Technology on Parallel and Distributed Laboratory,
College of Computer, National University of Defense Technology, Changsha, China
sherlock5204@163.com, {wangyijie,chengli09}@nudt.edu.cn

Abstract. Without class label, unsupervised feature selection methods choose a subset of features that faithfully maintain the intrinsic structure of original data. Conventional methods assume that the exact value of pairwise samples distance used in structure regularization is effective. However, this assumption imposes strict restrictions to feature selection, and it causes more features to be kept for data representation. Motivated by this, we propose Unsupervised Feature Selection via Local Total-order Preservation, called **UFSLTP**. In particular, we characterize a local structure by a novel total-order relation, which applies the comparison of pairwise samples distance. To achieve a desirable features subset, we map total-order relation into probability space and attempt to preserve the relation by minimizing the differences of the probability distributions calculated before and after feature selection. Due to the inherent nature of machine learning and total-order relation, less features are needed to represent data without adverse effecting on performance. Moreover, we propose two efficient methods, namely Adaptive Neighbors Selection(ANS) and Uniform Neighbors Serialization(UNS), to reduce the computational complexity and improve the method performance. The results of experiments on benchmark datasets demonstrate that the proposed method significantly outperforms the state-of-the-art methods. Compared to the competitors by clustering performance, it averagely achieves 31.01% improvement in terms of NMI and 14.44% in terms of Silhouette Coefficient.

Keywords: Unsupervised feature selection · Total-order relation · Local manifold structure

1 Introduction

There are plenty of high-dimensional data in many fields, such as pattern recognition [4], content distribution [24,25] and cloud computing [21], which presents great problems such as the curse of dimensionality, huge cost of computation. Therefore, it's vital to conduct feature dimension reduction, which mainly includes feature learning and feature selection. However, feature learning methods, such as t-SNE [13], PCA [1], aims to combine and integrate features, it will

I. V. Tetko et al. (Eds.): ICANN 2019, LNCS 11728, pp. 16–28, 2019.
https://doi.org/10.1007/978-3-030-30484-3_2

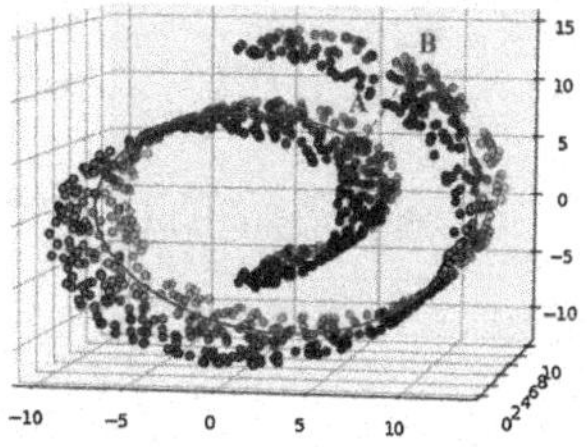

Fig. 1. An example of "Swiss roll". For two data points A and B on a nonlinear manifold, their Euclidean distance (length of dashed line) cannot accurately reflect their intrinsic similarity, as measured by the distance along the manifold (length of solid curve).

loss the practical physical significance of features. Therefore, the research will focus on feature selection. Meanwhile, as most data are unlabeled and labeling data is particularly expensive in both time and effort, unsupervised feature selection is challenging but significant for the effective analysis of data [8,22,23].

Recently, a variety of methods have been proposed to address the problems of unsupervised feature selection. Without class label, they attempt to choose a subset of features that can faithfully maintain the intrinsic structure derived from the original data [5,12,19]. The commonly used structures include, but not limit to, the global[1] structure [26,29,30], the local manifold structure [3,6,11,27], and discriminative information [18]. These structures can be captured by classic models, such as, stochastic neighbors (SNE) [13], linear combination of samples [5], local linear embedding (LLE) [11], and personalized structure [9], most of which are constructed by the linear relation or similarity between samples. However these will affect the effectiveness of structure, since the former neglects nonlinear relationship between instances, and the similarity measured in high-dimensional space might not be qualitatively meaningful [12], i.e., data samples in high-dimensional space are approximately equidistant from each other [14,17]. Obviously, the quality of selected features relies severely on the effectiveness of structure. Unfortunately, when the samples are distributed in a nonlinear manifold (e.g. Fig. 1), the structure constructed in traditional methods, especially the global structure, may not be that accurate as ideal [16]. All in all, the key challenge centers around how to construct an effective geometric structure to accurately present the intrinsic relationship between instances.

Most of the existing unsupervised feature selection methods, overwhelmingly build a structure by the exact value of distance. Despite the empirical availability of high learning performance, they inevitably impose strict restrictions to feature selection, it causes more features to be kept for data representation. In machine learning, the nearest class or cluster is referenced to label new data, thus it is of vital meaning to consider the comparison of distance for learning tasks.

[1] In the following, we term pairwise samples similarity as global structure in order to keep it consistent with local manifold structure.

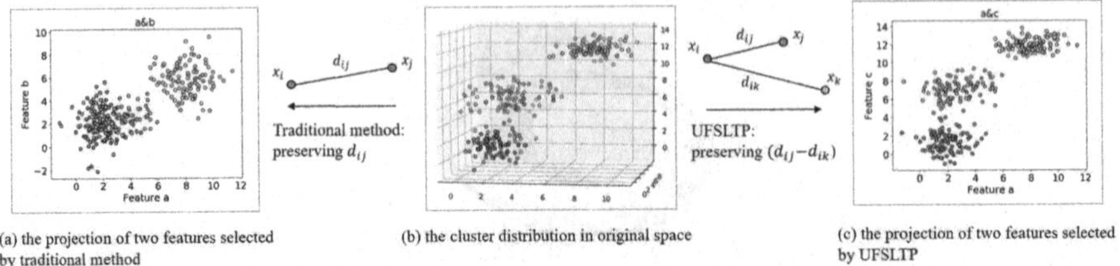

(a) the projection of two features selected by traditional method

(b) the cluster distribution in original space

(c) the projection of two features selected by UFSLTP

Fig. 2. An example of the comparision between UFSLTP and traditional algorithms. Without labels, some traditional methods obtain weights with similar value for [a, b, c], such as [0.9352, 0.9023, 0.9001]. If asked to select two features, they will select features a and b, which is obviously sub-optimal (a). However UFSLTP gets highly differentiated weights as [0.8729, 0.5409, 0.9357], therefore it will select features a and c(c).

Inspired by above observations, we propose to perform unsupervised feature selection via preserving the comparison of distance, rather than the exact value. And we from a concept of total-order relation on datasets to express the comparison between instances in terms of distance. By means of it, we propose an effective method, namely Unsupervised Feature Selection via Local Total-order Preservation (UFSLTP). An example of the contrast between UFSLTP and traditional algorithms is shown in Fig. 2. Due to the inherent nature of machine learning and total-order relation, less features are needed to represent data without adverse effect on performance. The major contributions of this work is summarized as follows:

- We formally define a local total-order relation on datasets, it helps to construct an effective local manifold structure.
- A novel unsupervised feature selection method UFSLTP is proposed. And by virtue of it, less features are needed to represent data without adverse effect on learning performance.
- We propose two efficient methods, namely Adaptive Neighbors Selection (ANS) and Uniform Neighbors Serialization (UNS), to reduce the computational complexity and improve the method performance.
- Comprehensive experiments demonstrate that compared to other methods in clustering, our UFSLTP averagely achieves 31.01% improvement in terms of NMI and 14.44% in terms of Silhouette Coefficient.

2 Related Work

In unsupervised scenarios, various of criteria are utilized to accomplish feature selection. A typical and simple criterion is the Low Variance [15], which eliminates the features having a variance score below the predefined threshold. However, the selected features are not guaranteed to be discriminant for labels [7,20]. From the perspective of this, there is a new criterion attempting to choose a subset of features that can faithfully maintain the intrinsic structure of data

[5,12,19]. The commonly used structures include but not limit to, the global structure [26,29,30], the local manifold structure [3,6,11,27], and discriminative information [18].

Obviously, the quality of selected features relies severely on the effectiveness of structure. To preserve global structure, SPEC [29] employs the spectrum of the graph induced from pairwise samples distance to measure feature relevance. SNFS [26] employs the concept of stochastic neighbors and selects the features best preserving such structure. What's more, SPFS [30] and USFSM [19] also select features from the alike view.

Recently, the methods by preserving local manifold structure have been increasingly popular. Laplacian Score (LS) [6] is computed to reflect the locality preserving power for each feature. Analogously, some typical scheme are proposed and widely applied, such as multi-cluster embedding (MCFS) [3], local linear embedding (LLE) [16], linear preserve projection (LPP) [7], and local tangent space alignment (LTSA) [28].

Based on the view of preserving discriminative information, pseudo-label based algorithms received great attention due to their excellent performance, such as UDFS [27], RSFS [18], SPFS [9] and so on. Without available class labels, such methods predominately attempt to generate pseudo-labels through linear regression or transformation. However, the pseudo-labels in such methods are always inaccurate, and will mislead the results.

As shown in [30], most of the classic feature selection methods proposed so far, can be interpreted from the perspective of similarity preservation. Whereas the similarity or distance measured in high-dimensional space might not be qualitatively meaningful for the curse of dimensionality, which will affect the effectiveness of structure and lead to an unideal feature subset.

In a word, the key challenge centers around constructing an effective geometric structure to accurately present the intrinsic relationship between instances.

3 Problem Formulation

In this section we present the concepts used in this work. Let $X \in \mathbb{R}^{n\times D}$ be the unlabeled dataset where each instance $x_i \in \mathbb{R}^{1\times d}$.

Definition 1. ***Total-order relation.*** *We formulate such property as total-order on X, identified as $x_j \geq_i x_k$: there is always $d_{ij}^T d_{ij} \geq d_{ik}^T d_{ik}$, where x_i, x_j, and x_k denote three different instances from X, and $d_{ij} = x_i - x_j$.*

The total-order relation on dataset is aimed at representing the relationship between data samples in terms of distance, i.e., a data sample is closer to a given sample than another. And the properties of it are as follows:

Corollary 1. ***The properties of total-order relation.*** *For a total-order relation, the following statements are true for all data points x_i, x_j, x_k from X:*
Inversion symmetry: *if $x_j \geq_i x_k$, $x_k \geq_i x_j$, then $x_j =_i x_k$.*
Transitivity: *if $x_j \geq_i x_k$ and $x_k \geq_i x_z$, then $x_j \geq_i x_z$.*
Completeness: *there is always either $x_j \geq_i x_k$ or $x_k \geq_i x_j$.*

In order to complete feature selection, we introduce an indicator vector $w = (w_1, w_2, \ldots, w_D), w_t \in \{0, 1\}$, then x_i changes into $x_i diag(w)$ after feature selection. With the above definitions, the pivotal problem of UFSLTP can be defined as follows. Given a dataset X, the task is to obtain a w by (1) calculating the total-order relation with $diag(w)$ for each instance when before and after feature selection; (2) minimizing the differences of the relation calculated before and after feature selection.

4 The UFSLTP Algorithm

4.1 The Objective Problem

In view of the definitions above, we denote the relative distance before feature selection as $d_{ijk} = d_{ij}^T d_{ij} - d_{ik}^T d_{ik}$, and that after feature selection as $d'_{ijk} = d_{ij}^T diag(w) d_{ij} - d_{ik}^T diag(w) d_{ik}$.

Definition 2. ***Probabilistic Total-order Relation.*** *For a total-order relation $x_j \geq_i x_k$, its probabilistic model is defined as follows:*

$$p_{ijk} = P(x_j \geq_i x_k) = \frac{1}{1 + e^{-d_{ijk}}}. \tag{1}$$

For the sake of more flexibility, we include a scale parameter δ^2 into the probability model p_{ijk}.

$$p_{ijk} = P(x_j \geq_i x_k) = \frac{1}{1 + e^{-\frac{d_{ijk}}{\delta^2}}}. \tag{2}$$

Also, we can get another model q_{ijk} generated from selected features:

$$q_{ijk} = P(x_j \geq_i x_k | w) = \frac{1}{1 + e^{-\frac{d'_{ijk}}{\delta^2}}}. \tag{3}$$

In such case, we get two distributions $p_i = [p_{i12}, p_{i13}, \cdots, p_{i(n-1)n}]$ and $q_i = [q_{i12}, q_{i13}, \cdots, q_{i(n-1)n}]$ for each instance. We try to minimize the differences of the two probability distributions for each x_i, and represent it by KL-divergence between p_i and q_i.

$$\forall i, KL(p_i \| q_i) = \sum_{j \neq i, k \neq i} p_{ijk} \log \frac{p_{ijk}}{q_{ijk}}. \tag{4}$$

Furthermore, we propose the criterion of feature selection: choose the set of features that can minimize the aggregated differences of the probability models calculated before and after feature selection. What's more, we relax the '0/1' constraint on w_t to real values in $[0, 1]$, where $\| \cdot \|_1$ is the L1-norm and λ is the parameter to control the L1 regularization:

$$f(w) = \min_w \sum_{i=1}^{n} \sum_{j,k \neq i} p_{ijk} \log \frac{p_{ijk}}{q_{ijk}} + \lambda \|w\|_1, \ s.t. \ w_t \in [0, 1], \forall t = 1, \ldots, D. \tag{5}$$

4.2 Optimization

Adaptive Neighbors Selection and Uniform Neighbors Serialization. For the efficiency of computation, we formulate local total-order relation, only adding a constrain to Definition 1 that x_j, x_k are all from the neighborhood set N_i of x_i (i.e., $x_j, x_k \in N_i$). Of course, the properties of it are all inherited.

Also, we propose two efficient methods, namely Adaptive Neighbors Selection(ANS) and Uniform Neighbors Serialization(UNS), which help to from an efficient local manifold structure. In the experiment, we obtain the neighbors for each instance by k-nearest neighbors. To ensure the adaptability in various of datasets, here we propose ANS by introducing a proportionality coefficient γ ($k = |N_i| = \gamma n$), the sensitivity of it will be discussed in experiment. UNS is proposed to further improve the performance of UFSLTP. UNS aims to uniformly sort the selected neighbors for each instance with respect to the distance, which gives us a sorted sequence of instances. Under the action of the transitivity of total-order relation, we can just perform the calculation between the adjacent instances in sorted sequence. Therefore, the final objective function is as follows:

$$f(w) = \min_{w} \sum_{i=1}^{n} \sum_{x_j \in N_i, k=j+1}^{|N_i|-1} p_{ijk} \log \frac{p_{ijk}}{q_{ijk}} + \lambda \|w\|_1, \ s.t. \ w_t \in [0,1], \forall t = 1, \ldots, D. \tag{6}$$

L-BFGS-B for UFSLTP. With gradient projection, L-BFGS-B can optimize nonlinear problems with bounds constraint, such as $\min_{x} f(x), \ s.t. \ l \leq x \leq u$ [2].

Let us denote the function in (6) as $\mathcal{L}$, we can get function value f_m and gradient vector g_m by $\frac{\partial \mathcal{L}_i}{\partial w_t}$ for each iteration:

$$f_m = \sum_{i=1}^{n} \sum_{j \neq i, k=j+1}^{|N_i|-1} p_{ijk} \log \frac{p_{ijk}}{q_{ijk}} + \lambda \|w\|_1. \tag{7}$$

$$\frac{\partial \mathcal{L}_i}{\partial w_t} = \sum_{j \neq i, k=j+1}^{|N_i|-1} - \frac{p_{ijk} q_{ijk} [(x_{it} - x_{jt})^2 - (x_{it} - x_{kt})^2]}{\delta^2} \times e^{-\frac{-d_{ijk}}{\delta^2}} + \lambda. \tag{8}$$

In each iteration, we compute the new step size η_m that satisfies:

$$f(w_{m+1}) \leq f(w_m) + \alpha \eta_m g_m^T d_m, \ |g_{m+1}^T| \leq \beta |g_m^T d_m|. \tag{9}$$

where d_m is the search direction, and α, β are parameters valuing 10^{-4} and 0.9 in our code, respectively. And our code terminates when:

$$\|P(w_m - g_m, l, u) - w_m\|_\infty \leq 10^{-5}, where \ P(x, l, u)_i = \begin{cases} l_i & if \ x_i < l_i. \\ x_i & if \ x_i \in [l_i, u_i]. \\ u_i & if \ x_i > u_i. \end{cases} \tag{10}$$

Algorithm 1. UFSLTP

Require: The dataset $X \in R^{n \times D}$, the starting point w, and an integer $r \leq 0$.
Ensure: F_{index}: The index list of the selected features.
1: Initialize $H_0 \leftarrow I$ and $m \leftarrow 0$.
2: Select neighbors for each sample x_i and sort them by the distance to x_i.
3: Compute p_{ijk} (2) for each sample and its neighbors, store the results into a list P.
4: **repeat**
5: Compute q_{ijk} (3) for each sample, store the results into a list Q.
6: Compute f_m using (7).
7: Compute the gradient vector g_m using (8).
8: Compute a search direction $d_m \leftarrow H_m g_m$ using a two-loop recursion.
9: Perform a line search along d_m satisfying the Wolfe conditions (9), subject to the bounds on the problem, to compute a step size η_m.
10: Set $w_{m+1} \leftarrow w_m + \eta_m d_m$.
11: **if** $m \leq r$ **then**
12: Discard the vector pair $\{s_{k-r}, y_{k-r}\}$.
13: **end if**
14: Save $s_m \leftarrow x_{m+1} - x_m$, $y_m \leftarrow g_{m+1} - g_m$ for the two-loop recursion.
15: Set $m \leftarrow m + 1$.
16: **until** the convergence test(10) is satisfied.
17: Sort all D features according to w_t $(t = 1, 2, \ldots, D)$ in descending order and selecting the features with w_t ranking top $\mu\%(\mu = 10, 20, \ldots, 100)$.

As what we can see from Algorithm 1, the details of solving the objective problem for UFSLTP (6) are shown in line 8–15. Line 2 describes ANS and UNS, and line 3–7 record the probability distributions and the results of f_m and g_m for each iteration.

4.3 Theoretical Analysis on Convergence and Complexity

The UFSLTP is solved by L-BFGS-B with Wolfe search, which has been proved the global convergence by Liu and Nocedal [10]. Besides, the experiments show its fast convergence, the iterations is often less than 25.

It is noteworthy that there are 6 portions in Algorithm 1, and the computational cost for each step is as follows:

- ANS and UNS: Considering k neighbors for each data, $O(n^2k)$ is needed.
- Computing probability distribution p: $O(2nk)$.
- Computing q, f, and g: $O(2nk) + O(2nkD)$ in each iteration.
- Two-loop recursion: $O(nl)$.
- Updating vector w: $O(D + 2nkD)$.
- Selecting top $\mu\%$ features: $O(DlogD)$.

Supposing the number of loop is c, while k, c and l are much less than n and D, then the total computational cost for our UFSLTP algorithm is: $O(n^2k + 2nk + 2cnk + 2cnkD + cnl + cD + 2ckD + DlogD) \sim O(n^2 + nD + DlogD)$.

Table 1. The details of the experimental datasets.

Datasets		No. of instance	No. of features	No. of classes
UCI datasets	SPECTF	267	44	2
	vehicle	846	18	4
	segmentation	2310	19	7
	optdigits	3823	64	10
	Forgs	7195	22	60
Large datasets	colon	62	2000	2
	nci9	60	9712	9
	Yale	165	1024	15

5 Experiments

5.1 Experimental Settings

We carry out the experiments on 8 real-world datasets. As shown in Table 1, there are 5 public standard real datasets taken from the UCI machine learning repository[2], and 3 datasets from ASU feature selection repository[3].

We compare UFSLTP with the following unsupervised feature selection algorithms. The contrast against them was made because they are respectively a typical representation of the algorithms designed from different standpoints.

- ***All-Fea:*** All features of the datasets are employed for clustering.
- ***LaplacianScore(LS):*** Selects features by local manifold structure [6].
- ***Multi-Cluster Feature Selection(MCFS):*** Selects features based on preserving the multi-cluster structure of data [3].
- ***Unsupervised Discriminative Feature Selection(UDFS):*** Selects features by preserving the structure based on discriminative information [27].
- ***Stochastic Neighbors-preserving Feature Selection(SNFS):*** Selects feature by preserving the structure based on stochastic neighbors [26].
- ***Unsupervised Personalized Feature Selection(UPFS):*** Selects features by preserving the personalized structure of original data [9].

For LS, MCFS and UDFS, we fix k, which specifies the size of neighborhood, at 5 for all datasets. To fairly compare different algorithms, we tune regularization parameters from $\{10^{-6}, 10^{-3}, 1, 10^3, 10^6\}$ for MCFS and UDFS. Because the feature numbers of different datasets are various, we set the number of selected features as $n \times \{10\%, 20\%, \ldots, 100\%\}$, with n denoting the total number of instances. We report the best results of the methods with different parameters.

Currently, there is no standard measure for unsupervised feature selection, hence we follow the typical ways to perform the evaluation: in terms of the

[2] http://archive.ics.uci.edu/ml/datasets.html.
[3] http://featureselection.asu.edu/datasets.php.

Table 2. Clustering results (NMI/SC) of different algorithms over 8 datasets.

Datasets	All-Fea	LS	MCFS	UDFS	SNFS	UPFS	UFSLTP
SPECTF	0.247	0.109	0.138	0.156	0.213	0.142	**0.243**
	0.454	0.411	0.478	0.512	0.467	0.463	**0.513**
vehicle	0.185	0.291	0.289	**0.347**	0.299	0.319	0.346
	0.442	0.395	0.503	0.445	0.418	0.362	**0.511**
segmentation	0.675	0.552	0.393	0.442	0.442	0.488	**0.556**
	0.429	0.461	0.488	0.400	0.380	0.405	**0.513**
optdigits	0.747	0.596	0.557	0.510	0.583	0.599	**0.649**
	0.183	0.205	0.190	0.208	0.210	0.167	**0.212**
Forgs	0.740	0.681	0.643	0.637	0.611	0.634	**0.684**
	0.234	0.226	0.215	0.197	0.228	0.176	**0.231**
colon	0.006	0.001	0.004	0.003	0.006	0.005	**0.008**
	0.231	0.225	0.230	0.234	**0.242**	0.219	0.237
Yale	0.493	0.463	0.480	0.470	0.516	0.514	**0.581**
	0.104	0.104	0.108	0.111	0.113	0.111	**0.141**
nci9	0.426	0.428	0.437	0.436	0.428	0.438	**0.462**
	0.050	0.052	0.052	0.044	0.052	0.042	**0.053**
Average	0.439	0.391	0.367	0.375	0.387	0.387	**0.441**
	0.266	0.0.260	0.283	0.269	0.264	0.243	**0.301**
Average improvement by UFSLTP	10.53%	75.00%	28.03%	33.61%	17.34%	21.52%	***31.01%***
	13.37%	14.24%	8.57%	13.90%	11.75%	24.78%	***14.44%***

clustering performance by Normalized Mutual Information(NMI) and Silhouette Coefficient(SC). The value of them range from 0 to 1, they reflect the clustering performance in terms of internal and external view, and a better features subset gets a larger value of NMI or SC. We use K-means as the clustering method, and repeat it 20 times with random initializations, the average results are reported.

5.2 Performance Evaluation

To evaluate UFSLTP in terms of clustering, the methods mentioned above are applied over all datasets. The average clustering results in terms of NMI and SC are shown in Table 2. In the last row, the value shows how much the performance is averagely improved by using UFSLTP compared with this method, it is calculated as follow:

$$100\% \times \frac{p\_v_{UFSLTP} - p\_v_{other}}{p\_v_{other}}. \tag{11}$$

where p_v_{UFSLTP} is the performance of UFSLTP, and p_v_{other} is the performance of the corresponding method.

And the values in italics show the averagely improved performance compared with all other baseline methods. As what we can see from it, the proposed UFSLTP outperforms other methods, achieving 31.01% improvement in terms of NMI and 14.44% in terms of Silhouette Coefficient.

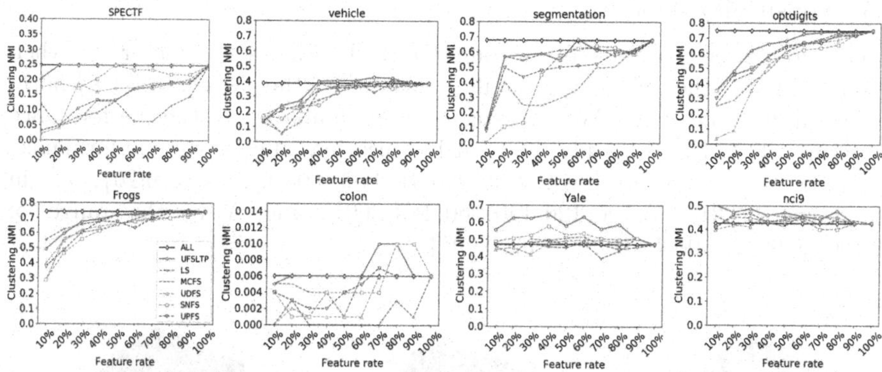

Fig. 3. Clustering NMI with various percentages of ranked features over 8 datasets.

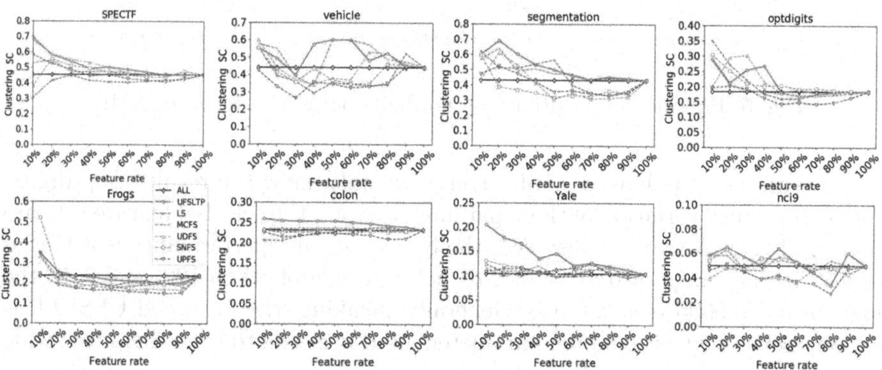

Fig. 4. Clustering SC with various percentages of ranked features over 8 datasets.

Furthermore, in order to check whether UFSLTP can rank and select the features considered as relevant in terms of clustering, we collect the results with different feature numbers, and present them in Figs. 3 and 4. From the data shown in them, the proposed UFSLTP always gets a better or stable value with less features than other methods, and the best percentage is between 20% and 60%. When the percentage is larger than that, the performance changes slightly or even decreases.

Considering the information in Table 2 and the figures, we can obtain that UFSLTP gets better clustering results with less features than other methods. The improvements can be attributed to the inherent nature of the total-order relation, which only restricts the comparison of pairwise samples distance.

5.3 Sensitivity Analysis

There are three parameters in our UFSLTP, the scale factor γ when perform ANS, the δ^2 in probability mapping, the λ controls L_1-norm for regularization item. We investigate their impact on the performance in terms of NMI. To study how their variation affects the performance, we vary γ in the range of $\{0.005, 0.01, 0.02, 0.05, 0.10, 0.15, 0.20\}$, δ^2 in the range of $\{60, 80, 100, 120, 140, 160, 180, 200\}$, and λ in the range of $\{0.0001, 0.0002, 0.0005, 0.001, 0.002, 0.005\}$.

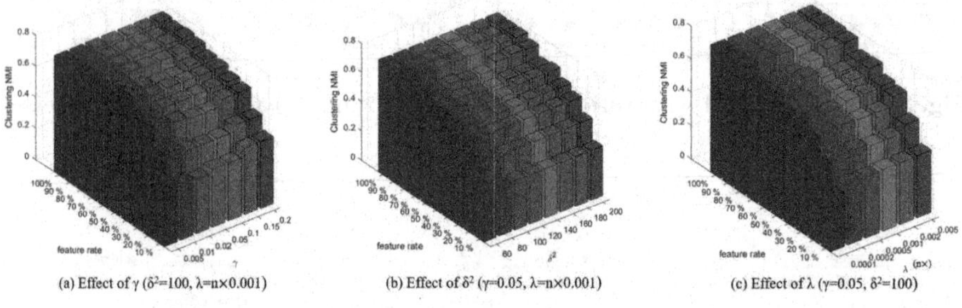

(a) Effect of γ (δ^2=100, λ=n×0.001) (b) Effect of δ^2 (γ=0.05, λ=n×0.001) (c) Effect of λ (γ=0.05, δ^2=100)

Fig. 5. Parameters sensitivity on optdigits dataset in terms of NMI.

Since all datasets have a similar trend, we only show the result of optdigits. The performance variation of these parameters w.r.t. the selected feature rate are shown in Fig. 5. As can be observed, the best clustering performance is achieved when γ in the range of 0.01 to 0.1, δ^2 in the range of 80 to 120, and λ in the range of $n \times 0.0005$ to $n \times 0.005$. Generally speaking, the proposed UFSLTP is not very sensitive to the model parameters, and it is safe to tune them in a wide range, which is appealing in practice.

6 Conclusion

In this paper, we propose a new unsupervised feature selection method UFSLTP. It aims to preserve a local structure characterized by a total-order relation, which uses the comparison of the pairwise samples distance rather than the exact value. Due to the inherent nature of machine learning and total-order relation, less features are needed to represent data without adverse effecting on performance. In comparison with six baseline approaches, the results of experiments on real-world datasets demonstrate that UFSLTP achieves better performance with less features than other methods in terms of clustering and supervised classification.

Acknowledgment. This work is supported by the National Key Research and Development Program of China(2016YFB1000101), the National Natural Science Foundation of China(Grant No.61379052), the Science Foundation of Ministry of Education of China(Grant No.2018A02002), the Natural Science Foundation for Distinguished Young Scholars of Hunan Province(Grant No.14JJ1026).

References

1. Abdi, H., Williams, L.J.: Principal component analysis. Wiley Interdisc. Rev. Comput. Stat. **2**(4), 433–459 (2010). https://doi.org/10.1002/wics.101
2. Byrd, R.H., Lu, P., Nocedal, J., Zhu, C.: A limited memory algorithm for bound constrained optimization. SIAM J. Sci. Comput. **16**(5), 1190–1208 (1995). https://doi.org/10.2172/204262
3. Cai, D., Zhang, C., He, X.: Unsupervised feature selection for multi-cluster data. In: Proceedings of the 16th ACM SIGKDD International Conference on Knowledge Discovery and Data Mining, pp. 333–342. ACM (2010). https://doi.org/10.1145/1835804.1835848
4. Chen, C.C., Juan, H.H., Tsai, M.Y., Lu, H.H.S.: Unsupervised learning and pattern recognition of biological data structures with density functional theory and machine learning. Sci. Rep. **8**(1), 557 (2018). https://doi.org/10.1038/s41598-017-18931-5
5. Du, L., Shen, Y.D.: Unsupervised feature selection with adaptive structure learning. In: Proceedings of the 21th ACM SIGKDD International Conference on Knowledge Discovery and Data Mining, pp. 209–218. ACM (2015). https://doi.org/10.1145/2783258.2783345
6. He, X., Cai, D., Niyogi, P.: Laplacian score for feature selection. In: Advances in Neural Information Processing Systems, pp. 507–514 (2006)
7. He, X., Niyogi, P.: Locality preserving projections. In: Advances in Neural Information Processing Systems, pp. 153–160 (2004). https://doi.org/10.1016/j.patcog.2011.05.014
8. Li, J., et al.: Feature selection: a data perspective. ACM Comput. Surv. (CSUR) **50**(6), 94 (2018). https://doi.org/10.1145/3136625
9. Li, J., Wu, L., Dani, H., Liu, H.: Unsupervised personalized feature selection. In: Thirty-Second AAAI Conference on Artificial Intelligence (2018)
10. Liu, D.C., Nocedal, J.: On the limited memory BFGS method for large scale optimization. Math. Program. **45**(1–3), 503–528 (1989). https://doi.org/10.1007/bf01589116
11. Liu, X., Wang, L., Zhang, J., Yin, J., Liu, H.: Global and local structure preservation for feature selection. IEEE Trans. Neural Netw. Learn. Syst. **25**(6), 1083–1095 (2013). https://doi.org/10.1109/tnnls.2013.2287275
12. Luo, M., Nie, F., Chang, X., Yang, Y., Hauptmann, A.G., Zheng, Q.: Adaptive unsupervised feature selection with structure regularization. IEEE Trans. Neural Netw. Learn. Syst. **29**(4), 944–956 (2017). https://doi.org/10.1109/tnnls.2017.2650978
13. Maaten, L.V.D., Hinton, G.: Visualizing data using t-SNE. J. Mach. Learn. Res. **9**, 2579–2605 (2008)
14. Parsons, L., Haque, E., Liu, H.: Subspace clustering for high dimensional data: a review. ACM SIGKDD Explor. Newsl. **6**(1), 90–105 (2004). https://doi.org/10.1145/1007730.1007731

15. Pedregosa, F., Varoquaux, G., Gramfort, A., et al.: Scikit-learn: machine learning in python. J. Mach. Learn. Res. **12**, 2825–2830 (2011). https://doi.org/10.1524/auto.2011.0951
16. Roweis, S.T., Saul, L.K.: Nonlinear dimensionality reduction by locally linear embedding. Science **290**(5500), 2323–2326 (2000). https://doi.org/10.1126/science.290.5500.2323
17. Sammut, C., Webb, G.I.: Encyclopedia of Machine Learning. Springer, Heidelberg (2011). https://doi.org/10.1007/978-0-387-30164-8
18. Shi, L., Du, L., Shen, Y.D.: Robust spectral learning for unsupervised feature selection. In: 2014 IEEE International Conference on Data Mining, pp. 977–982. IEEE (2014). https://doi.org/10.1109/icdm.2014.58
19. Solorio-Fernández, S., Martínez-Trinidad, J.F., Carrasco-Ochoa, J.A.: A new unsupervised spectral feature selection method for mixed data: a filter approach. Pattern Recogn. **72**, 314–326 (2017). https://doi.org/10.1016/j.patcog.2017.07.020
20. Wang, D., Nie, F., Huang, H.: Unsupervised feature selection via unified trace ratio formulation and K-means clustering (TRACK). In: Calders, T., Esposito, F., Hüllermeier, E., Meo, R. (eds.) ECML PKDD 2014. LNCS (LNAI), vol. 8726, pp. 306–321. Springer, Heidelberg (2014). https://doi.org/10.1007/978-3-662-44845-8_20
21. Wang, H., Shi, P., Zhang, Y.: Jointcloud: a cross-cloud cooperation architecture for integrated internet service customization. In: 2017 IEEE 37th International Conference on Distributed Computing Systems (ICDCS), pp. 1846–1855. IEEE (2017). https://doi.org/10.1109/icdcs.2017.237
22. Wang, Y., Li, S.: Research and performance evaluation of data replication technology in distributed storage systems. Comput. Math. Appl. **51**(11), 1625–1632 (2006). https://doi.org/10.1016/j.camwa.2006.05.002
23. Wang, Y., Li, X., Li, X., Wang, Y.: A survey of queries over uncertain data. Knowl. Inf. Syst. **37**(3), 485–530 (2013). https://doi.org/10.1007/s10115-013-0638-6
24. Wang, Y., Ma, X.: A general scalable and elastic content-based publish/subscribe service. IEEE Trans. Parallel Distrib. Syst. **26**(8), 2100–2113 (2014). https://doi.org/10.1109/tpds.2014.2346759
25. Wang, Y., Pei, X., Ma, X., Xu, F.: Ta-update: an adaptive update scheme with tree-structured transmission in erasure-coded storage systems. IEEE Trans. Parallel Distrib. Syst. **29**(8), 1893–1906 (2017). https://doi.org/10.1109/tpds.2017.2717981
26. Wei, X., Philip, S.Y.: Unsupervised feature selection by preserving stochastic neighbors. In: Artificial Intelligence and Statistics, pp. 995–1003 (2016). https://doi.org/10.1145/2694859.2694864
27. Yang, Y., Shen, H.T., Ma, Z., Huang, Z., Zhou, X.: L2, 1-norm regularized discriminative feature selection for unsupervised. In: Twenty-Second International Joint Conference on Artificial Intelligence (2011). https://doi.org/10.5591/978-1-57735-516-8/IJCAI11-267
28. Zhang, T., Yang, J., Zhao, D., Ge, X.: Linear local tangent space alignment and application to face recognition. Neurocomputing **70**(7–9), 1547–1553 (2007). https://doi.org/10.1016/j.neucom.2006.11.007
29. Zhao, Z., Liu, H.: Spectral feature selection for supervised and unsupervised learning. In: Proceedings of the 24th International Conference on Machine learning, pp. 1151–1157. ACM (2007). https://doi.org/10.1145/1273496.1273641
30. Zhao, Z., Wang, L., Liu, H., Ye, J.: On similarity preserving feature selection. IEEE Trans. Knowl. Data Eng. **25**(3), 619–632 (2011). https://doi.org/10.1109/tkde.2011.222

Discrete Stochastic Search and Its Application to Feature-Selection for Deep Relational Machines

Tirtharaj Dash(✉), Ashwin Srinivasan(✉), Ramprasad S. Joshi, and A. Baskar

Department of Computer Science and Information Systems, BITS Pilani, K. K. Birla Goa Campus, Goa 403726, India
{tirtharaj,ashwin,rsj,abaskar}@goa.bits-pilani.ac.in

Abstract. We use a model for discrete stochastic search in which one or more objects ("targets") are to be found by a search over n locations ("boxes"), where n is infinitely large. Each box has some probability that it contains a target, resulting in a distribution H over boxes. We model the search for the targets as a stochastic procedure that draws boxes using some distribution S. We derive first a general expression on the expected number of misses $\mathrm{E}[Z]$ made by the search procedure in terms of H and S. We then obtain an expression for an optimal distribution S^* to minimise $\mathrm{E}[Z]$. This results in a relation between: the entropy of H and the KL-divergence between H and S^*. This result induces a 2-partitions over the boxes consisting of those boxes with H probability greater than $\frac{1}{n}$ and the rest. We use this result to devise a stochastic search procedure for the practical situation when H is unknown. We present results from simulations that agree with theoretical predictions; and demonstrate that the expected misses by the optimal seeker decreases as the entropy of H decreases, with a maximum obtained for uniform H. Finally, we demonstrate applications of this stochastic search procedure with a coarse assumption about H. The theoretical results and the procedure are applicable to stochastic search over any aspect of machine learning that involves a discrete search-space: for example, choice over features, structures or discretized parameter-selection. In this work, the procedure is used to select features for Deep Relational Machines (DRMs) which are Deep Neural Networks (DNNs) defined in terms of domain-specific knowledge and built with features selected from large, potentially infinite-attribute space. Empirical results obtained across over 70 real-world datasets show that using the stochastic search procedure results in significantly better performances than the state-of-the-art.

Keywords: Deep Neural Network · Inductive Logic Programming · Relational learning · Stochastic search · Infinite-attribute space

I. V. Tetko et al. (Eds.): ICANN 2019, LNCS 11728, pp. 29–45, 2019.
https://doi.org/10.1007/978-3-030-30484-3_3

1 Introduction

Our interest in this paper is to obtain a distributional understanding of discrete stochastic search. By this, we mean the following: (a) The purpose of a discrete search is to find one or more objects (targets) that are in one or more of n locations (boxes). The object-locations are selected using some probability distribution over the boxes (we will call this H); and (b) The search procedure uses a distribution over the boxes (S) to select boxes, and determine if a target is in the box. We would like to provide answers to the questions like these: (1) Does minimising the number of false selections ("misses") by the search procedure necessarily mean that $H = S$?; (2) If the answer to (1) is "no", are some H's easier than others, for a search procedure seeking to minimise misses?; and (3) If the answer to (2) is "yes", how can a search procedure use knowledge of H (either complete, partial, or aggregate) to minimise misses?

Motivation for exploring this view of stochastic search is due to our interest in machine learning algorithms searching potentially infinite discrete spaces. These algorithms can be applied for solving problems concerning natural phenomena. One example of this kind of problem is prediction of carcinogenicity of chemicals [9] which forms the application area in this paper. In such cases, it is conceptually useful to think of targets being distributed according to some non-uniform distribution H. This machine learning setting of searching for targets in natural phenomena is different to the adversarial setting of a hide-and-seek game in which the purpose of the hider is to make search as difficult as possible for the seeker. It will be seen below that this corresponds to the special case of H being a uniform distribution, which results in the maximal number of misses by the optimal S. Nevertheless, in this paper, we will still refer to H as a "hider distribution", and to S as a "seeker distribution", with the caveat that this will not necessarily imply an adversarial setting.

Distributional models for search are of interest to machine learning for at least three reasons. First, when the search space is potentially infinite [3], the only reasonable techniques for searching will involve some form of sampling from known or unknown distributions. Second, practical machine learning often deals with good, rather than optimal solutions. This means that there may be more than one possible target, and finding any one of them should suffice. We can characterise what this means in terms of H, and how will this affect the choice of S. Third, in applications the boxes need not be independent. If this translates to some local smoothness assumptions about the locations of good solutions, then it can be used by the search procedure when devising an S. Based on the above, our contributions can be outlined as follows: (1) we develop a relation between H and S^*. Further, we address theoretically and experimentally the cases arising from non-uniform H's and from many good solutions; (2) The results are used to develop a sampling procedure for large discrete search spaces; (3) The sampling procedure is then used to select features for Deep Relational Machines (DRMs). DRMs are Deep Neural Networks (DNNs) defined in terms of domain-specific knowledge and are built with features selected from large, potentially infinite-attribute space [5,14]; (4) We empirically test the performance of DRM across over 70 real-world datasets. The results suggest that using the stochastic search procedure results in significantly better performances than the state-of-the-art.

The rest of the paper is organised as follows. Section 2 describes discrete search with a stationary H. In Sect. 2.1 we show how, if H is known completely, the optimal S need not necessarily be identical to H. In Sect. 2.2 we use the insights gained from previous section to devise a simple sampling strategy when H is not known but some meta-information about H is available. Section 3 contains results from simulations, supporting the theoretical results and an application of the "unknown H" situation to the problem of selecting relational features from a potentially infinite-attribute space for a Deep Neural Network (DNN). We evaluate the stochastic feature selection on over 70 datasets obtained from real-world biochemical problems. Section 4 concludes the paper. The proofs can be found in the Appendix.

2 A Distributional Model of Discrete Search

We start with a distributional model that is consistent with the description of the discrete search hide-and-seek game in [16] and [18]. We start with n boxes and one ball. The ball is thrown onto the boxes (and it must fall into one of them) with some probability. For us, this gives rise to the "hider distribution" H on the boxes. A stochastic search procedure is a sampling strategy that draws boxes at random using some "seeker distribution" S, until it succeeds eventually after m trials to find the ball. A miss can be understood as an event of selecting (opening) a box and not finding the ball. Here we will assume that if the ball is in a box opened, then it will be detected. There is a cost associated with this search, monotonic in the number of misses m. It is natural to expect that the expected cost to find the ball will depend on whether or not H is known. We sharpen this intuition using the ideal setting when H is known completely to the stochastic search procedure.

2.1 Hider Distribution Known

We will assume that if the ball is in a box, then it will be found. As with a generalised form of the hide-and-seek game, this can be changed to allow finding the ball with some probability even if it is there. Let Z be a random variable for number for misses by the search before finding the ball. We want to find the expected number of misses $\mathrm{E}[Z]|_{H,S}$.

Lemma 1 (Expected number of misses with a single ball). *Let H and S be discrete distributions denoted by $H = (h_1, h_2, \ldots, h_n)$, $S = (s_1, s_2, \ldots, s_n)$. Let $h_i, s_i > 0$ for $i = 1$ to n. Let the ball be in one of n boxes according to the hider distribution H. The search attempts to find the ball using the seeker distribution S. Then, the expected number of misses is:*

$$\mathrm{E}[Z]|_{H,S} \;=\; \mathrm{E}[Z] = \sum_{k=1}^{n} \frac{h_k}{s_k} - 1 \tag{1}$$

We note that $\mathrm{E}[Z]|_{H,S}$ is $n-1$ when $H = S$ or when S is a uniform distribution. Also, we state here that $\mathrm{E}[Z]|_{H,S} \geq (n-1)$ when H is uniform (see the appendix for a proof).

A generalisation of this expression can be derived when there is more than one ball and each box can contain not more than one ball. The expected number of misses is lower if it is sufficient for the search to find any one of the balls.

Lemma 2 (Expected number of misses with K balls). *Let H and S be discrete distributions as in Lemma 1. Let there be K balls in K of the n boxes according to the hider distribution H. The search attempts to find at least one ball using the seeker distribution S. Then, the expected number of misses is:*

$$\mathrm{E}[Z]|_{H,S} = \sum_{i,\sigma(i)\in \mathrm{P}(n,K)} \left(\prod_{k=1}^{K} h^{(k)}_{\sigma(i)}\right)\left\{\frac{1}{\left(\sum_{k=1}^{K} s^{(k)}_{\sigma(i)}\right)} - 1\right\},$$

where, $\sigma(i)$ is ith position in the permutation of $1, \ldots, n$.

All the results above are derived assuming sampling with replacement. The first reason for this assumption is simply mathematical convenience. Sampling without replacement, when all boxes have equal probability is governed by the hypergeometric distribution, yielding $(n-1)/2$ misses on average.

However, with non-uniform hider distributions, the appropriate seeker distribution is the more complex Wallenius non-central hypergeometric distribution, which is difficult to solve analytically (but numerical solutions are tractable in some cases: see [6]). Secondly, it can be argued that for real problems involving multiple rounds of experimentation, sampling with replacement is in fact the correct model, since hypotheses discarded in one experiment, may nevertheless become viable options on later ones. Thirdly, it is a well-known practicality, that the differences do not matter if n is large. These caveats notwithstanding, the results in the next section can be seen as upper-bounds on those obtainable when sampling is done without replacement (even with a non-central hypergeometric distribution).

The following result is a consequence of the fact that H and S are distributions:

Theorem 1 (Expected misses is convex). *Given a distribution H and a positive distribution S, $\mathrm{E}[Z]|_{H,S} = \sum_i \frac{h_i}{s_i} - 1$ is convex.*

It follows that there is an optimal seeker distribution S^* such that Eq. (1) is minimised.

Theorem 2 (Optimal S given H). *Let H be a discrete distribution as in Lemma 1. The optimal seeker distribution $S^* = (s_1^*, s_2^*, \ldots, s_n^*)$ where $s_i^* = \frac{\sqrt{h_i}}{\sum_{j=1}^{n}\sqrt{h_j}}$, $1 \leq i \leq n$.*

The following result follows for the special case of a uniform H (that is, H is $Unif(1, n)$):

Corollary 1 (S^* for Uniform H). *If $H \sim Unif(1,n)$ then $S^* \sim Unif(1,n)$ and $E[Z]|_{H,S^*} = n-1$.*

We note that this result is consistent with those presented in [16,18] for the hide-and-search game, where the adversarial nature of the game requires the hider to select a uniform distribution to maximise the expected misses by a seeker.

If H distribution is non-uniform, then we note the following.

Corollary 2. *Given a non-uniform hider distribution H and a corresponding optimal seeker distribution S^*,*

$$E[Z] = \sum_{i=1}^{n} \frac{h_i}{s_i^*} - 1 = \sum_{i=1}^{n} \left(\sqrt{h_i}\right)^2 - 1$$

With non-uniform H, E[Z] can get substantially lower than the $n-1$ value obtained for uniform H. For non-uniform H, we find the following.

Theorem 3. *Let H and S^* be defined as in Theorem 2. Let $KLD(U||V)$ denote the Kullback-Liebler divergence between distributions U and V. Then, $E[Z]|_{H,S^*} = 2^{2KLD(H||S^*)+Entropy(H)} - 1$.*

Based on the earlier result for uniform H, it is evident if H is uniform, entropy of H will be a maximum the KL-divergence between H and S^* will be 0. As entropy of H decreases (H is non-uniform), although the KLD term increases, the overall expression has a minimum for $S = S^*$. We provide some further intuition about the optimal seeker S^* for the case of a non-uniform H. In this case, some boxes will have higher than uniform probability of containing the target, and some will have less than uniform probability. In order to minimise misses, the seeker needs also to look at unlikely boxes. Specifically, an unlikely box has to be selected with higher probability than that used by H to avoid many misses if the box contains the target. In general therefore, the optimal S distribution needs to have higher probabilities on unlikely boxes than the hider; and to compensate, lower probabilities on the likely boxes. This pushes the seeker closer to the uniform. distribution, and therefore usually with higher entropy than H.

If, on the other hand, H is uniform then the seeker simply cannot use any higher entropy distribution and has no choice but to follow the hider's uniform distribution.

All these results require H to be known. In practice, the question is what can be done if H is not known. We consider this in the following section for the case of non-uniform H.

2.2 Unknown Hider Distribution

In almost all practical situations, we do not know H. What can be done in such cases? Based on the results of the previous section, we will begin by assuming, for efficient target identification, that H is non-uniform. We define a 2-partition of the locations based on H as follows: the U partition contains locations that have probability greater than uniform probability ($> \frac{1}{n}$) and the rest forms the V partition. We assume further:

- Any target location has probability greater than $\frac{1}{n}$. All targets are to be found in the "target partition". W.l.o.g. we can take the target partition to be U; and
- The size of the target partition is known to be the proportion p ($0 < p < 1$)

The sample size which with high probability will result in boxes from the target partition can be calculated.

Lemma 3 (Samples from the target partition). *Let H be a distribution over a set X. Let U denote the set of boxes $\{x : x \in X \text{ and } h(x) > 1/n\}$ and $L = X - U$. Without loss of generality, let the target(s) be in U, and let $p = |U|/|X|$ (> 0). Then a sample of size:*

$$s \geq \frac{\log(1-\alpha)}{\log(1-p)}$$

will contain at least one element of U with probability $\geq \alpha$.

(This use of s should not be confused with the search-distribution probability s_i for a location i). With the assumptions above, it is evident that the higher the number of targets, the greater the value of p, and the smaller the sample size s. That is, with many possible locations containing targets, it is easier to find at least one target location.[1] Of course, sampling only guarantees with high probability that there will be at least one box from the target partition. Thus, not all boxes in the sample will be from the target partition; and of those, not all may contain a target.

A procedure that uses the sample to search for the targets is in Procedure 1. The procedure takes as inputs: X, a set of boxes; p (> 0), the proportion of boxes in the target's partition; α, lower bound on probability of finding an element from the target's partition; t, an upper bound on the iterations of the sampler; function $Hider : X \to \{TRUE, FALSE\}$, s.t. $Hider(x)$ is $TRUE$ for box x if a ball is in box x; and $FALSE$ otherwise; and returns a box with a target and the number of misses.
Some issues with this procedure are apparent immediately:

- Since sampling is done with replacement, in the worst case, the procedure can end up drawing many more than $n-1$ samples before finding the hider, unless the bound t stops the procedure before this happens;

[1] We note that a similar argument is used in [7] to identify possibly good solutions in discrete event simulations; and is proposed for use in Inductive Logic Programming (ILP) in [17]. Both do not explicitly relate this to a distribution model, as is done here.

Procedure 1. The Sampling Procedure

```
procedure SAMPLER(X, p, α, t, Hider)
    done ← FALSE
    m ← 0
    s ← ⌈log(1−α)/log(1−p)⌉
    while ¬done do
        Sample ← Draw(Unif, s, X)        ▷ Draw a sample of s boxes from X
        X′ ← {x : x ∈ Sample and Hider(x) = TRUE}
        if X′ ≠ ∅ or m > t then
            done ← TRUE
        m ← m + 1
    x ← Draw(Unif, 1, X′)
    return (x, m)
```

- If $Hider(x) = FALSE$ for all $x \in B$ (that is, there is no ball), then the procedure will not terminate, until the bound t is reached; and
- This procedure does not take into account boxes already sampled (that is, boxes are drawn independently of each other).

Obvious corrections for the first two issues are either to bound the maximum rounds of sampling allowed; or to use sampling without replacement (in experiments in this paper, we adopt the former. One way in which t could be assigned is as follows. Let β denote a lower bound on the probability of obtaining a hider in t trials, each with sample s determined by p and α (that is, the probability of identifying a box with a ball is at least α). It is not hard to derive that if $t \geq \frac{\log(1-\beta)}{\log(1-\alpha)}$ then the probability of identifying a box with a ball in t trials will be at least β. The number of boxes after t rounds of sampling is clearly $s \times t$. To address the third issue, sampling can be made conditional on boxes already obtained (that is, adopting a Markov model): we do not pursue this further in this paper.

The procedure also assumes that there can be more than one box $x \in X$ with $Hider(x) = TRUE$, and that it is sufficient to find any one of these boxes. This assumption about multiple hiders often makes sense in practice, when we are happy with near-optimal solutions.

3 Empirical Evaluation

3.1 Simulations

The results from simulations are as follows:

Known hider distribution. Results of simulations with known H distributions are in Fig. 1. These results confirm the following:

1. The seeker distribution obtained in Theorem 2 have higher entropy than the hider distribution (as expected).

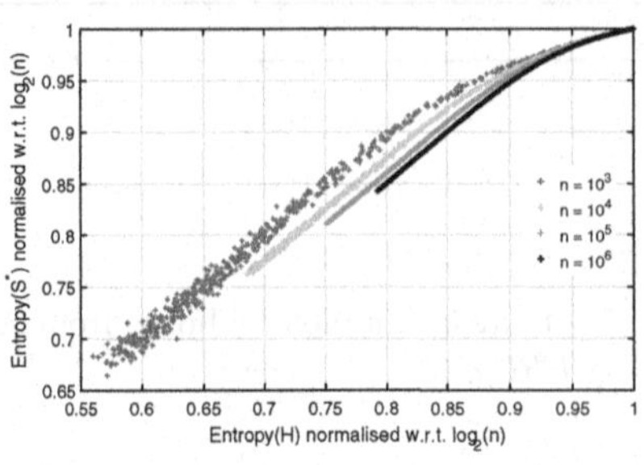

(a) Hider Entropy vs. Seeker Entropy

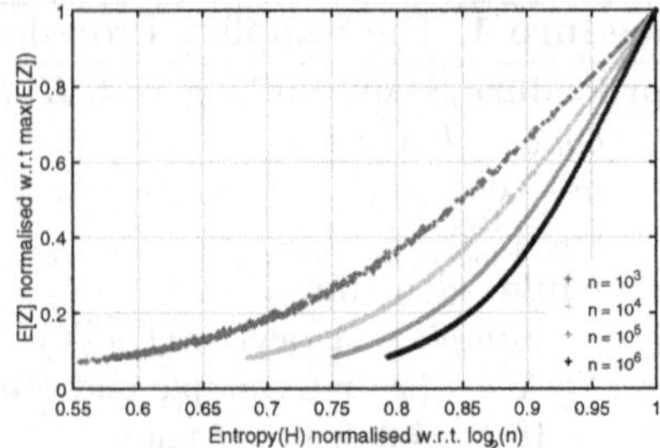

(b) Hider Entropy vs. Expected Seeker Misses

Fig. 1. Known hider distribution

2. For hider distributions other than the uniform, it is possible to obtain seeker distributions that make fewer expected misses than $n-1$ (which is the value obtained if the seeker knows the hider's distribution). Further, as predicted theoretically, this expected value is lower as n increases.
3. For low-entropy hiders, it is possible to obtain substantially low numbers of expected misses with the distribution obtained in Theorem 2.

Unknown hider distribution. Figure 2 shows the expected number of misses observed using Procedure 1 for varying values of n ($|X|$) and p, the proportion of boxes in the H's target partition. In all cases, $\alpha = 0.95$ (that is, we want to be 95% sure of obtaining at least one box from the H's target partition on each iteration of sampling in Procedure 1). We note the following:

1. The number of misses increases as the number of hidden objects (balls) decreases. This is as expected.
2. The expected number of misses: (a) is substantially less than the worst case of $n-1$; (b) decreases as p increases; and (c) decreases as n increases. The last finding may seem surprising in the first instance. However, we note that the sample size in Procedure 1 does not change with n, but the actual number of balls for a given abscissa is much larger for larger values n. A simple pigeonhole argument therefore suffices to explain the empirical result of finding balls quicker as n increases. This behaviour is also consistent with the theoretical case predicted when the hider is known (and observed empirically in Fig. 1).

3.2 Real-World Data

In this section we focus on real-world applications of the "unknown H" problem. Specifically, we will focus on problems arising in the area of structure-activity prediction. In this, data are in the form of arbitrary-sized graphs representing small molecules. The vertices in the graph are atoms, and the edges represent bonds, labelled as single, double, aromatic and so on. Each molecule is

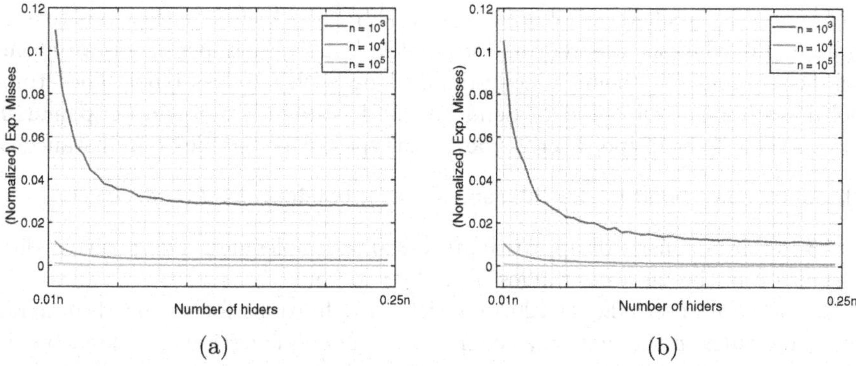

(a)

(b)

Fig. 2. Unknown hider distribution, with more than 1 hider: (a) $p = 0.1$; and (b) $p = 0.25$. That is, the proportion of boxes in the H's partition of the step-approximation is known to be 10% and 25% of the total number of boxes n. The number of balls is varied from 1% of n to 25% of n (X-axis). The expected number of misses is on the Y-axis.

labelled as belonging to one of several classes (for example *carcinogenic* or *non-carcinogenic*). Also available is a substantial body of bio-chemical knowledge in the form of definition of functional groups, ring structures, and so on. Given the graph-structure of a molecule, bio-chemical knowledge allows us to infer further relations that hold for the molecule. For example, it may follow that the molecule as several benzene rings, and that some of these were fused, and so on. Relational "features" are molecular fingerprints defined in terms of what is known biochemically. For example, one such fingerprint might be: *a molecule* m *has a 7-membered ring* r_1; *and* m *has a lactone ring* r_2; *and* r_1 *and* r_2 *are connected*. The area of Inductive Logic Programming (ILP [15]) has been used with success to discover features like these, given data and generic definitions of concepts like lactone rings (see for example [10]).

Deep Relational Machines, or DRMs ([14]), use relational features such as the ones above, as inputs to a deep neural network. While this form of neuro-symbolic modelling combines the power of deep learning and relational modelling, a difficulty is that the number of relational features given sufficiently complex domain knowledge can be very large (in principle, infinitely large). The question then arises of how to select suitable inputs for a DRM. Recently, it has been shown empirically that DRMs with even randomly drawn relational features can be surprisingly effective for classification problems [5]). We investigate whether the stochastic search procedure proposed here can do better.

Data and Domain Knowledge. The data consists of 73 datasets from the National Cancer Institute (NCI)[2] originating from an extensive experimental study on effectiveness of chemical compounds against various cell lines. The

[2] https://www.cancer.gov/.

effectiveness is labelled as an anti-cancer activity which is either positive or negative. This dataset was recently studied in [5,22]. Each instance is an atom-level description of a chemical compound along with its class label. The atom-label description is captured in `bond` fact and is defined as `bond(CompoundID, Atom1, Atom2, Atom1Type, Atom2Type, BondType)`. An example of an instance is:

`class(m1, pos). bond(m1, 29, 30, car, car, ar). bond(m1, 14, 11, car, c3, 1).` ...

The 73 datasets consist of approximately 220,000 molecules. The positive class distribution in the datasets ranges from 40% to 90%.

The domain knowledge ([2,20]) consists of definitions for various functional groups and rings in the molecular compounds. These definitions are described in multiple hierarchies. For instance: hydroxilamine is a amine group, methyl group is an inductive donating group, and halide is an inductive accepting group. The ring hierarchy consists of definitions for aromatic and non-aromatic rings. Functional groups are represented as `functional_group(CompoundID, Atom, Length, Type)` and rings are described as `ring(CompoundID, RingID, Atoms, Length, Type)`. These definitions are in turn used to infer the presence of higher level composite structures. These are: the presence of fused rings, connected rings, and substructures.

Algorithms and Machines. The relational features are generated using the procedure described in [21]. The structure and parameters of the deep net are learned using Adam Optimiser [11]. Specifically, for finding the structure of the deep net, a validation set was used which was randomly sampled from the training set.

All the experiments (feature construction and deep learning) are conducted in two Linux based machines with similar architectures: 64 GB main memory, 16 processing cores, 8 GB NVIDIA Graphics Processing Units. We used Python based Keras ([4]) with Tensorflow as backend ([1]) for implementation of Deep Neural Network models.

Method. The Deep Relational Machine (DRM) is built using the features sampled by the hide-and-seek procedure as described in Procedure 1. We assume the goodness of features is their Laplace score (the Laplace score of a feature is $\frac{p+1}{p+n+2}$ where p, n are the number of positive and negative instances for which the feature is $TRUE$); and any feature in the top 50-percentile of scores is acceptable as an input feature for the DRM (that is, $p = 0.5$). That is, target features are to be found in the top 50-percentile of possible relational features is taken to be a "hidden ball". This gives a small bias towards good features, but does not restrict the DRM from identifying better features by combination in its hidden layers. In all experiments, α is fixed at 0.95. Therefore, the value of the sample size (s) in Procedure 1 (Line 4) is 5. That is, the number of features sampled before selecting a good feature is very small.

For different numbers of input-features, each found by hide-and-seek sampling, we follow the procedure used in [5] to identify the structure and weights of the DRM. That is: (a) the network is a dense fully-connected multilayer perceptron; (b) the network structure is allowed to vary from 1 to 4 hidden layers: so, the simplest structure has 1 hidden layer and the complex most structure has 4 hidden layers; (c) the number of neurons in each hidden layer is selected from a set: {5, 10}; (d) the hidden neurons are activated by rectified linear function; (e) the output layer (two neurons representing the two classes) use the softmax activation; (f) the dropout rate is fixed at 0.50.; (g) loss function is defined by cross-entropy; and (h) The Adam Optimiser ([12]) with learning rate: 0.001; $\beta_1 : 0.9$; $\beta_2 : 0.999$; $\epsilon : 10^{-8}$; $decay : 0$ is used for training; and (i) we estimate the accuracy of the DRMs on the same independent test-sets as used in [5].

Results. The test results from comparing the Hide-and-Seek DRM (HS) and the Lifted Relational Neural Network (LRNN) [22] are in Fig. 3. The comparison suggests a significant improvement over the state-of-the-art results. In a recent study on the DRMs [5], it is shown that selecting features uniformly from a very large space can also result in better predictive performance. The performances of uniform random DRM (Rand) and the hide-seek DRM (HS) are compared with regard to different number of features in Fig. 4. It is evident that other than the last row, DRMs with hide-and-seek selection perform better than those with the uniform random sampling strategy employed in [5]. This suggests that if the number of input features are restricted to being small (due to limitations of hardware, or for reasons of efficiency), then hide-and-seek sampled features would be a better choice. It is curious that with a large number of input features (here, >3500 or so), there is no significant statistical advantage from hide-and-seek sampling. This may be due to the fact that the DRM has a sufficiently diverse set of input features from uniform selection to be able to construct good features in its intermediate hidden layers.

#Feats	LRNN-Wins	HS-Wins	P-value
50	65	8	< 0.01
100	60	13	< 0.01
250	36	37	< 0.01
500	24	49	< 0.01
1000	23	50	< 0.01
2500	23	50	< 0.01

Fig. 3. A comparison of the performance of Hide-Seek based DRM versus state-of-the-art result (LRNN [22]). A "win" on a problem means the DRM has a higher predictive accuracy, as estimated on an independent test set for that problem. There are 73 problems in all, and entries are numbers of wins for each DRM. The P-value denotes the probability that the performance of the two models is the same.

#Feats	Ties	Rand-Wins	HS-Wins	P-value
50	12	18	43	< 0.01
100	9	14	50	< 0.01
250	4	21	48	< 0.01
500	1	21	51	< 0.01
1000	4	25	44	< 0.01
2500	2	21	50	< 0.01
3800	1	33	39	0.22

Fig. 4. A comparison of the performance of DRMs using uniform random (Rand) sampling of features and hide-and-seek (HS) sampling. The last row contains 3800 features to match the average number of features in [5]. A "win" on a problem means the corresponding DRM has a higher predictive accuracy, as estimated on an independent test set for that problem. There are 73 problems in all, and entries are numbers of wins for each DRM. The P-value denotes the probability that the performance of the two kinds of DRMs is the same.

4 Conclusions

In this paper, we have attempted to clarify, in distributional terms, some of the conditions under which a seeker can expect to do well in a hide-and-seek game. If the game is adversarial, the seeker will not be able to find the ball for long period of time. In distributional terms, this comes down to selection a hiding location using a uniform distribution. The expected cost for the seeker is then a maximum ($= n - 1$, where n is the number of locations). For non-uniform hider distribution H, the number of guesses made by the seeker can be lower. But when is this a minimum? A natural assumption is this would occur when the seeker uses the same distribution as H. In fact, this is not the case, and our results here present evidence for this empirically and theoretically.

Our interests in non-uniform hider distributions arise from the intuition that for many problems in machine learning, data are from observational studies of phenomena for which an adversarial setting is not appropriate. Instead, the distribution of good solutions follows some distribution, usually non-uniform. This is especially so if the phenomena being studied are natural ones ("Nature is not adversarial": [13]). The results we have here are first steps in obtaining an alternative mathematical characterisation of applications in these domains. The results we have obtained for clause-selection in ILP are extremely promising, demonstrating how we are able to find good solutions by sampling very small fractions of the overall space. Further, the theoretical results and the proposed sampling procedure are applicable to stochastic search over any other aspect of machine learning that involves a discrete search-space: for example, structures or discretized parameter-selection.

Earlier studies such as [8,16,18,19] have formulated the discrete pursuit-evasion problem described in terms of hider and seekers. The principal motivation of these methods is to obtain a strategy for the hider to avoid detection by the seeker. Our emphasis has been on a distributional formulation, which has led to several results that are, to the best of our knowledge, not found in the literature of pursuit games. Specifically, this includes: our mathematical characterisation of the minimising seeker distribution for non-uniform hider distribution H and the existence of step-approximations to H. However, one result in common with the literature on pursuit games is this: if H is uniform, this would maximise the expected misses by the seeker.

In the application on real-world data, we have demonstrated how hide-and-seek sampling can help select good features for a deep relational machine, when the size of the input layer cannot be very large. In such cases, our results suggest that non-uniform sampling of features based on the results with an unknown hider distribution usually result in better performance than selection based an uniform sampling of features. Of course, feature-selection based on elaborate search may give even better performance: but the sampling based approach is very efficient (the numbers of features sampled before selecting one is very small). The Deep Networks built with the hide-and-seek sampling based features show significant improvement over the state-of-the-art deep network methods and therefore it may stand as a new baseline for comparison.

We see some other ways in which the work here can be extended. First, we have stayed with the classical discrete hide-and-seek setting, in which locations are unrelated. In practice, this is unrealistic, since relations amongst boxes may arise if we are happy with good solutions (as opposed to the best solution). If locations in the neighbourhood of a box containing a good solution are also likely to contain good solutions. We would like to characterise this as the seeker knowing something about the behaviour of H. Second, when the H is not known, we only use the size of the hiding partition (the proportion of boxes in which the ball has been hidden) when sampling. If more information is known, then it may be possible to sample more efficiently: for example, only from the hiding partition. This would us to address much more effectively problems for which there are very few hiders.

Acknowledgments. The second author (A.S.) is a Visiting Professorial Fellow, School of CSE, UNSW Sydney. This work is partially supported by DST-SERB grant EMR/2016/002766, Government of India.

Appendix: Proofs

Proof of Lemma 1

Proof. The ideal case is $\mathrm{E}[Z] = 0$. That is, on average, the search opens the correct box k on its first attempt. Now $\mathrm{P}(Z = 0|$ the ball is in box $k) = h_k s_k = h_k(1 - s_k)^0 s_k$. Since the ball can be in any of the n boxes, $\mathrm{P}(Z = 0) = \sum_{k=1}^{n} h_k(1 - s_k)^0 s_k$. More generally, for $Z = j$, the search opens wrong boxes j times, and $\mathrm{P}(Z = j) = \sum_{k=1}^{n} h_k(1 - s_k)^j s_k$. The expected number of misses can now be computed:

$$
\begin{aligned}
\mathrm{E}[Z]|_{H,S} &= \sum_{j=0}^{\infty} j \times \mathrm{P}(Z=j) \\
&= \sum_{j=0}^{\infty} j \sum_{k=1}^{n} h_k (1-s_k)^j s_k
\end{aligned}
$$

Swapping the summations over j and k, we get

$$
\begin{aligned}
\mathrm{E}[Z]|_{H,S} &= \sum_{k=1}^{n} h_k s_k \sum_{j=0}^{\infty} j (1-s_k)^j \\
&= \sum_{k=1}^{n} h_k s_k \frac{1-s_k}{s_k^2}
\end{aligned}
$$

This simplifies to:

$$
\mathrm{E}[Z]|_{H,S} = \sum_{k=1}^{n} \frac{h_k}{s_k} - 1
$$

Proof of Lemma 2

Proof. This extends the Lemma 1 (Expected Cost of Misses by the Seeker) to a general case of multiple (K) stationary hiders. The number of ways the K hiders can choose to hide in n boxes is ${}^nP_K$ and let $\mathsf{P}(n, K)$ denote a set of all such permutations. For example, $\mathsf{P}(3, 2) = \{(1, 2), (1, 3), (2, 1), (2, 3), (3, 1), (3, 2)\}$.

All the K hiders can hide in any one of these choices with probability $\left(h^{(1)}_{\sigma(i)} h^{(2)}_{\sigma(i)} \cdots h^{(K)}_{\sigma(i)}\right)$, where $h^{(k)}_{\sigma(i)}$ denotes the probability of the hider in kth place in the selected choice of $\sigma(i)$. Analogously, the seeker can find any one of these hiders with probability $\left(s^{(1)}_{\sigma(i)} + s^{(2)}_{\sigma(i)} + \cdots + s^{(K)}_{\sigma(i)}\right)$, and would not find the hider once is $1 - \left(s^{(1)}_{\sigma(i)} + s^{(2)}_{\sigma(i)} + \cdots + s^{(K)}_{\sigma(i)}\right)$. If the hider makes j such misses, then it is $\left\{1 - \left(s^{(1)}_{\sigma(i)} + s^{(2)}_{\sigma(i)} + \ldots s^{(K)}_{\sigma(i)}\right)\right\}^j$. Now, the expected misses for this multiple hider formulation is given as

$$
\mathrm{E}[Z] = \sum_{i,\sigma(i) \in \mathsf{P}(n,K)} \prod_{k=1}^{K} h^{(k)}_{\sigma(i)} \sum_{j=0}^{\infty} j \left(1 - \sum_{k=1}^{K} s^{(k)}_{\sigma(i)}\right)^j \sum_{k=1}^{K} s^{(k)}_{\sigma(i)}
$$

This further simplifies to

$$
\mathrm{E}[Z]|_{H,S} = \sum_{i,\sigma(i) \in \mathsf{P}(n,K)} \prod_{k=1}^{K} h^{(k)}_{\sigma(i)} \left(\frac{1}{\sum_{k=1}^{K} s^{(k)}_{\sigma(i)}} - 1\right)
$$

Proof of Theorem 1

Proof. The problem can be posed as a constrained optimisation problem in which the objective function that is to be minimized is

$$f = \sum_{i=1}^{n} \frac{h_i}{s_i} - 1$$

Our objective is to minimize the function f given any hider distribution H. Let us represent $\nabla f = \left(\frac{\partial f}{\partial s_1}, \frac{\partial f}{\partial s_2}, \ldots, \frac{\partial f}{\partial s_n}\right)$. In this problem, $\nabla f = \left(-\frac{h_1}{s_1^2}, -\frac{h_2}{s_2^2}, \ldots, -\frac{h_n}{s_n^2}\right)$. Now, computing the double derivative $\nabla^2 f$, we get

$$\nabla^2 f = \nabla(\nabla f) = 2\left(\frac{h_1}{s_1^3}, \frac{h_2}{s_2^3}, \ldots, \frac{h_n}{s_n^3}\right)$$

Since, $\forall i, h_i \geq 0, s_i \geq 0$, we can claim that $\nabla^2 f$ has all non-negative second derivative components. And, therefore f is convex.

Proof of Theorem 2

Proof. We will write $\mathrm{E}[Z]|_{H,S}$ as a function of S i.e. $f(S)$. Our objective is to minimise $f(S) = \sum_{i=1}^{n} \frac{h_i}{s_i}$ subject to constraint $\sum_{i=1}^{n} s_i = 1$. The corresponding dual form (unconstrained) of this minimisation problem can be written as

$$g(S, \lambda) = \sum_{i=1}^{n} \frac{h_i}{s_i} + \lambda\left(1 - \sum_{i=1}^{n} s_i\right)$$

To obtain the optimal values of S and λ, we set $\frac{\partial g}{\partial s_i} = 0$ for $i = 1, \ldots, n$, and $\frac{\partial g}{\partial \lambda} = 0$. This gives: $-\frac{h_i}{s_i^2} - \lambda = 0$ and $\sum_{i=1}^{n} s_i = 1$. From this: $s_i = -\frac{\sqrt{h_i}}{\sqrt{\lambda}}$, $\forall i$. Applying this quantity for s_i in $\sum_{i=1}^{n} s_i = 1$ and the value of the parameter $\lambda = -\frac{h_i}{s_i^2}$, we get: $-\frac{\sum_{i=1}^{n} \sqrt{h_i}}{-\frac{\sqrt{h_i}}{s_i}} = 1$. Simplifying the above, we obtain the desired optimal seeker distribution S^*: $s_i^* = \frac{\sqrt{h_i}}{\sum_{j=1}^{n} \sqrt{h_j}}$, $\forall i \in \{1, \ldots, n\}$.

Proof of Corollary 1

Proof. If S is non-uniform with $\forall s_i > 0$, we have $\mathrm{E}[Z]|H, S = \frac{1}{n} \sum_{i=1}^{n} \frac{1}{s_i} - 1 \geq \frac{n}{\sum_{i=1}^{n} s_i} - 1$ and the denominator is 1 because S is a distribution. So, S^* must be a uniform distribution and in this case, the quantity $\mathrm{E}[Z]|_{H,S} = \sum_{i=1}^{n} \frac{1/n}{1/n} - 1 = \sum_{i=1}^{n} 1 - 1 = n - 1$.

Proof of Corollary 2

Proof. The proof is as follows:

$$\sum_{i=1}^{n} \frac{h_i}{s_i^*} = \sum_{i=1}^{n} \frac{h_i}{\left(\frac{\sqrt{h_i}}{\sum_{j=1}^{j} \sqrt{h_j}}\right)} = \sum_{i=1}^{n} \sqrt{h_i} \sum_{j=1}^{j} \sqrt{h_j} = \sum_{i=1}^{n} \left(\sqrt{h_i}\right)^2$$

Hence, the result follows.

Proof of Theorem 3

Proof. The KL-divergence between the two distribution H and S^* is defined as:

$$\begin{aligned}
\mathrm{KLD}(H\|S^*) &= \sum_{i=1}^{n} h_i \log_2 \frac{h_i}{s_i^*} \\
&= \sum_{i=1}^{n} h_i \log_2 h_i - \sum_{i=1}^{n} h_i \log_2 \frac{\sqrt{h_i}}{\sum_{j=1}^{n}\sqrt{h_j}} \quad \text{(using Theorem 2)} \\
&= \frac{1}{2}\sum_{i=1}^{n} h_i \log_2 h_i + \log_2\left(\sum_{j=1}^{n}\sqrt{h_j}\right)\left(\sum_{i=1}^{n} h_i\right) \\
&= -\frac{1}{2} Entropy(H) + \log_2\left(\sum_{j=1}^{n}\sqrt{h_j}\right) \\
&= -\frac{1}{2} Entropy(H) + \log_2 \left(\mathrm{E}[Z]|_{H,S^*} + 1\right)^{\frac{1}{2}} \quad \text{(using Corollary 2)} \\
&= \frac{1}{2}\left[-Entropy(H) + \log_2\left(\mathrm{E}[Z]|_{H,S^*} + 1\right)\right]
\end{aligned}$$

Simplifying, we get:

$$\mathrm{E}[Z]|_{H,S^*} = 2^{2\mathrm{KLD}(H\|S^*)+Entropy(H)} - 1$$

Proof of Lemma 3

Proof. The probability that a randomly drawn box is not in the U partition is $(1-p)$. The probability that in a sample of s boxes, none are from the U partition is $(1-p)^s$, and therefore the probability that there is at least 1 box amongst the s from the U partition is $1-(1-p)^s$. We want this probability to be at least α. That is:

$$1-(1-p)^s \geq \alpha$$

With some simple arithmetic, it follows that

$$s \geq \frac{\log(1-\alpha)}{\log(1-p)}$$

References

1. Abadi, M., Agarwal, A., et al.: TensorFlow: large-scale machine learning on heterogeneous systems (2015). https://www.tensorflow.org/
2. Ando, H.Y., Dehaspe, L., Luyten, W., Van Craenenbroeck, E., Vandecasteele, H., Van Meervelt, L.: Discovering H-bonding rules in crystals with inductive logic programming. Mol. Pharm. **3**(6), 665–674 (2006). https://doi.org/10.1021/mp060034z
3. Blum, A.: Learning boolean functions in an infinite attribute space. Mach. Learn. **9**(4), 373–386 (1992). https://doi.org/10.1007/BF00994112
4. Chollet, F., et al.: Keras (2015). https://keras.io

5. Dash, T., Srinivasan, A., Vig, L., Orhobor, O.I., King, R.D.: Large-scale assessment of deep relational machines. In: Riguzzi, F., Bellodi, E., Zese, R. (eds.) ILP 2018. LNCS (LNAI), vol. 11105, pp. 22–37. Springer, Cham (2018). https://doi.org/10.1007/978-3-319-99960-9_2
6. Fog, A.: Sampling methods for wallenius' and fisher's noncentral hypergeometric distributions. Commun. Stat. Simul. Comput.® **37**(2), 241–257 (2008). https://doi.org/10.1080/03610910701790236
7. Ho, Y.C., Zhao, Q.C., Jia, Q.S.: Ordinal Optimization: Soft Optimization for Hard Problems. Springer, Boston (2007). https://doi.org/10.1007/978-0-387-68692-9
8. Kelly, F.: On optimal search with unknown detection probabilities. J. Math. Anal. Appl. **88**(2), 422–432 (1982)
9. King, R.D., Muggleton, S.H., Srinivasan, A., Sternberg, M.J.: Structure-activity relationships derived by machine learning: the use of atoms and their bond connectivities to predict mutagenicity by inductive logic programming. Proc. Nat. Acad. Sci. U.S.A. **93**(1), 438–42 (1996). https://doi.org/10.1073/pnas.93.1.438
10. King, R.D., Muggleton, S.H., Srinivasan, A., Sternberg, M.: Structure-activity relationships derived by machine learning: the use of atoms and their bond connectivities to predict mutagenicity by inductive logic programming. Proc. Nat. Acad. Sci. **93**(1), 438–442 (1996). https://doi.org/10.1073/pnas.93.1.438
11. Kinga, D., Adam, J.B.: A method for stochastic optimization. In: International Conference on Learning Representations (ICLR), vol. 5 (2015)
12. Kingma, D.P., Ba, J.: Adam: a method for stochastic optimization. arXiv preprint arXiv:1412.6980 (2014)
13. Lidbetter, T., Lin, K.: Searching for multiple objects in multiple locations. arXiv preprint arXiv:1710.05332 (2017)
14. Lodhi, H.: Deep relational machines. In: Lee, M., Hirose, A., Hou, Z.-G., Kil, R.M. (eds.) ICONIP 2013. LNCS, vol. 8227, pp. 212–219. Springer, Heidelberg (2013). https://doi.org/10.1007/978-3-642-42042-9_27
15. Muggleton, S., De Raedt, L.: Inductive logic programming: theory and methods. J. Logic Program. **19**, 629–679 (1994). https://doi.org/10.1016/0743-1066(94)90035-3
16. Ruckle, W.H.: A discrete search game. In: Raghavan, T.E.S., Ferguson, T.S., Parthasarathy, T., Vrieze, O.J. (eds.) Theory and Decision Library, pp. 29–43. Springer, Netherlands (1991). https://doi.org/10.1007/978-94-011-3760-7_4
17. Srinivasan, A.: A study of two probabilistic methods for searching large spaces with ILP. Technical report PRG-TR-16-00, Oxford University Computing Laboratory, Oxford (2000)
18. Stone, L.D.: Theory of Optimal Search, vol. 118. Elsevier, Amsterdam (1976)
19. Subelman, E.J.: A hide-search game. J. Appl. Probab. **18**(3), 628–640 (1981). https://doi.org/10.2307/3213317
20. Van Craenenbroeck, E., Vandecasteele, H., Dehaspe, L.: Dmax's functional group and ring library. https://dtai.cs.kuleuven.be/software/dmax/ (2002)
21. Vig, L., Srinivasan, A., Bain, M., Verma, A.: An investigation into the role of domain-knowledge on the use of embeddings. In: Lachiche, N., Vrain, C. (eds.) ILP 2017. LNCS (LNAI), vol. 10759, pp. 169–183. Springer, Cham (2018). https://doi.org/10.1007/978-3-319-78090-0_12
22. Šourek, G., Aschenbrenner, V., Železny, F., Kuželka, O.: Lifted relational neural networks. In: Proceedings of the 2015th International Conference on Cognitive Computation: Integrating Neural and Symbolic Approaches, vol. 1583, pp. 52–60. COCO 2015. CEUR-WS.org, Aachen, Germany, Germany (2015). http://dl.acm.org/citation.cfm?id=2996831.2996838

Joint Dictionary Learning for Unsupervised Feature Selection

Yang Fan[1], Jianhua Dai[2(✉)], Qilai Zhang[1], and Shuai Liu[2]

[1] College of Intelligence and Computing, Tianjin University, Tianjin, China
{fany,zql_wolf}@tju.edu.cn

[2] Hunan Provincial Key Laboratory of Intelligent Computing and Language Information Processing, Hunan Normal University, Changsha, Hunan, China
{jhdai,liushuai}@hunnu.edu.cn

Abstract. Unsupervised feature selection (UFS) as an effective method to reduce time complexity and storage burden has been widely applied to various machine learning tasks. The selected features should model data distribution, preserve data reconstruction and maintain manifold structure. However, most UFS methods don't consider these three factors simultaneously. Motivated by this, we propose a novel joint dictionary learning method, which handles these three key factors simultaneously. In joint dictionary learning, an intrinsic space shared by feature space and pseudo label space is introduced, which can model cluster structure and reveal data reconstruction. To ensure the sparseness of intrinsic space, the ℓ_1-norm regularization is imposed on the representation coefficients matrix. The joint learning of robust sparse regression model and spectral clustering can select features that maintain data distribution and manifold structure. An efficient algorithm is designed to solve the proposed optimization problem. Experimental results on various types of benchmark datasets validate the effectiveness of our method.

Keywords: Feature selection · Data distribution · Data reconstruction · Manifold structure · Joint dictionary learning

1 Introduction

With the rapid growth of contemporary information technology, data information is often represented by high dimensional features in machine learning, data mining and natural language processing [11]. In fact, not all features are relevant and important to the data processing tasks and many of them are unrelated, redundant or noisy. Feature selection aims to select the most representative features and eliminate redundant features from the original data, and it has been proved to be effective in handling high-dimensional data [6].

Many feature selection algorithms have been proposed for selecting the most representative features. From the perspective of the availability of label information, feature selection algorithms can be divided into supervised [10], semi-supervised [5] and unsupervised cases [1]. Supervised methods usually use label

I. V. Tetko et al. (Eds.): ICANN 2019, LNCS 11728, pp. 46–58, 2019.
https://doi.org/10.1007/978-3-030-30484-3_4

information to select discriminative features to distinguish instances from different labels. However, unsupervised feature selection, due to the lack of label information, is a difficult task to guide the search of relevant features.

In unsupervised scenario, data distribution, data reconstruction and local structure are the key factors for guiding feature selection [16]. Since the discriminative information is usually encoded in labels, how to select the discriminative features is an important but difficult task for unsupervised problem [8]. One common method is to utilize cluster labels (which can be regarded as pseudo labels) to select features that can best preserve the cluster structure, which can discriminate samples from different classes. Thus, data distribution, which can be reflected by cluster structure, is significant for unsupervised feature selection. From the perspective of data reconstruction, the selected features should be representative and can reconstruct the original data well. More specifically, it assumes that the original data can be approximated by performing a reconstruction function on the selected features [6]. Additionally, nearby samples should be divided into the same cluster, resulting in locality preserving needs to be considered. So far, there are very few algorithms taking into account these three main factors simultaneously [16].

In light of all these factors, we propose an effective unsupervised feature selection algorithm, i.e, Joint Dictionary Learning for Unsupervised Feature Selection (JDLUFS). We consider data reconstruction, data distribution and manifold structure simultaneously to select the most important and discriminative features for unsupervised learning. Unlike traditional unsupervised feature selection methods which use matrix factorization to generate pseudo labels, we apply dictionary learning to obtain sparse intrinsic space, which can reveal the data reconstruction and reconstruct more accurate pseudo labels. To select the discriminative features, A linear regression term is added into the objective function to maintain the cluster structure. Spectral clustering is utilized to uncover the data local structure. The main contributions of our work are as follows: (a) A joint dictionary learning method for unsupervised feature selection is proposed, and features that can model data distribution, preserve data reconstruction and maintain manifold structure are selected. (b) The ℓ_1-norm regularization is used to ensure the sparseness of intrinsic space and the $\ell_{2,1}$-norm regularization is added to achieve group sparsity and remove the irrelevant or noisy features. (c) An alternating minimization algorithm is developed to solve the optimization problem. Extensive experiments on different types of benchmark datasets demonstrate the effectiveness of the proposed model.

2 Related Work

In this section, we mainly review the existing unsupervised feature selection models for data distribution, data reconstruction, and local structure.

Unsupervised method based on data distribution first detect the cluster structure of samples and then directly select features that can best preserve the cluster structure. To maintain the distribution information, NDFS [8] performs spectral clustering to learn the cluster structure of samples, and adds $\ell_{2,1}$-norm regularization on the feature selection matrix to select the discriminative features. RUFS [11] combines robust clustering with robust feature selection to select the most important features, which can improve the robustness of the algorithm. Inspired by multi-view learning, CUFS [16] considers data distribution as one-view, and data reconstruction as the other view, in which the common redundant noisy features can be removed by co-regularized learning. Another type of unsupervised algorithm selects features from the perspective of data reconstruction, which defines feature relevance as the capability of features to approximate feature space via a reconstruction function [6]. Under the framework of matrix factorization, EUFS [12] directly embeds feature selection into a clustering algorithm through sparse learning and adds nonnegative orthogonal constraints to the cluster indicator matrix. CDLFS [15] utilizes dictionary learning instead of matrix factorization to learn the synthesis dictionary which can reconstruct samples and the analysis dictionary which can select features. REFS [6] embeds the reconstruction function learning process to feature selection.

In manifold learning, it is generally considered that high-dimensional data are nearly lying on a low-dimensional manifold [15]. To preserve the local geometric structure, the manifold regularization is often used in many unsupervised feature selection methods.

It can be seen that most existing methods don't consider data distribution, data reconstruction and local structure simultaneously. To address this issue, our proposed method seamlessly integrates these three key factors into a unified framework in which the dictionary learning replaces matrix factorization to reflect data reconstruction capabilities.

3 The Proposed Approach

Throughout this paper, matrices are denoted as boldface capital letters and vectors are written as boldface lowercase letters. The same as [17], we denote the i-th row and j-th column of a matrix $\mathbf{A} = [\mathbf{A}_{ij}]$ as $\mathbf{a}_i$ and $\mathbf{a}^j$, and its Frobenius norm and $\ell_{2,1}$-norm are denoted as $||\mathbf{A}||_F = \sqrt{\sum_i \sum_j \mathbf{A}_{ij}^2}$, and $||\mathbf{A}||_{2,1} = \sum_i \sqrt{\sum_j \mathbf{A}_{ij}^2}$, and $\mathrm{Tr}(\mathbf{A})$ is the trace of $\mathbf{A}$ if $\mathbf{A}$ is square. Let $\mathbf{X} \in \mathbb{R}^{d \times n}$ be the training data set, where d is feature number, n is the number of samples and each column $\mathbf{x}^i \in \mathbb{R}^{d \times 1}$ represents an instance. Denote the cluster indicator matrix $\mathbf{U} = [\mathbf{u}_i; \ldots; \mathbf{u}_n] \in \mathbb{R}^{n \times c}$, where c is the number of clusters and each row $\mathbf{u}_i \in \{0, 1\}^{1 \times c}$ is the cluster indicator vector for i-th sample.

3.1 Approach

To select the most representative features, we consider the key factors mentioned above in our model. Since matrix factorization can not reflect some data distribution priors in unsupervised learning, we adopt dictionary learning to maintain data reconstruction and obtain cluster labels, i.e, pseudo labels.

In cross-modality case, it is generally considered that related modalities share the same sparse representation, i.e., the intrinsic space. Inspired by the success of joint dictionary learning in cross-modality problems [14], we extend joint dictionary learning for UFS and consider the feature space $\mathbf{X}$ and the pseudo label space $\mathbf{U} \in \mathbb{R}^{n \times c}$ to be two modalities which share an intrinsic space $\mathbf{A} \in \mathbb{R}^{k \times n}$, where k is dictionary size, i.e, intrinsic space dimension. We introduce the dictionary $\mathbf{D}_x$ used to reconstruct the feature matrix $\mathbf{X}$ and the dictionary $\mathbf{D}_u$ used to reconstruct the pseudo label matrix $\mathbf{U}$. To maximize the connection between the two modalities in the intrinsic space and learn more accurate pseudo labels of samples, the extended joint dictionary learning model is defined as follows:

$$\begin{aligned} \min_{\mathbf{D}_x, \mathbf{D}_u, \mathbf{A}, \mathbf{U}} \quad & ||\mathbf{X} - \mathbf{D}_x \mathbf{A}||_F^2 + ||\mathbf{U}^T - \mathbf{D}_u \mathbf{A}||_F^2 + \beta ||\mathbf{A}||_1 \\ \text{s.t.} \quad & ||\mathbf{d}_{xi}||_2^2 \leq 1, ||\mathbf{d}_{ui}||_2^2 \leq 1, \forall i \end{aligned} \tag{1}$$

Under the framework of joint dictionary learning, the consistent intrinsic space of samples is adaptively learned by feature space and pseudo label space, and the accurate cluster labels are reconstructed by the intrinsic space. By leveraging the interactions between these two goals, we can preserve the data reconstruction well and capture accurate cluster structure. Additionally, we add the ℓ_1-norm to $\mathbf{A}$ to make the intrinsic space more sparse and improve generalization ability.

Because of the importance of discriminative information encoded in labels, it is very significant to select representative features that are more relevant to pseudo labels in unsupervised feature selection problems [8]. Since the cluster structure can reveal the data distribution of instances well, we introduce a feature selection matrix $\mathbf{W} \in \mathbb{R}^{d \times c}$ to preserve the cluster structure via linear sparse regression, by which the original features can be projected into corresponding clusters. The feature selection framework based on data distribution is formulated as:

$$\min_{\mathbf{W}} \quad \alpha ||\mathbf{U} - \mathbf{X}^T \mathbf{W}||_F^2 + \delta ||\mathbf{W}||_{2,1} \tag{2}$$

where δ is a regularization parameter used to balance the sparsity and regression error. The $\ell_{2,1}$-norm is imposed on the feature selection matrix $\mathbf{W}$ to achieve the group sparsity and remove noisy features. In detail, $||\mathbf{w}_i||_2$ shrinks to zero if i-th feature is less discriminative to the pseudo label $\mathbf{U}$. Hence, when $||\mathbf{w}_i||_2 = 0$, it indicates that the i-th feature is redundant and should be discarded. In other words, the larger the value of $||\mathbf{w}_i||_2$ is, the more important the i-th feature is. Therefore, we finally get the most important features by sorting feature weights $\mathbf{w}_i = ||\mathbf{w}_i||_2, i = 1, \ldots, d$ in descending order.

In the above models, we mainly aim to assist in maintaining data reconstruction and data distribution. Additionally, we expect that the obtained pseudo label space can also preserve the local geometric structure of the samples. In other words, similar samples should be grouped into the same cluster. Spectral analysis has been proven to maintain the manifold structure [9]. We further add the following function to force similar samples with similar cluster labels:

$$\min_{\mathbf{U}} \quad \gamma \text{Tr}(\mathbf{U}^T \mathbf{L} \mathbf{U}), \quad \text{s.t.} \quad \mathbf{U}^T \mathbf{U} = \mathbf{I}, \mathbf{U} \geq \mathbf{0} \tag{3}$$

where $\mathbf{L} \in \mathbb{R}^{n \times n}$ is a Laplacian matrix, $\mathbf{L} = \mathbf{D} - \mathbf{S}$, $\mathbf{D}$ is a diagonal matrix with its diagonal element defined as $\mathbf{D}_{ii} = \sum_{j=1}^{n} \mathbf{S}_{ij}$ and $\mathbf{S} \in \mathbb{R}^{n \times n}$ represents the sample similarity matrix which can be learned by heat kernel or cosine similarity. Here we use the heat kernel weighting method.

Putting (1), (2), and (3) together, the proposed approach JDLUFS is to solve the following optimization model:

$$\begin{aligned}
\min_{\mathbf{D}_x, \mathbf{D}_u, \mathbf{A}, \mathbf{W}, \mathbf{U}} \quad & ||\mathbf{X} - \mathbf{D}_x \mathbf{A}||_F^2 + ||\mathbf{U}^T - \mathbf{D}_u \mathbf{A}||_F^2 + \beta ||\mathbf{A}||_1 \\
+ \quad & \alpha ||\mathbf{U} - \mathbf{X}^T \mathbf{W}||_F^2 + \gamma \mathrm{Tr}(\mathbf{U}^T \mathbf{L} \mathbf{U}) + \delta ||\mathbf{W}||_{2,1} \\
\text{s.t.} \quad & ||\mathbf{d}_{xi}||_2^2 \leq 1, ||\mathbf{d}_{ui}||_2^2 \leq 1, \forall i, \mathbf{U}^T \mathbf{U} = \mathbf{I}, \mathbf{U} \geq \mathbf{0}
\end{aligned} \tag{4}$$

3.2 Optimization Algorithm

The optimization problem in (4) is non-convex with respect to $\mathbf{D}_x$, $\mathbf{D}_u$, $\mathbf{A}$, $\mathbf{W}$ and $\mathbf{U}$, but is convex for each variable while fixing the others. Thus we employ an alternating optimization strategy to derive the update rule for each variable. In the next subsection, we will give a clear description of the convergence of the optimization algorithm.

Update $\mathbf{D}_x$. As for the updating of $\mathbf{D}_x$, we fix other variables except $\mathbf{D}_x$ and remove the irrelevant items. Then we get the following optimization problem:

$$\hat{\mathbf{D}}_x = \arg\min_{\mathbf{D}_x} ||\mathbf{X} - \mathbf{D}_x \mathbf{A}||_F^2, \quad \text{s.t.} \quad ||\mathbf{d}_{xi}||_2^2 \leq 1, \forall i \tag{5}$$

We further introduce an auxiliary variable $\mathbf{H}$, and $\hat{\mathbf{D}}_x$ can be calculated by Alternating Direction Method of Multipliers (ADMM) algorithm [2]:

$$\begin{cases}
\mathbf{D}_x^{t+1} = \arg\min_{\mathbf{D}_x} ||\mathbf{X} - \mathbf{D}_x \mathbf{A}||_F^2 + \mu ||\mathbf{D}_x - \mathbf{H}^t + \mathbf{S}^t||_F^2 \\
\mathbf{H}^{t+1} = \arg\min_{\mathbf{H}} \mu ||\mathbf{D}_x^{t+1} - \mathbf{H}^t + \mathbf{S}^t||_F^2, \quad \text{s.t.} \quad ||\mathbf{h}_i||_2^2 \leq 1, \forall i \\
\mathbf{S}^{t+1} = \mathbf{S}^t + \mathbf{D}_x^{t+1} - \mathbf{H}^{t+1}, \quad \textit{update } \mu \textit{ if appropriate}
\end{cases} \tag{6}$$

Update $\mathbf{D}_u$. The optimization problem about $\mathbf{D}_u$ is similar to $\mathbf{D}_x$. We can update $\mathbf{D}_u$ similar to $\mathbf{D}_x$ by (6).

Update A. After fixing the other variables, the problem in (4) becomes:

$$\hat{\mathbf{A}} = \arg\min_{\mathbf{A}} ||\mathbf{X} - \mathbf{D}_x \mathbf{A}||_F^2 + ||\mathbf{U}^T - \mathbf{D}_u \mathbf{A}||_F^2 + \beta ||\mathbf{A}||_1 \tag{7}$$

The closed-form solution of the above formula is:

$$\hat{\mathbf{A}} = (\mathbf{D}_x^T \mathbf{D}_x + \mathbf{D}_u^T \mathbf{D}_u + \beta \mathbf{I})^{-1} (\mathbf{D}_x^T \mathbf{X} + \mathbf{D}_u^T \mathbf{U}) \tag{8}$$

Update U. Similar to the process of updating $\mathbf{A}$, we need to remove items that are not related to $\mathbf{U}$, resulting in the following equation:

$$\min_{\mathbf{U}^T \mathbf{U} = \mathbf{I}, \mathbf{U} \geq \mathbf{0}} \quad ||\mathbf{U}^T - \mathbf{D}_u \mathbf{A}||_F^2 + \alpha ||\mathbf{U} - \mathbf{X}^T \mathbf{W}||_F^2 + \gamma \mathrm{Tr}(\mathbf{U}^T \mathbf{L} \mathbf{U}) \tag{9}$$

To eliminate the orthogonal constraint of $\mathbf{U}$, we add a penalty term $\lambda||\mathbf{U} - \mathbf{I}||_F^2$ (In our experiment, $\lambda = 10^6$). Since $\mathbf{U} \geq \mathbf{0}$, we introduce the Lagrangian multiplier $\mathbf{\Phi} \in \mathbb{R}^{n\times c} \geq \mathbf{0}$, and the obtained Lagrangian function is:

$$\mathcal{F}(\mathbf{U}, \mathbf{\Phi}) = ||\mathbf{U}^T - \mathbf{D}_u\mathbf{A}||_F^2 + \alpha||\mathbf{U} - \mathbf{X}^T\mathbf{W}||_F^2 + \gamma\text{Tr}(\mathbf{U}^T\mathbf{L}\mathbf{U}) + \lambda||\mathbf{U} - \mathbf{I}||_F^2 - \text{Tr}(\mathbf{\Phi}^T\mathbf{U}) \tag{10}$$

Setting $\frac{\partial\mathcal{F}(\mathbf{U},\mathbf{\Phi})}{\partial\mathbf{U}} = 0$, we get:

$$\mathbf{\Phi} = 2(\mathbf{U} - \mathbf{A}^T\mathbf{D}_u^T) + 2\alpha(\mathbf{U} - \mathbf{X}^T\mathbf{W}) + 2\gamma\mathbf{L}\mathbf{U} + 4\lambda\mathbf{U}(\mathbf{U}^T\mathbf{U} - \mathbf{I}) \tag{11}$$

Then we can derive the update formula of $\mathbf{U}$ according to the Karush-Kuhn-Tuckre (KKT) condition $\mathbf{\Phi}_{ij}\mathbf{U}_{ij} = 0$:

$$\mathbf{U}_{ij} = \frac{(\mathbf{A}^T\mathbf{D}_u^T + \alpha\mathbf{X}^T\mathbf{W} + 2\lambda\mathbf{U})_{ij}}{(\mathbf{U} + \alpha\mathbf{U} + \gamma\mathbf{L}\mathbf{U} + 2\lambda\mathbf{U}\mathbf{U}^T\mathbf{U})_{ij}}\mathbf{U}_{ij} \tag{12}$$

Finally, we normalize $\mathbf{U}$ such that $(\mathbf{U}^T\mathbf{U})_{ii} = 1, i = 1, \ldots, c$.

Update W. Similar to the above methods, we get the subproblem of $\mathbf{W}$:

$$\hat{\mathbf{W}} = \arg\min_{\mathbf{W}} \alpha||\mathbf{U} - \mathbf{X}^T\mathbf{W}||_F^2 + \delta||\mathbf{W}||_{2,1} \tag{13}$$

The problem in (13) is non-smooth but is convex. In this paper, we solve the subproblem of $\mathbf{W}$ by using the Iterative Reweighed Least Square (IRLS) algorithm. Following [15], the objective problem can be rewritten as:

$$\begin{aligned}\mathbf{W}^{t+1} &= \arg\min_{\mathbf{W}} Q(\mathbf{W}|\mathbf{W}^t) \\ &= \arg\min_{\mathbf{W}} \text{Tr}((\mathbf{U} - \mathbf{X}^T\mathbf{W})^T(\mathbf{U} - \mathbf{X}^T\mathbf{W})) + \frac{\delta}{\alpha}\text{Tr}(\mathbf{W}^T\mathbf{G}^t\mathbf{W})\end{aligned} \tag{14}$$

where $\mathbf{G}$ is a diagonal matrix with the i-th diagonal element as $\mathbf{G}_{ii} = \frac{1}{2||\mathbf{w}_i^t||_2}$. Then let the derivative of the above expression be 0, i.e., $\frac{\partial Q(\mathbf{W}|\mathbf{W}^t)}{\partial\mathbf{W}} = 0$, we get:

$$\mathbf{X}(\mathbf{X}^T\mathbf{W} - \mathbf{U}) + \frac{\delta}{\alpha}\mathbf{G}^t\mathbf{W} = 0 \tag{15}$$

Obviously, the closed-form solution of $\mathbf{W}^{t+1}$ is:

$$\mathbf{W}^{t+1} = (\mathbf{X}\mathbf{X}^T + \frac{\delta}{\alpha}\mathbf{G}^t)^{-1}\mathbf{X}\mathbf{U} \tag{16}$$

To get the solution of $\mathbf{W}^{t+1}$, we have to calculate the inverse of $(\mathbf{X}\mathbf{X}^T + \frac{\delta}{\alpha}\mathbf{G}^t)$. Obviously, when the feature dimension is very high, the time consumption of (16) is unacceptable. Fortunately, when the number of instances is much smaller than its feature dimension, we can use the Woodbury matrix identity: $(\mathbf{A} + \mathbf{B}\mathbf{C}\mathbf{D})^{-1} = \mathbf{A}^{-1} - \mathbf{A}^{-1}\mathbf{B}(\mathbf{C}^{-1} + \mathbf{D}\mathbf{A}^{-1}\mathbf{B})^{-1}\mathbf{D}\mathbf{A}^{-1}$. Hence, we can further rewrite (16) as:

$$\mathbf{W}^{t+1} = \mathbf{G}^{t^{-1}}\mathbf{X}(\mathbf{X}^T\mathbf{G}^{t^{-1}} + \frac{\delta}{\alpha}\mathbf{I})^{-1}\mathbf{U} \tag{17}$$

Based on the above iterative criteria for $\mathbf{D}_x$, $\mathbf{D}_u$, $\mathbf{A}$, $\mathbf{W}$ and $\mathbf{U}$, the pseudo code of the proposed JDLUFS framework is summarized in Algorithm 1.

Algorithm 1. The JDLUFS algorithm.

Input: Data matrix $\mathbf{X} \in \mathbb{R}^{d \times n}$; Parameters $p, c, \alpha, \beta, \gamma$ and δ; Dictionary size k; Loss variation ratio σ; Maximum number of iterations N;
Output: t features from the dataset.

```
Initialize α = 1, λ = 10^6, D_x, D_u, W and U;
Compute affinity graph S and Laplacian matrix L;
repeat
    Â = (D_x^T D_x + D_u^T D_u + βI)^{-1} (D_x^T X + D_u^T U);
    Update D_x and D_u by calculating iteration problem (6);
    U_ij = (A^T D_u^T + αX^T W + 2λU)_ij / (U + αU + γLU + 2λUU^T U)_ij · U_ij
    Update W by solving (13) using IRLS;
until Up to the maximum number of iterations or loss variation ratio
Sort all d features according to ||w_i||_2 in descending order and select the top-t
    ranked features.
```

3.3 Time Complexity and Convergence Analysis

There are five subproblems in our algorithm: $\mathbf{D}_x$, $\mathbf{D}_u$, $\mathbf{A}$, $\mathbf{W}$ and $\mathbf{U}$. The time complexities of updating dictionaries $\mathbf{D}_x$ and $\mathbf{D}_u$ are $O(T_1(k^3+k^2d+d^2k+kdn))$ and $O(T_1(k^3+k^2c+c^2k+kcn))$, respectively, where T_1 indicates the iteration number in (6). $\mathbf{A}$ has a closed-form solution and the time complexity is $O(k^3+k^2d+kdn)$. For $\mathbf{W}$, we consider the relationship between the number of samples and the feature dimension, therefore the time complexity is $O(T_2(min(d^3,n^3)))$, where T_2 is the iteration number of the IRLS algorithm. In subproblem $\mathbf{U}$, we traverse each item in $\mathbf{U}$ and the time complexity is $O(cn^2)$.

In each iteration, the optimization problem for $\mathbf{A}$ and the transformed Lagrangian function for $\mathbf{U}$ are convex functions, so we can get the respective closed-form solutions. For dictionaries $\mathbf{D}_x$ and $\mathbf{D}_u$, the ADMM algorithm can guarantee the optimum solutions to update these two dictionaries and the detailed convergence proof of ADMM can be found in [2]. Additionally, the convergence proof of the IRLS algorithm for solving the subproblem of $\mathbf{W}$ has been intensively studied in [15]. Since our objective function has a lower bound 0, the proposed algorithm is guaranteed to converge to a stationary point.

4 Experiments

In this section, we conduct extensive comparative experiments to evaluate our algorithm in terms of both classification and clustering performance on six benchmark datasets[1], including one handwritten digital image dataset (USPS), one object image dataset (COIL20), two face image datasets (warpPIE10P and pixraw10P), one spoken letter dataset (ISOLET) and one cancer dataset (LUNG). Detailed information of the datasets is summarized in Table 1. All experiments are performed on a computer with CPU (i5-6500 @ 3.20 GHz) and 8 GB memory using MATLAB software.

[1] http://featureselection.asu.edu/datasets.php.

Table 1. Detailed information of the datasets

Dataset	Instances	Features	Classes	Domain	Selected features
USPS	9298	256	10	Image, Digit	$[50, 80, \ldots, 200]$
COIL20	1440	1024	20	Image, Object	$[50, 100, \ldots, 300]$
warpPIE10P	210	2420	10	Image, Face	$[50, 100, \ldots, 300]$
ISOLET	1560	617	26	Spoken letter	$[50, 100, \ldots, 300]$
LUNG	203	3312	5	Biological	$[50, 100, \ldots, 300]$
Pixraw10P	100	10000	10	Image, Face	$[50, 100, \ldots, 300]$

4.1 Experiment Setup

We compare JDLUFS with five representative unsupervised feature selection algorithms. The ideas of these algorithms are briefly shown as follows:

- Laplacian Score [4]: a filter algorithm which selects features that best preserve the local manifold structure by calculating the Laplacian Score.
- SPEC [13]: a filter model that selects features by using spectral clustering.
- RUFS [11]: a method which combines matrix factorization and local manifold learning and uses $\ell_{2,1}$-norm to maintain the robustness of the algorithm.
- EUFS [12]: an embedded method that embeds feature selection into a clustering algorithm through sparse learning.
- CUFS [16]: an approach which selects features with the ability to maintain data distribution and data reconstruction under matrix factorization framework.

For classification performance, we use the nearest neighbor classifier and record the classification accuracy. Two clustering evaluation metrics, Normalized mutual information (NMI) and Clustering Accuracy (ACC) [3], are employed to evaluate clustering performance. The lager the three metrics are, the better the performance is. Following the previous works [7,11], for all the methods, we specify the size of neighborhoods p as 5 to construct the Laplacian matrix for all datasets. For JDLUFS, we fix $\alpha = 1$ and $\lambda = 10^6$ and mainly investigate the influence of β, γ and δ. We also set the size of dictionary to be k times the original feature dimension and the range of k is from $\{0.2, 0.4, 0.6, 0.8\}$. To fairly compare all the methods, we tune the parameters by a "grid-search" strategy from $\{10^{-6}, 10^{-5}, \ldots, 10^6\}$ and record the best result. How to determine the optimal number of selected features is still an open question, thus we set the number of selected features for last five datasets as $\{50, 100, \ldots, 300\}$. Since the dimension of USPS is 256, we set the number of selected features for this dataset as $\{50, 80, \ldots, 200\}$. We record average results over different dimensions. In this experiment, we use the k-means clustering algorithm to evaluate the performance of selected features of different methods. We randomly initialize and repeat the clustering 20 times for each setting. Additionally, we adopt 10-fold cross-validation to ensure the reliability of the classification results.

As for the evaluation by classification and clustering, we report the average results with standard deviation (std) for all algorithms.

4.2 Results and Analysis

The classification and clustering results of different algorithms on the six benchmark datasets are shown in Table 2. We can have the following observations. Laplacian score performs well overall in terms of classification accuracy. Both SPEC and Laplacian take into account the manifold structure of samples, which illustrates the importance of local structure information. RUFS jointly performs robust cluster label learning and robust feature selection, which indicates proper

Table 2. Comparing results (mean% ± std) of several unsupervised feature selection algorithms on six benchmark datasets in terms of three metrics (Classification Accuracy, NMI and ACC). The best results are in boldface. The number in the parentheses is the size of dictionary k which is a multiple of the original feature dimension.

Dataset	Classification results (Classification Accuracy% ± std)					
	USPS	COIL20	warpPIE10P	ISOLET	LUNG	Pixraw10P
Laplacian	94.08 ± 3.65	85.94 ± 6.05	94.28 ± 3.56	76.56 ± 4.82	91.78 ± 1.17	87.50 ± 15.24
SPEC	78.66 ± 23.71	57.14 ± 21.19	97.19 ± 5.60	73.30 ± 8.03	89.77 ± 2.25	68.00 ± 20.06
RUFS	95.41 ± 5.70	94.31 ± 11.44	99.89 ± 3.56	84.04 ± 8.15	93.61 ± 1.65	97.83 ± 1.78
EUFS	95.47 ± 3.53	93.01 ± 8.83	99.75 ± 0.72	80.95 ± 10.15	93.13 ± 1.56	97.50 ± 4.34
CUFS	95.86 ± 1.82	93.49 ± 4.52	99.91 ± 0.44	84.16 ± 3.00	91.13 ± 1.40	99.00 ± 3.53
Ours (0.2)	96.01 ± 2.81	**95.22 ± 3.68**	99.92 ± 1.90	85.63 ± 3.81	94.14 ± 1.53	99.00 ± 2.80
Ours (0.4)	96.09 ± 2.88	95.06 ± 3.67	99.93 ± 1.88	86.57 ± 3.02	94.14 ± 1.53	**99.17 ± 2.99**
Ours (0.6)	**96.11 ± 2.86**	95.01 ± 3.61	**99.95 ± 1.82**	**86.77 ± 3.97**	**94.43 ± 1.56**	99.00 ± 2.89
Ours (0.8)	96.10 ± 2.76	94.89 ± 3.39	99.83 ± 1.83	85.03 ± 3.77	94.14 ± 1.63	99.00 ± 2.33
Clustering results (NMI% ± std)						
Laplacian	61.08 ± 4.88	65.68 ± 2.97	22.36 ± 2.57	70.62 ± 2.77	59.78 ± 6.60	79.43 ± 13.61
SPEC	47.85 ± 23.71	50.54 ± 21.19	52.77 ± 5.60	66.51 ± 8.03	59.09 ± 2.25	66.13 ± 20.06
RUFS	62.55 ± 3.52	73.38 ± 6.96	42.28 ± 4.21	76.62 ± 8.80	65.50 ± 5.17	87.35 ± 3.60
EUFS	62.27 ± 2.52	67.61 ± 2.16	**68.50 ± 12.91**	70.47 ± 6.37	59.11 ± 7.55	79.76 ± 4.88
CUFS	61.89 ± 1.69	71.63 ± 2.47	48.23 ± 4.99	75.23 ± 3.87	59.52 ± 2.61	81.95 ± 5.66
Ours (0.2)	62.98 ± 1.63	**73.98 ± 2.39**	44.50 ± 3.30	78.14 ± 4.44	67.15 ± 2.08	90.88 ± 6.22
Ours (0.4)	**63.03 ± 1.73**	73.87 ± 2.47	39.04 ± 3.17	77.74 ± 4.49	**67.38 ± 2.10**	90.48 ± 6.20
Ours (0.6)	62.94 ± 1.75	73.97 ± 2.49	41.23 ± 3.25	**78.53 ± 4.67**	66.90 ± 2.20	**91.42 ± 6.22**
Ours (0.8)	63.02 ± 1.66	73.87 ± 2.23	41.58 ± 3.22	77.63 ± 4.36	67.22 ± 2.29	90.94 ± 6.73
Clustering results (ACC% ± std)						
Laplacian	64.58 ± 4.28	53.19 ± 2.93	21.44 ± 1.54	55.49 ± 3.12	70.49 ± 8.68	66.22 ± 17.20
SPEC	50.38 ± 12.99	35.72 ± 10.04	42.98 ± 5.90	52.01 ± 4.06	64.85 ± 3.29	56.95 ± 10.41
RUFS	66.43 ± 3.10	61.01 ± 7.44	34.53 ± 2.31	62.03 ± 9.61	79.61 ± 4.39	81.20 ± 4.43
EUFS	66.46 ± 2.98	54.46 ± 1.92	**58.93 ± 10.31**	56.86 ± 6.66	71.71 ± 6.53	74.00 ± 5.04
CUFS	65.06 ± 2.03	60.52 ± 3.23	41.42 ± 3.76	62.15 ± 5.21	69.70 ± 2.46	75.97 ± 5.56
Ours (0.2)	**67.74 ± 2.47**	61.21 ± 3.75	37.10 ± 3.04	64.26 ± 4.92	82.34 ± 3.65	83.00 ± 5.35
Ours (0.4)	67.58 ± 2.70	61.24 ± 3.79	32,60 ± 3.99	64.92 ± 4.01	**83.15 ± 3.97**	83.35 ± 5.37
Ours (0.6)	67.49 ± 2.61	**61.71 ± 3.74**	34.37 ± 3.92	**65.59 ± 4.21**	79.38 ± 3.89	**84.22 ± 5.52**
Ours (0.8)	67.67 ± 2.57	61.43 ± 3.53	35.02 ± 4.02	63.46 ± 4.78	82.33 ± 3.10	83.57 ± 5.10

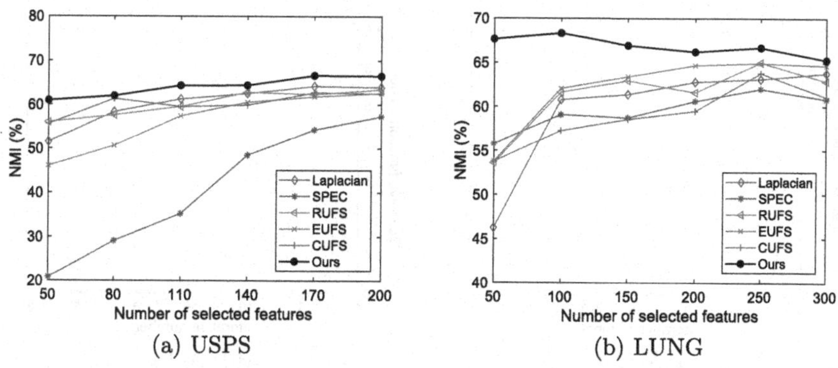

(a) USPS (b) LUNG

Fig. 1. Clustering performance (NMI) of all the methods on USPS and LUNG datasets.

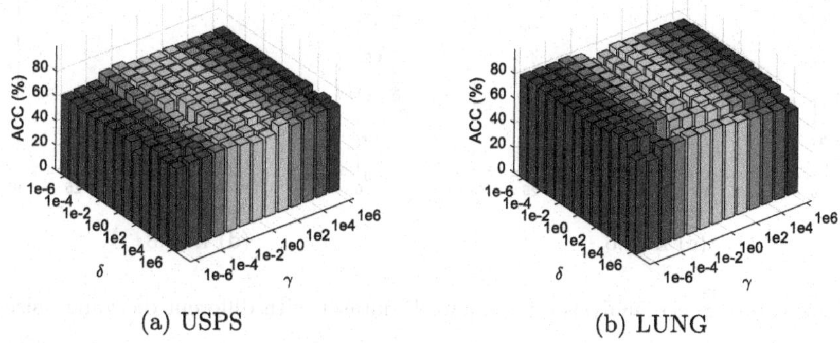

(a) USPS (b) LUNG

Fig. 2. Clustering accuracy with α and β fixed on USPS and LUNG datasets.

cluster label generation methods are significant for selecting discriminative features. EUFS achieves better clustering performance by directly embedding feature selection into the clustering algorithm and considering both data reconstruction capabilities and local structure. CUFS focuses on data distribution and data reconstruction simultaneously and achieves higher ACC and NMI than EUFS. JDLUFS achieves the best classification performance on 6 datasets, and the optimal clustering performance on 5 datasets, which can be mainly explained by the following reasons. First, using joint dictionary learning, the learned intrinsic space shared by feature space and pseudo label space can reconstruct features and cluster labels and minimize the reconstruction error. Second, we utilize linear sparse regression to capture cluster structure and maintain data distribution. Third, introduce the manifold regularization to reveal data local structure. Therefore, the three key factors are simultaneously integrated into our framework to guide feature selection. Additionally, for the dictionary size k, it can be observed that when $k = 0.4$ or $k = 0.6$, our model obtains the best results in most cases. As we continue to increase the dictionary size, the experimental

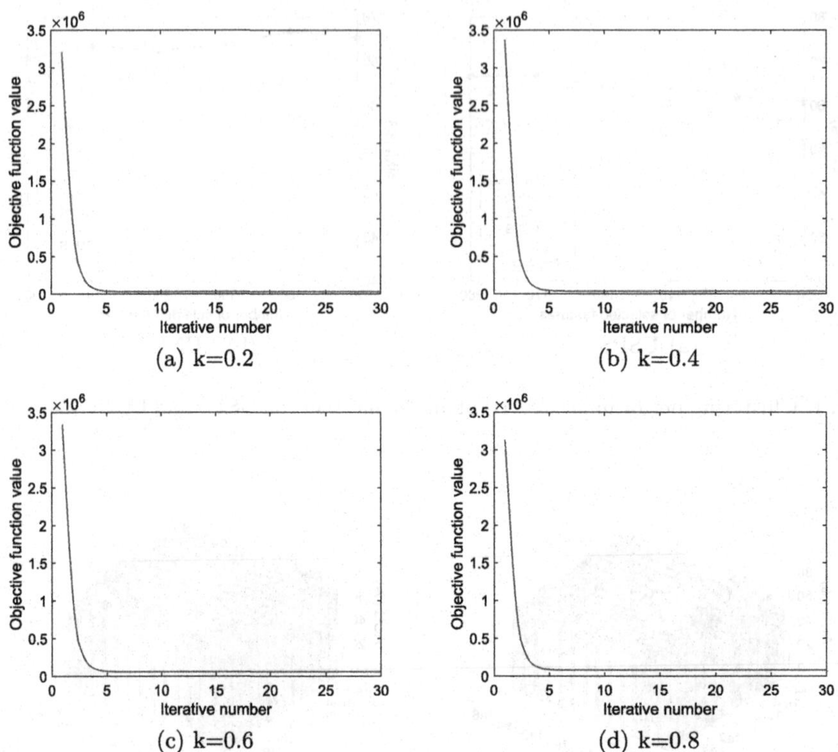

(a) k=0.2 (b) k=0.4 (c) k=0.6 (d) k=0.8

Fig. 3. Convergence analysis on Pixraw10P dataset with different dictionary sizes

results are not improved. Obviously, the intrinsic space dimension should not be too low or too high. Hence, the precision and storage consumption need to be considered simultaneously. In Fig. 1, we present the clustering performance in term of NMI as the number of selected features changes. Due to space limit, we only report the results on USPS and LUNG datasets. We can see that JDLUFS achieves better NMI than compared methods, which means our model tends to select representative features. However, the performance is comparatively sensitive to the number of selected features, which is still an open problem for many unsupervised feature selection algorithms.

4.3 Parameters Sensitivity and Convergence

JDLUFS has four parameters α, β, γ and δ. We always fix α and β to 1, and tune γ and δ from $\{10^{-6}, 10^{-5}, ..., 10^{6}\}$. The experimental results in terms of cluster accuracy on USPS and LUNG datasets are shown in Fig. 2. We can observe that the clustering performance doesn't vary much, which indicates that our method is not very sensitive to the parameters γ and δ with wide ranges. To verify the convergence of the proposed algorithm, we run JDLUFS on Pixraw10P dataset which has 10,000 features. Figure 3 shows the convergence curves of JDLUFS with different dictionary sizes k. The experimental results show that our algorithm converges within 30 iterations and is not sensitive to the dictionary size.

5 Conclusion

In this paper, we propose a joint dictionary learning method for unsupervised feature selection, which considers data distribution, data reconstruction and data local structure simultaneously and seamlessly integrates these three key factors into a unified framework. Compared with the existing unsupervised feature selection methods preserve data reconstruction via matrix factorization, we learn an intrinsic space shared by feature space and pseudo label space which can better reconstruct cluster labels and reduce reconstruction error. Moreover, we adopt linear sparse regression term to maintain the cluster structure of samples and $\ell_{2,1}$-norm is imposed on feature selection matrix to select the most discriminative features. Experiment results on benchmark datasets verify the effectiveness of the proposed method in classification and clustering performance. Future work will investigate if the proposed method can be extended to semi-supervised learning.

Acknowledgment. This work was partially supported by the National Natural Science Foundation of China (No. 61473259) and the Hunan Provincial Science & Technology Project Foundation (2018TP1018, 2018RS3065).

References

1. Alelyani, S., Tang, J., Liu, H.: Feature selection for clustering: a review. In: Aggarwal, C.C., Reddy, C.K. (eds.) Data Clustering: Algorithms and Applications, pp. 29–60. CRC Press, Boca Raton (2013)
2. Boyd, S.P., Parikh, N., Chu, E., Peleato, B., Eckstein, J.: Distributed optimization and statistical learning via the alternating direction method of multipliers. Found. Trends Mach. Learn. **3**(1), 1–122 (2011). https://doi.org/10.1561/2200000016
3. Cai, D., Zhang, C., He, X.: Unsupervised feature selection for multi-cluster data. In: Proceedings of the 16th ACM SIGKDD International Conference on Knowledge Discovery and Data Mining, pp. 333–342 (2010). https://doi.org/10.1145/1835804.1835848
4. He, X., Cai, D., Niyogi, P.: Laplacian score for feature selection. In: Advances in Neural Information Processing Systems, vol. 18, pp. 507–514 (2005)
5. Kong, X., Yu, P.S.: Semi-supervised feature selection for graph classification. In: Proceedings of the 16th ACM SIGKDD International Conference on Knowledge Discovery and Data Mining, pp. 793–802 (2010)
6. Li, J., Tang, J., Liu, H.: Reconstruction-based unsupervised feature selection: an embedded approach. In: Proceedings of the Twenty-Sixth International Joint Conference on Artificial Intelligence, pp. 2159–2165 (2017)
7. Li, J., Wu, L., Dani, H., Liu, H.: Unsupervised personalized feature selection. In: Proceedings of the Thirty-Second AAAI Conference on Artificial Intelligence (2018)

8. Li, Z., Yang, Y., Liu, J., Zhou, X., Lu, H.: Unsupervised feature selection using nonnegative spectral analysis. In: Proceedings of the Twenty-Sixth AAAI Conference on Artificial Intelligence (2012)
9. von Luxburg, U.: A tutorial on spectral clustering. Stat. Comput. **17**(4), 395–416 (2007). https://doi.org/10.1007/s11222-007-9033-z
10. Nie, F., Huang, H., Cai, X., Ding, C.H.: Efficient and robust feature selection via joint $\ell_{2,1}$-norms minimization. In: Advances in Neural Information Processing Systems, pp. 1813–1821 (2010). https://doi.org/10.1007/978-3-319-10690-8_12
11. Qian, M., Zhai, C.: Robust unsupervised feature selection. In: IJCAI 2013, Proceedings of the 23rd International Joint Conference on Artificial Intelligence, pp. 1621–1627 (2013)
12. Wang, S., Tang, J., Liu, H.: Embedded unsupervised feature selection. In: Proceedings of the Twenty-Ninth AAAI Conference on Artificial Intelligence, pp. 470–476 (2015)
13. Zhao, Z., Liu, H.: Spectral feature selection for supervised and unsupervised learning. In: Machine Learning, Proceedings of the Twenty-Fourth International Conference, pp. 1151–1157 (2007). https://doi.org/10.1145/1273496.1273641
14. Zhu, F., Shao, L., Yu, M.: Cross-modality submodular dictionary learning for information retrieval. In: Proceedings of the 23rd ACM International Conference on Conference on Information and Knowledge Management, pp. 1479–1488 (2014). https://doi.org/10.1145/2661829.2661926
15. Zhu, P., Hu, Q., Zhang, C., Zuo, W.: Coupled dictionary learning for unsupervised feature selection. In: Proceedings of the Thirtieth AAAI Conference on Artificial Intelligence, pp. 2422–2428 (2016)
16. Zhu, P., Xu, Q., Hu, Q., Zhang, C.: Co-regularized unsupervised feature selection. Neurocomputing **275**, 2855–2863 (2018). https://doi.org/10.1016/j.neucom.2017.11.061
17. Zhu, X., Zhu, Y., Zhang, S., Hu, R., He, W.: Adaptive hypergraph learning for unsupervised feature selection. In: Proceedings of the Twenty-Sixth International Joint Conference on Artificial Intelligence, pp. 3581–3587 (2017)

Comparison Between Filter Criteria for Feature Selection in Regression

Alexandra Degeest[1,2](✉), Michel Verleysen[2], and Benoît Frénay[3]

[1] Haute-Ecole Bruxelles Brabant - ISIB, 150 rue Royale, 1000 Brussels, Belgium
adegeest@he2b.be

[2] Machine Learning Group - ICTEAM, UCLouvain, Place du Levant 3, 1348 Louvain-La-Neuve, Belgium
michel.verleysen@uclouvain.be

[3] Faculty of Computer Science, NADI Institute - PReCISE Research Center, Université de Namur, Rue Grandgagnage 21, 5000 Namur, Belgium
benoit.frenay@unamur.be

Abstract. High-dimensional data are ubiquitous in regression. To obtain a better understanding of the data or to ease the learning process, reducing the data to a subset of the most relevant features is important. Among the different methods of feature selection, filter methods are popular because they are independent from the model, which makes them fast and computationally simpler than other feature selection methods. The key factor of a filter method is the filter criterion. This paper focuses on which properties make a good filter criterion, in order to be able to select one from the numerous existing ones. Six properties are discussed, and three filter criteria are compared with respect to the aforementioned properties.

Keywords: Feature selection · Filter criteria · Regression

1 Introduction

In regression problems, datasets are often high-dimensional. Therefore, selecting a reduced subset of the most relevant features is an important challenge for data analysis, to help fighting the curse of dimensionality, to ease the learning process, to increase interpretability of the original data, etc. Many works, in diverse domains such as healthcare, spam detection or marketing, focus on methods reducing the original subset of features in datasets [9,13,22,26,28]. Feature selection can roughly be classified into filters, wrappers and embedded methods. This paper focuses on filter methods, which have the advantage to be fast thanks to their independence from the model used. Indeed filters do not need to train any model during the selection process, contrarily to wrappers [16,17] or embedded methods [20]. They also lead to a selection of features that is independent from the models that will be subsequently used. To select the subset of the

I. V. Tetko et al. (Eds.): ICANN 2019, LNCS 11728, pp. 59–71, 2019.
https://doi.org/10.1007/978-3-030-30484-3_5

most relevant features for the problem at hand, filter methods need a sound relevance criterion. The choice of this criterion is therefore strategic for a successful filter-based feature selection process. The problem is that there exist many filter criteria with various properties. Among these criteria, this paper does not intend to present the best criterion to be used on every dataset but focuses instead on the essential properties of what makes a good filter criterion for feature selection in regression, and what are its strengths or weaknesses with respect to these properties. These properties are described and discussed in Sect. 3, after introducing feature selection with filters in Sect. 2. Several interesting filter criteria are described in Sect. 4 and compared in the light of these properties in Sect. 5. Finally, conclusions on these comparisons are given in Sect. 6.

2 Feature Selection with Filter Criteria

Feature selection helps to reduce the dimension of a dataset by removing redundant or less useful features. In the context of filter methods for feature selection, a good relevance criterion must first be selected. The relevance criterion measures the importance of the relationship between a feature, or a group of features, and the target. The target is the output variable depending on the problem at hand. This criterion is therefore the key factor of a successful dimension reduction process with filter methods.

Filter criteria are very diverse: for example, some are based on entropy, such as the mutual information (Sect. 4.1), while some are based on noise variance (Sect. 4.2) or regression quality (Sect. 4.3). The question raised by this paper is: "What is needed in a good filter criterion in order to obtain the subset of the most relevant features for the problem at hand?" These properties are listed in Sect. 3 and used for comparison of several relevance criteria in Sect. 5.

A complete feature selection process needs mainly two ingredients: a filter criterion, as already discussed, but also a search procedure, in order to find the best subset of features among all possible subsets (whose number grows exponentially with the number of initial features), without having to compute the filter criterion between all subsets of variables and the target. Several methods exist, such as forward search, greedy search, genetic algorithms, mRMR [23], etc. During this search procedure, the chosen relevance criterion is, again, strategic. For example, those search methods need a multivariate criterion to be able to measure the relevance between two features but also between a subset of features and the target. Indeed it is often believed that filters use univariate criteria only; this is not correct: several multivariate filter criteria exist, such as the mutual information (Sect. 4.1) and the noise variance (Sect. 4.2). This property is discussed in Sect. 3.2 and is used for comparison in Sect. 5.2.

3 Properties of a Relevance Criterion for Feature Selection in Regression

The choice of the relevance criterion used for feature selection, among the various existing ones, is strategic. This section describes the six essential properties of a good relevance criterion used as a filter during a feature selection process in regression. It also discusses the reasons why these properties are important. In order to demonstrate how to use these six properties, a comparison of the filter criteria presented in Sect. 4, with respect to these properties, is realised in Sect. 5.

3.1 Property 1: Ability to Detect Nonlinear Relationships

In real datasets, the relationship between variables is most generally nonlinear. Therefore, a good filter criterion for feature selection in regression should be able to detect nonlinear relations between variables, or groups of variables [11,14].

3.2 Property 2: Ability to Detect Multivariate Relationships

When looking for the best subset of features, a search procedure, such as a forward search, needs to evaluate the relations between groups of two, or more, features and the target. Indeed, measuring the relationship between one input feature and the target is not enough, as some features only contribute to the target when combined. An example of that would be when the target is determined by the product of two features. To achieve this multidimensional measurement, the filter criterion needs to be able to measure multivariate relations between groups of variables. This property is essential for feature selection methods with a filter criterion [6,24].

3.3 Property 3: Estimator Behaviour

Most filter criteria are defined as a statistical property of the data integrated over the domain space. The criteria are repeatedly evaluated at each step of the search procedure. However, the criteria themselves can usually not be evaluated exactly because of the integration over the domain space. An estimator is thus needed, whose computational complexity and statistical properties are therefore important and must be taken into account when choosing a criterion [3].

3.4 Property 4: Estimator Parameters

Filter criteria estimator often require an optimization parameter to be tuned. The influence of this parameter on the quality of the estimation, and therefore on the quality of the feature selection itself, might be important. For example, nearest-neighbours based estimators, such as the Kraskov estimator (see Sect. 4.1), need to choose the number of neighbours used in the estimation. This choice of parameter might be crucial, while its influence is sometimes underestimated in the literature. When comparing different estimators, the stability of the estimator with respect to an optimization parameter is an important property to take into account. This property is discussed in Sect. 5.4.

3.5 Property 5: Estimator Behaviour in Small Datasets

Data are ubiquitous. In many fields the number of data that can be collected might be huge, leading to the so-called "big data". In other fields however the number of data remains limited (for example because of collection costs), while the number of dimensions (features) might be large for every data [15]. The ratio "number of instances/dimensionality" is therefore an important concept in all machine learning methods. A small sample dataset is one with a low ratio "number of instances/dimensionality". When working with a small sample dataset, the estimator of the filter criterion needs to behave well to select the best subset of features. This property is discussed, and filter criteria are compared with respect to it, in Sect. 5.5, for small sample situations.

3.6 Property 6: Invariant Estimator

When comparing features or groups of features having a linear, or quasi-linear, relationship, some estimators evaluate differently linear relationships with different gradients of the relationship between the features and the target. However, the importance of a feature or a group of features should not depend on this gradient but only on the predictability, i.e. the quality of the information in the features used to predict the output. In feature selection, this would have the consequence to prefer some features with a greater gradient than features with a lower gradient. The independence of the estimator towards this gradient is discussed in Sect. 5.6.

4 Description of Three Popular Criteria

This section reviews three filter criteria, the mutual information, the noise variance and the adjusted coefficient of determination, with their most frequently used estimators, in order to illustrate the important properties of a good filter criterion presented in Sect. 3.

4.1 Mutual Information

Mutual information (MI) is a frequently used criterion for filter methods, in regression or classification [1,2,13,21,27]. Based on entropy, it is a symmetric measurement of the dependence between random variables, introduced by Shannon in 1948 [25]. It evaluates the importance of the relationship between a feature, or a group of features, and another one. It has been shown to be an efficient criterion to select relevant features in classification [11,23] and in regression [10,14]. This paper focuses on regression problems.

Let X and Y be two random variables, whose respective probability density functions are p_X and p_Y, and where X represents the features and Y the target. MI measures the reduction in the uncertainty on Y when X is known

$$I(X;Y) = H(Y) - H(Y|X) \tag{1}$$

where $H(Y) = -\int_Y p_Y(y)\log p_Y(y)dy$ is the entropy of Y and $H(Y|X) = \int_X p_X(x)H(Y|X=x)dx$ is the conditional entropy of Y given X. The mutual information between X and Y is equal to zero if and only if they are independent. If Y can be perfectly predicted as a function of X, then $I(X;Y) = H(Y)$.

With real datasets, MI cannot be directly computed because it is defined in terms of probability density functions, which are unknown when only a finite sample of data is available. Therefore, MI has to be estimated from the dataset [12]. The estimator introduced by Kraskov et al. [19] is based on a k-nearest neighbour method and results from the Kozachenko-Leonenko entropy estimator [18] $\hat{H}(X) = -\psi(k)+\psi(N)+\log c_d + \frac{d}{N}\sum_{i=1}^{N}\log \epsilon_k(i)$, where k is the number of neighbours, N is the number of instances in the dataset, d is the dimensionality, $c_d = (2\pi^{\frac{d}{2}})/\Gamma(\frac{d}{2})$ is the volume of the unitary ball of dimension d, Γ is the gamma function, $\epsilon_k(i)$ is twice the distance from the ith instance to its kth nearest neighbour and ψ is the digamma function. The Kraskov estimator of the mutual information is

$$\hat{I}(X;Y) = \psi(N) + \psi(K) - \frac{1}{k} - \frac{1}{N}\sum_{i=1}^{N}(\psi(\tau_x(i)) + \psi(\tau_y(i))) \tag{2}$$

where $\tau_x(i)$ is the number of points located no further than the distance $\epsilon_X(i,k)/2$ from the ith observation in the X space, $\tau_y(i)$ is the number of points located no further than the distance $\epsilon_Y(i,k)/2$ from the ith observation in the Y space and where $\epsilon_X(i,k)/2$ and $\epsilon_Y(i,k)/2$ are the projections into the X and Y subspaces of the distance between the ith observation and its kth neighbour.

When using MI for feature selection, the relationships between several subsets of features and the target Y are computed with a search procedure. Among these subsets, the one maximising the value of the estimated mutual information $\hat{I}(X;Y)$ (2) is selected.

4.2 Noise Variance

Noise variance is another popular filter criterion used for feature selection. Its aim is to evaluate the level of noise in a finite dataset. In regression, the noise represents the error in estimating the output variable as function of the input variables, under the hypothesis that a model could be built (by a machine learning regression model).

Let us consider a dataset with N instances, d features X_j, a target Y and N input-output pairs $(\mathbf{x}_i, y_i)$. The relationship between these input-output pairs is

$$y_i = f(\mathbf{x}_i) + \epsilon_i \quad i = 1, ..., N \tag{3}$$

where f is the unknown function between $\mathbf{x}_i$ and y_i, and ϵ_i is the noise or prediction error when estimating f. The principle is to select the subsets of features X_j which lead to the lowest prediction error, or lowest noise variance [14].

With real finite datasets, the noise variance has to be estimated, e.g. with the Delta Test, which is a widely used estimator [7,8]. The Delta Test δ is defined as

$$\delta = \frac{1}{2N} \sum_{i=1}^{N} [y_{NN(i)} - y_i]^2 \tag{4}$$

where N is the size of the dataset, $y_{NN(i)}$ is the output associated to $\mathbf{x}_{NN(i)}$, $\mathbf{x}_{NN(i)}$ being the nearest neighbour of the point $\mathbf{x}_i$.

For feature selection using the noise variance, and therefore the Delta Test estimator, the relationships between several subsets of features and Y are computed, again with a search procedure such as a greedy search. The search procedure selects the subset of features with the lowest value of the estimator δ.

4.3 Coefficient of Determination

The coefficient of determination R^2 is the proportion of the variance in the output variable that can be explained from the input variables; it ranges between 0% (unpredictable) and 100% (totally predictable). The definition of R^2 is

$$R^2 = 1 - \frac{SS_{res}}{SS_{tot}} \tag{5}$$

where $SS_{res} = \sum_i (y_i - f(\mathbf{x}_i))^2$ and $SS_{tot} = \sum_i (y_i - \overline{y})^2$ with i = 1, ..., n, and with $\overline{y}$ being the mean of the observed data. This coefficient statistically measures how well the regression approximates the target. Because R^2 automatically increases when features are added to the model, we use its alternative, the adjusted R^2, or R^2_{adj}, for feature selection in regression, which is more suitable for small sample sizes. Its definition is

$$R^2_{adj} = 1 - \frac{SS_{res}/(n-d-1)}{SS_{tot}/(n-1)} \tag{6}$$

where d is the number of selected features in the model and n the sample size. A low R^2_{adj} indicates that the data are not close to the fitted regression line and a high R^2_{adj} indicates the opposite.

The R^2_{adj} criterion used with a linear regression model cannot capture the nonlinear relationships between the features and the target. In order to use the R^2_{adj} in a nonlinear context, local linear approximations are considered [5]. In practice, for each point of the function f, a linear regression is computed with a number of neighbours k starting from 4. The R^2_{adj} is computed for every regression. For each value of k, an average of the R^2_{adj} on every point of f is computed. The best mean R^2_{adj} is then selected; it corresponds to a specific number of neighbours k.

The first step of the search procedure, the univariate step, selects the feature with the highest mean R^2_{adj} [5]. The multidimensional feature selection strategy, where the group of features with the highest mean R^2_{adj} is selected, is implemented similarly, but instead of evaluating the regression in two dimensions, R^2_{adj} evaluates the fitness of the local, multivariate regressions in three, four, five dimensions, depending on the step of the search process.

5 Analysis and Comparison

This section analyses and compares, in the context of feature selection in regression, the mutual information, the noise variance and the coefficient of determination (described in Sect. 4), with respect to the six properties listed and discussed in Sect. 3.

5.1 Comparison with Property 1: Non-linearity

The three filter criteria described in this paper can evaluate a nonlinear relationship between a group of features and the target. For the mutual information and the noise variance, it is intrinsically true. For R^2_{adj}, the implementation described in Sect. 4.3 uses local approximations of the regression and is therefore suitable for nonlinear relations between the features and the target as well. This important property is therefore non-discriminant for the three filter criteria compared in this section. This paper does not consider dependencies between features X_j and focuses on evaluating their interest for predicting a given target. Several approaches have been proposed to deal with redundancy in feature subsets, like e.g. mRMR [23].

5.2 Comparison with Property 2: Multivariate Criterion

The three filter criteria compared in this section are all able to evaluate the relationship between a group of features and the target for relevance, and between groups of features for redundancy, as shown in their respective equations (see Sect. 4). This second property is therefore also non-discriminant. This shows that these three criteria are all worth considering when doing feature selection.

5.3 Comparison with Property 3: Estimator Behaviour

The estimators of the three relevance criteria compared in this paper are all based on a k-nearest neighbour method. Therefore, their time complexity and their statistical properties are similar and less discriminant. Their respective behaviour during a forward search method for selecting features with small sample datasets is discussed in Sect. 5.5.

5.4 Comparison with Property 4: Estimator Parameters

Being all based on a k-nearest-neighbour method, the three estimators of the compared criteria all have one optimization parameter k. For the Kraskov estimator of the mutual information, this parameter is usually set between 6 and 8 [19]. For the Delta Test, the k parameter is, by definition, set to 1 and therefore does not need to be modified. For the mean R^2_{adj}, k is usually set higher than for the Kraskov estimator, in order to obtain stable results during the feature selection process.

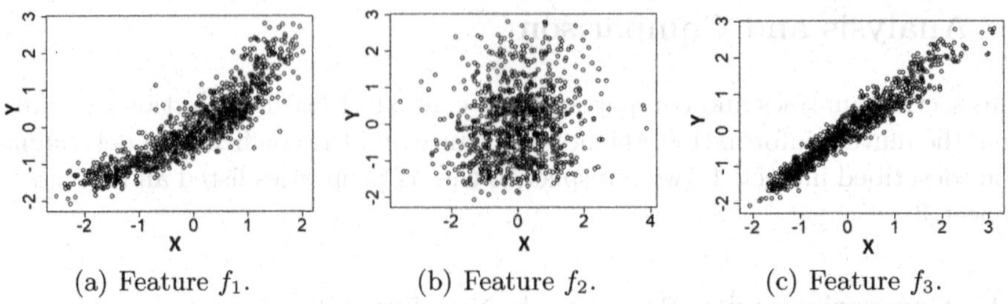

(a) Feature f_1. (b) Feature f_2. (c) Feature f_3.

Fig. 1. Three features of the dataset *Anthrokids*, where f_1 is the 1st feature, f_2 is the 11th feature and f_3 is the 19th feature of the dataset.

In order to evaluate the relation between the value of k and the value of the filter criterion, and in order to understand how to select k when using these estimators, the first step of a feature selection method has been performed on 3 features of the *Anthrokids*[1] dataset (Fig. 1), with a value of k neighbours ranging from 5 to approximately 200, both for the mutual information and the noise variance. Let us remark that this experiment has not been performed for the Delta Test, the value of k being set to 1 by definition.

Results are shown in Fig. 2: The MI value for the 3 features f_1 to f_3 in Fig. 2(a) and the mean R^2_{adj} for the same features in Fig. 2(b). Figure 2(a) shows a good stability of the mutual information estimator towards the value of k for these features. Figure 2(b) shows that the value of the highest mean R^2_{adj} is less stable than the values of the mutual information. But for a value of k higher than 50, the feature selection results are stable for R^2_{adj} as well, as the ranking of the features does not change for a k between 50 and 200, the feature f_1 being the first to be selected and the feature f_3 being the last to be selected by both criteria.

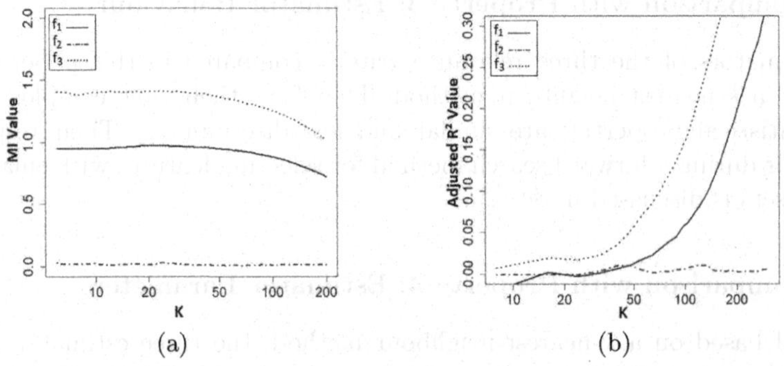

(a) (b)

Fig. 2. Evolution of (2(a)) MI values and (2(b)) R^2_{adj} values for three features f_1, f_2 and f_3 (corresponding respectively to the features 1, 11 and 19 of the dataset *Anthrokids* presented in Fig. 1) when k varies.

[1] https://research.cs.aalto.fi/aml/datasets.shtml.

5.5 Comparison with Property 5: Estimator Behaviour in Small Sample Datasets

Methods such as k-nearest-neighbours methods can suffer from a bias when comparing smooth and non-smooth features, especially in small sample [4,5]. However, the biases in the estimations are much more severe with the mutual information than with the noise variance or the adjusted R^2 [4,7].

Experiments have been performed on the real-world dataset *Anthrokids*. A forward search has been realised with three features of this dataset (Fig. 1). Results are presented in Fig. 3. The best feature selected in Fig. 3(a) is the one maximizing the mutual information value. In Fig. 3(b), it is the one minimizing the noise variance. And in Fig. 3(c), it is the one maximizing the adjusted R^2. For the three criteria, the first feature selected is the feature f_3. Results also show that the value of the mutual information and of the adjusted R^2 stabilises itself around a hundred instances (Figs. 3(a) and (c)). The values of the Delta Test measure are more stable, even in small sample. When comparing Figs. 3(a), (b) and (c), the adjusted R^2 measure and the MI measure presents the advantage to distinguish better the values between the features f_1 and f_3. For the Delta Test, these values are almost the same, contrarily to the adjusted R^2.

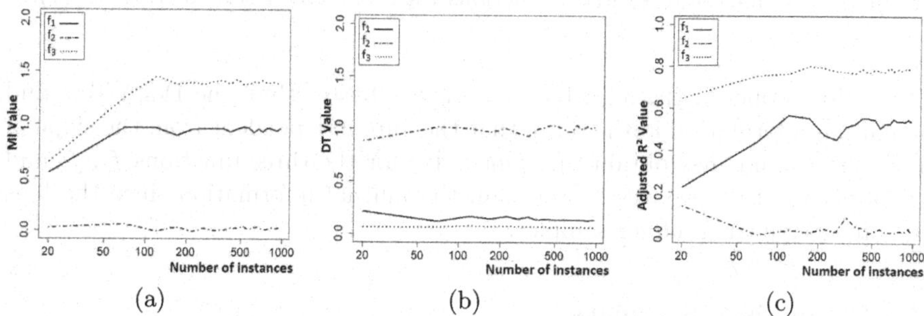

Fig. 3. Average values of (3(a)) MI measures, (3(b)) Delta Test measures and (3(c)) adjusted R^2 measures for three features of the dataset *Anthrokids*.

5.6 Comparison with Property 6: Estimator Invariance

In order to analyse the invariance of the estimator with respect to the gradient of the relation between a feature, or a group of features, and the target, an illustrative experiment has been realised on three linear functions with various slopes. Three different linear functions have been generated:

$$\begin{aligned} y_1 = f_1(\mathbf{x}) &= 2x_1 + x_2 + \epsilon \quad \text{where } \epsilon \sim \mathrm{N}(0,\ 0.1) \\ y_2 = f_2(\mathbf{x}) &= 4x_1 + 2x_2 + \epsilon \quad \text{where } \epsilon \sim \mathrm{N}(0,\ 0.1) \\ y_3 = f_3(\mathbf{x}) &= 6x_1 + 4x_2 + \epsilon \quad \text{where } \epsilon \sim \mathrm{N}(0,\ 0.1) \end{aligned} \tag{7}$$

Experiments have been performed with various sizes of samples, from small ones to larger ones. For each size, an average value of the estimators of the three criteria have been computed. The results of this experiment are presented in Fig. 4. The Delta Test (Fig. 4(b)) and the mutual information (Fig. 4(a)) show an influence of the gradient on the results. This influence disappears with a larger size of sample for the Delta Test. R^2_{adj} (Fig. 4(c)) shows no influence of the function gradient on the results as the three functions are almost superposed.

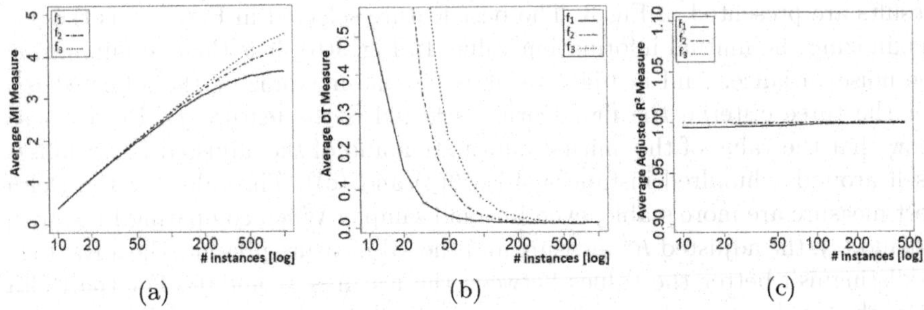

Fig. 4. Average value of (4(a)) the mutual information, (4(b)) the Delta Test and (4(c)) the adjusted R^2 for the three linear functions with different slopes described in (7).

For this property, the adjusted R^2 behaves better than the Delta Test and the mutual information in the sense that they are independent from the slope of the functions and they obtain the same value for the three functions f_1, f_2 and f_3. The Delta Test behaves better than the mutual information since the bias tends to disappear in larger samples.

5.7 Comparison Summary

Table 1 shows a summary of the comparison of the three filter criteria with respect to the six properties presented in Sect. 3, in a context of feature selection in regression. When analysing the ease of parameter optimization (P4), the Delta Test performs better than the mutual information and the adjusted R^2 because its only parameter k is set to 1 by definition. In the small sample scenario presented in this paper (P5), the Delta Test behaves better than the two other criteria. For the estimator invariance (P6), the adjusted R^2 behaves better than the Delta Test and the mutual information in the sense that this criterion is not influenced by the slope of the function between the features and the target.

Table 1. Comparison of mutual information with Kraskov, Delta Test and Adjusted R^2. A '+' indicates a good behaviour of the criterion towards this property. A '−' indicates a weakness of the criterion towards this property. The signs'+ +' or '− − ' are only there to show a difference between two criteria with a good (or bad) behaviour towards the property, when one of them is better (or worse) than the other one.

Properties	MI with Kraskov	Noise variance with DT	Adjusted R^2
P1: Non-linearity	+	+	+
P2: Multivariate	+	+	+
P3: Estimator Behaviour	+	+	+
P4: Estimator Parameters	+	+ +	−
P5: Estimator in Small Sample	−	+	−
P6: Estimator Invariance	−	−	+

6 Conclusions

This paper focuses on which properties make a good filter criterion for feature selection in regression. To illustrate the importance of these properties, it compares three filter criteria, with artificial and real datasets, to show their respective strengths and weaknesses with respect to each other. These properties could be used to analyse any other filter criterion used for feature selection or they could be used in situations where there is redundancy like mRMR or missing values in feature subsets.

References

1. Battiti, R.: Using mutual information for selecting features in supervised neural net learning. IEEE Trans. Neural Netw. **5**, 537–550 (1994). https://doi.org/10.1109/72.298224
2. Brown, G., Pocock, A., Zhao, M., Lujan, M.: Conditional likelihood maximisation: a unifying framework for mutual information feature selection. J. Mach. Learn. Res. **13**, 27–66 (2012)
3. Chandrashekar, G., Sahin, F.: A survey on feature selection methods. Comput. Electr. Eng. **40**, 16–28 (2014). https://doi.org/10.1016/j.compeleceng.2013.11.024
4. Degeest, A., Verleysen, M., Frénay, B.: Smoothness bias in relevance estimators for feature selection in regression. In: Proceedings of AIAI, pp. 285–294 (2018). https://doi.org/10.1007/978-3-319-92007-825
5. Degeest, A., Verleysen, M., Frénay, B.: About filter criteria for feature selection in regression. In: Rojas, I., Joya, G., Catala, A. (eds.) IWANN 2019. LNCS, vol. 11507, pp. 579–590. Springer, Cham (2019). https://doi.org/10.1007/978-3-030-20518-8_48
6. Doquire, G., Verleysen, M.: A comparison of multivariate mutual information estimators for feature selection. In: Proceedings of ICPRAM (2012). https://doi.org/10.5220/0003726101760185
7. Eirola, E., Lendasse, A., Corona, F., Verleysen, M.: The delta test: The 1-NN estimator as a feature selection criterion. In: Proceedings of IJCNN, pp. 4214–4222 (2014). https://doi.org/10.1109/IJCNN.2014.6889560

8. Eirola, E., Liitiäinen, E., Lendasse, A., Corona, F., Verleysen, M.: Using the delta test for variable selection. In: Proceedings of ESANN (2008)
9. François, D., Rossi, F., Wertz, V., Verleysen, M.: Resampling methods for parameter-free and robust feature selection with mutual information. Neurocomputing **70**(7–9), 1276–1288 (2007). https://doi.org/10.1016/j.neucom.2006.11.019
10. Frénay, B., Doquire, G., Verleysen, M.: Is mutual information adequate for feature selection in regression? Neural Netw. **48**, 1–7 (2013). https://doi.org/10.1016/j.neunet.2013.07.003
11. Frénay, B., Doquire, G., Verleysen, M.: Theoretical and empirical study on the potential inadequacy of mutual information for feature selection in classification. Neurocomputing **112**, 64–78 (2013). https://doi.org/10.1016/j.neucom.2012.12.051
12. Gao, W., Kannan, S., Oh, S., Viswanath, P.: Estimating mutual information for discrete-continuous mixtures. In: Advances in Neural Information Processing Systems, vol. 30, pp. 5986–5997. Curran Associates, Inc. (2017). http://arxiv.org/abs/1709.06212
13. Gómez-Verdejo, V., Verleysen, M., Fleury, J.: Information-theoretic feature selection for functional data classification. Neurocomputing **72**, 3580–3589 (2009). https://doi.org/10.1016/j.neucom.2008.12.035
14. Guillén, A., Sovilj, D., Mateo, F., Rojas, I., Lendasse, A.: New methodologies based on delta test for variable selection in regression problems. In: Workshop on Parallel Architectures and Bioinspired Algorithms, Canada (2008)
15. Helleputte, T., Dupont, P.: Feature selection by transfer learning with linear regularized models. In: Buntine, W., Grobelnik, M., Mladenić, D., Shawe-Taylor, J. (eds.) ECML PKDD 2009. LNCS (LNAI), vol. 5781, pp. 533–547. Springer, Heidelberg (2009). https://doi.org/10.1007/978-3-642-04180-8_52
16. Karegowda, A.G., Jayaram, M.A., Manjunath, A.S.: Feature subset selection problem using wrapper approach in supervised learning. Int. J. Comput. Appl. **1**(7), 13–17 (2010). https://doi.org/10.5120/169-295
17. Kohavi, R., John, G.H.: Wrappers for feature subset selection. Artif. Intell. **97**, 273–324 (1997). https://doi.org/10.1016/S0004-3702(97)00043-X
18. Kozachenko, L.F., Leonenko, N.: Sample estimate of the entropy of a random vector. Prob. Inform. Trans. **23**, 95–101 (1987)
19. Kraskov, A., Stögbauer, H., Grassberger, P.: Estimating mutual information. Phys. Rev. E **69**, 066138 (2004). https://doi.org/10.1103/PhysRevE.69.066138
20. Lal, T.N., Chapelle, O., Weston, J., Elisseeff, A.: Embedded methods. In: Guyon, I., Nikravesh, M., Gunn, S., Zadeh, L.A. (eds.) Feature Extraction. Studies in Fuzziness and Soft Computing, vol. 207, pp. 137–165. Springer, Heidelberg (2006). https://doi.org/10.1007/978-3-540-35488-86
21. Liu, A., Jun, G., Ghosh, J.: A self-training approach to cost sensitive uncertainty sampling. In: Buntine, W., Grobelnik, M., Mladenić, D., Shawe-Taylor, J. (eds.) ECML PKDD 2009. LNCS (LNAI), vol. 5781, pp. 10–10. Springer, Heidelberg (2009). https://doi.org/10.1007/978-3-642-04180-8_10
22. Paul, J., D'Ambrosio, R., Dupont, P.: Kernel methods for heterogeneous feature selection. Neurocomputing **169**, 187–195 (2015). https://doi.org/10.1016/j.neucom.2014.12.098
23. Peng, H., Long, F., Ding, C.: Feature selection based on mutual information: criteria of max-dependency, max-relevance, and min-redundancy. IEEE Trans. Pattern Anal. Mach. Intell. **27**, 1226–1238 (2005). https://doi.org/10.1109/TPAMI.2005.159

24. Schaffernicht, E., Kaltenhaeuser, R., Verma, S.S., Gross, H.-M.: On estimating mutual information for feature selection. In: Diamantaras, K., Duch, W., Iliadis, L.S. (eds.) ICANN 2010. LNCS, vol. 6352, pp. 362–367. Springer, Heidelberg (2010). https://doi.org/10.1007/978-3-642-15819-3_48
25. Shannon, C.E.: A mathematical theory of communication. Bell Syst. Tech. J. **27**, 379–423 (1948). https://doi.org/10.1002/j.1538-7305.1948.tb01338.x
26. Song, Q., Ni, J., Wang, G.: A fast clustering-based feature subset selection algorithm for high-dimensional data. IEEE Trans. Knowl. Data Eng. **25**(1), 1–14 (2013). https://doi.org/10.1109/TKDE.2011.181
27. Vergara, J.R., Estévez, P.A.: A review of feature selection methods based on mutual information. Neural Comput. Appl. **24**, 175–186 (2014). https://doi.org/10.1007/s00521-013-1368-0
28. Xue, B., Zhang, M., Browne, W., Yao, X.: A survey on evolutionary computation approaches to feature selection. IEEE Trans. Evol. Comput. **20** (2015). https://doi.org/10.1109/TEVC.2015.2504420

CancelOut: A Layer for Feature Selection in Deep Neural Networks

Vadim Borisov[1(✉)], Johannes Haug[1], and Gjergji Kasneci[1,2]

[1] Eberhard Karls University of Tübingen, Tübingen, Germany
{vadim.borisov,johannes-christian.haug,gjergji.kasneci}@uni-tuebingen.de
[2] SCHUFA Holding AG, Wiesbaden, Germany

Abstract. Feature ranking (FR) and feature selection (FS) are crucial steps in data preprocessing; they can be used to avoid the curse of dimensionality problem, reduce training time, and enhance the performance of a machine learning model. In this paper, we propose a new layer for deep neural networks - CancelOut, which can be utilized for FR and FS tasks, for supervised and unsupervised learning. Empirical results show that the proposed method can find feature subsets that are superior to traditional feature analysis techniques. Furthermore, the layer is easy to use and requires adding only a few additional lines of code to a deep learning training loop. We implemented the proposed method using the PyTorch framework and published it online (The code is available at: www.github.com/unnir/CancelOut).

Keywords: Deep learning · Feature ranking · Feature selection · Unsupervised feature selection · Machine learning explainability

1 Introduction

Feature importance and interpretability of machine learning (ML) models have received much attention in the recent years due to the fact that accurate estimations are not always enough to solve a data problem. An explanation of machine learning model outcomes may help not only to understand the model's results, but also to introduce new tests, better understand the data, and as a consequence from above, improve trust in the model, which is important when the model is used by specialists from other fields. However, most accurate and robust ML models usually cannot be interpreted [4].

One of the most effective ML methods nowadays is deep learning (DL), which can be explained in terms of the universal approximation theorem [2]. Which principally states that any compactly supported continuous function on $\mathbb{R}^n$ can be approximated with a single hidden layer feed-forward neural network (NN). However, due to DL's high inherent complexity, most DL models are primarily handled as a black box. Even though recent attempts have been made to address the issue of their interpretability and feature selection [1,4], existing methods are complicated.

I. V. Tetko et al. (Eds.): ICANN 2019, LNCS 11728, pp. 72–83, 2019.
https://doi.org/10.1007/978-3-030-30484-3_6

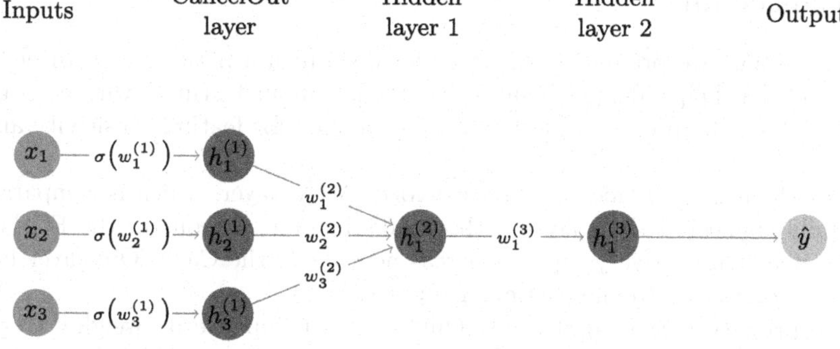

Fig. 1. A deep neural network with a CancelOut layer as an input layer.

2 Related Work

Many research articles on feature ranking (FR) and feature selection (FS) using DL propose the permutation method, which is based on the idea that if we remove or corrupt a feature from a dataset, the performance will change. By analyzing these changes, it is possible to determine if a feature is valuable or not. The obvious drawback of that idea is that it is computation-intensive, and in order to check n features, one need to train a DL model at least n times.

Another similar strategy was proposed in [1], where the dropout layer is exploited for feature ranking [12] for feature ranking. To analyze which features are important, an artificial NN model with a dropout layer must achieve minimum loss, and the dropout layer should learn small dropout rates for features that are important, while increasing the dropout rate for the rest of unimportant features. In this case, a model can be run once.

An interesting approach for quantifying the influence of individual input signals on the output computed by a deep neural network was proposed in the paper [6]. This method is based on the estimation of local linear models for each neuron in the network and the propagation and aggregation of these models into a net wide model.

The work in [9] introduces a similar idea to the linear models with elastic net regularization, but it employs a NN with multiple layers. This method regularizes input weights in a loss function using $l1$ and $l2$ norms together; without these terms the method is unstable.

Furthermore, many articles investigate an interpretation of a decision of the ANN for a single data sample [13]. However, this approach is hard to apply for feature ranking of a whole dataset.

The paper is divided into four sections. In Sect. 3, the proposed approach for feature ranking is introduced. Section 4 presents the implementation and result of the study. Finally, Sect. 5 contains a summary of the work.

3 CancelOut

In this Section, we present a new layer for deep neural networks - CancelOut, a method that helps identify a subset of relevant input features (variables) in a dataset. Also, the proposed method can be applied for feature sensitivity analysis.

CancelOut is an artificial neural network (ANN) layer, which is comparable to a fully connected (FC) layer with one distinction: neurons in the FC layer have connections to every input, whereas neurons in the CancelOut layer have only one connection to one particular input (Fig. 1).

The primary idea behind CancelOut layer is to update its weights (W_{CO}) during the training stage so that irrelevant features will be *canceled out* with a negative weight (Eq. 1). Otherwise, the best variables, which contribute more to a learning process, are going to be passed through with a positive weight.

$$CancelOut(\boldsymbol{X}) = \boldsymbol{X} \odot g(W_{CO}) \tag{1}$$

where $\odot$ indicates an element-wise multiplication, $\boldsymbol{X}$ is an input vector $\boldsymbol{X} \in \mathbb{R}_v^N$, W_{CO} is a weight vector $W_{CO} \in \mathbb{R}_v^N$, N_v is the feature size, and g is an activation function. Note, $g(x)$ denotes here element-wise application, e.g. $\boldsymbol{X} = \begin{bmatrix} a \\ b \\ c \end{bmatrix}$, then

$$g(\boldsymbol{X}) = g\left(\begin{bmatrix} a \\ b \\ c \end{bmatrix}\right) = \left(\begin{bmatrix} g(a) \\ g(b) \\ g(c) \end{bmatrix}\right).$$

3.1 Theoretical Justification of the CancelOut Layer

For simplicity, consider a three layers artificial neural network (Fig. 1) with *linear activation function* after layer $^{(2)}$ and $^{(3)}$, where the CancelOut layer with the sigmoid activation function σ is utilized as input layer (superscript $^{(1)}$). Note that bias terms in FC layers are omitted for simplicity reasons. Then the output of the network is given by:

$$\hat{y} = \boldsymbol{X} \odot \sigma(W_{CO}) \cdot W^{(2)} w_1^{(3)} \tag{2}$$

where $\boldsymbol{X} = [x_1, x_2, x_3]$, $W_{CO} \in \mathbb{R}^3, W^{(2)} \in \mathbb{R}^3$, and $w_1^{(3)} \in \mathbb{R}$. Note, $\cdot$ is the dot product between two vectors.

The Eq. 2 can be seen as a linear regression model:

$$\hat{y} = X\theta_1 + \theta_0 \tag{3}$$

where θ_1:

$$\theta_1 = \sigma(W_{CO}) \cdot W^{(2)} w_1^{(3)} \tag{4}$$

In case of multiple artificial neurons in the hidden layer$^{(2)}$ (Fig. 2), the output is given by:

$$\hat{y} = \boldsymbol{X} \odot \underbrace{\sigma(W_{CO}) \cdot W_1^{(2)} w_1^{(3)}}_{\theta_1} + \boldsymbol{X} \odot \underbrace{\sigma(W_{CO}) \cdot W_2^{(2)} w_2^{(3)}}_{\theta_2} \tag{5}$$

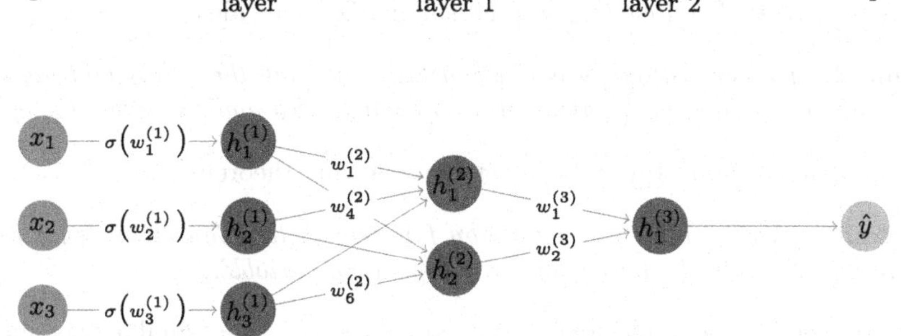

Fig. 2. A deep neural network with a CancelOut layer and two artificial neurons in the third layer.

From the Eq. 2 it can be seen that if the any value after the activation function $g(w_{CO}^{(1)}))$ in the CancelOut layer equals 0, than the corresponding input value x_n to $g(w_{CO}^{(1)}))$ is also 0. The following lemma summarizes this idea.

Lemma 1. *If a value after an activation function from the CancelOut layer is 0, a corresponding input variable does not affect the output of an ANN.*

As an illustration: let a value after the activation function from the CancelOut layer be 0.

$$\sigma(w_1^{(1)}) = 0 \tag{6}$$

Then $\hat{y}$ from Eq. 5 from the ANN 5, can be seen as:

$$\begin{aligned}\hat{y} &= \boldsymbol{X} \odot \sigma(W_{CO}) \cdot W_1^{(2)} w_1^{(3)} + \boldsymbol{X} \odot \sigma(W_{CO}) \cdot W_2^{(2)} w_2^{(3)} \\ &= \cancel{x_1 \sigma(w_1^{(1)}) w_1^{(2)} w_1^{(3)}} + x_2 \sigma(w_2^{(1)}) w_2^{(2)} w_1^{(3)} + x_3 \sigma(w_3^{(1)}) w_3^{(2)} w_1^{(3)} \\ &\quad + \cancel{x_1 \sigma(w_1^{(1)}) w_4^{(2)} w_2^{(3)}} + x_2 \sigma(w_2^{(1)}) w_5^{(2)} w_2^{(3)} + x_3 \sigma(w_3^{(1)}) w_6^{(2)} w_2^{(3)}\end{aligned} \tag{7}$$

Remark 1. Clearly, if $w_1^{(2)} = w_4^{(2)} = 0$ in the Eq. 7 and the bias[1] term is also zero, then a CancelOut weight $w_1^{(1)}$ does not represent beneficial information. In order to avoid this outcome, we suggest to consider these recommendations:

- a proper choice of activation function in a layer after the CancelOut layer helps to bypass that issue;
- regularization terms can be used in a loss function;
- finally, it is advisable to have numerous artificial neurons in the layer after the CancelOut layer, since it diminishes the chance that all neurons weights in the layer after $W^{(2)}$ the CancelOut layer be zeros.

[1] The bias term is omitted here, see Subsect. 3.1.

Moreover, if a weight w_i in the CancelOut layer is 0, then the gradient with respect to w_i is 0. The following lemma summarizes this idea.

Lemma 2. *If a value after an activation function from the CancelOut layer is approximately 0, then the gradient of the weight is also approximately 0.*

Combining Lemmas 1 and 2, we get the following theorem:

Theorem 1. *Values after the activation function in the CancelOut layer indicate contributions to the output of a corresponding variable.*

Consequently, the CancelOut layer ranks features in a similar way linear models do, e.g. the large the absolute values in the CancelOut layer the more a corresponding input variable contributes to the output. Also, compared to linear models, the CancelOut method takes into account linear and non-linear combinations of input data.

Remark 2. A zero coefficient in CancelOut values $\sigma(W_{CO}^{(1)})$ leads to fewer optimization parameters, hence, a model learns faster. This also helps to reduce, it helps to reduce the number of features, therefore mitigating overfitting. Moreover, feature selection with the CancelOut layer can be adopted in two scenarios; a user can either specify the number of features or extract features using a chosen threshold.

Our FR approach is similar to [9], but in our work, the input scalar $\sigma(W_{CO}^{(1)})$ is bound in the chosen interval (e.g. for the sigmoid activation function is $(0,1)$). Therefore our approach is more stable, and it is simpler to rank features since a user selects only a threshold. Besides, the CancelOut FR method does not require a penalty coefficient in a loss function.

3.2 CancelOut Layer Weights Initialization

A random weight initialization is not desired for the CancelOut layer, since it may give an advantage for one subset of features over another. Therefore, weights are initialized with uniformly distribution [5] with additional β coefficient:

$$W_{CO} \sim \mathcal{U}(-\frac{1}{\sqrt{n_{in}}} + \beta, \frac{1}{\sqrt{n_{in}}} + \beta) \tag{8}$$

where n_{in} is the size of the previous layer, and β is the coefficient which depends on the choice of an activation function.

We introduced β coefficient into Eq. 8 in order to control the initial output values after an activation function $g(W_{CO})$, it needs to be $g(W_{CO}) \neq 0$, because we assume that every feature is equally important e.g. for the logistic activation function $\beta \in [-3, \inf)$.

3.3 Loss Function

In order to accelerate the feature ranking process in the CancelOut layer, we introduce two regularization terms in a loss function (Eq. 9):

$$\mathbb{L}(X,Y) = \mathcal{L}(X,Y) - \lambda_1\, var(\frac{W_{CO}}{N_v}) + \lambda_2 \left\| \frac{W_{CO}}{N_v} \right\|_1 \tag{9}$$

where $\mathcal{L}$ is a selected loss function, for the classification task it can be seen as:

$$\mathcal{L}_{CE}(X,Y) = -\frac{1}{n}\sum_{i=1}^{n}(y^{(i)} \ln \psi(x^{(i)}) + \left(1 - y^{(i)}\right) \ln \left(1 - \psi(x^{(i)})\right)) \\ -\lambda_1\, var(\frac{W_{CO}}{N_v}) + \lambda_2 \left\| \frac{W_{CO}}{N_v} \right\|_1 \tag{10}$$

where $X = \{x^{(1)}, \ldots, x^{(n)}\}$ is the set of input examples in the training dataset, and $Y = \{y^{(1)}, \ldots, y^{(n)}\}$ is the corresponding set of labels. The $\psi(x)$ represents the output of the neural network given input x, λ_1 and λ_2 are user-specified parameter coefficients $\lambda_1 \in [0,1], \lambda_2 \in [0,1]$, N_v is a number of variables in a dataset, and W_{CO} are CancelOut weights.

The mean square error (MSE) loss can be utilized for regression tasks:

$$\mathcal{L}_{MSE}(X,Y) = \frac{1}{2n}\sum_{i=1}^{n}(y^{(i)} - \psi(x^{(i)}))^2 - \lambda_1\, var(\frac{W_{CO}}{N_v}) + \lambda_2 \left\| \frac{W_{CO}}{N_v} \right\|_1 \tag{11}$$

The variance of the weights from the CancelOut layer $var(\frac{W_{CO}}{N_v})$ helps to stimulate diversity in the CancelOut layer, there $l1$ norm is used to introduce sparsity in W_{CO} weights and to constrain the variation to small weights. Also, $l1$ penalty restricts the model from selecting correlated features. Lastly, our feature selection approach supports all losses and does not require the realization terms (Table 1).

Table 1. Datasets

Dataset	Samples	Features	Target
Statlog (Australian Credit Approval)	690	14 (continuous, nominal)	Binary
Diabetes	442	10 (continuous, nominal)	Regression
MNIST	70.000	784 (continuous)	Multiclass

4 Experimental Results

In this section, we perform several experiments to evaluate different aspects of our CancelOut layer. In a first experiment, we examine the performance of our algorithm for classification and regression tasks, using the Statlog (Australian Credit Approval) and Diabetes dataset [3] (Sect. 4.1). We choose these datasets, because they contain different feature types such as continuous and nominal. We compare the proposed features from a CancelOut NN with a Random Forest and a Gradient Boosting algorithm using k-fold cross-validations (stratified for the classification experiment).

In a second experiment, we add a dummy variable $(Y + \epsilon_1) \in X$ with normally distributed noise ϵ to the Australian Credit Approval dataset, in order to see if the proposed method is able to detect a feature that is highly correlated with the target feature (Sect. 4.2). Additionally, we introduce a "noisy" variable $X_{random} \sim N(0, 1) + \epsilon_2$ to assess, whether CancelOut discards irrelevant features. Note, $\epsilon_1 \neq \epsilon_2$.

Next, we compare feature importance characteristics from LASSO, SHAP [10], and CancelOut (Sect. 4.3). In a final experiment, we evaluate our model for the unsupervised scenario using a convolutional autoencoder (Sect. 4.4).

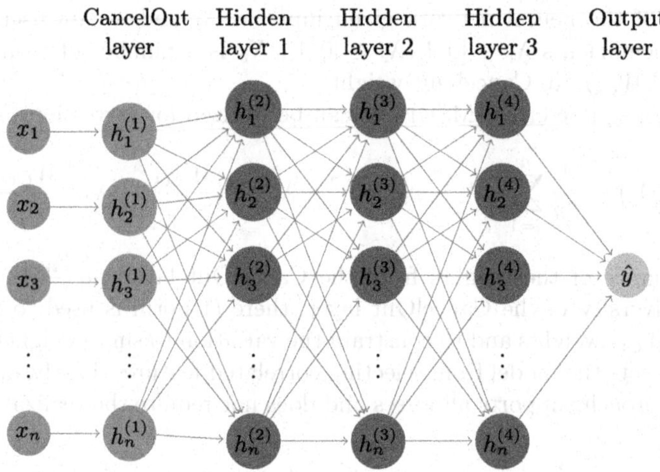

Fig. 3. A deep neural network architecture used for the experiments, where n is a number of variables.

In all experiments, we use a five layers DL model (Fig. 3) where the input layer is the CancelOut layer with the sigmoid activation function after each FC layer the ReLU activation function [5] was applied. Further, we use the optimization algorithm Adam [7] with learning rate 0.003, $\beta_1 = 0.9$, $\beta_2 = 0.999$, and $\epsilon = 10^{-9}$. We utilize the early stopping technique to control overfitting of our model.

4.1 Feature Ranking

Classification Example. We illustrate the AUC scores for different sizes of feature subsets [3] in Fig. 4. The results are obtained by five-fold stratified cross-validation on the Australian Credit Approval dataset using Naive Bayes (Fig. 4a) and decision trees (Fig. 4b). Our algorithm achieves consistently good predictions for both classifiers and all feature set sizes. Moreover, CancelOut obtains superior predictions for small feature subsets. The variability in AUC is similar for all algorithms.

Regression Example. To evaluate CancelOut in context of a regression problem, we apply linear regression (Fig. 4c) and decision trees regression (Fig. 4d) on the diabetes dataset. We illustrate the MSE for different sizes of the reduced feature set in Fig. 4. We obtain the MSE scores again by five-fold cross-validation. CancelOut has disadvantages for linear regression if the number of features is smaller than three. However, our algorithm obtains competitive results for the

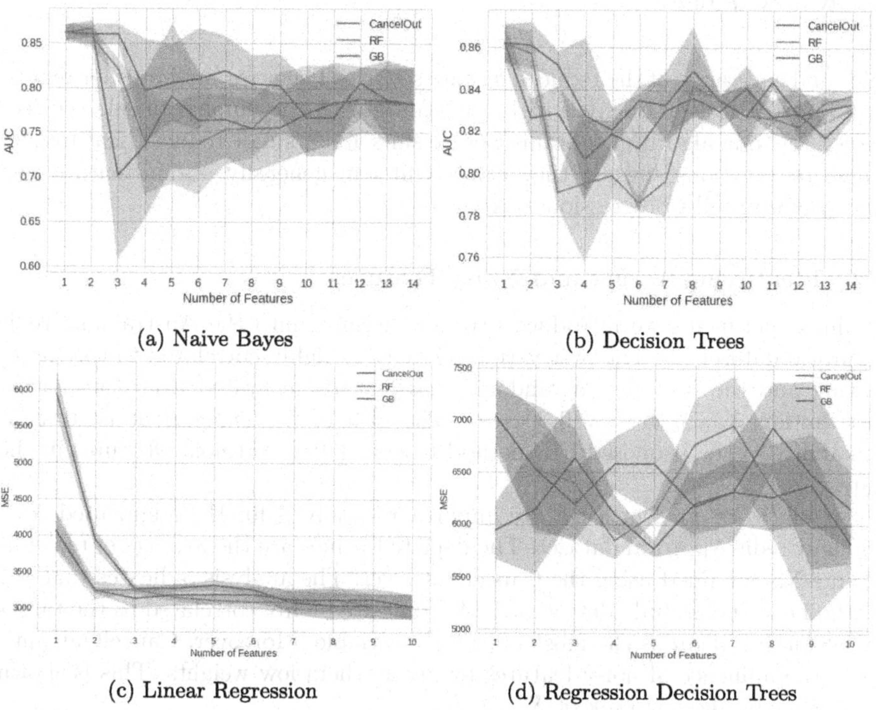

(a) Naive Bayes
(b) Decision Trees
(c) Linear Regression
(d) Regression Decision Trees

Fig. 4. A comparison of FS methods using Naive Bayes classifier (a) and decision trees (b) for the classification problem, and using linear regression (c) and decision trees regression (d) algorithms for the regression problem.

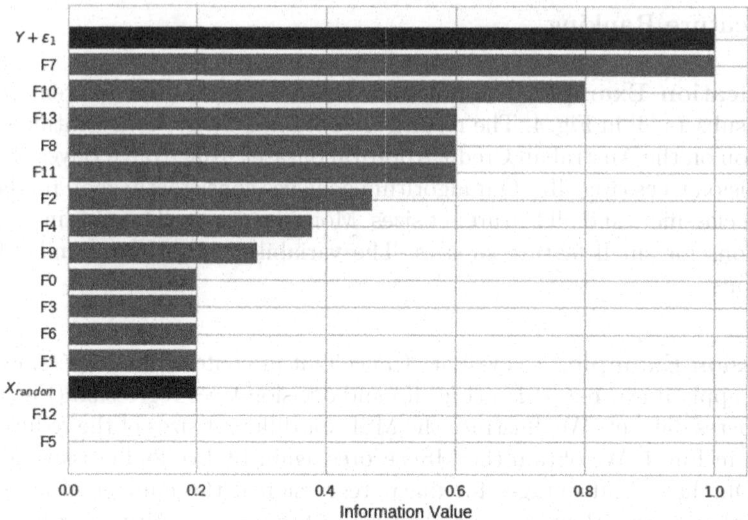

Fig. 5. A feature importance analysis for the Australian credit approval dataset [3] with two new features.

mid- and end-range of the reduced feature set size. The error measures for regression tasks with decision trees highly fluctuate with the number of selected features. Yet, our algorithm obtains best results for a small reduced feature set. These observations suggest that CancelOut can generally obtain feature sets that perform well in regression tasks.

4.2 Identifying Target and Noisy Features

In this experiment, we introduce two new features into the Australian Credit Approval dataset [3]. The first variable $Y + \epsilon_1$ is highly correlated to the target feature and the second is a random noise feature generated from the normal distribution $X_{random} \sim N(0, 1) + \epsilon_2$. The idea of the experiment is to show the ability of the proposed FR method to detect key and noisy features in the dataset.

In Fig. 5, we present a feature importance analysis for the augmented Australian Credit Approval dataset. The depicted values are the average of ten runs of an ANN obtained using the CancelOut layer. The analysis indicates that our method can successfully detect variables that are highly correlated to the target by evaluating them as the most important variable. Moreover, CancelOut mitigates the influence of noisy features by giving them low weights. This is shown exemplary by the low rank of X_{random}.

4.3 Evaluating Individual Feature Importance

We investigated several feature analysis methods for the diabetes dataset and summarized it into Fig. 6. The purpose of this comparison is to show that

CancelOut behaves comparable to other algorithms. Although there are differences in feature importance for the single features *age*, *sex*, *s2* and *s3*, the overall distribution of CancelOut weights is comparable to that of the SHAP and LASSO models.

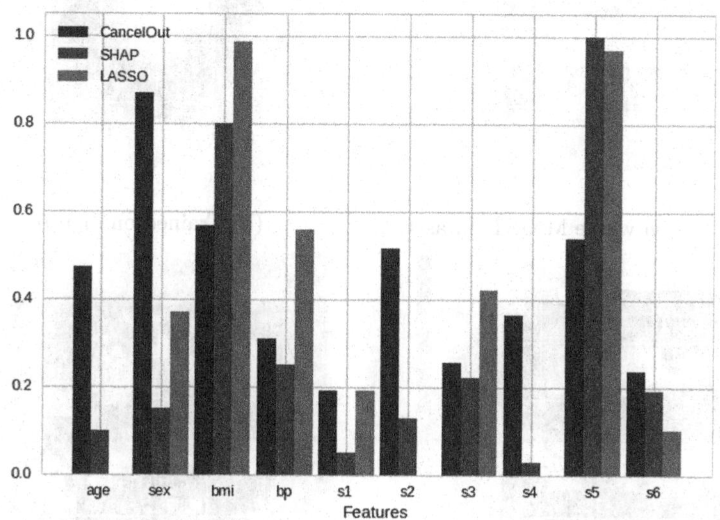

Fig. 6. A feature importance analysis for the diabetes dataset [3] using the proposed method (CancelOut), LASSO, and SHAP.

4.4 Unsupervised Feature Ranking Using Autoencoder

In this subsection, we demonstrate how the CancelOut layer can be utilized for unsupervised learning tasks with a convolutional autoencoder [11]. The architecture of the autoencoder consists of three convolutional neural network (CNN) layers in encoder and decoder parts, and the CancelOut as an input layer for the encoder. For this experiment, the MNIST dataset [8] is used.

Figure 7 shows CancelOut variable weights after training the convolutional autoencoder on the whole dataset (a), only on digit 0 (b), only on digit 3 (c), and only on digit 8 (c). CancelOut captures the most relevant regions of the picture for all four training sets. The information provided by CancelOut layer weights can help in model understanding, debugging, and adjustment, e.g. by introducing a "focus" on relevant features if a model performs poorly.

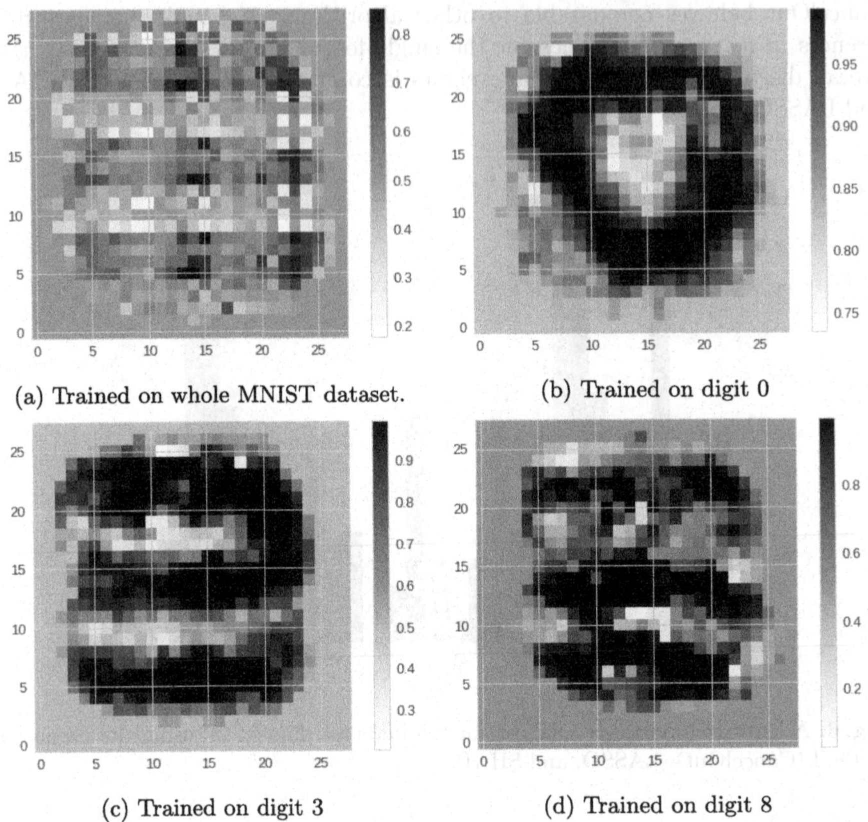

(a) Trained on whole MNIST dataset.

(b) Trained on digit 0

(c) Trained on digit 3

(d) Trained on digit 8

Fig. 7. $\sigma(W_{CO})$ values from the CancelOut layer after training using MNIST dataset: (a) the whole dataset, (b) images from 0 class, (c) images from 3 class, (c) images from 8 class.

5 Conclusion

In this paper, we introduced a novel feature ranking method using deep neural networks for various machine learning problems. The proposed method is extremely easy to implement, it can be done using all modern DL frameworks, and this method can be simply scaled. Due to the power of the neural networks, the presented approach learns linear and non-linear data dependencies. Also, the CancelOut layer can be applied for any data type and machine learning tasks, such as classification and regression problems or even for unsupervised problems as an input layer for an autoencoder. Finally, the proposed layer helps understand the data and its influence on the performance of DL models.

References

1. Chang, C.H., Rampasek, L., Goldenberg, A.: Dropout feature ranking for deep learning models. arXiv e-prints (2017)
2. Cybenko, G.: Approximation by superpositions of a sigmoidal function. Math. Control, Signals Syst. **2**(4), 303–314 (1989). https://doi.org/10.1007/BF02551274
3. Dua, D., Graff, C.: UCI machine learning repository (2017). http://archive.ics.uci.edu/ml
4. Gilpin, L.H., Bau, D., Yuan, B.Z., Bajwa, A., Specter, M., Kagal, L.: Explaining explanations: an overview of interpretability of machine learning. arXiv e-prints (2018)
5. Goodfellow, I., Bengio, Y., Courville, A.: Deep Learning. MIT Press, Cambridge (2016). http://www.deeplearningbook.org
6. Kasneci, G., Gottron, T.: LICON: a linear weighting scheme for the contribution ofInput variables in deep artificial neural networks. In: Proceedings of the 25th ACM International on Conference on Information and Knowledge Management, CIKM 2016, pp. 45–54. ACM, New York, NY, USA (2016). https://doi.org/10.1145/2983323.2983746
7. Kingma, D.P., Ba, J.: Adam: a method for stochastic optimization. arXiv e-prints (2014)
8. LeCun, Y., Cortes, C.: MNIST handwritten digit database (2010). http://yann.lecun.com/exdb/mnist/
9. Li, Y., Chen, C.Y., Wasserman, W.W.: Deep feature selection: theory and application to identify enhancers and promoters. J. Comput. Biol. **23**(5), 322–336 (2016). https://doi.org/10.1089/cmb.2015.0189. PMID: 26799292
10. Lundberg, S.M., Lee, S.I.: A unified approach to interpreting model predictions. In: Guyon, I., et al. (eds.) Advances in Neural Information Processing Systems, vol. 30, pp. 4765–4774. Curran Associates, Inc. (2017). http://papers.nips.cc/paper/7062-a-unified-approach-to-interpreting-model-predictions.pdf
11. Rumelhart, D.E., Hinton, G.E., Williams, R.J.: Learning internal representations by error propagation. In: Rumelhart, D.E., McClelland, J.L., (eds.) Parallel Distributed Processing: Explorations in the Microstructure of Cognition, vol. 1, pp. 318–362. MIT Press, Cambridge (1986). http://dl.acm.org/citation.cfm?id=104279.104293
12. Srivastava, N., Hinton, G., Krizhevsky, A., Sutskever, I., Salakhutdinov, R.: Dropout: a simple way to prevent neural networks from overfitting. J. Mach. Learn. Res. **15**, 1929–1958 (2014). http://jmlr.org/papers/v15/srivastava14a.html
13. Zhang, Q., Nian Wu, Y., Zhu, S.C.: Interpretable convolutional neural networks. arXiv e-prints (2017)

Adaptive-L_2 Batch Neural Gas

Nicomedes L. Cavalcanti Jr.[1(✉)], Marcelo Rodrigo Portela Ferreira[2], and Francisco de Assis Tenorio de Carvalho[1]

[1] Centro de Informática – CIn/UFPE, Av. Prof. Luiz Freire, s/n, Cidade Universitária, Recife, PE 50740-540, Brazil
{nlcj,fatc}@cin.ufpe.br

[2] Departamento de Estatística – CCEN/UFPB, João Pessoa, PB 58051-900, Brazil
marcelo@de.ufpb.br

Abstract. Neural Gas (NG) algorithms aim to find optimal data representations based on feature vectors. Unlike SOM, NG algorithms take into consideration the dissimilarities between prototypes in the original input space and not on a grid defined in advance. It has been successfully applied in vector quantization and clustering. However, conventional NG algorithms implicitly assume that the variables have the same importance in the clustering task. Nevertheless, some variables may be irrelevant and, among the important ones, some may be more or less important than others to the clustering task. This paper provides an adaptive batch NG algorithm that, in comparison with the traditional batch NG algorithm, has an additional step where it automatically computes the importance of the variables in the clustering task. Experiments with synthetic and real datasets show the usefulness of the proposed adaptive NG algorithm.

Keywords: Batch Neural Gas · Clustering · Adaptive Distances · Variable weight

1 Introduction

Clustering is an essential task in unsupervised learning. Clustering aims to organise a dataset in clusters such that objects in the same cluster have a high degree of similarity but are dissimilar concerning objects belonging to other clusters [12,22,25]. Clustering has been successfully used in different fields, including bioinformatics [21], image processing [24], and information retrieval [5].

Traditionally, the most popular cluster structures provided by clustering methods are partition and hierarchy. Hierarchical methods build a nested sequence of partitions of the input data with a graphical representation called dendrogram. Partitioning methods aim to obtain a single partition of the data into a fixed number of clusters according to some suitable clustering criteria based on dissimilarity, density, etc. [12].

This paper is concerned with a class of partitioning methods, the prototype-based clustering algorithms. Hard prototype-based partitioning methods, like

I. V. Tetko et al. (Eds.): ICANN 2019, LNCS 11728, pp. 84–95, 2019.
https://doi.org/10.1007/978-3-030-30484-3_7

k-means [15,16], assign each data point to exactly one cluster. Others algorithms, like fuzzy c-means [2], self-organizing maps (SOM) [13,14] and Neural Gas (NG) [17,18], have in common that each data point influences more than one prototype at a time. Besides, prototype-based partitioning methods have batch and sequential versions.

SOM has been successfully used for clustering and visualization. SOM consists of neurons arranged on a regular low-dimensional grid (the map) such that there are neighborhood relations among the neurons. To each neuron corresponds a prototype vector (model) which represents a subset of data units (cluster). One of the difficulties of the SOM is that it performs clustering assuming neighborhood relations between neurons in a discrete output grid defined in advance [14], that has to match the previous neighborhood relations between the data points. Unlike the SOM, NG algorithms [3,7,17,18] take into consideration the dissimilarities between prototypes in the original input space and not on a grid defined in advance.

Conventional NG algorithms implicitly assume that the variables have the same importance in the clustering task. However, some variables may be irrelevant and, among the important ones, some may be more or less important than others to the clustering task. For this purpose, several variations of the k-means algorithm have been proposed aiming to automatically learn the weights of the variables [1,4,11,20,23]. Concerning supervised and unsupervised sequential NG algorithms, it has been demonstrated that the optimization of parameterized distance functions can improve their performance [8,9].

The main contribution of this paper is to provide an adaptive batch neural gas algorithm that, in comparison with the traditional batch neural gas algorithm [3], has an additional step where it automatically computes the importance of the variables in the clustering task.

The rest of this paper has the following structure: Sect. 2 reviews on-line and batch neural gas; Sect. 3 presents the proposed adaptive neural gas algorithm. Section 4 shows the experiments performed to assess the proposed algorithm compared to k-means and the traditional on-line and batch neural gas algorithms. On Sect. 5 some conclusions are drawn and an outline for future research is proposed.

2 Neural Gas

This section reviews the basic on-line and batch neural gas algorithms [3,7,17,18]. Neural gas has been used successfully for vector quantization, clustering, pattern recognition, etc. In contrast to k-means, in NG algorithms, each object influences more than one prototype at a time, according to their mutual neighborhood. Moreover, unlike the SOM, in NG algorithms, no grid topology is imposed in advance.

2.1 On-Line Neural Gas

Let data points $\mathbf{x} \in \mathtt{R}^P$ distributed according to a distribution $P(\mathbf{x})$. The on-line NG aims to find prototypes $\mathbf{w}_r$ $(1 \leq r \leq C)$ that represent the data points such that the following cost function is minimized:

$$E_{\mathrm{NG}}(\mathbf{W}) = \frac{1}{2C(\lambda)} \sum_{r=1}^{C} \int h_\lambda(\mathcal{K}_r(\mathbf{x}_k, \mathbf{w}_r)) d^2(\mathbf{x}, \mathbf{w}_r)\, P(\mathbf{x})\, d\mathbf{x} \tag{1}$$

where

- A matrix $\mathbf{W} = (w_{rj})_{\substack{1 \le r \le C \\ 1 \le j \le P}}$ of representatives (prototypes) of the clusters;
- $d^2(\mathbf{x}, \mathbf{w}_r)$ is the squared Euclidean distance between data point $\mathbf{x}$ and prototype $\mathbf{w}_r$;
- $\mathcal{K}_r(\mathbf{x}, \mathbf{w}_r)$ is a hidden variable with the constraint that its values constitute a permutation of $\{0, \dots, C-1\}$ for each $\mathbf{x}$;
- h_λ is a Gaussian shaped curve with neighborhood radius $\lambda > 0$, that is computed as $h_\lambda(\mathcal{K}_r(\mathbf{x}, \mathbf{w}_r)) = \exp\{-\mathcal{K}_r(\mathbf{x}, \mathbf{w}_r)/\lambda\}$;
- $C(\lambda) = \sum_{r=1}^{C} h_\lambda(\mathcal{K}_r(\mathbf{x}, \mathbf{w}_r))$, is a normalization constant.

The training of the on-line NG evolves on mainly two steps, namely competition and representation. The competition step provides the rank of the prototypes sorted according to the distances as follows:

$$\mathcal{K}_r(\mathbf{x}, \mathbf{w}_r) = |\{\mathbf{w}_l : d(\mathbf{x}, \mathbf{w}_l) < d(\mathbf{x}, \mathbf{w}_r)\}| \\ (1 \le r, l \le C) \tag{2}$$

The representation step provides the prototypes whose computation has the form of a stochastic gradient descent, which results in:

$$\mathbf{w}_r = \mathbf{w}_r + \Delta\mathbf{w}_r \\ \Delta\mathbf{w}_r = \epsilon\, h_\lambda(\mathcal{K}_r(\mathbf{x}, \mathbf{w}_r))\, (\mathbf{x} - \mathbf{w}_r) \\ (1 \le r \le C) \tag{3}$$

where, the learning rate $\epsilon > 0$ controls the extent to which every $\mathbf{w}_r$ changes given a new data point $\mathbf{x}$. The neighborhood radius decreases during the training in such a way that at the beginning, the data point influences almost all prototypes and at the end, it influences only a few prototypes.

Assuming a clustering task, after the training of the NG algorithm, a partition of the data points into C clusters can be obtained as $P_r = \{\mathbf{x}_k \in \mathcal{D} : \mathcal{K}_r(\mathbf{x}_k, \mathbf{w}_r) \text{ is equal to } 0\}$ $(1 \le r \le C)$.

2.2 Batch Neural Gas

Batch NG algorithms have the advantage of converging faster than their on-line counterparts in most cases. Adaptation, in this case, only happens after all samples have been collected rather than at each sample, which for high dimensional data can become a computation burden.

Let $\Theta = \{\theta_1, \dots, \theta_N\}$ be a set of N objects described by P real-valued variables. Let $\mathcal{D} = \{\mathbf{x}_1, \dots, \mathbf{x}_N\}$ be a non-empty set, where the kth object θ_k $(1 \le k \le N)$ is represented by a vector $\mathbf{x}_k = (x_{k1}, \dots, x_{kP}) \in \mathrm{R}^P$.

The Batch Neural Gas (BNG) derives from the NG cost function for finite data sample as follows:

$$E_{\text{BNG}}(\mathbf{W}) = \sum_{r=1}^{C}\sum_{k=1}^{N} h_\lambda(\mathcal{K}_r(\mathbf{x}_k, \mathbf{w}_r))\, d^2(\mathbf{x}_k, \mathbf{w}_r) \tag{4}$$

where $d^2(\mathbf{x}_k, \mathbf{w}_r)$, $\mathcal{K}_r(\mathbf{x}_k, \mathbf{w}_r)$, $h_\lambda(\mathcal{K}_r(\mathbf{x}_k, \mathbf{w}_r))$ and λ are as before.

Assuming a clustering task and from an initial solution, the training of the batch NG also evolves on mainly two steps, namely competition and representation. As before, the competition step provides the rank of the prototypes sorted according to the distances as follows:

$$\begin{gathered}\mathcal{K}_r(\mathbf{x}, \mathbf{w}_r) = |\{\mathbf{w}_l : d(\mathbf{x}, \mathbf{w}_l) < d(\mathbf{x}, \mathbf{w}_r)\}| \\ (1 \le r, l \le C)\end{gathered} \tag{5}$$

The representation step provides the prototypes that are obtained from the minimization of the cost function E_{BNG} with respect to the prototypes. Thus, from $\frac{\partial E_{\text{BNG}}}{\partial \mathbf{w}_r} = 0$ and after some algebra, the cluster prototypes $\mathbf{w}_r$ $(1 \le r \le C)$ are obtained as follows:

$$\mathbf{w}_r = \frac{\sum_{k=1}^{N} h_\lambda(\mathcal{K}_{rk})\mathbf{x}_k}{\sum_{k=1}^{N} h_\lambda(\mathcal{K}_{rk})} \tag{6}$$

After the BNG training, a partition of the data points into C can be obtained according to $P_r = \{\mathbf{x}_k \in \mathcal{D} : \mathcal{K}_r(\mathbf{x}_k, \mathbf{w}_r) \text{ is equal to } 0\}$ $(1 \le r \le C)$.

3 Adaptive-L_2 Batch Neural Gas

This section presents the Adaptive-L_2 Batch Neural Gas algorithm. The proposed Adaptive-L_2 Batch Neural Gas (hereafter named ABNG) aims to provide:

- A vector $\mathbf{v} = (v_1, \ldots, v_P)$, where v_j is the relevance weight of the jth variable. The larger v_j is, the more important j^{th} variable is;
- A matrix $\mathbf{W} = (w_{rj})_{\substack{1 \le r \le C \\ 1 \le j \le P}}$ of representatives (prototypes) of the clusters, where $\mathbf{w}_r = (w_{r1}, \ldots, w_{rP})$ is the prototype of the cluster r $(1 \le r \le C)$, and w_{rj} $(1 \le j \le P)$ is the jth component of the cluster prototype $\mathbf{w}_r$;
- A matrix $\mathbf{K} = (\mathcal{K}_{rk})_{\substack{1 \le k \le N \\ 1 \le r \le C}}$, where $\mathcal{K}_{rk} = \mathcal{K}_r(\mathbf{x}_k, \mathbf{w}_r)$ are hidden variables with the constraint that their values constitute a permutation of $\{0, \ldots, C-1\}$ for each $\mathbf{x}_k$ [3].

Finally, after the training and assuming a clustering task, a partition $\mathcal{P} = \{P_1, \ldots, P_C\}$ of Θ into C non-empty clusters can be obtained.

The ABNG algorithm is derived from a modified version of the cost function of the BNG algorithm [3,7] as follows:

$$E_{\text{ABNG}}(\mathbf{v}, \mathbf{W}, \mathbf{K}) = \sum_{r=1}^{C} \sum_{k=1}^{N} h_\lambda(\mathcal{K}_{rk})\, d^2_{\mathbf{v}}(\mathbf{x}_k, \mathbf{w}_r) \tag{7}$$
$$= \sum_{r=1}^{C} \sum_{k=1}^{N} h_\lambda(\mathcal{K}_r(\mathbf{x}_k, \mathbf{w}_r))\, d^2_{\mathbf{v}}(\mathbf{x}_k, \mathbf{w}_r)$$
$$= \sum_{r=1}^{C} \sum_{k=1}^{N} h_\lambda(\mathcal{K}_r(\mathbf{x}_k, \mathbf{w}_r)) \sum_{j=1}^{P} v_j\, (x_{kj} - w_{rj})^2$$

where

- $d^2_{\mathbf{v}}$ is an adaptive squared Euclidean distance parameterized by $\mathbf{v}$, the vector of relevance weights of the variables, that is computed as follows:

$$d^2_{\mathbf{v}}(\mathbf{x}_k, \mathbf{w}_r) = \sum_{j=1}^{P} v_j\, (x_{kj} - w_{rj})^2 \tag{8}$$

- h_λ is a Gaussian shaped curve with neighborhood radius $\lambda > 0$, that is computed as $h_\lambda(\mathcal{K}_r(\mathbf{x}_k, \mathbf{w}_r)) = \exp\{-\mathcal{K}_r(\mathbf{x}_k, \mathbf{w}_r)/\lambda\}$.

For a given cycle, when the neighborhood λ radius is kept fixed, $\mathbf{v}$, $\mathbf{W}$ and $\mathbf{K}$ are computed interactively in three steps (weighting, representation, and competition) through the minimization of the cost function E_{ABNG}.

During the weighting step, the matrices $\mathbf{W}$ and $\mathbf{K}$ are kept fixed. Thus, the minimum of the cost function E_{ABNG} is obtained when $\mathbf{v}$ is a null vector. To avoid this trivial solution, a constraint on the components of $\mathbf{v}$ is needed. In previous work two main types of constraints are proposed: a product-to-one constraint [4] and a sum-to-one constraint [11]. Since the latter approach needs the tuning of a further parameter, in this paper, we will consider only the product-to-one constraint. Therefore, first, we use the method of Lagrange multipliers with the restriction that $\prod_{j=1}^{P} v_j = 1$ and obtain

$$\mathcal{L}_{\text{ABNG}}(\mathbf{v}, \mathbf{W}, \mathbf{K}) = \sum_{r=1}^{C} \sum_{k=1}^{N} h_\lambda(\mathcal{K}_r(\mathbf{x}_k, \mathbf{w}_r)) \sum_{j=1}^{P} v_j\, (x_{kj} - w_{rj})^2 - \omega \left(\prod_{j=1}^{P} v_j - 1 \right) \tag{9}$$

Then, we compute the partial derivatives of L_{ABNG} w.r.t. v_j $(1 \leq j \leq P)$ and ω, and after some algebra we obtain

$$v_j = \frac{\left\{ \prod_{h=1}^{P} \left[\sum_{r=1}^{C} \sum_{k=1}^{N} h_\lambda(\mathcal{K}_r(\mathbf{x}_k, \mathbf{w}_r))\, (x_{kh} - w_{rh})^2 \right] \right\}^{\frac{1}{P}}}{\sum_{r=1}^{C} \sum_{k=1}^{N} h_{\lambda(t)}(\mathcal{K}_r(\mathbf{x}_k, \mathbf{w}_r))\, (x_{kj} - w_{rj})^2} \tag{10}$$

During the representation step, $\mathbf{v}$ and $\mathbf{K}$ are kept fixed. The cost function E_{ABNG} is optimized with respect to the prototypes. Thus, from $\frac{\partial E_{\text{ABNG}}}{\partial \mathbf{w}_r} = 0$ and after some algebra, the cluster prototypes $\mathbf{w}_r$ $(1 \leq r \leq C)$ are obtained as follows:

$$\mathbf{w}_r = \frac{\sum_{k=1}^{N} h_\lambda(\mathcal{K}_{rk})\mathbf{x}_k}{\sum_{k=1}^{N} h_\lambda(\mathcal{K}_{rk})} \tag{11}$$

During the competition step, $\mathbf{v}$ and $\mathbf{W}$ are kept fixed. The cost function E_{ABNG} is optimized with respect to the matrix $\mathbf{K}$. First, we can rewrite E_{ABNG} as

$$E_{\text{ABNG}}(\mathbf{K}) = \sum_{k=1}^{N}\sum_{r=1}^{C} h_\lambda(\mathcal{K}_{rk})\, d^2_{\mathbf{v}}(\mathbf{x}_k, \mathbf{w}_r)$$

The cost function $E_{\text{ABNG}}(\mathbf{K})$ is minimized with respect to the matrix $\mathbf{K} = (\mathcal{K}_{rk})_{\substack{1\le k\le N\\ 1\le r\le C}}$ if, for each $\mathbf{x}_k \in \mathcal{D}$, $\sum_{r=1}^{C} h_\lambda(\mathcal{K}_{rk})\, d^2_{\mathbf{v}}(\mathbf{x}_k, \mathbf{w}_r)$ is minimized. According to Ref. [7] this is achieved if $\mathcal{K}_{rk}$, the rank of prototype $\mathbf{w}_r$ with respect to object $\mathbf{x}_k$, is sorted according to the (adaptive) distance used to compare objects and prototypes, i.e., if $\mathcal{K}_{rk}$ is computed as follows:

$$\mathcal{K}_{rk} = \mathcal{K}_r(\mathbf{x}_k, \mathbf{w}_r) = |\{\mathbf{w}_l : d_{\mathbf{v}}(\mathbf{x}_k, \mathbf{w}_l) < d_{\mathbf{v}}(\mathbf{x}_k, \mathbf{w}_r)\}| \tag{12}$$

where $|A|$ is the cardinal of a given set A.

Algorithm 1. ABNG algorithm

Require: : the data-set $\mathcal{D} = \{\mathbf{x}_1, \ldots, \mathbf{x}_n\}$; the number C of clusters; the number of iterations T_{max}; initial radius λ_i; final radius λ_f

Ensure: : the vector of relevance weights of the variables $\mathbf{v}$; the matrix of prototypes $\mathbf{W}$; the matrix $\mathbf{K}$ the partition $\mathcal{P}$

Initialization

Set $t \leftarrow 0$; Set $\lambda_{(t)} = \lambda_i \left(\frac{\lambda_f}{\lambda_i}\right)^{\frac{t}{T_{Max}}}$; Set $\mathbf{v}^{(t)} = (1, \ldots, 1)$;

For $(1 \le r \le C)$, randomly select C distinct prototypes $\mathbf{w}_r^{(t)} \in \mathcal{D}$;

For $(1 \le k \le N)$ and $(1 \le r \le C)$, compute $d_{\mathbf{v}^{(t)}}(\mathbf{x}_k, \mathbf{w}_r^{(t)})$;

For $(1 \le k \le N)$ and $(1 \le r \le C)$, compute $\mathcal{K}_{rk}^{(t)} = \mathcal{K}_r(\mathbf{x}_k, \mathbf{w}_r^{(t)}) = |\{\mathbf{w}_l^{(t)} : d_{\mathbf{v}^{(t)}}(\mathbf{x}_k, \mathbf{w}_l^{(t)}) < d_{\mathbf{v}^{(t)}}(\mathbf{x}_k, \mathbf{w}_r^{(t)})\}|$;

repeat

set $t = t + 1$; set $\lambda_{(t)} = \lambda_i \left(\frac{\lambda_f}{\lambda_i}\right)^{\frac{t}{T_{Max}}}$;

Step 1: weighting:

For $(1 \le j \le P)$, compute:

$v_j^{(t)} = \frac{\left\{\prod_{h=1}^{P}\left[\sum_{r=1}^{C}\sum_{k=1}^{N} h_{\lambda(t)}(\mathcal{K}_r(\mathbf{x}_k, \mathbf{w}_r^{(t-1)}))\,(x_{kh} - w_{rh}^{(t-1)})^2\right]\right\}^{\frac{1}{P}}}{\sum_{r=1}^{C}\sum_{k=1}^{N} h_{\lambda(t)}(\mathcal{K}_r(\mathbf{x}_k, \mathbf{w}_r^{(t-1)}))\,(x_{kj} - w_{rj}^{(t-1)})^2}$

Step 2: representation:

For $(1 \le r \le C)$, compute: $\mathbf{w}_r^{(t)} = \frac{\sum_{k=1}^{N} h_{\lambda(t)}(\mathcal{K}_r(\mathbf{x}_k, \mathbf{w}_r^{(t-1)}))\mathbf{x}_k}{\sum_{k=1}^{N} h_{\lambda(t)}(\mathcal{K}_r(\mathbf{x}_k, \mathbf{w}_r^{(t-1)}))}$

Step 3: competition:

For $(1 \le k \le N)$ and $(1 \le r \le C)$, compute $\mathcal{K}_{rk}^{(t)} = \mathcal{K}_r(\mathbf{x}_k, \mathbf{w}_r^{(t)}) = |\{\mathbf{w}_l^{(t)} : d_{\mathbf{v}^{(t)}}(\mathbf{x}_k, \mathbf{w}_l^{(t)}) < d_{\mathbf{v}^{(t)}}(\mathbf{x}_k, \mathbf{w}_r^{(t)})\}|$;

until $t > t_{max}$

Step 3: final assignment:

For $(1 \le r \le C)$, compute: $P_r = \{\mathbf{x}_k \in \mathcal{D} : \mathcal{K}_r(\mathbf{x}_k, \mathbf{w}_r^{(t)})$ is equal to $0\}$

Once reached the predetermined maximum number of cycles by the user, the last step of ABNG is to assign the objects to the clusters as follows:

$$P_r = \{\mathbf{x}_k \in \mathcal{D} : \mathcal{K}_r(\mathbf{x}_k, \mathbf{w}_r) \text{ is equal to } 0\} \; (1 \leq r \leq C) \tag{13}$$

4 Experiments

This section provides an experimental comparison between the proposed ABNG algorithm with conventional NG and BNG neural gas algorithms as well as k-means as a baseline algorithm.

4.1 Synthetic Datasets

To evaluate the ability of the proposed method for handling noise on data, the 3MC synthetic dataset (available at https://github.com/deric/clustering-benchmark) was considered. This dataset has 400 objects each described by 2 real-valued variables plus a class indicator variable. There are 3 well-defined clusters into this dataset. One cluster has a ring-like shape and the other two clusters have a rectangular shape. These clusters do not overlap.

During the experiments over 3MC, four scenarios were considered. The first scenario is the original 3MC dataset. In the second, third and fourth scenarios were added, respectively, one, five and ten noise variables. The noise variables follow a Gaussian distribution with mean set to $2\,\mu_1 + 2\,\mu_2$ and variance set to $(2\,\sigma_1^2 + 2\,\sigma_2^2)^2$ where μ_1 and μ_2 are the sampling mean of 3MC original two variables respectively and σ_1^2 and σ_2^2 are the sampling variance of 3MC original two variables respectively.

In each of the four scenarios considered here the four algorithms KM, NG, BNG, and ABNG were executed 30 times. The quality of the partitions provided by these algorithms was assessed with the Adjusted Rand index (AR) [10]. The AR index measures the similarity between an a priori partition and a partition provided by a clustering algorithm. AR takes its values from the interval $[-1, 1]$, where the value 1 indicates perfect agreement between partitions, whereas values near 0 (or negatives) correspond to cluster agreement found by chance [19]. For the learning rate parameter $\epsilon_{(t)} = \epsilon_i(\frac{\epsilon_f}{\epsilon_i})^{\frac{t}{T_{Max}}}$ of NG algorithm, we follow Ref. [17] and set suitable initial and final values, respectively as $\epsilon_i = 0.5$ and $\epsilon_f = 0.05$, for all 3MC datasets. For the neighbourhood radius $\lambda_{(t)} = \lambda_i(\frac{\lambda_f}{\lambda_i})^{\frac{t}{T_{Max}}}$ of BNG and ABNG algorithms, the initial and final values were set, respectively, as $\lambda_i = 199.00$ and $\lambda_f = 0.43$ for each 3MC dataset. The initial value was set such that $h_\lambda(C-1) = \exp\{-(C-1)/\lambda\} = 0.99$. In this way, each data point influences strongly all the prototypes, even the prototype of highest rank (the most dissimilar prototype). On the contrary, the final value was set such that $h_\lambda(C-1) = \exp\{-(C-1)/\lambda\} = 0.01$. In this way, each data point influences strongly only the prototypes of lower rank (the most similar prototypes). We also considered 400 cycles ($\mathrm{T_{Max}} = 400$).

Table 1 shows the performance of the algorithms in terms of AR index for the solution that presented the minimum value of the cost function among the 30 solutions. It can be observed that ABNG outperforms all the other algorithms considered here when noise variables are added to the original 3MC. The other algorithms have their AR index values severely compromised even when just one single noise variable was added to 3MC whereas ABNG showed robust performance in terms of AR index for all scenarios considered.

Table 1. AR index for the solution with minimum value of the cost function for 3MC dataset and versions of it with noise variables

Dataset + number of noise variables added	AR index			
	KM	NG	BNG	ABNG
3MC + 0	**0.80026**	0.80026	0.71435	0.73309
3MC + 1	−0.00434	−0.00472	−0.00351	**0.75255**
3MC + 5	0.00503	0.00284	0.00359	**0.65653**
3MC + 10	−0.00263	−0.00251	−0.00372	**0.60010**

The second column of Table 2 shows the final weight vector $\mathbf{v}$ computed by ABNG for the minimum value for cost function E_{ABNG} over 30 executions. Despite the addition of noise variables to the original 3MC dataset, ABNG was able to assign much higher weights to the first two original variables and comparatively much lower weights to the noise variables. This helps to explain how ABNG handles so well the scenarios where noise variables were added to 3MC data set.

Table 2. Final weight vectors $\mathbf{v}$ provided by the ABNG algorithm for 3MC datasets, with and without noise variables, for the minimum cost function E_{ABNG}

Dataset + number of noise variables added	Final weight vector $\mathbf{v}$ provided by the ABNG
3MC + 0	$(1.752, 0.570)$
3MC + 1	$(13.056, 12.192, 0.006)$
3MC + 5	$(374.961, 116.076, 0.121, 0.119, 0.127, 0.115, 0.108)$
3MC + 10	$(481.508, 625.415, 0.274, 0.244, 0.271, 0.298, 0.295, 0.264, 0.308, 0.308, 0.282, 0.289)$

4.2 UCI Machine Learning Repository Datasets

Fifteen datasets from the UCI Machine learning Repository [6], were considered in this study. Table 3, in which N is the number of objects, P is the number of variables, K is the number of a priori classes, summarizes these datasets.

Table 3. Summary of the datasets

Dataset	N	P	K
Breast Tissue	106	9	6
Cardiotocography	2126	22	3
Crowdsourced Mapping	10845	29	6
Ecoli	336	7	8
Glass identification	214	9	6
Image Segmentation	2310	16	7
Iris	150	4	3
Leaf-30c	310	14	30
Libras Movement	360	90	15
Mice Protein	1077	68	8
Thyroid Gland	215	5	3
Pima Diabetes	768	8	2
wdbc	569	32	2
Wine	178	13	3
Yeast	1484	8	10

The initial and final values of the learning rate parameter of NG algorithm were set, respectively, as $\epsilon_i = 0.5$ and $\epsilon_f = 0.05$, for all datasets. For the neighbourhood radius of NG, BNG, and ABNG algorithms, Table 4 provides suitable initial value λ_i and final value λ_f specifically for each dataset. We refer to the Sect. 4.1 for a discussion on setting these parameters.

K-means, NG, BNG and ABNG were run on these datasets 30 times, with C (the number of clusters) equal to K (the number of a priori classes). The quality of the partitions provided by these algorithms was also assessed with the Adjusted Rand index (AR) [10]. For each algorithm, Table 5 shows its performance in terms of AR index for the solution that presented the minimum value of the cost function among the 30 solutions, one for each run. It can be observed that ABNG was the best in 7 out of 15 datasets. In particular, ABGN outperformed BNG in 11 out 15 datasets and NG in 8 out 15 datasets. However, k-means outperformed the ABNG algorithm in 8 out of 15 datasets.

Table 4. Neighbourhood radius: initial and final values

Dataset	λ_i	λ_f
Breast cancer winsconsin	99.50	0.22
Breast Tissue	497.50	1.09
Cardiotocography	199.00	0.43
Crowdsourced Mapping	497.50	1.09
Ecoli	696.49	1.52
Glass identification	497.50	1.09
Image Segmentation	596.99	1.30
Iris	199.00	0.43
leaf-30c	2885.48	6.30
Libras movement	1392.99	3.04
Mice protein	696.49	1.52
Pima Diabetes	99.50	0.22
Thyroid Gland	199.00	0.43
Wine	199.00	0.43
Yeast	895.49	1.95

Table 5. AR index for the solution with minimum E

Dataset	CRand for minimum E			
	KM	NG	BNG	ABNG
BreastTissue	0.17452	0.09986	0.16429	**0.28897**
Cardiotocography	0.04578	0.04171	0.01984	**0.06277**
Crowdsourced Mapping	**0.10593**	0.10223	0.09496	0.10381
Ecoli	**0.42266**	0.41313	0.38940	0.38436
Glass identification	0.27023	**0.27389**	0.23341	0.19504
Image Segmentation	0.40342	0.32288	0.30691	**0.47409**
Iris	0.73024	0.73024	**0.75834**	0.71728
Leaf-30c	**0.31538**	0.30420	0.24062	0.26143
Libras Movement	**0.32728**	0.31527	0.21434	0.20981
Mice Protein	0.14491	**0.15681**	0.10680	0.14080
Thyroid Gland	0.57907	0.57907	0.36858	**0.84875**
Pima Diabetes	0.07439	0.07203	0.07619	**0.10680**
wdbc	0.49142	0.49142	0.49664	**0.71220**
Wine	0.37111	0.37111	0.37198	**0.77127**
Yeast	0.13361	**0.13867**	0.08646	0.12377

5 Conclusions

Conventional on-line and batch NG algorithms implicitly assume that the variables have the same importance in the clustering task. This paper proposes ABNG, an adaptive batch NG algorithm that computes the optimal weights of relevance of the variables in this task. These weights change at each iteration of the algorithm and are different from variable to variable. Therefore, the proposed algorithm is able to select the important variables for the clustering task.

Experiments with synthetic and real datasets from the UCI machine learning repository [6] showed the usefulness of the proposed new clustering method. The experiments with the synthetic datasets showed the ability of the proposed method for handling noise on data, in contrast with the conventional neural gas algorithms. The results with the real datasets, showed the overall good performance of the ABNG algorithm, specially for the datasets with variables of different relevance for the clustering task. Moreover, the proposed adaptive batch NG outperformed the conventional batch NG in 11 out of 15 datasets.

The adaptive batch NG algorithm of this paper takes into account the relevance weight of the variables globally for all clusters. In the near future, we aim to extent it to take into account the relevance weight of the variables locally for each cluster specifically.

Acknowledgment. The authors would like to thank the anonymous referees for their careful revision, and the CNPq, National Council for Scientific and Technological Development, Brazil (303187/2013-1), for its financial support.

References

1. de Amorim, R.C., Mirkin, B.: Minkowski metric feature weighting and anomalous cluster initializing in k-means clustering. Pattern Recogn. **45**, 1061–1075 (2012)
2. Bezdek, J.C.: Pattern Recognition with Fuzzy Objective Function Algorithms. Plenum, New York (1981)
3. Cottrell, M., Hammer, B., Hassenfuß, A., Vilmann, T.: Batch and median neural gas. Neural Netw. **19**(6), 762–771 (2006)
4. Diday, E., Govaert, G.: Classification automatique avec distances adaptatives. R.A.I.R.O. Informatique Comput. Sci. **11**(4), 329–349 (1977)
5. Djenouri, Y., Belhadi, A., Fournier-Viger, P., Lin, J.C.W.: Fast and effective cluster-based information retrieval using frequent closed itemsets. Inf. Sci. **453**, 154–167 (2018)
6. Dua, D., Taniskidou, E.K.: UCI Machine Learning Repository. University of California, School of Information and Computer Science, Irvine, CA (2017). http://archive.ics.uci.edu/ml
7. Hammer, B., Hassenfuß, A., Vilmann, T.: Magnification control for batch neural gas. Neurocomputing **70**, 1225–1234 (2007)
8. Hammer, B., Strickert, M., Villmann, T.: Supervised neural gas with general similarity measure. Neural Process. Lett. **21**, 21–44 (2005)
9. Hammer, B., Villmann, T.: Generalized relevance learning vector quantization. Neural Netw. **15**, 1059–1068 (2002)

10. Hubert, L., Arabie, P.: Comparing partitions. J. Classif. **3**, 193–218 (1985)
11. Hunag, J.Z., Ng, M.K., Li, Z.: Automated variable weighting in k-means type clustering. IEEE Trans. Pattern Anal. Mach. Intell. **27**(5), 657–668 (2005)
12. Jain, A.K.: Data clustering: 50 years beyond k-means. Pattern Recogn. Lett. **31**(8), 651–666 (2010)
13. Kohonen, T.: Self-Organizing Maps. SSINF, vol. 30. Springer, Heidelberg (1995). https://doi.org/10.1007/978-3-642-97610-0
14. Kohonen, T.: Essentials of the self-organizing map. Neural Netw. **37**, 52–65 (2013)
15. Lloyd, S.P.: Least squares quantization in PCM. IEEE Trans. Inform Theory **28**(2), 129–137 (1982)
16. MacQueen, J.: Some methods for classification and analysis of multivariate observations. In: LeCam, L.M., Neyman, J. (eds.) Proceedings of the 5th Berkeley Symposium on Mathematics Statistics, and Probability, pp. 281–297 (1967)
17. Martinetz, T., Berkovich, S.G., Schulten, K.J.: 'Neural-gas' network for vector quantization and its application to time-series prediction. IEEE Trans. Neural Networks **4**, 558–569 (1993)
18. Martinetz, T., Schulten, K.: A 'neural-gas' network learns topologies. In: Mäkisara, K., Simula, O., Kangas, J., Kohonen, T. (eds.) Artificial Neural Networks, pp. 397–402. Elsevier, North-Holland, Amsterdam (1991)
19. Milligan, G.W.: Clustering validation: results and implications for applied analysis. Max M. Fisher College of Business, Ohio State University (1996)
20. Modha, D.S., Spangler, W.S.: Feature weighting in k-means clustering. Mach. Learn. **52**(3), 217–237 (2003)
21. Pagnuco, I.A., Pastore, J.I., Abras, G., Brun, M., Ballarin, V.L.: Analysis of genetic association using hierarchical clustering and cluster validation indices. Genomics **109**(5–6), 438–445 (2017)
22. Saxena, A., et al.: A review of clustering techniques and developments. Neurocomputing **267**, 664–681 (2017)
23. Tsai, C.Y., Chiu, C.C.: Developing a feature weight self-adjustment mechanism for a k-means clustering algorithm. Comput. Stat. Data Anal. **52**, 4658–4672 (2008)
24. Wazarkar, S., Keshavamurthy, B.N.: A survey on image data analysis through clustering techniques for real world applications. J. Vis. Commun. Image Represent. **55**, 596–626 (2018)
25. Xu, R., Wunusch, D.I.I.: Survey of clustering algorithms. IEEE Trans. Neural Networks **16**(3), 645–678 (2005)

Application of Self Organizing Map to Preprocessing Input Vectors for Convolutional Neural Network

Hiroshi Dozono(✉) and Masafumi Tanaka

Saga University, 1 Honjyo, Saga 8408502, Japan
hiro@dna.ec.saga-u.ac.jp,
19625010@edu.cc.saga-u.ac.jp

Abstract. Recently, the applications of Artificial Intelligence are widely spread in many areas of research. They almost use tailor made classification engine of Deep Learning, and many of such engines uses Convolutional Neural Networks. In this paper, we propose a method for preprocessing the un-structured data to the 2 dimensional data suitable for CNN using Self Organizing Map. The performance is evaluated with the experiments using KDD cup 99 data as input vectors.

Keywords: Self Organizing Map · Convolutional Neural Network · Data compression

1 Introduction

Recently, Artificial Intelligence (AI) is applied to the applications of many areas, such as industrial, entertainment, educational, and so on. In these applications, Deep Learning (DL) [1] method which employs the neural network using deep layers are used. DLs are also applied to many researches of bio-medicine, chemistry, biology, security, and so on. One of reason why DLs are applied to many researches is existence of tailor made classification engines which are based on DL. Many of these engines are designed for image classification which employed deep Convolutional Neural Network (CNN) [2]. However, almost of real world data are not 2-dimensional array data which can be easily converted to image. It may be the vector of 1-dimensional array of large number of elements, multi-modal vectors which are composed of unstructured vectors, or multi-dimensional arrays more than 3 dimension. In some researches, the input data are simply converted to images with simply arranging the original data on 2-dimensional array, and applied to CNN for classification. In [3], processor level features are simply arranged on 2 dimensional array, and given to CNN for detecting Malware. Using this method, good performance of classification is reported in a certain degree, however the performance of CNN is considered not to be provided enough. CNN can extract the features of local region in the images with convolution. However, the effect of convolution may be meaningless because the input data are arranged on 2-dimensional array in meaningless way.

I. V. Tetko et al. (Eds.): ICANN 2019, LNCS 11728, pp. 96–100, 2019.
https://doi.org/10.1007/978-3-030-30484-3_8

In this paper, we propose a method for preprocessing the un-structured data to the 2 dimensional array suitable for CNN using Self Organizing Map (SOM) [4]. Conventionally, SOM is applied to the unsupervised clustering and visualization of the relationship of input vectors. In this paper, SOM is presented the vector of each element of all data as input vectors, because SOM is used to convert the unstructured data to 2 dimensional array. With using smaller map size compared with the original data, the input data can be compressed, and the time for computation in classification is expected to be shortened. After converting the input data to set of 2 dimensional arrays, the arrays are given to CNN for classification.

The experiments using KDD cup 99 data [5] are conducted to examine the performance of proposed method.

2 Method

2.1 Preprocessing of Input Data Using SOM

As for the conventional Self Organizing Map (SOM), the input vectors are given for each data in row data shown as (a) in Fig. 1. After learning, the input data is mapped to a winner unit, and the relationship among the data is visualized on the map.

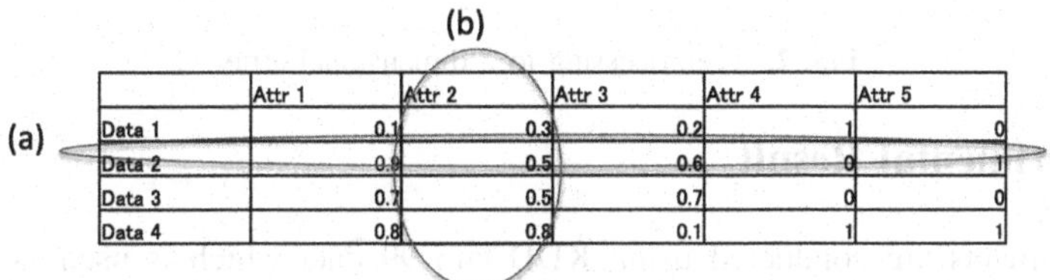

Fig. 1. Input data of SOM

For converting the input data to 2 dimensional array, the input data are given to SOM for each attribute in column as shown as (b) in Fig. 1. Before learning, the input data are normalized for each attribute. After learning SOM, the map represents the relationship among the attributes according to the set of input data. Thus, the layer composed of the element of n-th position in reference vectors represents the features of n-th input data arranged on 2 dimensional array of map size as shown in Fig. 2. If the size of map is taken as smaller than the number of attributes, input data is compressed. If the size is taken as larger, input data is extended including the relationship among the data.

The preprocessed data are given to CNN as image data after normalizing the values in 2 dimensional array between 0–255, and classification is conducted.

2.2 Algorithm

The brief algorithm is as follows.

1. For each attributes, the input data are normalized between 0 and 1.
2. Train SOM using the input vector composed of each attribute of all input data as shown as (b) in Fig. 1.
3. Extract each layer of the reference vectors on the map as the converted data of each input data as shown in Fig. 2, and convert the values from 0.0–1.0 to 0–255 as to convert to 8 bit grayscale image.
4. Classify the converted images using CNN.

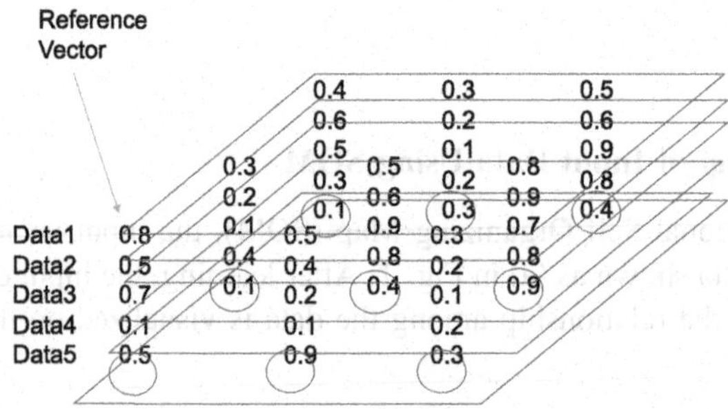

Fig. 2. Preprocessing to 2 dimensional array

3 Experimental Result

The experiments are conducted using KDD cup 99 data which is used as standard benchmark data for detection of malicious IP packets. As for the reason of computational resources, 10000 heading data in kddcup.data_10_percent is used, and the major 9 labels which include more than 10 data are used for classification. Each data is composed of 42 attributes including the label, and 38 numerical attributes are used after normalizing to the range 0 to 1 as mentioned in Sect. 2.

The experiments are conducted with changing the size of maps. For all cases, each data is learned in 100 iterations with changing the neighbor size from 1/2 of map size to 0, learning rate from 0.8 to 0.1. Figure 3 shows the preprocessed data which is converted to 4 × 4 images using the map of 4 × 4 units for 3 data labeled Normal, Neptune and Smurf in KDD cup 99 data.

Fig. 3. Preprocessed Images of 4 × 4

For each label, the input data is converted to the different image which can be easily identified by human.

After preprocessing using SOM, the converted images are given to CNN for the experiments of classification. For the comparison, the original data are converted to the image of 8 × 5 pixels with arranging 38 attributes in order and padding 0 to remainders.

CNN is implemented using Keras library with TensorFlow. The CNN with 6 layers which is composed of 4 convolution layers and 2 dense layers is used. 80% of the data are used for training and 20% of data are used for validation, and 3 cross validations are conducted for each case. All training data are presented to CNN in 5 epochs. Table 1 shows the results.

Table 1. Accuracies of classification

	Training data	Validation	Normal (1956)	Neptune (2114)	Smurf (5742)
Original data	0.996	0.997	0.995	1.000	0.999
2 × 2	0.981	0.980	0.997	1.000	0.666
3 × 3	0.995	0.995	0.995	1.000	1.000
4 × 4	0.993	0.993	0.998	1.000	0.999
8 × 5	0.994	0.994	0.997	1.000	0.999
8 × 8	0.996	0.994	0.996	0.999	0.999
16 × 16	0.994	0.995	0.986	1.000	1.000
Tear drop (19)	Port sweep (27)	Ip sweep (10)	Back (13)	Satan (!5)	Warez client (20)
0.982	0.963	0.855	0.983	0.880	0.833
0.000	0.000	0.000	0.000	0.282	0.000
1.000	0.877	0.870	0.942	0.812	0.282
0.544	0.914	0.652	0.800	0.812	0.410
0.982	0.827	0.783	0.958	0.838	0.462
1.000	0.889	0.841	0.783	0.812	0.821
0.947	0.877	0.841	0.958	0.897	0.936

The number in () in the first row denotes the number of data for each label. From 2nd row, each row denotes the result with changing the size of map. The first column denotes the accuracies for training data, the second column denotes those for validation data, and the remainder denotes the those for each labeled data. For all cases, the accuracies for training data and validation data are over 98%. The data of major 3 labels are classified in high accuracies for all cases, however accuracies of minor 6 labels degrade as the size of the images becomes smaller. Conversely, major 3 labels can be almost classified using only 4 elements in 2 × 2 images preprocessed by SOM.

4 Conclusion

In this paper, the preprocessing method of unstructured data to 2 dimensional array suitable for Convolutional Network using Self Organizing Map is proposed. The effectiveness is confirmed by the experiments using KDD cup 99 data. Practical accuracy can be achieved even if the original data are compressed to 1/10 number of elements.

As the future work, the preprocessing method of newly presented data should be considered. In current method, new data must be preprocessed by SOM with adding to training data. The method which can convert new data using the trained map should be developed. And, it may be possible to get better accuracy with converting the data to 3 or more dimensional data, and applying to CNN.

References

1. Caglar Gulcehre Deep Learning. http://deeplearning.net
2. FLDL Tutrial: Convolutional Neural Network. http://ufldl.stanford.edu/tutral/supervised/Convolutiona/Neural
3. Otani, G., Takase, H., Kobayashi, R., Kato, M.: Detection of Subspecific Malware Focusing on Processor Level Features, IPSJ-CSEC18080031 (2018)
4. Kohonen, T.: Self Organizing Maps. Springer, Heidelberg (2001). https://doi.org/10.1007/978-3-642-56927-2. ISBN 3-540-67921-9
5. KDD Cup 1999 Data. http://kdd.ics.uci.edu/databases/kddcup99/kddcup99.html

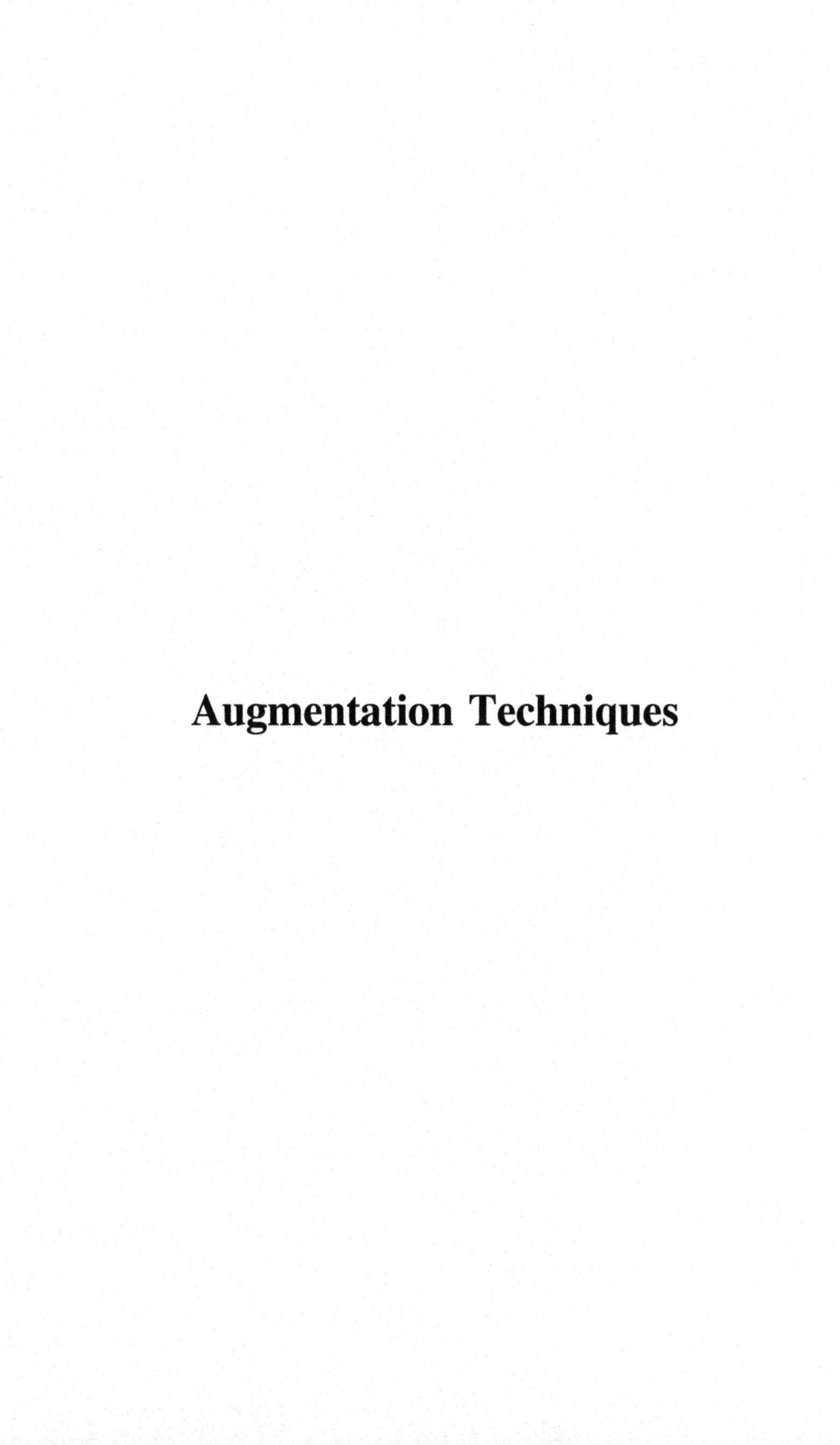

Augmentation Techniques

Hierarchical Reinforcement Learning with Unlimited Recursive Subroutine Calls

Yuuji Ichisugi[1(✉)], Naoto Takahashi[1], Hidemoto Nakada[1], and Takashi Sano[2]

[1] National Institute of Advanced Industrial Science and Technology (AIST), AIRC, Tsukuba, Japan
y-ichisugi@aist.go.jp

[2] Department of Computer and Information Science, Faculty of Science and Technology, Seikei University, Musashino, Japan

Abstract. Humans can set suitable subgoals to achieve certain tasks. They can also set sub-subgoals recursively if required. The depth of this recursion is apparently unlimited. Inspired by this behavior, we propose a new hierarchical reinforcement learning architecture called RGoal. RGoal solves the Markov Decision Process (MDP) in an augmented state-action space. In multitask settings, sharing subroutines between tasks makes learning faster. A novel mechanism called thought-mode is a type of model-based reinforcement learning. It combines learned simple tasks to solve unknown complicated tasks rapidly, sometimes in zero-shot time.

Keywords: Hierarchical reinforcement learning · Model-based reinforcement learning · Zero-shot learning · Computational neuroscience

1 Introduction

Humans can set suitable subgoals to achieve certain tasks (goals). They can also set sub-subgoals recursively if needed. For example, if you wish to get an object on a high shelf, it is necessary to set up a ladder first. In this case, "the ladder is set up" is a subgoal state. If the ladder is in a store room, it is necessary to go to the store room first to retrieve the ladder. In this case, "you are in the store room" becomes a sub-subgoal state. The depth of this recursion is apparently unlimited for humans. Inspired by this behavior, we propose a new hierarchical reinforcement learning architecture [2–6,8,9,11] called the *RGoal architecture*.

In RGoal, an agent's subgoal settings are similar to subroutine calls in programming languages. Each subroutine can execute primitive actions or recursively call other subroutines. The timing for calling another subroutine is learned by using a standard reinforcement learning method. Unlimited recursive subroutine calls accelerate learning because they increase the opportunity for the reuse of subroutines in multitask settings.

RGoal is strongly influenced by the previously proposed HDG [4] and MAXQ [6] architectures. MAXQ is a multi-layered hierarchical reinforcement

I. V. Tetko et al. (Eds.): ICANN 2019, LNCS 11728, pp. 103–114, 2019.
https://doi.org/10.1007/978-3-030-30484-3_9

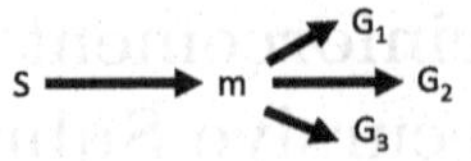

Fig. 1. Even though goals (G_1, G_2, and G_3) are different between tasks, the route from the state S to the subgoal m is common. If the tasks share that route as a subroutine, learning will be accelerated.

learning architecture with a fixed number of layers. It accelerates learning based on the following three features.

1. Subtask sharing: In multitask settings, sharing subroutines between tasks makes learning faster (Fig. 1).
2. Temporal abstraction: When learning complicated tasks, restricting the search space such that it only includes combinations of simple subroutines makes learning faster.
3. State abstraction: Abstracting states to such an extent that they do not affect the execution of subroutines makes learning faster.

RGoal provides the first feature through *value function decomposition* (Sect. 2.3) and the second feature through a novel mechanism called *thought-mode* (Sect. 2.7). Although we have not yet implemented the third feature, it should be possible through function approximation using neural networks.

In the future, by extending RGoal, we wish to construct a computational model of the mechanism of human planning based on the prefrontal cortex of the human brain. Therefore, RGoal is designed not only to be useful from an engineering perspective, but also to be a simple architecture that can be easily implemented in the neural circuits of the brain.

The remainder of the paper is organized as follows. First, we describe the architecture of RGoal in Sect. 2 and evaluate it in Sect. 3. We describe related works in Sect. 4. Finally, we present our conclusions in Sect. 5.

2 The RGoal Architecture

2.1 Landmarks and Subgoals

In this paper, we assume that the set of states that may become goals or subgoals on the environment is given beforehand. We refer to an element of this set as a *landmark*. Typically, landmarks are states of the environment that are salient to the agent.

In RGoal, a subroutine g is "a policy for reaching the subgoal state g from arbitrary states." We assume that an agent executing subroutine g will reach the corresponding state g within finite time. This assumption simplifies the theoretical framework and algorithm for RGoal, and facilitates the realization of the thought-mode described in Sect. 2.7. It must be possible to extend RGoal in the future such that each subroutine can have more than one terminal state, similar

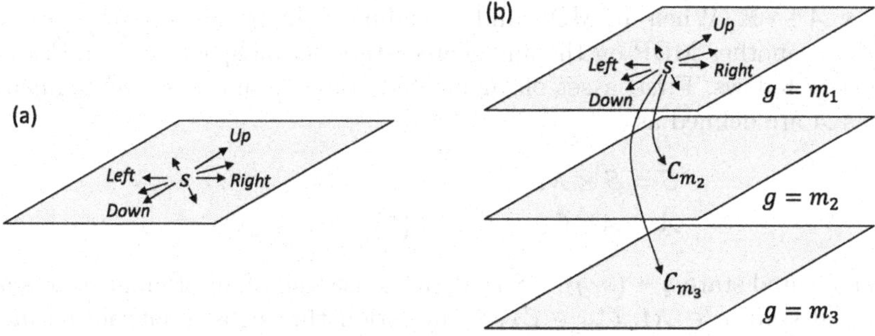

Fig. 2. (a) An example state-action space in a two-dimensional grid. (b) The augmented state-action space when a landmark set $\mathcal{M} = \{m_1, m_2, m_3\}$ is given. Possible actions include the subroutine calls $\mathcal{C}_{\mathcal{M}} = \{C_{m_1}, C_{m_2}, C_{m_3}\}$ and movements within the two-dimensional space.

to the MAXQ architecture [6]. Although the reusability of subroutines can be increased in this manner, it may also increase the calculation cost of action-value functions or decrease calculation accuracy.

An agent maintains a stack to remember subgoals. When an agent calls a subroutine g', the current subgoal g is pushed onto the stack. When the subroutine g' terminates (the agent reaches the corresponding state g'), the original subgoal g is popped from stack and reset as a new subgoal.

There is another design methodology that does not use a stack. In this methodology, an agent only remembers the original goal G. Whenever the final called subroutine terminates, the current subgoal is reset to G. Although we have confirmed that this methodology also works, we do not present its details in this paper.

Although the landmark set affects performance, a bad landmark set does not make a task unsolvable. If a landmark set only contains the goal state, the behavior of RGoal is the same as non-hierarchical reinforcement learning. If there are too many landmarks in the set, learning becomes very difficult. However, landmarks that are not worth using will be gradually filtered out as learning progresses.

2.2 The Augmented State-Action Space

The RGoal architecture learns the action-value function for the *Markov decision process (MDP)* in *the augmented state-action space* [9] described in this Section. Because the mathematical structure of this MDP is the same as typical MDPs, we can utilize various theoretical conclusions (e.g., convergence to an exact solution) and implementation techniques (e.g., function approximation and eligibility trace) to solve problems.

An MDP is defined as $< \mathcal{S}, \mathcal{A}, P, r >$, which consists of a set of states $\mathcal{S}$, set of actions $\mathcal{A}$, transition function $P : \mathcal{S} \times \mathcal{A} \rightarrow (\mathcal{S} \rightarrow [0, 1])$, and reward function

$r : \mathcal{S} \times \mathcal{A} \to \mathbb{R}$. When an MDP and a landmark set $\mathcal{M} = \{m_1, m_2, \cdots\} \subseteq \mathcal{S}$ are given, another MDP on the augmented state-action space $< \tilde{\mathcal{S}}, \tilde{\mathcal{A}}, \tilde{P}, \tilde{r} >$ is defined as follows. First, a set of augmented states $\tilde{\mathcal{S}}$ and a set of augmented actions $\tilde{\mathcal{A}}$ are defined as

$$\begin{aligned} \tilde{\mathcal{S}} &= \mathcal{S} \times \mathcal{M} \\ \tilde{\mathcal{A}} &= \mathcal{A} \cup \mathcal{C}_{\mathcal{M}}, \quad \mathcal{C}_{\mathcal{M}} = \{C_{m_1}, C_{m_2}, \cdots\}. \end{aligned} \tag{1}$$

An augmented state $\tilde{s} = (s, g) \in \tilde{\mathcal{S}}$ is a pair consisting of an original state s and a subgoal state $g \in \mathcal{M}$. $C_m \in \mathcal{C}_{\mathcal{M}}$ is an action that calls a subroutine m. In other words, C_m sets the landmark m as a new subgoal. Taking an action C_m changes the augmented state (s, g) to (s, m). A transition function $\tilde{P}(\tilde{s}'|\tilde{s}, \tilde{a})$ is defined based on the original transition function $P(s'|s, a)$ as follows:

$$\begin{aligned} \tilde{P}((s', g)|(s, g), a) &= P(s'|s, a) \\ \tilde{P}((s, m)|(s, g), C_m) &= 1. \end{aligned} \tag{2}$$

A reward function $\tilde{r}(\tilde{s}, \tilde{a})$ is defined based on the original reward function $r(s, a)$ as follows:

$$\begin{aligned} \tilde{r}((s, g), a) &= r(s, a) \\ \tilde{r}((s, g), C_m) &= R^{\mathcal{C}}, \end{aligned} \tag{3}$$

where the constant $R^{\mathcal{C}}$ is a hyperparameter that represents the cost of each subroutine call.

Figure 2 presents an example of an augmented state-action space. It contains the subgoal g, which represents the agent's inner state, as part of the state of the external environment. If the original state-action space is a two-dimensional space and n landmarks are given, the augmented state-action space looks like a building with n floors. At each step, the agent moves within the current floor or moves to another floor. In general, optimal policies do *not* execute any C_m. However, the execution of some C_m may make convergence to a suboptimal policy faster.

2.3 Value Function Decomposition

Decomposition of the action-value function in the augmented state-action space makes learning faster because parts of the decomposed functions are shared between different tasks. The details of this process are provided below.

Given a policy $\pi : \tilde{\mathcal{S}} \times \tilde{\mathcal{A}} \to [0, 1]$ and a goal $G \in \mathcal{M}$, the action-value function $Q^{\pi}_{G}(\tilde{s}, \tilde{a})$ is defined as

$$Q^{\pi}_{G}((s, g), \tilde{a}) = E^{\pi}_{G}[\Sigma_{t=0}^{\infty} r_{t+1} | \tilde{s}_0 = (s, g), \tilde{a}_0 = \tilde{a}], \tag{4}$$

which is the expected value of the summation of the sequence of rewards $r_1 = \tilde{r}(\tilde{s}_0, \tilde{a}_0), r_2 = \tilde{r}(\tilde{s}_1, \tilde{a}_1), \cdots$, which are obtained when taking an action $\tilde{a}$ at an initial state $\tilde{s}_0 = (s, g)$ and taking actions according to the policy π. We assume that the total reward obtained after reaching the goal state G is 0. In other words, tasks are episodic. In this paper, we assume that rewards are not discounted.

We assume that if an agent is using a policy π, the agent at a state (s, g) reaches the subgoal state (g, g) within finite time. Furthermore, an agent at the state (g, G) reaches the goal state (G, G) within finite time. When the stack contains only G and an agent reaches the subgoal state (g, g) from (s, g), the state is automatically set to (g, G) and the reward at the time is 0. Then, $Q_G^\pi(\tilde{s}, \tilde{a})$ can be decomposed into two parts (i.e., rewards obtained before and after reaching the subgoal g) as follows:

$$Q_G^\pi((s,g),\tilde{a}) = Q^\pi(s,g,\tilde{a}) + V_G^\pi(g), \tag{5}$$

where $Q^\pi(s,g,\tilde{a})$ is the expected value of the total rewards obtained when taking an action $\tilde{a}$ at an initial state (s, g) and taking actions according to the policy π until reaching (g, g). Additionally, $V_G^\pi(g)$ is the expected value of the total rewards after the state (g, G) until reaching (G, G), which can be efficiently calculated based on $Q^\pi(s, g, \tilde{a})$ as

$$\begin{aligned} V_G^\pi(g) &= \Sigma_{\tilde{a}}\pi((g,G),\tilde{a})Q_G^\pi((g,G),\tilde{a}) \\ &= \Sigma_{\tilde{a}}\pi((g,G),\tilde{a})(Q^\pi(g,G,\tilde{a}) + V_G^\pi(G)) \\ &= \Sigma_{\tilde{a}}\pi((g,G),\tilde{a})Q^\pi(g,G,\tilde{a}). \end{aligned} \tag{6}$$

(Note that $V_G^\pi(G) = 0$).

Because the function $Q^\pi(s, g, \tilde{a})$ does not depend on the original goal G, it can be shared between different tasks to make learning faster. The same argument holds when recursive calls are permitted.

2.4 Update Rule

The current implementation of RGoal represents an action-value function $Q(s, g, \tilde{a})$ as a table. The update rule for the table can be derived from a standard reinforcement learning method, Sarsa algorithm for $Q_G(\tilde{s}, \tilde{a})$:

$$Q_G(\tilde{s},\tilde{a}) \leftarrow Q_G(\tilde{s},\tilde{a}) + \alpha(r + Q_G(\tilde{s}',\tilde{a}') - Q_G(\tilde{s},\tilde{a})). \tag{7}$$

Consider the case where $\tilde{a}$ is $C_{g'}$, which represents a subroutine call g'. When the stack contains only G and prior to the subroutine call, the assumed route of the agent is $s \to g \to G$. After the subroutine call, the route is changed to $s \to g' \to g \to G$. Therefore, the following equation holds:

$$\begin{aligned} &Q_G(\tilde{s}',\tilde{a}') - Q_G(\tilde{s},\tilde{a}) \\ &= (Q(s',g',\tilde{a}') + V_g(g') + V_G(g)) - (Q(s,g,\tilde{a}) + V_G(g)) \\ &= Q(s',g',\tilde{a}') - Q(s,g,\tilde{a}) + V_g(g'). \end{aligned} \tag{8}$$

This equation also holds when $\tilde{a}$ is not a subroutine call, but is a primitive action. (Not that $g = g'$ and $V_g(g') = 0$, in such cases.) The same argument holds when recursive calls are permitted. From Eqs. (5), (7), (8), the update rule for $Q(s, g, \tilde{a})$ is derived as

$$Q(s, g, \tilde{a}) \leftarrow Q(s, g, \tilde{a}) + \alpha(r + Q(s', g', \tilde{a}') - Q(s, g, \tilde{a}) + V_g(g')). \quad (9)$$

Note that special treatment is required when $s = g$ (i.e., the agent reaches the subgoal g). Because $Q(s, g, \tilde{a}) = 0$ when $s = g$, by definition, the table values should not change in such cases.

2.5 Table Initialization

The elements of the table Q should be initialized as $Q(s, g, \tilde{a}) = 0$ if $s = g$.

If $s \neq g$, the initial values are arbitrary. However, the values do affect performance [7]. As an extreme case, we can restrict subroutine calls by setting $Q(s, g, C_m) = -\infty$ for some appropriate set of (s, g, m) to reduce the search space. If such a restriction is too strong, performance will become worse. However, this does not make a task unsolvable because the execution of primitive actions is not restricted. An engineer may design appropriate restrictions of subroutine calls to tune overall performance, similar to the task graph design in the MAXQ architecture [6].

2.6 Action Selection

The action-selection policy $\pi(\tilde{s}, \tilde{a})$ is derived from the action-value function $Q_G(\tilde{s}, \tilde{a})$. The current implementation uses a softmax action selection policy, which is defined as follows:

$$\begin{aligned}\pi((s, g), \tilde{a}) &= \frac{exp(\beta Q_G((s, g), \tilde{a}))}{\Sigma_{\tilde{a}'} exp(\beta Q_G((s, g), \tilde{a}'))} = \frac{exp(\beta Q(s, g, \tilde{a}) + \beta V_G(g))}{\Sigma_{\tilde{a}'} exp(\beta Q(s, g, \tilde{a}') + \beta V_G(g))} \\ &= \frac{exp(\beta Q(s, g, \tilde{a}))}{\Sigma_{\tilde{a}'} exp(\beta Q(s, g, \tilde{a}'))}. \end{aligned} \quad (10)$$

2.7 Thought-Mode

When learning complicated tasks, restricting the search space to include only combinations of simple subroutines makes learning faster. In this case, subroutines realize the temporal abstraction [5] of action sequences. In the RGoal architecture, a novel mechanism called thought-mode facilitates this behavior.

Suppose that the optimal routes between all neighboring pairs of landmarks have been already learned. Then, an approximate solution for the optimal route between distant landmarks can be obtained by connecting neighboring landmarks. For example, in Fig. 1, the route $S \rightarrow m \rightarrow G_1$ is an approximate solution for the route from S to G_1. Such solutions can be found without taking any actions within the environment [2–4]. The thought-mode of RGoal is a mechanism for finding approximate routes by repeating simulations of episodes within an agent's brain. This mechanism can be implemented with only a few small

```
procedure EPISODE(S, G, think-flag)
    s ← S;  g ← G;  stack ← empty
    Choose ã from s, g using policy derived from Q
    while s ≠ G do
        # Take action.
        if ã = RET then
            s' ← s;  g' ← stack.pop();  r ← 0
        else if ã is C_m then
            stack.push(g);  s' ← s;  g' ← m;  r ← R^C
        else
            if think-flag then
                s' ← g;  g' ← g;  r ← dummy
            else
                Take action ã, observe r, s';  g' ← g
        # Choose action.
        if s' = g' then
            ã' ← RET
        else
            Choose ã' from s', g' using policy derived from Q
        # Update.
        if s = g or (think-flag and ã is not C_m) then
            # Do nothing.
        else
            Q(s, g, ã) ← Q(s, g, ã) + α(r + Q(s', g', ã') − Q(s, g, ã) + V_g(g'))
        s ← s';  g ← g';  ã ← ã'
```

Fig. 3. Pseudo code for the RGoal algorithm, which is based on the Sarsa algorithm.

modifications to the RGoal algorithm. Because of its simplicity, we consider this mechanism to be a promising first step toward a computational model for the planning mechanism of the human brain.

The behavior of thought-mode is described below. If the selected action $\tilde{a}$ is a primitive action, the simulated state in the agent's brain is *immediately* changed from s to the current subgoal g. In such cases, the table element $Q(s, g, \tilde{a})$ is not updated. If $\tilde{a}$ is a subroutine call C_m, the behavior of thought-mode is the same as that of the normal mode. In such cases, the subgoal g is changed to m and the table element $Q(s, g, C_m)$ is updated normally.

The behavior described above can be regarded as a type of model-based reinforcement learning [1]. The learned value of $Q(s, g, \tilde{a})$ is used as a model of the environment that tells the agent how much reward will be obtained if the agent moves from s to g.

2.8 RGoal Algorithm

The pseudo code for the RGoal algorithm, which is based on the Sarsa algorithm, is presented in Fig. 3. This algorithm uses a flat table and stack with a single loop consisting entirely of simple operations.

3 Evaluation

RGoal performance was evaluated on a maze task. Here, we focus on convergence speed to suboptimal solutions, rather than exact solutions.

The map and landmark set are presented in Fig. 4. For each episode, the start S and goal G are randomly selected from the landmark set. When the agent reaches G, the episode ends and the next episode with a different start and goal begins.

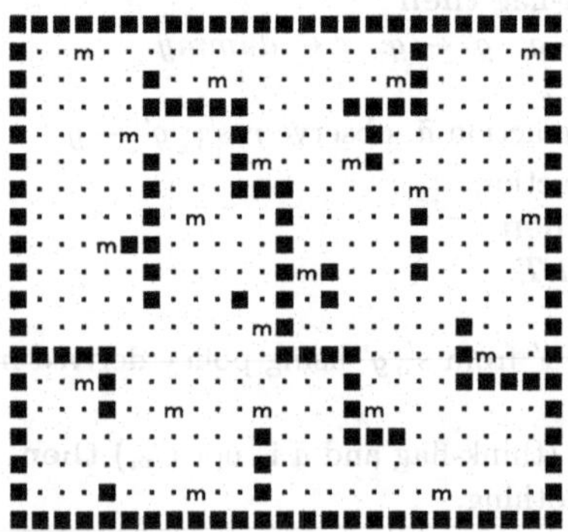

Fig. 4. Map of a maze on the 2D grid used for the evaluation. Twenty landmarks (denoted **m**) are placed on the map. For each episode, the start S and goal G are randomly selected from the landmark set.

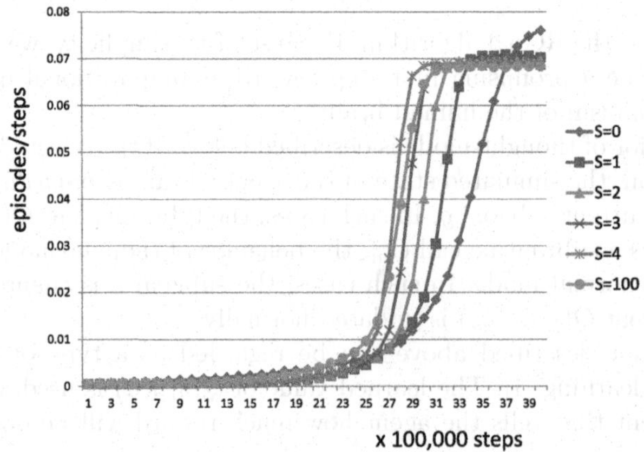

Fig. 5. Experiment 1. Relationship between the upper limit S of the stack depth and RGoal performance. $S = 0$ corresponds to non-hierarchical reinforcement learning. When $S = 1$, recursive calls are not allowed, as in the two-layered reinforcement learning. A greater upper limit results in faster convergence because it increases the opportunity for the reuse of subroutines.

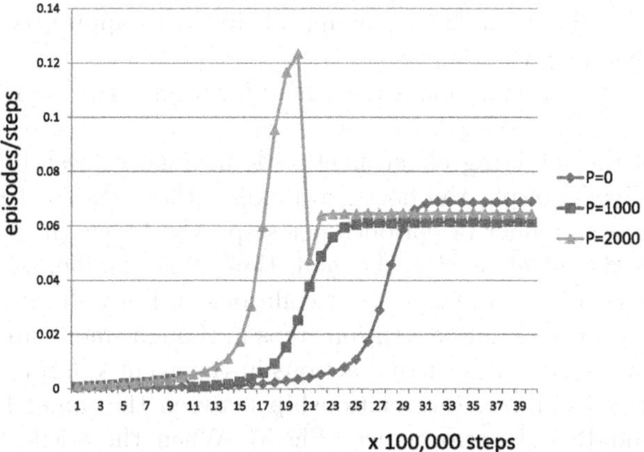

Fig. 6. Experiment 2. Relationship between the length P (times 1000 steps) of the pre-training phase and RGoal performance. In the pre-training phase, only pairs of the start and goal within Euclidean distances of eight are selected. $S = 100$. The graph also includes a change in the score during the pre-training phase. The greater the value of P, the faster the convergence speed.

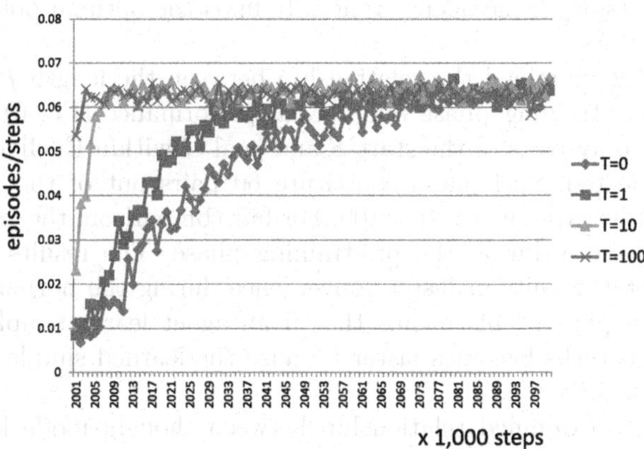

Fig. 7. Experiment 3. Relationship between thought-mode length T and RGoal performance. T is the number of simulations executed prior to the actual execution of each episode. $S = 100$, $P = 2000$. Here, we only plot the change in score after the pre-training phase. If thought-mode length is sufficiently long, approximate solutions are obtained in almost zero-shot time.

The reward for moving up, down, left, or right is -1, that for moving diagonally is $-\sqrt{2}$, that for hitting a wall is -1, and that for a subroutine call is $R^C = -1$. As mentioned earlier, rewards are not discounted.

The table elements of $Q(s, g, \tilde{a})$ are initialized to zero if $s = g$ and $-50 - n$ (n is small noise), otherwise. To make learning faster, subroutine calls are restricted to be executable only on landmarks by initializing some appropriate elements to $-\infty$, as described in Sect. 2.5.

The action-selection function is a softmax function with $\beta = 1$. The learning rate is $\alpha = 0.1$.

For each of the following experiments, the average values of 10 trials were calculated. For each graph, the horizontal axis is the number of steps and the vertical axis is the number of episodes per step. The larger the value of the y-axis, the faster the agent reaches the goal. Here, "the number of steps" means the number of moves within the map or collisions with a wall. Subroutine calls, returns from subroutines, and execution steps in thought-mode are not included because they are regarded as virtual actions in the agent's brain.

Experiment 1 examined the relationship between the upper limit S of the stack depth and RGoal performance (Fig. 5). When the stack depth reaches the upper limit, the agent does not make any further subroutine calls. $S = 0$ corresponds to non-hierarchical reinforcement learning. A greater upper limit results in faster convergence. However, at $S = 100$, the convergence is slightly slower than that at $S = 4$. The score after convergence is the best when $S = 0$. This is because if subroutines can be used, an agent may choose suboptimal routes through some landmarks. We have confirmed that even when subroutine calls can be used, if we optimize the search tendency by choosing a small value of β, then increasing β, the agent eventually finds the optimal policy that does not call subroutines.

Experiment 2 examined the relationship between the length P (times 1000 steps) of the pre-training phase and RGoal performance (Fig. 6). In the pre-training phase, only pairs of the start S and goal G within Euclidean distances of eight are selected. Such pairs constitute 60 pairs out of the $20\ 19 = 380$ total pairs. In this experiment, $S = 100$. For fair comparison, the graph includes changes in the score during the pre-training phase. The results show that a greater value of P results in faster convergence during the normal phase after the pre-training phase. This means that if an agent learns simple tasks first, learning difficult tasks becomes faster because the learned simple tasks can be reused as subroutines.

Experiment 3 examined relationship between thought-mode length T and RGoal performance (Fig. 7). T is the number of simulations in an agent's brain that are executed immediately before each actual execution of an episode in the environment. In this experiment, $S = 100$ and $P = 2000$. Here, we only plot changes in the score after 2,000,000 steps of the pre-training phase. The results show that if the thought-mode length is sufficiently long, approximate solutions for unknown tasks are obtained immediately (almost in zero-shot time) by combining knowledge from previously experienced simple tasks.

4 Related Work

Unlike previous hierarchical reinforcement learning architectures, RGoal is unique in that the caller and callee relation between subroutines is not pre-defined, but is learned within the framework of reinforcement learning. We have integrated several important ideas that were proposed in previous papers into a single simple architecture to realize the desired RGoal features.

RGoal has a very similar structure to the Hierarchical Distance to Goal (HDG) architecture [4]. HDG uses a dedicated algorithm for offline searching of routes by connecting distant landmarks. In contrast, RGoal accomplishes the same goal by using thought-mode, which is much easier to implement and is similar to human behavior.

The H-DYNA architecture [2,3] also utilizes planning with temporal abstraction, similar to the thought-mode in our architecture.

MAXQ [6] is an architecture for hierarchical reinforcement learning that can utilize layers deeper than two and handles subtask sharing through value function decomposition. In RGoal, decomposition becomes simpler based on the assumption that each subroutine terminates in a single state.

The R-MAXQ architecture [8] introduced the feature of model-based reinforcement learning into MAXQ. It straightforwardly leans and utilizes a model of the environment. In RGoal, the learned $Q(s, g, \tilde{a})$ is used as a model of the environment.

Derivation of a hierarchical policy using an augmented state-action space was proposed in [9]. The space in RGoal is simpler and visually understandable, thereby facilitating easier understanding of recursive subgoal settings.

The option-critic architecture [11] acquires options (subroutines) from agent experiences. In RGoal, the landmark set is given or supposed to be acquired as salient states experienced by the agent.

Because the theoretical framework of RGoal is simple, it is easy to extend. For example, techniques for accelerating learning, such as universal value function approximators [10] or hindsight experience replay [12], should be easily applicable.

5 Conclusion

We proposed a novel hierarchical reinforcement learning architecture that allows unlimited recursive subroutine calls. We integrated several important ideas that were proposed in previous papers into a single simple architecture. A novel mechanism called thought-mode combines learned simple tasks to solve unknown complicated tasks rapidly, sometimes in zero-shot time. Because of its simplicity, we consider RGoal to be a promising first step toward a computational model of the planning mechanism of the human brain. In the future, RGoal will be applicable to robots that purposefully use tools such as ladders. A dialogue system that makes purposeful speech is also one of the applications aimed at.

In the future, we will attempt to speed up learning by introducing state abstraction via function approximation and aim for more realistic application tasks. Detailed comparisons with other approaches are also important future work.

Acknowledgments. We gratefully acknowledge Yu Kohno and Tatsuji Takahashi for their helpful discussion.

This work was supported by JSPS KAKENHI Grant Number JP18K11488.

References

1. Sutton, R.S.: Integrated architectures for learning, planning, and reacting based on approximating dynamic programming. In: Proceedings of the Seventh International Conference on Machine Learning, pp. 216–224 (1990)
2. Singh, S.P.: Reinforcement learning with a hierarchy of abstract models. In: Proceedings of the Tenth National Conference on Artificial Intelligence, San Jose, California, pp. 202–207. AAAI Press (1992)
3. Singh, S.P.: Scaling reinforcement learning algorithms by learning variable temporal resolution models. In: Proceedings of the Ninth International Conference on Machine Learning, Aberdeen, Scotland, pp. 406–415. Morgan Kaufmann (1992)
4. Kaelbling, L.P.: Hierarchical learning in stochastic domains: preliminary results. In: Proceedings of the 10th International Conference on Machine Learning, San Francisco, California, pp. 167–173. Morgan Kaufmann (1993)
5. Sutton, R.S., Precup, D., Singh, S.P.: Between MDPs and semi-MDPs: a framework for temporal abstraction in reinforcement learning. Artif. Intell. **112**(1–2), 181–211 (1999)
6. Thomas, G.D.: Hierarchical reinforcement learning with the MAXQ value function decomposition. J. Artif. Intell. Res. **13**, 227–303 (2000)
7. Wiewiora, E.: Potential-based shaping and Q-value initialization are equivalent. J. Artif. Intell. Res. **19**, 205–208 (2003)
8. Jong, N., Stone, P.: Hierarchical model-based reinforcement learning: R-Max + MAXQ. In: Proceedings of ICML (2008)
9. Levy, K.Y., Shimkin, N.: Unified inter and intra options learning using policy gradient methods. In: Sanner, S., Hutter, M. (eds.) EWRL 2011. LNCS (LNAI), vol. 7188, pp. 153–164. Springer, Heidelberg (2012). https://doi.org/10.1007/978-3-642-29946-9_17
10. Schaul, T., Horgan, D., Gregor, K., Silver, D.: Universal value function approximators. In: Proceedings of the 32nd International Conference on Machine Learning (ICML 2015), pp. 1312–1320 (2015)
11. Bacon, P.-L., Harb, J., Precup, D.: The option-critic architecture. In: Proceedings of AAAI, pp. 1726–1734 (2017)
12. Andrychowicz, M., et al.: Hindsight experience replay. In: Advances in Neural Information Processing Systems, vol. 30, pp. 5055–5065 (2017)

Automatic Augmentation by Hill Climbing

Ricardo Cruz[1,2(✉)], Joaquim F. Pinto Costa[3], and Jaime S. Cardoso[1,2]

[1] INESC TEC, Porto, Portugal
{rpcruz,jaime.cardoso}@inesctec.pt
[2] Faculty of Engineering, University of Porto, Porto, Portugal
[3] Faculty of Sciences, University of Porto, Porto, Portugal
jpcosta@fc.up.pt

Abstract. When learning from images, it is desirable to augment the dataset with plausible transformations of its images. Unfortunately, it is not always intuitive for the user how much shear or translation to apply. For this reason, training multiple models through hyperparameter search is required to find the best augmentation policies. But these methods are computationally expensive. Furthermore, since they generate static policies, they do not take advantage of smoothly introducing more aggressive augmentation transformations. In this work, we propose repeating each epoch twice with a small difference in data augmentation intensity, walking towards the best policy. This process doubles the number of epochs, but avoids having to train multiple models. The method is compared against random and Bayesian search for classification and segmentation tasks. The proposal improved twice over random search and was on par with Bayesian search for 4% of the training epochs.

Keywords: Convolutional neural networks · Data augmentation · Computer vision · Learning to learn

1 Introduction

Data augmentation is the process of syntactically creating plausible new observations that could come from the original source. Data augmentation has become a staple of deep learning, in particular when it comes to computer vision [16]. Transformations such as rotation or shear are applied to create new images from existing images.

All these transformations require some sort of parametrization. The parameter choice is not always straight-forward, especially when it comes to continuous parameters like the aforementioned transformations. Unfortunately, the search methods that exist, as described in the next section, are highly expensive computationally, as they require training many models to try different parameter combinations which are then evaluated using the validation set.

I. V. Tetko et al. (Eds.): ICANN 2019, LNCS 11728, pp. 115–124, 2019.
https://doi.org/10.1007/978-3-030-30484-3_10

In this work, we propose a simple approach: slowly increase the amount of augmentation during training. This has the added benefit of accruing gains from gradually increasing the difficulty of the observations, a process known as curriculum learning [3].

2 State of the Art

There is a large intersection between hyperparameter search and automatic augmentation. An hyperparameter is any parameter that cannot be estimated by the normal estimation process of the model; this includes such disparate things as the learning rate, the size of the neural network or, in our case, how much rotation or shear to apply during data augmentation.

Several search heuristics exist to reduce the hyperparameter search space. These techniques involve training many models to find the best hyperparameter(s) $\theta^* = \arg_\theta \max s(f_\theta(X^{\text{val}}))$ such that a metric function s is maximized when a surrogate model f_θ, trained with θ augmentations, is evaluated using validation data X^{val}. Since hyperparameters are not independent, the problem becomes combinatorial.

Given a budget B of how many surrogate models to train, the problem becomes how best to sample an user-defined range $\theta \in [\underline{\theta}, \overline{\theta}]$. All the existing hyperparameter search methods consist in suggesting different sampling functions $\theta \sim \mathcal{F}_i$ for each model i, $1 \leq i \leq B$.

Grid search consists in dividing this range linearly, $\mathcal{F}_i = \underline{\theta} + \frac{i-1}{B}(\overline{\theta} - \underline{\theta})$. Another common approach is **random search**, which samples of an uniform distribution, $\mathcal{F} = \mathcal{U}(\underline{\theta}, \overline{\theta})$. It has been found to produce better results for a smaller B [4].

Other techniques exist that focus on the most promising parts of the search space. **Bayesian optimization** samples from the posterior distribution to best solve the exploration-exploitation trade-off problem involved. This distribution is generally modeled using a Gaussian Process, and an acquisition function chooses the next point to sample based on an expectation/variance combination (exploitation/exploration) [5]. **Successive halving** trains each model for a few epochs and then chooses the best-half performing models for the next $\mathcal{F}_{i+1}$ sampling [14]. **AutoAugment** uses an RNN as its $\mathcal{F}$ sampling function [9]. **Evolutionary algorithms** have also been used for hyperparameter search [21].

Fewer research exists into dynamically optimizing hyperparameters. Gradient-based algorithms do exist that allow minimizing a validation loss for particular problems, such as L2 regularization [17].

After a vector $\boldsymbol{\theta}$ is found, it is known as a *policy*. Most work find a single θ which specifies a limit on the augmentation; for example, if $\theta = 30$ for rotation, then, for each image, rotation is applied randomly using an Uniform $(-30, 30)$. This is how our experimental section will work. But other work find two hyperparameters for each transformation: the probability of the transformation being applied and its absolute magnitude [9].

3 Proposal

Our proposal consists in starting with no augmentation ($\theta_1 = 0$) and gradually make it more aggressive ($\theta_{t+1} > \theta_t$). The index refers to the iteration (or epoch). Please notice only a single model is being used. At each epoch t, the proposal is to perform the epoch twice, for $\theta_{t-1} - \varepsilon$ and $\theta_{t-1} + \varepsilon$, so that the impact of a small perturbation ε can be inferred using finite differences on the validation set. The procedure consists in the following steps:

1. Model f is trained for one (or more) epoch(s) without augmentation, obtaining weights w_1.
2. The weights are then forked in two, $w_{t+1}^{(1)}$ and $w_{t+1}^{(2)}$, which are obtained by minimizing the loss $\mathcal{L}$ for one epoch using the training set $X^{\text{tr}}(\boldsymbol{\theta}_t)$, augmented by vector $\boldsymbol{\theta}_t$, and labels y^{tr},
$$w_{t+1}^{(1)} = \arg\min_w \mathcal{L}(X^{\text{tr}}(\boldsymbol{\theta}_t - \boldsymbol{\Delta}), y^{\text{tr}} \mid w_t)$$
$$w_{t+1}^{(2)} = \arg\min_w \mathcal{L}(X^{\text{tr}}(\boldsymbol{\theta}_t + \boldsymbol{\Delta}), y^{\text{tr}} \mid w_t).$$
$\boldsymbol{\Delta}$ is a vector which is zero for all values except for a single one j, for which $\Delta_j = \varepsilon$. This j is chosen randomly in this work. This hyperparameter j is the one that is being tested.
3. The models are then evaluated and compared
$$\delta = s(f(X^{\text{val}} \mid w_{t+1}^{(2)}), y^{\text{val}}) - s(f(X^{\text{val}} \mid w_{t+1}^{(1)}), y^{\text{val}}),$$
so that
$$\boldsymbol{\theta}_{t+1} = \boldsymbol{\theta}_t - \boldsymbol{\Delta} \text{ and } w_{t+1} = w_{t+1}^{(1)} \quad \text{if } \delta < 0,$$
$$\boldsymbol{\theta}_{t+1} = \boldsymbol{\theta}_t + \boldsymbol{\Delta} \text{ and } w_{t+1} = w_{t+1}^{(2)} \quad \text{if } \delta > 0.$$
Possible ties ($\delta = 0$) are solved by using the validation loss.
4. Go back to (2).

An illustration of the process is provided in Fig. 1. The hyperparameter θ controls the range with how aggressive augmentation is applied, it controls the probability

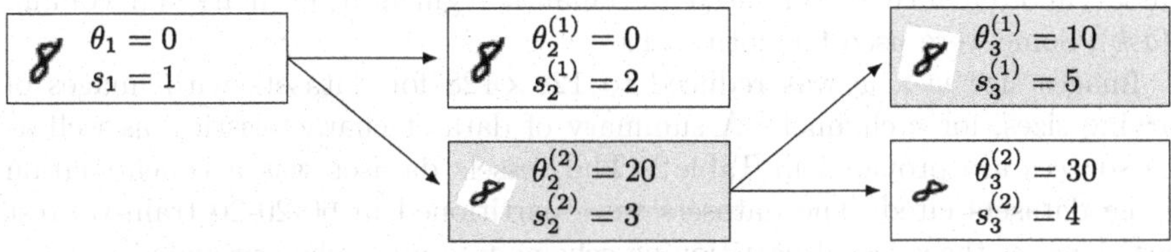

Fig. 1. Hyperparameter evolution where θ controls the rotation and s is the validation score.

distribution of how aggressive the augmentation will be. For example, a rotation of $\theta = 30$ means that the rotation of each image will be chosen randomly using an Uniform $(-30, 30)$.

The possible range of values for each hyperparameter θ is defined differently per transformations. For example, for rotation, the valid range is $[0, 180]$. See Table 1.

Table 1. The six transformations used in this work

Hyperparameter	Units	$\underline{\theta}$	$\overline{\theta}$	Example
none	–	–	–	
Rotation	degrees	0	180	
Translation x/y	pixels	0	width	
Shear	degrees	0	60	
Zoom out	factor	1/3	–	
Zoom in	factor	–	3	
Channel shift	value	0	50	
Brightness	value	0.5	2	

4 Experiments

Tranformations. The augmentation techniques that have been used are the six transformations provided by the Keras Pre-processing toolkit[1] – rotation, x/y translation, shear, zoom in/out, channel shift (add a constant to each layer), and brightness (multiply each layer by a constant). There are six transformations and seven hyperparameters since zoom is the same transformation with two hyperparameters defining the range. The ranges and an example from the MNIST dataset are illustrated in Table 1.

Datasets. A collection of 16 datasets was used (Table 2), most of which were from medical applications. Ten of these datasets were used for classification (with K classes) and ten of these were used for semantic segmentation (marked in column *Mask*). Some were used for both tasks.

Images size $w \times w$ was reduced to 128×128 for datasets with images of varying sizes, for c channels. A summary of dataset characteristics, as well as the sources are provided in Table 2. The vessels dataset was a concatenation of the datasets cited. The datasets were partitioned in 60-20-20 train-val-test partitions, or the original partitioning scheme was used when provided.

[1] https://github.com/keras-team/keras-preprocessing.

Table 2. Summary of the datasets used

Dataset	w	c	N	K?	*Mask?*	Source
breast-aesthetic	128	3	120	—	✓	[6]
cervix-huc	128	3	261	—	✓	[11]
cervix-kaggle	128	3	1503	—	✓	[1]
CIFAR-10	32	3	60 k	10	—	[15]
CIFAR-100	32	3	60 k	100	—	[15]
Fashion-MNIST	28	1	70 k	10	—	[26]
ISIC 2017	128	3	2750	3	✓	[8]
iris	128	3	2164	—	✓	[23]
MNIST	28	1	70 k	10	—	[18]
PH2	128	3	200	3	✓	[19]
smartskins	128	3	292	3	✓	[25]
STL10	96	3	13 k	10	—	[7]
SVHN	32	3	≈99 k	10	—	[20]
teeth	128	3	98	—	✓	[12]
vessels	128	3	88	—	✓	[2, 13, 24]
VOC 2012	128	3	≈12 k	20	✓	[10]

Tasks. Two different types of datasets were experimented with: classification and semantic segmentation, whenever the dataset allowed. In both cases, cross-entropy was used, and, to solve any class imbalance in the dataset, the loss was weighted by the inverse frequency of each class. The metrics used were balanced accuracy (classification), and the Jaccard index (segmentation).

Segmentation is an interesting problem given that the image and the binary mask must synchronously suffer from the same augmentation. Evidently, no brightness or channel shift is applied to the mask.

Architecture. The neural network used was made of convolution-maxpooling blocks, initially with a image of size $w \times w$ and halving the activation map at each layer until the activation was approximately 6×6, so that each block was applied $\lceil \log_2 \frac{w}{6} \rceil$ times, with the classification problem ending in K classes: $w \times w \times c \rightarrow w/2 \times w/2 \times 32 \rightarrow \cdots \rightarrow\approx 6 \times 6 \times 32 \rightarrow\approx 1152 \rightarrow 32 \rightarrow K$. The activation function used was ReLU, except for softmax for the last layer. For semantic segmentation, an U-Net architecture was used [22], which is composed of an encoding and a decoding phase. The encoding phase used is the same as the gray colored part, and the decoding phase is also the same in reverse, with up-sampling being used instead of max-pooling to double the activation map. Skip-layers are used to connect the first convolutional layer with the last, the second with the penultimate, and so forth, like in U-Net.

Table 3. Evaluation scores in percentage using the testing set (higher is better)

Classification (balanced accuracy)					
Dataset	None	Random	Bayesian	Proposal	Proposal*
CIFAR-10	64.1	70.0	73.6	**78.2**	*73.7*
CIFAR-100	27.4	27.3	*30.4*	**38.5**	18.5
Fashion-MNIST	91.4	83.7	*92.0*	*92.0*	**92.1**
ISIC 2017	48.7	46.7	**53.7**	*49.8*	43.0
MNIST	99.1	99.0	**99.5**	*99.4*	99.2
PH2	46.7	*62.8*	**64.7**	48.6	52.1
smartskins	32.7	34.3	35.9	**37.9**	*37.1*
STL10	57.2	*62.4*	58.5	**64.8**	56.8
SVHN	79.4	10.0	81.8	**87.1**	*85.6*
VOC 2012	12.7	28.9	**34.9**	*33.5*	30.8
# Top 1	**0**	**0**	**4**	**5**	**1**
# Top 2	*0*	*2*	*6*	*9*	*4*
Avg Rel Gain	0.0	8.5	26.6	27.2	14.6

bold: best method; *italic:* second-best.

Methods. We tested our **proposal** together with no augmentation (**none**) trained for 250 epochs, each epoch augmenting a total of 1,024 images in batches of 128 images. These methods were compared against state-of-the-art augmentation using **random** and **Bayesian** search. In these cases, 50 surrogate children were trained for 25 epochs each (the cost was therefore of 1,250 epochs), with the final child trained for 250 epochs. Bayesian search was performed using Expected Improvement as the acquisition function [5], modeled using a Gaussian Process with an RBF kernel, using as seed the first 10 of the 50 surrogate models trained.

Furthermore, a method called **proposal*** was added to the table, which is a static version of the **proposal**. This method takes the last policy found by the proposal method and applies that, and only that policy, to a model trained from scratch. The purpose of this exercise is to test if the gain from the proposed method came from the incremental nature of the method.

Reproducibility. The code was implemented in Keras and is available at http://github.com/rpmcruz/averse-segmentation.

5 Results

Tables 3 and 4 consider 10 datasets for each classification and segmentation tasks, respectively. Our proposal is compared against random and Bayesian search. Firstly, it is interesting to note that gains from data augmentation were much greater for classification than from segmentation. For each dataset, if we contrast the best performing method against apply no augmentation, then the average relative gains are of 32% and 3% for classification and segmentation, respectively. In fact, doing nothing (none) was three times in top-2 for segmentation.

Table 4. Evaluation scores in percentage using the testing set (higher is better)

Semantic segmentation (Jaccard index)					
Dataset	None	Random	Bayesian	Proposal	Proposal*
breast-aesthetic	95.6	90.6	*96.8*	95.9	**96.9**
cervix-huc	82.4	*84.5*	84.2	83.7	**84.9**
cervix-kaggle	92.6	91.1	*93.2*	**93.4**	*93.2*
iris	*99.1*	98.4	98.2	**99.2**	98.9
ISIC 2017	90.7	*91.5*	**91.7**	**91.7**	91.1
PH2	87.5	**91.3**	89.9	*90.7*	89.7
smartskins	**97.9**	94.6	96.7	96.2	*97.1*
teeth	*94.0*	91.5	91.0	**94.1**	93.0
vessels	67.7	75.4	**77.8**	*76.8*	73.6
VOC 2012	74.0	75.1	**78.7**	*77.8*	76.2
# Top 1	**1**	**1**	**3**	**4**	**2**
# Top 2	*3*	*3*	*5*	*7*	*4*
Avg Rel Gain	0.0	0.7	2.4	2.5	1.8

bold: best method; *italic:* second-best.

The proposal performed better in the vast majority of cases (top-2 was 90% and 70% of cases). The poor performance is explained by the vast search space from having 7 transformations, and the fact there is a bias towards conservative augmentation (centered in zero) performing better.

Furthermore, proposal* can be contrasted with the proposal column to understand whether the dynamic nature of the method contributed to its performance, as suggested by the curriculum learning literature [3]. In most cases, the results are not significantly different. However, this static version was 60% worse than the dynamic version.

In terms of training time, while the proposal would be expected to double the training time relative to the baseline, it actually increased training time by around 5.1 times, on average for all datasets, due to the way context switching of the training was implemented. The weights were saved and loaded from the disk each time a context switch was necessary, which could be improved. In any case, random search models were about 8.6 times worse than the baseline on average.

The hyperparameters evolved more or less stably as can be seen in the rotation examples from Fig. 2. It makes sense that rotation is not particularly useful when it comes to digit recognition. On the other hand, skin lesions do benefit from rotation.

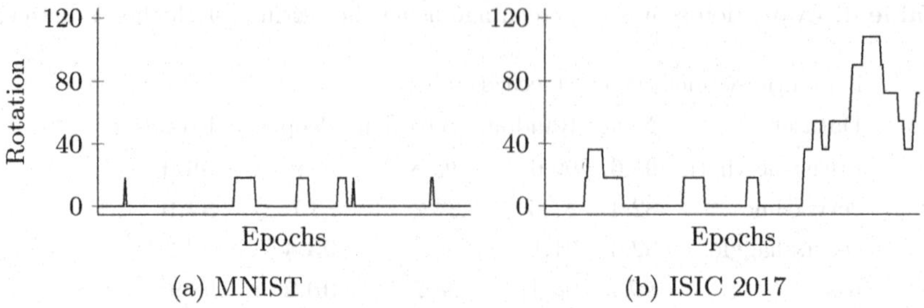

Fig. 2. Evolution of the *rotation* hyperparameter

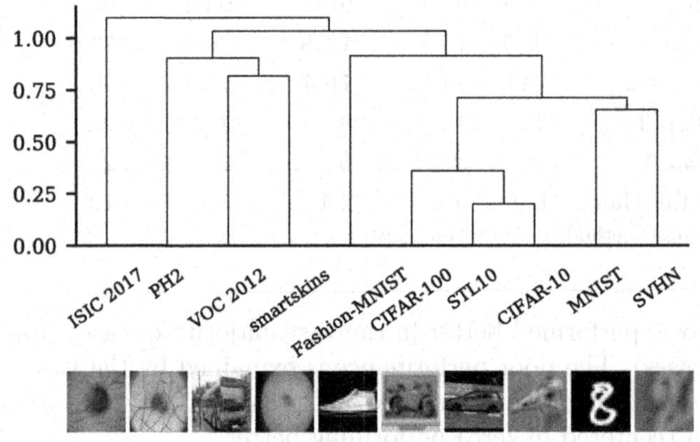

Fig. 3. Hierarchical clustering of the final augmentation policies

Considering the hyperparameters $\boldsymbol{\theta}$ at the final epoch, $t = 250$, found by the proposed method, a dendrogram was built to find which classification datasets performed similarly, using Euclidean distance (Fig. 3). Interestingly, all melanoma-related datasets (in the left of the dendrogram) had similar augmentations, and could easily form a cluster. Fashion-MNIST and VOC 2012 relate miscellaneous classes and are distanced similarly, as does MNIST and SVHN which relate numbers.

6 Conclusion

A problem has been identified: the magnitude to apply data augmentation is not always obvious. Finding the best parametrization using traditional search methods is intensive. The solution: a simple yet novel approach is to gradually allow for more aggressive augmentation, using the validation set as an oracle.

Each epoch is run twice with a slight difference in one of the augmentation parameters, and the best parameter is chosen for the next epoch. This method was contrasted against random and Bayesian search. It performed slightly better than Bayesian search in both classification and segmentation tasks for one-fifth the epochs, and twice the performance of random search.

As future work, a number of details could be improved. The index j, which was here chosen randomly, could be chosen using a multi-armed bandit heuristic. The timing of when to make augmentation more aggressive could be based on the loss plateauing, rather than the end of each epoch.

Acknowledgments. This work is financed by National Funds through the Portuguese funding agency, FCT – Fundação para a Ciência e a Tecnologia within project: UID/EEA/50014/2019, and the PhD grant "SFRH/BD/122248/2016" from FCT supported by POCH and the EU.

References

1. Intel & MobileODT cervical cancer screening, Kaggle competition (2017). https://www.kaggle.com/c/intel-mobileodt-cervical-cancer-screening. Accessed 1 Dec 2018
2. Retinal CHASE DB1 database (2017). https://blogs.kingston.ac.uk/retinal/chasedb1/. Accessed 1 Dec 2018
3. Bengio, Y., Louradour, J., Collobert, R., Weston, J.: Curriculum learning. In: Proceedings of the 26th Annual International Conference on Machine Learning, pp. 41–48. ACM (2009). https://doi.org/10.1145/1553374.1553380
4. Bergstra, J., Bengio, Y.: Random search for hyper-parameter optimization. J. Mach. Learn. Res. **13**, 281–305 (2012)
5. Bergstra, J.S., Bardenet, R., Bengio, Y., Kégl, B.: Algorithms for hyper-parameter optimization. In: Advances in Neural Information Processing Systems, pp. 2546–2554 (2011)
6. Cardoso, J.S., Cardoso, M.J.: Towards an intelligent medical system for the aesthetic evaluation of breast cancer conservative treatment. Artif. Intell. Med. **40**(2), 115–126 (2007). https://doi.org/10.1016/j.artmed.2007.02.007
7. Coates, A., Ng, A., Lee, H.: An analysis of single-layer networks in unsupervised feature learning. In: Proceedings of the Fourteenth International Conference on Artificial Intelligence and Statistics, pp. 215–223 (2011)
8. Codella, N.C., Gutman, D., Celebi, M.E., Helba, B., et al.: Skin lesion analysis toward melanoma detection: a challenge at the 2017 International Symposium on Biomedical Imaging (ISBI), hosted by the International Skin Imaging Collaboration (ISIC). In: 2018 IEEE 15th International Symposium on Biomedical Imaging (ISBI), pp. 168–172. IEEE (2018). https://doi.org/10.1109/ISBI.2018.8363547
9. Cubuk, E.D., Zoph, B., Mane, D., Vasudevan, V., Le, Q.V.: AutoAugment: learning augmentation policies from data (2018). arXiv preprint: arXiv:1805.09501
10. Everingham, M., Eslami, S.A., Van Gool, L., Williams, C.K., Winn, J., Zisserman, A.: The PASCAL visual object classes challenge: a retrospective. Int. J. Comput. Vis. **111**(1), 98–136 (2015). https://doi.org/10.1007/s11263-014-0733-5
11. Fernandes, K., Cardoso, J.S., Fernandes, J.: Transfer learning with partial observability applied to cervical cancer screening. In: Alexandre, L.A., Salvador Sánchez, J., Rodrigues, J.M.F. (eds.) IbPRIA 2017. LNCS, vol. 10255, pp. 243–250. Springer, Cham (2017). https://doi.org/10.1007/978-3-319-58838-4_27

12. Fernandez, K., Chang, C.: Teeth/Palate and interdental segmentation using artificial neural networks. In: Mana, N., Schwenker, F., Trentin, E. (eds.) ANNPR 2012. LNCS (LNAI), vol. 7477, pp. 175–185. Springer, Heidelberg (2012). https://doi.org/10.1007/978-3-642-33212-8_16
13. Hoover, A., Kouznetsova, V., Goldbaum, M.: Locating blood vessels in retinal images by piecewise threshold probing of a matched filter response. IEEE Trans. Med. Imaging **19**(3), 203–210 (2000)
14. Jamieson, K., Talwalkar, A.: Non-stochastic best arm identification and hyperparameter optimization. In: Artificial Intelligence and Statistics, pp. 240–248 (2016)
15. Krizhevsky, A., Hinton, G.: Learning multiple layers of features from tiny images. Technical report, Citeseer (2009)
16. Krizhevsky, A., Sutskever, I., Hinton, G.E.: ImageNet classification with deep convolutional neural networks. In: Advances in Neural Information Processing Systems, pp. 1097–1105 (2012)
17. Larsen, J., Hansen, L.K., Svarer, C., Ohlsson, M.: Design and regularization of neural networks: the optimal use of a validation set. In: Proceedings of the 1996 IEEE Signal Processing Society Workshop on Neural Networks for Signal Processing VI, pp. 62–71. IEEE (1996)
18. LeCun, Y., Cortes, C., Burges, C.: MNIST handwritten digit database. AT&T Labs [Online]. http://yann.lecun.com/exdb/mnist 2 (2010). https://doi.org/10.1109/MSP.2012.2211477
19. Mendonça, T., Ferreira, P.M., Marques, J.S., Marcal, A.R., Rozeira, J.: PH^2-a dermoscopic image database for research and benchmarking. In: 2013 35th Annual International Conference of the IEEE Engineering in Medicine and Biology Society (EMBC), pp. 5437–5440. IEEE (2013). https://doi.org/10.1109/EMBC.2013.6610779
20. Netzer, Y., Wang, T., Coates, A., Bissacco, A., Wu, B., Ng, A.Y.: Reading digits in natural images with unsupervised feature learning. In: NIPS Workshop on Deep Learning and Unsupervised Feature Learning, vol. 2011, p. 5 (2011)
21. Olson, R.S., Urbanowicz, R.J., Andrews, P.C., Lavender, N.A., Kidd, L.C., Moore, J.H.: Automating biomedical data science through tree-based pipeline optimization. In: Squillero, G., Burelli, P. (eds.) EvoApplications 2016, Part I. LNCS, vol. 9597, pp. 123–137. Springer, Cham (2016). https://doi.org/10.1007/978-3-319-31204-0_9
22. Ronneberger, O., Fischer, P., Brox, T.: U-Net: convolutional networks for biomedical image segmentation. In: Navab, N., Hornegger, J., Wells, W.M., Frangi, A.F. (eds.) MICCAI 2015, Part III. LNCS, vol. 9351, pp. 234–241. Springer, Cham (2015). https://doi.org/10.1007/978-3-319-24574-4_28
23. Sequeira, A.F., Monteiro, J.C., Rebelo, A., Oliveira, H.P.: MobBIO: a multimodal database captured with a portable handheld device. In: 2014 International Conference on Computer Vision Theory and Applications (VISAPP), vol. 3, pp. 133–139. IEEE (2014). https://doi.org/10.5220/0004679601330139
24. Staal, J., Abràmoff, M.D., Niemeijer, M., Viergever, M.A., Van Ginneken, B.: Ridge-based vessel segmentation in color images of the retina. IEEE Trans. Med. Imaging **23**(4), 501–509 (2004). https://doi.org/10.1109/TMI.2004.825627
25. Vasconcelos, M.J.M., Rosado, L., Ferreira, M.: Principal axes-based asymmetry assessment methodology for skin lesion image analysis. In: Bebis, G., et al. (eds.) ISVC 2014, Part II. LNCS, vol. 8888, pp. 21–31. Springer, Cham (2014). https://doi.org/10.1007/978-3-319-14364-4_3
26. Xiao, H., Rasul, K., Vollgraf, R.: Fashion-MNIST: a novel image dataset for benchmarking machine learning algorithms (2017). arXiv preprint: arXiv:1708.07747

Learning Camera-Invariant Representation for Person Re-identification

Shizheng Qin[1], Kangzheng Gu[1], Lecheng Wang[1], Lizhe Qi[2(✉)], and Wenqiang Zhang[1,2(✉)]

[1] Shanghai Key Laboratory of Intelligent Information Processing, School of Computer Science, Fudan University, Shanghai, People's Republic of China
{szqin17,kzgu17,wanglc17}@fudan.edu.cn

[2] Academy for Engineering and Technology, Fudan University, Shanghai, People's Republic of China
{qilizhe,wqzhang}@fudan.edu.cn

Abstract. Person re-identification (re-ID) problem aims to retrieve a person from an image gallery captured across multiple cameras. However, images of the same identity have variations due to the change in camera views. So learning a camera-invariant representation is one objective of re-identification. In this paper, we propose a camera-style transfer model for generating images, and a fake triplet loss for training the person feature embedding model. We train a StarGAN, a kind of generative adversarial networks, as our transfer model, which can transfer the style of an image from one camera to multiple different camera-styles by a generator network. So the image set is expanded with style-transferred images. However, style transferring yields image distortion, which misleads the training of feature embedding model. To overcome the influence of image distortion, we consider the gap between fake and real images, then we propose a fake triplet loss to capture the camera-invariant information of fake images. We do a series of experiments on the Market-1501, DukeMTMC-reID, and CUHK03 datasets, and show the effectiveness of our methods.

Keywords: Re-identification · Generative adversarial networks · StarGAN · Triplet loss

1 Introduction

Person re-identification (re-ID) is a task of retrieving cross-camera images of a specified pedestrian in a gallery. In the past few years, person re-ID attracts great attention due to its applications in many fields, such as video surveillance and group behavior analysis. However, person image often undergoes dramatic variations in pose, illumination, and background. The labels of poses and backgrounds are difficult to be obtained, while camera-ID is catched during collecting

I. V. Tetko et al. (Eds.): ICANN 2019, LNCS 11728, pp. 125–137, 2019.
https://doi.org/10.1007/978-3-030-30484-3_11

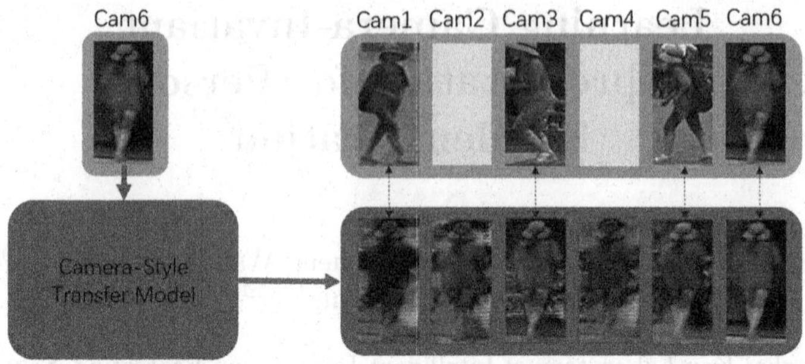

Fig. 1. The generation process of camera-style transferred images.

pedestrian images for re-ID tasks. As a result, we aim to extract camera-invariant features for re-ID problems.

Some previous works have attempted to catch camera-invariant features for re-ID problems. Triplet loss is one method of extracting camera-invariant features, which maps cross-camera images with the same identity to close features. However, an identity always keeps a single pose in a specific camera view, so human poses are entangled with camera views, which influence the performance of triplet loss. In addition, an image transfer model called CycleGAN (Cycle-constrained Generative Adversarial Network) is used to transfer camera-styles of images [20,21]. But they only use cross-entropy loss to train the feature embedding model and do not pay attention to the relevance of transferred images and original images. Moreover, the training of multiple CycleGANs in [20,21] is time-consuming.

In this paper, we propose a method that uses the idea of transferring camera-styles. We employ a unified generative adversarial network called StarGAN [1] as our camera-style transfer model, which transfer a person image to different images with other camera-styles. The transferred fake image retains the identity information and human pose of the original image. Instead of training multiple CycleGANs, we use a single StarGAN model to transfer person images.

The camera-style transfer model makes up a deficiency of re-ID datasets. For one pedestrian, he/she will appear in multiple camera views under various conditions, such as background and illumination, and this person has different poses in these scenes. While in real life, the person may appear in these scenes with the same pose, and most collected training dataset lacks these images. Some generated fake images are displayed in Fig. 1. As shown in Fig. 1, the fake images keep person poses, and the background and illumination are transformed into other styles. In addition, the person may not appear in some camera views, and our model can generate these images with corresponding camera-styles.

However, fake images generated by StarGAN suffer from noise and distortion, so there is a gap between generated fake images and collected real images. If simply ignoring the image gap and training feature embedding model, the performance of our embedding model will decline. To alleviate the influence of

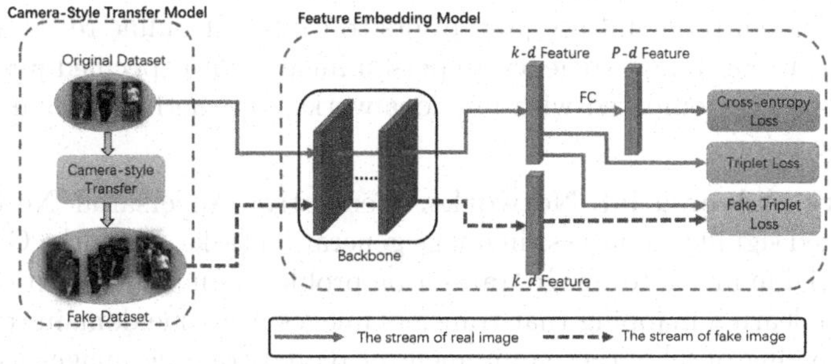

Fig. 2. The pipeline of our proposed method. Our method contains a camera-style transfer model and a feature embedding model. P is the number of identities in the training dataset.

image distortion, we apply a fake triplet loss to train a camera-invariant embedding model. The fake triplet loss is calculated with the features of fake and real images, so fake triplet loss studies the relevance between original images and transferred images. The entire architecture of our model is shown in Fig. 2.

Our proposed cross-camera re-ID method has the following advantages. First, we use a simple camera-style transfer model to generate fake images, and our model takes less training time and achieve a solid transfer performance. Second, we propose a fake triplet loss for training feature embedding models, and the fake triplet loss represents the gap between fake and real images. In a nutshell, our work has the following contributions:

- A StarGAN based cross-camera style transfer model for person re-identification. This model simplifies the process of generating camera-style transferred samples.
- A fake triplet loss on both real and fake images. This loss helps feature embedding models to learn camera-invariant feature and relieves the effect of distortion on camera-style transferred images.
- We evaluate our approach on three benchmark datasets. By comparison with some methods, the performance of our approach is competitive on the three datasets.

2 Related Work

Camera-Invariant Representation for Person Re-identification. The success of deep learning classification motivates the booming of deep re-ID models. In [17], Zheng et al. raise a single stream re-ID model called IDE (ID-feature Embedding) which is trained as an image classification model. The IDE model can be fine-tuned from ImageNet [6] pre-trained models. In [12], Schroff et al. propose triplet loss and show the outstanding performance of using triplet loss in feature embedding models. Moreover, Some researchers intend to extract camera-invariant embeddings with deep networks. In [15], Wu et al. build a model for predicting human pose and use pose priors to carry out online re-ID matching. In [9], Qian et al. attempt to generate person images with specified poses by the network of GAN. Compared with previous works, our method does not require human pose priors.

Generative Adversarial Networks. Generative Adversarial Networks [2] have obtained significant success in image generation tasks. Recently, GANs have also been used in image-to-image translation problems. In [5], a conditional GAN is applied to learn a mapping that transfers images from one domain to another. The shortcoming of [5] is the requirement of paired training images as supervision. CycleGAN [22] overcomes this problem by employing cycle-consistency loss on the framework of [5], which is trained by unpaired images from two domains. However, a CycleGAN model only transfers images between two fixed domains. More recently, Choi et al. [1] propose a framework called StarGAN that can transfer an image from one domain to multiple other domains, and we employ this model as our camera-style transfer model. In [19], Zhong et al. employ StarGAN and do unsupervised domain adaptation between two datasets, while we aim to extract camera-invariant feature in one dataset.

3 Proposed Method

The explanation of our method is structured as follows. First, we exhibit our utilization and modification of StarGAN in Sect. 3.1. Second, we introduce our fake triplet loss in Sect. 3.2, which intends to exploit camera-style transferred fake images in the training stage. Finally, we present the training details of our work in Sect. 3.3.

3.1 StarGAN in Camera-Style Translation

In this paper, we employ StarGAN as our camera-style transfer model, which transfer real images to different camera-styles. We consider camera views as person image domains and consider camera-ID labels as domain-ID labels. Then we train a StarGAN to transfer one person image from the camera domain C_i to other camera domains $\{C_{j \neq i}\}$.

The objective of StarGAN [1] is to train a single generator G that learns mappings among multiple domains. Given C domains $\{X^1, X^2, ..., X^C\}$, where $X^c = \{x_i^c\}_{i=1}^{\mathcal{N}_c}$ and c is the domain label, we train G to transfer an input image x^{C_j} in domain C_j to an output image y in domain C_k. The formal representation of an optimal generator G^* is $G^*(x^{C_j}, C_k) = y$, where the distribution of y is close to the real dataset X^{C_k}.

Moreover, a discriminator D is proposed to train the generator in an adversarial form. The output of D is two probability distributions $D : x \rightarrow \{D_r(x), D_d(x)\}$, where D_r denotes the reality level of images and D_d denotes the domain classification probabilities. To train the network, the adversarial loss L_{adv} is applied which can make the generated images indistinguishable from real images. Besides, a domain classification loss is decomposed into two terms L_{cls}^r

and L^f_{cls} to optimize the model with real images and fake images separately. L_{adv}, L^r_{cls} and L^f_{cls} are expressed as follows:

$$L_{adv} = E_x[\log D_r(x)] + E_{x,c}[\log(1 - D_r(G(x,c)))] \tag{1}$$

$$L^r_{cls} = E_{x,c}[-\log D_{cls}(c|x)] \tag{2}$$

$$L^f_{cls} = E_{x,c}[-\log D_{cls}(c|G(x,c))] \tag{3}$$

where c is the target domain of generator G.

To guarantee that transferred images contain the identity of original images, a reconstruction loss L_{rec} is applied to reconstruct the original image x from the transferred image $G(x,c)$. Generally, person images are the ROIs detected from large images by algorithms like DPM [3], so the person always located in the center of images. As a result, we add a mask to the reconstruction loss. The modified reconstruction loss loosens the limitation of cycle-consistency constraint [22], so the model is encouraged to ignore the variations over background parts. The modified reconstruction loss is expressed as:

$$L_{rec} = E_{x,c,c'}[||(x - G(G(x,c),c')) \odot M||_1] \tag{4}$$

where c' is the source domain of x, c is the target domain of x, $\odot$ denotes element-wise multiplication, and M is a mask.

The overall loss functions of StarGAN are expressed as:

$$L_D = -L_{adv} + \lambda_{cls} L^r_{cls} \tag{5}$$

$$L_G = L_{adv} + \lambda_{cls} L^f_{cls} + \lambda_{rec} L_{rec} \tag{6}$$

where L_D and L_G correspond to the loss functions of discriminator D and generator G; λ_{cls} and λ_{rec} are hyper-parameters that leverage the weights of domain classification loss and reconstruction loss.

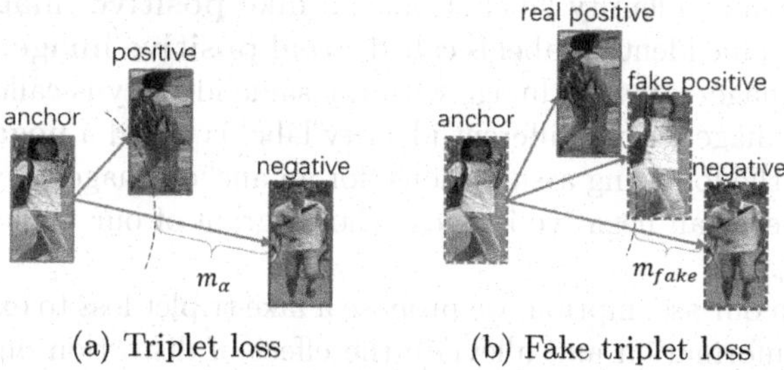

Fig. 3. The diagram of triplet loss and fake triplet loss. m_α and m_{fake} are the margins between anchor-positive distance and anchor-negative distance.

3.2 Fake Triplet Loss

The goal of a re-ID task is to learn a function f_θ which maps person images $x \in X$ to a feature space F. A metric function $D(x_i, x_j)$ measures the distance between features $f_\theta(x_i)$ and $f_\theta(x_j)$, and feature embedding models aim at enlarging $D(x_i, x_j)$ when the x_i and x_j belong to different identities and shortening $D(x_i, x_j)$ when the x_i and x_j belong to the same identity. In FaceNet [12], triplet loss is proposed to ensure that an anchor image x_a of one person is closer to positive images x_p of the same identity than other negative images x_n of other different identities. The formulated expression is written as:

$$D(x_a, x_p) + m_\alpha < D(x_a, x_n), (x_a, x_p, x_n) \in \mathcal{T} \tag{7}$$

where m_α denotes a given margin between the anchor-positive distance and the anchor-negative distance and $\mathcal{T}$ means the set of all triplets. Generally, $D(x_i, x_j) = ||x_i - x_j||_2$.

The number of triplets is so numerous that using all the triplets in the training phase is intractable. A sampling method samples P person identities from the dataset, then randomly samples K images for each identity. Therefore, a mini-batch with $P \times K$ person images is formed. Based on this sampling method, the triplet loss is formulated as:

$$L_{tri} = \sum_{i=1}^{P} \sum_{a=1}^{K} [m_\alpha - \min_{\substack{j=1..P \\ n=1..K \\ j \neq i}} D(x_a^i, x_n^j) + \max_{p=1..K} D(x_a^i, x_p^i)]_+ \tag{8}$$

where $[\cdot]_+$ denotes $max(0, \cdot)$ function. The schematic diagram of triplet loss is shown in Fig. 3(a).

Owing to the distortion of fake images, choosing fake images as anchor images will degrade the performance of feature embedding models, hence we do not directly apply triplet loss to fake images. For the convenience of description, we define some annotations for specific person images. Given an anchor image, a fake image with the same identity label is called a **fake positive image**, and a real image with the same identity label is called a **real positive image**. Analogously, for an anchor image, a person image with the same identity is called a **positive image** and an image with a different identity label is called a **negative image**. Then we make the following assumptions: for an anchor image, the fake positive images are closer than negative images. The diagram of our triplet assumption is shown in Fig. 3(b).

To constrain our assumption, we propose a fake triplet loss to exploit the fake person image information and alleviate the effect of distortion on fake images. The fake triplet loss is expressed as:

$$L_{fake} = \sum_{i=1}^{P} \sum_{a=1}^{K} [m_{fake} - \min_{\substack{j=1..P \\ n=1..K \\ j \neq i}} D(x_a^i, x_n^j) + \max_{p=1..K} D(x_a^{r,i}, x_p^{f,i})]_+ \tag{9}$$

where the superscripts of x^r or x^f denotes x belongs to the original dataset or the fake dataset. This loss will shorten the metric distance between an original image and corresponding camera-style transferred images, hence the feature embedding model can learn a camera-invariant embedding mapping between person images and features. To utilize our loss during the training phase, we first sample P identities, then sample K real images and K fake images for each identity.

3.3 Training Details

We train a StarGAN model to transfer person images. We follow the network structure and training strategy in [1]. Keeping the setting in [1], person images are resized to 128×128. The mask M, located on the center of images, is 64 by 128 pixels. For every image in the original training dataset, the generator produces C new training samples related to all C cameras. We refer to the generated images as camera-style transferred images or fake images. Since each fake image is transferred from a real image and contains the same identity information, we can try to tag fake images with the corresponding original image labels. During training the feature embedding model, we use the combination of original images and fake images to train our feature embedding model.

We use the ResNet-50 network [4] as the backbone of our feature embedding model. When trained with real images, our model is optimized by an additional label-smoothing cross-entropy loss, which is written as:

$$L_{cls} = -\frac{1}{N}\sum_{i=1}^{N} \log p(x_i)q'(x_i), q'(x_i) = (1-\epsilon)q(x_i) + \frac{\epsilon}{K} \tag{10}$$

where $\epsilon \in [0, 1]$ is a hyper-parameter, $p(x_i)$ is the predicted classification probability distribution of image x_i, $q(x_i)$ is the one-hot identity label of x_i and K is the number of identities.

The full objective of our feature embedding model is expressed as:

$$L = L_{tri} + L_{fake} + L_{cls} \tag{11}$$

We use two types of models as our feature embedding models in our training phase. The first type is the IDE model [17]. We follow the training strategy of IDE-model for fine-tuning the ImageNet pre-trained model. We pool the output of backbone to a $2048-d$ vector as the representation of a person image. The second type is the mid-level feature embedding model. This model fuses the features of final-layer and mid-layer in ResNet50, and outputs a $3072-d$ feature vector. We resize person images to 128×256 and add a fully-connected layer to map feature vectors into P dimensions for classification, where P is the number of identities in the training dataset.

4 Experiments

4.1 Datasets

We evaluate our method on Market-1501 [16], DukeMTMC-reID [10] and CUHK03 [7] datasets.

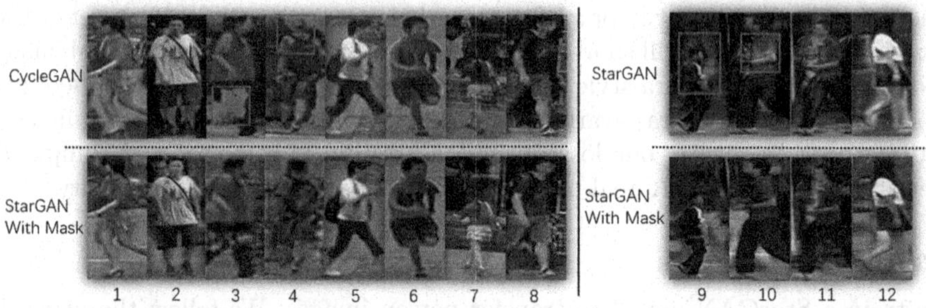

Fig. 4. The comparison of CycleGAN and StarGAN, and the comparison of original StarGAN and StarGAN with mask.

The Market-1501 dataset contains 32,668 bounding boxes of 1,501 identities captured from 6 different viewpoints. All bounding boxes are detected by DPM [3]. 12,936 images from 751 identities are used for training and 19,732 images from 750 identities are used for testing. In testing, 3,368 hand-drawn bounding boxes from 750 identities are used as queries.

DukeMTMC-reID is a newly published person re-ID dataset. It contains 36,411 labeled images of 1,404 identities collected from 8 cameras. The dataset is split into two parts: one part includes 16,522 training images from 702 identities, the other part includes 2,228 query images from other 702 identities and 17,661 gallery images.

The CUHK03 dataset contains 14,097 images of 1,467 identities. Identities are observed from 10 cameras. CUHK03 applies two ways to produce the cropped images: one is human annotation and the other is DPM detection. Our evaluation is based on the DPM detected images. We use the new training/testing protocol in [18] to select 767 identities for training and the rest 700 for testing.

We transfer one image to C new images for each dataset, where C is the number of cameras in the dataset.

4.2 The Comparison of CycleGAN and StarGAN

We compare the generative performance of CycleGAN and StarGAN in the camera-style transfer process. We follow the model architecture and training strategy in [20,21]. For CycleGAN, to achieve style transferring for the total of 6 cameras in Market1501 dataset, each pair of cameras need a CycleGAN model. So we train $\binom{6}{2} = 15$ CycleGAN model to generate transferred images. For StarGAN, we need only one model to learn all the transformations among 6 cameras. The size of the generated images is 128×128. We display the generated images in Fig. 4. As exhibited in Fig. 4, images generated by StarGAN have less noise and distortion. Our transfer model works better on drawing body contours (Shown in Fig. 4-{1,2,3,4}), and our model produces less noise and distortion (Shown in Fig. 4-{5,6,7,8}). Besides, the training of our model spends less time.

Table 1. The comparison of using different m_{fake}

m_{fake} value	Rank-1	mAP
0.10	88.09	73.24
0.05	87.86	73.39
0.00	**89.10**	**74.44**
−0.05	88.51	74.20
−0.10	87.38	72.05

Table 2. The comparison of triplet loss and fake triplet loss

L_{tri} dataset	L_{fake} dataset	Rank-1	mAP
real	–	88.36	74.19
real+fake	–	85.96	68.94
real	real+fake	**89.10**	**74.44**

Training our transfer model on one TITAN Xp takes 12 h, while training 15 CycleGAN takes about $9 \times 15 = 135$ h.

Furthermore, we compare the generated images of original StarGAN and the modified StarGAN. We modify the reconstruction loss with adding a mask. The images are shown in Fig. 4. While most generated images are similar, some images contains difference. The origin loss forces transferred images to match the background, while the person part is distorted, which weaken the quality of images.

4.3 The Influence of Fake Triplet Loss

To leverage between the distortion of fake images and the camera-invariant information of fake images, we select a list of values assigned to m_{fake} and train the IDE model with two triplet loss functions. The results of applying fake triplet loss on the IDE model is shown in Table 1.

When training the embedding model with fake triplet loss, if the similarity between the anchor image and the negative image is bigger than the similarity between the anchor and the fake positive plus m_{fake}, the fake triplet loss will try to enlarge the distance between anchor and the negative image. Although "fake" images contain the "real" identities information, they still have gaps compared to real ones. So, it is necessary for model to tolerant such gaps in a certain degree. Therefore, we need such m_{fake} to do some trade-off. Due to the results in Table 1, we can see that choosing 0.00 as the value of m_{fake} will achieve a better performance. This result signifies that the generated fake positive images are closer to an anchor image than negative images, even fake images involve some image distortion.

Furthermore, the performance of choosing fake images as anchor images in triplet loss is tested. As shown in Table 2, directly applying triplet loss on fake images will degrade the performance of feature embedding models. These results indicate that using fake triplet loss will indeed relieve the effect of distortion in fake images.

4.4 Ablation Study of Loss Functions

We conduct some experiments on the Market-1501 dataset to indicate the availability of our proposed approach. As shown in Table 3, the baseline approach with L_{cls} and L_{tri} can achieve 89.49% on Rank-1 accuracy. After adding our fake triplet loss, the performance of the IDE model on Rank-1 accuracy can reach 90.70%. And our approach with the mid-level model can achieve 92.73% on Rank-1 accuracy, which is a competitive result on Market-1501.

Table 3. The results of ablation study

Model	L_{cls}	L_{tri}	L_{fake}	Rank-1	mAP
IDE	√			86.73	69.87
IDE		√		88.36	74.19
IDE	√	√		89.49	74.95
IDE		√	√	89.10	74.44
IDE	√	√	√	**90.70**	**76.48**
mid-level	√	√		90.53	76.79
mid-level	√	√	√	**92.73**	**79.41**

Table 4. Augment dataset with incremental schema

Dataset	Rank-1	mAP
Real	89.49	74.95
Real+Fake1,2,3	90.35	74.84
Real+Fake4,5,6	90.08	75.27
Real+Fake1,2,3+Fake4,5,6	90.71	76.75
Real+Fake1,2,3,4,5,6	90.70	76.48

4.5 Flexibility for the Number of Cameras

In general, a single StarGAN could only learn a fixed number of styles, which means that in Re-ID problems the number of cameras must be fixed, and results in some inflexibility of algorithms. However, our algorithm could adapt to the changing of camera numbers by introducing an incremental schema.

Suppose we only have 3 cameras (Cam 1, 2 and 3) in the beginning. So we train a StarGAN to transfer images between 3 cameras. When we get new data from extra cameras (Cam 4, 5, 6), we just train another StarGAN to adapt newly added cameras.

Our experiments (Table 4) show that separately training different models to augment the dataset incrementally can achieve the same performance (90.71%) as train a single model containing all transformations among all 6 cameras (90.70%). That means our method is flexible enough to deal with a variable number of cameras. And no matter we augment the dataset incrementally or uniformly, the more camera we have, the better performance we get. (90.35% for only use camera 1, 2, 3, and 90.08% for only use camera 4, 5, 6, versus 90.7% for use all 6 cameras).

4.6 Results

We compare our method with some re-ID methods on Market-1501, DukeMTMC-reID, and CUHK03 datasets in Table 5. First, we train the IDE model with our approach on all datasets and obtain competitive results compared with state-of-the-art methods. Specifically, our approach achieves 90.70% for Market-1501, 80.83% for DukeMTMC-reID and 61.21% for CUHK03 in Rank-1 accuracy.

Moreover, we train the mid-level model with our proposed method. We achieve Rank-1 accuracy 92.73% for Market-1501, Rank-1 accuracy 82.36% for DukeMTMC-reID and Rank-1 accuracy 62.00% for CUHK03.

Table 5. The overall results on three datasets

Method	Market-1501		DukeMTMC-reID		CUHK03	
	Rank-1	mAP	Rank-1	mAP	Rank-1	mAP
BOW+kissme [16]	44.4	20.8	25.1	12.2	6.4	6.4
SVDNet [14]	82.3	62.1	76.7	56.8	41.5	37.3
CamStyle [20,21]	88.12	68.72	75.27	53.48	–	–
CamStyle+RE [20,21]	89.49	71.55	78.32	57.61	–	–
PoseTransfer [8]	87.65	68.92	78.52	56.91	41.6	38.7
ContrAttn [13]	83.79	74.33	–	–	46.71	46.87
PSE [11]	88.6	72.6	79.2	60.6	–	–
PoseNormalize [9]	89.43	72.58	73.58	53.20	–	–
IDE	89.49	74.95	79.94	63.30	60.14	55.08
IDE + Ours	**90.70**	**76.48**	**80.83**	**63.66**	**61.21**	**55.55**
mid-level	90.53	76.79	80.57	64.02	60.93	55.34
mid-level + Ours	**92.73**	**79.41**	**82.36**	**65.69**	**62.00**	**56.65**

5 Conclusion

In this paper, we exploit the domain transfer capability of StarGAN to generate camera-style transferred images. Then we propose fake triplet loss, an effective loss function for learning discriminative representation, to train our feature embedding models. This loss can alleviate the distortion of fake images and exploit the camera-invariant identity information hidden in fake images. Experiments on Market-1501, DukeMTMC-reID and CUHK03 datasets show that our method can improve the performance of feature embedding models.

References

1. Choi, Y., Choi, M., Kim, M., Ha, J.W., Kim, S., Choo, J.: StarGAN: unified generative adversarial networks for multi-domain image-to-image translation. In: Proceedings of the IEEE Conference on Computer Vision and Pattern Recognition, pp. 8789–8797 (2018). https://doi.org/10.1109/CVPR.2018.00916
2. Creswell, A., White, T., Dumoulin, V., Arulkumaran, K., Sengupta, B., Bharath, A.A.: Generative adversarial networks: an overview. IEEE Signal Process. Mag. **35**(1), 53–65 (2017). https://doi.org/10.1109/MSP.2017.2765202
3. Felzenszwalb, P., McAllester, D., Ramanan, D.: A discriminatively trained, multiscale, deformable part model (2008). https://doi.org/10.1109/CVPR.2008.4587597
4. He, K., Zhang, X., Ren, S., Sun, J.: Deep residual learning for image recognition. In: Proceedings of the IEEE Conference on Computer Vision and Pattern Recognition, pp. 770–778 (2016). https://doi.org/10.1109/CVPR.2016.90
5. Isola, P., Zhu, J.Y., Zhou, T., Efros, A.A.: Image-to-image translation with conditional adversarial networks. In: Proceedings of the IEEE Conference on Computer Vision and Pattern Recognition, pp. 1125–1134 (2017). https://doi.org/10.1109/CVPR.2017.632
6. Krizhevsky, A., Sutskever, I., Hinton, G.E.: ImageNet classification with deep convolutional neural networks. In: Advances in Neural Information Processing Systems, pp. 1097–1105 (2012). https://doi.org/10.1145/3065386
7. Li, W., Zhao, R., Xiao, T., Wang, X.: DeepReID: deep filter pairing neural network for person re-identification. In: Proceedings of the IEEE Conference on Computer Vision and Pattern Recognition, pp. 152–159 (2014). https://doi.org/10.1109/CVPR.2014.27
8. Liu, J., Ni, B., Yan, Y., Zhou, P., Cheng, S., Hu, J.: Pose transferrable person re-identification. In: Proceedings of the IEEE Conference on Computer Vision and Pattern Recognition, pp. 4099–4108 (2018). https://doi.org/10.1109/CVPR.2018.00431
9. Qian, X., et al.: Pose-normalized image generation for person re-identification. In: Ferrari, V., Hebert, M., Sminchisescu, C., Weiss, Y. (eds.) ECCV 2018. LNCS, vol. 11213, pp. 661–678. Springer, Cham (2018). https://doi.org/10.1007/978-3-030-01240-3_40
10. Ristani, E., Solera, F., Zou, R., Cucchiara, R., Tomasi, C.: Performance measures and a data set for multi-target, multi-camera tracking. In: Hua, G., Jégou, H. (eds.) ECCV 2016. LNCS, vol. 9914, pp. 17–35. Springer, Cham (2016). https://doi.org/10.1007/978-3-319-48881-3_2
11. Saquib Sarfraz, M., Schumann, A., Eberle, A., Stiefelhagen, R.: A pose-sensitive embedding for person re-identification with expanded cross neighborhood re-ranking. In: Proceedings of the IEEE Conference on Computer Vision and Pattern Recognition, pp. 420–429 (2018). https://doi.org/10.1109/CVPR.2018.00051
12. Schroff, F., Kalenichenko, D., Philbin, J.: FaceNet: a unified embedding for face recognition and clustering. In: Proceedings of the IEEE Conference on Computer Vision and Pattern Recognition, pp. 815–823 (2015). https://doi.org/10.1109/CVPR.2015.7298682

13. Song, C., Huang, Y., Ouyang, W., Wang, L.: Mask-guided contrastive attention model for person re-identification. In: Proceedings of the IEEE Conference on Computer Vision and Pattern Recognition, pp. 1179–1188 (2018). https://doi.org/10.1109/CVPR.2018.00129
14. Sun, Y., Zheng, L., Deng, W., Wang, S.: SVDNet for pedestrian retrieval. In: Proceedings of the IEEE International Conference on Computer Vision, pp. 3800–3808 (2017). https://doi.org/10.1109/ICCV.2017.410
15. Wu, Z., Li, Y., Radke, R.J.: Viewpoint invariant human re-identification in camera networks using pose priors and subject-discriminative features. IEEE Trans. Pattern Anal. Mach. Intell. **37**(5), 1095–1108 (2015). https://doi.org/10.1109/TPAMI.2014.2360373
16. Zheng, L., Shen, L., Tian, L., Wang, S., Wang, J., Tian, Q.: Scalable person re-identification: a benchmark. In: Proceedings of the IEEE International Conference on Computer Vision, pp. 1116–1124 (2015). https://doi.org/10.1109/ICCV.2015.133
17. Zheng, L., Zhang, H., Sun, S., Chandraker, M., Yang, Y., Tian, Q.: Person re-identification in the wild (2017). https://doi.org/10.1109/CVPR.2017.357
18. Zhong, Z., Zheng, L., Cao, D., Li, S.: Re-ranking person re-identification with k-reciprocal encoding. In: Proceedings of the IEEE Conference on Computer Vision and Pattern Recognition, pp. 1318–1327 (2017). https://doi.org/10.1109/CVPR.2017.389
19. Zhong, Z., Zheng, L., Li, S., Yang, Y.: Generalizing a person retrieval model hetero- and homogeneously. In: Ferrari, V., Hebert, M., Sminchisescu, C., Weiss, Y. (eds.) ECCV 2018. LNCS, vol. 11217, pp. 176–192. Springer, Cham (2018). https://doi.org/10.1007/978-3-030-01261-8_11
20. Zhong, Z., Zheng, L., Zheng, Z., Li, S., Yang, Y.: Camera style adaptation for person re-identification. In: Proceedings of the IEEE Conference on Computer Vision and Pattern Recognition, pp. 5157–5166 (2018). https://doi.org/10.1109/CVPR.2018.00541
21. Zhong, Z., Zheng, L., Zheng, Z., Li, S., Yang, Y.: CamStyle: a novel data augmentation method for person re-identification. IEEE Trans. Image Process. **28**(3), 1176–1190 (2019). https://doi.org/10.1109/TIP.2018.2874313
22. Zhu, J.Y., Park, T., Isola, P., Efros, A.A.: Unpaired image-to-image translation using cycle-consistent adversarial networks. In: Proceedings of the IEEE International Conference on Computer Vision, pp. 2223–2232 (2017). https://doi.org/10.1109/ICCV.2017.244

PA-RetinaNet: Path Augmented RetinaNet for Dense Object Detection

Guanghua Tan(✉), Zijun Guo, and Yi Xiao

Hunan University, Changsha 410000, China
guanghuatan@gmail.com, guozj_727@hnu.edu.cn, yixiao1984@gmail.com

Abstract. Object detection methods can be divided into two categories that are the two-stage methods with higher accuracy but lower speed and the one-stage methods with lower accuracy but higher speed. In order to inherit the advantages of both approaches, a novel dense object detector, called Path Augmented RetinaNet (PA-RetinaNet), is proposed in this paper. It not only achieves a better accuracy than the two-stage methods, but also maintains the efficiency of the one-stage methods. Specifically, we introduce a bottom-up path augmentation module to enhance the feature exaction hierarchy, which shortens the information path between lower feature layers and topmost layers. Furthermore, we address the class imbalance problem by introducing a Class-Imbalance loss, where the loss of each training sample is weighted by a function of its predicted probability, so that the trained model focuses more on hard examples. To evaluate the effectiveness of our PA-RetinaNet, we conducted a number of experiments on the MS COCO dataset. The results show that our method is 4.3% higher than the existing two-stage method, while the speed is similar to the state-of-the-art one-stage methods.

Keywords: Object detection · Convolutional neural network · Class imbalance

1 Introduction

In recent years, object detection has achieved significant progress, with the use of deep neural networks (DNN). The most advanced DNN detectors currently are divided into two categories: two-stage approaches and one-stage approaches. The two-stage approaches, such as Faster R-CNN [1], R-FCN [2] and FPN [3], typically generates a set of sparse object candidate boxes in the first phase, and then further classifies and regresses the candidate boxes in the second phase. The two-stage approaches have achieved the top performances on the challenging COCO benchmark [4]. The one-stage approaches, *e.g.*, YOLO [5,6], SSD [7,8],

Supported by the National Key R&D Program of China (2018YFB0203904), National Natural Science Foundation of China (61602165) and Natural Science Foundation of Hunan Province (2018JJ3074), NSFC from PRC (61872137, 61502158), Hunan NSF (2017JJ3042).

I. V. Tetko et al. (Eds.): ICANN 2019, LNCS 11728, pp. 138–149, 2019.
https://doi.org/10.1007/978-3-030-30484-3_12

to uniformly sample the object locations on a picture according to scales and aspect ratios. The efficiency of the one-stage method calculation makes it highly concerned. However, their detection accuracy is always lower than the two-stage methods. One of the main reasons is due to class imbalance [9].

The two-stage methods address class imbalance through cascading and heuristic sampling. The first proposal stage (such as Selective Search [10], RPN [1]) filters out the background samples and controls the number of candidate object locations to a small extent (*e.g.*, 2k). In the second classification stage, heuristic sampling, such as fixed foreground-background ratio (1:3) or online hard example mining (OHEM) [11], is used to maintain the balance between foreground and background.

Instead, the one-stage methods must process a larger set of candidate locations that are periodically sampled on an image. In practice, a large number of locations are often enumerated to densely cover spatial locations, scales, and aspect ratios. Therefore, this is extremely caused to the class imbalance problem. To solve it, some methods have been proposed. In order to reduce the false detections caused by class imbalance, Zhang *et al.* [12] designed a maximum output labeling mechanism. Kong *et al.* [13] use the objectness prior constraint on convolutional feature maps to significantly reduce the search space of objects. Lin *et al.* [9] solve the class imbalance problem by reconstructing the standard cross entropy loss, focus the training on a sparse set of hard examples and down-weights the loss assigned to well-classified examples.

In this paper, we have improved the RetinaNet [9] by adding a path augmentation module to shorten the information propagation path while using low-level features for precise positioning. Also, we propose a new loss function based on cross entropy loss. With the predicted probability of a certain class in the training process, this loss function changes dynamically. The scaling factor we introduced only related to prediction probability, can automatically down-weight of easy examples, making the model more focal on hard examples. Extensive experiments show that our proposed method can train a high-accuracy, quickly one-stage detector that outperforms the sampling heuristics or hard example mining, the previous state-of-the-art one-stage detector. Our method achieves 42.5% AP on MS coco test-dev with ResNet-101 [14].

The main contributions of this work are summarized as follows. (1) We improve the RetinaNet framework for object detection by adding a bottom-up path augmentation module. This shortens the information propagation path, using low-level features for accurate location. (2) To address the class imbalance problem, we design a new loss, named Class-Imbalance loss (CIL). During the training, the loss function changes dynamically, and the scaling factor only related to predicted probability can automatically down-weight of the easy examples, making the model pay more attention to the hard examples. (3) The method we proposed, named PA-RetinaNet, achieves the state-of-the-art results on MS COCO [4].

2 Related Work

Classical Object Detectors. Early object detection methods use the sliding-window paradigm that apply hand-crafted features and classifiers on dense image grids to find objects. Viola and Jones [15] use Haar and AdaBoost algorithms to cascade and weight a series of weak classifiers into a strong classifier for face detection, achieving satisfactory accuracy with high efficiency. DPM [16] is a very successful object detection algorithm, and won the PASCAL VOC (2007, 08, 09) consecutive detection champion and it was once an important part of many classifiers, segmentation, human poses, and behavioral classifications. However, with the re-emergence of deep learning, the CNN-based detector has quickly become the dominant object detection field, which can be roughly divided into two categories, *i.e.*, the two-stage approaches and one-stage approaches.

Two-Stage Approaches. More recent approaches like R-CNN [17] use region proposal methods (*e.g.*, Selective Search [10], EdgeBoxes [18], RPN [1]) to first generate potential bounding boxes in an image and then run a classifier on these proposed boxes. Its worth to noting that the two-stage approaches (*e.g.*, R-CNN [19], SPPnet [20], Fast RCNN [17] to Faster R-CNN [1]) in several challenging datasets (*e.g.*, MS COCO [4]) has achieved remarkable performance. After that, many effective techniques are proposed to further improve the performance, such as architecture diagram [2], training strategy [11,21], contextual reasoning [8,22] and multiple layers exploiting [13,23–25].

One-Stage Approaches. The complex pipelines of the two-stage methods are slow and hard to optimize because each individual component must be trained separately. Therefore, one-stage methods have attracted much attention because of its efficiency. OverFeat [26] is one of the first proposed one-stage object detectors based on deep networks for classification, localization and detection. In recent years, Redmon *et al.* [5] propose You Only Look Once (YOLO), which can use a single feedforward convolutional network to directly predict object classes and locations. After that, YOLOv2 [6] is put forward to further enhance the previous version. Liu *et al.* [8] spreads out anchors of different scales to multiple layers to focus on predicting objects of a certain scale, this method was called SSD. DSDD [7] uses deconvolution to introduce additional context into SSD for the promotion of the accuracy. Lin *et al.* [9] propose focal loss to deal with the class imbalanceand design RetinaNet to improve the detection accuracy. Although the one-stage methods have made good progress, its accuracy still lags behind the two-stage methods.

The design of our PA-RetinaNet detector inherits and improves the structure of RetinaNet. Adding a bottom-up path, which shortens the information propagation path and makes low-layer information easier to propagate, yields a satisfying effect.

Class Imbalance. As [9], most one-stage object detection methods are troubled by the large class imbalance problem in the training process. An image only has a few locations containing objects, but these detectors need evaluate $10^4 - 10^5$ candidate locations. So the class imbalance problem may cause the inefficient training even overwhelm training and degenerate models. Hard negative mining [8,11,15] is usually used to solve this problem, however, less effective. On the contrary, we introduce a Class-Imbalance loss to deal with the problem a one-stage detector must face.

3 Network Architecture

Our overall network architecture is illustrated in Fig. 1. Our PA-RetinaNet consists of a backbone network, a path augmentation module and two parallel subnetworks with specific tasks. The backbone adopts the Feature Pyramid Network (FPN) [3], an existing convolutional network, to calculate a feature map of an entire input image. A path augmentation module is augmented to make low-layer information easier to propagate. The two sub-networks are used for object classification and bounding box regression, respectively.

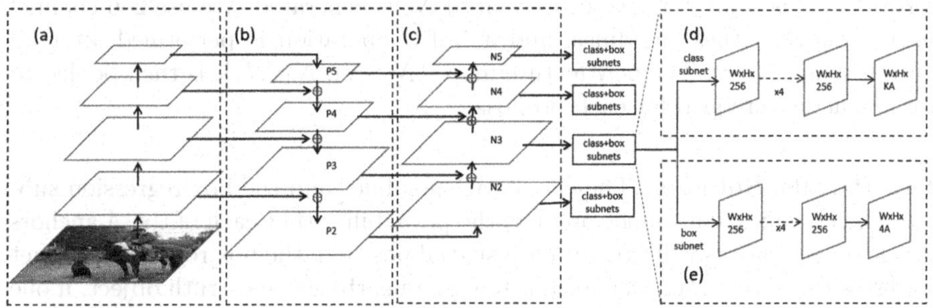

Fig. 1. PA-RetinaNet architecture. (a) ResNet. (b) Feature Pyramid Network(FPN). (c)Bottom-up path augmentation. (d) Class subnet. (e) Box subnet. $\oplus$ stands for lateral connection.

Backbone Network. We adopt Feature Pyramid Network (FPN) [3] as the backbone network of our PA-RetinaNet. FPN augments a standard convolutional network with a top-down pathway and lateral connections, allowing the network to efficiently construct a rich, multi-scale feature pyramid from a single resolution input image, as show in Fig. 1(a)–(b). Each level of the pyramid can be used to detect objects at a different scale.

Path Augmentation. The low-level feature map mainly perceiving the image's edge, corner and other details and local information, while the high-level feature map mainly reflecting the semantical information of the whole objects. Inspired by [27], a bottom-up path is augmented to make low-layer information easier to propagate. Therefore, adding a bottom-up path is necessary to propagate semantically strong features and enhance the reasonable classification capability of all features in FPN [3].

According to the definition in FPN [3], layers of the same network stage can generate feature maps of the same spatial size, each feature level corresponds to one stage. We use ResNet [14] as our basic structure and represent feature levels of FPN as $\{P_2; P_3; P_4; P_5\}$. The path augmentation module from the lowest P_2 to P_5. Their space size is gradually down-sampled to 1/4 of the previous layer size as shown in Fig. 1(c). We use $\{N_2; N_3; N_4; N_5\}$ to represent newly generated feature maps corresponding to $\{P_2; P_3; P_4; P_5\}$. Note that N_2 is P_2.

As shown in Fig. 1, $\oplus$ represents the lateral connection of the lower-layer coarse feature map P_{i+1} and the higher-layer fine feature map N_i, generating a new feature map N_{i+1}. Each feature map N_i is first down-sampled by a 3×3 convolutional layer with stride 2, which gives the same resolution as P_{i+1} and is added to it by a lateral connection. Then, the fused feature map generates N_{i+1} through another 3×3 convolutional layer as input to the next two sub-networks. This is an iterative process until N_5 is generated. We use 256-channel feature maps in these modules, and a ReLU operation is performed after all convolutional layers. The new feature map, $\{N_2; N_3; N_4; N_5\}$, is then pooled to obtain the feature grid for each proposal.

Two Parallel Subnets. The classification subnet and the box regression subnet. The classification subnet predicts the probability that each of the A anchors and K object classes will exist at each spatial position, the box regression subnet regresses the offset from each anchor box to a nearby ground-truth object, if one exists. The two subnets are both a small FCN [28]. They are attached to each FPN level; parameters of the same subnet are shared across all pyramid levels, but not shared in different subnet. In the classification subnet, the input feature map of 256 channels is obtained from the given layer. The subnet first applies four 3×3 conv layers, each conv layer has 256 filters, and each one is followed by ReLU activations, then a 3×3 conv layer with KA filters, and finally the sigmoid activations outputs KA binary predictions for per spatial location, see Fig. 1(d). The design of the box regression subnet is identical to the classification subnet except that it terminates in $4A$ linear outputs per spatial location, shown in Fig. 1(e).

Loss Function. Lin *et al.* [9] propose the focal loss, which introduces a modulating factor with tunable focusing parameter $\gamma \geq 0$, takes a lot of experimentation to get the best value, to some extent, it is empirical.

In this paper, we propose a new loss function that is only related to the predicted probability, similar as [9], and still perform the binary classification based on the cross entropy (CE) loss function:

$$CE(p, y) = \begin{cases} -log(p) & if\ y = 1 \\ -log(1-p) & otherwise. \end{cases} \tag{1}$$

Here, $p \in [0,\ 1]$ is the predicted probability for the class with label $y = 1$.

We introduce a scaling factor $\beta = \begin{cases} 1 - p^{\frac{1}{p}-1} & if\ y = 1 \\ 1 - (1-p)^{\frac{1}{1-p}-1} & otherwise. \end{cases}$ that is only related to the predicted probability of a certain class in the training process, define the loss as:

$$CIL(p, y) = -\beta \times CE(p, y) = \begin{cases} (1 - p^{\frac{1}{p}-1})log(p) & if\ y = 1 \\ (1 - (1-p)^{\frac{1}{1-p}-1})log(1-p) & otherwise. \end{cases} \tag{2}$$

As shown in Fig. 2, compare with the focal loss[1], when $p \rightarrow 0$, our loss is significantly greater than the focal loss, which makes our model pay more concerned with hard, misclassified examples than Lin *et al.* [9]; On the contrary, when $p \rightarrow 1$, the two are almost the same.

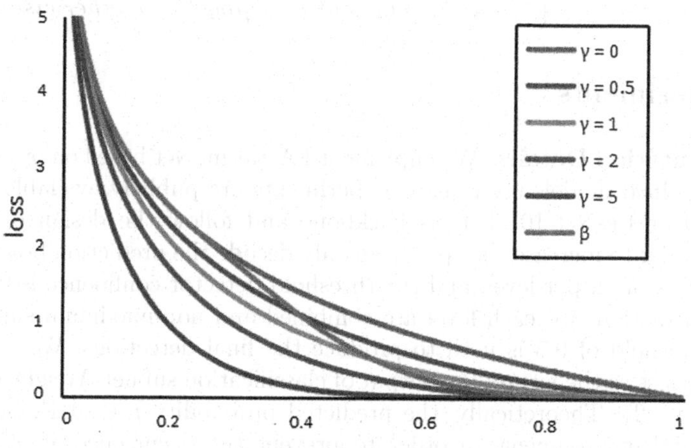

Fig. 2. Comparison of difference loss. We introduce a novel loss, named Class-Imbalance loss, is described by the green curve (β). Other curves visualize the focus loss functions corresponding to different focusing parameters $\gamma = \{0, 0.5, 1, 2, 5\}$.

The scaling factor β can reduce the loss weight of the easy examples and also extend the loss weight range of the examples. Compared with the standard

[1] Lin *et al.* [9] found $\gamma = 2$ to work best through a large number of experiments. The function in this paper is mainly compared with the focal loss at $\gamma = 2$.

cross entropy loss function, when the example classification probability $p \approx 0.9$, the loss weight of the example is reduced by about 100 times; when the example classification probability $p \approx 0.969$, the loss weight of the example is reduced by about 1000 times; when the example classification probability $p = 0.9$, the loss of the example is reduced by 2 times; when the example classification probability $p = 0.1$, the loss weight coefficient of the example is 0.999. When $p \approx 0.9$ and $p \approx 0.969$, the Class-Imbalance loss function and the focus loss function have little difference for the loss weight adjustment, but when $p \leq 0.5$, the loss weight of the Class-Imbalance loss function for misclassified example is obviously higher than the focus loss function, which plays a great positive effect in correcting misclassified examples.

A common way to solve the class imbalance problem is to introduce a weighting factor $\alpha \in [0, 1]$. The precision is slightly improved compared to $CIL(p, y)$ without adding a weighting factor. Therefore, we also introduce a weighting factor α for $y = 1$ and $1-\alpha$ for otherwise in our experiments. The final expression of our Class-Imbalance loss is:

$$\begin{aligned} CIL(p, y) &= -\alpha\beta \times CE(p, y) \\ &= \begin{cases} \alpha(1 - p^{\frac{1}{p}-1})log(p) & if\ y = 1 \\ (1-\alpha)(1-(1-p)^{\frac{1}{1-p}-1})log(1-p) & otherwise. \end{cases} \end{aligned} \tag{3}$$

4 Experiments

Implementation Details. We implement PA-RetinaNet based on pytorch [30]. The pre-trained models used in the experiments are publicly available. We use ResNet-50 or ResNet-101 [14] as backbone and follow the design of anchors in [9]. In order to increase the speed, we only decode the prediction box with the highest score of 1k per level, and the threshold detector confidence is 0.05. The highest predictions for each level are combined and non-maximum suppression with a threshold of 0.5 is used to produce the final detections. We use Class-Imbalance loss as the loss on the output of classification subnet. Weighting factor α is set to 0.25. Theoretically, the predicted probability $p \in [0, 1]$, but in the experimental environment, in order to prevent the occurrence of infinity, we clamp the predicted probability $p \in [1e-4, 1.0-1e-4]$.

Dataset and Metrics. COCO [4] dataset is one of the most challenging datasets in object detection because of its data complexity.There are 118 k images in the training set, 5 k images in the verification machine, test-dev set and test-challenge set each contain 20 k images. The label of the test subset is not public. This data set contains 80 classes. We trained our model on the train2017 subset, conducted the ablation experiment on the val2017 subset, and conducted the comparison experiment on the test-dev. We follow the standard evaluation metrics, *i.e.*, AP, AP_{50}, AP_{75}, AP_S, AP_M and AP_L.

Ablation Studies. First, we analyze what role the bottom-up path augmentation plays in training. Then we analyze the importance of our Class-Imbalance loss function. Our ablation study are performed on the val-2017 subset, based on the RetinaNet framework [9], followed by focal loss function (FL) or Class-Imbalance loss function (CIL), and a bottom-up path enhancement module (BUPA). The study is shown in Table 1. We initialize RetinaNet with resnet-50 [14].

(1) Bottom-up Path Augmentation (BUPA). Bottom-up path augmentation module facilitates easier propagation of low-layer. With or without Class-Imbalance loss function,bottom-up path augmentation module can achieve better performance. The improvement to large-scale instances is the most significant. This verifies that the information from lower feature levels is also useful.

(2) Class-Imbalance Loss (CIL). With or without bottom-up path augmentation, class-imbalance loss consistently improves detection AP by more than 1.7 and 4.9 respectively. This improvement means that our class-imbalance loss can focus more on the hard examples, which proves the effectiveness of our loss function.

Table 1. Ablation experiments for PA-RetinaNet and Class-Imbalance Loss (CIL). All models are trained and tested on coco 2017. All ablation experiments use default values: anchors for 3 scales and 3 aspect ratios, ResNet-50 backbone, and a 600 pixel train and test image scale. Based on RetinaNet [9], we gradually add or replace focal loss (FL), bottom-up path augmentation(BUPA), Class-Imbalance loss (CIL)for ablation studies

RetinaNet	FL	BUPA	CIL	AP	AP_{50}	AP_{75}	AP_S	AP_M	AP_L
√	√			34.3	53.2	36.9	16.2	37.4	47.4
√	√	√		35.7	57.3	38.0	18.6	39.4	51.7
√			√	36.0	55.2	38.7	17.4	39.6	49.7
√		√	√	39.2	59.4	41.1	20.8	43.9	54.1
				+4.9	+6.2	+4.2	+4.6	+6.5	+6.7

Table 2. Speed comparison of PA-RetinaNet and RetinaNet on MS COCO test-dev set.

Methods	Backbone	Scale	Time
RetinaNet [9]	ResNet-50	600	92
RetinaNet [9]	ResNet-101	600	118
PA-RetinaNet(ours)	ResNet-50	600	96
PA-RetinaNet(ours)	ResNet-101	600	123

Fig. 3. Visualization results of PA-RetinaNet on COCO validation set.

Comparison to State of the Art. We compare PA-RetinaNet with the state-of-the-art detectors in Tables 2 and 3. Compared to existing one-stage methods, our results are top ranked, while the speed is similar to them. Compared to recent two-stage methods, PA-RetinaNet achieves a 4.3 point gap above Mask R-CNN [29] based on ResNet-101.

Visualization. In Fig. 3, we present some detection examples on coco dataset with our PA-RetinaNet model. Only detection bounding boxes with scores greater than 0.6 are displayed.

Table 3. Detection results on MS COCO test-dev set. Bold fonts indicate the best performance.

Methods	Backbone	AP	AP_{50}	AP_{75}	AP_S	AP_M	AP_L
Two-stage:							
Faster R-CNN [1]	VGG-16	21.7	35.9	-	-	-	-
R-FCN [2]	ResNet-101	29.9	51.9	-	10.9	32.8	45.0
Mask R-CNN [29]	ResNet-101	38.2	60.3	41.7	20.1	41.1	50.2
One-stage:							
YOLOv2 [6]	DarkNet-19	21.6	44.0	19.2	5.0	22.4	35.5
SSD300* [8]	VGG-16	25.1	43.1	25.8	6.6	25.9	41.4
SSD321 [7]	ResNet-101	28.0	45.4	29.3	6.2	28.3	49.3
DSSD321 [7]	ResNet-101	28.0	46.1	29.2	7.4	28.1	47.6
SSD512* [8]	VGG-16	28.8	48.5	30.3	10.9	31.8	43.5
SSD513 [7]	ResNet-101	31.2	50.4	33.3	10.2	34.5	49.8
DSSD513 [7]	ResNet-101	33.2	53.3	35.2	13.0	35.4	51.1
RetinaNet [9]	ResNet-101	39.1	59.1	42.3	21.8	42.7	50.2
PA-RetinaNet(ours)	ResNet-50	40.1	61.9	44.0	22.9	42.8	50.9
PA-RetinaNet(ours)	ResNet-101	**42.5**	**63.6**	**46.3**	**26.6**	**45.5**	**53.6**

5 Conclusion

In this paper, we propose PA-RetinaNet, an upgrade to the RetinaNet architecture, to make low-layer information easier to propagate and a new Class-Imbalance loss to address the class imbalance problem. These changes are evaluated on MS COCO [4], and achieve state-of-the-art results. In the future, we plan to employ PA-RetinaNet to detect some other specific kinds of objects, *e.g.*, vehicle, pedestrian, and face, and introduce a rough-fine (Supercategory - category) classification mechanism in our PA-RetinaNet to further improve the performance.

Acknowledgments. This project is an improvement on yhenon's work, thanks for the code provided by yhenon (https://github.com/yhenon/pytorch-retinanet).

References

1. Ren, S., He, K., Girshick, R., et al.: Faster R-CNN: towards real-time object detection with region proposal networks (2015). https://doi.org/10.1109/TPAMI.2016.2577031
2. Dai, J., Li, Y., He, K., et al.: R-FCN: Object Detection Via Region-based Fully Convolutional Networks (2016)
3. Lin, T., Dollár, P., Girshick, R., et al.: Feature pyramid networks for object detection (2016). https://doi.org/10.1109/CVPR.2017.106

4. Lin, T.-Y., et al.: Microsoft COCO: common objects in context. In: Fleet, D., Pajdla, T., Schiele, B., Tuytelaars, T. (eds.) ECCV 2014. LNCS, vol. 8693, pp. 740–755. Springer, Cham (2014). https://doi.org/10.1007/978-3-319-10602-1_48
5. Redmon, J., Divvala, S., Girshick, R., et al.: You only look once: unified, real-time object detection (2015). https://doi.org/10.1109/CVPR.2016.91
6. Redmon, J., Farhadi, A.: YOLO9000: better, faster, stronger. In: 2017 IEEE Conference on Computer Vision and Pattern Recognition (CVPR), pp. 6517–6525 (2017)
7. Fu, C.Y., Liu, W., Ranga, A., et al.: DSSD: Deconvolutional Single Shot Detector (2017)
8. Liu, W., et al.: SSD: single shot multibox detector. In: Leibe, B., Matas, J., Sebe, N., Welling, M. (eds.) ECCV 2016. LNCS, vol. 9905, pp. 21–37. Springer, Cham (2016). https://doi.org/10.1007/978-3-319-46448-0_2
9. Lin, T.Y., Goyal, P., Girshick, R., et al.: Focal loss for dense object detection. IEEE Trans. Pattern Anal. Mach. Intell. **PP**(99), 2999–3007 (2017). https://doi.org/10.1109/TPAMI.2018.2858826
10. Uijlings, J.R.R., van de Sande, K.E.A.: Selective search for object recognition. Int. J. Comput. Vis. **104**(2), 154–171 (2013). https://doi.org/10.1007/s11263-013-0620-5
11. Shrivastava, A., Gupta, A., Girshick, R.: Training region-based object detectors with online hard example mining. In: 2016 IEEE Conference on Computer Vision and Pattern Recognition (CVPR), pp. 761–769 (2016). https://doi.org/10.1109/CVPR.2016.89
12. Zhang, S., Zhu, X., Lei, Z., et al.: S^3FD: single shot scale-invariant face detector (2017). https://doi.org/10.1109/ICCV.2017.30
13. Kong, T., Sun, F., Yao, A., et al.: RON: reverse connection with objectness prior networks for object detection (2017). https://doi.org/10.1109/CVPR.2017.557
14. He, K., Zhang, X., Ren, S., et al.: Deep residual learning for image recognition (2015). https://doi.org/10.1109/CVPR.2016.90
15. Viola, P., Jones, M.: Rapid object detection using a boosted cascade of simple features. In: IEEE Computer Society (2001). https://doi.org/10.1109/CVPR.2001.990517
16. Felzenszwalb, P.F., Girshick, R., McAllester, D., Ramanan, D.: Object detection with discriminatively trained part based models. PAMI **32**(9), 1627–1645 (2010)
17. Girshick, R.: Fast R-CNN. In: Computer Science (2015). https://doi.org/10.1109/ICCV.2015.169
18. Zitnick, C.L., Dollár, P.: Edge boxes: locating object proposals from edges. In: Fleet, D., Pajdla, T., Schiele, B., Tuytelaars, T. (eds.) ECCV 2014. LNCS, vol. 8693, pp. 391–405. Springer, Cham (2014). https://doi.org/10.1007/978-3-319-10602-1_26
19. Girshick, R., Donahue, J., Darrell, T., Malik, J.: Rich feature hierarchies for accurate object detection and semantic segmentation. In: CVPR, pp. 580–587 (2014)
20. He, K., Zhang, X., Ren, S., et al.: Spatial pyramid pooling in deep convolutional networks for visual recognition. IEEE Trans. Pattern Anal. Mach. Intell. **37**(9), 1904–1916 (2014). https://doi.org/10.1007/978-3-319-10578-9_23
21. Wang, X., Shrivastava, A., Gupta, A.: A-Fast-RCNN: hard positive generation via adversary for object detection. In: 2017 IEEE Conference on Computer Vision and Pattern Recognition (CVPR), pp. 3039–3048 (2017). https://doi.org/10.1109/cvpr.2017.324

22. Bell, S., Zitnick, C.L., Bala, K., et al.: Inside-outside net: detecting objects in context with skip pooling and recurrent neural networks (2015). https://doi.org/10.1109/CVPR.2016.314
23. Cai, Z., Fan, Q., Feris, R.S., Vasconcelos, N.: A unified multi-scale deep convolutional neural network for fast object detection. In: Leibe, B., Matas, J., Sebe, N., Welling, M. (eds.) ECCV 2016. LNCS, vol. 9908, pp. 354–370. Springer, Cham (2016). https://doi.org/10.1007/978-3-319-46493-0_22
24. Kong, T., Yao, A., Chen, Y., et al.: HyperNet: towards accurate region proposal generation and joint object detection (2016). https://doi.org/10.1109/CVPR.2016.98
25. Shrivastava, A., Sukthankar, R., Malik, J., et al.: Beyond Skip Connections: Top-down Modulation For Object Detection (2016)
26. Sermanet, P., Eigen, D., Zhang, X., et al.: OverFeat: Integrated Recognition, Localization And Detection Using Convolutional Networks. Eprint Arxiv (2013)
27. Liu, S., Qi, L., Qin, H., et al.: Path aggregation network for instance segmentation (2018). https://doi.org/10.1109/CVPR.2018.00913
28. Long, J., Shelhamer, E., Darrell, T.: Fully convolutional networks for semantic segmentation. IEEE Trans. Pattern Anal. Mach. Intell. **39**(4), 640–651 (2014). https://doi.org/10.1109/TPAMI.2016.2572683
29. He, K., Gkioxari, G., Dollar, P., et al.: Mask R-CNN. IEEE Trans. Pattern Anal. Mach. Intell. **PP**(99), 1 (2017). https://doi.org/10.1109/TPAMI.2018.2844175
30. Pytorch homepage. https://pytorch.org

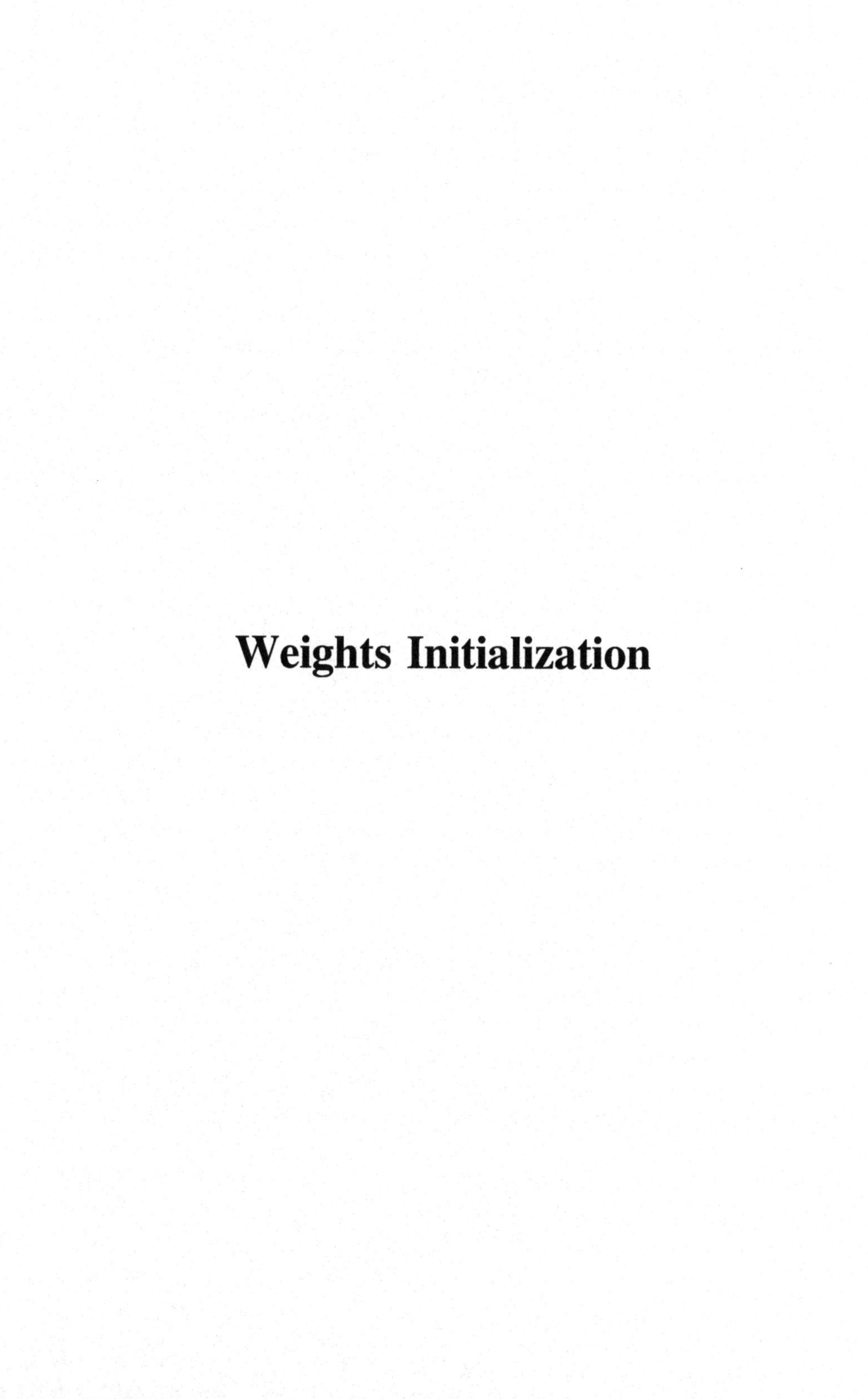

Weights Initialization

Singular Value Decomposition and Neural Networks

Bernhard Bermeitinger[1,2(✉)], Tomas Hrycej[1], and Siegfried Handschuh[1,2]

[1] Chair of Data Science, Institute of Computer Science, University of St.Gallen, St.Gallen, Switzerland
{bernhard.bermeitinger,siegfried.handschuh}@unisg.ch
[2] University Passau, Passau, Germany
{bernhard.bermeitinger,siegfried.handschuh}@uni-passau.de

Abstract. Singular Value Decomposition (SVD) constitutes a bridge between the linear algebra concepts and multi-layer neural networks—it is their linear analogy. Besides of this insight, it can be used as a good initial guess for the network parameters, leading to substantially better optimization results.

Keywords: Singular Value Decomposition · Neural network · Deep neural network · Initialization · Optimization · Conjugate gradient

1 Motivation

The utility of multi-layer neural networks is frequently being explained by their capability of extracting meaningful features in their hidden layers. This view is particularly appropriate for large size applications such as corpus-based semantics analyses where the number of training examples is too low for making the problem fully determined in terms of a direct mapping from the input to the output space.

This capability of feature extraction is mostly implicitly attributed to using nonlinear units in contrast to a linear mapping. The prototype of such linear mapping is linear regression, using multiplication of an input pattern by a regression matrix to get an estimate of the output pattern, omitting the possibility of using a sequence of two (or more) matrices corresponding to the use of a hidden layer of linear units. This possibility is usually considered to be obsolete with the argument that a product of two matrices is also a matrix and the result is thus equivalent to using a single matrix.

This argument, although superficially correct, hides the possibility of using a matrix of deliberately chosen low rank, which leads to the correct treatment of under-determined problems.

A key to understanding the situation is Singular Value Decomposition (SVD). In the following, it will be shown that SVD can be interpreted as a linear analogy of a neural network with one hidden layer and that it can be used for generating

I. V. Tetko et al. (Eds.): ICANN 2019, LNCS 11728, pp. 153–164, 2019.
https://doi.org/10.1007/978-3-030-30484-3_13

a good initial solution for optimizing nonlinear multi-layer neural networks. Saxe et al. [5] support this theory from the opposite direction: they showed empirically that the optimized results from a nonlinear network are very similar to the results coming from an SVD. McCloone et al. [4] have an interesting approach on how to support optimization by SVD in various network architectures (namely Multi-Layer Perceptron and RBF networks). However, our interest is in pointing out the direct relationship between SVD and a shallow multi-layer neural network with a low dimensional hidden layer. The low dimensionality of the hidden layer has the function of feature extraction.

The work of Xue et al. [8] is decreasing the number of parameters within a neural network significantly by replacing a layer's weight matrix by two layers which weight matrices are constructed using SVD. Similar to our approach, this results effectively in initializing the two layers using the resulting matrices from SVD (1). Still, it is used to decrease the model size rather than showing that this initialization is already good guess for finding the (near-) optimal solution.

2 Singular Value Decomposition

SVD is a powerful concept of linear algebra. It is a decomposition of an arbitrary matrix A of size $m \times n$ into three factors:

$$A = USV^T \tag{1}$$

where U and V are orthonormal and S is of identical size as A, consisting of a diagonal matrix D_0 and a zero matrix. For $m < n$, it is $[S_0, 0]$, for $m > n$ it is $[S_0, 0]^T$. In the further discussion, only the case of $m < n$ will be considered as the opposite case is analogous.

SVD is then simplified to

$$A = USV^T = U\left[S_0, 0\right]\left[V_0, V_x\right]^T = US_0V_0^T \tag{2}$$

by omitting redundant zero terms. This form is sometimes called *economical.*

For the economical form (2), the decomposition with $r = \min(m, n)$ has $mr + r + nr = (m + n + 1)\, r$ nonzero parameters. The orthonormality of U and V imposes $2r$ unity norm constraints, and $r\,(r - 1)$ orthogonality constraints, resulting in a total number of

$$2r + r\,(r - 1) = r^2 + r \tag{3}$$

constraints.

The number of free parameters amounts to

$$(m + n + 1)\, r - r^2 - r \tag{4}$$

which is

$$(m + n + 1)\, m - m^2 - m = mn, \quad \text{for } m < n \tag{5}$$

and, analogically,

$$(m+n+1)\,n - n^2 - n = mn, \quad \text{for } m > n \tag{6}$$

So, the economical form of SVD possesses the same number of free parameters as the original matrix A.

The number of nonzero singular values in S_0 is equal to the rank r of matrix A. An interesting case arises if the matrix A is not full rank, that is, if $r < \min(m,n)$. Then, some diagonal elements of S_0 are zero. Reordering the diagonal elements of S_0 (and, correspondingly the columns of U and V_0) so that its nonzero elements are in the field S_1 and zero elements in S_2, the decomposition further collapses to

$$A = US_0V_0^T = [U_1, U_2]\begin{bmatrix} S_1 & 0 \\ 0 & S_2 \end{bmatrix}[V_1, V_2]^T = U_1S_1V_1^T \tag{7}$$

Then, with the help of orthogonality of U_1 and V_1, the matrix can be decomposed into the sum

$$A = USV^T = \sum_{k=1}^{r} s_k u_k v_k^T \tag{8}$$

An important property of SVD is its capability for a matrix approximation by a matrix of lower rank. In analogy to the partitioning the singular values with the help of S_1 and S_2 to nonzero and zero ones, they can be partitioned to large and small ones. Selecting the $\hat{r}$ largest singular values makes (8) to an approximation $\hat{A}$ of matrix A. This approximation has the outstanding property of being that with the minimum L_2 matrix norm of the difference $\hat{A} - A$

$$\left\|\hat{A} - A\right\|_2 \tag{9}$$

out of all matrices of rank $\hat{r}$.

The L_2 matrix norm of M is defined as an induced norm by the L_2 vector norm, so that it is defined as

$$\left\|M\right\|_2 = \max_x \frac{\left\|Mx\right\|_2}{\left\|x\right\|_2} \tag{10}$$

In many practical cases, a relatively small number $\hat{r}$ leads to approximations very close to the original matrix. Equation 8 shows that this property can be used for an economical representation of a $m \times n$ matrix A by only $\hat{r}\,(m+n+1)$ numerical values. The optimum approximation property is shown below to be relevant for the mapping approximation discussed below.

A further important application of SVD is an explicit formula for a matrix pseudo-inverse. Pseudo-inverse A^+ is the analogy of an inverse matrix for the case of non-square matrices, with the property

$$AA^+A = A \tag{11}$$

It can be easily computed with the help of SVD:

$$X^{+} = V S_{\mathrm{inv}}^{T} U^{T} \tag{12}$$

with S_{inv} being a matrix of the same dimension as S with inverted non-zero elements $\frac{1}{s_{ii}}$ on the diagonal.

3 SVD and Linear Regression

One of the applications of the pseudo-inverse (11) is a computing scheme for least squares. The linear regression problem is specified by input/output column vector pairs (x_i, y_i), seeking the best possible estimates

$$\hat{y}_i = B x_i + a \tag{13}$$

in the sense of least squares.

The bias vector a can be received by extending the input patterns x_i by a unity constant. For simplicity, it will be omitted in the ongoing discussion.

The solution amounts to solving the equation

$$Y = BX \tag{14}$$

with matrices Y and X made of the corresponding column vectors. The optimum is found with the help of the pseudo-inverse X^{+} of X. In the over-determined case (typical for linear regression), the least squares solution is

$$B = YX^{+} = YX^{T}\left(XX^{T}\right)^{-1} \tag{15}$$

In the under-determined case, there is an infinite number of solutions with zero approximation error. The following solution has the minimum matrix norm of B:

$$B = YX^{+} = Y\left(X^{T}X\right)^{-1} X^{T} \tag{16}$$

Both (15) and (16) use the pseudo-inverse that can be easily computed with help of SVD according to (12).

4 SVD and Mappings of a Given Rank

Both the full SVD (1) and its reduced rank form (7) are products of a dense matrix U, a partly or fully diagonal matrix S, and a dense matrix V^{T}. This suggests the possibility of viewing them as a product of two dense matrices US and V^{T}, or U and SV^{T}. All these matrices are full rank, even if the original matrix B was not due to the under-determination.

The product US and V^{T} is the sequence of two linear mappings. The latter matrix maps the n-dimensional input space to an intermediary space of dimension $\hat{r}$, the former the intermediary space to the m-dimensional output space. Since $n > \hat{r}$ and $m > \hat{r}$, the intermediary space represents a bottleneck similar to a hidden layer of a neural network. The orthogonal columns of V can be viewed as hidden features compressing the information in the input space. This relationship to neural networks be followed in Sect. 5.

The reasons to search for such a compressed mapping are different for the over-determined and the under-determined problems.

4.1 Over-Determined Problems

Suppose for an over-determined problem with input matrix X and output matrix Y, the best linear solution is sought. The columns of X and Y correspond to the training examples. The least-square-optimum solution is the linear regression

$$y = Bx + a \tag{17}$$

with matrix B from (15). The bias vector a can be received by extending the matrix X by a unit row and applying the pseudo-inversion of such an extended matrix. The last column of such an extended regression matrix corresponds to the column bias vector a.

The linear regression matrix is $m \times n$ for input dimension n and output dimension m, its SVD is as in (1).

With more than n independent training examples, the regression matrix B and also the matrix S are full rank with singular values on the diagonal of S.

There may be reasons for assuming that there are random data errors, without which the rank of B would not be full. This would amount to the assumption that some of the training examples are, in fact, linearly dependent or even identical and only the random data errors make them different. To ensure correct generalization, it would then be appropriate to assume a lower rank of the regression matrix. This will suggest using the approximating property of SVD with a reduced singular value set. Leaving out the components with small singular values may be equivalent to removing the data noise. Taking a matrix S_{mod} with $\hat{r}$ largest singular values while zeroing the remaining ones (see, e.g., [7]) results in a matrix according to (7):

$$B_{\text{mod}} = U_{\text{mod}} S_{\text{mod}} V_{\text{mod}}^T \tag{18}$$

that has the least matrix L_2 norm

$$\left\| B - B_{\text{mod}} \right\|_2 \tag{19}$$

out of all existing matrices B_{mod} with rank $\hat{r}$. The L_2 matrix norm is induced by the L_2 vector norm, as defined in Eq. 10. The definition (10) of the L_2 matrix norm has an implication for the accuracy of the forecasts with help of R and R_{mod}:

$$\left\| B - B_{\text{mod}} \right\|_2 = \max_x \frac{\left\| (B - B_{\text{mod}})\, x \right\|_2}{\left\| x \right\|_2} = \max_x \frac{\left\| y - y_{\text{mod}} \right\|_2}{\left\| x \right\|_2} \tag{20}$$

The vector norm of the forecast error equal to the square root of the mean square error is obviously minimal for a given norm of the input vector. In other words, the modified, reduced-rank regression matrix has the least maximum forecast deviation from the original regression matrix relative to the norm of the input vector x.

4.2 Under-Determined Problems

A different situation is if the linear regression is under-determined. This is frequently the case in high-dimensional applications such as computer vision and corpus-based semantics—the number of training examples may be substantially lower than the dimensions of the input. The training examples span a subspace of the input vector space. Using this training information, new patterns can only be projected onto this subspace. The projection operator, using the same definition of the input matrix X as above, is given as:

$$\hat{x} = XX^{+}x = X\left(X^{T}X\right)^{-1}X^{T}x \tag{21}$$

This can be viewed as a pattern-specific weighting of training examples by a weight vector w_x

$$\hat{x} = Xw_x^T \tag{22}$$

To recall the corresponding output, the same weight vector can be used:

$$\hat{y} = Yw_x^T = YX^{+}x = Y\left(X^{T}X\right)^{-1}X^{T}x \tag{23}$$

This is equivalent to solving the regression problem

$$Y = RX \tag{24}$$

with help of the pseudo-inverse (see, e.g., [3]) of X, which is (16) in the under-determined case.

The regression matrix R is, as usual, of size $m \times n$. If the input dimension m exceeds the number of training examples the regression matrix R solving Eq. 24 is not full rank. Its SVD will exhibit some zero singular values and can be reduced, without a loss of information, to a reduced form:

$$B_{\text{red}} = U_{\text{red}}S_{\text{red}}V_{\text{red}}^T \tag{25}$$

5 SVD and Linear Networks

Before establishing the relationship between SVD and nonlinear neural networks, let us consider hypothetical multi-layer networks with linear units of the form $g(x) = x$ in the hidden layer.

Suppose a network with one hidden layer of predefined size p is used to represent a mapping from input x to output y. Suppose now that the best linear mapping from input x to output y is

$$y = Bx \tag{26}$$

The best approximation with a rank limitation to $\hat{r}$ and is, according to (7):

$$y = U_1 S_1 V_1^T x \tag{27}$$

This expression can be viewed as a network with one linear hidden layer of width $p = \hat{r}$. The weight matrix between the input and the hidden layers is

$$V_1^T \tag{28}$$

and that between the hidden and the output layers is

$$U_1 S_1 \tag{29}$$

This network has the property of being the best approximation of the mapping from the input to the output between all networks of this size with orthonormal (in the hidden layer) and orthogonal (in the output layer) weight vectors.

This optimality is not strictly guaranteed to be reached if relaxing the orthogonality constraints. The difference between the orthogonal and the non-orthogonal solutions depends on the ratio between the input and the output widths, and on the relative width of the hidden layer in the following way.

How serious this optimality gap may be can be assessed observing the fraction of the number of orthogonality constraints to the number of parameters. If this fraction is small, the number of independent parameters is close to the number of all parameters and the influence of the orthogonality constraints is small.

With hidden layer size r (equal to the rank of the linear mapping), the total number of constraints is $r^2 + r$. With $m < n$ and $n = qm, q \geq 1$, the total number of parameters is $(m + qm + 1)\, r$. The fraction, and its approximation for realistic values of $r \gg 1$ is then

$$\frac{r^2 + r}{(m + qm + 1)\, r} = \frac{r + 1}{m + qm + 1} \approx \frac{r}{(1 + q)\, m} \tag{30}$$

This fraction decreases with the ratio $\frac{m}{r}$ (the degree of *feature compression* by the network) and the ratio q. Since both ratios will usually be large in practical problems of the mentioned domain, the distance to the optimality after relaxing the orthogonality constraints can be expected to be small.

6 SVD and Initializing Nonlinear Neural Networks

Most popular hidden units possess a linear or nearly linear segment. A *sigmoid* unit

$$s(x) = \frac{1}{1 + e^{-x}} \tag{31}$$

is nearly linear around the point $x = 0$ where its derivative is equal to 0.25. Rescaling this unit to the symmetric form

$$f(x) = 2s(2x) - 1 = \frac{2}{1 + e^{-2x}} - 1 \tag{32}$$

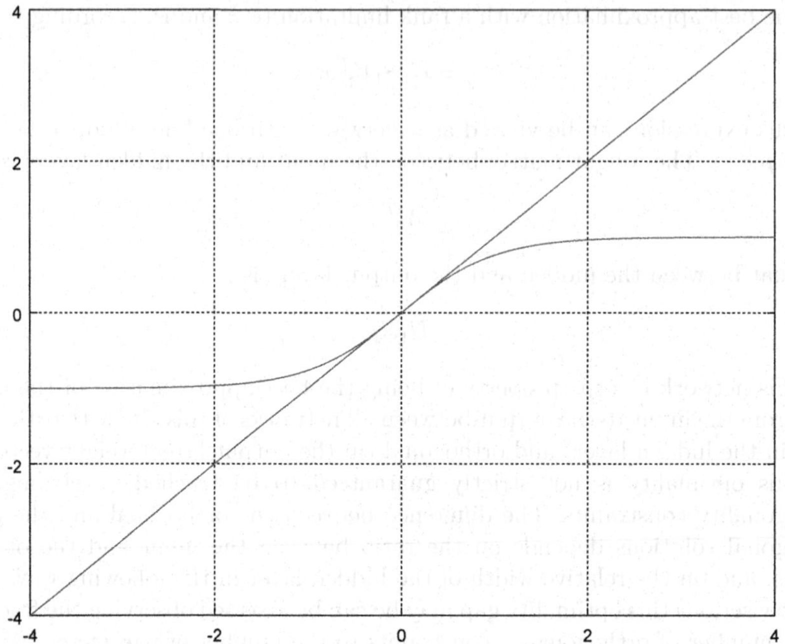

Fig. 1. Plot of Eq. 32

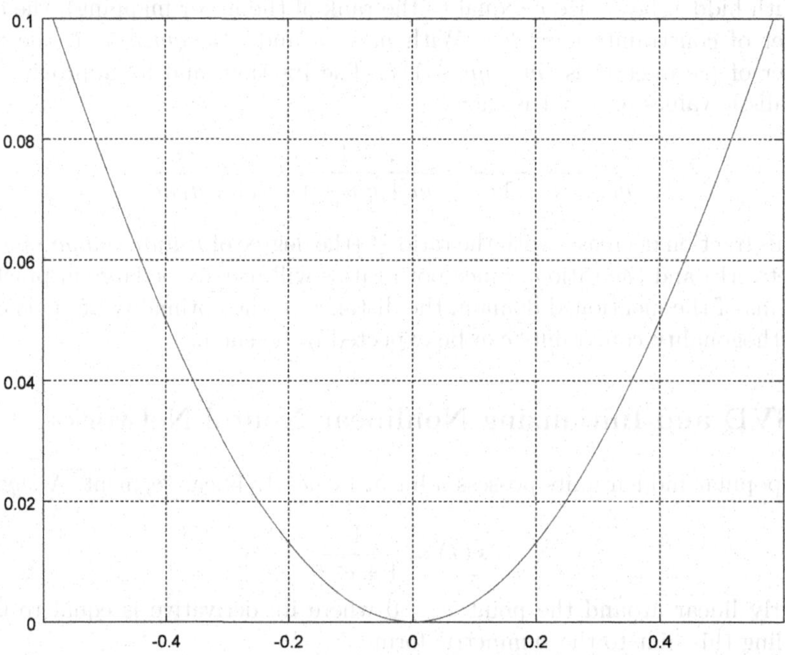

Fig. 2. Plot of relative deviation between a linear function and sigmoid

we obtain a nonlinear function the derivative of which is unity around $x = 0$, plotted in Fig. 1.

Its relative deviation from the linear function $g(x) = x$ is below ten percent for $q|x| < 0.58$ (see Fig. 2). So, a neural network with one hidden layer using the sigmoid activation function (32) behaves like a linear network for small activation values of the hidden layer.

This fact can be used for finding a good initial guess of parameters of a nonlinear neural network with a single hidden layer. The in-going weights into the hidden and output layers are (28) and (29), respectively.

7 Computing Experiments

A series of computing experiments have been carried out to assess the real efficiency of using SVD as a generator of the initial state of neural network parameters. To provide a meaningful interpretation of the mean square figures attained, all problems have been deliberately defined to have a minimum at zero. To justify the use of the hidden layer as a feature extractor, its width should be smaller than the minimum of the input and output sizes. The dimensions have been chosen so that the full regression would be under-determined (as typical for the application types mentioned above), but the use of a hidden layer with a smaller width makes it slightly over-determined. So, the effect of overfitting, harmful for generalization, is excluded.

The software used for SVD computation was the Python module *SciPy* [2]. Neural networks were optimized by several methods implemented in the popular framework *Keras* [1]: *Stochastic Gradient Descent* (SGD), selected because of its widespread use, as well as *Adadelta* and *RMSprop*, which seem to be the most efficient ones for the problems considered.

Typical Keras-methods are first order and there is a widespread opinion in the neural network community that second-order methods are not superior to the first order ones. However, there are strong theoretical and empirical arguments in favor of the second-order methods from numerical mathematics. So the conjugate gradient method (CG), as implemented in SciPy, has also been applied. Since the SciPy/Keras interface failed to work for this method[1], efficient Keras-based network evaluation procedures could not be used. So, for the largest problems, the CG method had to be omitted.

The performance of the optimization methods has been compared with the help of the number of gradient calls. All methods have been used with the default settings of Keras and SciPy.

Three problem sizes denoted as A, B, and C have been used. Using different size classes will make it possible to discern possible dependencies on the problem size if there are any. The largest size of class C is still substantially below that of huge networks such as *VGG-19* [6] used in image classification. The computing

[1] Since we use TensorFlow as Keras' backend execution engine, the resulting computation graph would have been cut into two different executions for each optimization step which causes a too high computational overhead.

effort for making method comparison with such huge sizes would be excessive for the goals of this study. However, we believe the size is sufficient for showing trends relevant for very large network sizes.

The three size classes are characterized by their input and output dimensions as well as by the size of the training set. The concrete network sizes, parameter numbers, and numbers of constraints (output values to be reached times the number of training examples) are given in Table 1. The column "# constraints" shows the number of constraints imposed by the reference outputs to be fitted. It is the product of the output dimension and the training set size. Comparing the number of constraints with the number of parameters defines the over-determination or the under-determination of the problem (e.g., a problem with more constraints than parameters is over-determined).

The results for the different size classes are given in Table 2. For each network architecture, three different parametrizations with corresponding training sets have been generated, all with a known mean square error minimum of zero. For every variant, an SVD has been computed and used to determine the network initialization. For comparison, five different random network initializations have been generated. The results below are geometric means of minima reached (means from three optimization runs for SVD initializations, and means from $3 \cdot 5 = 15$ runs for random initializations).

Table 1. Test problem definitions

Type	#input	#output	#hidden	#training	#parameters	#constraints
A	100	50	20	80	3070	4000
B	300	150	60	240	27210	36000
C	1000	500	200	800	300700	400000

Table 2. Mean square minima reached by various optimization methods with random and SVD-based initial parameter sets

Algorithm	Init.	Size class A		Size class B		Size class C	
		#iter.	$F_{opt} \times 10^{-3}$	#iter.	$F_{opt} \times 10^{-3}$	#iter.	$F_{opt} \times 10^{-3}$
SVD	—	—	10.200	—	10.559	—	10.814
SGD	Random	2000	30.361	2000	90.402	2000	177.095
RMSprop	Random	2000	0.040	2000	0.096	2000	0.260
Adadelta	Random	2000	1.290	2000	6.748	2000	31.076
CG	Random	637	0.002	821	0.012	—	—
SGD	SVD	2000	1.779	2000	4.145	2000	7.254
RMSprop	SVD	2000	0.030	2000	0.085	2000	0.248
Adadelta	SVD	2000	0.062	2000	0.511	2000	2.086
CG	SVD	316	0.000	233	0.021	—	—

The results of four optimization methods are given in the randomly initialized variant and in the variant initialized with help of the SVD solution.

The first row, labeled with algorithm "SVD", shows the minima reached by the SVD solution without any subsequent optimization. It is obvious that the SVD-based initialization is pretty good. Its mean square error minimum is substantially better than the weakest Keras-method *SGD* with random initialization. For the largest problem size class, SVD without optimization is also superior to Adadelta with random initialization.

An SVD-based initialization with a subsequent optimization lets *SGD* reach an acceptable minimum, with even better results using *Adadelta*. The best Keras-method, *RMSprop*, was clearly inferior to the conjugate gradient (*CG*), although CG stopped the optimization substantially earlier that the fixed iteration number of RMSprop. For both these methods, the improvement by SVD-based initialization was weak (for CG only in the number of iterations). This is not unexpected: good optimization methods are able to find the representations similar to the SVD by themselves, solving a closely related problem with a different numerical procedure.

8 Conclusion and Discussion

SVD constitutes a bridge between the linear algebra concepts and multi-layer neural networks—it is their linear analogy. Besides this insight, it can be used as a good initial guess for the network parameters. The quality of this initial guess may be, for large problems, better than weakly performing (but widely used) methods such as SGD ever reach.

It has to be pointed out that as long as the network uses nonlinear hidden units, simply using this initial guess as ultimate network parameters makes little sense: it would be preferable to make the units linear, and use the SVD matrices directly to represent the desired input-output mapping.

Unfortunately, there seems to be no analogous generalization for networks with multiple hidden layers. With a hidden layer sequence of monotonically decreasing width (for example, from the input towards the output) it would be possible to proceed iteratively, by successively adding hidden layers of decreasing width.

The procedure would start by defining the first hidden layer z_1 (the one with the largest dimension) and initializing its weights with the help of SVD. Then, the following iterations over the desired number of hidden layers would be performed:

1. Analyzing the mapping between the output of the last hidden layer considered and the output layer $z_i \rightarrow y$ (with $z_0 = x$) using SVD.
2. Finding an initial guess of parametrization for the incoming weights to z_{i+1}.
3. Optimizing the weights of such extended nonlinear network by some appropriate optimization method.

This is a formal generalization of the procedure for the network with a single hidden layer z_1, as presented above.

However, it is difficult to find a founded justification for this procedure, as it is equally difficult to find a founded justification for using multiple fully connected hidden layers at all—although there seems to be empirical evidence in favor of this. Of course, there are good justifications for using special architectures such as convolutional networks, which are motivated, e.g., by spatial operators in image processing.

References

1. Chollet, F., et al.: Keras (2015). https://keras.io
2. Jones, E., Oliphant, T., Peterson, P., et al.: SciPy: open source scientific tools for Python (2001). http://www.scipy.org/
3. Kohonen, T.: Self-Organization and Associative Memory. SSINF, vol. 8, 3rd edn. Springer, Heidelberg (1989). https://doi.org/10.1007/978-3-642-88163-3. https://www.springer.com/de/book/9783540513872
4. McLoone, S., Brown, M.D., Irwin, G., Lightbody, A.: A hybrid linear/nonlinear training algorithm for feedforward neural networks. IEEE Trans. Neural Networks **9**(4), 669–684 (1998). https://doi.org/10/dwvsrs
5. Saxe, A.M., McClelland, J.L., Ganguli, S.: Exact solutions to the nonlinear dynamics of learning in deep linear neural networks. arXiv 1312.6120 (2013). http://arxiv.org/abs/1312.6120
6. Simonyan, K., Zisserman, A.: Very deep convolutional networks for large-scale image recognition. arXiv 1409.1556, September 2014. http://arxiv.org/abs/1409.1556
7. Trefethen, L.N., Bau III, D.: Numerical Linear Algebra, vol. 50. SIAM (1997). ISBN 978-0-898713-61-9
8. Xue, J., Li, J., Gong, Y.: Restructuring of deep neural network acoustic models with singular value decomposition. In: Bimbot, F., et al. (eds.) INTERSPEECH 2013, 14th Annual Conference of the International Speech Communication Association, Lyon, France, 25–29 August 2013, pp. 2365–2369. ISCA (2013). https://isca-speech.org/archive/interspeech_2013/i13_2365.html

PCI: Principal Component Initialization for Deep Autoencoders

Aiga Suzuki[1,2(✉)] and Hidenori Sakanashi[1,2]

[1] National Institute of Advanced Industrial Science and Technology, 1-1-1 Umezono, Tsukuba, Ibaraki 305–8560, Japan
{ai-suzuki,h.sakanashi}@aist.go.jp

[2] University of Tsukuba, 1-1-1 Tennodai, Tsukuba, Ibaraki 307–8577, Japan

Abstract. An autoencoder (AE) is one of the important neural network methods for dimensionality reduction problems. Unfortunately, however, deep AEs have the drawback in trainability which often makes obtaining a good performance a difficult task owing to their model complexity. This paper proposes a simple weight initialization algorithm called the principal component initialization (PCI) method to improve and stabilize the generalization performance of deep AEs in one shot. PCI uses orthogonal bases of the original data space obtained with principal component analysis and transposed ones as initial weights of the AEs. The proposed method significantly outperforms the current de facto standard initialization method for image reconstruction tasks.

Keywords: Weight initialization · Deep Autoencoders

1 Introduction

Autoencoders (AEs) has become a powerful dimensionality reduction method in the recent decade in the context of "deep learning" since Hinton et al. demonstrated the success of the deep AE model [5]. However, deep AEs have a lack of trainability because of the gradient vanishing problem and the high complexity of the model parameters. Several studies have attempted to tackle this problem. For example, Hinton et al. [5] proposed a layerwise pretraining method for deep AEs using the deep belief network (DBN), i.e., the deep restricted Boltzmann machine (RBM). This approach is an efficient weight initialization method that has been reported as a good alternative to overcome trainability problems [3]. However, such successful initialization methods based on pretraining [3,5] require a massive amount of computation because they have to perform complex iterative optimizations for each layer.

This paper proposes a one-shot weight initialization method for deep AEs, called "Principal Component Initialization" (PCI) to improve the generalization performance and the convergence of learning transitions without the iterative training of entire networks. The key to the proposed method is the well-known parallels between PCA and AEs. Several studies reported that the PCA can

I. V. Tetko et al. (Eds.): ICANN 2019, LNCS 11728, pp. 165–169, 2019.
https://doi.org/10.1007/978-3-030-30484-3_14

be interpreted as a special case of shallow AE [2,8]. Further, Karakida et al. reported that RBMs—commonly used for pretraining of AEs—have the same dynamics as the principal component analysis on their steady-state solution calculated with contrastive divergence algorithms [6]. We could make an intuitive assumption as follows: *Knowledge derived from a PCA could be used for efficient weight initialization.* Mathias et al. proposed a weight initialization method for shallow AEs by transferring the PCA result; however, their method is slightly complicated, and it does not provide the mechanism for initializing deep AEs. Our method can be employed for deep AEs in a more straightforward manner owing to tied-weight learning [3]. The experimental result demonstrates that the proposed method significantly improves reconstruction errors with reduced representations calculated in AEs.

2 Methodology

2.1 Comparison Between PCA and AEs

Both PCA and AE—the important methods in this study–are dimensionality reduction methods in the sense of machine learning. PCA is a factor decomposition method used to calculate an orthogonal subspace of the original data space to ensure that the given data is well-represented with coordinates on the subspace. $X = (\boldsymbol{x}_1, \cdots, \boldsymbol{x}_N) \in \mathbb{R}^{D \times N}$ denotes a data matrix of D-dimensional samples. PCA finds a decomposition $X = WY$ where $W \in \mathbb{R}^{D \times M}$ is the M-dimensional orthogonal basis matrix of projection subspace and $Y \in \mathbb{R}^{M \times N}$ denotes a reduced M-dimensional representation of an original data matrix X. A *maximum variance* solution of PCA can be calculated as a eigendecomposition problem of the covariance matrix of data matrix $\Sigma := \langle (\boldsymbol{x} - \langle \boldsymbol{x} \rangle)(\boldsymbol{x} - \langle \boldsymbol{x} \rangle)^T \rangle$ by setting $W = V_M$, where V_M contains M eigenvectors with the largest eigenvalues of Σ. For an input $\boldsymbol{x}$, PCA calculates the reduced representation as $\boldsymbol{y} = W^T \boldsymbol{x}$, which means a projection onto the obtained orthogonal bases W.

AE is a fully connected neural network used for the data transformation problem. AEs can be divided into two parts: One is an encoder, which transforms D-dimensional inputs into M-dimensional intermediate representation. The other is a decoder, which transforms M-dimensional intermediate representations into D-dimensional space as to reconstruct the inputs. AEs serve as a dimensionality reduction model in the case of $M < D$ because the low-dimensional intermediate representations calculated in the encoder retain the information for reconstructing the inputs. Here, we consider a two-layered AE with D-dimensional inputs and M-dimensional intermediate representation, denoted as (D-M). The encoder's dimensionality reduction for input $\boldsymbol{x}$ is calculated as $\boldsymbol{y} = \phi(W\boldsymbol{x} + \boldsymbol{b})$ where ϕ denotes a nonlinear function called the activation function, e.g., $\mathrm{ReLU}(x) = \max(0, x)$, $W \in \mathbb{R}^{M \times D}$, and $\boldsymbol{b} \in \mathbb{R}^M$ denotes weight parameters and bias parameter, respectively. The decoder reconstructs the input $\boldsymbol{x}$ from the reduced representation $\boldsymbol{y}$ as $\boldsymbol{x}' = \phi(W'\boldsymbol{y} + b')$, where $W' \in \mathbb{R}^{D \times M}$ and $b' \in \mathbb{R}^D$ are decoder weights and bias parameters, respectively. AEs obtain a good transformation to calculate intermediate representations, that means trainable parameters W, b, W', b', by optimizing them as to reconstruct the input as $\boldsymbol{x} = \boldsymbol{x}'$.

2.2 Proposed Method: Principal Component Initialization

The key to the proposed method (PCI) is that the calculation of the reduced representation of PCA and AE are similar, except for an activation function and a bias parameter of AEs. On both models, the primary mechanism of dimensionality reduction is the product of the weight matrix W. In our proposed method, the encoder weight matrix of AEs $W \in \mathbb{R}^{M \times D}$, which has M intermediate neurons, is initialized as V_M, i.e., the bases of M-dimensional projection subspace of PCA. The decoder weights are initialized as the transpose of V_M because the decoder weights serve well in transposed constraints $W' = W^T$, known as the tied-weight learning [3]. The remaining bias parameters are initialized with Gaussian initialization, e.g., the He's initialization [4].

For deep AEs, which for example, have 4-layers (D-M_1-M_2), the weight matrix of first encoder and decoder $W^{(1)} \in \mathbb{R}^{M_1 \times D}, W^{(1)'} \in \mathbb{R}^{D \times M_1}$ are initialized first as $W^{(1)} = V_{M_1}, W^{(1)'} = V_{M_1}^T$ in the same manner as a two-layered AE. Subsequently, the weight matrix of the second layers $W^{(2)} \in \mathbb{R}^{M_2 \times M_1}, W^{(2)'} \in \mathbb{R}^{M_1 \times M_2}$ are initialized with the PCI for the transformed input by using the initialized first encoder, which means that the PCA result of the transformed M_1-dimensional intermediate representations $(\boldsymbol{y}_i = V_{M_1}\boldsymbol{x}_i + \boldsymbol{b})_{i=1}^N$. For all layers in AEs, the proposed method successively initializes their weights by fixing previous layers weights, as in Hinton's layerwise pretraining method, mentioned in Sect. 1.

3 Experiments and Results

We compared the reconstruction errors from reduced intermediate representations for AEs that are initialized with He's initialization [4]; i.e., the de facto standard weight initialization method for ReLU networks and our proposed method PCI. Experimental datasets are MNIST, CIFAR-10, and CIFAR-100, which are the high-dimensional image dataset, and they are used in many studies on dimensionality reduction problems. We trained all AEs using the Adam optimization algorithm [7] with parameters $\alpha = 0.001, \beta_1 = 0.9, \beta_2 = 0.999$, and $\epsilon = 10^{-8}$ until training loss plateaus were obtained.

We calculated a test MSE loss with the 90th percentile values of the converged learning processes as a representative value for the evaluation, and we averaged over 10 different realizations for the random conditions. To evaluate the improvement in training speed, we also calculated the ratio $e_{\mathrm{PCI}}/e_{\mathrm{He}}$ of epochs to reach to the 90th percentile losses for two initialization conditions (PCI and He's initialization). Table 1 shows the results of two two-layered shallow AEs (D-100) and (D-10), and two deep AEs (D-100-50-10) and (D-500 − 500 − 200-100), mentioned in [5], where D indicates input dimensionality that is 784 for MNIST and

3072 for CIFAR-10/100. For all data and AE structures, the proposed method achieves better reconstruction losses than He's initialization method, which is statistically significant ($p < 0.01$, $n = 10$, non-parametric Wilcoxon signed-rank test). As a notable fact, the proposed method decreased the standard deviation of the losses, which suggests that PCI also improves the stability of the resulting trained model. Epochs to achieve the same generalization have also been massively decreased for all conditions, especially in the case of shallow networks, i.e., (D-100) and (D-10).

Table 1. MSE losses and convergence speed for test data. Each metrics following ± indicate the standard deviation of 10 realizations.

MNIST	(D-100)	(D-10)	(D-100-50-10)	(D-500-500-200-10)
He's initialization	41.39 ± 2.501	255.9 ± 45.48	106.3 ± 7.297	76.13 ± 16.05
PCI *(Ours)*	27.61 ± 0.008	161.2 ± 0.009	93.75 ± 3.932	43.36 ± 0.422
p-value	0.0050	0.0051	0.0051	0.0051
e_{PCI}/e_{He}	0.014 ± 0.0022	0.024 ± 0.021	0.178 ± 0.129	0.078 ± 0.070
CIFAR-10	(D-100)	(D-10)	(D-100-50-10)	(D-500-500-200-10)
He's initialization	717.4 ± 172.7	952.0 ± 13.23	375.9 ± 28.15	393.4 ± 46.35
PCI *(Ours)*	139.5 ± 5.076	355.4 ± 0.009	340.2 ± 15.29	314.8 ± 17.93
p-value	0.0051	0.0051	0.0469	0.0051
e_{PCI}/e_{He}	0.038 ± 0.014	0.045 ± 0.0010	0.351 ± 0.362	0.185 ± 0.186
CIFAR-100	(D-100)	(D-10)	(D-100-50-10)	(D-500-500-200-10)
He's initialization	885.1 ± 192.0	1075.1 ± 69.27	387.4 ± 24.12	374.1 ± 28.13
PCI *(Ours)*	138.7 ± 3.498	345.8 ± 5.945	346.9 ± 19.02	301.6 ± 8.395
p-value	0.0051	0.0051	0.0093	0.0051
e_{PCI}/e_{He}	0.044 ± 0.012	0.045 ± 0.0010	0.454 ± 0.423	0.092 ± 0.078

4 Discussion and Conclusion

This paper proposed a PCA-based efficient weight initialization method, named as a principal component initialization (PCI), for deep AEs. The proposed method used projection bases obtained in PCA as initial weights of AEs to improve the efficiency for learning better reduced representations. In the experiments, we compared a reconstruction loss from the learned reduced representation of AEs. The proposed method demonstrated significantly better results than the conventionally used He's initialization algorithm in the image reconstruction tasks.

As future work, the effects of non-linearity of a dataset on the performance of PCI should be investigated to prove that PCI can work well for an extremely non-linear dataset. Akinduko et al. reported that, in the study of similar initialization from PCA to the self-organizing map model, random initializations outperformed PCA initialization in the case of significant non-linear tasks [1]. It is not clear whether the proposed method performs well for a significantly non-linear dataset. Further, as an improvement of our method, it is expected for PCI to be able to automatically lead the optimal number of intermediate neurons of AEs by eigenvalues of principal components, which correspond to the variances of principal subspaces.

References

1. Akinduko, A.A., Mirkes, E.M., Gorban, A.N.: SOM: stochastic initialization versus principal components. Inf. Sci. **364**, 213–221 (2016). https://doi.org/10.1016/j.ins.2015.10.013
2. Baldi, P., Hornik, K.: Neural networks and principal component analysis: learning from examples without local minima. Neural Netw. **2**(1), 53–58 (1989). https://doi.org/10.1016/0893-6080(89)90014-2
3. Bengio, Y., Lamblin, P., Popovici, D., Larochelle, H.: Greedy layer-wise training of deep networks. In: Advances in Neural Information Processing Systems, pp. 153–160 (2007)
4. He, K., Zhang, X., Ren, S., Sun, J.: Delving deep into rectifiers: surpassing human-level performance on ImageNet classification. In: Proceedings of the IEEE International Conference on Computer Vision, pp. 1026–1034 (2015). https://doi.org/10.1109/ICCV.2015.123
5. Hinton, G.E., Salakhutdinov, R.R.: Reducing the dimensionality of data with neural networks. Science **313**(5786), 504–507 (2006)
6. Karakida, R., Okada, M., Amari, S.i.: Dynamical analysis of contrastive divergence learning: restricted Boltzmann machines with Gaussian visible units. Neural Netw. **79**, 78–87 (2016). https://doi.org/10.1016/j.neunet.2016.03.013
7. Kingma, D.P., Ba, J.: Adam: a method for stochastic optimization. arXiv preprint arXiv:1412.6980 (2014)
8. Oja, E.: Simplified neuron model as a principal component analyzer. J. Math. Biol. **15**(3), 267–273 (1982). https://doi.org/10.1007/BF00275687

Improving Weight Initialization of ReLU and Output Layers

Diego Aguirre(✉) and Olac Fuentes

University of Texas at El Paso, El Paso, TX 79968, USA
{daguirre6,ofuentes}@utep.edu

Abstract. We introduce a data-dependent weight initialization scheme for ReLU and output layers commonly found in modern neural network architectures. An initial feedforward pass through the network is performed using an initialization set (a subset of the training data set). Using statistics obtained from this pass, we initialize the weights of the network, so the following properties are met: (1) weight matrices are orthogonal; (2) ReLU layers produce a predetermined fraction of nonzero activations; (3) the outputs produced by internal layers have a predetermined variance; (4) weights in the last layer are chosen to minimize the squared error in the initialization set. We evaluate our method on popular architectures (VGG16, VGG19, and InceptionV3) and faster convergence rates are achieved on the ImageNet data set when compared to state-of-the-art initialization techniques (LSUV, He, and Glorot).

Keyword: Weight initialization

1 Introduction

Because of its success solving challenging problems, deep learning has become a very active area of research. Throughout the years, techniques to train and improve the quality of these models have been presented. The research community has been aggressively pushing the sate-of-the-art by developing new architectures, regularization techniques, and more efficient and effective optimization algorithms. New resources, such as powerful GPUs, have allowed us to train and use deeper networks that are currently the only solution we have to tackle challenging problems.

In recent years, the research community has put a strong emphasis in developing new network architectures [8,9,19,19,23] and regularization techniques [10,17,21,22]. Relatively little attention has been given to weight initialization. This might be explained by the increasing number of decisions that have to be made during the architecture design phase. To name a few, the deep learning practitioner has to determine the number of hidden layers in the network, the number of units per layer, the type of layers, the cost function, the optimization algorithm, and an appropriate selection of regularization techniques. With so many decisions to be made, selecting the initial weights of the network may,

I. V. Tetko et al. (Eds.): ICANN 2019, LNCS 11728, pp. 170–184, 2019.
https://doi.org/10.1007/978-3-030-30484-3_15

at first glance, seem like a minor detail. However, weight initialization is an important step that has a strong impact on the training time of a network and the quality of the resulting model. In fact, improper weight initialization can prevent gradient descent from converging [7].

Many researchers pre-train their models on other data sets (such as ImageNet) due to their large size. The reasoning behind this practice is that the first layers in the network learn to perform feature-extraction tasks that are useful for many similar problems. Thus, pre-training a model on a large data set allows the network to learn robust feature extraction mechanisms that then serve as the initial weights of the network when training it on the original task's data set. Doing this has shown to work well in practice. However, He et al. [6] show that, although ImageNet pre-training speeds up convergence early in training, doing this does not necessarily help the resulting model generalize or perform better.

In the following sections, we present a taxonomy of weight initialization techniques, and survey the most representative examples in each category. We also present a novel weight initialization technique that achieves better convergence rates when compared to other modern weight initialization schemes. This new scheme uses an initialization set extracted from the training data to initialize the weights in such a way that the following desirable properties are attained:

- The weight vectors associated to different units in the same layer are orthogonal, allowing to decouple the behavior of individual units.
- ReLU layers produce a predetermined fraction of non-zero activations, which prevents dead units or units that have linear behavior.
- The outputs produced by each internal layer have a predetermined constant variance, preventing vanishing or exploding gradients.
- Weights in the last layer are chosen to minimize the error in the initialization set, which starts the optimization process in a good region of the search space.

We present experiments using modern deep learning architectures (VGG16 [16], VGG19 [16], and InceptionV3 [20]) applied to the ImageNet [4] data set. We compare our algorithm with three state-of-the-art initialization techniques and show that it provides faster convergence.

2 Weight Initialization Techniques

Weight initialization techniques can be divided into three main groups: *Data Independent*, *Data Dependent*, and *Pre-Training* approaches, depending on the amount of information derived from available data.

Data Independent Weight Initialization Techniques. Techniques in this category are the ones that do not make use of any training data to determine the initial parameter values of a network. They usually work by sampling numbers from a normal/uniform distribution and using such numbers as the initial values of the network's parameters. Multiple heuristics have been proposed to select the variance and mean when a normal distribution is used, or the minimum and maximum values when sampling from a uniform distribution. A simple and commonly-used heuristic consists of using a normal distribution with zero mean and unit variance. However, this often leads to poor convergence in deep networks, as it makes the variances in the activations of hidden units increase with depth. Glorot et al. [5] propose to use a standard deviation of $\sqrt{\frac{2}{n_{in}+n_{out}}}$ to initialize linear layers, where n_{in} is the number of inputs the layer is fed and n_{out} is the number of outputs it produces. The idea behind this method is to try to keep the variance of the input gradient and the output gradient the same by initializing the weights to numbers that are not *too small* nor *too big*. A similar analysis was performed by He et al. [7] for ReLU activations. He et al. show that Glorot's initialization does not work well for ReLU layers, and empirically demonstrates it building a 30-layer network that converges under He Initialization, but not under Glorot's. In this approach, a variance of $Var(W_i) = 2/n_{in}$ is used for ReLU layers.

Data Dependent Weight Initialization Techniques. While Glorot and He initializations make reasonable assumptions about the input data, other techniques explicitly exploit available training data to initialize the network's weights. An example is the layer-sequential unit-variance (LSUV) initialization scheme proposed by Mishkin et al. [12]. In this approach, weights are pre-initialized using orthonormal matrices. Then, an initialization set is extracted from the training data and used in an iterative process where the weights of a layer are updated until unit variance in the layer's activations is obtained. At each iteration, the layer's activations are calculated using the initialization set and the layer's weights are updated by dividing them over the activations' standard deviation.

LSUV initialization was tested on different architectures, and the results showed that it allows for the training of very deep networks using standard gradient descent. The overhead added is minimal since running this scheme is equivalent to processing a single mini-batch, which is done thousands of times when training deep neural networks. LSUV initialization works well with multiple activation functions (such as linear, ReLU, maxout, etc.), and outperforms more sophisticated systems such as FitNets [13]. Mishkin et al. also show that LSUV reduces the need for batch normalization [10].

Another data-dependent scheme used within a larger, more elaborate process is *Weight Normalization (WN)* [14]. WN is a weight reparameterization process that allows gradient descent to converge more rapidly. This is done by reparameterizing each neuron's weight vector w in terms of another vector v and a scalar parameter g as follows:

$$w = \frac{\mathrm{g}}{||v||} v$$

The idea is to perform stochastic gradient descent on v and g directly. This reparameterization step has the effect of forcing the Euclidean norm of the weight vector w to be g. To properly initialize g, v, and the biases b, Salimans et al. propose to use a data dependent approach. Based on their experiments, Salimans et al. propose to sample elements of v from a normal distribution with 0 mean and a standard deviation of 0.05. To initialize a neuron's g and b parameters, they propose to use an initialization set X, and perform an initial feedforward pass through the network, where each neuron computes the following:

$$\mathrm{y}_{\mathrm{pre}} = \frac{v \cdot x}{||v||} \qquad \mathrm{y} = f(\frac{\mathrm{y}_{\mathrm{pre}} - \mu(\mathrm{y}_{\mathrm{pre}})}{\sigma(\mathrm{y}_{\mathrm{pre}})})$$

To fix the initialization set statistics of all pre-activations $\mathrm{y}_{\mathrm{pre}}$ in the batch, parameters b and g are initialized as follows:

$$\mathrm{g} = \frac{1}{\sigma(\mathrm{y}_{\mathrm{pre}})} \qquad \mathrm{b} = \frac{-\mu(\mathrm{y}_{\mathrm{pre}})}{\sigma(\mathrm{y}_{\mathrm{pre}})}$$

To test the performance of this technique, WN was applied to four different models covering applications in image recognition, generative modelling, and deep reinforcement learning. In all cases, WN showed a faster convergence rate.

Pre-training Weight Initialization Techniques. Weight initialization techniques in this category usually start by initializing the weights randomly and pre-train the network on another task. An example of this is training the model using a large data set (like ImageNet) before using the task's data to fine-tune parameter values. Another example of this type of techniques is presented by Sudowe et al. [18]. Sudowe et al. propose to collect large amounts of unlabeled data and use it to pretrain the network in a self-supervised way. The artificial task they created to pretrain an image classification network is called *Patch Task*, and it is described as follows. Given a patch of pixels extracted from the input, the model is trained to predict its origin out of k possible locations in the original image. The original image is divided into k locations, where each location is a discrete position within the image. Thus, the task is similar to solving a jigsaw puzzle with only one piece missing.

Once the network is trained on this artificial task, the weights are reused when training the network to solve its primary task. When evaluated, it was shown that this method outperforms traditional random initialization and closely matches reusing weight matrices obtained training on the ImageNet dataset.

3 Proposed Initialization Scheme

3.1 Initialization of ReLU Layers

Like Mishkin et al. [12], we also propose to initialize the parameters of layers using orthonormal matrices, and force the output of a layer to have a predetermined standard deviation s using an initialization set. The innovation in our approach is the incorporation of a hyperparameter called the *active fraction* (f) that allows the deep learning practitioner to specify how likely it should be for a unit in a ReLU layer to produce non-zero activation. Our scheme can be seen as a three-step process: (1) Orthogonalization, (2) ReLU Adaptation, and (3) Standarization. The following subsections describe each of the steps.

Orthogonalization Step. An adequate initialization scheme should try to exploit the representational capacity of a network. To accomplish this, we initialize the units/filters of a layer using weight vectors that are orthogonal to each other, as described by Saxe et al. in [15].

ReLU Adaptation Step. The ReLU activation function has shown to be a very effective and easy way to introduce non-linearity in a network [3]. Due to their strong performance, ReLU layers and their variations (leaky ReLU, parametric ReLU, etc.) are very common in modern deep learning architectures. We propose to incorporate a hyperparameter called the *active fraction* f that can be used to determine how likely it is for a ReLU unit to produce a non-zero value.

To accomplish this, an initialization set of size n is fed to the network to compute the layer's output before the ReLU operation is applied. Let H be the pre-ReLU activation tensor, where $H_{i,j}$ is the output for instance i and unit j. To obtain the desired behavior, b_j, the bias for unit j must be equal to minus the $\lfloor(1-f)n\rfloor$-th order statistic of column j of H.[1]

Standarization Step. Mishkin et al. [12] propose to initialize the weights of a layer in such a way that the activations produced by the layer have unit variance. We build on this idea by incorporating a hyperparameter s that allows the deep learning practitioner to specify the desired standard deviation of a layer's activations. We do this by computing the layer's output after the ReLU operation is applied using the initialization set. We divide the weight and biases tensors by the corresponding standard deviation of the produced output and multiply that by s.

3.2 Initialization of Output Layers

To initialize the output layer(s) of the network, we also feed an initialization set to the network and compute the output H produced by the last hidden layer. If the network's output is $Y' = HW$, we propose to initialize W by setting it to H^*Y, where Y is the network's expected output for the initialization set and H^* is the pseudo-inverse of H. If softmax is used, we replace Y with the corresponding logits the network is to produce. In essence, we are computing the best least-squares solution to $Y = HW$.

[1] In practice, we find the kth statistic by sorting the columns of H, but a slightly faster $(O(n))$ vs. $(O(n \log n))$ implementation is possible using *quickselect*.

Algorithm 1 shows the complete weight initialization algorithm. The input X, Y represent the intialization set, h is a vector containing the layer sizes (where h_0 is the dimensionality of the input), f is the active fraction and σ_g is the desired standard deviation for all hidden units. Notice that the pseudocode assumes all layers are fully-connected, but the same initialization scheme can be applied to any layer that uses the ReLU function.

Algorithm 1. Weight Initialization

```
procedure INITIALIZE(X, Y, h, f, σ_g)
    H^(0) ← X
    n ← len (h)
    for i = 1 to n do
        W^(i) ← randn(0, 1)_[h_{i-1} × h_i]        ▷ random matrix of size h_{i-1} × h_i
        W^(i) ← Orthonormalization(W^(i))          ▷ orthogonalize
        P ← H^(i-1) W^(i)
        P ← sort(P)                                ▷ sort each column of P in ascending order
        b^(i) ← −P[⌊(1 − f)h_i⌋]
        s = σ(P)                                   ▷ vector of column-wise standard deviations
                                                   ▷ Scale weights and bias to obtain σ_g standard deviation
        for j = 1 to h_i do
            W^(i)_[:,j] ← W^(i)_[:,j] σ_g / s_j
            b^(i) ← b^(i)_j σ_g / s_j
        H^(i) ← relu(H^(i-1) W^(i) + b^(i))
    W^(n) ← (H^(n))^* Y
    b^(n) ← 0
    return W^(1), ..., W^(n), b^(1), ..., b^(n)
```

3.3 Overhead

Our initialization technique adds operations that are not performed by standard weight initialization schemes. To analyze this overhead, we need to consider the running time of: (1) the feed-forward pass performed on the initialization set; (2) the creation of orthonormal weight matrices; (3) the algorithm used to find the kth statistic in every column of activation matrices; (4) the operations performed on weight values to produce the predetermined goal standard deviation; and (5) the algorithm used to compute the pseudo-inverse necessary for the initialization of the output layer.

The size of the initialization set is considerably smaller than the size of the complete training set. In our experiments, we set the size of the initialization set to be about 4% of the size of the complete training set. Thus, the cost of the feed-forward pass performed on the initialization set is a small fraction of the time it takes to complete a full epoch. Generating orthonormal matrices using the approach described in [15] requires computing the singular value decomposition (SVD) of each weight matrix in the network. The running time of this is $O(min(h_i h_{i+1}^2, h_{i+1} h_i^2))$, where h_i represents the number of units in layer i. Finding the kth statistic in every column of activation matrices can be done using *quickselect*, which runs in $O(n)$, where n (in our context) is the size of the initialization set. To produce the goal standard deviation, we first compute the standard deviation of the activations of a given unit, which takes $O(n)$, where n is the size of the initialization set. Once this is done, every weight is divided by this value and multiplied by the goal standard deviation. This steps takes $O(n)$, where n is the number of inputs the unit receives. Finally, the cost of initializing the output layer is determined by the time it takes to compute the Moore-Penrose inverse, which is dominated by the cost of computing the SVD of the activation matrix of the last hidden layer. As previously stated, the running time of performing this operation is $O(min(mn^2, nm^2))$ for an m-*by*-n matrix. In our context, n is the number of samples in the initialization set, and m is the number of units in the last hidden layer. Thus, for $n > m$, the initialization process takes time $O(n)$ with constant factors depending on the network's architecture.

Empirically, we observed that the running time of the initialization process is about 3 to 6 times of that of processing a training mini-batch of the same size as the initialization set.

4 Experimental Results

We designed two sets of experiments. The purpose of the first set was to analyze how the performance of our method is affected by its hyperparameters. In the second set, we compared our method to popular weight initialization techniques, including Glorot, He, and LSUV. The following subsections describe in detail the evaluation process of each set of experiments.

Table 1. Hyperparameter values

Hyperparameter	Values
Initialization set size	128, 256, 512, 1024, 2048
Active fraction	0.1, 0.2, 0.3, 0.4, 0.5, 0.6, 0.7, 0.8, 0.9
Learning rate	0.01, 0.001, 0.0001
Goal standard deviation	0.1, 0.2, 0.3, 0.4, 0.5, 0.6, 0.7, 0.8, 0.9, 1.0, 1.1, 1.2, 1.3, 1.4, 1.5, 1.6, 1.7, 1.8, 1.9, 2.0, 2.1, 2.2, 2.3, 2.4, 2.5, 2.6, 2.7, 2.8, 2.9, 3.0

4.1 Hyperparameter Evaluation

We were mostly interested in understating how the learning rate, the size of the initialization set, and the active fraction hyperparameters affect the performance of our technique. To accomplish this, we constructed a small convolutional neural network and used our approach to initialize it multiple times using different hyperparameter values. After initialization, the network was trained for 50 epochs using gradient descent and categorical crossentropy as the loss function. We used a mini-batch size of 128 and used the CIFAR10/100 [11] data sets. We exhaustively ran experiments using all combinations of hyperparameter values as defined in Table 1. The architecture of the convolutional network is described in Table 2. All convolutional layers are composed of 3 × 3 filters with a stride of 1.

Table 2. Convolutional neural network architecture

Layer #	Type	Properties
1	Convolutional 2D - ReLU	Number of filters: 32
2	Convolutional 2D - ReLU	Number of filters: 32
3	MaxPooling 2D	Pool size: 2 × 2
4	Dropout	Rate = 0.25
5	Convolutional 2D - ReLU	Number of filters: 64
6	Convolutional 2D - ReLU	Number of filters: 64
7	MaxPooling 2D	Pool size: 2 × 2
8	Dropout	Rate: 0.50
9	Dense - ReLU	Number of units: 512
10	Dropout	Rate: 0.50
11	Softmax	

Initialization Set Size Results. Due to the large number of conducted experiments, Table 3 only presents a subset of them. We kept the results where the learning rate, the active fraction, and goal standard deviation were set to 0.01, 0.8, and 1.0, respectively, as they are representative of the behavior observed with other hyperparameter values. We also only show the results obtained using CIFAR100 as they are very similar to the ones obtained using CIFAR10.

Table 3. CIFAR100 - Initialization set results

Initialization set size	Loss after initialization	Test accuracy after initialization	Loss after 1 epoch	Test accuracy after 1 epoch	Loss after 50 epochs	Test accuracy after 50 epochs
128	4.535	0.043	4.059	0.088	2.180	0.431
256	4.566	0.041	4.396	0.042	2.287	0.4083
512	14.872	0.010	15.956	0.01	15.956	0.01
1024	4.479	0.065	4.459	0.033	2.254	0.412
2048	**4.410**	**0.110**	**4.050**	**0.104**	**2.132**	**0.439**

The results show that, as expected, larger initialization set sizes produce better initial accuracies and lower loss values. However, this behavior is not monotonic; when the initialization set size is exactly the same as the number of neurons in the last hidden layer, performance is extremely poor. This is due to the way the Moore-Penrose pseudo-inverse is computed. When we have more instances in the set than units in the layer, the algorithm solves an over-determined system of equations. When this happens, the pseudo-inverse algorithm finds the least-squares fit solution. If we have more units than examples in the set and thus deal with an underdetermined system of equations, the pseudo-inverse algorithm finds a solution that minimizes the L2 norm of the solution variables. In both cases, the pseudo-inverse algorithm has a regularizing effect on the weight values. If the number of examples in the set is the same as the number of units, the matrix is square and (usually) invertible, thus the solution overfits the initialization set and does not have any regularization effect on the weights, which leads to poor generalization.

Active Fraction Results. Table 4 (CIFAR100) only shows a subset of the results as well. We kept the results where the learning rate, initialization set size, and goal standard deviation were set to 0.001, 2048, and 1.0, respectively. The results suggest that a value between 0.6 and 0.9 should be used. We say that ReLU units *die* when pushed into a state where they no longer produce a non-zero value. We speculate that a higher active fraction allows ReLU units to become active most of the time, preventing them from dying as the training process occurs while still introducing non-linearity into the network.

Table 4. CIFAR100 - Active fraction results

Active fraction	Loss after initialization	Test accuracy after initialization	Loss after 1 epoch	Test accuracy after 1 epoch	Loss after 50 epochs	Test accuracy after 50 epochs
0.1	4.674	0.026	4.593	0.018	4.572	0.027
0.2	4.521	0.052	4.564	0.035	4.342	0.075
0.3	4.476	0.067	4.537	0.049	3.996	0.122
0.4	4.452	0.084	4.514	0.057	3.649	0.164
0.5	4.448	0.093	4.494	**0.071**	3.502	0.188
0.6	4.436	0.099	**4.483**	0.063	3.392	0.205
0.7	**4.419**	**0.108**	4.495	0.046	3.313	0.215
0.8	4.420	0.106	4.504	0.042	**3.296**	**0.218**
0.9	4.438	0.098	4.498	0.049	3.320	0.213

Table 5. CIFAR100 - Learning rate results

Learning Rate	Loss after initialization	Test Accuracy after initialization	Loss after 1 epoch	Test Accuracy after 1 epoch	Loss after 50 epochs	Test Accuracy after 50 epochs
0.01	4.410	0.110	**4.050**	**0.104**	**2.132**	**0.439**
0.001	4.410	0.110	4.504	0.042	3.296	0.218
0.0001	4.410	0.110	4.464	0.064	4.231	0.079

Learning Rate Results. For Table 5, we kept the results where the active fraction, initialization set size, and goal standard deviation were set to 0.8, 2048, and 1.0, respectively. The results suggest that a large learning rate should be used with our approach. We hypothesize that gradient values are small when using our approach, as our weights are chosen to minimize the network's initial loss value. Therefore, a large learning rate is favored.

Table 6. CIFAR100 - Standard deviation results

Goal standard deviation	Loss after initialization	Test accuracy after initialization	Loss after 1 epoch	Test accuracy after 1 epoch	Loss after 50 epochs	Test accuracy after 50 epochs
0.1	4.418	0.109	4.438	0.053	2.487	0.385
0.2	4.425	0.104	4.392	0.071	2.356	0.396
0.3	4.414	0.108	4.341	0.081	2.304	0.408
0.4	4.432	0.105	4.329	0.075	2.270	0.410
0.5	4.425	0.105	4.274	0.062	2.226	0.418
0.6	4.412	0.110	4.200	0.090	2.166	0.438
0.7	4.422	0.110	4.194	0.087	2.233	0.420
0.8	4.421	0.107	4.148	0.085	2.237	0.421
0.9	4.419	0.108	4.075	0.101	2.167	0.434
1.0	4.426	0.109	4.110	0.087	2.227	0.423
1.1	4.419	0.112	3.992	0.109	2.185	0.433
1.2	4.425	0.111	3.959	0.112	2.132	0.445
1.3	4.418	0.109	3.925	0.106	2.192	0.429
1.4	4.426	0.104	3.916	0.111	2.160	0.436
1.5	**4.411**	**0.119**	3.861	0.123	2.192	0.432
1.6	4.424	0.107	3.872	0.122	2.176	0.432
1.7	4.422	0.108	3.853	0.116	**2.126**	**0.448**
1.8	4.417	0.108	3.830	0.120	2.131	0.441
1.9	4.420	0.109	3.814	0.120	2.152	0.436
2.0	4.422	0.110	3.796	0.127	2.176	0.432
2.1	4.416	0.110	3.782	0.129	2.192	0.426
2.2	4.414	0.111	3.760	0.129	2.130	0.438
2.3	4.428	0.107	3.815	0.126	2.144	0.443
2.4	4.420	0.108	3.815	0.122	2.210	0.426
2.5	4.420	0.110	**3.737**	**0.136**	2.148	0.437
2.6	4.417	0.109	3.843	0.122	2.140	0.441
2.7	4.419	0.105	3.764	0.128	2.135	0.446
2.8	4.421	0.108	3.806	0.127	2.187	0.429
2.9	4.425	0.106	3.864	0.118	2.188	0.429
3.0	4.414	0.110	3.751	0.126	2.159	0.436

Standard Deviation Results. For Table 5, we kept the results where the active fraction was set to 0.8, the initialization set size was 2048, and the learning rate was kept constant at 0.01. The results, presented in Table 6, are very similar across all standard deviation values. We tried values distant from 1, such as 0.1, 0.001, 10, and 100, and we observed significantly worse performance. We conclude that a value between 0.8 and 3 is appropriate. The complete set of results is publicly available online [2].

4.2 Other Initialization Techniques

Table 7. VGG16 - ImageNet - Initialization and one epoch results

Learning rate	Initialization method	Loss after initialization	Test accuracy after initialization	Loss after 1 epoch	Test accuracy after 1 epoch
0.1	Ours	**6.884**	**0.008**	16.096	0.001
0.1	LSUV	7.400	0.001	16.099	0.001
0.1	Glorot	6.910	0.001	**6.910**	0.001
0.1	He	7.389	0.001	16.099	0.001
0.01	Ours	**6.884**	**0.008**	**3.915**	**0.233**
0.01	LSUV	7.400	0.001	4.043	0.205
0.01	Glorot	6.910	0.001	6.654	0.006
0.01	He	7.389	0.001	4.000	0.218
0.001	Ours	**6.884**	**0.008**	**4.519**	**0.156**
0.001	LSUV	7.400	0.001	5.243	0.088
0.001	Glorot	6.910	0.001	6.909	0.001
0.001	He	7.389	0.001	5.144	0.098
0.0001	Ours	**6.884**	**0.008**	**5.325**	**0.086**
0.0001	LSUV	7.400	0.001	6.201	0.029
0.0001	Glorot	6.910	0.001	6.909	0.001
0.0001	He	7.389	0.001	6.395	0.018

We compared our method to the following state-of-the-art initialization techniques: Glorot, He, and LSUV. We tested all initialization schemes on the following model architectures: VGG16, VGG19, and InceptionV3. We used ImageNet for all experiments with images resized to 256 × 256. When using our initialization approach, we used an initialization set of size 256 for hidden layers, an initialization set of size 8192 for the output layers, a value of 0.8 for the *active fraction* hyperparameter, and a goal standard deviation (s) of 1.0. For LSUV, we also used an initialization set of size 256 for hidden layers, and an initialization set of size 8192 for the output layers. We only trained the models for 1 epoch

Table 8. VGG19 - ImageNet - Initialization and one epoch results

Learning rate	Initialization method	Loss after initialization	Test accuracy after initialization	Loss after 1 epoch	Test accuracy after 1 epoch
0.1	Ours	**6.888**	**0.006**	16.102	0.001
0.1	LSUV	7.430	0.001	16.105	0.001
0.1	Glorot	6.910	0.001	**6.910**	0.001
0.1	He	7.238	0.001	16.102	0.001
0.01	Ours	**6.888**	**0.006**	**3.828**	**0.232**
0.01	LSUV	7.430	0.001	4.068	0.206
0.01	Glorot	6.910	0.001	6.909	0.001
0.01	He	7.238	0.001	4.138	0.196
0.001	Ours	**6.888**	**0.006**	**4.487**	**0.159**
0.001	LSUV	7.430	0.001	5.120	0.095
0.001	Glorot	6.910	0.001	6.909	0.001
0.001	He	7.238	0.001	5.179	0.092
0.0001	Ours	**6.888**	**0.006**	**5.269**	**0.090**
0.0001	LSUV	7.430	0.001	6.162	0.026
0.0001	Glorot	6.910	0.001	6.909	0.001
0.0001	He	7.238	0.001	6.232	0.026

as we were mostly interested in comparing the strategies in the early stages of the training process. Because we know that the learning rate plays an important role, we repeated the experiments with the following learning rates: 0.1, 0.01, 0.001, and 0.0001.

Tables 7, 8, and 9 present the test loss and test accuracy after initialization (but before training) and after one epoch of training tested on the above-mentioned models and initialization schemes.

We also trained VGG16 on ImageNet for 10 epochs using all initialization techniques to analyze how these methods compare as the training process advances. We used a learning rate of 0.01, a mini batch size of 32, regular stochastic gradient descent, and categorical crossentropy as the loss function. Figure 1 shows the accuracy achieved on the test set after every training epoch.

Our experiments confirm the results obtained by He et al. [7]. Glorot initialization does not work well with ReLU layers. It consistently performs worse than the rest of the techniques. Our results also show that our method initializes the network in a desirable area in the parameter space; where the initial test accuracy is high and the loss is low. In all experiments, our method outperformed the other techniques in both loss and test set accuracy. We also observed better accuracies as the training process advanced. Our code is freely available in our GitHub repository [1].

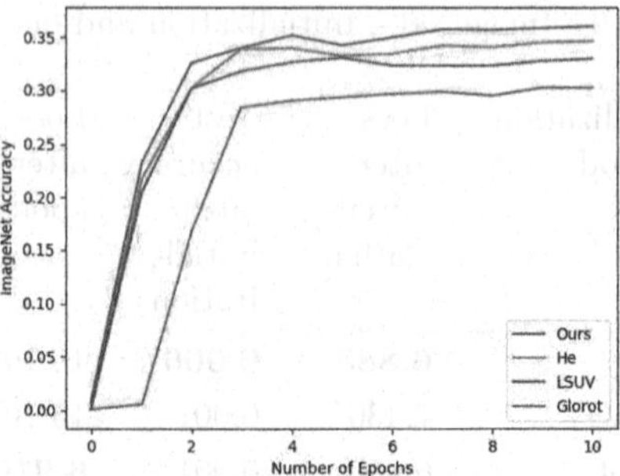

Fig. 1. VGG16 - ImageNet - 10 training epochs results

Table 9. InceptionV3 - ImageNet - Initialization and one epoch results

Learning rate	Initialization method	Loss after initial-ization	Test accuracy after initial-ization	Loss after 1 epoch	Test accuracy after 1 epoch
0.1	Ours	**6.875**	**0.016**	**2.744**	**0.407**
0.1	LSUV	7.430	0.001	3.060	0.355
0.1	Glorot	6.911	0.001	2.986	0.372
0.1	He	7.160	0.001	2.977	0.367
0.01	Ours	**6.875**	**0.016**	**3.326**	**0.300**
0.01	LSUV	7.430	0.001	3.904	0.222
0.01	Glorot	6.911	0.001	3.677	0.251
0.01	He	7.160	0.001	4.000	0.206
0.001	Ours	**6.875**	**0.016**	**5.302**	**0.072**
0.001	LSUV	7.430	0.001	5.891	0.036
0.001	Glorot	6.911	0.001	5.803	0.039
0.001	He	7.160	0.001	11.605	0.002
0.0001	Ours	**6.875**	**0.016**	**6.799**	**0.007**
0.0001	LSUV	7.430	0.001	7.010	0.003
0.0001	Glorot	6.911	0.001	6.936	0.004
0.0001	He	7.160	0.001	7.277	0.001

5 Conclusion

In this paper, we propose a new weight initialization technique, where we use statistics obtained from a subset of the training set to initialize the network's weights. We used orthonormal vectors to initialize the units of a layer, and introduce a hyperparameter called *active fraction* that allows the deep learning practitioner to define a prior on the behavior of ReLU layers. Similar to LSUV, we also incorporate a weight standarization step, where we force the output of each layer to have a predetermined standard deviation. Lastly, we show that initializing the last layer using the Moore-Penrose pseudo-inverse of the representation produced by the last hidden layer introduces a regularizing effect on the weights while minimizing the initial loss value. Future work includes studying the behavior of our method in other domains beyond image classification, analyzing its behavior in relation to optimization algorithms that employ adaptive learning rates such as Adam and RMSprop, and extending it to work on recurrent networks.

References

1. Aguirre, D.: Weight initialization code repository (2019). https://github.com/aguirrediego/weight-initialization-relu-and-output-layers
2. Aguirre, D.: Weight initialization results (2019). http://bit.ly/2W3iEIr
3. Arora, R., Basu, A., Mianjy, P., Mukherjee, A.: Understanding deep neural networks with rectified linear units. arXiv preprint arXiv:1611.01491 (2016)
4. Deng, J., Dong, W., Socher, R., Li, L.J., Li, K., Fei-Fei, L.: ImageNet: a large-scale hierarchical image database. In: IEEE Conference on Computer Vision and Pattern Recognition, CVPR 2009, pp. 248–255. IEEE (2009). https://doi.org/10.1109/CVPR.2009.5206848
5. Glorot, X., Bengio, Y.: Understanding the difficulty of training deep feedforward neural networks. In: Proceedings of the Thirteenth International Conference on Artificial Intelligence and Statistics, pp. 249–256 (2010)
6. He, K., Girshick, R., Dollár, P.: Rethinking imagenet pre-training. arXiv preprint arXiv:1811.08883 (2018)
7. He, K., Zhang, X., Ren, S., Sun, J.: Delving deep into rectifiers: surpassing human-level performance on imagenet classification. In: Proceedings of the IEEE International Conference on Computer Vision, pp. 1026–1034 (2015). https://doi.org/10.1109/ICCV.2015.123
8. He, K., Zhang, X., Ren, S., Sun, J.: Deep residual learning for image recognition. In: Proceedings of the IEEE Conference on Computer Vision and Pattern Recognition, pp. 770–778 (2016). https://doi.org/10.1109/CVPR.2016.90
9. Hu, J., Shen, L., Sun, G.: Squeeze-and-excitation networks. arXiv preprint arXiv:1709.01507 (2017). https://doi.org/10.1109/CVPR.2018.00745
10. Ioffe, S., Szegedy, C.: Batch normalization: accelerating deep network training by reducing internal covariate shift. In: International Conference on Machine Learning, pp. 448–456 (2015)
11. Krizhevsky, A., Nair, V., Hinton, G.: The CIFAR-10 dataset. http://www.cs.toronto.edu/~kriz/cifar.html (2014)

12. Mishkin, D., Matas, J.: All you need is a good init. arXiv preprint arXiv:1511.06422 (2015)
13. Romero, A., Ballas, N., Kahou, S.E., Chassang, A., Gatta, C., Bengio, Y.: FitNets: hints for thin deep nets. arXiv preprint arXiv:1412.6550 (2014)
14. Salimans, T., Kingma, D.P.: Weight normalization: a simple reparameterization to accelerate training of deep neural networks. In: Advances in Neural Information Processing Systems, pp. 901–909 (2016)
15. Saxe, A.M., McClelland, J.L., Ganguli, S.: Exact solutions to the nonlinear dynamics of learning in deep linear neural networks. arXiv preprint arXiv:1312.6120 (2013)
16. Simonyan, K., Zisserman, A.: Very deep convolutional networks for large-scale image recognition. arXiv preprint arXiv:1409.1556 (2014)
17. Srivastava, N., Hinton, G., Krizhevsky, A., Sutskever, I., Salakhutdinov, R.: Dropout: a simple way to prevent neural networks from overfitting. J. Mach. Learn. Res. **15**(1), 1929–1958 (2014)
18. Sudowe, P., Leibe, B.: PatchIt: self-supervised network weight initialization for fine-grained recognition. In: BMVC (2016). https://doi.org/10.5244/C.30.75
19. Szegedy, C., Ioffe, S., Vanhoucke, V., Alemi, A.A.: Inception-v4, inception-ResNet and the impact of residual connections on learning. In: AAAI, vol. 4, p. 12 (2017)
20. Szegedy, C., Vanhoucke, V., Ioffe, S., Shlens, J., Wojna, Z.: Rethinking the inception architecture for computer vision. In: Proceedings of the IEEE Conference on Computer Vision and Pattern Recognition, pp. 2818–2826 (2016). https://doi.org/10.1109/CVPR.2016.308
21. Ulyanov, D., Vedaldi, A., Lempitsky, V.: Instance normalization: the missing ingredient for fast stylization. arXiv preprint arXiv:1607.08022 (2016)
22. Yamada, Y., Iwamura, M., Kise, K.: Shakedrop regularization. arXiv preprint arXiv:1802.02375 (2018)
23. Zoph, B., Vasudevan, V., Shlens, J., Le, Q.V.: Learning transferable architectures for scalable image recognition. In: Proceedings of the IEEE Conference on Computer Vision and Pattern Recognition, pp. 8697–8710 (2018). https://doi.org/10.1109/CVPR.2018.00907

Parameters Optimisation

Post-synaptic Potential Regularization Has Potential

Enzo Tartaglione(✉), Daniele Perlo, and Marco Grangetto

Computer Science Department, University of Torino, 10149 Turin, TO, Italy
{enzo.tartaglione,daniele.perlo,marco.grangetto}@unito.it

Abstract. Improving generalization is one of the main challenges for training deep neural networks on classification tasks. In particular, a number of techniques have been proposed, aiming to boost the performance on unseen data: from standard data augmentation techniques to the ℓ_2 regularization, dropout, batch normalization, entropy-driven SGD and many more.

In this work we propose an elegant, simple and principled approach: post-synaptic potential regularization (PSP). We tested this regularization on a number of different state-of-the-art scenarios. Empirical results show that PSP achieves a classification error comparable to more sophisticated learning strategies in the MNIST scenario, while improves the generalization compared to ℓ_2 regularization in deep architectures trained on CIFAR-10.

Keywords: Regularization · Generalization · Post-synaptic potential · Neural networks · Classification

1 Introduction

In the last few years artificial neural network (ANN) models received huge interest from the research community. In particular, their potential capability of solving complex tasks with extremely simple training strategies has been the initial spark, while convolutional neural networks (CNNs), capable of self-extracting relevant features from images, have been the fuel for the burning flame which is the research around ANNs. Furthermore, thanks to the ever-increasing computational capability of machines with the introduction of GPUs (and, recently, TPUs) in the simulation of neural networks, ANNs might be embedded in many portable devices and, potentially, used in everyday life.

State-of-the-art ANNs are able to learn very complex classification tasks: from the nowadays outdated MNIST [15], moving to CIFAR-10 and then even the ImageNet classification problem. In order to overcome the complexity of these learning tasks, extremely complex architectures have been proposed: some examples are VGG [22] and ResNet [10]. However, due to their extremely high number of parameters, these models are prone to over-fitting the data; hence,

I. V. Tetko et al. (Eds.): ICANN 2019, LNCS 11728, pp. 187–200, 2019.
https://doi.org/10.1007/978-3-030-30484-3_16

they are not able to generalize as they should. In this case, the simple learning strategies (like SGD) alone are no longer able to guarantee the network to learn the relevant features from the training set and other strategies need to be adopted.

In order to improve the generalization of ANNs, several approaches have been proposed. One of the most typical relies on the introduction of a "regularization" term, whose aim is to add an extra constraint to the overall objective function to be minimized. Recently, other approaches have been proposed: from the introduction of different optimizers [13] to data augmentation techniques, the proposal of new techniques like dropout [24] and even changing the basic architecture of the ANN [10].

In this work, we propose a regularization term inspired by a side effect of the ℓ_2 regularization (also known as *weight decay*) on the parameters. In particular, we are going to show that, naturally, weight decay makes the post-synaptic potential dropping to zero in ANN models. From this observation, a post-synaptic potential regularization (PSP) is here proposed. Differently from ℓ_2 regularization, its effect on the parameters is not local: parameters belonging to layers closer to the input feel the effect of the regularization on the forward layers. Hence, this regularization is aware of the configuration of the whole network and tunes the parameters using a global information and, unlike activation function research techniques [19], it is low-complexity. We show that the standard ℓ_2 regularization is a special case of the proposed regularizer as well. Empirically we show that, when compared to the standard weight decay regularization, PSP generalizes better.

The rest of this paper is organized as follows. In Sect. 2 we review some of the most relevant regularization techniques aiming at improving generalization. Next, in Sect. 3 we introduce our proposed regularization, starting from some simple considerations on the effect of the ℓ_2 regularization on the post synaptic potential and analyzing the potential effects on the learning dynamics. Then, in Sect. 4 we show some empirical results and some extra insights of the proposed regularization. Finally, in Sect. 5 the conclusions are drawn.

2 Related Work

Regularization is one of the key features a learning algorithm should particularly take care of in deep learning, in order to prevent data over-fit and boosting the generalization [8]. Even though such a concept is more general and older than the first ANN models [26], we are going to focus on what regularization for deep architectures (trained on finite datasets via supervised learning) is. We can divide the regularization strategies in our context under four main categories [14]:

- regularization via *data*: some examples include (but are not limited to) the introduction of gaussian noise to the input [7], dropout to the input [24], data augmentation [1,4] and batch normalization [11].
- regularization via *network architecture*: in this case, the architecture is properly selected in order to fit the particular dataset we are aiming to train. It can

involve the choice of single layers (pooling, convolutional [15], dropout [24]), it can involve the insertion of entire blocks (residual blocks [10]), the entire structure can be designed on-purpose [2,5,9] or even pruned [25,29]. Recently, an empirical study on new activation functions has been proposed [19]. Ramachandran *et al.* proposed a search technique to investigate the performance over a combination of activation functions. Its outcome is the best-fitting activation function for the training problem, according to the ANN architecture used. Recently, it was shown that models with multiple outputs and shared layers may also act as a regularizing technique [20].
- regularization via *optimization*: an optimizer can determine the nature of the local minima and avoid "bad" local minima (if any [12]), boosting the generalization [3,13]. The initialization also seemed to cover an important role [6], together with early-stopping [18] techniques.
- regularization via *regularization term*: here a regularization term is added to the loss, and a global objective function is minimized. This will be the scope of our work.

One of the ground-breaking regularization techniques, proposed few years ago, is *dropout*. Srivastava *et al.* [24] proposed, during the training process, to stochastically set a part of the activations in an ANN to zero according to an a-priori set dropout probability. Empirically it was observed that, applying dropout on a fully-connected architecture, was significantly improving the generalization, while its effectiveness was less evident in convolutional architectures. Such a technique, however, typically requires a longer training time, and sometimes a proper choice of the dropout probability may change the effectiveness of the technique. However, dropout has many variants aiming to the same goal: one of the most used is dropconnect by Wan *et al.* [28].

A completely different approach to boost the generalization is to focus the attention on some regions of the loss functions. It has been suggested by Lin *et al.* [16] that "sharp" minima of the loss function does not generalize as well as "wide" minima. According to this, the design of an optimizer which does not remain stuck in sharp minima helps in the generalization. Towards this end, some optimizers like SGD or Adam [13] are already implicitly looking for these kind of solutions. Recently, a specially-purposed optimizer, *Entropy-SGD*, designed by Chaudhari *et al.* [3], showed good generalization results. However, more sophisticated optimizers increase the computational complexity significantly.

A regularization technique, proposed about 30 years ago by Weigend *et al.* and just recently re-discovered, is *weight elimination* [29]: a penalty term is added to the loss function and the total objective function is minimized. The aim of the regularization term is here to estimate the "complexity" of the model, which is minimized together with the loss function. The learning complexity for an object increases with its number of parameters: there should exist an optimal number of parameters (or, in other words, configuration) for any given classification problem. Supporting this view, while using their *sensitivity-driven regularization* [25] aiming to sparsify deep models, Tartaglione *et al.* observed an improvement of the generalization for low compression ratios.

Any of the proposed regularization techniques, however, is typically used jointly with the ℓ_2 regularization. Such a technique is broadly used during most of the ANN trainings and, despite its simple formulation, under a wide range of different scenarios, it improves the generalization. Furthermore, many recent works suggest that there is a correspondence between ℓ_2 regularization and other techniques: for example, Wager *et al.* [27] showed an equivalence between dropout and weight decay. Is there something else to understand about ℓ_2 regularization? What's under the hood? This will be our starting point, to be discussed more in details in Sect. 3.2.

3 Post-synaptic Potential Regularization

In this section we first analyze the effect of weight decay on the output of any neuron in an ANN model. We show that ℓ_2 regularization makes the post-synaptic potential drop to zero. Hence, a regularization over the post-synaptic potential is formulated (PSP). Next, the parameters update term is derived and some considerations for multi-layer architectures are drawn. Finally, we show the concrete effect of post-synaptic potential regularization on both the output of a single neuron and its parameters.

3.1 Notation

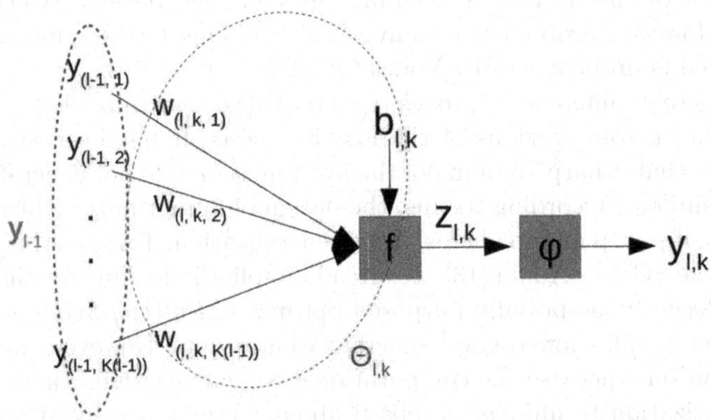

Fig. 1. Representation of the k-th neuron of the l-th layer of an ANN. The input $\mathbf{y}_{l-1}$ is weighted by the parameters $\Theta_{l,k}$, passes through some affine function $f(\cdot)$ producing the post-synaptic potential $z_{l,k}$ which is fed to the activation function $\varphi(\cdot)$, producing the output $y_{l,k}$

In this section we introduce the notation to be used in the rest of this work. Let us assume we work with an acyclic, multi-layer artificial neural network composed of N layers, where layer $l = 0$ is the input layer and $l = N$ the output layer. The ensemble of all the trained parameters in the ANN will be indicated as $\mathbf{\Theta}$. Each of the l layers is made of K_l neurons (or filters for convolutional layers). Hence, the k-th neuron ($k \in [1, K_l]$) in the l-th layer has:

- $y_{l,k}$ as its own output.
- $\mathbf{y}_{l-1}$ as input vector.
- $\theta_{l,k}$ as its own parameters: $\mathbf{w}_{l,k}$ are the weights (from which we identify the j-th as $w_{l,k,j}$) and $b_{l,k}$ is the bias.

Each of the neurons has its own activation function $\varphi_{l,k}(\cdot)$ to be applied after some affine function $f_{l,k}(\cdot)$ which can be convolution, dot product, adding residual blocks, batch normalization or any combination of them. Hence, the output of a neuron can be expressed by

$$y_{l,k} = \varphi_{l,k}\left[f_{l,k}\left(\theta_{l,k}, \mathbf{y}_{l-1}\right)\right] \tag{1}$$

We can simplify (1) if we define the *post-synaptic potential* (or equivalently, the pre-activation potential) $z_{l,k}$ as

$$z_{l,k} = f_{l,k}\left(\theta_{l,k}, \mathbf{y}_{l-1}\right) \tag{2}$$

As we are going to see, the post-synaptic potential will be central in our method and analysis and encloses the true essence of the proposed regularization strategy. A summary of the introduced notation is graphically represented in Fig. 1.

3.2 Effect of Weight Decay on the Post-synaptic Potential

Most of the learning strategies use the well-known ℓ_2 regularization term

$$R_{\ell_2}(\mathbf{\Theta}) = \frac{1}{2}\sum_l\sum_k\sum_j \theta^2_{l,k,j} \tag{3}$$

Equation (3) is minimized together with the loss function $L(\cdot)$; hence, the overall minimized function is

$$J(\mathbf{\Theta}, \hat{\mathbf{y}}) = \eta L(\mathbf{\Theta}, \hat{\mathbf{y}}) + \lambda R_{\ell_2}(\mathbf{\Theta}) \tag{4}$$

where $\hat{\mathbf{y}}$ is the desired output and η, λ are positive real numbers, and commonly in range $(0, 1)$. All the update contributions are computed using the standard back-propagation strategy. Let us focus here, for sake of simplicity, on the regularization term (3). Minimizing it corresponds to adopt the commonly named *weight decay* strategy for which we have the following update rule:

$$\theta^{t+1}_{l,k,j} := (1-\lambda)\theta^t_{l,k,j} \tag{5}$$

This generates a perturbation of the output for the corresponding neuron resulting in a perturbation of the post-synaptic potential:

$$\Delta z_{l,k} = z_{l,k}^{t+1} - z_{l,k}^{t} \tag{6}$$

How does the ℓ_2 regularization affect $z_{l,k}$?

Clearly, minimizing (3) means that $\theta_{l,k,j} \rightarrow 0 \forall l,k,j$. Now, if we have an input pattern for our network $\mathbf{y}_0$, it is straightforward, according to (2) and (5), that $z_{l,k} \rightarrow 0$, as all the parameters will be zero.

Under this assumption, we can say that the weight decay strategy implicitly aims to focus on peculiar regions of the mostly-used activation functions: in the case we use *sigmoid* or *hyperbolic tangent*, we have the maximum value for the derivative for $z_{l,k} \approx 0$; while for the ReLU activation we are close to the function's derivative discontinuity. Is this the real essence of weight decay and one of the reasons it helps in the generalization?

Starting from these very simple observation, we are now going to formulate a regularization term which explicitly minimizes $|z_{l,k}|$.

3.3 Post-synaptic Regularization

In the previous section we have observed that, in the typical deep learning scenario, weight decay minimizes the post-synaptic potential, focusing the output of the neuron around some particular regions, which might help in the signal back-propagation and, indirectly, favor the generalization.

If we wish to explicitly drive the output $y_{l,k}$ of the neuron, or better, its post-synaptic potential, we can impose an ℓ_2 regularization on $z_{l,k}$:

$$R = \frac{1}{2}\sum_{l}\sum_{k}(z_{l,k})^2 \tag{7}$$

where k is an index ranging for all the neurons in the l-th layer. We can split (7) for each of the k neurons in the l-th layer:

$$R_{l,k} = \frac{1}{2}(z_{l,k})^2 \tag{8}$$

In case we desire to apply the regularization (8), we can use the chain rule to check what is the update felt by the parameters of our model:

$$\frac{\partial R_{l,k}}{\partial \theta_{l,k,j}} = \frac{\partial R_{l,k}}{\partial z_{l,k}} \cdot \frac{\partial z_{l,k}}{\partial \theta_{l,k,j}} = z_{l,k} \cdot \frac{\partial z_{l,k}}{\partial \theta_{l,k,j}} \tag{9}$$

Expanding (9), we have

$$\frac{\partial R_{l,z}}{\partial \theta_{l,k,j}} = \frac{\partial z_{l,k}}{\partial \theta_{l,k,j}} \cdot \left(b_{l,k} + \sum_{i} w_{l,k,i} y_{(l-1,i)}\right) \tag{10}$$

Here we need to differentiate between bias and weight cases: if $\theta_{l,k,j}$ is the bias then (10) can be easily written as

$$\frac{\partial R_{l,k}}{\partial b_{l,k}} = b_{l,k} + \sum_i w_{l,k,i} y_{(l-1,i)} \tag{11}$$

while, if $\theta_{l,k,j}$ is one of the weights,

$$\begin{aligned}
\frac{\partial R_{l,k}}{\partial w_{l,k,j}} &= \frac{\partial z_{l,k}}{\partial w_{l,k,j}} \cdot \left[w_{l,k,j} \frac{\partial z_{l,k}}{\partial w_{k,j}} + \left(b_{l,k} + \sum_{i \neq j} w_{l,k,i} y_{(l-1,i)} \right) \right] \\
&= w_{l,k,j} \left(\frac{\partial z_{l,k}}{\partial w_{l,k,j}} \right)^2 + \left(b_{l,k} + \sum_{i \neq j} w_{l,k,i} y_{(l-1,i)} \right) \frac{\partial z_{l,k}}{\partial w_{l,k,j}} \\
&= w_{l,k,j} \left(\frac{\partial z_{l,k}}{\partial w_{l,k,j}} \right)^2 + C_{l,k,j} \frac{\partial z_{l,k}}{\partial w_{l,k,j}}
\end{aligned} \tag{12}$$

where $C_{l,k,j}$ is the contribution to $z_{l,k}$ from all the parameters except for $w_{l,k,j}$. From (12) it is possible to recover the usual weight decay assuming $\frac{\partial z_{l,k}}{\partial w_{l,k,j}} = 1$ and $C_{l,k,j} = 0$.

The variation in the parameter value, according to (9), is

$$\Delta \theta_{l,k,j} = -\lambda z_{l,k} \frac{\partial z_{l,k}}{\partial \theta_{l,k,j}} \tag{13}$$

where $\lambda \in (0, 1)$ as usual. As we are minimizing (7), we can say that $z_{l,k}$ is a bounded term. Furthermore, looking at $y_{(l-1,j)}$, we need to distinguish between two cases:

- $l = 1$: in this case, $y_{(0,j)}$ represents the input, which we impose to be a bounded quantity.
- $l \neq 1$: here we should recall that $y_{(l-1,j)}$ is the output of the $(l-1)$-th layer: if we minimize the post-synaptic potentials also in those layers, for the commonly-used activation functions, we guarantee it to be a bounded quantity.

Hence, as a product of bounded quantities, also (13) is a limited quantity.

However, what we aim to minimize is not (8), but the whole summation in (7). If we explicitly wish to write what the regularization contribution to the parameter $\theta_{l,k,j}$ is, we have

$$\frac{\partial R_{p,h}}{\partial \theta_{l,k,j}} = z_{p,h} \cdot \frac{\partial z_{p,h}}{\partial \theta_{l,k,j}} \tag{14}$$

Here, three different cases can be analyzed:

- $p < l$: in this case, the gradient term is $\frac{\partial z_{p,h}}{\partial \theta_{l,k,j}} = 0$ and the entire contribution is zero.

- $p = l$: here, the gradient term $\frac{\partial z_{p,h}}{\partial \theta_{l,k,j}} = y_{(l-1,j)}$ if $h = k$, zero otherwise.
- $p > l$: this is the most interesting case: regularization on the last layers affects all the previous ones, and such a contribution is automatically computed using back-propagation.

Hence, in the most general case, the total update contribution resulting from the minimization of (7) on the j-th weight belonging to the k-th neuron at layer l is indeed

$$\Delta\theta_{l,k,j} = -\lambda \left[z_{l,k} \frac{\partial z_{l,k}}{\partial \theta_{l,k,j}} + \sum_{p=l+1}^{L} \frac{\partial R_p}{\partial \theta_{l,k,j}} \right] \tag{15}$$

where

$$\frac{\partial z_{l,k}}{\partial \theta_{l,k,j}} = \begin{cases} 1 & if\ \theta_{l,k,j}\ is\ bias \\ y_{(l-1,j)} & if\ \theta_{l,k,j}\ is\ weight \end{cases} \tag{16}$$

In this section we have proposed a post-synaptic potential regularization which explicitly minimizes $z_{l,k}$ in all the neurons of the ANN. In particular, we have observed that the update term for the single parameter employs a global information coming from forward layers, favoring the regularization. In the next section, results from some simulations in which PSP regularization is tested are shown.

4 Experiments

In this section we show the performance reached by some of the mostly-used ANNs with our post-synaptic potential regularization (PSP) and we compare it to the results obtained with weight decay. We have tested our regularization on three different datasets: MNIST, Fashion-MNIST and CIFAR-10 on LeNet5, ResNet-18 [10], MobileNet v2 [21] and All-CNN-C [23]. The proposed hyper-parameters have been selected using grid search. All the simulations are performed using the standard SGD with CUDA 8 on a Nvidia Tesla P-100 GPU. Our regularization has been implemented using PyTorch 1.1.[1]

4.1 Simulations on MNIST

As very first experiments, we attempted to train the well-known LeNet-5 model over the standard MNIST dataset [15] (60k training images and 10k test images, all the images are 28 × 28 pixels, grey-scale). We use SGD with a learning parameter $\eta = 0.1$, mini-batch size 100. The training lasts here 50 epochs. In Fig. 2a, we show a typically observed scenario in our experimental setting, where we compare standard SGD with no regularization, the effect of ℓ_2 and ℓ_1 regularization ($\lambda = 0.0001$), the effect of dropout on the network (having $p = 0.5$) and our pre-activation signal potential regularization (PSP, $\lambda = 0.001$). The results are shown in Table 1, that reports the obtained classification errors, averaged on 10 different runs along with the corresponding standard deviation. While the

[1] All the source code is publicly available at https://github.com/enzotarta/PSP.

weight decay average performance is 0.74%, PSP performance is 0.55%. Please note that this result is deemed statistically significant since the t-test rejects the null hypothesis that there's no difference between the means with p-value in order of 10^{-5}. We would like to emphasize that, using this simple training strategy, the performance reached on LeNet-5 is among the best recorded, nevertheless having a much lower computational complexity [3]. We find interesting the behavior of $\langle z^2 \rangle$ for all the three techniques (Fig. 2b). In the case of standard SGD, the averaged $\langle z^2 \rangle$ value, as it is not controlled, typically grows until the gradient on the loss will not be zero. For ℓ_2 regularization, interestingly, it slowly grows until it reaches a final plateau. Finally, in PSP regularization, the $\langle z^2 \rangle$ value is extremely low, and still slowly decreases. According to the results in Fig. 2a, this is helping in the generalization.

At this point we can have a further look at what is happening at the level of the distribution of the parameters layer-by-layer. A typical trained parameters distribution for LeNet5, trained on MNIST, is shown in Fig. 3. While ℓ_2 regularization typically shrinks the parameters around zero, PSP regularization does not constrain the parameters with the same strength, while still constrains the pre-activation signal (Fig. 2b). However, contrarily to this, the first convolutional layer, with ℓ_2 regularization, is less constrained around zero than with PSP (Fig. 3a). Such a behavior can be explained by (15): all the regularization contributions coming from all the forward layers (in this case, conv2, fc1 and fc2) affect the parameters in conv1, which are directly conditioning all the z computed in forward layers.

4.2 Simulations on Fashion-MNIST

We have decided, as a further step, to test LeNet-5 on a more complex dataset: hence, we have chosen the Fashion-MNIST dataset [30]. It is made of 10 classes of 28 × 28 grey-scale images representing various pieces of clothing. They are divided in 60k examples for the training set and 10k for the test set. Such a dataset has two main advantages: the problem dimensionality (input, output) is the same as MNIST; hence, the same ANN can be used for both problems, and it is not as trivial as MNIST to solve.

Table 1. Classification error on LeNet-5 for MNIST and Fashion-MNIST evaluated on an average of 10 runs (error % ± standard deviation)

Regularization	MNIST	Fashion-MNIST
ℓ_2	0.74(±0.06)	8.28(±0.73)
PSP	**0.55**(±0.05)	**7.88**(±0.28)
ℓ_1	1.02(±0.26)	9.56(±0.64)
Dropout	0.63(±0.08)	8.22(±0.25)

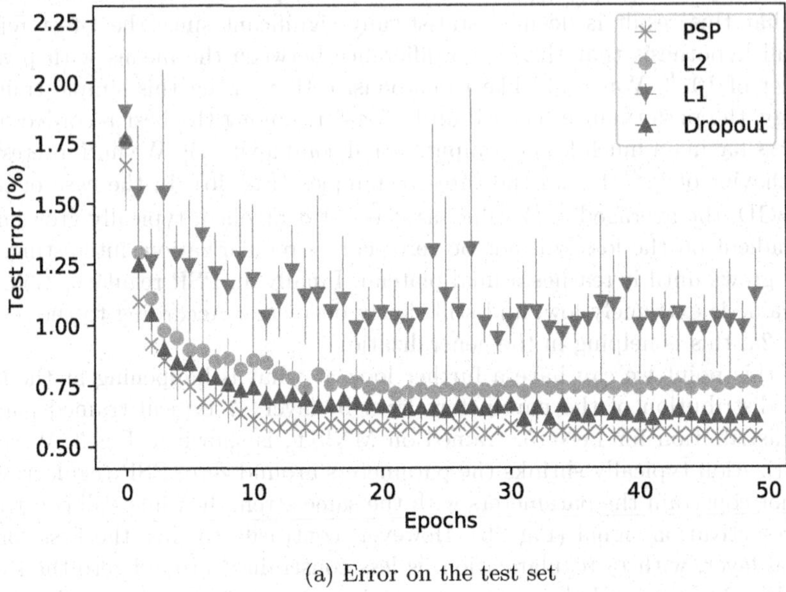

(a) Error on the test set

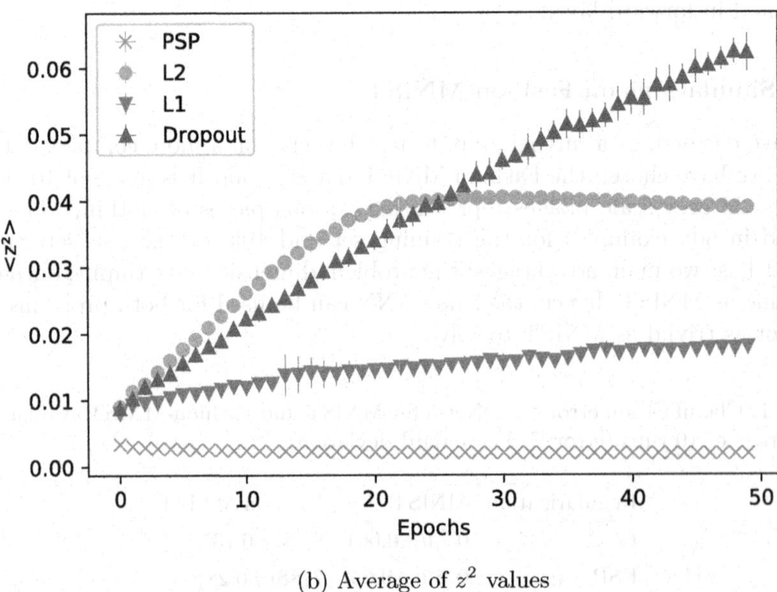

(b) Average of z^2 values

Fig. 2. Performance comparison in LeNet5 trained on MNIST between ℓ_2 regularization, ℓ_1 regularization, dropout and post synaptic potential regularization (PSP). All the plots show an average on 10 runs.

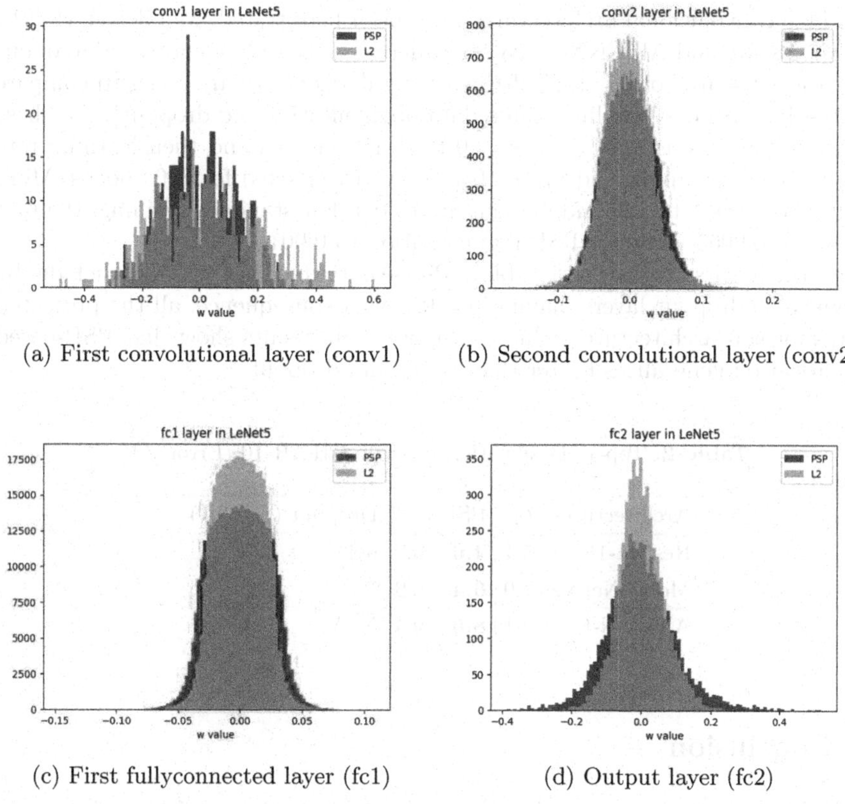

(a) First convolutional layer (conv1) (b) Second convolutional layer (conv2)

(c) First fullyconnected layer (fc1) (d) Output layer (fc2)

Fig. 3. Typical distribution of the parameters in a LeNet5 trained on MNIST with ℓ_2 regularization and with post synaptic potential regularization (PSP).

Training results are shown in Table 1. The simulations are performed with $\eta = 0.1$, batch size 100 and $\lambda = 0.0001$ for both ℓ_2 and ℓ_1 regularization while $\lambda = 0.001$ for PSP. The training lasts here 150 epochs. Here, the difference in the generalization between ℓ_2 and PSP is wider than the one presented for MNIST: we are able, with the same architecture, to improve the performance by around the 1% without any other heuristics.

4.3 Simulations on CIFAR-10

Moving towards deep architectures, we decided to use CIFAR-10 as dataset. It is made of 32×32 color images (3 channels) divided in 10 classes. The training set is made of 50k images and the test set of 10k samples. This dataset is a good compromise to make the first tests on deep architectures as the training is performed from scratch.

Three convolutional architectures have been here tested: MobileNet v2 [21], ResNet-18 [10] and All-CNN-C [23]. In order to separate the contribution of our regularizer towards other state-of-the-art regularizers, we are going to compare our results with our baseline (same data augmentation, no dropout). All these networks were pre-trained with $\eta = 0.1$ for 150 epochs and then learning rate decay policy was applied (drop to 10% every 100 epochs) for 300 epochs. Minibatch size was set to 128 and momentum to 0.9. For standard training, the ℓ_2 λ was set to 0.0005 while for PSP regularization to 0.001.

All the results are shown in Table 2. Please note that ALL-CNN-C includes by design some dropout layers, having $p = 0.5$; as a consequence, all the presented results for this architecture includes dropout. Our results show that PSP-based regularization generalizes better than ℓ_2, ℓ_1 and dropout.

Table 2. Top-1 classification error on CIFAR-10 (Error %)

Architecture	ℓ_2	PSP	ℓ_1	Dropout ($p = 0.1$)
ResNet-18	5.1	**4.6**	6.2	6.4
MobileNet v2	7.0	**6.4**	6.9	7.7
All-CNN-C	9.1	**8.6**	9.4	N/A

5 Conclusion

In this work we have proposed a post-synaptic potential regularizer for supervised learning problems. Starting from the observation that weight decay indirectly shrinks the post-synaptic potential to zero, we have formulated the new PSP regularization. Contrarily to weight decay, it uses a global information coming from other parameters affecting the post-synaptic potential. We have also shown that ℓ_2 regularization is a special case of our PSP regularization. Looking at the computational complexity, if the Autograd [17] package is used for back-propagation, no significant computational overhead is added.

Empirical results show that PSP regularization improves the generalization on both simple and more complex problems, boosting the performance also on deep architectures. Future work includes the application of PSP to recurrent neural networks, tests on networks using non-linear activation functions and the definition of a proper decay policy for PSP regularization.

References

1. Calimeri, F., Marzullo, A., Stamile, C., Terracina, G.: Biomedical data augmentation using generative adversarial neural networks. In: Lintas, A., Rovetta, S., Verschure, P.F.M.J., Villa, A.E.P. (eds.) ICANN 2017. LNCS, vol. 10614, pp. 626–634. Springer, Cham (2017). https://doi.org/10.1007/978-3-319-68612-7_71

2. Caruana, R.: Multitask learning. Mach. Learn. **28**(1), 41–75 (1997). https://doi.org/10.1007/978-1-4615-5529-2_5
3. Chaudhari, P., et al.: Entropy-SGD: biasing gradient descent into wide valleys. arXiv preprint arXiv:1611.01838 (2016)
4. Cui, X., Goel, V., Kingsbury, B.: Data augmentation for deep neural network acoustic modeling. IEEE/ACM Trans. Audio Speech Lang. Process. (TASLP) **23**(9), 1469–1477 (2015). https://doi.org/10.1109/icassp.2014.6854671
5. Elsken, T., Metzen, J.H., Hutter, F.: Neural architecture search: a survey. arXiv preprint arXiv:1808.05377 (2018)
6. Glorot, X., Bengio, Y.: Understanding the difficulty of training deep feedforward neural networks. In: Proceedings of the Thirteenth International Conference on Artificial Intelligence and Statistics, pp. 249–256 (2010)
7. Goldberg, P.W., Williams, C.K., Bishop, C.M.: Regression with input-dependent noise: a Gaussian process treatment. In: Advances in Neural Information Processing Systems, pp. 493–499 (1998)
8. Goodfellow, I., Bengio, Y., Courville, A.: Deep Learning. MIT Press (2016). https://doi.org/10.1007/s10710-017-9314-z
9. Gulcehre, C., Moczulski, M., Visin, F., Bengio, Y.: Mollifying networks. arXiv preprint arXiv:1608.04980 (2016)
10. He, K., Zhang, X., Ren, S., Sun, J.: Deep residual learning for image recognition. In: Proceedings of the IEEE Conference on Computer Vision and Pattern Recognition, pp. 770–778 (2016). https://doi.org/10.1109/cvpr.2016.90
11. Ioffe, S., Szegedy, C.: Batch normalization: accelerating deep network training by reducing internal covariate shift. arXiv preprint arXiv:1502.03167 (2015)
12. Kawaguchi, K.: Deep learning without poor local minima. In: Advances in Neural Information Processing Systems, pp. 586–594 (2016)
13. Kingma, D.P., Ba, J.: Adam: a method for stochastic optimization. arXiv preprint arXiv:1412.6980 (2014)
14. Kukacka, J., Golkov, V., Cremers, D.: Regularization for deep learning: a taxonomy. CoRR abs/1710.10686 (2017). http://arxiv.org/abs/1710.10686
15. LeCun, Y., Bottou, L., Bengio, Y., Haffner, P., et al.: Gradient-based learning applied to document recognition. Proc. IEEE **86**(11), 2278–2324 (1998). https://doi.org/10.1109/5.726791
16. Lin, H.W., Tegmark, M., Rolnick, D.: Why does deep and cheap learning work so well? J. Stat. Phys. **168**(6), 1223–1247 (2017). https://doi.org/10.1007/s10955-017-1836-5
17. Maclaurin, D., Duvenaud, D., Adams, R.P.: Autograd: effortless gradients in numpy. In: ICML 2015 AutoML Workshop (2015)
18. Prechelt, L.: Automatic early stopping using cross validation: quantifying the criteria. Neural Networks **11**(4), 761–767 (1998). https://doi.org/10.1016/s0893-6080(98)00010-0
19. Ramachandran, P., Zoph, B., Le, Q.V.: Searching for activation functions. arXiv preprint arXiv:1710.05941 (2017)
20. Reyes, O., Ventura, S.: Performing multi-target regression via a parameter sharing-based deep network. Int. J. Neural Syst. (2019). https://doi.org/10.1142/S012906571950014X
21. Sandler, M., Howard, A., Zhu, M., Zhmoginov, A., Chen, L.C.: MobileNetV2: inverted residuals and linear bottlenecks. In: Proceedings of the IEEE Conference on Computer Vision and Pattern Recognition, pp. 4510–4520 (2018). https://doi.org/10.1109/cvpr.2018.00474

22. Simonyan, K., Zisserman, A.: Very deep convolutional networks for large-scale image recognition. arXiv preprint arXiv:1409.1556 (2014)
23. Springenberg, J.T., Dosovitskiy, A., Brox, T., Riedmiller, M.: Striving for simplicity: the all convolutional net. arXiv preprint arXiv:1412.6806 (2014)
24. Srivastava, N., Hinton, G., Krizhevsky, A., Sutskever, I., Salakhutdinov, R.: Dropout: a simple way to prevent neural networks from overfitting. J. Mach. Learn. Res. **15**(1), 1929–1958 (2014)
25. Tartaglione, E., Lepsøy, S., Fiandrotti, A., Francini, G.: Learning sparse neural networks via sensitivity-driven regularization. In: Advances in Neural Information Processing Systems, pp. 3882–3892 (2018)
26. Tikhonov, A.N.: On the stability of inverse problems. Dokl. Akad. Nauk SSSR. **39**, 195–198 (1943)
27. Wager, S., Wang, S., Liang, P.S.: Dropout training as adaptive regularization. In: Advances in Neural Information Processing Systems, pp. 351–359 (2013)
28. Wan, L., Zeiler, M., Zhang, S., Le Cun, Y., Fergus, R.: Regularization of neural networks using DropConnect. In: International Conference on Machine Learning, pp. 1058–1066 (2013)
29. Weigend, A.S., Rumelhart, D.E., Huberman, B.A.: Back-propagation, weight-elimination and time series prediction. In: Connectionist Models, pp. 105–116. Elsevier (1991). https://doi.org/10.1016/B978-1-4832-1448-1.50016-0
30. Xiao, H., Rasul, K., Vollgraf, R.: Fashion-MNIST: a novel image dataset for benchmarking machine learning algorithms (2017)

A Novel Modification on the Levenberg-Marquardt Algorithm for Avoiding Overfitting in Neural Network Training

Serdar Iplikci[1(✉)], Batuhan Bilgi[2], Ali Menemen[2], and Bedri Bahtiyar[1]

[1] Department of Electrical and Electronics Engineering, Kinikli Campus, Pamukkale University, Denizli, Turkey
{iplikci,bedribahtiyar}@pau.edu.tr

[2] Akgün Electrical and Electronics Engineering Company, Denizli, Turkey
{batuhan.bilgi,ali.menemen}@akgunelk.com

Abstract. In this work, a novel modification on the standard Levenberg-Marquardt (LM) algorithm is proposed for eliminating the necessity of the validation set for avoiding overfitting, thereby shortening the training time while maintaining the test performance. The idea is that training points with smaller magnitudes of training errors are much liable to cause overfitting and that they should be excluded from the training set at each epoch. The proposed modification has been compared to the standard LM on three different problems. The results shown that even though the modified LM does not use the validation data set, it reduces the training time without compromising the test performance.

Keywords: Neural networks · Levenberg-Marquardt algorithm · Overfitting · Validation data set

1 Introduction

Overfitting is one of the most important problems in the machine learning area of research, especially in training neural networks, that degrades the generalization capability of the model under investigation. In the literature, there are several techniques to overcome overfitting problem namely, Early Stopping (ES) [1], Weight Decay [2], Noise Injection [3] and Optimized Approximation [4]. On the other hand, as the training algorithms, gradient-based methods such as Steepest Descend, Conjugate Gradient, and Levenberg–Marquardt (LM) [5] have been the most widely preferred optimization methods for training neural networks. The choice of the optimization method together with the method for avoiding overfitting is very important due to the its impact on the generalization performance [6]. Among others, the LM with ES is the mostly used one due to its advantages over other options. In this paper, we proposed a novel modification on LM for avoiding overfitting that provides an acceptable test performance without using the validation data set. This paper is organized as follows: in the next Section, the standard LM algorithm is reviewed. In Sect. 3, the proposed

I. V. Tetko et al. (Eds.): ICANN 2019, LNCS 11728, pp. 201–207, 2019.
https://doi.org/10.1007/978-3-030-30484-3_17

modification is given in detail. Next, the comparison results for three different examples have been given in Sect. 4. Finally, the paper concludes with the conclusions in Sect. 5.

2 Training a Feed-Forward Neural Network with LM

Given a data set $\mathfrak{D} = \{\mathbf{t}_i, y_i\}_{i=1}^{N}$, where $\mathbf{t}_i \in \mathbb{R}^R$ is the ith input vector and $y_i \in \mathbb{R}$ is the corresponding output, our goal is to find the parameters of the best feed-forward neural network with one hidden layer and S hidden neurons. The input-output relationship of the network is of the form, $\hat{y}_i(\mathbf{x}) = \mathbf{W}^c\mathbf{h}(\mathbf{W}^g\mathbf{t}_i + \mathbf{b}^h) + b^c$, where $\mathbf{x}$ is the vector of all adjustable parameters (weights and biases), $\mathbf{h}$ is the $S \times 1$ vector of hyperbolic tangent activation functions, $\mathbf{W}^g$ is the $S \times R$ matrix of input weights, $\mathbf{b}^h$ is the $S \times 1$ vector of hidden biases, $\mathbf{W}^c$ is the $1 \times S$ vector of output weights and b^c is the scalar output bias [7]. To prevent the neural network from overfitting, the most commonly used technique is ES, where the data set is divided into three subsets namely training, validation and testing. Training is terminated at the Lth increase in $f_{\text{val}}(\mathbf{x})$ in a row, at the end of which the best neural network is the one that has the best validation performance, as seen in Fig. 1. As the training algorithm, LM uses the update direction as $\mathbf{p}_k = -\left[\mathbf{J}^T(\mathbf{x}_k)\mathbf{J}(\mathbf{x}_k) + \mu_k\mathbf{I}\right]^{-1}\mathbf{J}^T(\mathbf{x}_k)\mathbf{e}(\mathbf{x}_k)$. In LM, the regulation term μ_k may change at every epoch. In this study, we have adopted a conventional way, which is to multiply/divide by $\mu_{scal} = 10$. For more details on the strategies for changing the regulation term in LM, one may refer to [8].

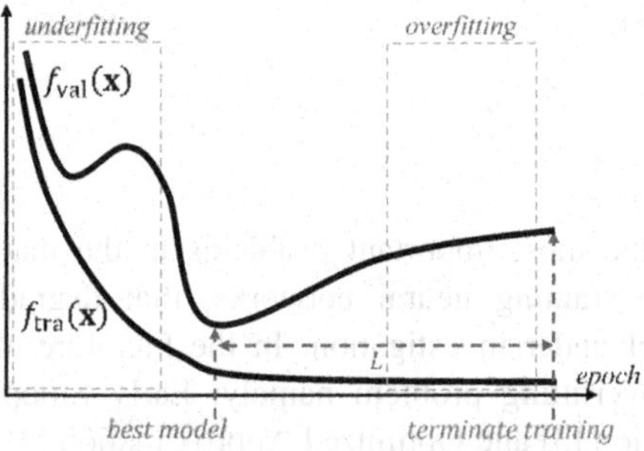

Fig. 1. Finding the best model by early stopping based on the validation performance.

3 Motivation and the Modified LM Algorithm

The main idea in the proposed modification on LM is that training points with smaller magnitudes of training errors, especially the ones within the interval $[-\epsilon \quad +\epsilon]$, are much likely to cause overfitting and thus they should be excluded from the training set in the current training epoch, thereby shortening the training time while maintaining the test performance. In the standard LM algorithm, consider $e_i(\mathbf{x}_k)$, which is the training error at the kth epoch for the ith training data point. Let E be the set of the indices of the

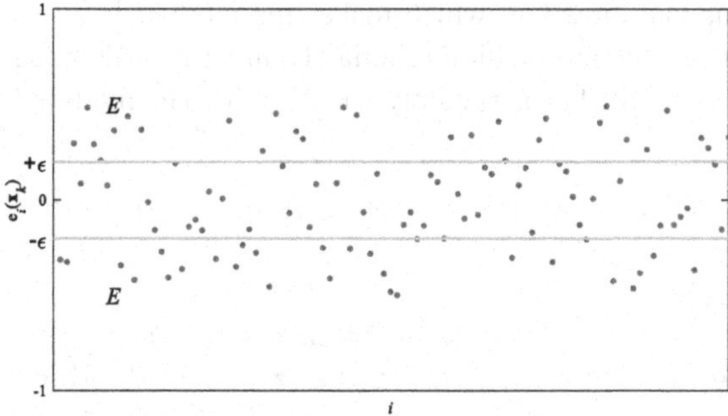

Fig. 2. Training errors in and out of the set E

training data points outside the interval $[-\epsilon \quad +\epsilon]$, i.e., $E = \{\, i, \quad \epsilon < |e_i(\mathbf{x}_k)|\, \}$, then there are N_E data points in the set E. If we plot $e_i(\mathbf{x}_k)$ for $i = 1, 2, \ldots, N_{\mathrm{tra}}$, as seen in Fig. 2, it can be seen that for a specified ϵ, $N_{\mathrm{tra}} - N_E$ errors lie within the interval $[-\epsilon \quad +\epsilon]$ and the remaining N_E data points are outside the interval.

During the standard LM training, for a specified ϵ small enough, training data points within the interval $[-\epsilon \quad +\epsilon]$ may cause overfitting in the current training epoch. Therefore, if the training data points within the interval $[-\epsilon \quad +\epsilon]$ are excluded from the training data set at each epoch, then overfitting can somewhat be avoided. The main idea of the modification is that, at each epoch, we work only with N_E data points in E, since the excluded data points in the interval $[-\epsilon \quad +\epsilon]$ have much more influence on the overfitting. As we work with only the data points in E, instead of using the Jacobian matrix $\mathbf{J}(\mathbf{x}_k)$ and the error vector $\mathbf{e}(\mathbf{x}_k)$ to calculate $\mathbf{p}_k$, we use their subsets $\mathbf{J}_E(\mathbf{x}_k)$ and $\mathbf{e}_E(\mathbf{x}_k)$, respectively. In other words, the update direction is calculated as, $\mathbf{p}_k = -\left[\mathbf{J}_E^T(\mathbf{x}_k)\mathbf{J}_E(\mathbf{x}_k) + \mu_k \mathbf{I}\right]^{-1} \mathbf{J}_E^T(\mathbf{x}_k)\mathbf{e}_E(\mathbf{x}_k)$, where $\mathbf{e}_E(\mathbf{x}_k)$ is the $N_E \times 1$ vector of errors in E and $\mathbf{J}_E(\mathbf{x}_k)$ is the $N_E \times n$ Jacobian matrix corresponding to the data points in E. Another modification is proposed on the update condition; in the standard LM, if $f_{tra}(\mathbf{x}_k + \mathbf{p}_k) < f_{tra}(\mathbf{x}_k)$ is satisfied then the parameters are updated, i.e. $\mathbf{x}_{k+1} \leftarrow \mathbf{x}_k + \mathbf{p}_k$. On the other hand, in the modified LM, the update is made according to the number of elements in the sets E and E_p, where E_p is defined as the set of indices of the training data points outside the interval $[-\epsilon \quad +\epsilon]$ when the parameters are updated with $\mathbf{p}_k$, that is to say, $E_p = \{\, i, \quad \epsilon < |e_i(\mathbf{x}_k + \mathbf{p}_k)|\, \}$. Thus, if N_{E_p} (the number of elements in E_p) is less than N_E, then the update is made, which forces the data points towards the interval $[-\epsilon \quad +\epsilon]$. To select the value of ϵ, it is initialized with a proper value and then adapted at each training epoch, which is another modification in the algorithm. This adaptation is made as follows: In the standard LM, if $f_{tra}(\mathbf{x}_k + \mathbf{p}_k) < f_{tra}(\mathbf{x}_k)$ is satisfied, then the parameters are updated and the μ_k is divided by μ_{scal}; otherwise, no update is made and μ_k is multiplied by μ_{scal}. On the other hand, in the modified LM, if $N_{E_p} < N_E$, then the update is made, the parameter μ_k is decreased as $\mu_k \leftarrow \mu_k / \mu_{scal}$ and also ϵ is decreased as $\epsilon \leftarrow \epsilon - \Delta\epsilon$; otherwise, no update is made, μ_k is increased as $\mu_k \leftarrow \mu_k \times \mu_{scal}$ and ϵ is increased as $\epsilon \leftarrow \epsilon + \Delta\epsilon$. Thus, the parameter ϵ is adapted according to the update direction, which makes the interval $[-\epsilon \quad +\epsilon]$ flexible. The last modification is on the termination criteria. Training is terminated if the maximum number of epochs is reached or E is empty, i.e. $N_E = 0$. The modified LM algorithm is given below:

```
Determine x_0, μ_0, μ_max, μ_scal, k_max, ρ_1, ρ_2, L, ε and Δε; k = 0;
f_tra* = ∞; MainLoop = TRUE
while MainLoop
  k ← k+1; Calculate f_tra(x_k), e(x_k) and J(x_k);   Find the
  set E of e(x_k) satisfying ε<|e(x_k)|.  Find e_E(x_k), the
  subset of e(x_k) with indices in E. Find J_E(x_k), the sub-
  set of J(x_k) with indices in E. InnerLoop = TRUE;
 while InnerLoop
   p_k = -[J_E^T(x_k)J_E(x_k)+μ_k I_E]^-1 J_E^T(x_k)e_E(x_k). Find the set E_p of
   e(x_k+p_k) satisfying ε<|e(x_k+p_k)|
   if length(E_p)<length(E)
     x_k+1 = x_k+p_k; μ_k ← μ_k/μ_scal; ε ← ε-Δε; InnerLoop = FALSE
   else
     μ_k ← μ_k×μ_scal; ε ← ε+Δε
     if μ_k<μ_max; InnerLoop = FALSE; MainLoop = FALSE; end
   end
 end
 Calculate f_tra(x_k+1)
 if f_tra(x_k+1)<f_tra*; f_tra* = f_tra(x_k+1); x*=x_k+1. end
 if k_max<k | N_E=0; MainLoop = FALSE;   end
end
```

4 Examples

We have compared our modified LM algorithm with the standard LM algorithm with respect to training time and test performance on three different regression examples. For all examples, the parameters are set as follows: $\mu_0 = 1$, $\mu_{\max} = 10^{10}$, $\mu_{\mathrm{scal}} = 10$, $k_{\max} = 100$, $\sigma_1 = 10^{-10}$, $\sigma_2 = 10^{-10}$, $L = 10$, $\epsilon = 0.02$ and $\Delta\epsilon = 0.02$. Moreover, all input variables and output variable in the data sets are normalized to the interval $[0 \quad 1]$; afterwards, they are corrupted by additive white noise with zero mean and 0.05 standard deviation. In all examples, 60% of data is used for training, 20% is used for validation and 20% is used for testing, respectively. For a fair comparison, conditions for the algorithms under comparison are totally same, i.e., initial parameters of the neural networks and training sets are all same at every simulation. The only difference is that the classical LM uses the validation data set, while modified LM does not. After each training phase, the test performances of the methods are obtained by the same test data set. For each case, the simulations are repeated 100 times by starting the neural networks with different initial parameters, and then training times and test performances for each algorithm are stored. Afterwards, we obtained the average values of training times and test performances for the algorithms.

The first example is Sun Spot data, which contains monthly mean total sunspot number from 1749 to 2015, which adds up to 3193 data points in total [9]. Based on R previous months, the mean sun spot number in the next month is predicted. In the simulations R is increased from 5 to 50 by one and S (number of hidden neurons) is increased from 5 to $S_{\max}$. For each case, i.e. (R, S) pair, networks are started with the same random initial parameters, then trained with standard LM and modified LM and their training times and test performances are stored. This is repeated 100 times and average values of the training times and test performances are tabulated in Table 1.

Table 1. Results for the Sun Spot Data

	Av. Training time (sec.)	Av. Test performance $f_{\mathrm{tst}}(\mathbf{x})$
Standard LM	52.747	2.4221
Modified LM	25.290	2.4165

Results show that modified LM provides nearly the same test performance as that of the standard LM, while reducing the average training time by half.

Another example is Box and Jenkins' data that has one input variable $u(n)$, and one output variable $y(n)$, with 286 data points. It is assumed that $y_n = f\left(y_{n-1}, \ldots, y_{n-n_y}, u_{n-1}, \ldots, u_{n-n_u}\right)$ for proper choices of n_y and n_u [10]. In the simulations n_y and n_u are increased from 1 to 3 by one and S is increased from 5 to $S_{\max}$. For each case, i.e. $\left(n_y, n_u, S\right)$ triplets, networks are started with the same random initial parameters, then trained with standard LM and modified LM and their training times and test performances are stored. This is repeated 100 times and average values of the training times and test performances are tabulated in Table 2.

Table 2. Results for the Box-Jenkins process

	Av. Training time (sec.)	Av. Test performance $f_{\mathrm{tst}}(\mathbf{x})$
Standard LM	0.9199	0.2910
Modified LM	0.1873	0.2909

Results show that modified LM provides satisfactory test performance, while reducing the average training time to its 1/5.

The last example is Continuously Stirred Tank Reactor (CSTR) which is a third-order nonlinear process, the dynamics of which is given by a set of differential equations as $\dot{x}_1(t) = 1 - 4x_1(t) + 0.5x_2^2(t)$, $\dot{x}_2(t) = 3x_1(t) - x_2(t) - 1.5x_2^2(t) + u(t)$, $\dot{x}_3(t) = x_2^2(t) - x_3(t)$ and $y(t) = x_3(t)$, where $u(t)$ is the input signal, $y(t)$ is the output of the process [11]. During the data collection phase, the magnitude of the control signal is made random between $u_{\min} = 0$ and $u_{\max} = 0$ in each Runge-Kutta time-step of $T_s = 0.1$sec. to obtain a persistently exciting data set of 5000 data points. It is assumed that $y_n = f(y_{n-1}, \ldots, y_{n-n_y}, u_{n-1}, \ldots, u_{n-n_u})$ for proper choices of n_y and n_u. In the tests, n_y and n_u are increased from 1 to 4 by one and S is increased from 5 to $S_{\max}$. For each case, i.e. (n_y, n_u, S) triplets, networks are started with the same random initial parameters, then trained with standard LM and modified LM and their training times and test performances are stored. This is repeated 100 times and average values of the training times and test performances are tabulated in Table 3. Results show that modified LM provides the same test performance as that of the standard LM, while reducing the average training time to its 1/3.

Table 3. Results for the CSTR process

	Av. Training time (sec.)	Av. Test performance $f_{\text{tst}}(\mathbf{x})$
Standard LM	31.7114	3.7540
Modified LM	11.1304	3.7513

5 Conclusions

In this paper, a novel modification on the standard LM algorithm is proposed for eliminating the need of the validation set for avoiding overfitting, thereby reducing the training time without any deterioration in the test performance. Accordingly, the modified algorithm works with less data than standard LM, and hence it improves the computational time and complexity. The proposed modification has been compared to the standard LM on three different problems. The results shown that even though the modified LM does not use the validation data set, it reduces the training time considerably without compromising the test performance.

Acknowledgements. This work is supported by Pamukkale University Scientific Research Projects Council under the grand number 2018KRM002-035.

References

1. Sarle, W.S.: Stopped Training and Other Remedies for Overfitting. In: 27th Symposium on the Interface, pp. 352–360 (1995). https://doi.org/10.1.1.42.3920
2. Poggio, T., Girosi, F.: Networks for Approximation and Learning. Proc. IEEE **78**(9), 1481–1497 (1990). https://doi.org/10.1109/5.58326
3. Zur, R.M., Jiang, Y., Pesce, L.L., Drukker, K.: Noise Injection for Training ANNs: A Comparison with Weight Decay and Early Stopping. Medical Phys. **36**(10), 4810–4818 (2009). https://doi.org/10.1118/1.3213517
4. Liu, Y., Starzyk, J.A., Zhu, Z.: Optimized Approximation Algorithm in Neural Networks without Overfitting. IEEE Trans. Neural Networks **19**(6), 983–995 (2008). https://doi.org/10.1109/TNN.2007.915114
5. Nocedal, J., Wright, S.: Numerical Optimization. Springer Series in Operations Research and Financial Engineering. Springer, New York (2006)

6. Piotrowski, A.P., Napiorkowski, J.J.: A comparison of methods to avoid overfitting in NNs training in the case of catchment runoff modelling. J. Hydrol. **476**, 97–111 (2013). https://doi.org/10.1016/j.jhydrol.2012.10.019
7. Hagan, M.T., Demuth, H.B., Beale, M.: Neural Network Design. PWS Publishing Co., Boston (1996)
8. Kwak, Y., Hwang, J., Yoo, C.: A new damping strategy of Levenberg-Marquardt algorithm for Multilayer Perceptrons. Neural Network World **21**(4), 327–340 (2011). https://doi.org/10.14311/NNW.2011.21.020
9. Sunspot Index and Long-term Solar Observations. http://www.sidc.be/silso
10. Purwar, S., Kar, I.N., Jha, A.N.: On-line system identification of complex systems using chebyshev neural networks. Appl. Soft Comput. **7**, 364–372 (2007). https://doi.org/10.1016/j.asoc.2005.08.001
11. Wu, W., Chou, Y.S.: Adaptive feedforward and feedback control of nonlinear time-varying uncertain systems. Int. J. Control **72**(12), 1127–1138 (1999). https://doi.org/10.1080/002071799220489

Sign Based Derivative Filtering for Stochastic Gradient Descent

Konstantin Berestizshevsky(✉) and Guy Even

School of Electrical Engineering, Tel Aviv University, Tel Aviv, Israel
konsta9@mail.tau.ac.il, guy@eng.tau.ac.il

Abstract. We study the performance of stochastic gradient descent (SGD) in deep neural network (DNN) models. We show that during a single training epoch the signs of the partial derivatives of the loss with respect to a single parameter are distributed almost uniformly over the minibatches. We propose an optimization routine, where we maintain a moving average history of the sign of each derivative. This history is used to classify new derivatives as "exploratory" if they disagree with the sign of the history. Conversely, we classify the new derivatives as "exploiting" if they agree with the sign of the history. Each derivative is weighed according to our classification, providing control over exploration and exploitation. The proposed approach leads to training a model with higher accuracy as we demonstrate through a series of experiments.

Keywords: Optimization · Gradients · Deep learning · Neural networks

1 Introduction

In supervised machine learning, the training of a machine learning model is generally a lengthy iterative optimization procedure. During this procedure, a loss function, which corresponds to the incorrectness of the model, is minimized.

The loss optimizer is an algorithm that iteratively minimizes the model's loss function over the training set, by adjusting the model's parameters. One of the most common optimization algorithms is "Minibatch Stochastic Gradient Descent" (Minibatch-SGD) [3]. In this approach, a subset of training examples (a minibatch) is used to produce the loss value with respect to the loss function and the current model parameters. Next, the gradient, that is the set of the partial derivatives of the loss function w.r.t. all the model parameters, is computed for each training example using backpropagation [14]. The gradients of the different training examples in a minibatch are averaged, resulting in a single derivative for every parameter.

For practical reasons and for better generalization, minibatch sizes are usually as small as 4 orders of magnitude smaller than the size of the training set [5]. As a result, the gradients of each minibatch are very different. In this work, Sect. 3, we demonstrate that only slightly more than half of the minibatches yield

I. V. Tetko et al. (Eds.): ICANN 2019, LNCS 11728, pp. 208–219, 2019.
https://doi.org/10.1007/978-3-030-30484-3_18

derivatives with a sign that complies with the sign of the average derivative for the whole dataset. This means that gradients from minibatches are very noisy and the question that arises is why should the model parameters be updated based on such noisy information.

The goal of this study is to devise a training routine that allows control over the noise of the gradients, such that the training will either converge faster or to higher accuracy. Specific contributions of this paper are:

1. An optimization algorithm that controls the degree of noise created by the minibatch-SGD.
2. Empirical evidence for the noise of the minibatch-SGD.

This paper is organized as follows. Section 2 presents relevant previous research on the optimization algorithms in machine learning. Section 3 presents a key observation about the noisiness of the minibatch-SGD, which serves as the motivation for the proposed technique. Section 4 presents the proposed derivative filtering (DF) optimization algorithm. Section 5 describes the experimental setup, including the datasets, the architectures and the training routines that were involved in the empirical examination of the DF algorithm. Section 6 presents the results of the experiments. Section 7 discusses interesting further research directions and Sect. 8 concludes the paper.

2 Related Work

Parameter update strategies were investigated in order to modify the parameters of the model in a way that ensures high accuracy and fast convergence time. SGD modification such as the momentum [16] were introduced in order to speedup the gradient descent and to avoid sharp updates due to noisy gradients. Other studies proposed update strategies that involved tracking the sizes of the gradients and of the model parameters, and applying proportional updates (AdaGrad [4], AdaDelta [20], RMSProp [19], Adam [11]). For example, the AdaGrad approach maintains a separate learning rate for each trainable parameter in the model, its idea was recently developed into an online adaptive method [12]. Adam optimization algorithm continuously maintains the first and the second moments of the gradients across the mini batches and updates the parameters using these estimates. Interestingly, the most recent state-of-the-art results on CIFAR, SVHN and ImageNet, PASCAL VOC, and MS-COCO datasets were obtained with variants of Residual Neural Networks (ResNet s) [5], and the optimization algorithm they used was the regular SGD. Recently proposed SGD with warm restarts (SGDR) [13] showed a better convergence rate.

Other than the optimizer, the operation of Batch-Normalization [10], greatly reduces the convergence time during training. The batch normalization operation, applied after every linear layer, reduces the model's internal covariate shift. Without the batch normalization, the internal covariate shift naturally takes place since different layers often perform updates in contradicting directions and hence constantly change the distribution of activations observed by the succeeding layers. [6] showed that batch-normalization, weight-decay, and learning rate are related, and proposed alternative norms (L^1 and L^∞) for better convergence.

The noise induced by the minibatch-SGD was found to be proportional to $\eta|T|/b$ where η is the learning rate, $|T|$ is the number of training examples and b is the size of the minibatch [18]. In deep neural networks, the amount of noise injected in the parameter update steps is often amplified by additive Gaussian noise [15], or even by a multiplicative noise [7]. In our work, we attempt to control the noise induced by the minibatch gradients, rather than to introduce extra noise.

The signs of the gradient were explored in a context of gradient compression for the parallel SGD training [2,17]. In these works, the sign of the derivatives provided crucial information for the optimization process, allowing to compress their magnitude without a significant impact on the training progress. Our work, on the other hand, attempts to exploit the signs of the gradients to control the noise created by the small minibatches.

3 SGD is Noisy

For the rest of the paper, we refer to partial derivatives in the gradient simply as *derivatives*. This is not to be confused with the gradients, which are vectors of derivatives.

The vanilla SGD procedure provides noisy update steps, determined by the small size of the minibatches, which do not capture the direction of Gradient Descent (GD) minima. On the one hand, these noisy updates provide the optimization with exploratory capability, which greatly improves the generalization ability of the model, as we discussed in Sect. 2. On the other hand, the noisy updates may slow down the training progress.

To demonstrate the above-mentioned phenomenon, we produced a decently difficult synthetic binary classification dataset (100k training samples, 2 classes) and trained a 3-layer fully-connected neural network on it. The training was performed with a minibatch size equal to the size of the dataset (e.g. a single parameter update per epoch). Next, at each epoch, we observed the gradients of randomly drawn minibatches of size 100 and sought for a correlation between these small minibatches and the dataset-sized minibatch. Figure 1 shows the distribution of the mean batch derivatives w.r.t the last fully-connected layer parameters. Namely, the values of the elements in the gradient of the last layer are shown in a form of distribution quantized into 40 bins. Each bin is split into a red and a green column. The green column shows the number of derivatives in a minibatch, for which the derivative averaged across the entire dataset is positive. The red column shows the number of derivatives in a minibatch, for which the derivative averaged across the entire dataset negative.

The distribution presented in Fig. 1 shows, that in almost half of the minibatches the sign of the average derivative does not correspond to the sign of that derivative when averaged across the entire dataset. The implication is that almost half of the updates in the epoch are in the "wrong" direction, rendering them exploratory steps rather than optimization steps.

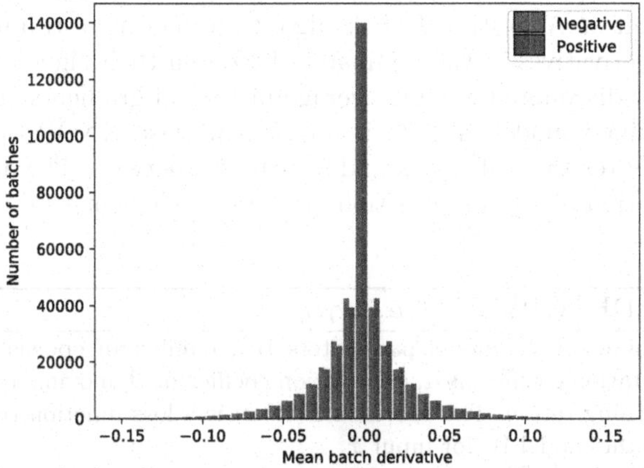

Fig. 1. Distribution of mean derivative values. The x-axis stands for the mean derivative value in batch (batch-size 100) and is split into 40 bins. Each bin contains two bars which show the number of batches whose mean derivative value fell in that bin. The red (leftmost) bar shows the amount of the examples in the bin for which the GD's derivative is negative, whereas the green (rightmost) bar shows the number of the examples in the bin for which the GD's derivative is positive. (Color figure online)

4 Sign Based Derivative Filtering

The core idea of the proposed training algorithm is to distinguish between two types of derivatives based on their **sign**. The derivatives that comply with the sign of the recently observed derivatives are denoted **exploiting** derivatives, whereas the derivatives that do not comply with the sign of previously observed derivatives are denoted **exploratory** derivatives. To keep track of the recent derivatives, a discounted moving average is maintained. Setting the history discount factor γ to 0 degenerates the history to contain the gradients of the previous iteration.

To leverage the noise of the SGD minibatches, the exploiting derivatives are multiplied by α and the exploratory derivatives are multiplied by β. This modulation reweighs the derivatives prior to updating the model parameters, and controls the exploitation-to-exploration ratio. Setting $\alpha/\beta > 1$ prioritizes the exploiting derivatives, thereby reduces the impact of the noisy gradients. Setting $\alpha/\beta = 1$ degenerates the DF algorithm to a baseline minibatch SGD. It is important to notice that since the coefficients α and β are applied to the gradients, they affect the learning rate. Hence the choice of two hyperparameters rather than a single hyperparameter α for exploitation and $1 - \alpha$ for exploitation, allows using values larger than 1, such that the global learning rate is not reduced.

The proposed optimization algorithm is denoted Derivative Filtering (DF) and we present it as Algorithm 1. This algorithm presents a training procedure that reweighs derivatives in the minibatch, based on their sign compared to an iteration-level γ-discounted moving average history of gradients. The algorithm returns the trained model. The $\odot$ is an element-wise XNOR operation. The function $sign(x)$ returns 1 if $x \geq 0$, and returns 0 otherwise. The multiplications and the application of $sign(x)$ function are strictly element-wise.

Algorithm 1. $\mathrm{DF}(X, W_0, \mathcal{L}, T, b, \alpha, \beta, \gamma, \eta)$

1: **Input:** training set X, model parameters W_0, number of epochs T, minibatch-size b, exploitation coefficient α, exploration coefficient β, moving average discount factor γ, learning rate η. The provided $\mathcal{L}(W, x)$ is a loss function that returns the loss value of the model W for input x.
2: **Initialize:** $H_0 \leftarrow \frac{1}{|X|}\sum_{x \in X} \nabla_W \mathcal{L}(W_0, x))$
3: **Initialize:** $V_0 \leftarrow 0$
4: **for** $t = 0$ **to** $T - 1$ **do**
5:     **for** $B \subseteq X, |B| = b$ **do**
6:         $\tilde{G}_t \leftarrow \frac{1}{b}\sum_{x \in B} \nabla_W \mathcal{L}(W_t, x))$
7:         $M_t \leftarrow sign(\tilde{G}_t) \odot sign(H_t)$
8:         $G_t \leftarrow \alpha \cdot M_t \cdot \tilde{G}_t + \beta \cdot (1 - M_t) \cdot \tilde{G}_t$
9:         $V_{t+1} \leftarrow 0.9 V_t - \eta G_t$
10:         $W_{t+1} \leftarrow W_t + V_{t+1}$
11:         $H_{t+1} \leftarrow \gamma \cdot H_t + (1 - \gamma) \cdot \tilde{G}_t$
12:     **end for**
13: **end for**
14: **return** W_T

Lines 9–10 perform the model's parameter update using momentum with coefficient 0.9. Line 11 maintains a moving average of the non-modulated gradients.

We note that the initial bias introduced by the exponential moving average does not require special attention here since the number of training iterations is large (60 thousand iterations per training in the datasets we consider) and the influence of the initial biased moving average is negligible.

5 Experimental Setup

To examine the effect of the derivative filtering on the training, we performed an empirical study. The DF (Algorithm 1) was implemented using Tensorflow [1] framework, and its effect was observed during the training on image classification datasets. Specifically, we experimented with $\alpha, \beta \geq 1$ in order not to slow down the training, since these coefficients directly affect the learning rate. Note that the baseline for comparison (i.e., a non-DF training using Momentum-SGD) is obtained by setting $\alpha = \beta$.

Datasets. CIFAR-10 and CIFAR-100 are the two image classification datasets we used. Each of these datasets contains $50k$ training examples and $10k$ test examples, where each example is a labeled RGB color image of the size 32×32. The labels in CIFAR-10 and CIFAR-100 correspond to 10 and 100 classes, respectively.

Models. The deep neural network models we trained are from the ResNet family [5]. We chose this architecture family due to its widespread success and the fact that its core idea contributed to a series of architectures that followed such as DenseNet [8] and Deep Networks with stochastic depth [9]. The ResNet architecture consists of building blocks, each of which contains 2 convolutional layers with a skip connection which allows passing the input of the building block "as is" to the output of this building block. Batch normalization in ResNet was applied after the convolutional operation before any other operation (such as non-linear activation or addition with the skip connection) takes place. Specifically, we focused on two variants of ResNet models: ResNet-20 and ResNet-110, containing 20 and 110 layers, respectively. The reasoning behind this choice is to examine the DF algorithm both on shallow and deep models.

Training Routine. During the training, we employed a standard data augmentation and the optimization was done using DF (Algorithm 1). Learning rate initialized to 0.1 and reduced by a factor of 10 at epochs 80 and 120. Training time: 150 epochs, minibatch size: 128. For statistically stable results, every training was repeated 10 times (with differently randomized initial weights) and the average accuracy, as well as the standard deviation of the accuracy, are reported.

6 Results

Our initial experiments showed degradation in test accuracy when employing DF with $\frac{\alpha}{\beta} < 1$. This result can be explained by the fact that the vanilla SGD (corresponding to $\frac{\alpha}{\beta} = 1$) optimizes the model using extremely noisy gradients. Hence, further amplification of the (exploratory) derivatives would cause the optimization to diverge. The Appendix contains results for such choices of parameters. On the other hand, we received promising results using $\alpha/\beta > 1$.

Test accuracies obtained using DF with $\alpha/\beta \geq 1$ from ResNet-20 and ResNet-110 models are presented in Tables 1 and 2, respectively. In these tables, we depict 12 models, trained with DF $(\frac{\alpha}{\beta}, \gamma) \in \{1, 2, 4\} \times \{0, 0.01, 0.5, 0.99\}$. The models that achieved the highest test accuracy appear in bold. Compared to the vanilla Momentum-SGD training ($\alpha/\beta = 1, \gamma = 0$), the setting that achieved the highest test accuracy was DF with a high discount factor ($\gamma = 0.99$) and the exploitation favoring ratio of $\alpha/\beta = 2$. The gains of this setup of parameters ($\alpha/\beta = 2$, $\gamma = 0.99$), in terms of the final test accuracy, are summarized in Table 3.

In addition, we observed how different parameters affect test accuracy throughout the training process. Test accuracy plots, as a function of training epoch, for various γ values and for $\alpha/\beta = 2, 4$ are presented in Figs. 2 and 3 for the models ResNet-20 and ResNet-110, respectively. The plots present the average accuracy trend, obtained from 10 differently initialized models.

Table 1. Test accuracy of ResNet-20 on CIFAR-10 and CIFAR-100 datasets. The presented accuracies are average across 10 differently randomized and trained models. The corresponding standard deviation (σ) is reported for every result.

ResNet 20	CIFAR-10				CIFAR-100			
	$\gamma = 0$	$\gamma = 0.01$	$\gamma = 0.5$	$\gamma = 0.99$	$\gamma = 0$	$\gamma = 0.01$	$\gamma = 0.5$	$\gamma = 0.99$
$\alpha/\beta = 1$	91.05%	**90.93%**	90.97%	90.98%	66.22%	65.89%	66.07%	**66.27%**
	$\sigma = .35\%$	$\sigma = .24\%$	$\sigma = .15\%$	$\sigma = .13\%$	$\sigma = .38\%$	$\sigma = .34\%$	$\sigma = .39\%$	$\sigma = .47\%$
$\alpha/\beta = 2$	91.24%	91.07%	91.07%	**91.50%**	65.89%	66.10%	66.07%	**67.40%**
	$\sigma = .27\%$	$\sigma = .32\%$	$\sigma = .29\%$	$\sigma = .19\%$	$\sigma = .88\%$	$\sigma = .50\%$	$\sigma = .54\%$	$\sigma = .43\%$
$\alpha/\beta = 4$	91.10%	**91.14%**	90.95%	90.98%	65.91%	66.05%	66.57%	**67.07%**
	$\sigma = .17\%$	$\sigma = .2\%$	$\sigma = .26\%$	$\sigma = .31\%$	$\sigma = .51\%$	$\sigma = .65\%$	$\sigma = .40\%$	$\sigma = .29\%$

Table 2. Test accuracy of ResNet-110 on CIFAR-10 and CIFAR-100 datasets. The presented accuracies are average across 10 differently randomized and trained models. The corresponding standard deviation (σ) is reported for every result.

ResNet 110	CIFAR-10				CIFAR-100			
	$\gamma = 0$	$\gamma = 0.01$	$\gamma = 0.5$	$\gamma = 0.99$	$\gamma = 0$	$\gamma = 0.01$	$\gamma = 0.5$	$\gamma = 0.99$
$\alpha/\beta = 1$	91.29%	91.14%	91.04%	**91.55%**	**67.31%**	67.04%	65.98%	66.96%
	$\sigma = 1\%$	$\sigma = .88\%$	$\sigma = .89\%$	$\sigma = .70\%$	$\sigma = 1\%$	$\sigma = 1.7\%$	$\sigma = 2\%$	$\sigma = 2\%$
$\alpha/\beta = 2$	91.52%	91.24%	91.30%	**92.43%**	67.73%	68.06%	68.68%	**71.17%**
	$\sigma = .83\%$	$\sigma = 1\%$	$\sigma = .94\%$	$\sigma = .51\%$	$\sigma = 2.7\%$	$\sigma = 1.5\%$	$\sigma = 1.2\%$	$\sigma = 1\%$
$\alpha/\beta = 4$	92.00%	91.80%	**92.42%**	91.77%	**69.77%**	69.31%	68.94%	69.11%
	$\sigma = .74\%$	$\sigma = .87\%$	$\sigma = .49\%$	$\sigma = .76\%$	$\sigma = .84\%$	$\sigma = 2\%$	$\sigma = 1.3\%$	$\sigma = 2.3\%$

Table 3. Test accuracy achieved by models trained by a Momentum SGD without derivative filtering (left column) and by models trained with the best parameter setup of the DF (right column).

		no DF $\alpha/\beta = 1$	DF ($\gamma = 0.99$) $\alpha/\beta = 2$
ResNet-20	CIFAR-10	91.05%, $\sigma = .35\%$	91.50%, $\sigma = .19\%$
	CIFAR-100	66.22%, $\sigma = .38\%$	67.40%, $\sigma = .43\%$
ResNet-110	CIFAR-10	91.29%, $\sigma = 1\%$	92.43%, $\sigma = .51\%$
	CIFAR-100	67.31%, $\sigma = 1\%$	71.17%, $\sigma = 1\%$

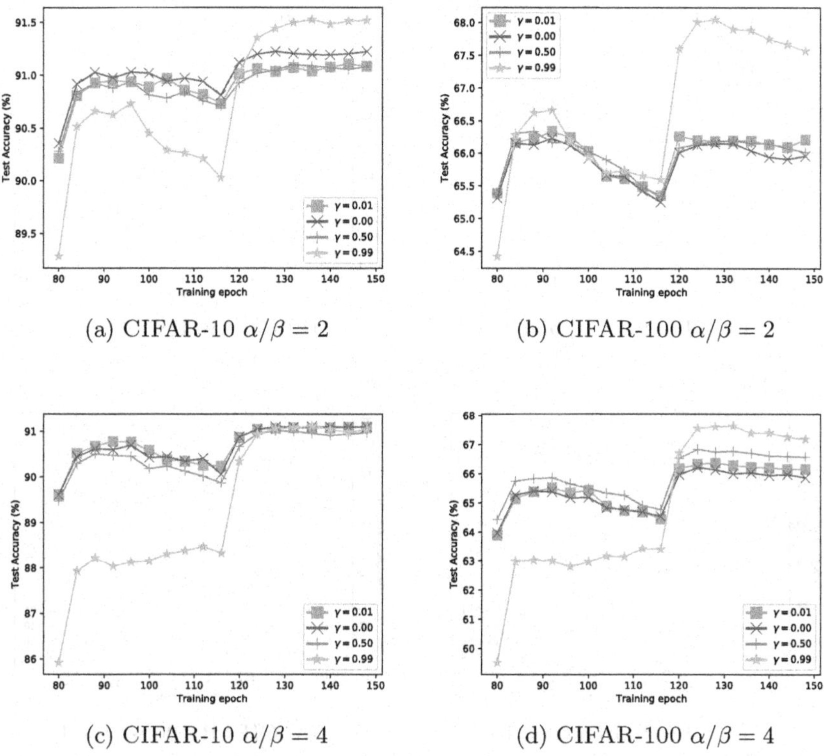

(a) CIFAR-10 $\alpha/\beta = 2$

(b) CIFAR-100 $\alpha/\beta = 2$

(c) CIFAR-10 $\alpha/\beta = 4$

(d) CIFAR-100 $\alpha/\beta = 4$

Fig. 2. Test accuracy curve for DF training (Algorithm 1) and ResNet-20 architecture.

7 Discussion and Future Work

We mark batches as "exploratory" per parameter if the sign of the derivative of the loss does not agree with the sign of the discounted average of the derivative. We scale the derivative based on whether it categorised as exploratory or not. Our experiments demonstrate that this idea leads to improved test-accuracy. Final results showed that the best choice of ratio between the scaling factors α (for "exploitation") and β (for "exploration") is two. Such tuning of parameters is not rare in the literature. In fact, some of the most advanced optimization algorithms employ numerous manually determined parameters (c.f. Adam optimizer [11] employs β_1, β_2; momentum-accelerated SGD [16] requires the momentum value to be set manually). It would be interesting to devise an adaptive method for setting this parameter.

This work focused on a general training setup, employing minibatches of conventional sizes. In the light of the popular large scale distributed training, which often employs large batch sizes, it is tempting to investigate how the proposed DF algorithm (Algorithm 1) can accommodate large minibatches. In the case of large minibatches, the gradients are less exploratory and therefore may require $\alpha/\beta < 1$. In addition, given the fact that categorizing and scaling derivatives

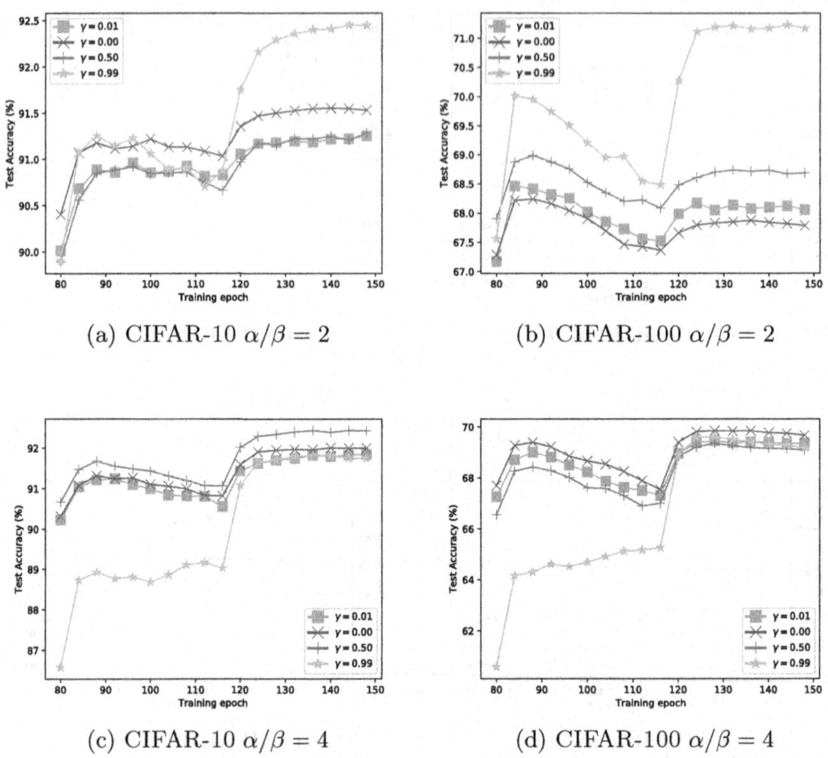

(a) CIFAR-10 $\alpha/\beta = 2$

(b) CIFAR-100 $\alpha/\beta = 2$

(c) CIFAR-10 $\alpha/\beta = 4$

(d) CIFAR-100 $\alpha/\beta = 4$

Fig. 3. Test accuracy during DF training (Algorithm 1) and ResNet-110 architecture.

based on signs imposes a biasing of the gradient estimates, a theoretical analysis of the convergence rate for the DF algorithm is of separate interest.

8 Conclusions

In this paper we unveiled a new way of handling a stream of gradient information provided by the minibatch-SGD training. We temporally weighted each partial derivative in a gradient according to its sign change relative to the history of recent minibatches. It was done by introducing three coefficients α, β, γ. The α/β ratio modulates the exploiting ability of the training, whereas the discount factor γ acts similarly to a low pass filter, smoothing fluctuations of the gradients. Moreover, we showed that when the DF approach is applied with large discount factor (which translates into a strong smoothing of the gradients) and with $\alpha > \beta$, the trained model reaches higher classification accuracy.

The results of our experiments showed, that the proposed technique can act as a regularizer, namely slowing down the training in its initial stages, but eventually reaching a higher level of generalization. Namely, our empirical findings exhibit $0.3\% - 3.6\%$ accuracy improvement on CIFAR-10 and CIFAR-100 datasets.

Acknowledgments. We thank Nissim Halabi, Moni Shahar and Daniel Soudry for useful conversations.

Appendix

See Fig. 4.

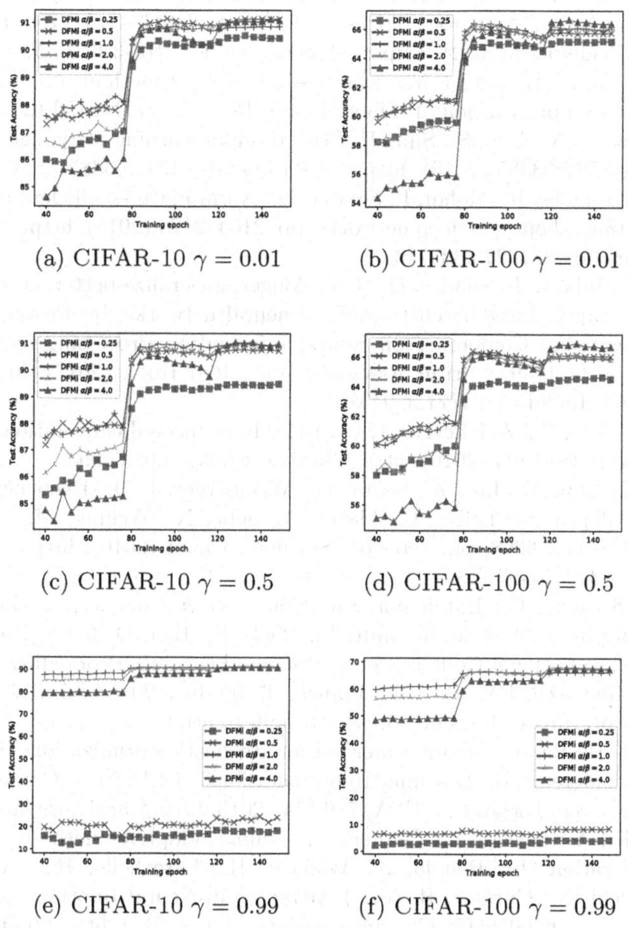

(a) CIFAR-10 $\gamma = 0.01$ (b) CIFAR-100 $\gamma = 0.01$

(c) CIFAR-10 $\gamma = 0.5$ (d) CIFAR-100 $\gamma = 0.5$

(e) CIFAR-10 $\gamma = 0.99$ (f) CIFAR-100 $\gamma = 0.99$

Fig. 4. Test accuracy curve for DF of ResNet-20 models using both exploration favoring ratios ($\alpha/\beta < 1$) and exploitation favoring ratios ($\alpha/\beta > 1$). Poor performance is observed for exploration favoring strategy.

References

1. Abadi, M., et al.: TensorFlow: large-scale machine learning on heterogeneous systems (2015). Software http://tensorflow.org/
2. Bernstein, J., Wang, Y.X., Azizzadenesheli, K., Anandkumar, A.: signSGD: compressed optimisation for non-convex problems. In: Proceedings of Machine Learning Research, PMLR, Stockholmsmässan, Stockholm Sweden, 10–15 July 2018, vol. 80, pp. 560–569 (2018)
3. Bottou, L.: Stochastic gradient descent tricks. In: Montavon, G., Orr, G.B., Müller, K.-R. (eds.) Neural Networks: Tricks of the Trade. LNCS, vol. 7700, pp. 421–436. Springer, Heidelberg (2012). https://doi.org/10.1007/978-3-642-35289-8_25
4. Duchi, J., Hazan, E., Singer, Y.: Adaptive subgradient methods for online learning and stochastic optimization. J. Mach. Learn. Res. **12**, 2121–2159 (2011)
5. He, K., Zhang, X., Ren, S., Sun, J.: Deep residual learning for image recognition. CoRR abs/1512.03385 (2015). http://arxiv.org/abs/1512.03385
6. Hoffer, E., Banner, R., Golan, I., Soudry, D.: Norm matters: efficient and accurate normalization schemes in deep networks, pp. 2164–2174 (2018). http://dl.acm.org/citation.cfm?id=3326943.3327143
7. Hoffer, E., Hubara, I., Soudry, D.: Train longer, generalize better: closing the generalization gap in large batch training of neural networks. In: Proceedings of the 31st International Conference on Neural Information Processing Systems, NIPS 2017, pp. 1729–1739. Curran Associates Inc., Red Hook (2017). http://dl.acm.org/citation.cfm?id=3294771.3294936
8. Huang, G., Liu, Z., Weinberger, K.Q.: Densely connected convolutional networks. CoRR abs/1608.06993 (2016). http://arxiv.org/abs/1608.06993
9. Huang, G., Sun, Y., Liu, Z., Sedra, D., Weinberger, K.Q.: Deep networks with stochastic depth. In: Leibe, B., Matas, J., Sebe, N., Welling, M. (eds.) ECCV 2016. LNCS, vol. 9908, pp. 646–661. Springer, Cham (2016). https://doi.org/10.1007/978-3-319-46493-0_39
10. Ioffe, S., Szegedy, C.: Batch normalization: accelerating deep network training by reducing internal covariate shift. In: Bach, F., Blei, D. (eds.) Proceedings of the 32nd International Conference on Machine Learning. Proceedings of Machine Learning Research, PMLR, Lille, France, 07–09 July 2015, vol. 37, pp. 448–456 (2015). http://proceedings.mlr.press/v37/ioffe15.html
11. Kingma, D.P., Ba, J.: Adam: a method for stochastic optimization. In: 3rd International Conference on Learning Representations, ICLR 2015, Conference Track Proceedings, San Diego, CA, USA, 7–9 May 2015. http://arxiv.org/abs/1412.6980
12. Levy, Y.K., Yurtsever, A., Cevher, V.: Online adaptive methods, universality and acceleration. In: Bengio, S., Wallach, H., Larochelle, H., Grauman, K., Cesa-Bianchi, N., Garnett, R. (eds.) Advances in Neural Information Processing Systems 31, pp. 6500–6509. Curran Associates, Inc. (2018). http://papers.nips.cc/paper/7885-online-adaptive-methods-universality-and-acceleration.pdf
13. Loshchilov, I., Hutter, F.: SGDR: stochastic gradient descent with restarts. CoRR abs/1608.03983 (2016). http://arxiv.org/abs/1608.03983
14. Nawi, N.M., Ransing, R.S., Salleh, M.N.M., Ghazali, R., Hamid, N.A.: An improved back propagation neural network algorithm on classification problems. In: Zhang, Y., Cuzzocrea, A., Ma, J., Chung, K., Arslan, T., Song, X. (eds.) FGIT 2010. CCIS, vol. 118, pp. 177–188. Springer, Heidelberg (2010). https://doi.org/10.1007/978-3-642-17622-7_18

15. Neelakantan, A., et al.: Adding gradient noise improves learning for very deep networks. arXiv preprint arXiv:1511.06807 (2015)
16. Qian, N.: On the momentum term in gradient descent learning algorithms. Neural Netw. **12**(1), 145–151 (1999). https://doi.org/10.1016/S0893-6080(98)00116-6
17. Seide, F., Fu, H., Droppo, J., Li, G., Yu, D.: 1-bit stochastic gradient descent and application to data-parallel distributed training of speech DNNs. In: Interspeech 2014, September 2014
18. Smith, S.L., Le, Q.V.: A Bayesian perspective on generalization and stochastic gradient descent. CoRR abs/1710.06451 (2017). http://arxiv.org/abs/1710.06451
19. Tieleman, T., Hinton, G.: Lecture 6.5 - RMSProp. Technical report (2012). https://www.cs.toronto.edu/~tijmen/csc321/slides/lecture_slides_lec6.pdf
20. Zeiler, M.D.: ADADELTA: an adaptive learning rate method. CoRR abs/1212.5701 (2012). http://arxiv.org/abs/1212.5701

Architecture-Aware Bayesian Optimization for Neural Network Tuning

Anders Sjöberg[1,2(✉)], Magnus Önnheim[1,2], Emil Gustavsson[1,2], and Mats Jirstrand[1,2]

[1] Fraunhofer-Chalmers Centre, 412 88 Gothenburg, Sweden
anders.sjoberg@fcc.chalmers.se
[2] Fraunhofer Center for Machine Learning, Gothenburg, Sweden

Abstract. Hyperparameter optimization of a neural network is a non-trivial task. It is time-consuming to evaluate a hyperparameter setting, no analytical expression of the impact of the hyperparameters are available, and the evaluations are noisy in the sense that the result is dependent on the training process and weight initialization. Bayesian optimization is a powerful tool to handle these problems. However, hyperparameter optimization of neural networks poses additional challenges, since the hyperparameters can be integer-valued, categorical, and/or conditional, whereas Bayesian optimization often assumes variables to be real-valued. In this paper we present an architecture-aware transformation of neural networks applied in the kernel of a Gaussian process to boost the performance of hyperparameter optimization.

The empirical experiment in this paper demonstrates that by introducing an architecture-aware transformation of the kernel, the performance of the Bayesian optimizer shows a clear improvement over a naïve implementation and that the results are comparable to other state-of-the-art methods.

Keywords: Hyperparameter optimization · Gaussian process · Transformation · Neural networks

1 Introduction

Designing a well-functioning neural network architecture is not a trivial task. The hyperparameters [2], which describe the architecture of a neural network, can be large in quantity and have a non-linear impact of the performance. To evaluate a hyperparameter setting one needs to train the model, with the specified setting, and test it on validation data. Since the training of a neural network model is very

This research was supported by the project *Root Cause Analysis of Quality Deviations in Manufacturing using Machine Learning (RCA-ML)* in the funding program *The smart digital factory* (DNR 2016-04472), administered by VINNOVA, the Swedish Government Agency for Innovation Systems. It was also developed in the Fraunhofer Cluster of Excellence *Cognitive Internet Technologies.*

I. V. Tetko et al. (Eds.): ICANN 2019, LNCS 11728, pp. 220–231, 2019.
https://doi.org/10.1007/978-3-030-30484-3_19

time consuming it is intractable to systematically test all possible configurations. In other words, we are facing a non-linear expensive black-box optimization problem.

To tackle such black-box problems, surrogate methods are often employed, and the subclass of Bayesian optimization has shown to be a powerful tool in many applications (e.g., [10,12,19]). The Bayesian procedure is to construct a probabilistic model of a black box function, and after each function evaluation exploit the posterior distribution to make a decisions about where to next evaluate the function. Bayesian methods generally depend on a prior distribution, and in this case, we need to choose a prior over functions, assumed to capture the behavior of the black box function. Gaussian process (GP) is an efficient and powerful family of prior distributions of functions [17], and in this paper we utilize the properties of GPs to optimize the architecture of neural networks.

An additional challenge of neural networks, as compared to standard black-box optimization, is that the hyperparameters can be conditioned by another. That is, some hyperparameters need only to be specified if other parameters are active or have a certain value. For example, a neural network with only one layer does not have parameters associated with a second to third layer. Given a joint set of all the hyperparameters, e.g., the number of layers and the number of neurons for each layer, respectively, will result in many points with inactive hyperparameters. A common strategy is to give a default value to the inactive parameters and let the surrogate model ignore those values (for a GP having a zero distance between these points) [5]. With this approach one can construct conditional kernels [15]. Equivalently, in this paper we describe it with a general transformation T in the kernel of a GP. More precisely, we construct a transformation $T : \mathcal{B}^D \rightarrow \mathcal{X}$, where $\mathcal{B}^D$ is a box where the GP is defined and $\mathcal{X}$ is the set of hyperparameters for a neural network. Furthermore, since many of the hyperparameters are integers and/or categorical then many of the points in the box will map to the same configuration under the transformation T. That is, two distinct points $x_i, x_j \in \mathcal{B}^D$ can be equal under the transformation, i.e., $T(x_i) = T(x_j)$. By utilizing this transformation in the kernel of a GP all points that describes the same configuration will have the same mean and variance.

The paper is organized as follows. We begin in Sect. 2 with a short summary of the relevant background on Bayesian optimization and GPs. In Sect. 3 we describe the proposed transformation in detail and how it is employed in the special case of hyperparameter optimization of neural networks. In Sect. 4 we present some numerical results of our proposed idea and in Sect. 5 we conclude with some final remarks and some proposed future work.

1.1 Contribution

Our main contribution in this paper is the idea/construction of a general transformation T in the kernel of a GP that is well-suited for hyperparameter optimization of neural networks. This transformation can handle continuous, integer-valued, categorical, and conditional hyperparameters. We include feasibility projection into the transformation that project infeasible hyperparameter configurations of neural networks to feasible configurations, which in turn reduces the problem. The inclusion of the transformation T introduces some difficulties for the gradient based local search methods commonly used for optimizing the acquisition function. By modifying these methods to pattern search algorithms that are interacting with the transformation we solve the problem. Lastly, we introduce a parameterization of neural network that decreases the size of the hyperparameter set that in turn simplifies the hyperparameter optimization problem.

2 Bayesian Optimization

Consider the problem to

$$\begin{aligned} & \underset{\boldsymbol{x}}{\text{minimize}} && f(\boldsymbol{x}) \\ & \text{subject to} && \boldsymbol{x} \in \mathcal{X} \subseteq \mathbb{R}^D, \end{aligned} \tag{1}$$

where f is assumed to be prohibitively expensive to evaluate, so that, e.g., a direct gradient based search is intractable. One approach to approximately solve (1) is by iteratively replacing f by surrogate models, inferred from past function evaluations, and using these model to propose new candidate values for $\boldsymbol{x}$. The Bayesian optimization approach fits into this framework by considering f to be a random function, according to some prior distribution, and interpreting function evaluations as sample data for calculating posterior distributions, in turn yielding posterior distributions of the function values at $\boldsymbol{x} \in \mathcal{X}$. Of course, having access to a full distribution of function values at every point $\boldsymbol{x}$, it is not obvious how to select the next candidate point to evaluate, requiring the choice of an *acquisition function* for estimating the benefit of evaluating a point x. To completely specify a Bayesian optimization algorithm we thus have to answer two questions:

1. How do we choose the prior distribution for f?
2. How do we choose the acquisition function?

In Sects. 2.1 and 2.2 we describe our approach to answering these to questions.

2.1 Gaussian Processes

A Gaussian process is an extension of the multivariate Gaussian distribution to an infinite-dimensional stochastic process for which any finite combination of dimensions is a Gaussian distribution. That is, a GP (on $\mathcal{X}$) is a distribution over functions on the form $f : \mathcal{X} \to \mathbb{R}$, specified by its mean function $m : \mathcal{X} \to \mathbb{R}$ and its covariance function $k : \mathcal{X} \times \mathcal{X} \to \mathbb{R}$:

$$f(\boldsymbol{x}) \sim GP(m(\boldsymbol{x}), k(\boldsymbol{x}, \boldsymbol{x}')).$$

The prior mean function m is often assumed to be zero function $m(\boldsymbol{x}) = 0$. There are, however, alternative priors that are used, e.g., in [3]. Further, for predictive purposes the covariance function is often assumed to be given by a *kernel*, i.e., an a priori selected form of k. The particular characteristic of the function $f(\boldsymbol{x})$, e.g., smoothness, amplitude, additive noise can then be specified by the choice of kernel k, and we will in the sequel only consider the popular Matèrn 5/2-kernel [19]:

$$k_{M52}(\boldsymbol{x}, \boldsymbol{x}') = \theta_0 \left(1 + \sqrt{5r^2(\boldsymbol{x}, \boldsymbol{x}')} + \frac{5}{3} r^2(\boldsymbol{x}, \boldsymbol{x}')\right) \exp - \sqrt{5r^2(\boldsymbol{x}, \boldsymbol{x}')} \quad (2)$$

where

$$r^2(\boldsymbol{x}, \boldsymbol{x}') = \sum_{d=1}^{D} \frac{(x_d - x'_d)^2}{\theta_d^2}, \quad (3)$$

and θ_i, $i = 0, \ldots, D$, are hyperparameters to the covariance function. Several other kernels are commonly used, we refer the reader to [17] for an overview.

Suppose that we have evaluated a black box function $f_{\text{black box}}(\boldsymbol{x})$ at t points $\boldsymbol{x}_1, \ldots, \boldsymbol{x}_t \in \mathcal{X}$. Let the corresponding objective values be summarized by the set $\mathcal{D}_{1:t} = \{(\boldsymbol{x}_i, y_i)\}_{i=1}^t$, where $y_i = f_{\text{black box}}(\boldsymbol{x}_i) + \epsilon_i$ and $\epsilon_i \sim \mathcal{N}(0, \sigma^2_{\text{noise}})$ is additive noise with variance σ^2_{noise}. Then the predictive distribution of the GP is

$$P(y_{t+1} | \mathcal{D}_{1:t}, \boldsymbol{x}_{t+1}) = \mathcal{N}(\mu_t(\boldsymbol{x}_{t+1}), \sigma_t^2(\boldsymbol{x}_{t+1})), \quad (4)$$

where

$$\mu_t(\boldsymbol{x}_{t+1}) = \boldsymbol{k}^T [K + \sigma^2_{\text{noise}} I]^{-1} \boldsymbol{y}_{1:t}, \quad (5a)$$

$$\sigma_t^2(\boldsymbol{x}_{t+1}) = k(\boldsymbol{x}_{t+1}, \boldsymbol{x}_{t+1}) [K + \sigma^2_{\text{noise}} I]^{-1} \boldsymbol{k}, \quad (5b)$$

with $\boldsymbol{y}_{1:t} = (y_1, \ldots, y_t)$ as column vector with all the objective evaluations, K as the covariance matrix defined as

$$K = \begin{pmatrix} k(\boldsymbol{x}_1, \boldsymbol{x}_1) & \cdots & k(\boldsymbol{x}_1, \boldsymbol{x}_t) \\ \vdots & \ddots & \vdots \\ k(\boldsymbol{x}_t, \boldsymbol{x}_1) & \cdots & k(\boldsymbol{x}_t, \boldsymbol{x}_t) \end{pmatrix}, \quad (6)$$

and $\boldsymbol{k} = (k(\boldsymbol{x}_{t+1}, \boldsymbol{x}_1), \ldots, k(\boldsymbol{x}_{t+1}, \boldsymbol{x}_t))$ as column covariance vector. See [17] for detailed derivation.

It should be clear from the above that the choice of prior can have a strong effect on performance of a Bayesian optimizer. Hence, one runs the risk of replacing the hard-to-optimize function f with hard-to-tune hyperparameters of the GP priors. This problem can however be circumvented somewhat, by additionally placing a prior on the set of GP hyperparameters (e.g., the kernel function k), and using Markov Chain Monte Carlo (MCMC) sampling [7] of GP hyperparameters for a full Bayesian treatment. This carries the computational cost of running an MCMC sampler, which should be balanced against the computational cost of additional evaluations of f.

2.2 Acquisition Function

The purpose of the acquisition function $a : \mathcal{X} \rightarrow \mathbb{R}^+$ is to guide the search to the optimum. Generally acquisition functions are defined such that a high acquisition value corresponds to a potentially low function value. In our case, the acquisition function uses the predictive distribution generated by the Gaussian process to compute the utility of performing an evaluation of a certain point in $\mathcal{X}$. That is, the next point $\boldsymbol{x}_{t+1}$ to be evaluated by f is simply $\boldsymbol{x}_{t+1} = \arg\max_{\boldsymbol{x}\in\mathcal{X}} a(\boldsymbol{x})$. Typically, acquisition functions depend on previous observations and the hyperparameters of the Gaussian process, i.e. σ^2_{noise} and the hyperparameters θ_i of the kernel, and we denote this dependency by $a(\boldsymbol{x}; \mathcal{D}_{1:t}, \boldsymbol{\theta})$. Several popular acquisition functions are under the GP prior solely described by the predictive mean, from Eq. (5a) including the dependencies, $\mu(\boldsymbol{x}; \mathcal{D}_{1:t}, \boldsymbol{\theta})$, and the predictive variance function, from Eq. (5b) including the dependencies, $\sigma^2(\boldsymbol{x}; \mathcal{D}_{1:t}, \boldsymbol{\theta})$.

One popular acquisition function is the *Expected Improvement* (EI) [12]:

$$a_{\text{EI}}(\boldsymbol{x}; \mathcal{D}_{1:t}, \boldsymbol{\theta}) = \sigma(\boldsymbol{x}; \mathcal{D}_{1:t}, \boldsymbol{\theta}) \left(\gamma(\boldsymbol{x})\Phi(\gamma(\boldsymbol{x})) + \phi(\gamma(\boldsymbol{x}))\right), \tag{7}$$

where $\Phi(\cdot)$ and $\phi(\cdot)$ are the c.d.f and the p.d.f, respectively, of a standard Gaussian distribution, $\boldsymbol{x}_{\text{best}} = \arg\min_{\boldsymbol{x}\in\{\boldsymbol{x}_1,\ldots,\boldsymbol{x}_t\}} f_{\text{black box}}(\boldsymbol{x})$, and

$$\gamma(\boldsymbol{x}) = \frac{f_{\text{black box}}(\boldsymbol{x}_{\text{best}}) - \mu(\boldsymbol{x}; \mathcal{D}_{1:t}, \boldsymbol{\theta})}{\sigma(\boldsymbol{x}; \mathcal{D}_{1:t}, \boldsymbol{\theta})}. \tag{8}$$

We will in the sequel only use Expected Improvement as acquisition function, however we note that there is a large literature regarding other choices (e.g., [4,8]).

3 Transformation

The hyperparameter set $\mathcal{X}$ of a neural network usually includes conditional, categorical, and integer hyperparameters. This implies that the common assumption in Bayesian optimization that the feasible set $\mathcal{X}$ of (1) is a (scaled) hypercube is not satisfied. However, we may of course apply a transformation

$$T : B^D \rightarrow \mathcal{X}, \tag{9}$$

where B is a box in $\mathbb{R}^D$. If T is surjective, we can replace (1) by the equivalent problem to

$$\begin{aligned} \underset{\boldsymbol{x}}{\text{minimize}} \quad & f(T(\boldsymbol{x})) \\ \text{subject to} \quad & \boldsymbol{x} \in B^D, \end{aligned} \tag{10}$$

which is a problem with only continuous variables, and attempt to apply Bayesian optimization to this problem. An issue with this approach is illustrated in the following example.

Example 1. Let $f(x) = x^2$, $\mathcal{X} = \{0,1\} \subset \mathbb{R}^1$, and let T be the rounding of $[0,1]$ to the nearest point in $\mathcal{X}$, i.e., $T : [0,1] \to \{0,1\}$, $T(x) = [x]$. Suppose that we have evaluated each point in $\mathcal{X}$ once, so that $\mathcal{D}_{1:2} = \{(0,0),(1,1)\}$. Then, although the function is fully determined by the sampled values, a Gaussian process as described above will retain some uncertainty regarding the value, say, $f(T(1/4))$. The effect is that we may spend unnecessary function evaluations in a region where the black-box function is fully determined when optimizing f.

The core issue in the example above is that the Gaussian process is defined naïvely on B^D, rather than on $\mathcal{X}$. To define a Gaussian process on $\mathcal{X}$ we note that the Matèrn kernel is well defined for *any* pseudometric space (X,d), by simply replacing the rescaled Euclidean metric in (3) by the metric d on X. Moreover, since $\mathcal{X} \subset \mathbb{R}^D$, we can take the restriction of the Euclidean metric on $\mathbb{R}^D$, rescaled as in (3), as a metric on $\mathcal{X}$. Doing so would however require optimization of the acquisition function a over $\mathcal{X}$ for generating new candidate points during the optimization process, and for ease of implementation we instead define a Gaussian process on B^D by defining a family of pseudometrics d', parametrized by θ as in (3), on B^D

$$d'(\boldsymbol{x},\boldsymbol{x}';\theta) := d(T(\boldsymbol{x}),T(\boldsymbol{x}');\theta), \tag{11}$$

It follows that the Gaussian process on B^D has the property that, $k(\boldsymbol{x},\boldsymbol{x}') = \theta_0$ whenever $T(\boldsymbol{x}') = T(\boldsymbol{x})$. In other words, optimizing (10), using (11) to define a kernel, is algorithmically equivalent to optimizing (1) using the corresponding Gaussian process on $\mathcal{X}$, assuming the acquisition function is optimized exactly.

We point out that using a pseudometric to define a Matèrn kernel on B^D, the covariance matrix K in (6) is only guaranteed to be positive semi-definite, rather than positive definite. However, when $\sigma_{\text{noise}} > 0$, $K + \sigma^2_{\text{noise}} I$ is indeed positive definite, and the Gaussian process update (5) is well defined.

3.1 A Transformation for Neural Networks

We describe the definition of our constructed transformation T, in (9), that is suited for neural networks, component-wise for continuous, integer, categorical, and conditional hyperparameters:

- Continuous hyperparameters are assumed to be normalized to the unit interval, standard procedure [20], and the transformation is simply the identity map.
- Integer hyperparameters, with domain $\{a,\dots,b\}$, are transformed by rounding, similar to [6], i.e.:

$$\begin{aligned} T : [a-1/2, b+1/2] &\to \{a,\dots,b\} \\ x &\mapsto [x]. \end{aligned}$$

- Categorical hyperparameters are assumed to be represented via one-hot encoded, i.e., a categorical hyperparameter with C values is parametrized by

an element of $\{0,1\}^C$. The transformation is then a map $T : [0,1]^C \to \{0,1\}^C$, as in [6], such that $T(x)_i = 1$, where i is the largest component of x (with ties broken by taking the smallest i), and $T(x_j) = 0$ for $j \neq i$.
- Conditional hyperparameters are given a default value under the transformation T for inactive hyperparameters, and otherwise treated according to their as in the above. Note that when utilizing such a transformation T points that only differ in inactive hyperparameters are transformed to the same point.

While working with hyperparameters of neural networks some configurations might end up in infeasible points. For example, changing the hyperparameters "pooling size" and "convolutional filter size" in a convolutional neural network might result in a too aggressive down-sampling of the data, so that nothing of the data remains. We solve this problem by amending the construction of the transformation T above to include feasibility projections; a hyperparameter configuration that leads to an infeasible network architecture is transformed to a "nearby" configuration. In the case of convolutional neural network above, an infeasible point will be transformed to the point where the number of layers are equal to the feasible amount of layers, i.e., the layer before the data got down-sampled too much.

3.2 Parameterization of Neural Network

Even though one replaces the black-box function $f(\boldsymbol{x})$ with a Gaussian process, that is cheap to evaluate, the global optimization of the acquisition function can still be a non-trivial task. Therefore, if we can decrease the size of the hyperparameter set, but still preserve, at least close to, the best performance it would simplify optimization of the acquisition function. Furthermore, given that we will use a distance-based kernel of the Gaussian processes, we wish, if possible, to choose a parametrization such that a change in i:th and j:th components of $\boldsymbol{x}$ have a comparable effect on f. The latter, however, is not a trivial task. How the hyperparameters of a neural network affect the performance is an open research problem. Nevertheless, an intuitive idea, based on the result in [16], is to reduce the number of points that govern the number of neurons per layer. In [16] it is shown that the number of linear regions of a deep neural network, with rectified linear activations, grows exponentially with the number of layers, and polynomially in the width the layers. To match the effect of width and depth we take a parametrization such that the width is exponential in the corresponding parameter value. That is, instead of choosing an exact number neurons per layer, we choose a relative exponential amount of neurons compared to the previous layer: either we double the number of neurons, keep the same amount, or reduce it by half to the next layer. This way we reduce the hyperparameter governing the number of neurons at layer $i \geq 2$ down to three values, respectively, while keeping a comparable effect on representational capacity of the neural network, as measured by the possible number of linear regions, of width- and depth-related variables.

3.3 Optimization of Acquisition Function Under Transformation

A common procedure [20] to optimize the acquisition function is to start with initialization of randomized points, uniformly or from a Sobol sequence, in the hypercube and thereafter utilize local search, commonly by utilization of gradients, on each of the randomized points. However, when we are applying the transformation T, some variables are in fact integers, reflected in the fact that the acquisition function is constant for large areas of the categorical, integer-valued and inactive conditional hyperparameter will have the same value. That is, in those dimensions there will be large plateaus, where the partial derivative for that dimension will be zero, see Fig. 1 as an example. These plateaus complicate the local search and solely gradient-based can get stuck completely. Therefore, we implement a pattern search [21] based strategy for local search, described below.

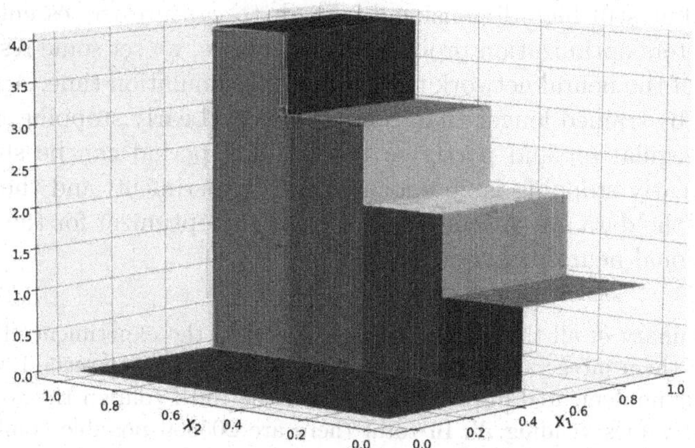

Fig. 1. An illustration of integer-valued and conditional variable. The variable x_1 govern if the variable x_2 is active or not. As long as $x_1 > 0.5$ then x_2 is active and this variable is an integer-valued variable. This illustrates the large plateaus that can occur in the hyperparameter set of a neural network under the transformation T.

For local search we separate the continuous hyperparameters from the categorical, integer-valued, and conditional hyperparameters. The continuous variables are updated with gradient ascent while non-continuous variables are fixed. Non-continuous variables are then updated, keeping the continuous variables fixed, by evaluating neighboring points if they differ under the transformation T, maintaining a Tabu list of previously visited points. An alternation between the two updates is utilized until local maximum has been found or a maximum number of evaluations has been reached.

The transformation T is applied during the initialization phase of the Bayesian optimizer as well, such that only points that differ under the transformation are evaluated. Furthermore, we use an adapted probability distribution weighted according to the number of points for each layer, i.e., the initialization of points in the acquisition function will have more points with more layers since they make up more of the hyperparameter space under the transformation T. Lastly, to increase that probability that there are some potentially good initialization points for the optimization task of the acquisition function, n points with high acquisition score from previous iteration are stored and used together with a new randomized initialization from the adapted probability distribution at each iteration.

4 Experimental Results

Consider the problem to find the best suited convolutional neural network for CIFAR-10 [14] image recognition task. The hyperparameters we consider are summarized in Table 1. We choose to not have a very high-dimensional hyperparameter set so that the experiment can be run multiple times in a reasonable time frame, but still high-dimensional enough to capture the essential part of hyperparameters optimization problem. Furthermore, we set some restriction on the training of the neural network to decrease the simulation time. A neural network cannot be trained longer than ten minutes and early stopping is included, partly as a regularizer and partly so the training period can be shorter than 10 min. The early stopping is 20 epochs in this experiment, and the validation set is 20% of the data set. Adam [13] is used as the optimizer for the training of the convolutional neural network.

Table 1. Summary of all the hyperparameters used in the experiment. There are 13 in total, all of them integers, and seven of them conditional. The second column indicates the value implemented during training and the third column the corresponding parameterized values yielding $\mathcal{X}$. In total there are 205800 possible combinations of hyperparameters.

Hyperparameter	Implementation	Parametrization	Conditional
Number of convolutional layers	$\{1, 2, 3\}$	$\{1, 2, 3\}$	No
Neurons in convolutional layer 1	$\{2^4, 2^5, \ldots, 2^8\}$	$\{4, \ldots, 8\}$	No
$\frac{\text{Neurons in layer } i}{\text{Neurons in layer } i-1}, i = 2, 3$	$\{1/2, 1, 2\}$	$\{-1, 0, 1\}$	Yes
Filter size in layer i	$\{2, 3, 4\}$	$\{2, 3, 4\}$	Yes
Pooling size after layer i	$\{2, 3\}$	$\{2, 3\}$	Yes
Number of dense layers	$\{1, 2\}$	$\{1, 2\}$	No
Neurons in dense layer 1	$\{2^4, 2^5, \ldots, 2^8\}$	$\{4, \ldots, 8\}$	No
$\frac{\text{Neurons in dense layer 2}}{\text{Neurons in dense layer 1}}$	$\{1/2, 1, 2\}$	$\{-1, 0, 1\}$	Yes

We consider five different models:

- Random search, that cannot pick an already chosen hyperparameter configuration.

- Regular GP, from the library pyGPGO [11].
- GP modified with transformation T and random search as optimizer of the acquisition function.
- GP modified with transformation T and local search as optimizer of the acquisition function.
- Tree Parzen Estimator (TPE) [2], from the library hyperopt [1].

All models get 150 evaluation points, whereof 50 are initialization points. For the three GPs we choose expected improvement, see Eq. (7), as the acquisition function, matern52, see Eq. (2), as the covariance function, NUTS [9] as the MCMC-sampler for the hyperparameters of the GP implemented in the library pymc3 [18], 10 NUTS samples used for each iteration, i.e., 10 GPs constructed. The results of the empirical experiment are visualized in Fig. 2.

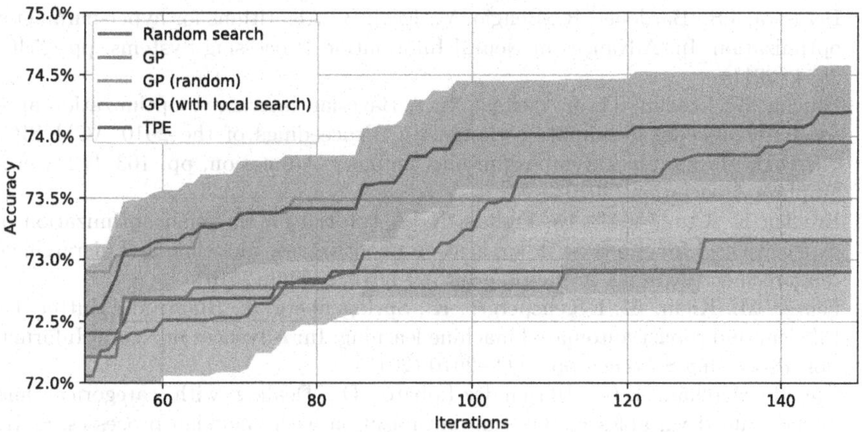

Fig. 2. Average accuracy ± a half standard deviation of the best hyperparameter configuration found on the data set CIFAR-10 for the five different models; Random search, GP, GP (random), GP (with local search), and TPE, for 8, 4, 6, 9, and 10 runs, respectively. Due to differences in the initialization phase the methods start at different accuracy levels (after 50 initialization points). One can see that TPE and GP with local search perform the best and that Random search and standard GP show worst performance.

5 Conclusion and Future Work

By introducing an architecture-aware transformation of the kernel, the performance of our architecture-aware Bayesian optimizer shows a clear improvement over a naïve implementation, which performs comparably to the baseline of random search. We achieve comparable, but slightly worse, results to the state-of-the-art method TPE. However, we note that there is significant room for improving the Bayesian optimizer by, e.g., varying the acquisition function. Further, the results show that the choice of the acquisition function optimizer has a strong effect on performance, which indicates yet another possibility for improvement.

Future work include evaluating the proposed idea with transformations in the kernel of Gaussian processes on other data sets and other types of neural network architectures. Categorical and continuous variables are easily included in the proposed framework, and the next step is to analyze the performance when having mixed variable types (e.g., adding learning rate and type of activation functions).

References

1. Bergstra, J., Yamins, D., Cox, D.D.: Hyperopt: a Python library for optimizing the hyperparameters of machine learning algorithms. In: Proceedings of the 12th Python in Science Conference, pp. 13–20. Citeseer (2013)
2. Bergstra, J.S., Bardenet, R., Bengio, Y., Kégl, B.: Algorithms for hyper-parameter optimization. In: Advances in Neural Information Processing Systems, pp. 2546–2554 (2011)
3. Brochu, E., Brochu, T., de Freitas, N.: A Bayesian interactive optimization approach to procedural animation design. In: Proceedings of the 2010 ACM SIGGRAPH/Eurographics Symposium on Computer Animation, pp. 103–112. Eurographics Association (2010)
4. Brochu, E., Cora, V.M., De Freitas, N.: A tutorial on Bayesian optimization of expensive cost functions, with application to active user modeling and hierarchical reinforcement learning. arXiv preprint arXiv:1012.2599 (2010)
5. Feurer, M., Klein, A., Eggensperger, K., Springenberg, J., Blum, M., Hutter, F.: Efficient and robust automated machine learning. In: Advances in Neural Information Processing Systems, pp. 2962–2970 (2015)
6. Garrido-Merchán, E.C., Hernández-Lobato, D.: Dealing with categorical and integer-valued variables in Bayesian optimization with Gaussian processes. arXiv preprint arXiv:1805.03463 (2018)
7. Hastings, W.K.: Monte Carlo sampling methods using Markov chains and their applications. Biometrika **57**(1), 97–109 (1970). https://doi.org/10.1093/biomet/57.1.97
8. Hernández-Lobato, J.M., Hoffman, M.W., Ghahramani, Z.: Predictive entropy search for efficient global optimization of black-box functions. In: Advances in Neural Information Processing Systems, pp. 918–926 (2014)
9. Hoffman, M.D., Gelman, A.: The No-U-Turn sampler: adaptively setting path lengths in Hamiltonian Monte Carlo. J. Mach. Learn. Res. **15**(1), 1593–1623 (2014)
10. Huang, D., Allen, T.T., Notz, W.I., Zeng, N.: Global optimization of stochastic black-box systems via sequential kriging meta-models. J. Global Optim. **34**(3), 441–466 (2006)
11. Jiménez, J., Ginebra, J.: pyGPGO: Bayesian optimization for Python. J. Open Source Softw. **2**, 431 (2017)
12. Jones, D.R., Schonlau, M., Welch, W.J.: Efficient global optimization of expensive black-box functions. J. Global Optim. **13**(4), 455–492 (1998)
13. Kingma, D.P., Ba, J.: Adam: a method for stochastic optimization. arXiv preprint arXiv:1412.6980 (2014)
14. Krizhevsky, A., Nair, V., Hinton, G.: The CIFAR-10 dataset, p. 4 (2014). http://www.cs.toronto.edu/kriz/cifar.html

15. Lévesque, J.C., Durand, A., Gagné, C., Sabourin, R.: Bayesian optimization for conditional hyperparameter spaces. In: 2017 International Joint Conference on Neural Networks (IJCNN), pp. 286–293. IEEE (2017)
16. Montufar, G.F., Pascanu, R., Cho, K., Bengio, Y.: On the number of linear regions of deep neural networks. In: Advances in Neural Information Processing Systems, pp. 2924–2932 (2014)
17. Rasmussen, C., Williams, C.: Gaussian Processes for Machine Learning. Adaptive Computation and Machine Learning. MIT Press, Cambridge (2006)
18. Salvatier, J., Fonnesbeck, C., et al.: PyMC3: Python probabilistic programming framework. Astrophysics Source Code Library (2016)
19. Snoek, J., Larochelle, H., Adams, R.P.: Practical Bayesian optimization of machine learning algorithms. In: Advances in Neural Information Processing Systems, pp. 2951–2959 (2012)
20. Snoek, J.R.: Bayesian optimization and semiparametric models with applications to assistive technology. Ph.D. thesis, University of Toronto (2013)
21. Torczon, V.: On the convergence of pattern search algorithms. SIAM J. Optim. **7**(1), 1–25 (1997)

Non-convergence and Limit Cycles in the Adam Optimizer

Sebastian Bock(✉) and Martin Weiß

OTH Regensburg, Prüfeninger Str. 58, 93049 Regensburg, Germany
{sebastian2.bock,martin.weiss}@oth-regensburg.de

Abstract. One of the most popular training algorithms for deep neural networks is the Adaptive Moment Estimation (Adam) introduced by Kingma and Ba. Despite its success in many applications there is no satisfactory convergence analysis: only local convergence can be shown for batch mode under some restrictions on the hyperparameters, counterexamples exist for incremental mode. Recent results show that for simple quadratic objective functions limit cycles of period 2 exist in batch mode, but only for atypical hyperparameters, and only for the algorithm without bias correction. We extend the convergence analysis to all choices of the hyperparameters for quadratic functions. This finally answers the question of convergence for Adam in batch mode to the negative. We analyze the stability of these limit cycles and relate our analysis to other results where approximate convergence was shown, but under the additional assumption of bounded gradients which does not apply to quadratic functions. The investigation heavily relies on the use of computer algebra due to the complexity of the equations.

Keywords: Adam optimizer · Convergence · Computer algebra · Dynamical system · Limit cycle

1 Introduction

Adaptive Moment Estimation (Adam), originally presented by Kingma and Ba [6] is probably the most widely used training algorithm for neural networks, especially convolutional neural networks. Implementations exist in all popular machine learning frameworks like Tensorflow or PyTorch. In order to make the presentation self-contained and to motivate our contribution we first explain the variant of the Adam algorithm used in this paper (Algorithm 1): Adam constitutes a first order method for minimization of $f = f(w) : \mathbb{R}^n \to \mathbb{R}$, so only gradient information is used. Plain gradient descent $w_{t+1} = w_t - \alpha \nabla_w f(w_t)$, with a learning rate $\alpha > 0$, termed backpropagation in the neural network language, is easy to understand and implement but has several drawbacks (see [7] for a basic exposition): First, convergence is only local and cannot guarantee a global optimum due to the nonlinearity of the objective function. Second, the learning rate must be chosen small enough but an upper bound usually cannot

I. V. Tetko et al. (Eds.): ICANN 2019, LNCS 11728, pp. 232–243, 2019.
https://doi.org/10.1007/978-3-030-30484-3_20

be given for real life problems, so users resort to trial and error. Third, convergence can be very slow for ill-conditioned problems, i.e. objective functions with a large ratio of the largest and smallest eigenvalues of the Hessian.

The first issue is a fundamental boundary in nonlinear optimization. Adaptation of a single learning rate is not addressed by Adam either, rather individual learning rates for the components of f are computed relative to a common learning rate, based on so called moments of the function f: The gradient $\nabla f(w)$ is not directly used as a descent direction but passed through a linear filter with parameter β_1 giving an exponential moving average m_t, the first moment. The componentwise square of the gradient is passed through another linear filter with parameter β_2 giving an exponential moving average v_t, the second moment. (The symbols $\otimes, \oplus$ and $\oslash$ denote the component-wise multiplication and division of vectors, as well as component-wise addition of vectors and scalar, so $\nabla f(w_t) \otimes \nabla f(w_t)$ gives the component-wise squares. We also denote the componentwise square root of a nonnegative vector x with the symbol $\sqrt{x}$.) Typical values used in practice and suggested in [6] without theoretical justification are $\beta_1 = 0.9$, $\beta_2 = 0.999$. The vector $-m_t \oslash \sqrt{v_t}$ is then used as the iteration direction, with roughly similar componentwise scaling. To avoid division by zero, a small positive term ε is added in the denominator.

Algorithm 1. Adam Optimization

Require: $\alpha \in \mathbb{R}^+$, $\varepsilon \in \mathbb{R}$ $\beta_1, \beta_2 \in (0,1)$, $w_0 \in \mathbb{R}^n$, objective function $f(w) \in C^2(\mathbb{R}^n, \mathbb{R})$

$m_0 = 0$

$v_0 = 0$

$t = 0$

while w not converged **do**

$\quad m_{t+1} = \beta_1 m_t + (1-\beta_1)\nabla f(w_t)$

$\quad v_{t+1} = \beta_2 v_t + (1-\beta_2)\nabla f(w_t) \otimes \nabla f(w_t)$

$\quad w_{t+1} = w_t - \alpha \frac{\sqrt{1-\beta_2^{t+1}}}{(1-\beta_1^{t+1})} m_{t+1} \oslash \sqrt{v_{t+1} \oplus \varepsilon}$

$\quad t = t+1$

end while

In the course of time, several variations of the Adam optimizer were developed. The main points worth noting about Algorithm 1 are: If a constant value F is used as an input in the equations for m_t and v_t instead of $\nabla f(w_t)$ then m_t and v_t will converge, but not to F and F^2 respectively, as one would like to have in an replacement for the raw gradient terms. To remedy this, a so-called bias correction is used to compensate the geometric sum up to time t, dividing m_{t+1} by $(1-\beta_1^{t+1})$, and v_{t+1} by $\sqrt{1-\beta_2^{t+1}}$. All referenced publications with the exception of [4] apply a bias correction in the learning rate α_t; we use the same bias correction as described in [6, Sect. 2].

Originally Kingma and Ba [6] used $\sqrt{v} \oplus \varepsilon$ and a bias correction. Other publications like [3,9] do not use an ε to avoid division by zero, probably assuming that $\nabla f(w_0) \neq 0$ in all components, so effectively the initial value is set to some small ε. We use the variant with ε in the denominator; otherwise the initial value $v_0 = 0$ would have to be excluded in all results, and one could not talk about stability of a fixed point $w_\star$ of the iteration corresponding to a minimum of the objective function.

Also we use $\sqrt{v \oplus \varepsilon}$ as in [2], instead of $\sqrt{v} \oplus \varepsilon$ as in the original publication [6]. Our variant has the advantage that the iteration is continuously differentiable for all $v \geq 0$ whereas the ε outside of the square root leads to a non differentiable exception set. The numerical differences of the two variants are marginal and described in more detail in [2].

Despite its apparent success the theoretical basis for Adam is weak: The first moment cannot be shown to be a descent direction, so the objective value does not decrease in each iteration. The original proof published in [6] is wrong as has been noted by several authors, see [1,9,10]. Of course a faulty proof does not imply that the Adam optimizer does not converge, and indeed local convergence can be shown for batch mode under reasonable restrictions on the hyperparameters α, β_1, β_2, see [2]. In [9] an example is given where the regret does not converge, neither do the arguments of the objective function, but this counterexample does not use batch mode, rather two cyclically alternating objective functions during the iteration. Our counterexample function is much simpler, but the proof relies on computer algebra.

Results exist which show ε-bounds on the gradients, $\|\nabla f(w_t)\| < \varepsilon$ for $\varepsilon > 0$ arbitrarily small for all t sufficiently large, see [3]. Other results show asymptotic bounds on the regret or that the function values come close to the minimum, $f(w_t) - f(w_\star) < \varepsilon$, see [3] again for example. To the best of the authors' knowledge, [2] is the only (partial) result on weight convergence in the standard mathematical definition $\lim_{t\to\infty} w_t = w_\star$, however only in a local sense.

Contrary to these results the preprint [4] shows that 2-cycles exist for the Adam optimizer without bias correction for the simple case of a scalar quadratic objective function $f(w) = \frac{1}{2}w^2$. Quadratic objective functions are a natural benchmark for any optimization algorithm in convex analysis: The standard gradient descent algorithm converges for learning rate small enough, see [8], so this behaviour should be replicated by more sophisticated gradient motivated adaptive algorithms like Adam. However [4, Proposition 3.3] only deals with the case $\beta_1 = 0$ which means that the first moments are not adapted at all – this case hardly can be called an adaptive moment algorithm any more.

We extend the results of [4] to the general case of hyperparameters $\alpha > 0$, $0 < \beta_1 < 1$, $0 < \beta_2 < 1$, and show existence of 2-limit-cycles for scalar objective functions $f(w) = \frac{1}{2}cw^2$, $c > 0$, which easily generalizes by diagonalization to strictly convex quadratic functions $f(w) = \frac{1}{2}w^\perp Cw$ with C positive definite; we denote the transpose by $w^\perp$. This is done for the Adam algorithm in batch mode only, but also for bias correction. We assume that the gradient of $f : \mathbb{R}^n \to \mathbb{R}$ exists and is continuous; the Hessian is needed for some results.

We give numerical evidence that for typical values of β_1, β_2 near 1 these 2-cycles are unstable, and stable for β_1, β_2 near 0. The analysis of the limit cycles is not exhaustive: more 2-cycles may exist, and cycles of larger period. However our results suffice to clarify the global non-convergence of Adam even for strictly convex functions under the fairly standard assumptions of bounds on the Hessian $\nabla^2 f(w)$ like $0 < lI_n \le \nabla^2 f(w) \le LI_n$ for all $w \in \mathbb{R}^n$.

The outline of the paper is as follows: In Sect. 2 we define our variant of the Adam algorithm and explain the steps of our proof. In Sect. 3 these steps are carried out. The Maple code used can be obtained from GitHub[1]. Section 4 shows numerical simulations suggesting that a Hopf bifurcation occurs, before we state some conclusions and relate our results to other research.

2 Outline of the Proof

We denote $x = (m, v, w)$ the state of the Adam iteration, and interpret the algorithm as discrete time dynamical system $x_{t+1} = T(t, x_t; p)$ with $T = T(t, x; p) = T(t, m, v, w; \alpha, \beta_1, \beta_2, \varepsilon)$ to express the dependence of the iteration on the state $x = (m, v, w)$ and the hyperparameters $p = (\alpha, \beta_1, \beta_2, \varepsilon)$.

We write Adam without bias correction in the same way as $\bar{T} = \bar{T}(x; p) = \bar{T}(m, v, w; \alpha, \beta_1, \beta_2, \varepsilon)$. This gives an autonomous dynamical system; the right hand side does not explicitly depend on t. The difference between the two systems is denoted by $\Theta(t, x; p)$, so we have analogous to [2]

$$x_{t+1} = T(t, x_t; p) = \bar{T}(x_t; p) + \Theta(t, x_t, p) \tag{1}$$

with

$$\bar{T}(x_t; p) = \begin{bmatrix} \beta_1 m_t + (1-\beta_1)\, g(w_t) \\ \beta_2 v_t + (1-\beta_2)\, g(w_t) \otimes g(w_t) \\ w_t - \alpha\left(m_{t+1} \oslash \sqrt{v_{t+1} \oplus \varepsilon}\right) \end{bmatrix} \tag{2}$$

and

$$\Theta(t, x_t; p) = \begin{bmatrix} 0 \\ 0 \\ -\alpha\left(\frac{\sqrt{1-\beta_2^{t+1}}}{1-\beta_1^{t+1}} - 1\right)\left(m_{t+1} \oslash \sqrt{v_{t+1} \oplus \varepsilon}\right) \end{bmatrix} \tag{3}$$

2.1 Steps of the Proof

We show that for the objective function $f(w) = \frac{1}{2}cw^2$ with $c > 0$ 2-cycles occur for a wide range of hyperparameters in the Adam iteration without bias correction, and that iterations of the bias corrected algorithm converge to this limit cycle if it is stable. We proceed in several steps, analyzing simplified variants of Adam first, then adding complexity in each step. The analysis uses Maple as a computer algebra system and some continuity and disturbance arguments because the naive approach of applying the `solve` command to find 2-cycles fails – the equations are too complicated.

[1] https://github.com/SebastianB3/Cycles-in-Adam.

1. We start with the scalar case $f(w) = \frac{1}{2}cw^2$, $c > 0$. We obtain analytical expressions for 2-limit-cycles $\bar{T}^2(x; \alpha, \beta_1, \beta_2, \varepsilon) = x$ of the autonomous system with $\varepsilon = 0$.
2. Calculating the eigenvalues of $\bar{T}^2$ we find that these do not depend on the learning rate α and the factor c in the objective function. For some typical values of the hyperparameters we give evidence that these limit cycles are often attractive. We have not managed to give analytical estimates for stable eigenvalues using CAS so far.
3. Using the implicit function theorem we show that for a neighbourhood of $\varepsilon_\star = 0$ there exists a unique limit cycle of the autonomous system with $\varepsilon > 0$. By continuity of the eigenvalues, these limit cycles are also attractive for ε small enough.
4. We apply a disturbance estimate to show that locally solutions of $T(t, x; p)$ converge to the limit cycles of $\bar{T}(x; p)$. The proof is essentially the same as in [2, Theorem V.1.] and holds for cycles of any integer length.

3 Existence of 2-Limit-Cycles in Adam

Step 1: We show that limit cycles of period 2 exist for Adam without bias correction, i.e. the autonomous system $\bar{T}$. A 2-cycle corresponds to a non-constant solution of $\bar{T}(\bar{T}(x; p); p)) = x$, so we try to solve this system of equations with Maple. This fails, so we do not use arbitrary parameters but fix $\varepsilon = 0$. Now Maple succeeds and returns

$$\tilde{m} = \frac{1}{2}\frac{c\left(\beta_1 - 1\right)^2\alpha}{\left(\beta_1 + 1\right)^2}, \quad \tilde{v} = \frac{1}{4}\frac{\alpha^2\left(\beta_1^2 - 2\beta_1 + 1\right)c^2}{\left(\beta_1 + 1\right)^2}, \quad \tilde{w} = \frac{1}{2}\frac{\alpha\left(\beta_1 - 1\right)}{\beta_1 + 1} \tag{4}$$

with $(-\tilde{m}, \tilde{v}, -\tilde{w})$ the other point on the 2-cycle. Note that $\tilde{m} \neq 0$, so we have a 2-cycle indeed. We abbreviate these points as $\tilde{x}_1$ and $\tilde{x}_2$. The v components of $\tilde{x}_1$ and $\tilde{x}_2$ are identical. This limit 2-cycle exists for all $\beta_1 \neq \pm 1$, that is for all reasonable Adam hyperparameters. Maple also returns more 2-cycles depending on the roots of $2\beta_1\beta_2 - 2\beta_2^2 - 2\beta_1 + 2\beta_2$, we have not analyzed these. We could not determine cycles of greater period $q \in \mathbb{N}$ by solving $\bar{T}^q(x) = x$.

Step 2: But we can determine the stability of the limit cycle using the Eigenvalues of the Jacobian of $\bar{T}^2(\tilde{x}_1)$, which are the same as those of $\bar{T}^2(\tilde{x}_2)$. The Jacobian, with no easy interpretation, is computed by Maple as:

$$\begin{bmatrix} -\left(\beta_1 + 2\right)\beta_1 & 2\frac{(\beta_1+1)\beta_2}{\alpha c} & c\left(\beta_1 - 1\right)\left(\beta_1 + 2\beta_2 - 1\right) \\ -2\left(\beta_2 - 1\right)\alpha\beta_1 c & 3{\beta_2}^2 - 2\beta_2 & 2\frac{c^2(\beta_1-1)(\beta_1+3/2\beta_2-1/2)(\beta_2-1)\alpha}{\beta_1+1} \\ 2\frac{\beta_1(\beta_1+1)(1-\beta_1-2\beta_2)}{c(\beta_1-1)} & 2\frac{(2\beta_1+3\beta_2-1)(\beta_1+1)\beta_2}{c^2\alpha(\beta_1-1)} & 2{\beta_1}^2 + \left(8\beta_2 - 6\right)\beta_1 + 6{\beta_2}^2 - 6\beta_2 + 1 \end{bmatrix}$$

Using Maple we obtain a very lengthy expression for the eigenvalues which does *not* depend on α or c, but on β_1 and β_2 only. Details can be seen in the supplementary code. This is surprising as most algorithms show dependence on the learning rate, and one might assume that the behaviour at a limit cycle is different at least for $\alpha \to 0$ and $\alpha \to \infty$.

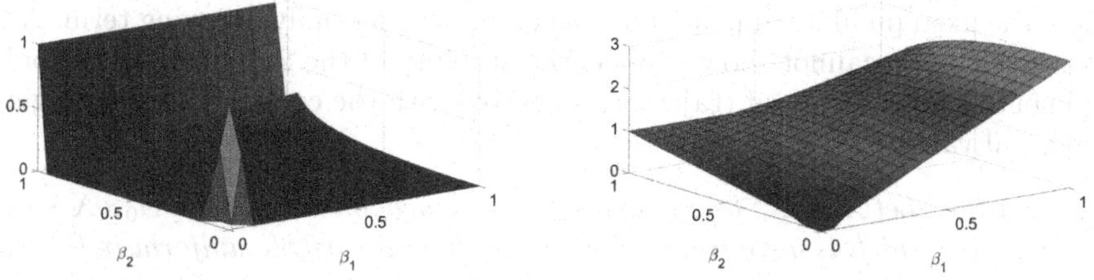

Fig. 1. Absolute magnitude of real and complex eigenvalues

Plotting the absolute values of the eigenvalues over β_1 and β_2 we can see that these limit cycles are often attractive, see Fig. 1. Local attractivity holds if the absolute values are less than 1: This is the case for the real eigenvalue, see left plot, but the magnitude approaches 1 as β_2 approaches 1 – consider the standard value $\beta_2 = 0$ suggested in [6]. The pair of complex conjugate eigenvalues can be stable as well as unstable – unstable again for β_1 and β_2 near 1. This is good news: For typical β_1, β_2 the limit cycle will not turn up in numerical simulations as it is unstable. We have not managed to give analytical estimates for stable eigenvalues using CAS so far.

Step 3: Now we show that the limit cycle also exists for $\varepsilon > 0$ sufficiently small. We fix the hyperparameters α, β_1, β_2 and consider the function

$$F(x, \varepsilon) = \bar{T}(\bar{T}(x; \alpha, \beta_1, \beta_2, \varepsilon); \alpha, \beta_1, \beta_2, \varepsilon) - x$$

Consider a state $\tilde{x}$ on a 2-cycle for $\tilde{\varepsilon} = 0$ as in step 1, then $F(\tilde{x}, 0) = 0$, that is we have a zero of F. If $\frac{\partial F}{\partial x}(\tilde{x}, 0)$ is invertible, then the Implicit Function Theorem shows that in a neighbourhood of $\tilde{\varepsilon} = 0$ there exists a unique zero $x(\varepsilon)$ with $F(x(\varepsilon), \varepsilon) = 0$. This zero of F corresponds to a 2-cycle of $\bar{T}$ with hyperparameter ε. (We always have $\varepsilon > 0$, but on a non-trivial 2-cycle we have shown that $v > 0$ by the explicit term for $\tilde{x}_1$ and $\tilde{x}_2$ in (4), so even a small reduction of ε would be allowed.) Calculating the determinant with Maple we get

$$\det\left(\frac{\partial F}{\partial x}(\tilde{x}, 0)\right) = 8(\beta_1 + 1)(\beta_2 - 1)(\beta_1 + \beta_2)$$

which is non-zero for all relevant $0 < \beta_1, \beta_2 < 1$ So the limit cycle exists for small $\varepsilon < \hat{\varepsilon}$, let us call this upper bound

$$\hat{\varepsilon} = \hat{\varepsilon}(\alpha, \beta_1, \beta_2) \tag{5}$$

for reference and by continuous dependence of the eigenvalues on the matrix, these limit cycles are also attractive.

Step 4: We apply a disturbance estimate to show that $\bar{T}(x; \alpha, \beta_1, \beta_2, \varepsilon)$ and $T(t, x; \alpha, \beta_1, \beta_2, \varepsilon)$ have asymptotically the same limit cycles. The following theorem is a variation of [2, Theorem V.1.] and holds for cycles of any integer length. The proof is very similar and omitted for brevity. The difference between the variants is that here we do not use an estimate of the type $\|\Theta(t, \tilde{x})\| \leq C\beta^t \|\tilde{x} - x_\star\|$

where the fixed point $x_\star$ appears but rather an exponentially decaying term $C\beta^t$. Consequently we cannot show exponential stability of the 2-limit-cycle but only exponential convergence of trajectories nearby, with the constants depending on the initial value.

Theorem 1. *Let $X \subset \mathbb{R}^n$ be a closed set, $\|\cdot\|$ a norm on $\mathbb{R}^n$. Let $T : \mathbb{N}_0 \times X \to X$ be a mapping which is a contraction w.r.t. the second variable uniform in $t \in \mathbb{N}_0$, i.e. there exists $L < 1$ with*

$$\|T(t,x) - T(t,y)\| \leq L\,\|x-y\| \quad \forall x,y \in X, t \in \mathbb{N}_0$$

Furthermore assume that the difference between $T(t+1,\cdot)$ and $T(t,\cdot)$ is exponentially bounded: There exist $C \geq 0$, $0 < \beta < 1$ such that

$$\|T(t+1,x) - T(t,x)\| \leq C\beta^t \;\; \forall x \in X, k \in \mathbb{N}_0$$

Then T has a unique fixed-point $x_\star$ in X: $T(t,x_\star) = x_\star$ for all $t \in \mathbb{N}_0$. For all $x_0 \in X$, the sequence defined by $x_{t+1} = T(t,x_t)$, $t \in \mathbb{N}_0$, converges to $x_\star$ exponentially.

To apply this theorem to the 2-limit-cycle we have to estimate the difference between two iterations of Adam with and without bias correction:

$$\left\|T(t+1,T(t,x)) - \bar{T}(\bar{T}(x))\right\|$$

We use the fact from [2] that

$$\|\Theta(t,x)\| = \left\|T(t,x) - \bar{T}(x)\right\| \leq C\beta^t\,\|x - x_\star\|$$

as well as

$$\|\Theta(t,x)\| = \left\|T(t,x) - \bar{T}(x)\right\| \leq C\beta^t\,\|x\|$$

Using this we estimate

$$\begin{aligned}\left\|T(t+1,T(t,x)) - \bar{T}(\bar{T}(x))\right\| &\leq \left\|T(t+1,T(t,x)) - \bar{T}(T(t,x))\right\| + \\ &\quad \left\|\bar{T}(T(t,x)) - \bar{T}(\bar{T}(x))\right\| \\ &\leq C\beta^{t+1}\,\|T(t,x)\| + L\left\|T(t,x) - \bar{T}(x)\right\|\end{aligned}$$

where L is a local Lipschitz constant near the limit cycle. The Lipschitz continuity exists because $\bar{T}$ is continuously differentiable. We continue the estimate

$$\begin{aligned}&\leq C\beta^{t+1}\,\|T(t,x)\| + LC\beta^t\,\|x\| \\ &= C\beta^{t+1}\left\|\bar{T}(x) + \Theta(t,x)\right\| + LC\beta^t\,\|x\| \\ &\leq C\beta^{t+1}\left\|\bar{T}(x)\right\| + C^2\beta^{t+1}\beta^t\,\|x\| + LC\beta^t\,\|x\| \\ &\leq \tilde{C}\beta^t \max\{\left\|\bar{T}(x)\right\|, \|x\|\}\end{aligned}$$

with $\tilde{C} \geq \max\{C^2, LC\}$. As we consider only states x near the limit cycle $\tilde{x}_1$, $\tilde{x}_2$ we can locally bound the term $\left\|\bar{T}(x)\right\|$ by continuity of $\bar{T}$.

We summarize our findings in the following theorem.

Theorem 2. *Consider the Adam-Optimizer as defined in Algorithm 1 and objective function $f(w) = \frac{1}{2}cw^2$, $c > 0$. Then the algorithm is locally convergent under the assumptions stated in [2]. However there exist solutions that converge to the 2-limit-cycles of the algorithm without bias correction; so the algorithm does not converge globally to the minimum $w_\star = 0$.*

4 Numerical Simulations: Discrete Limit Cycles

In [4, Proposition 3.3] the authors show the existence of a discrete limit cycle for the Adam. This discrete limit cycle depends on the learning rate α and $\beta_1 = 0$. Therefore we demand $0 < \beta_1 < 1$ this limit cycle does not affect the local convergence proof of [2]. But we found in some numerical experiments few limit cycles which alter the convergence of Adam.

First, we will recall the hyperparameter bound of [2]

$$\frac{\alpha \max_{i=1}^{n}(\mu_i)}{\sqrt{\epsilon}}(1-\beta_1) < 2\beta_1 + 2 \tag{6}$$

with μ_i the i-th eigenvalue of the Hessian $\nabla^2 f(w_\star)$. This bound is marked in the Experiments with a red cross and depicts in every of our Experiments the bifurcation position. The $\epsilon_{\text{mach}} = 2^{-52} \approx 2.2204 \cdot 10^{-16}$ is the machine accuracy of IEEE floating point arithmetic with double precision (Table 1).

Table 1. Parameters of the different limit cycles

	Experiment 1	Experiment 2	Experiment 3
c	10	1	1
α	0.001	0.5	0.8
β_1	0.9	0.2	0.5
β_2	0.999	0.5	0.6
ε	10^{-8}	10^{-6}	0.01
m_0	$-1.281144718 \cdot 10^{-5}$	0	0
v_0	$5.925207756 \cdot 10^{-8}$	0	0
w_0	$2.434174964 \cdot 10^{-5}$	ϵ_{mach}	ϵ_{mach}

In the first Experiment, we found a 2-limit-cycle close the parameters suggested by [6]. A plot between the three main values m_t, v_t, w_t looks like a fountain and we can see, that the values of m_t and w_t become more diffuse with increasing v_t (see Fig. 2 left). By looking closely to w_t, it attracts attention that w_t is reaching the solution 0 but leaving it again (see Fig. 2 right). One of the eigenvalues of the corresponding Jacobian is greater than 1, so the solution is not a stable 2-limit-cycle. The other real valued 2-limit-cycles also are not stable. Therefore we reach in Experiment 1 a limit-cycle with a higher order than 2 (see Fig. 3).

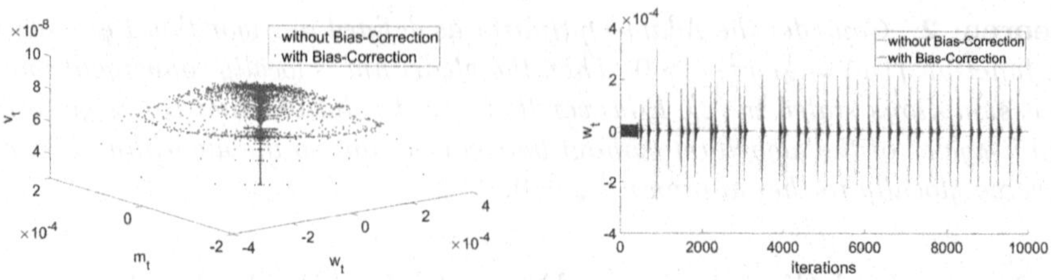

Fig. 2. Discrete limit cycle with the parameters suggested by [6] (Experiment 1)

In the following we will only consider w and α. By the fact that m_t and v_t are only auxiliary variables depending on the history of w, they are less important than w and α. In order to clarify this aspect, reference is made at this point to page 3 in [6]. There is a definition for v_t without v_{t-1} and thus a definition of w without m and v is possible. In addition, the following remark gives an insight into the dependency from m_t to the history of w in 2-limit-cycles.

Remark 1. We assume a 2-limit-cycle and therefore we can write $m_t = m_{t+2}$. With this knowledge, we can rewrite the m_t-update rule.

$$\begin{bmatrix} -\beta_1 & 1 \\ 1 & -\beta_1 \end{bmatrix} \begin{bmatrix} m_t \\ m_{t+1} \end{bmatrix} = (1-\beta_1) \begin{bmatrix} g(w_t) \\ g(w_{t+1}) \end{bmatrix}$$

Defining $\beta_1 \in (0,1)$ the system is uniquely solvable and thus m_t does not have more information for the system than w. The same applies to v_t.

If we are iterating over α from 10^{-4} to 0.001 we reach Fig. 3 and see a Hopf bifurcation. With inequality (6) we can calculate exactly the coordinate of the bifurcation (see the red cross in Fig. 3).

$$\alpha_{\text{Bifurcation}} = \frac{(2\beta_1 + 2)\sqrt{\epsilon}}{(1-\beta_1)\max_{i=1}^{n}(\mu_i)} = 0.00038$$

In the second Experiment we can see that it is possible that even if we are starting closely to the solution $w_0 = \epsilon_{\text{mach}}$ we are ending in a stable cycle far away. By iterating over α from 10^{-4} to 0.01 we can see a pitchfork bifurcation of the Adam. With $\alpha = 0.5$ stable, the eigenvalues of the corresponding Jacobian are $\lambda_1 \approx 0.0113983$ and $\lambda_{2,3} \approx -0.7606667 \pm 0.5465392\,\mathrm{i}$. In absolute value all three eigenvalues are smaller than 1 and so we reach a stable 2-limit-cycle between $w_1 = 1/6$ and $w_2 = -1/6$.

In contrast to the implicit function argument, Experiment 3 uses $\varepsilon = 0.01 \gg \epsilon_{\text{mach}}$. In Fig. 5 on the left side one can see that starting at $\alpha = 0.6$ Adam converges to a 2-limit-cycle. At around $\alpha = 0.7$ Adam shows a chaotic behaviour. On the right side one can see the behaviour of the parameters m, v and w at $\alpha = 0.8$. It visualizes the chaotic behaviour and reminds of the shape of a Lorenz system.

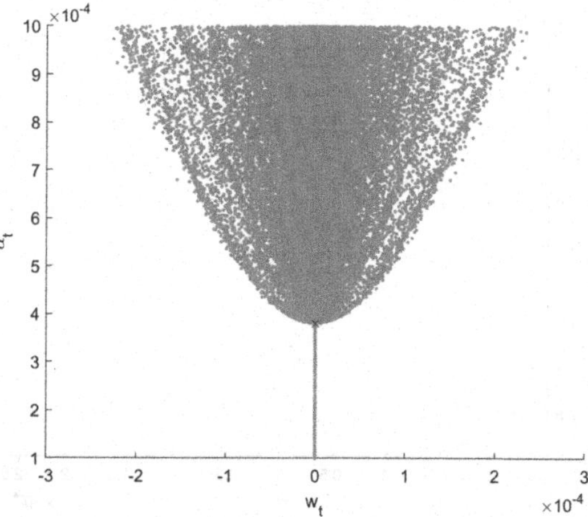

Fig. 3. Hopf bifurcation (Experiment 1) (Color figure online)

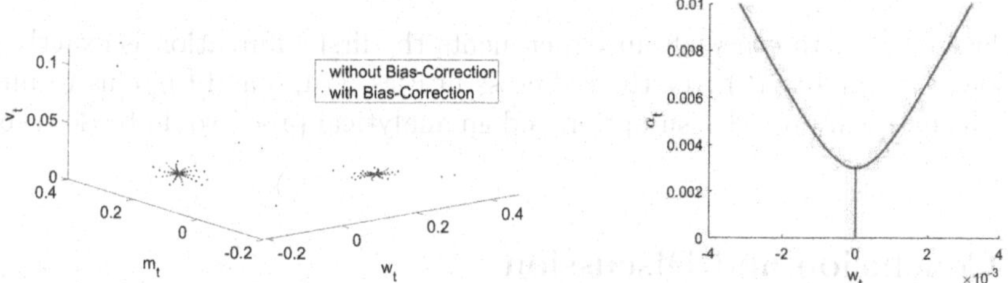

Fig. 4. Discrete limit cycle starting near the solution (Experiment 2) (Color figure online)

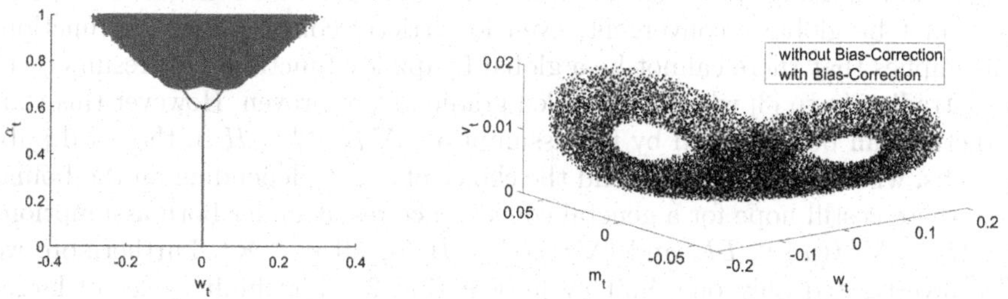

Fig. 5. Discrete limit cycle with a large ε (Experiment 3) (Color figure online)

Even if we want to minimize a multidimensional problem we can detect such a bifurcation. For example, with $f(w) : \mathbb{R}^2 \to \mathbb{R}, f(w) = w^{\perp}Cw$ and

$$C = \begin{bmatrix} 1.1184 & 0.5841 \\ 0.5841 & 3.8816 \end{bmatrix} = Q^{\perp} \begin{bmatrix} 1 & 0 \\ 0 & 4 \end{bmatrix} Q$$

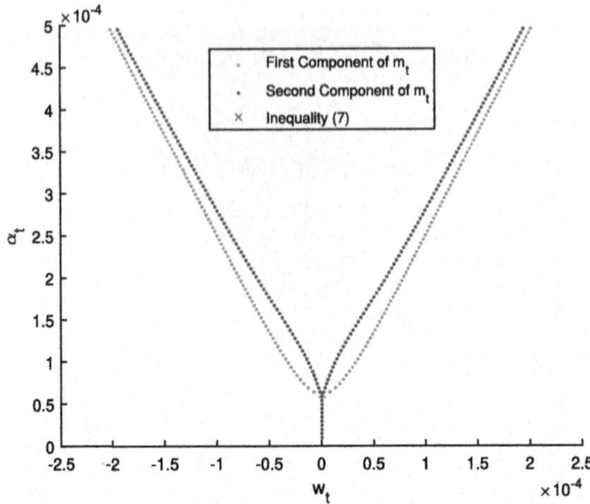

Fig. 6. Bifurcation in a multidimensional optimization (Color figure online)

we obtain Fig. 6. In every of our experiments the first bifurcation is exactly on the solved inequality (6) (see the red cross in Figs. 3, 4, 5 and 6). This result is only an empirical proved assumption and an analytical proof would be desirable.

5 Conclusion and Discussion

The results can be extended easily by a diagonalization argument and change of coordinates to strictly convex quadratic functions $\frac{1}{2}w^{\perp}Cw + b^{\perp}w + a$ with $w \in \mathbb{R}^n$. But already the scalar quadratic function shows that the Adam dynamics cannot be globally convergent, even for strictly convex objective function. This implies that there cannot be a global Lyapunov function. Our results seem in contradiction to [3] where ε-bounded gradients are proven. However this contradiction can be explained by the assumption $\|\nabla f(w)\| \leq H$ in the cited publications, which we do not use, and the choice of β_1, β_2 depending on the bound ε. So there is still hope for a general convergence result under both assumptions $0 < lI_n \leq \nabla^2 f(w) \leq LI_n$ and $\|\nabla f(w)\| \leq H$ for all $w \in \mathbb{R}^n$. Furthermore we have investigated only one limit cycle of period 2. More limit cycles of larger period might exist, so restrictions on objective function and hyperparameters that eliminate this 2-limit-cycle might miss other or even create other limit cycles. The computer algebraic methods used in this paper seem hopeless even for period 3, so probably completely other methods are necessary.

Our results also have no direct implication on efforts to prove convergence of Adam in the incremental mode under additional assumptions. However the lack of a Lyapunov function suggests that Lyapunov based proofs like [5] for the stochastic heavy ball algorithm, cannot be transferred to Adam in the stochastic or incremental setting.

Acknowledgements. This paper presents results of the project "LeaP – Learning Poses" supported by the Bavarian Ministry of Science and Art under Kap. 15 49 TG 78.

References

1. Bock, S.: Rotationsermittlung von Bauteilen basierend auf neuronalen Netzen. M.Sc. thesis, Ostbayerische Technische Hochschule Regensburg (2017, unpublished)
2. Bock, S., Weiß, M.G.: A proof of local convergence for the Adam optimizer. In: International Joint Conference on Neural Networks IJCNN 2019, Budapest (2019)
3. Chen, X., Liu, S., Sun, R., Hong, M.: On the convergence of a class of Adam-type algorithms for non-convex optimization. In: Proceedings of the 7th International Conference on Learning Representations, New Orleans, LA (2019)
4. da Silva, A.B., Gazeau, M.: A general system of differential equations to model first order adaptive algorithms (2018). https://arxiv.org/pdf/1810.13108
5. Gadat, S., Panloup, F., Saadane, S.: Stochastic heavy ball. Electron. J. Statist. **12**(1), 461–529 (2018). https://doi.org/10.1214/18-EJS1395
6. Kingma, D.P., Ba, J.L.: Adam: a method for stochastic optimization. In: Proceedings of the 3rd International Conference on Learning Representations, San Diego, CA (2015)
7. Luenberger, D.G., Ye, Y.: Linear and Nonlinear Programming. ISOR, vol. 228, 4th edn. Springer, Cham (2016). https://doi.org/10.1007/978-3-319-18842-3
8. Nesterov, J.E.: Introductory Lectures on Convex Optimization: A Basic Course, Applied Optimization, vol. APOP 87. Kluwer Acad. Publ., Boston (2004)
9. Reddi, J.S., Kale, S., Kumar, S.: On the convergence of Adam and beyond. In: 6th International Conference on Learning Representations, Vancouver, BC, Canada (2018)
10. Rubio, D.M.: Convergence analysis of an adaptive method of gradient descent. M.Sc. thesis, University of Oxford, Oxford (2017)

Pruning Networks

Learning Internal Dense But External Sparse Structures of Deep Convolutional Neural Network

Yiqun Duan(✉) and Chen Feng

School of Engineering, The University of British Columbia (Okanagan Campus), Kelowna, BC V1V 1V7, Canada
{yiqun.duan,chen.feng}@ubc.ca

Abstract. Recent years have witnessed two seemingly opposite developments of deep convolutional neural networks (CNNs). On the one hand, increasing the density of CNNs (e.g., by adding cross-layer connections) achieves better performance on basic computer vision tasks. On the other hand, creating sparsity structures (e.g., through pruning methods) achieves a more slim network structure. Inspired by modularity structures in the human brain, we bridge these two trends by proposing a new network structure with internally dense yet externally sparse connections. Experimental results demonstrate that our new structure could obtain competitive performance on benchmark tasks (*CIFAR10, CIFAR100, and ImageNet*) while keeping the network structure slim.

Keywords: Hierarchical CNN · Evolutionary algorithms · Neural network structure

1 Introduction

Deep Convolutional Neural Networks (e.g. [12,18,20,28]) have recently made remarkable success in visual tasks. The very intuitive idea of improving a neural network at the earlier period is to enlarge the scale of the network. However, follow-up papers have shown that when the feedforward network structure has reached a certain depth, neither the best test accuracy nor training accuracy will increase as the network depth increases [15]. An important observation is that by increasing network density and adding long distance connections, the network could be improved such as ResNet [12] and DenseNet [15] have shown. These long-distance connections could create shortcuts between layers in different depth. By propagating loss directly, the network could become deeper and more accurate.

As the network becomes denser, deeper, and more accurate, its scale increases up to millions of parameters. Thus, reducing the network scale and complexity becomes a crucial research task for real-world applications. One promising solution is to increase the network sparsity by pruning redundant connections. For

I. V. Tetko et al. (Eds.): ICANN 2019, LNCS 11728, pp. 247–262, 2019.
https://doi.org/10.1007/978-3-030-30484-3_21

instance, by pruning connections with tiny weights and fine-tuning the pruned network, [11] could reduce the network complexity while only sacrificing about 1% of model accuracy. Similar solutions to create sparsity include channel pruning [14] and structure sparsity [36].

In neuroscience, studies concentrating on the brain structure reveal that neuron connections in human brain perform a locally dense but externally sparse property that the closer two regions are, the denser the connections between them will be [4,9,34]. Also, studies show that while sensory information arrives at the cortex, it is fed up through hierarchical regions from primary area V1 up to higher areas such as V2, V4 and IT [2]. Inside of each cortex layer, tightly packed pyramidal cells consist of basic locally dense structures in the brain.

Based on neuroscientific considerations, the brain does not form connections between every neuron. Instead, the brain forms local modules which consist of internally dense connected neurons inside and forms connections between these dense modules to save space and become more efficient. These internally dense yet externally sparse properties could also be introduced into neural network structures. Thus, we could bridge the trends of being dense and being sparse together in neural network structures. Intuitively, we could acquire good performance while keeping the network structure slim by introducing this brain inspired structure.

We introduce an internally dense yet externally sparse neural network structure by prefixing dense modules and evolving sparse connections between them. The basic building blocks of this network structures are several internally dense modules, where each module consists of several densely connected [15] bottleneck layers to simulate the tightly packed cells. After that, we could form sparse connections between these dense modules for the whole network structure. To give more convincing guidance for forming sparse connections rather than manually design connections based on experience, we design an evolutionary training algorithm (Sect. 3.3) to search optimized connections Moreover, besides merely creating parallel connections between modules, our algorithm could create long-distance connections between the input module and the output module by a transit layer.

The main contribution of this paper is to introduce biologically-inspired internally dense yet externally sparse properties into convolutional neural network by prefixing dense modules and forming sparse connections between dense modules. Instead of empirically constructing module connections, we design an evolutionary training algorithm to search optimized connections. This structure could reach compared slim network structures while keeping competitive model performance on image classification tasks (Exp. Sect. 4.3). We give a detailed analysis of how different sparse connections and different module properties will contribute to the final performance. Moreover, we reveal contribution proportion on the final performance of each connection by several contrast experiments. Thus, we could give intuitive guidance for designing hierarchical network structures.

2 Related Works

Network Architectures Are Becoming Denser

The exploration of network architectures has been an important foundation for all Deep Learning tasks. At the early period of deep learning, increasing the depth of a network might promise a good result as the network structure moved from LeNet to VGG (e.g. [18,20,28]). Since people realize that the increasing depth of the network amplifies problems such as over-fitting and gradient-vanishing [3], parallel structures [32,39] and densely connected layers [15] have been introduced to increase network capacity. In this paper, we refer to the dense block in [15] while constructing internal densely connected modules.

Deep Neural Network Compression

Besides increasing model capacity, deep neural network compression is another active domain concentrating on acquiring slim models by eliminating network redundancy. These methods could be summarized by the three basic aspects: **1. Numerical approximation of kernels**, which includes binarization [7,25], quantization [40], weight sharing or coding method [10] and mainly uses numerical method to approximate kernel with smaller scale; **2. Sparse regularization on kernels**, which mainly prunes connections based on regularization on kernels, such as weights/channel pruning [14,23] and structure sparsity learning [22,36]; **3. Decomposition of kernels**, which mainly uses smaller groups of low-rank kernel instead of a larger whole kernel, such as [6,8,17] and [37]. Instead of pre-training then pruning the whole network structure, we use an evolutionary programming method to determine sparse connections between dense modules, while keeping the modules slim. Competitive performances are obtained.

Neural Network Structure Search

At early period, papers [1,5,24,31] have developed methods that evolve both topologies and weights on simple neural networks. Recently, papers concentrate on evolving structures have risen again along with the rapid development of deep learning. Genetic CNN [38] concentrates on using genetic algorithm to evolve skip-connections on a straight forward convolutional neural network. Then, Google [26] shows great potential about structure search on image classification tasks. Google also proposed a state-of-the-art deep neural network structure NasNet [41] to search both the parameters and the structures. However, the huge scale of these networks still remains a problem. In our paper, the evolving algorithm is a tool to reveal properties of internally dense yet externally sparse structures. Moreover, we analyze how each connections could contribute to the final model performance.

3 Methodology

In order to introduce internal dense yet external sparse properties into deep convolutional neural networks, we proposed a new network structure which prefixes internal dense modules and evolves sparse connections between dense modules. We define M as the set of dense modules. For a clear identification of these dense modules, we divide these dense modules into D layers, where each layer contains W modules. In particular, we define a dense module in the set M as $M_{d,w}, d \in \{0, 1, ...D\}, w \in \{0, 1, ...W\}$, where index d denotes the depths in layer wise and w denotes the module index among all of the others in the same depth. These modules M are sparsely connected by directed edges/connections. We define P as the adjacency matrix to represent these directed connections between modules. Clearly, the whole neural network structure can be defined as a directed graph $G(M, P)$, where M denotes the set of internal dense modules $M_{d,w}$, P denotes the adjacency matrix, which is used to represent sparse connections between modules.

For example, Fig. 1 shows a set of dense modules in subfigure Fig. 1(a) with depth $D = 4$ and $W = 3$. We use an adjacency matrix P to represent connections between modules as it shows in Fig. 1(b). In this example, firstly a 3*3 convolutional layer processed the input images into some feature maps. Then the feature maps are divided into several groups in channel wise. Each group is sent into a dense module as the input feature maps. After the features flow through sparse dense convolutional neural networks, the outputs are concatenated together for final output layer.

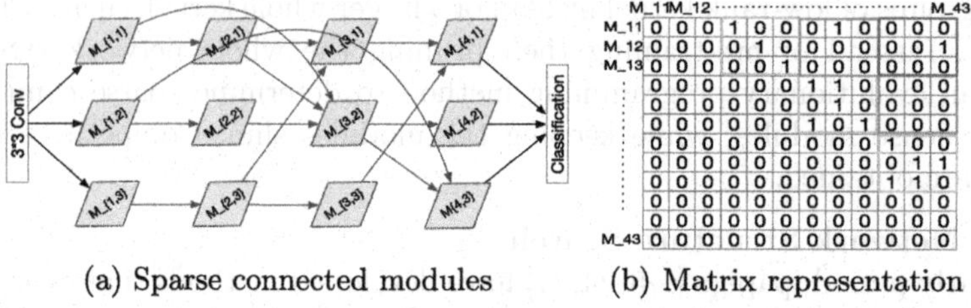

	M_11	M_12										M_43
M_11	0 0 0	1 0 0	0 1 0	0 0 0								
M_12	0 0 0	0 1 0	0 0 0	0 0 1								
M_13	0 0 0	0 0 1	0 0 0	0 0 0								
	0 0 0	0 0 0	1 1 0	0 0 0								
	0 0 0	0 0 0	0 1 0	0 0 0								
	0 0 0	0 0 0	1 0 1	0 0 0								
	0 0 0	0 0 0	0 0 0	1 0 0								
	0 0 0	0 0 0	0 0 0	0 1 1								
	0 0 0	0 0 0	0 0 0	1 1 0								
	0 0 0	0 0 0	0 0 0	0 0 0								
	0 0 0	0 0 0	0 0 0	0 0 0								
M_43	0 0 0	0 0 0	0 0 0	0 0 0								

(a) Sparse connected modules (b) Matrix representation

Fig. 1. Example of a network's structure obtained by fixing the dense modules M in advance and using the adjacency matrix P to represent sparse connections between modules. Figure (a) denotes the network structure. Figure (b) denotes the adjacency matrix corresponding to Fig. (a), where red rectangle area denotes connections with distance 1, green rectangle denotes connections with distance 2, blue area denotes connections with distance 3. (Color figure online)

Naturally, three main questions occur: 1. What is the exact structure and definition of a dense module $M_{d,w}$? 2. What does a connection represent in this convolutional neural network? 3. How shall we connect these dense modules and decide the adjacency matrix P?

The exact structure of an internal dense module $M_{d,w}$ is defined in Sect. 3.1. In Sect. 3.2, we answer the second question by specifying a connection in neural networks. In Sect. 3.3, we solve the problem of connecting these modules by evolving sparse connections between them.

3.1 Build Internal Densely Connected Modules

In this section, we will introduce the detailed structure of a dense module $M_{d,w}$. From a high level, a dense module $M_{d,w}$ receives feature maps from other dense modules as its input, then outputs down-scaled feature maps. In other words, we densely connect our *bottleneck layers* and a *transit layer* as the main structure inside a dense module as it is shown in Fig. 2.

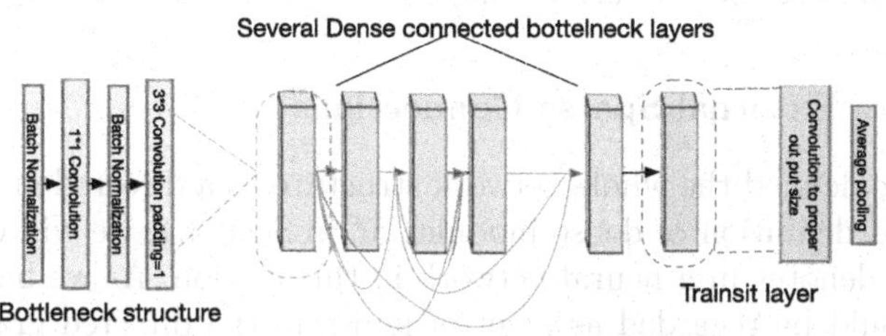

Fig. 2. An example of structure for a prefixed dense module as shown above, where yellow layer represents several densely connect bottleneck layers (it means each intermediate output has a direct connection to the output layer). The detailed structure of a bottleneck layer is shown left. After the final layer, the green layer represents a transition layer to control the feature map size. The depth of dense blocks in our experiment usually varied from 6 to 20. (Color figure online)

This structure uses a *bottleneck layer* as the basic building block of the dense module. Following [15, 33], we design our own bottleneck layer as below. A bottleneck layer consists of sequential layers as follows: {BN - 1*1conv -BN - 3*3conv}, where BN denotes a batch normalization layer [16] which could normalize the feature maps by adjusting and scaling after activation functions. The BN layer is followed by a 1*1 convolution layer which keeps the feature map size the same. Then it is followed by a BN layer and a 3*3 convolution layer with zero padding. The bottleneck layer l keeps the output feature map size unchanged and controls the channel number of the feature maps always be constant number k (the meaning of k will be explained later).

In that case, the bottleneck layers could be densely connected [15] to increase density of dense module $M_{d,w}$. The densely connectivity could be presented as $x_l = H_l(x_0, x_1, x_2, ...x_{l-1})$, where H_l represents nonlinear operation on feature maps in bottleneck layer l and $(x_0, x_1, x_2, ...x_{l-1})$ represents the concatenation (channel-wise) of all previous outputs. It means that the input of layer l depends on outputs of every previous layers. As each bottleneck layer produces feature maps with k channels, the layer l has concatenated input feature maps with $k_0 + k \times (l-1)$ channels, where k_0 is the channel number of input feature maps in this dense module. In that case, as layer number l goes deeper, the channel number of input feature maps will grow rapidly as defined above. Following [15], we define k as the growth rate of the module, which could control the module scale. In experiments of this paper, we keep the growth rate k the same for all dense modules M.

We define a transit layer as the output layer of every dense module $M_{d,w}$. The transit layer consists of sequential layers {BN - Relu -1*1conv - Average-pooling}, where BN is the batch normalization layer introduced above, Relu is the activation function. The 1*1 convolution layer controls the output feature map channels as a constant number k_0 for all dense modules M. The average pooling layer mainly down scale the feature map size for final classification task. It should be noted that, the transit layer could control the output feature maps of dense modules to have a certain shape.

3.2 Explore External Sparse Connections

Since we have defined the whole network structure as a directed graph $G(M, P)$ and explained definition of dense modules M in Sect. 3.1, we will explain what a connection denotes in a neural network in this section. As we have explained before, M could be regarded as a set of nodes in the directed graph $G(M, P)$ and P is the adjacency matrix to represent the directed connections between modules M. The directed connections denote the feature map flow in our neural networks. Once there is a connection between two modules, it means one module will accept the output feature map of the other module as part of its inputs. For example, in Fig. 1, the module $M_{3,1}$ receives two directed connections from $M_{2,1}$ and $M_{2,3}$, it means module $M_{3,1}$ receives feature maps both from $M_{2,1}$ and $M_{2,3}$. Similarly, the module $M_{3,1}$ sends a directed connection to $M_{4,1}$, this means $M_{3,1}$ send output feature maps to $M_{4,1}$ as one of its inputs.

According to the *transit layers* defined in Sect. 3.1, output feature maps of all modules have the same channel number k_0. However, the sizes of feature maps from different depth are different. So, how can we make a module to accept output feature maps from different depth of feature maps? After the example, we will introduce how we exactly make a module to accept changeable feature maps from multiple other dense modules.

Methods for Local Connections with Same Depth

Here we define the distance as the difference $d_1 - d_2$ of two connected modules M_{d_1,w_1} and M_{d_2,w_2} in depth. If the distance of the connection is 1 (e.g., connection between $M_{3,3}$ and $M_{2,3}$ in Fig. 1), we call it a local connection. As we defined in Sect. 3.1, each output feature map of a dense module with same depth shares the same feature map size and the same channel number k_0. If there is only one local connection, we could naturally follow the down sampling flow of deep CNN and directly send the feature map output of the previous depth to the current module as: $O_{d,w} = M_{d,w}(O_{d-1,w_2})$, where O_{d-1,w_2} denotes the output feature map of previous depth M_{d-1,w_2}.

But what if the module $M_{d,w}$ has several local connections? We use an *Addition Method* to connect multiple feature map inputs which could be defined as: $O_{d,w} = M_{d,w}(O_{d-1,w_1} + O_{d-1,w_2} ...)$, where O_{d_1,w_1} and $O_{d_1,w_2}...$ denote the multiple input feature maps. These additional methods directly add all the input feature maps from local connections and fit the required input feature map size of $M_{d,w}$. Actually we also try the *Concatenation Methods* which concatenate all input feature maps channel wise and use a single transit layer introduced in Sect. 3.1 to reduce the channel number to required k_O. The experiment results show that the two connection methods have very similar results on the same structure. As addition methods don't need extra transit layers when changing the input feature map numbers, we choose addition methods as our connection methods.

Methods for Long Distance Connections from Different Depth

Within the same definition of distance above, a typical example of multiple long distance connections is as shown in Fig. 1, where $M_{4,3}$ receives directed connections from both $M_{3,2}$ (with depth 3) and $M_{1,2}$ (with depth 1). It should be noted that the existence of long distance connections means that feature maps could flow through different numbers of dense modules in this network structure. Here we also use the addition methods introduced above. Since the fact that the output feature maps of all the modules have same channel number k_O, the only problem for adding feature maps from different depth is the different feature map size. In that case, before addition, we implement an average pooling layer T_d according to the depth d to change the feature map size into current requirement of a module. After that, we could add all the adjusted input feature maps as the input of $M_{d,w}$. The math process can be define as $O_{d,w} = M_{d,w}(T_{d_1}(O_{d_1,w_1}) + T_{d_2}(O_{d_2,w_2})...)$, where $O_{d,w}$ denotes the output feature map of module $M_{d,w}$ and T_d denotes the pooling layer from depth d. In this case, we can achieve long distance connections.

3.3 Evolution Algorithm to Search External Sparse Connections

Since we've answered the question of what is a dense module in Sect. 3.1 and how the modules are connected in Sect. 3.2, this section will introduce how we decide the connection topologies.

One crucial problem in creating sparse connections between dense modules is that there has not been a convincing theory on what can be called an efficient connection. In that case, we decide to make the neural network evolving optimized sparse connections by itself. In this paper, we use a genetic algorithm [29] to search the proper connections. We take the adjacency matrix P as shown above as the gene for evolving. In each iteration, the genetic algorithm generates several new 'individuals' with genes from the mutation of the best 'individual' in last iteration. The set of generated 'individuals' is called 'population'. Genetic algorithm evolves by selecting best performance individual in every iteration.

Encoding: Here we take the adjacent matrix P to represent connection topology during training. In implementation details, we use a connection list of each module to reduce the storage space.

Initial State: The initial adjacency matrix is shown as Fig. 3-*Initial State* which only has direct local connections. We randomly initialize the weights value of modules at the first iteration in the training process. Since a deep neural network needs a long time to train, restricted to our computation capacity, we set the

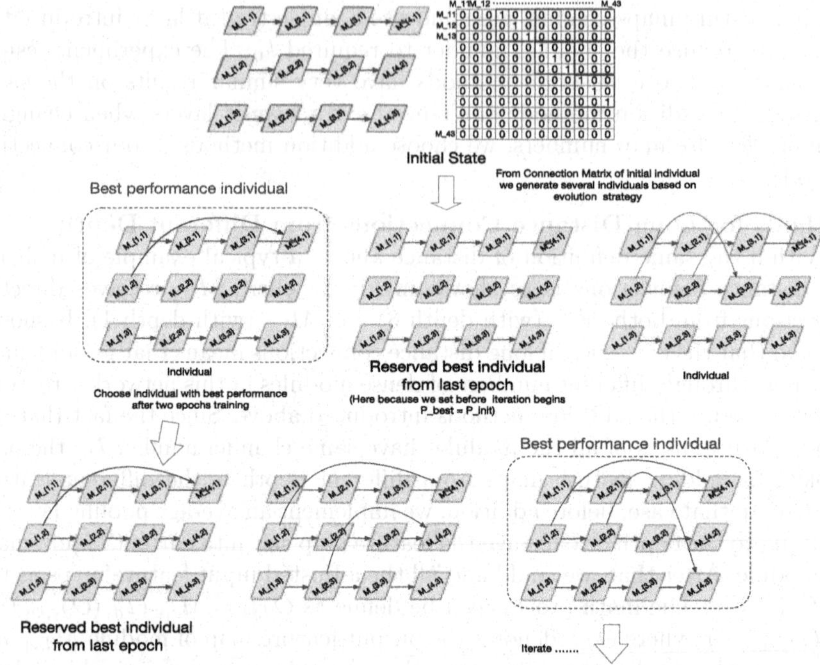

Fig. 3. An example of the Network Structure Evolving. *Initial state* denotes the initial adjacency matrix P. As we set before first iteration $P_{best} = P_{init}$, based on P_{best} we generate 2 individuals below. All together these 3 individuals form the population which to be trained simultaneously in iteration 1. Then, we choose the individual with the best performance, and based on that we form population for iteration 2. Following this principle we keep the network evolving.

population between 2 to 3 individuals. We define the adjacency matrix of the initial individual state as P_{init}, the best performance individual of the previous iteration as P_{best}, and others as P_i at beginning of each iteration. An example of evolving process is shown in Fig. 3.

Evolution Strategy: At each iteration, the mutation function will generate several new individuals based on the best individual from the previous iteration P_{best}. The mutation function could be defined as:

$$P_1, P_2... = Mutation(P_{best}) \tag{1}$$

Where it accepts P_{best} as its input, then generates several mutation individuals $P_1, P_2...$ based on P_{best}. The mutation function randomly picks two possible connections and changed their connectivity based on the input adjacency matrix. It means that, if we randomly pick an unconnected connection, we set it connected. And for already connected connection, we set it disconnected. Then we treat the set of $P_{best}, P_1, P_2...$ as population in this iteration and separately resume training the whole network under these connection conditions for an epoch and choose

Algorithm 1. Evolutionary Connectivity Algorithm

procedure EVOLVE($G(M, P_{init}), Data, n$) ▷ *Data*: Training data, $G(M, P_{init})$: Given network structure with modules M and initial adjacency matrix P_{init}, n: Total iteration
  $P_{best} \leftarrow P_{init}$
  for n iterations **do**
    $P_1, P_2 ... P_{k-1}, P_k \leftarrow Mutation(P_{best})$ ▷ k,Number of individuals in a generation, $P_k = P_{best}$
    $checkpoint \leftarrow G(M, P_{best})$
    for k iterations **do**
      Resume weights of M in the *Checkpoint*: $G(M, P_k) \leftarrow checkpoint$
      train $G(M, P_k)$ on *Data* and get validation accuracy
      if $P_k.accuracy > P_{best}.accuracy$ **then**
        $P_{best} \leftarrow P_k$
        $best - check \leftarrow G(M, P_k)$
      end if
    end for
    Resume weights of M in the $best - check$: $G(M, P_{best}) \leftarrow best - check$
  end for
  Return P_{best}
end procedure

the individual with the best accuracy as P_{best} of current iteration. Adjacency matrix of the best performance individual P_{best} will remain to next iteration. And based on it we mutate new individuals. The whole process is shown in Algorithm 1.

4 Experiments

In this section, we apply several experiments to reveal interesting phenomena and properties of the internally dense yet externally sparse deep neural network structures. All of the experiments in this section are based on CIFAR10, CIFAR100 and ImageNet datasets for image classification tasks. Section 4.1 shows the efficiency of the evolutionary algorithm by several repeatability experiments. Section 4.2 discusses how the growth rate of each module will affect the model performance. Section 4.3 gives our performance benchmark compared to state-of-the-art models. At last, we do a detailed discussion about which connections are important for the whole model in Sect. 4.4.

4.1 Evolving Sparse Connections

This experiment is used to prove the efficiency of the Evolutionary Connectivity Algorithm introduced in Sect. 3.3. We evaluate the network structure efficiency on the classification task using benchmark dataset CIFAR10. In implementation details, we prefix the dense modules having 4 different depth, where in each depth, it has 3 modules. The total of 12 modules M have the growth rate k of 12. The dense modules in depth 1, 2, 3, 4 respectively have 6, 12, 24, 16 bottleneck layers inside each module. The input feature map channels of each dense module k_0 is 32. The preprocessed images firstly flow through a 3*3 convolution layer and generate feature maps with 96 channels. Then the feature maps are divided into 3 feature map groups with 32 channels each. And the three groups are separately fed to input dense modules with depth 1 $(M_{1,1}, M_{1,2}, M_{1,3})$.

Through the training process, the network evolves sparse connections between prefixed dense modules according to the Evolutionary Connectivity Algorithm 1. We set the total iteration number to be 160, with weight decay of 5e−4. The training uses SGD with momentum 0.9 for gradient descent. The learning rate strategy is the same as most of the papers that during epoch 0–90 the learning rate is 0.1, during 90–140 learning rate is 0.01, and during 140–160 learning rate is 0.001. It should be noted that changing the learning rate will lead to accuracy 'step jumps' such as Figs. 4, 5 and 6 show. Restricted to our computation power, we set the number of individuals generated in each iteration to be 2. The training curves of P_{best} are shown in Fig. 4. All the experiments are trained on NVIDIA AWS P3.x2large instance.

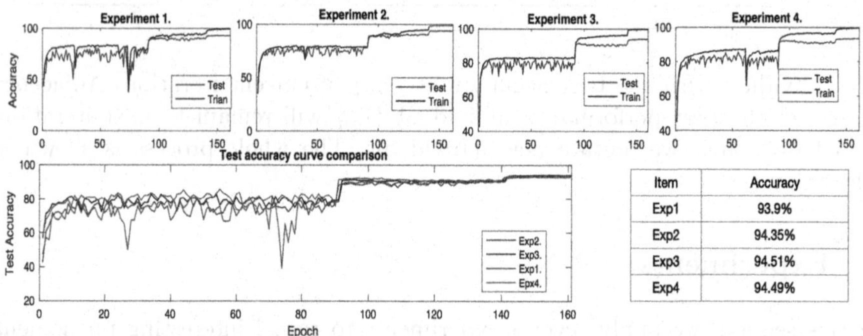

Item	Accuracy
Exp1	93.9%
Exp2	94.35%
Exp3	94.51%
Exp4	94.49%

Fig. 4. Several Repeatable Experiments on Sparse Connection Evolving. The upper four figures denote the training curve & testing curve of each experiment. The lower figure denotes the comparison of test accuracy of each experiment. All accuracy step jumps are caused by learning rate change strategy in Sect. 4.1.

According to the repeatable experiment results, although randomness of forming the early generations may lead to variation and fluctuation on the testing performance curve, the training curve will finally converge to the same trend. This shows the *repeatability* of our algorithm. Based on these experiments, we found that the optimized adjacency matrix is not unique to achieve good performances. The evolving results are shown in Fig. 5. However, we could still find some similarity between those evolving results of these experiments. It denotes that the modules with shallow depth are more likely to form a long-distance connection. This means that the distance between the input and the output are shortened under that situation. This perfectly fits a current trend observed by various papers [6,12,15,27,32,33] that skip/direct connections are important.

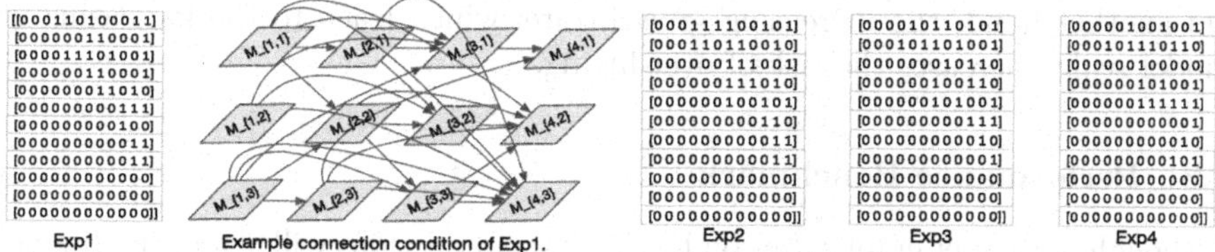

Fig. 5. Connection Matrix with Best Performance on each Experiment. We also give an example connection status of Exp1.

4.2 How Growth Rate of the Dense Module Influences the Final Result

As we mentioned above in Sect. 3.1, growth rate k is an important parameter which controls the model scale. In order to figure out the influence of growth rate k, this subsection introduces the contrast experiment by controlling all other factors the same except the growth rate k in the prefix dense modules. The prefixed modules and training parameters are the same as those used in experiment Sect. 4.1. We train the network with the same strategy and the same device above. The results are shown in Fig. 6.

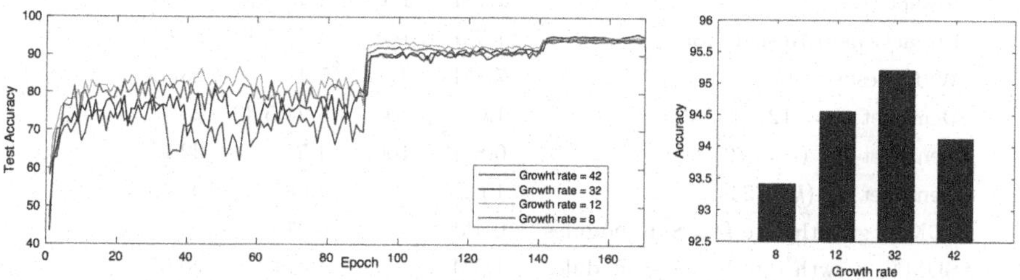

Fig. 6. Test Accuracy Curve Comparison on Different Growth Rate. Each color represents test accuracy curve of experiments on different growth rate.

Clearly, the networks with smaller growth rate converge faster and have flatter curve shapes compared to those with larger growth rates at the earlier period of training. It means that the modules with smaller scale are easier to train while the connections of this network evolving. We can also see that, although modules with smaller growth rates converge really fast, the final test accuracy is not as high as those modules with larger growth rate. However, experiment results also demonstrate that the network redundancy is not the 'larger the better'. As it shows in Fig. 6, after the growth rate is larger than 32, the test accuracy will not increase anymore. It is also rational because if the capacity of each module is too large, the unstable input features may make the network harder to train. On another hand, the increasing growth rate, which leads to the increasing of model scale, increases the risk of over-fitting.

4.3 Performance Benchmark

Although our paper emphasizes on how sparse connections will change the model performance, we still give performance scores on the benchmark dataset as shown in Tables 1 and 2. Since the aim of this paper is to obtain slim structures while keeping the model's capacity and achieve internally dense yet externally sparse network structures, the test accuracy on both *ImageNet* and *CIFAR* is not that high compared to state-of-the-art models. However, we still get competitive results on both datasets.

Table 1. Test error rate performance on CIFAR dataset. Note results with * are the best result run by ourselves.

Method	Params	Depth	CIFAR-10	CIFAR-100
Network in network [21]	–	–	8.81	35.68
VGG19 [28]	–	–	6.58	27.09
Highway Network [30]	–	–	7.72	32.29
DFN [35]	3.9M	50	6.40	27.61
Fractal Net [19]	38.6M	21	5.22	23.30
Resnet [12]	1.7M	110	5.46 5.58*	27.62
Pre-activated Resnet [13]	1.7M	164	4.72 5.12*	25.6
Wide Resnet [39]	7.4M	32	5.4	23.55
Densenet ($k = 12$) [15]	1M	40	5.24 5.43*	24.42 24.98*
Densenet-BC ($k = 12$)	0.8M	100	4.51	22.27
Densenet121 ($k = 24$)	15.2M	121	4.68*	21.49*
SDMN, growth rate $k = 8$, 6 modules	0.4M	–	6.97*	–
SDMN, growth rate $k = 8$, 8 modules	1.3M	–	6.59*	25.6*
SDMN, growth rate $k = 8$, 12 modules	2.3M	–	5.97*	24.8*
SDMN, growth rate $k = 12$, 12 modules	3.7M	–	5.35*	23.41*
SDMN, growth rate $k = 32$, 12 modules	22M		4.79*	21.9*

4.4 Separable of Sparse Connections

In this subsection, we discuss which connections are important based on one of our evolved adjacency matrices. We separately cut off one sparse connection

Table 2. Test accuracy rate performance on ImageNet dataset, compared with slim network models.

Model	Params	Top1/Top5 Acc.
MobileNetV1	4.2M	70.6%/89.5%
ShuffleNet (2x)	4.4M	70.9%/89.8%
MobileNetV2 (1.4)	6.9M	74.7%/â
NASNet-A (N = 4, F = 44)	5.1M	74.0%/91.3%
Sparse-Dense-Modules (k = 12)	3.7M	71.1%/90.0%

from the whole network structure each time and test the remaining accuracy on *CIFAR10* dataset. Then we come up with a matrix, which suggests the accuracy decreasing while losing each connection. The matrix is shown in Fig. 7.

The red rectangle area denotes the direct connections; the green and blue rectangle area denote the long-distance connections. According to the accuracy loss distribution, local and direct connections are of vital importance for a neural network. This is rational because the deep learning method needs a compared invariant forward and backward feature flow path for loss propagation. We can also see the accuracy loss is larger along the diagonal to the high left of the matrix. It means that connections within shallow depth play a more important role in conducting features/patterns than deeper connections. It is also rational because the shallower connections simultaneously mean the features that flow through such connections have not been extract to some level of abstraction.

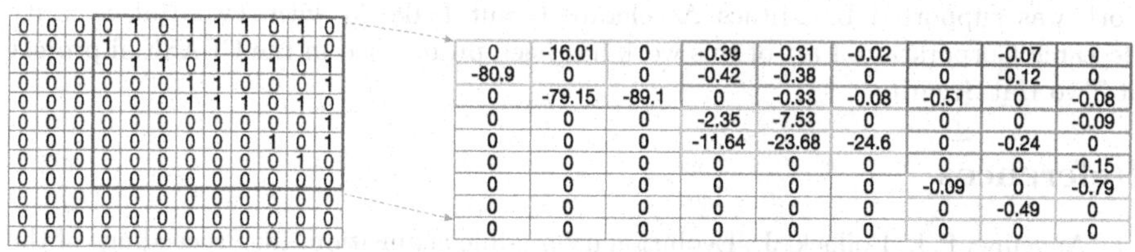

Fig. 7. Example connection matrix shows the selected best connection from a typical experiment. Right part of the figure shows how much accuracy will loss if we cut off the corresponding connection in the connection matrix. (Color figure online)

5 Conclusions and Future Work

In this paper, we firstly introduce locally dense but externally sparse structures of deep convolutional neural network by prefixing some dense modules M and evolving sparse connections between them. Experiment results demonstrate that evolving sparse connections between dense modules could reach competitive results on benchmark datasets. In order to analyze the properties of these biologically plausible structures, we apply several sets of contrast experiments and show in *Experiment* section. By changing the growth rate of each dense module, we analyze how model scale will influence the model performance. Similar to most of the related works, redundancy of each dense module is not 'the larger the better', where the test accuracy will first increase with the growth rate increasing, but finally drop while the growth has reached some thresholds. We also analyze the contribution of each connection to the whole model by disconnecting each connection and separately testing the accuracy of the model with the disconnected connection. It shows that local connections are important for baseline accuracy, while long-distance connections could improve the accuracy by small steps.

The combination of being dense and being sparse is an interesting area. The internally dense and externally sparse structures also coincide with the modularity in human brain. We demonstrate the feasibility of these structures and give a simple algorithm to search best connections. We also notice that the connection matrix is not unique for reaching good performance. We will concentrate on revealing the relationship between these similar connection matrices and the corresponding features behind it. In this case, we may acquire state-of-the-art performance on other datasets and tasks in our future work. Moreover, as these structures have various direct paths between input and output, separating a network into several small networks without big accuracy loss is also a promising topic.

Acknowledgment. We thank the anonymous reviewers for their comments. This work was supported by Mitacs Accelerate Grant IT08175 with Two Hat Security Research Corporation. Part of this work has been prototyped in the CEASE.ai project at Two Hat Security.

References

1. Angeline, P.J., Pollack, J.: Evolutionary module acquisition. In: Proceedings of the Second Annual Conference on Evolutionary Programming, pp. 154–163. Citeseer (1993). https://doi.org/10.1007/978-3-540-24650-3_17
2. Belliveau, J., et al.: Functional mapping of the human visual cortex by magnetic resonance imaging. Science **254**(5032), 716–719 (1991). https://doi.org/10.1126/science.1948051
3. Bengio, Y., Simard, P., Frasconi, P.: Learning long-term dependencies with gradient descent is difficult. IEEE Trans. Neural Networks **5**(2), 157–166 (1994). https://doi.org/10.1109/72.279181
4. Betzel, R.F., et al.: The modular organization of human anatomical brain networks: accounting for the cost of wiring. Netw. Neurosci. **1**(1), 42–68 (2017). https://doi.org/10.1162/NETN_a_00002
5. Braun, H., Weisbrod, J.: Evolving neural feedforward networks. In: Albrecht, R.F., Reeves, C.R., Steele, N.C. (eds.) Artificial Neural Nets and Genetic Algorithms, pp. 25–32. Springer, Vienna (1993). https://doi.org/10.1007/978-3-7091-7533-0_5. https://doi.org/10.1109/72.80206

6. Chollet, F.: Xception: deep learning with depthwise separable convolutions. arXiv preprint, pp. 1610–02357 (2017). https://doi.org/10.1109/CVPR.2017.195
7. Courbariaux, M., Hubara, I., Soudry, D., El-Yaniv, R., Bengio, Y.: Binarized neural networks: training deep neural networks with weights and activations constrained to +1 or −1. arXiv preprint arXiv:1602.02830 (2016)
8. Denton, E.L., Zaremba, W., Bruna, J., LeCun, Y., Fergus, R.: Exploiting linear structure within convolutional networks for efficient evaluation. In: Advances in Neural Information Processing Systems, pp. 1269–1277 (2014)
9. Gazzaniga, M.S.: Brain modularity: towards a philosophy of conscious experience (1988)
10. Han, S., Mao, H., Dally, W.J.: Deep compression: compressing deep neural networks with pruning, trained quantization and Huffman coding. arXiv preprint arXiv:1510.00149 (2015). https://doi.org/10.1145/2351676.2351678
11. Han, S., Pool, J., Tran, J., Dally, W.: Learning both weights and connections for efficient neural network. In: Advances in Neural Information Processing Systems, pp. 1135–1143 (2015)
12. He, K., Zhang, X., Ren, S., Sun, J.: Deep residual learning for image recognition. In: Proceedings of the IEEE Conference on Computer Vision and Pattern Recognition, pp. 770–778 (2016). https://doi.org/10.1109/CVPR.2016.90
13. He, K., Zhang, X., Ren, S., Sun, J.: Identity mappings in deep residual networks. In: Leibe, B., Matas, J., Sebe, N., Welling, M. (eds.) ECCV 2016. LNCS, vol. 9908, pp. 630–645. Springer, Cham (2016). https://doi.org/10.1007/978-3-319-46493-0_38
14. He, Y., Zhang, X., Sun, J.: Channel pruning for accelerating very deep neural networks. In: International Conference on Computer Vision (ICCV), vol. 2, p. 6 (2017)
15. Huang, G., Liu, Z., Weinberger, K.Q., van der Maaten, L.: Densely connected convolutional networks. In: Proceedings of the IEEE Conference on Computer Vision and Pattern Recognition, vol. 1, p. 3 (2017). https://doi.org/10.1109/CVPR.2017.243
16. Ioffe, S., Szegedy, C.: Batch normalization: accelerating deep network training by reducing internal covariate shift. arXiv preprint arXiv:1502.03167 (2015)
17. Kim, Y.D., Park, E., Yoo, S., Choi, T., Yang, L., Shin, D.: Compression of deep convolutional neural networks for fast and low power mobile applications. arXiv preprint arXiv:1511.06530 (2015)
18. Krizhevsky, A., Sutskever, I., Hinton, G.E.: ImageNet classification with deep convolutional neural networks. In: Advances in Neural Information Processing Systems, pp. 1097–1105 (2012). https://doi.org/10.1145/3065386
19. Larsson, G., Maire, M., Shakhnarovich, G.: FractalNet: ultra-deep neural networks without residuals. arXiv preprint arXiv:1605.07648 (2016)
20. LeCun, Y., Bottou, L., Bengio, Y., Haffner, P.: Gradient-based learning applied to document recognition. Proc. IEEE **86**(11), 2278–2324 (1998). https://doi.org/10.1109/5.726791
21. Lin, M., Chen, Q., Yan, S.: Network in network. arXiv preprint arXiv:1312.4400 (2013)
22. Mao, H., et al.: Exploring the regularity of sparse structure in convolutional neural networks. arXiv preprint arXiv:1705.08922 (2017)
23. Park, J., et al.: Faster CNNs with direct sparse convolutions and guided pruning. arXiv preprint arXiv:1608.01409 (2016)
24. Pujol, J.C.F., Poli, R.: Evolving the topology and the weights of neural networks using a dual representation. Appl. Intell. **8**(1), 73–84 (1998). https://doi.org/10.1023/a:1008272615525

25. Rastegari, M., Ordonez, V., Redmon, J., Farhadi, A.: XNOR-Net: ImageNet classification using binary convolutional neural networks. In: Leibe, B., Matas, J., Sebe, N., Welling, M. (eds.) ECCV 2016. LNCS, vol. 9908, pp. 525–542. Springer, Cham (2016). https://doi.org/10.1007/978-3-319-46493-0_32
26. Real, E., Aggarwal, A., Huang, Y., Le, Q.V.: Regularized evolution for image classifier architecture search. arXiv preprint arXiv:1802.01548 (2018)
27. Redmon, J., Farhadi, A.: YOLOv3: an incremental improvement. arXiv preprint arXiv:1804.02767 (2018)
28. Simonyan, K., Zisserman, A.: Very deep convolutional networks for large-scale image recognition. arXiv preprint arXiv:1409.1556 (2014)
29. Srinivas, M., Patnaik, L.M.: Genetic algorithms: a survey. Computer **27**(6), 17–26 (1994). https://doi.org/10.1109/2.294849
30. Srivastava, R.K., Greff, K., Schmidhuber, J.: Highway networks. arXiv preprint arXiv:1505.00387 (2015)
31. Stanley, K.O., Miikkulainen, R.: Evolving neural networks through augmenting topologies. Evol. Comput. **10**(2), 99–127 (2002). https://doi.org/10.1162/106365602320169811
32. Szegedy, C., Ioffe, S., Vanhoucke, V., Alemi, A.A.: Inception-v4, inception-ResNet and the impact of residual connections on learning. In: AAAI, vol. 4, p. 12 (2017)
33. Szegedy, C., Vanhoucke, V., Ioffe, S., Shlens, J., Wojna, Z.: Rethinking the inception architecture for computer vision. In: Proceedings of the IEEE Conference on Computer Vision and Pattern Recognition, pp. 2818–2826 (2016). https://doi.org/10.1109/CVPR.2016.308
34. Sztarker, J., Tomsic, D.: Brain modularity in arthropods: individual neurons that support "what" but not "where" memories. J. Neurosci. **31**(22), 8175–8180 (2011). https://doi.org/10.1523/jneurosci.6029-10.2011
35. Wang, J., Wei, Z., Zhang, T., Zeng, W.: Deeply-fused nets. arXiv preprint arXiv:1605.07716 (2016)
36. Wen, W., Wu, C., Wang, Y., Chen, Y., Li, H.: Learning structured sparsity in deep neural networks. In: Advances in Neural Information Processing Systems, pp. 2074–2082 (2016)
37. Xie, G., Wang, J., Zhang, T., Lai, J., Hong, R., Qi, G.J.: IGCV 2: interleaved structured sparse convolutional neural networks. arXiv preprint arXiv:1804.06202 (2018). https://doi.org/10.1109/CVPR.2018.00922
38. Xie, L., Yuille, A.: Genetic CNN. In: Proceedings of the IEEE International Conference on Computer Vision, pp. 1379–1388 (2017)
39. Zagoruyko, S., Komodakis, N.: Wide residual networks. arXiv preprint arXiv:1605.07146 (2016). https://doi.org/10.5244/C.30.87
40. Zhou, A., Yao, A., Guo, Y., Xu, L., Chen, Y.: Incremental network quantization: towards lossless CNNs with low-precision weights. arXiv preprint arXiv:1702.03044 (2017)
41. Zoph, B., Vasudevan, V., Shlens, J., Le, Q.V.: Learning transferable architectures for scalable image recognition (2017)

Using Feature Entropy to Guide Filter Pruning for Efficient Convolutional Networks

Yun Li, Luyang Wang, Sifan Peng, Aakash Kumar, and Baoqun Yin(✉)

Department of Automation, University of Science and Technology of China, Hefei, China
{yli001,ly1105,sifan,akb}@mail.ustc.edu.cn
bqyin@ustc.edu.cn

Abstract. The rapid development of convolutional neural networks (CNNs) is usually accompanied by an increase in model volume and computational cost. In this paper, we propose an entropy-based filter pruning (EFP) method to learn more efficient CNNs. Different from many existing filter pruning approaches, our proposed method prunes unimportant filters based on the amount of information carried by their corresponding feature maps. We employ entropy to measure the information contained in the feature maps and design features selection module to formulate pruning strategies. Pruning and fine-tuning are iterated several times, yielding thin and more compact models with comparable accuracy. We empirically demonstrate the effectiveness of our method with many advanced CNNs on several benchmark datasets. Notably, for VGG-16 on CIFAR-10, our EFP method prunes 92.9% parameters and reduces 76% float-point-operations (FLOPs) without accuracy loss, which has advanced the state-of-the-art.

Keywords: Convolutional neural networks · Filter pruning · Entropy · Features selection module

1 Introduction

In recent years, we have witnessed a rapid development of deep neural networks in many computer vision tasks such as image classification [6], semantic segmentation [16,19] and object detection [3]. However, as the CNN architectures tend to be deeper and wider to get superior performance, the number of parameters and convolution operations also increase rapidly. For instance, Resnet-164 has nearly 2 million parameters and VGG-16 requires more than 500 MB storage space. These cumbersome models significantly exceed the computing limitation of current mobile devices.

Considerable research efforts have been devoted to compressing large CNN architectures. Pruning is an intuitive CNN compression strategy and it mostly focuses on removing unimportant network connections. The current pruning

I. V. Tetko et al. (Eds.): ICANN 2019, LNCS 11728, pp. 263–274, 2019.
https://doi.org/10.1007/978-3-030-30484-3_22

methods usually include directly deleting weight values of filters [4,22] and totally pruning some filters [7,12,15,24]. The weight value pruning methods introduce non-structured sparsity in the parameter tensors and require dedicated sparse matrix operation libraries. In contrast, the filter level pruning is a naturally structured way of pruning without introducing sparsity and thus does not require sparse libraries or specialized hardware. Therefore, filter pruning attracts more attention in accelerating CNN architectures.

However, most of the previous researches on filter pruning only focus on the activation values or the scale factors weighted on the output of filters and fail to consider the amount of information carried by the feature maps. The feature maps are the most direct reflection of the usefulness of convolution filters. Previous works [12,14] have shown that feature maps are sparse and a considerable number of feature maps output by the middle layers of CNN are most of zeros or zero matrices. Regardless of the given scale factor, the feature maps with all zero values cannot make contribution to the accuracy of the model. On the other hand, if given a small scale factor, a feature map containing a large amount of information will be pruned, which may lead to some important information loss.

In this paper, we propose an entropy-based filter pruning (EFP) method to address the above-mentioned problem. Our EFP selects unimportant filters based on the amount of information contained in their corresponding feature maps. We employ entropy [21] to measure the information carried by feature maps, since it plays a central role in information theory as measures of information and uncertainty. Some similar works proposed to prune the network based on entropy. [13] proposed to calculate the filter entropy, and failed to consider that the amount of information in the filter is unexplained compared with the feature map. [17] calculated the entropy of the global mean of the feature map, which is a rough measure and ignores the spatial information in the feature map. However, our proposed feature entropy method is different from them and can overcome their weakness, since we choose to expand the feature maps by row and calculate their spatial information entropy to weigh the effectiveness of the corresponding filters. Then, we design features selection module to extract the output of every filter and determine their entropy weights. These modules are placed between every two adjacent convolutional layers of a well-trained network, as shown in Fig. 1. Those filters whose output feature maps are given small weights will be pruned. After pruning, we fine-tune the compact model to restore performance and can even achieve a higher accuracy in many cases. Finally, the pruning and fine-tuning process are repeated for several times to get an even more compact network. Furthermore, we also research the correspondence between the entropy pruning ratio and the number of filters to explore the distribution of information in each convolutional layer of a CNN architecture.

We evaluate our method on several benchmark datasets and different CNN architectures. For VGG-16 on CIFAR-10, we achieve 92.9% of parameters pruning and 76% float-point-operations (FLOPs) reduction with 0.04% accuracy improvement, which has advanced the state-of-the-art. For the less redundant

ResNet-56 and ResNet-164, we also gain 50.8% and 52.9% parameters reduction, respectively, without notable accuracy loss.

2 Related Work

Most previous works on deep CNN compression can be roughly divided into 4 categories, matrix decomposition, weight quantization, architecture learning and model pruning.

Matrix decomposition was proposed to approximate weight matrix of deep CNN tensor with sparse decomposition and low-rank matrix [23], using techniques like Singular Value Bounding [10]. While these methods can reduce the computational cost, the compression of the parameters is very limited.

Some works [1,2,4] proposed to quantize the filter weights. The network weights were quantized to several groups and all the weights in the same group shared the same value, only the effective weights and indices need to be stored. This method can achieve a large compression ratio in terms of parameters. However, the FLOPs of the network cannot be reduced, since shared weights need to be restored to the original positions during the process of calculation.

Some other works [8,25] proposed to learn the CNN architecture automatically. [25] trained RNN with reinforcement learning to maximize the expected accuracy of the generated architectures on a validation set. [8] designed AutoML for Model Compression which leverages reinforcement learning to sample the model design space and achieves the model compression. The search space of these strategies is extremely large and they need to train models for a long time to determine the best strategy.

Pruning is an intuitive model compression method. [4] proposed an iterative connection pruning method by pruning unimportant connections whose weights are below the threshold. [22] regularized the structures by group Lasso penalty leading to a compact structure. However, pruning weights always bring unstructured models which are not implementation friendly and the FLOPs reduction is very limited. To overcome these limitations, some filter pruning methods have been explored. [9,12,15] leveraged L1-based methods to select unimportant filters and channels. [18] used statistics information from next layer to evaluate and prune filters. [24] utilized LSTM to select convolutional layers and then evaluated the filters of selected layers. [7] proposed a soft filter pruning method which updates the filters to be pruned after each training epoch. These methods usually require less dedicated libraries or hardwares, as they pay attention to pruning the network structures instead of individual connection of filters. Our proposed entropy-based method also falls into this category, achieving not only parameters reduction but also FLOPs saving without special libraries designed.

3 Method

In this section, we will give a detailed description of our entropy-based filter pruning method. First, we introduce how to determine the entropy weights of feature maps in Sect. 3.1. Next, our feature maps selection and filter pruning strategies are presented in Sect. 3.2. Finally, the analysis of computational cost compression is illustrated in Sect. 3.3.

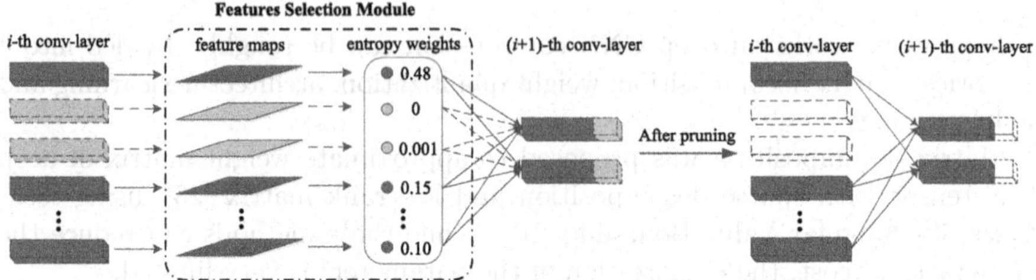

Fig. 1. Illustration of our proposed method which prunes filters based on entropy. We insert features selection module between each two adjacent convolutional layers of the well-trained network (left side). For the i-th layer, the output feature maps of convolution filters are extracted and input to the entropy module to determine their entropy weights. Then those feature maps with smaller weights indicate that they contain less information and the corresponding filters will be pruned (right side). Meanwhile, the corresponding channels of each filter in $(i+1)$-th layer will also be pruned to be consistent with input. All the convolutional layers are pruned in parallel.

3.1 Determining Entropy Weights of Feature Maps

Most of the previous works [9,12,15] determine the importance of filters by L1 sparsity or scale factors and ignore the amount of information carried by the feature maps. Some previous works [12,14] have shown that quite a number of feature maps output by the intermediate layers of CNN are zero matrices or most of zeros, which reveals that not all the filters in the model are useful.

To judge the effectiveness of filters, we employ entropy to measure the information in feature maps. Entropy plays a central role in information theory as measures of information and uncertainty and it is proportional to the amount of information [17]. Considering that the outputs of different convolutional layers have significant differences in the amount of information, the weights of feature maps are determined in each layer independently. Specially, to avoid the contingent result of a single image, we randomly select a large number of images from the training dataset to calculate the average entropy weights of filters. Let H_i/W_i denote the height/width of the output feature maps and m_i be the number of filters of the i-th convolutional layer, in which one filter generates one feature map. N denotes the number of images randomly fed into the network. For n-th image, let $X_{i,k}^{(n)}$ be the k-th output feature map matrix of layer i, expanded by row and forms a feature map vector:

$$\hat{X}_{i,k}^{(n)} = \left(x_{i,k,1}^{(n)},\, x_{i,k,2}^{(n)},\, \cdots,\, x_{i,k,L_i}^{(n)}\right), \tag{1}$$

in which $L_i = H_i \times W_i$. Normalize $\hat{X}_{i,k}^{(n)}$ by Eq. (2), we gain $P_{i,k}^{(n)}$.

$$p_{i,k,l}^{(n)} = \frac{x_{i,k,l}^{(n)} - \min_{l}\left\{x_{i,k,l}^{(n)}\right\}}{\max_{l}\left\{x_{i,k,l}^{(n)}\right\} - \min_{l}\left\{x_{i,k,l}^{(n)}\right\}} \tag{2}$$

$$P_{i,k}^{(n)} = \left(p_{i,k,1}^{(n)}, p_{i,k,2}^{(n)}, \cdots, p_{i,k,L_i}^{(n)}\right) \tag{3}$$

Next, for n-th image and i-th convolutional layer, the entropy of the the k-th feature map vector is defined as:

$$E_{i,k}^{(n)} = -q_i \sum_{l=1, f_{i,k,l}^{(n)}>0}^{L_i} f_{i,k,l}^{(n)} \ln f_{i,k,l}^{(n)}, k = 1, 2, \cdots, m_i, \tag{4}$$

in which $f_{i,k,l}^{(n)} = p_{i,k,l}^{(n)} / \sum_{l=1}^{L_i} p_{i,k,l}^{(n)}$, $q_i = 1/\ln L_i$.

Then, for the output of the i-th convolutional layer, the entropy weight of the k-th feature map can be defined as:

$$w_{i,k}^{(n)} = \frac{E_{i,k}^{(n)}}{\sum\limits_{k=1}^{m_i} E_{i,k}^{(n)}}, \tag{5}$$

in which $0 \leq w_{i,k}^{(n)} \leq 1$, $\sum_{k=1}^{m_i} w_{i,k}^{(n)} = 1$.

Afterwards, we get the average entropy weight of the the k-th feature map:

$$w_{i,k} = \frac{\sum\limits_{n=1}^{N} w_{i,k}^{(n)}}{N}, \tag{6}$$

in which $0 \leq w_{i,k} \leq 1$, $\sum_{k=1}^{m_i} w_{i,k} = 1$.

Eventually, using the the algorithm described above, we can determine all the entropy weights of feature maps in each convolutional layer.

3.2 Filter Pruning Strategies

In order to identify the less useful filters from a well-trained model, the features selection module is designed and inserted between each two adjacent convolutional layers of the model. As shown in Fig. 1, the output of i-th convolutional layer is fed into entropy weights module to determine the weights of every feature map via the algorithm described in Sect. 3.1. The low weights indicate there is less information in these feature maps and the corresponding filters of i-th convolutional layer are less useful. Then we can prune the feature maps with low weights by removing all their incoming and outgoing connections. By doing so, all the less important filters of the i-th layer and feature maps fed into the $(i+1)$-th layer are pruned, as well as the corresponding channels of each filter in the $(i+1)$-th layer.

Determining Pruning Thresholds. In each convolution layer, it is essential to determine the pruning threshold based on the given entropy pruning ratio. Firstly, entropy weights of feature maps in each layer are sorted in ascending order. Then they are accumulated from the smallest weights until the given entropy pruning ratio is exceeded. The last superimposed weight is used as the threshold of the corresponding layer, and all the feature maps and corresponding filters whose entropy weights are lower than the threshold will be pruned. After that, we obtain a more compact network with fewer parameters, less storage and less run time consumption.

Iterative Pruning and Fine-Tuning. There may be some temporary accuracy loss after pruning, but it can be largely compensated by the following fine-tuning process. After that, we can even achieve a higher accuracy than the original one. For the whole network pruning, previous works usually prune and fine-tune the filters layer by layer [4,18], or retrain the network after each pruning and fine-tuning process [15]. Considering that these strategies are quite time-consuming, our method prunes all layers in parallel, followed by fine-tuning to compensate any loss of accuracy. Moreover, we prune and fine-tune the network iteratively and there is no need to retrain the network from scratch again. The experiments on VGGNet indicate that this strategy is effective. With several iterations, we can achieve a large degree of compression and even lead to a better result.

Adjustment Strategy for Residual Architectures. The proposed filter pruning method can be easily applied to plain CNN architectures such as VGGNet and AlexNet. However, some adjustment strategies are required when it is used to prune complex architectures with cross layer connections such as residual networks [6]. For these architectures, the output of the building block's last convolutional layer and the identity mapping must be same in size and number of feature maps, which makes them difficult to be pruned. As can be seen from part b of Fig. 2, our features selection modules are placed after the first and second convolutional layers. For the third convolutional layer of the bottleneck block, we only prune the channels of each filter to make them consistent with the input feature maps and do not reduce the number of filters, since the output of it must match the identity maps and there are fewer parameters contained in these 1×1 filters.

3.3 Analysis of Computational Cost Compression

According to Sect. 3.1, the ith convolutional layer takes as input a $W_{i-1} \times H_{i-1} \times m_{i-1}$ tensor of feature maps and produces a $W_i \times H_i \times m_i$ tensor, where m_{i-1} and m_i are the numbers of feature maps. Let us assume the ith convolutional layer is parameterized by $K_i \times K_i \times m_{i-1} \times m_i$, where K_i is the spatial dimension of every filter. Standard convolutions have the computational cost of $K_i \times K_i \times m_{i-1} \times m_i \times W_i \times H_i$. Let r_i denote the entropy pruning rate of i-th layer and $\hat{r}_i$ be the corresponding filter pruning rate. Then the number of filters of the i-th layer will be reduced from m_i to $m_i\,(1 - \hat{r}_i)$, and the channels of filters in

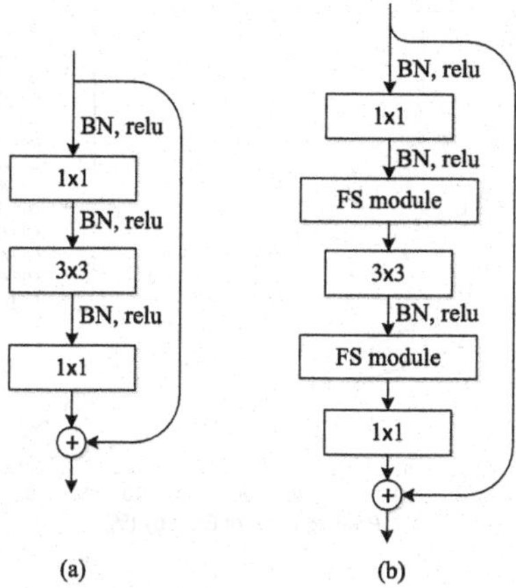

Fig. 2. Illustration of the strategy to prune residual networks. (a) Original bottleneck block of ResNet, (b) bottleneck block with features selection (FS) modules. The BN layer is placed before each convolutional layer, and FS module is placed after ReLU.

this layer are reduced from m_{i-1} to $m_{i-1}\left(1-\hat{r}_{i-1}\right)$. Afterwards, we can get the compression ratio in computational cost for this pruned layer:

$$\begin{aligned} &1-\frac{{K_i}^2 \times m_{i-1}\left(1-\hat{r}_{i-1}\right) \times m_i\left(1-\hat{r}_i\right) \times W_i \times H_i}{{K_i}^2 \times m_{i-1} \times m_i \times W_i \times H_i} \\ &=1-\left(1-\hat{r}_{i-1}\right)\left(1-\hat{r}_i\right). \end{aligned} \tag{7}$$

4 Experiments

We evaluate our proposed EFP on several benchmark datasets and networks: VGG-16 on CIFAR10 and CIFAR100, ResNet-56 on CIFAR-10, ResNet-164 on CIFAR-100. Both CIFAR datasets [11] contain 50000 training images and 10000 test images. The CIFAR-10 dataset is categorized into 10 classes, and the CIFAR-100 is categorized into 100 classes. All the experiments are implemented with PyTorch [20] framework on NVIDIA GTX TITAN Xp GPU. Moreover, our method is compared with several state-of-the-art methods [7,9,12,15].

4.1 Implementation Details

Experimental Setting. In the experiments, the initial models are trained from scratch to calculate the accuracies as their baselines. During the training process, all images are cropped randomly into 32×32 with four paddings and horizontal flip is also applied. We use mini-batch size 100 to train and mini-batch size 1000 to test VGGNet, and use mini-batch size 64 to train and mini-batch size 256 to test ResNet. All the models are trained and fine-tuned using SGD for 180 epochs on two datasets. During training and fine-tuning processes, the initial learning

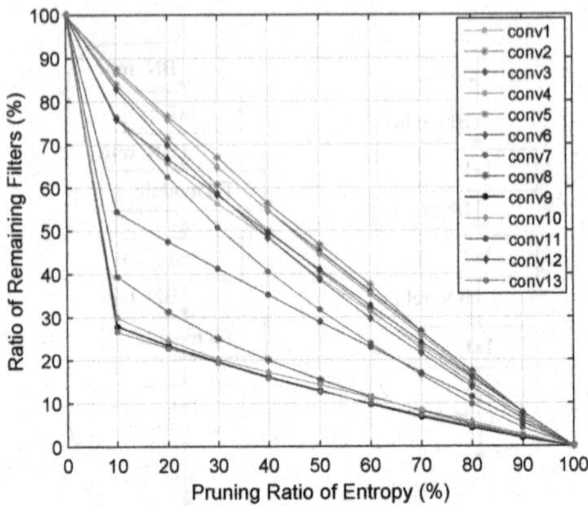

Fig. 3. The pruning results of VGG-16 on CIFAR-10 with entropy pruning rate from 10% to 100%.

rate is set to 0.1, and is divided by 10 at 50% and 75% of the total number of epochs, following the setting in [15]. Besides, the weight initialization described by [5] is also applied.

Entropy Pruning Rate and Filter Pruning Rate. We use our entropy-based method to prune less important filters. In our experiments, 1000 images randomly selected from the datasets are fed into the pre-trained network to gain the average entropy weights of feature maps. Then, we give entropy pruning rates for every convolutional layer to calculate the pruning thresholds via the method described in Sect. 3.2. Figure 3 shows the filter pruning results of VGG-16 on CIFAR-10 with entropy pruning rate from 10% to 100%. The pruning results reveal that information distribution varies between different convolution layers. For some convolutional layers of VGG-16, pruning only 10% information entropy can lead to more than 70% filters reduction.

4.2 Pruning VGGNet

To evaluate the effectiveness of our proposed method on VGG-16, we test it on CIFAR-10 and CIFAR-100 datasets.

VGG-16 on CIFAR-10. Considering that convolutional layers of VGGNet are different in robustness [12] and information concentration, we give each convolution layer a separate pruning ratio. According to the number of filters and the results shown in Fig. 3, the layers of VGG-16 are divided into 3 levels, the layers with less than 128 filters, the layers with 256 filters and the layers with 512 filters. For a given entropy pruning rate r, the rates are set to $0.5r$, r and $1.5r$ for the three levels, respectively. We set $r = 10\%$ and prune VGG-16 model iteratively. As shown in Table 1(a), our proposed EFP achieves a better performance than the other filter pruning methods. With only one iteration, our

Table 1. Pruning results of VGGNet on CIFAR-10 and CIFAR-100. "Baseline" and "Param. baseline" denote the normal accuracy and number of parameters of the original model, respectively. In "Method" column, "iter-1" declares the first iteration of pruning. The pruned ratio of parameters and FLOPs are also shown in column-7&8.

(a) Pruning results of VGG-16 on CIFAR-10						
Method	Baseline	Accuracy	Param. baseline	Parameters	Pruned	Flops saved
Li *et al.* [12]	93.25%	93.30%	1.5×10^7	5.4×10^6	64.0%	34.2%
Slimming [15]	93.66%	93.80%	–	–	88.5%	51.0%
Ours (iter-1)	93.72%	**93.97%**	1.5×10^7	3.5×10^5	76.4%	49.5%
Ours (iter-4)	93.72%	93.76%	1.5×10^7	1.0×10^5	**92.9%**	**76.0%**
(b) Pruning results of VGG-16 on CIFAR-100						
Method	Baseline	Accuracy	Param. baseline	Parameters	Pruned	Flops saved
Slimming [15]	73.26%	73.48%	–	–	**75.1%**	37.1%
Ours (iter-1)	73.60%	**73.82%**	1.5×10^7	9.6×10^6	34.4%	26.2%
Ours (iter-2)	73.60%	73.61%	1.5×10^7	6.4×10^6	56.4%	**44.0%**

method can prune 50% parameters and even achieve 0.25% accuracy improvement. After four iterations, the parameters saving can be up to 92.9% and the FLOP reduction is 76% with 0.04% accuracy improvement, which has advanced the state-of-the-art.

VGG-16 on CIFAR-100. We use the same setting on VGG-16 to evaluate our method on CIFAR-100. As can be seen from Table 1(b), our model can achieve 44% FLOPs reduction with only two iterations, which is better than the result of [15]. The pruning ratio is not as high as it in CIFAR-10. It is possibly due to the fact that CIFAR-100 contains more classes and it needs more information to classify targets.

4.3 Pruning ResNet

For ResNet architectures, two models ResNet-56 and ResNet-164 with bottleneck structure are utilized to evaluate the proposed method. In bottleneck blocks, the BN layer and ReLU are placed before each convolutional layer. Considering that there are skip connections in the ResNet structures and the information can be shared across the network, we use the same entropy pruning ratio to prune all the layers. Moreover, the feature information can be shared across the network through skip connection, making ResNet structures less sensitive to large-scale pruning, so we prune ResNet-56 and ResNet-164 in a one-shot manner.

ResNet-56 on CIFAR-10. We first prune a medium depth network ResNet-56 on CIFAR-10. The result is compared with several state-of-the-art methods. As shown in Table 2(a), we can gain almost the equal accuracy with the original

Table 2. Pruning results of ResNet on CIFAR-10 and CIFAR-100 datasets. In "Method" column, "10%" is the one-shot pruning ratio of entropy weights.

(a) Pruning results of Resnet-56 on CIFAR-10

Method	Baseline	Accuracy	Param. baseline	Parameters	Pruned	Flops saved
Li *et al.* [12]	93.04%	93.06%	8.5×10^5	7.3×10^5	13.7%	27.6%
He *et al.* [9]	92.80%	91.80%	–	–	–	50.0%
He *et al.* [7]	93.59%	93.35%	–	–	–	52.6%
Ours (15%)	94.12%	**94.11%**	5.9×10^5	4.3×10^5	25.7%	29.4%
Ours (30%)	94.12%	93.31%	5.9×10^5	2.9×10^5	**50.8%**	**53.9%**

(b) Pruning results of Resnet-164 on CIFAR-100

Method	Baseline	Accuracy	Param. baseline	Parameters	Pruned	Flops saved
Slimming1 [15]	76.63%	77.13%	–	–	15.5%	33.3%
Slimming2 [15]	76.63%	76.09%	–	–	29.7%	50.6%
Ours (10%)	76.96%	**77.59%**	1.7×10^6	1.3×10^6	23.5%	24.0%
Ours (20%)	76.96%	77.14%	1.7×10^6	1.0×10^6	41.2%	46.8%
Ours (30%)	76.96%	76.59%	1.7×10^6	8.0×10^5	**52.9%**	**58.7%**

model with about 26% parameters pruned and 30% FLOPs reduced. Moreover, our EFP can also prune 50.8% parameters and 53.9% FLOPs with only 0.79% accuracy drop. It can be observed that unlike VGGNet has a large number of parameters and FLOPs, the bottleneck designed ResNet has less redundancy in parameters and calculations.

ResNet-164 on CIFAR-100. For the deeper network ResNet-164, we adopt the same setting with ResNet-56. Table 2(b) shows that our method outperforms Network Slimming [15]. For ResNet-164, Network Slimming can prune 15% parameters without accuracy loss. When they prune about 30% parameters, there will be 0.54% accuracy drop. However, our proposed method can outperform the original model by 0.18% with 41.2% parameters pruned and 46.8% FLOPs reduced. When we prune 30% entropy weights, our method achieves 52.94% parameters pruned and 58.7% FLOPs saved with only 0.37% accuracy drop.

To comprehensively understand the impact of our proposed method on the model, we test model compression ratio and accuracy of different entropy pruning rates. As shown in Fig. 4, the accuracy of the pruned model first rises above the baseline model and then drops as the entropy pruning rate increases. When the entropy pruning ratio is under 25%, almost 50% parameters are pruned, and our method brings no accuracy loss and even achieves slight accuracy improvement. This result shows our proposed EFP can reduce redundant information and improve the effective expression of features.

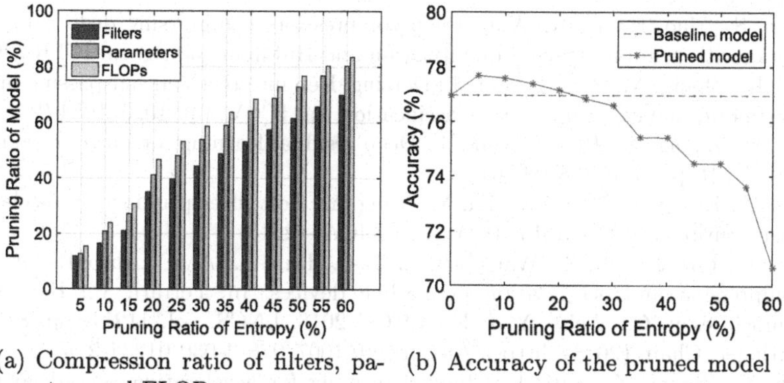

(a) Compression ratio of filters, parameters and FLOPs

(b) Accuracy of the pruned model

Fig. 4. Pruning results of ResNet-164 on CIFAR-100 regarding different entropy pruning ratios.

5 Conclusion

In this paper, we propose a simple yet effective method, which evaluates the usefulness of convolution filters based on the information contained in the feature maps output by these filters. Our method introduces entropy to measure the amount of information carried by feature maps and evaluate the importance of corresponding convolution filters. Features selection module is designed to formulate pruning strategies. To fit different network structures, some pruning strategies are proposed and address the problem of the dimension mismatch in resnets during pruning. Moreover, the distribution of information in every convolutional layer of CNNs is also discussed and the results demonstrate that in some layers most filters make limited contribution to the performance of the model. Extensive experiments show the superiority of our approach compared to the existing methods. Notably, for VGG-16 on CIFAR-10, our proposed method can prune 92.9% parameters and meanwhile lead to 76% FLOPs reduction without accuracy loss, and this performance has advanced recent state-of-the-art methods.

Acknowledgments. This work was supported by the Equipment Pre-Research Foundation of China under grant No. 61403120201.

References

1. Chen, W., Wilson, J., Tyree, S., Weinberger, K., Chen, Y.: Compressing neural networks with the hashing trick. In: ICML, pp. 2285–2294 (2015)
2. Courbariaux, M., Hubara, I., Soudry, D., El-Yaniv, R., Bengio, Y.: Binarized neural networks: training deep neural networks with weights and activations constrained to +1 or −1. arXiv preprint arXiv:1602.02830 (2016)
3. Girshick, R., Donahue, J., Darrell, T., Malik, J.: Rich feature hierarchies for accurate object detection and semantic segmentation. In: CVPR, pp. 580–587 (2014)

4. Han, S., Mao, H., Dally, W.J.: Deep compression: compressing deep neural networks with pruning, trained quantization and Huffman coding. In: ICLR (2016)
5. He, K., Zhang, X., Ren, S., Sun, J.: Delving deep into rectifiers: surpassing human-level performance on imagenet classification. In: ICCV, pp. 1026–1034 (2015)
6. He, K., Zhang, X., Ren, S., Sun, J.: Deep residual learning for image recognition. In: CVPR, pp. 770–778 (2016)
7. He, Y., Kang, G., Dong, X., Fu, Y., Yang, Y.: Soft filter pruning for accelerating deep convolutional neural networks. In: IJCAI (2018)
8. He, Y., Lin, J., Liu, Z., Wang, H., Li, L.-J., Han, S.: AMC: AutoML for model compression and acceleration on mobile devices. In: Ferrari, V., Hebert, M., Sminchisescu, C., Weiss, Y. (eds.) ECCV 2018. LNCS, vol. 11211, pp. 815–832. Springer, Cham (2018). https://doi.org/10.1007/978-3-030-01234-2_48
9. He, Y., Zhang, X., Sun, J.: Channel pruning for accelerating very deep neural networks. In: ICCV (2017)
10. Jia, K., Tao, D., Gao, S., Xu, X.: Improving training of deep neural networks via singular value bounding. In: CVPR 2017, pp. 3994–4002 (2017)
11. Krizhevsky, A., Hinton, G.: Learning multiple layers of features from tiny images. Technical report, Citeseer (2009)
12. Li, H., Kadav, A., Durdanovic, I., Samet, H., Graf, H.P.: Pruning filters for efficient convnets. In: ICLR (2017)
13. Li, Y., et al.: Exploiting kernel sparsity and entropy for interpretable CNN compression. In: CVPR (2019)
14. Liu, B., Wang, M., Foroosh, H., Tappen, M., Pensky, M.: Sparse convolutional neural networks. In: CVPR, pp. 806–814 (2015)
15. Liu, Z., Li, J., Shen, Z., Huang, G., Yan, S., Zhang, C.: Learning efficient convolutional networks through network slimming. In: ICCV, pp. 2755–2763 (2017)
16. Long, J., Shelhamer, E., Darrell, T.: Fully convolutional networks for semantic segmentation. In: CVPR, pp. 3431–3440 (2015)
17. Luo, J.H., Wu, J.: An entropy-based pruning method for CNN compression. arXiv preprint arXiv:1706.05791 (2017)
18. Luo, J.H., Wu, J., Lin, W.: ThiNet: a filter level pruning method for deep neural network compression. In: ICCV (2017)
19. Noh, H., Hong, S., Han, B.: Learning deconvolution network for semantic segmentation. In: ICCV, pp. 1520–1528 (2015)
20. Paszke, A., Gross, S., Chintala, S., Chanan, G.: Pytorch: tensors and dynamic neural networks in Python with strong GPU acceleration (2017)
21. Shannon, C.E.: A mathematical theory of communication. Bell Syst. Tech. J. **27**(3), 379–423 (1948)
22. Wen, W., Wu, C., Wang, Y., Chen, Y., Li, H.: Learning structured sparsity in deep neural networks. In: Advances in Neural Information Processing Systems, pp. 2074–2082 (2016)
23. Yu, X., Liu, T., Wang, X., Tao, D.: On compressing deep models by low rank and sparse decomposition. In: CVPR, pp. 7370–7379 (2017)
24. Zhong, J., Ding, G., Guo, Y., Han, J., Wang, B.: Where to prune: using LSTM to guide end-to-end pruning. In: IJCAI, pp. 3205–3211 (2018)
25. Zoph, B., Le, Q.V.: Neural architecture search with reinforcement learning. arXiv preprint arXiv:1611.01578 (2016)

Simultaneously Learning Architectures and Features of Deep Neural Networks

Tinghuai Wang[1(✉)], Lixin Fan[1], and Huiling Wang[2]

[1] Nokia Technologies, Espoo, Finland
wang.tinghuai@gmail.com
[2] Tampere University, Tampere, Finland

Abstract. This paper presents a novel method which simultaneously learns the *number of filters* and *network features* repeatedly over multiple epochs. We propose a novel pruning loss to explicitly enforces the optimizer to focus on promising candidate filters while suppressing contributions of less relevant ones. In the meanwhile, we further propose to enforce the diversities between filters and this diversity-based regularization term improves the trade-off between model sizes and accuracies. It turns out the interplay between architecture and feature optimizations improves the final compressed models, and the proposed method is compared favorably to existing methods, in terms of both models sizes and accuracies for a wide range of applications including image classification, image compression and audio classification.

1 Introduction

Large and deep neural networks, despite of their great successes in a wide variety of applications, call for compact and efficient model representations to reduce the vast amount of network parameters and computational operations, that are resource-hungry in terms of memory, energy and communication bandwidth consumption. This need is imperative especially for resource constrained devices such as mobile phones, wearable and Internet of Things (IoT) devices. Neural network compression is a set of techniques that address these challenges raised in real life industrial applications.

Minimizing network sizes without compromising original network performances has been pursued by a wealth of methods, which often adopt a three-phase learning process, i.e. training-pruning-tuning. In essence, network features are first learned, followed by the pruning stage to reduce network sizes. The subsequent fine-tuning phase aims to restore deteriorated performances incurred by undue pruning. This ad hoc three phase approach, although empirically justified e.g. in [12,14,17,20,22], was recently questioned with regards to its efficiency and effectiveness. Specifically [3,15] argued that the network *architecture* should be optimized first, and then *features* should be learned from scratch in subsequent steps.

I. V. Tetko et al. (Eds.): ICANN 2019, LNCS 11728, pp. 275–287, 2019.
https://doi.org/10.1007/978-3-030-30484-3_23

In contrast to the two aforementioned opposing approaches, the present paper illustrates a novel method which simultaneously learns both the *number of filters* and *network features* over multiple optimization epochs. This integrated optimization process brings about immediate benefits and challenges—on the one hand, separated processing steps such as training, pruning, fine-tuning etc, are no longer needed and the integrated optimization step guarantees consistent performances for the given neural network compression scenarios. On the other hand, the dynamic change of network architectures has significant influences on the optimization of features, which in turn might affect the optimal network architectures. It turns out the interplay between architecture and feature optimizations plays a crucial role in improving the final compressed models.

2 Related Work

Network pruning was pioneered [4,6,11] in the early development of neural network, since when a broad range of methods have been developed. We focus on neural network compression methods that prune filters or channels. For thorough review of other approaches we refer to a recent survey paper [2].

Li *et al.* [12] proposed to prune filters with small effects on the output accuracy and managed to reduce about one third of inference cost without compromising original accuracy on CIFAR-10 dataset. Wen *et al.* [20] proposed a structured sparsity regularization framework, in which the group lasso constrain term was incorporated to penalize and remove unimportant filters and channels. Zhou *et al.* [22] also adopted a similar regularization framework, with tensor trace norm and group sparsity incorporated to penalize the number of neurons. Up to 70% of model parameters were reduced without scarifying classification accuracies on CIFAR-10 datasets. Recently Liu *et al.* [14] proposed an interesting network slimming method, which imposes L1 regularization on channel-wise *scaling factors* in batch-normalization layers and demonstrated remarkable compression ratio and speedup using a surprisingly simple implementation. Nevertheless, network slimming based on scaling factors is not guaranteed to achieve desired accuracies and separate fine-tunings are needed to restore reduced accuracies. Qin *et al.* [17] proposed a functionality-oriented filter pruning method to remove less important filters, in terms of their contributions to classification accuracies. It was shown that the efforts for model retraining is moderate but still necessary, as in the most of state-of-the-art compression methods.

DIVNET adopted Determinantal Point Process (DPP) to enforce diversities between individual neural activations [16]. Diversity of filter weights defined in (4) is related to orthogonality of weight matrix, which has been extensively studied. An example being [5], proposed to learn Stiefel layers, which have orthogonal weights, and demonstrated its applicability in compressing network parameters. Interestingly, the notion of diversity regularized machine (DRM) has been proposed to generate an ensemble of SVMs in the PAC learning framework [21], yet its definition of diversity is critically different from our definition in (4), and its applicability to deep neural networks is unclear.

3 Simultaneous Learning of Architecture and Feature

The proposed compression method belongs to the general category of filter-pruning approaches. In contrast to existing methods [3,12,14,15,17,20,22], we adopt following techniques to ensure that simultaneous optimization of network architectures and features is a technically sound approach. First, we introduce an explicit *pruning loss* estimation as an additional regularization term in the optimization objective function. As demonstrated by experiment results in Sect. 4, the introduced pruning loss enforces the optimizer to focus on promising candidate filters while suppressing contributions of less relevant ones. Second, based on the importance of filters, we explicitly *turn-off* unimportant filters below given percentile threshold. We found the explicit shutting down of less relevant filters is indispensable to prevent biased estimation of pruning loss. Third, we also propose to enforce the diversities between filters and this diversity-based regularization term improves the trade-off between model sizes and accuracies, as demonstrated in various applications.

Our proposed method is inspired by network slimming [14] and main differences from this prior art are two-folds: (a) we introduce the pruning loss and incorporate explicit pruning into the learning process, without resorting to the multi-pass pruning-retraining cycles; (b) we also introduce filter-diversity based regularization term which improves the trade-off between model sizes and accuracies.

3.1 Loss Function

Liu *et al.* [14] proposed to push towards zero the scaling factor in batch normalization (BN) step during learning, and subsequently, the insignificant channels with small scaling factors are pruned. This sparsity-induced penalty is introduced by regularizing L1-norm of the learnable parameter γ in the BN step *i.e.*,

$$g(\gamma) = |\gamma| \,; \text{ where } \hat{z} = \frac{z_{in} - \mu_B}{\sqrt{\sigma^2 + \epsilon}}; z_{out} = \gamma \hat{z} + \beta, \tag{1}$$

in which z_{in} denote filter inputs, μ_B, σ the filter-wise mean and variance of inputs, γ, β the scaling and offset parameters of batch normalization (BN) and ϵ a small constant to prevent numerical un-stability for small variance. It is assumed that there is always a BN filter appended after each convolution and fully connected filter, so that the scaling factor γ is directly leveraged to prune unimportant filters with small γ values. Alternatively, we propose to directly introduce scaling factor to each filter since it is more universal than reusing BN parameters, especially considering the networks which have no BN layers.

By incorporating a filter-wise sparsity term, the object function to be minimized is given by:

$$L = \sum_{(\mathbf{x},y)} loss(f(\mathbf{x}, \mathbf{W}), y) + \lambda \sum_{\gamma \in \Gamma} g(\gamma), \tag{2}$$

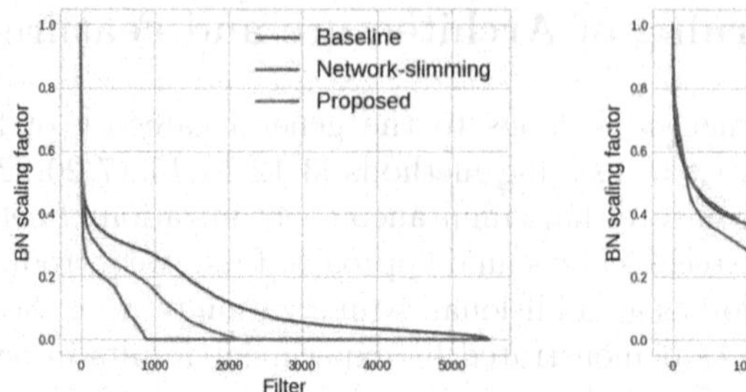

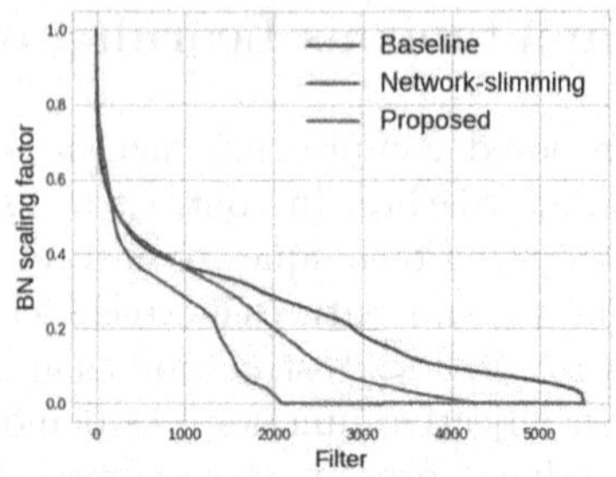

Fig. 1. Comparison of scaling factors for three methods, *i.e.*, baseline with no regularization, network-slimming [14], and the proposed method with diversified filters, trained with CIFAR-10 and CIFAR-100. Note that the pruning loss defined in (3) are 0.2994, 0.0288, 1.3628×10^{-6}, respectively, for three methods. Accuracy deterioration are 60.76% and 0% for network-slimming [14] and the proposed methods, and the baseline networks completely failed after pruning, due to insufficient preserved filters at certain layers.

where the first term is the task-based loss, $g(\gamma) = ||\gamma||_1$ and $\varGamma$ denotes the set of scaling factors for all filters. This pruning scheme, however, suffers from two main drawbacks: (1) since scaling factors are equally minimized for all filterers, it is likely that the pruned filters have unignorable contributions that should not be unduly removed. (2) the pruning process, *i.e.*, architecture selection, is performed independently w.r.t. the feature learning; the performance of pruned network is inevitably compromised and has to be recovered by single-pass or multi-pass fine-tuning, which impose additional computational burdens.

An Integrated Optimization

Let $\mathbf{W}, \check{\mathbf{W}}, \hat{\mathbf{W}}$ denote the sets of neural network weights for, respectively, all filters, those pruned and remained ones i.e. $\mathbf{W} = \{\check{\mathbf{W}} \bigcup \hat{\mathbf{W}}\}$. In the same vein, $\varGamma = \{P(\varGamma) \bigcup R(\varGamma)\}$ denote the sets of scaling factors for all filters, those removed and remained ones respectively.

To mitigate the aforementioned drawbacks, we propose to introduce two additional regularization terms to Eq. 2,

$$
\begin{aligned}
L(\hat{\mathbf{W}}, R(\varGamma)) = &\sum_{(\mathbf{x},y)} loss(f(\mathbf{x}, \hat{\mathbf{W}}), y) + \lambda_1 \sum_{\gamma \in R(\varGamma)} g(\gamma) \\
&- \lambda_2 \frac{\sum_{\gamma \in R(\varGamma)} \gamma}{\sum_{\gamma \in \varGamma} \gamma} - \lambda_3 \sum_{l \in L} Div(\hat{\mathbf{W}}^l),
\end{aligned} \tag{3}
$$

where $loss(\cdot, \cdot)$ and $\sum_{\gamma \in R(\varGamma)} g(\gamma)$ are defined as in Eq. 2, the third term is the pruning loss and the forth is the diversity loss which are elaborated below. $\lambda_1, \lambda_2, \lambda_3$ are weights of corresponding regularization terms.

Estimation of Pruning Loss

The second regularization term in (3) i.e. $\gamma^R := \frac{\sum_{\gamma \in R(\varGamma)} \gamma}{\sum_{\gamma \in \varGamma} \gamma}$ (and its compliment $\gamma^P := \frac{\sum_{\gamma \in P(\varGamma)} \gamma}{\sum_{\gamma \in \varGamma} \gamma} = 1 - \gamma^R$) is closely related to performance deterioration incurred by undue pruning[1]. The scaling factors of pruned filters $P(\Gamma)$, as in [14], are determined by first ranking all γ and taking those below the given percentile threshold. Incorporating this pruning loss enforces the optimizer to increase scaling factors of promising filters while suppressing contributions of less relevant ones.

The rationale of this pruning strategy can also be empirically justified in Fig. 1, in which scaling factors of three different methods are illustrated. When the proposed regularization terms are added, clearly, we observed a tendency for scaling factors being dominated by few number of filters — when 70% of filters are pruned from a VGG network trained with CIFAR-10 dataset, the estimated pruning loss $\frac{\sum_{\gamma \in P(\Gamma)} \gamma}{\sum_{\gamma \in \Gamma} \gamma}$ equals 0.2994, 0.0288, 1.3628×10^{-6}, respectively, for three compared methods. Corresponding accuracy deterioration are 60.76% and 0% for network-slimming [14] and the proposed methods. Therefore, retraining of pruned network is no longer needed for the proposed method, while [14] has to retain the original accuracy through single-pass or multi-pass of pruning-retraining cycles.

Turning off Candidate Filters

It must be noted that the original loss $\sum_{(\mathbf{x},y)} loss(f(\mathbf{x}, \mathbf{W}), y)$ is independent of the pruning operation. If we adopt this loss in (3), the estimated pruning loss might be seriously biased because of undue assignments of γ not being penalized. It seems likely some candidate filters are assigned with rather small scaling factors, nevertheless, they still retain decisive contributions to the final classifications. Pruning these filters blindly leads to serious performance deterioration, according to the empirical study, where we observe over 50% accuracy loss at high pruning ratio.

In order to prevent such biased pruning loss estimation, we therefore explicitly shutdown the outputs of selected filters by setting corresponding scaling factors to absolute zero. The adopted loss function becomes $\sum_{(\mathbf{x},y)} loss(f(\mathbf{x}, \hat{\mathbf{W}}), y)$. This way, the undue loss due to the biased estimation is reflected in $loss(f(\mathbf{x}, \hat{\mathbf{W}}), y)$, which is minimized during the learning process. We found the turning-off of candidate filters is indispensable.

Online Pruning. We take a global threshold for pruning which is determined by percentile among all channel scaling factors. The pruning process is performed over the whole training process, *i.e.,* simultaneous pruning and learning. To this end, we compute a linearly increasing pruning ratio from the first epoch (0%) to the last epoch (100%) where the ultimate pruning target ratio is applied. Such an approach endows neurons with sufficient evolutions driven by diversity term and pruning loss, to avoid mis-pruning neurons prematurely which produces crucial features. Consequently our architecture learning is seamlessly integrated with feature learning. After each pruning operation, a narrower and more compact network is obtained and its corresponding weights are copied from the previous network.

[1] In the rest of the paper we refer to it as the estimated pruning loss.

Algorithm 1. Proposed algorithm

procedure ONLINE PRUNING
  Training data $\leftarrow \{x_i, y_i\}_{i=1}^N$
  Target pruning ratio $\mathbf{Pr}_N \leftarrow \mathbf{p}\%$
  Initial network weights $W \leftarrow$ *method by [7]*
  $\Gamma \leftarrow \{0.5\}$
  $\hat{W} \leftarrow W$
  $P(\Gamma) \leftarrow \emptyset$
  $R(\Gamma) \leftarrow \Gamma$
  for each *epoch* $n \in \{1, \ldots, N\}$ **do**
    Current pruning ratio $\mathbf{Pr}_n \in [0, \mathbf{Pr}_N]$
    Sort Γ
    $P(\Gamma) \leftarrow$ *prune filters w.r.t.* $\mathbf{Pr}_n$
    $R(\Gamma) \leftarrow \Gamma \setminus P(\Gamma)$
    Compute $L(\hat{\mathbf{W}}, R(\Gamma))$ *in Eq.* (2)
    $\hat{\mathbf{W}} \leftarrow$ *SGD*
    $\check{\mathbf{W}} \leftarrow \hat{\mathbf{W}} \setminus \check{\mathbf{W}}$

Filter-Wise Diversity

The third regularization term in (3) encourages high diversities between filter weights as shown below. Empirically, we found that this term improves the trade-off between model sizes and accuracies (see experiment results in Sect. 4).

We treat each filter weight, at layer l, as a weight (feature) vector $\mathbf{W}_i^l$ of length $w \times h \times c$, where w, h are filter width and height, c the number of channels in the filter. The *diversity* between two weight vectors of the same length is based on the *normalized cross-correlation* of two vectors:

$$div(\mathbf{W}_i, \mathbf{W}_j) := 1 - |\langle \bar{\mathbf{W}}_i, \bar{\mathbf{W}}_j \rangle|, \tag{4}$$

in which $\bar{\mathbf{W}} = \frac{\mathbf{W}}{|\mathbf{W}|}$ are normalized weight vectors, and $\langle \cdot, \cdot \rangle$ is the dot product of two vectors. Clearly, the diversity is bounded $0 \le div(\mathbf{W}_i, \mathbf{W}_j) \le 1$, with value close 0 indicating low diversity between highly correlated vectors and values near 1 meaning high diversity between uncorrelated vectors. In particular, diversity equals 1 also means that two vectors are orthogonal with each other.

The *diversities* between N filters at the same layer l is thus characterized by a *N-by-N* matrix in which elements $d_{ij} = div(\mathbf{W}_i^l, \mathbf{W}_j^l), i, j = \{1, \cdots, N\}$ are pairwise diversities between weight vectors $\mathbf{W}_i^l, \mathbf{W}_j^l$. Note that for diagonal elements d_{ii} are constant 0. The *total diversity* between all filters is thus defined as the sum of all elements

$$Div(\mathbf{W}^l) := \sum_{i,j=1,1}^{N,N} d_{i,j}. \tag{5}$$

Table 1. Results on CIFAR-10 dataset

Models/Pruning ratio	0.0	0.5	0.6	0.7	0.8
VGG-19 (Base-line)	0.9366	–	–	–	–
VGG-19 (Network-slimming)	–	–	–	0.9380	NA
VGG-19 (Ours)	–	0.9353	0.9394	0.9393	0.9302
ResNet-164 (Base-line)	0.9458	–	–	–	–
ResNet-164 (Network-slimming)	–	–	0.9473	NA	NA
ResNet-164 (Ours)	–	0.9478	0.9483	0.9401	NA

Table 2. Results on CIFAR-100 dataset

Models/Pruning ratio	0.0	0.3	0.4	0.5	0.6
VGG-19 (Base-line)	0.7326	–	–	–	–
VGG-19 (Network-slimming)	–	–	0.7348	–	–
VGG-19 (Ours)	–	0.7332	0.7435	0.7340	0.7374
ResNet-164 (Base-line)	0.7663	–	–	–	–
ResNet-164 (Network-slimming)	–	–	0.7713	–	0.7609
ResNet-164 (Ours)	–	0.7716	0.7749	0.7727	0.7745

4 Experiment Results

In this section, we evaluate the effectiveness of our method on various applications with both visual and audio data.

4.1 Datasets

For visual tasks, we adopt ImageNet and CIFAR datasets. The ImageNet dataset contains 1.2 million training images and 50,000 validation images of 1000 classes. CIFAR-10 [10] which consists of 50 K training and 10 K testing RGB images with 10 classes. CIFAR-100 is similar to CIFAR-10, except it has 100 classes. The input image is 32×32 randomly cropped from a zero-padded 40×40 image or its flipping. For audio task, we adopt ISMIR Genre dataset [1] which has been assembled for training and development in the ISMIR 2004 Genre Classification contest. It contains 1458 full length audio recordings from Magnatune.com distributed across the 6 genre classes: Classical, Electronic, JazzBlues, MetalPunk, RockPop, World.

4.2 Image Classification

We evaluate the performance of our proposed method for image classification on CIFAR-10/100 and ImageNet. We investigate both classical plain network, VGG-Net [18], and deep residual network *i.e.,* ResNet [8]. We evaluate our method on two popular network architecture *i.e.*, VGG-Net [18], and ResNet [8]. We take variations of the original VGG-Net, *i.e.*, VGG-19 used in [14] for comparison purpose. ResNet-164 which has 164-layer pre-activation ResNet with bottleneck structure is adopted. As base-line networks, we compare with the original networks without regularization terms and their counterparts in network-slimming [14]. For ImageNet, we adopt VGG-16 and ResNet-50 in order to compare with the original networks.

To make a fair comparison with [14], we adopt BN based scaling factors for optimization and pruning. On CIFAR, we train all the networks from scratch using SGD with mini-batch size 64 for 160 epochs. The learning rate is initially set to 0.1 which is reduced twice by 10 at 50% and 75% respectively. Nesterov momentum [19] of 0.9 without dampening and a weight decay of 10^{-4} are used. The robust weight initialization method proposed by [7] is adopted. We use the same channel sparse regularization term and its hyperparameter $\lambda = 10^{-4}$ as defined in [14].

Table 3. Accuracies of different methods before (orig.) and after pruning (pruned). For CIFAR10 and CIFAR100, 70% and 50% filters are pruned respectively. Note that 'NA' indicates the baseline networks completely failed after pruning, due to insufficient preserved filters at certain layers.

CIFAR10	Methods			CIFAR100	Methods		
	BASE	SLIM [14]	OURS		BASE	SLIM [14]	OURS
ACC orig.	0.9377	0.9330	0.9388	ACC orig	0.7212	0.7205	0.75
ACC pruned	NA	0.3254	0.9389	ACC pruned	NA	0.0531	0.7436
γ^P	0.2994	0.0288	1.36e−6	γ^P	0.2224	0.0569	4.75e−4

Overall Performance. The results on CIFAR-10 and CIFAR-100 are shown in Tables 1 and 2 respectively. On both datasets, we can observe when typically 50–70% filters of the evaluated networks are pruned, the new networks can still achieve accuracy higher than the original network. For instance, with 70% filters pruned VGG-19 achieves an accuracy of 0.9393, compared to 0.9366 of the original model on CIFAR-10. We attribute this improvement to the introduced diversities between filter weights, which naturally provides discriminative feature representations in intermediate layers of networks.

As a comparison, our method consistently outperforms network-slimming without resorting to fine-tuning or multi-pass pruning-retraining cycles. It is also worth-noting that our method is capable of pruning networks with prohibitively high ratios which are not possible in network-slimming. Take VGG-19 network on CIFAR-10 dataset as an example, network-slimming prunes as much as 70%, beyond which point the network cannot be reconstructed as some layers are totally destructed. On the contrary, our method is able to reconstruct a very narrower network by pruning 80% filters while producing a marginally degrading accuracy of 0.9302. We conjecture this improvement is enabled by our simultaneous feature and architecture learning which can avoid pruning filters prematurely as in network-slimming where the pruning operation (architecture selection) is isolated from the feature learning process and the performance of the pruned network can be only be restored via fine-tuning.

The results on ImageNet are shown in Table 4 where we also present comparison with [9] which reported top-1 and top-5 errors on ImageNet. On VGG-16, our method provides 1.2% less accuracy loss while saving additionally 20.5M parameters and 0.8B FLOPs compared with [9]. On ResNet-50, our method saves 5M more parameters and 1.4B more FLOPs than [9] while providing 0.21% higher accuracy.

Table 4. Results on ImageNet dataset

Models	Top-1	Top-5	Params	FLOPs
VGG-16 [9]	31.47	11.8	130.5M	7.66B
VGG-16 (Ours)	30.29	10.62	44M	6.86B
VGG-16 (Ours)	31.51	11.92	23.5M	5.07B
ResNet-50 [9]	25.82	8.09	18.6M	2.8B
ResNet-50 (Ours)	25.61	7.91	13.6M	1.4B
ResNet-50 (Ours)	26.32	8.35	11.2M	1.1B

Ablation Study. In this section we investigate the contribution of each proposed component through ablation study.

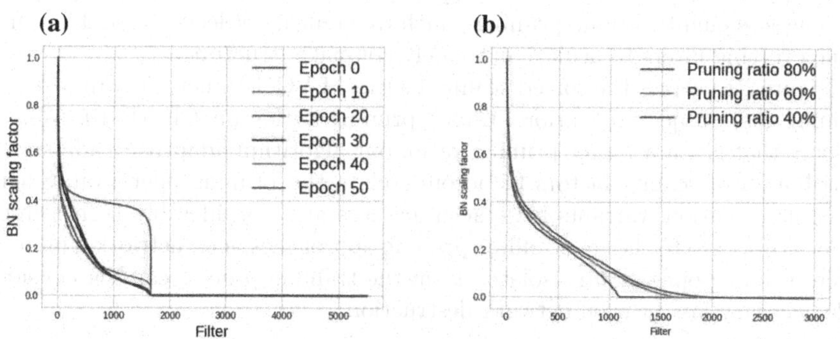

Fig. 2. (a) Scaling factors of the VGG-19 network at various epochs during training trained with diversified filters (b) Sorted scaling factors of VGG-19 network trained with various pruning ratios on CIFAR-10.

Filter Diversity. Figure 2(a) shows the sorted scaling factors of VGG-19 network trained with the proposed filter diversity loss at various training epochs. With the progress of training, the scaling factors become increasingly sparse and the number of large scaling factors, *i.e.,* the area under the curve, is decreasing. Figure 1 shows the sorted scaling factors of VGG-19 network for the baseline model with no regularization, network-slimming [14], and the proposed method with diversified filters, trained with CIFAR-10 and CIFAR-100. We observe significantly improved sparsity by introducing filter diversity to the network compared with network-slimming, indicated by *nsf*. Remember the scaling factors essentially determine the importance of filters, thus, maximizing *nsf* ensures that the deterioration due to filter pruning is minimized. Furthermore, the number of filters associated with large scaling factor is largely reduced, rendering more irrelevant filter to be pruned harmlessly. This observation is quantitatively confirmed in Table 3 which lists the accuracies of three schemes before and after pruning for both CIFAR-10 and CIFAR-100 datasets. It is observed that retraining of pruned network is no longer needed for the proposed method, while network-slimming has to restore the original accuracy through single-pass or multi-pass of pruning-retraining cycles. Accuracy deterioration are 60.76% and 0% for network-slimming and the proposed method respectively, whilst the baseline networks completely fails after pruning, due to insufficient preserved filters at certain layers.

Online Pruning. We firstly empirically investigate the effectiveness of the proposed pruning loss. After setting $\lambda_3 = 0$, we train VGG-19 network by switching off/on respectively (set $\lambda_2 = 0$ and $\lambda_2 = 10^{-4}$) the pruning loss on CIFAR-10 dataset. By adding the proposed pruning loss, we observe improved accuracy of 0.9325 compared to 0.3254 at pruning ratio of 70%. When pruning at 80%, the network without pruning loss can not be constructed due to insufficient preserved filters at certain layers, whereas the network trained with pruning loss can attain an accuracy of 0.9298. This experiment demonstrates that the proposed pruning loss enables online pruning which dynamically selects the architectures while evolving filters to achieve extremely compact structures.

Figure 2(b) shows the sorted scaling factors of VGG-19 network trained with pruning loss subject to various target pruning ratios on CIFAR-10. We can observe that given a target pruning ratio, our algorithm adaptively adjusts the distribution of scaling factors to accommodate the pruning operation. Such a dynamic evolution warrants little accuracy loss at a considerably high pruning ratio, as opposed to the static offline pruning approaches, *e.g.*, network-slimming, where pruning operation is isolated from the training process causing considerable accuracy loss or even network destruction.

4.3 Image Compression

The proposed approach is applied on end-to-end image compression task which follows a general autoencoder architecture as illustrated in Fig. 3. We utilize general scaling layer which is added after each convolutional layer, with each

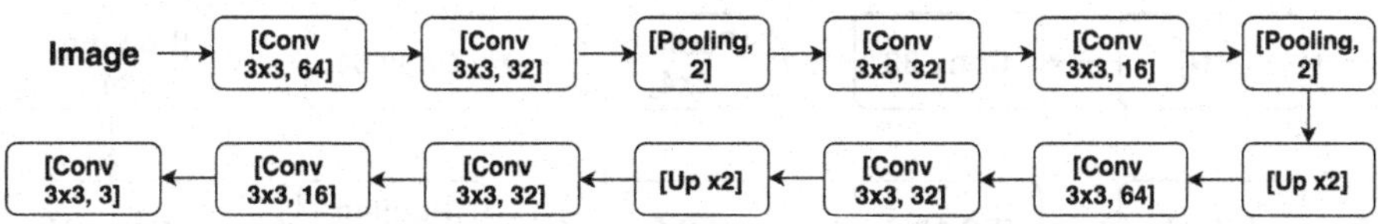

Fig. 3. Network architecture for image compression.

Table 5. Results of image compression on CIFAR-100 dataset

Models	PSNR	Params	Pruned (%)	FLOPs	Pruned (%)
Base-line	30.13	75888	–	46M	–
Ours	29.12 (−3%)	43023	43%	23M	50%
Ours	28.89 (−4%)	31663	58%	17M	63%

Table 6. Results of music genre classification on ISMIR Genre dataset

Models	Accuracy	Params	Pruned (%)	FLOPs	Pruned (%)
Base-line	0.808	106506	–	20.3M	–
Ours	0.818 (+1%)	8056	92.5	4M	80.3
Ours	0.798 (−1.3%)	590	99.5	0.44M	98.4

scaling factor initialized as 1. The evaluation is performed on CIFAR-100 dataset. We train all the networks from scratch using Adam with mini-batch size 128 for 600 epochs. The learning rate is set to 0.001 and MSE loss is used. The results are listed in Table 5 where both parameters and floating-point operations (FLOPs) are reported. Our method can save about 40%–60% parameters and 50%–60% computational cost with minor lost of performance (PSNR).

4.4 Audio Classification

We further apply our method in audio classification task, particularly *music genre classification*. The preprocessing of audio data is similar with [13] and produces Mel spectrogram matrix of size 80×80. The network architecture is illustrated in Fig. 4, where the scaling layer is added after both convolutional layers and fully connected layers. The evaluation is performed on ISMIR Genre dataset. We train all the networks from scratch using Adam with mini-batch size 64 for 50 epochs. The learning rate is set to 0.003. The results are listed in Table 6 where both parameters and FLOPs are reported. Our approach saves about 92% parameters while achieves 1% higher accuracy, saving 80% computational cost. With a minor loss of about 1%, 99.5% parameters are pruned, resulting in an extreme narrow network with $\times 50$ times speedup.

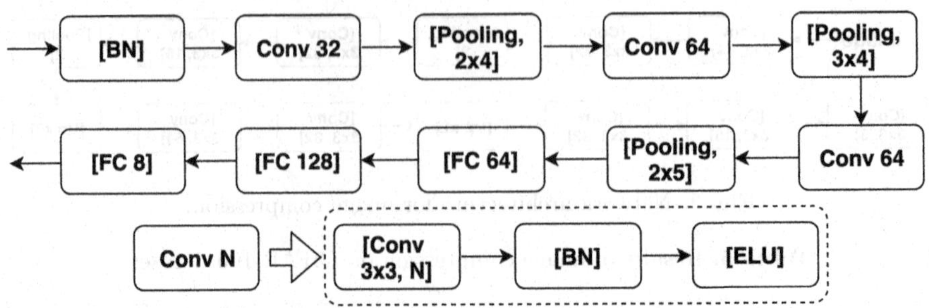

Fig. 4. Network architecure for music genre classification.

5 Conclusions

In this paper, we have proposed a novel approach to simultaneously learning architectures and features in deep neural networks. This is mainly underpinned by a novel pruning loss and online pruning strategy which explicitly guide the optimization toward an optimal architecture driven by a target pruning ratio or model size. The proposed pruning loss enabled online pruning which dynamically selected the architectures while evolving filters to achieve extremely compact structures. In order to improve the feature representation power of the remaining filters, we further proposed to enforce the diversities between filters for more effective feature representation which in turn improved the trade-off between architecture and accuracies. We conducted comprehensive experiments to show that the interplay between architecture and feature optimizations improved the final compressed models in terms of both models sizes and accuracies for various tasks on both visual and audio data.

References

1. Cano, P., et al.: ISMIR 2004 audio description contest (2006)
2. Cheng, Y., Wang, D., Zhou, P., Zhang, T.: A survey of model compression and acceleration for deep neural networks. ArXiv e-prints, October 2017
3. Crowley, E.J., Turner, J., Storkey, A., O'Boyle, M.: Pruning neural networks: is it time to nip it in the bud? ArXiv e-prints arXiv:1810.04622, October 2018
4. Han, S., Pool, J., Tran, J., Dally, W.: Learning both weights and connections for efficient neural network. In: Advances in Neural Information Processing Systems, pp. 1135–1143 (2015)
5. Harandi, M., Fernando, B.: Generalized BackPropagation. Étude De Cas: Orthogonality. ArXiv e-prints (2016)
6. Hassibi, B., Stork, D.G.: Second order derivatives for network pruning: optimal brain surgeon. In: Advances in Neural Information Processing Systems, pp. 164–171 (1993)
7. He, K., Zhang, X., Ren, S., Sun, J.: Delving deep into rectifiers: surpassing human-level performance on ImageNet classification. In: Proceedings of the IEEE International Conference on Computer Vision, pp. 1026–1034 (2015)

8. He, K., Zhang, X., Ren, S., Sun, J.: Deep residual learning for image recognition. In: Proceedings of the IEEE Conference on Computer Vision and Pattern Recognition, pp. 770–778 (2016)
9. Huang, Z., Wang, N.: Data-driven sparse structure selection for deep neural networks. In: Ferrari, V., Hebert, M., Sminchisescu, C., Weiss, Y. (eds.) ECCV 2018. LNCS, vol. 11220, pp. 317–334. Springer, Cham (2018). https://doi.org/10.1007/978-3-030-01270-0_19
10. Krizhevsky, A., Hinton, G.: Learning multiple layers of features from tiny images. Technical report, Citeseer (2009)
11. LeCun, Y., Denker, J.S., Solla, S.A.: Optimal brain damage. In: Advances in Neural Information Processing Systems, pp. 598–605 (1990)
12. Li, H., Kadav, A., Durdanovic, I., Samet, H., Graf, H.P.: Pruning filters for efficient ConvNets. ArXiv e-prints, August 2016
13. Lidy, T., Schindler, A.: Parallel convolutional neural networks for music genre and mood classification. In: MIREX 2016 (2016)
14. Liu, Z., Li, J., Shen, Z., Huang, G., Yan, S., Zhang, C.: Learning efficient convolutional networks through network slimming. In: ICCV, pp. 2736–2744 (2017). http://arxiv.org/abs/1708.06519
15. Liu, Z., Sun, M., Zhou, T., Huang, G., Darrell, T.: Rethinking the value of network pruning. ArXiv e-prints arXiv:1810.05270, October 2018
16. Mariet, Z., Sra, S.: Diversity networks: neural network compression using determinantal point processes. ArXiv e-prints arXiv:1511.05077, November 2015
17. Qin, Z., Yu, F., Liu, C., Zhao, L., Chen, X.: Interpretable convolutional filter pruning. ArXiv e-prints, October 2018
18. Simonyan, K., Zisserman, A.: Very deep convolutional networks for large-scale image recognition. arXiv preprint arXiv:1409.1556 (2014)
19. Sutskever, I., Martens, J., Dahl, G., Hinton, G.: On the importance of initialization and momentum in deep learning. In: International Conference on Machine Learning, pp. 1139–1147 (2013)
20. Wen, W., Wu, C., Wang, Y., Chen, Y., Li, H.: Learning structured sparsity in deep neural networks. In: NIPS, vol. 521, no. 12, pp. 61–64 (2016)
21. Yu, Y., Li, Y.f., Zhou, Z.h.: Diversity regularized machine. In: IJCAI, pp. 1603–1608 (2011)
22. Zhou, H., Alvarez, J.M., Porikli, F.: Less is more: towards compact CNNs. In: Leibe, B., Matas, J., Sebe, N., Welling, M. (eds.) ECCV 2016. LNCS, vol. 9908, pp. 662–677. Springer, Cham (2016). https://doi.org/10.1007/978-3-319-46493-0_40

Learning Sparse Hidden States in Long Short-Term Memory

Niange Yu[1], Cornelius Weber[2], and Xiaolin Hu[1(✉)]

[1] State Key Laboratory of Intelligent Technology and Systems, Beijing National Research Center for Information Science and Technology, Department of Computer Science and Technology, Tsinghua University, Beijing 100084, China
niangeyu@gmail.com, xlhu@tsinghua.edu.cn

[2] Department of Informatics, University of Hamburg, Hamburg, Germany
weber@informatik.uni-hamburg.de

Abstract. Long Short-Term Memory (LSTM) is a powerful recurrent neural network architecture that is successfully used in many sequence modeling applications. Inside an LSTM unit, a vector called "memory cell" is used to memorize the history. Another important vector, which works along with the memory cell, represents hidden states and is used to make a prediction at a specific step. Memory cells record the entire history, while the hidden states at a specific time step in general need to attend only to very limited information thereof. Therefore, there exists an imbalance between the huge information carried by a memory cell and the small amount of information requested by the hidden states at a specific step. We propose to explicitly impose sparsity on the hidden states to adapt them to the required information. Extensive experiments show that sparsity reduces the computational complexity and improves the performance of LSTM networks (The source code is available at https://github.com/feiyuhug/SHS_LSTM/tree/master).

Keywords: Recurrent neural network (RNN) · Long Short-Term Memory (LSTM) · Language modeling · Image captioning · Network acceleration

1 Introduction

Recurrent neural networks (RNNs) are widely used in sequence modeling problems. Generally, a recurrent unit takes actions along a given sequence of inputs and, step-by-step, produces a sequence of outputs. The current actions attend to the current inputs or predictions, while a memory records history. Modern recurrent units like LSTM [8] or Gated Recurrent Unit (GRU) [5] use gate mechanisms to control the communication between the memory and the externals. By selectively retrieving messages from the inputs, and writing and erasing some

We acknowledge support by NSFC (61621136008) and German Research Foundation (DFG) under project CML (TRR 169).

I. V. Tetko et al. (Eds.): ICANN 2019, LNCS 11728, pp. 288–298, 2019.
https://doi.org/10.1007/978-3-030-30484-3_24

contents in the memory with gates, those recurrent units can learn to process sequences with complex interdependencies. Their applications span a wide range such as language modeling [15], machine translation [20], speech recognition [6] and image captioning [21].

The memory in a recurrent unit is in charge of the whole history of the sequence, but taking an action (such as prediction) at one step should only require to attend to a specific part of the memory. In an LSTM unit, a hidden state h is learned to carry the message from the memory c and used to make the prediction. Since h should learn to get rid of a large part of the information in c that is unrelated to the current step, a general priority can be set that h should be "lighter" than c. However, the hidden state h and memory c are two vectors that share the same dimension. "Lighter" in this context has two meanings: one is that h should carry less information than c, reflecting the focus of the current step, which may not require all information that is kept in memory. The other is that the computational complexity with h should be lower, since h will be passed on to further processing steps. We achieve both targets by imposing sparsity on h.

Sparse coding has been subject to many modelling studies, and physiological recordings from sensory neurons indicate that it is employed in several modalities in the sensory cortex [17]. Forming part of efficient coding [4], sparse distributions have also been found in the underlying causes of natural stimuli [2]. Hence, imposing sparse coding on a network state representation may bias the network to encode compact representations of the causes of sensory stimuli.

Let us refer to the dimensions of the memory cell as "channels". In vanilla LSTM units, the output gates modulate the channels softly by multiplying with a value in $(0, 1)$, which does not affect the dimensionality of h. We zero out many output gates that are lower than a threshold, as to close many channels in h. In this way, sparsity is imposed on h. While the hidden state h is central in the computational graph of the LSTM unit, the computational complexity of a time step is reduced in proportion to the sparsity ratio of h.

We conduct extensive experiments on language modeling and image captioning tasks. By adjusting the sparsification strength, an optimal sparsity ratio on h can always be found that improves both the prediction accuracy and inference efficiency over the baseline. Unlike weight regularization, the proposed hidden state sparsification method does not reduce the number of adaptable network parameters θ, i.e. weights. We will show in Sect. 4.1 that hidden state sparsification can be combined with weight sparsification methods [16,23] for additional merit.

2 Related Works

Many works have been proposed to accelerate neural networks. Dynamic networks with conditional computations inside reduce the computational cost by exploring certain computation paths for each input [3,14,19]. Lin et al. propose to selectively prune some channels in a feed-forward convolutional neural network (CNN) according to the current inputs. They use an external network to generate pruning actions that are learned by a reinforcement learning algorithm [11]. For RNN acceleration, Jernite et al. propose to update only a fraction of hidden states to reduce computational cost at each step. An external module is learned to determine which hidden states to update [9]. This method has only been successfully applied to the vanilla RNN and GRU. In our method, a subset of channels in the hidden state is selected to open for each input, and this selection process is modulated by the output gate of an LSTM unit, which incurs no extra computational cost.

Another line of works proposed sparsity on weight matrices to reduce computational cost [7,16,22], which is different from the proposed hidden states sparsification method.

3 Methods

The computation for an LSTM unit can be formulated as:

$$\mathrm{LSTM}: x_t, h_{t-1}, c_{t-1} \rightarrow h_t, c_t \tag{1}$$

where subscripts denote time steps. At time step t, it takes an input x_t and updates the hidden state ($h_{t-1} \rightarrow h_t$) and memory cell ($c_{t-1} \rightarrow c_t$). The computation inside is with four gates: "input", "forget", "output" and "input modulation" (denoted as i_t, f_t, o_t, g_t respectively),

$$i_t = \mathrm{sigm}(W_{ix}x_t + W_{ih}h_{t-1} + b_i), \tag{2}$$

$$f_t = \mathrm{sigm}(W_{fx}x_t + W_{fh}h_{t-1} + b_f), \tag{3}$$

$$o_t = \mathrm{sigm}(W_{ox}x_t + W_{oh}h_{t-1} + b_o), \tag{4}$$

$$g_t = \tanh(W_{gx}x_t + W_{gh}h_{t-1} + b_g), \tag{5}$$

$$c_t = f_t \odot c_{t-1} + i_t \odot g_t, \tag{6}$$

$$h_t = o_t \odot \tanh(c_t). \tag{7}$$

The memory cell $c_t \in \mathbb{R}^n$ is a vector that stores the long-term memory, and $h_t \in \mathbb{R}^n$ is the hidden state that is usually used to predict the output y_t (see Eq. (16)). "sigm" is the sigmoid function, "tanh" is the hyperbolic tangent function and $\odot$ denotes element-wise multiplication.

Multiple LSTM units can be stacked into a hierarchical network, in which the output of each unit is fed into the next upper unit. The original input x_t is fed into the bottom-most unit, and the final output is taken from the top-most unit. Let superscripts denote layers, the computation inside the LSTM unit in the l-th layer at time step t ($1 \leq l \leq L, 1 \leq t \leq T$) can be formulated as [24], where T denotes the unrolled time steps.

$$\mathrm{LSTM}: h_t^{l-1}, h_{t-1}^l, c_{t-1}^l \rightarrow h_t^l, c_t^l, \tag{8}$$

$$\begin{pmatrix} i_t^l \\ f_t^l \\ o_t^l \\ g_t^l \end{pmatrix} = \begin{pmatrix} \mathrm{sigm} \\ \mathrm{sigm} \\ \mathrm{sigm} \\ \tanh \end{pmatrix} T_{2n,4n} \begin{pmatrix} h_t^{l-1} \\ h_{t-1}^l \end{pmatrix}, \tag{9}$$

$$c_t^l = f_t^l \odot c_{t-1}^l + i_t^l \odot g_t^l, \tag{10}$$
$$h_t^l = o_t^l \odot \tanh(c_t^l). \tag{11}$$

The input is h_t^{l-1} which is from the lower layer for $l > 1$, or x_t for $l = 1$. The computations with four gates are fused in (9), where $T_{2n,4n} : \mathbb{R}^{2n} \rightarrow \mathbb{R}^{4n}$ is an affine transform $(Wx + b)$ which contributes the most to the computational costs.

Equation (10) is the memory update function. Note that there is no non-linear or parameterized transformation at the memory update. Some parts of the memory may be kept over many steps, which add LSTM model long-term dependencies. However, in many scenarios, such as in sequence generation tasks, the LSTM needs to make a prediction at every time step. The prediction targets at different steps are usually different, which may be in conflict with the shared memory. Since the output gate o_t^l connects the memory and the prediction layer, our idea is that it should learn to attend to different parts of the memory for different predictions, so to resolve the conflicts.

We empirically find that the output gate values learned implicitly in LSTM are widely distributed ("baseline" shown in the left column of Fig. 2), which may not produce distinct attention over the memory for different predictions.

In order to impose sparsity, we introduce an L1-norm loss term over the output gate at layer l as

$$\mathcal{L}^S(o^l(x,\theta)) = \sum_{1 \leq b \leq B} \sum_{1 \leq t \leq T} |o_t^l(x^{(b)})|. \tag{12}$$

Unlike weight regularization, the output gate sparsification is data-dependent. Sparsification refers to a training batch $x^{(b)}(1 \leq b \leq B)$, where B is the batch size. $o_t^l(x^{(b)})$ is computed in Eq. (9) and T denotes the unrolled time steps. The sparsity loss term is added to the classification loss term $\mathcal{L}^{XE}(\theta)$ for the adaptation of model parameters θ by supervised learning, which will be described in the following sections. Denoting the model weights as w, the updating function for w via stochastic gradient decent (SGD) is

$$w \leftarrow w - \Big(\eta \frac{\partial \mathcal{L}^{XE}(\theta)}{\partial w} + \sum_{1 \leq l \leq L} \lambda_l \frac{\partial \mathcal{L}^S(o^l(x,\theta))}{\partial w}\Big), \tag{13}$$

where η is the learning rate and λ_l are the coefficients that control the strength of the sparsity term at each LSTM layer $(1 \leq l \leq L)$.

By increasing λ_l, more output gate channels would be driven to zero. We empirically found that introducing a threshold function ψ after the gates could obtain better performance:

$$\tilde{o}_t^l(x_t^{(b)}) = \psi(o_t^l(x_t^{(b)}), \xi) = \begin{cases} o_t^l(x_t^{(b)}), & o_t^l(x_t^{(b)}) > \xi \\ 0 \quad , & o_t^l(x_t^{(b)}) <= \xi \end{cases}, \tag{14}$$

where $\xi \geq 0$. The threshold function is appended after the output gates, both in training and testing. As a consequence, the hidden state function defined in Eq. (11) is reformulated as:

$$h_t^l = \tilde{o}_t^l \odot \tanh(c_t^l). \tag{15}$$

During training, the sparsity of the output gates would increase gradually and become stable after several epochs. The final sparsity that can be reached is determined by $\lambda_l (1 \leq l \leq L)$ and ξ. Higher values for λ_l and ξ both increase the sparsity.

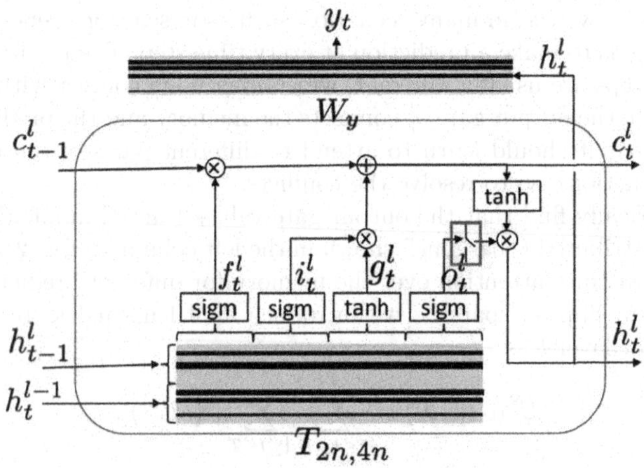

Fig. 1. Sparse LSTM. Given sparse hidden state vectors (h_{t-1}^l, h_t^{l-1}) and h_t^l, only a few rows of the respective transformation matrices $T_{2n,4n}$ and W_y are used. (Color figure online)

Taking the unit in the top-layer of the LSTM network as an example, the computational graph of the LSTM unit with the sparse hidden state is shown in Fig. 1. Compared with a classical LSTM unit, a threshold layer is appended behind the output gate (shown inside the red box). The major computational burden in the LSTM unit is two affine transformations: one is defined in Eq. (9) and the other is the output layer

$$y_t = W_y h_t^l. \tag{16}$$

The input vectors of both affine transformations are from the sparse hidden states. The dimensions set to zero in the input vector would zero out the corresponding rows in the weight matrices ($T_{2n,4n}$ and W_y) as shown in the two shaded blocks in Fig. 1, where gray indicates zero rows and black indicates nonzero rows. Only nonzero rows in the weight matrices take part in the affine transformations Eqs. (9) and (16). The computational complexity of the two affine transformations is reduced in proportion to the sparsity ratio of h_t^l and (h_{t-1}^l, h_t^{l-1}) respectively.

4 Experiments

4.1 Language Modeling

The language modeling experiments are conducted on the Penn Treebank dataset [13]. We start by implementing the proposed method in a two-layer LSTM network proposed in [24]. The dimensions of both the LSTM memory and the word embedding in the input layer are 1500. Given the next word y_t^* as target output, the cross-entropy loss that we minimize as part of Eq. (13) is:

$$\mathcal{L}^{XE}(\theta) = -\sum_{t=1}^{T} \log(p_t^{(\theta)}(y_t^*|(y_{1:t-1}^*))), \tag{17}$$

We use the PyTorch implementation of the publicly available baseline model[1]. The distribution of the output gates o in the baseline model (i.e. $\xi = 0, \lambda = 0$) is shown in Fig. 2. At the training, we set $\xi = 0.1$, and use the output gate sparsification to squeeze more gates under ξ as to increase sparsity. The distributions of the output gates with $\lambda_1/\lambda_2 = 1e^{-6}$ and $\lambda_1/\lambda_2 = 1.6e^{-6}/4.8e^{-6}$ are shown in Fig. 2. The distribution can be further pushed close to zero if λ continues to increase.

Table 1. Learning sparse output gates from scratch.

Method	$\xi, \lambda_1/\lambda_2(10^{-6})$	Test perplexity	Output width (1st, 2nd) LSTM	Mult-add[a] reduction	Time (ms)/ speed-up
Baseline	$(0.0, 0.0/0.0)$	77.88	(1500, 1500)	1.00×	81.7/1×
Ours	$(0.1, 0.4/0.4)$	77.14	(720, 953)	1.56×	53.3/1.53×
	$(0.1, 1.0/1.0)$	**76.97**	(436, 797)	1.89×	44.6/1.83×
	$(0.1, 1.6/1.6)$	77.05	(344, 706)	2.09×	38.2/2.14×
	$(0.1, 1.6/4.8)$	77.85	**(261, 344)**	**2.75**×	**29.9/2.73**×

[a]The reduction of multiplication-add operations in matrix multiplications.

With ξ fixed to 0.1, we search for the optimal λ. The results are shown in Table 1. All the models are trained from scratch in the same setting with the baseline. "Test Perplexity" denotes the perplexity on the test set; lower is better. We find that $\lambda_1/\lambda_2 = 1e^{-6}$ gets the best perplexity (the improvement is -0.91 compared to the baseline), with λ_1/λ_2 higher or lower than this value would lead to inferior results. "Output width" denotes the remaining (non-zero) output channels at each LSTM layer. Notably, models with sparse output largely reduce the computational complexity. For $\lambda_1/\lambda_2 = 1.6e^{-6}/4.8e^{-6}$, the output channel dimension is reduced to 17%(261/1500) in the first layer and to 23%(344/1500)

[1] https://github.com/pytorch/examples/tree/master/word_language_model.

in the second layer, thereby totally reducing Multi-add operations by a factor of 2.75. We measure the inference time on an Intel® Core™ i7-6850K @ 3.60 GHz CPU processor with OpenBLAS library for matrix-multiplication operations. Testing the time by unrolling the LSTM unit for 100 steps, the maximum speed-up is 2.73×.

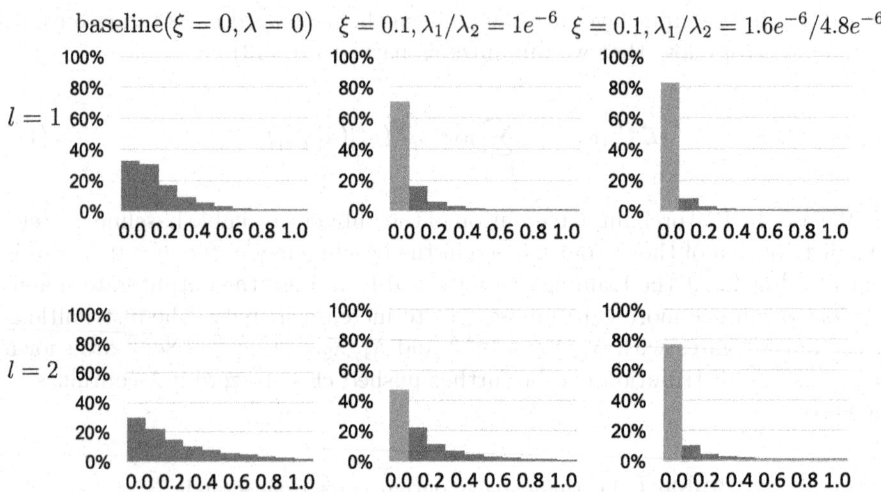

Fig. 2. Distributions of the output gate values o_t^l as defined in Eq. (9) for three pre-trained models. $l = 1$ and $l = 2$ stands for the first and second layers respectively. The values are calculated with a batch size of 50 and with 35 unrolled steps ($t = 1, ..., 35$) on the test set.

Next, we evaluate whether our state sparsification method combined with weight sparsification yields additional benefit. Intrinsic Sparse Structures (ISS) [22] is a recently proposed weight-sparsifying LSTM acceleration method, which yields an impressive performance on the Penn Treebank dataset. Based on group Lasso regularization, it reduces the dimension of the memory, the hidden state and the related weight matrices by structured weight pruning. Our method can be embedded into ISS easily by adjusting ξ to control the output width. The experimental results are listed in Table 2. The third column lists the memory size and the output width of the learned model. ISS+Ours ($\xi = 0.20$) achieves the highest speed-up ratio of 6.28× with slightly lower test perplexity (78.37) than the baseline (ISS) (78.57) or ISS alone (78.65).

4.2 Image Captioning

We experiment our methods with the image captioning model *Google NIC* [21] as a baseline. Google NIC is an encoder-decoder framework which uses a CNN as an encoder to extract features from images and then uses an LSTM decoder

Table 2. ISS with sparse hidden states

Method	Test perplexity	Memory/Output width (1st, 2nd) LSTM	Mult-add reduction	Time (ms)/ Speed-up
Baseline[a]	78.57	(1500, 1500)/ (1500, 1500)	1.00×	81.7/1.00×
ISS	78.65	(373, 315)/ (373, 315)	7.48×	14.1/5.79×
ISS+Ours ($\xi = 0.10$)	**76.27**	(379, 536)/ (229, 445)	5.99×	17.2/4.75×
ISS+Ours ($\xi = 0.20$)	78.37	(194, 542)/ (63, 375)	**8.63**×	**13.0/6.28**×

[a]The baseline is different from the baseline in Table 1.

to generate sentences. The CNN image features are input to the LSTM at the beginning step. The LSTM network generates the sentence word by word with one word per step and stops when the "stop token" is predicted or when it reaches the maximum length.

Formally, the inputs for the LSTM are

$$x_1 = \text{CNN}(I), \tag{18}$$
$$x_t = W_e y_{t-1}, (t \in 2, 3, ..., T), \tag{19}$$

where I denotes the raw image and x_1 is input once at $t = 1$. y_{t-1} is the one-hot representation of the input word (from the target sentence at training or the previous prediction at inference). $W_e \in \mathcal{R}^{V \times E}$ is the word embedding matrix for a vocabulary of size V. Words are predicted using Softmax:

$$p_t = \text{Softmax}(h_t). \tag{20}$$

The predicted word y_t is sampled from p_t. h_t is the hidden state defined in Eq. (7). Given a ground-truth sentence $y^*_{1:T}$, the cross-entropy loss that we minimize as part of Eq. (13) is:

$$\mathcal{L}^{XE}(\theta) = -\sum_{t=1}^{T} \log(p_t^{(\theta)}(y_t^* | (\text{CNN}(I), y^*_{1:t-1}))). \tag{21}$$

The model is trained and evaluated on MSCOCO [12], which is a widely used benchmark for image captioning. MSCOCO has 123,000 images with five captions annotated for each image. We use the publicly available split [10], where the validation set and test set each has 5,000 images. The remaining 113,000 images are used for training.

Table 3 shows the results. All listed models use ResNet101 or ResNet152 as an encoder. Compared with state-of-the-art methods [1,18], our Google NIC implementations (NIC 512/NIC 1024/NIC 2048) achieve new best results on BLEU4 and METEOR scores, on par with ROUGE-L, but not winning on CIDEr. Note that while the other works involve dedicated attention networks with learnt attention weights, our model uses only simple sparsification, which by focusing activations has an attention-like effect.

Table 3. The results of Google NIC with different memory size and ξ on the MSCOCO Karpathy test split. B4, M, R-L and C stand for BLEU4, METEOR, ROUGE-L and CIDEr respectively. Time is in ms.

Model	Time	B4	M	R-L	C
[18]	–	31.3	26.0	54.3	101.3
[1]	–	33.4	26.1	**54.4**	**105.4**
NIC 512	239	**33.5**	25.8	**54.4**	101.7
NIC 1024	503	32.6	26.0	54.1	101.8
NIC 2048	1070	32.3	26.1	53.9	102.1
NIC 2048 ($\xi = 0.3$)	721	33.3	**26.4**	**54.4**	103.0
NIC 2048 ($\xi = 0.4$)	616	32.9	**26.4**	**54.4**	103.3
NIC 2048 ($\xi = 0.5$)	436	32.7	26.0	53.9	102.9

Finally, we adjust the parameter ξ directly to close more channels in the output gates without using the output gate sparsification of Eq. (12). The results with $\xi = 0.3, 0.4, 0.5$ on the image caption task are listed in Table 3. It is found that the optimal setting for ξ is 0.4 which improves the CIDEr from 102.1 to 103.3 while speeding up by a factor of $1.74\times$ (1070 ms/616 ms).

5 Conclusion

We explore novel sparse LSTM networks in which the activations of the output gates are sparsified. This reduces the amount of information that is passed on for further processing, while not impacting on the memory of the LSTM cells. Experiments were conducted on three tasks including language modeling and image captioning. The proposed method obtains better performance on all tasks at lower computational costs. On the Penn Treebank language modeling experiments, we found that sparse hidden states can work together with weight sparsifying regularization methods to achieve better results than when using them individually.

References

1. Anderson, P., et al.: Bottom-up and top-down attention for image captioning and visual question answering. In: IEEE Conference on Computer Vision and Pattern Recognition (CVPR) (2018). https://doi.org/10.1109/cvpr.2018.00636

2. Barlow, H.: What is the computational goal of the neocortex? In: Koch, C., Davis, J. (eds.) Large-Scale Neuronal Theories of the Brain, pp. 1–22. The MIT Press, Cambridge (1994)
3. Campos, V., Jou, B., Giró-i Nieto, X., Torres, J., Chang, S.F.: Skip RNN: learning to skip state updates in recurrent neural networks. arXiv preprint arXiv:1708.06834 (2017)
4. Chalk, M., Marre, O., Tkačik, G.: Toward a unified theory of efficient, predictive, and sparse coding. Proc. Natl. Acad. Sci. **115**(1), 186–191 (2018). https://doi.org/10.1101/152660
5. Cho, K., van Merriënboer, B., Bahdanau, D., Bengio, Y.: On the properties of neural machine translation: encoder-decoder approaches. In: Proceedings of SSST@EMNLP 2014, Eighth Workshop on Syntax, Semantics and Structure in Statistical Translation, pp. 103–111 (2014). https://doi.org/10.3115/v1/w14-4012
6. Graves, A., Mohamed, A.r., Hinton, G.: Speech recognition with deep recurrent neural networks. In: 2013 IEEE International Conference on Acoustics, Speech and Signal Processing (ICASSP), pp. 6645–6649. IEEE (2013). https://doi.org/10.1109/icassp.2013.6638947
7. Han, S., Pool, J., Tran, J., Dally, W.: Learning both weights and connections for efficient neural network. In: Advances in Neural Information Processing Systems, pp. 1135–1143 (2015)
8. Hochreiter, S., Schmidhuber, J.: Long short-term memory. Neural Comput. **9**(8), 1735–1780 (1997). https://doi.org/10.4324/9781315174105-4
9. Jernite, Y., Grave, E., Joulin, A., Mikolov, T.: Variable computation in recurrent neural networks. arXiv preprint arXiv:1611.06188 (2016)
10. Karpathy, A., Fei-Fei, L.: Deep visual-semantic alignments for generating image descriptions. In: IEEE Conference on Computer Vision and Pattern Recognition (CVPR), pp. 3128–3137 (2015). https://doi.org/10.1109/cvpr.2015.7298932
11. Lin, J., Rao, Y., Lu, J., Zhou, J.: Runtime neural pruning. In: Advances in Neural Information Processing Systems, pp. 2178–2188 (2017)
12. Lin, T.-Y., et al.: Microsoft COCO: common objects in context. In: Fleet, D., Pajdla, T., Schiele, B., Tuytelaars, T. (eds.) ECCV 2014. LNCS, vol. 8693, pp. 740–755. Springer, Cham (2014). https://doi.org/10.1007/978-3-319-10602-1_48
13. Marcus, M.P., Marcinkiewicz, M.A., Santorini, B.: Building a large annotated corpus of English: the penn treebank. Comput. Linguist. **19**(2), 313–330 (1993)
14. McGill, M., Perona, P.: Deciding how to decide: dynamic routing in artificial neural networks. arXiv preprint arXiv:1703.06217 (2017)
15. Mikolov, T., Karafiát, M., Burget, L., Černocký, J., Khudanpur, S.: Recurrent neural network based language model. In: Eleventh Annual Conference of the International Speech Communication Association (2010)
16. Narang, S., Elsen, E., Diamos, G., Sengupta, S.: Exploring sparsity in recurrent neural networks. arXiv preprint arXiv:1704.05119 (2017)
17. Olshausen, B.A., Field, D.J.: Sparse coding of sensory inputs. Curr. Opinion Neurobiol. **14**(4), 481–487 (2004). https://doi.org/10.1016/j.conb.2004.07.007
18. Rennie, S.J., Marcheret, E., Mroueh, Y., Ross, J., Goel, V.: Self-critical sequence training for image captioning. In: IEEE Conference on Computer Vision and Pattern Recognition (CVPR), pp. 7008–7024 (2017). https://doi.org/10.1109/cvpr.2017.131
19. Shazeer, N., et al.: Outrageously large neural networks: the sparsely-gated mixture-of-experts layer. arXiv preprint arXiv:1701.06538 (2017)

20. Sutskever, I., Vinyals, O., Le, Q.V.: Sequence to sequence learning with neural networks. In: Advances in Neural Information Processing Systems, pp. 3104–3112 (2014)
21. Vinyals, O., Toshev, A., Bengio, S., Erhan, D.: Show and tell: a neural image caption generator. In: IEEE Conference on Computer Vision and Pattern Recognition (CVPR), pp. 3156–3164. IEEE (2015). https://doi.org/10.1109/cvpr.2015.7298935
22. Wen, W., et al.: Learning intrinsic sparse structures within long short-term memory. arXiv preprint arXiv:1709.05027 (2017)
23. Yu, N., Qiu, S., Hu, X., Li, J.: Accelerating convolutional neural networks by group-wise 2D-filter pruning. In: 2017 International Joint Conference on Neural Networks (IJCNN), pp. 2502–2509. IEEE (2017). https://doi.org/10.1109/ijcnn.2017.7966160
24. Zaremba, W., Sutskever, I., Vinyals, O.: Recurrent neural network regularization. arXiv preprint arXiv:1409.2329 (2014)

Multi-objective Pruning for CNNs Using Genetic Algorithm

Chuanguang Yang[1,2], Zhulin An[1(✉)], Chao Li[1], Boyu Diao[1], and Yongjun Xu[1]

[1] Institute of Computing Technology, Chinese Academy of Sciences, Beijing 100190, China
{yangchuanguang,anzhulin,lichao,diaoboyu2012,xyj}@ict.ac.cn
[2] University of Chinese Academy of Sciences, Beijing 100049, China

Abstract. In this work, we propose a heuristic genetic algorithm (GA) for pruning convolutional neural networks (CNNs) according to the multi-objective trade-off among error, computation and sparsity. In our experiments, we apply our approach to prune pre-trained LeNet across the MNIST dataset, which reduces 95.42% parameter size and achieves 16 times speedups of convolutional layer computation with tiny accuracy loss by laying emphasis on sparsity and computation, respectively. Our empirical study suggests that GA is an alternative pruning approach for obtaining a competitive compression performance. Additionally, compared with state-of-the-art approaches, GA can automatically pruning CNNs based on the multi-objective importance by a pre-defined fitness function.

Keywords: Genetic algorithm · Convolutional neural networks · Multi-objective pruning

1 Introduction

Vision application scenarios often have different requirements in terms of multi-objective importance about error, computational cost and storage for convolutional neural networks (CNNs), but state-of-the-art pruning approaches do not take this into account. Thus, we develop the genetic algorithm (GA) that can iteratively prune redundant parameters based on the multi-objective trade-off by a two-step procedure. First, we prune the network by taking the advantages of swarm intelligence. Next, we retrain the elite network and reinitialize the population by the trained elite. Compared with state-of-the-art approaches, our approach obtains a comparable result on sparsity and a significant improvement on computation reduction. In addition, we detail how to adjust the fitness function for obtaining diverse compression performances in practical applications.

I. V. Tetko et al. (Eds.): ICANN 2019, LNCS 11728, pp. 299–305, 2019.
https://doi.org/10.1007/978-3-030-30484-3_25

2 Proposed Approach

2.1 Evaluation Regulation

Similar to general evolutionary algorithms, we design a fitness function f to evaluate the comprehensive performance of a genome. In our method, f is defined by the weighted average of error rate e, computation remained rate c and sparsity s. And our target is to minimize the fitness function as follows:

$$\begin{aligned} &\min f = \min(\lambda_1 e + \lambda_2 c + \lambda_3 (1 - s)) \\ &s.t.\ 0 \leqslant e, c, s, \lambda_1, \lambda_2, \lambda_3 \leqslant 1, \lambda_1 + \lambda_2 + \lambda_3 = 1 \end{aligned} \tag{1}$$

The coefficients λ_1, λ_2, and λ_3 adjust the importance of the three objectives. e, c and s denote the percentage of misclassified samples, remained multiplication-addition operations (FLOPs) and zeroed out parameters, respectively. From the experimental analyses in Sect. 3, treating the multi-objective nature of the problem by linear combination and scalarization is indeed effective and consistent to our expectation, albeit more sophisticated fitness function may further improve the results.

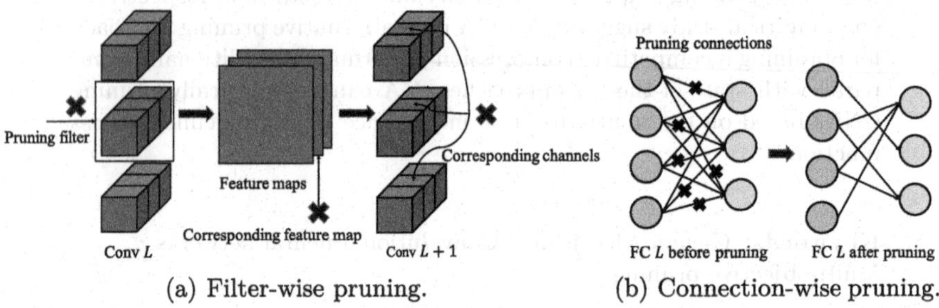

(a) Filter-wise pruning. (b) Connection-wise pruning.

Fig. 1. Pruning techniques of CONV layer (a) and FC layer (b) in mutation phase. For the current CONV layer, we carry out a filter-wise pruning based on mutation rate P_{mc}, and then a corresponding channel-wise pruning will also take place for the next CONV layer. For the current FC layer, we carry out a connection-wise pruning based on mutation rate P_{mf}.

2.2 Heuristic Pruning Procedure

Genetic Encoding and Initialization. A CNN is encoded to a genome including M parameter genes that denoted by $\theta^1, \theta^2, ..., \theta^M$, where M denotes the depth of the CNN, θ^m denotes the mth layer parameter with a 4D tensor of size $F_m C_m H_m W_m$ in convolutional (CONV) layer, or a 2D tensor of size $O_m I_m$ in fully-connected (FC) layer, where F_m, C_m, H_m and W_m denote the size of filters, input channels, height and width of kernels, O_m and I_m denote the size of output and input features, respectively. We apply N times mutations on a pre-trained CNN to generate the initial population consisting of N genomes.

Selection. We straightforward select the top K genomes with minimum fitness to reproduce next generation. It is worth mentioning that we have attempted a variety of selection operations, such as tournament selection, roulette-wheel selection and truncation selection. Our empirical results indicate that different selection operations finally obtain the similar performance but the vanilla selection which we adopt has the fastest convergence speed.

Algorithm 1. Multi-objective Pruning by GA

Input: pre-trained CNN parameter $\theta_{initial}$, maximum number of iterations G, population size N, number of selected genomes K, crossover rate P_c, mutation rate P_{mc} and P_{mf}, number of interval iterations T

Output: parameter of elite genome $\hat{\theta}^G$

for $i = 1 \rightarrow N$ **do**
    $\mathcal{P}_i^{g=0} \leftarrow \text{MUTATION}(\theta_{initial}, P_{mc}, P_{mf})$
end for
for $g = 1 \rightarrow G$ **do**
    $\mathcal{F}_{1,\dots,N}^{g-1} \leftarrow f(\mathcal{P}_{1,\dots,N}^{g-1})$
    $elite \leftarrow argmax_{i \in \{1,\dots,N\}} \mathcal{F}_i^{g-1}$
    $\hat{\theta}^{g-1} \leftarrow \mathcal{P}_{elite}^{g-1}$
    $\mathcal{P}_{1,\dots,K}^{g} \leftarrow \text{SELECTION}(\mathcal{P}_{1,\dots,N}^{g-1}, \mathcal{F}_{1,\dots,N}^{g-1}, K)$
    $\mathcal{P}_{1,\dots,N-1}^{g} \leftarrow \text{CROSSOVER}(\mathcal{P}_{1,\dots,K}^{g}, P_c)$
    $\mathcal{P}_{1,\dots,N-1}^{g} \leftarrow \text{MUTATION}(\mathcal{P}_{1,\dots,N-1}^{g}, P_{mc}, P_{mf})$
    $\mathcal{P}_{1,\dots,N}^{g} \leftarrow \mathcal{P}_{1,\dots,N-1}^{g} \cup \{\hat{\theta}^{g-1}\}$
    if $mod(g, T) = 0$ **then**
        $\hat{\theta}^g \leftarrow argmax_{\theta \in \mathcal{P}_{1,\dots,N}^{g}} f(\theta)$
        $\hat{\theta}^g \leftarrow train(\hat{\theta}^g)$
        for $i = 1 \rightarrow N-1$ **do**
            $\mathcal{P}_i^{g} \leftarrow \text{MUTATION}(\hat{\theta}^g, P_{mc}, P_{mf})$
        end for
        $\mathcal{P}_{1,\dots,N}^{g} \leftarrow \mathcal{P}_{1,\dots,N-1}^{g} \cup \{\hat{\theta}^{g}\}$
    end if
end for
$\hat{\theta}^G \leftarrow train(\hat{\theta}^G)$

Crossover. Crossover operations are occurred among the selected genomes based on the crossover rate P_c. We employ the classical microbial crossover inspired by bacterial conjugation. For each crossover, we choose two genomes randomly, from which the one with lower fitness is called Winner genome, and the other one is called Loser genome. Then, each gene in Loser genome is copied from Winner genome based on 50% probability. Thus, Winner genome can remain unchanged to preserve the good performance, and Loser genome can be modified to generate possibly better performance by the infection of Winner genome. One potential strength of microbial crossover is implicitly remaining the elite genome to the next generation, since the fittest genome can win any tournaments against any genomes.

Mutation. Mutation performs for every genome except for the elite with mutation rate P_{mc} and P_{mf} in each CONV layer and FC layer, respectively. Follow [5], we employ the coarse-grained pruning on CONV layers and fine-grained pruning on FC layers, both of which are sketched in Fig. 1.

Main Procedure. After each heuristic pruning process including selection, crossover and mutation with T iterations, we retrain the elite genome so that the remained weights can compensate for the loss of accuracy, and then reinitialize the population by the trained elite genome. The above procedures are repeated iteratively until the fitness of the elite genome is convergence. Algorithm 1 illustrates the whole procedures of multi-objective pruning by GA.

3 Experimental Results and Analyses

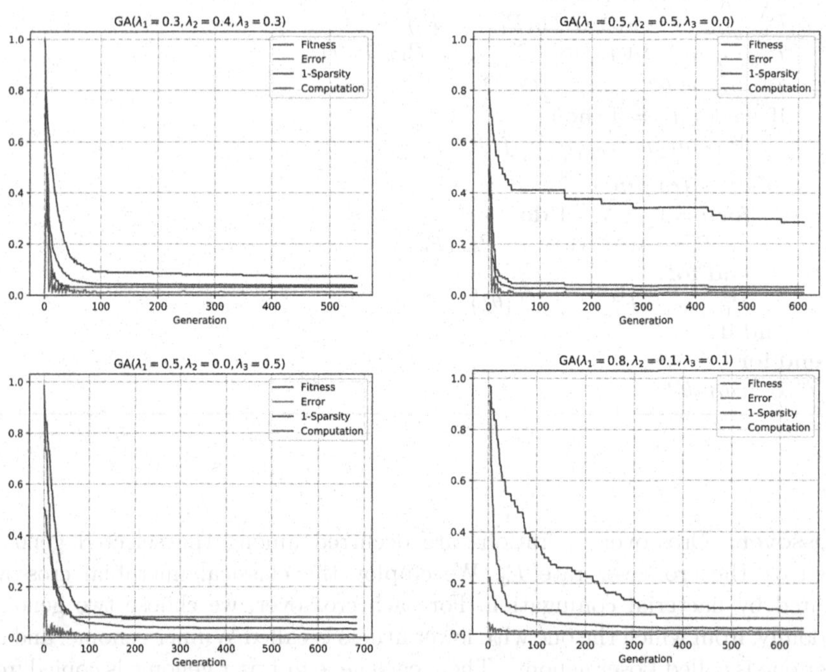

Fig. 2. Pruning process of GA with different $\lambda_1 \sim \lambda_3$. The blue, orange, green, red curves reflect the indicator of fitness, error, sparsity and FLOPs of the elite, respectively (Color figure online)

Table 1. Comparison against the pruning approaches evaluated on MNIST dataset. Note that bold entries represent the emphases on objectives laid by GA.

Approach	Error:e	Computation:c	Sparsity:s	Accuracy change
LeNet Baseline [4]	0.8%	100%	0%	–
LNA [8]	0.7%	–	90.5%	+0.1%
SSL [9]	0.9%	25.64%	75.1%	−0.1%
TSNN [10]	0.79%	13%	95.84%	+0.01%
SparseVD [6]	0.75%	45.66%	92.58%	+0.05%
StructuredBP [7]	0.86%	9.53%	79.8%	−0.06%
l_0 Regularization [2]	1.0%	23.22%	99.14%	−0.2%
RA-2-0.1 [3]	0.9%	–	97.7%	−0.1%
Ours:				
GA($\lambda_1 = 0.3, \lambda_2 = 0.4, \lambda_3 = 0.3$)	0.93%	**6.22%**	**94.30%**	−0.13%
GA($\lambda_1 = 0.5, \lambda_2 = 0.5, \lambda_3 = 0$)	0.87%	**6.10%**	71.63%	−0.07%
GA($\lambda_1 = 0.5, \lambda_2 = 0, \lambda_3 = 0.5$)	0.89%	9.00%	**95.42%**	−0.09%
GA($\lambda_1 = 0.8, \lambda_2 = 0.1, \lambda_3 = 0.1$)	**0.85%**	8.16%	91.00%	−0.05%

The hyper-parameter settings of GA are as follows: population size $N = 30$, number of selected genomes $K = 5$, crossover rate $P_c = 0.6$, mutation rate $P_{mc} = 0.1$ and $P_{mf} = 0.15$, iteration number $T = 5$. Albeit we find that further hyper-parameter tuning can obtain better results, such as increasing population size or diminishing mutation rate, but corresponding with more time cost.

Comprehensive comparison against state-of-the-art approaches on LeNet[1] across the MNIST [1] is summarized in Table 1. We highlight in particular that different pruning performances can be obtained by adjusting $\lambda_1 \sim \lambda_3$. Meanwhile, we empirically analyze the effectiveness by custom $\lambda_1 \sim \lambda_3$ with corresponding curves which are exhibited in Fig. 2. Note that CONV layers and FC layers are the main source of computation and parameter size, respectively. And λ_1 cannot be set too tiny in order to ensure the low error.

1. $\boldsymbol{\lambda_1 = 0.3, \lambda_2 = 0.4, \lambda_3 = 0.3}$. With the approximate weights for $\lambda_1 \sim \lambda_3$ as our baseline, which reach the overall optimal compression performance but with relatively higher error rate.
2. $\boldsymbol{\lambda_1 = 0.5, \lambda_2 = 0.5, \lambda_3 = 0}$. This setting aims at high-speed inference for CNN. In this case, computation achieves maximum reduction, but sparsity is hard to optimize because GA pays less attention to pruning FC layers which are not the main source of computation.
3. $\boldsymbol{\lambda_1 = 0.5, \lambda_2 = 0, \lambda_3 = 0.5}$. This setting aims at a CNN with low storage. In this case, we obtain the utmost sparsity and high-level computation reduction simultaneously. Albeit CONV layers only play an unimportant role in the

[1] https://github.com/tensorflow/models/tree/master/tutorials/image/cifar10.

overall parameter size, it can also obtain the high-level sparsity because of the tractability with coarse granularity pruning. Thus, λ_3 can also indirectly facilitate computation reduction.

4. $\boldsymbol{\lambda_1 = 0.8, \lambda_2 = 0.1, \lambda_3 = 0.1}$. This setting aims at minimal performance loss. In this case, error curve is always at the low level resulting in that GA is conservative to pruning both CONV and FC layers. Hence, parameter and FLOPs curves are slower to fall compared with baseline.

Compared with other approaches, albeit we do not obtain a minimal sparsity, our computation achieves outstanding reduction because of coarse granularity pruning. While some approaches with larger sparsity always employ fine granularity pruning, which is very tractable for facilitating sparsity but not essentially reducing the FLOPs of sparse weight tensors. Furthermore, our approach can perform a multi-objective trade-off according to the actual requirements whereas state-of-the-art approaches are unable to achieve this task.

4 Conclusion

We propose the heuristic GA to prune CNNs based on the multi-objective trade-off, which can obtain a variety of desirable compression performances. Moreover, we develop a two-step pruning framework for evolutionary algorithms, which may open a door to introduce the biological-inspired methodology to the field of CNNs pruning. As a future work, GA will be further investigated and improved to prune more large-scale CNNs.

References

1. MNIST dataset. http://yann.lecun.com/exdb/mnist/. Accessed 23 Mar 2019
2. Louizos, C., Welling, M., Kingma, D.P.: Learning sparse neural networks through l_0 regularization. In: Proceedings of the International Conference on Learning Representations (2018)
3. Dong, X., Liu, L., Li, G., Zhao, P., Feng, X.: Fast CNN pruning via redundancy-aware training. In: Kůrková, V., Manolopoulos, Y., Hammer, B., Iliadis, L., Maglogiannis, I. (eds.) ICANN 2018. LNCS, vol. 11139, pp. 3–13. Springer, Cham (2018). https://doi.org/10.1007/978-3-030-01418-6_1
4. LeCun, Y., Bottou, L., Bengio, Y., Haffner, P., et al.: Gradient-based learning applied to document recognition. Proc. IEEE **86**(11), 2278–2324 (1998). https://doi.org/10.1109/5.726791
5. Mao, H., et al.: Exploring the granularity of sparsity in convolutional neural networks. In: Proceedings of the IEEE Conference on Computer Vision and Pattern Recognition Workshops, pp. 13–20 (2017). https://doi.org/10.1109/cvprw.2017.241
6. Molchanov, D., Ashukha, A., Vetrov, D.: Variational dropout sparsifies deep neural networks. In: Proceedings of the 34th International Conference on Machine Learning, vol. 70, pp. 2498–2507. JMLR.org (2017)

7. Neklyudov, K., Molchanov, D., Ashukha, A., Vetrov, D.P.: Structured Bayesian pruning via log-normal multiplicative noise. In: Advances in Neural Information Processing Systems, pp. 6775–6784 (2017)
8. Srinivas, S., Babu, V.: Learning neural network architectures using backpropagation. In: Wilson, R.C., Hancock, E.R., Smith, W.A.P. (eds.) Proceedings of the British Machine Vision Conference (BMVC), pp. 104.1–104.11. BMVA Press, September 2016. https://doi.org/10.5244/C.30.104
9. Wen, W., Wu, C., Wang, Y., Chen, Y., Li, H.: Learning structured sparsity in deep neural networks. In: Advances in Neural Information Processing Systems, vol. 29, pp. 2074–2082 (2016)
10. Srinivas, S., Subramanya, A., Babu, R.V.: Training sparse neural networks. arXiv preprint arXiv:1611.06694 (2016)

Dynamically Sacrificing Accuracy for Reduced Computation: Cascaded Inference Based on Softmax Confidence

Konstantin Berestizshevsky(✉) and Guy Even

School of Electrical Engineering, Tel Aviv University, Tel Aviv, Israel
konsta9@mail.tau.ac.il, guy@eng.tau.ac.il

Abstract. We study the tradeoff between computational effort and classification accuracy in a cascade of deep neural networks. During inference, the user sets the acceptable accuracy degradation which then automatically determines confidence thresholds for the intermediate classifiers. As soon as the confidence threshold is met, inference terminates immediately without having to compute the output of the complete network. Confidence levels are derived directly from the softmax outputs of intermediate classifiers, as we do not train special decision functions. We show that using a softmax output as a confidence measure in a cascade of deep neural networks leads to a reduction of 15%–50% in the number of MAC operations while degrading the classification accuracy by roughly 1%. Our method can be easily incorporated into pre-trained non-cascaded architectures, as we exemplify on ResNet. Our main contribution is a method that dynamically adjusts the tradeoff between accuracy and computation without retraining the model.

Keywords: Deep learning · Neural networks · Efficient inference

1 Introduction

State-of-the-art Deep Neural Networks (DNNs) usually consist of hundreds of layers and millions of trainable weights. At inference time, this translates into billions of multiply-accumulate operations (MACs) for a single input [19]. The training process of models is a computationally intensive task that is performed once. After training is completed, the trained model is used for inference. Inference requires fewer computations than training, however, the inference is performed multiple times. Hence, reducing the amount of computation during the inference is an interesting ongoing goal [13]. Moreover, modern DNNs usually apply the same number of operations for every inputs, and the natural question that arises is whether this amount of computation is indeed required [17].

In this paper, we focus on the computational effort spent on inference in DNNs. For simplicity, we measure the computational effort in the number of multiply-accumulate operations (MACs). Many claim that the computational effort required for classifying images should depend on the image [9,11,17,20].

I. V. Tetko et al. (Eds.): ICANN 2019, LNCS 11728, pp. 306–320, 2019.
https://doi.org/10.1007/978-3-030-30484-3_26

We claim that the required computational effort for classification is an intrinsic yet hidden property of the inputs. Namely, some images are much easier to classify than others, but the required computational effort needed for classification is hard to predict before classification is completed.

The desire to spend the "right" computational effort in classification leads to the first goal in this work.

Goal 1. *Given a model M, design a model M' in which the computational effort during the classification of an input x is proportional to the likelihood of misclassifying x using M.*

Misclassification likelihood indicates and measures the hardness of an input. The question we pose is whether we can (almost) preserve accuracy while reducing the computational effort required to classify "easy" instances. The two extreme cases are: (1) Consider a distribution of inputs D for which the misclassification likelihood is very low (say 1%) in model M. We view D as a distribution of "easy" inputs, and would like the new model M' to classify $x \in D$ while spending a fraction of the computational effort compared to M. (2) Consider a distribution of inputs D' for which the misclassification likelihood is high (say, 25%) in model M. We view D' as a distribution of "hard" inputs, and would like the new model M' to classify inputs from D' almost as accurately as M does. The computational effort of M' for inputs in D' is only slightly higher than that of M (c.f., an overhead of 1% in the computation). The principle behind our goal is that an efficient model should achieve a high classification accuracy faster for "easy" instances than for "harder" ones.

A motivation to reduce the computational effort during the inference can be exemplified by systems with non-constant power consumption or throughput. Examples of such settings are: (1) As the battery drains in a mobile device, one would like to enter a "power saving mode" in which less power is spent per classification. (2) If the input rate increases in a real-time system (e.g., due to a burst of inputs), then one must spend less time per input [4]. (3) Timely processing in a data center during spikes in query arrival rates may require reducing the computational effort per query [2,5].

Dynamic changes in the computational effort or the throughput lead to the second goal in this work.

Goal 2. *Introduce the ability to dynamically control the computational effort while sacrificing accuracy as little as possible. Such changes in the computational effort should not involve retraining of the DNN.*

1.1 Contribution

We propose an architecture that is based on a cascade of DNNs [3] depicted in Fig. 1. The cascade comprises multiple DNNs (e.g., three DNNs), called *component DNNs*. The cascade is organized sequentially so that the next component DNN is fed by the previous component. Hence previous computations are reused and further refined by the next component. Classification takes place by invoking the component DNNs one-by-one and stopping the computation as soon as the confidence level reaches the desired level. Our setting is applicable to general multiclass classification in general architectures that terminate with a softmax function.

The stopping decision is based on the softmax output of each component DNN. We define a simple confidence threshold, based on the softmax output, that allows for trading off (a small) decrease in accuracy for (a substantial) reduction in computational effort. The resulting approach has several advantages over the previous work [3,17,18]. The main contribution of our work is:

Dynamically change the compromise between accuracy and computational effort without retraining the cascaded model.

In addition, we show how a cascaded architecture can be obtained from an ordinary feed-forward DNN while requiring only small fine-tuning (see Sect. 6). We demonstrate the performance of our models on various image classification datasets: (i) A computation reduction of 34% that sacrifices 1.2% accuracy with respect to the CIFAR-10 test set. (ii) A computation reduction of 16% that sacrifices 0.7% accuracy with respect to the CIFAR-100 test set. (iii) A computation reduction of 54% that sacrifices 1.4% accuracy with respect to the SVHN test set. (iv) A computation reduction of 17% that sacrifices 1.3% accuracy with respect to the IMAGENET validation set.

Finally, our experimentation demonstrates a monotone relation between softmax values and classification accuracy in intermediate classifiers (see Sect. 7.3).

2 Related Work

The two principle techniques that we employ are *cascaded classification* and *confidence estimation.* We elaborate on the recent usage of these techniques hereinafter.

2.1 Cascaded Classification

Cascaded classification is suggested in the seminal work of Viola and Jones [21]. As opposed to voting or stacking ensembles in which classification is derived from the outputs of multiple experts (e.g., majority), the decision in a cascaded architecture is based on the last expert. A cascaded neural network architecture for computer vision is presented in [24]. In their work, as the complexity of the input increases, the evaluation is performed with increased resolution and increased number of component DNNs in the cascade. The works of Wang *et al.* [22,23] presents the skipping approach, where each input can take a path composed of a subset of layers of the original architecture. Skipping of layers requires training of switches that decide whether skipping of layers takes place. The work by Lerox *et al.* [15] presented the idea of early stopping in a setting in which the cascaded DNNs are distributed among multiple devices.

Reinforcement learning is employed by Odena *et al.* [16] in a cascade of meta-layers to train controllers that select computational modules per meta-layer.

2.2 Confidence Estimation

Uncertainty measures of classifiers are discussed in [6,7]. These works address the issue of the degree of confidence that a classifier has about its output. The confidence of an assembly of algorithms is investigated by Fagin *et al.* [8] in general setup. Fagin *et al.* define instance optimality and suggest to terminate the execution according to a criterion based on a threshold.

Rejection refers to the event that a classifier is not confident about its outcome, and hence, the output is rendered unreliable. Geifman and El-Yaniv [10] describe a selective classification technique, in which a classifier and a rejection-function are trained together. The goal is to obtain coverage (i.e., at least one classifier does not reject) while controlling the risk via rejection functions. They proposed a softmax-response mechanism for deriving the rejection function and discussed how the true-risk of a classifier (i.e., the average loss of all the non-rejected samples) can be traded-off with its coverage (i.e., the mass of the non-rejected region in the input space). Our work adopts the usage of the softmax response as a confidence rate function, however, it differs in a way we apply the confidence threshold. Namely, we propose a cascade of classifiers that terminates as soon as the desired confidence threshold is reached.

The ability of the softmax output to reflect the true confidence of the classifier was investigated by Gu *et al.* [12]. The authors propose the temperature scaling technique in order to calibrate the softmax output, making it highly correlated with the expected accuracy.

2.3 Combined Approach: Cascaded Inference with Confidence Estimation

The work of Cambazoglu *et al.* [4] presents an additive ensemble machine learning approach with early exits in a context of the web document ranking. In the additive approach, the sum of the outputs of a prefix of the classifiers provides the current output confidence.

The work of Teerapittayanon *et al.* [20] presents the BranchyNet approach, in which a neural network architecture has multiple branches, each branch consists of a few convolutional layers terminated by a classifier and a softmax function. The approach in [20] does not help to reduce the amount of computation that takes place outside the "main path". The confidence of an output vector y in BranchyNet is derived from the entropy function $entropy(y) = -\sum_c y_c \log y_c$. Finally, in [20], automatic setting of threshold levels is not developed, and the gains of their approach were not examined on large datasets.

Cascaded classification with dedicated linear confidence estimations (rather than softmax) appears in the Conditional Deep Learning (CDL) of [17], however, this approach was not examined on large datasets and did not discuss an automatic setting of confidence thresholds. Cascaded classification with confidence estimation appears also in the SACT mechanism [9], an extension of the prior work by Graves [11] that deals with recurrent neural networks. Confidence estimation is based on the summation of the halting scores. Computation is terminated as soon the cumulative halting score reaches a threshold. An interesting aspect of SACT architecture is the feature of spatial adaptivity. Namely, different computational efforts are spent on different regions of the input image.

Recently, Bolukbasi *et al.* [3] proposed an adaptive-early-exit cascaded classification architecture. The computation may terminate after each convolutional layer. For every convolutional layer k, a special decision function γ_k is trained to whether an exit should be chosen. One of the drawbacks of this approach is that the decision functions must be re-trained per value of the acceptable accuracy degradation.

3 Cascaded Inference (CI)

3.1 Cascaded Architecture

A cascade of DNNs is a chain of convolutional layers with branching between layers to a classifier (see Fig. 1). Early termination in cascaded DNN components means that intermediate feature maps are evaluated by classifiers. These classifiers attempt to classify the feature map and output a confidence measurement of their classification. If the confidence level is above a threshold, then execution terminates, and the classification of the intermediate feature map is output. See Fig. 1 for an example of a cascaded architecture based on three convolutional layers. Each component in a cascaded architecture consists of convolutional layers followed by a branching that leads to (1) a classifier, and (2) the next component.

In our experimentation, we employ ResNet block layers [14] as component DNNs in our cascade. Moreover, in Sect. 6 we show how a large pre-trained model (ResNet-50-v2) can be quickly transformed into a cascaded architecture.

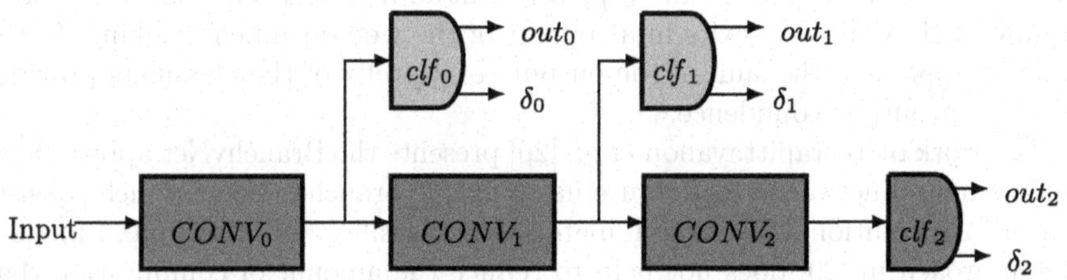

Fig. 1. An example of a cascaded architecture of three component DNNs with early termination. A cascade of convolutional layers ($CONV_0, \ldots, CONV_2$) ends with a classifier clf_2. Early termination is enabled by introducing the classifiers clf_i after convolutional layers. Each classifier outputs a classification out_i and a its confidence δ_i.

It is tempting to adjust the aforementioned topology of the cascade for even higher computational reuse. For example, the out_i output of the classifier can be fed to the following component (namely to the $CONV_{i+1}$). Such an adjustment, however, is not applicable in the case when the $CONV$ layers are pre-trained in a non-cascaded setup, losing a major advantage of the method we propose.

3.2 Early Termination Based on Confidence Threshold

The usage of the threshold for determining early termination in the cascade is listed as Algorithm 1. The algorithm applies the component DNNs one by one and stops as soon as the confidence measure reaches the confidence threshold of this component. This approach differs from previous cascaded architectures in which a combination (e.g., sum) of the confidence measures of the components is used to control the execution [4,9].

Instead of having D per-component thresholds, one could suggest using a single global threshold for the whole cascade. Another alternative is to set $D \cdot C$ thresholds for every (component, class) pair. We empirically compared the three aforementioned approaches and found the first one (per component thresholds) to be the most effective, which therefore became the approach of our choice.

Algorithm 1. $\mathrm{CI}(M, \hat{\delta}, x)$- Cascaded Inference. Early termination takes place as soon as the confidence level reaches the confidence threshold.

Input: cascaded model M, thresholds $\hat{\delta}$, input x
for $m = 0$ **to** $D-1$ **do**
    $(out_m(x), \delta_m(x)) \leftarrow M_m(x)$
    if $\delta_m(x) \geq \hat{\delta}_m$ **then**
        return $out_m(x)$
    end if
end for
return $out_{D-1}(x)$

3.3 Softmax Confidence

Every component DNN is terminated by a classifier with one or more FC layers followed by a softmax function. Let $z_m \in \mathbb{R}^C$ denote the input to the softmax function in the m'th component of the cascade. Let $s_m \in [0,1]^C$ denote the softmax vector in the m'th component. The softmax vector is defined as follows.

Definition 1 (softmax). $s_m[i] = \frac{e^{z_m[i]}}{\sum_{c=0}^{C-1} e^{z_m[c]}}$.

Definition 2 (confidence measure). *The confidence measure* $\delta_m \in [0,1]$ *is defined by* $\delta_m \triangleq \max_c\{s_m[c] \mid 0 \leq c \leq C-1\}$.

Definition 3 (predicted class). *The predicted class* $out_m \in \{0, \ldots, C-1\}$ *is defined to be the class* c *such that* $s_m[c] = \delta_m$.

4 Training Procedure

In this section we present the training procedure of the component DNNs.

Consider a cascaded architecture with D components. We denote this cascade by $M = (M_0, \ldots, M_{D-1})$, where M_m denotes the m'th component in the cascade. Let $\Theta_{conv} = \{\theta_{conv_0}, \ldots, \theta_{conv_{D-1}}\}$ denote the weights and biases of the convolutional layers of the component DNNs $(M_1, \ldots, M_{D-1})$. Let $\Theta_{clf} = \{\theta_{clf_0}, \ldots, \theta_{clf_{D-1}}\}$ denote the weights and biases of the classifiers of the component DNNs $(M_1, \ldots, M_{D-1})$.

Let $L_M(out_m, T)$ denote a loss function of the cascade M with respect to the output of the m'th component, averaged over the labeled dataset T. In order to train the cascade M, we propose a backtrack-training (Algorithm 2) $\text{BT}(M, T)$.We emphasize that the training procedure first optimizes all the convolutional weights together with the weights of the last classifier. Only then, do we optimize the weights of the classifiers clf_i, for $0 \leq i \leq D-2$ (i.e., classifiers of intermediate components). Our approach differs from previous training procedures [20,22] in which the loss functions associated with all the classifiers were *jointly optimized.* This difference has two following advantages: (1) the longest computational path of the cascade is trained independently of the intermediate loss functions, hence the maximum achievable accuracy of the model is not compromised. (2) A pre-trained, non-cascaded, architecture can be transformed into a cascade and then trained according to lines 4–7 of the $\text{BT}(M, T)$ algorithm to fine-tune only the intermediate classifiers.

Algorithm 2. $\text{BT}(M, T)$ - An algorithm for a backtrack training of the cascade $M = \{M_0, \ldots, M_{D-1}\}$. The output is the trained weights of the cascade M

1: **Input:** cascaded model M, training set T
2: Let $\Theta_{deep} = \Theta_{conv} \cup \theta_{clf_{D-1}}$
3: $\Theta_{deep} = \arg\min_{\Theta_{deep}} \{L_M(out_{D-1}, T)\}$.
4: **for** $m = 0$ **to** $D-2$ **do**
5: $\quad \theta_{clf_m} = \arg\min_{\theta_{clf_m}} \{L_M(out_m, T)\}$.
6: **end for**
7: **return** $\Theta_{conv} \cup \Theta_{clf}$

5 Setting of Confidence Thresholds

In this section, we present an automatic methodology for setting the confidence threshold $\hat{\delta}_m$ for every component M_m given an acceptable accuracy degradation ϵ. We note that the hyper-parameter ϵ is a single parameter for the whole cascade, and the automatic methodology we present determines an individual confidence threshold for every component in the cascade. The important attribute of the automatic setting of the confidence thresholds is that one can change them on the fly during the inference stage.

Let $T_m(\delta) \subseteq T$ denote the subset of inputs for which the confidence measure of the mth component is at least δ.

$$T_m(\delta) \triangleq \{(x, y) \mid \delta_m(x) \geq \delta\}.$$

Let $\gamma_m(\delta)$ denote the number of times the classification output by component M_m is correct for inputs in $T_m(\delta)$.

$$\gamma_m(\delta) \triangleq \sum_{(x,y) \in T_m(\delta)} \mathbb{1}\{out_m(x) = y\}.$$

Let $\alpha_m(\delta)$ denote the accuracy of component M_m with respect to $T_m(\delta)$.

$$\alpha_m(\delta) \triangleq \begin{cases} \frac{\gamma_m(\delta)}{|T_m(\delta)|} & \text{if } |T_m(\delta)| > 0 \\ 0 & \text{otherwise} \end{cases}$$

Let α_m^* denote the maximum accuracy for component M_m.

$$\alpha_m^* \triangleq \max_{\delta \in [0,1]} \alpha_m(\delta).$$

For an acceptable accuracy degradation $\epsilon > 0$, we define the confidence threshold $\delta_m(\epsilon)$ by

$$\delta_m(\epsilon) \triangleq \min \{\delta \mid \alpha_m(\delta) \geq \alpha_m^* - \epsilon\}.$$

When a cascaded inference is performed using $\mathrm{CI}(M, \hat{\delta}, x)$ (Algorithm 1), the confidence threshold vector $\hat{\delta}$ is set as follows. Choose an $\epsilon \in [0, 1]$, and set $\hat{\delta}_m \leftarrow \delta_m(\epsilon)$, for every m. We remark that (i) the threshold for the last component should be zero, and (ii) one could use separate datasets for training the weights and setting the confidence threshold.

In some applications, the desired accuracy metric is "top-K", meaning that a prediction is regarded as correct if the top K most confident predictions of a classifier contain the ground truth class. To choose appropriate thresholds for the top-K metric, the only change to the methodology above is to set $\delta_m(x)$ to be the sum over the top K elements in the softmax vector.

6 Experimental Setup

In order to examine the usefulness of cascaded inference we performed experiments on CIFAR-10, CIFAR-100 and SVHN datasets using ResNet-110 architecture and on IMAGENET dataset using ResNet-50-v2 architecture. The transformation of the ResNet architecture into a cascade was done by dividing it into three stages; the choice of the layers after which a new stage begins was based on the structure of the architecture (i.e., between distinct layer blocks, differently color-coded in Fig. 3 of [14]). Each component DNN consists of a stage and a classifier. The analysis of the overhead introduced by our transformation

Table 1. Number of MAC operations required for a single inference in ordinary ResNet models and in their cascaded counterparts.

	ResNet-110	ResNet-50-v2
non-Cascaded	253,953,214	4,037,883,817
Cascade - total	253,978,670	4,044,633,979
component DNN 0	86,000,922	1,817,092,009
component DNN 1	84,068,170	1,467,571,177
component DNN 2	83,909,578	759,970,793
Computation increase	0.01%	0.17%

is depicted in Table 1. According to this analysis, the increase in the number of MACs, caused by the transformation of the ResNet into a cascade of 3 component DNNs, is less than 0.2%.

We trained the cascaded ResNet-110 from scratch with respect to algorithm 2. Simple data augmentation was employed only for CIFAR models as in [14]. The optimization of every classifier was performed with Stochastic Gradient Descent (SGD) for 160 epochs in CIFAR datasets and for 50 epochs for SVHN dataset. Learning rate was scheduled as described in [14].

For the IMAGENET experiments, we transformed the official pre-trained[1] Tensorflow [1] ResNet-50-v2 model into a cascaded architecture by introducing additional classifiers after every layer block. We then followed lines 4–7 of the BT(M, T) algorithm (Algorithm 2) to train the two new classifiers, each of which has 2 FC layers, while freezing all the pre-trained weights. Source code, for reproducing our IMAGENET results, is publicly available[2]. This fine tuning of the pre-trained model took less than 20 h per classifier using 4 GPUs.

7 Results

7.1 Confidence Threshold Effect

We trained the cascaded versions of ResNet-110 and ResNet-50-v2 models as described in Sect. 6. We evaluated the performance using various ϵ values. The tradeoff between the test-accuracy and the number of MACs required for a single inference is shown in Fig. 2. The MAC counts were obtained analytically by summing up the linear operations in the convolutional layers and the FC layers, excluding activations and batch normalization. Quantitative results that appear in Table 2 demonstrate the ability of the cascaded architectures to trade as little as 1.3% of accuracy for a reduction of 16%–53% of the computational effort. Note the reduced effect on accuracy for IMAGENET when accuracy is measured with respect to the top-5 classifications compared to the top-1 classification (see last two lines in Table 2).

[1] https://github.com/tensorflow/models/tree/master/official/resnet.

[2] https://github.com/AnonymousConferenceCode/Cascaded_Inference.

Table 2. Accuracy-computation tradeoffs. - Column 1 lists the tested datasets. Columns 2–4 list the accuracy of classifier clf_i, for $i \in \{0, 1, 2\}$, with respect to the complete test set. Columns 5–10 list the accuracy of our cascaded architecture for different values of ϵ - the acceptable accuracy degradation (see Sect. 6 for the details of which network was used for each dataset). Computational reduction by the cascade for each ϵ is relative to the computational effort of the non-cascaded architecture $M_{0,1,2}$ and is defined by $1 - \frac{\#MAC\_Count(Cascade(\epsilon))}{\#MAC\_Count(M_{0,1,2})}$.

Dataset	Accuracy of $M_{0,\ldots,m-1}$			Accuracy(top), computation reduction(bottom)					
	M_0	$M_{0,1}$	$M_{0,1,2}$	$\epsilon = 0\%$	$\epsilon = 1\%$	$\epsilon = 2\%$	$\epsilon = 4\%$	$\epsilon = 7\%$	$\epsilon = 8\%$
CIFAR-10	77.50%	81.40%	93.10%	93.10%	92.70%	**91.90%**	91.10%	87.32%	86.35%
				6%	27%	**34%**	42%	50%	52%
CIFAR-100	48.10%	50.00%	70.50%	70.50%	70.65%	70.50%	70.30%	69.94%	**69.78%**
				1%	4%	7%	10%	15%	**16%**
SVHN	89.80%	85.20%	97.03%	97.03%	**95.60%**	94.00%	91.30%	89.76%	89.80%
				0%	**54%**	59%	64%	66%	66%
				$\epsilon = 0\%$	$\epsilon = 1\%$	$\epsilon = 2\%$	$\epsilon = 5\%$	$\epsilon = 6\%$	$\epsilon = 7\%$
IMAGENET top-1	46.69%	62.76%	76.51%	76.51%	76.51%	76.50%	75.90%	75.56%	**75.19%**
				0%	3%	7%	14%	15%	**17%**
IMAGENET top-5	70.22%	84.31%	93.21%	93.21%	92.84%	**92.02%**	88.54%	87.30%	86.13%
				0%	11%	**17%**	28%	31%	33%

7.2 Comparison with Bolukbasi *et al.*

Figure 2e and Table 3 compare the top-5 accuracy-to-computation tradeoffs of our cascaded inference against adaptive cascaded inference over ResNet-50 with early exits [3]. We translated the speedups presented in [3] from time to MAC-count speedups for the purpose of comparison to our work (to exclude the impact of software and hardware environments differences). Our model demonstrates higher accuracy for any given computational effort, in addition to being able to dynamically adjust to different accuracy-to-computation tradeoffs.

Table 3. Comparison of cascaded inference to [3] on IMAGENET top-5 metric. Column 1 lists the accuracy lost relative to the original ResNet-50 model. Columns 2 and 3 list the speedups of the work by Bolukbasi *et al.* and of our cascaded inference with respect to the full ResNet-50 model. Speedup is $\frac{old\_MACs}{new\_MACs} - 1$.

Accuracy reduction	Bolukbasi et al. 2017 speedup	Our Cascade speedup
1%	8%	20%
2%	18%	27%
5%	22%	41%

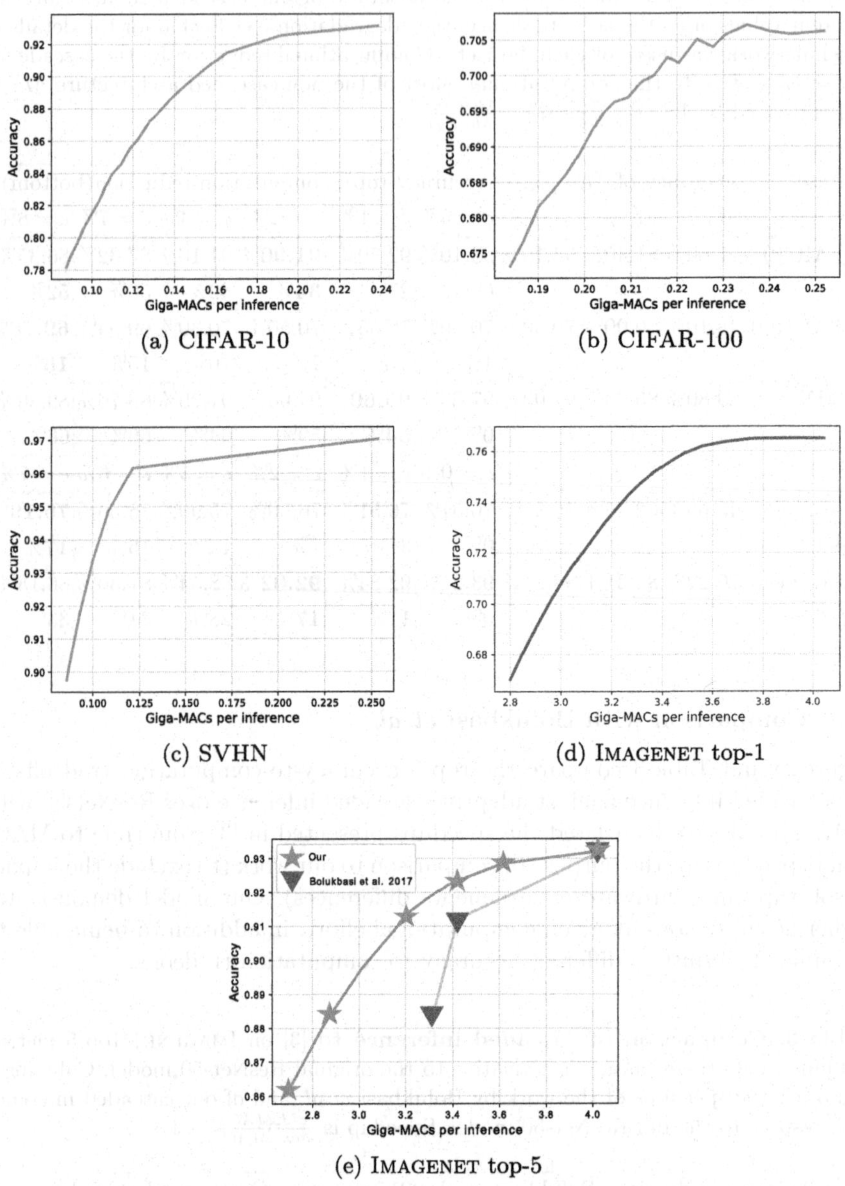

Fig. 2. Cascaded inference with early termination test accuracy vs. average number of MAC operations per inference. The measured points on the curves are obtained by considering variable values of $\epsilon \in \{20\%, \ldots, 1\%, 0\%\}$.

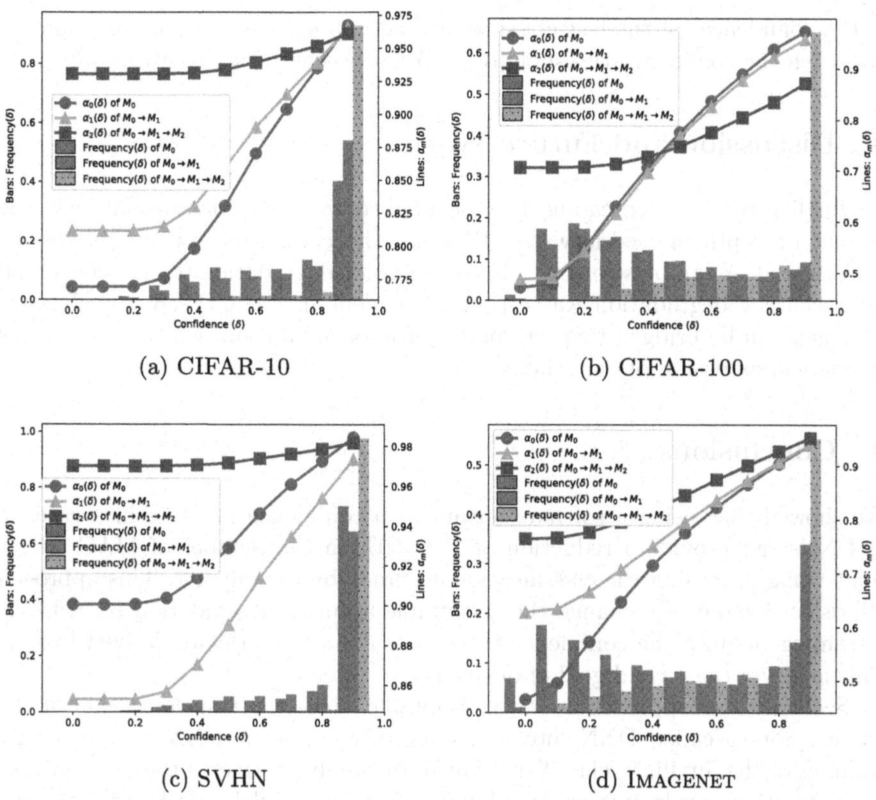

(a) CIFAR-10

(b) CIFAR-100

(c) SVHN

(d) IMAGENET

Fig. 3. Softmax as a confidence measure. The line plots show the accuracy $\alpha_m(\delta)$ of each classifier in the cascade independently. The bar plot presents the frequency of the different confidence levels sampled over the test set. All plots were obtained by separately testing the three component DNNs of the cascaded ResNet.

7.3 Softmax as a Confidence Measure

For the cascaded ResNet models, we analyzed the accuracy $\alpha_m(\delta)$ (see definition in Sect. 5) of each classifier independently. The accuracy $\alpha_m(\delta)$ was measured for $\delta \in [0, 1]$ using the test-set rather than to the training set. The plots in Fig. 3 show how the choice of the threshold provides control over the test accuracy. Note that the range of $\alpha_m(\delta)$ starts with the accuracy of clf_m and ends with the accuracy that corresponds to the highest confidence measure. The almost linear behavior of $\alpha_m(\delta)$ as a function of δ justifies basing the confidence threshold on the softmax output. We note that these results were obtained without applying softmax calibration techniques.

In addition, we examined the frequency of the different confidence levels observed at the output of each classifier in a cascade. This observation is presented in the form of a bar-plot distribution in Fig. 3. The distribution of the first two components of the cascade is relatively uniform. Whereas the distribution of the confidences of the last classifier has no importance since in our inference approach the confidence threshold of the last classifier is set to $\hat{\delta}_{D-1} = 0$.

8 Discussion and Future Work

As further research, cascading can be applied to RNNs or alternatively, the impact of depth of feed-forward DNNs on the confidence estimation can be investigated. A gap between the allowed accuracy degradation (ϵ) and the actual test accuracy degradation was especially evident in the CIFAR-100 dataset. This gap can be bridged by performing softmax-calibration, which can serve as a practical extension of our study.

9 Conclusions

We showed that using a softmax output as a confidence measure in a cascade of DNNs can provide a reduction of 15%–50% in the number of MAC operations while degrading the classification accuracy by roughly 1%. This approach allows to dynamically change the acceptable accuracy degradation (ϵ) without retraining because the confidence thresholds are automatically derived from ϵ. This achieves the second goal of our work.

Secondly, our approach is easily adoptable, since the transformation of the trained non-cascaded DNN into a cascade of component DNNs requires only training of the auxiliary classifiers, which are small relative to the original network. In other words, non-cascaded state-of-the-art models can be transformed into a cascade of component DNNs with very little training involved. Once the transformation is complete, these models will benefit from less computation during inference.

Finally, we observed a monotone, almost linear, relation between the softmax function and the test accuracy. This implies that the softmax output is a good estimate of the neural network confidence. Our approach explicitly demands lower computational effort for inputs that indicate higher confidence. This achieves the first goal of this work.

Acknowledgments. We thank Nissim Halabi, Moni Shahar and Daniel Soudry for useful conversations.

References

1. Abadi, M., et al.: TensorFlow: large-scale machine learning on heterogeneous systems (2015). Software available http://tensorflow.org/
2. Bodik, P.: Automating datacenter operations using machine learning. Ph.D. thesis, Berkeley, CA, USA (2010). aAI3555582
3. Bolukbasi, T., Wang, J., Dekel, O., Saligrama, V.: Adaptive neural networks for efficient inference, pp. 527–536 (2017)

4. Cambazoglu, B.B., et al.: Early exit optimizations for additive machine learned ranking systems. In: Proceedings of the Third ACM International Conference on Web Search and Data Mining, WSDM 2010, pp. 411–420. ACM, New York (2010). https://doi.org/10.1145/1718487.1718538
5. Chang, S., Lee, S.h., Kwak, N.: URNet: User-Resizable Residual Networks with Conditional Gating Module (2019). arXiv preprint: arXiv:1901.04687
6. Cordella, L.P., De Stefano, C., Tortorella, F., Vento, M.: A method for improving classification reliability of multilayer perceptrons. IEEE Trans. Neural Netw. **6**(5), 1140–1147 (1995). https://doi.org/10.1109/72.410358
7. De Stefano, C., Sansone, C., Vento, M.: To reject or not to reject: that is the question-an answer in case of neural classifiers. IEEE Trans. Syst. Man Cybern. Part C (Appl. Rev.) **30**(1), 84–94 (2000). https://doi.org/10.1109/5326.827457
8. Fagin, R., Lotem, A., Naor, M.: Optimal aggregation algorithms for middleware. J. Comput. Syst. Sci. **66**(4), 614–656 (2003). https://doi.org/10.1016/S0022-0000(03)00026-6
9. Figurnov, M., et al.: Spatially adaptive computation time for residual networks. In: 2017 IEEE Conference on Computer Vision and Pattern Recognition (CVPR), pp. 1790–1799, July 2017. https://doi.org/10.1109/CVPR.2017.194
10. Geifman, Y., El-Yaniv, R.: Selective classification for deep neural networks. In: Proceedings of the 31st International Conference on Neural Information Processing Systems, NIPS 2017, pp. 4885–4894. Curran Associates Inc., USA (2017)
11. Graves, A.: Adaptive computation time for recurrent neural networks. arXiv preprint: arXiv:1603.08983 (2016)
12. Guo, C., Pleiss, G., Sun, Y., Weinberger, K.: On calibration of modern neural networks. In: ICML 2017, April 2017
13. Han, S., et al.: EIE: efficient inference engine on compressed deep neural network. ACM SIGARCH Comput. Archit. News **44** (2016). https://doi.org/10.1145/3007787.3001163
14. He, K., Zhang, X., Ren, S., Sun, J.: Deep residual learning for image recognition, June 2016
15. Leroux, S., et al.: The cascading neural network: building the internet of smart things. Knowl. Inf. Syst. **52**(3), 791–814 (2017). https://doi.org/10.1007/s10115-017-1029-1
16. Odena, A., Lawson, D., Olah, C.: Changing model behavior at test-time using reinforcement learning. arXiv preprint: arXiv:1702.07780 (2017)
17. Panda, P., Sengupta, A., Roy, K.: Conditional deep learning for energy-efficient and enhanced pattern recognition. In: 2016 Design, Automation Test in Europe Conference Exhibition (DATE), pp. 475–480, March 2016
18. Stamoulis, D., et al.: Designing adaptive neural networks for energy-constrained image classification. In: ICCAD 2018, pp. 23:1–23:8. ACM (2018). https://doi.org/10.1145/3240765.3240796
19. Sze, V., Chen, Y., Yang, T., Emer, J.S.: Efficient processing of deep neural networks: a tutorial and survey. Proc. IEEE **105**(12), 2295–2329 (2017). https://doi.org/10.1109/JPROC.2017.2761740
20. Teerapittayanon, S., McDanel, B., Kung, H.T.: BranchyNet: fast inference via early exiting from deep neural networks. In: ICPR, pp. 2464–2469, December 2016. https://doi.org/10.1109/ICPR.2016.7900006
21. Viola, P., Jones, M.: Rapid object detection using a boosted cascade of simple features. In: Proceedings of the 2001 IEEE Computer Society Conference on Computer Vision and Pattern Recognition, CVPR 2001, vol. 1, p. I, December 2001. https://doi.org/10.1109/CVPR.2001.990517

22. Wang, X., Yu, F., Dou, Z., Gonzalez, J.E.: SkipNet: Learning dynamic routing in convolutional networks. arXiv preprint: arXiv:1711.09485 (2017)
23. Wang, Z., Sun, F., Lin, J., Wang, Z., Yuan, B.: SGAD: Soft-guided adaptively-dropped neural network. arXiv preprint: arXiv:1807.01430 (2018)
24. Wu, S., Li, G., Chen, F., Shi, L.: Training and inference with integers in deep neural networks. In: 6th International Conference on Learning Representations, ICLR 2018, Vancouver, BC, Canada, 30 April–3 May 2018, Conference Track Proceedings (2018)

Light-Weight Edge Enhanced Network for On-orbit Semantic Segmentation

Junxing Hu[1,2](✉), Ling Li[1,2], Yijun Lin[1,2], Fengge Wu[1], and Junsuo Zhao[1]

[1] Institute of Software Chinese Academy of Sciences (ISCAS), Beijing, China
junxing2017@iscas.ac.cn

[2] University of Chinese Academy of Sciences, Beijing, China

Abstract. On-orbit semantic segmentation can produce the target image tile or image description to reduce the pressure on transmission resources of satellites. In this paper, we propose a fully convolutional network for on-orbit semantic segmentation, namely light-weight edge enhanced network (LEN). For the model to be pruned, we present a new model pruning strategy based on unsupervised clustering. The method is performed according to the l_1-norm of each filter in the convolutional layer. And it effectively guides the pruning of filters and corresponding feature maps in a short time. In addition, the LEN uses a trainable edge enhanced module called enhanced domain transform to further optimize segmentation performance. The module fully exploits multi-level information of the object to generate the edge map and performs edge-preserving filtering on the coarse segmentation. Experimental results suggest that the models produce competitive results while containing only 1.53 M and 1.66 M parameters respectively on two public datasets: Inria Aerial Image Labeling Dataset and Massachusetts Buildings Dataset.

Keywords: Semantic segmentation · Model pruning · Enhanced domain transform

1 Introduction

Due to the limitation of transmission bandwidth, there are few images acquired by satellites can be transmitted to the ground, and most of them are useless. It is necessary to conduct on-orbit processing of remote sensing (RS) images. Semantic segmentation performing pixel-level prediction is suitable for RS image understanding. Based on the results of on-orbit semantic segmentation, only transmitting the useful images, target image tiles or image description can effectively reduce the pressure on satellite bandwidth. TianZhi-2 satellite equipped with computing resources supports deep learning and will be launched soon. Limited by computational capability and energy, it is necessary to reduce resource consumption while improving the performance of the segmentation method.

Classical machine learning methods require manual feature engineering or interactive operations, which cannot be applied to satellites. Deep learning based

I. V. Tetko et al. (Eds.): ICANN 2019, LNCS 11728, pp. 321–333, 2019.
https://doi.org/10.1007/978-3-030-30484-3_27

methods promote the development of semantic segmentation. Maggiori et al. [1] use a model based on FCN to combine features at different resolutions. Bischke et al. [2] propose a cascaded multi-task loss to preserve segmentation boundaries. Khalel and El-Saban [3] exploit stacked models where each model enhances the results of the previous one. However, these models are large and not accurate enough. The model pruning and segmentation optimization are required.

Model Pruning. Many compression methods for deep learning models have been proposed. Han et al. [4] prune redundant connections determined by the given threshold. The method results in sparse convolutional kernels which require sparse libraries. Zhou et al. [5] incorporate sparse constraints into the objective function. Wen et al. [6] present a structured sparsity learning method to regularize filters and layer depth of models. Li et al. [7] use the l_1-norm as an effective measure and we also use it in our work. They prune and retrain each layer independently, and then compare the testing accuracies of the pruned model before and after retraining to observe its sensitivity to pruning. The process of retraining can take thousands of hours and the method requires artificial determination of the pruning ratio for each layer. Different from it, we exploit the clustering based method to obtain the light-weight model in a short time.

Segmentation Optimization. The edge prediction of the target usually has a great influence on the overall segmentation result. Lin et al. [8] improve the edge prediction to optimize the segmentation by using the fully connected Conditional Random Fields (CRFs). Bertasius et al. [9] propose predicting boundaries by exploiting object-level features from a pre-trained model for object classification. But they consider the edge detection and semantic segmentation as two separate tasks. In contrast, Chen et al. [10] exploit domain transform as an edge-preserving filter to improve the segmentation result. However, they only use several layers from low-level stages which contain limited edge information.

Based on such prior studies, we present the light-weight edge enhanced network (LEN) for the on-orbit semantic segmentation of RS images. The main contributions of this work can be summarized as follows:

- First, a new pruning strategy is proposed to produce the light-weight model. By clustering filters according to the sum of absolute weights, the pruning ratio of each convolutional layer is computed automatically to guide the compression. The method does not require long-term sensitivity analysis of pruning and excessive human intervention.
- Second, the enhanced domain transform uses multi-scale edge features to filter the coarse segmentation by combining multi-stage convolutional layers. It makes the LEN pay more attention to the edge prediction and thereby produce more accurate segmentation results.

Experimental results show that the models regain close to and even outperform the original performance while all achieving more than 95% parameters reduction on two most widely used datasets: Inria Aerial Image Labeling Dataset (Inria) [1] and Massachusetts Buildings Dataset (Mass) [11].

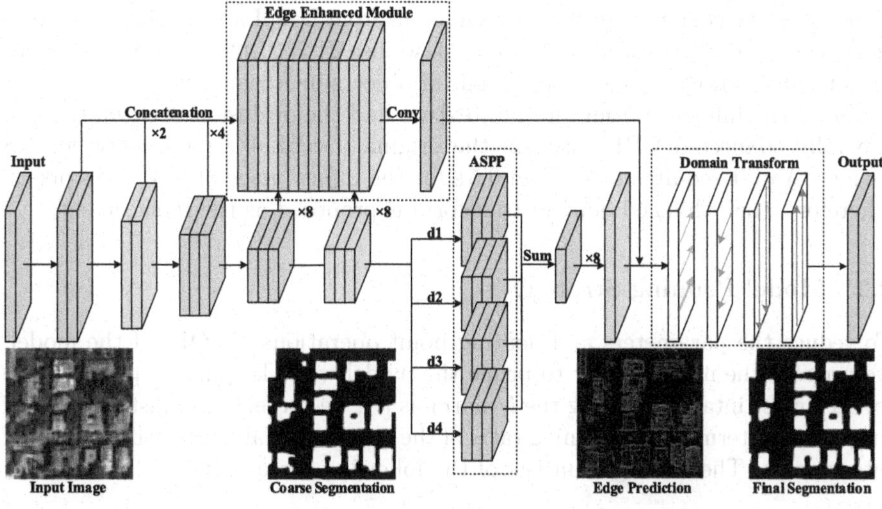

Fig. 1. The overall structure of the proposed model. '×' indicates the up-sampling.

2 Proposed Methods

In this section, we introduce the method for semantic segmentation of RS images. We first prune this backbone model, then integrate the enhanced domain transform into the light-weight network to optimize its segmentation performance.

2.1 Overall Structure

As shown in Fig. 1, the proposed method mainly consists of two components. First, VGG based DeepLab v2 [12] is used as the backbone model since we have verified its superiority in five current fully convolutional networks in the previous work [13]. Second, we use the enhanced domain transform to further optimize the segmentation. This component is detailed in Sect. 2.3.

Atrous Convolution for Remote Sensing Images. In RS images, some targets are extremely small while some others are large. Moreover, many targets are unevenly distributed (buildings, roads, and forests), and the sharpness of their boundaries are different. The atrous convolution is suitable for segmenting these RS images. DeepLab v2 uses the atrous convolution with dilation d, which enlarges the kernel K with a $k \times k$ size to $k_e \times k_e$ as the following formula:

$$k_e = k + (k-1)(d-1) \quad (1)$$

The method fills consecutive filter values with $d-1$ zeros to avoid increasing parameters of the model. Furthermore, the Atrous Spatial Pyramid Pooling (ASPP) exploits different dilation to capture multi-scale information of targets. It extends conv6 as four parallel branches with multiple dilations and sums them to produce the coarse segmentation. Different from DeepLab v2 using large dilations as $d1 = 6, d2 = 12, d3 = 18, d4 = 24$, we use $d1 = 2, d2 = 4, d3 = 8, d4 = 12$ in our model for capturing more details of objects in RS images.

Since the influence from internal texture and the occlusion between targets, the fully connected CRFs used in the original DeepLab v2 is useless for RS images. And it requires more than 0.5 s for the input image of 513×513 pixels. Therefore, the enhanced domain transform is proposed as the replacement.

2.2 Model Pruning Strategy

To reduce the parameters and floating point operations (FLOP) of the model, we propose the new strategy to prune the model while keeping its performance levels almost intact. By using the l_1-norm as [7], we present the clustering based method to determine the pruning ratio of the convolutional layer with less human intervention. The strategy consists of the following three parts.

Measure the Importance of the Filter. As the first part of the model compression, it is crucial to determine the pruning object and the corresponding importance measure. To avoid producing sparse connectivity patterns and the additional regularization as [5,6], we use the filter of the convolutional layer as the pruning object following [7]. For the jth filter of the ith convolutional layer $f_{i,j}$, the l_1-norm $l_{i,j}$, i.e., absolute weights sum $\sum |f_{i,j}|$ is calculated as follows:

$$l_{i,j} = \sum |f_{i,j}| = \sum_{n=1}^{c_i} \sum |K_n| \tag{2}$$

where c_i is the number of input channels in the ith convolutional layer, K_n is the nth kernel of the filter $f_{i,j}$. The more important filter has a larger l_1-norm.

Determine the Pruning Ratio by Clustering. Different from [7], to simplify the sensitivity analysis of pruning and reduce human intervention, we propose directly calculating the pruning ratio of each layer in the original model by using the unsupervised clustering method.

Choose a Suitable Clustering Method. We compare several common clustering methods, such as the k-means clustering [14], the fuzzy c-means clustering (FCM) [15] and the density-based clustering (DBSCAN) [16]. In this task, the FCM produces the degree of membership for the filter in the cluster. It is not conducive to the repeatability of the experiment. Moreover, since the sample (filter) only has one dimension feature, and the DBSCAN usually predicts some samples as outliers, it is also not suitable for clustering filters. Therefore, we choose the k-means for subsequent processing.

Calculate the Pruning Ratio. We propose the procedure of computing the pruning ratio for the ith convolutional layer as follows:

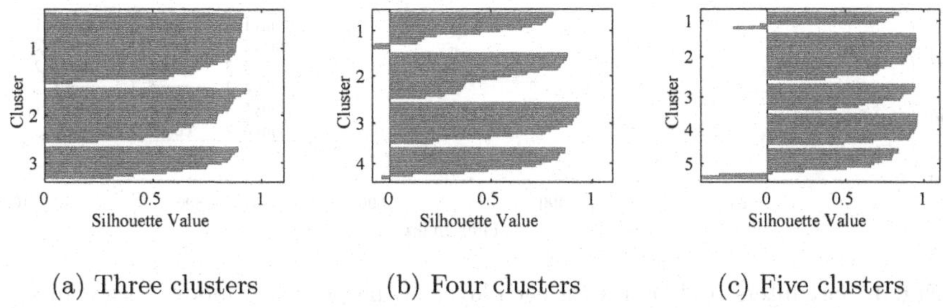

(a) Three clusters (b) Four clusters (c) Five clusters

Fig. 2. Silhouette plots for the conv1_1 with a different number of clustering centers.

(1) Compute the l_1-norm $l_{i,j}$ of the jth filter.
(2) Sort filters of the layer according to the l_1-norm.
(3) Prune 50% smallest filters of the layer and directly evaluate the pruned model without retraining. The layer with small accuracy loss (e.g., $\leq$5%) of the pruned model can be compressed more, otherwise less compression.
(4) Cluster the filters into Z_i categories by $l_{i,j}$, and a_z is the zth category. The (Z_i+1)-quantiles are used as initial centers for the reproducibility.
(5) Sort these clusters by $l_{i,j}$, and a_1 corresponds to the smallest value.
(6) Calculate the pruning ratio p_i using the following formula:

$$p_i = \begin{cases} \dfrac{\sum_{z=1}^{Z_i-1} num(a_z)}{o_i}, & \text{more compression on the layer, } Z_i \geq 3; \\ \dfrac{num(a_1)}{o_i}, & \text{less compression on the layer.} \end{cases} \tag{3}$$

where o_i denotes the number of output channels for the ith convolutional layer, $num(.)$ is the function for counting filter numbers.

Note: In step (3), the segmentation results usually have a lager visible deterioration when the loss of accuracy is greater than 5%. In step (4), silhouettes [17] and the gap statistic [18] are used to determine the optimal number of clusters (Z_i). For example, Fig. 2 illustrates silhouette plots for the conv1_1 layer of the proposed model on Inria. In the silhouette plot, the silhouette value ranges from -1 to 1. The value -1 indicates the point is assigned to the wrong cluster and the value 1 is the opposite. The figures indicate that three clusters are better separated than others for conv1_1. In addition, Fig. 3 shows the l_1-norm of sorted filters for each layer in the model trained on the Inria. Since the shape of each curve is approximately similar, it is reasonable to exploit the clustering with the same setting (Z_i) for all layers. This part runs very fast, especially when the validation set used in step (3) is small.

Prune and Retrain the Model. As our model has many convolutional layers, pruning and retraining it layer-by-layer is very time-consuming. According to pruning ratios of convolutional layers generated by the clustering, we prune

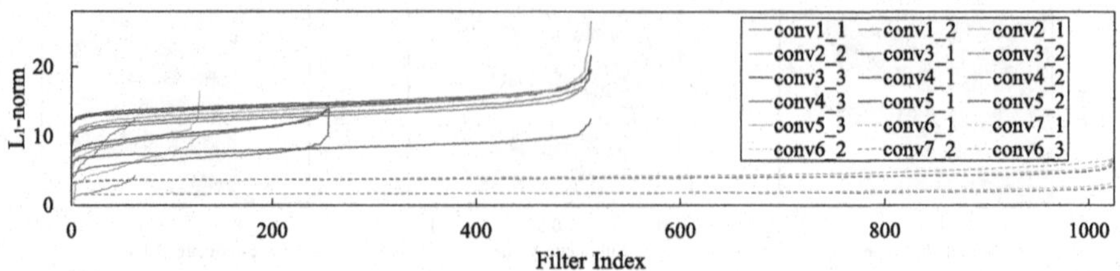

Fig. 3. Sort filters by l_1-norm for each layer of the proposed model on the Inria.

filters and connecting feature maps across multiple layers at once. After that, we retrain the pruned model until the accuracy is recovered and even better.

2.3 Enhanced Domain Transform

Since the misclassification usually occurs at the edge of the target, we present the enhanced domain transform (EDT) to optimize the segmentation performance by edge filtering. As illustrated in Fig. 1, the EDT is mainly composed of two parts: the edge enhanced module and domain transform (DT).

Edge Enhanced Module. As one input of the EDT, this module is used to generate the edge map. Different from natural images with fewer and simpler edges of targets, RS images have more complex edges. Inspired by [19] which exploits richer convolutional features to fulfill the edge detection task, we propose utilizing all of the low-level convolutional layers containing multi-scale structural information to predict the enhanced edge map. By using the structure as [10], the feature maps are resized to the original size by bilinear interpolation. The concat layer is used to concatenate feature maps. The convolutional layer with 1×1 kernel size and ReLU is used to produce the edge map with a single channel.

Domain Transform. After obtaining the coarse segmentation and the edge map, we use the trainable DT to conduct edge-preserving filtering following [10]. Figure 1 shows the forward propagation. The DT recursively filters the coarse segmentation (2-D signals) in a separable way through T iterations. Specifically, it implements 1-D filtering sequentially in four directions (i.e., left-to-right, right-to-left, top-to-bottom and bottom-to-top) at each iteration. Let x/y denote the input/output, and g be the edge map, the left-to-right filtering on the 1-D signals of length M is computed recursively as follows:

$$y_m = (1 - w_m)x_m + w_m y_{m-1} \tag{4}$$

$$w_m = exp(-\frac{\sqrt{2}}{\sigma_t}(1 + g_m \frac{\sigma_s}{\sigma_r}))$$

$$\sigma_t = \sqrt{3}\sigma_s \frac{2^{T-t}}{\sqrt{4^T - 1}}$$

where $m = 2, ..., M$, $t = 1, ..., T$, w_m is the mth weight corresponding to the x_m, σ_s and σ_r are the standard deviation of the filter kernel over the input's spatial domain and the edge map's range, σ_t is computed by σ_s at the tth iteration.

During back-propagation, the DT back-propagates the segmentation errors at y_m onto x_m and g_m to update them simultaneously. Corresponding to the forward pass above, the derivatives are calculated as follows:

$$\begin{aligned} \frac{\partial L}{\partial x_m} &\leftarrow (1 - w_m)\frac{\partial L}{\partial y_m} \\ \frac{\partial L}{\partial y_{m-1}} &\leftarrow \frac{\partial L}{\partial y_{m-1}} + w_m \frac{\partial L}{\partial y_m} \\ \frac{\partial L}{\partial g_m} &\leftarrow -\frac{\sqrt{2}\,\sigma_s}{\sigma_t\ \sigma_r} w_m \frac{\partial L}{\partial w_m} \\ \frac{\partial L}{\partial w_m} &\leftarrow \frac{\partial L}{\partial w_m} + (y_{m-1} - x_m)\frac{\partial L}{\partial y_m} \end{aligned} \tag{5}$$

where $m = M, ..., 2$, which is opposite to the forward propagation. We use the same T as [10], but adjust σ_s and σ_r according to our datasets.

3 Experimental Results

3.1 Dataset

We experiment separately on two public building datasets. The available subset of Inria [1] contains 180 images of size 5000 × 5000 pixels, which has 36 images for each of five cities. The first 5 images of each city are used for testing and the remaining 155 images for training as [1]. Mass [11] contains 141 (train) and 10 (test) images of size 1500 × 1500 pixels. These datasets are labeled as two classes at the pixel level: building and non-building. 512 × 512 patches with 12 pixels overlap are extracted from original images. In the end, Inria has 15500 (train) and 2500 (test) images. Mass has 1201 (train) and 90 (test) images because those patches with a large blank area are discarded.

3.2 Training Pipeline

The models implemented with Caffe are pre-trained on the PASCAL VOC-2012 datasets [20]. We use a "poly" policy with initial learning rate e-3, momentum 0.9 and weight decay 5e-4. The performance is measured by Intersection over Union (IoU) and accuracy. All models are trained for 100 epochs and the best results are reported during the training process. Since Inria is larger and more convincing, we perform the experiments on Inria as three steps: (1) Train DeepLab v2 as baseline models. (2) Prune models by using the clustering based method and the method in [7] as a comparison. (3) Add the EDT to the pruned models and compare them with DT. Moreover, Mass is used to verify the proposed methods.

Table 1. The segmentation results (%) of three versions of DeepLab v2 on two datasets.

Method	Inria (IoU)		Inria (Accuracy)		Mass (IoU)		Mass (Accuracy)	
	no CRFs	CRFs	no CRFs	CRFs	no CRFs	CRFs	no CRFs	CRFs
DeepLab_R	**75.21**	71.32	**96.10**	95.60	**61.70**	41.86	**91.79**	88.68
DeepLab_L	**74.86**	70.92	**96.08**	95.58	**62.46**	45.05	**91.61**	89.13
DeepLab_S	**76.13**	72.93	**96.27**	95.87	**63.15**	47.40	**91.69**	89.62

Table 2. Compare the different number of clusters. 'number' denotes the number of layers that are judged to use the specified clusters. 'value' is the average of evaluation values for 21 layers, and the largest value corresponds to the optimal clustering.

Criterion	Three clusters		Four clusters		Five clusters	
	Number	Value	Number	Value	Number	Value
Silh (Inria)	**12**	**0.69**	7	0.65	2	0.67
Gap (Inria)	**20**	**0.87**	0	0.79	1	0.75
Silh (Mass)	**10**	**0.70**	2	0.68	9	0.69
Gap (Mass)	**19**	**0.97**	0	0.89	2	0.85

3.3 Baseline Model Results

As indicated in Table 1, we train DeepLab v2 as the baseline and compare its three versions: ResNet-101 based model (DeepLab_R), VGG-16 based model with large dilations (DeepLab_L) and with small dilations (DeepLab_S) as described in Sect. 2.1. For two datasets, DeepLab_S achieves better results than DeepLab_L because the smaller dilation facilitates the prediction of details. And the ResNet model may not be suitable for our task. Moreover, we find that the fully-connected CRFs makes results worse caused by occlusion, so we use the DeepLab_S without the fully-connected CRFs as the baseline model.

3.4 Model Pruning Results

Clustering Based Method. First, we prune 50% filters with the smallest l_1-norm of each layer from the models independently. We evaluate the pruned models directly as shown in Fig. 4(a)(b)(c)(f). Note that these figures also contain results at other pruning ratios (from 10% to 90%), which are used in the contrast experiments. For results at 50% pruning ratio, we set the upper limit of the loss of IoU is 30% and 5% for accuracy. Then the first seven layers (from conv1_1 to conv3_3) of models for both datasets are judged to be used with small pruning ratios, while large pruning ratios for the remaining layers.

Second, the k-means is used to cluster sorted filters in each layer of the original models. We use silhouettes (Silh) and the gap statistic (Gap) to find the optimal number of clusters from three to five for all layers. Table 2 shows that three clusters are better separated than four and five for both models.

Table 3. Pruning ratios (%) obtained by pruning strategies (rounded to the nearest ten). '1'-'21' indicate 21 convolutional layers from conv1_1 to conv7_4. 'Acc' is accuracy. 'PS_1'-'PS_7' are different pruning strategies for the model trained on Inria.

Pruning Strategy (PS)	1	2	3	4	5	6	7	8	9	10	11	12	13	14	15	16	17	18	19	20	21
PS_Mass (cluster, large)	70	60	80	70	80	80	80	**80**	**90**	**90**	**80**	**90**	**90**	**90**	**90**	**80**	**90**	**70**	**90**	**80**	**90**
PS_Mass (cluster, small)	**30**	**40**	**40**	**30**	**30**	**30**	**30**	40	50	40	40	40	60	50	50	30	30	20	40	40	50
PS_1 (cluster, large)	80	60	60	80	80	80	80	**80**	**80**	**80**	**90**	**90**	**90**	**90**	**90**	**90**	**90**	**90**	**90**	**90**	**90**
PS_1 (cluster, small)	**50**	**30**	**30**	**30**	**30**	**30**	**30**	40	30	30	40	40	50	50	60	50	60	50	70	50	60
PS_2 (cluster, same)	50	50	30	30	30	30	30	80	80	80	90	90	90	90	90	90	90	90	90	90	90
PS_3 (retraining, IoU)	50	50	30	30	70	50	50	70	70	70	90	90	90	90	90	90	90	90	90	90	90
PS_4 (retraining, same)	50	50	30	30	50	50	50	70	70	70	90	90	90	90	90	90	90	90	90	90	90
PS_5 (retraining, Acc)	50	50	30	20	50	40	30	50	50	30	40	50	50	90	90	90	90	90	90	90	90
PS_6 (before, IoU)	0	0	0	0	0	0	0	0	0	0	0	0	0	80	90	70	10	60	20	0	70
PS_7 (no guidance)	0	0	0	0	0	0	0	0	0	0	0	0	0	50	50	50	50	50	50	50	50

Table 4. Performance of pruned models. 'LW_i' is the light-weight model produced by PS_i. 'Pruned' denotes the pruning ratio of the parameter and FLOP separately.

Model	IoU (%)	Acc (%)	Parameter	Pruned (%)	FLOP	Pruned (%)
LW (Mass)	60.74	91.25	1.66×10^6	95.61	5.13×10^{10}	87.27
LW_1 (Inria)	74.30	95.93	1.53×10^6	95.95	5.13×10^{10}	87.29
LW_2	73.94	95.88	1.52×10^6	95.98	4.79×10^{10}	88.12
LW_3	73.59	95.80	1.37×10^6	96.38	3.61×10^{10}	91.04
LW_4	74.11	95.85	1.47×10^6	96.11	3.95×10^{10}	90.21
LW_5	74.59	95.96	5.77×10^6	84.74	8.06×10^{10}	80.01
LW_6	76.27	96.27	2.46×10^7	34.81	2.92×10^{11}	27.56
LW_7	76.26	96.26	2.52×10^7	33.31	2.97×10^{11}	26.38

Finally, based on the above results, the pruning ratio of each layer can be calculated automatically as shown by the bold numbers in Table 3. 'PS_Mass' is the pruning strategy for the model on Mass and 'PS_1' on Inria. The entire process takes only a few minutes and no human decision is required.

Contrast Experiments. Following [7], we retrain the pruned models on Inria and test them as shown in Fig. 4(d)(e), which runs for more than one thousand hours on the TITAN Xp GPU. The sensitivity to the pruning of each layer can be observed by comparing the performance of the corresponding pruned model before and after retraining. Then we manually set the pruning ratio for each layer. Table 3 also shows these pruning strategies as follows:

PS_2. Use the same pruning ratio for layers in the same stage as [7], i.e., change the pruning ratio from 30% to 50% of the second layer (conv1_2) in PS_1.

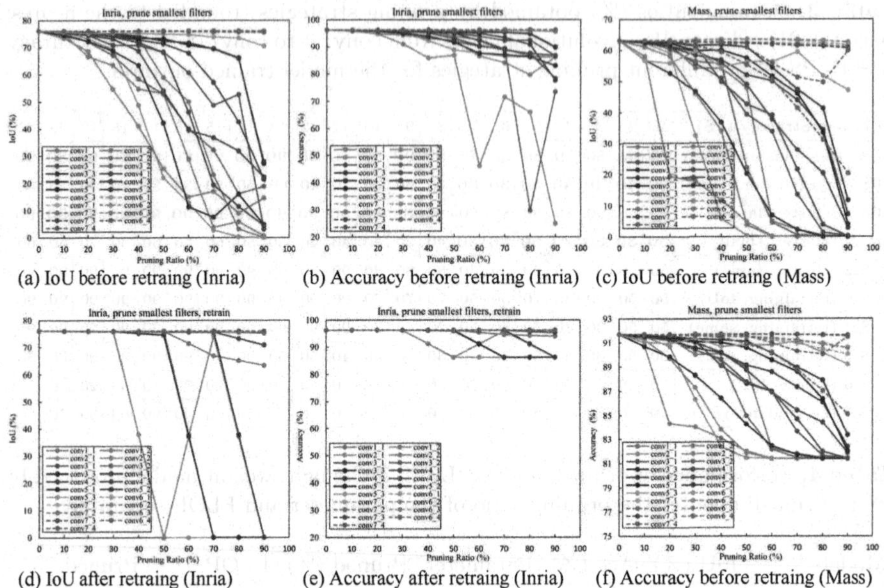

(a) IoU before retraing (Inria) (b) Accuracy before retraing (Inria) (c) IoU before retraing (Mass)

(d) IoU after retraing (Inria) (e) Accuracy after retraing (Inria) (f) Accuracy before retraing (Mass)

Fig. 4. The IoU and accuracies of the pruned models on Inria and Mass.

PS_3. Prune the model according to the sensitivities to pruning of layers, guided by the IoU of the pruned model after retraining as shown in Fig. 4(d).

PS_4. Change the pruning ratio from 70% to 50% of the fifth layer (conv3_3) in PS_3 as PS_2 does.

PS_5. Different from PS_3, prune the model by using the accuracy of the pruned model after retraining as shown in Fig. 4(e).

PS_6. Figure 4(a) indicates that pruning some layers (e.g., conv6_1) without retraining even makes the IoU higher, so we prune these layers directly.

PS_7. As a comparison with PS_6, empirically prune 50% filters for each of high-level layers (from conv6_1 to conv7_4) without guidance from Fig. 4.

As shown in Table 4, the light-weight model on Mass which is produced by the clustering based pruning method achieves more than 95% parameters reduction while regaining close to the original accuracy (91.69%). Then we compare several light-weight models on Inria. The pruning ratio of our model (LW_1) is greater than 95% which is similar to LW_2, LW_3, LW_4, but the segmentation performance is better than them. And we find that using the same pruning ratio for layers in the same stage as [7] is useless in our task. In addition, LW_5 shows little improvement on segmentation with the smaller pruning ratio. So IoU is more instructive than accuracy. LW_6 and LW_7 achieve the better results but their pruning ratios are much smaller than others. And LW_6 outperforms LW_7 with smaller parameters indicating that it is reliable to prune the model based

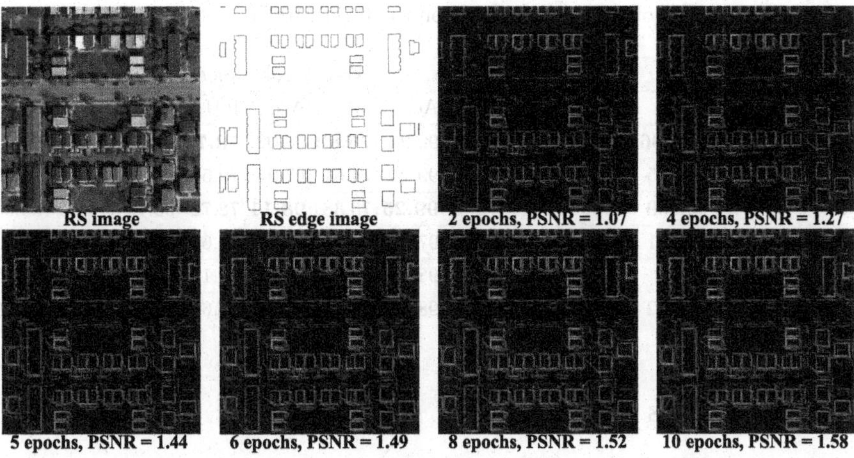

Fig. 5. Use the PSNR to compare the edge map generated from different epochs.

Table 5. Performance (%) of models with different components on two datasets.

Method	Inria		Mass	
	IoU	Acc	IoU	Acc
LW with EDT (LEN)	**75.33**	**96.13**	**63.55**	**91.58**
LW with DT	74.89	96.06	62.34	91.27

on data rather than human experience. Therefore, the clustering based pruning strategy is faster and more efficient in this task.

3.5 Segmentation Results

We integrate the EDT into the light-weight models and fine-tune the new models from them to optimize their segmentation. Note that the EDT has almost no influence on increasing parameters of the models which are 1.66M for Mass and 1.53M for Inria. Figure 5 illustrates that the generated edge map becomes clearer and the Peak Signal-to-Noise Ratio (PSNR) is larger as the number of epochs increases during the training phase. Table 5 shows that the models with EDT perform better than DT for both datasets because of richer edge information. And the LEN on Mass even achieves better IoU than the original (63.15%). Table 6 indicates the comparison of LEN with other methods on Inria. By using 700×700 pixels images with 100 pixels overlap for testing, the LEN is further optimized and even superior to other methods with the larger model sizes. Therefore, the LEN produces the competitive results which regain close to and even outperform the original with more than 95% parameter reduction.

Table 6. Results (%) of different methods on the Inria. '100' denotes 100 pixels overlap.

Method	Austin		Chicago		Kitsap		West Tyrol		Vienna		Overall	
	IoU	Acc	IoU	Acc	IoU	Acc	IoU	Acc	IoU	Acc	IoU	Acc
LEN (100)	**78.70**	**96.86**	**69.80**	92.54	66.31	99.22	**75.82**	98.02	**79.76**	94.10	**75.65**	**96.15**
LEN	78.54	96.85	69.57	92.52	66.36	99.24	74.51	97.94	79.54	94.11	75.33	96.13
Stacked [3]	77.29	96.69	68.52	92.4	72.84	**99.25**	75.38	**98.11**	78.72	93.79	74.55	96.05
Multi [2]	76.76	93.21	67.06	**99.25**	**73.3**	97.84	66.91	91.71	76.68	**96.61**	73	95.73
MLP [1]	61.2	94.2	61.3	90.43	51.5	98.92	57.95	96.66	72.13	91.87	64.67	94.42
FCN [1]	47.66	92.22	53.62	88.59	33.7	98.58	46.86	95.83	60.6	88.72	53.82	92.79

4 Conclusions

In this paper, we have proposed the light-weight edge enhanced network for on-orbit semantic segmentation. By using the clustering based pruning strategy, the models are well compressed without longtime retraining and produce competitive results. In addition, the method uses the edge enhanced module to exploit more useful edge information from multi-level layers. It improves the edge prediction of targets and the overall segmentation performance simultaneously. Experimental results show that the proposed models have a small number of parameters while performing well on two public datasets. These models will be deployed on the TianZhi-2 satellite which will be launched soon for on-orbit testing.

References

1. Maggiori, E., Tarabalka, Y., Charpiat, G., Alliez, P.: Can semantic labeling methods generalize to any city? The Inria aerial image labeling benchmark. In: IEEE IGARSS, pp. 3226–3229 (2017). https://doi.org/10.1109/IGARSS.2017.8127684
2. Bischke, B., Helber, P., et al.: Multi-task learning for segmentation of building footprints with deep neural networks. arXiv preprint: arXiv:1709.05932 (2017)
3. Khalel, A., El-Saban, M.: Automatic pixelwise object labeling for aerial imagery using stacked U-Nets. arXiv preprint: arXiv:1803.04953 (2018)
4. Han, S., Pool, J., Tran, J., Dally, W.: Learning both weights and connections for efficient neural network. In: Advances in NIPS, pp. 1135–1143 (2015)
5. Zhou, H., Alvarez, J.M., Porikli, F.: Less is more: towards compact CNNs. In: Leibe, B., Matas, J., Sebe, N., Welling, M. (eds.) ECCV 2016, Part IV. LNCS, vol. 9908, pp. 662–677. Springer, Cham (2016). https://doi.org/10.1007/978-3-319-46493-0_40
6. Wen, W., Wu, C., Wang, Y., Chen, Y., Li, H.: Learning structured sparsity in deep neural networks. In: Advances in NIPS, pp. 2074–2082 (2016)
7. Li, H., Kadav, A., Durdanovic, I., Samet, H., Graf, H.P.: Pruning filters for efficient ConvNets. In: International Conference on Learning Representations (2017)
8. Lin, G., Milan, A., Shen, C., Reid, I.: RefineNet: multi-path refinement networks for high-resolution semantic segmentation. In: Proceedings of the IEEE Conference on CVPR, pp. 1925–1934 (2017). https://doi.org/10.1109/CVPR.2017.549

9. Bertasius, G., Shi, J., Torresani, L.: High-for-low and low-for-high: efficient boundary detection from deep object features and its applications to high-level vision. In: ICCV, pp. 504–512 (2015). https://doi.org/10.1109/ICCV.2015.65
10. Chen, L.C., Barron, J.T., Papandreou, G., Murphy, K., Yuille, A.L.: Semantic image segmentation with task-specific edge detection using CNNs and a discriminatively trained domain transform. In: Proceedings of the IEEE Conference on CVPR, pp. 4545–4554 (2016). https://doi.org/10.1109/CVPR.2016.492
11. Hinton, G.E., Mnih, V.: Machine learning for aerial image labeling (2013)
12. Chen, L.C., Papandreou, G., Kokkinos, I., Murphy, K., Yuille, A.L.: DeepLab: semantic image segmentation with deep convolutional nets, atrous convolution, and fully connected CRFs. IEEE Trans. PAMI **40**(4), 834–848 (2018)
13. Hu, J., Li, L., Lin, Y., Wu, F., Zhao, J.: A Comparison and Strategy of Semantic Segmentation on Remote Sensing Images. arXiv preprint: arXiv:1905.10231 (2019)
14. MacQueen, J.: Some methods for classification and analysis of multivariate observations. In: Proceedings of the Fifth Berkeley Symposium on Mathematical Statistics and Probability, vol. 1(14), pp. 281–297 (1967)
15. Bezdek, J.C., Ehrlich, R., Full, W.: FCM: the fuzzy c-means clustering algorithm. Comput. Geosci. **10**(2–3), 191–203 (1984)
16. Ester, M., Kriegel, H.P., Sander, J., Xu, X.: A density-based algorithm for discovering clusters in large spatial databases with noise. In: KDD 1996, vol. 34, pp. 226–231 (1996)
17. Rousseeuw, P.J.: Silhouettes: a graphical aid to the interpretation and validation of cluster analysis. J. Comput. Appl. Math. **20**, 53–65 (1987). https://doi.org/10.1016/0377-0427(87)90125-7
18. Tibshirani, R., Walther, G., Hastie, T.: Estimating the number of clusters in a data set via the gap statistic. J. R. Stat. Soc. Ser. B (Stat. Methodol.) **63**(2), 411–423 (2001). https://doi.org/10.1111/1467-9868.00293
19. Liu, Y., Cheng, M. M., Hu, X., Wang, K., Bai, X.: Richer convolutional features for edge detection. In: CVPR, pp. 3000–3009 (2017). https://doi.org/10.1109/CVPR.2017.622
20. Everingham, M., Eslami, S.A., Van Gool, L., Williams, C.K., Winn, J., Zisserman, A.: The Pascal visual object classes challenge: a retrospective. Int. J. Comput. Vis. **111**(1), 98–136 (2015). https://doi.org/10.1007/s11263-014-0733-5

Local Normalization Based BN Layer Pruning

Yuan Liu[1], Xi Jia[1], Linlin Shen[1(✉)], Zhong Ming[2], and Jinming Duan[3]

[1] Computer Vision Institute, Shenzhen University, Shenzhen, Guangdong, China
{liuyuan20162,jiaxi}@email.szu.edu.cn,
llshen@szu.edu.cn

[2] Big Data Institute, Shenzhen University, Shenzhen, Guangdong, China
mingz@szu.edu.cn

[3] School of Computer Science, University of Birmingham, Birmingham, England
j.duan@bham.ac.uk

Abstract. Compression and acceleration of convolutional neural network (CNN) have raised extensive research interest in the past few years. In this paper, we proposed a novel channel-level pruning method based on gamma (scaling parameters) of Batch Normalization layer to compress and accelerate CNN models. Local gamma normalization and selection was proposed to address the over-pruning issue and introduce local information into channel selection. After that, an ablation based beta (shifting parameters) transfer, and knowledge distillation based fine-tuning were further applied to improve the performance of the pruned model. The experimental results on CIFAR-10, CIFAR-100 and LFW datasets suggest that our approach can achieve much more efficient pruning in terms of reduction of parameters and FLOPs, e.g., 8.64× compression and 3.79× acceleration of VGG were achieved on CIFAR, with slight accuracy loss.

Keywords: Convolutional neural network (CNN) ·
Model compression and acceleration · Pruning · Knowledge distillation

1 Introduction

In the past few years, deep learning has achieved remarkable success in computer vision, especially in image classification. A lot of CNN architectures, such as VGG [1], Inception [2], ResNet [3] and DenseNet [4], have been proposed. It is still difficult to deploy CNN for real-time applications in edge-computing devices with limited resources (e.g. CPU, memory, bandwidth and energy), such as embedded devices, smart phones, wearable devices, drones, etc. Denil *et al.* [5] showed that DNN with a small minority of parameters after compression can

The work is supported by National Natural Science Foundation of China (Grant No. 61672357 and U1713214), and the Science and Technology Project of Guangdong Province (Grant No. 2018A050501014).

I. V. Tetko et al. (Eds.): ICANN 2019, LNCS 11728, pp. 334–346, 2019.
https://doi.org/10.1007/978-3-030-30484-3_28

achieve comparable performance. Based on such theory, network pruning is developed to make the DNN model more compact and slim with slight cost of accuracy. Generally, pruning is exerted on a trained DNN model to remove the unnecessary weights or channels for parameters and FLOPs reduction. The majority of parameters and the calculation overhead are from the fully-connected and the convolution layers, respectively. To get a well-pruned performance, the DNN model is usually trained with ℓ_1 regularization for sparsity constraint.

In this paper, we developed a Batch Normalization (BN) layer based network pruning approach including three contributions:

1. For the approach proposed by Liu *et al.* [6] with high pruning ratio, most and even all of the channels in the deep layers could be pruned and this is so called "over-pruning". To address such issue and make the pruning more balanced, we proposed local gamma (scaling parameters) normalization and selection.
2. To relieve the potential loss brought by ignoring and simply removing the corresponding beta of pruned channels, we proposed ablation based beta (shifting parameters) transfer.
3. To further improve the performance of pruned neural network models, we proposed knowledge distillation based fine-tuning.

2 Related Works

2.1 Knowledge Distillation

Knowledge distillation attempts to extract knowledge from a deeper and more complex teacher model, and then transfer it to a shallower and simpler student model so that it can obtain similar performance. To this end, extracting and transferring knowledge are the two key points of knowledge distillation.

Jimmy *et al.* [7] claimed that the input of the teacher model's softmax layer contains comprehensive supervision information, which can be considered as an effective generalization of the knowledge learned by the neural network. Therefore they transformed the training problem into a regression problem.

Hinton *et al.* [8] calculated Kullback-Leibler divergence loss between the output of teacher model's and student model's softmax layers. They suggest that the output of softmax layer represents the prediction probabilities of each class and indicates the correlation between classes, which is so called "soft label". In order to obtain a better probability distribution, they introduced a hyper-parameter τ called "Temperature". However, it is hard to converge when the number of classes is big, e.g. face recognition [9].

Mirzadeh *et al.* [10] proposed a two-step distillation. They found out that student model performance degrades when the gap between student and teacher is large. Therefore, they alleviated this shortcoming by two-step distillation with a intermediate-sized model called "Teacher Assistant", which is considered to bridge the gap between student and teacher models. Their experiments confirmed the effectiveness of the proposed approach.

2.2 Pruning

Network pruning has been proposed to reduce the complexity of neural network and address the over-fitting issue. In the early research of pruning, LeCun *et al.* [11] and Hassibi *et al.* [12] reduced the number of connections between neurons based on Hessian of the loss function, and their works showed that pruning can bring better accuracy improvement than the regularization methods such as weight decay. In view of granularity, we can categorize pruning into connection-level and channel-level pruning.

Connection-level pruning is unstructured but fine-grained. Han *et al.* [13] introduced a simple method to prune the parameters whose values are lower than a predefined threshold and then fine-tune the network with a L_2 regularization term. Based on the previous works, Han *et al.* [14] proposed a method to address the sparse matrix issue produced by connection-level pruning. Although such unstructured pruning can greatly reduce the redundancy of parameters, it actually cannot lead to faster inference since most hardwares exploit regular structures in computation to achieve high throughput, and therefore the connection-level pruning requires specialized hardware and software to achieve theoretical acceleration.

Channel-level pruning is structured but coarse-grained. The works proposed by Li *et al.* [15], He *et al.* [16], Luo *et al.* [17], Liu *et al.* [6], and Ye *et al.* [18] are typical cases of channel-level pruning. Li *et al.* [15] introduced l_0 regularization to the filters to make them sparse and then pruned those filters with small l_1 norm. Luo *et al.* [17] used greedy algorithm to minimize the output loss of each layer. With structured pruning, neural network can be easily deployed without any modification to the existing deep learning framework. He *et al.* [16] used a LASSO regression for channel selection, which used a l_1 regularization to measure the loss between the output before and after pruning. Liu *et al.* [6] proposed a channel-level pruning called "Network Slimming" by leveraging the scaling factors gamma in BN layers to measure the importance of channels in each layer. Then they used a global pruning strategy which firstly sorts the absolute values of gamma across all BN layers in ascending order and then prunes the channels with small gamma absolute value in a certain proportion. After that, they transferred the remained parameters to a new model and fine-tuned it.

3 Methods

In this section, we firstly introduce a Batch Normalization based channel-level pruning method and its potential drawback. Then, we introduce a Batch Normalization based channel-level pruning method with local gamma normalization and selection, ablation based beta transfer, and knowledge distillation based fine-tuning.

3.1 Batch Normalization

Batch Normalization [19] is proposed to improve the performance and training stability of DNN. The main idea is to normalize the inputs of each layer such that they have standard gaussian distribution for each batch, and then scale (by γ) and shift (by β) the results by learning.

$$\hat{x_i} \leftarrow \frac{x_i - \mu_B}{\sqrt{\sigma_B^2 + \epsilon}} \tag{1}$$

$$BN_{\gamma,\beta}(x_i) \leftarrow \gamma_i \hat{x_i} + \beta_i \tag{2}$$

where μ_B and σ_B denote the mean and variance of the mini-batch respectively, $\hat{x_i}$ and $BN_{\gamma,\beta}(x_i)$ are the normalized result of the ith input and the ith final output of the Batch Normalization.

3.2 Batch Normalization Based Channel-Level Pruning

In the proposed approach of Liu *et al.* [6], the global pruning strategy will lead to a critical issue. We did a statistics on the gamma values of each BN layer and showed the results in Fig. 1. As shown in Fig. 1, the distribution of gamma in each BN layer is quite different, where the line within the box, upper and lower whisker denote average, maximum and minimum value, respectively. Take the BN layers No. 9, 11 and 12 for example, their maximum and average gamma are very small, i.e. all their channels will be pruned when the global pruning ratio is set high. This is so called "over-pruning issue".

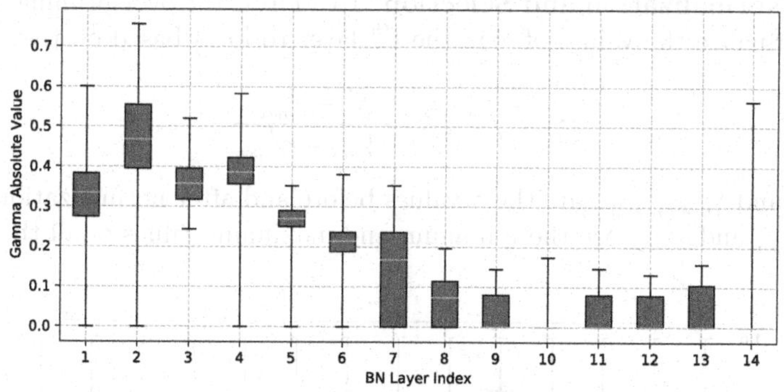

Fig. 1. The distribution of gamma in each BN layer

Another drawback of Liu *et al.* is that they didn't take the corresponding β of the pruned γ into account, i.e. the corresponding β are simply pruned even when β are large. According to Eq. 2, β is the parameter that shift the normalized input after scaling, i.e. γ and β jointly defined the final output of BN layer. When the β of pruned channels are large enough, the BN output will have great influence to the subsequent convolution layer.

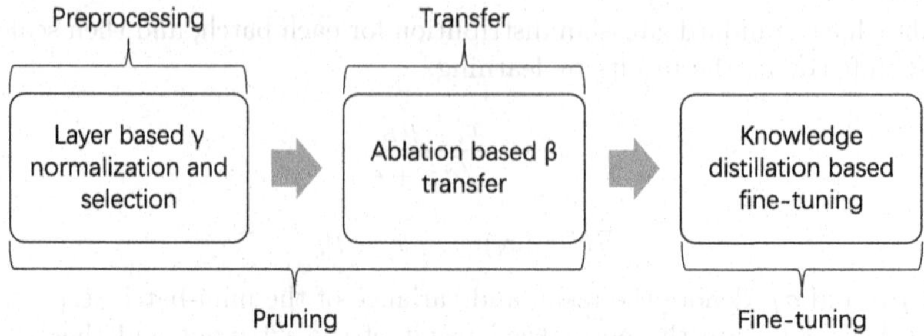

Fig. 2. Flow chart of our method

3.3 Our Method

As shown in the Fig. 2, our method includes three stages: (1) local γ normalization and selection, (2) ablation based β transfer, and (3) knowledge distillation based fine-tuning. Particularly, Pruning includes two stages: Preprocessing and Transfer. In Preprocessing, we collect the channel number of each BN layer via local γ normalization and selection, which will be used to construct a new slim model. Then, we transfer the retained parameters with ablation based β transfer, from the old model to the new one in the stage of Transfer. Fine-tuning is used to improve the accuracy of the new slim model, where we apply the proposed knowledge distillation based fine-tuning.

Local γ Normalization and Selection. To address the over-pruning issue, we firstly normalize the values of γ in the lth layer to $[0, 1]$ based on the min-max rule:

$$\gamma^l_{normalized} = \frac{\gamma^l - \gamma^l_{min}}{\gamma^l_{max} - \gamma^l_{min}} \tag{3}$$

where γ^l and $\gamma^l_{normalized}$ are the γ values before and after normalization respectively, γ^l_{min} and γ^l_{max} are the minimum and maximum values of all the γ^l.

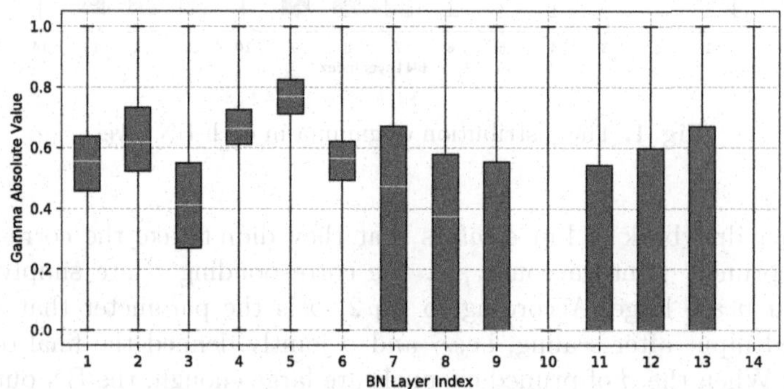

Fig. 3. The distribution of gamma after local normalization in each BN layer

Then, we sort all the normalized γ across all the BN layers. Finally, we prune the channels with smallest γ according to the pruning ratio ρ.

We applied local normalization to the gamma of each BN layer and showed the result in Fig. 3. As shown in Fig. 3, the distribution of gamma after local normalization is more balanced compared to Fig. 1, and all the maximum gamma of each BN layer are normalized to 1. Due to the local min-max normalization, we can guarantee that there will be at least one channel retained after pruning. The global sort ignores the local relative information, which exactly lead to over-pruning issue. We believe local normalization introduces local relative information into channel selection, which makes the pruning more balanced.

Ablation Based β Transfer. According to Eq. 2, γ and β are used to scale and shift the normalized feature map, respectively. If the γ is treated as zero, then the feature map is only defined by the β. In such way, we can treat the BN output of pruned channels as constant feature maps. In the convolution operation of the following convolution layer, such constant feature maps will be convolved and added together with the rest channels. Therefore, the influence of such constant maps shouldn't be ignored, especially when the corresponding β are large enough.

Ye *et al.* [18] proposed an approach to absorb the corresponding β into the following convolution layer. However, they only considered the case of ReLU activation. For the activation function like PReLU, we utilize the retained parameters of PReLU for non-linear mapping. The method we proposed is presented as below and visualized in Fig. 4:

* If the subsequent convolution layer is followed by a non-BN layer:

$$x^{l+1} = \sigma(w^{l+1} * x^l + b^{l+1}) \tag{4}$$

where x^l denotes the output of current BN layer, x^{l+1}, σ, w^{l+1} and b^{l+1} are output, activation function, weight and bias of the subsequent convolution layer respectively.
Then let β^l of the BN layer (the lth layer) be absorbed in the convolution layer (the $(l+1)^{th}$ layer)'s bias (b^{l+1})

$$b_{new}^{l+1} = b^{l+1} + \sum^{a}(I(\beta^l) \cdot \sigma(\beta^l) \sum^{i} \sum^{j} w_{:,a,i,j}^{l+1}) \tag{5}$$

where b^{l+1} and w^{l+1} are the bias and weight of the subsequent convolution layer. β^l and $I(\beta^l)$ are the values of β and bool matrix of discarded β index in current BN layer. Specially, $w_{:,a,i,j}^{l+1}$ denotes the filters with a input channels and kernel size $i \times j$.

$$x^{l+1} \approx \sigma_{\neg I(\beta^l)}(w^{l+1} * x^l + b_{new}^{l+1}) \tag{6}$$

where $\neg I(\beta^l)$ is the negative matrix of $I(\beta^l)$.

* If the subsequent convolution layer is followed by a BN layer, then the convolution layer's bias doesn't work. Therefor, we absorb β into *running_mean* of next BN layer:

$$x^{l+2} = \sigma(\gamma^{l+2} \cdot \mathcal{BN}_{\mu^{l+2}}(w^{l+1} * x^l + b^{l+1}) + \beta^{l+2}) \tag{7}$$

where x^{l+2}, γ^{l+2}, $\mathcal{BN}_{\mu^{l+2}}(\cdot)$ and β^{l+2} are the output, γ, normalization by mean μ and β of the BN layer behind the subsequent convolution layer respectively, w^{l+1} and b^{l+1} are the weight and bias of subsequent convolution layer. Then let β^l of the BN layer (the lth layer) be absorbed in the BN layer (the $(l+2)^{th}$ layer)'s running mean (μ^{l+2})

$$\mu_{new}^{l+2} = \mu^{l+2} - \sum^{a}(I(\beta^l) \cdot \sigma(\beta^l) \sum^{i}\sum^{j} w_{:,a,i,j}^{l+1}) \tag{8}$$

where μ^{l+2} is the running mean of the BN layer behind the subsequent convolution layer.

$$x^{l+2} \approx \sigma_{\neg I(\beta^l)}(\gamma^{l+2} \cdot \mathcal{BN}_{\mu_{new}^{l+2}}(w^{l+1} * x^l + b^{l+1}) + \beta^{l+2}) \tag{9}$$

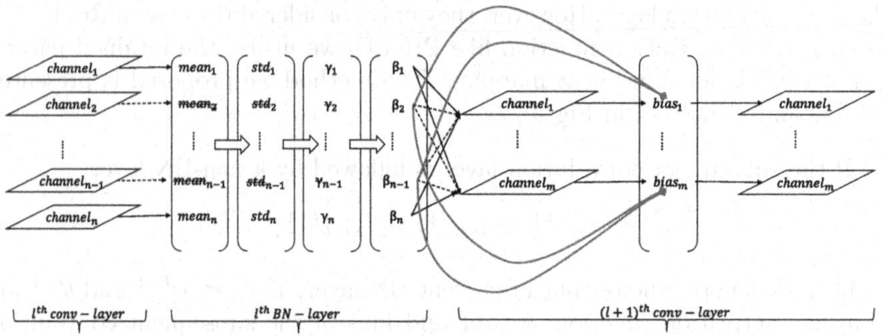

(1) If the subsequent convolution layer is followed by a non-BN layer

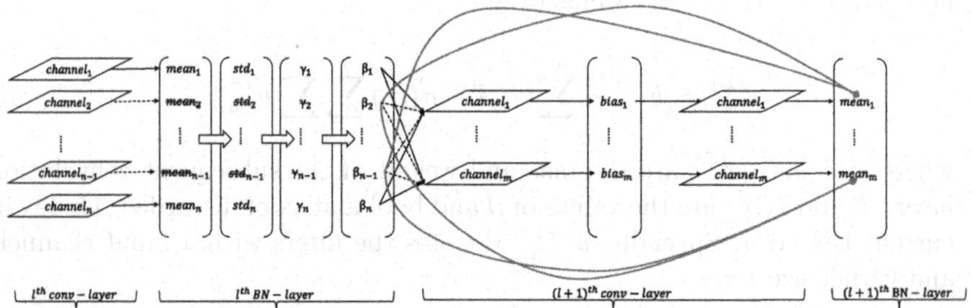

(2) If the subsequent convolution layer is followed by a BN layer

Fig. 4. Consider all the parameters as ice, the ice β melts and flows through the subsequent convolution layer(s) and is frozen into the (1) *bias* or (2) *running_mean*. The blue lines denote the convolution output of corresponding channels and filters. (Color figure online)

Knowledge Distillation Based Fine-Tuning. In fine-tuning process, we use knowledge distillation [7] to help the pruned model restore the accuracy as much as possible. The total loss of fine-tuning includes classification loss ($\mathcal{L}(\cdot)$) with ground-truth label, and regression loss (mean square error, MSE) with teacher model's output. The hyperparameter ξ is used to control the ratio between the classification and regression loss. The fine-tuning objective function is given as below:

$$min \frac{1}{n} \sum_{i=1}^{n} [\xi \cdot \mathcal{L}(\mathcal{H}_{\mathrm{s}}(x_i), y_i) + \frac{(1-\xi)}{2} (\mathcal{H}_{\mathrm{s}}(x_i) - \mathcal{H}_{\mathrm{t}}(x_i))^2] \tag{10}$$

where n, x_i and y_i, $\mathcal{H}(\cdot)$ are the number of samples, input, ground-truth label of the ith sample and network mapping function, respectively, the subscripts s and t denote student model and teacher model. We select the models trained without ℓ_1 regularization (sparsity constraint) as our teacher models.

Since distillation is hard to converge when the number of classes is big [9], the fine-tuning objective function of models for face recognition is given as below:

$$min \frac{1}{n} \sum_{i=1}^{n} [\xi \cdot \mathcal{L}(\mathcal{H}_{\mathrm{s}}(x_i), y_i) + \frac{(1-\xi)}{2} (\mathcal{H}_{\mathrm{s}}^{\mathrm{feature}}(x_i) - \mathcal{H}_{\mathrm{t}}^{\mathrm{feature}}(x_i))^2] \tag{11}$$

where $\mathcal{H}_{*}^{\mathrm{feature}}(\cdot)$ denotes the mapping function of neural network for the face feature output.

4 Experiments and Results

4.1 Datasets

CIFAR. Both CIFAR-10 and CIFAR-100 datasets consist of 60,000 32 × 32 colour images, including 50,000 training images and 10,000 test images. CIFAR-10 images are from 10 classes while CIFAR-100 images are from 100 classes.

CASIA-WebFace & LFW. The CASIA-WebFace consists of 49,4414 color face images from 10,575 classes. The duplicate subjects in CASIA-WebFace and LFW were removed. CASIA-WebFace + LFW is a suitable combination for large scale face recognition in the wild. The LFW dataset contains more than 13,000 images of faces collected from the web.

4.2 Models

VGG. We select two variants [20,21] of VGG-16 [1] as representatives of plain CNN to validate our method on CIFAR-10 and CIFAR-100. Both variants introduce Batch Normalization layer into VGG-16, while the variant No. 1 [20] adds two more convolution layers and remains only one fully-connection layer, No. 2 [21] introduce Dropout into the model. In our experiments of VGG-16, the variant No. 1 and No. 2 are the same with Liu's [6] and Li's [15], respectively.

ResNet. We select ResNet-164-pre-activation [22] as a representative of Residual CNN to validate our method on CIFAR-10 and CIFAR-100. The basic convolution block of the model is $BN \rightarrow Activation \rightarrow Convolution$, instead of $Convolution \rightarrow Activaiton \rightarrow BN$. To compare with the results of Li *et al.* [15] directly, we also apply our method to ResNet-56 [3].

SphereFace. We select SphereFace20 [23] with Batch Normalization to validate our method on CASIA-WebFace and LFW.

4.3 Hyperparameters

In CIFAR dataset, random crop, mirror, and normalization are applied to the samples and we optimize all the models for 160 epochs by SGD-momentum-nesterov with initial learning rate of 0.1, momentum of 0.9, weight decay of 0.0001, l_1 regularization penalty of 0.0001 and reduce the learning rate by cosine annealing of SGDR. The same data augmentations, momentum and learning rate scheduler are reserved in fine-tuning for 60 epochs, the initial learning rate, l_1 regularization penalty and weight decay are changed respectively to 0.01, 0, 0. However, the loss ratio of knowledge distillation should vary with the pruning ratio, we usually set the loss ratio equal to the pruning ratio.

In CASIA-WebFace dataset, only mirror and normalization are applied to the samples and the models are trained for 28 epochs by SGD-momentum-nesterov with initial learning rate of 0.05, momentum of 0.9, weight decay of 0.0005, l_1 regularization penalty of 0.0001 and the learning rate is reduced by 0.1 at the 16th and 24th epochs. The same data augmentations, momentum and weight decay are used in fine-tuning for 28 epochs, the initial learning rate and l_1 regularization penalty are changed respectively to 0.0001, 0. And the learning rate is reduced by cosine annealing of SGDR. For all the BN layers, we initialize γ and β to 0.5 and 0 respectively.

4.4 Results

As shown in the Table 1, when the pruning ratio was set as 70%, the model pruned with our local γ normalization and selection achieved 6.19% error on CIFAR-10 dataset, without any additional process. While ablation based β transfer and knowledge distillation based fine tuning can further reduce the error rate

Table 1. ResNet control experiment on CIFAR10

Model	Test error (%)	Ablation based β transfer	Knowledge distillation
ResNet	6.19		
	6.07 (−0.12)	✓	
	5.61 (−0.58)		✓
	5.41 (**−0.78**)	✓	✓

Table 2. Performance on CIFAR-10

	VGG16				ResNet164			
	ρ (%)	Error (%)	Params (M)	FLOPs ($\times 10^8$)	ρ (%)	Error (%)	Params (M)	FLOPs ($\times 10^8$)
Liu [6]	0	6.34	20.04	7.97	0	5.42	1.70	4.99
	70	6.20	**2.30**	3.91	40	5.08	1.44	3.81
					60	5.27	1.10	2.75
Ours	0	6.33	20.04	7.97	0	5.32	1.72	5.00
	70	**5.96**	2.32	**3.83**	40	**4.96**	1.00	2.28
					60	5.07	**0.61**	**1.33**

to 6.07% and 5.61%, respectively, combination of the two processes reduced the error rate to 5.41%. Therefore, in the following experiments, both ablation based β transfer and knowledge distillation were applied after the γ based pruning.

Table 3. Performance on CIFAR-100

	VGG16				ResNet164			
	ρ (%)	Error (%)	Params (M)	FLOPs ($\times 10^8$)	ρ (%)	Error (%)	Params (M)	FLOPs ($\times 10^8$)
Liu [6]	0	26.74	20.08	7.97	0	23.37	1.73	4.99
	50	26.52	5.00	5.01	40	22.87	1.46	3.33
					60	23.91	1.21	2.47
Ours	0	26.42	20.08	7.97	0	23.37	1.74	5.00
	50	**25.87**	**4.94**	**4.07**	40	**22.51**	1.02	2.09
					60	23.31	**0.63**	**1.32**

Tables 2 and 3 show the performance of our approach applied to prune a variant of VGG-16 [20] and ResNet-164-preactivation [22] on CIFAR-10 and CIFAR-100, with different pruning ratios ρ. The performance of Liu *et al.* [6] is also included for comparison. One can observe from the two tables that our pruning approach can achieve comparable accuracy with Liu's approach, but with much higher reduction in number of parameters and FLOPs. Take ResNet for example, when prunning ratio is set as 60%, the sizes of our pruned model for CIFAR-10 and CIFAR-100 are 0.61M and 0.63M, respectively, which are roughly half the size of the models pruned by Liu's approach. Similar conclusions can also be suggested for FLOPs. Regarding to the performance of ResNet on CIFAR-100 database, while significantly higher reduction in number of parameters and FLOPs were achieved, our approach achieved even better performance than Liu's work in terms of test error.

Table 4 lists the performance of another variant of VGG16 [21] and ResNet56 [3] on CIFAR-10 without accuracy loss, together with that of Li *et al.* [15] and Luo *et al.* [17]. The experimental results of Li are from their paper while Luo's are from our implementation. Li's channel-level pruning is layer-wise, where Pruned-A is to prune each layer with fixed pruning ratio and skip some pruning-sensitive layers while Pruned-B is to prune the layers of different depths with

Table 4. Comparison with other channel-level pruning on CIFAR-10 without accuracy loss

Method	VGG16			
	Pruning ratio or Policy	Error (%)	Params (M)	Speedup
Li [15]	0	6.75	15.00	1×
	Pruned-A	6.60	5.40	1.52×
Luo [17] (our impl.)	0	6.31	14.99	1×
	50	6.24	4.09	2.04×
Ours	65	**6.20**	**1.98**	**2.24**×
Method	ResNet56			
	Pruning ratio or Policy	Error (%)	Params (M)	Speedup
Li [15]	0	6.96	0.85	1×
	Pruned-B	6.94	0.73	1.37×
Luo [17] (our impl.)	0	6.00	0.86	1×
	40	5.99	0.51	1.62×
Ours	50	**5.96**	**0.42**	**1.99**×

different pruning ratio and skip more pruning-sensitive layers. Li's FLOPs is only counted from convolution and fully-connection layers while ours is from the whole neural network, hence we use speedup instead of FLOPs to measure acceleration. Luo's channel-level pruning is also layer-wise but convolution-layer-only, they use greedy algorithm to obtain a minimum subset of filters in convolution layers. However, Luo takes global average pooling layer in place of fully-connection layers for VGG16, which we don't consider as pruning and we didn't take it into our implementation. As shown in the table, without accuracy loss on VGG16 and ResNet56, our method achieves 86.79% and 51.46% reduction in parameters while 55.25% and 49.87% reduction in FLOPs, respectively.

Table 5. Performance on LFW

Model	ρ (%)	Error (%)	Parameters (M)	FLOPs ($\times 10^8$)
SphereFace20	0	1.00	22.68	35.04
	30	1.20	19.55	24.23
	40	1.27	18.34	21.53
	50	1.33	17.23	18.65

Table 5 lists the performance on LFW for SphereFace20 using our approach, when the network was trained using CASIA-WebFace. As shown in the table, our approach can reduce around 24% of the parameters and 47% of the FLOPs, when the pruning ratio was set as 50%, with a cost of 0.33% increase in classification error.

5 Conclusion

We have proposed a Batch Normalization based channel-level pruning method with local normalization and selection, ablation based β transfer and knowledge distillation based fine-tuning. Our approach firstly normalize the values of γ at each BN layer and then prune the channels whose γ values are smaller than a layer adaptive threshold. After channel pruning, ablation based β transfer, and knowledge distillation based fine tuning are also applied to further improve the performance of pruned model. The experimental results on CIFAR-10, CIFAR-100 and LFW clearly suggest that our approach can achieve much efficient pruning in terms of reduction in parameters and FLOPs. Take ResNet for example, when pruning ratio is set as 60%, the sizes of our pruned model for CIFAR-10 and CIFAR-100 are 0.61M and 0.63M, respectively, which are roughly half the size of the models pruned by Liu's approach. Similar conclusions can also be suggested for FLOPs. Compared to other channel-level pruning [15,17] without accuracy loss on VGG16 and ResNet56, our method achieves 86.79% and 51.46% reduction in parameters while 55.25% and 49.87% reduction in FLOPs, respectively.

References

1. Simonyan, K., Zisserman, A.: Very deep convolutional networks for large-scale image recognition. arXiv preprint: arXiv:1409.1556 (2014)
2. Szegedy, C., et al.: Going deeper with convolutions. In: Proceedings of the IEEE Conference on Computer Vision and Pattern Recognition, pp. 1–9 (2015)
3. He, K., Zhang, X., Ren, S., Sun, J.: Deep residual learning for image recognition. In: Proceedings of the IEEE Conference on Computer Vision and Pattern Recognition, pp. 770–778 (2016)
4. Huang, G., Liu, Z., Van Der Maaten, L., Weinberger, K.Q.: Densely connected convolutional networks. In: CVPR, vol. 1, p. 3 (2017)
5. Denil, M., Shakibi, B., Dinh, L., De Freitas, N., et al.: Predicting parameters in deep learning. In: Advances in Neural Information Processing Systems, pp. 2148–2156 (2013)
6. Liu, Z., Li, J., Shen, Z., Huang, G., Yan, S., Zhang, C.: Learning efficient convolutional networks through network slimming. In: 2017 IEEE International Conference on Computer Vision (ICCV), pp. 2755–2763. IEEE (2017)
7. Ba, J., Caruana, R.: Do deep nets really need to be deep? In: Ghahramani, Z., Welling, M., Cortes, C., Lawrence, N.D., Weinberger, K.Q. (eds.) Advances in Neural Information Processing Systems 27, pp. 2654–2662. Curran Associates, Inc. (2014)
8. Hinton, G., Vinyals, O., Dean, J.: Distilling the knowledge in a neural network. arXiv preprint: arXiv:1503.02531 (2015)
9. Luo, P., Zhu, Z., Liu, Z., Wang, X., Tang, X., et al.: Face model compression by distilling knowledge from neurons. In: AAAI, pp. 3560–3566 (2016)
10. Mirzadeh, S.I., Farajtabar, M., Li, A., Ghasemzadeh, H.: Improved knowledge distillation via teacher assistant: bridging the gap between student and teacher. arXiv preprint: arXiv:1902.03393 (2019)

11. LeCun, Y., Denker, J.S., Solla, S.A.: Optimal brain damage. In: Advances in Neural Information Processing Systems, pp. 598–605 (1990)
12. Hassibi, B., Stork, D.: Second order derivaties for network prunning: optimal brain surgeon. In: Advances in NIPS 5, pp. 164–171 (1993)
13. Han, S., Pool, J., Tran, J., Dally, W.: Learning both weights and connections for efficient neural network. In: Advances in Neural Information Processing Systems, pp. 1135–1143 (2015)
14. Han, S., Mao, H., Dally, W.J.: Deep compression: Compressing deep neural networks with pruning, trained quantization and Huffman coding. arXiv preprint: arXiv:1510.00149 (2015)
15. Li, H., Kadav, A., Durdanovic, I., Samet, H., Graf, H.P.: Pruning filters for efficient convnets. arXiv preprint: arXiv:1608.08710 (2016)
16. He, Y., Zhang, X., Sun, J.: Channel pruning for accelerating very deep neural networks. In: International Conference on Computer Vision (ICCV), vol. 2 (2017)
17. Luo, J.H., Wu, J., Lin, W.: Thinet: A filter level pruning method for deep neural network compression. arXiv preprint: arXiv:1707.06342 (2017)
18. Ye, J., Lu, X., Lin, Z., Wang, J.Z.: Rethinking the smaller-norm-less-informative assumption in channel pruning of convolution layers. arXiv preprint: arXiv:1802.00124 (2018)
19. Ioffe, S., Szegedy, C.: Batch normalization: Accelerating deep network training by reducing internal covariate shift. arXiv preprint: arXiv:1502.03167 (2015)
20. foolwood: pytorch-slimming (2018). https://github.com/foolwood/pytorch-slimming
21. szagoruyko: cifar.torch (2014). https://github.com/szagoruyko/cifar.torch
22. He, K., Zhang, X., Ren, S., Sun, J.: Identity mappings in deep residual networks. In: Leibe, B., Matas, J., Sebe, N., Welling, M. (eds.) ECCV 2016, Part IV. LNCS, vol. 9908, pp. 630–645. Springer, Cham (2016). https://doi.org/10.1007/978-3-319-46493-0_38
23. Liu, W., Zhang, Y.M., Li, X., Yu, Z., Dai, B., Zhao, T., Song, L.: Deep hyperspherical learning. In: Advances in Neural Information Processing Systems, pp. 3950–3960 (2017)

Search for an Optimal Architecture

On Practical Approach to Uniform Quantization of Non-redundant Neural Networks

Alexander Goncharenko[1,2(✉)], Andrey Denisov[1,2], Sergey Alyamkin[1], and Evgeny Terentev[3]

[1] Expasoft LLC, Novosibirsk, Russia
expasoft@expasoft.ru
[2] Novosibirsk State University, Novosibirsk, Russia
[3] Microtech, Moscow, Russia
https://expasoft.com/, https://english.nsu.ru/, https://microtech.ai

Abstract. The neural network quantization is highly desired procedure to perform before running the neural networks on mobile devices. Quantization without fine-tuning leads to accuracy drop of the model, whereas commonly used training with quantization is done on the full set of the labeled data and therefore is both time- and resource-consuming. Real life applications require simplification and acceleration of the quantization procedure that will maintain the accuracy of full-precision neural network, especially for modern mobile neural network architectures like Mobilenet-v1, MobileNet-v2 and MNAS.

Here we present two methods to significantly optimize the training with the quantization procedure. The first one is introducing the trained scale factors for discretization thresholds that are separate for each filter. The second one is based on mutual rescaling of consequent depth-wise separable convolution and convolution layers. Using the proposed techniques, we quantize the modern mobile architectures of neural networks with the set of train data of only ∼10% of the total ImageNet 2012 sample. Such reduction of the train dataset size and a small number of trainable parameters allow to fine-tune the network for several hours while maintaining the high accuracy of the quantized model (the accuracy drop was less than 0.5%). The ready-for-use models and code are available at: https://github.com/agoncharenko1992/FAT-fast-adjustable-threshold.

Keywords: Machine learning · Quantization · Distillation · Neural networks

1 Introduction

Mobile neural network architectures [6,18,21] allow running AI solutions on the mobile devices due to the small size of models, low memory consumption, and

I. V. Tetko et al. (Eds.): ICANN 2019, LNCS 11728, pp. 349–360, 2019.
https://doi.org/10.1007/978-3-030-30484-3_29

high processing speed while providing a relatively high level of accuracy in the image recognition tasks. In spite of their high computational efficiency, these networks continuously undergo the further optimization to meet the requirements of edge devices. One of the promising optimization directions is to use quantization to int8, which is natively supported by the mobile processors. From a practical point of view, at the moment there is only one TF-lite framework[1] which allows the usage of quantized neural networks. It applies int8 quantization, either with or without training. Both methods have the certain advantages and disadvantages.

Quantization of the neural network without training is a fast process as in this case a pre-trained model is used. However, the accuracy of the resultant network is particularly low compared to the one typically obtained in the commonly used mobile architectures of neural networks [11]. On the other hand, quantization with training is a resource-intensive task which results in the low applicability of this approach.

The current article suggests a method which allows speeding up the procedure of training with quantization and at the same time preserves a high accuracy of results for 8-bit discretization.

2 Related Work

In general case the procedure of neural network quantization implies the discretization of weights and input values of each layer. Mapping from the space of float32 values to the space of signed integer values with n significant digits is defined by the following formulae:

$$S_w = \frac{2^n - 1}{T_w} \tag{1}$$

$$T_w = max|W| \tag{2}$$

$$W_{int} = \lfloor S_w \cdot W \rceil \tag{3}$$

$$\begin{aligned} W_q &= clip(W_{int}, -(2^{n-1} - 1), 2^{n-1} - 1) \\ &= min(max(W_{int}, -(2^{n-1} - 1)), 2^{n-1} - 1) \end{aligned}$$

Here $\lfloor \rceil$ is rounding to the nearest integer number, W – weights of some layer of the neural network, T – quantization threshold, max calculates the maximum value across all axes of the tensor. Input values can be quantized both to signed and unsigned integer numbers depending on the activation function on the previous layer.

$$S_i = \frac{2^n - 1}{T_i} \tag{4}$$

[1] https://www.tensorflow.org/lite.

$$T_i = max|I| \quad (5)$$

$$I_{int} = \lfloor S_i \cdot I \rceil \quad (6)$$

$$I_q^{signed} = clip(I_{int}, -(2^{n-1} - 1), 2^{n-1} - 1) \quad (7)$$

$$I_q^{unsigned} = clip(I_{int}, 0, 2^n - 1) \quad (8)$$

After all inputs and weights of the neural network are quantized, the procedure of convolution is performed in a usual way. It is necessary to mention that the result of operation must be in higher bit capacity than the operands. For example, in Ref. [9] the authors use a scheme where weights and activations are quantized to 8-bits while accumulators are 32-bit values.

Potentially the quantization threshold can be calculated on the fly, which, however, can significantly slow down the processing speed on a device with the low system resources. It is one of the reasons why the quantization thresholds are usually calculated beforehand in a calibration procedure. A set of data is provided to the network input to find the desired thresholds (in the example above - the maximum absolute value) of each layer. The calibration dataset contains the most typical data for the certain network and this data does not have to be labeled according to the procedure described above.

2.1 Quantization with Knowledge Distillation

The knowledge distillation method was proposed by Hinton [5] as an approach to neural network quality improvement. Its main idea is training of neural networks with the help of the pre-trained network. In Refs. [14,15] this method was successfully used in the following form: a full-precision model was used as a model-teacher, and the quantized neural network - as a model-student. Such paradigm of learning gives not only a higher quality of the quantized network inference, but also allows reducing the bit capacity of the quantized data while keeping an acceptable level of accuracy.

2.2 Quantization Without Fine-Tuning

Some frameworks allow using the quantization of neural networks without fine-tuning. The most known examples are TensorRT[2], Tensorflow [1] and Distiller framework from Nervana Systems[3]. However, in the last two models the calculation of quantization coefficients is done on the fly, which can potentially slow down the operation speed of neural networks on the mobile devices. In addition, to the best of our knowledge, the TensorRT framework does not support quantization of neural networks with the architectures like MobileNet.

[2] https://developer.nvidia.com/tensorrt - NVIDIA TensorRT™ platform, 2018.

[3] https://github.com/NervanaSystems/distiller.

2.3 Quantization with Training/Fine-Tuning

One of the main focus points of research publications over the last years is the development of methods that allow to minimize the accuracy drop after the neural network quantization. The first results in this field were obtained in Refs. [4,7,16,22]. The authors used the Straight Through Estimator (STE) [3] for training the weights of neural networks into 2 or 3 bit integer representation. Nevertheless, such networks had substantially lower accuracy than their full-precision analogs.

The most recent achievements in this field are presented in Refs. [13,23] where the quality of trained models is almost the same as for the original architectures. Moreover, in Ref. [23] the authors emphasize the importance of the quantized networks ensembling which can potentially be used for binary quantized networks. In Ref. [9] the authors report the whole framework for modification of the network architecture allowing the further launch of learned quantized models on the mobile devices.

In Ref. [2] the authors use the procedure of threshold training which is similar to the method suggested in our work. However, the reported approach has substantial shortcomings that prevent its usage for fast conversion of the pre-trained neural network on the mobile devices. First of all there is a requirement to train the threshold on the full ImageNet dataset [17], and second of all there are no examples demonstrating the accuracy of networks which are considered to be the standards for the mobile platforms.

In the current paper we propose a novel approach to set the quantization threshold with the fast fine-tuning procedure on a small set of unlabeled data that allows to overcome the main drawbacks of the known methods. We demonstrate the performance of our approach on the modern mobile neural network architectures (MobileNet-v2, MNAS).

3 Method Description

Under the certain conditions (see Fig. 1) the processed model can significantly degrade during the quantization process. The presence of outliers for weights distribution shown in Fig. 1 forces to choose a high value for thresholds that leads to accuracy degradation of the quantized model.

The outliers can appear due to several reasons, namely specific features of the calibration dataset such as class imbalance or non-typical input data. They also can be a natural feature of the neural network, that are, for example, weight outliers formed during training or the reaction of some neurons on the features with the maximum value.

Overall it is impossible to avoid the outliers completely because they are closely associated with the fundamental features of the neural networks. However, there is a chance to find a compromise between the value of threshold and distortion of other values during quantization, and thus get a better quality of the quantized neural network.

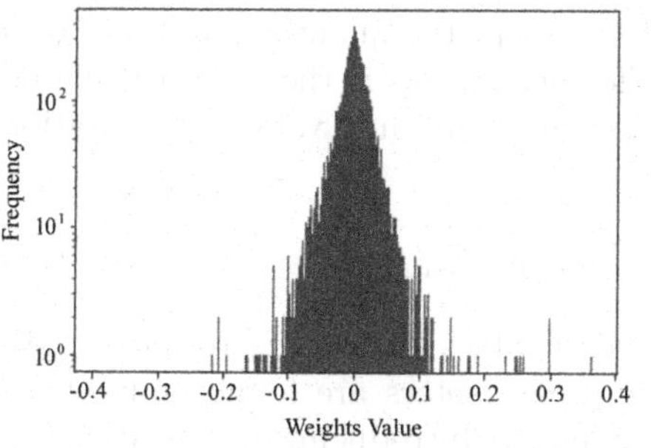

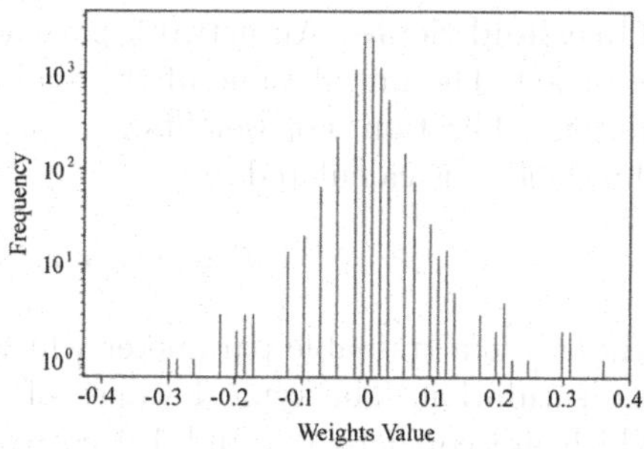

Fig. 1. Distribution of weights of ResNet-50 neural network before the quantization procedure (on the left) and after it (on the right). The number of values appeared in bins near zero increased significantly.

3.1 Quantization with the Threshold Fine-Tuning

Differentiable Quantization Threshold. In Refs. [3,7,22] it is shown that the Straight Through Estimator (STE) can be used to define a derivative of a function which is non-differentiable in the usual sense (*round*, *sign*, *clip*, etc.). Therefore, the value which is an argument of this function becomes differentiable and can be trained with the method of steepest descent, also called the gradient descent method. Such variable is a quantization threshold and its training can directly lead to the optimal quality of the quantized network. This approach can be further optimized through some modifications as described below.

Batch Normalization Folding. Batch normalization (BN) layers play an important role in training of neural networks because they speed up the train procedure convergence [8]. Before making the quantization of neural network weights, we suggest to perform the batch normalization folding with the network weights similar to the method described in Ref. [9]. As a result, we obtain the new weights calculated by the following formulae:

$$W_{fold} = \frac{\gamma W}{\sqrt{\sigma^2 + \varepsilon}} \tag{9}$$

$$b_{fold} = \beta - \frac{\gamma \mu}{\sqrt{\sigma^2 + \varepsilon}} \tag{10}$$

where μ is moving average, σ is moving deviation, γ and β are learnable batchnorm parameters.

We apply quantization to weights which were fused with the BN layers because it simplifies the discretization and speeds up the neural network inference. Further in this article the folded weights will be implied (unless specified otherwise).

Threshold Scale. All network parameters except the quantization thresholds are fixed. The initial value of thresholds for activations is the value calculated during calibration. For weights it is the maximum absolute value. Quantization threshold T is calculated as

$$T = clip(\alpha, min_{\alpha}, max_{\alpha}) \cdot T_{max} \tag{11}$$

where α is a trainable parameter which takes values from min_{α} to max_{α} with the saturation. The typical values of these parameters are found empirically, which are equal to 0.5 and 1.0 correspondingly. Introducing the scale factor simplifies the network training since the update of thresholds is done with the different learning rates for different layers of the neural network as they can have various orders of values. For example, values on the intermediate layers of VGG network [20] may increase up to 7 times in comparison with the values on the first layers.

Therefore the quantization procedure can be formalized as follows:

$$T_{adj} = clip(\alpha, 0.5, 1) \cdot T_i \tag{12}$$

$$S_I = \frac{2^n - 1}{T_{adj}} \tag{13}$$

$$I_q = \lfloor I \cdot S_I \rceil \tag{14}$$

The similar procedure is performed for weights. The current quantization scheme has two non-differentiable functions, namely *round* and *clip*. The derivatives of these functions can be defined as:

$$I_q = \lfloor I \rceil \tag{15}$$

$$\frac{dI_q}{dI} = 1 \tag{16}$$

$$X_c = clip(X, a, b) \tag{17}$$

$$\frac{dX_c}{dX} = \begin{cases} 1, if\ X \in [a, b] \\ 0, otherwise \end{cases}$$

Bias quantization is performed similar to Ref. [9]:

$$b_q = clip(\lfloor S_i \cdot S_w \cdot b \rceil, -(2^{31} - 1), 2^{31} - 1) \tag{18}$$

Training of Asymmetric Thresholds. Quantization with the symmetric thresholds described in the previous sections is easy to implement on the certain devices, however, it uses an available spectrum of integer values inefficiently which significantly decreases the accuracy of quantized models. The authors in Ref. [9] effectively implemented quantization with the asymmetric thresholds for mobile devices, so it was decided to adapt the described above training procedure for the asymmetric thresholds.

There are left (T_l) and right (T_r) range limits for asymmetric thresholds. However, for quantization procedure it is more convenient to use other two values: left limit and width, and train these parameters. If the left limit is equal to 0, then scaling of this value has no effect. That is why a shift for the left limit is introduced. It is calculated as:

$$R = T_r - T_l \tag{19}$$

$$T_{adj} = T_l + clip(\alpha_T, min_{\alpha_T}, max_{\alpha_T}) \cdot R \tag{20}$$

The coefficients min_{α_T}, max_{α_T} are set empirically. They are equal to -0.2 and 0.4 in the case of signed variables, and to 0 and 0.4 in the case of unsigned. The range width is selected in a similar way. The values of min_{α_R}, max_{α_R} are also empiric and equal to 0.5 and 1.

$$R_{adj} = clip(\alpha_R, min_{\alpha_R}, max_{\alpha_R}) \cdot R \tag{21}$$

Vector Quantization. Sometimes due to the high range of weight values it is possible to perform the discretization procedure more softly, using the different thresholds for different filters of the convolutional layer. Therefore, instead of a single quantization factor for the whole convolutional layer (scalar quantization) there is a group of factors (vector quantization). This procedure does not complicate the realization on devices, however, it allows increasing the accuracy of the quantized model significantly. The considerable improvement of accuracy is observed for the models with the architecture using the depth-wise separable convolutions. The most known networks of this type are MobileNet-v1 [6] and MobileNet-v2 [18].

3.2 Training on the Unlabeled Data

Most articles related to the neural network quantization use the labeled dataset for training the discretization thresholds or directly the network weights. In the proposed approach it is recommended to discard the initial labels of train data which significantly speeds up the transition from a trained non-quantized network to a quantized one as it reduces the requirements to the train dataset. We also suggest to optimize the root-mean-square error (RMSE) between the outputs of the quantized and original networks before applying the softmax function, while leaving the parameters of the original network unchanged.

The suggested above technique can be considered as a special type of quantization with the distillation [14] where all components related to the labeled data are absent.

The total loss function L is calculated by the following formula:

$$L(x; W_T, W_A) = \alpha H(y, z^T) + \beta H(y, z^A) + \gamma H(z^T, z^A) \tag{22}$$

In our case α and β are equal to 0, and

$$H(z^T, z^A) = \sqrt{\sum_{i=1}^{N} \frac{(z_i^T - z_i^A)^2}{N}} \tag{23}$$

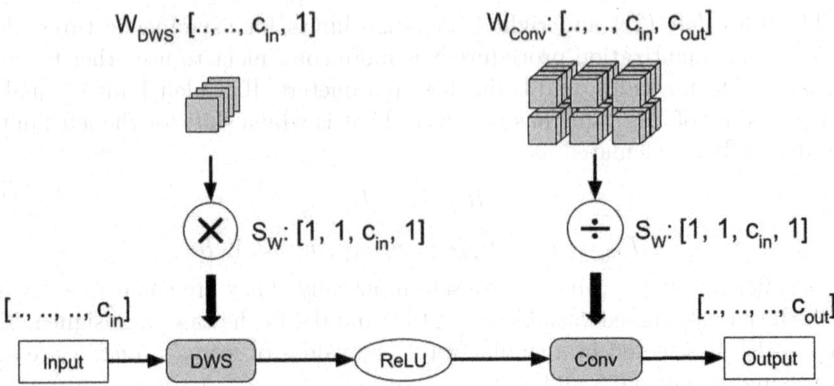

Fig. 2. Scaling the filters of DWS + Convolution layers where the output of DWS + Convolution remains unchanged. Numbers in square brackets denote the dimension of the scaling factors. W_{DWS} represents the weights of the DWS layer, and W_{CONV} - the weights of the convolution layer. Note that the scaling factor $S_W > 0$.

where:

- z^T is the output of non-quantized neural network,
- z^A is the output of quantized neural network,
- N is batch size,
- y is the label of x example.

3.3 Quantization of the Depth-Wise Separable Convolution

During the quantization of models having the depth-wise separable convolution layers (or DWS-layers) it was noticed that for some models (MobileNet-v2, MNasNet with the lower resolution of input images) the vector quantization gives much higher accuracy than the scalar quantization. Besides, the usage of vector quantization instead of scalar only for DWS-layers gives the accuracy improvement.

In contrast to the scalar quantization, the vector quantization takes into account the distribution of weights for each filter separately - each filter has its own quantization threshold. If we perform the rescaling of values so that the quantization thresholds become identical for each filter, then the procedures of scalar and vector quantization of the scaled data become equivalent.

For some models this approach may be inapplicable because any non-linear operations on the scaled data as well as addition of the data having the different scaling factors are not allowed. Scaling the data can be made for the particular case $DWS \rightarrow [ReLU] \rightarrow Conv$ (see Fig. 2). In this case only the weights of the model change.

Scaling the Weights for MobileNet-V2 (with ReLU6). As it is mentioned above, the described method is not applicable for models which use the non-linear activation functions. In the case of MobileNet, there is the ReLU6 activation function between the convolutional operations. When scaling the weights of a DWS-filter, the output of the DWS-layer is also scaled. One way to keep the result of the neural network inference unchanged is to modify the ReLU6 function, so that the saturation threshold for the *k-th* channel is equal to $6 \cdot S_W[k]$. However, it is not suitable for the scalar quantization technique.

In practice, the output data for some channels of a DWS-layer X_k may be less than 6.0 on a large amount of input data of the network. It is possible to make the rescaling for these channels, but with the certain restrictions. The scaling factor for each of these channels must be taken so that the output data for channels X_k does not exceed the value 6.0.

If $X_k < 6$ and $X_k \cdot S_W[k] < 6$, then

$$min(6, X_k \cdot S_W[k]) = S_W[k] \cdot min(6, X_k) \tag{24}$$

Consequently:

$$ReLU6(X_k \cdot S_W[k]) = S_W[k] \cdot ReLU6(X_k) \tag{25}$$

We propose the following scheme of scaling the DWS-filter weights.

1. Find the maximum absolute value of weights for each filter of a DWS-layer.
2. Using the set of calibration data, determine the maximum values reached by each channel of the output of the DWS-layer (before applying ReLU6).
3. Mark the channels where the output values exceed 6.0 or are close to it as "locked". The corresponding filters of the DWS layer must stay unchanged. We propose to lock the channels where the output data is close to the value 6.0, because it could reach this value if we use a different calibration dataset. In this article we consider 5.9 as the upper limit.
4. Calculate the maximum absolute value of weights for each of the locked filters $T(w_i^{fixed})$. The average of these maximum values $T_0 = \overline{T(w_i^{fixed})}$ becomes a control value that is used for scaling the weights of non-locked filters. The main purpose of such choice is to minimize the difference between the thresholds of different filters of the DWS-layer.
5. Find the appropriate scaling factors for the non-locked channels.
6. Limit these scaling factors so that the maximum values on the DWS-layer output for non-locked channels do not exceed the value 6.0.

4 Experiments and Results

4.1 Experiments Description

Researched Architectures. The procedure of quantization for architectures with the high redundancy is practically irrelevant because such neural networks are hardly applicable for the mobile devices. The current work is focused on the experiments on the architectures which are actually considered to be a standard for mobile devices (MobileNet-v2 [18]), as well as on more recent ones (MNasNet [21]). All architectures are tested using the 224 × 224 spatial resolution.

The Training Procedure. As it is mentioned above in the Sect. 3.2 ("Training on the unlabeled data"), we use RMSE between the original and quantized networks as a loss function. Adam optimizer [10] is used for training, and cosine annealing [12] with the reset of optimizer parameters - for the learning rate. Training is carried out on approximately 10% part of the ImageNet dataset [17]. Testing is done on the validation set. 100 images from the training set are used as the calibration data. Training takes approximately 5 h (6-8 epochs depending on the network) on Nvidia GeForce GTX 1080 Ti, and 50 h on the same graphic card when training with the quantization from scratch.

4.2 Results

The quality of network quantization is represented in the Tables 1 and 2.

Table 1. Quantization in the 8-bit scalar mode.

Architecture	Symmetric thresholds, %	Asymmetric thresholds, %	Original accuracy, %
MobileNet v2	8.1	19.86	71.55
MNas-1.0	72.42	73.46	74.34
MNas-1.3	74.92	75.30	75.79

Experimental results show that the scalar quantization of MobileNet-v2 has a very poor accuracy. A possible reason of such quality degradation is the usage of ReLU6 activation function in the full-precision network. The negative influence of this function on the process of network quantization is mentioned in Ref. [19]. In the case of using the vector procedure of thresholds calculation, the accuracy of quantized MobileNet-v2 network and other researched neural networks is almost the same as the original one.

For implementation, the Tensorflow framework [1] is chosen because it is rather flexible and convenient for the further porting to mobile devices. The pre-trained networks are taken from Tensorflow[4] repository. To verify the results, the program code and quantized scalar models in the .lite format, ready to run on the mobile phones, are presented in the repository specified in the abstract.

Table 2. Quantization in the 8-bit vector mode.

Architecture	Symmetric thresholds, %	Asymmetric thresholds, %	Original accuracy, %
MobileNet v2	71.11	71.39	71.55
MNas-1.0	73.96	74.25	74.34
MNas-1.3	75.56	75.72	75.79

[4] https://github.com/tensorflow/tensorflow/blob/master/tensor-flow/lite/g3doc/models.md - the image classification (Quantized Models).

The algorithm described in the Sect. 3.3 ("Quantization of the depth-wise separable convolution") gives the following results. After performing the scalar quantization of the original MobileNetV2 model, its accuracy becomes low (the top-1 value is about 1.6%). Applying the weights rescaling before the quantization increases the accuracy of the quantized model up to 67% (the accuracy of the original model is 71.55%[5]). To improve the accuracy of the quantized model we use fine-tuning of weights for all filters and biases. Fine-tuning is implemented via the trainable point-wise scale factors where each value can vary from 0.75 to 1.25. The intuition behind this approach is to compensate the disadvantages of the linear quantization by slight modification of weights and biases, so some values can change their quantized state. As a result, fine-tuning improves the accuracy of the quantized model up to 71% (without training the quantization thresholds). Fine-tuning procedures are the same as described in the Sect. 4.1.

5 Conclusion

This paper demonstrates the methodology of the neural network quantization with fine-tuning. The quantized networks obtained with the help of our method demonstrate a high accuracy that is proved experimentally. Our work shows that setting a quantization threshold as multiplication of the maximum threshold value and the trained scaling factor, and also training on a small set of unlabeled data allow using the described method of quantization for fast conversion of the pre-trained models to the mobile devices.

References

1. Abadi, M., et al.: TensorFlow: large-scale machine learning on heterogeneous distributed systems. arXiv preprint: arXiv:1603.04467 (2016)
2. Baskin, C., et al.: Nice: noise injection and clamping estimation for neural network quantization. arXiv preprint: arXiv:1810.00162 (2018)
3. Bengio, Y., Leonard, N., Courville, A.C.: Estimating or propagating gradients through stochastic neurons for conditional computation. arXiv preprint: arXiv:1308.3432 (2013)
4. Courbariaux, M., Bengio, Y., David, J.: Training deep neural networks with low precision multiplications. In: International Conference on Learning Representations (ICLR 2015) (2015)
5. Hinton, G., Vinyals, O., Dean, J.: Distilling the knowledge in a neural network. arXiv preprint: arXiv:1503.02531 (2015)
6. Howard, A.G., et al.: MobileNets: efficient convolutional neural networks for mobile vision applications. arXiv preprint: arXiv:1704.04861 (2017)
7. Hubara, I., Courbariaux, M., Soudry, D., El-Yaniv, R., Bengio, Y.: Binarized neural networks. In: Advances in Neural Information Processing Systems (NIPS 2016), pp. 4107–4115 (2016)

[5] The network accuracy is measured on a full validation set ImageNet2012 which includes single-channel images.

8. Ioffe, S., Szegedy, C.: Batch normalization: accelerating deep network training by reducing internal covariate shift. In: International Conference on Machine Learning (ICML 2015) (2015)
9. Jacob, B., et al.: Quantization and training of neural networks for efficient integer-arithmetic only inference. In: Conference on Computer Vision and Pattern Recognition (CVPR 2018) (2018)
10. Kingma, D.P., Ba, J.L.: Adam: a method for stochastic optimization. In: International Conference on Learning Representations (ICLR 2015) (2015)
11. Lee, J.H., Ha, S., Choi, S., Lee, W., Lee, S.: Quantization for rapid deployment of deep neural networks. arXiv preprint: arXiv:1810.05488 (2018)
12. Loshchilov, I., Hutter, F.: SGDR: stochastic gradient descent with warm restarts. In: International Conference on Learning Representations (ICLR 2017) (2017)
13. McDonnell, M.D.: Training wide residual networks for deployment using a single bit for each weight. In: International Conference on Learning Representations (ICLR 2018) (2018)
14. Mishra, A., Marr, D.: Apprentice: using knowledge distillation techniques to improve low-precision network accuracy. arXiv preprint: arXiv:1711.05852 (2017)
15. Mishra, A., Nurvitadhi, E., Cook, J.J., Marr, D.: WRPN: wide reduced-precision networks. arXiv preprint: arXiv:1709.01134 (2017)
16. Rastegari, M., Ordonez, V., Redmon, J., Farhadi, A.: XNOR-Net: ImageNet classification using binary convolutional neural networks. In: Leibe, B., Matas, J., Sebe, N., Welling, M. (eds.) ECCV 2016, Part IV. LNCS, vol. 9908, pp. 525–542. Springer, Cham (2016). https://doi.org/10.1007/978-3-319-46493-0_32
17. Russakovsky, O., et al.: ImageNet large scale visual recognition challenge. arXiv preprint: arXiv:1409.0575 (2014)
18. Sandler, M., Howard, A., Zhu, M., Zhmoginov, A., Chen, L.: Inverted residuals and linear bottlenecks: mobile networks for classification, detection and segmentation. In: IEEE Conference on Computer Vision and Pattern Recognition (CVPR 2018) (2018)
19. Sheng, T., Feng, C., Zhuo, S., Zhang, X., Shen, L., Aleksic, M.: A quantization-friendly separable convolution for MobileNets. arXiv preprint: arXiv:1803.08607 (2018)
20. Simonyan, K., Zisserman, A.: Very deep convolutional networks for large-scale image recognition. In: International Conference on Learning Representations (ICLR 2015) (2015)
21. Tan, M., Chen, B., Pang, R., Vasudevan, V., Le, Q.V.: MnasNet: platform-aware neural architecture search for mobile. arXiv preprint: arXiv:1807.11626 (2018)
22. Zhou, S., Wu, Y., Ni, Z., Zhou, X., Wen, H., Zou, Y.: DoReFa-Net: training low bitwidth convolutional neural networks with low bitwidth gradients. arXiv preprint: arXiv:1606.06160 (2016)
23. Zhu, S., Dong, X., Su, H.: Binary ensemble neural network: more bits per network or more networks per bit? arXiv preprint: arXiv:1806.07550 (2018)

Residual Learning for FC Kernels of Convolutional Network

Alexey Alexeev[1,2](✉), Yuriy Matveev[2], Anton Matveev[2], and Dmitry Pavlenko[3]

[1] ArmiSoft Ltd., Saint-Petersburg, Russia
aaalexeev@corp.ifmo.ru
[2] ITMO University, Saint-Petersburg, Russia
matveev@speechpro.com, aush.tx@gmail.com
[3] State University, Saint-Petersburg, Russia
dmit10@mail.ru
https://armisoft.net

Abstract. One of the most important steps in training a neural network is choosing its depth. Theoretically, it is possible to construct a complex decision-making function by cascading a number of shallow networks. It can produce a similar in accuracy result while providing a significant performance cost benefit. In practice, at some point, just increasing the depth of a network can actually decrease its performance due to overlearning. In literature, this is called "vanishing gradient descent".

Vanishing gradient descent is observed as a vanishing decrease of magnitudes of gradients of weights for each subsequent layer, effectively preventing the weight from changing its value in the lower layers of a deep network when applying the backward propagation of errors algorithm.

There is an approach called Residual Network (ResNet) to solve this problem for standard convolutional networks. However, the ResNet solves the problem only partially, as the resulting network is not sequential, but is an ensemble of shallow networks with all drawbacks typical for them.

In this article, we investigate a convolutional network with fully connected layers (so-called network in network architecture, NiN) and suggest another way to build an ensemble of shallow networks. In our case, we gradually reduce the number of parallel connections by using sequential network connections.

This allows to eliminate the influence of the vanishing gradient descent and to reduce the redundancy of the network by using all weight coefficients and not using residual blocks as ResNet does.

For this method to work it is not required to change the network architecture, but only needed to properly initialize its weights.

Keywords: Object detection · CNN · NiN · ResNet · Vanishing gradient descent

This work was financially supported by the Government of the Russian Federation (Grant 08-08).

I. V. Tetko et al. (Eds.): ICANN 2019, LNCS 11728, pp. 361–372, 2019.
https://doi.org/10.1007/978-3-030-30484-3_30

1 Introduction

Recently, the set of commonly used image processing methods has changed significantly, and these days the main part of it consists of fast and scalable convolutional neural networks (CNN) [1,2]. CNN allowed to solve many challenging image processing tasks, such as pattern recognition [3] and object detection [4–9]. The use of a fully connected network as a convolution kernel, as in NiN [10] (Fig. 1) has proven to be useful for large strides [11], which is impossible for classical networks due to the aliasing effect [12,13], and also due to loss of spatial information in terminal layers as a result of pooling. The stride length can be chosen equal to the length of a convolution window [11], significantly reducing amount of convolutional levels. The convolution kernels can be set up with a required amount of layers. Similar to classical networks, for convolution kernels with large number of layers the decrease in gradient becomes noticeable when training a network with the backpropagation algorithm. This effect is more pronounced, the lower the level of the network. With an even greater increase in the number of layers, the opposite effect occurs when the performance of the network becomes worse than in its variation with lower depth. This can be explained by the fact that the lower layers lose their ability to be trained, but the higher layers are already trained with the data from the previous stages.

Investigating networks like ResNet [14] we discovered, that in spite of lower actual depth and presence of multiple shallow networks in ensemble [15], these networks have a good generalization ability even with large number of internal parameters; they also do not degrade with increase of depth until a certain threshold. Based on our analysis of such networks, their applicability to NiN type networks, and also possibility to transform a set of shallow networks to a single sequential architecture, we have developed an approach, when, instead of parallel Identity functions, like connections of residual blocks in ResNet, the identity functions are embedded in useful connections of a fully connected network itself, with their subsequent gradual and natural weakening in the process of network training.

Our solution demonstrates that a network can be trained and not to be saturated even with large number of layers in each fully connected convolution kernel. Performance of a middle-sized neural network (with up to 30 layers) in terms of its Loss error level, appears to be higher comparing to other networks with lower depth. Very deep networks (with up to 150 layers) show similar results, but converge much slower. As for standard networks, convergence halts very fast for networks with high and even middle depth.

2 Related Work

Effects of vanishing and exploding gradients are very important for neural networks. This problem mostly occurs when modeling long-term dependencies in recurrent neural networks. In [16] it is shown that simple initialization of the matrix of a recurrent neural network as a unit matrix solves the problem of vanishing gradients and makes it possible to model long-term connections.

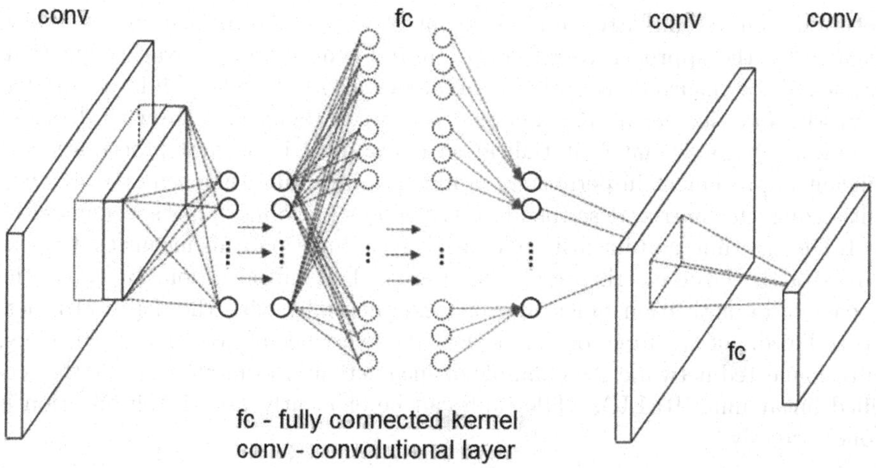

Fig. 1. Architecture of network in network, NiN

A similar approach was taken in [17], where in the baseline version an update matrix of a hidden state of a recurrent network was fixed as a unit matrix during training.

Using a unit matrix allows to preserve distances and, particularly, the length of the gradient between layers, making training smoother. In some publications, this restriction is not so strict and a unitary matrix is chosen. The most simple and obvious way to achieve that would be to replace the matrix with the closest unitary at each step of training, but this would be computationally inefficient. [18] proposed a method of parametrization of a set of unitary matrices. This idea was developed further in [19] and, based on [20] a method of parameterization of a subset of unitary matrices was suggested, making it possible to find a balance between computational complexity and the number of parameters. In [21] another method was suggested with a requirement not to step outside of the set of unitary matrices.

The type of matrix of a neural network layer is extremely important for solving the vanishing gradients problem. However, as number of layers grows, it is also important to account for an activation function. All aforementioned methods consider only the matrix. In [22] it was suggested how to select an architecture and initialize a network, and also how to choose an activation functions, for data, distributed with (μ, σ) at input, to have the same expected value and standard deviation, while also being stable, meaning that for a small deviation of parameters (μ, σ) these characteristics at the output closely approach the initial (μ, σ). This way it is possible to build fully connected networks of arbitrary size not worrying about the problem of vanishing gradients.

In publications [23–30] neural networks are investigated from the point of view of mean field theory and of their spectra of layer matrices. There are several important conclusions from these papers. First, recurrent and fully connected networks behave similarly from the point of view of mean field theory, which means that the approach to initialization and choosing an activation function, developed for recurrent neural networks, can also be used for fully connected networks and vice versa, and differences between them decrease with depth of a network. Second, matrix initialization is the most important procedure. Significant improvement in performance and training stability is achieved if, when initializing, the matrix, described in these papers (Jacobian), has spectrum close to 1. Disregarding non-linearity of an activation function, this means that eigenvalues of the layer matrix should be close to 1 at initialization. However, the impact of an activation function grows exponentially with the depth of a network. Third, not any function can be used for a very deep (more than 1000 layers) fully connected network. An example of such activation function can be the rectified linear unit (RELU), while tanh can be efficiently used if initialization is done correctly.

3 Description of the Network

Referencing the approach for standard CNN in [31] we have developed a method for networks with fully connected kernels, which does not employ residual blocks, but partially solves the problem of vanishing gradient descent and uses shallow networks only at the first period of training, the step, when gradient increases significantly.

Let's look at a simple case of connections between layers of a fully connected kernel of a convolutional network, when the weight matrix between layers is square.

In this case the output of the layer L_{n+1} is

$$\boldsymbol{x}_{l+1} = \sigma(\boldsymbol{W}_1\boldsymbol{x}_l) = \sigma((\boldsymbol{W}_0 + \boldsymbol{S}_n)\boldsymbol{x}_l) = \sigma(\boldsymbol{W}_0\boldsymbol{x}_l + \boldsymbol{S}_n\boldsymbol{x}_l) \tag{1}$$

where σ is a non-linear transformation leaky RELU, $\boldsymbol{W}_0 \in \boldsymbol{R}^{nxn}, w_{0ii} = 0$ for each i, $\boldsymbol{W}_1 \in \boldsymbol{R}^{nxn}, w_{1ii} = \lambda$ for each i, λ is a constant, $\boldsymbol{S}_n = diag(\lambda) = \lambda I$ is the scalar matrix.

Matrix $\boldsymbol{S}_n$ is analogous to the residual learning Identity in the case of $\lambda = 1.0$, provides lossless transferring of data between layers, and also, during training, reduces the impact of vanishing descent while calculating gradient.

If a leaky RELU was chosen as the activation function, the parameter λ equal to 1.0, and, considering that x_l is a positive vector and weights $\boldsymbol{W}_1$ besides the main diagonal, are very small, then the Eq. 1 becomes equivalent to the standard equation for residual networks with only one layer inside (we do not use more than one level in the same block)

$$\boldsymbol{x}_{l+1} = \sigma(\boldsymbol{W}_0\boldsymbol{x}_l + \boldsymbol{S}_n\boldsymbol{x}_l) \approx \sigma(\boldsymbol{W}_0\boldsymbol{x}_l) + \boldsymbol{I}_n\boldsymbol{x}_l \approx \sigma(\boldsymbol{W}_0\boldsymbol{x}_l) + \boldsymbol{x}_l \tag{2}$$

From this equation we can conclude that data from the very first layer of the network (raw image data) flows throughout the whole network to the final layer of each fully connected convolution kernel, making the network calculate residual $\mathcal{F}(\boldsymbol{x}) := \mathcal{H}(\boldsymbol{x}) - \boldsymbol{x}$ as in [14], where, in our case, $\mathcal{F}(\boldsymbol{x}) \equiv \sigma(\boldsymbol{W}_0\boldsymbol{x}_l)$, $\mathcal{H}(\boldsymbol{x}) \equiv \boldsymbol{x}_{l+1}$ and $\boldsymbol{x} \equiv \boldsymbol{x}_l$.

In general, the amount of connections is determined by the amount of neurons in the layer L_n, or in the layer L_{n+1} if it has fewer neurons, and the connections are chosen in parallel and only once when initializing the network. Weights for those connections are fixed and equal to λ. All other connections are standard weighted connections, allowing the network to be trained. Figure 2 illustrates standard weight and Identity connections on the left. For the sake of simplicity, standard connections are only visible for the top-right neurons of each diagram. The results of training are on the right of the figure. All Identity connections are only partially transitioned to standard connection, which is highlighted in semibold. In the case when there is a difference in amount of neurons between layers, some Identity connections are left unused.

This type of connections are established between all layers of fully connected kernels, including the very first layer, directly connected to the image. If it is not done, training performance becomes noticeably worse due to violation of the Identity principle for the connections between the input and the output of the network.

Our network, similar to ResNet, first creates a set of simple networks, which comes with drawbacks. In our case, natural adjustment of weights during training (including ones initialized as 1) leads to a partial transit from parallel to sequential networks. Thus, at the beginning of training, we can clearly see a uniform gradient increase while transitioning from parallel to sequential connected layers. Analyzing how gradient grows at the early stages of training, we see that it demonstrates a larger increase for all layers of the network, comparing to the same network with standard initialization. It is important to point out that all utilized Identity connections after training have the same role as all other connections in the network, thus not introducing additional redundancy.

4 Experiments

In this section, we provide analysis of the Loss parameter for various network configurations, based on publically available database of road signs [32]. It is important to point out that the problem being solved is detection (multi-class classification and regression), and not classification as in Self-Normalizing network [22]. This distinction can influence measurements of the Loss value, which is shown below.

4.1 Network Parameters

Structures of deep and shallow networks are shown in Table 1. Each of the columns C shows a level on convolution and each of the rows R is a level in a fully connected convolution kernel for each level of convolution. Overall depth of a network is determined as the sum of levels of a fully connected network for each level of convolution $\sum_{i=1}^{C} Num(r_i)$, where $r \in R$.

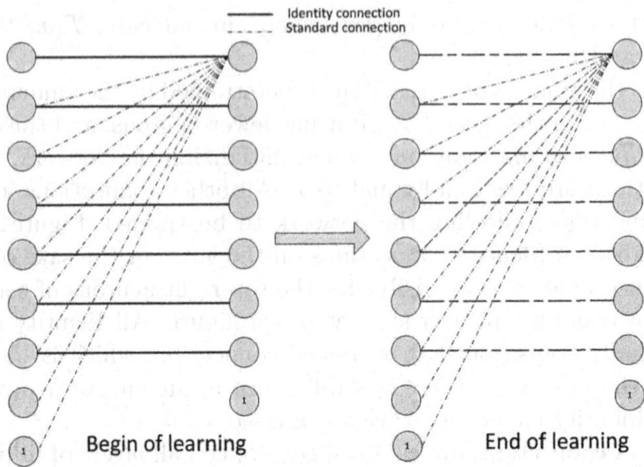

Fig. 2. Identity connections (left) are partially transformed to standard ones (right)

For an error function we chose MSE (Mean squared error), initial value of batch = 16, increasing during training, learning rate of 0.001, the leaky RELU activation function, ADAM optimization, no regularization and initial weights are

$$w_{ij} = \sqrt{\frac{2}{N_{l-1}}} N(\mu, \sigma^2) \tag{3}$$

Initial value of λ for the weight matrix W_1 from the Eq. 1 is set at 0.1 at the beginning and is gradually increasing towards the target value (we tested on values 0.5 and 1.0) in 10 iterations.

Table 1. Network composition

Network composition			
	Conv3D 1, 6 × 6, stride 6	Conv3D 2, 4 × 4, stride 4	Conv3D 3, 2 × 2, stride 1
1	FC 1, 24, lrelu	FC 1, 128, lrelu	FC 1, 256, lrelu
2	FC 2, 16, lrelu	FC 2, 64, lrelu	FC 2, 128, lrelu
3	FC 3, 16, lrelu	FC 3, 64, lrelu	FC 3, 128, lrelu
.	...	...	...
16	FC 7, 16, lrelu	FC 7, 64, lrelu	FC 7, 128, lrelu
17	FC 7, 16, lrelu	FC 7, 64, lrelu	FC 7, 150, lrelu

4.2 Improving Convergence in Shallow Networks

For shallow networks (the first and the last rows in the Table 1 for each level of convolution. Number of levels is $3 * 2 = 6$) the suggested initialization method provides just a minor decrease in the Loss value comparing to shallow networks with standard initialization (Fig. 3a). Significant here is that using the method, while a number of weights of the matrix W_1 is being used as Identity, it does not lead to degradation of training for shallow networks. This means that our method can be applied to shallow networks as well. For comparison with deep networks we provide results of work of depth residual network-31, which has even lower Loss value, on the same figure.

4.3 Training Deep Networks

For deep networks (all rows in Table 1, number of levels is $3 * 17 = 51$) our method provides a lower value of the Loss parameter, comparing to the deep networks with standard initialization (Fig. 3b). A standard network is prone to a rapid decline in training efficiency, while in our case the network continues to improve under training much further and its Loss value reaches a lower floor than a shallow network. We probed a couple of values for the scaling parameter λ. For the value of 1 at the beginning of training the error is very high, but it gradually resolves to norm. When we pick other values, for example 0.5, convergence suffers. It is possible to improve convergence by applying smaller weights outside of the main diagonals of the weight matrices (in Fig. 3b for 51 depth, labeled lw). Such if, after initializing in the usual way (the Eq. 3) we divide values of weights, for example, by 100 or more, then the network converges much faster and the Loss value is lower. For the same initial conditions even a deeper network can be used (Fig. 3b for 150 levels), but worth noting that it does not deliver any improvements in performance. The reason for that, most likely, is the aforementioned conclusion that not any activation function can perform efficiently for deep networks. The figure demonstrates a comparison to the shallow standard network-6. It loses to the networks with less than 51 levels, which use the Identity function and lower values of weights outside of the main diagonal.

4.4 Analysis of Weights Changing During Deep Networks Training

We have recorded changes in weights of each network level throughout training. For each iteration we calculate a Frobenius norm of the matrix W_0 via Eq. 1

$$\|x\|_F = \sqrt{Tr(\boldsymbol{W}_0 \boldsymbol{W}_0^T)} \tag{4}$$

where Tr - trace operator.

Figure 4 demonstrates the dynamic across uniformly chosen levels of a network ($conv1 = \{1, 8, 15\}, conv2 = \{18, 25, 32\}, conv3 = \{35, 42, 49\}$). For the standard deep network (Fig. 4a), changes in weights happen differently across levels of convolution. After some time, changes halt and the network is not

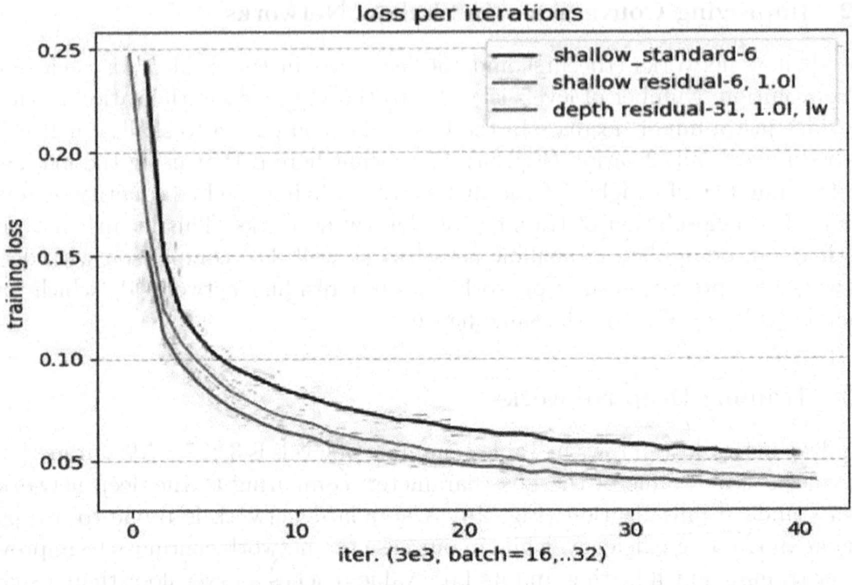

(a) Learning of shallow networks

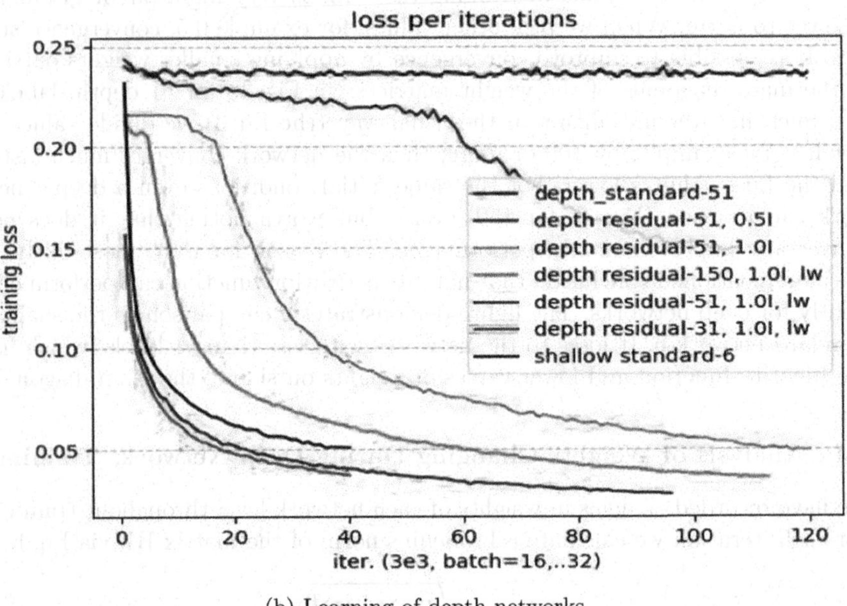

(b) Learning of depth networks

Fig. 3. (a) Dynamic of the Loss value change for shallow network with 6 levels and for depth network-31 for comparison. (b) Dynamic of the Loss value changes for deep networks with 31, 51, and 150 levels. An example for residual network with $\lambda = 0.5$ and $\lambda = 1.0$. The best convergence rate and the lowest Loss value is for the network with small initial weight outside of the main diagonal (lw-low weights)

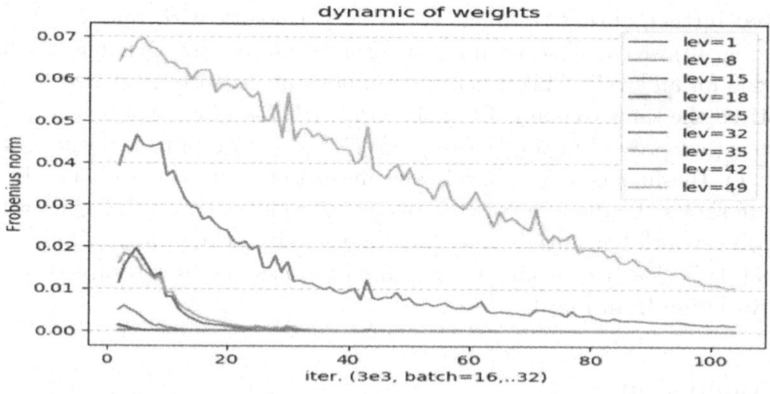

(a) Learning of standard depth networks with 51 layers

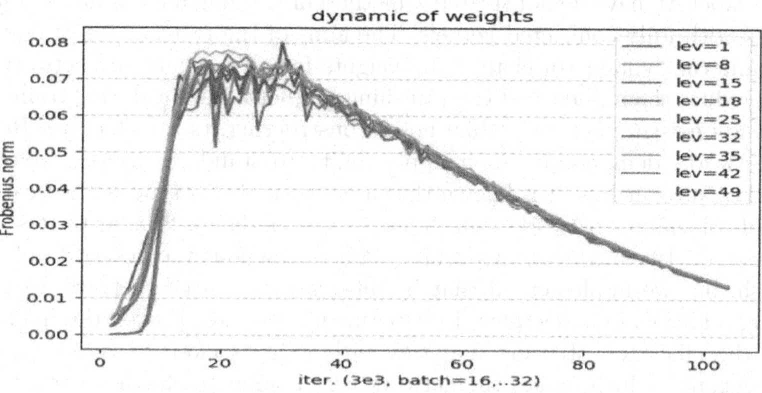

(b) Learning of residual depth networks with 51 layers

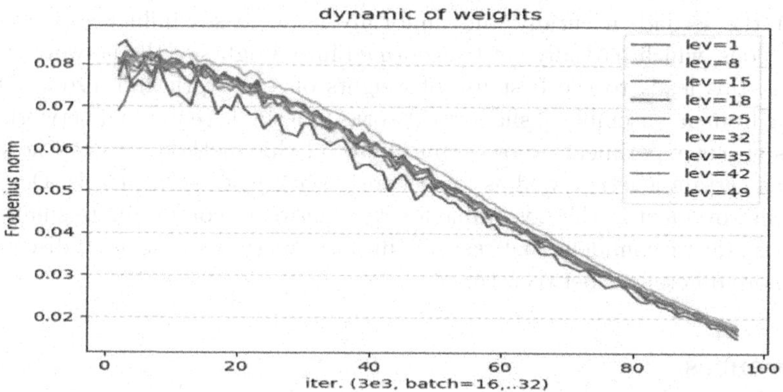

(c) Learning of residual depth networks with 51 layers and low weights

Fig. 4. Dynamics of networks weights changing at each level during training. (a) Standard deep network. (b) Residual deep network. (c) Residual deep network with low weights besides main diagonal of weights matrix. For (b) and (c) Frobenius norm has close values during training for all network levels. For (c) data do not have a transition period

improved further during training. For a deep network with initialization proposed (Fig. 4b) we can observe uniform absolute and relative dynamic of changes in weights for all levels. This fact is very important because the network is deep. We noticed the same dynamic for a network with 150 levels. For a network with 530 levels (not present in the picture), after some period of time during training weights on the first couple of levels become frozen and do not change further. Figure 4c shows the dynamic of changes in the weights for the same network as in Fig. 4b network but initialized by low values in its weights matrix beside main diagonal. It is clear that using low weights produces the best results comparing to the variation from Fig. 4c.

5 Conclusion

In this paper we have demonstrated a method of training a convolutional neural network with fully connected kernels. The aims of the method are to provide a more uniform dynamic of changes in weights for all levels of the network, and also to reduce the influence of the vanishing gradient descent during training for an already existing network while not reconstructing its architecture. ResNet-type networks demonstrate their applicability to standard deep convolutional networks. Nevertheless, it is known that a network of this type is identical to an ensemble of shallow networks, which leads to redundancy. Similar to ResNet we also used identity matrices for pushing data throughout the network from start to finish, but we implemented that by integrating it in the network itself, not creating additional connections. In experiments we have proven the hypothesis about the efficiency of using matrices with weights close to zero except the main diagonal, which makes the network very similar to ResNet. However, our network differs from ResNet in that its training is done in two steps. At the first step, it provides fast convergence by training first network levels more efficiently, and at the second, naturally and uniformly it decreases influence of Identity connections, which partially get transformed into weights of the network. In our opinion, this leads to the best use of weights of a network and also results in shifting from an ensemble of shallow networks to a single sequential network. The results of our experiments show applicability of this method for deep networks (up to a certain level) as well as for networks with just several levels. Despite a small improvement in the Loss value for deep networks comparing to small-sized networks, we are confident that research in this direction is crucial for discovering even more differences between them.

References

1. Agarwal, S., Terrail, J.O.D., Jurie, F.: Recent advances in object detection in the age of deep convolutional neural networks, CoRR, vol. abs/1809.03193 (2018)
2. Zhao, Z., Zheng, P., Xu, S., Wu, X.: Object detection with deep learning: a review, CoRR, vol. abs/1807.05511 (2018)

3. Krizhevsky, A., Sutskever, I., Hinton, G.E.: ImageNet classification with deep convolutional neural networks. In: Pereira, F., Burges, C.J.C., Bottou, L., Weinberger, K.Q. (eds.) Advances in Neural Information Processing Systems 25, pp. 1097–1105. Curran Associates, Inc. (2012)
4. Ren, S., He, K., Girshick, R., Sun, J.: Faster R-CNN: towards real-time object detection with region proposal networks, ArXiv e-prints, June 2015
5. Redmon, J., Divvala, S.K., Girshick, R.B., Farhadi, A.: You only look once: unified, real-time object detection, CoRR, vol. abs/1506.02640 (2015)
6. Redmon, J., Farhadi, A.: Yolov3: an incremental improvement, arXiv (2018)
7. Lin, T., Goyal, P., Girshick, R.B., He, K., Dollár, P.: Focal loss for dense object detection, CoRR, vol. abs/1708.02002 (2017)
8. Liu, W., et al.: SSD: single shot multibox detector, CoRR, vol. abs/1512.02325 (2015)
9. Wong, A., Shafiee, M.J., Li, F., Chwyl, B.: Tiny SSD: a tiny single-shot detection deep convolutional neural network for real-time embedded object detection, CoRR, vol. abs/1802.06488 (2018)
10. Lin, M., Chen, Q., Yan, S.: Network in network, CoRR, vol. abs/1312.4400 (2013)
11. Alexeev, A., Matveev, Y., Kukharev, G.: A3Net: fast end-to-end object detector on neural network for scenes with arbitrary size. In: Robotics and Technical Cybernetics, vol. 3, pp. 43–52, September 2018
12. Zeiler, M.D., Fergus, R.: Visualizing and understanding convolutional networks, CoRR, vol. abs/1311.2901 (2013)
13. Gong, Y., Poellabauer, C.: Impact of aliasing on deep CNN-based end-to-end acoustic models. In: Proceedings of Interspeech 2018, pp. 2698–2702 (2018)
14. He, K., Zhang, X., Ren, S., Sun, J.: Deep residual learning for image recognition, CoRR, vol. abs/1512.03385 (2015)
15. Veit, A., Wilber, M.J., Belongie, S.J.: Residual networks are exponential ensembles of relatively shallow networks, CoRR, vol. abs/1605.06431 (2016)
16. Le, Q.V., Jaitly, N., Hinton, G.E.: A simple way to initialize recurrent networks of rectified linear units, CoRR, vol. abs/1504.00941 (2015)
17. Li, S., Li, W., Cook, C., Zhu, C., Gao, Y.: Independently recurrent neural network (IndRNN): building a longer and deeper RNN, CoRR, vol. abs/1803.04831 (2018)
18. Arjovsky, M., Shah, A., Bengio, Y.: Unitary evolution recurrent neural networks, CoRR, vol. abs/1511.06464 (2015)
19. Jing, L., et al.: Tunable efficient unitary neural networks (EUNN) and their application to RNN, CoRR, vol. abs/1612.05231 (2016)
20. Mathieu, M., LeCun, Y.: Fast approximation of rotations and Hessians matrices, CoRR, vol. abs/1404.7195 (2014)
21. Wisdom, S., Powers, T., Hershey, J., Le Roux, J., Atlas, L.: Full-capacity unitary recurrent neural networks. In: Lee, D.D., Sugiyama, M., Luxburg, U.V., Guyon, I., Garnett, R. (eds.) Advances in Neural Information Processing Systems 29, pp. 4880–4888. Curran Associates, Inc. (2016)
22. Klambauer, G., Unterthiner, T., Mayr, A., Hochreiter, S.: Self-normalizing neural networks, CoRR, vol. abs/1706.02515 (2017)
23. Pennington, J., Schoenholz, S.S., Ganguli, S.: Resurrecting the sigmoid in deep learning through dynamical isometry: theory and practice, CoRR, vol. abs/1711.04735 (2017)
24. Schoenholz, S.S., Gilmer, J., Ganguli, S., Sohl-Dickstein, J.: Deep information propagation, CoRR, vol. abs/1611.01232 (2016)
25. Yang, G., Pennington, J., Rao, V., Sohl-Dickstein, J., Schoenholz, S.S.: A mean field theory of batch normalization, CoRR, vol. abs/1902.08129 (2019)

26. Gilboa, D., et al.: Dynamical isometry and a mean field theory of LSTMs and GRUs, CoRR, vol. abs/1901.08987 (2019)
27. Chen, M., Pennington, J., Schoenholz, S.S.: Dynamical isometry and a mean field theory of RNNs: gating enables signal propagation in recurrent neural networks. In: Dy, J.G., Krause, A. (eds.) Proceedings of the 35th International Conference on Machine Learning, ICML 2018, Stockholmsmässan, Stockholm, Sweden, 10–15 July 2018. JMLR Workshop and Conference Proceedings, vol. 80, pp. 872–881. JMLR.org (2018)
28. Schoenholz, S.S., Pennington, J., Sohl-Dickstein, J.: A correspondence between random neural networks and statistical field theory, CoRR, vol. abs/1710.06570 (2017)
29. Xiao, L., Bahri, Y., Sohl-Dickstein, J., Schoenholz, S., Pennington, J.: Dynamical isometry and a mean field theory of CNNs: how to train 10,000-layer vanilla convolutional neural networks. In: Dy, J., Krause, A. (eds.) Proceedings of the 35th International Conference on Machine Learning, Stockholmsmässan, Stockholm Sweden, 10–15 July 2018. Proceedings of Machine Learning Research, vol. 80, pp. 5393–5402. PMLR (2018)
30. Pennington, J., Schoenholz, S.S., Ganguli, S.: The emergence of spectral universality in deep networks. In: Storkey, A.J., Pérez-Cruz, F. (eds.) International Conference on Artificial Intelligence and Statistics, AISTATS 2018, Playa Blanca, Lanzarote, Canary Islands, Spain, 9–11 April 2018. Proceedings of Machine Learning Research, vol. 84, pp. 1924–1932. PMLR (2018)
31. Zagoruyko, S., Komodakis, N.: DiracNets: training very deep neural networks without skip-connections, CoRR, vol. abs/1706.00388 (2017)
32. Shakhuro, V.I., Konushin, A.S.: Russian traffic sign images dataset. Comput. Opt. **40**(2), 294–300 (2016)

A Novel Neural Network-Based Symbolic Regression Method: Neuro-Encoded Expression Programming

Aftab Anjum[1], Fengyang Sun[1], Lin Wang[1](✉), and Jeff Orchard[2]

[1] Shandong Provincial Key Laboratory of Network Based Intelligent Computing, University of Jinan, Jinan 250022, China
wangplanet@gmail.com

[2] David R. Cheriton School of Computer Science, University of Waterloo, Waterloo, ON N2L 3G1, Canada

Abstract. Neuro-encoded expression programming (NEEP) that aims to offer a novel continuous representation of combinatorial encoding for genetic programming methods is proposed in this paper. Genetic programming with linear representation uses nature-inspired operators (e.g., crossover, mutation) to tune expressions and finally search out the best explicit function to simulate data. The encoding mechanism is essential for genetic programmings to find a desirable solution efficiently. However, the linear representation methods manipulate the expression tree in discrete solution space, where a small change of the input can cause a large change of the output. The unsmooth landscapes destroy the local information and make difficulty in searching. The neuro-encoded expression programming constructs the gene string with recurrent neural network (RNN) and the weights of the network are optimized by powerful continuous evolutionary algorithms. The neural network mappings smoothen the sharp fitness landscape and provide rich neighborhood information to find the best expression. The experiments indicate that the novel approach improves training efficiency and reduces test errors on several well-known symbolic regression problems.

Keywords: Genetic programming · Symbolic regression · Neural network · Gene expression programming · Evolutionary algorithm

1 Introduction

Symbolic regression (SR) [27] is to find an explicit function for simulation of user-defined data. Compared to implicit numerical (linear or nonlinear) regression analysis, SR can construct a function for a complex data without any prior knowledge and generally has powerful interpretability due to clear mathematical formula. Currently, genetic programming methods with linear representation [3, 10, 25] are mainly used to solve SR, which adopts a number of nature-inspired operators such as mutation and crossover to manipulate expressions and has presented decent performances on various applications.

A. Anjum and S. Sun—Contribute equally to this article.

I. V. Tetko et al. (Eds.): ICANN 2019, LNCS 11728, pp. 373–386, 2019.
https://doi.org/10.1007/978-3-030-30484-3_31

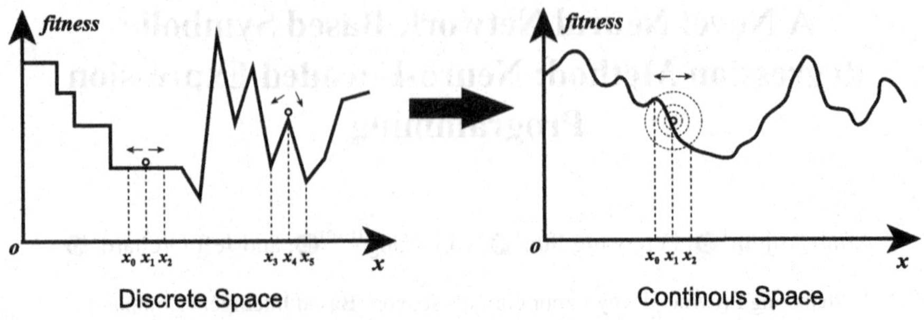

Fig. 1. A sketch plot of comparison between discrete and continuous space. The discrete space shows two types of fitness landscape features. Plateau is that the fitness values around point x_1 is the same as central point. The neighborhood of x_4 is extremely sharp and fluctuant. Instead, the continuous space shows that the central point can obtain a slope in a small or large neighborhood.

However, the linear representation approaches encode the expressions in discrete manner, which considers it as a combinatorial problem. Compared to continuous problems, the combinatorial problem do not provide sufficient and useful neighborhood information to aid searching [19,28]. In addition, the local structure of the combinatorial problem are hard "sharp" style and the fitness landscape is not smooth where a minute change of the genotype can instill a substantial change of the phenotype [8,30] and may cause oscillation of converging process [4] (Fig. 1). All the factors above make it difficult to find a desirable function fitting data for linear representation methods.

Recently neural networks have achieved great success in generative tasks [13,23, 32]. In particular, neural networks have demonstrated considerable potential for generating texts or strings [2]. The genetic programming methods (such as gene expression programming) can decode a string to an expression tree that is equivalent to a mathematical function. Then the two facts make it possible to use neural networks to generate expressions, which converts the purely discrete encoding to continuous encoding and alleviates the aforementioned difficulties in solution space.

Therefore, we propose a neuro-encoded expression programming (NEEP), which constructs the mathematical functions with neural networks generating expression string. Instead of the discrete way, a small change in continuous weights vector only triggers similar form of function and makes slow-varying effects. Therefore, the continuous neural network mappings smoothen and soften the hard sharp discrete fitness landscape and provide more flexible local information. In this manner, the NEEP can adopt powerful continuous optimizers to finely adjust the weights of network and find better function.

2 Related Works

2.1 Symbolic Regression

The purpose of symbolic regression is to find an explicit function, which is the primary difference with numerical regression. For a predefined data, SR finds an explicit function $f : \mathbf{x} \rightarrow y$ that approximates the data with minimum error.

2.2 Genetic Programming

There are several types of methods that can be used to solve SR, e.g., analytic programming [39], fast function extraction [21], grammar evolution [26] and genetic programming [16]. Genetic programming methods (such as gene expression programming and standard genetic programming) are one type of the commonly used methods to solve symbolic regression. Standard genetic programming (GP) [16] tunes the tree structure of expression directly by nature-inspired operators, e.g., crossover is the exchange in subtrees of two chromosomes at certain nodes. GPs maintain good patterns but suffer from the explosion of tree size. Gene expression programming (GEP) [10,36] constructs chromosomes with linear expression strings and provides an efficient way to encode syntactically correct expressions. For readers' better understanding of our method, we introduce more details about GEP.

Gene expression programming encodes the expression tree structure into fixed length linear chromosomes. Structurally, GEP genes consist of head and tail. Head consists of function symbols and terminal symbols and tail contains terminal symbols only. GEP uses the population of linear expression strings, selects them according to their fitness values and introduces genetic variation through genetic operators.

The encoding design [40] has a significant influence on the performance of gene expression programming since it determines the search space as well as the mapping between genotypes and phenotypes. Traditional GEP adopts the K-expression representation [10], which converts a linear string to an expression tree by using a breadth-first travelling procedure. Li et al. [37] introduced new enhancements (P-GEP), which improve the encoding design by suggesting the depth-first technique of converting the string into the expression Tree. P-GEP increases the searching efficiency, but it is not scalable for complex problems. Automatically defined functions (ADF) [15] were, for the first time, introduced by Koza as a way of reusing code in genetic programming. Ferreira [9] introduced improvements (GEP-ADF) to encode the subfunctions into the expression tree which makes the GEP more flexible and robust. However, these encoding improvements are still based on discrete space, which lacks of sufficient neighborhood information. To the best of our knowledge, there are few approaches encoding the expression string in a continuous manner. Therefore, the difficulties from discrete encoding are yet to be solved.

2.3 Neural Network on Generation Task

Neural network has achieved success on generation task such as image [13], audio [23] and text [2] generation. In particular, several studies on text/string generation by neural networks are reviewed in this part. Bowman et al. [2] proposed an RNN-based variational autoencoder (VAE) language model that incorporates distributed latent representations of entire sentences in a continuous space and explicitly models holistic properties of sentences. Wang et al. [32] generated texts based on generative adversarial networks (GANs). This method builds discriminator with a convolutional neural network and constructs generator with RNN and VAE to solve the problem that GANs always emit the similar data.

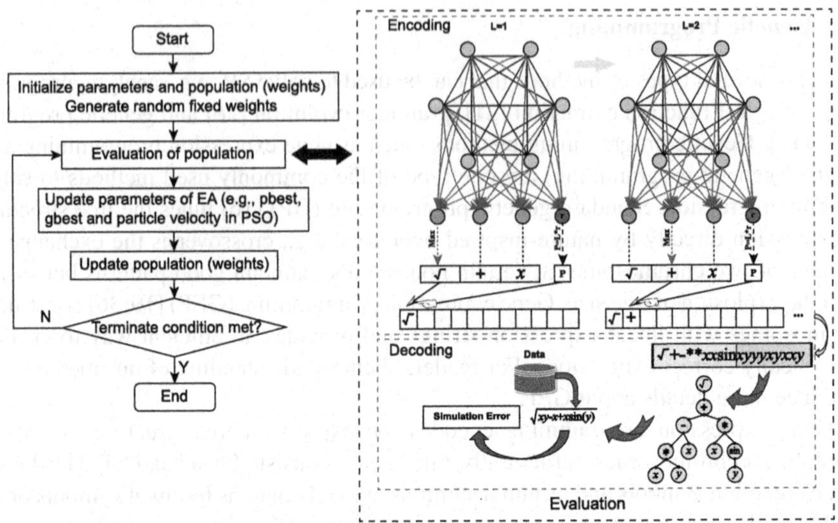

Fig. 2. The framework for neuro-encoded expression programming in a general description. The black dashed square represents the fitness evaluation of the evolutionary algorithm. The neural encoding in evaluation is the main contribution of this study, which uses the neural network to encode the expression string. The network structure details is seen in Fig. 3. The first light-colored segment of linear string is the head part and the second part is tail. The string is decoded into a function in breadth-first scheme as GEP. The simulation error will return back to the evolutionary algorithm as the fitness value in optimization.

To our knowledge, there is little research that uses neural network to solve symbolic regression by generating expression strings in spite of its success on generating texts. Liskowski et al. [18] proposed a method in which neural networks play a "pre-training" role to detect possible patterns in data, and then aids in finding the function rather than generating expression strings directly. Yin et al. [38] proposed a novel self-organizing reservoir computing methods by gene regulatory network. This method can process arbitrary sequences of inputs such as speech recognition, whereas generating expression is not a sequential problem and there is no external "formula" input for training. Another type of interesting works are word embedding methods [17], however in reality we do not have enough formula data to learn their underlying similarity.

3 Methodology

The neuro-encoded expression programming (NEEP) adopts an evolutionary algorithm (EA) to optimize the network connection weights, then use the neural network to generate the expression string, and the K-expression method to decode the string into a function and then calculate the simulation error (Fig. 2). The main contribution of this paper is the method for encoding and generating the expression tree, which is based on the output of a neural network.

3.1 General Framework

The first step of this method is initializing the parameters (e.g., pbest and gbest in particle swarm optimization [14], distribution mean and step size in covariance matrix adaptation evolution strategy [1]) and population (all the net weights to be optimized) of the evolutionary algorithm. When evaluating each network weights vector, the weights are inserted into a recurrent neural network that generates the expression strings composed of function operators (such as +, −, ∗, /) and terminal symbols (e.g., variables). After that, these strings are decoded into expression trees, which are equivalent to mathematical functions. By putting the data into the expression, we can compare its value and to the target value. We use the resulting error as the fitness value of each individual network in population. Then, we update all the necessary parameters in the evolutionary algorithm (e.g., update pbest, gbest and velocity according to fitness in PSO) and update the current solutions set (weights to be optimized). We repeat the above process until the termination condition is met (Fig. 2).

3.2 Encoding

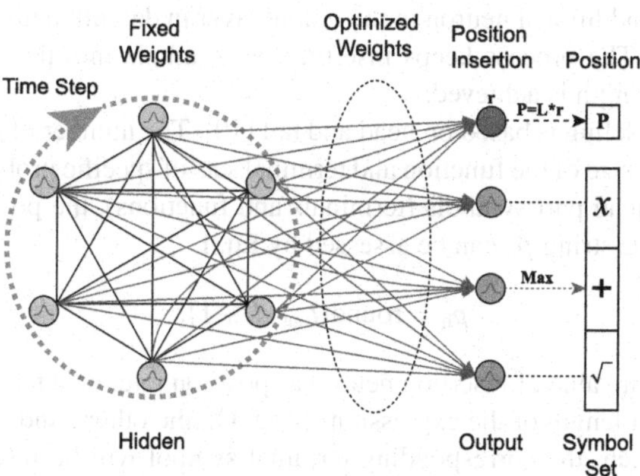

Fig. 3. The architecture of the encoder demonstrated in Fig. 2. The black lines in the dashed circle represent the fixed hidden weights of the recurrent neural network. The blue arrows are the output weights to be updated. After all the time steps, the model obtains the outputs and each output neuron corresponds to a function or terminal symbol. Then the output neuron with maximum value will trigger the single symbol at certain position. L is the current length of the expression string and r is the output value as position rate in $[0,\ 1]$. P denotes the position where the triggered symbol will be inserted. This general formula is interpreted into two cases of Eqs. 1 and 2. (Color figure online)

Inspired by biological brain, neural network presents flexible learning and powerful representation capability [33] and has been widely designed and applied in various fields [12,34]. The fully connected recurrent neural network [33] thus acts as the encoder which specifies the linear expression string. The neural network consists of hidden neurons and the output neurons, and all the hidden neurons are fully connected with each other. As is shown in Fig. 3, there are no formal input neurons in the network because no external information is input into the network during the generation of the string. Instead of back propagation, we use an evolutionary algorithm to optimize the weights between the output neurons and all the hidden neurons (see optimization part). The Gaussian shape function $f = e^{-x^2}$ is chosen as the activation function of the hidden and output neurons instead of a sigmoid function because of premature convergence during encoding the string.

Firstly, for symmetry, each neuron is initialized to zero. The hidden weights are uniformly randomized before the evolution and keep constant during the evolution. This fixed weights are the same for all the neural networks. As the behavior of the network can be chaotic, a small change in the initial condition could produce a significant difference in the later state [20]. As shown in [31], to reduce the instability we introduce fixed weights among all the hidden neurons and the remaining weights are still capable of finding the underlying pattern. All the other weights between the hidden and output neurons are uniformly randomized and are further optimized by evolutionary algorithms. After each time step, the output neurons are updated. Then, after all the time step the output neuron with the maximum value indicates which function or terminal symbol will be inserted into the expression string at a certain position. The position is determined by an additional neuron in the output layer in default, naming it the position insertion neuron. The process keeps inserting the symbols into the expression string until the desired length is achieved.

The string modeling is based on head and tail [10]. The number of output neurons is determined by the size of the function and terminal sets of specific problem. For position identification of head part symbols (terminals and functions), the position insertion in the head part of the string p_{h} can be assessed by Eq. 1.

$$p_{\mathrm{h}} = \mathrm{round}(i_{\mathrm{out}} \cdot L + 1), \tag{1}$$

where i_{out} is output value of insertion neuron as position rate, which is distributed in (0, 1]. L is the current length of the expression string. On the other hand, if L is larger than the head size h then, the corresponding terminal symbol will be inserted at a certain point of the tail part according to the value of position insertion neuron i_{out}. The value of position insertion neuron in the tail part p_{t} can be calculated by the given Eq. 2.

$$p_{\mathrm{t}} = \mathrm{round}(i_{\mathrm{out}} \cdot (L - h + 1) + h). \tag{2}$$

The whole process of symbol injection can be seen the encoding part in Fig. 2.

3.3 Decoding

The decoder is the translator which transfers the information from the string into the expression tree. The translation starting position is always the first position of the gene, whereas the last position of the gene does not necessarily coincide with the termination point.

Let us consider the encoded gene "$\sqrt{}$+-**xxsin$xyyyxyxxy$" as represented in Fig. 2. This encoded gene can be translated into the expression tree by the breadth-first technique which is further decoded into the mathematical function. The fitness value of each mathematical function/expression is calculated by measuring how well it fits the data, using mean square error (MSE) between the predicted values and the desired values. The decoding process is the same as in GEP (see more details in [10]).

3.4 Optimization

In the NEEP framework, we can choose different evolutionary algorithms to optimize the neural network for producing the most accurate expression. Three versions of NEEP are proposed in this work, which is GA-NEEP (based on GA, genetic algorithm [11]), PSO-NEEP (based on PSO, particle swarm optimization [14]), CMAES-NEEP (based on CMA-ES, covariance matrix adaptation evolution strategy [1]). In all the evolutionary algorithms, the population (chromosomes or particles) are the weight vectors, their values are uniformly randomized and then insert into the neural network for encoding the expression strings.

We do not use back propagation (BP) because the problem is different from conventional supervised learning. The evolved function is not fixed during the calculation of derivative of weights. It is quite hard to obtain gradients with a uniform BP for all the problems and evolved functions. On the other hand, evolutionary algorithms [5] can conduct efficient optimization by approximating search direction without gradient information and become an appropriate choice of optimizer.

3.4.1 Genetic Algorithm

Genetic algorithm (GA) [11] is the search and optimization procedure inspired by the natural selection process of genetic. For evolving the population selection, crossover and mutation operators are used for creating better offspring than the parents. GA is a robust optimization method that is easy to implement and requires few problem information. In this study, the individuals are the weight vectors whose values are randomly created. Each weight vector is put into the corresponding neural network and then obtains its fitness value. GA is adopted in this work as a baseline method.

3.4.2 Partials Swarm Optimization

Partials swarm optimization (PSO) [14,35] is a global numerical algorithm inspired by birds foraging. In PSO the particle migrate towards the direction of a combination of their former velocity personal best and global best and update its position. In this work, the particles are the weight vectors, and their values are randomly created. For the evaluation of these particles, they are inserted into the neural network and calculate their fitness values. PSO has shown robustness and efficiency in finding global optima.

3.4.3 Covariance Matrix Adaptation Evolution Strategy

Covariance matrix adaptation evolution strategy (CMA-ES) [1] is a leading stochastic and derivative-free method for continuous optimization of non-linear, non-convex functions. The CMA-ES samples candidate points with a multivariate normal distribution. It updates the mean vector and covariance matrix so that it encourages reproducing previously successful search steps based on the maximum-likelihood principle. The CMA-ES has shown advantageous convergence property when compared to many other evolutionary algorithms for a wide class of problems. CMSA-ES is adopted in this study as one of the optimizers because of the mentioned advantages and powerful performances.

4 Experiments

This section explores the performance of the proposed NEEP, and will not devise more sophisticated wrappers around GEP to improve the encoding way. The analysis will be limited to synthetic and benchmark regression problems. The three proposed methods are compared with standard GEP and standard GP. The problem configurations are outlined in Table 1, and the algorithm settings are described in the following subsection. Finally, the convergence behaviors and test accuracy are discussed.

4.1 Benchmark Configurations

We evaluated the proposed methods, GEP and GP on 14 synthetic benchmark problems [7,22,24] and 2 UCI data sets [6]. The Poly10 function is from [29]. All the benchmark problems are listed in Table 1. Function Poly10 and Sphere5 use the function set below

$$\{+, -, *, /\}.$$

The other functions use the function set below

$$\{+, -, *, /, \sin, \cos, e^n, \ln(|n|)\}.$$

The division is protected by $f = x/(y+\varepsilon)$, where ε is a very small number (e.g., 1E-100). Other benchmark details are listed in Table 1. All these difficult benchmark problems are commonly used due to their unique structural complexities with respect to objective formula. Several large scale benchmarks (e.g., 10 variables) for symbolic regression are considered one of the hard cases due to the difficulty of finding the solution in larger search space.

4.2 Compared Algorithm Configurations

Standard GEP and GP [16], which both are classic and powerful models in the field of genetic programming methods, are compared with the three instances of the proposed method (marked as GA-NEEP, PSO-NEEP, and CMAES-NEEP). For a fair comparison, all common parameters in the listed methods are initialized with the same value. All the algorithms in the experiments used a population size of 100, and the number of generations 500. Other parameters of GA, PSO and CMA-ES were specified by default. For GP, we used tournament size of 3, maximum tree depth of 10, maximum tree length of 61, maximum mutation depth of 4, maximum crossover of depth 10, maximum grow depth of 1 and minimum grow depth of 1. For GEP, we used header length of 30,

Table 1. Test problems used in this paper. $U[a, b, c]$ is c samples uniformly randomized in $[a, b]$ for the variable. $E[a, b, c]$ are mesh points which are spaced equally with an interval of c, from a to b inclusive.

Name	Variables	Function	Training set	Testing set
Sphere5	5	$x_1^2+x_2^2+x_3^2+x_4^2+x_5^2$	$U[1, 11, 1000]$	$U[1, 11, 1000]$
Dic1	10	$x_1+x_2+x_3+x_4+x_5$	$U[1, 11, 1000]$	$U[1, 11, 1000]$
Dic3	10	$x_1+\frac{x_2x_3}{x_4}+\frac{x_3x_4}{x_5}$	$U[1, 11, 1000]$	$U[1, 11, 1000]$
Dic4	10	$x_1x_2+x_2x_3+x_3x_4x_5+x_5x_6$	$U[1, 11, 1000]$	$U[1, 11, 1000]$
Dic5	10	$\sqrt{x_1}+\sin(x_2)+\log_e(x_3)$	$U[1, 11, 1000]$	$U[1, 11, 1000]$
Nico9	2	$x_1^4-x_1^3+x_2^2/2-x_2$	$U[-5, 5, 1000]$	$U[-5, 5, 1000]$
Nico14	6	$(x_5x_6)/(x_1/x_2x_3/x_4)$	$U[-5, 5, 1000]$	$U[-5, 5, 1000]$
Nico16	4	$32-3\frac{\tan(x_1)}{\tan(x_2)}\frac{\tan(x_3)}{\tan(x_4)}$	$U[-5, 5, 1000]$	$U[-5, 5, 1000]$
Nico20	10	$\sum_{i=1}^{5}\frac{1}{x_i}$	$U[-5, 5, 1000]$	$U[-5, 5, 1000]$
Poly10	10	$x_1x_2+x_2x_3+x_3x_4+x_4x_5+x_5x_6$ $+x_1x_7x_9+x_3x_6x_{10}$	$U[-1, 1, 250]$	$U[-1, 1, 250]$
Pagie1	2	$\frac{1}{1+x_1^{-4}}+\frac{1}{1+x_2^{-4}}$	$E[-5, 5, 0.4]$	$E[-4.95, 5.05, 0.4]$
Nguyen6	1	$\sin(x)+\sin(x+x^2)$	$U[-1, 1, 20]$	$U[-1, 1, 20]$
Nguyen7	1	$\ln(x+1)+\ln(x^2+1)$	$U[0, 2, 20]$	$U[0, 2, 20]$
Vlad3	2	$e^{-x}x^3(\cos x\sin x)(\cos x\sin^2 x-1)(y-5)$	$x: E[0.05, 10, 0.1]$ $y: E[0.05, 10.05, 2]$	$x: E[-0.5, 10.5, 0.05]$ $y: E[-0.5, 10.5, 0.5]$
Energy	8	Energy efficiency of buildings		
Concrete	8	Concrete compressive strength		

a crossover rate of 0.7, mutation rate of 0.1, IS transposition of 0.1, RIS transposition of 0.1, and the inversion rate of 0.1. For the three proposed methods (GA-NEEP, PSO-NEEP and CMAES-NEEP), we used header length of 30, hidden neurons 40, time steps of 10, the initial fixed weights sparsity of 0.5 and the initial optimizing weight range of $[-2, 2]$.

4.3 Results and Discussions

Table 2 summarizes the test errors obtained by GEP, GP and the three versions of NEEP on all the benchmark problems. The median and standard deviation are summarized over the 50 independent repeated trials for each of the 16 benchmarks function. It can be observed that the proposed methods (GA-NEEP, PSO-NEEP, CMAES-NEEP) significantly outperformed GEP and GP on 14 out of 16 problems according to the median of MSE, and perform competitively on the remaining problems. In particular, CMAES-NEEP reported dramatically lower MSE and more stable performance (according to their standard deviation values) on all the high dimensional data (Poly10, Dic1, Dic3, Dic4, Dic5, Nico20), while GEP and GP failed to locate the global optimum for these problems because the solution expressions of a high dimensional problem become overwhelming or extremely complicated. Therefore, such problems may become tough for the traditional GEP and GP due to their lack of capability to encode a complex function in a single string.

Table 2. Median, standard deviation and corresponding ranks of testing errors of the five compared algorithms. All differences are statistically significant according to a Wilcoxon test with a confidence level of 95%. Symbols − and + represent that the proposed method is respectively significantly worse than and better than the other two methods (GP and GEP). The other cases are marked with =.

	GEP	GP	GA-NEEP	PSO-NEEP	CMAES-NEEP
Sphere5	4.87e+04±6.58e+07	**3.93e+02**±1.40e+02	7.71e+02±4.46e+02	6.27e+02±4.35e+02	6.30e+02±1.17e+02
rank	5	1	4	2	3
			=	=	=
Dic1	6.00e+02±4.91e+07	1.55e+01±1.30e+01	2.04e+01±1.58e+01	2.83e+00±1.40e+01	**4.97e-30**±7.67e-02
rank	5	3	4	2	1
			=	+	+
Dic3	4.96e+02±5.58e+15	1.29e+02±2.61e+01	1.44e+02±2.39e+01	**1.18e+02**±2.51e+01	1.20e+02±1.30e+02
rank	5	3	4	1	2
			=	+	+
Dic4	7.00e+04±1.28e+11	6.68e+03±1.40e+04	3.01e+04±1.50e+04	5.12e+03±1.66e+04	**3.62e+03**±1.79e+03
rank	5	3	4	2	1
			=	=	+
Dic5	6.80e+00±1.35e+19	8.96e-01±8.70e-01	1.00e+00±2.61e-01	5.99e-01±2.50e-01	**5.54e-01**±1.21e-01
rank	5	3	4	2	1
			=	+	+
Nico9	4.80e+04±1.85e+19	**3.64e+02**±6.39e+03	1.32e+04±2.07e+05	1.27e+03±3.80e+03	2.65e+03±5.62e+04
rank	5	1	4	2	3
			=	=	=
Nico14	1.18e+07±1.47e+19	1.20e+07±6.95e+07	**1.18e+07**±1.12e+07	1.18e+07±1.93e+10	1.18e+07±5.89e+06
rank	3	5	1	4	2
			=	=	=
Nico16	4.47e+09±1.20e+18	4.48e+09±2.74e+11	**4.46e+09**±3.69e+11	4.91e+09±5.25e+12	4.46e+09±1.36e+13
rank	3	4	1	5	2
			=	-	=
Nico20	7.54e+02±1.21e+19	1.86e+03±4.64e+04	6.85e+02±2.15e+04	**5.19e+02**±5.52e+04	6.80e+02±1.54e+06
rank	4	5	3	1	2
			+	+	=
Poly10	5.48e-01±7.29e+00	3.24e-01±5.24e-02	3.21e-01±6.11e-02	3.21e-01±3.48e-02	**3.17e-01**±2.83e-02
rank	5	4	2	3	1
			=	+	+
Pagie1	9.61e-01±1.58e+19	1.26e-01±1.14e-01	1.95e-01±4.03e-02	1.24e-01±3.42e-02	**1.21e-01**±2.58e-02
rank	5	3	4	2	1
			=	=	=
Nguyen6	2.10e-01±2.57e+19	1.54e-01±1.61e-01	1.10e-01±1.22e-01	1.40e-02±3.28e-02	**4.41e-03**±1.47e-02
rank	5	4	3	2	1
			+	+	+
Nguyen7	2.63e-01±1.41e+19	3.92e-02±1.35e-01	3.30e-02±7.07e-01	2.19e-03±8.33e-02	**1.15e-03**±4.86e-03
rank	5	4	3	2	1
			+	+	+
Vlad3	7.63e+00±2.57e+20	1.22e+00±1.52e+12	**9.47e-01**±Inf	1.05e+00±Inf	1.01e+00±1.04e+33
rank	5	4	1	3	2
			+	=	+
Energy	1.06e+02±3.81e+18	2.58e+01±3.78e+01	4.52e+01±2.20e+01	**2.17e+01**±7.48e+00	2.34e+01±6.57e+00
rank	5	3	4	1	2
			=	+	+
Concrete	3.39e+02±5.78e+18	2.26e+02±6.63e+01	2.21e+02±2.66e+01	1.80e+02±3.41e+01	**1.66e+02**±3.38e+01
rank	5	4	3	2	1
			=	+	+
Avg. Rank	4.69	3.38	3.06	2.25	1.63

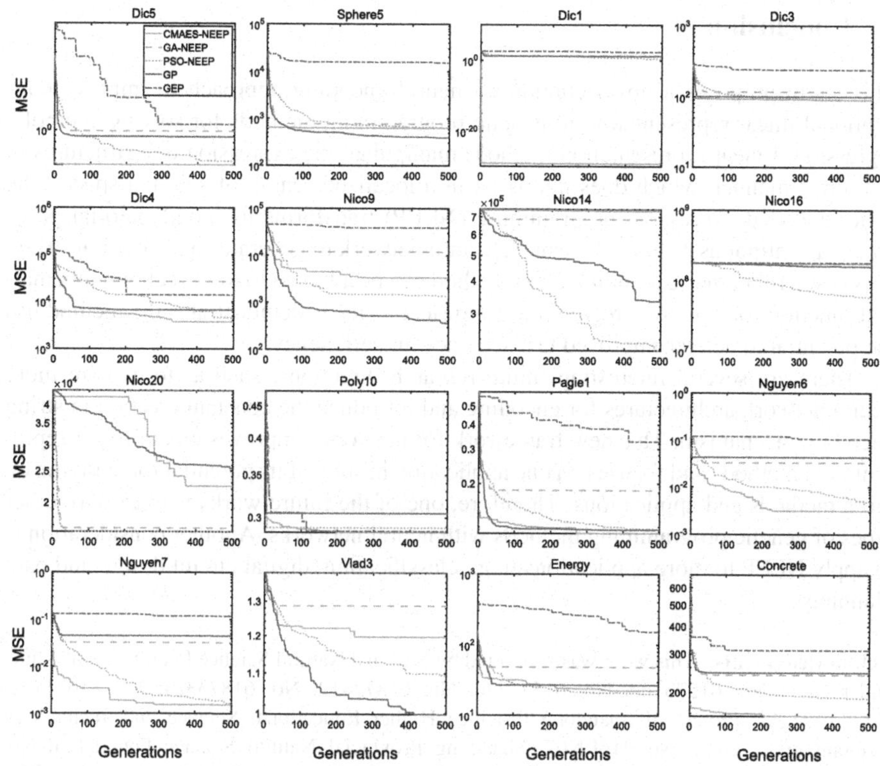

Fig. 4. Evolution of the average best training errors of 50 independent trials for all compared algorithms.

For the two regression data sets Concrete and Energy, the convergence curves in Fig. 4 and test errors in Table 2 reveal that CMAES-NEEP and PSO-NEEP have remarkable performance and high stability among all the compared methods. According to the convergence curves, in some functions (Nico16, Dic1, Dic3) these methods illustrate premature convergence and get stuck at a local optimum during evolution. For Nico9 and Sphere5 problem, GP sits as the best method among all the compared algorithms, due to its property of reusability of existing nodes during the encoding of the expression tree. On the other hand, GEP stands at the worst, and all other proposed methods show the competitive results concerning GP.

According to the test error results and the convergence curves, we can observe that the proposed method has shown more stable performance and faster training speed on most of the listed benchmark functions. In addition, we can obtain a rough conclusion that among the three evolutionary algorithms, CMA-ES is the most powerful, PSO is the second, and GA is the last one. These ranks also conform the general impression of their performances on many artificial benchmark functions in evolutionary computation. Therefore, it is important for NEEP to choose a strong optimizer for searching better neural networks.

5 Conclusion

This study proposes a novel continuous neural encoding approach to improve conventional linear representation in genetic programming methods for solving symbolic regression. Linear representation methods manipulate the expression tree structures in a discrete manner, which does not assist in a localized search of solution space. The neuro-encoded expression programming (NEEP) transforms the combinatorial problem to a continuous problem by using a neural network to generate an expression string, thus powerful numerical optimization method can be adopted to find a better mathematical function for symbolic regression. Empirical analysis demonstrates the method has the potential to deliver improved test accuracy and efficiency.

There are several interesting future research directions, such as to explore more neural network architectures for encoding and introduce the constant creation in string encoding mechanism. This new framework for now only improves one of linear representation methods and focuses on one application in spite of its potential for applying on more methods and applications. Therefore, one of the future works is to explore other types of genetic programming methods with neural networks. Another consideration is to apply NEEP to more applications (e.g., classification, digital circuit design and path planning).

Acknowledgments. This work was supported by National Natural Science Foundation of China under Grant No. 61573166, No. 61572230, No. 61872419, No. 61873324, No. 81671785, No. 61672262. Project of Shandong Province Higher Educational Science and Technology Program under Grant No. J16LN07. Shandong Provincial Natural Science Foundation No. ZR2019MF040, No. ZR2018LF005. Shandong Provincial Key R&D Program under Grant No. 2019GGX101041, No. 2018GGX101048, No. 2016ZDJS01A12, No. 2016GGX101001, No. 2017CXZC1206. Taishan Scholar Project of Shandong Province, China.

References

1. Auger, A., Hansen, N.: A restart CMA evolution strategy with increasing population size. In: 2005 IEEE Congress on Evolutionary Computation, vol. 2, pp. 1769–1776 (2005). https://doi.org/10.1109/CEC.2005.1554902
2. Bowman, S.R., Vilnis, L., Vinyals, O., Dai, A., Jozefowicz, R., Bengio, S.: Generating sentences from a continuous space. In: Proceedings of the 20th SIGNLL Conference on Computational Natural Language Learning, pp. 10–21 (2016). https://doi.org/10.18653/v1/K16-1002
3. Brameier, M.F., Banzhaf, W.: Basic concepts of linear genetic programming. In: Linear Genetic Programming, pp. 13–34. Springer, Boston (2007). https://doi.org/10.1007/978-0-387-31030-5_2
4. Chatzarakis, G.E., Li, T.: Oscillation criteria for delay and advanced differential equations with nonmonotone arguments. Complexity **2018**, 1–18 (2018). https://doi.org/10.1155/2018/8237634
5. Chen, C.L.P., Zhang, T., Chen, L., Tam, S.C.: I-Ching divination evolutionary algorithm and its convergence analysis. IEEE Trans. Cybern. **47**(1), 2–13 (2017). https://doi.org/10.1109/TCYB.2015.2512286
6. Dheeru, D., Karra Taniskidou, E.: UCI machine learning repository (2017)

7. Dick, G.: Sensitivity-like analysis for feature selection in genetic programming. In: Proceedings of the Genetic and Evolutionary Computation Conference, pp. 401–408. ACM (2017). https://doi.org/10.1145/3071178.3071338
8. Fan, P., Xin, W., Ouyang, Y.: Approximation of discrete spatial data for continuous facility location design. Integr. Comput. Aided Eng. **21**(4), 311–320 (2014). https://doi.org/10.3233/ICA-140466
9. Ferreira, C.: Automatically defined functions in gene expression programming. In: Nedjah, N., Mourelle, L.M., Abraham, A. (eds.) Genetic Systems Programming. SCI, vol. 13, pp. 21–56. Springer, Heidelberg (2006). https://doi.org/10.1007/3-540-32498-4_2
10. Ferreira, C.: Gene expression programming: a new adaptive algorithm for solving problems. Complex Syst. **13**(2), 87–129 (2001). https://doi.org/10.1007/3-540-32849-1
11. Holland, J.H.: Adaptation in Natural and Artificial Systems: An Introductory Analysis with Applications to Biology, Control, and Artificial Intelligence. MIT Press, Cambridge (1992)
12. Huang, W., Oh, S.K., Pedrycz, W.: Hybrid fuzzy wavelet neural networks architecture based on polynomial neural networks and fuzzy set/relation inference-based wavelet neurons. IEEE Trans. Neural Netw. Learn. Syst. **29**(8), 3452–3462 (2018). https://doi.org/10.1109/TNNLS.2017.2729589
13. Kataoka, Y., Matsubara, T., Uehara, K.: Image generation using generative adversarial networks and attention mechanism. In: IEEE/ACIS 15th International Conference on Computer and Information Science (ICIS), pp. 1–6 (2016). https://doi.org/10.1109/ICIS.2016.7550880
14. Kennedy, J., Eberhart, R.: Particle swarm optimization. In: Proceedings of the International Conference on Neural Networks, ICNN 1995, vol. 4, pp. 1942–1948 (1995). https://doi.org/10.1109/ICNN.1995.488968
15. Koza, J.R., Andre, D., Bennett III, F.H., Keane, M.A.: Use of automatically defined functions and architecture-altering operations in automated circuit synthesis with genetic programming. In: Proceedings of the First Annual Conference on Genetic Programming, pp. 132–140 (1996)
16. Langdon, W.B., Poli, R., McPhee, N.F., Koza, J.R.: Genetic programming: an introduction and tutorial, with a survey of techniques and applications. In: Fulcher, J., Jain, L.C. (eds.) Computational Intelligence: A Compendium. SCI, vol. 115, pp. 927–1028. Springer, Heidelberg (2008). https://doi.org/10.1007/978-3-540-78293-3_22
17. Levy, O., Goldberg, Y.: Neural word embedding as implicit matrix factorization. In: Advances in Neural Information Processing Systems, pp. 2177–2185 (2014)
18. Liskowski, P., Błądek, I., Krawiec, K.: Neuro-guided genetic programming: prioritizing evolutionary search with neural networks. In: Proceedings of the Genetic and Evolutionary Computation Conference, pp. 1143–1150 (2018). https://doi.org/10.1145/3205455.3205629
19. Maehara, T., Marumo, N., Murota, K.: Continuous relaxation for discrete DC programming. Math. Programm. **169**(1), 199–219 (2018). https://doi.org/10.1007/s10107-017-1139-2
20. Manjunath, G., Jaeger, H.: Echo state property linked to an input: exploring a fundamental characteristic of recurrent neural networks. Neural Comput. **25**(3), 671–696 (2013). https://doi.org/10.1162/NECO_a_00411
21. McConaghy, T.: FFX: fast, scalable, deterministic symbolic regression technology. In: Riolo, R., Vladislavleva, E., Moore, J. (eds.) Genetic Programming Theory and Practice IX. Genetic and Evolutionary Computation, pp. 235–260. Springer, New York (2011). https://doi.org/10.1007/978-1-4614-1770-5_13
22. McDermott, J., et al.: Genetic programming needs better benchmarks. In: Proceedings of the 14th Annual Conference on Genetic and Evolutionary Computation, pp. 791–798 (2012). https://doi.org/10.1145/2330163.2330273
23. Mogren, O.: C-RNN-GAN: continuous recurrent neural networks with adversarial training (2016). arXiv preprint: arXiv:1611.09904

24. Nicolau, M., Agapitos, A., O'Neill, M., Brabazon, A.: Guidelines for defining benchmark problems in genetic programming. In: 2015 IEEE Congress on Evolutionary Computation (CEC), pp. 1152–1159 (2015). https://doi.org/10.1109/CEC.2015.7257019
25. Oltean, M., Grosan, C.: Evolving evolutionary algorithms using multi expression programming. In: The 7th European Conference on Artificial Life, vol. 2801, pp. 651–658 (2003). https://doi.org/10.1007/978-3-540-39432-7_70
26. O'Neill, M., Ryan, C.: Under the hood of grammatical evolution. In: Proceedings of the 1st Annual Conference on Genetic and Evolutionary Computation, vol. 2, pp. 1143–1148 (1999)
27. Orzechowski, P., La Cava, W., Moore, J.H.: Where are we now?: A large benchmark study of recent symbolic regression methods. In: Proceedings of the Genetic and Evolutionary Computation Conference, pp. 1183–1190 (2018). https://doi.org/10.1145/3205455.3205539
28. Pardalos, P.M., Prokopyev, O.A., Busygin, S.: Continuous approaches for solving discrete optimization problems. In: Appa, G., Pitsoulis, L., Williams, H.P. (eds.) Handbook on Modelling for Discrete Optimization. International Series in Operations Research & Management Science, vol. 88, pp. 39–60. Springer, Boston (2006). https://doi.org/10.1007/0-387-32942-0_2
29. Poli, R.: A simple but theoretically-motivated method to control bloat in genetic programming. In: Ryan, C., Soule, T., Keijzer, M., Tsang, E., Poli, R., Costa, E. (eds.) EuroGP 2003. LNCS, vol. 2610, pp. 204–217. Springer, Heidelberg (2003). https://doi.org/10.1007/3-540-36599-0_19
30. Rothlauf, F.: Analysis and design of representations for trees. In: Representations for Genetic and Evolutionary Algorithms, pp. 141–215. Springer, Heidelberg (2006). https://doi.org/10.1007/3-540-32444-5_6
31. Sussillo, D., Abbott, L.F.: Generating coherent patterns of activity from chaotic neural networks. Neuron **63**(4), 544–557 (2009). https://doi.org/10.1016/j.neuron.2009.07.018
32. Wang, H., Qin, Z., Wan, T.: Text generation based on generative adversarial nets with latent variables. In: Phung, D., Tseng, V.S., Webb, G.I., Ho, B., Ganji, M., Rashidi, L. (eds.) 2018 Pacific-Asia Conference on Knowledge Discovery and Data Mining, pp. 92–103 (2018). https://doi.org/10.1007/978-3-319-93037-4_8
33. Wang, L., Orchard, J.: Investigating the evolution of a neuroplasticity network for learning. IEEE Trans. Syst. Man Cybern. Syst. (2017). https://doi.org/10.1109/TSMC.2017.2755066
34. Wang, L., Yang, B., Chen, Y., Zhang, X., Orchard, J.: Improving neural-network classifiers using nearest neighbor partitioning. IEEE Trans. Neural Netw. Learn. Syst. **28**(10), 2255–2267 (2017). https://doi.org/10.1109/TNNLS.2016.2580570
35. Wang, L., Yang, B., Orchard, J.: Particle swarm optimization using dynamic tournament topology. Appl. Soft Comput. **48**, 584–596 (2016). https://doi.org/10.1016/j.asoc.2016.07.041
36. Wang, L., Yang, B., Wang, S., Liang, Z.: Building image feature kinetics for cement hydration using gene expression programming with similarity weight tournament selection. IEEE Trans. Evol. Comput. **19**(5), 679–693 (2015). https://doi.org/10.1109/TEVC.2014.2367111
37. Xin, L., Chi, Z., Weimin, X., Peter, C.N.: Prefix gene expression programming. In: Late Breaking Paper at Genetic and Evolutionary Computation Conference, pp. 25–29 (2005)
38. Yin, J., Meng, Y., Jin, Y.: A developmental approach to structural self-organization in reservoir computing. IEEE Trans. Auton. Mental Dev. **4**(4), 273–289 (2012). https://doi.org/10.1109/TAMD.2012.2182765
39. Zelinka, I., Oplatkova, Z., Nolle, L.: Analytic programming-symbolic regression by means of arbitrary evolutionary algorithms. Int. J. Simul. Syst. Sci. Technol. **6**(9), 44–56 (2005)
40. Zhong, J., Feng, L., Ong, Y.S.: Gene expression programming: a survey. IEEE Comput. Intell. Mag. **12**(3), 54–72 (2017). https://doi.org/10.1109/MCI.2017.2708618

Compute-Efficient Neural Network Architecture Optimization by a Genetic Algorithm

Sebastian Litzinger(✉), Andreas Klos, and Wolfram Schiffmann

Faculty of Mathematics and Computer Science,
FernUniversität in Hagen, Hagen, Germany
{sebastian.litzinger,Andreas.Klos,Wolfram.Schiffmann}@fernuni-hagen.de

Abstract. A neural network's topology greatly influences its generalization ability. Many approaches to topology optimization employ heuristics, for example genetic algorithms, oftentimes consuming immense computational resources. In this contribution, we present a genetic algorithm for network topology optimization which can be deployed effectively in low-resource settings. To this end, we utilize the TensorFlow framework for network training and operate with several techniques reducing the computational load. The genetic algorithm is subsequently applied to the MNIST image classification task in two different scenarios.

Keywords: Neural networks · Neural Architecture Search · Genetic algorithms

1 Introduction

Since an ANN's topology greatly influences its ability to generalize, topology optimization is a viable means to improve an ANN's performance. In order to find ANN topologies that facilitate high generalization performance we have to explore a huge search space including: hidden layers (types and dimensions), activation function, weight initialization, loss function, training algorithm, epochs, mini-batch size, stopping criterion, Neural Architecture Search (NAS) algorithm.

This paper is dedicated to a NAS algorithm based on genetic algorithms (GAs), which was first introduced in 1989 [12]. In [10] a hierarchical representation for architecture search is introduced. The first level is composed of primitive nodes, e.g. convolution, max pooling etc., which are assembled to more complex nodes in each subsequent level. This algorithm was applied using 200 GPUs for 1.5 days and is therefore considered as computationally demanding.

Besides, in [13] a gradient based evolution of Convolutional Neural Networks (CNNs) is proposed. The search space is restricted to reduce the computational demands and facilitate the analysis on consumer hardware. To favor small CNNs a penalty term, based on the number of multiply-accumulate operations, is added to the normal fitness value. Unfortunately, the processing time till termination and the purpose of upscaling the images, e.g. MNIST [9], is left unconsidered.

I. V. Tetko et al. (Eds.): ICANN 2019, LNCS 11728, pp. 387–392, 2019.
https://doi.org/10.1007/978-3-030-30484-3_32

In [3] topologies and learning parameters of CNNs are selected based on GA and Dynamic Structured Grammatical Evolution (DSGE). The fitness evaluation is composed of two steps: mapping from genotype to phenotype and training of the ANN. Furthermore, the correlation between average fitness and the number of layers per generation is examined. The analysis lacks the reference of the used hardware and the required time to achieve the results. Additionally, some special tweaks of the final training procedure were necessary to achieve the results. Moreover, in [4] CNNs are evolved by a GA and grammatical evolution. To facilitate the introduced NAS in low-resource settings the search space was heavily restricted. Two fitness measures are applied to prevent sticking to local optima. The first fitness value is based on the prediction accuracy acquired during the training. The second one is a penalty term and is influenced by a similarity measure between newly created and the remaining individuals. Unfortunately, the computation time required to reach the shown results is not stated.

If we had unrestricted compute resources we could make all the necessary design decisions automatically. Unfortunately, in a realistic setup we have to find a path through the space of opportunities and target our search to a low-resource hardware setup. The main objectives of our research are: 1. development of a GA for the topology optimization of ANNs with regard to classification accuracy and/or model size, 2. implementation of the fitness evaluation component in TensorFlow (TF), 3. application of various techniques lowering the computational effort when training a network or restricting the GA's search space. Thereby, the non expert user is enabled to obtain ANNs tailored to the problem at hand, with little demands on the available hardware resources.

The paper is structured as follows: In Sect. 2, the GA implementation and our chosen parametrization are outlined. In Sect. 3 the results are presented. Section 4 recapitulates our contribution and gives an outlook on our future work.

2 GA Implementation and Parametrization

This section is structured as follows: First, our GA for NAS is described. Then, its interaction with TF is presented and an overview of ANN training techniques incorporated into the GA is provided. Finally, the GA's parametrization and several methods to lower the computational load are introduced.

GAs approximate optimal solutions to a certain problem by iteratively attempting to improve solutions from a subset of solutions already developed. In the context of NAS, a solution represents an ANN's architecture. In this paper a solution's fitness is primarily regarded as the classification accuracy on the test set. As an ANN's ability to generalize is advanced by keeping the number of free parameters low [15], this value should also be considered when an ANN's fitness is determined. That way, selection and population update can be adapted to specific goals, e.g., they can be based on the number of free parameters after reaching a certain accuracy and thus guide the algorithm to finding an architecture capable of delivering a desired accuracy while being kept as small as possible. Aside from better generalization ability, smaller ANNs require less computation power for training and prediction takes less time.

New solutions evolve by *mutation*, i,e., one of the properties changes, or by *recombination* (often *crossover*) with a second solution from the population; the new solution thus inherits characteristics from each of the two original solutions. In the present context, a mutation is one of the following operations: inserting or deleting a layer, modifying a layer (depending on layer type: number of neurons, dimension of convolution kernel, stride, number of feature maps, type of zero padding, aggregation operation) or switching two layers. Optionally, the degree of mutation decays exponentially during the course of the GA's execution. Thus, in the early phase architectures are developed which differ significantly from previous ones and exploration of the solution space advances quickly. Later, when execution nears termination, modifications become subtle so that solutions developed so far are refined in order to closely approximate an optimal solution.

Training success of ANNs can vary due to stochastic elements like weight initialization. It is therefore conceivable that a network may deliver significantly better performance when retrained from scratch. This consideration is reflected in our GA which provides the opportunity to repeatedly train a network with a certain architecture based on two factors: An architecture may be re-evaluated if it has surpassed a given accuracy value when first evaluated, thereby scrutinizing the most promising architectures. Furthermore, the maximum number of training runs during the evaluation phase can be tied to the ANN's number of free parameters, allowing more training runs the fewer free parameters a network has. The repeated training of ANNs necessitates extensive computations. We utilize TF which offers various techniques, e.g., early stopping and instruments to improve a network's training and thus ultimately its predictive performance.

We have chosen the TF Estimator API to create the GA's evaluation component. An object describing the ANN's architecture is fed into the estimator model function, where it forms the basis for generating the ANN. The ANN is then trained, evaluated and finally, its test set accuracy is returned.

Our GA discovered an architecture suitable for classification of MNIST. The training set is divided in 55,000 training and 5000 validation images. Before running the GA, adequate parameter values for network training as well as for the GA have been determined. In this endeavor, we adopted the network architecture used to classify the MNIST dataset from the TF documentation [1] and recorded loss, accuracy, and execution time for various training algorithms and learning rates.

3 Results

We employed the GA to find a suitable ANN topology covering two scenarios: 1. matching the accuracy of the ANN in [1] with the smallest count of free parameters. 2. surpassing the accuracy of the ANN in [1] while not exceeding its number of free parameters.

In the first scenario, the GA completed 2000 iterations in 47 h on a Nvidia GeForce GTX 1050 Ti. The best architecture is shown in Table 1. It contains 5 hidden layers and reaches a test set accuracy of 0.9940 (i.e. a test error rate of 0.60%) with 61,787 free parameters, which is about 1.9% the size of the ANN in [1] featuring 3,274,634 free parameters.

Table 1. Best architecture found for first scenario

Layer type	Dimensions	Kernel	Stride	Feature maps
Input	28 × 28			
Convolutional	14 × 28	5 × 5	2 × 1	52
Avg. pooling	14 × 28	2 × 3	1 × 1	
Convolutional	14 × 28	3 × 2	1 × 1	50
Convolutional	7 × 14	5 × 3	2 × 2	24
Convolutional	4 × 14	2 × 5	2 × 1	33
Dense	10			

Here, the GA demonstrates its ability to reveal small yet well-performing architectures – an essential capability when designing an ANN which will operate under firm real-time constraints and must produce predictions rapidly. By regarding the number of free parameters as the decisive fitness criterion after reaching a certain test set accuracy, the GA was steered to favor ANNs with convolutional and pooling layers as hidden layers, since these layer types add fewer free parameters to the ANN than dense layers. Consequently, the only dense layer is the ANN's output layer.

In the second scenario, a higher computational load is to be expected due to larger ANN size. Therefore, we implemented further techniques to mitigate this effect: weight sharing and layer freezing. After an ANN's evaluation, its weights are stored and when being selected in a subsequent iteration of the GA, the evolved ANN retrieves its ancestor's weights up to the layer where a change in ANN architecture has occurred. These weights are then exempted from training, so the computational load for ANN training lessens. The comparative experiments we have performed to quantify the effect of employing these techniques show that runtime drops to $<\frac{1}{3}$. Moreover, in the second scenario we introduced another layer type – the residual unit [8]. To determine the influence of some of the parameters, the GA was executed several times, each time under slightly different configurations: 1. high mutation rate, no decay of mutation increment/decrement values, 2. high mutation rate, no decay of mutation increment/decrement values, number of GA iterations greatly increased (8000), 3. high recombination rate, no decay of mutation increment/decrement values, 4. high mutation rate, decay of mutation increment/decrement values, 5. high mutation rate, no decay of mutation increment/decrement values, local response normalization (LRN). The evolved architectures of the best performing ANNs are obtained within days utilizing single Nvidia Pascal consumer graphics cards.

The result from configuration 1 (4 residual, 2 conv. and 2 dense layers, 2,689,180 free parameters), reaches a 0.31% test error rate. In configuration 2, the best architecture is composed of 4 residual, 6 conv., 1 pooling and 2 dense layers (1,071,154 free parameters) and achieves a slightly higher test error rate of 0.32%. Despite the deeper architecture, the ANN contains roughly 40% of the best ANN's number of free parameters. Configuration 3 results in an architecture consisting of 1 residual, 2 conv., 1 pooling and 4 dense layers (1,984,664 free parameters). The most notable difference is the larger number of dense layers compared to the other architectures. However, this does not lead to a lower test error rate. The results from configuration 4 show that the decay of the mutation operators' values does not have any impact on the quality of results. The architecture features 2 residual, 4 conv., 1 pooling and 3 dense layers (1,850,248 free parameters) and accomplishes a 0.32% test set error. In configuration 5, the application of LRN provided slightly worse results (best test error rate 0.37%)

and led to a significantly higher runtime of the GA. It should therefore not be employed in low-resource settings.

In [9] an overview of test error rates on the MNIST dataset attained with various machine learning methods is given. ANNs, and CNNs in particular, achieve the lowest values. In [6], a multi-layer perceptron with 12 million free parameters reaches 0.35% test error rate. To prevent the ANN from overfitting, data augmentation is applied to the input. A CNN with six convolutional layers obtaining 0.35% test error rate is presented in [7]. The very best test error rates of 0.23% and 0.27% are accomplished in [5], where multi-column deep ANNs are deployed. In each of these cases, input data is preprocessed, which incurs additional resource consumption. All in all, 2 of the 69 entries in [9] outperform the best ANN encountered by the proposed GA. In [4], the authors list the most competitive recent results on MNIST obtained without data augmentation. The best ANN accomplishes a test error rate of 0.24%, while 12 of the 37 list entries achieve error rates below 0.4%, 3 of which even reach error rates <0.31%. This demonstrates that our endeavor to reduce resource consumption does not impair the quality of the results developed by our GA. Table 2 shows results obtained on the MNIST dataset by other NAS approaches. The best accuracy of 0.28% test error rate is achieved by [11] featuring the genetic DCNN designer and data augmentation. It took 30 GPU days (10 generations à 3 days) on a Nvidia Titan XP to produce the corresponding architecture. DENSER [2] reaches a 0.30% test error rate with an approach based on evolutionary computation comprising not only ANN topology optimization but also hyperparameter tuning. Furthermore, for the best result data augmentation was applied. In [4], the authors reach a test error rate of 0.37% with a grammatical neuroevolution procedure and report worse results for a genetic algorithm. AmoebaNet-A [14] employs a tournament selection evolutionary algorithm with a focus on the age of an individual, preferring younger over older ones, which yields a test error rate of ≈0.50%. In [13], an architecture generated via differential evolution reaches a 1.34% test error rate. Compared to other approaches, our proposal thus combines competitive accuracy (0.31% test error rate vs. 0.28% best test error rate obtained in [11]) with moderate computational effort (a few days on a Pascal consumer card) while refraining from hyperparameter optimization or data augmentation as in [2], which offers the possibility to further improve the results. Moreover, we have shown that with our proposed technique, one can trade accuracy for lower ANN complexity. Thus, architectures can be created which reach a user-specified target accuracy and at the same time allow for rapid predictions or can be deployed to computationally less powerful devices.

Table 2. Results of other NAS methods

Work	Test set accuracy
Ma and Xia [11]	99.72%
Assunção et al. [2]	99.70%
Proposed approach	99.69%
Baldominos et al. [4]	99.63%
Real et al. [14]	≈99.50%
Mitschke et al. [13]	98.67%

4 Conclusions

We have presented a GA for NAS and placed a strong focus on efficiency by employing various techniques to lower the computational effort. That way, we aim to facilitate NAS in low-resource settings. Furthermore, it has been demonstrated that the GA is capable of producing competitive results on the MNIST dataset with fairly low resource commitment. This especially holds true in comparison to other NAS methods, where the only approaches delivering (marginally) better results necessitate more extensive computations as well as the application of further techniques such as data augmentation or hyperparameter optimization.

References

1. Abadi, M., et al.: TensorFlow: large-scale machine learning on heterogeneous systems (2015). https://www.tensorflow.org/tutorials/estimators/cnn
2. Assunção, F., et al.: DENSER: deep evolutionary network structured representation. CoRR abs/1801.01563 (2018). http://arxiv.org/abs/1801.01563
3. Assunção, F., Lourenço, N., Machado, P., Ribeiro, B.: Evolving the topology of large scale deep neural networks. In: Castelli, M., Sekanina, L., Zhang, M., Cagnoni, S., García-Sánchez, P. (eds.) EuroGP 2018. LNCS, vol. 10781, pp. 19–34. Springer, Cham (2018). https://doi.org/10.1007/978-3-319-77553-1_2
4. Baldominos, A., Saez, Y., Isasi, P.: Evolutionary convolutional neural networks: an application to handwriting recognition. Neurocomputing **283**, 38–52 (2018)
5. Ciresan, D.C., Meier, U., Schmidhuber, J.: Multi-column deep neural networks for image classification. In: Proceedings of the IEEE Conference on Computer Vision and Pattern Recognition, pp. 3642–3649 (2012)
6. Ciresan, D.C., et al.: Deep, big, simple neural nets for handwritten digit recognition. Neural Comput. **22**(12), 3207–3220 (2010)
7. Ciresan, D.C., et al.: Flexible, high performance convolutional neural networks for image classification. In: Walsh, T. (ed.) Proceedings of the Twenty-Second International Joint Conference on Artificial Intelligence, pp. 1237–1242 (2011)
8. He, K., et al.: Deep residual learning for image recognition. CoRR abs/1512.03385 (2015). http://arxiv.org/abs/1512.03385
9. LeCun, et al.: The MNIST database of handwritten digits. http://yann.lecun.com/exdb/mnist/. Accessed 21 Sept 2018
10. Liu, H., et al.: Hierarchical representations for efficient architecture search. CoRR abs/1711.00436 (2017). http://arxiv.org/abs/1711.00436
11. Ma, B., et al.: Autonomous deep learning: a genetic DCNN designer for image classification. CoRR abs/1807.00284 (2018). http://arxiv.org/abs/1807.00284
12. Miller, G., et al.: Designing neural networks using genetic algorithms. In: Proceedings of the 3rd International Conference on Genetic Algorithms, pp. 379–384. Morgan Kaufmann Publishers Inc., San Francisco (1989)
13. Mitschke, N., et al.: Gradient based evolution to optimize the structure of convolutional neural networks. In: Proceedings of the 25th IEEE Conference on Image Processing (ICIP), pp. 3438–3442 (2018)
14. Real, E., et al.: Regularized evolution for image classifier architecture search. CoRR abs/1802.01548 (2018). http://arxiv.org/abs/1802.01548
15. Schwartz, D., et al.: Exhaustive learning. Neural Comput. **2**, 371–382 (1990)

Controlling Model Complexity in Probabilistic Model-Based Dynamic Optimization of Neural Network Structures

Shota Saito[1,2(✉)] and Shinichi Shirakawa[1]

[1] Yokohama National University, Yokohama, Kanagawa, Japan
saito-shota-bt@ynu.jp, shirakawa-shinichi-bg@ynu.ac.jp
[2] SkillUp AI Co., Ltd., Tokyo, Japan
s_saito@skillupai.com

Abstract. A method of simultaneously optimizing both the structure of neural networks and the connection weights in a single training loop can reduce the enormous computational cost of neural architecture search. We focus on the probabilistic model-based dynamic neural network structure optimization that considers the probability distribution of structure parameters and simultaneously optimizes both the distribution parameters and connection weights based on gradient methods. Since the existing algorithm searches for the structures that only minimize the training loss, this method might find overly complicated structures. In this paper, we propose the introduction of a penalty term to control the model complexity of obtained structures. We formulate a penalty term using the number of weights or units and derive its analytical natural gradient. The proposed method minimizes the objective function injected the penalty term based on the stochastic gradient descent. We apply the proposed method in the unit selection of a fully-connected neural network and the connection selection of a convolutional neural network. The experimental results show that the proposed method can control model complexity while maintaining performance.

Keywords: Neural networks · Structure optimization · Stochastic natural gradient · Model complexity · Stochastic relaxation

1 Introduction

Deep neural networks (DNNs) are making remarkable progress in a variety of tasks, such as image recognition and machine translation. While various neural network structures have been developed to improve predictive performance, the selection or design of neural network structures remains the user's task. In general, tuning a neural network structure improves model performance. It is, however, tedious, because the user must design an appropriate structure for the target task through trial-and-error.

To automate neural network structure design processes, methods called neural architecture search have been developed. A popular approach is to regard

I. V. Tetko et al. (Eds.): ICANN 2019, LNCS 11728, pp. 393–405, 2019.
https://doi.org/10.1007/978-3-030-30484-3_33

the structure parameters (e.g., the numbers of layers and units, the type of layers, and the connectivity) as the hyperparameters and optimized them through black-box optimization methods, such as the evolutionary algorithms [15,19] and Bayesian optimization [9]. Another approach trains the neural network that generates the network architecture using policy gradient-based reinforcement learning methods [23]. However, these approaches require huge computational resources; several works conducted the experiments using more than 100 GPUs [15,23], as the evaluation of a candidate structure requires model training and takes several hours in the case of DNNs.

To solve the computational bottleneck, alternative methods that simultaneously optimize both the structure and the connection weights in a single training loop have been proposed [10,14,17]. These methods are promising because they can find structures with better prediction performance using only one GPU. In this paper, we employ the *dynamic structure optimization* framework introduced in [17] as the baseline algorithm. This framework considers the probability distribution of structure parameters and simultaneously optimizes both the distribution parameters and weights based on gradient methods.

The above-mentioned methods concentrate on finding neural network structures demonstrating high prediction performance; that is, they search for a structure that minimizes validation or training error. The structures found based on such criteria might become resource-hungry. To deploy such neural networks using limited computing resources, such as mobile devices, a compact yet high-performing structure is required. Several studies introduced the model complexity-based objective function, such as the total number of weights and/or FLOPs. Tan et al. [20] introduced latency (delay time with respect to (w.r.t.) data transfer) to the objective function as the penalty in the policy gradient-based neural architecture search and searched for a platform-aware structure. Additionally, multi-objective optimization methods have been applied to obtain the structures over a trade-off curve of the performance and model complexity [3,4]. However, such methods require greater computational resource, as existing methods are based on hyperparameter optimization.

For the purpose of obtaining compact structures, regularization-based connection pruning methods have been investigated. Han et al. [5] used L2 norm regularization of weights and iterate the weight coefficient-based pruning and retraining. This method obtained a simpler structure with the same performance as the original structure. Liu et al. [11] proposed channel-wise pruning for use with convolutional neural networks (CNNs) with the addition of new weights for each channel; the weights are penalized through L1 norm regularization. In general, regularization-based pruning methods impose a penalty on the weight values. It is, therefore, difficult to directly use aspect of the network size, such as the number of weight parameters or units, as the penalty.

In this paper, we introduce a penalty term for controlling model complexity in the dynamic structure optimization method [17]. In accordance with the literature [17], we assume the binary vector as the structure parameters that can use to represent the network structure, such as the selection of units or connections between layers. Further, we consider the multivariate Bernoulli distribution and formulate the objective function to be minimized as the expectation of loss function under the distribution. Then the penalty term w.r.t. the number of weights or units is incorporated into the loss to control the model complexity. To investigate the effects of the proposed penalty term, we apply this method in the unit selection of a fully-connected neural network and the connection selection of densely connected CNN (DenseNet) [7]. The experimental result shows that the proposed method can control the model complexity and preferentially remove insignificant units and connections to maintain the performance.

2 The Baseline Algorithm

We will now briefly explain the dynamic structure optimization framework proposed in [17]. Neural networks are modeled as $\phi(W, M)$ by two types of parameters: the vector of connection weights W and the structure parameter M. The structure parameter $M \in \mathcal{M}$ determines d hyperparameters, such as the connectivity of each layer or the existence of units. Let us consider that the structure parameter M is sampled from the probabilistic distribution $p(M \mid \theta)$, which is parameterized by a vector $\theta \in \Theta$ as a distribution parameter. We denote the loss to be minimized as $\mathcal{L}(W, M) = \int l(z, W, M) p(z) \mathrm{d}z$, where $l(z, W, M)$ and $p(z)$ indicate the loss of a datum z and the probability distribution of z, respectively.

Instead of directly optimizing $\mathcal{L}(W, M)$, the *stochastic relaxation* of M is considered; that is, the following expected loss under $p(M \mid \theta)$ is minimized:

$$\mathcal{G}(W, \theta) = \int \mathcal{L}(W, M) p(M \mid \theta) \mathrm{d}M, \tag{1}$$

where $\mathrm{d}M$ is a reference measure on $\mathcal{M}$. To optimize W and θ, we use the following vanilla (Euclidian) gradient w.r.t. W and the natural gradient w.r.t. θ:

$$\nabla_W \mathcal{G}(W, \theta) = \int \nabla_W \mathcal{L}(W, M) p(M \mid \theta) \mathrm{d}M, \tag{2}$$

$$\tilde{\nabla}_\theta \mathcal{G}(W, \theta) = \int \mathcal{L}(W, M) \tilde{\nabla}_\theta \ln p(M \mid \theta) p(M \mid \theta) \mathrm{d}M, \tag{3}$$

where $\tilde{\nabla}_\theta = F(\theta)^{-1} \nabla_\theta$ is the so-called natural gradient [2] and $F(\theta)$ is the Fisher information matrix of $p(M \mid \theta)$. Optimizing θ using (3) works the same way as information geometric optimization (IGO) [13], which is a unified framework for probabilistic model-based evolutionary algorithms. Different from the IGO, Shirakawa et al. [17] proposed the simultaneously updating of W and θ with the gradient directions using (2) and (3), and produced dynamic structure optimization. In practice, the gradients (2) and (3) are approximated by Monte-Carlo methods using the mini-batch data samples and the λ structure parameters sampled from $p(M \mid \theta)$.

3 Introducing Penalty Term in Dynamic Structure Optimization

In this section, we introduce a penalty term to dynamic structure optimization to control model complexity. We focus on the case that the structure parameter can be treated as a binary vector, as was done in [17].

Representation of Structure Parameter. We denote neural networks as $\phi(W, M)$ modeled by the two parameters: W is the weight vector, and $M = (m_1, \ldots, m_d)^{\mathrm{T}} \in \mathcal{M} = \{0,1\}^d$ is a d-dimensional binary vector that determines neural network structures. We consider the multivariate Bernoulli distribution defined by $p(M \mid \theta) = \prod_{i=1}^{d} \theta_i^{m_i}(1-\theta_i)^{1-m_i}$ to be the probability distribution for the random variable M, where $\theta = (\theta_1, \ldots, \theta_d)^{\mathrm{T}}$, $\theta_i \in [0,1]$ refers to the parameters of the Bernoulli distribution. For instance, in the connection selection, the parameter m_i determines whether or not the i-th connection appears, and θ_i corresponds to the probability that m_i becomes one.

Incorporating Penalty Term into Objective Function. We denote the original loss function of neural network models by $\mathcal{L}(W, M)$, which depends on W and M. To penalize the complicated structure, we introduce the penalty term $\mathcal{R}(M)$, which depends on M, and obtain the objective function represented by $\mathcal{L}(W, M) + \epsilon\mathcal{R}(M)$, where ϵ is a penalty coefficient. In this paper, we particularly focus on the case that the penalty term can be represented by the weighted sum of m_i, $i = 1, \ldots d$, namely $\mathcal{R}(M) = \sum_{i=1}^{d} c_i m_i$ where c_i indicates the coefficient representing the model complexity that corresponds to the i-th bit. Here, we assume that the model complexity increases if the bit m_i becomes one. This is a reasonable assumption because the binary vector is usually used to determine the existences of connections, layers, and units. Therefore, we can consider that the model complexity increases as the number of '1' bits increases.

As both the original loss and the penalty term are not differentiable w.r.t. M, we employ stochastic relaxation by taking the expectation of the objective function. The expected objective function incorporated with the penalty term under the Bernoulli distribution $p(M \mid \theta)$ is given by

$$\mathcal{G}(W, \theta) = \sum_{M \in \mathcal{M}} \mathcal{L}(W, M) p(M \mid \theta) + \epsilon \sum_{i=1}^{d} c_i \theta_i. \tag{4}$$

When $\epsilon = 0$, the minimization of $\mathcal{G}(W, \theta)$ recovers the same algorithm with [17].

Gradients for Weights and Distribution Parameters. To simultaneously optimize W and θ, we derive the gradients of $\mathcal{G}(W, \theta)$ w.r.t. W and θ. The vanilla gradient w.r.t. W is given by $\nabla_W \mathcal{G}(W, \theta) = \sum_{M \in \mathcal{M}} \nabla_W \mathcal{L}(W, M)$ since the penalty term $\mathcal{R}(M)$ does not depend on W. Note that the gradient $\nabla_W \mathcal{L}(W, M)$ can be computed through back-propagation.

Regarding the distribution parameters θ, we derive the natural gradient [2], defined by the product of the inverse of Fisher information matrix and the vanilla gradient, that is the steepest direction of θ when the KL-divergence is considered as the pseudo distance of θ. Since we are considering the Bernoulli distribution, $F(\theta)^{-1}$ can be obtained analytically by $F(\theta)^{-1} = \mathrm{diag}(\theta(1-\theta))$, where the product of vectors indicates the element-wise product. We then obtain the analytical natural gradients of the log-likelihood and the penalty term as $\tilde{\nabla}_\theta \ln p(M \mid \theta) = M - \theta$ and $\tilde{\nabla}_\theta \sum_{i=1}^{d} c_i \theta_i = c\theta(1-\theta)$, respectively, where $c = (c_1, \ldots, c_d)^{\mathrm{T}}$ is the vector representation of the model complexity coefficients and $\tilde{\nabla}_\theta = F(\theta)^{-1}\nabla_\theta$ indicates the natural gradient operator. As a result, we obtain the following gradient:

$$\tilde{\nabla}_\theta \mathcal{G}(W,\theta) = \sum_{M \in \mathcal{M}} \mathcal{L}(W,M)(M-\theta) + \epsilon c\theta(1-\theta). \tag{5}$$

Gradient Approximation. In practice, the analytical gradients are approximated by Monte-Carlo method using λ samples $\{M_1, \ldots, M_\lambda\}$ drawn from $p(M \mid \theta)$. Moreover, the loss $\mathcal{L}(W, M_i)$ is also approximated using $\bar{N}$ mini-batch samples $\mathcal{Z} = \{z_1, \ldots, z_{\bar{N}}\}$. Referring to [17], we use the same mini-batch between different M_i to obtain an accurate ranking of losses. The approximated loss is given by $\bar{\mathcal{L}}(W, M_i) = \bar{N}^{-1} \sum_{z \in \mathcal{Z}} l(z, W, M_i)$, where $l(z, W, M_i)$ represents the loss of a datum. The gradient for W is estimated by Monte-Carlo method using λ samples:

$$\nabla_W \mathcal{G}(W,\theta) \approx \frac{1}{\lambda}\sum_{i=1}^{\lambda} \nabla_W \bar{\mathcal{L}}(W, M_i). \tag{6}$$

We can update W using any stochastic gradient descent (SGD) method with (6).

To update the distribution parameters θ, we transform the loss value $\bar{\mathcal{L}}(W, M_i)$ into the ranking-based utility u_i as was done in [17]: $u_i = 1$ if $\bar{\mathcal{L}}(W, M_i)$ is in top $\lceil \lambda/4 \rceil$, $u_i = -1$ if it is in bottom $\lceil \lambda/4 \rceil$, and $u_i = 0$ otherwise. The ranking-based utility transformation makes the algorithm invariant to the order preserving transformation of $\mathcal{L}$. We note that this utility function transforms the original minimization problem into a maximization problem. With this utility transformation, the approximation of (5) is given by $\tilde{\nabla}_\theta \mathcal{G}(W,\theta) \approx \frac{1}{\lambda}\sum_{i=1}^{\lambda} u_i(M_i - \theta) - \epsilon c\theta(1-\theta)$. As a result, the update rule for θ at the t-th iteration is given by

$$\theta^{(t+1)} = \theta^{(t)} + \eta_\theta \left(\sum_{i=1}^{\lambda} \frac{u_i}{\lambda}(M - \theta^{(t)}) - \epsilon c \theta^{(t)}(1-\theta^{(t)}) \right), \tag{7}$$

where η_θ is the learning rate for θ. If we use the binary vector to select input units and set $c = (1, \ldots, 1)^{\mathrm{T}}$, the algorithm works as feature selection [16]. The method introduced in this paper targets model complexity control and can be applied in cases where each bit corresponds to a different number of weights by introducing the model complexity coefficient c. The optimization procedure of the proposed method is shown in Algorithm 1.

Algorithm 1: The training procedure of the proposed method.

Input: Training data $\mathcal{D}$ and hyperparameters $\{\lambda, \eta_\theta, \epsilon'\}$
Output: Optimized parameters of W and θ
begin
  Initialize the weight and distribution parameters as $W^{(0)}$ and $\theta^{(0)}$
  $t \leftarrow 0$
  while *not stopping criterion is satisfied* **do**
    Get $\bar{N}$ mini-batch samples from $\mathcal{D}$
    Sample $M_1, \dots, M_\lambda$ from $p(M \mid \theta^{(t)})$
    Compute the losses $\bar{\mathcal{L}}(W, M_i)$ for $i = 1, \dots, \lambda$
    Update the distribution parameters to $\theta^{(t+1)}$ by (7)
    Restrict the range of $\theta^{(t+1)}$
    Update the weight parameters to $W^{(t+1)}$ using (6) by any SGD
    $t \leftarrow t + 1$

Prediction for Test Data. As was proposed in [17], there are two options for predicting new data using optimized θ and W. In the first method, the binary vectors are sampled from $p(M \mid \theta)$, and the prediction results are averaged. This stochastic prediction method will produce an accurate prediction, but it is not a desirable to obtain a compact structure. The second way is to deterministically select the binary vector as $M^* = \operatorname{argmax}_M p(M \mid \theta)$ such that $m_i = 1$ if $\theta_i \geq 0.5$; otherwise, $m_i = 0$. In our experiment, we use the second option, deterministic prediction, and report our results.

Implementation Remark. We restrict the range of θ within $[1/d, 1 - 1/d]$ to retain the possibility of generating any binary vector. To be precise, if the updated θ through (7) falls outside this range, the values of θ are set at the boundary value. In addition, the coefficient of ϵ is normalized as $\epsilon = \epsilon' / \max(c)$. The natural gradient corresponding to $\mathcal{L}$ is bounded within the range of $[-1, 1]^d$ due to the utility transformation. In the above normalization, the one corresponding to the penalty term is bounded within $[0, \epsilon'/4]^d$. Therefore, both the gradients are at approximately the same scale regardless of their encoding scheme (i.e., the usage of M).

4 Experiment and Result

We apply the proposed method to the two neural network structure optimization problems with image classification datasets: unit selection of fully-connected neural networks and connection selection of DenseNet [7]. All algorithms are implemented using Chainer framework [21] (version 4.5.0) and CuPy backend [12] (version 4.5.0) and run on a single NVIDIA GTX 1070 GPU in the experiment of unit selection and on a single NVIDIA GTX 1080Ti GPU in the experiment of connection selection. In both experiments, weights are optimized using the SGD with Nesterov's momentum. The coefficient of the momentum and the weight decay are set to 0.9 and 10^{-4}, respectively. Based on [7,17], the learning rate for weights is divided by 10 at 1/2 and 3/4 of the maximum number of epochs. The weight parameters are initialized by He's initialization [6]. We used the cross-entropy loss of $l(z, W, M)$. The experimental setting of the proposed method is based on [17]; the sample size is $\lambda = 2$, the learning rate is $\eta_\theta = 1/d$, and the initial distribution parameters is $\theta^{(0)} = 0.5$.

4.1 Unit Selection of the Fully-Connected Neural Network

Experimental Setting. In this experiment, we use a fully-connected neural network with three hidden layers of 784 units as the base structure, and we select the units in each hidden layer. The MNIST dataset, which is a 10 class handwritten digits dataset consisting of 60,000 training and 10,000 test data of 28×28 gray-scaled images, is used. We use the pixel values as the inputs and determine the existence of the units in hidden layers according to the binary vector M. The i-th unit is active if $m_i = 1$ and inactive if $m_i = 0$. The output of the i-th unit is represented by $m_i F(X_i)$, where F and X_i denote the activation function and the input for the activation of the i-th unit, respectively. We use rectified linear unit (ReLU) and softmax activation as F in hidden layers and in an output layer, respectively. When $m_i = 0$, the connections to/from the i-th unit can be omitted; that is, the active number of weights decreases. The dimension of θ, the total number of hidden units, is $d = 2352$. This task is simple, but we can check how the proposed penalty term works.

We set the mini-batch size to $\bar{N} = 32$ and the number of training epochs to 500 in the proposed method, while the mini-batch size to $\bar{N} = 64$ and the number of training epochs is set to 1000 in other methods. Under these settings, the number of data samples used in one iteration and the number of iterations for parameters update become identical in all methods, where the number of iterations is about 9.5×10^5. We initialize the learning rate for W by 0.01. In this experiment, we change the coefficient ϵ' as 2^{-6}, 2^{-7}, 2^{-8}, 2^{-9}, 0, -2^{-3}, and -2^0 to check the effect of the penalty term.[1] Since each bit decides whether or not its corresponding unit is active, we simply use the same coefficients of model complexity for each unit, $c = (1, \ldots, 1)^\mathrm{T}$.

To evaluate the proposed method's performance, we report the experimental result of the fixed neural network structures with the various numbers of units. We manually and uniformly remove the units in the hidden layers and control the number of weights. As the network structures are stochastically sampled in the training phase of the dynamic structure optimization, our method is somewhat similar to that of stochastic network models, such as Dropout [18]. We also report the result using Dropout with a dropout rate of 0.5 for comparison. Note that the aim of a dropout is to prevent overfitting; thus, all units are kept in the test phase.

[1] The negative value of ϵ' encourages the increase of the number of active units.

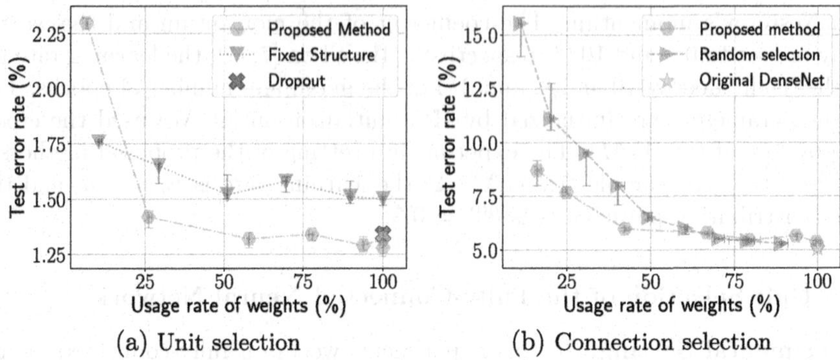

(a) Unit selection (b) Connection selection

Fig. 1. The relationship between the weight usage rate and test error rates of (a) unit selection of the fully-connected neural network and (b) the connection selection of DenseNet. The median values and 25% and 75% quantile values of each over five independent trials are plotted.

Result and Discussion. Figure 1(a) shows the relation between the weight usage rate and test error rates of the proposed method, the fixed structure, and Dropout. The median values and the 25% and 75% quantile values of each over five independent trials are plotted.

Comparing the proposed method and fixed structure, the proposed method outperforms the fixed structure over the 25% usage rate of weights. In the fixed structure, the error rate gradually increases as the usage rate of weights decreases. The performance of the proposed method deteriorates when its weights usage rate is approximately 6%. This indicates that the proposed method can control the usage rate of weights by changing the penalty coefficient of ϵ' and remove the units while still maintaining its performance. The structures obtained by the different ϵ' settings create a trade-off curve between the model complexity and performance.

Comparing the proposed method and the original structure (i.e., the fixed structure with the 100% weight usage rate), the proposed method outperforms the original structure in the usage rate of 25% to 100%. Remarkably, when $\epsilon' < 0$, although all units are selected after the training procedure (i.e., the structure is the same as the original structure), the performance improves. Additionally, dropout training also improves performance. Based on these results, stochastic training appears to improve prediction performance. Dropout, however, cannot control the weight usage rate, but the proposed method can reduce the number of used weights without significant performance deterioration.

Table 1 shows a summary of median values of the number of selected units in each layer. We observe that the proposed method preferentially removes units in the second and third hidden layers. Therefore, the proposed method removes the units selectively rather than at random.

Table 1. The numbers of selected units in each hidden layer in the unit selection experiment.

Weight usage rate	1st layer	2nd layer	3rd layer
6.6% ($\epsilon' = 2^{-6}$)	92	31	24
26.1% ($\epsilon' = 2^{-7}$)	340	141	126
57.8% ($\epsilon' = 2^{-8}$)	599	380	379
77.7% ($\epsilon' = 2^{-9}$)	704	544	567
93.7% ($\epsilon' = 0$)	770	717	724
100% ($\epsilon' = -2^{-3}$)	784	784	784

Table 2. The numbers of selected connections in each block in the connection selection experiment.

Weight usage rate	1st block	2nd block	3rd block
15.8% ($\epsilon' = 2^{-2}$)	36	6	20
24.1% ($\epsilon' = 2^{-3}$)	45	8	49
42.3% ($\epsilon' = 2^{-4}$)	57	39	67
67.5% ($\epsilon' = 2^{-5}$)	59	61	76
80.3% ($\epsilon' = 2^{-6}$)	65	64	80
100% ($\epsilon' = -2^{0}$)	91	91	91

The computational time for training by the proposed method is almost the same as that required by the fixed structure. Even if we run several different penalty coefficient ϵ' settings to obtain additional trade-off structures, the total computational time of the structure search more or less increases several times over. This is reasonable more than the hyperparameter optimization-based structure optimization.

4.2 Connection Selection of DenseNet

Experimental Setting. We use DenseNet [7] as the base network structure; it is composed of several dense blocks and transition layers. The dense block consists of L_{block} layers, each of which implements a non-linear transformation with batch normalization (BN) [8] followed by the ReLU activation and the 3×3 convolution. In the dense block, the l-th layer receives the outputs of all the preceding layers as inputs that are concatenated on the channel dimension. The size of the output feature-maps in the dense block is the same as that of the input feature-maps. The transition layer is located between the dense blocks and consists of the batch normalization, ReLU activation, and the 1×1 convolution layer, which is followed by 2×2 average pooling. The detailed structure of DenseNet can be found in [7]. Unlike [7], however, we do not use Dropout.

We optimize the connections in the dense blocks using the CIFAR-10 dataset, which contains 50,000 training and 10,000 test data of 32×32 color images in the 10 different classes. During the preprocessing and data augmentation, we use the standardization, padding, and cropping for each channel, and this is followed by randomly horizontal flipping. The setting details are the same as in [17].

We determine the existence of the connections between the layers in each dense block according to the binary vector M. As was done in [17], we use a simple DenseNet structure with a depth of 40 that contains three dense blocks with $L_{\text{block}} = 12$ and two transition layers. In this setup, the dimension of M and θ becomes $d = 273$. We vary the coefficient ϵ' as 2^{-2}, 2^{-3}, 2^{-4}, 2^{-5}, 2^{-6}, 0, -2^{-3}, and -2^{0} to assess the effect of the penalty term. Additionally, we set the coefficients of the model complexity c_i to match the number of weights corresponding to the i-th connection.

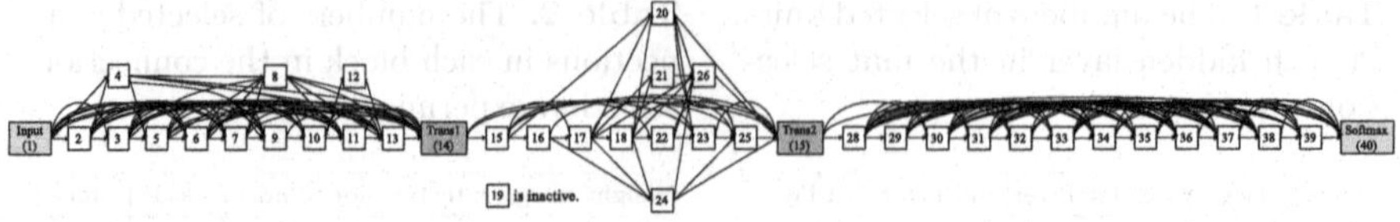

Fig. 2. The obtained DenseNet structure in the case of $\epsilon' = 2^{-4}$ on a typical single run. The numbers in the cells represent the depth of each layer in the original DenseNet structure. Cells placed in the same column locate the same depth, and the depth of this DenseNet structure is 32.

For the proposed method, we set the mini-batch size to $\bar{N} = 32$ and the number of training epochs to 300. For the other methods, the mini-batch size is set to $\bar{N} = 64$ and the number of training epochs to 600. With these settings, the number of iterations for parameter updates become identical in all methods, where the number of iterations is about 4.7×10^5. We initialize the learning rate for W by 0.1.

We also report the result when the connections are removed randomly. We repeatedly sample the binary vector M such that the weight usage rate becomes the target percentage, and then we train the fixed network.

Result and Discussion. Figure 1(b) shows the relations between the weight usage rate and test error rate. Comparing the proposed method and random selection, the proposed method outperforms the random selection in the 15% to 40% weight usage rate. In the random selection method, important connections might be lost when the usage rate of weights is less than 40%. In contrast, the proposed method can selectively remove the number of weights without increasing the test errors, so it does not eliminate important connections. However, the difference between the test error rates of the random selection and the proposed method is not significant when the weight usage rate exceeds 60%. This result indicates that a small number of connections in DenseNet can be randomly removed without performance deterioration, meaning that DenseNet might be redundant; the proposed method can moderate increase of the test error rate within 1% in the 40% weight usage rate.

Table 2 summarizes the median values of the number of selected connections in each block. The proposed method preferentially remove the connections in the first and second blocks when $\epsilon' = 0$ to 2^{-5}, but these deletions do not have a significant impact on performance. When $\epsilon' = 2^{-4}$ to 2^{-2}, the proposed method actively removes the connections in the second block, so the obtained structure can reduce the performance deterioration more than random selection.

Figure 2 shows the structure obtained by the proposed method when $\epsilon' = 2^{-4}$ on a typical single run. As we can see, the second block in this structure, which is between 'Trans1' and 'Trans2' cells, becames sparser and wider than the first and third blocks. Interestingly, the second block became a wide structure through removing the connections between its layers. This result might suggest that wide structures may be able to improve performance with limited computing resources. Several works, such as [22], report that widening layers improves the predictive performance; our findings may also support these wide networks. We would like to emphasize that it is not easy to manually design a structure, such as that shown in Fig. 2, due to the differing connectivities in each block.

Finally, we note that the amount of computational time required by our structure for training is not significantly greater than that required by random selection, meaning that our proposed structure optimization is computationally efficient.

5 Conclusion

In this paper, we propose a method of controlling model complexity by adding a penalty term to the objective function involved in the dynamic structure optimization of DNNs. We incorporate a penalty term dependent on structure parameters into the loss function and consider its expectation under the multivariate Bernoulli distribution to be the objective function. We derive a modified update rule that enables us to control model complexity.

In the experiment on unit selection, the proposed method outperforms the fixed structure in terms of a 25 to 100% weight usage rate. In the connection selection experiment, the proposed method also outperforms random selection in the small number of weights and preferentially removing insignificant connections during the training. Upon checking the obtained structure, it is found that the intermediate block became a wide structure.

As the increased amount of the computational time required by the proposed method is not significant, we can take the trade-off between model complexity and performance with an acceptable computational cost. Our method requires training only once, whereas the pruning methods, such as that in [11], require the retraining after pruning.

In future work, we will apply the proposed method to the architecture search method for more complex neural network structures, such as that proposed in [1]. Additionally, we should evaluate the proposed penalty term using different datasets. Another possible future work is modifying the proposed method so that it can use other types of the model complexity criteria, such as FLOPs of neural networks.

Acknowledgment. This work is partially supported by the SECOM Science and Technology Foundation.

References

1. Akimoto, Y., Shirakawa, S., Yoshinari, N., Uchida, K., Saito, S., Nishida, K.: Adaptive stochastic natural gradient method for one-shot neural architecture search. In: International Conference on Machine Learning (ICML), pp. 171–180 (2019)
2. Amari, S.: Natural gradient works efficiently in learning. Neural Comput. **10**(2), 251–276 (1998). https://doi.org/10.1162/089976698300017746

3. Dong, J., Cheng, A., Juan, D., Wei, W., Sun, M.: PPP-Net: platform-aware progressive search for pareto-optimal neural architectures. In: International Conference on Learning Representations (ICLR) Workshop (2018)
4. Elsken, T., Metzen, J.H., Hutter, F.: Efficient multi-objective neural architecture search via Lamarckian evolution. In: International Conference on Learning Representations (ICLR) (2019)
5. Han, S., Pool, J., Tran, J., Dally, W.J.: Learning both weights and connections for efficient neural networks. In: Neural Information Processing Systems (NIPS) (2015)
6. He, K., Zhang, X., Ren, S., Sun, J.: Delving deep into rectifiers: surpassing human-level performance on ImageNet classification. In: IEEE International Conference on Computer Vision (ICCV), pp. 1026–1034 (2015). https://doi.org/10.1109/ICCV.2015.123
7. Huang, G., Liu, Z., van der Maaten, L., Weinberger, K.Q.: Densely connected convolutional networks. In: IEEE Conference on Computer Vision and Pattern Recognition (CVPR), pp. 2261–2269 (2017). https://doi.org/10.1109/CVPR.2017.243
8. Ioffe, S., Szegedy, C.: Batch normalization: accelerating deep network training by reducing internal covariate shift. In: International Conference on Machine Learning (ICML), pp. 448–456 (2015)
9. Kandasamy, K., Neiswanger, W., Schneider, J., Poczos, B., Xing, E.: Neural architecture search with Bayesian optimisation and optimal transport. In: Neural Information Processing Systems (NIPS) (2018)
10. Liu, H., Simonyan, K., Yang, Y.: DARTS: differentiable architecture search. In: International Conference on Learning Representations (ICLR) (2019)
11. Liu, Z., Li, J., Shen, Z., Huang, G., Yan, S., Zhang, C.: Learning efficient convolutional networks through network slimming. In: IEEE International Conference on Computer Vision (ICCV), pp. 2736–2744 (2017)
12. Okuta, R., Unno, Y., Nishino, D., Hido, S., Loomis, C.: CuPy: a NumPy-compatible library for NVIDIA GPU calculations. In: Workshop on Machine Learning Systems (LearningSys) in the 31st Annual Conference on Neural Information Processing Systems (NIPS) (2017)
13. Ollivier, Y., Arnold, L., Auger, A., Hansen, N.: Information-geometric optimization algorithms: a unifying picture via invariance principles. J. Mach. Learn. Res. **18**(18), 1–65 (2017)
14. Pham, H., Guan, M., Zoph, B., Le, Q.V., Dean, J.: Efficient neural architecture search via parameters sharing. In: International Conference on Machine Learning (ICML), pp. 4095–4104 (2018)
15. Real, E., et al.: Large-scale evolution of image classifiers. In: International Conference on Machine Learning (ICML), pp. 2902–2911 (2017)
16. Saito, S., Shirakawa, S., Akimoto, Y.: Embedded feature selection using probabilistic model-based optimization. In: Genetic and Evolutionary Computation Conference (GECCO) Companion, pp. 1922–1925 (2018). https://doi.org/10.1145/3205651.3208227
17. Shirakawa, S., Iwata, Y., Akimoto, Y.: Dynamic optimization of neural network structures using probabilistic modeling. In: The 32nd AAAI Conference on Artificial Intelligence (AAAI-18), pp. 4074–4082 (2018)
18. Srivastava, N., Hinton, G., Krizhevsky, A., Sutskever, I., Salakhutdinov, R.: Dropout: a simple way to prevent neural networks from overfitting. J. Mach. Learn. Res. **15**, 1929–1958 (2014)

19. Suganuma, M., Shirakawa, S., Nagao, T.: A genetic programming approach to designing convolutional neural network architectures. In: Genetic and Evolutionary Computation Conference (GECCO), pp. 497–504 (2017). https://doi.org/10.1145/3071178.3071229
20. Tan, M., et al.: MnasNet: platform-aware neural architecture search for mobile. In: The IEEE Conference on Computer Vision and Pattern Recognition (CVPR), June 2019
21. Tokui, S., Oono, K., Hido, S., Clayton, J.: Chainer: a next-generation open source framework for deep learning. In: Workshop on Machine Learning Systems (LearningSys) in Neural Information Processing Systems (NIPS), pp. 1–6 (2015)
22. Zagoruyko, S., Komodakis, N.: Wide residual networks. In: British Machine Vision Conference (BMVC), pp. 87.1-87.12 (2016). https://doi.org/10.5244/C.30.87
23. Zoph, B., Le, Q.V.: Neural architecture search with reinforcement learning. In: International Conference on Learning Representations (ICLR) (2017)

Confidence Estimation

Predictive Uncertainty Estimation with Temporal Convolutional Networks for Dynamic Evolutionary Optimization

Almuth Meier(✉) and Oliver Kramer

Computational Intelligence Group, Department of Computer Science, University of Oldenburg, Oldenburg, Germany
{almuth.meier,oliver.kramer}@uni-oldenburg.de

Abstract. Prediction strategies in dynamic evolutionary optimization aim at estimating the moving optimum after a change of the fitness function. Considering the predicted optimum for re-initialization of the population, the evolution strategy is led into the direction of the next optimum. We propose a new way to control the influence of the prediction depending on its estimated uncertainty. In addition, we construct a new benchmark generator for dynamic optimization problems, Dynamic Sine Benchmark, tailored to prediction approaches. For prediction of the moving optimum and uncertainty estimation we apply a temporal convolutional network (TCN) with Monte Carlo dropout. In the experimental study, we compare our approach to known prediction and re-initialization strategies. The results show the advantage of the new re-initialization strategy and TCNs with uncertainty estimation for complex problems up to a certain dimensionality.

Keywords: Evolutionary optimization · Dynamic optimization · Prediction · Temporal convolutional network · Predictive uncertainty

1 Introduction

Dynamic optimization is the task of optimizing a fitness function $f(\mathbf{x}, t) \rightarrow \mathbb{R}$ that changes over time $t \in \mathbb{N}$, with $\mathbf{x} \in \mathbb{R}^d$ and problem dimensionality d. Besides approaches from control theory, common techniques for solving dynamic optimization problems are evolution strategies (ES), see, e.g., [9] for an introduction, and [10] for a recent contribution in machine learning. During a change period $c \in \mathbb{N}$, the fitness function undergoes no change and the ES can behave like for a stationary problem. Due to their good convergence properties, ES have to adapt their population after a fitness function change in order to find the new optimum position $\mathbf{o}_c$ that might be far from the previous optimum $\mathbf{o}_{c-1}$. To cope with this, different approaches exist [15], like random re-initialization of the population and prediction. Prediction approaches mostly aim at predicting the new optimum position $\hat{\mathbf{o}}_\mathbf{c}$ and incorporate $\hat{\mathbf{o}}_\mathbf{c}$ into the population. The prediction is based on training data provided by the ES, i.e., the best solutions $\mathbf{x}_i^*$ found for previous change periods i, with $1 \leq i \leq c-1$.

I. V. Tetko et al. (Eds.): ICANN 2019, LNCS 11728, pp. 409–421, 2019.
https://doi.org/10.1007/978-3-030-30484-3_34

For dynamic ES, different prediction approaches have been proposed, e.g., autoregression [6,24], Kalman filter [19], recurrent neural network [13], and others, e.g., [3,18,20,24]. They have in common that they might hamper the optimization in case the predicted optimum differs much from the true one. If all individuals were re-initialized around the falsely predicted optimum the ES possibly needs some extra generations to find a promising region in the solution space. Ideally, the closer the prediction is to the true optimum, the more individuals should be placed near to the prediction. As the true optimum is not known, it would be useful to have at least an estimate $\hat{\mathbf{u}}_c$ for the predictive uncertainty, i.e., the uncertainty of the predicted optimum $\hat{\mathbf{o}}_c$.

To our knowledge, there exists only the work by Rossi et al. [19] that takes into account predictive uncertainty. They utilize a linear Kalman filter as prediction model. Based on the estimated prediction error they adapt the number of individuals that are placed around the predicted optimum. As new strategy for population re-initialization we propose to sample not only some as in [19] but all new individuals from confidence intervals around the prediction. The width of the intervals depends on the uncertainty estimate. We also propose to use a prediction model that might be able to capture more difficult problem dynamics: a temporal convolutional network equipped with Monte Carlo dropout. Since in preliminary experiments TCNs seemed to be easier and more stable to train we do not employ recurrent neural networks that other works propose [13]. However, also recurrent neural networks can be extended by uncertainty estimation.

The paper is structured as follows. In Sect. 2, we explain predictive uncertainty estimation for Kalman filters and neural networks. We present our ES framework and propose new re-initialization strategies in Sects. 3 and 4, respectively. In Sect. 5, we describe the experimental setup, and discuss the results in Sect. 6. A conclusion summarizes the most important findings in Sect. 7.

2 Predictive Uncertainty Estimation

2.1 Kalman Filter

The Kalman filter [7] is a linear time series model that is based on the assumption that the state of a system is observable by noisy measurements. It can be applied to both estimating the true state variables $\boldsymbol{a}_{c-1}$ underlying noisy observations and predicting the next state $\hat{\boldsymbol{a}}_c$ for that not yet observations are available. It is a recursive model. First, an a priori estimation of the next system state $\hat{\boldsymbol{a}}_c^-$ and its error covariance $\hat{\boldsymbol{E}}_c^-$ is computed. After obtaining an observation for the next time step the filter model is optimized so that the a posteriori covariance error is minimized. With the updated model the a posteriori estimation for state $\hat{\boldsymbol{a}}_c$ and its error covariance $\hat{\boldsymbol{E}}_c$ are computed. For further details on Kalman filter see, e.g., Rossi et al. [19].

In the context of dynamic optimization, Rossi et al. [19] employ the a priori state estimation $\hat{\boldsymbol{a}}_c^-$ as the predicted optimum $\hat{\mathbf{o}}_c$ of the changed fitness function and the a priori error variance, i.e., the diagonal of $\hat{\boldsymbol{E}}_c^-$, as an estimate for the predictive uncertainty $\hat{\mathbf{u}}_c$. The observations are the solutions $\mathbf{x}_i^*$ found by the ES for previous change periods i, with $1 \leq i \leq c-1$.

2.2 Temporal Convolutional Network

TCNs are a kind of convolutional neural network (CNN) specialized to time series data. In contrast to fully-connected NNs, that consist of layers of neurons and weighted connections between them, TCNs are based on the concept of filters that are sliding over the input time series. A complete TCN is constructed by stacking layers of filters. Among different TCN architectures, we chose the one proposed by Bai et al. [1], see that work for a detailed explanation on TCNs.

By design, artificial neural networks (NNs) output only a point prediction $\hat{\mathbf{y}}$ for a given input $\mathbf{x} \in \mathbb{R}^d$. In order to get an estimate for the uncertainty of the output, NNs of any type can be combined with Monte Carlo (MC) dropout without changing the network architecture [5]. With MC dropout, neurons are dropped not only during training but also for prediction. After training the NN, for a given input the output and its uncertainty are predicted by conducting m so-called Monte Carlo runs. The NN output is computed m times for the same input with other neurons dropped in each run. This leads to m different network outputs for the given input. The average output and its variance, i.e., predictive mean and predictive variance, respectively, are computed as follows:

$$\mathrm{E}\left[\hat{\mathbf{y}}\right] = \frac{1}{m}\sum_{i=1}^{m} n_i(\mathbf{x}) \tag{1}$$

$$\mathrm{Var}\left[\hat{\mathbf{y}}\right] = \frac{1}{m}\sum_{i=1}^{m} q_i(\mathbf{x}) + n_i(\mathbf{x})^2 - \mathrm{E}\left[\hat{\mathbf{y}}\right]^2 \tag{2}$$

where $n_i(\mathbf{x})$ denotes the network output of the ith MC run for input $\mathbf{x}$. The predictive variance represents the uncertainty of the prediction. It consists of the sample variance plus noise $q_i(\mathbf{x})$ that is inherently present in the data, i.e., aleatoric uncertainty [8]. Aleatoric uncertainty is data-dependent and can automatically be learned by the NN without further information. Only an additional output layer for $q(\mathbf{x})$ and a corresponding loss function are required. For more information on uncertainty estimation for deep NNs, see [5,8,16].

In order to estimate the uncertainty of the TCN prediction in dynamic optimization we combine the TCN with MC dropout. The ES employs the predictive mean $\mathrm{E}\left[\hat{\mathbf{y}}\right]$ as predicted optimum $\hat{\mathbf{o}}_c$ and the predictive variance $\mathrm{Var}\left[\hat{\mathbf{y}}\right]$ as predictive uncertainty $\hat{\mathbf{u}}_c$.

3 TCN Prediction for Dynamic ES

ES are stochastic population-based optimization algorithms. Each individual in the population is a position in the solution space and represents a possible solution. Originally stemming from stationary optimization, ES need a few extensions to deal with dynamic problems. Here, we describe the adaptations we make to apply prediction to an ES variant controlling mutation strength s by Rechenberg's 1/5th success rule [17], see Algorithm 1.

If the fitness function does not change, the ES behaves like for stationary optimization. It generates λ offspring individuals by recombination and mutation (Line 13), and selects the best μ individuals from the parent and the offspring population (Line 14). To recognize a change in the fitness function, the ES needs a detection mechanism (Line 7). We implement this by comparing fitness values from succeeding generations for some individuals from the population and random points in the solution space. If a change occurred, the mutation strength is reset to its initial value and the best solution $\mathbf{x}^*_{c-1}$ found for the previous change period is stored (Lines 9–10). Based on solutions found so far, the prediction model is trained, and the next optimum position $\hat{\mathbf{o}}_c$ and its uncertainty $\hat{\mathbf{u}}_c$ are predicted (Line 11). Then, the predicted optimum is employed to re-initialize the population (Line 12), and the new individuals are inserted as immigrants into the old population. After the next selection step the population again has its original size μ.

Algorithm 1. Dynamic $(\mu+\lambda)$-ES with Prediction

1: $\mathbf{P} \leftarrow$ initialize_population() # randomly within solution space
2: $s \leftarrow$ initialize_mutation_strength() # initial value
3: $\mathbf{O} \leftarrow [\,]$ # list of found optima
4: $c \leftarrow 1$ # index of change period
5: **for** generations **do**
6: $s \leftarrow$ adapt_mutation_strength() # Rechenberg's 1/5th rule [17]
7: **if** change_detected() **then**
8: $c \leftarrow c + 1$ # count change period
9: $s \leftarrow$ reset_mutation_strength() # initial value
10: $\mathbf{O}$.append($\mathbf{x}^*_{c-1}$) # add solution to list
11: $\hat{\mathbf{o}}_c$, $\hat{\mathbf{u}}_c \leftarrow$ train_and_predict($\mathbf{O}$)
12: $\mathbf{P} \leftarrow$ reinitialize_population($\mathbf{P}$, $\hat{\mathbf{o}}_c$, $\hat{\mathbf{u}}_c$)
13: **P'** $\leftarrow$ create_λ_offspring_individuals($\mathbf{P}$, s) # recombination, mutation
14: $\mathbf{P} \leftarrow$ select_best_μ_individuals($\mathbf{P}$, **P'**)

4 Re-initialization Strategies

Population re-initialization after a change is important to support exploration abilities of the ES. Different re-initialization strategies exist both for dynamic optimization with [3,6,20] and without prediction [4,15,22]. We propose new re-initialization strategies for ES with prediction (`pUNC`, `pDEV`, `pRND`): one with and two without predictive uncertainty estimation. The pattern for the strategies' names is as follows. The first letter signifies whether a prediction model is applied (`p`) or not (`n`). The last letters denote the respective strategy. In this section we denote the ith immigrant of change period c by $\mathbf{x}_c$ instead of $\mathbf{x}_{c_i}$.

nRND. The new individuals $\mathbf{x}_c$ are randomly sampled within the lower bound $\mathbf{x}_l$ and upper bound $\mathbf{x}_u$ of the solution space: $\mathbf{x}_c \sim \mathcal{U}(\mathbf{x}_l, \mathbf{x}_u)$ [23].

nVAR. The new individuals are the old ones with additional noise: $\mathbf{x}_c = \mathbf{x}_{c-1} + \varepsilon$. The noise is sampled with $\varepsilon \sim \mathcal{N}\left(\mathbf{0}, \frac{1}{4d}\|\mathbf{x}_{c-1} - \mathbf{x}_{c-2}\|_2^2\right)$ and depends on the difference between the current position $\mathbf{x}_{c-1}$ and the position of the nearest individual $\mathbf{x}_{c-2}$ in the previous population [23].

nPRE. This strategy does not require a separate prediction model but serves itself as a simple prediction approach [23]. For each individual $\mathbf{x}_{c-1}$ its next position $\hat{\mathbf{x}}_c$ is predicted with $\hat{\mathbf{x}}_c = \mathbf{x}_{c-1} + (\mathbf{x}_{c-1} - \mathbf{x}_{c-2})$ where $\mathbf{x}_{c-2}$ is defined as in nVAR. The individuals are re-initialized at their predicted positions that are perturbed with noise ε as in nVAR: $\mathbf{x}_c = \hat{\mathbf{x}}_c + \varepsilon$.

pKAL. The only approach that considers uncertainty $\hat{\mathbf{u}}_c$ of prediction $\hat{\mathbf{o}}_c$, is the work of Rossi et al. [19] with a Kalman filter prediction model. The new individuals $\mathbf{x}_c$ are sampled from $\mathbf{x}_c \sim \mathcal{N}(\hat{\mathbf{o}}_c, \hat{\mathbf{u}}_c)$. Rossi et al. [19] propose to re-initialize only $\lfloor h \cdot \mu \rfloor$ individuals around the predicted optimum, the remaining ones are re-initialized with a standard method, e.g., nRND. With increasing uncertainty, h decreases, where $h = \frac{\chi}{1+\hat{u}_{\max}}$, $0 < \chi < 1 + \hat{u}_{\max}$. Here $\hat{u}_{\max}$ denotes the maximum entry of $\hat{\mathbf{u}}_c$, μ the population size, and χ a selectable constant. We set $\chi = 0.1$ since this setting turned out to be good in the original work.

pUNC. In contrast to pKAL, we propose to locate *all* individuals around the predicted optimum with $\mathbf{x}_c \sim \mathcal{N}\left(\hat{\mathbf{o}}_c, z \cdot \boldsymbol{\sigma}^2\right)$ and $\boldsymbol{\sigma}^2 = \sqrt{\hat{\mathbf{u}}_c}$ leading to a larger spread in dimensions with high uncertainty. Employing $\sqrt{\hat{\mathbf{u}}_c}$ instead of $\hat{\mathbf{u}}_c$ for variance $\boldsymbol{\sigma}^2$ empirically shows better results; for pKAL this is not found. With $z = 1$ this is the 68.27% confidence interval. Since other intervals possibly result in better samplings, we sample from various intervals $z \in \{0.01, 0.1, 1.0, 10.0\}$.

pDEV. In order to examine whether the uncertainty estimation of the Kalman filter and the TCN, respectively, are useful we also propose a simpler kind of uncertainty estimation. Here, the deviation of the predicted and found optimum is interpreted as uncertainty $\sigma = \sqrt{\frac{1}{d}\|\mathbf{x}^*_{c-1} - \hat{\mathbf{o}}_{c-1}\|_2^2}$. We sample with different z values like in pUNC: $\mathbf{x}_c \sim z \cdot \mathcal{N}\left(\hat{\mathbf{o}}_c, \sigma^2\right)$. In contrast to pKAL and pUNC, here only one uncertainty estimate for all d dimensions is available.

pRND. Our last strategy does not consider predictive uncertainty and is only for the sake of comparison. The predicted optimum is randomly perturbed with different scales $z \in \{0.01, 0.1, 1.0, 10.0\}$: $\mathbf{x}_c \sim z \cdot \mathcal{N}(\hat{\mathbf{o}}_c, \mathbf{I})$, where $\mathbf{I}$ is the identity.

5 Experimental Setup

We equip the same base ES (Algorithm 1) with five different prediction approaches: no prediction model (`npm`), a linear autoregressive model (`ar`) [6], TCN without (`tcn`) and with uncertainty estimation (`unc`), and a Kalman filter (`kal`). We combine the prediction approaches with following re-initialization strategies:

- `npm` with `nRND`, `nVAR`, and `nPRE`
- `ar` and `tcn` with `pRND`, and `pDEV`
- `kal` and `unc` with `pRND`, `pDEV`, `pKAL`, and `pUNC`

Settings for the ES. We employ a (50+100)-ES with mutation strength set to 1.0 initially. After a change, 50 immigrants are generated according to the respective re-initialization strategy and inserted into the population. The fitness function changes each 30th generation and the ES is conducted for 554 change periods. We chose this number in order to get a number of training data that is divisible by the batch size of the TCNs. All experiments are repeated 20 times.

Settings for the Prediction Models. We predict the next optimum after each change but re-train the prediction models only every 75 changes to circumvent excessive runtimes. For training, we use 128 training patterns each consisting of 50 input time steps and one expected output. The training data are scaled into range $[-1, 1]$ and overall 5 training phases are conducted. We train the TCNs with the Adam optimizer for 100 epochs and conduct during training and prediction 50 and 10 Monte Carlo runs, respectively. Since the training patterns have a window size of 50 time steps, the TCN has 4 layers [1]. In preliminary experiments, we tuned the hyperparameters of the TCNs. The best setting is: 27 filters, filter size 6, learning rate 0.001, batch size 32, and dropout probability 0.1. Our code can be found on GitHub: https://github.com/almuthmeier/DynOpt.

5.1 Benchmarks

We compare the algorithms on the Dynamic Sine Benchmark (DSB), proposed in this paper, and the Moving Peaks Benchmark (MPB). We initialize the benchmarks for dimensions $d \in \{2, 5, 10, 20\}$. The solution space is within $[0, 100]^d$.

Dynamic Sine Benchmark. There exist various benchmarks for dynamic optimization [15], e.g., MPB [2], CEC competition benchmarks [11], and the Free Peaks benchmark [12]. But they mostly are not tailored to prediction approaches since the optimum movement either is not predictable or the dynamic is simple, e.g., noisy linear. Since in real-world applications the optimum might not follow simple relationships, but, e.g., in control problems, would have rather complex oscillations, we propose a new benchmark generator with quantifiable complexity: Dynamic Sine Benchmark (DSB).

In each dimension w of the solution space the optimum movement follows a separate trigonometric function

$$\zeta_w(c) = \tau + \prod_{i=1}^{\rho} \left(\iota_i \cdot \sin\left(\beta_i \cdot \kappa \cdot (c-1) + \gamma_i\right)\right)$$

which is composed by multiplying ρ sine functions with randomly parametrized amplitude ι_i, frequency β_i, phase shift γ_i, and vertical movement τ. In change period c the optimum is located at $\mathbf{o}_c = [\zeta_1(c), \zeta_2(c), \ldots, \zeta_d(c)]$. To generate optimum positions for P change periods, for each dimension w the respective function ζ_w is evaluated for $c \in [1, \ldots, P]$. Here, κ (step size) determines the distance between the points at which ζ_w is evaluated. Step size κ requires a careful choice to cover the important parts of function ζ_w. DSB can be combined with any stationary fitness function f_s. The fitness for individual $\mathbf{x}$ in generation t is $f(\mathbf{x}, t) = f_s(\mathbf{x} - (\mathbf{o}_c - \mathbf{o}_{f_s}))$ if generation t belongs to change period c and $\mathbf{o}_{f_s}$ denotes the global optimum of the unmoved function f_s.

In order to quantify the benchmark's complexity we introduce the concepts of curviness and velocity. The curviness specifies the number of extremes ζ_w has within the base time interval $[0, 2\pi]$, i.e., how many changes in the direction of the optimum movement take place. By this means, the curviness indicates the difficulty for the prediction model to track the optimum. The velocity is the median distance between succeeding optimum positions and represents the problem difficulty for the ES. In case the velocity is much higher than the mutation strength, an ES without prediction might need many more generations to find the new optimum position. In DSB, all functions ζ_w are generated with the same curviness and velocity in order to ensure that the complexity of DSB instances with different dimensionality only depends on the number of dimensions.

In the experimental study, we combine DSB with the well-known fitness functions Sphere (unimodal), Rastrigin (multimodal), and Rosenbrock (non-separable). The parameterization is: curviness 10, velocity 0.5, $\rho = 4$, $\kappa = \frac{\pi}{30}$.

Moving Peaks Benchmark. The Moving Peaks Benchmark (MPB) [2] is a standard test set in evolutionary dynamic optimization. It consists of multiple peaks with randomly changing positions, heights, and widths. We use a variant, where the noise of the linear optimum movement is controlled with a correlation factor η, see, e.g., [14] for an explanation. The optimum movement may employ jumps when the height of a so far local optimum becomes the global optimum. We instantiate MPB with ten peaks and noise $\nu \in \{0.0, 0.01, 0.05\}$, $\eta = 1 - \nu$.

5.2 Metrics

We measure both the performance of the ES ($\overline{\text{BOG}}$, BEBC, RCS) and the accuracy of the prediction models (ACC). The metrics are computed with respect to the generations, in which a prediction is conducted. Best of generation ($\overline{\text{BOG}}$) is a frequent performance measure in dynamic optimization [15]. It averages the fitness of the best found solutions over all generations and runs of the experiment, and represents the behavior of the ES during the whole run. Low values are desirable for minimization problems. Also best error before change (BEBC) [21] is a well-known performance measure for dynamic optimization. It averages the fitness difference between the best solution of a change period and the true optimum over all P change periods. Therefore, it ignores, e.g., fitness peaks during the early generations of a change period. The best value for BEBC is 0. Relative convergence speed (RCS) [13] measures how fast the ES approaches the global optimum relatively to the other algorithms included in the comparison. It ranges from 0 (best value) to 1 (worst value). We introduce prediction accuracy (ACC) as root mean squared error of the predicted and true optimum positions over all change periods. The best ACC value is 0.

6 Experimental Results

Both for DSB and MPB we first identify for each prediction model the best re-initialization strategy. Due to space restrictions the results are not included in this paper. The main finding from this is that re-initialization strategy `pKAL` nearly always is outperformed by our uncertainty-based strategy `pUNC`.

In the next paragraphs, we compare the different prediction approaches combined with the identified settings. We conduct pairwise Mann-Whitney U tests with significance level $\alpha = 0.05$ to examine statistical significance. The resulting Tables 1, 2 and 3 contain '▼' ('△'), if the algorithm of the respective row achieves a significantly lower (larger) value than the algorithm in the respective column regarding the specific metric on the given benchmark. In the columns, the order of metrics listed for each algorithm is $\overline{\text{BOG}}$, BEBC, RCS, ACC. The symbol '–' signifies a non-significant test result. With '·' we indicate that the ACC measure is not computed for `npm`, since `npm` has no prediction model. The algorithm name consists of the prediction model followed by the re-initialization strategy.

6.1 Dynamic Sine Benchmark

No prediction, i.e. `npm`, is nearly always worst except for good RCS values compared to `ar`, see Table 2. `ar` is outperformed by the other approaches as well. Though it does not take into account predictive uncertainty, `tcn` is superior to `kal`. The comparison of `tcn` and `unc` shows that `tcn` is nearly never better than `unc`. Strategy `unc` outperforms `tcn` on lower dimensions ($d \in \{2, 5\}$) and has even for higher dimensions ($d = 10$) a better $\overline{\text{BOG}}$. On Rastrigin, `tcn` and `unc` behave very similarly but also here `unc` achieves a better $\overline{\text{BOG}}$ for $d \in \{2, 5\}$.

Overall, the order of performance reaches from best to worst `unc`, `tcn`, `kal`, `ar`, `npm`. The results emphasize the advantage of uncertainty estimation since `kal-pUNC` and `unc-pUNC` outperform their respective counterparts that do not use predictive uncertainty. The fact that `tcn` outperforms `kal` shows that, in case a prediction approach is not suited to the kind of problem dynamic, even uncertainty estimation cannot compensate the weaknesses of the prediction approach.

Table 1. `tcn-pDEV` and `unc-pUNC` on Sphere, various dimensionalities

Algorithm	Dim.	unc-pUNC
tcn-pDEV	2	△ △ △ △
	3	△ △ △ –
	4	△ △ △ △
	5	△ △ △ –
	6	△ △ △ –
	7	△ △ △ –
	8	△ – △ –
	9	△ – – –
	10	△ – △ –
	11	△ – – –
	12	– – – –
	13	– – – –
	14	– – – –
	15	– ▼ – –
	16	– ▼ – –
	17	– – – –
	18	– ▼ – △
	19	– ▼ ▼ ▼
	20	– – △ –

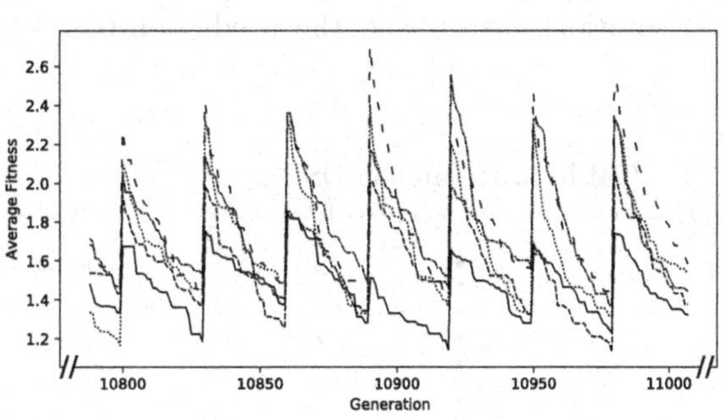

Fig. 1. Best fitness for selected generations on Sphere function ($d = 10$), averaged over runs, with `npm-nVAR` -·-·-, `ar-pDEV` - -, `tcn-pDEV` ---, `kal-pUNC` ······, `unc-pUNC` —.

In addition, a smaller advantage of uncertainty could be observed for multimodal and high dimensional problems.

We examine on the Sphere function, up to which dimensionality predictive uncertainty provides useful information. From Table 1 it is obvious that `unc` outperforms `tcn` for lower dimensions and the use of predictive uncertainty decreases with increasing dimensions. From $d = 12$, `unc` has no advantage over `tcn`. Strategy `unc` outperforms `tcn` especially regarding $\overline{\text{BOG}}$ and becomes worse first for BEBC. This finding is confirmed by Fig. 1 that shows for all prediction approaches the best average fitness achieved in the respective generation. Due to restricted space not all generations are shown. It can be observed that `unc` often starts with a lower fitness value than `tcn` after a change. Thus, considering predictive uncertainty for re-initialization prevents high fitness peaks during the first generations of change periods.

6.2 Moving Peaks Benchmark

Autoregressive prediction (`ar`), is worse than all other approaches. It only outperforms `npm` regarding $\overline{\text{BOG}}$. No prediction (`npm`) outperforms the other approaches frequently regarding BEBC. The reason for this might be that the prediction-based approaches follow a local optimum but not the global one. Therefore, they have lower fitness values at the beginning of the change period resulting in lower $\overline{\text{BOG}}$ and RCS. In contrast to that, `npm` shows more diversity in the population. Hence, it is more likely to explore the global optimum leading to a better BEBC.

On the multimodal Rastrigin function these effects do not appear, see Table 2. Possibly, this can be explained by the fitness landscape. MPB is rather flat with some small peaks whereas Rastrigin has everywhere strong slopes enabling the ES to find promising directions in the solution space. Therefore, `npm` might find good solutions faster, and the prediction-based approaches could easier leave

Table 2. Results on DSB

Algorithm	Benchmark	Dim.	ar-pDEV	tcn-pDEV	kal-pUNC	unc-pUNC
npm-nVAR	sphere	2	△ – – ·	△ △ △ ·	△ – △ ·	△ △ △ ·
		5	△ – ▼ ·	△ △ △ ·	△ △ △ ·	△ △ △ ·
		10	△ – ▼ ·	△ △ △ ·	△ △ △ ·	△ △ △ ·
		20	△ △ ▼ ·	△ △ △ ·	△ △ – ·	△ △ △ ·
	rosenbrock	2	△ – ▼ ·	△ △ △ ·	△ △ – ·	△ △ △ ·
		5	△ – ▼ ·	△ △ △ ·	△ △ △ ·	△ △ △ ·
		10	△ △ ▼ ·	△ △ △ ·	△ △ △ ·	△ △ △ ·
		20	△ △ ▼ ·	△ △ △ ·	△ △ – ·	△ △ △ ·
	rastrigin	2	▼ – – ·	△ △ △ ·	△ △ △ ·	△ △ △ ·
		5	– – ▼ ·	△ – – ·	– – ▼ ·	△ △ – ·
		10	△ – ▼ ·	△ △ – ·	△ – ▼ ·	△ △ – ·
		20	△ – – ·	△ △ △ ·	△ – ▼ ·	△ △ △ ·
ar-pDEV	sphere	2		△ △ △ △	△ – △ △	△ △ △ △
		5		△ △ △ △	△ △ △ △	△ △ △ △
		10		△ △ △ △	△ △ △ △	△ △ △ △
		20		△ △ △ △	△ △ △ ▼	△ △ △ △
	rosenbrock	2		△ △ △ △	△ △ △ △	△ △ △ △
		5		△ △ △ △	△ △ △ △	△ △ △ △
		10		△ △ △ △	△ △ △ △	△ △ △ △
		20		△ △ △ △	△ △ △ ▼	△ △ △ △
	rastrigin	2		△ △ △ △	△ △ △ △	△ △ △ △
		5		△ – △ △	– – – ▼	△ – △ △
		10		△ △ △ △	– – ▼ ▼	△ △ △ △
		20		△ △ △ –	▼ – ▼ ▼	△ △ △ –
tcn-pDEV	sphere	2			▼ ▼ ▼ ▼	△ △ △ △
		5			▼ ▼ ▼ ▼	△ △ △ –
		10			▼ ▼ ▼ ▼	△ – – –
		20			▼ ▼ ▼ ▼	– – ▼ –
	rosenbrock	2			▼ ▼ ▼ ▼	△ ▼ – –
		5			▼ ▼ ▼ ▼	△ △ △ –
		10			▼ ▼ ▼ ▼	△ – – –
		20			▼ ▼ ▼ ▼	– – – △
	rastrigin	2			▼ ▼ ▼ ▼	△ – △ –
		5			▼ ▼ ▼ ▼	△ – – –
		10			▼ ▼ ▼ ▼	– – – –
		20			▼ ▼ ▼ ▼	– – – –
kal-pUNC	sphere	2				△ △ △ △
		5				△ △ △ △
		10				△ △ △ △
		20				△ △ △ △
	rosenbrock	2				△ △ △ △
		5				△ △ △ △
		10				△ △ △ △
		20				△ △ △ △
	rastrigin	2				△ △ △ △
		5				△ △ △ △
		10				△ △ △ △
		20				△ △ △ △

Table 3. Results on MPB

Algorithm	Noise	Dim.	ar-pRND	tcn-pRND	kal-pUNC	unc-pUNC
npm-nRND	0.00	2	△ △ – ·	△ – ▼ ·	△ △ – ·	△ – ▼ ·
		5	▼ ▼ ▼ ·	– ▼ ▼ ·	△ – – ·	– ▼ – ·
		10	– – – ·	△ △ △ ·	△ – △ ·	– – – ·
		20	△ ▼ – ·	△ ▼ – ·	△ ▼ △ ·	△ ▼ △ ·
	0.01	2	△ △ △ ·	△ △ △ ·	△ △ △ ·	△ △ △ ·
		5	– ▼ – ·	– – – ·	– – – ·	– ▼ – ·
		10	△ ▼ – ·	△ ▼ △ ·	△ ▼ △ ·	△ ▼ △ ·
		20	– ▼ – ·	△ ▼ △ ·	△ – △ ·	△ ▼ △ ·
	0.05	2	△ ▼ ▼ ·	△ ▼ ▼ ·	– ▼ ▼ ·	△ – – ·
		5	△ – – ·	△ – △ ·	– – – ·	△ – △ ·
		10	△ ▼ △ ·	△ ▼ △ ·	△ △ △ ·	△ ▼ △ ·
		20	– ▼ – ·	– ▼ – ·	△ ▼ △ ·	△ ▼ △ ·
ar-pRND	0.00	2		– – – –	– – – –	– – ▼ ▼
		5		– – – –	△ △ △ △	△ △ – –
		10		△ △ △ △	△ △ △ △	– – △ –
		20		– – – △	△ △ △ –	△ △ – –
	0.01	2		△ △ △ –	△ △ △ △	△ △ △ △
		5		– – – –	– – – –	– – – –
		10		– – △ –	△ △ △ –	– – △ –
		20		– – – △	△ △ △ –	– – – –
	0.05	2		– – – ▼	– – – –	– – △ –
		5		– – – –	– – – –	– – △ –
		10		▼ ▼ – –	△ △ △ –	– – △ –
		20		– – – –	△ △ △ –	– – △ –
tcn-pRND	0.00	2			△ – – △	– – – –
		5			△ △ △ △	△ △ △ △
		10			– – – –	– – – –
		20			△ △ △ –	△ △ △ ▼
	0.01	2			△ △ △ △	△ △ – △
		5			– – – –	– – – –
		10			△ △ △ ▼	– – – –
		20			△ △ △ –	– – – –
	0.05	2			– – – △	△ △ – △
		5			– – – –	– – – –
		10			△ △ △ –	△ △ △ –
		20			△ △ △ –	– – – △
kal-pUNC	0.00	2				▼ ▼ ▼ ▼
		5				▼ ▼ ▼ ▼
		10				▼ ▼ ▼ –
		20				▼ ▼ – –
	0.01	2				▼ ▼ ▼ ▼
		5				▼ ▼ – –
		10				▼ ▼ ▼ –
		20				▼ ▼ ▼ –
	0.05	2				△ △ △ –
		5				– – – –
		10				▼ ▼ ▼ –
		20				– – – –

their tracked local optimum. This might lead to a better RCS for `npm` on Rastrigin than on MPB, and to a better BEBC for the prediction-based approaches.

In contrast to DSB, on MPB `tcn` is almost always outperformed by `kal`. Prediction approach `unc` seems to have advantages over `tcn` only on low dimensions. Interestingly, `tcn` sometimes outperforms `unc` regarding RCS. `kal` is the best prediction approach. It outperforms even `unc` regarding $\overline{\text{BOG}}$ and BEBC showing its superiority for problems with linear dynamic. Only for high noise (0.05) the differences are not obvious. The overall order of performance on MPB is from best to worst `kal`, `unc`, `tcn`, `npm`, `ar`.

7 Conclusion

In this paper, we proposed a new re-initialization strategy to consider predictive uncertainty for population re-initialization. We applied a temporal convolutional network (TCN) with Monte Carlo dropout as new prediction model with uncertainty estimation for dynamic optimization. Besides, we constructed Dynamic Sine Benchmark, a new benchmark generator for dynamic problems tailored to prediction approaches.

The results show the advantage of TCNs with uncertainty estimation on rather complex problems whereas Kalman filters are superior on noisy linear problem dynamics. Our new re-initialization strategy turned out to outperform the existing one that considers predictive uncertainty. We could show that predictive uncertainty only has a positive effect on the ES, if the prediction approach is combined with the proper re-initialization strategy. In general, the effect vanishes with increasing problem dimensionality. Especially for the multimodal Rastrigin function with higher dimensionality no large differences between prediction approaches with and without uncertainty estimation could be observed.

Acknowledgments. This research is funded by the German Research Foundation through the Research Training Group SCARE (DFG-GRK 1765/2).

References

1. Bai, S., Kolter, J.Z., Koltun, V.: An empirical evaluation of generic convolutional and recurrent networks for sequence modeling. CoRR abs/1803.01271 (2018)
2. Branke, J.: Memory enhanced evolutionary algorithms for changing optimization problems. In: Congress on Evolutionary Computation (CEC), pp. 1875–1882 (1999). https://doi.org/10.1109/CEC.1999.785502
3. Bu, C., Luo, W., Yue, L.: Continuous dynamic constrained optimization with ensemble of locating and tracking feasible regions strategies. IEEE Trans. Evol. Comput. **21**(1), 14–33 (2017). https://doi.org/10.1109/TEVC.2016.2567644
4. Cruz, C., González, J.R., Pelta, D.A.: Optimization in dynamic environments: a survey on problems, methods and measures. Soft Comput. **15**(7), 1427–1448 (2011). https://doi.org/10.1007/s00500-010-0681-0
5. Gal, Y.: Uncertainty in deep learning. Ph.D. thesis, Cambridge University (2016)

6. Hatzakis, I., Wallace, D.: Dynamic multi-objective optimization with evolutionary algorithms: a forward-looking approach. In: Genetic and Evolutionary Computation Conference (GECCO), pp. 1201–1208 (2006). https://doi.org/10.1145/1143997.1144187
7. Kalman, R.E.: A new approach to linear filtering and prediction problems. J. Basic Eng. **82**(1), 35–45 (1960). https://doi.org/10.1115/1.3662552
8. Kendall, A., Gal, Y.: What uncertainties do we need in Bayesian deep learning for computer vision? In: Advances in Neural Information Processing Systems (NIPS), pp. 5580–5590 (2017)
9. Kramer, O.: A Brief Introduction to Continuous Evolutionary Optimization. SAST. Springer, Cham (2014). https://doi.org/10.1007/978-3-319-03422-5
10. Krause, O., Arbonès, D.R., Igel, C.: CMA-ES with optimal covariance update and storage complexity. In: Advances in Neural Information Processing Systems (NIPS), pp. 370–378 (2016)
11. Li, C., Mavrovouniotis, M., Yang, S., Yao, X.: Benchmark generator for the IEEE WCCI-2014 competition on evolutionary computation for dynamic optimization problems. Technical report, De Montfort University (2013)
12. Li, C., Nguyen, T.T., Zeng, S., Yang, M., Wu, M.: An open framework for constructing continuous optimization problems. IEEE Trans. Cybern. **49**, 1–15 (2018)
13. Meier, A., Kramer, O.: Prediction with recurrent neural networks in evolutionary dynamic optimization. In: Sim, K., Kaufmann, P. (eds.) EvoApplications 2018. LNCS, vol. 10784, pp. 848–863. Springer, Cham (2018). https://doi.org/10.1007/978-3-319-77538-8_56
14. Moser, I., Chiong, R.: Dynamic function optimization: the moving peaks benchmark. In: Alba, E., Nakib, A., Siarry, P. (eds.) Metaheuristics for Dynamic Optimization. Studies in Computational Intelligence, vol. 433, pp. 35–59. Springer, Heidelberg (2013). https://doi.org/10.1007/978-3-642-30665-5_
15. Nguyen, T.T., Yang, S., Branke, J.: Evolutionary dynamic optimization: a survey of the state of the art. Swarm Evol. Comput. **6**, 1–24 (2012). https://doi.org/10.1016/j.swevo.2012.05.001
16. Oehmcke, S., Zielinski, O., Kramer, O.: Direct training of dynamic observation noise with UMarineNet. In: Kůrková, V., Manolopoulos, Y., Hammer, B., Iliadis, L., Maglogiannis, I. (eds.) ICANN 2018. LNCS, vol. 11139, pp. 123–133. Springer, Cham (2018). https://doi.org/10.1007/978-3-030-01418-6_13
17. Rechenberg, I.: Evolutionsstrategie: Optimierung technischer Systeme nach Prinzipien der biologischen Evolution. Frommann-Holzbog, Stuttgart (1973)
18. Rong, M., Gong, D., Zhang, Y., Jin, Y., Pedrycz, W.: Multidirectional prediction approach for dynamic multiobjective optimization problems. IEEE Trans. Cybern. **49**, 1–13 (2018). https://doi.org/10.1109/TCYB.2018.2842158
19. Rossi, C., Abderrahim, M., Díaz, J.C.: Tracking moving optima using Kalman-based predictions. Evol. Comput. **16**(1), 1–30 (2008). https://doi.org/10.1162/evco.2008.16.1.1
20. Simões, A., Costa, E.: Prediction in evolutionary algorithms for dynamic environments. Soft Comput. **18**(8), 1471–1497 (2014). https://doi.org/10.1007/s00500-013-1154-z
21. Trojanowski, K., Michalewicz, Z.: Searching for optima in non-stationary environments. In: Congress on Evolutionary Computation (CEC), pp. 1843–1850 (1999). https://doi.org/10.1109/CEC.1999.785498
22. Woldesenbet, Y.G., Yen, G.G.: Dynamic evolutionary algorithm with variable relocation. IEEE Trans. Evol. Comput. **13**(3), 500–513 (2009). https://doi.org/10.1109/TEVC.2008.2009031

23. Zhou, A., Jin, Y., Zhang, Q., Sendhoff, B., Tsang, E.: Prediction-based population re-initialization for evolutionary dynamic multi-objective optimization. In: Obayashi, S., Deb, K., Poloni, C., Hiroyasu, T., Murata, T. (eds.) EMO 2007. LNCS, vol. 4403, pp. 832–846. Springer, Heidelberg (2007). https://doi.org/10.1007/978-3-540-70928-2_62
24. Zhou, A., Jin, Y., Zhang, Q.: A population prediction strategy for evolutionary dynamic multiobjective optimization. IEEE Trans. Cybern. **44**(1), 40–53 (2014)

Sparse Recurrent Mixture Density Networks for Forecasting High Variability Time Series with Confidence Estimates

Narendhar Gugulothu(✉), Easwar Subramanian, and Sanjay P. Bhat

TCS Research, Hyderabad, India
{narendhar.g,easwar.subramanian,sanjay.bhat}@tcs.com

Abstract. Accurate forecasting of a high variability time series has relevance in many applications such as supply-chain management, price prediction in stock markets and demand forecasting in the energy segment. Most often forecasts of such time series depend on many factors ranging from weather to socio-economic attributes such as GDP or average income. Dependence on such features can cause the underlying time series to be highly variable in nature and possess non-stationary shifts. Most traditional forecasting methods fail to capture such trend shifts and high variability present in the data. Further, for certain applications, it may be necessary to estimate the confidence of the forecasts. In this work, we propose two variants of recurrent mixture density network (RMDN), for time series forecasting, that have the ability to handle high-dimensional input features, capture trend shifts and high variability present in the data, and provide a confidence estimate of the forecast. To this end, we first pass the high-dimensional time series data through a feedforward layer, which performs dimensionality reduction or feature selection in an unsupervised manner by inducing sparsity on the weights of the feedforward layer. The resultant low-dimensional time series is then fed through recurrent layers to capture temporal patterns. These recurrent layers also aid in learning the latent representation of the input data. Thereafter, a mixture density network (MDN) is used to model the variability and trend shifts present in the input and it also estimates the confidence of the predictions. The models are trained in an end-to-end fashion and the efficacy of the proposed models is demonstrated on three publicly available datasets from energy markets.

Keywords: Recurrent mixture density networks · Sparse neural networks · Highly variable time series · Forecasting · Confidence estimation of prediction · Dimensionality reduction

1 Introduction

In applications such as supply-chain logistics, stock price prediction or load forecasting in energy markets, it is imperative for the prediction model to be accurate

I. V. Tetko et al. (Eds.): ICANN 2019, LNCS 11728, pp. 422–433, 2019.
https://doi.org/10.1007/978-3-030-30484-3_35

and posses the ability to handle high-dimensional data with trend shifts and variability. Among the applications listed above, we choose load-forecasting task as a test-bed to demonstrate the features of our proposed models since the desiderata listed above are very useful in energy market applications. For example, accuracy in load prediction is critical for maintaining the balance between supply and demand of electricity. Any imbalance in the energy network can be costly to all the players in the market [9]. Further, energy consumption pattern of retail or wholesale customers are typically highly variable in nature with trend shifts that depend on various factors such as weather, historical consumption patterns and other socio-economic indicators. Also, dependence of the consumption pattern on these factors results in high-dimensional data. The ability of a model to provide the confidence estimate of its forecast is useful for power generators and electricity brokers to manage demand volatility and imbalances better [18].

To achieve the above mentioned desiderata, we propose two variants of sparse recurrent mixture density networks for time series prediction that output p-step ahead forecast. Specifically, we consider long short-term memory (LSTM) [17] and encoder-decoder (ED) [28,30] as the two underlying recurrent architectures. We use a feedforward dimensionality reduction layer to handle high-dimensional input data by imposing sparsity constraint on the weights of feedforward layer, which effectively results in unsupervised feature selection [13,27]. RNNs (LSTM or ED architectures) are used to capture the temporal patterns present in the time series data. Finally, mixture density networks [4] are used to model the trend shifts and variability present in the data and provide a confidence estimate of the prediction. The performance of the proposed architectures are tested on three publicly available electricity load forecasting datasets. Specifically, we used mean squared error (MSE) and mean absolute percentage error (MAPE) as quantitative metrics to compare the efficacy of the proposed models in time series forecasting.

We claim that the proposed sparse recurrent neural network based mixture density networks for forecasting high variability time series have following features:

- Performs automatic feature selection of the high-dimensional input data in an unsupervised fashion by using feedforward dimensionality reduction layer.
- Captures the temporal patterns present in the data with the help of underlying RNNs present in the models.
- Captures trend shifts and variability present in the input data with the help of the mixture density networks.
- Provides a confidence estimate of the forecast.

Further, because of the RNNs present in the proposed networks, these models have the ability to provide p-step ahead forecast of an input time series with reliable accuracy.

The outline of the paper is as follows. In Sect. 2, a brief summary of related work is presented. A detailed description of the sparse RMDN models are given in Sect. 3. Experimental setup and dataset description are elaborated in Sect. 4. Results are showcased in Sect. 5, and findings are summarized in Sect. 6.

2 Related Work

Recurrent neural networks, especially those based on long short-term memory [17] or gated recurrent units [7], have gained popularity in the recent years for sequential modeling tasks due to their ability to capture temporal patterns. These models have achieved state-of-the-art performance on sequence modeling tasks such as machine translation [7], speech recognition [12], remaining useful life estimation [14] and anomaly detection [13,15,16,19,26].

RNN-based networks are capable of capturing long-term dependencies, and hence are relevant in forecasting problems. Recently, recurrent mixture density network (RMDN) based models have outperformed other existing RNN based approaches on tasks like sequence generation [11], trajectory generation [33,34], surgical motion prediction [8], visual attention [2] and in anomaly detection [16]. The use of MDNs along with LSTMs for modeling the variance of predicted demand in supply-demand logistics has also been explored [21]. The LSTMs along with MDNs have been used to predict taxi demand [31]. However, these models do not have any inherent mechanism to handle high-dimensional data. Our work uses a feedforward layer to automatically select salient features of the data. In addition, we also propose an encoder-decoder based sparse RMDN architecture that is known to be better at generating sequences than LSTM-based architectures.

As mentioned in the introduction, the MDN-based architectures proposed in this exposition are tested on datasets pertaining to electricity demand from energy markets. Popular approaches to load forecasting problems have generally been based on econometric [3,25] and time series [1,10] methods. Of late, data driven models [23] that use deep neural networks [6,24] have gained importance due to their generalizability and superior prediction capability. However, these approaches follow a two-stage process to handle high-dimensional data. The first stage has the mechanism to find out important features from high-dimensional data and the second stage uses the important features as input to the forecasting model. For instance, the authors of [6] have used random forest, while [5] has used wrapper and embedding based recursive feature elimination technique to get important features in the first stage. The important features obtained from the first stage are then fed as input to the LSTM-based forecasting models in the second stage. Nevertheless, to the best of our knowledge, the models proposed in the studies mentioned above neither have an inherent mechanism to handle high-dimensional data nor do they provide confidence estimates of the forecasted demand. We propose to address these issues through the sparse recurrent MDN architectures proposed in this work.

3 Sparse Recurrent MDN Models for Forecasting

In this section, we introduce two variants of recurrent MDN architectures that can be used in forecasting tasks. Let $\mathbf{x}_{1,\ldots,T}$ denote a time series of length T, where each $\mathbf{x}_t \in \mathbb{R}^d$, d being the input dimension. The objective of the forecasting model is to predict future points of a time series $\mathbf{y}$ given the historical data for the time series $\mathbf{x}$. In other words, the model is required to provide a prediction $\mathbf{y}'_{t+1,...,t+p}$ of $\mathbf{y}_{t+1,...,t+p}$ given the input $\mathbf{x}_{1,...,t}$ with the help of a non-linear mapping function f_{net}, where p is the prediction length.

Popular neural networks for time series prediction include long short-term memory (LSTM) and encoder-decoder (ED). An LSTM is a recurrent neural network with a cell or memory, an input gate, an output gate, and a forget gate. The role of the cell is to extract temporal relations of the input sequence, while the gates regulate the information flow in and out of the LSTM cell. An ED is a seq2seq learning model [28,30] that contains a pair of RNNs (called encoder and decoder) which are trained simultaneously. Given the input time series the encoder learns a latent representation $\mathbf{z}_t$ of the time series. The decoder, which has the same structure as the encoder, decodes the hidden state $\mathbf{z}_t$ to predict $\mathbf{y}'_{t+1,...,t+p}$. As we will see later, both LSTM and ED based models do not capture trend shifts very well. It is also difficult to capture variability very well when these networks are trained using a mean squared error objective function, which is equivalent to maximum likelihood estimation under the assumption that the underlying distribution is Gaussian (and hence unimodal). Furthermore, LSTM and ED models do not have an inherent mechanism to handle high-dimensional data and perform unsupervised feature selection. We bring in sparse recurrent MDNs to address these shortcomings.

3.1 Sparse Recurrent MDN: Architecture

The sparse recurrent MDNs that we present in this exposition are schematically depicted in Figs. 1(a) and (b) for 1-step ahead forecasting. The MDN models a mixture of Gaussians with the latent representation $\mathbf{z}_t$ of the input time series data $\mathbf{x}_{1,...,t}$. If the latent representation $\mathbf{z}_t$ of the input time series is obtained using standard LSTM, then we call the model as **sparse LSTM-MDN**. If $\mathbf{z}_t$ is obtained using standard ED then we refer to the model as **sparse ED-MDN**. Every forecasted point of the time series is associated with its own mixture of Gaussians. Let K be the total number of mixtures, then each component $k \in \{1, \cdots, K\}$ in the mixture is associated with coefficients ρ_k, mean μ_k and standard deviation σ_k.

The mathematical description of the proposed sparse MDN models is as follows. The input sequence is first passed through a feedforward layer with r units and weight matrix $\mathbf{W}_f$. The output of the feedforward layer for input $\mathbf{x}^i$ at time step t (of dimension $1 \times d$) is given by

$$\hat{\mathbf{x}}_t^i = f_{ReLU}(\mathbf{W}_f \cdot (\mathbf{x}_t^i)^T + \mathbf{b}_f), \tag{1}$$

where $f_{ReLU}(\cdot) = \max(\cdot, 0)$ and $\mathbf{W}_f$ is $r \times d$. The reduction in dimensionality is achieved by choosing the number of units in feedforward layer $r \leq \frac{d}{2}$. The feature selection in an unsupervised manner from the feedforward layer is achieved by imposing a Lasso penalty [29] on the weights of feedforward layer to make the input connections sparse. The L_1 constraint or the Lasso penalty induces sparsity

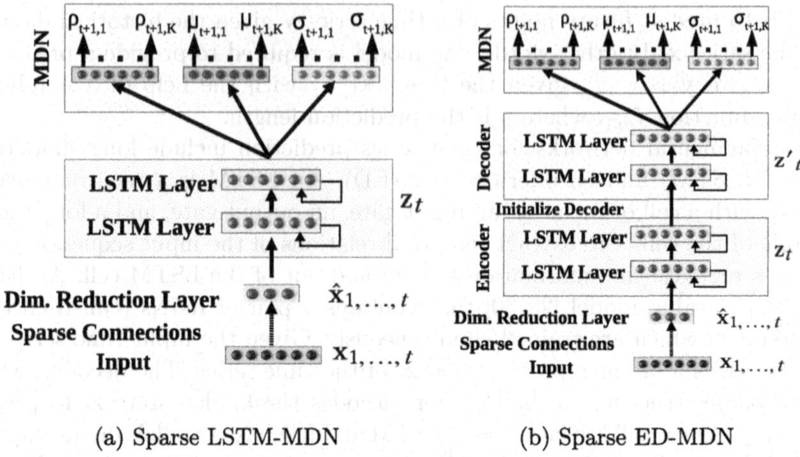

(a) Sparse LSTM-MDN (b) Sparse ED-MDN

Fig. 1. Proposed sparse RMDNs for 1-step ahead forecasting with two LSTM layers.

on the weights $\mathbf{W}_f$ of the fully connected feedforward layer by restricting a fraction of the weights in $\mathbf{W}_f$ to be close to zero and thus results in unsupervised feature selection. In contrast to our end-to-end training process, [5,6] use a two-stage process to achieve dimensionality reduction and feature selection. Note that, convolutions can also be used to achieve the dimensionality reduction as in [20,22,32].

The intermediate term $\hat{\mathbf{x}}^i$ is then fed to the subsequent LSTM or ED layers. Let $\mathbf{z}_t$[1] denote the latent representation of the input obtained by the LSTM or ED. The parameters of the mixture of K Gaussians are estimated as follows:

$$\begin{aligned} \rho_{t',K}(\mathbf{z}_t) &= \text{softmax}(\mathbf{W}_\rho \cdot \mathbf{z}_t + \mathbf{b}_\rho) \\ \mu_{t',K}(\mathbf{z}_t) &= \mathbf{W}_\mu \cdot \mathbf{z}_t + \mathbf{b}_\mu \\ \sigma_{t',K}(\mathbf{z}_t) &= \exp(\mathbf{W}_\sigma \cdot \mathbf{z}_t + \mathbf{b}_\sigma) \end{aligned} \quad (2)$$

where $t' \in [t+1, \cdots, t+p]$, and $\mathbf{W}_\rho, \mathbf{W}_\mu, \mathbf{W}_\sigma$ are the learned parameters of the MDN with $\mu_{\cdot,k}$ and $\sigma_{\cdot,k}$ representing mean and standard deviation of the kth Gaussian component respectively. The coefficients $\rho_{t',k}$ play the role of probabilities. The softmax ensures that each value $\rho_{t',k} \in [0,1]$ and $\sum_{k=1}^{K} \rho_{t',k} = 1$ at any time step t' and exp function is used to ensure that the standard deviation term σ is always positive. The outputs of the MDN as formulated in (2) model the conditional distribution of the future values $\mathbf{y}_{t+1,\dots,t+p}$ to be predicted given the latent representation $\mathbf{z}_t$ expressed as follows:

$$P(\mathbf{y}_{t+1,\dots,t+p} | \mathbf{x}_{1,\dots,t}; \mathbf{z}_t) = \prod_{t'=t+1}^{t+p} \sum_{k=1}^{K} \rho_{t',k}(\mathbf{z}_t) \mathcal{N}\Big(\mathbf{y}_{t'}; \mu_{t',k}(\mathbf{z}_t), \sigma_{t',k}(\mathbf{z}_t)\Big) \quad (3)$$

[1] In case of ED, $\mathbf{z}_t$ comes from decoder.

Thus, the MDN layer outputs a well-defined joint probability distribution obtained for all the time steps in the forecast time horizon. The model parameters are learned by minimizing the negative log-likelihood of the distribution in (3) as shown below:

$$\mathcal{L}_{RMDN} = -\frac{1}{N}\sum_{i=1}^{N} \log P\Big(\mathbf{y}^i_{t+1,\ldots,t+p}|\mathbf{x}^i_{1,\ldots,t};\mathbf{z}^i_t\Big), \tag{4}$$

where superscript i denotes the ith sample, and N is the total number of samples in the train set. It is to be noted that ρ, μ and σ depends upon the latent representation $\mathbf{z}_t$ of the input time series obtained using the parameters of LSTM or ED.

The final loss function along with the L_1 constraint or the Lasso penalty on the weights of the feedforward dimensionality layer is thus given by

$$\mathcal{L} = \mathcal{L}_{RMDN} + \frac{\lambda}{d \times r}||\mathbf{W}_f||_1, \tag{5}$$

The regularization parameter λ controls the level of sparsity in $\mathbf{W}_f$.

Since mixture of Gaussian distribution model a wide class of distributions, we believe RMDNs are better equipped to capture trend shifts and variability in the data. To get prediction at time t, we select a mixture k with the one having more probability $\rho_{t,k}$. We consider selected mixture's mean $\mu_{t,k}$ as the prediction and $\sigma_{t,k}$ as the confidence estimate of the prediction.

4 Performance Evaluation

We compare the performance of the proposed sparse recurrent MDNs, namely, *sparse LSTM-MDN* and *sparse ED-MDN* with the traditional RNN based forecasting approaches, namely *Standard LSTM* and *Standard ED*. We also consider following variants of the proposed sparse RMDN models in our comparison.

- Standard LSTM and ED with feedforward dimensionality reduction layer called as *sparse LSTM* and *sparse ED* respectively.
- Sparse LSTM-MDN and sparse ED-MDN without the feedforward dimensionality reduction layer referred to as *LSTM-MDN* and *ED-MDN* respectively.
- An ensemble of the predictions from eight forecasting approaches considered in this exposition referred to as *Ensemble*.

The evaluation of the proposed models was done on three energy market datasets with MSE and MAPE as metrics. We also evaluated the proposed models using weighted MAPE metric, but the results are similar to MAPE. Hence, they are not reported in this paper.

4.1 Datsets Description

AEMO Dataset[2]**:** This dataset is from the Australian energy market operator (AEMO) and has load information corresponding to five regions of the Australian energy market. Of these, we considered data from a single region spanning September 2014 to July 2015. The load information is available at half-hour interval with corresponding weather data. The task is to predict day-ahead load of the region at half-hour frequency based on weather, calendar and past consumption values as features in input data.

UMass Smart HomeA Dataset[3]**:** This dataset contains three year electricity consumption records of a household. Data is available every half-hour, between years 2014 and 2016. We considered measurements from January to April 2014. Apart from overall load consumption, the dataset contains readings of 31 electrical appliances from the household and weather information of the region. Further, since the weather details are available only at one-hour interval other features were also sampled at the same frequency. The recordings of 17 appliances were zero and hence were discarded. The task is to predict day-ahead consumption of the household at hourly frequency given past consumption and other features of the input data.

PowerTAC Dataset[4]**:** PowerTAC is an annual trading agent tournament that simulates crucial elements of a smart-grid system. As a part of the PowerTAC environment, retail customers of varied nature are simulated whose energy consumption pattern depends on a large range of factors from weather to tariff subscribed. For the purpose of this work, we simulated data from three customer models from the PowerTAC environment called *MedicalCenter-1, CentervilleHomes and BrooksideHomes*. This dataset has energy usage at one-hour intervals along with corresponding weather and calendar information. The task is to predict day-ahead load at an hourly frequency.

Table 1. Datasets details.

Dataset	Window length	Prediction length	Input dimensions	Total windows	Sampling rate (hrs)
AEMO	144	48	31	690	0.5
HomeA	72	24	53	217	1.0
PowerTAC	72	21	24	1270	1.0

4.2 Training Details

In our training process, each dataset is divided into train, validation and test sets. Input sequence of length t were generated by dividing a large time series data into

[2] https://www.aemo.com.au/.
[3] http://traces.cs.umass.edu/index.php/Smart/Smart.
[4] http://powertac.org/.

small subsequences or windows of length t with shift s. Categorical features like time-of-day were represented using one-hot encoding. Min-max normalization was performed for all features on the train, validation and test sets by obtaining minimum and maximum values from the train set data. The exact values of these parameters are presented in Table 1.

We use Adam optimizer for optimizing the weights of the networks in all our experiments. We chose the best architecture as the one with least negative log likelihood for mixture density networks as in Eq. (5) and the one with least mean squared error for non-MDN models on the hold-out validation set. To this end, a grid search over several hyper-parameter values were performed. Specifically, we considered the following choices for various hyper-parameters: number of layers $L \in \{1, 2, 3\}$, number of hidden units h per layer in the range of 50–300 in steps of 50, number of units in the feedforward layer $r \in \{\frac{d}{5}, \frac{d}{4}, \frac{d}{3}, \frac{d}{2}\}$, learning rate $l_r \in \{0.01, 0.001, 0.0001\}$, $\lambda \in \{0.01, 0.001, 0.0001\}$, number of mixtures in the mixture of Gaussians $K \in \{2, 3, 4, 5\}$, and a dropout rate of 0.3 over feedforward connections of the RNN.

Table 2. Performance comparison of proposed sparse RMDN based forecasting models.

Approach	Dataset									
	AEMO		HomeA		MedicalCenter-1		CentervilleHomes		BrooksideHomes	
	MSE	MAPE	MSE	MAPE	MSE	MAPE	MSE	MAPE	MSE	MAPE
Standard LSTM	0.00159	9.03186	0.01182	46.98303	0.00559	17.71834	0.00159	12.6512	0.00276	30.47902
Standard ED	0.00237	11.03585	0.01172	44.10512	0.00586	17.5974	0.00165	13.35113	0.00275	29.24932
Sparse LSTM	**0.00137**	**8.66642**	0.01113	42.77446	0.00596	18.5316	0.00162	12.1824	**0.00256**	28.94780
Sparse ED	0.00170	9.25787	0.01177	43.95304	0.00619	18.5024	0.00154	13.02479	0.00273	31.45647
LSTM-MDN	0.00227	10.36923	0.01295	28.36924	0.00559	**17.22558**	0.00157	12.06838	0.0028	28.93074
ED-MDN	0.00199	9.37978	0.01381	35.16026	0.00587	17.26241	0.00155	12.17745	0.00277	28.51284
Sparse LSTM-MDN	0.00167	9.14346	0.01188	**25.64572**	0.00553	18.54566	**0.00150**	**11.96106**	0.00281	**26.81967**
Sparse ED-MDN	0.00176	9.19194	**0.01170**	29.37821	**0.00536**	18.84936	0.00153	12.42076	0.00299	27.03677
Ensemble	**0.00134**	**8.07125**	**0.01015**	34.10546	**0.00510**	**17.11900**	**0.00139**	**11.74229**	**0.00242**	27.27441

5 Results

The performance of our models are summarized in Table 2 and Fig. 2. The results reported in Table 2 are obtained by performing the experiments once. Predictions from the forecasting models along with their ground truths are plotted in Fig. 2. More specifically, predictions μ for the MDN-based forecasting models along with a one-sigma confidence band at the estimated confidence σ are plotted in Fig. 2. One can form the following inferences from the results.

1. Sparse LSTM and sparse ED outperformed standard LSTM and standard ED in both metrics on most of the datasets, thus showing the efficacy of having feedforward dimensionality reduction layer with L_1 penalty on its weights to reduce the dimensions. Recall that feedforward layer with sparsity constraint on its weights $\mathbf{W}_f$ performs unsupervised feature selection, thus resulting in improved performance.

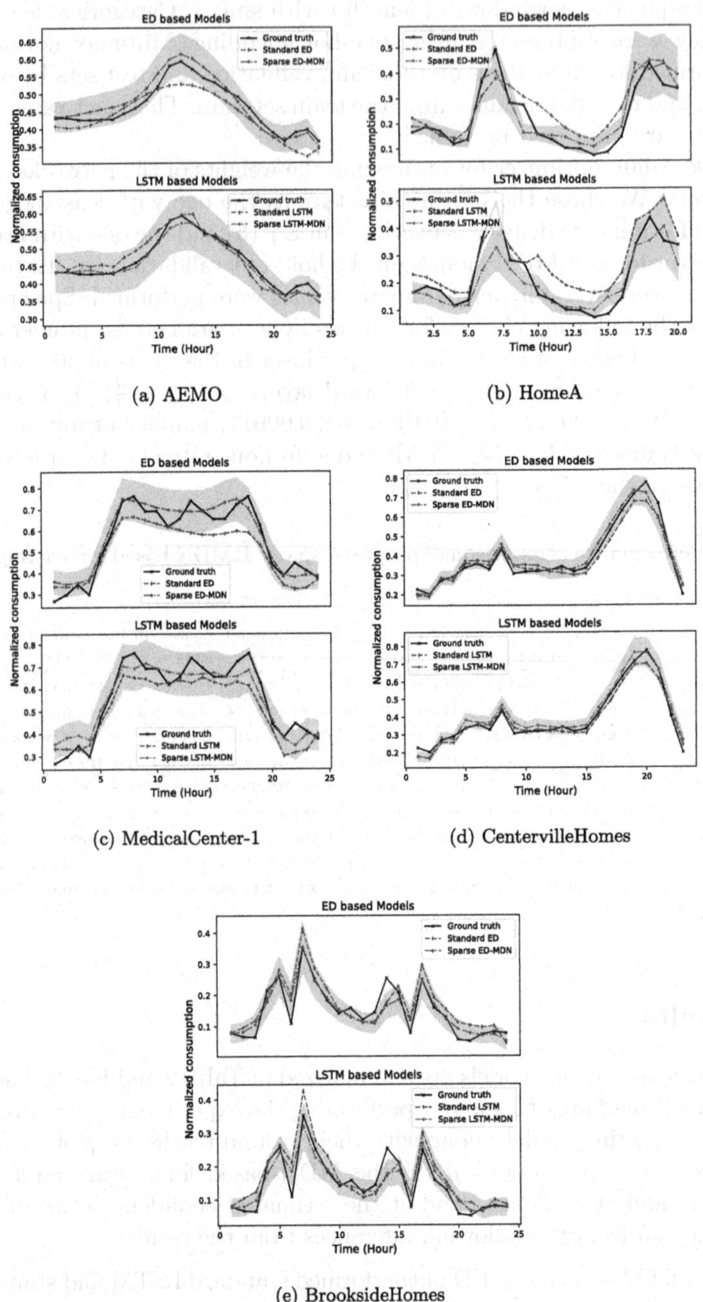

(a) AEMO (b) HomeA

(c) MedicalCenter-1 (d) CentervilleHomes

(e) BrooksideHomes

Fig. 2. Comparison of proposed sparse Recurrent Mixture Density Networks and standard RNN based models with the ground truth for forecasting. We did not plot the predictions from other models for the sake of clarity.

2. LSTM-MDN and ED-MDN are performing better than standard LSTM and standard ED in MAPE metric on most of the datasets. They are also performing better than Sparse LSTM and sparse ED, which demonstrates the ability of MDNs to model the variability and trend shifts present in the data.
3. Sparse LSTM-MDNs and sparse ED-MDNs based forecasting models are performing better than other forecasting approaches on most of the datasets. As discussed earlier, this suggests that sparse RMDNs based forecasting approaches are superior in capturing the variability of the load or demand profile and handling high-dimensional data better than other approaches.
4. Sparse RMDN based forecasting models are performing better than all other approaches in terms of MSE metric on all datasets except AEMO dataset. The AEMO dataset differs from the other datasets we have used in that it exhibits lesser variability. Both these observations suggest that sparse RMDNs are better suited to peaks and high variability than their non-sparse, non-MDN counterparts.
5. One can observe from the Figs. 2(b), (c) and (d) that the estimated confidence σ is low whenever the error between the predicted demand and ground truth is low and the σ is high otherwise. The model thus provides a confidence measure on its prediction ability which is very useful in many real-world applications.
6. The *Ensemble* formed using the eight proposed forecasting models is performing better than all other baselines and it is very robust.
7. While the sparsity constraint improves the performance of both the ED and LSTM models, the improvement depends on the dataset and the performance metric, and does not show a clear trend.

6 Conclusion

We proposed two variants of sparse RMDN models, namely, sparse LSTM-MDN and sparse ED-MDN, for the forecasting problem. These models perform point-wise dimensionality reduction using the feedforward layer and capture the temporal patterns using the underlying RNNs. These architectures can handle variability and trend shifts present in the data and also output a confidence estimate for the forecast. Performance of these two sparse RMDN models were compared with their non-sparse, non-MDN counterparts on three public datasets. Apart from scoring high on chosen performance measures, the results suggest that using the feedforward layer for feature selection improves the ability to handle high-dimensional data. We end this note by remarking that the applicability of these models is not restricted to datasets from energy markets but can be used in other domains like supply-chain logistics, manufacturing, retail or transportation.

References

1. Amarawickrama, H., Hunt, L.: Electricity demand for Sri Lanka: a time series analysis. Energy **33**(5), 724–739 (2008). https://doi.org/10.1016/j.energy.2007.12.008

2. Bazzani, L., Larochelle, H., Torresani, L.: Recurrent mixture density network for spatiotemporal visual attention. arXiv preprint arXiv:1603.08199 (2016)
3. Beenstock, M., Goldin, E., Nabot, D.: The demand for electricity in Israel. Energy Econ. **21**(2), 168–183 (1999). https://doi.org/10.1016/s0140-9883(98)00005-x
4. Bishop, C.M.: Mixture density networks. Technical report, Citeseer (1994)
5. Bouktif, S., Fiaz, A., Ouni, A., Serhani, M.: Optimal deep learning LSTM model for electric load forecasting using feature selection and genetic algorithm: comparison with machine learning approaches. Energies **11**(7), 1636 (2018)
6. Cheng, Y., Xu, C., Mashima, D., Thing, V.L.L., Wu, Y.: PowerLSTM: power demand forecasting using long short-term memory neural network. In: Cong, G., Peng, W.-C., Zhang, W.E., Li, C., Sun, A. (eds.) ADMA 2017. LNCS (LNAI), vol. 10604, pp. 727–740. Springer, Cham (2017). https://doi.org/10.1007/978-3-319-69179-4_51
7. Cho, K., et al.: Learning phrase representations using RNN encoder-decoder for statistical machine translation. arXiv preprint arXiv:1406.1078 (2014)
8. DiPietro, R., Hager, G.D.: Unsupervised learning for surgical motion by learning to predict the future. arXiv preprint arXiv:1806.03318 (2018)
9. Douglas, A., Breipohl, A., Lee, F., Adapa, R.: Risk due to load forecast uncertainty in short term power system planning. IEEE Trans. Power Syst. **13**(4), 1493–1499 (1998). https://doi.org/10.1109/59.736296
10. Gonzalez-Romera, E., Jaramillo-Moran, M., Carmona-Fernandez, D.: Monthly electric energy demand forecasting based on trend extraction. IEEE Trans. Power Syst. **21**(4), 1946–1953 (2006). https://doi.org/10.1109/tpwrs.2006.883666
11. Graves, A.: Generating sequences with recurrent neural networks. arXiv preprint arXiv:1308.0850 (2013)
12. Graves, A., Rahman, M.A., Hinton, G.: Speech recognition with deep recurrent neural networks. In: IEEE International Conference on Acoustics, Speech and Signal processing (ICASSP), pp. 6645–6649. IEEE (2013)
13. Gugulothu, N., Malhotra, P., Vig, L., Shroff, G.: Sparse neural networks for anomaly detection in high-dimensional time series. In: AI4IOT Workshop in Conjunction with ICML, IJCAI and ECAI, July 2018
14. Gugulothu, N., TV, V., Malhotra, P., Vig, L., Agarwal, P., Shroff, G.: Predicting remaining useful life using time series embeddings based on recurrent neural networks. Int. J. Prognostics Health Manage. IJPHM. arXiv preprint arXiv:1709.01073 (2017)
15. Gugulothu, N., et al.: On practical aspects of using RNNs for fault detection in sparsely-labeled multi-sensor time series. In: PHM Society Conference, vol. 10 (2018)
16. Guo, Y., Liao, W., Wang, Q., Yu, L., Ji, T., Li, P.: Multidimensional time series anomaly detection: a GRU-based Gaussian mixture variational autoencoder approach. In: Asian Conference on Machine Learning, pp. 97–112 (2018)
17. Hochreiter, S., Schmidhuber, J.: Long short-term memory. Neural Comput. **9**(8), 1735–1780 (1997)
18. Ketter, W., Collins, J., Weerdt, M.: The 2018 Power Trading Agent Competition (2017). https://papers.ssrn.com/sol3/papers.cfm?abstract_id=3087096/
19. Malhotra, P., Ramakrishnan, A., Anand, G., Vig, L., Agarwal, P., Shroff, G.: LSTM-based encoder-decoder for multi-sensor anomaly detection. arXiv preprint arXiv:1607.00148 (2016)
20. Morales, F.J.O., Roggen, D.: Deep convolutional and LSTM recurrent neural networks for multimodal wearable activity recognition. In: Sensors (2016)

21. Mukherjee, S., et al.: ARMDN: associative and recurrent mixture density networks for eRetail demand forecasting. arXiv preprint arXiv:1803.03800 (2018)
22. Oehmcke, S., Zielinski, O., Kramer, O.: Input quality aware convolutional LSTM networks for virtual marine sensors. Neurocomputing **275**, 2603–2615 (2018). https://doi.org/10.1016/j.neucom.2017.11.027
23. Oğcu, G., Demirel, O.F., Zaim, S.: Forecasting electricity consumption with neural networks and support vector regression. Procedia Soc. Behav. Sci. **58**, 1576–1585 (2012). https://doi.org/10.1016/j.sbspro.2012.09.1144
24. Polson, M., Sokolov, V.: Deep learning for energy markets. arXiv preprint arXiv:1808:05527 (2014)
25. Samouilidis, J.E., Mitropoulos, C.: Energy and economic growth in industrializing countries: the case of Greece. Energy Econ. **6**(3), 191–201 (1984). https://doi.org/10.1016/0140-9883(84)90016-1
26. Saurav, S., et al.: Online anomaly detection with concept drift adaptation using recurrent neural networks. In: Proceedings of the ACM India Joint International Conference on Data Science and Management of Data, CoDS-COMAD 2018, pp. 78–87. ACM, New York (2018). https://doi.org/10.1145/3152494.3152501
27. Scardapane, S., Comminiello, D., Hussain, A., Uncini, A.: Group sparse regularization for deep neural networks. Neurocomputing **241**, 81–89 (2017). https://doi.org/10.1016/j.neucom.2017.02.029
28. Sutskever, I., Vinyals, O., Le, Q.V.: Sequence to sequence learning with neural networks. In: Advances in Neural Information Processing Systems, pp. 3104–3112 (2014)
29. Tibshirani, R.: Regression shrinkage and selection via the lasso. J. Roy. Stat. Soc. Ser. B (Methodol.) **58**, 267–288 (1996)
30. Vincent, P., Larochelle, H., Bengio, Y., Manzagol, P.A.: Extracting and composing robust features with denoising autoencoders. In: Proceedings of the 25th International Conference on Machine Learning, ICML 2008, pp. 1096–1103. ACM, New York (2008). https://doi.org/10.1145/1390156.1390294
31. Xu, J., Rahmatizadeh, R., Bölöni, L., Turgut, D.: Real-time prediction of taxi demand using recurrent neural networks. IEEE Trans. Intell. Transp. Syst. **19**(8), 2572–2581 (2018). https://doi.org/10.1109/TITS.2017.2755684
32. Xu, Y., Kong, Q., Huang, Q., Wang, W., Plumbley, M.D.: Convolutional gated recurrent neural network incorporating spatial features for audio tagging. In: International Joint Conference on Neural Networks IJCNN, pp. 3461–3466 (2017). https://doi.org/10.1109/IJCNN.2017.7966291
33. Zhang, H., Heiden, E., Julian, R., He, Z., Lim, J.J., Sukhatme, G.S.: Auto-conditioned recurrent mixture density networks for complex trajectory generation. arXiv preprint arXiv:1810.00146 (2018)
34. Zhao, Y., Yang, R., Chevalier, G., Shah, R., Romijnders, R.: Applying deep bidirectional LSTM and mixture density network for basketball trajectory prediction. CoRR abs/1708.05824 (2017). http://arxiv.org/abs/1708.05824

A Multitask Learning Neural Network for Short-Term Traffic Speed Prediction and Confidence Estimation

Yanyun Tao[1], Xiang Wang[1(✉)], and Yuzhen Zhang[2]

[1] School of Rail Transportation, Soochow University, Suzhou 215005, China
{taoyanyun, wangxiang}@suda.edu.cn
[2] The First Affiliated Hospital of Soochow University, Suzhou 215006, China

Abstract. To improve predictive accuracy on short-term traffic speed, we proposed a multitask learning neural network (MLNN). MLNN carries out the speed prediction task for three short-terms by the combination of convolution neural network (CNN) and gated recurrent units' network (GRU), and accomplishes the confidence estimation task on predicted speed with the confidence network. A multitask loss function with weighted sub loss terms for multitask learning is employed. In the experiment, our method was tested on the data set of Shanghai Expressway at 2014. Conventional methods such as auto-regressive integrated moving average (ARIMA) and Gaussian maximum likelihood (GML), and time series models, recurrent neural network (RNN), GRU and long short-term memory (LSTM), were also used to compare. The results show that MLNN with square loss obtained the smallest mean squared error (MSE) on most cases. For four road types, MLNN obtained the overall smallest mean absolute percentage error (MAPE) on these cases. We also proved that as compared to single-term prediction, multitask learning outperformed 12.4% in MSE and 9.91% in MAPE for 10-min and 15-min prediction. To improve the forecast on low speed, MAP-loss term is additionally used in multitask loss function. It efficiently improved the predictive accuracy on low speed. The confidence estimation network gave a 89.93% estimation accuracy on the predicted speed, efficiently avoiding the inaccurate speed prediction.

Keywords: Short-term speed prediction · Spatial-temporal features · Multitask learning · Neural network · Confidence estimation · Multitask loss function

1 Introduction

Traffic congestion has become a bottleneck restricting the economic and social development of the city. Due to the time cost and economic loss caused by traffic congestion every year, it is imminent to give accurate prediction on traffic congestion. With the decrease in prediction time granularity, the difficulty of traffic flow prediction is greatly increased. Since 1970s, uni-variate time series models have been widely used for short-term traffic flow prediction, especially auto-regressive integrated moving average (ARIMA) model [1] and exponential smoothing (ES) model [2]. The results

I. V. Tetko et al. (Eds.): ICANN 2019, LNCS 11728, pp. 434–449, 2019.
https://doi.org/10.1007/978-3-030-30484-3_36

showed that this model can obtain limited accuracy. As the volume of traffic data becomes large, data-driven approaches for short-term prediction on traffic speed are promising. In recent years, many experts have tried machine learning methods to solve traffic problems, not only prediction on flow but also on speed. For instance, a forecast model based on Gaussian maximum likelihood (GML) estimation method is proposed by Lin [3]. As compared to non-parametric regression (NPR) [4], ARIMA and neural network (NN), GML obtained the best performance. To deal with new traffic data added, online-support vector regression (SVR) is proposed for short-term traffic flow prediction [5].

Deep learning models have attracted many researches to solve traffic problems. Jia et al. [6] established deep belief net (DBN) to predict short-term traffic flow, adopted greedy unsupervised learning to train model and fine-tune the data through the marked data. Wang et al. [7] proposed the traffic speed prediction model based on long short-term memory (LSTM) with remote sensor data. Polson et al. [8] designed a deep learning architecture with L_1 regularization and a sequence of tanh layers. To give the prediction on traffic congestion, Tan et al. [9] proposed a model with deep learning. Its predicted accuracy on peak traffic congestion is about 85%. Fu et al. [10] proposed recurrent neural network (RNN), LSTM and gated recurrent units (GRU), to predict short-term traffic flow, and the result showed improvement of LSTM and GRU perform over ARIMA model. LSTM has also been applied in network-wide traffic speed prediction [11], travel time prediction [12] and mixed traffic trajectory prediction [13]. In addition, convolution neural network (CNN), which learns the data of traffic flow as an image, is employed to predict the state of large-scale traffic network [14].

For short-term traffic speed prediction, the spatial-temporal features extraction is a critical issue. Many works used deep learning models to extract spatial or temporal information from history traffic data. However, this is not enough. The important temporal information may not be further extracted because shorter-term data cannot be collected. In addition, no matter how high the quality of built model, the inaccurate prediction cannot be fully avoided. It is better to provide a credit probability of the predicted speed, which can avoid the inaccurate prediction as possible. For time series uncertainty estimation, Zhu et al. proposed a Bayesian deep model to give confident prediction [15]. Gal conducted deep study on uncertainty in deep learning [16].

To improve the predicted accuracy and give the confidence estimation, multitask learning (MTL) [17, 18] is used in this study. It has been proved that learning the tasks jointly greatly improves over independent task learning (ITL) when the tasks are related. Huang et.al used DBN with a MTL layer for supervised prediction [19]. They grouped regression tasks on different roads and stations, which are spatially correlated with each other. Besides using multitask, spatial correlation for one node can be achieved by collecting more data of spatially related nodes. As compared to spatially correlated multitask, time-dependent multitasks may be more beneficial. The speed forecasting task can be decomposed into two heterogeneous multitask with several time-related sub multitask. The heterogeneous multitask are the confidence estimation task and the speed prediction task. Time-dependent sub multitask are within the heterogeneous multitask. They are simultaneous, not sequential. Hence, multitask learning is more appropriate than transfer learning. In this work, we propose a multitask learning neural network (MLNN) to accomplish prediction tasks.

2 Problem Formulation

First, we give notations in short-term traffic speed prediction. Traffic node indicates a spatial location of ground loop detector on road. The target node denotes the critical traffic node, on which it is worthy of speed prediction. Up/down-stream nodes denote the traffic nodes are spatially before or after the target node.

Spatial Dependencies. Figure 1 shows spatial-temporal dependency of traffic nodes. The traffic state of target node is significantly related to neighbouring nodes in a period. The traffic congestion of downstream nodes gradually spreads to the target node and upstream nodes. It achieves at its peak later.

Temporal Dependencies. For a node, the traffic speed at current time is related to the speed at the short time before. A low traffic speed of target node occurring at 8am affected that from 8 am to 8:30am, leading to a traffic congestion during this period.

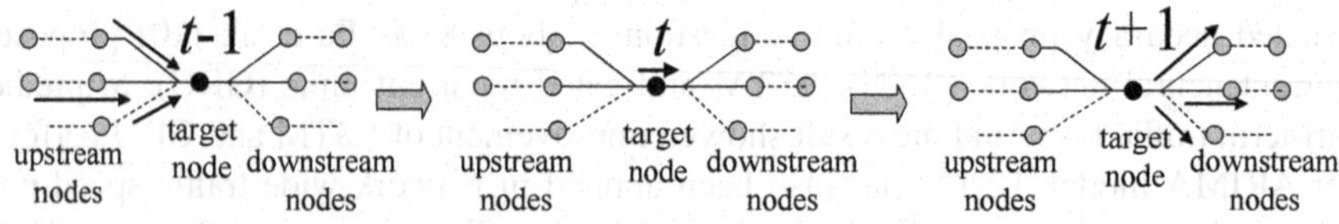

Fig. 1. Spatial-temporal relationship of traffic nodes

Let t be the current time and $t + \xi_i$ $(i = 1, 2, \ldots, m)$ be the short-term time after t. ξ_i indicates a short-term, which is i times of 5-min, and m denotes the number of short-terms to be predicted. The interval between t and $t - 1$ is 5-min. The short-term traffic speed prediction problem is formulated as follows.

$$\begin{aligned} & Z = [Z^S, Z^C] = [\min\{e(y^s_{t+\xi_i}, f^s(x_t))\}, \min\{e(y^c_{t+\xi_i}, f^c(x_t))\}] \\ & \xi_i = 5 \cdot i \ (i = 1, 2 \ldots, m) \\ & x_t = \{s_t, s_{t-1}, \ldots s_{t-\tau+1}, r_t, r_{t-1}, \ldots r_{t-\tau+1}\} \\ & s_t, r_t \in \mathbb{R} \end{aligned} \tag{1}$$

Here, Z^s and Z^c are accuracy functions of speed prediction and confidence estimation; x_t is the input and τ is number of time steps before t; $s_{t-\tau+1}$ and $r_{t-\tau+1}$ denote the speed of target node and its related nodes at the time $t - \tau + 1$, respectively. $e(y, x)$ denotes the error of x to y, e.g. *mean squared error* (*mse*); $y^s_{t+\xi_i}$ and $y^c_{t+\xi_i}$ indicate the observed speed of target node and the confidence label at the time $t + \xi_i$, respectively; $f^s(x_t)$ and $f^c(x_t)$ are the predicted speed and the estimated confidence.

3 MLNN

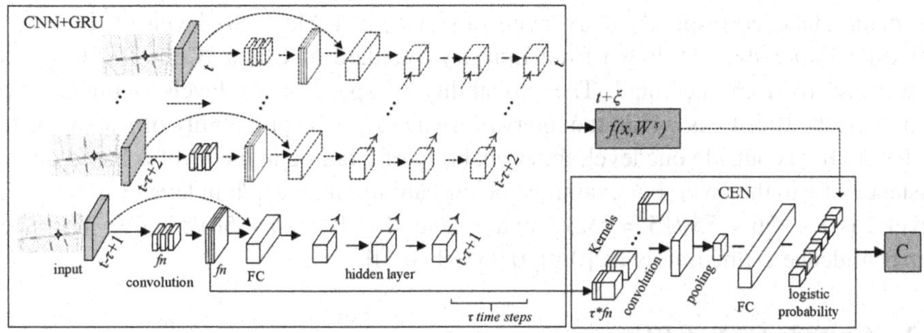

Fig. 2. MLNN structure

A multitask learning neural network (MLNN), composed by CNN+GRU and confidence estimation network (CEN), is proposed to address problem (1). The architecture of MLNN is shown in Fig. 2.

3.1 Input Data and Multitask Labels

The raw data of a node is a 1-dimension (1D) time series data of a traffic node at 5-min interval. We extracted data from target node, five up- and downstream nodes at 5 time steps (i.e. $t-4$, $t-3$, $t-2$, $t-1$, t). Hence, each extracted data has 11*5 spatial-temporal features (11 spatial features for 5 time steps). For each time step, the samples are arranged in a (3*4) matrix form. This is because the spatial layout of 11 nodes is a network.

In CNN+GRU, CNN deals with spatial features, while GRU performs on temporal features. CNN receives the data of (3*4) matrix and runs for 5 time steps. The input of 5 time steps is shown in Fig. 3. *s* indicates the target node, and *r_up_i* and *r_down_i* denote the up- and downstream-node *i*.

$$X^{t}=\begin{bmatrix} s^{t} & r\_up\_5^{t} & r\_up\_4^{t} & r\_up\_3^{t} \\ r\_up\_2^{t} & r\_up\_1^{t} & r\_down\_1^{t} & r\_down\_2^{t} \\ r\_down\_3^{t} & r\_down\_4^{t} & r\_down\_5^{t} & 0 \end{bmatrix} \cdots X^{t-4}=\begin{bmatrix} s^{t-4} & r\_up\_5^{t-4} & r\_up\_4^{t-4} & r\_up\_3^{t-4} \\ r\_up\_2^{t-4} & r\_up\_1^{t-4} & r\_down\_1^{t-4} & r\_down\_2^{t-4} \\ r\_down\_3^{t-4} & r\_down\_4^{t-4} & r\_down\_5^{t-4} & 0 \end{bmatrix}$$

Fig. 3. Input of five time steps

Table 1. Service level of highway-express 80 km/h.

Level	1	2	3	4	5	6
Speed (km/h)	(0, 40)	[40, 55)	[55, 64)	[64, 72)	[72, 80)	[80, +∞)

Two labels are designed for solving problem (1). One label is a six-probability vector for the confidence estimation task, and the other label is a vector of observed speed (km/h) for speed prediction tasks at 5-,10- and 15-min, respectively. Confidence estimation label corresponds to six levels of service in Table 1. Six levels of service for 80 km/h Expressway is drawn from Industry Standard of China "Code for design of urban and road engineering". The probability of speed at six levels is obtained as follow: if the speed v is within the interval of one level, the probability of v at this level is 100%. If v is outside one level, the probability of v falling in the level is based on the distance of v to the level. For example, the probability of 56 km/h in level-3 is 100%, at level-2 is 1 – (56 – 55)/15 = 93.3% and at level-4 is 1 – (64 – 56)/8 = 0%. The label for confidence estimation is as [0, 0, 0.933, 1, 0, 0].

3.2 Cascade CNN+GRU

A cascade CNN+GRU is designed to accomplish speed prediction task. In this cascade, CNN contains one convolution layer with identity mapping and a fully connected layer (FC). GRU contains three layers, namely input layer, hidden layer and the output layer. The input layer of GRU is exactly the output layer of CNN.

The input to CNN is a single channel. Each time step generates *fn* feature maps. The activation function *f*() is ReLU, the size of kernel is [2, 2], the stride of kernels is 1 and the number of output channels is *fn*. The pooling layer is not used in CNN+GRU. This is because the pooling probably ignores important relation information of traffic nodes during fitting speed of target node. Fully connected layer (FC) with dropout combines feature maps to implement transformations. The dropout is a regularization method that makes some neuron nodes inactive with some probability.

In CNN+GRU, the output of CNN is a vector at each time step. GRU runs τ time steps to obtain temporal features from CNN outputs. In GRU, only update gate z and reset gates r are reserved. The larger the value of the update gate, the more the state information of the previous moment is brought into the current state. Reset gate controls the degree of forgetting the state information of the previous moment. The more the value of reset gate is, the more it is forgotten.

3.3 CEN

CEN estimates the confidence by calculating the probability of predicted speed falling in service levels (Table 1). It has two convolution layers, one max pooling layer, a FC layer with dropout and a logistic output layer. CEN shares the first convolution layer with CNN+GRU.

In the second convolution layer, each kernel has τ*fn* input channels, receiving feature maps of τ time steps from the previous layer. The stride of kernels in the second convolution layer is also set to 1. Following the convolution layers, the max-pooling is used. The size of pooling window is [2, 2], reducing input feature map into half size. The stride is set to [2, 2], and the padding is "SAME".

In the output layer, *softmax* function is not adopted to calculate the probability for multiple outputs. This is because credit probability of predicted speed belonging to different levels must be independent and non-competitive. Hence, we employ the logistics function to provide independent probabilities. Let $f_l(x, W^c)$ be the probability of level-l and $f(x, W^S)$ be the predicted speed. W^S and W^C denote the weights of CNN +GRU and CEN. The confidence on the predicted speed is of the form.

$$C = \{f_l(x, W^c) \mid f(x, W^s) \in l\} \quad (2)$$

Here, $f(x, W^s)$ falls in level l, and the confidence is the l-th probability. For example, a probability vector [0.02, 0.01, 0.54, 0.98, 0.04, 0.09] is obtained on the predicted speed 71 km/h, which falls in level-4. The confidence the predicted speed is 0.98, the 4-th element in the probability vector.

4 Multitask Learning

4.1 Multitask Learning and Corporation

MLNN carries out the regression task for traffic speed prediction and a confidence estimation task at multiple short-term times. The regression task is to fit the observed speed without distinguishing the category of road types and give the predicted speed. The confidence estimation task provides the credible probability estimation on the predicted speed, which is a limited dependent variable regression. Each task contains three sub tasks, which are responsible for 5-, 10- and 15-min speed prediction and confidence estimation, respectively. Time-related information sharing can improve the accuracy of longer-term speed prediction and heterogeneous information sharing improve the forecasting credibility. Figure 4 is the schematic of multitask learning.

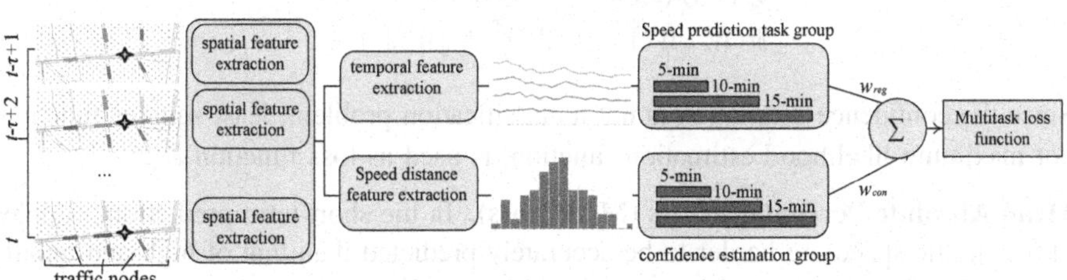

Fig. 4. Multitask learning

Generally, the speed prediction task and confidence estimation task are heterogeneous multitask. They are worth learning from each other and improve each other. The speed prediction task minimized the distance of samples to a hyper-plane by extracting common features from most samples, while the confidence estimation task increases the dissimilarity gap by extracting features from distant samples and reduces the similarity variation by extracting features from near samples. Two tasks are mutual complementary. Within the speed prediction task, sub tasks for three short-term prediction are strongly time-dependent correlated. For instance, the task of 15-min prediction can learn beneficial information from 5-min task. Three sub tasks within the confidence estimation task are the same as ones in the regression task. Through joint learning of time-dependent sub tasks and heterogeneous multitask, more informative representations can be achieved.

4.2 Multitask Loss Function

For multitask learning, multitask loss function is a weighted combination of loss terms of sub tasks. Each loss term is the optimization objective of one sub task. The loss function L of MLNN with multiple sub loss terms is of the form:

$$L = \omega_s \sum_{i=1}^{N} \ell^S(y_i^s, f(x_i, W^s)) + \omega_c \sum_{i=1}^{N} \ell^C(y_i^c, f(x_i, W^c)) + \lambda \cdot \Re(W^c, W^s) \quad (3)$$

Here, N is the number of samples, $x_i \in \mathbb{R}^{3\times4\times5}$ is the input, $y_i^s \in \mathbb{R}^3$ is the observed speed of three short-term prediction tasks, and $y_i^c \in [0,1] \in \mathbb{R}^{6\times3}$ is the probability label for confidence estimation. The first term ℓ^S is the loss of CNN+GRU and ℓ^C is the loss term of confidence estimation network; ω_c and ω_s are weight parameters of two tasks ℓ^C and ℓ^S, which indicate the importance of multitask. The third term $\lambda \cdot \Re(W^c, W^s)$ is the L_2 regularizer.

Square Loss (L_2 Loss). L_2 is a conventional loss function, which is used for multitask and regularizer. Loss terms using L_2 loss are of the form.

$$\begin{aligned} \ell^S(y_i^s, f(x_i, W^s)) &= \left\| f(x_i, W^s) - y_i^s \right\|^2 \\ \ell^C(y_i^c, f(x_i, W^c)) &= \left\| f(x_i, W^c) - y_i^c \right\|^2 \\ \Re(W^c, W^s) &= \left(\|W^c\|^2 + \|W^s\|^2\right) \end{aligned} \quad (4)$$

Since the confidence estimation is not a classification problem, least squares function, not maximum likelihood estimation function, is used as loss function ℓ^C.

Mean Absolute Percentage Loss (MAP Loss). In the short-term prediction, samples of low traffic speed are harder to be accurately predicted than that of high and middle speed. Actually, the predictive accuracy on low traffic speed is very important to the traffic management, since it always pay more attentions to the congestion state (i.e., low speed). To improve the accuracy on low speed, MAP loss is used in multitask loss function. It penalizes the loss only from high speed, while keeping the loss of low speed samples unchanged. The first term ℓ^S in L can be changed as follows.

$$\ell^S(y_i^s, f(x_i, W^s)) = \left| 1 - \frac{f(x_i, W^s)}{y_i^s} \right| \quad (5)$$

Here, μ is set to 10 that enlarges the weight of loss term. The second and third terms in (10) are not changed.

5 Experiments

5.1 Data Collection

Our data set for test is collected from Shanghai Expressway at the Shanghai Traffic Information Center, from March 1 to 14, 2014, Shanghai Expressway geomagnetic loop data. A total of 3,304 in-path loops are located on the expressway, and the loop detector collects data every 5 min. The volume of daily data can reach 1 million. Each data contains a loop code, a recording time, section speed, section flow rate, section occupancy rate and other related information.

First, the quality control on the dataset is conducted. The abnormal data includes some invalid data in the recording results, abnormality in the monitoring equipment, or abnormality in external factors, causing quality problems in the recording process. For example, erroneous data-morning and evening rush hour, the flow rate and occupancy rate displayed by the detector is 0; the missing data-the loop detector does not record data at a certain moment. Then, the data of loop detectors is grouped according to the group. The loop group is defined as a section on the road network. The flow rate is the sum of the loop flow rates in the group, and the speed is the weighted sum of the loop speeds in the group.

According to road topology, the traffic data are grouped into normal type, merge type, diverge type and ramp type, denoted as S1, S2, S3, S4 and S5. For each road type, training set has 15200 samples and test set has 3800 samples.

5.2 Parameters

All experiments are performed on a PC with a GPU of NVIDIA 1060i. The parameters of MLNN are given in Table 2. In the loss function, ω_c, ω_s and λ are set to 200, 1 and 0.02. ω_c is a large value because the loss term of confidence estimation is a small dimension. Batch size is equals to the number of samples. This is because both the number of training samples and features are not too large. We tested many times that this batch size leads to a good convergence. We can set learning rate to 0.01 and 0.001. It found that the validation error decreases during training when learning rate is 0.01, the error decreases too slowly while learning rate is 0.001. The number of iterations is set to 500. This setting is drawn from the truth that validation error cannot be decreased after 500 iterations during training.

In the experiment, ARIMA with parameters $(p, d, q) = (2,2,2)$, GML, CNN, RNN, GRU and LSTM are compared to two MLNNs. In the following tables, MLNN-S indicates MLNN for a single-term prediction, and MLNN-M denotes MLNN for multiple short-term speed prediction. Mean squared error (MSE) is a typical measure of predictive accuracy, and mean absolute percentage error (MAPE) is a measure of relative error, which biases to low speed samples.

Table 2. MLNN parameters.

Hyper parameters			
Input	3*4	Iteration	500
Learning rate	0.01	Batch size	All samples
ω_c	200	Dropout	0.5
ω_s	1	λ	0.02
CNN+GRU parameters			
conv	4*cov(2,2,1,1)	# hidden nodes	50
FC	96	Output	3
Time step	5	Activation	ReLU
CEN parameters			
conv	8*cov2(2,2,1,5*4)	Pooling	8*max_pooling([2,2],[2,2])
FC	96	Output	3*6

6 Results and Discussion

6.1 Analysis on Spatial and Temporal Features

Figure 5(a) (b), (c) and (d) are plots of the predicted speed curve in the training step and five time-step outputs of CNN for three runs. CNN 1–5 indicate output of CNN at $t-4$, $t-3$, $t-2$, $t-1$, t. As plots show, the predicted curve is strongly related to outputs of CNN at $t-4$, $t-3$ and $t-2$. This illustrates that GRU makes full use of five time-step information for the speed prediction. Figure 5(e) shows hot maps of features extracted from four kernels of CNN. Red grids denote the largest value of convolution/pooling and green grids are the smallest value. The larger value of grid, the more importance of corresponding feature. In Fig. 5(e), elements (1,3) and (2,1) in most 3*4 matrices obtained the largest value, e.g. kernel 1, kernel 2 and kernel 3 at $t-4$, kernel 1, kernel 2 and kernel 4 at $t-3$, and kernel 3 at t. Elements (1,1), (2,2) and (2,3) in some matrices attained a large value. It is noted that these elements mentioned above involved the downstream node-1, -2 and upstream node-1, -2. Hence, we inferred that the upstream node-1, -2 and downstream node-1, -2 probably have the largest effect on the speed of target node. This result is assistant with the hypothesis that adjacent nodes have the strongest correlation with the target node under S1 road type.

Figure 6 gave scatter plots of MLNN-M vs MLNN-S, ARIMA, RNN and GRU on S5 for 5-min and on S2 for 15-min prediction. It can be observed that the predicted speed of MLNN-S is overall the nearest to the identity line at 5-min prediction. However, for 5-min prediction on low speed, MLNN-M and ARIMA yielded a better prediction than MLNN-S. In this case, MLNN-S gave higher predicted value than that of observed samples, while the other methods under-predicted. On high- or middle-speed, MLNN-M obviously outperformed the other methods. For 15-min prediction, the predicted data of ARIMA were far away from the identity line. It is noted that MLNN-S is poorer than MLNN-M on low speed prediction. Hence, MLNN-S doesn't suffices. Meanwhile, MLNN-M outperformed RNN and GRU in these cases.

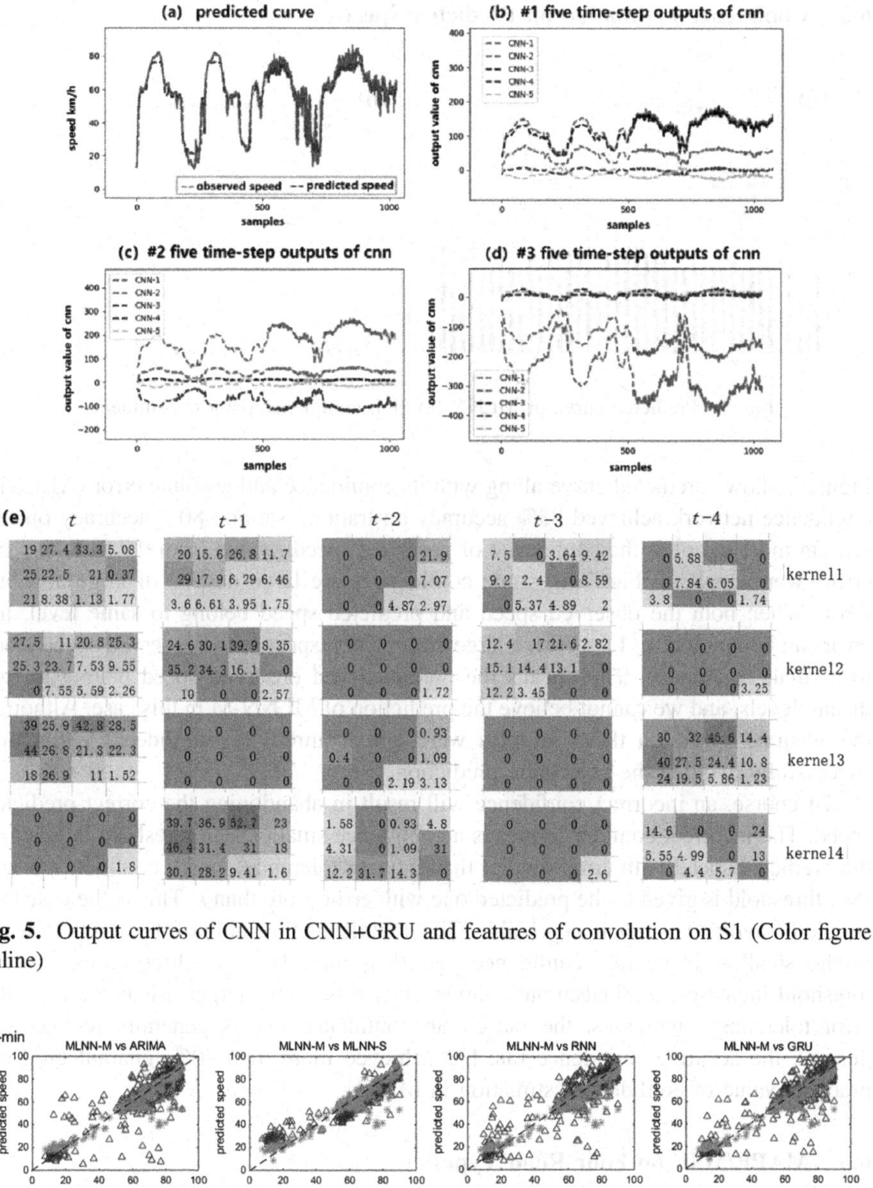

Fig. 5. Output curves of CNN in CNN+GRU and features of convolution on S1 (Color figure online)

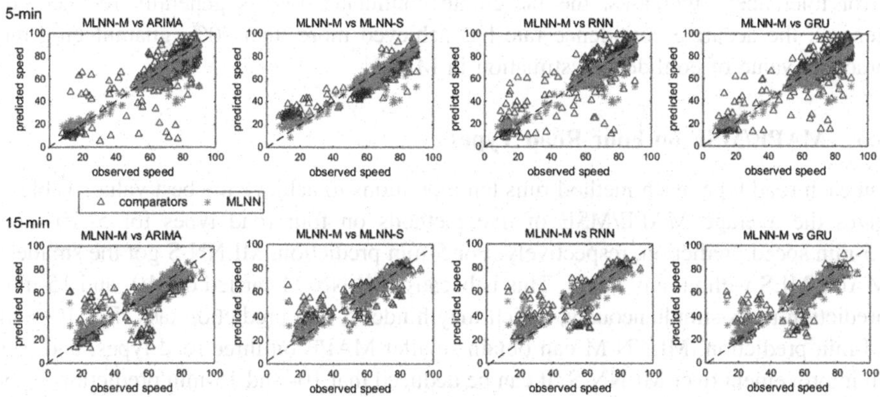

Fig. 6. Scatter plots of methods on S5 for 5- and S2 for 15-min prediction

6.2 Confidence Estimation on Predicted Speed

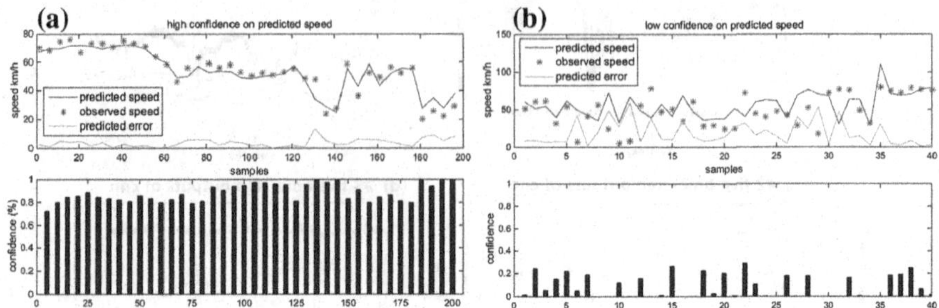

Fig. 7. Predicted curve of MLNN (a) high confidence (b) low confidence

Figure 7 shows predicted curve along with its confidence and absolute error (AE). The confidence network achieved 83% accuracy on training set and 80% accuracy on test set. On most samples, the confidence of predicted speed ranged from 0.7 to 1, and the errors were small. In Fig. 7(a), some confidences are large despite of large absolute error. When both the observed speed and predicted speed belong to same level, the error can be ignored. In Fig. 7(b), a large error with respect to the observed speed leads to a small confidence. This means the predicted and observed speed belong to two distant levels, and we cannot believe the prediction of MLNN-M in this case. Although the accurate speed on these samples were not acquired, the confidence estimation successfully avoided the inaccurate prediction.

Of course, an incorrect confidence will result in abandoning the correct predicted speed. The incorrect confidence means a confidence smaller than threshold is given to the predicted speed with error smaller than ε (error tolerance), and a confidence larger than threshold is given to the predicted one with error more than ε. This is the case that should be avoided as much as possible. The confidence threshold of 0.3 and 0.35 leads to the smallest inaccurate confidence rate (less than 10%) in three cases. As the threshold increases, the inaccurate confidence rate becomes larger. Meanwhile, as the error tolerance ε increases, the inaccurate confidence rate is generally reduced. In general, the accurate confidence rate has achieved more than 90%, guaranteeing the practical value of confidence estimation in MLNN.

6.3 MAPE/MSE on Four Road Types

On each road type, each method runs ten repetitions to achieve the best value. Table 3 gives the average MAPE/MSE of five methods on four road types for 5-,10- and 15-min speed prediction, respectively. For 5-min prediction, MLNN-S got the smallest MAPE/MES without any doubt. This is because MLNN-M carried out 10- and 15-min prediction tasks simultaneously, which may hinder 5-min prediction task. For 10- and 15-min prediction, MLNN-M can obtain smaller MAPE on three road types, and had an improvement over MLNN-S. It can be deduced that 10- and 15-min prediction tasks learned more useful features from 5-min prediction task. MLNN-S got better MAPE than MLNN-M only on S1. This is because as compared to the other types, the temporal dependency is apparently weaker than the spatial dependency in S1.

For 5-min prediction, CNN has obtained better results than MLNN-M at S1 and S2 in terms of MAPE. These are attributed to the ability of CNN in extracting spatial features for hard samples. When to perform 5-min prediction, the shorter-term information (e.g. the information of 2-,3-,4-min before the given time) cannot be further acquired. In this case, the spatial features become important for accurate prediction. Another reason for this is that the temporal dependency of S1 and S2 is poorer than on that of S3 and S4. In addition, RNN, GRU and LSTM can obtain good results in some cases. Conventional methods, ARIMA and GML, gave accurate prediction on some cases. ARIMA obtained the best result on S3 for 15-min prediction. However, on S1 and S4, ARIMA cannot got good accuracy.

Table 3. MAPE/MSE on four road types.

Model		MAPE				MSE			
		S1	S2	S3	S4	S1	S2	S3	S4
ARIMA	5-min	14.94	14.15	13.68	18.41	11.45	8.584	7.994	11.46
GML		13.55	13.62	14.92	21.97	5.800	8.702	9.661	3.575
LSTM		10.70	12.42	12.22	8.826	3.423	8.123	7.676	2.101
GRU		10.01	9.93	10.99	9.18	2.157	4.877	5.811	1.911
RNN		10.35	10.23	11.43	9.86	1.989	4.892	5.452	2.000
CNN		**8.255**	9.034	23.34	10.27	4.100	6.868	8.089	2.187
MLNN-S		9.412	**5.922**	**9.378**	**5.64**	**1.212**	**2.289**	**3.498**	**1.293**
MLNN-M		10.05	10.54	10.30	10.03	2.127	4.812	5.278	2.118
ARIMA	10-min	17.35	16.43	14.84	21.84	7.448	9.849	7.684	14.38
GML		13.23	14.52	15.01	26.32	6.832	10.96	11.11	4.621
LSTM		15.92	14.48	13.20	11.09	5.852	9.762	9.020	4.324
GRU		13.29	13.04	13.92	11.80	3.233	8.097	8.427	3.000
RNN		13.05	13.39	13.79	12.27	5.382	7.999	7.493	3.162
CNN		19.71	16.55	19.06	14.54	5.523	10.57	11.83	4.589
MLNN-S		**12.40**	13.70	13.19	13.02	2.801	8.261	7.717	3.357
MLNN-M		12.91	**11.11**	**11.60**	**10.27**	**2.376**	**5.278**	**6.775**	**2.762**
ARIMA	15-min	19.10	18.60	13.58	21.99	16.54	13.02	**7.562**	15.83
GML		23.58	16.29	15.89	28.17	7.925	13.20	12.12	5.651
LSTM		15.62	14.76	13.45	15.77	7.101	11.59	9.723	4.832
GRU		16.05	16.27	17.01	13.91	4.160	10.84	10.89	3.832
RNN		15.98	16.35	16.48	14.15	3.604	10.62	9.576	3.689
CNN		16.06	17.13	34.24	14.73	7.910	13.22	23.23	4.598
MLNN-S		**14.97**	16.31	15.47	14.80	3.432	10.68	9.393	4.084
MLNN-M		15.11	**14.35**	**13.08**	**12.91**	**3.232**	**8.298**	8.971	**3.642**

6.4 MAP Loss Term Comparison

Although two MTNN with L_2 loss yielded a smaller MAPE than that of the other methods on 5-, 15-min prediction, they got inaccuracy on low speed in some cases. L_2 loss can well deal with emergencies in traffic because of its sensitivity to outliers. However, it is unbiased to low speed samples. Owing to the sensitivity to small value, MAP loss is able to improve the predictive accuracy on low speed despite of more loss on normal samples. Table 4 shows the MAPE comparison between different loss term used in MLNN-M. Shrink loss punishes only the loss of easy samples without changing the loss of hard samples. L_3 loss and L_1 loss, are also compared.

Table 4. MAPE comparison between loss functions.

Multitask loss function	S1	S2	S3	S4	S5	S1	S2	S3	S4	S5
	5-min prediction					15-min prediction				
MAP-loss	6.97	**6.49**	7.99	8.59	**10.7**	13.3	**14.1**	13.3	14.1	**18.0**
L_3 loss	13.8	12.8	14.2	15.3	15.8	19.2	18.3	15.3	18.3	24.3
L_2 loss	10.1	10.5	10.3	10.0	17.3	15.1	14.4	13.1	**12.9**	23.9
L_1 loss	**6.66**	6.72	**7.94**	**6.29**	17.1	**12.3**	14.3	**12.9**	14.1	21.6
Shrinkloss	7.37	11.9	11.8	11.0	15.2	14.3	16.6	15.4	15.2	23.2

Observed from Table 4, MLNN+MAP loss yielded a comprehensive improvement over MLNN+L_2 loss and L_3 loss on MAPE at 5-min prediction. Meanwhile, MLNN+MAP loss did not give a large penalty on MSE. It yielded only average 2.97% increase in MSE on five road types. The loss of MSE must be worth MAPE reduction. It is noted that L_1 loss obtained smaller MAPE than MAP-loss for 5-min prediction on three road types. Shrinkloss punishes easy samples and keeps hard samples unchanged. However, easy samples of high speed may be ignored such that the MAPE cannot be reduced overall.

Figure 8 shows loss function comparison on low- and high-speed prediction on ramp section (S5). As compared to the other methods, the predicted points of MAP-loss is nearest to the identity line at low speed area. Hence, MAP-loss achieved the most accurate low speed prediction in these cases. Meanwhile, MAP loss yields a higher accuracy than the other loss function without increasing a large error with respect to middle- or high speed samples. Although MLNN+MAP loss still gave poorer MAPE than that of RNN and GRU in some cases, it has achieved as accurate prediction as RNN and GRU on low speed and outperformed RNN and GRU on middle-speed prediction. This can be observed from Fig. 8.

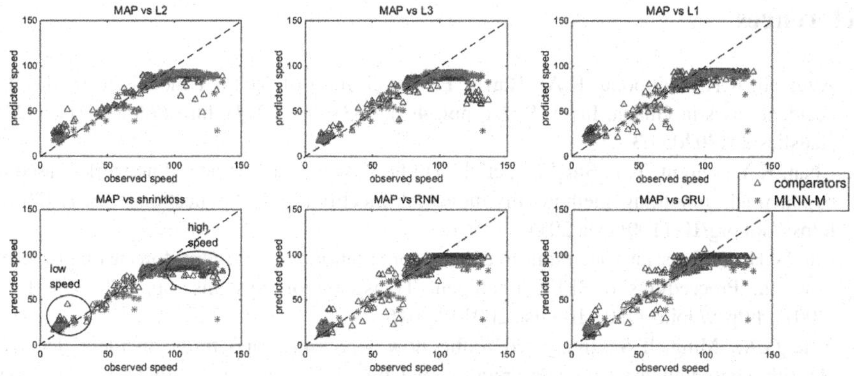

Fig. 8. Correlation between MAP loss and the other loss functions

7 Conclusion and Future Works

To solve multiple short-term (e.g., 5-, 10- and 15 min) prediction on traffic speed of different road types, we proposed MLNN. Features extracted from convolution layers were analyzed and it was found that the downstream node-1, -2 and upstream node-1, -2 may be more useful. In terms of MAPE/MSE, MLNN-S is the best one at 5-min prediction while MLNN-M was best at 10-, and 15-min prediction. The confidence estimation network gave a highly accurate confidence estimation on predicted speed. To further improve the forecast on congestion state of traffic, MAP loss function is used to make multitask learning bias to low speed. The results show that MLNN using L_2 loss obtained the smallest MSE on most cases, and MLNN using MAP loss can efficiently improve the accuracy 41% over L_2 loss in terms of MAPE for 5-min prediction, and 8.1% for 15-min prediction.

The future work has three research prospects. The first prospect is to find the other traffic data sources such as PeMS and GPS data of Shanghai taxi [20] to validate our method. Currently, we have no other sources except Shanghai Expressway to test the effectiveness of method. The second prospect is to conduct ablation study demonstrating the sensitivity of the hyper-parameters of MLNN. The final prospect is to employ road-type attention and further improve the accuracy on low speed samples.

Acknowledgments. This work is supported by the National Natural Science Foundation of China (Grant No. 61872259), the Natural Science Foundation of Jiangsu Province (Grant No. BK20160324) and the Natural Science Foundation of Jiangsu Colleges and Universities (Grant No.16KJB580009).

References

1. Avuglah, R.K., Adupoku, K.A., Harris, E.: Application of ARIMA models to road traffic accident cases in Ghana. Int. J. Stat. Appl. **4**(5), 233–239 (2014). https://doi.org/10.5923/j.statistics.20140405.03
2. Chan, K.Y., Dillon, T.S., Singh, J., et al.: Traffic flow forecasting neural networks based on exponential smoothing method. In: Industrial Electronics & Applications. IEEE (2011). https://doi.org/10.1109/iciea.2011.5975612
3. Lin, W.H.: A Gaussian maximum likelihood formulation for short-term forecasting of traffic flow. In: Proceedings of IEEE Intelligent Transportation Systems, pp. 150–155. IEEE (2001). https://doi.org/10.1109/itsc.2001.948646
4. Yan, G.X., Ming, T.S.: Integrated traffic flow forecasting and traffic incident detection algorithm based on non-parametric regression. China J. Highw. Transp. **16**(1), 82–86 (2003). https://doi.org/10.3321/j.issn:1001-7372.2003.01.020
5. Castro-Neto, M., Jeong, Y.S., Jeong, M.K., Han, L.D.: Online-SVR for short-term traffic flow prediction under typical and atypical traffic conditions. Expert Syst. Appl. **36**(3), 6164–6173 (2009). https://doi.org/10.1016/j.eswa.2008.07.069
6. Jia, Y., Wu, J., Du, Y.: Traffic speed prediction using deep learning method. In: Proceedings of IEEE International Conference on Intelligent Transportation Systems, pp: 1217–1222 (2016). https://doi.org/10.1109/itsc.2016.7795712
7. Ma, X., Tao, Z., Wang, Y.: Long short-term memory neural network for traffic speed prediction using remote microwave sensor data. Transp. Res. Part C Emerg. Technol. **54**, 187–197 (2015). https://doi.org/10.1016/j.trc.2015.03.014
8. Polson, N.G., Sokolov, V.O.: Deep learning for short-term traffic flow prediction. Transp. Res. Part C Emerg. Technol. **79**, 1–17 (2017). https://doi.org/10.1016/j.trc.2017.02.024
9. Tan, J., Wang, S.: Research on prediction model for traffic congestion based on deep learning. Appl. Res. Comput. **32**(10), 2951–2954 (2015). https://doi.org/10.3969/j.issn.1001-3695.2015.10.016
10. Fu, R., Zhang, Z., Li, L.: Using LSTM and GRU neural network methods for traffic flow prediction. In: 31st Youth Academic Annual Conference of Chinese Association of Automation, pp. 324–328 (2017). https://doi.org/10.1109/yac.2016.7804912
11. Cui, Z., Ke, R., Wang, Y.: Deep bidirectional and unidirectional LSTM recurrent neural network for network-wide traffic speed prediction (2018). arXiv:1801.02143
12. Duan, Y., Lv, Y., Wang, F.Y.: Travel time prediction with LSTM neural network. In: Proceedings of IEEE 19th International Conference on Intelligent Transportation Systems (ITSC). IEEE (2016). https://doi.org/10.1109/itsc.2016.7795686
13. Cheng, H., Sester, M.: Mixed traffic trajectory prediction using LSTM–based models in shared space. In: Mansourian, A., Pilesjö, P., Harrie, L., van Lammeren, R. (eds.) AGILE 2018. LNGC, pp. 309–325. Springer, Cham (2018). https://doi.org/10.1007/978-3-319-78208-9_16
14. Ma, X., Dai, Z., He, Z., et al.: Learning traffic as images: a deep convolutional neural network for large-scale transportation network speed prediction. Sensors **17**(4), 818–825 (2017). https://doi.org/10.3390/s17040818
15. Zhu, L., Laptev, N.: Deep and confident prediction for time series at uber. In: 2017 IEEE International Conference on Data Mining Workshops (ICDMW) (2017). https://doi.org/10.1109/icdmw.2017.19
16. Gal, Y.: Uncertainty in deep learning, Ph.D. dissertation, Ph.D thesis, University of Cambridge (2016)

17. Baxter, J.: A model of inductive bias learning: AI access foundation. J. Artif. Intell. Res. **12** (2000). https://doi.org/10.1613/jair.731
18. Chen, J., Tan, L., Liu, J., et al.: A convex formulation for learning shared structures from multiple tasks. In: Proceedings of the 26th Annual International Conference on Machine Learning - ICML 2009 (2009). https://doi.org/10.1145/1553374.1553392
19. Huang, W., Song, G., Hong, H., et al.: Deep architecture for traffic flow prediction: deep belief networks with multitask learning. IEEE Trans. Intell. Transp. Syst. **15**(5), 2191–2201 (2014). https://doi.org/10.1109/tits.2014.2311123
20. Huang, H.Y., Luo, P.E., Li, M., et al.: Performance evaluation of SUVnet with real-time traffic data. IEEE Trans. Veh. Technol. **56**(6), 3381–3396 (2007). https://doi.org/10.1109/tvt.2007.907273

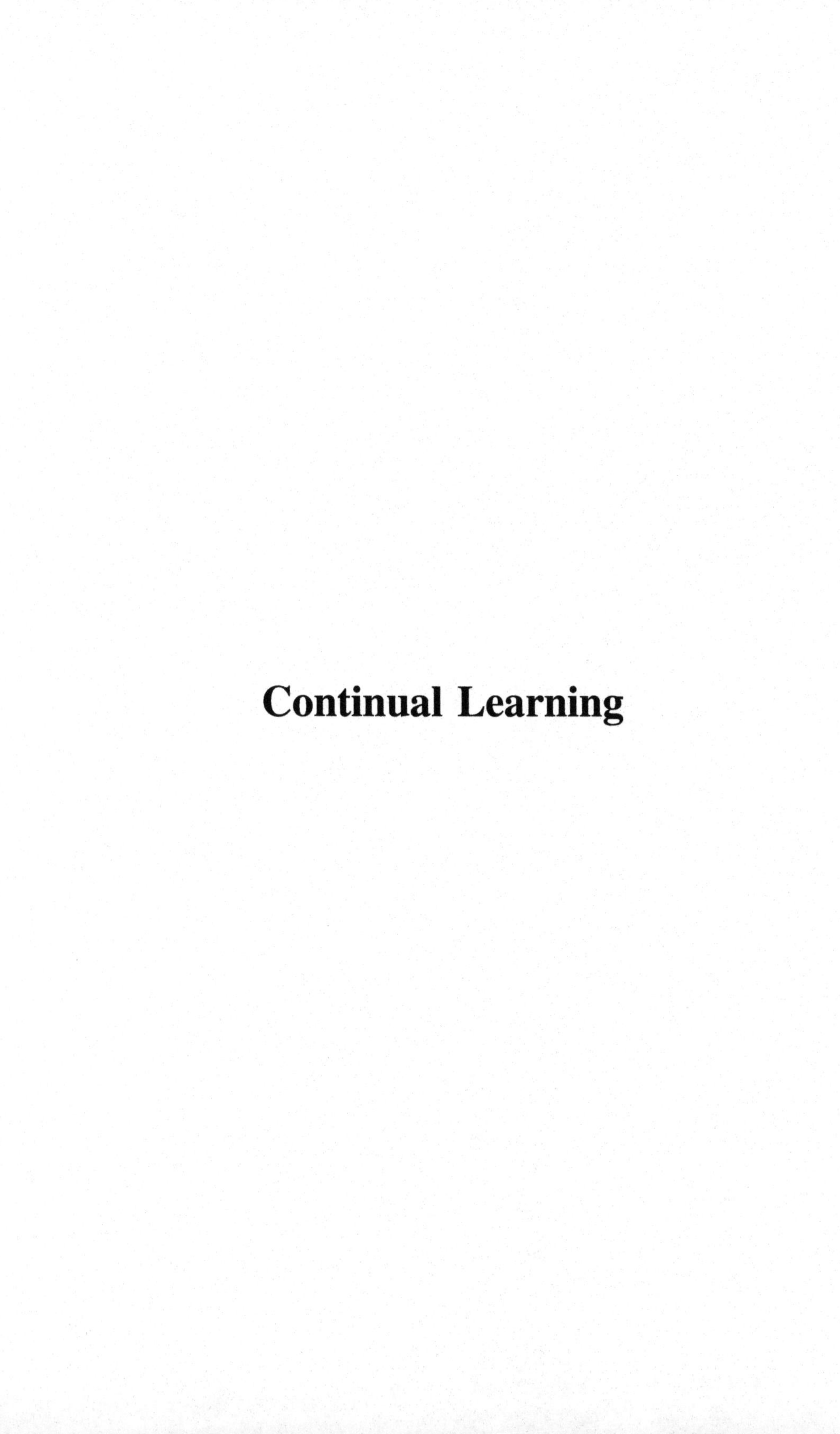

Continual Learning

Central-Diffused Instance Generation Method in Class Incremental Learning

Mingyu Liu and Yijie Wang(✉)

Science and Technology on Parallel and Distributed Laboratory,
College of Computer, National University of Defense Technology, Changsha, China
{liumingyu13,wangyijie}@nudt.edu.cn

Abstract. Class incremental learning is widely applied in the classification scenarios as the number of classes is usually dynamically changing. Meanwhile, class imbalance learning often occurs simultaneously in class incremental learning when the new class emerges. Previous studies mainly proposed different methods to handle this problem. But these methods focus on classification tasks with a fixed class set and cannot adjust the peripheral contour features of the original instance distribution. As a result, the classification performance degrades seriously in an open dynamic environment, and the synthetic instances are always clustered within the original distribution. In order to solve class imbalance learning effectively in class incremental learning, we propose a Central-diffused Instance Generation Method to generate the instances of minority class as the new class emerging, called CdIGM. The key is to randomly shoot direction vectors of fixed length from the center of new class instances to expand the instance distribution space. The vectors diffuse to form a distribution which is optimized to satisfy properties that produce a multi-classification discriminative classifier with good performance. We conduct the experiments on both artificial data streams with different imbalance rates and real-world ones to compare CdIGM with some other proposed methods, e.g. SMOTE, OPCIL, OB and SDCIL. The experiment results show that CdIGM averagely achieves more than 4.01%, 4.49%, 8.81% and 9.76% performance improvement over SMOTE, OPCIL, OB and SDCIL, respectively, and outperforms in terms of overall and real-time accuracy. Our method is proved to possess the strength of class incremental learning and class imbalance learning with good accuracy and robustness.

Keywords: Machine learning · Class incremental learning · Class imbalance learning · Supervised learning

1 Introduction

Incremental learning is a learning paradigm which generally makes use of the information from the new instances to update the original model. In a real dynamic environment, new classes of the emerging instances may appear at any

I. V. Tetko et al. (Eds.): ICANN 2019, LNCS 11728, pp. 453–465, 2019.
https://doi.org/10.1007/978-3-030-30484-3_37

time while these instances keep arriving. For this dynamic environment, class incremental learning is proposed as a machine learning framework to handle the new class instances incrementally [6,18]. It focuses on enabling the learning system to incorporate instances of classes which have never been seen previously into a continuous training process as new instances appear successively [11,20]. However, the current research based on class incremental learning is relatively limited. It has been applied in real world, especially for classification scenarios where the number of classes is dynamically changing, such as data stream anomaly detection, text classification [14], sound classification [13], etc.

Class incremental learning always involves class imbalance learning during the stream training process [2]. In many real incremental scenarios, the distribution between new class instances and the existing ones is not well balanced. In other words, the current classification model contains much more instances than those of the unseen class which emerges the first time. The class imbalance learning mainly exists in the task of supervised machine learning. And it is commonly seen in real world applications, such as intrusion detection in computer networks and fault diagnosis of control monitoring systems. The class with most instances is typically referred to as the majority class, and the other one as the minority class. Conventional learning algorithms in machine learning and data mining typically do not work well for class imbalance problems since they regard the overall classification accuracy as the learning target and their goal is to minimize the overall error rate, which implicitly treats all misclassification costs equally [5,17]. As a result, these algorithms may pay too much attention to the majority classes and produce trivial results, typically classifying all test instances as the majority classes [3,19]. Additionally, the new class is the one of greater interest during the process of class incremental learning. It cannot be regarded as a minority class of conventional learning. Therefore, how to solve the class imbalance learning effectively during the process of class incremental learning is a meaningful research.

Many techniques have been proposed to deal with class imbalance problem, among which ensemble learning methods have been proved more effective than other algorithms. But these methods are poor at dealing with the emerging class scenario. On the other hand, many methods for learning from data streams are also available on class incremental learning, but they do not solve the class imbalance problems well. Some research focuses on discovering emerging new classes which can be defined as anomaly classes in data stream [10,23]. One class learning aims to build a classification model from a training set which mainly consists of positive class only [4,21]. And one shot learning focuses on the field of image and vision and learning from one or few training examples, just like finishing the training process by a shot [7,8]. Although these two issues have been well studied independently in the past decades, the research on simultaneously solving both problems is limited.

Our work focuses on handling class imbalance problem during the process of class incremental learning. We propose a **C**entral-**d**iffused **I**nstance **G**eneration **M**ethod called **CdIGM** to achieve class imbalance learning with good classification performance in class incremental learning. The contributions of this work are summarized as follows:

- We propose a class incremental learning method which makes use of several emerging new class instances to diffuse the random direction vectors to enlarge the class distribution on data streams. And the instance distribution of the existing classes can adapt with arrival of new classes.
- Two long separate research areas, class imbalance learning and class incremental learning, are bridged together in this paper. We validate that our method can handle the class imbalance problem by conducting experiments.
- We conduct different kinds of experiments based on the synthetic dataset and real-world benchmark datasets respectively. The results can significantly prove the effectiveness of our method.

The rest of this paper is organized as follows: Sect. 2 describes the related work about class imbalance learning and class incremental learning; Sect. 3 provides the details of the proposed method; and experimental results are presented in Sect. 4; the final conclusion is provided in Sect. 5.

2 Related Works

2.1 Class Imbalance Learning

Most existing algorithms dealing with imbalanced data streams require processing data in batches, such as MuSeRA [15] proposed by Chen et al. Among limited class imbalance solutions strictly for online processing, two online ensemble learning methods—OOB and UOB are proposed by Wang [16]. However, the resampling rate in these two methods does not consider the size ratio between classes, there exists an issue that the resampling rate is not consistent with the imbalance degree in data and varies with the number of classes.

SMOTE [1] is a synthetic over-sampling method to solve imbalanced learning. It mainly calculates the similarity between instance feature distributions based on a few existing class instances, and then creates synthetic instances [12]. But this algorithm synthesizes new instances for the minority classes based on "interpolation". It results in that the synthetic instance space is limited to the "internal" of the original instance and cannot change the peripheral contour features of the original instance distribution. It also means that this algorithm has little influence on the decision boundary in the classification problem.

2.2 Class Incremental Learning

Class incremental learning is a branch of incremental learning which strengthens a previously trained classifier to deal with emerging new class. The problem of Streaming Classification Under Emerging New Class (SENC) is a class incremental learning problem in the data stream context. SENC-MaS is proposed as a framework for Streaming classification with Emerging New Class emerging by class Matrix Sketching modelling [10]. An algorithm called SENC-Forest is proposed for effectively solving class incremental learning problems [9]. The algorithm can detect the previous exceptions and new classes in the data stream. These approaches achieved good performance, but most of them are based on distance or tree structure and few of them focus on imbalanced learning.

Zhu proposed a new instance generation method to generate pseudo instances which are optimized to satisfy properties that produce a good performing discriminative classifier [22]. However, the GPI algorithm is used to generate the corresponding pseudo instances space from only one instance. And the process of generating pseudo instances suffers a higher cost.

3 Class Incremental Learning via CdIGM

To address the class imbalance problem in class incremental learning, we propose a central-diffused instance generation method called **CdIGM** to generate minority class so that the scales of the instances in each class become approximately the same. Our method synthesizes the instances of the minority class from its center to form a new distribution. As a result, the instance distribution can effectively upgrade the current multi-classifier of existing classes to a classifier for both the existing classes and the new class.

3.1 Framework

Let $X = R^d$ be the space of all supervised instances, $Y = \{1, 2, \cdots, K\}$ be the class label set, and $N = \{n_1, n_2, n_3, \ldots, n_K\}$ be the number set of the instances in the class i $(i \in Y)$, which d is the dimension of the instance and K is the number of the total classes.

Algorithm 1. Framework of Class Incremental Learning

Input: Sequence: S_K; number set: N; the number of the existing classes: M.
Output: Weight W for prediction.

Receive M supervised instance sets $\left\{\{(x_i, y_j)\}_{i=1}^{n_j}\right\}_{j=1}^{M}$ from sequence S_K;
$T \leftarrow \left\{\{(x_i, y_j)\}_{i=1}^{n_j}\right\}_{j=1}^{M}$;
$W \leftarrow$ Train multi-classification model for T;
repeat
    Receive a new instance set $\{(x_i, y_{M+1})\}_{i=1}^{n_{M+1}}$ from sequence S_K;
    $S \leftarrow \{(x_i, y_{M+1})\}_{i=1}^{n_{M+1}}$;
    $T \leftarrow CdIGM(W, S)$;
    $M \leftarrow M + 1$;
    $W \leftarrow Update(W, T)$;
until $M = K$;

During the process of class incremental learning, we define a sequence $S_K = \left\{\{(x_i, y_j)\}_{i=1}^{n_j}\right\}_{j=1}^{K}$, where $x_i \in X$ is the instance when the number of the emerging classes is j; and $y_j \in Y$ is the class label of x_i.

The final goal for class incremental learning is to find a map $f: X \rightarrow Y$, so as to minimize the loss over the sequence S_K:

$$\sum_{j=1}^{K} I\left(f(x_i) \neq y_j\right), i \in \{1, 2, \ldots, n_j\}, \tag{1}$$

where $I(\cdot)$ is an indicator function which returns 1 when the argument is true, and returns 0 otherwise; and f predicts the labels of instances. The framework of class incremental learning is summarized in Algorithm 1.

3.2 Central-Diffused Instance Generation Method (CdIGM)

We can obtain the following information from the instance distributions of each class. It can be used to update the existing model when a new class emerges in our proposed method:

- Centers of existing classes. Let $C = [c_1, c_2, \ldots, c_K]$ be the center set estimated for all K classes. The center vector set C is easy to calculate as $c_i = \frac{1}{n_i}\sum_{j=1}^{n_i} x_{i,j}$, where $c_i \in C, n_i \in N$ are defined above.
- Maximum distance from the center of each existing class. Let $\mathrm{D} = [d_1, d_2, \ldots, d_K]$ be the maximum distance set estimated for all K classes as well. The maximum distance set D is calculated as $d_i = \underset{j \in \{1,2,\ldots,n_i\}}{Max} |x_{i,j} - c_i|$.

The proposed method is described in the following steps, which is also shown in Algorithm 2 in detail:

- Firstly, after receiving the instances of a new emerging class from the data stream, we update the center vector set C by absorbing this new central point c_{new}. The central point c_{new} is the starting point to generate instances.
- Secondly, we generate the direction vectors randomly which are randomly initialized with different lengths and normalize each direction vector's length to the step length L in order to generate instances evenly.
- We adopt two different ways to generate instances by judging whether the center c_{new} falls into the distribution of any existing class.
- If not, we loop to generate instances for each direction vector evenly until the synthetic instance q which is also the end of the vector falls into the distribution of any known class. In addition, the length of the entire vector cannot be extended beyond the limit length $MaxL$. After extending all the direction vectors, the synthetic instance set G is formed.
- If yes, we suppose c_{new} falls into the distribution of class K. We choose to generate instances for each direction vector within the distribution of class K until the synthetic instance falls out of this distribution to get the new synthetic instance set G. Then the synthetic instance set G_K of class K should update by removing G from itself.
- Eventually, we iterate to merge the new synthetic instance set with the old one to form a final synthetic instance set.

Algorithm 2. Central-diffused Instance Generation Method

Input: Current weight: W; new class instance set: S; number of random vectors: P; step length: L

Output: Synthetic instance sets: T

Calculate center c_{new} for the new instance set $S = \{(x_i, y_M)\}_{i=1}^{n_M}$;
$C \leftarrow C \cup \{c_{new}\}$;
$G = \{c_{new}\}$;
Generate direction vector set $DV = \{dv_1, dv_2, \ldots, dv_P\}$ randomly;
Normalize each vector's length to get $NDV = \left\{L \cdot \frac{dv_1}{|dv_1|}, L \cdot \frac{dv_2}{|dv_2|}, \ldots, L \cdot \frac{dv_P}{|dv_P|}\right\} = \{ndv_1, \ldots, ndv_P\}$;
if c_{new} falls out of the distribution of any existing class:
    for $i = 1 : P$ **do**
        repeat
            $q = c_{new} + ndv_i$;
            Send q into the current multi-classifier W;
            if q falls into the distribution of any existing class:
                break;
            else
                $G \leftarrow G \cup \{q\}$;
        until $|q - c_M| > MaxL$;
        $G_M \leftarrow G \backslash \{q\}$;
        $T \leftarrow T \cup G_M$;
else
    $K \leftarrow$ the class which distribution c_{new} falls in;
    for $i = 1 : P$ **do**
        repeat
            $q = c_{new} + ndv_i$;
            if q falls out of the distribution of K:
                break;
            else
                $G \leftarrow G \cup \{q\}$;
        $G_M \leftarrow G \backslash \{q\}$;
        $G_K \leftarrow G_K \backslash G_M$;
        $T \leftarrow T \cup G_M$;
return Synthetic instance set T;

3.3 Parameter Adjustment

In our proposed method, two main parameters should be determined: the number of random direction vectors P; and the step length L. P determines the exact shape of the distribution, and L affects the density of distribution in some ways. The generated instances of the minority class should obey the following properties in order to maintain a high classification performance. The properties are shown in the following paragraphs.

Property 1. *The number of generated instances for minority class should be roughly the same as the average number of instances for the existing majority classes.*

The most direct characteristic of imbalanced problem is the difference between the scales of the existing classes and the new emerging one. Our method CdIGM is adopted to generate instances for the emerging class to make the number of instances in each dataset become approximately the same. Based on this property, the number of the generated instances is limited as following.

$$n_{gen} = \frac{1}{M}\sum_{i=1}^{M} n_i, n_i \in N, \tag{2}$$

where M is the number of the existing classes.

Property 2. *The upper limit of the direction vector's length should be roughly the same as the average maximum distance of the existing majority classes.*

We cannot let the direction vectors extend infinitely. So $MaxL$ is defined as the upper limit of the direction vector's length. Although we have controlled the number of generated instances according to Property 1, the distribution of generated instances directly affects the spatial density of instances, which also needs to be limited. So, all generated instances are limited within a radius of $MaxL$ as a cluster.

$$MaxL = \frac{1}{M}\sum_{i=1}^{M} d_i, d_i \in D, \tag{3}$$

where D is the set of the maximum distance in each class.

Property 3. *The number of generated instances of the minority class is ideally evaluated as the direction vectors can be extended to $MaxL$.*

Not all direction vectors can extend to the maximum length $MaxL$. If they fall into the distribution region of any other existing classes in advance, they will stop extending. To approximate the number of generated instances for the minority class, we make the assumption that the number equals approximately to the ideal case in which the direction vectors can be extended to $MaxL$.

Under this assumption, the number of generated instances for minority class can be calculated as:

$$n_{gen} \approx P \cdot \frac{MaxL}{L}, \tag{4}$$

where P is the number of random vectors; L is the step length; and $MaxL$ is the upper limit of the direction vector's length.

According to (2) (3) (4), we can deduce the relationship between P and L:

$$L \cdot \sum_{i=1}^{M} n_i \approx P \cdot \sum_{i=1}^{M} d_i \tag{5}$$

4 Experiments and Evaluation

This section describes class imbalance data stream used in the experiment, including 3 artificial data streams and 7 real-world data streams, and explains the algorithm settings and experimental designs for a clear understanding in the following analysis.

4.1 Configuration

Data Stream

To facilitate a deep understanding and accurate analysis, artificial data streams (named ADS) are generated as desired types of class imbalance data streams. We produce 3 ten-class data streams (each class has 1000 instances) with the same multivariate normal distribution of 5 dimensions but different imbalance rates. The imbalance rate (IR), i.e. the ratio of a minority class to a majority one, is a direct factor that affects any algorithm's performance. A smaller rate means a smaller chance to collect the minority class instances, and thus a harder case for classification.

In addition, we still conduct experiments on 7 real-world multi-class data streams, i.e., *glass, iris, segment, svmguide2, vehicle, vowel, minst.* These multi-class benchmark datasets cover different application fields and varying degrees of complexity. And we take 80% of the dataset for training, and the remaining 20% for testing.

Table 1 summarizes the characteristics of the data streams, including the number of total class, the number of features, number of total instances, the number of existing classes, and the imbalance rate. Here, the existing classes act as a root model. During the process of class incremental learning, the new class keeps arriving in the form of data stream and iteratively updates the root model. In our experiments, we set the number of existing number to roughly half the number of total class.

Table 1. The information of data streams used in experiments

Data	Total class	Feature	Total instances	Existing classes	Imbalance rate
ADS1	10	5	10000	5	30%
ADS2	10	5	10000	5	20%
ADS3	10	5	10000	5	10%
Glass	6	9	214	3	
Iris	3	4	150	2	
Segment	7	19	2310	4	
Svmguide2	3	20	391	2	
Vehicle	4	18	846	2	
Vowel	11	10	528	6	
Minst	10	780	60000	5	

Competitors and Parameters

In order to test the classification performance of our method, we compare CdIGM with other proposed methods:

- SMOTE—calculates the similarity between sample feature distributions based on a few existing class instances, and then creates synthetic samples;

- OPCIL—generates pseudo instances which are optimized to satisfy properties that produce a good performing discriminative classifier;
- OB—achieves online ensemble learning by online bagging which can adjust the learning bias from the majority to the minority class effectively and adaptively through resampling;
- SDCIL—divides the input space into different subregions and determines the class of the testing instances by judging the distribution where they finally fall in practice.

There are some parameters that need to be specified. In particular, we use 5 algorithms(including our method) to conduct the experiments. The parameters of different algorithms are summarized in Table 2.

Table 2. Parameters setting

Algorithms	Parameters
CdIGM	$P = 100$ L changes automatically according to (5)
SMOTE	Number of neighbors $k = 5$ Distance d = Euclidean distance
OPCIL	$m = 1$ is used as the default
OB	K follows the $Poisson(\lambda{=}1)$ distribution
SDCIL	$\nu = 0.3$ s is determined by the modified MIES algorithm automatically

Evaluation

To evaluate the classification performance of our method, the overall accuracy is assessed over one entire data stream which is the average over 5 times on each dataset. In addition, we also assess the real-time accuracy of the classifier in each new class emerging step as soon as the classifier has been updated on 3 ADS data streams with different imbalance rates to show the change trend of the performance in class incremental learning.

4.2 Results

Figure 1 demonstrates the real-time accuracy trend on 3 ADS data streams with each algorithm. We use line graphs to find out the change trend with the class number increasing by using different methods based on the same data stream. All trends are downward but the decline ranges of different methods are not the same. At any stage of the new class emerging, CdIGM presents the best classification performance with the least performance degradation among all the competitor methods. This illustrates the strong robustness of our method.

For each data stream, the experiment is repeated 5 times. Table 3 exhibits the overall performance of all methods on different data streams. CdIGM is the

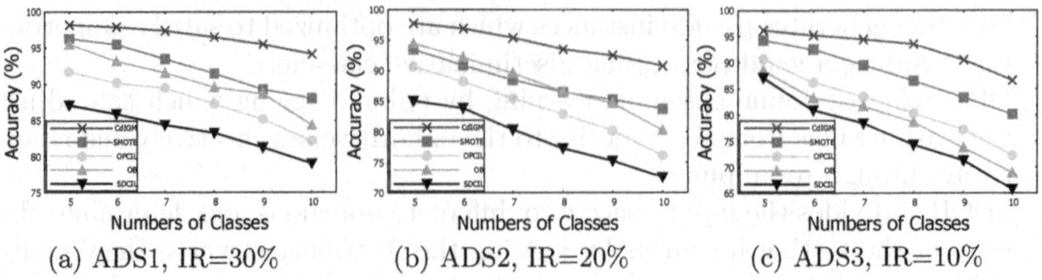

(a) ADS1, IR=30% (b) ADS2, IR=20% (c) ADS3, IR=10%

Fig. 1. Real-time accuracy on artificial data streams with different imbalance rate

best performer among these competitors in all artificial data streams. Among these 3 ADSs with different imbalance rates (30%, 20% and 10%), the overall classification performance decreases with the decline of imbalance rates. As the imbalance rates decrease from 30% to 10%, the overall accuracy decreases by 7.59%, 7.92%, 9.91%, 15.48% and 13.37% over CdIGM, SMOTE, OPCIL, OB and SDCIL, respectively.

Table 3. Overall accuracy on data streams in experiments

Data	CdIGM	SMOTE	OPCIL	OB	SDCIL
ADS1	**94.23 ± 0.084**	88.11 ± 0.108	82.25 ± 0.486	84.49 ± 0.393	79.18 ± 0.296
ADS2	**90.84 ± 0.035**	83.89 ± 0.075	76.26 ± 0.349	80.34 ± 0.486	72.67 ± 0.834
ADS3	**86.64 ± 0.079**	80.19 ± 0.234	72.34 ± 0.495	69.01 ± 0.199	65.81 ± 0.474
Glass	**91.33 ± 0.934**	85.29 ± 0.278	87.52 ± 1.134	84.19 ± 0.157	82.58 ± 0.837
Iris	**93.24 ± 0.259**	90.58 ± 1.147	92.11 ± 0.824	89.99 ± 0.938	85.46 ± 0.630
Segment	74.13 ± 1.597	**78.43 ± 0.392**	73.90 ± 0.957	63.65 ± 0.295	71.96 ± 0.301
Svmguide2	**88.15 ± 0.949**	84.36 ± 0.395	80.65 ± 0.284	74.99 ± 0.851	80.03 ± 0.047
Vehicle	**87.21 ± 0.385**	82.11 ± 0.884	78.45 ± 0.955	80.34 ± 0.751	76.03 ± 0.937
Vowel	**79.31 ± 0.753**	68.48 ± 0.438	74.57 ± 0.418	64.23 ± 0.281	58.92 ± 0.431
Minst	**65.45 ± 0.413**	61.44 ± 0.294	60.17 ± 0.538	59.75 ± 0.369	55.51 ± 0.199

The average online AUC results (± for standard deviation) are shown in Table 4. The online AUC is generated by predicting each instance before it is used for training the classifier. In summary, the preliminary results indicate that our proposed method is sufficiently flexible to deal with class imbalance problem.

From Table 3, it is observed that CdIGM gets the highest accuracy mostly based on the real-world data streams. Specifically, our method CdIGM is better than SMOTE on 6 of 7 real-world data streams except for *segment.* But CdIGM remains the second best on this data stream. Significantly, CdIGM performs better than the other 3 competitors on all real-world data streams. After calculation, CdIGM averagely achieves more than 4.01%, 4.49%, 8.81% and 9.76% performance improvement over SMOTE, OPCIL, OB and SDCIL, respectively.

Table 4. Average online AUC

	CdIGM	SMOTE	OPCIL	OB	SDCIL
ADS1	.7720 ± .0229	.5944 ± .0637	.6348 ± .0372	.5716 ± .0975	.5214 ± .0356
ADS2	.7270 ± .0436	.5547 ± .0435	.5498 ± .0598	.5275 ± .0309	.5439 ± .0607
ADS3	.6834 ± .0444	.5174 ± .0344	.6048 ± .0355	.5648 ± .0372	.5571 ± .0368

5 Conclusion

The class imbalance learning between the new emerging class and the old existing classes makes it a difficult task to produce a good performing discriminative classifier in class incremental learning. In this paper, we proposed a **C**entral-**d**iffused **I**nstance **G**eneration **M**ethod called **CdIGM** for instances of minority class in class incremental learning. It mainly eliminates the bad effects of class imbalance learning in class incremental learning. The key is to randomly shoot direction vectors of fixed length from the center of these new class instances to expand the instance distribution space. Based on this, it can form a distribution which is optimized to satisfy properties that produce a multi-classification discriminative classifier with good performance. Substantial experimental results show that CdIGM significantly outperforms the other 4 competitors on 3 artificial data streams with different imbalance rates and 7 real-world data streams in terms of overall and real-time accuracy.

Acknowledgements. This work is supported by the National Key Research and Development Program of China (2016YFB1000101), the National Natural Science Foundation of China (Grant No.61379052), the Science Foundation of Ministry of Education of China (Grant No. 2018A02002), the Natural Science Foundation for Distinguished Young Scholars of Hunan Province (Grant No. 14JJ1026). The corresponding author is Yijie Wang and her email is wangyijie@nudt.edu.cn.

References

1. Chawla, N.V., Bowyer, K.W., Hall, L.O., Kegelmeyer, W.P.: Smote: synthetic minority over-sampling technique. J. Artif. Intell. Res. **16**(1), 321–357 (2002). https://doi.org/10.1613/jair.953
2. Dong, Q., Gong, S., Zhu, X.: Imbalanced deep learning by minority class incremental rectification. IEEE Trans. Pattern Anal. Mach. Intell. **PP**(99), 1 (2018). https://doi.org/10.1109/tpami.2018.2832629
3. Huang, C., Li, Y., Chen, C.L., Tang, X.: Learning deep representation for imbalanced classification. In: Computer Vision & Pattern Recognition (2016). https://doi.org/10.1109/cvpr.2016.580
4. Khan, S.S., Madden, M.G.: One-class classification: taxonomy of study and review of techniques. Knowl. Eng. Rev. **29**(3), 345–374 (2014). https://doi.org/10.1017/s026988891300043x

5. Khoshgoftaar, T.M., Golawala, M., Hulse, J.V.: An empirical study of learning from imbalanced data using random forest. In: IEEE International Conference on TOOLS with Artificial Intelligence, pp. 310–317 (2008). https://doi.org/10.1109/ictai.2007.46
6. Kuzborskij, I., Orabona, F., Caputo, B.: From n to n+1: Multiclass transfer incremental learning, pp. 3358–3365 (2013). https://doi.org/10.1109/cvpr.2013.431
7. Lake, B.M., Salakhutdinov, R., Tenenbaum, J.B.: One-shot learning by inverting a compositional causal process. In: International Conference on Neural Information Processing Systems (2013)
8. Li, F.F., Rob, F., Pietro, P.: One-shot learning of object categories. IEEE Trans. Pattern Anal. Mach. Intell. **28**(4), 594–611 (2006). https://doi.org/10.1109/tpami.2006.79
9. Mu, X., Kai, M.T., Zhou, Z.H.: Classification under streaming emerging new classes: a solution using completely-random trees. IEEE Trans. Knowl. Data Eng. **29**(8), 1605–1618 (2016). https://doi.org/10.1109/tkde.2017.2691702
10. Mu, X., Zhu, F., Du, J., Lim, E.P., Zhou, Z.H.: Streaming classification with emerging new class by class matrix sketching. In: AAAI, pp. 2373–2379 (2017)
11. Muhlbaier, M.D., Topalis, A., Polikar, R.: Learn ++.nc: combining ensemble of classifiers with dynamically weighted consult-and-vote for efficient incremental learning of new classes. IEEE Trans. Neural Netw. **20**(1), 152 (2009). https://doi.org/10.1109/tnn.2008.2008326
12. Pruengkarn, R., Wong, K.W., Fung, C.C.: Imbalanced data classification using complementary fuzzy support vector machine techniques and smote. In: IEEE International Conference on Systems (2017). https://doi.org/10.1109/smc.2017.8122737
13. Rabaoui, A., Davy, M., Rossignol, S., Lachiri, Z.: Improved one-class SVM classifier for sounds classification. In: 2007 IEEE Conference on Advanced Video and Signal Based Surveillance, AVSS 2007, pp. 117–122 (2007). https://doi.org/10.1109/avss.2007.4425296
14. Sebastiani, F.: Machine learning in automated text categorization. ACM Comput. Surv. **34**(1), 1–47 (2002). https://doi.org/10.1145/505282.505283
15. Sheng, C., He, H., Kang, L., Desai, S.: MuSeRA: multiple selectively recursive approach towards imbalanced stream data mining. In: International Joint Conference on Neural Networks (2010). https://doi.org/10.1109/ijcnn.2010.5596538
16. Wang, S., Minku, L.L., Yao, X.: A learning framework for online class imbalance learning. In: Computational Intelligence & Ensemble Learning (2013). https://doi.org/10.1109/ciel.2013.6613138
17. Wang, Y., Li, S.: Research and performance evaluation of data replication technology in distributed storage systems. Comput. Math. Appl. **51**(11), 1625–1632 (2006). https://doi.org/10.1016/j.camwa.2006.05.002
18. Wang, Y., Li, X., Li, X., Wang, Y.: A survey of queries over uncertain data. Knowl. Inf. Syst. **37**(3), 485–530 (2013). https://doi.org/10.1007/s10115-013-0638-6
19. Wang, Y., Ma, X.: A general scalable and elastic content-based publish/subscribe service. IEEE Trans. Parallel Distrib. Syst. **26**(8), 2100–2113 (2014). https://doi.org/10.1109/tpds.2014.2346759
20. Wang, Y., Pei, X., Ma, X., Xu, F.: TA-update: an adaptive update scheme with tree-structured transmission in erasure-coded storage systems. IEEE Trans. Parallel Distrib. Syst. **29**(8), 1893–1906 (2017). https://doi.org/10.1109/tpds.2017.2717981

21. Yao, C., Zou, J., Luo, Y., Li, T., Bai, G.: A class-incremental learning method based on one class support vector machine (2018). https://doi.org/10.1088/1742-6596/1267/1/012007
22. Zhu, Y., Kai, M.T., Zhou, Z.H.: New class adaptation via instance generation in one-pass class incremental learning. In: IEEE International Conference on Data Mining, pp. 1207–1212 (2017). https://doi.org/10.1109/icdm.2017.163
23. Zhu, Y., Ting, K.M., Zhou, Z.H.: Multi-label learning with emerging new labels. In: IEEE International Conference on Data Mining, pp. 1371–1376 (2017). https://doi.org/10.1109/icdm.2016.0188

Marginal Replay vs Conditional Replay for Continual Learning

Timothée Lesort[1,2(✉)], Alexander Gepperth[3], Andrei Stoian[2], and David Filliat[1]

[1] Flowers Laboratory (ENSTA ParisTech & Inria), Palaiseau, France
lesort@ensta.fr
[2] Thales, Theresis Laboratory, Palaiseau, France
[3] Fulda University of Applied Sciences, Fulda, Germany

Abstract. We present a new replay-based method of continual classification learning that we term "conditional replay" which generates samples and labels together by sampling from a distribution conditioned on the class. We compare conditional replay to another replay-based continual learning paradigm (which we term "marginal replay") that generates samples independently of their class and assigns labels in a separate step. The main improvement in conditional replay is that labels for generated samples need not be inferred, which reduces the margin for error in complex continual classification learning tasks. We demonstrate the effectiveness of this approach using novel and standard benchmarks constructed from MNIST and FashionMNIST data, and compare to the regularization-based *elastic weight consolidation* (EWC) method [17,34].

Keywords: Continual learning · Generative models · Generative replay

1 Introduction

This contribution is in the context of incremental, continual or lifelong learning, subject that is gaining increasing recent attention [8,26] and for which a variety of different solutions have recently been proposed (see below). Briefly put, the problem consists of repeatedly re-training a deep neural network (DNN) model with new sub-tasks, or continual learning tasks (CLTs), (for example: new visual classes) over long time periods, while avoiding the abrupt degradation of previously learned abilities that is known under the term "catastrophic interference" or "catastrophic forgetting" [6,8,28]. Please see Fig. 1 for a visualization of the problem setting. Is has long been known that catastrophic forgetting (CF) is a problem for connectionist models [6] of which modern DNNs are a specialized instance, but only recently there have been efforts to propose workable solutions to this problem for deep learning models [3,15,17,19,32]. A recent article [27] demonstrates empirically that most proposals fail to eliminate CF when common-sense application constraints are imposed (e.g., restricting prior access to data from new sub-tasks, or imposing constant, low memory and execution time requirements).

I. V. Tetko et al. (Eds.): ICANN 2019, LNCS 11728, pp. 466–480, 2019.
https://doi.org/10.1007/978-3-030-30484-3_38

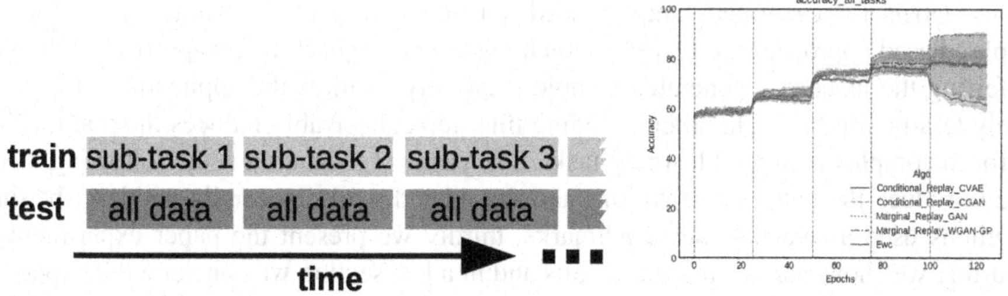

Fig. 1. Left: The problem setting of continual learning as investigated in this article. DNN models are trained one after the other on a sequence of sub-tasks (of which three are shown here), and are continuously evaluated on a test set consisting of the union of all sub-task test sets. This gives rise to results as shown exemplarily on the right-hand side of the figure, i.e., plots of test set accuracy over time for different models, where boundaries between sub-tasks (5 in this case) are indicated by vertical lines.

One aspect of the problem seems to be that gradient-based DNN training is greedy, i.e., it tries to optimize all weights in the network to solve the current task only. Previous tasks, which are not represented in the current training data, will naturally be disregarded in this process. While approaches such as [17, 19] aim at "protecting" weights that were important for previous tasks, one can approach the problem from the other end and simply include samples from previous tasks in the training process each time a new task is introduced.

This is the *generative replay* approach, which is in principle model-agnostic, as it can be performed with a variety of machine learning models such as decision trees, support vector machines (SVMs) or deep neural networks (DNNs). It is however unfeasible for, e.g., embodied agents or embedded devices performing object recognition, to store all samples from all previous sub-tasks. Because of this, generative replay proposes to train an additional machine learning model (the so-called *generator*). Thus, the "essence" of previous tasks comes in the form of trained generator parameters which usually require far less space than the samples themselves. A downside of this and similar approaches is that the time complexity of adapting to a new task is not constant but depends on the number of preceding tasks that should be replayed. Or, conversely, if continual learning should be performed at constant time complexity, only a fixed amount of samples can be generated, and thus there will be forgetting, although it won't be catastrophic.

In this paper we decide to investigate two different types of generative models: Generative adversarial networks (GAN) and variational auto-encoder (VAE). On one hand GAN are known to generate samples of high quality but on the other hand VAE directly maximize the likelihood of the learned distribution while training. It was then interesting to experiment both of them to compare their performances.

This article proposes and evaluates a particular method for performing replay using DNNs, termed "conditional replay", which is similar in spirit to [34] but presents important conceptual improvements (see next section). The main advantage of conditional replay is that samples can be generated conditionally, i.e., based on a provided label.

Thus, labels for generated samples need not be inferred in a separate step as other replay-based approaches, e.g., [34], which we term *marginal replay* approaches. Since inferring the label of a generated sample inevitably requires the application of a possibly less-than-perfect classifier, avoiding this step conceivably reduces the margin for error in complex continual learning tasks. The paper organization is the following, first we introduce the paper contributions and the related works, secondly we describe the methods used as well as the benchmarks, thirdly we present the paper experiments, fourthly we show and discuss our results and in a last section we conclude the paper.

1.1 Contribution

The original contributions of this article can be summarized as follows (Figs. 2, 3 and Table 1):

- **Conditional replay as a method for continual classification learning.** We experimentally establish the advantages of conditional replay in the field of continual learning by comparing conditional and marginal replay models on a common set of benchmarks.
- **Improvement of marginal learning.** We furthermore propose an improvement of marginal replay as proposed in [34] by using generative adversarial networks (GANs, see [10]).
- **New experimental benchmarks for generative replay strategies.** To measure the merit of these proposals, we use two experimental settings that have not been previously considered for benchmarking generative replay: rotations and permutations. In addition, we promote the "10-class-disjoint" task as an important benchmark for continual learning as it is impossible to solve for purely discriminative methods (at no time, samples from different classes are provided for training so no discrimination can happen).
- **Comparison of generative replay to EWC.** We show the principled advantage that generative replay techniques have with respect to regularization methods like EWC in a "one class per task" setting, which is after all a very common setting in practice and in which discriminatively trained models strongly tend to assign the same class label to every sample regardless of content.

Table 1. Hyperparameters for MNIST and Fashion MNIST all models (all CL settings have the same training hyper parameters with Adam)

Method	Epochs	LR classifier	LR generator	beta1	beta2	Batch Size
Marginal replay	25	0.01	2e−4	5e−1	0.999	64
Conditional replay	25	0.01	2e−4	5e−1	0.999	64
EWC	25	0.01	–	5e−1	0.999	64

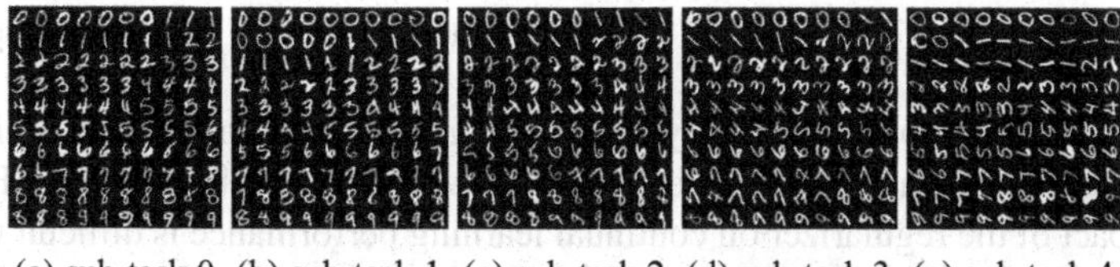

(a) sub-task 0 (b) sub-task 1 (c) sub-task 2 (d) sub-task 3 (e) sub-task 4

Fig. 2. MNIST training data for rotation sub-tasks.

Fig. 3. MNIST training data for permutation-type CLTs.

1.2 Related Work

The field of continual learning is growing and has been recently reviewed in, e.g., [8,26]. In the context of neural networks, principal recent approaches include ensemble methods [2,5,22,24,30–32,41], regularization approaches [1,3,4,7,12,15,17,19, 23,37], dual-memory systems [9,14,29], distillation-based approaches [16,22,35] and generative replay methods [13,14,21,34,38]. In the context of single-memory DNN methods, regularization approaches are predominant: whereas it was proposed in [11] that the popular Dropout regularization can alleviate catastrophic forgetting, the EWC method [17] proposes to add a term to the DNN energy function that protects weights that are deemed to be important for the previous sub-task(s). Whether a weight is important or not is determined by approximating and analyzing the Fisher information matrix of the DNN. A somewhat related approach is pursued with the incremental moment matching (IMM, see [19]) technique, where weights are transferred between DNNs trained on successive sub-tasks by regularization techniques, and the Fisher information matrix is used to "merge" weights for current and past sub-tasks. Other regularization-oriented approaches are proposed in [3,37] which focus on enforcing sparsity of neural activities by lateral interactions within a layer, or in [15]. Concerning recent advances in generative replay improving upon [34]: Several works propose the use of generative models in continual learning of classification tasks [13,33,38,39] but their results does not provide comparison between different types of generative models. [21] propose a conditional replay mechanism similar to the one investigated here, but their goal is the sequential learning of data generation and not classification tasks. Generally, each approach to continual learning has its advantages and disadvantages:

- ensemble methods suffer from little to no interference between present and past knowledge as usually different networks or sub-networks are allocated to different learning tasks. The problem with this approach is that, on the one hand, model complexity is not constant, and more seriously, that the task from which a sample is coming from must be known at inference time in order to select the appropriate (sub-)network.

- regularization approaches are very diverse: in general, their advantage is simplicity and (often) a constant-time/memory behavior w.r.t. the number of tasks. However, the impact of the regularizer on continual learning performance is difficult to understand, and several parameters need to be tuned whose significance is unclear (i.e., the strengths of the regularization terms)
- distillation approaches can achieve very good robustness and continual learning performance, but either require the retention of past samples, or the occurrence of samples from past classes in current training data to be consistent. Also, the strength of the various distillation loss regularizers needs to be tuned, usually by cross-validation.
- generative replay and dual-memory systems show very good and robust continual learning performance, although time complexity of learning depends on the number of previous tasks for current generative replay methods. In addition, the storage of weights for a sufficiently powerful generator may prove very memory-consuming, so this approach cannot be used in all settings.

2 Methods

A basic notion in this article is that of a continual (or sequential) learning task (CLT or SLT, although we will use the abbreviation CLT in this article), denoting a classification problem that is composed of two or more sub-tasks which are presented sequentially to the model in question. Here, the CLTs are constructed from two standard visual classification benchmarks: MNIST and Fashion MNIST, either by dividing available classes into several sub-tasks, or by performing per-sample image processing operations that are identical within, and different between, sub-tasks. All continual learning models are then trained and evaluated in an identical fashion on all CLTs, and performances are compared by a simple visual inspection of classification accuracy plots.

2.1 Benchmarks

MNIST. [18] is a common benchmark for computer vision systems and classification problems. It consists of gray scale 28×28 images of handwritten digits (ten balanced classes representing the digits 0–9). The train, test and validation sets contain 55.000, 10.000 and 5.000 samples, respectively.

Fashion MNIST. [40] consists of grayscale 28×28 images of clothes. We choose this dataset because it claims to be a "more challenging classification task than the simple MNIST digits data [40]" while having the same data dimensions, number of classes, balancing properties and number of samples in train, test and validation sets.

2.2 Continual Learning Tasks (CLTs)

All CLTs are constructed from the underlying MNIST and FashionMNIST benchmarks, so the number of samples in train and test sets for each sub-task depend on the precise way of constructing them, see below (Fig. 4).

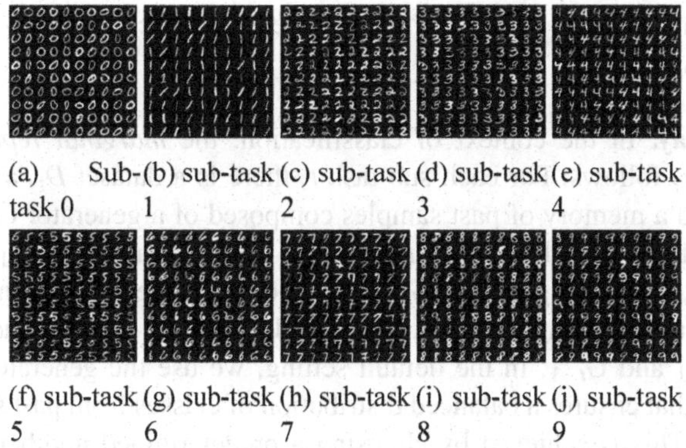

(a) Sub-task 0 (b) sub-task 1 (c) sub-task 2 (d) sub-task 3 (e) sub-task 4

(f) sub-task 5 (g) sub-task 6 (h) sub-task 7 (i) sub-task 8 (j) sub-task 9

Fig. 4. Samples of MNIST training data for the disjoint CLT. Each sub-task adds one more visual class, a principle which carries over identically to FashionMNIST.

Rotations. New sub-tasks are generated by choosing a random rotation angle $\beta \in [0, \pi/2]$ and then performing a 2D in-plane rotation on all samples of the original benchmark. As both benchmarks we use contain samples of 28×28 pixels, no information loss is introduced by this procedure. We limit rotation angles to $\pi/2$ because larger rotations could mix MNIST classes like 6 and 9. Each sub-task in rotation-based CLTs contains all 10 classes of the underlying benchmark, leading to 55.000 and 10.000 samples, respectively, in the train and test sets of each sub-task.

Permutations. New sub-tasks are generated by defining a random pixel permutation scheme, and then applying it to each data sample of the original benchmark. Each sub-task in permutation-based CLTs contains all 10 classes of the underlying benchmark, leading to 55.000 and 10.000 samples, respectively, in the train and test sets of each sub-task.

Disjoint Classes. For each benchmark, this CLT has as many sub-tasks as there are classes in the benchmark (10 in this article). Each sub-task contains the samples of a single class, i.e., roughly 6.000 samples in the train set and 1.000 samples in the test set. As the classes are balanced for both benchmarks, this does not unduly favor certain classes. This CLT presents a substantial challenge for machine learning methods since a normal DNN would, for each sub-task, learn to map all samples to a single class label irrespective of content. Selective discrimination between any two classes is hard to obtain except if replay is involved, because then a classifier actually "sees" samples from different classes at the same time.

2.3 Models

In this article, we compare a considerable number of deep learning models: unless otherwise stated, we employ the Rectified Linear Unit (ReLU) transfer function, cross-entropy loss for classifier training, and the Adam optimizer.

EWC. We re-implemented the algorithm described in [17], choosing two hidden layers with 200 neurons each.

Marginal Replay. In the context of classification, the *marginal replay* [21,34,38] method works as follows: For each sub-task t, there is a dataset D_t, a classifier C_t, a generator G_t and a memory of past samples composed of a generator G_{t-1} and a classifier C_{t-1}. The latter two allow the generation of artificial samples D_{t-1} from previous sub-tasks. Then, by training C_t and G_t on D_t and D_{t-1}, the model can learn the new sub-task t without forgetting old ones. At the end of the sub-task, C_t and G_t are frozen and replace C_{t-1} and G_{t-1}. In the default setting, we use the generator for marginal replay in a way that ensures a balanced distribution of classes from past sub-tasks D_{t-1}, see also Fig. 7. This is achieved by choosing a predetermined number of samples N to be added for all sub-tasks t, and letting the generator produce tN previous samples at sub-task t. Thus, the number of generated samples increases linearly over time. We choose to evaluate two different models for the generator: WGAN-GP as used in [34] and the original GAN model [10] since it is a competitive baseline [20].

Conditional Replay. The conditional replay method is derived from *marginal replay*: instead of saving a classifier and a generator, the algorithm only saves a generator that can generate conditionally (for a certain class). Hence, for each sub-task t, there is a dataset D_t, a classifier C_t and two generators G_t and G_{t-1}. The goal of G_{t-1} is to generate data from all the previous sub-tasks during training on the new sub-task. Since data is generated conditionally, samples automatically have a label and do not require a frozen classifier. We follow the same strategy as for marginal replay (previous paragraph) for choosing the number of generated samples at each sub-task. However, conditional replay does not require this: it can, in principle, keep the number of generated samples constant for each sub-task since it is trivially possible to generate a balanced distribution of $\frac{N}{t}$ samples per class, from t different classes, via conditional sample generation. C_t and G_t learn from generated data D_{t-1} and D_t. At the end of a sub-task t, C_t is able to classify data from the current and previous sub-tasks, and G_t is able to sample from them also. We choose to use two different popular conditional models: CGAN described in [25] and CVAE [36].

3 Experiments

We conduct experiments using all models and CLTs described in the previous section. Each class (regardless of the CLT) is presented for 25 epochs, Results are presented either based on the time-varying classification accuracy on the *whole* test set, or on the class (from the test set) that was presented first. In the first case, accuracy should ideally increase over time and reach its maximum after the last class has been presented. In the second case, accuracy should be stable if the model does not forgot or decrease over time, reflecting that some information about the first class is forgotten. We distinguish two major experimental goals or questions:

- Establishing the performance of the newly proposed methods (marginal replay with GAN, conditional replay with CGAN or CVAE) w.r.t. the state of the art. To this

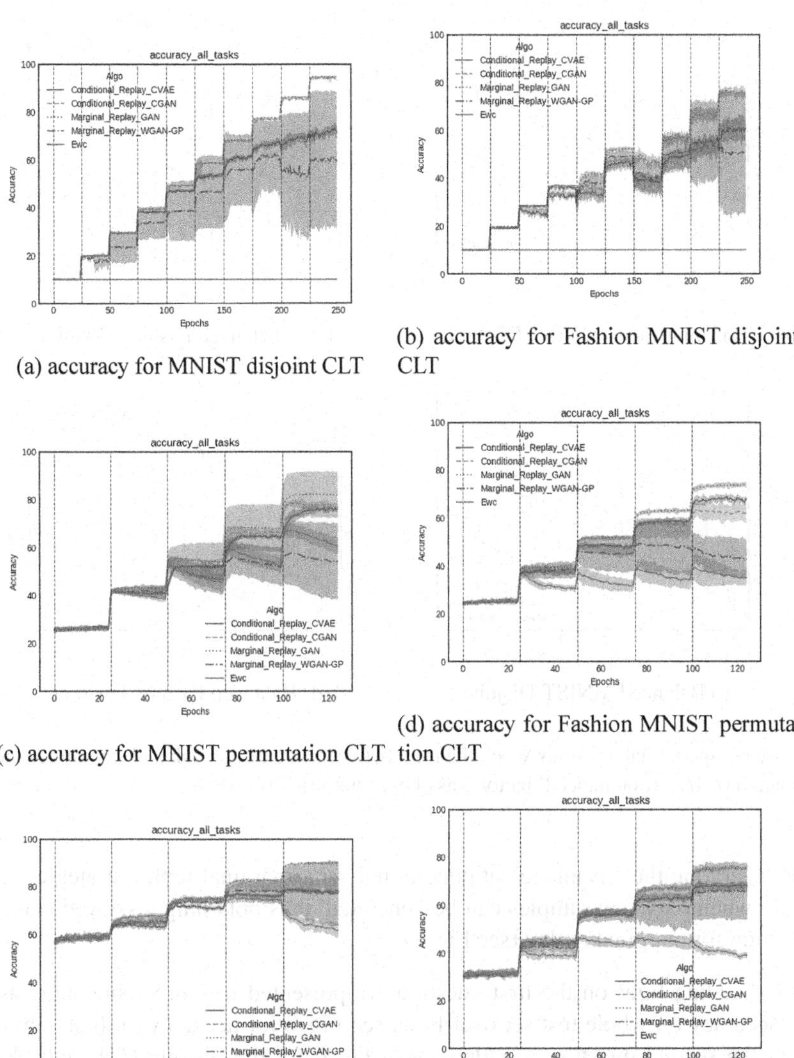

(a) accuracy for MNIST disjoint CLT

(b) accuracy for Fashion MNIST disjoint CLT

(c) accuracy for MNIST permutation CLT

(d) accuracy for Fashion MNIST permutation CLT

(e) accuracy for MNIST rotation CLT

(f) accuracy for Fashion MNIST rotation CLT

Fig. 5. Test set accuracies during training on different CLTs, shown for all sub-tasks (indicated by dotted lines).

effect, we conduct experiments that increase the number of generated samples over time in a way that ensures an effectively balanced class distribution (see Fig. 7). We do this both for marginal and conditional replay in order to ensure a fair comparison, although technically conditional replay can generate balanced distribution even with a constant number of generated samples.

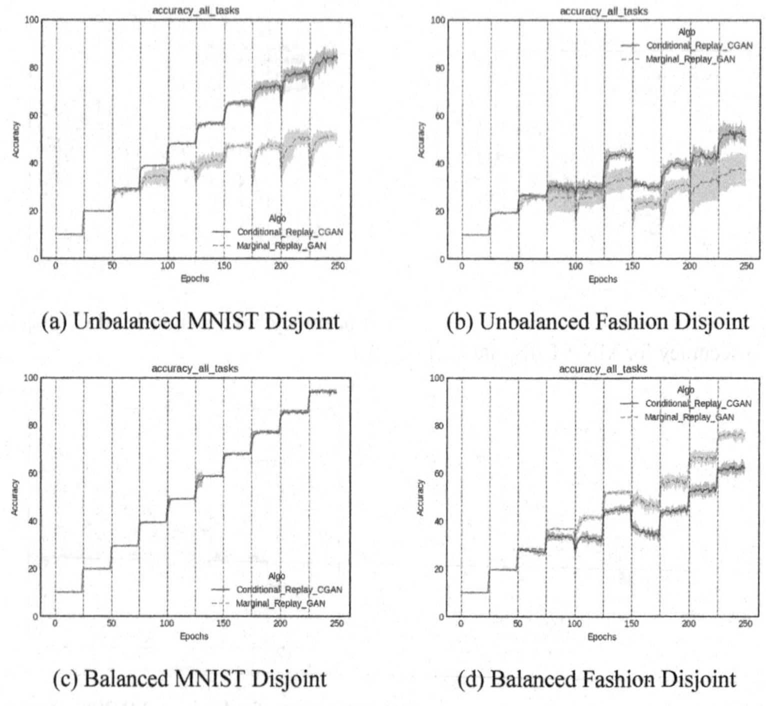

(a) Unbalanced MNIST Disjoint

(b) Unbalanced Fashion Disjoint

(c) Balanced MNIST Disjoint

(d) Balanced Fashion Disjoint

Fig. 6. We compare final accuracy when the ratio between size of old task and size of new task is 1 (balanced) or 1/10 (unbalanced, factor was chosen empirically).

- demonstrating the advantages of conditional w.r.t. marginal replay strategies, especially when only few samples can be generated, thus obtaining a skewed class distribution for marginal replay (see Fig. 7).

Results shedding light on the first question are presented in Fig. 5 (showing classification accuracy on whole test set over time, see Fig. 8 for accuracy on first sub-task), whereas the second question is addressed in Fig. 6 for the disjoint CTL only due to space limitations.

4 Results and Discussion

From the experiments described in the previous section, we can state the following principal findings:

Replay Methods Outperform EWC. As can be observed from Fig. 5, the novel methods we propose (marginal replay with GAN and WGAN-GP, conditional replay with CGAN and conditional replay with CVAE) outperform EWC, on all CLTs, sometimes by a large margin. Particular attention should be given to the performance of EWC: while generally acceptable for rotation and permutation CLTs, it completely fails for

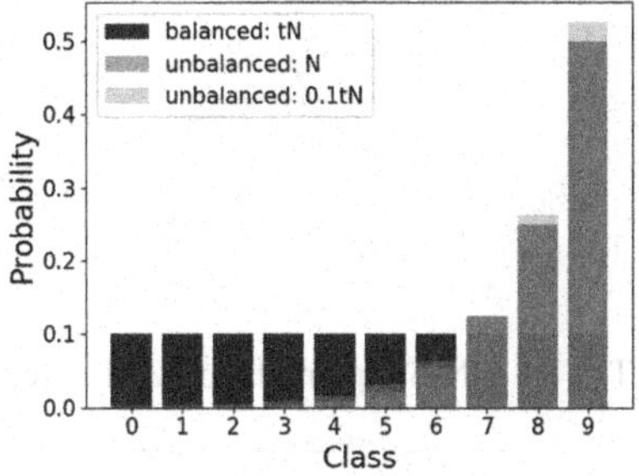

Fig. 7. Why marginal replay must linearly increase the number of generated samples: distribution of classes produced by the generator of a marginal replay strategy after sequential training of 10 sub-tasks (of 1 class each). This essentially corresponds to the "disjoint" type of CLTs. Shown are three cases: "*balanced*: tN" (blue bars) where tN samples are generated for each sub-task t, "unbalanced: N" (orange bars) where the number of generated samples is constant and equal to the number of newly trained samples N for each sub-task, and "unbalanced: $0.1tN$" where $0.1tN$ samples are generated. We observe that, in order to ensure a balanced distribution of classes, the number of generated samples must be re-scaled, or, in other words, must increase linearly with the number of sub-tasks. (Color figure online)

the disjoint CLT. This is due to the fact that there is only one class in each sub-task, making EWC try to map all samples to the currently presented class label regardless of input, since no replay is available to include samples from previous sub-tasks (as outlined before in Sect. 1.1).

Marginal Replay with GAN Outperforms WGAN-GP. The clear advantage of GAN over WGAN-GP is the higher stability of the generative models. This is not only observable in Fig. 5, but also when measuring performance on the first sub-task only during the course of continual learning (see Fig. 8).

Conditional Replay Can Be Run at Constant Time Complexity. A very important point in favour of conditional replay is run-time complexity, as expressed by the number of samples that need to be generated each time a new sub-task is trained. Since the generators in marginal replay strategies generate samples regardless of class, the distribution of classes will be proportional to the distribution of classes during the last training of the generator, which leads to an unbalanced class distribution over time, with the oldest classes being strongly under-represented (see Fig. 7). This is avoided by increasing the number of generated samples over time for marginal replay, leading to a balanced class distribution (see also Fig. 7) while vastly increasing the number of samples. Conditional replay, on the other hand, can selectively generate samples from a defined class, thus constructing a class-balanced dataset without needing to increase the number of generated samples over time. In the interest of accuracy, it can of course make sense to increase the number of generated samples over time, just as for marginal replay. This, however, is a deliberate choice and not something required by conditional replay itself.

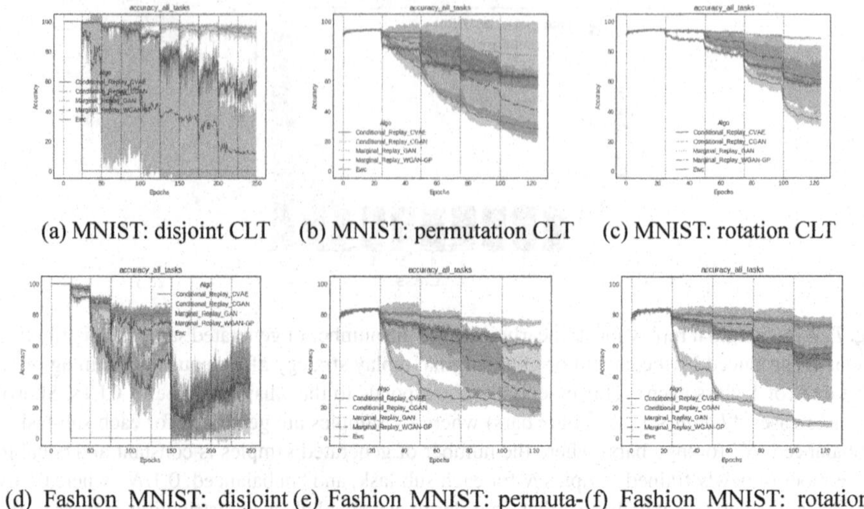

(a) MNIST: disjoint CLT (b) MNIST: permutation CLT (c) MNIST: rotation CLT

(d) Fashion MNIST: disjoint CLT (e) Fashion MNIST: permutation CLT (f) Fashion MNIST: rotation CLT

Fig. 8. Comparison of the accuracy of each approach on the first sub-task. This is another, very intuitive measure of how much is forgotten during continual learning. Means and standard deviations computed over 8 seeds.

Marginal Replay Outperforms Conditional Replay When Many Samples Can Be Generated. From Fig. 5, it can be observed that marginal replay outperforms conditional replay by a small margin. This comes at the price of having to generate a large number of samples, which will become unfeasible if many classes are involved in the retraining.

Conditional Replay is Superior When Few Samples are Generated. The results of Fig. 6 show that conditional replay is superior to marginal replay when generating fewer samples at each sub-task (more precisely: $0.1tN$ samples instead of tN, for sub-task t and number of new samples per sub-task N). This can be understood quite easily: since we generate only $0.1tN$ samples instead of tN samples at each sub-task, marginal replay produces an unbalanced class distribution, see Fig. 7, which strongly impairs classification performance. This is a principal advantage that conditional replay has over marginal replay: generating balanced class distributions while having much more control over the number of generated samples.

5 Conclusions

Summary. We have proposed several of performing continual learning with replay-based models and empirically demonstrated (on novel benchmarks) their merit w.r.t. the state of the art, represented by the EWC method. A principal conclusion of this article is that conditional replay methods show strong promise because they have competitive performance, and they impose less restrictions on their use in applications. Most notably, they can be used at constant time complexity, meaning that the number of generated samples does not need to increase over time, which would be problematic in applications with many sub-tasks and real-time constraints.

Concerning the Benchmarks. While one might argue that MNIST and FashionMNIST are too simple for a meaningful evaluation, this holds only for non-continual learning scenarios. In fact, recent articles [27] show that MNIST-related CLTs are still a major obstacle for most current approaches to continual learning under realistic conditions. So, while we agree that MNIST and FashionMNIST are not suitable benchmarks in general anymore, we must stress the difficulty of MNIST-related CLTs in continual learning, thus making these benchmarks very suitable indeed in this particular context. The use of intrinsically more complex benchmarks, such as CIFAR, SVHN or ImageNet is at present not really possible since generative methods are not really good enough for replaying these data [21].

Next Steps. Future work will include a closer study of conditional replay: in particular, we would like to better understand why they exhibit better performance w.r.t marginal replay in cases where the number of generated samples is restricted to be low. In addition, it would be interesting to study the continual learning behavior of conditional replay models when a fixed number of generated samples is imposed at each sub-task, for various CLTs. The latter topic is interesting because the success of replay-based continual learning methods in applications will depend on whether the number of generated samples (and thereby time and memory complexity) can be reduced to manageable levels.

Observations. An interesting point is that the disjoint type CLTs pose enormous problems to conventional machine learning architectures, and therefore represent a very useful benchmark for continual learning algorithms. If each of a CLT's sub-tasks contains a single visual class, training them one after the other will induce no between-class discrimination at all since every training step just "sees" a single class. Replay-based methods nicely bridge this gap, allowing continual learning while allowing between-class discrimination. To our mind, any application-relevant algorithm for continual learning therefore must include some form of experience replay.

Outlook. Ultimately, the goal of our research is to come up with replay-based models where the effort spent on replaying past knowledge is small compared to the effort of training with new samples, which will require machine learning models that are, intrinsically, less prone to catastrophic forgetting than DNNs are.

References

1. Aljundi, R., Babiloni, F., Elhoseiny, M., Rohrbach, M., Tuytelaars, T.: Memory aware synapses: learning what (not) to forget. In: Ferrari, V., Hebert, M., Sminchisescu, C., Weiss, Y. (eds.) ECCV 2018. LNCS, vol. 11207, pp. 144–161. Springer, Cham (2018). https://doi.org/10.1007/978-3-030-01219-9_9
2. Aljundi, R., Chakravarty, P., Tuytelaars, T.: Expert gate lifelong learning with a network of experts. In: Proceedings of the IEEE Conference on Computer Vision and Pattern Recognition, pp. 3366–3375 (2017)
3. Aljundi, R., Rohrbach, M., Tuytelaars, T.: Selfless sequential learning. In: International Conference on Learning Representations (2019). https://openreview.net/forum?id=Bkxbrn0cYX
4. Chaudhry, A., Dokania, P.K., Ajanthan, T., Torr, P.H.S.: Riemannian walk for incremental learning: understanding forgetting and intransigence. In: Ferrari, V., Hebert, M., Sminchisescu, C., Weiss, Y. (eds.) ECCV 2018. LNCS, vol. 11215, pp. 556–572. Springer, Cham (2018). https://doi.org/10.1007/978-3-030-01252-6_33
5. Fernando, C., et al.: PathNet: evolution channels gradient descent in super neural networks. arXiv preprint arXiv:1701.08734 (2017)
6. French, R.: Catastrophic forgetting in connectionist networks. Trends Cognit. Sci. **3**(4), 128 (1999)
7. Gepperth, A., Wiech, F.: Simplified computation and interpretation of fisher matrices in incremental learning with deep neural networks. In: ICANN (2019, Submitted)
8. Gepperth, A., Hammer, B.: Incremental learning algorithms and applications. In: European Symposium on Artificial Neural Networks (ESANN) (2016)
9. Gepperth, A., Karaoguz, C.: A bio-inspired incremental learning architecture for applied perceptual problems. Cognit. Comput. **8**(5), 924–934 (2016). https://doi.org/10.1007/s12559-016-9389-5
10. Goodfellow, I., et al.: Generative adversarial nets. In: Ghahramani, Z., Welling, M., Cortes, C., Lawrence, N.D., Weinberger, K.Q. (eds.) Advances in Neural Information Processing Systems, vol. 27, pp. 2672–2680. Curran Associates, Inc. (2014). http://papers.nips.cc/paper/5423-generative-adversarial-nets.pdf
11. Goodfellow, I.J., Mirza, M., Xiao, D., Courville, A., Bengio, Y.: An empirical investigation of catastrophic forgetting in gradient-based neural networks (2013). https://doi.org/10.1088/1751-8113/44/8/085201. http://arxiv.org/abs/1312.6211
12. Hinton, G.E., Srivastava, N., Krizhevsky, A., Sutskever, I., Salakhutdinov, R.R.: Improving neural networks by preventing co-adaptation of feature detectors, pp. 1–18 (2012). arXiv:1207.0580
13. Kamra, N., Gupta, U., Liu, Y.: Deep generative dual memory network for continual learning. ArXiv e-prints, arXiv:1710.10368, October 2017
14. Kemker, R., Kanan, C.: FearNet: brain-inspired model for incremental learning. arXiv preprint arXiv:1711.10563 (2017)
15. Kim, H., Kim, S., Lee, J.: Keep and learn: continual learning by constraining the latent space for knowledge preservation in neural networks. CoRR abs/1805.10784 (2018). http://arxiv.org/abs/1805.10784
16. Kim, H.-E., Kim, S., Lee, J.: Keep and learn: continual learning by constraining the latent space for knowledge preservation in neural networks. In: Frangi, A.F., Schnabel, J.A., Davatzikos, C., Alberola-López, C., Fichtinger, G. (eds.) MICCAI 2018. LNCS, vol. 11070, pp. 520–528. Springer, Cham (2018). https://doi.org/10.1007/978-3-030-00928-1_59
17. Kirkpatrick, J., et al.: Overcoming catastrophic forgetting in neural networks (2016). https://doi.org/10.1073/pnas.1611835114. http://arxiv.org/abs/1612.00796

18. LeCun, Y., Bottou, L., Bengio, Y., Haffner, P.: Gradient-based learning apllied to document recognition (1998). http://ieeexplore.ieee.org/document/726791/#full-text-section
19. Lee, S.W., Kim, J.H., Jun, J., Ha, J.W., Zhang, B.T.: Overcoming catastrophic forgetting by incremental moment matching. In: Advances in Neural Information Processing Systems, pp. 4655–4665 (2017)
20. Lesort, T., Goudou, J.F., Filliat, D.: Training discriminative models to evaluate generative ones (2018)
21. Lesort, T., Caselles-Dupré, H., Garcia- Ortiz, M., Stoian, A., Filliat, D.: Generative models from the perspective of continual learning. arXiv e-prints arXiv:1812.09111, December 2018
22. Li, Z., Hoiem, D.: Learning without forgetting. IEEE Trans. Pattern Anal. Mach. Intell. **40**(12), 2935–2947 (2018)
23. Liu, X., Masana, M., Herranz, L., Van de Weijer, J., Lopez, A.M., Bagdanov, A.D.: Rotate your networks: better weight consolidation and less catastrophic forgetting. In: 2018 24th International Conference on Pattern Recognition (ICPR), pp. 2262–2268. IEEE (2018)
24. Mallya, A., Lazebnik, S.: PackNet: adding multiple tasks to a single network by iterative pruning. In: Proceedings of the IEEE Conference on Computer Vision and Pattern Recognition, pp. 7765–7773 (2018)
25. Mirza, M., Osindero, S.: Conditional generative adversarial nets (2014)
26. Parisi, G.I., Kemker, R., Part, J.L., Kanan, C., Wermter, S.: Continual lifelong learning with neural networks: a review. arXiv preprint arXiv:1802.07569 (2018)
27. Pfülb, B., Gepperth, A.: A comprehensive, application-oriented study of catastrophic forgetting in DNNS. In: International Conference on Learning Representations (ICLR) (2019, Accepted)
28. Pfülb, B., Gepperth, A., Abdullah, S., Kilian, A.: Catastrophic forgetting: still a problem for DNNs. In: Kůrková, V., Manolopoulos, Y., Hammer, B., Iliadis, L., Maglogiannis, I. (eds.) ICANN 2018. LNCS, vol. 11139, pp. 487–497. Springer, Cham (2018). https://doi.org/10.1007/978-3-030-01418-6_48
29. Rebuffi, S.A., Kolesnikov, A., Sperl, G., Lampert, C.H.: iCaRL: incremental classifier and representation learning. In: Proceedings of the CVPR (2017)
30. Ren, B., Wang, H., Li, J., Gao, H.: Life-long learning based on dynamic combination model. Appl. Soft Comput. **56**, 398–404 (2017)
31. Rusu, A.A., et al.: Progressive neural networks. arXiv preprint arXiv:1606.04671 (2016)
32. Serrà, J., Suris, D., Miron, M., Karatzoglou, A.: Overcoming catastrophic forgetting with hard attention to the task. In: The 35th International Conference on Machine Learning (ICML 2018) (2018). https://arxiv.org/abs/1801.01423
33. Shah, H., Javed, K., Shafait, F.: Distillation techniques for pseudo-rehearsal based incremental learning. arXiv preprint arXiv:1807.02799 (2018)
34. Shin, H., Lee, J.K., Kim, J., Kim, J.: Continual learning with deep generative replay. In: Advances in Neural Information Processing Systems, pp. 2990–2999 (2017)
35. Shmelkov, K., Schmid, C., Alahari, K.: Incremental learning of object detectors without catastrophic forgetting. In: Proceedings of the IEEE International Conference on Computer Vision, pp. 3400–3409 (2017)
36. Sohn, K., Lee, H., Yan, X.: Learning structured output representation using deep conditional generative models. In: Cortes, C., Lawrence, N.D., Lee, D.D., Sugiyama, M., Garnett, R. (eds.) Advances in Neural Information Processing Systems 28, pp. 3483–3491. Curran Associates, Inc. (2015)
37. Srivastava, R.K., Masci, J., Kazerounian, S., Gomez, F., Schmidhuber, J.: Compete to compute. In: NIPS, pp. 2310–2318 (2013)
38. Wu, C., Herranz, L., Liu, X., Wang, Y., van de Weijer, J., Raducanu, B.: Memory replay GANs: learning to generate images from new categories without forgetting. arXiv preprint arXiv:1809.02058 (2018)

39. Wu, Y., et al.: Incremental classifier learning with generative adversarial networks. CoRR abs/1802.00853 (2018). http://arxiv.org/abs/1802.00853
40. Xiao, H., Rasul, K., Vollgraf, R.: Fashion-MNIST: a novel image dataset for benchmarking machine learning algorithms, pp. 1–6 (2017). http://arxiv.org/abs/1708.07747
41. Yoon, J., Yang, E., Lee, J., Hwang, S.J.: Lifelong learning with dynamically expandable networks. arXiv preprint arXiv:1708.01547 (2017)

Simplified Computation and Interpretation of Fisher Matrices in Incremental Learning with Deep Neural Networks

Alexander Gepperth(✉) and Florian Wiech

University of Applied Sciences Fulda, 36037 Fulda, Germany
alexander.gepperth@cs.hs-fulda.de

Abstract. Import recent advances in the domain of incremental or continual learning with DNNs, such as Elastic Weight Consolidation (EWC) or Incremental Moment Matching (IMM) rely on a quantity termed the *Fisher information matrix* (FIM). While the results obtained in this way are very promising, the use of the FIM relies on the assumptions that **(a)** the FIM can be approximated by its diagonal, and **(b)** that FIM diagonal entries are related to the variance of a DNN parameter in the context of Bayesian neural networks. In addition, the FIM is notoriously difficult to compute in automatic differentiation (AD) systems frameworks like TensorFlow, and existing implementations require an excessive use of memory due to this problem. We present the Matrix of SQuares (MaSQ), computed similarly as the FIM, but whose use in EWC-like algorithms follows directly from the calculus of derivatives and requires no additional assumptions. Additionally, MaSQ computation in AD frameworks is much simpler and more memory-efficient FIM computation. When using MaSQ together with EWC we show superior or equal performance to FIM/EWC on a variety of benchmark tasks.

1 Introduction

This article describes a study in the context of incremental or continual learning with deep neural networks (DNNs). Essentially, this means that a DNN is not trained once, on a single task D, but successively on two or more sub-tasks $D_1, \ldots, D_n$, one after another. Learning tasks of this type, which we term Sequential Learning Tasks (SLTs) (see Fig. 1a), are potentially very common in real-world applications. They occur wherever DNNs need to update their capabilities on-site and over time: gesture recognition, network traffic analysis, or face and object recognition in mobile robots. In such scenarios, neural networks have long been known to suffer from a problem termed "catastrophic forgetting" (CF) (e.g., [4]) which denotes the abrupt and near-complete loss of knowledge from previous sub-tasks $D_1, \ldots, D_{k-1}$ after only a few training iterations on the current sub-task D_k (see Fig. 1b compared to Fig. 1c). In this article, we focus on SLTs from the visual domain with two sub-tasks each, as DNNs show pronounced CF behavior even when only two sub-tasks are involved.

I. V. Tetko et al. (Eds.): ICANN 2019, LNCS 11728, pp. 481–494, 2019.
https://doi.org/10.1007/978-3-030-30484-3_39

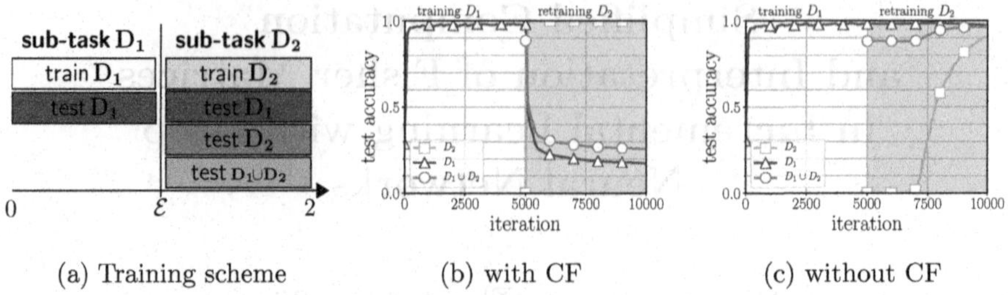

(a) Training scheme (b) with CF (c) without CF

Fig. 1. Schema of incremental training experiments conducted in this article (a) and representative outcomes with (b) and without CF (c). The sequential learning tasks used in this study only have two sub-tasks: D_1 and D_2. During training (white background) and re-training (gray background), test accuracy is measured on D_1 (blue, △), D_2 (red, ○) and $D_1 \cup D_2$ (green, □). The blue curve allows to determine the presence of CF by simple visual inspection: if there is significant degradation w.r.t. the red curve, then CF has occurred. (Color figure online)

1.1 Related Work

The field of incremental learning is large, e.g., [16] and [6]. Recent systematic comparisons between different DNN approaches to avoid CF are performed in, e.g., [11,22] or [18]. Principal recent approaches to avoid CF include ensemble methods [2,21], dual-memory systems [5,10,19,23] and regularization approaches. Whereas [7] suggest Dropout for alleviating CF, the EWC method [13] proposes to add a term to the energy function that protects weights that are important for the previous sub-task(s). Importance is determined by a quantity that is claimed to approximate the Fisher information matrix of the DNN within a framework of Bayesian neural networks inspired by works on the natural gradient in DNNS [17]. A related approach is pursued by the Incremental Moment Matching technique (IMM) (see [15]), where weights from DNNs trained on current and past sub-tasks are "merged" using a similar approximation to the Fisher information matrix. Other regularization-oriented approaches are proposed in [1,24] and [12] which focus on enforcing sparsity of neural activities by lateral interactions within a layer.

Algorithms like EWC are in fact related to very old works on pruning neural network weights [8,9,20], where the same goal is pursued: to estimate how "important" a weight is for the performance of the neural network by analyzing gradient information.

1.2 Motivation and Goals of the Article

We have been extensively analyzing [18] the performance of recently proposed algorithms for incremental learning like EWC or IMM, see Sect. 1.1. While doing so, we found that the computation of the FIM required for both methods is both computationally expensive, as well as conceptually questionable since the mathematical justification is at best unclear, and contains assumptions (diagonality of the FIM) that are neither proven nor empirically demonstrated. So the goal of the article is to propose a drop-in replacement for the FIM in regularization-based approaches to incremental learning like EWC or IMM that is both efficient to compute, and has a solid theoretical foundation which requires no unclear assumptions. The Matrix of SQuares (MaSQ) that we propose here has all of these properties, and we wish to empirically verify that incremental learning with EWC works just as well when using the MaSQ.

2 Methods

2.1 Dataset and Construction of Sequential Learning Tasks

We construct several sequential learning tasks (SLTs) from **MNIST** [14], a common benchmark for visual classification problems. It consists of 70.000 gray scale images of handwritten digits (0–9) of size 28×28, containing 55.000 training and 10.000 test samples that are approximately equally distributed over 10 classes. While MNIST may be considered too simple as an outright classification problem, we recently showed [18] that virtually all approaches to incremental or continual learning fail on simple two-task SLTs constructed from MNIST already, so MNIST-derived SLTs definitely do constitute adequate benchmarks here. We construct three types of two-task SLTs (defined by sub-tasks D_1 and D_2) from MNIST, which we term DP10-10 ("permuted"), D9-1 ("disjoint 9-1") and D5-5 ("disjoint 5-5"). The constructions given below apply equally to training, test and validation sets contained in MNIST.

Permuted SLT (DP10-10). This SLT is created by defining sub-task D_1 as the original MNIST benchmark containing all 10 classes, and adding sub-task D_2 as a copy of D_1 where copied samples all have their pixels spatially permuted in the same fashion. This is a benchmark that is widely used in studies on incremental learning, which we include for reference. As we could show [18], caution is required when using this benchmark as it seems to intrinsically facilitate incremental learning, probably because the patterns in D_1 and D_2 have very little overlap.

Disjoint SLTs (D9-1 and D5-5). These SLTs are created by defining D_1 as all samples from zero to eight (zero to four for D5-5) classes from MNIST, whereas D_2 is defined by the remaining classes (one for D9-1, five for D5-5).

2.2 DNN Models and Hyper-parameters

We employ simple fully-connected DNNs with EWC regularization, consisting of $L \in \{2, 3\}$ layers, all having an identical size of $S \in \{200, 400, 800\}$, and using the standard ReLU transfer function. We distinguish two learning rate parameters $\epsilon_1 = 0.001$ and $\epsilon_2 \in \{0.001, 0.0001, 0.00001, 1e-06\}$ for the two sub-tasks. Presence and effect of EWC regularization is governed by the balancing parameter $\lambda \in \{0, \frac{0.1}{\epsilon_1}, \frac{1}{\epsilon_1}, \frac{10}{\epsilon_1}\}$. Since we are dealing with classification problems, cross-entropy is used as a loss function $\mathcal{L}^{\text{CE}}$. Mini-batch size in stochastic gradient descent (SGD) optimization is always set to $B = 100$.

2.3 Elastic Weight Consolidation with FIM and MaSQ

In [13,15], the EWC loss function for training on sub-task D_2 is given as

$$\mathcal{L} = \frac{\lambda}{2}\mathcal{L}^{\text{CE}} + \sum_k F_k(\theta_k - \theta_k^{D_1})^2 \tag{1}$$

where the complete parameter set of a DNN (weight and biases) is denoted by $\boldsymbol{\theta}$, F_k describes the diagonal entries of the FIM (or MaSQ entries, see below), and $\boldsymbol{\theta}^{D_1}$ represents the complete set of stored parameters (again weights and biases) after having trained the DNN on sub-task D_1. In order to best describe our implementation of EWC (with FIM or MaSQ), we change the notation from the abstract parameter vector $\boldsymbol{\theta}$ of the DNN (as used in [13]) in favor of explicitly denoting the DNN weight matrices W^i and the bias vectors $\boldsymbol{b}^i, i \in \{0, \ldots, L-1\}$. The EWC loss function used for re-training on D_2 then reads, in this notation:

$$\begin{aligned}\mathcal{L} = \mathcal{L}^{\text{CE}} &+ \frac{\lambda}{2}\sum_{i=0}^{L-1}\sum_{kl} F_{kl}^{W^i}\left(W_{kl}^i - W_{kl}^{i,D_1}\right)^2 \\ &+ \frac{\lambda}{2}\sum_{i=0}^{L-1}\sum_{k} F_{k}^{b^i}\left(b_{k}^i - b_{k}^{i,D_1}\right)^2\end{aligned} \tag{2}$$

where we introduce the "lagged variables" W^{i,D_1}, $\boldsymbol{b}^{i,D_1}$ as specified in [13], and the coefficient matrices F^{W^i} and coefficient vectors $\boldsymbol{F}^{b^i}$ that correspond to FIM diagonal elements or MaSQ entries for the different weight matrices and bias vectors, both computed after training on D_1 is completed.

We implement the EWC algorithm for a two-task SLT by the following strategy:

- train the DNN normally on D_1, using a balancing parameter of $\lambda = 0$
- copy weight matrices and bias vectors to the set of lagged variables
- perform a single pass through the training data (one epoch) without modifying weights or biases, for FIM or MaSQ computation (only the gradients are required)
- train the DNN on D_2, keeping the previous values of weights and biases, and using either FIM or MaSQ with a nonzero EWC balancing parameter λ
- test on D_2 and $D_1 \cup D_2$ during re-training on D_2

2.4 A Critical Discussion of FIM Derivation and Computation

The expression given in [13,15,17] for computing the FIM reads (again denoting the ensemble of DNN parameters as $\boldsymbol{\theta}$ as in [13]):

$$\mathcal{F}_{ij} \equiv \frac{1}{N}\sum_n \left(\frac{\partial \mathcal{L}}{\partial \theta_i}\frac{\partial \mathcal{L}}{\partial \theta_j}\bigg|_{\boldsymbol{x}_n}\right), \tag{3}$$

where the expectation value is taken over all N training samples, indexed by n.

In [13,15], the FIM is assumed to be diagonal, so these authors use only the quantity

$$\boldsymbol{F} \equiv diag\,(\mathcal{F}_{ij}) \tag{4}$$

$$F_j \equiv \frac{1}{N}\sum_n \left(\frac{\partial \mathcal{L}}{\partial \theta_j}\Big|_{x_n}\right)^2, \tag{5}$$

although this simplification is not proven, nor is it, given the generality of Eq. (3), very likely to hold in general. In our notation, the FIM (with diagonal assumption) is written as

$$\boldsymbol{F}^{W^i}_{jk} \equiv \frac{1}{N}\sum_n \left(\frac{\partial \mathcal{L}}{\partial W^i_{jk}}\Big|_{x_n}\right)^2 \tag{6}$$

$$\boldsymbol{F}^{b^i}_{j} \equiv \frac{1}{N}\sum_n \left(\frac{\partial \mathcal{L}}{\partial b^i_{j}}\Big|_{x_n}\right)^2$$

We will verify FIM diagonality experimentally in Sect. 3.3.

A second point we like to raise is the utilization of the FIM diagonal in the EWC mechanism, given in its general form in Eq. (1), which is simply postulated in [13] and roughly justified as FIM diagonal entries F_k being equivalent to the certainty of parameter θ_k, and thus being a measure for its inverse variance in a Bayesian NN picture in [15]. The main justification of using FIM diagonal entries in [13,15] seems to be that the obtained results are very promising and give good results. We feel, however, that perhaps even better results could be obtained when using quantities in the EWC loss of Eq. (1) whose computation requires no diagonality assumptions, and whose use in Eq. (1) is justified by some rigorously provable mathematical principle. This is exactly what we propose with MaSQ, which will be detailed in the next section.

2.5 MaSQ Computation and Theoretical Justification

As in [13], the DNN loss function $\mathcal{L}$ is considered to depend on a parameter vector $\boldsymbol{\theta}$, which, in reality, is a concatenation of all (flattened) weight matrices W^i and bias vectors $\boldsymbol{b}^i$ of the DNN. Since DNN loss functions are assumed to be differentiable almost everywhere at least once, we can apply the standard theory of differential calculus which states that a differentiable function such as $\mathcal{L}$ can be locally approximated by linear functions in all directions $\boldsymbol{\delta} \in \mathbb{R}^n$, see, e.g., [3]:

$$\forall \boldsymbol{\delta} \in \mathbb{R}^n : \mathcal{L}(\boldsymbol{\theta} + h\boldsymbol{\delta}) = \mathcal{L}(\boldsymbol{\theta}) + h\boldsymbol{J} \cdot \boldsymbol{\delta} + \frac{\eta(h\boldsymbol{\delta})}{h} \tag{7}$$

where we define a deviation parameter h, the gradient $\boldsymbol{J}$, $J_k = \frac{\partial \mathcal{L}}{\partial \theta_k}$ and a function $\eta(h\boldsymbol{\delta})$ that goes to zero faster than h as $h \to 0$. This formula indicates that $\mathcal{L}$ gets better and better approximated by the linear function $\mathcal{L}(\boldsymbol{\theta} + J \cdot \boldsymbol{\delta})$ as $h \to 0$. So, for sufficiently small h, the rate of change of $\mathcal{L}(\boldsymbol{\theta})$ as a reaction to small changes in a parameter θ_k are given by the gradient entry J_k. Identifying the parameters that contribute most to changes of $\mathcal{L}$ is then reduced to ranking the entries of $\boldsymbol{J}$ by their absolute value. Using the squared value for ranking is possible as well, since squaring is an operation that does not change the ranking.

Since gradients in DNN training are computed as training set (with N samples) expectation values over per-sample gradients J_{nk}, samples being denoted by $\boldsymbol{x}_n$,

$$J_k = \frac{1}{N}\sum_n J_{nk} = \frac{1}{N}\sum_n \left(\frac{\partial \mathcal{L}}{\partial \theta_k}\bigg|_{\boldsymbol{x}_n}\right), \tag{8}$$

the squared gradients are then obtained as

$$F_k \equiv J_k^2 = \left(\frac{1}{N}\sum_n \frac{\partial \mathcal{L}}{\partial \theta_k}\bigg|_{\boldsymbol{x}_n}\right)^2, \tag{9}$$

The squared entries of $\boldsymbol{J}$ can thus be directly used to punish changes to certain parameters more than changes to other parameters, since a higher value of J_k^2 will, by the definition of differentiable functions given in Eq. (7), depend quadratically on the modulus of the linear rate of change J_k of $\mathcal{L}$ upon small changes to the parameter θ_k. For this argument, it is immaterial whether the square or the modulus of J_k is used, although squares punish deviations for critical parameters more strongly. The squared entries J_k^2 thus form the Matrix of SQuares (MaSQ). Its entries F_k can be re-written in terms of the individual weight matrices and bias vectors as

$$\boldsymbol{F}_{jk}^{W^i} \equiv \left(\frac{1}{N}\sum_n \frac{\partial \mathcal{L}}{\partial W_{jk}^i}\bigg|_{\boldsymbol{x}_n}\right)^2 \tag{10}$$

$$\boldsymbol{F}_{j}^{b^i} \equiv \left(\frac{1}{N}\sum_n \frac{\partial \mathcal{L}}{\partial b_{j}^i}\bigg|_{\boldsymbol{x}_n}\right)^2$$

in order to be inserted into the EWC loss function (2). When comparing Eqs. (10) and (6), we note that MaSQ and FIM are actually computed in quite a similar fashion, as expectation values over loss gradients. However, FIM requires to square the gradients prior to taking the expectation value over training samples, whereas it is the other way round for MaSQ. Since, in practice, gradients are summed up over mini-batches and averaged after having traversed all training samples, FIM and MaSQ are equivalent for batch sizes of $B = 1$.

Memory Consumption of FIM and MaSQ When Using TensorFlow. For $B > 1$ automatic differentiation frameworks like TensorFlow run into problems because they cannot compute per-sample gradients, which is required for FIM computation. So current reference implementations[1] use a workaround that

[1] https://github.com/stokesj/EWC.

consists of duplicating weight matrices and bias vectors B times, and then taking the gradient w.r.t each of the copies, which gives the per-sample gradients, although at the cost of a B-fold increase in memory consumption. MaSQ, in contrast, performs the squaring operation after having taken the average and thus does not require per-sample gradients to be computed.

3 Experiments

All DNN training is performed using stochastic gradient descent, and the Adam optimization strategy in particular. Training on D_1 or D_2 is always performed for 5000 iterations which, for MNIST, comes down to approximately 10 epochs. This value is empirically chosen, longer training times do not improve results. The code of our experiments is available on GitHub[2]. It is written in Python 3.6 using TensorFlow 1.12. The code is tested with GPU support, but will probably run without GPU support as well although much more slowly.

We perform our experiments in several steps:

- **Verification of incremental learning capacity of EWC/MaSQ.** In Sect. 3.1, we test whether EWC learning on all three SLTs works with MaSQ. In order to make sure that results are generalizable (i.e., do not depend on a particular choice of hyper-parameters), we perform extensive hyper-parameter optimization w.r.t. DNN topology, and re-training learning rate.
- **Consistency check.** In Sect. 3.2 we ensure that our EWC implementation is correct, by performing incremental learning experiments for the DNNs that performed best in the experiments of Sect. 3.1. This time, however, we work with a batch size of 1 for MaSQ computation, in which case, as outlined in Sect. 2.5, it corresponds exactly to the FIM as computed in [13].
- **Numerical comparison of FIM and MaSQ.** In Sect. 3.4, we compare the numerical values computed for FIM and MaSQ on the same SLT to determine whether there are significant deviations. The reasoning for this is as follows: If there are no significant deviations between FIM and MaSQ, it is not surprising if there are no differences in EWC performance. However, if there are deviations but EWC works nevertheless with MaSQ, then we can conclude that MaSQ is a valid alternative to FIM.
- **Empirical check of FIM diagonality assumption.** In Sect. 3.3, we check numerically whether the diagonal assumption made in [13,15] holds, at least approximately.

3.1 Verification of Incremental Learning Capacity of EWC/MaSQ

For these experiments, we adhere to the full experimental paradigm outlined in Sect. 2.3, computing the MaSQ using a batch size of 1000. While training on all SLTs, hyper-parameter optimization is performed by exhaustively varying

[2] www.github.com/EWC.

Table 1. Tabulated results of test accuracies for best DNN hyper-parameter settings, grouped by SLT. Evaluation is conducted using the "best" (above) or "last" (below) strategies, see text for details. Results for $\lambda = 0$ are not given for the "best" strategy since it is inappropriate in this case (the test accuracy has no peak except at the beginning, which is meaningless). Entries of -1 for the size of layer 3 mean that this layer is absent.

b	SLT	L1	L2	L3	ϵ_2	accuracy in %	acc. in % for $\lambda = 0$
e	DP10-10	800	800	200	1e−05	96.94	x
s	D9-1	800	400	400	1e−04	96.93	x
t	D5-5	800	800	−1	1e−05	87.81	x
l	SLT	L1	L2	L3	ϵ_2	acc. in %	acc. in % for $\lambda = 0$
a	DP10-10	800	800	200	1e−04	96.84	89
s	D9-1	800	400	400	1e−05	96.27	30
t	D5-5	800	800	−1	1e−05	87.29	49

the parameters given in Sect. 2.2 within the given ranges, using classification accuracy as a selection criterion. We distinguish two possibilities for determining the quality of a particular training/retraining run: while always relying on the test accuracy on the whole dataset $D_1 \cup D_2$, one may consider the best or the last value of the re-training interval (assuming test accuracy is evaluated after each mini-batch iteration). While it is intuitive to use the best value, using the last value makes sense, too, since this quantity requires no extra effort to compute and is usually more robust to variations of the re-training interval. For completeness, the results given in Table 1 list both possibilities.

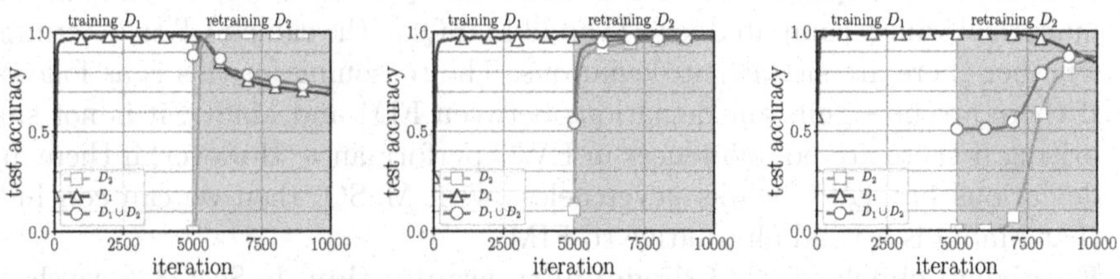

Fig. 2. Incremental learning performance of best DNNs (using EWC with MaSQ) resulting from hyper-parameter search EWC, applying the "best" criterion for evaluating an experiment. From left to right: D5-5, DP10-10, D9-1.

3.2 Consistency Check

We select, for each SLT, the DNN that performed best in the hyper-parameter selection strategy of the previous section, using the "best" criterion. We then

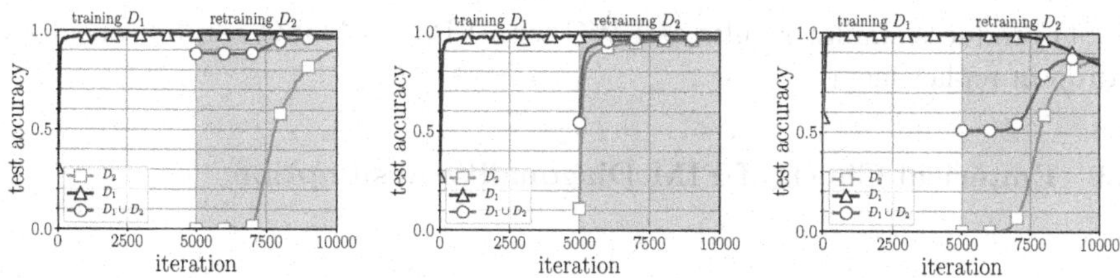

Fig. 3. Incremental learning performance of best DNNs (using EWC with MaSQ) resulting from hyper-parameter search EWC, applying the "last" criterion for evaluating an experiment. From left to right: D5-5, DP10-10, D9-1.

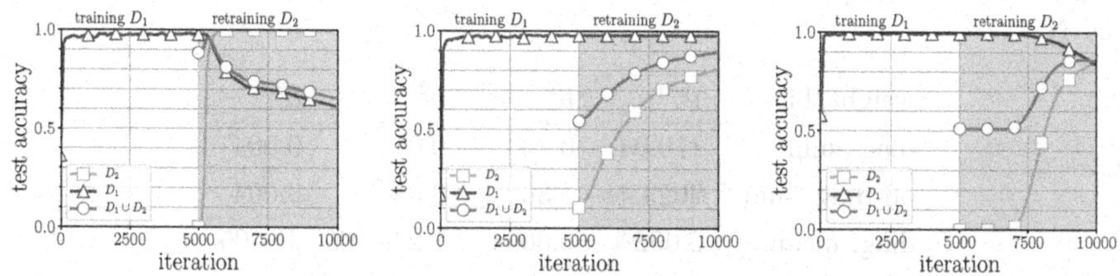

Fig. 4. Incremental learning performance of a DNN with fixed parameters with EWC, using the FIM instead of MaSQ. From left to right: D5-5, DP10-10, D9-1. To be compared to Figs. 2, 3 since the same hyper-parameters are used for each type of SLT.

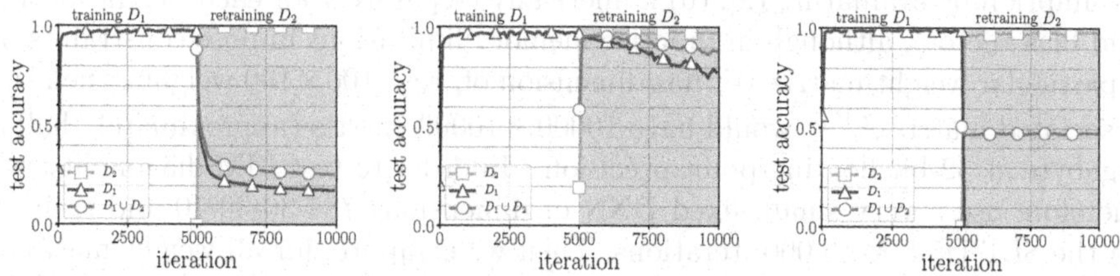

Fig. 5. Incremental learning performance of a DNN with fixed parameters without the EWC mechanism; i.e., setting $\lambda = 0$. From left to right: D5-5, DP10-10, D9-1. Strong forgetting can be observed for all SLTs. To be compared to Figs. 2, 3 since the same hyper-parameters are used for each type of SLT.

evaluate these three DNNs two times: one time with EWC turned off (balancing parameter $\lambda = 0$), and the second time with EWC turned on (using $\lambda = \frac{1}{\epsilon_2}$) but the batch size for MaSQ computation set to 1. In this case, the MaSQ and the FIM are identical, so we essentially perform EWC learning using the FIM. The results are given in Figs. 5, 4. We first observe in Fig. 5 that accuracy after re-training drops strongly for the D5-5 and D9-1 SLTs when turning off EWC. For DP10-10, forgetting is less strong, an effect already known from previous studies for this SLT [18]. In contrast, using the FIM together with EWC reduces forgetting for all SLTs and produces results that are very close to those obtained when using the MaSQ instead of FIM, see Figs. 2, 3. This shows that EWC with

MaSQ produces similar results as EWC with FIM, so MaSQ can be considered a drop-in replacement.

3.3 Empirical Check of FIM Diagonality Assumption

Table 2. Comparison of diagonal and off-diagonal entries of the FIM computed for SLT D5-5. For weight matrices W^1 and W^2, computation was too memory-consuming. We see that the average diagonal entry is, as a rule, several orders of magnitude larger than the off-diagonal entries. However, for the sums of diagonal and off-diagonal entries, this picture is reversed, a problem that grows worse with increasing number of weights in a DNN.

weight/bias→	W^3	$\boldsymbol{b}^1$	$\boldsymbol{b}^2$	$\boldsymbol{b}^3$
diag. sum	170.04	0.33	0.01	0.004
off-diag. sum	2023.41	1.36	0.04	0.004
diag. mean	0.002	0.0004	1.24e−06	4e−05
off-diag. mean	2.5e−07	1.7e−06	5.8e−08	4e−07

It is in principle rather simple to verify whether the FIM supports a diagonal assumption by evaluating Eq. (6) numerically (separately for each weight matrix and bias vector), although in practice memory limitations impose constraints: if a particular weight matrix W^i has dimension of, e.g., 100×100 weights, then the associated matrix $\mathcal{F}^{W^i_{kj}}$ would have 10000×10000 entries (approximately half a gigabyte at 32-bit floating point precision). In order to test FIM diagonality, we therefore use a very small, fixed DNN of dimensions 784-30-30-10 and train it on the SLT D5-5 for 5.000 iterations. Then we compute, for all weight matrices and bias vectors, the FIM $\mathcal{F}_{kl}$ defined in Eq. (3), with the parameter vector $\boldsymbol{\theta}$ being restricted to parameters from a particular weight matrix or bias vector.

The results for this very small DNN are given, for all SLTs, in Table 2. They show that, while individual diagonal entries of the full FIM are indeed much larger than off-diagonal entries, but that the sum of off-diagonal entries for exceeds the sum of diagonal entries. In an EWC-like mechanism including off-diagonal elements, these off-diagonal elements would therefore outweigh the diagonal elements, thus rendering the diagonal assumption questionable.

3.4 Numerical Comparison of FIM and MaSQ

In order to perform a numerical comparison between the FIM and the MaSQ, we analyze both quantities for all weight matrices W^i and bias vectors $\boldsymbol{b}^i$ in the DNNs, again using the hyper-parameters of the DNNs that performed best in the hyper-parameter optimization of Sect. 3.1. The results for SLTs D5-5, D9-1 and DP10-10 are given in Figs. 6, 7, 8, respectively. We find a pronounced difference in maximal values of about a factor of 2, uniformly through all weight matrices, bias vectors and SLTs. This indicates that the FIM and the MaSQ are indeed substantially different quantities, and that the fact of EWC working with MaSQ is not because the MaSQ is equal, or proportional, to the FIM.

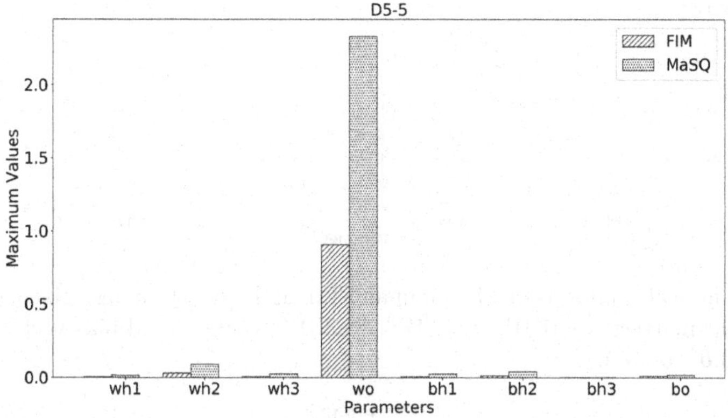

Fig. 6. Numerical comparison of maximal FIM and MaSQ values, given separately for all weight matrices (wh1:W^1, wh2:W^2, wh3:W^3, wo:W^4) and bias vectors (bh1:$\boldsymbol{b}^1$, bh2:$\boldsymbol{b}^2$, bh3:$\boldsymbol{b}^3$, bo:$\boldsymbol{b}^4$).

4 Discussion and Principal Conclusions

In this investigation, we introduce the Matrix of SQuares (MaSQ) as a drop-in replacement for the Fisher Information Matrix (FIM) in EWC-type incremental DNN learning algorithms. MaSQ is simple to compute and has a simple, mathematically well-founded interpretation.

MaSQ is Effective in Preventing Catastrophic Forgetting. By the results of Sect. 3.1, we find that using MaSQ performs at least as good as FIM on all considered tasks, and that both effectively prevent catastrophic forgetting if correct parameter choices are made, which we do by an exhaustive search procedure.

MaSQ and FIM Are Different. Results of Sect. 3.4 indicate that the MaSQ and the FIM are really numerically different, so similar performance cannot be explained by numerical similarity, but rather by the fact that the use of the MaSQ is motivated by intuitive considerations about gradients of differentiable functions, in this case the DNN loss function $\mathcal{L}$.

The FIM Diagonal Assumption is Problematic. As we show for a simple setting in Sect. 3.3, the assumption that the FIM is diagonal is justified at first glance since diagonal elements are uniformly larger by at least an order of magnitude than off-diagonal elements. This is not really surprising since diagonal

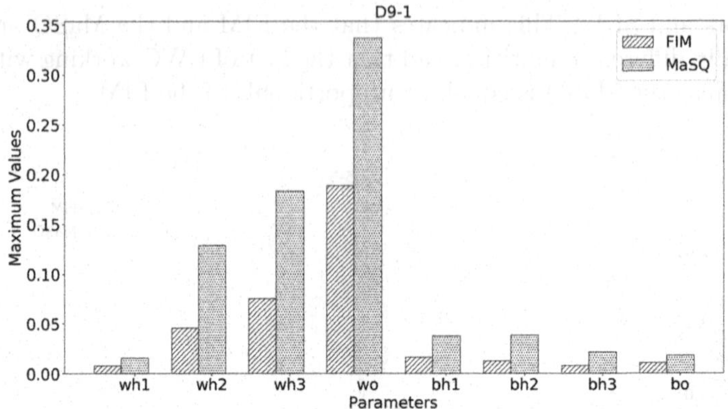

Fig. 7. Numerical comparison of maximal FIM and MaSQ values, given separately for all weight matrices (wh1:W^1, wh2:W^2, wh3:W^3, wo:W^4) and bias vectors (bh1:$\boldsymbol{b}^1$, bh2:$\boldsymbol{b}^2$, bh3:$\boldsymbol{b}^3$, bo:$\boldsymbol{b}^4$).

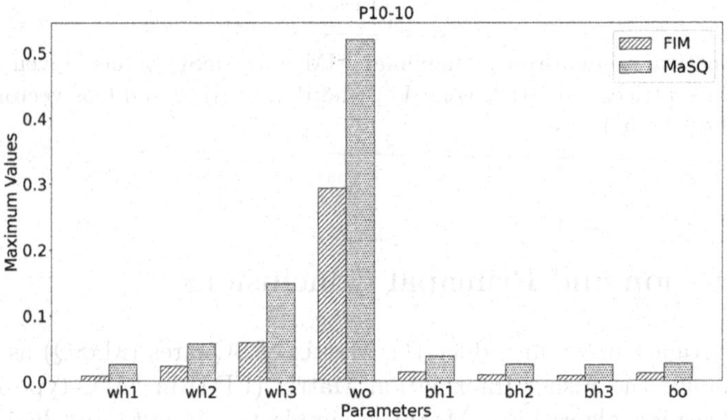

Fig. 8. Numerical comparison of maximal FIM and MaSQ values, given separately for all weight matrices (wh1, wh2, wh3, wo) and bias vectors (bh1, bh2, bh3, bo).

elements can only be positive due to the squaring, whereas off-diagonal elements have no such constraints and show lower average value simply because of this fact. We argue, however, that in an EWC-like mechanism using off-diagonal elements as well, these will have a much stronger impact since their number is far greater. Thus, neglecting the off-diagonal elements is not really justified when using the FIM for incremental EWC learning.

MaSQ is Efficient and Mathematically Well-Founded. This is not really a problem when using the MaSQ, since it requires no diagonality assumption, and its use in EWC-like algorithms can be rigorously motivated from the calculus of derivatives. The fact that MaSQ computation is much more memory-efficient in frameworks like TensorFlow is an interesting by-product of our investigation.

Why FIM is Problematic. Even when leaving aside the issue of the diagonal assumption in FIM computation, one may ask whether there is really a big difference between Eqs. (3) and (10): computing the expectation of squares or the square of the expectation does not really seem a noteworthy difference. However, when considering Jensen's inequality (which, as a particular case, states that for any convex function f and an integrable random variable X: $f(E(X)) \leq E(f(X)))$, we can very easily construct cases where FIM would grossly overestimate the importance of a weights that is actually irrelevant. For example, let us consider the case where a weight's MaSQ value, i.e., $E[dL/dW])^2$, gives approximately 0, reflecting that W is unimportant w.r.t to the loss function. By Jensen's inequality, the corresponding FIM entry, that is, $E[(dL/dW)^2]$, can be arbitrarily large since it is the upper bound on the MaSQ value. This case occurs when there are both positive and negative contributions to the gradient that approximately cancel: with FIM, we would have assigned high importance to a weight that is actually useless.

Probabilistic Interpretation of MaSQ. What is often confusing is that the FIM is computed in terms of the loss function, yet is attributed a probabilistic meaning. To resolve this, is must be recalled that, in the probabilistic view of machine learning the loss function is defined as the log likelihood of the data under the model: minimizing the loss corresponds to maximizing this likelihood. From this probabilistic interpretation of the loss function, a probabilistic interpretation of the FIM and its various approximations may be motivated. MaSQ, on the other hand, relies solely on multi-variate calculus for its interpretation and treats the loss like any other multi-variate function, making it much clearer to see what MaSQ values actually mean: if they are high, the corresponding model parameter is important w.r.t. the loss, which may or may not have a probabilistic interpretation.

5 Future Work

A straightforward corollary of this article is that all algorithms that make use of the FIM should work just as well or better when using MaSQ. In particular, we will test this approach for the very promising IMM [15] algorithm that strongly relies on FIM. All things considered, MaSQ should actually show better performance for EWC and its variants, so another line of investigation will consist of analyzing and comparing MaSQ/EWC performance and comparing this to existing work in terms of accuracy, but also speed and memory consumption.

References

1. Aljundi, R., Rohrbach, M., Tuytelaars, T.: Selfless sequential learning. In: ICLR (2018)
2. Fernando, C., et al.: PathNet: evolution channels gradient descent in super neural networks. arXiv preprint arXiv:1701.08734 (2017)
3. Forster, O.: Analysis 1, vol. 12. Springer, Heidelberg (2004). https://doi.org/10.1007/978-3-642-18491-8

4. French, R.: Catastrophic forgetting in connectionist networks. Trends Cogn. Sci. **3**(4), 128–135 (1999). https://doi.org/10.1016/S1364-6613(99)01294-2
5. Gepperth, A., Karaoguz, C.: A bio-inspired incremental learning architecture for applied perceptual problems. Cogn. Comput. **8**, 924–934 (2015)
6. Gepperth, A., Hammer, B.: Incremental learning algorithms and applications. In: European Symposium on Artificial Neural Networks (ESANN), pp. 357–368 (2016)
7. Goodfellow, I.J., Mirza, M., Xiao, D., Courville, A., Bengio, Y.: An empirical investigation of catastrophic forgetting in gradient-based neural networks. arXiv preprint arXiv:1312.6211 (2013). https://doi.org/10.1088/1751-8113/44/8/085201
8. Hassibi, B., Stork, D.G., Wolff, G.J.: Optimal brain surgeon and general network pruning. In: IEEE International Conference on Neural Networks, pp. 293–299. IEEE (1993)
9. Karnin, E.D.: A simple procedure for pruning back-propagation trained neural networks. IEEE Trans. Neural Networks **1**(2), 239–242 (1990)
10. Kemker, R., Kanan, C.: FearNet: brain-inspired model for incremental learning, pp. 1–16. arXiv preprint arXiv:1711.10563 (2017)
11. Kemker, R., McClure, M., Abitino, A., Hayes, T.L., Kanan, C.: Measuring catastrophic forgetting in neural networks. In: Thirty-Second AAAI Conference on Artificial Intelligence (2018)
12. Kim, H.-E., Kim, S., Lee, J.: Keep and learn: continual learning by constraining the latent space for knowledge preservation in neural networks. In: Frangi, A.F., Schnabel, J.A., Davatzikos, C., Alberola-López, C., Fichtinger, G. (eds.) MICCAI 2018. LNCS, vol. 11070, pp. 520–528. Springer, Cham (2018). https://doi.org/10.1007/978-3-030-00928-1_59
13. Kirkpatrick, J., et al.: Overcoming catastrophic forgetting in neural networks. Proc. Natl. Acad. Sci. **114**(13), 3521–3526 (2017)
14. LeCun, Y., Bottou, L., Bengio, Y., Haffner, P., et al.: Gradient-based learning applied to document recognition. Proc. IEEE **86**(11), 2278–2324 (1998)
15. Lee, S.W., Kim, J.H., Jun, J., Ha, J.W., Zhang, B.T.: Overcoming catastrophic forgetting by incremental moment matching. In: NIPS, pp. 1–16 (2017)
16. Parisi, G.I., Kemker, R., Part, J.L., Kanan, C., Wermter, S.: Continual lifelong learning with neural networks: a review. Neural Networks **113**, 54–71 (2019)
17. Pascanu, R., Bengio, Y.: Revisiting natural gradient for deep networks. arXiv preprint arXiv:1301.3584 (2013)
18. Pfülb, B., Gepperth, A.: A comprehensive, application-oriented study of catastrophic forgetting in DNNs. In: International Conference on Learning Representations (ICLR) (2019)
19. Rebuffi, S.A., Kolesnikov, A., Sperl, G., Lampert, C.H.: iCaRL: incremental classifier and representation learning. In: Proceedings of the IEEE Conference on Computer Vision and Pattern Recognition, pp. 2001–2010 (2017)
20. Reed, R.: Pruning algorithms-a survey. IEEE Trans. Neural Networks **4**(5), 740–747 (1993)
21. Ren, B., Wang, H., Li, J., Gao, H.: Life-long learning based on dynamic combination model. Appl. Soft Comput. J. **56**, 398–404 (2017). https://doi.org/10.1016/j.asoc.2017.03.005
22. Serrà, J., Surís, D., Miron, M., Karatzoglou, A.: Overcoming catastrophic forgetting with hard attention to the task. arXiv preprint arXiv:1801.01423 (2018)
23. Shin, H., Lee, J.K., Kim, J., Kim, J.: Continual learning with deep generative replay. In: NIPS (2017)
24. Srivastava, R.K., Masci, J., Kazerounian, S., Gomez, F., Schmidhuber, J.: Compete to compute. In: NIPS, pp. 2310–2318 (2013)

Active Learning for Image Recognition Using a Visualization-Based User Interface

Christian Limberg[1,2(✉)], Kathrin Krieger[1], Heiko Wersing[2], and Helge Ritter[1]

[1] Neuroinformatics Group, Bielefeld University, Universitätsstraße 25, 33615 Bielefeld, Germany
{climberg,kkrieger,helge}@techfak.uni-bielefeld.de
[2] HONDA Research Institute Europe GmbH, Carl-Legien-Straße 30, 63073 Offenbach, Germany
heiko.wersing@honda-ri.de

Abstract. This paper introduces a novel approach for querying samples to be labeled in active learning for image recognition. The user is able to efficiently label images with a visualization for training a classifier. This visualization is achieved by using dimension reduction techniques to create a 2D feature embedding from high-dimensional features. This is made possible by a querying strategy specifically designed for the visualization, seeking optimized bounding-box views for subsequent labeling. The approach is implemented in a web-based prototype. It is compared in-depth to other active learning querying strategies within a user study we conducted with 31 participants on a challenging data set. While using our approach, the participants could train a more accurate classifier than with the other approaches. Additionally, we demonstrate that due to the visualization, the number of labeled samples increases and also the label quality improves.

Keywords: Active learning · Classification · Pattern recognition · Image recognition · Object recognition · User interface · Visualization · Dimension reduction

1 Motivation

In a classification task, there are machine learning models that can be trained incrementally and samples can be labeled step-wise by the user. Active learning [14] is an efficient training technique, where the samples, which are predicted to deliver the highest improvement for the classifier, are chosen for being labeled. There are several approaches for selecting the samples to be queried. However, it depends on the actual data which approach yields the best accuracy [16].

Having this in mind, we try to find a more efficient way for applying active learning. The common practice is to ask the human for a label of one single sample at a time [15]. Since this is a monotonous task and therefore often leads to mislabeled samples, we want to intervene already at this point by using a

I. V. Tetko et al. (Eds.): ICANN 2019, LNCS 11728, pp. 495–506, 2019.
https://doi.org/10.1007/978-3-030-30484-3_40

labeling user interface which is not only capable of boosting the performance of the classifier and increase the number of labeled samples, but also gives the human a more pleasurable experience while training the classifier. Another goal is to give the human a better idea about the inner representation of the trained model. This insight may lead to a better understanding where strengths and weaknesses of a feature representation are. To facilitate human labeling of high-dimensional samples, we use dimension reduction techniques to visualize the data in a 2D feature embedding space. We use this for improving active querying in an image recognition task.

There are some approaches towards machine learning using such a visualization. Recently, Cavallo et al. [1] introduced an approach for not only visualizing high-dimensional data, but also changing both the data in the feature embedding space and in high-dimensional space. For instance, after changing data in feature embedding space it can be explored what effect this has in the high-dimensional data and vice versa. Iwata et al. [6] introduced an approach where the user can relocate the data in a visualization to be more representative for him. This can be useful if data is clustered in different categories and a category should be located in one region of the visualization space. It is also useful for ordering data, if it has a natural ordering like numbers or letters.

More related to active learning, there are approaches using scatter plots for visualizing data to facilitate labeling. Huang et al. [5] improved the labeling process of text documents showing the human visualizations of the feature space. The text data is visualized by t-SNE [13], force-directed graph layout and chord diagrams. Liao et al. [9] used semi-supervised metric learning to train a visualization of video data. In both approaches, the data is displayed next to the scatter plot for labeling. The querying of samples is done manually by the user, so there is no active learning strategy involved directly, which we want to accomplish for image recognition.

We introduce an active querying technique which utilizes the visualization and enables an efficient training by finding bounding-box views in the visualization for labeling images. Within a user study on a challenging outdoor object data set, we show that using a visualization is favorable and that using our adaptive interface together with the proposed querying method is more efficient than state-of-the-art approaches.

2 Active Learning

Active learning is an efficient technique for training a classifier incrementally. One variant of it is pool-based active learning, where the features $\mathbf{X}$ with labels $\mathbf{Y}$ are divided in an unlabeled pool $\mathbf{U}$ and a labeled pool $\mathbf{L}$. A querying function selects the most relevant samples from $\mathbf{U}$ to be labeled by an oracle, which is in most cases a human annotator. As the training progresses, samples from the unlabeled pool $\mathbf{U}$ are labeled and put in the labeled pool $\mathbf{L}$. Simultaneously, the classifier c is trained online with the new labeled samples.

There were many research contributions in the past proposing querying methods for high performance gain of the classifier. An often used approach is Uncertainty Sampling (US), originally proposed by Lewis et al. [8].

In US the classifier's confidence estimation c_p of the samples from the unlabeled pool are used to select those with the lowest certainty for querying: $argmin_{u \in \mathbf{U}} c_p(u)$. Another technique is query by committee (QBC) [17], where the query is chosen that maximizes the disagreement of the classifiers. In our evaluation we use the vote entropy for measuring the disagreement of classifiers: $argmax_{u \in \mathbf{U}} - \sum_i \frac{V(y_i)}{C} log \frac{V(y_i)}{C}$ where y_i is a particular label and $V(y_i)$ is the number of classifiers voted for this label, C is the number of classifiers in the committee. In our evaluation we chose a linear Support Vector Machine, a Decision Tree and Logistic Regression as a committee of diverse classifiers.

3 Dimension Reduction for Visualization

There are many dimension reduction approaches to visualize a high-dimensional feature space in lower dimensions. Their training is usually unsupervised. An early approach is Principal Component Analysis (PCA) [4], where a small set of linearly uncorrelated variables having the highest variance in the data, called principal components, are extracted. Multidimensional Scaling (MDS) [19] is a technique for dimension reduction, which preserves the spatial relation of the high-dimensional data in the lower-dimensional space. A Self Organizing Map (SOM) [7], introduced by Kohonen in 1982, can be used for dimension reduction. By applying competitive learning SOMs can preserve topological properties in the lower dimensional map.

In 2008, van der Maaten et al. proposed t-SNE [13], which is a variant of Stochastic Neighbor Embedding (SNE) [3]. By modeling data points as pairwise probabilities in both the original space and the embedding, using a gradient decent method to minimize the sum of Kullback-Leibler divergences, it is possible to create an embedding of high quality. Especially if there are classes with different variances in high-dimensional space, t-SNE delivers reasonable results. Our preliminary experiments also show, that t-SNE is delivering best results compared to PCA and MDS for image data where classes consist of objects showed from different viewing positions, like in the OUTDOOR data set [12] that we will also use in our evaluation. Because of these advantages, we use t-SNE as a dimension reduction technique in our experiments, but basically every other approach can be used as well.

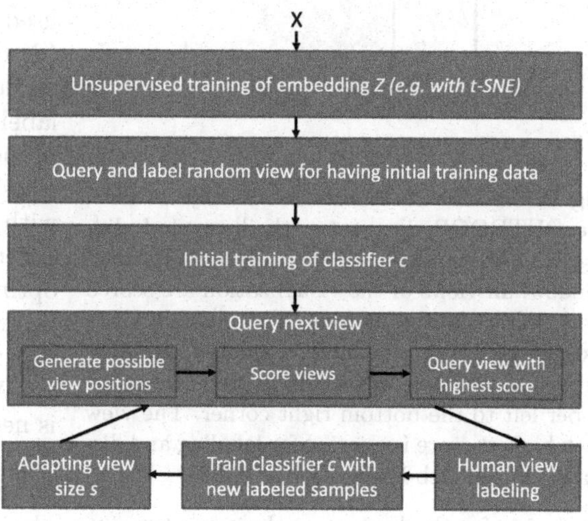

Fig. 1. General workflow diagram describing active learning using a visualization.

4 Adaptive Visualization View Querying (A2VQ)

The underlying idea is to query the samples within a bounding-box view of the visualization which we denote as a view $\mathbf{v}$. The goal of our approach is to query the optimal view for labeling of its enclosed samples.

In the following we introduce the Adaptive Visualization View Querying (A2VQ) approach for querying in active learning using an adaptive visualization. The overall workflow is illustrated in Fig. 1. First, we use the t-SNE algorithm to reduce the high dimensionality of $\mathbf{X}$ (usually a high dimensional feature description of an image using e.g. a CNN) to 2D for visualization. We normalize the output by applying feature scaling so that values of each of the two dimensions are between 0 and 1, naming this normalized embedding feature space $\mathbf{Z}$. In the following we refer $\mathbf{Z}_i$ as the visualization of sample $\mathbf{U}_i$.

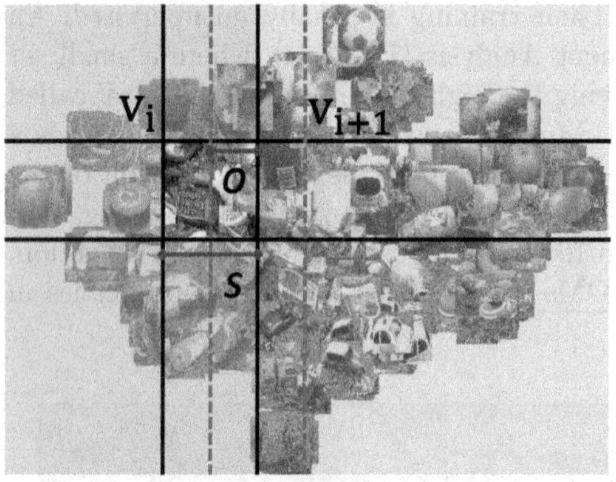

Fig. 2. t-SNE visualization of 50 objects from the OUTDOOR data set with illustrated sliding window approach. In one iteration of sliding window, all views of the visualization are scored by A2VQ's scoring function. The possible views are generated by moving the squared template with side length s in overlap o steps from the upper left to the bottom right corner. The view with highest score is queried for labeling and displayed in our web-based user interface.

Since we assume to have no label information at the beginning, active training starts with an empty $\mathbf{L}$. So labeling of one or more randomly generated views is necessary to initially train a classifier for our approach. Then confidences for samples of $\mathbf{U}$ are calculated by the classifier, used to query the optimal view (described in detail in the next section). The queried view can be labeled e.g. by a user with our proposed user interface. Then the classifier is trained incrementally with the newly labeled samples. After this training epoch, a new optimal view is queried with the retrained classifier and the process repeats.

We think, a querying method is necessary for an efficient labeling because a visualization of more complex data sets can be confusing for the human as there are too many classes and the images are highly overlapping as one can see in Fig. 2. Also we want to be able to actively query the samples which the classifier demands for efficient training.

4.1 Visualization View Querying

To query the optimal view we use a sliding window technique to cycle through a grid of possible bounding-box views that arises from a view size s and overlap amount o. The first view is positioned at $(0, 0)$ in $\mathbf{Z}$. By shifting the square $s - o$

in each dimension (illustrated in Fig. 2), there is a total number of $(1+\frac{1-s}{s-o})^2$ views to be evaluated. We therefore calculate a scoring function $r(\mathbf{v})$ for each view:

$$r(\mathbf{v}) = \frac{\sum_{u \in \mathbf{U_v}} (1 - c_p(u))}{m} \tag{1}$$

where $\mathbf{U_v}$ are the samples lying in the particular view, $c_p(u)$ is the classifier's confidences of the most certain class for sample u and m is the number of samples in the view with the most enclosed samples. By dividing by m not only the classifier's confidences of the view's samples are taken into account, but also the number of samples in the view. We do this for not querying views with few outlier samples with low confidences, as they can occur for instance at border areas in a t-SNE visualization (see Fig. 2). After calculating r for each view generated by the sliding window approach, the view with the highest score r is queried for labeling.

4.2 User Interface

The samples of the optimal view can be labeled with our user interface, also available at github[1] together with all implemented querying techniques. By applying an affine transformation the view is shown in full size with the corresponding sample images as scatter plot symbols. The resulting display is shown in Fig. 3. Due to the visualization most neighboring samples will receive the same label. Interactive selection techniques (see Fig. 3) allow economic labeling of the samples within the view.

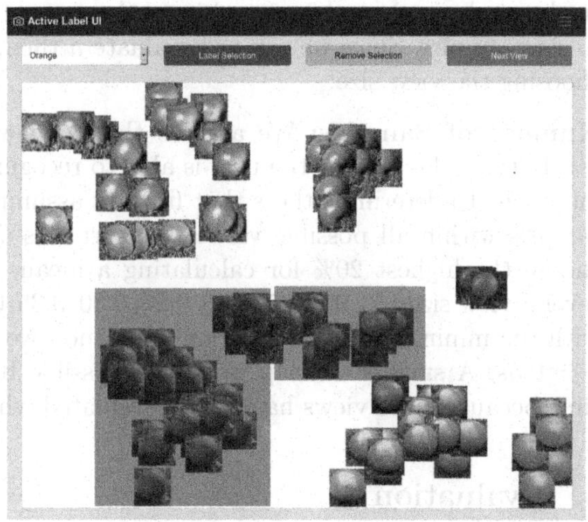

Fig. 3. Querying user interface showing a view queried by A2VQ. The user can label samples via selecting their thumbnails by dragging rectangles in the visualization. The class name can be entered in an input formula. With the button *Label* the selected samples are labeled and removed from the view. The button *Remove Selection* removes the rectangles. There are certain possible labeling strategies, like label everything, label only the biggest clusters or label only outliers. With a click on the button *Query next view* the classifier is retrained with the new labeled samples and a new view is queried with A2VQ.

4.3 Adaptive View Size

In addition to querying the best view for labeling, there is the question of finding the best view size s. A small s would not be efficient for labeling and a too large s

[1] https://github.com/limchr/A2VQ.

makes it impossible for the human to recognize the images because there are too many. We investigated two heuristics for finding a suitable view size.

Number of Classes: In this heuristic we assume that showing the user about $c = 3$ different classes within a view results in best usability. We incrementally increase or shrink s we use a heuristic that is evaluated after each labeled view:

$$s = s + \sigma(\lambda * (c - n)) - 0.5 \tag{2}$$

where λ is the learning rate, n are the number of individual classes in the view after removing outlier classes with less than 5 samples and σ is the sigmoid function. Using the learning rate inside the sigmoid function, which is centered vertically by subtracting 0.5, enables us to incrementally change the view size to match c.

Preliminary (automated) experiments showed, that adjusting view size with upper heuristic converges to a proper view size with $\lambda = 0.05$. However, in our automated experiments we assumed that the user has perfect ability in labeling the samples and that he labels all samples within a view, whereas in our user study we also train ambiguous objects. So we want to give the human the change to skip samples. Since we can not evaluate n then, we used another heuristic for choosing the view size:

Number of Samples: We assume that a view should not have more than $b = 100$ samples so that the user is able to recognize them while using our label interface. To determine the s that fits this assumption, we count the number of samples within all possible views. We sort this array in descending order and choose the highest 20% for calculating a mean, naming it m. We do this for several view sizes $\{0.10, 0.15, 0.20, 0.25, 0.30, 0.35, 0.40\}$ and choose the view size with the minimum $|b - m|$. In our user study we evaluated $s = 0.25$ and chose $o = 0.5s$. A smaller overlap would be possible but requires longer calculation time because more views have to be evaluated while querying.

5 Evaluation

5.1 Experiment

We did a user study for comparing A2VQ to the baselines US, QBC and random querying (RAND).

Participants. 31 participants (*gender*: 16 males, 13 females, 2 others. *status*: 27 students, 2 employees, 2 others) joined the study. The median of their age was 28 years. The participants were paid 5 € for completing the whole study which took 30 to 45 min. Three of the participants refused the money. The protocol was approved by the Bielefeld University Ethics Committee.

User Interfaces. In the study, participants labeled images with two different user interfaces. For A2VQ they used the already described user interface (see Fig. 3). Participants were told, that it is not necessary to label all images within one view because we wanted to give them the ability to skip samples in all approaches. If none of the images within a view could be labeled, the view with the next higher score was displayed. A classic user interface was used for labeling with US, QBC and RAND (see Fig. 4). To label an image, participants had to choose a label from the upper left drop down menu and click the *Label* button. If they were not sure about the label of an image, they could click the *Skip* button. After skipping an image we use DBQE [11] to prevent the querying of similar ambiguous images again, to speed up training.

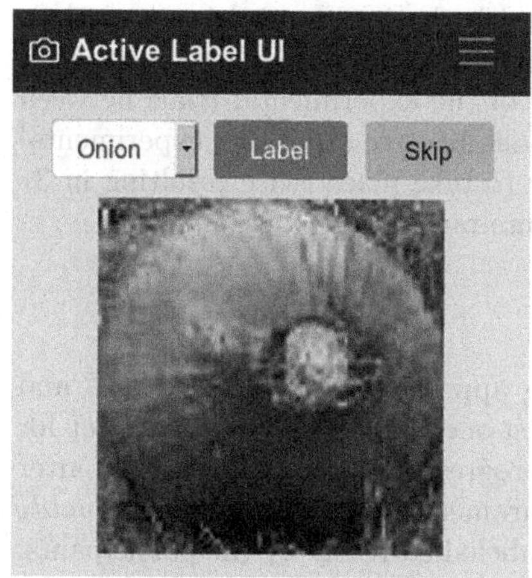

Fig. 4. Classic labeling interface for comparing with the baseline approaches US, QBC and RAND.

Data Set. We chose the OUTDOOR data set [12] for labeling in the experiment. The data set consists of 5000 images showing objects of 50 classes in a garden environment. Since this are too many classes to be labeled properly within a feasible time, we decided to reduce the data set to only seven classes. To make the labeling challenging for the participants, we selected object classes which might look very similar: *Onion*, *Orange*, *Potato*, *RedApple*, *RedBall*, *Tomato* and *YellowApple*. As a preprocessing step, the objects are cropped using a color segmentation. For feature extraction we used the penultimate layer of the VGG19 CNN [18] trained for the imagenet competition, resulting in a 4096 dimensional feature vector. For evaluation we used a 80/20 train-test split. The test images are used to evaluate the classifier's performance. The images of the train set were presented in the user interfaces and labeled by the participants. We have chosen a 1 nearest Neighbor classifier with the same parameters for all the approaches. For estimating classifier confidences c_p we chose relative similarity [10]. The classifier is trained in an online fashion after each labeled image in the classic labeling interface, or after each labeled image batch in A2VQ.

Task and Procedure. At the beginning participants signed an informed consent. They read the global task instructions telling them that the main task is to label images to train a service robot to distinguish objects. Afterwards, they performed four experimental trials. They all followed the same procedure. First, participants had to read specific task instructions. It contained information about which of the two user interfaces they will use in the following trial and how to interact with it. Before using the user interface for the first time, they watched a short video about the user interface's usage. Thereafter, the trial started and participants had to label images for five minutes. They were told to be as fast as possible but also as accurate as possible. After five minutes the trial was stopped automatically by the system.

Data Recording. Whenever a participant labeled an image with any of the tested approaches, several information were saved. We saved the time in milliseconds since the start of the experiment, the index of the labeled image, the given label, the ground truth label and the classifier's 0/1 accuracies on both train and test set.

Experimental Design. Since each participant labeled once with each approach, they performed four trials in which they labeled the same images. Therefore, it is likely that participants become familiar with the images and improve their labeling performance during the experiment. To avoid such effects having an impact on the analysis, we varied the order of the experimental trials between the 31 participants. There are 24 different possibilities to order four experimental trials. Seven of them were chosen randomly to take place twice resulting in 31 orders which were matched to the participants randomly.

5.2 Analysis

We investigated the impact of the querying approaches A2VQ, US, QBC and RAND on three different parameters. The first one is the *classifier's accuracy* for the test data set. The accuracy's temporal progress and the final accuracy after 5 min of training was explored. The second parameter was the *human label quality* which describes how much of the data was labeled correctly by the participants. Finally, we analyzed whether the querying approaches have an impact on the *number of samples* which are labeled during five minutes.

We aimed at analyzing whether there are significant differences in the three parameters influenced by the querying approaches. Therefore, we first checked whether the data meets the assumptions to perform an ANOVA with repeated measures. Inspection of box-plots showed outliers in all three parameters' data. Furthermore the data were not normally distributed as assessed by Shapiro-Wilk's test ($p < .05$). According to this, we performed a two-sided Friedman's test (with $\alpha = .05$) instead of the ANOVA. For each of the three parameters, which showed significant results in Friedman's test, we checked which of the querying approaches differs significantly from each other (see Table 1). Hence, we conducted multiple comparisons with a Bonferroni correction. Statistical tests were conducted with IBM, SPSS Statistics, Version 23.

5.3 Results and Discussion

Classifier's Accuracy. Figure 5 shows the temporal progress of the classifier's accuracy on the test data during training. A2VQ had a slower increase of accuracy in early training while having a higher accuracy at the end (4.8% better than US). The slow rise might be because labeling with A2VQ is comparable

Table 1. Overview of means, medians and standard deviation as well as results of Friedman's test.

	M	Mdn	SD	$\chi^2(3)$	p
Classifier's accuracy in %	0.73	0.74	0.15	10.869	.012*
Human label quality in %	0.79	0.81	0.11	9.311	.025*
Number of labeled samples	148.63	62	171.13	60.650	<.001*

Note: An asterisk marks significant differences between the querying approaches on a level of $\alpha = .05$.

with a depth-first search in a tree. Contrariwise the other approaches are rather comparable with a breadth-first search, having a representation of each object class early in training. Most of the time QBC performed better then US, which performed better than RAND. All baseline approaches started to converge near the end of the experiment.

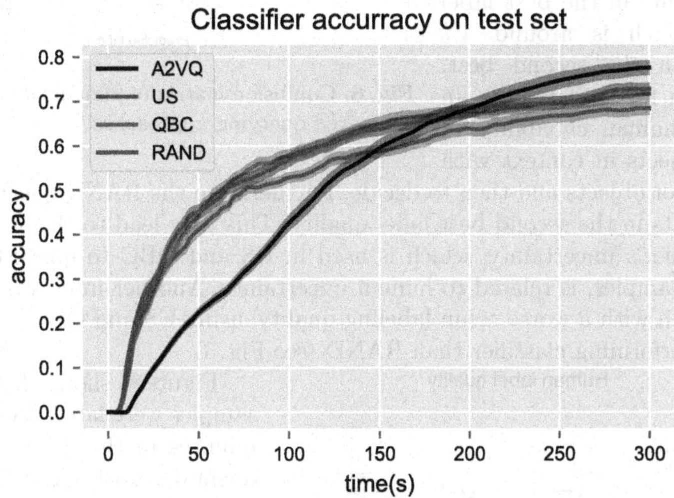

Fig. 5. Classifier's accuracy on held out test set while active training.

Friedman's test, comparing the accuracies of the different approaches after five minutes training, showed significant results. Post hoc tests revealed significant differences between A2VQ and QBC with p = .021 and between A2VQ and RAND with p = .002. This implies A2VQ delivers a better accuracy than RAND and QBC after five minutes training. Even if we did not find any significant differences between A2VQ and US, we can state that in our study A2VQ had the best mean accuracy compared with the other approaches after training the classifier for five minutes.

Human Label Quality. In Fig. 6, a confusion matrix is displayed showing the true labels and the labels given by the participants averaged over all approaches. The labeling task was challenging for the participants who were not perfect oracles while labeling. This is especially noticeable at classes *RedApple*, *RedBall* and *Tomato* with a label quality of 80% and below.

To compare the label accuracy of the participants between the tested approaches, we performed Friedman's test. Results were significant and, therefore, we performed multiple comparisons with a Bonferroni correction. There were significant differences between A2VQ and all baseline approaches (A2VQ and US with $p = .005$, A2VQ and QBC with $p < .021$, A2VQ and RAND with $p = .030$). Figure 7 demonstrates the results. Using A2VQ results in the best label quality, which is around 4% better than the second best. The reason for this may be an improved human capability to see the objects in context with similar other objects and then to decide. Furthermore the RAND querying approach results in the second best label quality. This may lead to the assumption that classifier's uncertainty, which is used in US and QBC to query the most uncertain samples, is related to human uncertainty. Another interesting insight is, that even with a worse mean labeling quality, using US and QBC resulted in a better performing classifier than RAND (see Fig. 5).

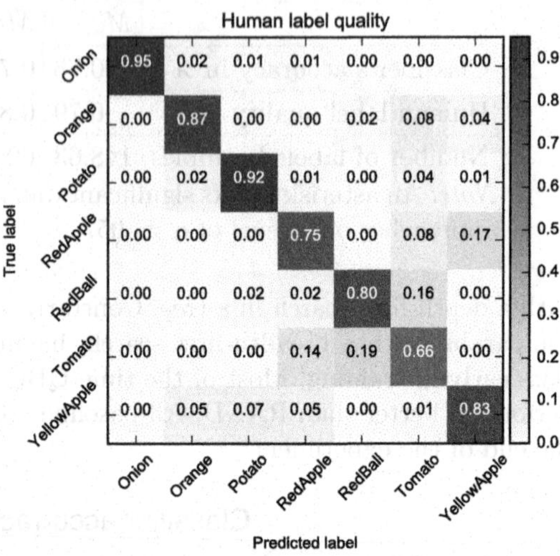

Fig. 6. Confusion matrix of human labels from all compared querying approaches.

Figure 8 shows how many samples were labeled within five minutes in the different experimental trials. The figure indicates, that people could label more samples using A2VQ while the number of labeled samples of the baseline approaches were comparable. The result of the statistical tests confirmed this observations. This outcome is as expected, because with A2VQ people can label multiple images with the same label while in baseline approaches just one image can be labeled at a time.

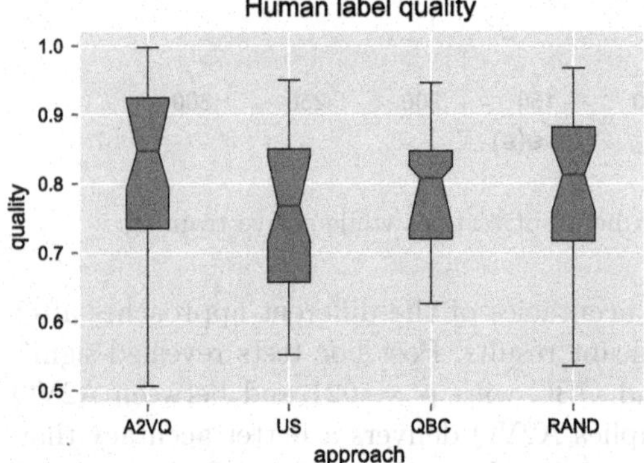

Fig. 7. Human label quality for tested approaches.

6 Conclusion

In this paper we have proposed to use dimension reduction techniques for applying active learning with a visualization. Therefore we introduced the querying approach A2VQ which queries optimal views for labeling by the user. We developed a user interface which implements A2VQ and was also evaluated in a user study. For the used OUTDOOR data set, the study showed that using A2VQ improves the classifier's accuracy, the number of labeled samples and also the label quality compared to US, QBC and random querying.

There are some possible directions for interesting further research in this field. The user study showed that baseline methods have the advantage to faster respond at the start of training. When training samples can be ambiguous, we showed that the used DQBE [11] approach has a huge impact in boosting the speed by querying only meaningful samples. However, our study showed that after 100 s the fast increase in accuracy of the baseline methods saturates. So it may be worth to evaluate a hybrid model, that first uses a baseline technique to query a few samples of each class for the fast training of an initial classifier. Following this, A2VQ could be used to label in depth. Using A2VQ also results in a higher label quality, as our study showed. Therefore, it may also correct former contradictions in labels, since we think that seeing patterns in contrast to other patterns facilitate to give the correct label.

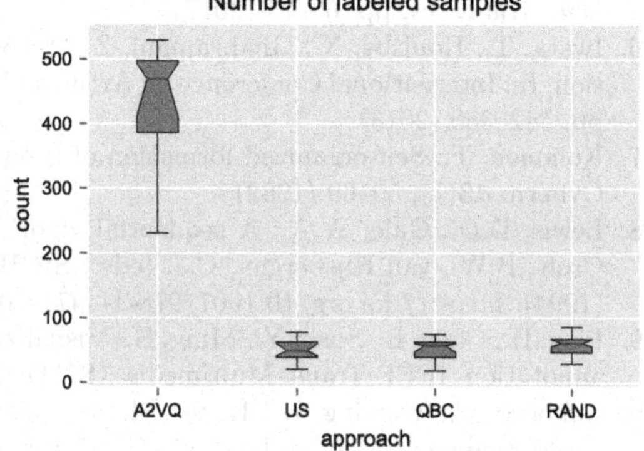

Fig. 8. Number of labeled samples of the different approaches.

It may be possible to use semi-supervised dimension reduction techniques [20] for a better visualization. Doing so, after each trained view not only the classifier is retrained, but also the visualization is regenerated with new label information.

In the near future we will integrate A2VQ together with the labeling interface within a service robot [2], which interacts in a smart lobby environment. By showing the user interface on the robot's front touch screen we want to allow the user not only to teach the robot objects by a finger swipe, but also give him a feeling what the robot's internal representation of the objects might be.

References

1. Cavallo, M., Demiralp, Ç.: A visual interaction framework for dimensionality reduction based data exploration. In: Conference on Human Factors in Computing Systems CHI, p. 635 (2018)

2. Hasler, S., Kreger, J., Bauer-Wersing, U.: Interactive incremental online learning of objects onboard of a cooperative autonomous mobile robot. In: Cheng, L., Leung, A.C.S., Ozawa, S. (eds.) ICONIP 2018. LNCS, vol. 11307, pp. 279–290. Springer, Cham (2018). https://doi.org/10.1007/978-3-030-04239-4_25
3. Hinton, G.E., Roweis, S.T.: Stochastic neighbor embedding. In: Advances in Neural Information Processing Systems (NIPS), pp. 857–864 (2003)
4. Hotelling, H.: Analysis of a complex of statistical variables into principal components. J. Educ. Psychol. **24**(6), 417 (1933)
5. Huang, L., Matwin, S., de Carvalho, E.J., Minghim, R.: Active learning with visualization for text data. In: ACM Workshop on Exploratory Search and Interactive Data Analytics, pp. 69–74 (2017)
6. Iwata, T., Houlsby, N., Ghahramani, Z.: Active learning for interactive visualization. In: International Conference on Artificial Intelligence and Statistics AISTATS, pp. 342–350 (2013)
7. Kohonen, T.: Self-organized formation of topologically correct feature maps. Biol. Cybern. **43**(1), 59–69 (1982)
8. Lewis, D.D., Gale, W.A.: A sequential algorithm for training text classifiers. In: Croft, B.W., van Rijsbergen, C.J. (eds.) SIGIR 1994, pp. 3–12. Springer, London (1994). https://doi.org/10.1007/978-1-4471-2099-5_1
9. Liao, H., Chen, L., Song, Y., Ming, H.: Visualization-based active learning for video annotation. IEEE Trans. Multimedia **18**(11), 2196–2205 (2016)
10. Limberg, C., Wersing, H., Ritter, H.: Efficient accuracy estimation for instance-based incremental active learning. In: European Symposium on Artificial Neural Networks (ESANN), pp. 171–176 (2018)
11. Limberg, C., Wersing, H., Ritter, H.: Improving active learning by avoiding ambiguous samples. In: Kůrková, V., Manolopoulos, Y., Hammer, B., Iliadis, L., Maglogiannis, I. (eds.) ICANN 2018. LNCS, vol. 11139, pp. 518–527. Springer, Cham (2018). https://doi.org/10.1007/978-3-030-01418-6_51
12. Losing, V., Hammer, B., Wersing, H.: Interactive online learning for obstacle classification on a mobile robot. In: International Joint Conference on Neural Networks (IJCNN), pp. 1–8 (2015)
13. Maaten, L.v.d., Hinton, G.: Visualizing data using t-SNE. J. Mach. Learn. Res. **9**, 2579–2605 (2008)
14. Ramirez-Loaiza, M.E., Sharma, M., Kumar, G., Bilgic, M.: Active learning: an empirical study of common baselines. Data Min. Knowl. Disc. **31**(2), 287–313 (2017)
15. Settles, B.: Active learning. Synth. Lect. Artif. Intell. Mach. Learn. **6**(1), 1–114 (2012)
16. Settles, B., Craven, M.: An analysis of active learning strategies for sequence labeling tasks. In: Conference on Empirical Methods in Natural Language Processing (EMNLP), pp. 1070–1079 (2008)
17. Seung, H.S., Opper, M., Sompolinsky, H.: Query by committee. In: Conference on Computational Learning Theory (COLT), pp. 287–294 (1992)
18. Simonyan, K., Zisserman, A.: Very deep convolutional networks for large-scale image recognition. CoRR abs/1409.1556 (2014)
19. Torgerson, W.S.: Multidimensional scaling: I. Theory and method. Psychometrika **17**(4), 401–419 (1952)
20. Zhang, D., Zhou, Z., Chen, S.: Semi-supervised dimensionality reduction. In: SIAM International Conference on Data Mining, pp. 629–634 (2007)

Basic Evaluation Scenarios for Incrementally Trained Classifiers

Rudolf Szadkowski(✉), Jan Drchal, and Jan Faigl

Department of Computer Science, Faculty of Electrical Engineering, Czech Technical University in Prague, Technická 2, 166 27 Prague 6, Czech Republic
{szadkrud,drchajan,faiglj}@fel.cvut.cz
https://comrob.fel.cvut.cz/

Abstract. Evaluation of incremental classification algorithms is a complex task because there are many aspects to evaluate. Besides the aspects such as accuracy and generalization that are usually evaluated in the context of classification, we also need to assess how the algorithm handles two main challenges of the incremental learning: the concept drift and the catastrophic forgetting. However, only catastrophic forgetting is evaluated by the current methodology, where the classifier is evaluated in two scenarios for class addition and expansion. We generalize the methodology by proposing two new scenarios of incremental learning for class inclusion and separation that evaluate the handling of the concept drift. We demonstrate the proposed methodology on the evaluation of three different incremental classifiers, where we show that the proposed methodology provides a more complete and finer evaluation.

Keywords: Incremental learning · Classification · Catastrophic forgetting · Concept drift · Methodology

1 Introduction

Evaluation of incremental learning algorithms is a complex task since there are many possible evaluation scenarios. Each scenario can evaluate multiple aspects of the incremental algorithm such as accuracy convergence, robustness against catastrophic forgetting (CF), or concept drift (CD) handling. Testing multiple aspects at once, however, does not usually help in the identification of the particular issues of the examined learning algorithm. Therefore, we need some basic evaluating scenarios, each addressing a specific aspect of the incremental learning algorithm, to tackle one issue at the time.

An incrementally trained classifier is a classifier that is being trained on consecutive tasks. Each task, the classifier is fed with labeled samples which cannot be stored but must be integrated into the classifier during the training. Such multiple training over the long period has two main challenges that are called *concept drift* and the *catastrophic forgetting* [2]. The symptom of catastrophic

I. V. Tetko et al. (Eds.): ICANN 2019, LNCS 11728, pp. 507–517, 2019.
https://doi.org/10.1007/978-3-030-30484-3_41

forgetting is a decrease of classifier performance, where the performance is measured on the previously trained tasks [4]. Such evaluation of the performance decrease is used as a metric for many proposed incremental algorithms [3,6,9], where authors introduce *incremental class learning* and *data permutation* scenarios [4].

In the incremental class learning scenario, the classifier is learning a different class each task, while in the data permutation scenario, the classifier learns on the same classes but with shuffled feature-vector components. Both scenarios examine how well is the classifier able to aggregate the new data without forgetting the learned class distributions, but it does not examine the algorithm adaptability to the concept drift. The concept drift is a consequence of a non-stationary environment where the class distribution changes in time [10]. The distribution change detection is still an open problem, and its solutions are dependent on the type of the concept drift [1,13]. A scenario where the concept drift is evident has to be designed to evaluate the concept drift handling on different incremental algorithms. An example of such evident concept drift is when the previously presented sample is presented again but with a different label [7,13]. The change of label requires the classifier to un-train the old label on the sample, and then train the new label. Such an operation should be tested during the evaluation of an incremental algorithm.

The evaluation methodology for incrementally trained classifiers observed from various papers [3,6,7,12] can be generally divided into three steps:

1. Test the basic properties of the classifier (e.g., accuracy, generalization, how fast it converges) within just one task.
2. Test the behavior of the classifier in the *minimal incremental classification problem*, where we have two tasks during which we train the classifier on given samples of two classes.
3. Test scalability by adding more classes and by increasing the number of tasks.

The main contribution of this paper relates to the second step for which we introduce basic evaluation scenarios. We show that there are 2^9 possible scenarios that can be inferred from the basic presuppositions for the minimal incremental classification problem. In the context of the incremental algorithm evaluation, we filter symmetric and redundant scenarios to get four basic evaluation scenarios. We propose the following basic evaluation scenarios (depicted in Fig. 1): class addition (`ADD`), expansion (`EXP`), inclusion (`INC`), and separation (`SEP`). Scenarios `ADD` and `EXP` correspond to *incremental class learning* and *data permutation* [4], respectively, which are used to evaluate how the algorithm handles the catastrophic forgetting. The new scenarios `INC` and `SEP` introduce the label change described in various concept drift cases [7,13]. The benefit of using these basic scenarios is that they are easy to construct with existing datasets (e.g., MNIST [8]) and the classifier can be considered as a black box. Furthermore, by evaluating the classifier with each basic scenario, we can analyze its properties separately. The proposed evaluation is demonstrated on multiple incremental classifiers.

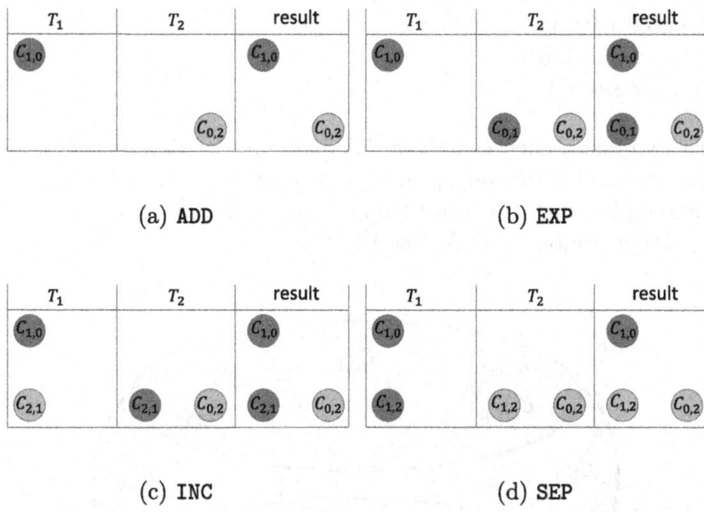

(a) ADD (b) EXP

(c) INC (d) SEP

Fig. 1. Illustration of four basic evaluation scenarios for evaluation of the catastrophic forgetting and concept drift handling. Each scenario has two consecutive tasks T_1, T_2 during which the classifier trains on the presented samples. The third right-most part of each sub-figure depicts the target state of the classes after the classifier is trained on T_1 and T_2. The blue and orange disks represent sample clusters labeled with the first l_1 and the second l_2 label, respectively. (a) All scenarios extends the ADD scenario which starts at T_1 with training on the cluster of the samples labeled with l_1 (blue) and ends with training on the cluster labeled with l_2 (orange). (b) In the EXP at T_2, we expand the class l_1 with new samples. (c) In the INC, the samples labeled as l_2 at T_1 are relabeled as l_1 at T_2. (d) In the SEP, a part of the class l_1 is relabeled as l_2 at T_2. Each disk contains the base set name defined in Sect. 2. (Color figure online)

The rest of the paper is organized as follows. The formal definition and inference of scenarios are provided in Sect. 2. The evaluated incremental algorithms are introduced in Sect. 3 and the evaluation results are reported in Sect. 4 with a detailed discussion and interpretation of the evaluation results in Sect. 4.1. The paper is concluded in Sect. 5.

2 Basic Scenarios of Incremental Classification

The incrementally trained classifier is being trained during consecutive tasks T_1, T_2, T_3, ..., where for each consecutive task T_i, the classifier F^{T_i} is trained on batch $D^{T_i} = \{(\boldsymbol{x}^j, l^j)\}_{1 \leq j \leq m}$ of m labeled samples. Samples $\boldsymbol{x} \in X$ are labeled by one of n labels $l \in L = \{L_1, \ldots, L_n\}$. We are interested in the *minimal incremental classification problem* where we have just two tasks T_1, T_2 and two labels L_1, L_2. Having just two labels, during each task T_i, each sample $\boldsymbol{x} \in X$ is in one of three *states* $S = \{S_1, S_2, S_0\}$; the sample $\boldsymbol{x}$ is either

- S_1: presented with the first label,
- S_2: or the second label,
- S_0: or not presented.

Having just two tasks, each sample $\boldsymbol{x} \in X$ has *tuple of states* $(s, s') \in S^2$, where s and s' are states of $\boldsymbol{x}$ during T_1 and T_2, respectively. Let a *base set* $C_{s,s'} \subset X$ be a set of samples with the state tuple (s, s'). All nine base sets are pairwise disjoint, and their union gives X (see Fig. 2).

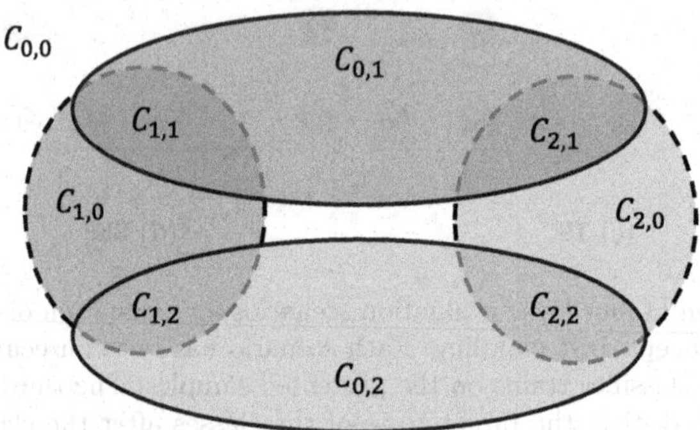

Fig. 2. Illustration of possible intersections of labeled sets that are presented during tasks T_1 (dashed border) and task T_2 (full line border). Sets labeled by the first and second labels l_1, l_2 are distinguished by the blue and orange color, respectively. For example, we can see that the base sets $C_{1,1}$ and $C_{2,2}$ are presented to the classifier at T_1 and T_2 while the base sets $C_{1,0}$ and $C_{2,0}$ are presented only at T_1. Note that this is a scenario where all base sets are non-empty. (Color figure online)

Each base set $C_{s,s'}$ is either empty or non-empty. The base sets $C_{1,1}$, $C_{1,2}$, $C_{2,1}$, and $C_{2,2}$ are sets that contain samples that are sampled twice (in T_1 and then in T_2). If samples are taken from a continuous probability distribution, the base sets with samples presented twice are always empty (the probability of sampling the same point twice is zero). However, in the context of the classifier evaluation, we present to a classifier the same sample $\boldsymbol{x}$ with different labels l, l' to examine whether the classifier can change its model in such a way, that after the task T_2, the classifier labels $\boldsymbol{x}$ as l'. Thus, in the evaluation scenarios, the base sets $C_{1,1}$, $C_{1,2}$, $C_{2,1}$, and $C_{2,2}$ can be non-empty.

Let *scenario* be an assignment function $r : S^2 \rightarrow \{0, 1\}$, where $r(s, s') = 1$ if $C_{s,s'}$ is non-empty else $r(s, s') = 0$. There are 2^9 scenarios, which we prune with the following constraints. First, we consider that labels are symmetric and assume that the base set $C_{0,0}$ is always non-empty. Second, in the context of the incremental algorithm evaluation, we want to measure how well the classifier can classify samples trained only in T_1 despite changes in T_2. The base set $C_{1,0}$ (or $C_{2,0}$) is a set of samples that are trained only in T_1, and the base sets with samples that change labels in T_2 are $C_{0,2}, C_{0,1}, C_{2,1}$, and $C_{1,2}$. The combination of non-empty $C_{1,0}$ with each of the above mentioned four base sets gives us four basic evaluation scenarios. Additionally, $C_{0,2}$ is non-empty in all four basic scenarios to ensure that after the task T_2, there are always two classes to classify. The basic evaluation scenarios are listed in Table 1 and illustrated in Fig. 1.

Table 1. Basic evaluation scenarios: class addition (ADD), expansion (EXP), inclusion (INC), and separation (SEP). Each presented scenario evaluates certain feature of incremental learning algorithm which handles catastrophic forgetting (CF) or concept drift (CD).

Scenario	Non-empty sets	Tested feature	Possible problem
ADD	$C_{1,0}, C_{0,2}$	Adding a new class	CF
EXP	$C_{1,0}, C_{0,2}, C_{0,1}$	Expanding a class	CF
INC	$C_{1,0}, C_{0,2}, C_{2,1}$	Untraining a class	CF, CD
SEP	$C_{1,0}, C_{0,2}, C_{1,2}$	Untraining part of a class	CF, CD

Thus the evaluation of a binary classifier $F^{T_i} : X \to \{1, 2\}$ is the examination of its performance for T_1 and T_2 in all basic scenarios, i.e.,

$$F^{T_1}(\boldsymbol{x}) = \begin{cases} 1 & \text{if } x \in \{C_{1,0} \cup C_{1,1} \cup C_{1,2}\} \\ 2 & \text{if } x \in \{C_{2,0} \cup C_{2,2} \cup C_{2,1}\} \end{cases}, \tag{1}$$

$$F^{T_2}(\boldsymbol{x}) = \begin{cases} 1 & \text{if } x \in \{C_{1,0} \cup C_{1,1} \cup C_{2,1} \cup C_{0,1}\} \\ 2 & \text{if } x \in \{C_{2,0} \cup C_{2,2} \cup C_{1,2} \cup C_{0,2}\} \end{cases}. \tag{2}$$

3 Incremental Classifiers

We introduce three incremental classifiers: ENS, ENSGEN, and ENSGENDEL, to present the proposed evaluation using the minimal scenarios listed in Table 1. The ENS is an ensemble of two multilayer perceptrons (MLPs), where each MLP is trained to classify its respective class. Each MLP is trained independently in the ADD scenario, and thus it should be robust to catastrophic forgetting. The ENS is trained each task with Algorithm 1 and the label prediction is made by $F(\boldsymbol{x}) = \arg\max_{l \in L} f_l(\boldsymbol{x})$.

The ENSGEN is an extension of ENS where we generate (replay) samples from autoencoder. The technique where we generate samples to prevent catastrophic forgetting is called the *memory replay* [11]. Many implementations of the memory replay (i.e., sample generation) use autoencoders, e.g., [14]. For each label $l \in \{L_1, L_2\}$, we have an autoencoder that is composed of the encoder $e_l : X \to Z$ and decoder $d_l : Z \to X$, where we call $Z = [0, 1]^N$ the *latent space*. The autoencoder $d_l \circ e_l$ is trained on samples labeled with l (along with the classifier f_l), and during the next task, we let the autoencoder to generate samples that resemble the samples from the previous task. The sample generation method $\text{GENERATE}(d, f)$ is defined as

$$\text{GENERATE}(d, f) := \{d(\boldsymbol{z}) | \boldsymbol{z} \in \text{SAMPLE\_UNIFORMLY}(Z); f(d(\boldsymbol{z})) > 0.9\}, \quad (3)$$

where $\text{SAMPLE\_UNIFORMLY}(Z)$ gets M random samples of the latent space, which are first decoded by decoder d and then filtered by the classifier f. The update method of the ENS can be used also for the ENSGEN for which Algorithm 1 is modified as follows. Line 4 and Line 5 of Algorithm 1 are modified to

$$A_{L_1} \leftarrow A^{o}_{L_1} \cup \text{GENERATE}(d_{L_1}, f_{L_1}), \quad (4)$$
$$A_{L_2} \leftarrow A^{o}_{L_2} \cup \text{GENERATE}(d_{L_2}, f_{L_2}). \quad (5)$$

The condition in the minimization iterator (Line 7, Algorithm 1) is changed to

$$\exists \boldsymbol{x} \in A_l : ||\boldsymbol{x} - d_l(e_l(\boldsymbol{x}))|| > \theta, \quad (6)$$

where we prioritize training of the autoencoder $d_l \circ e_l$ over the classifier f_l for two reasons. First, preliminary experiments showed that the classifier f_l is easier to train. Second, if the autoencoder is not well trained, then the GENERATE(d, f) method returns a small amount of samples in (4) and (5). The optimization of the autoencoder $d_l \circ e_l$ is implemented by adding

$$\mathcal{J}_l' \leftarrow \frac{1}{|A_l|} \sum_{\boldsymbol{x} \in A_l} ||\boldsymbol{x} - d_l(e_l(\boldsymbol{x}))||, \quad (7)$$

$$d_l, e_l \leftarrow \text{MINIMIZE}(\mathcal{J}_l, d_l, e_l). \quad (8)$$

after Line 9 of Algorithm 1.

On the other hand, the ENSGEN classifier can fail to relabel some of the samples from task T_1 in the INC and SEP scenarios. The samples that need to be relabeled ($C_{2,1}$ and $C_{1,2}$) can be within the cluster of the generated samples (see (4) and (5)). The cost functions of the autoencoder $e \circ d$ and classifier f are both smooth (differentiable), thus by minimizing the cost function over the set of samples A_l (see Line 8, in Algorithm 1 and (7)), we also minimize the cost in the *close neighborhood*[1] of samples A_l. Therefore, if two sets of samples share the close neighborhood but have conflicting minimization objectives (e.g., the two sets have different labels), the minimization process will slow down. We propose an extension of ENSGEN: the ENSGENDEL classifier, that "subtracts" the close neighborhood of the new samples $A^{o}_{l'}$ from the generated samples of label l. Hence, it cannot happen the classifier f_l will be trained to label $A^{o}_{l'}$ as l. The modification of ENSGEN is to replace Line 4 and Line 5 of Algorithm 1 to

$$A_{L_1} \leftarrow A^{o}_{L_1} \cup \{\boldsymbol{x} \in \text{GENERATE}(d_{L_1}, f_{L_1}) | \forall \boldsymbol{a} \in A^{o}_{L_2} : ||\boldsymbol{x} - \boldsymbol{a}|| > \varepsilon\}, \quad (9)$$
$$A_{L_2} \leftarrow A^{o}_{L_2} \cup \{\boldsymbol{x} \in \text{GENERATE}(d_{L_2}, f_{L_2}) | \forall \boldsymbol{a} \in A^{o}_{L_1} : ||\boldsymbol{x} - \boldsymbol{a}|| > \varepsilon\}, \quad (10)$$

where ε is the minimum distance between the generated and new samples.

[1] In a metric space X, a neighborhood of the point $\boldsymbol{x}$ is defined as a ball of the radius r with $\boldsymbol{x}$ in the center: $\mathcal{B}_d(\boldsymbol{x}, r) = \{\boldsymbol{y} | d(\boldsymbol{x}, \boldsymbol{y}) < r; \boldsymbol{y} \in X\}$, where d is a metric function. A close neighborhood is a neighborhood with a very small radius r.

Algorithm 1. Update method for ensemble classifier ENS. The algorithm can be used as an update method for the ENSGEN or ENSGENDEL using the modifications described in Sect. 3.

Variables During one task, the algorithm gets a dataset batch $D = \{(\boldsymbol{x}^1, l^1), (\boldsymbol{x}^2, l^2), \dots\}$, where $\boldsymbol{x} \in X$ and $l \in \{L_1, L_2\}$. The dataset is used to train two binary classifiers f_{L_1}, f_{L_2}, where $f_l : X \to [0,1]$. Parameters M and θ are the maximum epoch and threshold, respectively.

Result f_{L_1}, f_{L_2}: updated binary classifiers

function UPDATE(D, θ, f_{L_1}, f_{L_2})
  $A_{L_1^\circ} \leftarrow \{\boldsymbol{x} | l = L_1; (\boldsymbol{x}, l) \in D\}$ ▷ Separate samples by the label into two sets
  $A_{L_2^\circ} \leftarrow \{\boldsymbol{x} | l = L_2; (\boldsymbol{x}, l) \in D\}$
  $A_{L_1} \leftarrow A_{L_1}^\circ$ ▷ See Eqs. 4, 5 and Eqs. 9, 10
  $A_{L_2} \leftarrow A_{L_2}^\circ$
  for (l, l') **in** $\{(L_1, L_2), (L_2, L_1)\}$ **do**
    for M **times if** $\exists \boldsymbol{x} \in A_l : (1 - f_l(s)) > \theta$ **do**

$$\mathcal{J}_l \leftarrow -\frac{1}{|A_{L_1}|+|A_{L_2}|}\left(\sum_{\boldsymbol{x} \in A_l} \ln(f_l(\boldsymbol{x})) + \sum_{\boldsymbol{x} \in A_{l'}} \ln(1 - f_l(\boldsymbol{x}))\right)$$

      $f_l \leftarrow$ MINIMIZE($\mathcal{J}_l, f_l$)
    end for
  end for
end function

4 Results

In this section, we report how the proposed evaluation scenarios (see Sect. 2) can improve the analysis of incremental classifiers that is demonstrated on the classifiers described in Sect. 3. Moreover, to set a baseline, we also train a single MLP classifier SNG with the layer sizes 728-500-500-2 with the softmax layer and cross-entropy loss function. The ENS classifier has $\theta = 0.1$, $M = 1000$, and two binary MLPs, each has the layer sizes 728-500-250-125-1. The ENSGEN and ENSGENDEL classifiers have $\theta = 7$, $M = 10$, $\varepsilon = 0.1$, and two autoencoders, each composed of encoder and decoder with the layer sizes 784-500-200-8 and 8-200-500-784, respectively. A rectifier is used as the activation function for all hidden layers. The output layers of the encoder and MLP in ENS have a sigmoid activation function. All neural networks are trained with Adam [5] with the learning rate set to 0.0001. All the hyperparameters were found empirically.

Different scenarios are created by using the MNIST [8] dataset which has roughly 7000 samples per MNIST class (zero, one, ..., nine), where each MNIST sample is a 28×28 image of a digit. The dataset is divided into a training and testing set with the ratio 6 to 1. We construct scenarios by assigning some of the MNIST classes to the base sets $C_{i,j}$. Two assignment configurations are described in Table 2: the 021 assignment which is made from easily distinguishable digits (zeroes, twos, and ones), and the 197 assignment which contains digits that are harder to distinguish (ones, nines, and sevens). The classifiers are trained on scenarios created from the training set, and the evaluation is calculated on the scenarios created from the testing set. The results are shown in Tables 3 and 4.

Table 2. Configurations of the assignment of the MNIST classes to base sets that are used in the basic evaluation scenarios. The MNIST dataset has ten classes represented by the number 0 to 9. Since base sets $C_{0,1}$, $C_{2,1}$, and $C_{1,2}$ never appear together in the same scenario, the same MNIST class can be assigned to them.

Assignment	$C_{1,0}$	$C_{0,2}$	$C_{0,1}$	$C_{2,1}$	$C_{1,2}$
021	0	2	1	1	1
197	1	9	7	7	7

Table 3. Accuracy of classifiers after being trained on both tasks. The classifier accuracy is evaluated with respect to testing datasets for tasks T_1 and T_2 (see first and third columns in Fig. 1). The column T_2 shows the overall performance of the classifier, where the higher accuracy is always better. The low values in the T_1 column indicate the catastrophic forgetting since the classifier performs worse on the previous task. However, for the `INC` and `SEP` scenarios, values lower than one are expected because a classifier needs to forget (relabel) some of the previously presented samples.

Assignment	Classifier	`ADD`		`EXP`		`INC`		`SEP`	
		T_1	T_2	T_1	T_2	T_1	T_2	T_1	T_2
021	`SNG`	0.00	0.51	0.00	0.68	0.01	0.68	0.00	0.68
	`ENS`	0.69	0.84	0.00	0.68	0.00	0.68	0.22	0.48
	`ENSGEN`	0.99	0.98	0.96	0.98	0.46	0.98	0.58	0.90
	`ENSGENDEL`	0.99	0.98	0.95	0.97	0.45	0.98	0.47	0.98
197	`SNG`	0.00	0.47	0.07	0.62	0.54	0.97	0.00	0.64
	`ENS`	1.00	0.88	0.99	0.99	0.91	0.69	0.99	0.53
	`ENSGEN`	1.00	0.99	0.99	0.97	0.54	0.97	0.72	0.85
	`ENSGENDEL`	1.00	0.99	0.99	0.97	0.54	0.97	0.70	0.87

4.1 Discussion

The overall accuracy of the classifiers can be compared from the results in Table 3, where the regular evaluation on the `ADD` and `EXP` scenarios [3,6,7,12] is extended with the proposed `INC` and `SEP` scenarios. In the 197 assignment of the `INC` scenario, we can see that the `ENS` classifier is unable to relabel some of the previously presented samples (the accuracy in the T_1 column should be at most roughly 0.5, but it is 0.91 in the case of the `ENS` classifier). Such a low performance at relabeling is most likely caused by the similarity of the digits used in the 197 assignment (ones, nines, and sevens) because in the 021 assignment, the `ENS` classifier can relabel the previously presented samples (the `ENS` has 0 accuracy in the T_1 column of the `INC` scenario). With the `SEP` scenario, we can distinguish the performance of the `ENSGEN` and `ENSGENDEL` classifiers, which have almost identical results in all other scenarios. Thus we gain more information about the evaluated classifiers by evaluation with the proposed scenarios `SEP` and `INC`.

Table 4. The accuracy of each evaluated classifier calculated after the task T_2 for each respective base set $C_{i,j}$. The intuitive interpretation of the table values is as follows: the $C_{1,0}$ column represents the ratio of $C_{1,0}$ that the classifier is able to "remember" after T_2, the $C_{2,1}$ and $C_{1,2}$ columns represent the ratio of the respective base set that the classifier was able to relabel during T_2, the $C_{0,1}$ and $C_{0,2}$ columns are just accuracies evaluated on the respective base set.

Assignment	Classifier	ADD		EXP			INC			SEP		
		$C_{1,0}$	$C_{0,2}$	$C_{1,0}$	$C_{0,2}$	$C_{0,1}$	$C_{1,0}$	$C_{0,2}$	$C_{2,1}$	$C_{1,0}$	$C_{0,2}$	$C_{1,2}$
021	SNG	0.00	1.00	0.01	0.99	0.99	0.01	0.99	0.98	0.00	1.00	1.00
	ENS	0.70	0.98	0.00	0.99	0.99	0.00	0.99	1.00	0.03	0.78	0.60
	ENSGEN	1.00	0.98	0.96	1.00	0.99	0.99	1.00	0.98	1.00	0.97	0.78
	ENSGENDEL	1.00	0.98	0.99	0.99	0.98	0.98	0.99	0.99	1.00	0.98	0.98
197	SNG	0.00	1.00	0.07	0.97	0.91	1.00	0.96	0.95	0.00	1.00	1.00
	ENS	1.00	0.76	1.00	0.99	0.98	0.99	0.98	0.09	1.00	0.55	0.00
	ENSGEN	1.00	0.99	1.00	0.97	0.97	1.00	0.97	0.96	1.00	0.97	0.57
	ENSGENDEL	1.00	0.99	0.99	0.99	0.96	0.99	0.98	0.94	1.00	0.98	0.63

The regular evaluation listed in Table 3 is good for a comparison of multiple classifiers. However, for a finer analysis of the classifiers, we propose to evaluate the accuracy on each base set, like it is shown in Table 4, where the column $C_{1,0}$ shows how well the classifier "remembers" the base set $C_{1,0}$ after the task T_2. The accuracies in the column $C_{1,0}$ show that the classifiers ENSGEN and ENSGENDEL remember the previously learned samples almost perfectly. Other interesting columns are $C_{2,1}$ and $C_{1,2}$, which show how well the classifier relabel the previously trained samples. In assignment 021 of the SEP scenario, the ENSGEN classifier has been able to relabel only 0.78 of samples, while ENSGENDEL has been able to relabel almost all of them. Such explicit information is lost in the regular overall evaluation (see Table 3) because the regular evaluation is evaluated over multiple base sets.

The results in assignment 197 are worse than results in assignment 021 in most of the cases. From this difference, we can draw a lesson that it is important to try more assignments, as it is pointed out in [12] because each MNIST class (or any other class of different dataset) has different qualities. The quantity is another aspect to consider: in this paper, the base sets are of equal cardinality (roughly). Scenarios with the base sets that have different cardinalities could evaluate the classifier robustness against unbalanced data. Thus, it is good practice to use basic evaluation scenarios with multiple different assignments for a thorough examination of the incremental classifier.

5 Conclusion

In this paper, we propose a generalization of the current methodology for incremental classifier evaluation by proposing four basic evaluation scenarios: class addition, expansion, inclusion, and separation. Three incremental classifiers are presented to demonstrate the methodology within the proposed evaluation scenarios. Each classifier has been evaluated with the proposed methodology, and we assess how well the classifier handles the catastrophic forgetting and the concept drift issues. Moreover, the proposed generalization allows us to design a finer evaluation that can test particular aspects of incremental learning; such are remembering the previously trained samples or selective relabeling of the previously learned samples. Such a detailed methodology for incremental learning evaluation should improve the development of incremental classifiers, and therefore, researchers are encouraged to consider it in their developments.

Acknowledgments. This work was supported by the Czech Science Foundation (GAČR) under research project No. 18-18858S.

References

1. Freund, Y., Mansour, Y.: Learning under persistent drift. In: Ben-David, S. (ed.) EuroCOLT 1997. LNCS, vol. 1208, pp. 109–118. Springer, Heidelberg (1997). https://doi.org/10.1007/3-540-62685-9_10
2. Gepperth, A., Hammer, B.: Incremental learning algorithms and applications. In: European Symposium on Artificial Neural Networks (ESANN), pp. 357–368 (2016)
3. Goodfellow, I.J., Mirza, M., Xiao, D., Courville, A., Bengio, Y.: An empirical investigation of catastrophic forgetting in gradient-based neural networks (2013). arXiv e-prints: arXiv:1312.6211
4. Kemker, R., Abitino, A., McClure, M., Kanan, C.: Measuring catastrophic forgetting in neural networks. CoRR abs/1708.02072 (2017)
5. Kingma, D.P., Ba, J.: Adam: a method for stochastic optimization. CoRR abs/1412.6980 (2015)
6. Kirkpatrick, J., et al.: Overcoming catastrophic forgetting in neural networks. Proc. Natl. Acad. Sci. **114**(13), 3521–3526 (2017). https://doi.org/10.1073/pnas.1611835114
7. Lane, T., Brodley, C.E.: Approaches to online learning and concept drift for user identification in computer security. In: Proceedings of the Fourth International Conference on Knowledge Discovery and Data Mining, KDD 1998, pp. 259–263. AAAI Press (1998)
8. LeCun, Y., Cortes, C.: MNIST handwritten digit database (2010). http://yann.lecun.com/exdb/mnist/, cited on 2019-29-01
9. Lee, S., Kim, J., Ha, J., Zhang, B.: Overcoming catastrophic forgetting by incremental moment matching. CoRR abs/1703.08475 (2017)
10. Moreno-Torres, J.G., Raeder, T., Alaiz-Rodríguez, R., Chawla, N.V., Herrera, F.: A unifying view on dataset shift in classification. Pattern Recogn. **45**(1), 521–530 (2012). https://doi.org/10.1016/j.patcog.2011.06.019
11. Parisi, G.I., Kemker, R., Part, J.L., Kanan, C., Wermter, S.: Continual lifelong learning with neural networks: a review. Neural Netw. **113**, 54–71 (2019). https://doi.org/10.1016/j.neunet.2019.01.012
12. Pfülb, B., Gepperth, A., Abdullah, S., Kilian, A.: Catastrophic forgetting: still a problem for DNNs. In: Kůrková, V., Manolopoulos, Y., Hammer, B., Iliadis, L., Maglogiannis, I. (eds.) ICANN 2018, Part I. LNCS, vol. 11139, pp. 487–497. Springer, Cham (2018). https://doi.org/10.1007/978-3-030-01418-6_48

13. Wang, K., Zhou, S., Fu, C.A., Yu, J.X.: Mining changes of classification by correspondence tracing. In: Proceedings of the SIAM International Conference on Data Mining, pp. 95–106. SIAM (2003). https://doi.org/10.1137/1.9781611972733.9
14. Wu, Y., Chen, Y., Wang, L., Ye, Y., Liu, Z., Guo, Y., Zhang, Z., Fu, Y.: Incremental classifier learning with generative adversarial networks. CoRR abs/1802.00853 (2018)

Embedding Complexity of Learned Representations in Neural Networks

Tomáš Kuzma(✉) and Igor Farkaš

Faculty of Mathematics, Physics and Informatics,
Comenius University, Bratislava, Slovakia
{kuzma,farkas}@fmph.uniba.sk

Abstract. In classification tasks, the set of training examples for each class can be viewed as a limited sampling from an ideal infinite manifold of all sensible representants of this class. A layered artificial neural network model trained for such a task can then be interpreted as a stack of continuous transformations which gradually mold these complex manifolds from the original input space to simpler dissimilar internal representations on successive hidden layers – the so-called *manifold disentanglement hypothesis*. This, in turn, enables the final classification to be made in a linear fashion. We propose to assess the extent of this separation effect by introducing a class of measures based on the *embedding complexity* of the internal representations, with evaluation of the KL-divergence of t-distributed stochastic neighbour embedding (t-SNE) appearing as the most suitable method. Finally, we demonstrate the validity of the disentanglement hypothesis by measuring embedding complexity, classification accuracy and their relation on a sample of image classification datasets.

Keywords: Neural networks · Manifold disentanglement · Embedding complexity

1 Introduction

As an analogue to biological neural networks found in nature, artificial neural networks are constructed as graphical models of directionally connected units – neurons. While biological neurons can have complex and time dependent behaviours, artificial neurons are usually (but not always, for example *spiking neural networks*) modelled in an extremely simplified fashion:

- the output of an artificial neuron is represented by a single scalar real value (basically a frequency, or more precisely a time-average of virtual spike trains)
- each input synapse is given a single real-valued coefficient, *weight*
- output of a neuron is determined by an *activation function* on the weighted-sum of the inputs

This work was supported by grants VEGA 1/0796/18 and KEGA 042UK-4/2019.

I. V. Tetko et al. (Eds.): ICANN 2019, LNCS 11728, pp. 518–528, 2019.
https://doi.org/10.1007/978-3-030-30484-3_42

This simplified model is then trained by a variety of mostly similarly simple, often biologically-implausible methods (usually variants of error back-propagation).

Parts of biological neural networks, for example in the mammalian visual cortex [3,4], are structured in a simple layered fashion – each layer of neurons takes its inputs directly from the previous layer. This leads to a simple formulation of a neural network, called the *feedforward neural network*, which is easy to conceptualize and implement and also leads to increased computational efficiency due to the apparent potential for parallelization. Overwhelming proportion of neural models used in practice are either directly of this type, contain only small modifications (e.g. in residual networks each layer also connects to some of the indirectly preceding layers), or are constructed of blocks of this type (e.g. RNNs).

This simple layered construction also lends itself to a reinterpretation of the mechanics of a neural network – instead of viewing individual connected units, we can view the activations of entire layers of neurons at once as vectors in a n-dimensional space, where n is the number of units of a particular layer. The transition between each pair of successive layers then consists of two portions: a simple linear transformation (by the complete matrix of individual neuron weights) and an activation function (assuming that it's shared across the layer), which is almost always monotonous and continuous. The transition between two layers can then be viewed as a smooth non-linear transformation.

This interpretation allows us to examine the process of classifying an input from a *manifold perspective*. Each sample from the dataset represents a point in a high-dimensional space, belonging to a certain class. While the number of samples of a class in a practical dataset is usually limited, we may consider any such set a sampling from an infinite set of potential inputs (e.g. all images of dogs). This ideal infinite set S is then assumed to be continuous (a smoothness prior), i.e. for any input x and real positive ϵ there is an x' also in the set S, which is close to x (i.e. $\|x - x'\| \leq \epsilon$). This ideal set then forms a *low-dimensional manifold* in the input space and the classification problem can be viewed as partitioning the input space such that no partition contains parts of more than one manifold.

Complex classifiers usually construct this partition in multiple stages, with the interim stages transforming and simplifying the input and the final stage performing the partition in a less complex way. In the case of conventional artificial neural network classifiers, the final layer has one output neuron for each of the classes, and the classification is determined by which neuron has the largest activation.[1] This in turn produces a Voronoi-esque partition of the output space, whereas the preceding layers disentangle [1] the class manifolds from their complex structure in the input space into separable regions in the output space.

[1] Output neurons usually have softmax activation, but this is immaterial for the argmax selection, wherein any strictly-increasing function produces the same results.

2 Datasets

To study the process of untangling class manifolds, datasets of medium complexity are required. The complexity should be high enough so that the problem cannot be solved in the input space by a simple classifier, but a complex transformation, such as by an artificial neural network, is necessary. However, at the same time, the untransformed or partially transformed inputs cannot be inscrutable to available embedding methods as to remain interpretable. These restrictions led us to select two suitable datasets, both inadvertently being visual tasks.

2.1 MNIST

MNIST [6] is the quintessential basic dataset for optical character recognition, consisting of 50 000 training and 10 000 testing images in ten classes (digits). Each input is a grayscale 28 × 28 pixel bitmap of a hand-written digit, preprocessed to be centered and upright. Few examples:

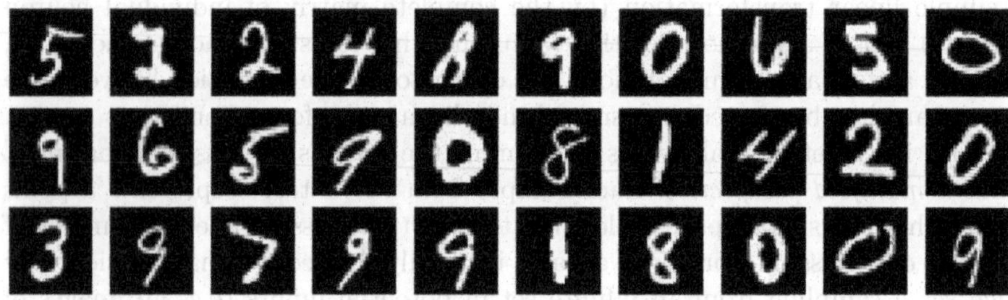

2.2 SVHN

The *StreetView House Numbers dataset* [8] (further referred to only as SVHN) is a more challenging task for digit recognition, which adds color, distracting surroundings, blurring and oblique perspectives. Each input image is a full-color 32 × 32 cutout from a StreetView photo, including the following random samples:

3 Models

To evaluate the manifold disentanglement process, we will employ simple (deep) feed-forward networks that are minimally powerful enough to satisfactorily classify the selected datasets. For simplicity, we will only use fully-connected layers of 100 neurons and use the same activation function at each hidden layer, one of:

- logistic sigmoid:
$$\text{logsig}(x) := \frac{1}{1+\exp(-x)}$$
- hyperbolic tangent:
$$\tanh(x) := \frac{\exp(x)-\exp(-x)}{\exp(x)+\exp(-x)}$$
- softsign function (introduced in [2]):
$$\text{softsign}(x) := \frac{x}{1+|x|}$$
- rectified linear units (ReLU):
$$\text{relu}(x) := \begin{cases} x, & \text{if } x \geq 0 \\ 0, & \text{otherwise} \end{cases}$$

With final classification layer having a neuron for each class with a *softmax* activation. All of these networks can be satisfactorily trained within a 100 epochs using simple stochastic gradient descent with momentum.

4 Methods

To assess the progress of the manifold disentanglement process we propose to measure the *embedding complexity*, i.e. how difficult is to embed the activation vectors for a balanced sample of training inputs to a lower dimensional space. To utilize both numeric and visual examination of the resulting quality of embeddings, we chose to realize the embedding into an output space of two dimensions. We examined several popular embedding methods (in order of increasing sophistication):

- PCA – Principal Component Analysis
- LLE – Locally-Linear Embedding [9] (not pictured)
- MDS – Multi-Dimensional Scaling [5]
- Isomap [10]
- t-SNE – t-distributed Stochastic Neighbour Embedding [7]

Figure 1 shows the differences in the resulting embedding. As the t-SNE embedding proves to be qualitatively superior, we will resort to only using this method. The method is also powerful enough that in the case of the MNIST dataset it manages to mostly separate the clusters even directly on the input data, therefore further qualitative comparisons will be restricted to the SVHN dataset.

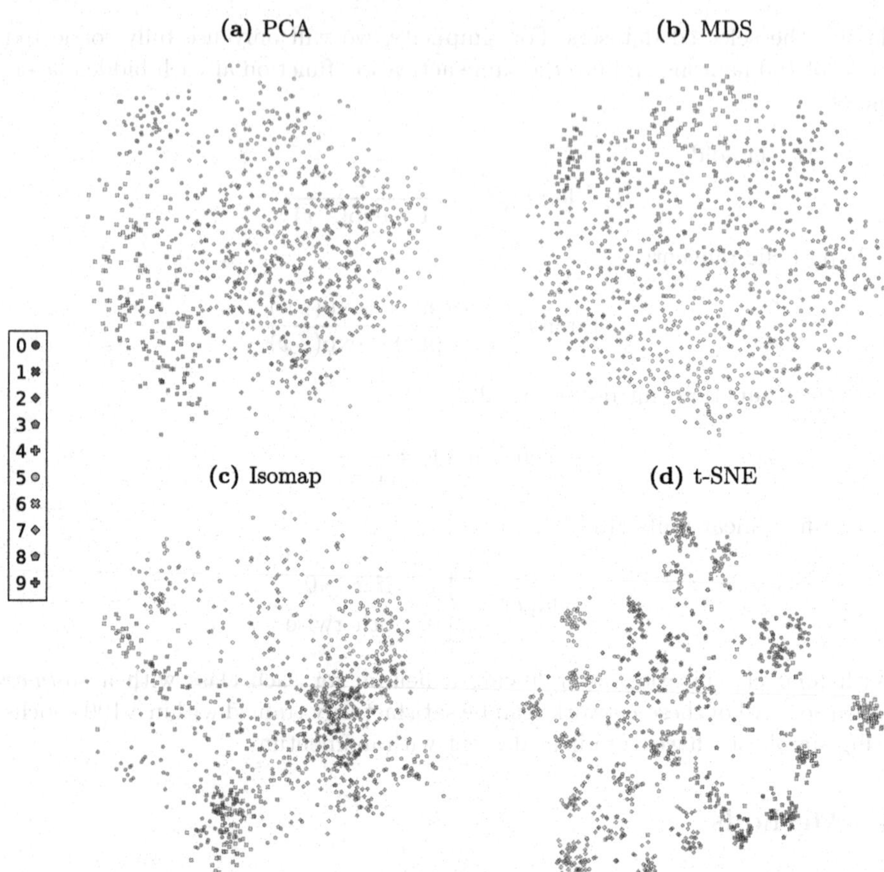

Fig. 1. A comparison of embedding methods applied to the final 7th hidden layer with a softsign activation, in a network classifying images of the StreetView House Numbers dataset. A thousand input images, one hundred from each of the classes, were provided as inputs for this network. Each of the inputs gradually transforms to an activation vector of one hundred real numbers, represented in this plot by a single point of the final embedding. The t-SNE method showcases its clearly superior clustering ability.

4.1 t-SNE

The *t-distributed Stochastic Neighbour Embedding* by [7], or *t-SNE*, is a popular non-linear embedding method, which is based on preserving the *stochastic neighbourhood* of elements, i.e. for every (oriented) pair of datapoints, we assign a probability (hence *stochastic*) that the two datapoints are close. This is in contrast to more conventional methods which usually use a fixed neighbourhood, either an adjustable parameter of the algorithm (e.g. k nearest neighbours in Locally-Linear Embedding or Isomap), or optimized to satisfy an internal condition, or factor all data points into consideration (e.g. Multi-dimensional Scaling or Principal

Component Analysis). This probability is modelled using Gaussian distributions in the *input* space (with x_i being the i-th input point):

$$p_{j|i} := \frac{1}{\sqrt{2\pi\sigma_i^2}} \cdot \exp\left(-\frac{\left\|x_i - x_j\right\|^2}{2\sigma_i^2}\right)$$

$$\hat{p}_{j|i} := \frac{p_{j|i}}{\sum_{k \neq m} p_{k|m}}$$

$$\hat{p}_{i,j} := \frac{\hat{p}_{i|j} + \hat{p}_{j|i}}{2}$$

where the $p_{j|i}$ represents the (directed) probability that j is a neighbour i, the $\hat{p}_{j,i}$ is the normalized neighbourhood score and the $\hat{p}_{i,j}$ is its symmetric (undirected) version. (The σ_i parameter is programmatically tuned for a desired *perplexity*.)

The original, less successful SNE variant also uses Gaussian distribution in the output space y_i, which doesn't take into account the difference in the number of dimensions between the spaces (i.e. embedding). The improved t-SNE method uses a t-Student distribution with a single degree of freedom (also called the Cauchy distribution), with a heavy-tail which alleviates this quantitative difference:

$$q_{i,j} = q_{j|i} = q_{i|j} := \frac{1}{1 + \|y_i - y_j\|^2}$$

$$\hat{q}_{i,j} := \frac{q_{i,j}}{\sum_{k \neq m} q_{k,m}}$$

The disparity between the distributions of probabilities in the input and output spaces is quantified by the *Kullback-Leibner* or *KL-divergence*:

$$KL := -\sum_{i \neq j} p_{i,j} \log \frac{q_{i,j}}{p_{i,j}}$$

The desired embedding is then produced by minimizing this divergence with respect to the placement of points in the output space. This turns out to be a convex optimization problem well-suited for a range of gradient-based methods.

5 Results

For each combination of dataset (MNIST or SVHN) and model (one to seven layers, one of the four activation functions), we train five independent networks (or *runs*). We then sample activations of each hidden neuron for 100 randomly selected input samples for each of the 10 input classes (MNIST and SVHN both), totalling 1000 activation vectors for each layer. In each independent run, we then embed those activation into two dimensions using t-SNE and measure the resulting KL-divergence as the hardness score. For a quantitative overview, we plot the result of all runs into a single bar chart, with the averaged value shown as the bold line and individual runs as translucent overlapping rectangles (this is an alternate version of a boxplot, which puts the greatest emphasis on the mean value). To better visualize the qualitative differences between the embeddings, we also plot the actual embeddings (for a single run; see Figs. 5, 7 and 8).

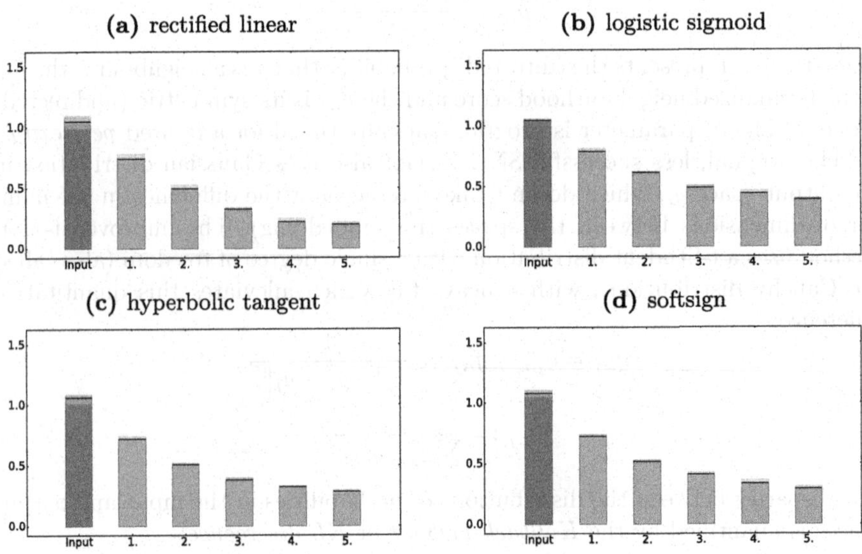

Fig. 2. The hardness score (KL-divergence) of the embedding of the activations of successive layers of a five-layer network classifying MNIST digits with four choices of the activation function. Transforming the inputs through the layers of the network makes subsequent embedding much easier.

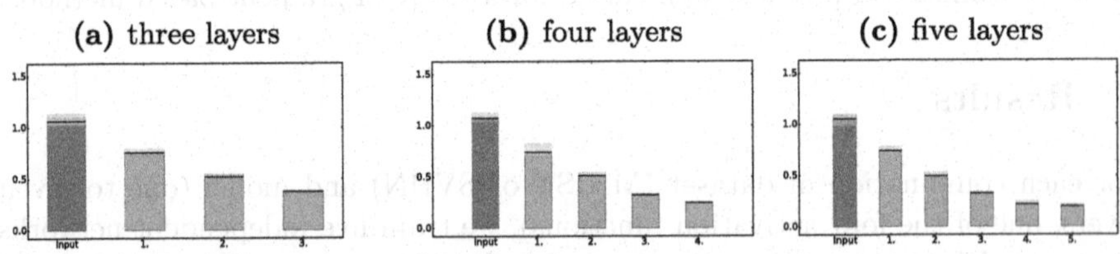

Fig. 3. The same dataset, MNIST, transformed by networks having three to five hidden layers of rectified linear units (ReLU) in total. Fewer layers lead to a quick decrease in hardness, but the final embedding is easier in larger networks.

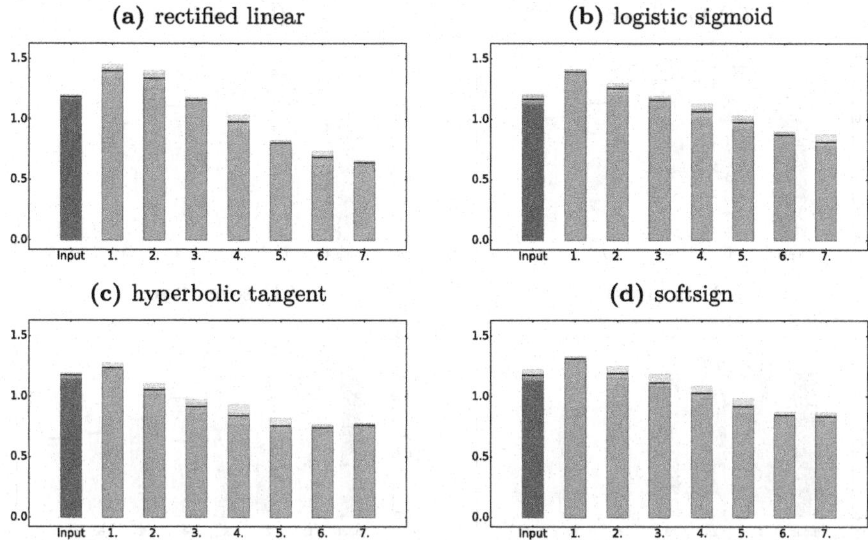

Fig. 4. Hardness scores for seven layer networks with inputs from the SVHN dataset. While the embedding is much harder, the decreasing trend still persists.

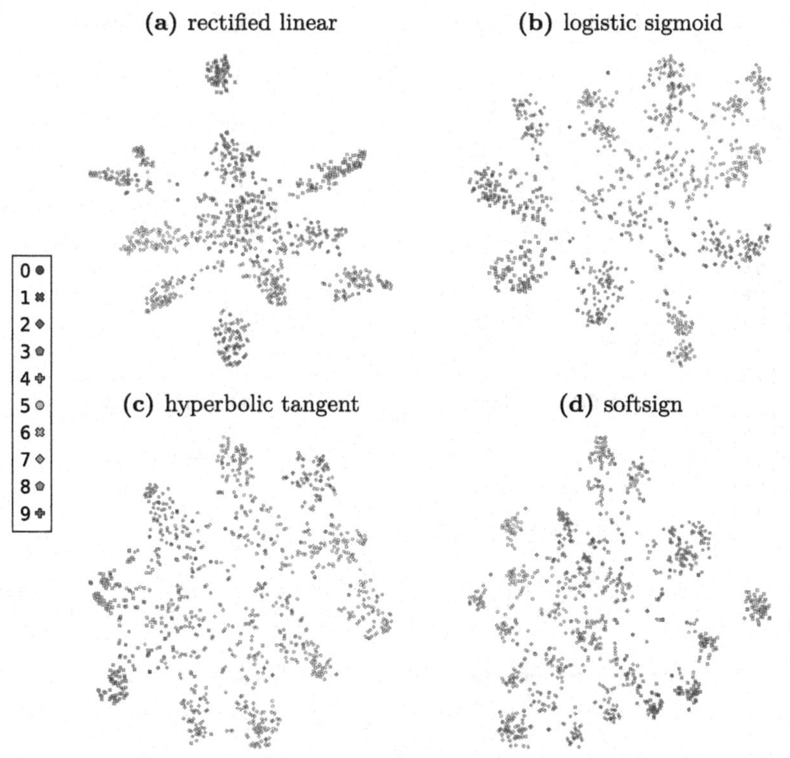

Fig. 5. Embeddings of a single run of SVHN in seven layer networks.

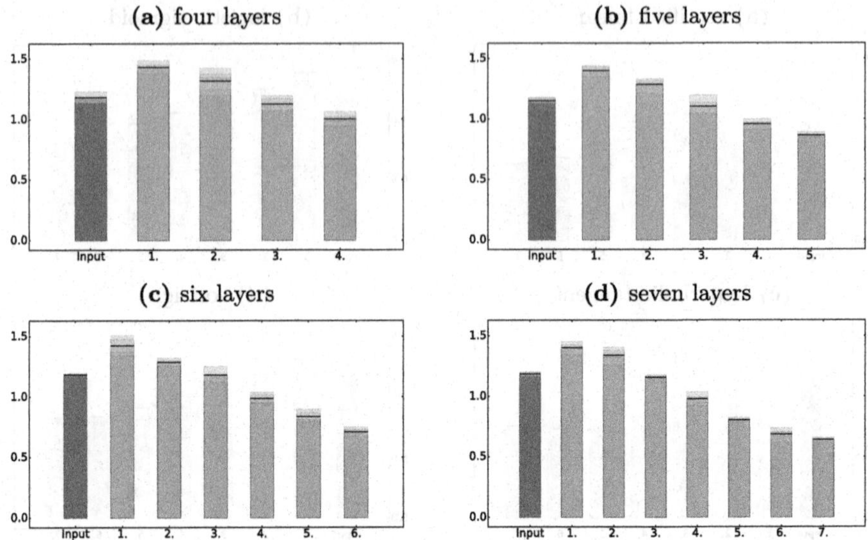

Fig. 6. Four to seven layers of rectified linear units on the SVHN dataset. Smaller networks on this complex task lead to embeddings that are much worse.

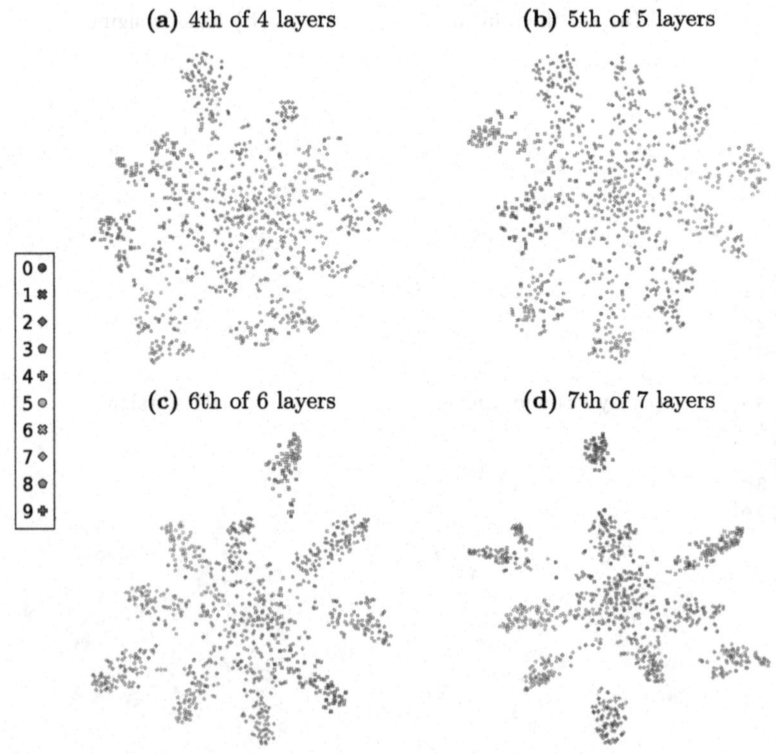

Fig. 7. Actual embeddings of the final layers of networks evaluated above.

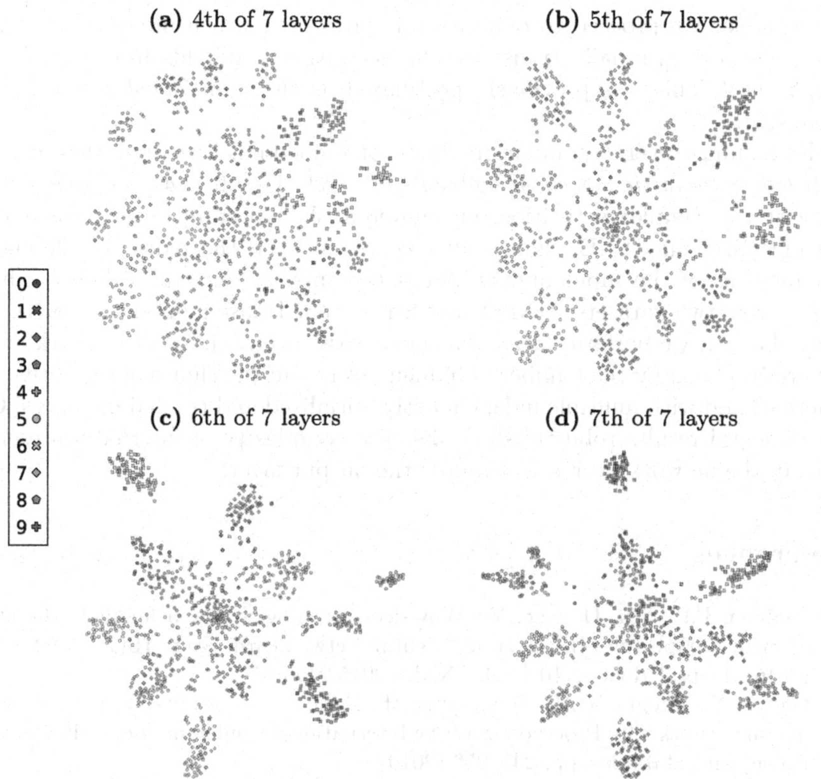

Fig. 8. Embeddings of the activations of the last four layers of a seven layer network, with inputs from the SVHN dataset. Clusterings computed on the higher layers are not only better scoring, but also visually more focused.

The embedding complexity scores, measured by the *KL-divergence* of the *t-SNE* embeddings, are plotted in Figs. 2 and 3 for the MNIST dataset (all runs). For the more challenging SVHN dataset, the selected scores for multiple runs and selected resulting embeddings for a single run are depicted in Figs. 4, 5, 6, 7, 8.

6 Conclusion

In this paper, we propose a novel method for gaining both quantitative and qualitative insight into the inner workings of deep neural networks, by examining the complexity of embedding their *learned representations* – the activations of their hidden layers. The inputs of modern machine learning tasks, especially of the visual variety, are highly complex and cannot be easily embedded to a low-dimensional space. In classification tasks, however, the activations of the final hidden layer are classified in a linear fashion (linear weighting usually followed by softmax and winner-takes-all classification), and therefore must be easily embeddable. We proceed to quantify this process in which intermediate layers of the network gradually transform the activation manifolds from complex to simple ones. This was previously postulated as the *manifold disentanglement hypothesis.*

Examining several popular methods of embedding, we find that only *t-distributed stochastic neighbour embedding (t-SNE)* is sufficiently capable of dealing with the complex activations encountered. We measure the criterion explicitly optimized in t-SNE, the *KL-divergence* between the pairwise "closeness" distributions of the input and output datapoints, as our embedding hardness score across two datasets, MNIST and StreetView House numbers (SVHN). For every dataset, we perform measurements across several different network architectures (defined by the number of hidden layers and the choice of the activation function) and with multiple independently initialized and trained instances. Our experimental results robustly show that the complexity of internal representations in the network decreases towards the output layer.

References

1. Brahma, P.P., Wu, D., She, Y.: Why deep learning works: a manifold disentanglement perspective. IEEE Trans. Neural Netw. Learn. Syst. **10**(27), 1997–2008 (2016). https://doi.org/10.1109/TNNLS.2015.2496947
2. Glorot, X., Bengio, Y.: Understanding the difficulty of training deep feedforward neural networks. In: Proceedings of the International Conference on Artificial Intelligence and Statistics, pp. 249–256 (2010)
3. Hubel, D.H., Wiesel, T.N.: Receptive fields of single neurons in the cat's striate cortex. J. Physiol. **148**, 574–591 (1959). https://doi.org/10.1113/jphysiol.1959.sp006308
4. Hubel, D.H., Wiesel, T.N.: Receptive fields, binocular interaction and functional architecture in the cat's visual cortex. J. Physiol. **60**, 106–154 (1962). https://doi.org/10.1113/jphysiol.1962.sp006837
5. Kruskal, J.B.: Multidimensional scaling by optimizing goodness of fit to a non-metric hypothesis. Psychometrika **29**(1), 1–27 (1964). https://doi.org/10.1007/BF02289565
6. LeCun, Y., Cortes, C.: MNIST handwritten digit database (2010). http://yann.lecun.com/exdb/mnist/
7. van der Maaten, L., Hinton, G.: Visualizing data using t-SNE. J. Mach. Learn. Res. **9**, 2579–2605 (2008)
8. Netzer, Y., Wang, T., Coates, A., Bissacco, A., Wu, B., Ng, A.Y.: Reading digits in natural images with unsupervised feature learning. In: NIPS Workshop on Deep Learning and Unsupervised Feature Learning 2011 (2011)
9. Roweis, S.T., Saul, L.K.: Nonlinear dimensionality reduction by locally linear embedding. Science **290**(5500), 2323–2326 (2000). https://doi.org/10.1126/science.290.5500.2323
10. Tenenbaum, J.B., Silva, V.d., Langford, J.C.: A global geometric framework for nonlinear dimensionality reduction. Science **290**(5500), 2319–2323 (2000). https://doi.org/10.1126/science.290.5500.2319

Metric Learning

Joint Metric Learning on Riemannian Manifold of Global Gaussian Distributions

Qinqin Nie[1], Bin Zhou[2], Pengfei Zhu[1](✉), Qinghua Hu[1], and Hao Cheng[1]

[1] College of Intelligence and Computing, Tianjin University, Tianjin 300350, China
{nieqinqin,zhupengfei,huqinghua,chenghao}@tju.edu.cn

[2] National Key Laboratory of Science and Technology on Aerospace Automatic Control Institute, Beijing 100854, China

Abstract. In many computer vision tasks, images or image sets can be modeled as a Gaussian distribution to capture the underlying data distribution. The challenge of using Gaussians to model the vision data is that the space of Gaussians is not a linear space. From the perspective of information geometry, the Gaussians lie on a specific Riemannian Manifold. In this paper, we present a joint metric learning (JML) model on Riemannian Manifold of Gaussian distributions. The distance between two Gaussians is defined as the sum of the Mahalanobis distance between the mean vectors and the log-Euclidean distance (LED) between the covariance matrices. We formulate the multi-metric learning model by jointly learning the Mahalanobis distance and the log-Euclidean distance with pairwise constraints. Sample pair weights are embedded to select the most informative pairs to learn the discriminative distance metric. Experiments on video based face recognition, object recognition and material classification show that JML is superior to the state-of-the-art metric learning algorithms for Gaussians.

Keywords: Gaussians · Riemannian Manifold · Joint metric learning

1 Introduction

Gaussian distributions have been widely used to represent the data variability of images or videos in many computer vision tasks, e.g., face recognition [26], image classification [11], person re-identification [16]. Gaussians that precisely capture both the first- and second-order information are experimentally verified to achieve superior performance to those using either zero-order [22] or first order information [8], or their combination [30]. To involve more variations, each image or image set can be represented by a Gaussian mixture model (GMM) as well [29]. Nakayama et al. proposed a global Gaussian approach for scene categorization by representing a distribution using a Gaussian in the entire feature space [17]. Matsukawa et al. presented a hierarchical Gaussian descriptor for person re-identification by modeling the region as a set of multiple Gaussian distributions [16]. Li et al. used a collection of Gaussians as visual words to represent the universal probability distribution of features from all classes [13].

In the light of information geometry, a set of Gaussians lie on a specific Manifold. The space $N(d)$ of d-dimensional Gaussians $\mathcal{N}(\mu, \Sigma)$, where μ is the mean vector and

I. V. Tetko et al. (Eds.): ICANN 2019, LNCS 11728, pp. 531–542, 2019.
https://doi.org/10.1007/978-3-030-30484-3_43

Σ is the covariance matrix, forms a Riemannian Manifold equipped with the Fisher metric rather than a Euclidean space. As the space of Gaussians forms a manifold space, the traditional distance metrics in Euclidean space cannot apply. To measure the difference between global Gaussian distributions, similarity or dissimilarity measures are defined, e.g., Kullback-Leibler Divergence (KLD), Bhattacharyya Distance (BD), Hellinger Distance (HD) and distance based on Lie Group (LGD). Although Gaussians can well capture the variations in data, the (dis) similarity measures for Gaussians lack discrimination ability for accurate matching. Hence, distance metrics should be learned for Gaussians to boost the recognition performance [25,26].

The challenge of metric learning for Gaussian distributions lies in how to well exploit both the first- and second-order information while respect the geometry property of Gaussians. Most existing metric learning methods emphasize on the second-order information while ignore the first-order statistics, which has proved to be important in classification tasks [18]. The covariance matrices, i.e., the second-order information, form a Riemannian manifold of symmetric positive definite (SPD) matrices. For SPD manifold, distance metrics are learned on the original manifold [4,6], in the tangent space [7] or the high-dimensional Hilbert space [5]. Additionally, the performance of metric learning is significantly affected by the pairwise constraints, e.g., positive (similar) and negative (dissimilar) sample pairs. Most existing metric learning methods, especially the ones for Gaussians, ignored the importance of different sample pairs.

Towards addressing the above issues, we propose a joint metric learning (JML) model on Riemannian Manifold of global Gaussian distributions. The distance between two Gaussians is defined as the sum of the Mahalanobis distance between the mean vectors and the log-Euclidean distance between the covariance matrices. The contribution of this paper can be summarized in three aspects:

- A novel joint metric learning model is proposed for Gaussian distributions. The distance metrics of the first-order and second-order are simultaneously optimized in the similar manner, which fuses the complementary information of both orders effectively.
- The weights of sample pairs (i.e., pairs of Gaussians) are embedded to select the most simply Gaussian pairs for metric learning. Compared with the traditional metric learning methods that treats all pairs equally, JML takes the difference of sample pairs into account.
- Experiments on video based face recognition, object recognition and classification show that JML outperforms the state-of-the-art metric learning algorithms.

2 Related Work

2.1 Learning with Global Gaussian Distributions

There are generally three categories of learning methods in terms of Gaussian distributions. The first one learns on the Manifold of Global Gaussian distributions directly. Gong et al. proposed shape of Gaussians, which is embedded into an affine group and the Riemannian metric is used to measure the distance [3]. Gaussians are also identified as SPD matrices by embedding them in the Siegel group [1] or the Riemannian symmetric space [15]. Wang et al. proposed a global Gaussian distribution embedding network by plugging Gaussian distribution into deep CNN in an end-to-end manner [27]. The second kind of methods first map the Gaussians to a vector space and then apply the classical discriminative learning methods in the Euclidean space. Serra et al. represented an image as a weighted Pyramid of Gaussians of local descriptors, and mapped the covariance matrix on the tangent space to concatenate the mean for classification [20]. Wang et al. embedded Gaussian distributions into the space of SPD matrices and then projected SPD manifold to the tangent space by logarithm operator [23]. Li et al. equipped the space of $n-$dimensional Gaussians with a Lie group structure and embedded it by matrix logarithm into a linear space [11]. The third one maps the Gaussian to the high-dimensional Hilbert Space using kernels derived for Gaussian distributions [4,26]. Kernel based methods involve great computation burden and therefore lack scalability in large-scale tasks.

2.2 Metric Learning for Gaussian Distributions

Metric learning aims to learn a discriminative metric by pulling similar sample pairs together and enlarging the distance between two samples in dissimilar pairs. Almost all existing methods focus on metric learning for Gaussian mixture model (GMM) rather than global Gaussian distributions. Li et al. presented a earth mover's distance methodology for image matching with Gaussian mixture models [12]. Wang et al. derived a series of provably positive definite probabilistic kernels for Gaussians and mapped them to a high-dimensional reproducing kernel Hilbert space (RKHS), where the classical kernel discriminative analysis algorithms can be applied [26]. To exploit the weights of the components in each GMM, a graph embedding method was developed by constructing the adjacency graph using the distance between Gaussians [25]. The problem with metric learning for GMM lies in that it is time-consuming to model images or videos by mixture Gaussians and therefore matching with GMM lacks efficiency.

3 Global Gaussian Distributions Modeling

Gaussian distribution is the most common probability distribution model. It is often used to describe random variations such as noise, feature distribution, pixel gray scale and so on. Gaussian distributions are widely used in identification and classification in that it captures both the first- and second-order statistics. For an image or image set, it can be modelled as a Gaussian distribution. As shown in Fig. 1, for an image set classification tasks, a handcrafted feature vector can be extracted from each image of an image set. We can also use convolutional neural network to extract the fully connected layer as deep features. For an image, the output matrix $\mathbf{X} \in \mathbb{R}^{m_i \times d}$ of the final convolution layer is used as the deep features, where m_i is the size of feature map and d is the number of kernels. For an image set, m_i means the number of images in this set and d represents the dimension of the feature vectors.

To build a Gaussian distribution $\mathcal{N}(\mu, \Sigma)$, the first order statistics (mean) μ and the second order statistics (covariance matrix) $\mathbf{\Sigma}$ should be computed.

$$\mu = \frac{1}{m} \sum_{i=1}^{m} x_i, \tag{1}$$

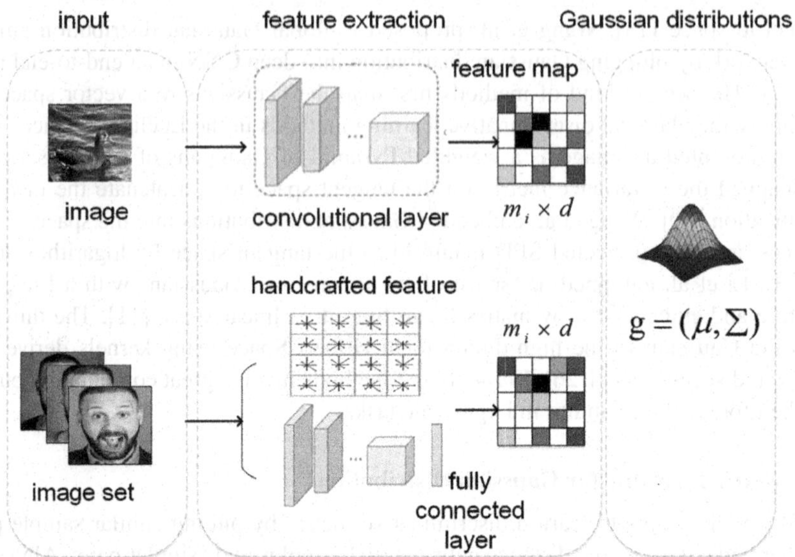

Fig. 1. Global Gaussian distribution modelling of images and image sets. For an image set, handcrafted features and deep features (fully connected layer) can be extracted for each image. For an image, we use convolutional neural network to extract the output of the final convolution layer as deep features. Thus, a feature matrix $\mathbf{X} \in \mathbb{R}^{\mathrm{m_i \times d}}$ can be extracted for both an image or image set.

$$\mathbf{\Sigma} = \frac{1}{m}\sum_{j=1}^{m}(x_j - \mu)^T(x_j - \mu), \tag{2}$$

where μ represent mean statistic of the set, $\mu \in \mathbb{R}^d$, $\mathbf{\Sigma} \in \mathbb{R}^{d \times d}$ represent covariance statistic. The average vector μ roughly reflects the average of the overall features, while the covariance matrix describes the correlation of different features. The space of Gaussians forms a Riemannian manifold, where the classical discriminative learning methods in Euclidean space cannot apply.

For a Gaussian distribution, there are two component, i.e. mean μ and covariance matrix $\mathbf{\Sigma}$. For μ, the distance between the means can be measured by Mahalanobis distance (MD). For $\mathbf{\Sigma}$, as covariance matrices forms a Riemannian Manifold of SPD matrices, i.e., SPD manifold. Two most widely used Riemannian metric on SPD manifold, i.e., affine invariant metric (AIM) and Log-Euclidean metric (LEM), are qualified to derive the truce geodesic on the SPD manifold. Compared with AIM that is computationally expensive, LEM breaks the computation limitations while keeps good theoretical properties. Hence, LEM based distance, i.e., Log-Euclidean distance (LED) has been widely used and achieved superior performance. The Mahalanobis distance (MD) is used to calculate the similarity between means:

$$MD(\mu_i, \mu_j) = \sqrt{(\mu_i - \mu_j)^T(\mathbf{\Sigma}_i^{-1} + \mathbf{\Sigma}_j^{-1})(\mu_i - \mu_j)}. \tag{3}$$

Log-Euclidean distance (LED) is used to measure the difference between two covariance matrices,

$$LED(\mathbf{\Sigma}_i, \mathbf{\Sigma}_j) = \|log(\mathbf{\Sigma}_i) - log(\mathbf{\Sigma}_j)\|_F \,. \tag{4}$$

The joint distance between two Gaussian distribution is defined as:

$$d(g_i, g_j) = MD(\mu_i, \mu_j) + LED(\mathbf{\Sigma}_i, \mathbf{\Sigma}_j). \tag{5}$$

Equation (5) fuses the distances of the first and second statistics.

4 Proposed Approach

4.1 Model

Given an image or image set, a feature matrix $\mathbf{X}_i \in \mathbb{R}^{m_i \times d}$ can be extracted by using handcrafted features or deep features. By computing the mean and covariance matrix of $\mathbf{X}_i$, an image or image set can be modelled by a Gaussian distribution $\mathcal{N}(\mu_i, \mathbf{\Sigma}_i)$ The Mahalanobis distance between the means can be defined as:

$$d_\mu = (\mu_i - \mu_j)^T \mathbf{A}(\mu_i - \mu_j) = tr(\mathbf{AT}_{ij}), \tag{6}$$

where $\mathbf{T}_{ij} = (\mu_i - \mu_j)^T(\mu_i - \mu_j)$ and $\mathbf{A}$ is a $d \times d$ SPD matrix. When $\mathbf{A}$ is an identity matrix, the distance metric in Eq. (6) is the classical Euclidean distance. Here $\mathbf{A}$ is the distance metric we need to learn for the first-order statistics of Gaussians. For covariance matrices, the distances in Euclidean space, e.g., Euclidean distance and Mahalanobis distance cannot apply. A set of covariance matrices form a SPD manifold. Hence, the distance that measures the difference between two points on the SPD manifold can be utilized. The most widely used distance metric on SPD manifold is log-Euclidean distance. For Gaussian distribution modelling, firstly a set of covariance matrices are computed for a set of images or features (denoted as $\mathbf{\Sigma} = \{\mathbf{\Sigma}_1, \mathbf{\Sigma}_2, ..., \mathbf{\Sigma}_n\}$). Let $f : \mathit{\Sigma}_+^d \to \mathit{\Sigma}_+^r$ be a smooth mapping from original SPD manifold to a new manifold $\mathit{\Sigma}_+^r$. Thus, for a point $\mathbf{\Sigma}_i$, the mapping of tangent space from $\mathit{\Sigma}_+^d$ to $\mathit{\Sigma}_+^r$ is defined as:

$$TF(\mathbf{\Sigma}_i) : T_{\mathbf{\Sigma}_i}\mathit{\Sigma}_+^d \to T_{f(\mathbf{\Sigma}_i)}\mathit{\Sigma}_+^r, \tag{7}$$

where the mapping $TF(\mathbf{\Sigma}_i)$ is an injection and mapping f is a smooth map [7]. Thus if we can find a transformation $\mathbf{M} \in R^{d \times r}$ of point $\mathbf{\Sigma}_i$ from original tangent space $T_{\mathbf{\Sigma}_i}\mathit{\Sigma}_+^d$ to space $T_{f(\mathbf{\Sigma}_i)}\mathit{\Sigma}_+^r$, geodesic distance between $\mathbf{\Sigma}_i$, $\mathbf{\Sigma}_j$ on original SPD manifold can be represented as:

$$d_{\mathbf{\Sigma}}(\mathbf{\Sigma}_i, \mathbf{\Sigma}_j) = \left\|\mathbf{M}^T \log(\mathbf{\Sigma}_i)\mathbf{M} - \mathbf{M}^T \log(\mathbf{\Sigma}_j)\mathbf{M}\right\|_F^2, \tag{8}$$

where $\mathbf{MM^T}$ is a rank-r symmetric positive semi-definite (SPSD) matrix ensuring that the converted space is a tangent space of SPD matrices in the logarithm domain. Let $\mathbf{C} = \log(\mathbf{\Sigma})$, and $\mathbf{Q} = \mathbf{MM}^T$. We can rewrite the formulation (8) as:

$$\begin{aligned} d_{\mathbf{\Sigma}}(\mathbf{C}_i, \mathbf{C}_j) &= tr((\mathbf{C}_i - \mathbf{C}_j)^T \mathbf{Q}(\mathbf{C}_i - \mathbf{C}_j)\mathbf{Q}) \\ &= tr(\mathbf{B}(\mathbf{C}_i - \mathbf{C}_j)(\mathbf{C}_i - \mathbf{C}_j)), \end{aligned} \tag{9}$$

where $\mathbf{Q}$ is a rank-r SPSD matrix, so $\mathbf{B} = \mathbf{Q}\mathbf{Q}$ is also a rank-r SPSD matrix. We can see that metric in Eq. (9) involves the parameter $\mathbf{B}$, which will be learned for more discriminative matching or classification. If we further let $\mathbf{H}_{ij} = (\mathbf{T}_i - \mathbf{T}_j)^T(\mathbf{T}_i - \mathbf{T}_j)$, the distance in terms of the second-order statistics becomes:

$$d_{\mathbf{\Sigma}}(g_i, g_j) = tr(\mathbf{B}\mathbf{H}_{ij}). \tag{10}$$

Here we can see that the distance of covariance matrices shares similar formula with that of the means in Eq. (6). This motivates us to solve the distance metrics jointly.

Considering the difference between the first-order and second-order statistics, the weighted joint distance between two Gaussians is defined as follows:

$$d(g_i, g_j) = r d_{\mu}(g_i, g_j) + (1 - r) d_{\mathbf{\Sigma}}(g_i, g_j), \tag{11}$$

where r is a constant between 0 and 1.

When the label information is available or the side information (e.g., pairwise constraints) is given, we can get two sets of sample pairs, one set P consisting of similar sample pairs while the other set N with dissimilar ones. Motivated by geometric mean metric learning in [28], different from the traditional metric learning methods that minimize the distance over all similar pairs while enlarging that over all dissimilar pairs, the distance metrics $\mathbf{A}$ and $\mathbf{B}$ are learned by minimizing the geodesic distance of similar pairs and the interpoint geodesic distance (described by $\mathbf{A}^{-1}$ and $\mathbf{B}^{-1}$) of dissimilar ones. The joint metric learning model is formulated as follows:

$$\min\Big(\sum_{ij \in P} d(g_i, g_j) + \sum_{ij \in N} d^{-1}(g_i, g_j)\Big)\Big), \tag{12}$$

where g_i and g_j represent two Gaussians, $\sum_{ij \in P} d(g_i, g_j)$ represents the geodesic distance of similar pairs and $\sum_{ij \in N} d^{-1}(g_i, g_j)$ represent the interpoint geodesic distance of dissimilar ones. By minimizing $\sum_{ij \in P} d(g_i, g_j)$, the distance between a pair of Gaussians with similar labels is decreased, while the minimization of $\sum_{ij \in N} d^{-1}(g_i, g_j)$ attempts to enhance the difference between samples with different labels. For metric learning, a large number of sample pairs are generated firstly. However, not all sample pairs are necessary for metric learning and the importance of samples also varies greatly during the metric learning process. To this end, we embed the weight of sample pairs into the metric learning model.

$$\min \left\{ \begin{array}{l} \sum_{ij \in P} (rtr(\alpha_{ij}^{v} \mathbf{A}\mathbf{T}_{ij}) + (1 - r) tr(\alpha_{ij}^{v} \mathbf{B}\mathbf{H}_{ij})) + \\ \sum_{ij \in N} (rtr(\beta_{ij}^{v} \mathbf{A}^{-1}\mathbf{T}_{ij}) + (1 - r) tr(\beta_{ij}^{v} \mathbf{B}^{-1}\mathbf{H}_{ij})) \end{array} \right\} \tag{13}$$

$$s.t. \sum_{ij \in P} \alpha_{ij} = 1, \sum_{ij \in N} \beta_{ij} = 1, \forall ij, \alpha_{ij} \geq 0, \beta_{ij} \geq 0.$$

where α_{ij} and β_{ij} are the weights for similar pairs and dissimilar pairs, respectively.

4.2 Optimization and Algorithm

For the objective function in Eq. (13), there are four variables $\{\mathbf{A}, \mathbf{B}, \alpha, \beta\}$ to solve. Alternation minimization is used to solve the optimization problem. When $\mathbf{A}$ and $\mathbf{B}$ are fixed, we can set the derivation of Eq. (13) with respect to α and β to zero. We can get the closed-form solution to α_{ij} and β_{ij} as follows:

$$\alpha_{ij} = \frac{(rtr(\mathbf{AT}_{ij}) + (1-r)tr(\mathbf{BH}_{ij}))^{\frac{-1}{v-1}}}{\sum\limits_{ij \in P} (rtr(\mathbf{AT}_{ij}) + (1-r)tr(\mathbf{BH}_{ij}))^{\frac{-1}{v-1}}}. \tag{14}$$

$$\beta_{ij} = \frac{(rtr(\mathbf{A}^{-1}\mathbf{T}_{ij}) + (1-r)tr(\mathbf{B}^{-1}\mathbf{H}_{ij}))^{\frac{-1}{v-1}}}{\sum\limits_{ij \in N} (rtr(\mathbf{A}^{-1}\mathbf{T}_{ij}) + (1-r)tr(\mathbf{B}^{-1}\mathbf{H}_{ij}))^{\frac{-1}{v-1}}}. \tag{15}$$

Note that $tr(\mathbf{A}^{-1}\mathbf{T}_{ij})$, $tr(\mathbf{B}^{-1}\mathbf{H}_{ij})$, $tr(\mathbf{A}^{-1}\mathbf{T}_{ij})$, and $tr(\mathbf{B}^{-1}\mathbf{H}_{ij})$ are all non-negative. We can ensure that α_{ij} and β_{ij} satisfy the non-negative constraints.

When the weight vectors α and β are solved, we get the following two subproblems with respect to $\mathbf{A}$ and $\mathbf{B}$

$$f(\mathbf{A}) = \min_{\mathbf{A} \succ 0} tr(\mathbf{AP1}) + tr(\mathbf{A}^{-1}\mathbf{N1}), \tag{16}$$

$$f(\mathbf{B}) = \min_{\mathbf{B} \succ 0} tr(\mathbf{BP2}) + tr(\mathbf{B}^{-1}\mathbf{N2}), \tag{17}$$

where $\mathbf{P1} = \sum\limits_{ij \in P} \alpha_{ij}^{v}\mathbf{T}_{ij}$, $\mathbf{P2} = \sum\limits_{ij \in P} \alpha_{ij}^{v}\mathbf{H}_{ij}$, $\mathbf{N1} = \sum\limits_{ij \in N} \beta_{ij}^{v}\mathbf{T}_{ij}$, $\mathbf{N2} = \sum\limits_{ij \in N} \beta_{ij}^{v}\mathbf{H}_{ij}$. In order to compute the total loss, we defined as follows:

$$f(\mathbf{A}, \mathbf{B}) = rf(\mathbf{A}) + (1-r)f(\mathbf{B}) \tag{18}$$

$\mathbf{P1}$ and $\mathbf{P2}$ might be non-invertible or near singular, that is, $\mathbf{P1}^{-1}$ and $\mathbf{P2}^{-1}$ might not exist or be unsolvable. Following the regularization strategy in [28], a LogDet Divergence regularization is imposed on $\mathbf{A}$ to get a stable solution.

$$F(\mathbf{A}) = \min_{\mathbf{A} \succ 0} \lambda D_{ld}(\mathbf{A}, \mathbf{A}_0) + tr(\mathbf{AP1}) + tr\left(\mathbf{A}^{-1}\mathbf{N1}\right), \tag{19}$$

where $\mathbf{A}_0$ is the prior of $\mathbf{A}$, λ is regular coefficient and $D_{sld}(\mathbf{A}, \mathbf{A}_0)$ is the LogDet Divergence.

$$D_{sld}(\mathbf{A}, \mathbf{A}_0) = tr\left(\mathbf{A}\mathbf{A}_0{}^{-1}\right) + tr\left(\mathbf{A}^{-1}\mathbf{A}_0\right) - 2d. \tag{20}$$

We can rewrite the objective function of the regularized version

$$\begin{aligned} F_R(\mathbf{A}) = \min_{\mathbf{A} \succ 0} & tr\left(\mathbf{A}\left(\mathbf{P1} + \lambda\mathbf{A}_0{}^{-1}\right)\right) \\ & + tr\left(\mathbf{A}^{-1}\left(\mathbf{N1} + \lambda\mathbf{A}_0\right)\right) - 2d \end{aligned} \tag{21}$$

and the solution is

$$\mathbf{A}_R = \left(\mathbf{P1} + \lambda\mathbf{A}_0{}^{-1}\right)^{-1} \#_{1/2} \left(\mathbf{N1} + \lambda\mathbf{A}_0\right). \tag{22}$$

When the regularization parameter $\lambda = 0$, $\mathbf{A}_R = \mathbf{A}$.

From the Riccati equation we can know that the solution of this minimum problem is the midpoint of geodesic curve joining $\mathbf{P1}^{-1}$ and $\mathbf{N1}$. For the regularized version, the solution becomes the midpoint of geodesic curve joining $\left(\mathbf{P1} + \lambda\mathbf{A_0}^{-1}\right)^{-1}$ and $(\mathbf{N1} + \lambda\mathbf{A}_0)$. When we consider the weight of the distance between two positive points and that between two negative points, a weight parameter t can be introduced to balance the two distances.

$$F_w(\mathbf{A}) = \min_{\mathbf{A}\succ 0} (1-t)\,\delta_R^2\left(\mathbf{A}, \mathbf{P1}^{-1}\right) + t\delta_R^2(\mathbf{A}, \mathbf{N1}), \tag{23}$$

where δ_R denotes the Riemannian distance on SPD matrices,

$$\delta_R(\mathbf{X}, \mathbf{Y}) = \left\|\log\left(\mathbf{Y}^{-1/2}\mathbf{X}\mathbf{Y}^{-1/2}\right)\right\|_F. \tag{24}$$

It can be proved that the new objective function is still geodesic convex and thus the solution is

$$\mathbf{A} = \mathbf{P1}^{-1}\#_t\mathbf{N1} = \mathbf{P1}^{-1/2}\left(\mathbf{P1}^{1/2}\mathbf{N1}\mathbf{P1}^{1/2}\right)^t\mathbf{P1}^{-1/2}, \tag{25}$$

where t is a positive constant.

Thus, by combining regularization and weighting, we get the final solution of matrix $\mathbf{A}$

$$\mathbf{A}_{final} = \left(\mathbf{P1} + \lambda\mathbf{A_0}^{-1}\right)^{-1}\#_t(\mathbf{N1} + \lambda\mathbf{A}_0), \tag{26}$$

where $\lambda \geq 0$ and $0 \leq t \leq 1$ is the regularization parameter and weight parameter, respectively.

Similarly, we can get the solution to $\mathbf{B}$, i.e.,

$$\mathbf{B}_{final} = (\mathbf{P2} + \lambda\mathbf{A}_0^{-1})^{-1}\#_t(\mathbf{N2} + \lambda\mathbf{A}_0). \tag{27}$$

The algorithm of joint metric learning on Riemannian manifold of Gaussian distributions is summarized in Algorithm 1.

Algorithm 1. JML

Input: A set of Gaussians, $g_i, i = 1, 2, ..., n, \varepsilon = 0.001, T = 5$
Output: Distance Metric matrix $\mathbf{A}$, $\mathbf{B}$;
Step1: Initialized $\mathbf{A}$, $\mathbf{B}$ using an identify matrix;
Step2: For t =1,2,...,T, repeat
2.1 Computer α_{ij} and β_{ij} using (14), (15) ;
2.2 Computer $\mathbf{A}$ and $\mathbf{B}$ using (26), (27) ;
2.3 If $t \geq 2$ and $\left|f(\mathbf{A}, \mathbf{B})^t - f(\mathbf{A}, \mathbf{B})^{t-1}\right| < \varepsilon$ go to **Step3**
Step3: Output the matrix $\mathbf{A}$, $\mathbf{B}$.

4.3 Convergence and Complexity

For the optimization problem in Eq. (13), we use alternation minimization to solve the problem. For each subproblem with respect to $\mathbf{A}$, $\mathbf{B}$, α, β, a closed-form solution is derived. It has been shown in [19], for general convex problem, the alternating minimization approach would converge to the correct solution. We experimentally find that JML can converge fast in few iterations. The main computation burden is solving the inverse of a $d \times d$ matrix. Therefore, the time complexity is $o(d^3)$.

5 Experiments

5.1 Datasets

To ensure a broad assessment of the different approaches, four common public datasets are used to conduct comparative experiments.

ETH-80 [10] contains 3,280 high-resolution color images. We randomly select half of the data set as the training set and others as the test set. For each image is resized to 20×20. Intensity feature of the dataset is utilized in the experiment. UIUC contains 216 images and 18 categories, each category includes 12 images [14]. For the sake of extracting local features, which the size of the feature is $m_i \times 512$, each image throughs a VGG-VD16 model pre-trained on ImageNet dataset and employs the outputs from the last convolution layer as local features. We randomly select 6 images to form the training set and use the rest as the test set. YouTube Celebrities (YTC) dataset is a collection of celebrities from YouTube [9]. In the experiment, in order to divide the training and test sets, we adopt the method in [7] by randomly selecting 3 images set objects as train set and 6 image sets of the test to ensure all the images used. Flickr material dataset (FMD) [21] contains 1000 images and 10 categories [21]. We randomly select half for the training set and the other half for the test set. The feature extraction strategy is took the same as UIUC dataset.

5.2 Parameter Setting and Performance Comparison

For our method, there are three parameters: r, t, and v. In our experiments, we set r from 0 to 1 at 0.1 intervals. Respectively, to the solution of A and B with Eq. (26), Eq. (27), we set t from 0.3 to 0.8 at 0.1 intervals. Considering v is a index parameter, from the Eq. (14), in order to solve α_{ij}, β_{ij}, $v \neq 1$. In the experiment, v is set from 2 to 4, it was found that α_{ij} set to 3 is more suitable. To prevent $\mathbf{\Sigma}_i$ matrix singularity, a small positive perturbation $(0.001 \times tr(\mathbf{\Sigma}_i))$, is added to the covariance matrix the same as [7]. For fair comparison of competitive methods, we exploit the source codes provided by the authors and the parameters are empirically tuned by the original papers. For MMD, a set-based method which are directly applicable for image set classification, PCA was adopted to learn the linear subspace of each image set. We select 95% of data energy with PCA to reduce the dimension. For the linear AHISD and CHISD [2], we employ PCA to learn 98% of the data energy. While for non-linear, there are two parameters τ, the error penalty term of the SVM C, we set τ between 1 and 5 and $C = 100$ the same as [2]. MAD mainly consists of three parameters: the number of local models n_i, the number of between-class NN local models $k^{'}$ and the dimension of MDA embedding space $4l$. Parameters is tuned the same as original paper (i.e., for YTC $n_i = 9, k^{'} = 10, l = 70$) [24].

The performance comparison on four datasets, i.e., ETH-80, FMD, UIUC and YTC, is shown in Table 1. Here JML(A) means that we only learn the distance metric using the fist-order statistics while JML(B) means that the distance metrics are learned for covariances matrices. JML(A+B) means that the distance metrics for both the mean and covariance matrices are learned jointly. LEML and SPDML learn distance metric based on SPD manifold. MMD and MDA are based on nonlinear manifold assumption while AHISD and CHISD are linear subspace based methods. Compare with the state-of-the-art metric learning algorithms, our proposed JML achieve superior performance. Besides, compared with learning distance metric for the first-order and second-order statistics separately, joint metric learning boosts the performance in that it combine the complementary information of both orders.

Table 1. Accuracies of different methods on four datasets

Method	ETH-80	FMD	UIUC	YTC
MMD	85.75	60.60	62.78	69.60
MDA	87.75	63.50	67.31	64.72
AHISD(linear)	72.50	46.72	55.37	64.65
AHISD(non-linear)	72.00	46.72	55.37	64.65
CHISD(linear)	79.75	47.52	65.09	67.24
CHISD(non-linear)	72.50	63.90	65.65	68.09
SPDML-AIRM	90.75	63.42	62.00	67.50
SPDML-Stein	90.75	66.80	61.12	68.10
LEML	93.50	66.60	62.96	69.85
JML(A)	77.50	68.40	75.56	70.96
JML(B)	90.00	64.88	66.05	61.99
JML(A+B)	**100.0**	**70.13**	**78.47**	**73.76**

In order to prove to the effect of adaptive pair weights, we compare the performance of JML and JML with equal weights. The recognition accuracy showed that the adaptive weights improve the accuracy by 2.25%, 2.43%, 2.21%, and 2.96% on four datasets, which verifies the effectiveness of adaptive weight learning (Table 2).

Table 2. Compare equal weight and adaptive pair weights on four datasets

Method	ETH-80	FMD	UIUC	YTC
Equal weight JML	0.975	67.77	76.26	70.92
Adaptive weight JML	100	70.13	78.47	73.76

6 Conclusions and Future Work

In this paper, we proposed a joint metric learning (JML) model for global Gaussian distributions. The distance between Gaussians are defined as the sum of the sum of the Mahalanobis distance of the first-order statistics and the log-Euclidean distance (LED) of the second order statistics. JML effectively combines the information of the means and covariance matrices by joint metric learning and embeds the weights of Gaussian pairs into the learning model. Experiments on video based face recognition, object recognition, and material classification show that our proposed JML achieves superior performance compared with the state-of-the-art metric learning algorithms. In the future, we will extend JML to Gaussian mixture models.

Acknowledgements. This work was supported by the National Natural Science Foundation of China under Grants 61502332, 61876127 and 61732011, Natural Science Foundation of Tianjin Under Grants 17JCZDJC30800, Key Scientific and Technological Support Projects of Tianjin Key R&D Program 18YFZCGX00390 and 18YFZCGX00680.

References

1. Calvo, M., Oller, J.M.: A distance between multivariate normal distributions based in an embedding into the Siegel group (1990). https://doi.org/10.1016/0047-259X(90)90026-E
2. Cevikalp, H., Triggs, B.: Face recognition based on image sets. In: CVPR, pp. 2567–2573 (2010). https://doi.org/10.1109/CVPR.2010.5539965
3. Gong, L., Wang, T., Liu, F.: Shape of Gaussians as feature descriptors. In: CVPR, pp. 2366–2371 (2009). https://doi.org/10.1109/CVPR.2009.5206506
4. Harandi, M., Salzmann, M., Hartley, R.: Dimensionality reduction on spd manifolds: the emergence of geometry-aware methods. TPAMI (2017). https://doi.org/10.1109/TPAMI.2017.2655048
5. Harandi, M.T., Sanderson, C., Hartley, R., Lovell, B.C.: Sparse coding and dictionary learning for symmetric positive definite matrices: a kernel approach. In: Fitzgibbon, A., Lazebnik, S., Perona, P., Sato, Y., Schmid, C. (eds.) ECCV 2012. LNCS, pp. 216–229. Springer, Heidelberg (2012). https://doi.org/10.1007/978-3-642-33709-3_16
6. Huang, Z., Wang, R., Shan, S., Chen, X.: Projection metric learning on Grassmann manifold with application to video based face recognition. In: CVPR, pp. 140–149 (2015). https://doi.org/10.1109/CVPR.2015.7298609
7. Huang, Z., Wang, R., Shan, S., Li, X., Chen, X.: Log-Euclidean metric learning on symmetric positive definite manifold with application to image set classification. In: ICML, pp. 720–729 (2015)
8. Jegou, H., Perronnin, F., Douze, M., Sánchez, J., Perez, P., Schmid, C.: Aggregating local image descriptors into compact codes. TPAMI **34**(9), 1704–1716 (2012). https://doi.org/10.1109/tpami.2011.235
9. Kim, M., Kumar, S., Pavlovic, V., Rowley, H.: Face tracking and recognition with visual constraints in real-world videos. In: CVPR, pp. 1–8 (2008). https://doi.org/10.1109/CVPR.2008.4587572
10. Leibe, B., Schiele, B.: Analyzing appearance and contour based methods for object categorization. In: CVPR, vol. 2, pp. 402–409 (2003). https://doi.org/10.1109/CVPR.2003.1211497
11. Li, P., Wang, Q., Zeng, H., Zhang, L.: Local log-Euclidean multivariate Gaussian descriptor and its application to image classification. TPAMI **39**(4), 803–817 (2017). https://doi.org/10.1109/TPAMI.2016.2560816

12. Li, P., Wang, Q., Zhang, L.: A novel earth mover's distance methodology for image matching with Gaussian mixture models. In: ICCV, pp. 1689–1696 (2013). https://doi.org/10.1109/ICCV.2013.212
13. Li, P., Zeng, H., Wang, Q., Shiu, S.C., Zhang, L.: High-order local pooling and encoding Gaussians over a dictionary of Gaussians. TIP **26**(7), 3372–3384 (2017). https://doi.org/10.1109/TIP.2017.2695884
14. Liao, Z., Rock, J., Wang, Y., Forsyth, D.: Non-parametric filtering for geometric detail extraction and material representation. In: CVPR, June 2013. https://doi.org/10.1109/CVPR.2013.129
15. Lovri, M., Min-Oo, M., Ruh, E.A.: Multivariate normal distributions parametrized as a riemannian symmetric space. JMVA **74**(1), 36–48 (2000). https://doi.org/10.1006/jmva.1999.1853
16. Matsukawa, T., Okabe, T., Suzuki, E., Sato, Y.: Hierarchical Gaussian descriptor for person re-identification. In: CVPR, pp. 1363–1372 (2016). https://doi.org/10.1109/CVPR.2016.152
17. Nakayama, H., Harada, T., Kuniyoshi, Y.: Global Gaussian approach for scene categorization using information geometry. In: CVPR, pp. 2336–2343 (2010). https://doi.org/10.1109/CVPR.2010.5539921
18. Nchez, J., Perronnin, F., Mensink, T., Verbeek, J.: Image classification with the fisher vector: theory and practice. IJCV **105**(3), 222–245 (2013). https://doi.org/10.1007/s11263-013-0636-x
19. Niesen, U., Shah, D., Wornell, G.W.: Adaptive alternating minimization algorithms. TIT **55**(3), 1423–1429 (2008). https://doi.org/10.1109/tit.2008.2011442
20. Serra, G., Grana, C., Manfredi, M., Cucchiara, R.: Gold: Gaussians of local descriptors for image representation. CVIU **134**, 22–32 (2015). https://doi.org/10.1016/j.cviu.2015.01.005
21. Sharan, L., Rosenholtz, R., Adelson, E.H.: Material perception: what can you see in a brief glance? J. Vis. **9**(8), 784 (2009)
22. Wang, J., Yang, J., Yu, K., Lv, F., Huang, T., Gong, Y.: Locality-constrained linear coding for image classification. In: CVPR, pp. 3360–3367 (2010). https://doi.org/10.1109/CVPR.2010.5540018
23. Wang, Q., Li, P., Zhang, L., Zuo, W.: Towards effective codebookless model for image classification. PR **59**(C), 63–71 (2016). https://doi.org/10.1016/j.patcog.2016.03.004
24. Wang, R., Chen, X.: Manifold discriminant analysis. In: CVPR, pp. 429–436 (2009). https://doi.org/10.1109/CVPRW.2009.5206850
25. Wang, W., Wang, R., Huang, Z., Shan, S., Chen, X.: Discriminant analysis on Riemannian Manifold of Gaussian distributions for face recognition with image sets. TIP **27**(1), 151–163 (2018). https://doi.org/10.1109/TIP.2017.2746993
26. Wang, W., Wang, R., Huang, Z., Shan, S., Chen, X.: Discriminant analysis on Riemannian Manifold of Gaussian distributions for face recognition with image sets. In: CVPR, pp. 2048–2057 (2015). https://doi.org/10.1109/CVPR.2015.7298816
27. Wang, W., Wang, R., Shan, S., Chen, X.: Discriminative covariance oriented representation learning for face recognition with image sets. In: CVPR, pp. 5599–5608 (2017). https://doi.org/10.1109/CVPR.2017.609
28. Zadeh, P.H., Hosseini, R., Sra, S.: Geometric mean metric learning. In: ICML, pp. 2464–2471 (2016)
29. Zhou, X., Cui, N., Li, Z., Liang, F., Huang, T.S.: Hierarchical Gaussianization for image classification. In: ICCV, pp. 1971–1977 (2009). https://doi.org/10.1109/ICCV.2009.5459435
30. Zhou, X., Yu, K., Zhang, T., Huang, T.S.: Image classification using super-vector coding of local image descriptors. In: Daniilidis, K., Maragos, P., Paragios, N. (eds.) ECCV 2010. LNCS, vol. 6315, pp. 141–154. Springer, Heidelberg (2010). https://doi.org/10.1007/978-3-642-15555-0_11

Multi-task Sparse Regression Metric Learning for Heterogeneous Classification

Haotian Wu[1], Bin Zhou[2], Pengfei Zhu[1](✉), Qinghua Hu[1], and Hong Shi[1]

[1] College of Intelligence and Computing, Tianjin University, Tianjin 300350, China
{wuhaotian,zhupengfei,huqinghua,serena}@tju.edu.cn

[2] National Key Laboratory of Science and Technology on Aerospace Automatic Control Institute, Beijing 100854, China

Abstract. With the ubiquitous usage of digital devices, social networks and industrial sensors, heterogeneous data explosively increase. Metric learning can boost the classification performance via jointly learning a set of distance metrics from heterogeneous data. The metric learning algorithms are affected by the noisy doublets, i.e., the similar and dissimilar sample pairs. It is also a challenging issue to balance commonality and individuality for multi-view metric learning. To address the above issues, in this paper, we propose a novel multi-task group sparse regression metric learning (MT-SRML) for heterogeneous classification. Metric learning is formulated as sparse regression problem. The group sparse regularization on the repression coefficients of the doublets can restrain the effect of the noisy sample pairs jointly for multiple views. Experiments on heterogeneous data show that the proposed MT-SRML outperforms the state-of-the art metric learning algorithms in terms of both accuracy and efficiency.

Keywords: Heterogeneous data · Metric learning · Sparse regression · Multi-task learning

1 Introduction

With the development of digital devices, industrial sensors and the ubiquitous of social networks, there are explosive growth of heterogeneous data from different sources. In the field of information technology, a web page can be described either by the text information in the web page or by the image information attached to the anchor chain of the web page. In computer vision, images are often described with different types of descriptors (such as HOG [4], SIFT [17] and LBP [21]). As shown in Fig. 1, different types of local descriptors, including LBP, GIST and EDH, are extracted for an image labeled as a bird. Heterogeneous data contain complementary information, which can be combined together to boost the recognition or clustering performance. To match heterogeneous data, great efforts have been devoted to learn a unified representation of the information in different sources so we can use heterogeneous data more accurately and efficiently [1,3]. For multi-view learning, the key challenge is how to balance the

I. V. Tetko et al. (Eds.): ICANN 2019, LNCS 11728, pp. 543–553, 2019.
https://doi.org/10.1007/978-3-030-30484-3_44

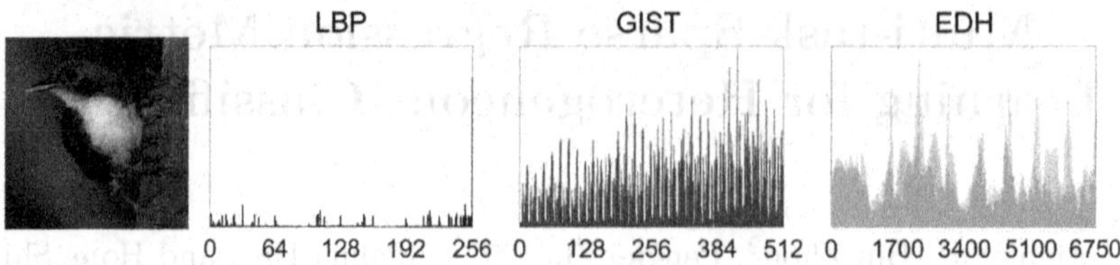

Fig. 1. An example of multi-view learning

commonality and individuality of different views so that the multi-view information can be well fused.

Distance metric learning aims to learn a distance metric to measure the difference between two samples. Compared with the distance metric learning that defines generalized or task-driven metrics, metric learning exploits the label information to learn a discriminative distance metric, which can boost the classification and regression performance. Metric learning has been widely applied in real-world applications including face recognition [11], face identification [8], image classification [11] and person re-identification [30]. Eric P. Xing proposed a global distance metric learning algorithm (PGDM) [29] based on probability by solving a constrained convex problem. Hu [10] proposed a multi-view deep metric learning (MvDML) approach by jointly learning an optimal combination of multiple distance metrics on multi-view representations.

Compared with traditional single-view data, heterogeneous data contain more information which helps improve the classification or regression performances. Existing metric learning methods, such as ITML (Information-Theoretic Metric Learning) and GMML (Geometric Mean Metric Learning), achieve good performance in traditional single view learning tasks. However, they fail to jointly exploit the complementary information from the heterogeneous data if they are directly applied to multi-view tasks.

In this paper, we propose a novel multi-task group sparse regression metric learning (MT-SRML) for heterogeneous classification. We use a 2-degree polynomial kernel for sample pairs in each tasks to get the sample pair relationships in the feature space. Inspired by multi-task dictionary learning, MT-SRML jointly learns distance metrics from heterogeneous data and imposes a group sparse regularization item on the coefficient vectors. The proposed model aims to fuse the discriminative capabilities of different views to help improve the efficiency and accuracy of classification results. Experiments on four benchmark datasets show that MT-SRML outperforms the state-of-the art metric learning algorithms, and achieves much better performance than single view learning.

The remainder of this paper is organized as follows. In Sect. 2, we give a brief review of metric learning and sparse regression. The proposed algorithm is described in Sect. 3. Data sets used in the experiments and the results are presented in Sect. 4. Conclusion are summarized in Sect. 5.

2 Related Work

2.1 Metric Learning

Metric learning aims to learn a distance function to improve the performance in the tasks of classification and regression. Good distance metrics are crucial to many computer vision tasks, such as image classification, face recognition and person re-identification tasks. In this section, we give a brief review of traditional metric learning approaches.

Early metric learning approaches use Euclidean distance to measure relationships of sample pairs. These methods only consider the local attributes of samples and ignore the discriminative capabilities of different sample features. The Mahalanobis distance overcomes the incompatibility of the traditional methods to the structure of samples. It considers the correlation between the different dimensional features of the samples and accomplishes the distance metric learning by calculating the covariance matrix between the samples. Most metric learning methods are based on Mahalanobis distance. In [27], the author proposed the LMNN (Large Margin Nearest Neighbor) method in 2009 to improve the performance of kNN (k-Nearest Neighbor) by maximizing the marginal distances of different categories. The ITML (Information-Theoretic Metric Learning) method proposed in [5] aims to minimize the relative entropy between two multivariate Gaussian distribution, leading to a Bregman optimization problem. The work in [19] presents a multiple kernel learning technique for integrating heterogeneous data into a single, unified similarity space to learn a holistic similarity measure on multiple modalities of data. Method HMML (Heterogeneous Multi-Metric Learning) [33] proposes a multiple-metric learning algorithm to learn jointly a set of optimal homogenous/heterogeneous metrics in order to fuse the data collected from multiple sensors for classification. The work in [28] raised a general framework of multi-modal distance metric learning based on the multi-wing harmonium model in which an optimal distance metric can be learned under proper supervision. In [24], Quadrianto formulated an objective function that express the intuitive concept that matching samples are mapped closely together in the output space. It addressed the problem of metric learning for multi-view data, namely the construction of embedding projections from data in different representations into a shared feature space.

Due to the impact of deep learning on traditional metric learning methods, many approaches have been extended to deep metric learning methods. [9] proposed a deep metric learning method using triplet network, which aims to learn useful representations by distance comparisons. In person re-identification field, [31] uses a "siamese" deep neural network to jointly learn different features and metric in a unified framework.

2.2 Sparse Regression

In statistics, the problem of regression is that of learning a function that allows to estimate a certain quantity of interest from several observed variables, known

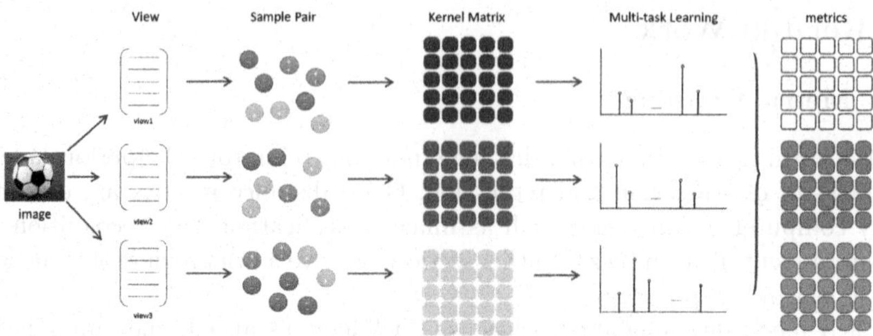

Fig. 2. The flowchart of multi-task sparse regression metric learning model.

as covariates, features or independent variables. However, in many modern applications, under the high-dimension-low-sample-size settings, heterogeneous data is sometimes largely redundant, making it hard to find the linear function. Dictionary learning aims to find the proper representation of data sets by means of reduced dimensionality subspaces, which can help relieve the pressure of learning tasks and reduce the involved computation and storage costs. One of the earliest dictionary learning works appeared for image representation. In 1997, [22] proposed a maximum likelihood (ML) dictionary learning method for natural images under the sparse approximation assumption, which is called the sparse coding. In [2], the author proposed an algorithm base on dictionary learning called KSVD, which learns an over-complete dictionary from a training set of natural image patches for sparse coding. [23] proposed a joint learning and dictionary construction method with consideration of the linear classifier performance and applied the method to object categorization and FR.

During the last few years, sparsity has become a general principle for modeling, and sparse coding has been successfully applied to tasks such as image and video denoising, inpainting, demosaicing, super-resolution [7] and segmentation [18]. Donoho [6] obtains parallel results in a general setting, where the dictionary can arise from two or several bases, frames, or even less structured systems. Jain [12] rised a novel framework based on sparse regression to automatically trim the redundant parameters, dealing with Blood Pressure (BP) monitoring problems. In [13], Kowalski proposed sparse expansion methods that explicitly introduce a notion of structured sparsity and combined this approach with multilayered signal expansion approaches, which aim at decomposing signals as sums of significantly different components.

3 Multi-task Sparse Regression Metric Learning

In this section, we propose a multi-task sparse regression metric learning model and algorithm.

3.1 Sample Pair Kernel

Suppose we have a heterogeneous training set $X = [X_1^m, ..., X_J^m]$, where $m = 1, ..., M$ denotes each view/feature of the data and $j = 1, ..., J$ denotes each category of the data. $x_i \in X$ represents the ith training sample, and scalar y_i represents the class label of x_i. We extract two samples from the training set and form a sample pair (x_i, x_j), and we assign a label h to this doublet as follows: $h = -1$ if $y_i = y_j$ and $h = 1$ if $y_i \neq y_j$. In our experiments, we generate sample pairs according to their categories and Euclidean distances between them. Then we use a 2-degree polynomial kernel method for the selected sample pairs. Let u_i denote the sample pair (x_{i1}, x_{i2}). The 2-degree polynomial kernel is defined as:

$$\begin{aligned} &\mathbf{K}(u_i, u_j) \\ &= tr\left((x_{i1} - x_{i2})(x_{i1} - x_{i2})^T (x_{j1} - x_{j2})(x_{j1} - x_{j2})^T\right) \\ &= \left((x_{i1} - x_{i2})^T (x_{j1} - x_{j2})\right)^2 \end{aligned} \tag{1}$$

We record the labels of all the doublets as $\mathbf{z}$.

3.2 Model and Optimization

The flowchart of the proposed metric learning model is given in Fig. 2. For an image, different types of feature descriptors can be extracted to construct a multi-view learning task. Then sample pairs are generated from each view and kernel matrices are calculated by the predefined sample pair kernels. A multi-task sparse regression problem is solved and the regression coefficients are obtained for all views. Finally, a set of distance metrics for each view are got. The multi-task sparse regression metric learning model is formulated as follows:

$$\begin{aligned} &\min \textstyle\sum_{i=1}^{m} \|\mathbf{z} - \mathbf{a}_i\mathbf{K}_i\|_2^2 + \lambda R(\mathbf{a}_1, ..., \mathbf{a}_i, ..., \mathbf{a}_m) \\ &s.t.\mathrm{i} = 1, 2, ..., \mathrm{M}. \end{aligned} \tag{2}$$

Here $\mathbf{z}$ represents the decision space information of doublets samples and we suppose (1) generated N doublets samples. $\mathbf{a_i}$ is the reconstruction coefficient vectors associated with each view of the heterogeneous data and $\mathrm{i} = 1, 2, ..., \mathrm{M}$. K is the 2-degree polynomial kernel for doublets sample pairs calculated by (1). λ is a positive constant and R is the joint regularization item imposed on $\mathbf{a_i}$. Our model is formulated as the solution to the following problem of multi-task sparse regression metric learning with ℓ_2 mixed-norm regularization, then we rewrite (2) as:

$$\begin{aligned} &\min \textstyle\sum_{i=1}^{m} \|\mathbf{z} - \mathbf{a}_i\mathbf{K}_i\|_2^2 + \lambda \sum\limits_{n=1}^{N} \|\mathbf{a}^n\|_2 \\ &s.t.\mathrm{i} = 1, 2, ..., \mathrm{M}. \end{aligned} \tag{3}$$

As for model optimization, we chose the popularly applied Accelerated Proximal Gradient (APG) model [20] to efficiently solve problem (3). The proposed APG algorithm aims to learn the coefficient vector $\mathbf{a}$ by updating a weight matrix sequence $\hat{A}_t = a_{m,t}^n$ and an aggregation matrix sequence $\hat{V}_t = v_{m,t}^n$ where $t \geq 1$.

For the generalized gradient mapping step, given the current matrix $\hat{V}_t$, we update $\hat{A}_t$ according to the result in [25] as follows:

$$\begin{aligned} \hat{a}_{m,t+1} &= \hat{v}_{m,t} - \eta \nabla_{m,t}, \quad m = 1, ..., M \\ \hat{a}^n_{t+1} &= \left[1 - \frac{\lambda\eta}{\left\|\hat{a}^n_{t+1}\right\|_2}\right]_+ \hat{a}^n_{t+1}, \quad n = 1, ..., N \end{aligned} \tag{4}$$

where $\nabla_{m,t} = -\mathbf{z} + \mathbf{K}_m \hat{v}_{m,t}$, η is the step size parameter which is set to 0.002, and $[\cdot]_+ = \max(\cdot, 0)$.

For the aggregation step, we construct a linear combination of $\hat{A}_t$ and $\hat{A}_{t+1}$ to update $\hat{V}_{t+1}$ as follows:

$$\hat{V}_{t+1} = \hat{A}_{t+1} + \tfrac{\alpha_{t+1}(1-\alpha_t)}{\alpha_t}(\hat{A}_{t+1} - \hat{A}_t) \tag{5}$$

where the sequence $\{\alpha_t\}$ is set to $\alpha = 2/(t+2)$ [26].

3.3 Metric Learning and Classification

After the above steps, we aim to learn the discriminative matrix $\mathbf{D}$ for Mahalanobis distance. Define $\mathbf{T}_i = (x_{i1} - x_{i2})(x_{i1} - x_{i2})^T$, then the metric learning can be formulated as follows:

$$\mathbf{D}_m = \textstyle\sum_{i=1}^N a_m \mathbf{T}_i, \quad m = 1, ..., M \tag{6}$$

Due to the particularity of heterogeneous data, we need to jointly consider the influence of each view/feature. We define the weights that measure the confidence of different views as $1/m$. We calculate the Mahalanobis distance of each view by the discriminative matrix $\mathbf{D}$. Then we combine the distance matrix calculated from each view and get a final distance matrix.

The details of our method MT-SRML are given in Algorithm 1.

4 Experiments

To evaluate the effectiveness of our proposed MT-SRML method, we apply it to four heterogeneous data and compare with existing state-of-the-art methods. The details of our experiments are as follows.

4.1 Datasets

The heterogeneous data employed are as follows:

handwritten:[1] This dataset contains 2000 images of 10 categories from 0 to 9. It contains 6 types of descriptors exacted: Pix, Fou, Fac, ZER, KAR and MOR.

[1] https://archive.ics.uci.edu/ml/datasets/Multiple+Features.

Algorithm 1. The algorithms of our proposed MT-SRML

Require:

Generate sample pairs (x_{i1}, x_{i2}),$i = 1, 2, ..., N$. and kernel $\mathbf{K}$

Compute sample relation $\mathbf{z}$.

Initialization: Properly initialize $\hat{v}_{m,0}$ and $\hat{a}_{m,0}$. Set $\alpha_0 = 1$, $t \leftarrow 0$ and $\eta \leftarrow 0.002$

repeat:

$\quad \hat{a}_{m,t+1} = \hat{v}_{m,t} - \eta \nabla_{m,t}$

$\quad \hat{a}^n_{t+1} = \left[1 - \frac{\lambda\eta}{\|\hat{a}^n_{t+1}\|_2}\right]_+ \hat{a}^n_{t+1}, \quad n = 1, ..., N$

$\quad \alpha_{t+1} = \frac{2}{t+2}$

$\quad \hat{V}_{t+1} = \hat{A}_{t+1} + \frac{\alpha_{t+1}(1-\alpha_t)}{\alpha_t}(\hat{A}_{t+1} - \hat{A}_t)$

$\quad t \leftarrow t + 1$

until convergence

Ensure:

$\mathbf{D}_m = \sum_{i=1}^{N} a_m \mathbf{T}_i, \quad m = 1, ..., M$

Table 1. Comparison with metric learning methods on heterogeneous data

Method	handwritten	Caltech101	MSRA	football
kNN	0.941 ± 0.015	0.882 ± 0.012	0.700 ± 0.092	0.631 ± 0.077
ITML	0.948 ± 0.013	0.915 ± 0.016	0.769 ± 0.057	0.580 ± 0.078
LMNN	0.922 ± 0.020	0.830 ± 0.061	0.767 ± 0.098	0.416 ± 0.053
LDML	0.944 ± 0.012	0.882 ± 0.012	0.700 ± 0.092	0.627 ± 0.078
GMML	0.939 ± 0.011	0.881 ± 0.013	0.702 ± 0.095	0.651 ± 0.070
HMML	0.927 ± 0.013	0.921 ± 0.013	0.798 ± 0.044	0.522 ± 0.093
EMGMML	0.839 ± 0.012	0.919 ± 0.007	0.802 ± 0.030	0.702 ± 0.088
Ours	$\mathbf{0.983 \pm 0.006}$	$\mathbf{0.925 \pm 0.010}$	$\mathbf{0.905 \pm 0.050}$	$\mathbf{0.864 \pm 0.034}$

MSRA: [16] This dataset has 210 images labeled with 7 classes: tree, building, airplane, cow, face, car and bicycle. There are 6 types of descriptors exacted: CENT, CMT, GIST, HOG, LBP and SIFT.

football:[2] This dataset contains 248 football players on Twitter labeled with 20 communities, which means 20 categories. There are 6 views describing relationships between two users: follows, followed by, mentions, mentioned by, retweets and retweeted by.

Caltech101-7: [14] This dataset is a subset of Caltech101. It contains 7 classes with 1474 images: faces, motorbikes, dollar-bill, garfield, snoopy, stop-sign, and windsor-chair. There are 6 features used in this dataset: Gabor, WM, CENTRIST, HOG, GIST and LBP.

[2] http://mlg.ucd.ie/aggregation/index.html.

4.2 Comparison Methods

We compared our method with state-of-the-art metric learning methods. The details of the methods are as follows:

kNN (k-nearest neighbor classification): kNN completes classification tasks by measuring the distance between different eigenvalues. For each feature, we use Euclidean distance to distinguish different categories.

ITML (Information-Theoretic Metric Learning) [5]: This method learns a Mahalanobis distance by formulating the problem as that of minimizing the differential relative entropy between two multivariate Gaussians under constraints on the distance function.

LMNN (Large Margin Nearest Neighbors) [27]: This method learns Mahalanobis metric with the goal that the k-nearest neighbors always belong to the same class while examples from different classes are separated by a large margin.

LDML (Logistic Discriminant Metric Learning) [8]: This method propose a logistic discriminant approach which learns the metric from a set of labelled image pairs.

HMML (Heterogeneous Multi-Metric Learning) [33]: This method learns an optimal heterogeneous metric to improve the classification performance.

GMML (Geometric Mean Metric Learning) [32]: The method learns a Euclidean metric by formulating it as a surprisingly simple optimization problem.

EMGMML (Efficient Multi-modal Geometric Mean Metric Learning) [15]: The method learns a distinctive distance metric for each view by minimizing the distance between similar pairs while maximizing the distance between dissimilar pairs.

4.3 Experimental Analysis

Due to the particularity of heterogeneous data, we first conduct our method on every feature of four datasets. As shown in Table 2, the first six rows represent 6 different features of our datasets while the last row shows the result of our

Table 2. Comparison on each feature of heterogeneous datasets

Feature	football	handwritten	MSRA	Caltech101
1	0.814	0.975	0.143	0.733
2	0.747	0.768	0.643	0.829
3	0.814	0.778	0.833	0.829
4	0.651	0.560	0.738	0.959
5	0.628	0.910	0.738	0.860
6	0.512	0.583	0.452	0.949
All	**0.864**	**0.983**	**0.905**	**0.971**

method on the entirety heterogeneous data. The result shows that our jointly learning method achieves a remarkable effect on heterogeneous data.

As shown in Table 1, we compared our method with other 7 multi-view metric learning methods. Among these approaches, HMML (Heterogeneous Multi-Metric Learning) and EMGMML (Efficient Multi-modal Geometric Mean Metric Learning) are designed for heterogeneous data. As for the other 5 approaches, we preprocess the heterogeneous data in an unified method. We combine each feature of the heterogeneous data for these single-view metric learning methods as input. We can see from Table 1 that our method outperforms all the comparisons on these four heterogeneous datasets which proves our MT-SRML method is more appropriate than the other method when dealing with heterogeneous data.

5 Conclusions

In this paper, we proposed a novel multi-task sparse regression metric learning (MT-SRML), which aims to jointly learn distance metrics from heterogeneous data. Metric learning is formulated as a sample pair regression task. A two-degree polynomial kernels is introduced to measure the relation of sample pairs. Metric learning for heterogeneous data is modelled as a multi-task sparse regression problem. The proposed model jointly learns a set of distance metrics from heterogeneous data to fuse the discriminative capabilities of different views to help improve the efficiency and accuracy of classification. Experiments on four heterogeneous datasets validated the superiority of the proposed model to the state-of-the-art metric learning algorithms.

Acknowledgements. This work was supported by the National Natural Science Foundation of China under Grants 61502332, 61876127 and 61732011, Natural Science Foundation of Tianjin Under Grants 17JCZDJC30800, Key Scientific and Technological Support Projects of Tianjin Key R&D Program 18YFZCGX00390 and 18YFZCGX00680.

References

1. Abiteboul, S., Cluet, S., Milo, T.: Correspondence and translation for heterogeneous data. In: Afrati, F., Kolaitis, P. (eds.) ICDT 1997. LNCS, vol. 1186, pp. 351–363. Springer, Heidelberg (1997). https://doi.org/10.1007/3-540-62222-5_56. https://doi.org/10.1016/s0304-3975(01)00128-1
2. Aharon, M., Elad, M., Bruckstein, A.: K-SVD: an algorithm for designing overcomplete dictionaries for sparse representation. IEEE Trans. Signal Process. **54**(11), 4311–4322 (2006). https://doi.org/10.1109/TSP.2006.881199
3. Castano, S., De Antonellis, V., Sabrina, D.C.D.V.: Global viewing of heterogeneous data sources. IEEE Trans. Knowl. Data Eng. **13**(2), 277–297 (2002). https://doi.org/10.1109/69.917566
4. Dalal, N.: Histgrams of oriented gradients for human detection. In: Proceedings of CVPR (2005). https://doi.org/10.1109/ISISE.2008.308

5. Davis, J.V., Kulis, B., Jain, P., Sra, S., Dhillon, I.S.: Information-theoretic metric learning. In: ICML, pp. 209–216 (2007). https://doi.org/10.1145/1273496.1273523
6. Donoho, D.L., Michael, E.: Optimally sparse representation in general (nonorthogonal) dictionaries via l1 minimization. Proc. Natl. Acad. Sci. U.S.A. **100**(5), 2197–2202 (2003). https://doi.org/10.1073/pnas.0437847100
7. Elad, M., Aharon, M.: Image denoising via sparse and redundant representations over learned dictionaries. IEEE Trans. Image Process. **15**(12), 3736–3745 (2006). https://doi.org/10.1109/TIP.2006.881969
8. Guillaumin, M., Verbeek, J., Schmid, C.: Is that you? Metric learning approaches for face identification. In: IEEE International Conference on Computer Vision, pp. 498–505 (2009). https://doi.org/10.1109/ICCV.2009.5459197
9. Hoffer, E., Ailon, N.: Deep metric learning using triplet network. In: Feragen, A., Pelillo, M., Loog, M. (eds.) SIMBAD 2015. LNCS, vol. 9370, pp. 84–92. Springer, Cham (2015). https://doi.org/10.1007/978-3-319-24261-3_7
10. Hu, J., Lu, J., Tan, Y.P.: Sharable and individual multi-view metric learning. IEEE Trans. Pattern Anal. Mach. Intell. **PP**(99), 1 (2017). https://doi.org/10.1109/TPAMI.2017.2749576
11. Huang, Z., Wang, R., Shan, S., Chen, X.: Projection metric learning on Grassmann manifold with application to video based face recognition. In: Computer Vision and Pattern Recognition, pp. 140–149 (2015). https://doi.org/10.1109/TPAMI.2017.2749576
12. Jain, M., Kumar, N., Deb, S., Majumdar, A.: A sparse regression based approach for cuff-less blood pressure measurement. In: IEEE International Conference on Acoustics, Speech and Signal Processing, pp. 789–793 (2016). https://doi.org/10.1109/ICASSP.2016.7471783
13. Kowalski, M.: Sparse regression using mixed norms. Appl. Comput. Harmonic Anal. **27**(3), 303–324 (2009). https://doi.org/10.1016/j.acha.2009.05.006
14. Li, F.F., Fergus, R., Perona, P.: Learning generative visual models from few training examples: an incremental Bayesian approach tested on 101 object categories. In: Conference on Computer Vision and Pattern Recognition Workshop, CVPRW 2004, p. 178 (2004). https://doi.org/10.1109/CVPR.2004.109
15. Liang, J., Hu, Q., Zhu, P., Wang, W.: Efficient multi-modal geometric mean metric learning. Pattern Recogn. **75**, 188–198 (2017). https://doi.org/10.1016/j.patcog.2017.02.032
16. Liu, T., et al.: Learning to detect a salient object. IEEE T-PAMI **33**(2), 353–367 (2010). https://doi.org/10.1109/TPAMI.2010.70
17. Lowe, D.G.: Object recognition from local scale-invariant features. In: ICCV, p. 1150 (1999). https://doi.org/10.1109/ICCV.1999.790410
18. Mairal, J., Bach, F., Ponce, J., Sapiro, G., Zisserman, A.: Discriminative learned dictionaries for local image analysis. In: IEEE Conference on Computer Vision and Pattern Recognition, CVPR 2008, pp. 1–8 (2008). https://doi.org/10.1109/CVPR.2008.4587652
19. McFee, B., Lanckriet, G.: Learning multi-modal similarity. J. Mach. Learn. Res. **12**, 491–523 (2011). https://doi.org/10.1049/iet-cta.2010.0271
20. Nesterov, Y.: Gradient methods for minimizing composite objective function. Core Discuss. Pap. **140**(1), 125–161 (2007). https://doi.org/10.1007/s10107-012-0629-5
21. Ojala, T., Harwood, I.: A comparative study of texture measures with classification based on feature distributions. Pattern Recogn. **29**(1), 51–59 (1996). https://doi.org/10.1016/0031-3203(95)00067-4

22. Olshausen, B.A., Field, D.J.: Sparse coding with an overcomplete basis set: a strategy employed by V1? Vision Res. **37**(23), 3311–3325 (1997). https://doi.org/10.1016/s0042-6989(97)00169-7
23. Pham, D.S., Venkatesh, S.: Joint learning and dictionary construction for pattern recognition. In: IEEE Conference on Computer Vision and Pattern Recognition, CVPR 2008, pp. 1–8 (2008). https://doi.org/10.1109/CVPR.2008.4587408
24. Quadrianto, N., Lampert, H.C.: Learning multi-view neighborhood preserving projections. In: International Conference on Machine Learning, ICML 2011, Bellevue, Washington, USA, 28 June–July 2011, pp. 425–432 (2011). https://doi.org/10.1145/2733373.2806349
25. Schmidt, M.W., Berg, E.V.D., Friedlander, M.P., Murphy, K.P.: Optimizing costly functions with simple constraints: a limited-memory projected quasi-Newton algorithm. Hansen Int. **5**(2–3), 355–357 (2009). https://doi.org/10.1080/00218460008029313
26. Tseng, P.: On accelerated proximal gradient methods for convex-concave optimization. SIAM J. Optim. (2008). https://doi.org/10.4236/ns.2011.31012
27. Weinberger, K.Q., Saul, L.K.: Distance metric learning for large margin nearest neighbor classification. J. Mach. Learn. Res. **10**, 207–244 (2009). https://doi.org/10.1007/s10845-008-0108-2
28. Xie, P., Xing, E.P.: Multi-modal distance metric learning. In: International Joint Conference on Artificial Intelligence, pp. 1806–1812 (2013). https://doi.org/10.3233/IDA-163196
29. Xing, E.P., Ng, A.Y., Jordan, M.I., Russell, S.: Distance metric learning, with application to clustering with side-information. In: International Conference on Neural Information Processing Systems, pp. 521–528 (2002). https://doi.org/10.1063/1.4908605
30. Xiong, F., Gou, M., Camps, O., Sznaier, M.: Person re-identification using kernel-based metric learning methods. In: Fleet, D., Pajdla, T., Schiele, B., Tuytelaars, T. (eds.) ECCV 2014. LNCS, vol. 8695, pp. 1–16. Springer, Cham (2014). https://doi.org/10.1007/978-3-319-10584-0_1
31. Yi, D., Lei, Z., Liao, S., Li, S.Z.: Deep metric learning for person re-identification, pp. 34–39 (2014). https://doi.org/10.1109/ICPR.2014.16
32. Zadeh, P., Hosseini, R., Sra, S.: Geometric mean metric learning. In: ICML, pp. 2464–2471 (2016)
33. Zhang, H., Huang, T.S., Nasrabadi, N.M., Zhang, Y.: Heterogeneous multi-metric learning for multi-sensor fusion. In: FUSION, pp. 1–8 (2011)

Fast Approximate Geodesics for Deep Generative Models

Nutan Chen[1(✉)], Francesco Ferroni[2], Alexej Klushyn[1], Alexandros Paraschos[1], Justin Bayer[1], and Patrick van der Smagt[1]

[1] Machine Learning Research Lab, Volkswagen Group, Munich, Germany
nutan.chen@gmail.com

[2] Autonomous Intelligent Driving GmbH, Munich, Germany

Abstract. The length of the geodesic between two data points along a Riemannian manifold, induced by a deep generative model, yields a principled measure of similarity. Current approaches are limited to low-dimensional latent spaces, due to the computational complexity of solving a non-convex optimisation problem. We propose finding shortest paths in a finite graph of samples from the aggregate approximate posterior, that can be solved exactly, at greatly reduced runtime, and without a notable loss in quality. Our approach, therefore, is hence applicable to high-dimensional problems, e.g., in the visual domain. We validate our approach empirically on a series of experiments using variational autoencoders applied to image data, including the Chair, FashionMNIST, and human movement data sets.

Keywords: Deep generative model · Geodesic · A* search

1 Introduction

Estimating the similarity between data points is central to data processing pipelines. In computer vision it is employed for matching points from frames [32] and for visual place recognition [27], where it is used for the visual detection of places despite visual changes due to weather or lighting conditions. For a method to be successful, certain invariances have to either be used as an inductive bias or presented through data. This necessitates for highly expressive models.

Recently, deep learning has enabled training generative models on large-scale databases, as typically found in computer vision [7,22]. Such models have been used for similarity estimation from the perspective of Riemannian manifolds in the context of Gaussian process latent variable models [34]. As such non-parametric approaches scale poorly with data set size, several authors [2,9,10] proposed the marriage of Riemannian manifold-based metric learning with deep generative models. This results in a principled measure of similarity between two members of the data distribution by relating it to the shortest path, or, geodesic between two corresponding points in latent space. A downside of this approach is that the geodesic has to be obtained as the solution to a non-linear

I. V. Tetko et al. (Eds.): ICANN 2019, LNCS 11728, pp. 554–566, 2019.
https://doi.org/10.1007/978-3-030-30484-3_45

optimisation problem. Consequently, there is high computational demand and no guarantee of the quality of the solution. The representation of this shortest path is also not obvious, as it is continuous in nature but ultimately has to be represented in a discrete fashion.

In contrast, local and global descriptors [26] do not suffer from said computational challenges. As their representation is a vector over real numbers, it is compactly represented as an array of floating point numbers, paving the way for efficient indexing techniques for nearest neighbour lookup [5,21].

This work takes a step in making Riemannian manifold based approaches faster, and hence applicable in high-dimensional settings. We show that spanning the latent space with a discrete and finite graph allows us to apply a classic search algorithm, A*, to obtain accurate approximations of the geodesic, that are superior to the previously proposed ODE and neural network based approaches in terms of computation performance, without loss in quality. Once the graph has been built, estimating the geodesic is bounded for any pair of points.

We apply the proposed framework to a toy example, that of a visual pendulum, to foster intuition of the approach, as it can be easily visualised. The practical applicability to more challenging data sets is then illustrated for the Chair, FashionMNIST and human motion capture data sets.

2 Related Work

A wide range of approaches has been proposed for estimating the similarity between data points. Typically, distance metrics are assumed to be given, however they often come with certain assumptions about the data. For example instances of the Minkowski distance require the data to be invariant to rotation under the $L2$-norm. The Mahalanobis distance is a popular choice when the data are multivariate Gaussian distributed, as it is invariant to translation and scaling.

Transforming the data can further allow applying a known metric, even when the data does not directly fulfill all the assumptions. In [17,36], the authors proposed the use of linear transformations for supervised learning. To enable an accurate measurement of even more complicated data, non-linear transformations based on neural networks were introduced in [31]. Additionally, transformations of time-series data to constant-length spaces have been proposed in [4], which allow applying similarity measures using recurrent neural networks.

To alleviate the problem of manually specifying a distance metric, learning distances directly from data has been proposed [12,24,35,38]. This is especially useful in high-dimensional spaces, where obtaining a meaningful distance metric is challenging. Traditional metrics may not even be qualitatively meaningful, since the ratio of the distances of the nearest and farthest neighbours to a given data point is almost 1 for a wide variety of distributions [1].

In recent work, [34] suggested perceiving the latent space of Gaussian process latent variable models as a Riemannian manifold, where the distance between two data points is given as the shortest path along the data manifold. Treating the latent space as a Riemannian manifold enables the use of interpolation [28] and trajectory-generation [11] algorithms between given points, with the advantage that the observable-space trajectory remains sufficiently close to the previously used training data [2,9,10,25]. The geodesics, i.e. the length-minimising curve given the curvature of the manifold, have been approximated by neural networks [9,10] or represented by ODEs [2].

Beside interpolation, using the geometry of the manifold has been proposed and used in other approaches based on generative models. For instance, in [14] the authors used task manifolds for meta-learning and in [19] the authors developed a constant-curvature manifold prior for adversarial autoencoders used for graph data.

Similarly to our approach, ISOMAP [33], computes the distance between two points using a graph and uses it for modelling the latent space. Our method, in contrast, computes the geodesic for trained models and, therefore, enables its use in state-of-the-art deep generative models, e.g., VAEs and GANs [18].

3 Methods

In this section, first, we provide the necessary background approaches that our work is based on, i.e., the variational autoencoders and the associated Riemannian geometry, and, second, we provide a detailed description of our approach.

3.1 Variational Autoencoders

Latent-variable models (LVMs) are defined by

$$p(\mathbf{x}) = \int p(\mathbf{x}|\mathbf{z})\, p(\mathbf{z})\, \mathrm{d}\mathbf{z}, \tag{1}$$

where the observable data $\mathbf{x} \in \mathbb{R}^{N_x}$ are represented through latent variables $\mathbf{z} \in \mathbb{R}^{N_z}$, that are based on hidden characteristics in $\mathbf{x}$. The integral of Eq. (1) is usually intractable and has to be approximated through sampling [15,20] or variational inference (VI) [23,29]. Using VI, the problem is rephrased as the maximisation of the evidence lower bound (ELBO), i.e.,

$$\ln p(\mathbf{x}) \geq \mathbb{E}_{q(\mathbf{z})}\left[\ln \frac{p(\mathbf{x}|\mathbf{z})\, p(\mathbf{z})}{q(\mathbf{z})}\right] =: \mathcal{L}_{\mathrm{ELBO}}, \tag{2}$$

where $p(\mathbf{x}|\mathbf{z})$ is the likelihood, $p(\mathbf{z})$ the prior, and $q(\mathbf{z})$ approximates the intractable posterior. The distribution parameters of $q(\mathbf{z}) = q_\phi(\mathbf{z}|\mathbf{x})$ and $p(\mathbf{x}|\mathbf{z}) = p_\theta(\mathbf{x}|\mathbf{z})$ can be expressed by neural networks to obtain the variational autoencoder (VAE) [23,29]. A tighter bound was proposed in the importance-weighted autoencoders (IWAEs) [8] through importance sampling, i.e.,

$$\mathcal{L}_{\mathrm{IWAE}} = \mathbb{E}_{\mathbf{z}_1,\ldots,\mathbf{z}_K \sim q_\phi(\mathbf{z}|\mathbf{x})}\left[\ln \frac{1}{K}\sum_{k=1}^{K} \frac{p_\theta(\mathbf{x}|\mathbf{z}_k)\, p_\theta(\mathbf{z}_k)}{q_\phi(\mathbf{z}_k|\mathbf{x})}\right], \tag{3}$$

where $\ln p(\mathbf{x}) \geq \mathcal{L}_{\mathrm{IWAE}} \geq \mathcal{L}_{\mathrm{ELBO}}$. In our experiments we used IWAEs.

3.2 Riemannian Geometry in Variational Autoencoders

A Riemannian space is a differentiable manifold M with an additional metric to describe its geometric properties. This enables assigning an inner product in the tangent space at each point $\mathbf{z}$ in the latent space through the corresponding metric tensor $\mathbf{G} \in \mathbb{R}^{N_z \times N_z}$, i.e.,

$$\langle \mathbf{z}', \mathbf{z}' \rangle_{\mathbf{z}} := \mathbf{z}'^T \, \mathbf{G}(\mathbf{z}) \, \mathbf{z}', \tag{4}$$

with $\mathbf{z}' \in T_{\mathbf{z}}M$ and $\mathbf{z} \in M$. $T_{\mathbf{z}}M$ is the tangent space. Treating the latent space of a VAE as a Riemannian manifold allows us to compute the *observation space distance* of latent variables. Assuming we have a trajectory $\gamma : [0, 1] \rightarrow \mathbb{R}^{N_z}$ in the Riemannian (latent) space that is transformed by a continuous function $f(\gamma(t))$ (decoder) to an N_x-dimensional Euclidean (observation) space. The length of this trajectory in the observation space, referred to as the Riemannian distance, is defined by

$$L(\gamma) = \int_0^1 \phi(t) \, \mathrm{d}t, \qquad \phi(t) = \sqrt{\langle \dot{\gamma}(t), \dot{\gamma}(t) \rangle_{\gamma(t)}}\,, \tag{5}$$

with the Riemannian velocity $\phi(t)$ and $\dot{\gamma}(t)$ denoting the time-derivative of the trajectory. The metric tensor is defined as $\mathbf{G} = \mathbf{J}^T \mathbf{J}$, with $\mathbf{J}$ as the Jacobian of the decoder. The trajectory which minimises the Riemannian distance $L(\gamma)$ is referred to as the shortest path geodesic. We integrate the metric tensor with n equidistantly spaced sampling points along γ to approximate the distance, i.e.,

$$\tilde{L}(\gamma) \approx \frac{1}{n} \sum_{i=1}^{n} \phi(t_i). \tag{6}$$

In our approach, we use a stochastic approximation of the Jacobian, as presented in [30],

$$\mathbf{J}(\mathbf{z}) = \lim_{\sigma \rightarrow 0} \frac{1}{\sigma} \mathbb{E}[f(\mathbf{z} + \epsilon) - f(\mathbf{z})], \tag{7}$$

with $\epsilon \sim \mathcal{N}(0, \sigma^2 I)$, to reduce the computation time.

3.3 Graph-Based Geodesics

Obtaining the geodesic is a challenging task, as for minimizing Eq. (5), we need the Hessian of the decoder during the optimisation process. Computing it is a time consuming optimisation procedure that scales poorly with the dimensionality of the observable and the latent space, intractable for a lot of applications. In addition, computing the Hessian limits the selection of the neural network's activation function [2,9]. To bypass the above-mentioned hurdles we introduce a graph-based approach, where a discrete and finite graph is built in the latent space using a binary tree data structure, a k-d tree, with edge weights based on Riemannian distances. Once the graph has been built, geodesics can

Algorithm 1. Graph based geodesic

```
1. Graph building process
Train IWAE
Sample n_nodes nodes
Build a graph using K-D tree
for i ← 1 to n_nodes do
   for k ← 1 to n_neighbours do
      Index j is the k-th neighbour
      if edge^(ij) or edge^(ji) empty then
         edge^(ij) = L(γ^(ij))
      end if
   end for
end for

2. Path search process
Given two points z^(i)
if z^(i) ∉ nodes then
   Insert z^(i) into the graph in K-D tree
   for k ← 1 to n_neighbours do
      Index j is the k-th neighbour
      edge^(ij) = L(γ^(ij))
   end for
end if
Search geodesic using A*
return path nodes
```

be approximated by applying a classic search algorithm, A* [13]. Our approach is summarized in Algorithm 1.

Building the Graph. The graph is structured as a k-d tree, a special case of binary space partitioning trees, where each leaf node corresponds to a k-dimensional vector. The nodes of the graph are obtained by encoding the observable data $\mathbf{X} = \{\mathbf{x}^{(1)}, \ldots, \mathbf{x}^{(N)}\}$ into their latent representations $\mathbf{z}^{(i)}$. This is done by using the respective mean values of the approximate posterior $q_\phi(\mathbf{z}^{(i)}|\mathbf{x}^{(i)})$. Each node is connected by an undirected edge to its k-nearest neighbours. The edge weights are set to Riemannian distances $L(\gamma)$, where γ is the straight line between the related pair of nodes.

Approximating Geodesics. A classic graph-traversing method to obtain the shortest path between nodes is A* search. It is an iterative algorithm that, given a graph $\mathcal{G}$, maintains a sorted list of nodes that can be visited in the current state. The list is typically initialised with the starting node and is being sorted according to the estimated cost of including node n into the optimal path. The estimated cost is computed by $f(n) = g(n) + h(n)$, where $g(n)$ is the cost of the path from the starting node n_{start} to n and $h(n)$ is a heuristic function that estimates the remaining cost from n to the target node n_{target}.

The cost function we use in our approach is the Riemannian distance between two subsequent nodes on the path, whereas the distance on the Remannian manifold with Euclidean interpolation on the latent space is used as heuristic. A*, in order to operate, requires a heuristic function that underestimates the true cost. It can be shown that the proposed heuristic fulfills this requirement. The performance of the algorithm is optimal among any other similar algorithm to the number of nodes that are being expanded. When the target node is reached, the algorithm terminates. The result is the shortest path through the graph regarding the Riemannian distance. This path approximates the geodesic well as shown in Sect. 4.

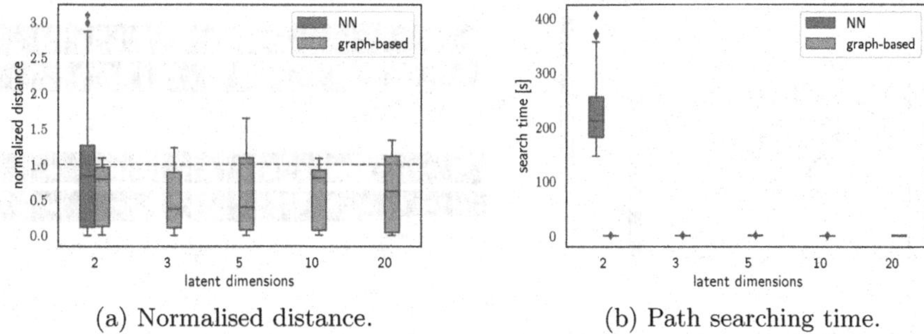

(a) Normalised distance. (b) Path searching time.

Fig. 1. Box plot of distances and searching time using 100 pairs of randomly selected data points. The box plot illustrates the median, as well as [25, 75] and [5, 95] percentiles. Our approach produces shorter distances and scales well to higher latent dimensions. (a) The geodesic distances are normalised to enable comparison across different generative models. The normalised distance is computed by $d_{\text{norm}} = d_{\text{Geod.}}/\text{mean}(d_{\text{Eucl.}})$. (b) The mean of the graph-based A* searching time is 0.09 s.

4 Results

We present an empirical evaluation of our graph-based approach for approximating geodesics in deep generative models. We compare the geodesics to Euclidean trajectories and show that following the geodesic leads to a smoother interpolation in the observation space. Additionally, we compare the graph-based approximation to a neural network (NN) based method, proposed in [9], to show that our approach does not degrade the approximation of the geodesic and scales significantly better.

In our comparisons, the NN-based method approximates the curve γ with NNs, which weights are updated during the minimisation of the trajectory length $L(\gamma)$. Euclidean interpolation is linear interpolation in the latent space. Piecewise Euclidean interpolation uses A* search on a graph in which the edges are the distances in the latent space. The distances of Euclidean and piecewise Euclidean interpolations are computed in Riemannian manifold after interpolation.

We use the magnification factor (MF) [6] to show the sensitivity of the generative models in 2D latent space and evaluate the approximated geodesic. The $\text{MF}(\mathbf{z}) =: \sqrt{\det \mathbf{G}(\mathbf{z})}$ can be interpreted as the scaling factor when moving from the Riemannian (latent) to the Euclidean (observation) space, due to the change of variables.

4.1 Pendulum Experiment

The pendulum dataset contains 16×16-pixel images of a simulated pendulum and has $T = 15 \cdot 10^3$ images for two different joint angle ranges, $R_1 = [0, 150)$ and $R_2 = [180, 330)$ degrees. To avoid overfitting, we augmented the dataset by adding 0.05 Gaussian noise to each pixel. We present our results using $\{2, 3, 5, 10, 20\}$ latent dimensions for the IWAE and used 15 samples for the

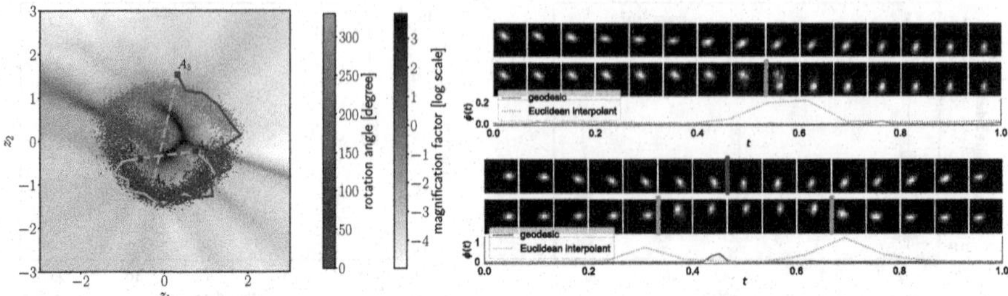

Fig. 2. (left) Latent space and MF of pendulum in two dimensions. With blue and magenta we show the approximate geodesics and with orange the Euclidean interpolations. (right) The respective reconstructed images. The upper images series is the reconstruction using the geodesic and the lower the Euclidean interpolation. The geodesic reconstruction is significantly smoother, as we can also see from the velocity ϕ. (Color figure online)

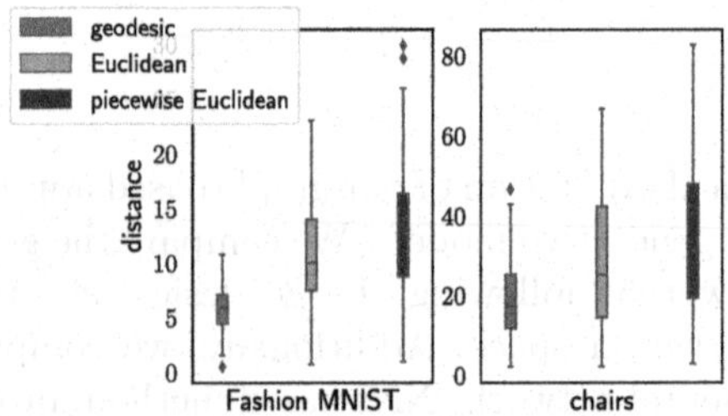

Fig. 3. The distribution of distances in Fashion MNIST and chairs from 100 randomly sampled trajectories based on geodesic, Euclidean interpolation or piecewise Euclidean interpolation. Both of the datasets are with 20D latent space.

importance weighting step. After training, 1000 points were chosen to build the graph. Each node had four nearest neighbours based on the distance in the latent space. We generated 100 random pairs of data points, as shown in Fig. 1, for computing the distances and search time. We show that with the increasing latent dimensionality, the search time does not increase, as it is dependent solely on the number of nodes. Comparing to [10] and [2], our approach does not require second-order derivatives and is significantly faster. The [2] approach takes more time than the NN-based method, so we only used latter for this comparison.

Two of the generated geodesic and Euclidean interpolant trajectories, in the case of two latent dimensions are illustrated in Fig. 2. Our approach finds a trajectory in the latent space which is significantly longer than a simple Euclidean interpolation, but significantly smoother as it does not cross a region of large MF. The effects of crossing such a region are shown in Fig. 2(right).

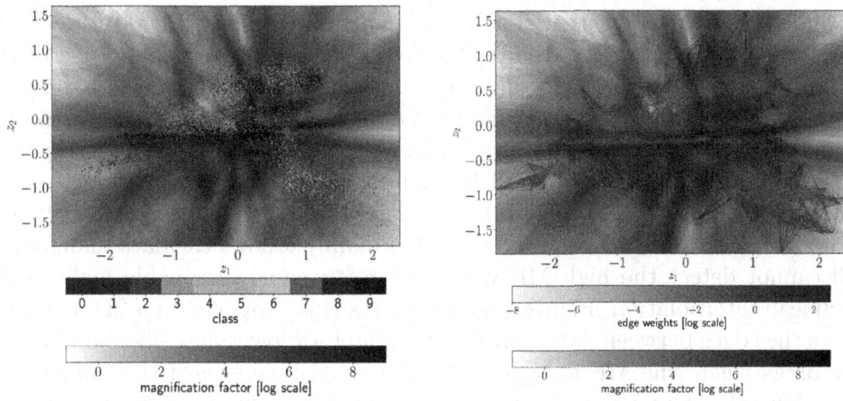

Fig. 4. (left) MF of Fashion MNIST using a 2D latent space. Points are sampled from the validation dataset. (right) Respective graph of Fashion MNIST. The edges are weighted by the geodesic distance. Darker color signifies a transition with a higher MF.

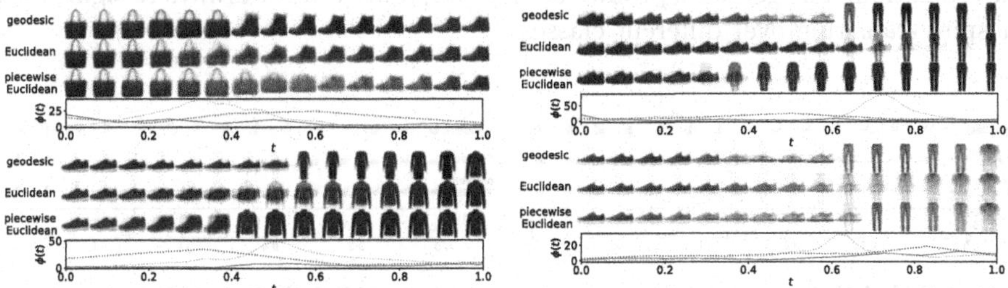

Fig. 5. Reconstruction of Fashion MNIST with 20 latent dimensions. The geodesic outperforms Euclidean interpolation by producing interpolations that visually stay on the manifold and the objects are recognisable.

4.2 Fashion MNIST

For the Fashion MNIST [37] evaluation, we used the standard training set, i.e. 28×28 pixel images, for fitting an IWAE consisting of eight 128-neuron layers with ReLU activation [16]. We use 20 latent dimensions for our evaluations. Additionally, standard augmentation strategies were used, e.g., horizontal flipping and jitter, and 20% dropout, to avoid overfitting. To generate the nodes of the geodesic graph, we randomly selected 2000 validation data points, encoded into the latent space. For each node, we selected the 20 nearest data samples, based on a Euclidean distance. For each edge we calculated the velocity and geodesic of the trajectory, using fifteen interpolation points.

As shown in Fig. 3, we sampled 100 trajectories between data points and calculated the geodesic distance and a distance based on Euclidean interpolation. The search time of 100 trajectories between data points is 0.018 s$\pm$0.010 (mean $\pm$ STD). The Euclidean-based trajectories result in consistently higher MF values, for all latent dimensions used. Therefore, the Euclidean-based trajectories cross more areas with high MF, resulting in fewer smooth transitions in the observational space. However, following the geodesic, smoothness is not guaranteed. There are cases where it is unavoidable for certain trajectories to cross an area of high magnification factor. Rather, following the geodesic can be interpreted as the minimisation of the overall Riemannian distance for a trajectory and it is expected that the MF will be lower than a simple Euclidean interpolation. Although piecewise Euclidean interpolation mainly follows the data manifold, it still cannot detect the high MF values; therefore, it is reasonable higher than Euclidean interpolation. Figure 4 demonstrates this property on a 2D manifold, where the edges between data samples are lighter for lower magnification factors. The areas where the MF is high, the edges are darker even if the samples are adjacent in the observational space. In such situations, the graph-based approach will therefore produce a more complex trajectory, but with a lower MF.

In Fig. 5 we present visual examples of such trajectories. The image reconstructions are produced from the decoder of the VAE by moving through the latent space along the trajectory specified by either the geodesic or Euclidean interpolation. The geodesic produces images that are almost always recognisable, despite transiting over different classes.

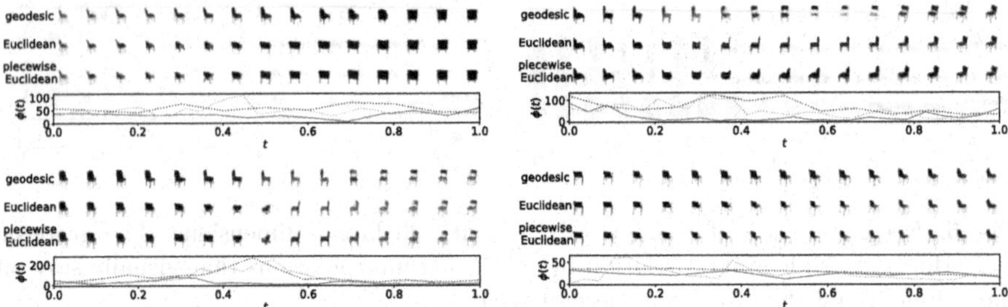

Fig. 6. Reconstruction of Chairs dataset, with 20 latent dimensions. The geodesic produces a smoother interpolation in the observation space, as we can observe by both the image sequences and the velocity ϕ.

4.3 Chairs

For the chairs dataset [3], we split chair sequences 80/20 for training and validation, using 74400 and 11966 images respectively. The zoom factor was set to 1.3 and the images rescaled to 64×64 pixels. We generated the geodesic graph in exactly as for Fashion MNIST. In Fig. 7 we present a comparison of the graph building time, the average distance of the geodesic, and the trajectory search time to the number nodes and neighbors. Our approach scales well to the increase of the number of nodes and neighbors.

Additionally, we compare the performance of our approach to Euclidean-based interpolation in Fig. 3, using 2000 nodes and 20 neighbors. Our approach outperforms the Euclidean-based, producing consistently lower MF values. Reconstructions are shown in Fig. 6.

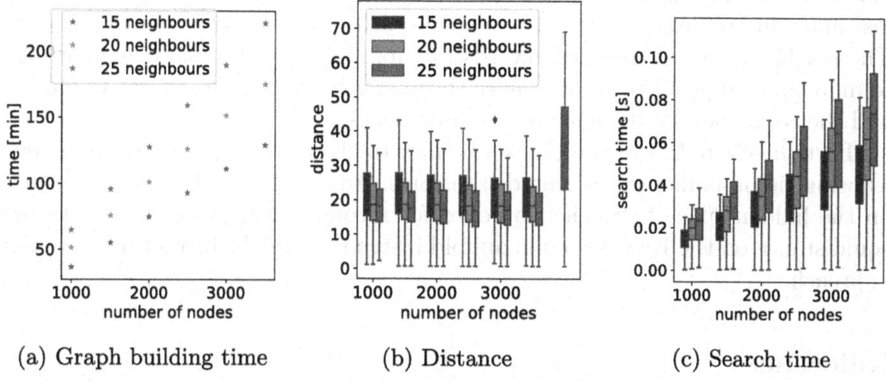

(a) Graph building time (b) Distance (c) Search time

Fig. 7. (a) The effects of the graph architectures for 20 latent dimensional latent space of the Chair dataset. (b) Geodesic distances using a different amount of neighbours in comparison to the Euclidean distance shown in red. (c) Search time averaged over 100 interpolations for a different number of neighbours. (Color figure online)

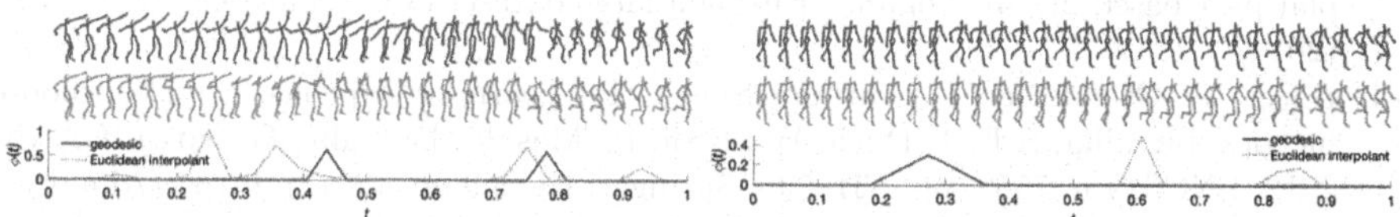

Fig. 8. Interpolation of human motions using three latent dimensions. Our approach produces a smoother interpolation in comparison to the Euclidean.

4.4 Human Motions

We evaluate our approach in a different domain, i.e., the CMU human motion dataset[1], that includes various movements. We selected walking (subject 35), jogging (subject 35), balancing (subject 49), punching (subject 143) and waving (subject 143). The input data is a 50-dimensional vector of the joint angles. In Fig. 8 we present the results using three latent dimensions. We observe that the Euclidean interpolation generates trajectories crossing high MF regions. However, using the geodesic we are able to find similar gestures between the classes and, subsequently, generate smoother interpolations.

[1] http://mocap.cs.cmu.edu/.

5 Conclusion and Future Work

In this paper, we demonstrate how the major computational demand of applying Riemannian geometry to deep generative models, can be sidestepped by solving a related graph-based shortest path problem instead. Although our approach is only approximate, in our experiments on a wide variety of data sets show little loss in quality of interpolations while linear paths are consistently outperformed. The machinery paves the way towards the application of Riemannian geometry to more applied problems that require the expressivity of deep generative models and the robustness of distance based approaches.

Further research in this topic can be how to efficiently choose the nodes such as using sigma points of unscented transform. Additionally, we use equidistance on the hidden space between two nodes for reconstruction. However, if we use equidistance on the Riemannian manifold instead, we might further improve our approach.

References

1. Aggarwal, C.C., Hinneburg, A., Keim, D.A.: On the surprising behavior of distance metrics in high dimensional space. In: Van den Bussche, J., Vianu, V. (eds.) ICDT 2001. LNCS, vol. 1973, pp. 420–434. Springer, Heidelberg (2001). https://doi.org/10.1007/3-540-44503-X_27
2. Arvanitidis, G., Hansen, L.K, Hauberg, S.: Latent space oddity: on the curvature of deep generative models. In: ICLR (2018)
3. Aubry, M., Maturana, D., Efros, A., Russell, B., Sivic, J.: Seeing 3D chairs: exemplar part-based 2D–3D alignment using a large dataset of CAD models. In: CVPR (2014)
4. Bayer, J., Osendorfer, C., van der Smagt, P.: Learning sequence neighbourhood metrics. In: Villa, A.E.P., Duch, W., Érdi, P., Masulli, F., Palm, G. (eds.) ICANN 2012. LNCS, vol. 7552, pp. 531–538. Springer, Heidelberg (2012). https://doi.org/10.1007/978-3-642-33269-2_67
5. Beygelzimer, A., Kakade, S., Langford, J.: Cover trees for nearest neighbor. In: ICML, pp. 97–104 (2006)
6. Bishop, C.M., Svensen, M., Williams, C.K.: Magnification factors for the SOM and GTM algorithms. In: Proceedings Workshop on Self-Organizing Maps (1997)
7. Brock, A., Donahue, J., Simonyan, K.: Large scale GAN training for high fidelity natural image synthesis. arXiv (2018)
8. Burda, Y., Grosse, R.B., Salakhutdinov, R.: Importance weighted autoencoders. CoRR, abs/1509.00519 (2015)
9. Chen, N., Klushyn, A., Kurle, R., Jiang, X., Bayer, J., van der Smagt, P.: Metrics for deep generative models. In: AISTATS, pp. 1540–1550 (2018)
10. Chen, N., Klushyn, A., Paraschos, A., Benbouzid, D., van der Smagt, P.: Active learning based on data uncertainty and model sensitivity. IEEE/RSJ IROS (2018)

11. Crouch, P., Leite, F.S.: The dynamic interpolation problem: on Riemannian manifolds, Lie groups, and symmetric spaces. J. Dynam. Control Syst. **1**(2), 177–202 (1995)
12. Davis, J.V., Kulis, B., Jain, P., Sra, S., Dhillon, I.S.: Information-theoretic metric learning. In: ICML, pp. 209–216 (2007)
13. Doran, J.E., Michie, D.: Experiments with the graph traverser program. Proc. R. Soc. Lond. A **294**(1437), 235–259 (1966)
14. Flennerhag, S., Moreno, P.G., Lawrence, N.D., Damianou, A.: Transferring knowledge across learning processes. arXiv (2018)
15. Gelfand, A.E., Smith, A.F.: Sampling-based approaches to calculating marginal densities. J. Am. Stat. Assoc. **85**(410), 398–409 (1990)
16. Glorot, X., Bordes, A., Bengio, Y.: Deep sparse rectifier neural networks. In: AISTATS, pp. 315–323 (2011)
17. Goldberger, J., Roweis, S.T., Hinton, G.E., Salakhutdinov, R.: Neighbourhood components analysis. In: NIPS, pp. 513–520 (2004)
18. Goodfellow, I., et al.: Generative adversarial nets. In: NIPS, pp. 2672–2680 (2014)
19. Grattarola, D., Zambon, D., Alippi, C., Livi, L.: Learning graph embeddings on constant-curvature manifolds for change detection in graph streams. arXiv (2018)
20. Hastings, W.K.: Monte Carlo sampling methods using Markov chains and their applications (1970)
21. Indyk, P., Motwani, R., Raghavan, P., Vempala, S.: Locality-preserving hashing in multidimensional spaces. In: ACM Symposium on the Theory of Computing, pp. 618–625 (1997)
22. Kingma, D.P., Dhariwal, P.: Glow: generative flow with invertible 1x1 convolutions. arXiv preprint arXiv:1807.03039 (2018)
23. Kingma, D.P., Welling, M.: Auto-encoding variational Bayes. CoRR (2013)
24. Kulis, B., et al.: Metric learning: a survey. Found. Trends® Mach. Learn. **5**(4), 287–364 (2013)
25. Kumar, A., Sattigeri, P., Fletcher, T.: Semi-supervised learning with GANs: manifold invariance with improved inference. In: NIPS, pp. 5534–5544 (2017)
26. Lowe, D.G.: Object recognition from local scale-invariant features. In: ICCV, pp. 1150–1157 (1999)
27. Lowry, S.M., et al.: Visual place recognition: a survey. IEEE Trans. Robot. **32**(1), 1–19 (2016)
28. Noakes, L., Heinzinger, G., Paden, B.: Cubic splines on curved spaces. IMA J. Math. Control Inf. **6**(4), 465–473 (1989)
29. Rezende, D.J., Mohamed, S., Wierstra, D.: Stochastic backpropagation and approximate inference in deep generative models, pp. 1278–1286 (2014)
30. Rifai, S., et al.: Higher order contractive auto-encoder. In: Gunopulos, D., Hofmann, T., Malerba, D., Vazirgiannis, M. (eds.) ECML PKDD 2011. LNCS (LNAI), vol. 6912, pp. 645–660. Springer, Heidelberg (2011). https://doi.org/10.1007/978-3-642-23783-6_41
31. Salakhutdinov, R., Hinton, G.E.: Learning a nonlinear embedding by preserving class neighbourhood structure. In: AISTATS, pp. 412–419 (2007)
32. Scharstein, D., Szeliski, R.: A taxonomy and evaluation of dense two-frame stereo correspondence algorithms. IJCV **47**(1–3), 7–42 (2002)
33. Tenenbaum, J.B., De Silva, V., Langford, J.C.: A global geometric framework for nonlinear dimensionality reduction. Science **290**(5500), 2319–2323 (2000)

34. Tosi, A., Hauberg, S., Vellido, A., Lawrence, N.D.: Metrics for probabilistic geometries. In: UAI, pp. 800–808 (2014)
35. Weinberger, K.Q., Blitzer, J., Saul, L.K.: Distance metric learning for large margin nearest neighbor classification. In: NIPS, pp. 1473–1480 (2006)
36. Weinberger, K.Q., Saul, L.K.: Distance metric learning for large margin nearest neighbor classification. JMLR **10**, 207–244 (2009)
37. Xiao, H., Rasul, K., Vollgraf, R.: Fashion-MNIST: a novel image dataset for benchmarking machine learning algorithms (2017)
38. Xing, E.P., Jordan, M.I., Russell, S.J., Ng, A.Y.: Distance metric learning with application to clustering with side-information. In: NIPS, pp. 521–528 (2003)

Spatial Attention Network for Few-Shot Learning

Xianhao He(✉), Peng Qiao, Yong Dou, and Xin Niu

National Laboratory for Parallel and Distributed Processing,
National University of Defense Technology, Changsha, China
{hexianhao18,pengqiao,yongdou,xinniu}@nudt.edu.cn

Abstract. Metric learning is one of the feasible approaches to few-shot learning. However, most metric learning methods encode images through CNN directly, without considering image contents. The general CNN features may lead to hard discrimination among distinct classes. Based on observation that feature maps correspond to image regions, we assume that image regions relevant to target objects should be salient in image features. To this end, we propose an effective framework, called Spatial Attention Network (SAN), to exploit spatial context of images. SAN produces attention weights on clustered regional features indicating the contributions of different regions to classification, and takes weighted sum of regional features as discriminative features. Thus, SAN highlights important contents by giving them large weights. Once trained, SAN compares unlabeled data with class prototypes of few labeled data in nearest-neighbor manner and identifies classes of unlabeled data. We evaluate our approach on three disparate datasets: *mini*ImageNet, Caltech-UCSD Birds and *mini*DogsNet. Experimental results show that when compared with state-of-the-art models, SAN achieves competitive accuracy in *mini*ImageNet and Caltech-UCSD Birds, and it improves 5-shot accuracy in *mini*DogsNet by a large margin.

Keywords: Few-Shot Learning · Attention module · Discriminative features

1 Introduction

Recently, deep learning models such as AlexNet [10], VGG [18] and ResNet [6] have achieved great success in image classification tasks [2]. However, these models are trained in a supervised manner using large amounts of labeled data. Moreover, these models can only recognize images from specific classes appearing in training data. Furthermore, in a case that we have few training samples from some classes, models trained using these data would perform poorly due to overfitting. Many attempts such as fine-tuning [25], data augmentation [10] and dropout [20] are proposed to alleviate overfitting, however, this problem

I. V. Tetko et al. (Eds.): ICANN 2019, LNCS 11728, pp. 567–578, 2019.
https://doi.org/10.1007/978-3-030-30484-3_46

still exists. Focusing on above issues, One- or Few-Shot Learning aims to learn new knowledge from one or few instances under the inspiration of human's quick learning ability.

Few-Shot Learning has attracted much attention recently, and most of existing few-shot approaches adopt meta-learning training strategy that learns a task-agnostic knowledge from various tasks and quickly adapts to new target tasks. These methods can be grouped in three categories: **learning an optimization algorithm** with initialization and parameters update [3,11,15], **generative models** [17] that produce images or features to enlarge scarce dataset and **metric-learning** [9,21,22] that embeds instances into a new space and compares embeddings via distance function. The prior two techniques either fine-tune parameters on target problems with learnt initialization and update, or are hard to manipulate the quality of produced examples. Therefore, our work is focused on metric-learning.

Previous works in metric-learning have achieved satisfactory results, but most of these methods directly embed an image into new vector space [21,22] with little consideration of spatial context in image. We assume that exploiting spatial information of image can bring improvement in few-shot classification. Specifically, Luo et al. [12] observe that a position in feature map relies on an image region. It means that we can view feature map as a set of cells, each of which is a vector with dimension of channel size. These cells include spatial context and correspond to different receptive fields of input image. Based on this observation, we cluster feature map and obtain clusters of cells. We believe that cells containing relevant contents would belong to the same cluster. Later, these clusters are processed by attention module to produce a set of attention weights on feature map cells. The weighted sum of cells is output as image feature. Therefore, we associate salient regions in image with output feature by attention weights. The architecture described above is called Spatial Attention Network (SAN). Inspired by [19], we compute class prototypes of labeled data. Prediction on unlabeled data depends on the nearest prototype of labeled data.

Overall, our contribution can be summarized that we **(i)** propose an architecture called Spatial Attention Network (SAN) to produce a set of weights representing how much attention the model needs to pay on different image regions, **(ii)** evaluate our model on three standard benchmarks of few-shot learning, and SAN achieves comfortable results in comparison with previous state-of-the-art methods, and **(iii)** visualize clusters of image contents, attention module and discriminative features to understand what SAN learns.

2 Related Work

2.1 Few-Shot Meta-learning

Meta-Learning aims to teach a learner model "how to learn". These methods in few-shot learning are trained on few training instances from different tasks to learn a learner that tackles a variety of learning tasks in testing. In [15], Ravi and Larochelle propose a LSTM-based meta-learner to learn an optimization algorithm to update parameters in another classification learner in few-shot mechanism. In MAML [3], Finn et al. promote the above meta-learner, and provide a model-agnostic method that initializes learned parameters of specific model and updates these parameters with small gradient steps and few training data. Li et al. [11] propose Meta-SGD that has faster and easier training procedure than method in Meta-LSTM [15], and components of an optimizer (initialization, update direction and learning rate) are inclusively learned. Our proposed approach utilizes meta-learning in training stage.

2.2 Few-Shot Metric Learning

Previous works [9,16,19] use a large number of training samples to learn a neural network that appropriately embeds images into a new vector space. Some distance functions (cosine or Euclidean distance) can be used to classify unlabeled data. For examples, in new embedding space, if one unlabeled instance has the nearest distance with one labeled instance, they would share identical class. Another approach in [21] employs distance measure that is learned on neural networks instead of cosine or Euclidean distance. Furthermore, in some cases [21,22], their proposed networks adopt meta-learning training method to boost accuracy in testing.

2.3 Attention Modules

Recently, attention modules have widely existed in computer vision tasks such as image classification [4,23,27], image caption [24,26] and object detection [5]. Although attention modules have unfixed structures in applications, their aim is to learn from training data to capture key regions of an image. In zero-shot learning, [8] proposed attention network instructed by class semantic descriptions to focus on effective image patches, and these patches are relevant to class semantic descriptions. Our approach has similar intention with [8], however, SAN has different attention structure and is supervised by class-level label only.

3 Methodology

At this section, we describe the details of our network architecture and define the task of few-shot classification. We assume that the whole dataset can be divided into D_{base} and D_{novel}. Each category of D_{base} is rich in image examples, while each category of D_{novel} has fewer images. We ensure that D_{base} and D_{novel} have disjoint label space. For D_{novel} set, we randomly sample Q disparate classes with M examples for each class, and these data consist of *support set*. In testing episodes, *query* images are made up of n samples with prior knowledge that they have identical label space $\{label_1, label_2, \cdots, label_Q\}$ with *support set*, and images in *query set* are unseen in *support set*. The task of Q-way, M-shot classification is to assign labels $\{y_i, y_i \in \{label_1, label_2, \cdots, label_Q\}\}_{i=1}^{n}$ to images $\{x_i\}_{i=1}^{n}$ in *query set*.

An overview of our network architecture is presented in Fig. 1. Our network has two stages: *feature extractor* stage and *few-shot learning* stage. In *feature extractor* stage, we train a ConvNet based on D_{base} to learn extracting features from input images. In *few-shot learning* stage, attention module is trained to identify informative regions related to target objects.

3.1 Feature Extractor

To extract features from input images, we train a ConvNet based on D_{base} from scratch. ConvNet has two components: feature extractor $G(\cdot|\theta)$ and classifier W_{base}, where θ and W_{base} are trainable parameters. ConvNet is made up of stacked feature maps which contain regional information of input image. At this stage, we ignore these feature maps and choose the last d-dimensional vector $z = G(x|\theta) \in \mathbb{R}^d$ to represent the feature of input image x. W_{base} is a set of weight vectors $\{w_i \in \mathbb{R}^d\}_{i=1}^{C_{base}}$, where each vector represents the classifier of that category. Therefore, the probability of input image x belonging to the i-th category is as follow:

$$p_i = \frac{e^{z^T \cdot w_i}}{\sum_{j=1}^{C_{base}} e^{z^T \cdot w_j}} \tag{1}$$

We employ sum of cross entropy loss of all images as loss function.

3.2 Few-Shot Learning

The purpose of SAN is to find informative regions of input image. To achieve this goal, we fully exploit spatial context of an image via clustering and attention module (see Fig. 1).

Clustering. For a given feature map with size of $W \times H \times C$, where W, H and C represent width, height and channels of the feature map respectively, a set of feature map cells $S = \{\mathrm{f}_1, \mathrm{f}_2, \cdots, \mathrm{f}_{W \times H}\}, \mathrm{f}_i \in \mathbb{R}^C$ diversely correspond to $W \times H$ patches in the input image. We assume that the feature map cells containing related parts of object are "closer" in c-dimensional vector space. For example, distance between f_1 and f_2 is shorter than distance between f_1 and f_3 or f_2 and f_3 with the assumption that f_1 and f_2 cover the regions of a bird's wing and tail respectively, while f_3 contains background patch. Therefore, we cluster feature map cells and obtain the clusters $\{c_1, c_2, \cdots, c_k\}$, where k is a hyper-parameter indicating the number of clusters. For every $\mathrm{f}_j \in c_i$, we add these features to generate $\mathrm{F}_i = \sum_{j \in c_i} \mathrm{f}_j$. The feature $\mathrm{F}_i (i = 1, 2, \cdots, k)$ incorporates relevant regions of an image. Finally, the sequence of $\{\mathrm{F}_1, \mathrm{F}_2, \cdots, \mathrm{F}_k\}$ is output. Notice that, due to the property of clustering algorithm, the above sequence is unordered. For example, both x_1 and x_2 are images of bird. After clustering, the bird's wing of x_1 is included in c_1 while that of x_2 in c_2, which causes the order of $\{\mathrm{F}_1, \mathrm{F}_2, \cdots, \mathrm{F}_k\}$ various from different images.

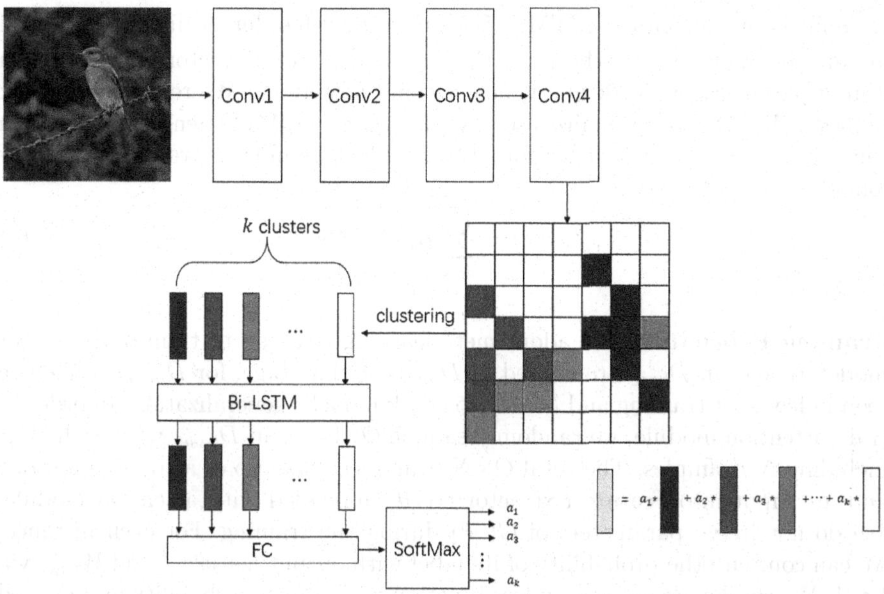

Fig. 1. An illustration of the overview architecture of proposed spatial attention network. It consists of feature extractor and attention module. The figure illustrates an example of attention module applied on one layer in Conv4 Block. Feature map cells drawn with identical color belong to identical cluster. The output feature (gray) is weighted sum of regional features.

Attention Module. In a specific layer of ConvNet, feature map cells that correspond to target objects are included in $\{\mathrm{F}_1, \mathrm{F}_2, \cdots, \mathrm{F}_k\}$, and the sequence $\{\mathrm{F}_1, \mathrm{F}_2, \cdots, \mathrm{F}_k\}$ involves spatial context of input image. The essence of attention module is to highlight effective contents in the sequence. Inspired by [14] which employes sequential model to tackle image regions, we thus proposed a method applying bi-directional LSTM which reduces the impact of sequence order to exploit contextual relations in $\{\mathrm{F}_1, \mathrm{F}_2, \cdots, \mathrm{F}_k\}$ and generates attention weights $\alpha_i (i = 1, 2, \cdots, k)$ assigned to $\mathrm{F}_i (i = 1, 2, \cdots, k)$. The bi-directional LSTM and attention weights are defined as follow.

$$\overrightarrow{h}_i, \overrightarrow{c}_i = \mathrm{LSTM}(\mathrm{F}_i, \overrightarrow{h}_{i-1}, \overrightarrow{c}_{i-1}) \tag{2}$$

$$\overleftarrow{h}_i, \overleftarrow{c}_i = \mathrm{LSTM}(\mathrm{F}_i, \overleftarrow{h}_{i+1}, \overleftarrow{c}_{i+1}) \tag{3}$$

$$\hat{\alpha_i} = g(\left[\overrightarrow{h}_i, \overleftarrow{h}_i\right]) \tag{4}$$

$$\alpha_i = \frac{e^{\hat{\alpha_i}}}{\sum_{j=1}^{k} e^{\hat{\alpha_j}}} \tag{5}$$

$\overrightarrow{h}_i$ and $\overleftarrow{h}_i$ are outputs of LSTM at the i-th step with different direction. $\overrightarrow{h}_i$ and $\overleftarrow{h}_i$ are concatenated together, and then the concatenated vector is put through a multiple neural network $g(\cdot)$ which outputs a score $\hat{\alpha_i}$. We resort to softmax function (Eq. 5) that normalizes scores $\{\hat{\alpha_1}, \hat{\alpha_2}, \cdots, \hat{\alpha_k}\}$ and generates attention weights $\{\alpha_1, \alpha_2, \cdots, \alpha_k\}$. Therefore, the final feature in this layer is obtained as follow.

$$f = \sum_{i=1}^{k} \alpha_i \cdot \mathrm{F}_i \tag{6}$$

Training Procedure. We adopt meta-learning strategy to train our few-shot model. Images in D_{base} are viewed as D_{novel} at this stage, for D_{novel} cannot be seen in few-shot training and is used to check model's generalization. In order to train attention module, we randomly sample Q classes in D_{base}, with each class including N examples. The total $Q \times N$ examples make up of a training episode and are input into Feature Extractor $G(\cdot|\theta)$ appended with attention module. We do not freeze parameters of $G(\cdot|\theta)$ during the training. For each instance, we can compute the probability of its label with output feature f and W_{base} via Eq. 1. We employ cross-entropy loss function with above probability and ground truth label at this stage.

Prediction on Novel Classes. For Q-way, M-shot classification in D_{novel}, we need to compute class prototypes of *support set*. The details of class prototype can be seen in [19]. At prediction phase, output features of unlabeled *query* data and class prototypes of labeled *support* data would be compared in nearest-neighbor manner to determine classes for unlabeled data.

4 Experiment

In this section, we firstly describe our experimental design. Then we conduct the experiment about exploring how to choose cluster number k. We present experimental results evaluated on three few-shot learning benchmark datasets with appropriate cluster number. Finally, visualization is posted to understand what SAN learns.

4.1 Experimental Design

We conduct 5-way 1 and 5-shot classification in all our experiments. In one training episode, we randomly choose 5 classes with 16 images for each class. With regard to one testing episode, we reference to experiments in [17]. Besides randomly sampling 5 classes with 1 image (5 images in 5-shot setting) for each class as *support set*, the remaining unseen images for each sampled classes make up of *query set* on both 1 and 5-shot tasks. Average accuracy is computed on 10 such testing episodes.

In all experiments, we train our model using Adam optimization with initial learning rate 10^{-3}. The learning rate is multiplied by 0.5 after every 1,000 training episodes. We use weight decay 10^{-4}. Simple ConvNet is selected as feature extractor. ConvNet has 4 convolutional blocks, each of which is consisted of 3 $\times$ 3 convolutions with 64 filters, batch normalization, ReLU non-linearity, and 2 $\times$ 2 max-pooling. ConvNet takes images of 84 $\times$ 84 as input. To evaluate our method on deep network, we also try ResNet as backbone network, which takes images of 224 $\times$ 224 as input. Attention module is applied on the last CNN feature map. Our implementation of all experiments is based on PyTorch [1].

4.2 Comparison

Dataset Description. Three public benchmark datasets in our experiments are *mini*ImageNet, Caltech-UCSD Birds and *mini*DogsNet. *Mini*ImageNet dataset is consisted of 60,000 color images, which contains 100 classes with 600 examples for each class. We follow the split introduced by [17], with 80 for training, and the remaining 20 classes for testing. Caltech-UCSD Birds (CUB) is a fine-grained classification dataset which includes 12K images with 200 categories of wild birds. We conduct an experiment on CUB to evaluate the performance of our proposed approach on fine-grained few-shot classification. For 200 categories of bird species, we randomly split them into 150 for training and 50 for testing. *Mini*DogsNet is an alternative fine-grained classification dataset. We follow [7] to create the dataset which contains 100 classes of dogs randomly selected from ImageNet dog categories. To mimic the experimental setting on *mini*ImageNet, we divide *mini*DogsNet into 80 for training and 20 for testing.

Discussion on Cluster Number. In order to explore the effect of different cluster number k on accuracy in various tasks, we test the hyper-parameter in $\{2, 5, 7, 10, 15, 20\}$. For simplicity, the experiment is conducted on 5-way 1-shot classification in three datasets and our backbone network is ConvNet. We can perceive that choosing $k = 10, 7, 10$ leads to best accuracies in these datasets, respectively. The result is shown in Table 1 and visualization about clusters of image contents is presented in Fig. 2. In later experiments, we thus select $k = 10$ for *mini*ImageNet and *mini*DogsNet, $k = 5$ for CUB.

Table 1. 5-way 1-shot accuracies with different cluster k

Dataset	$k = 2$	$k = 5$	$k = 7$	$k = 10$	$k = 15$	$k = 20$
*mini*ImageNet	49.33	52.82	53.82	54.16	47.31	45.63
CUB	56.37	61.53	63.13	60.57	58.74	50.14
*mini*DogsNet	45.39	45.78	45.74	46.32	45.07	45.47

5-Way 1/5-Shot Result. We post our experimental results in Table 2. The state-of-the-art models are implemented by simple ConvNet that is described above. It is obvious that our proposed method achieves competitive results (54.16% on 1-shot classification and 69.35% on 5-shot classification) in *mini*ImageNet dataset. For evaluation on fine-grained dataset, SAN achieves the highest 1-shot accuracy in CUB, but does not overtake Relation Net on 5-shot learning. In *mini*DogsNet, our method achieves the highest results on both 1 and 5-shot classification, and enhances 5-shot result by a large margin. Furthermore, backbone network based on ResNet can boost classification performance because of its strong ability on feature representation.

Table 2. 5-way 1-shot/5-shot accuracy results

Method	*mini*ImageNet	CUB	*mini*DogsNet
Matching Network [22]	45.91/57.66	49.34/59.31	46.01/57.38
Prototypical Network [19]	49.42/68.20	51.31/70.77	–
Meta-Learner LSTM [15]	43.44/60.60	40.43/49.65	38.37/53.65
MAML [3]	48.70/63.11	55.92/72.09	31.52/59.66
MACO [7]	41.09/58.32	60.76/74.96	39.10/54.45
RELATION NET [21]	**57.02/71.07**	62.45/**76.11**	–
SAN(ConvNet)	54.16/69.35	**63.13**/72.70	**46.32/64.37**
SAN(ResNet)	58.17/75.92	66.47/78.46	57.39/71.08

4.3 Visualization

In order to figure out what attention module learns, we conduct the following three visualizations and analyze why Spatial Attention Network works in few-shot classification.

Image Contents Clustering. We firstly observe that whether relevant image contents are gathered together by clustering. Specifically, last feature map of ResNet has size of $7 \times 7 \times 512$, and we divide input image into 7×7 regions. We assume that clusters of feature map cells approximate to clusters of these regions. Visualization results can be seen in Fig. 2. Note that relevant image contents belong to one or several clusters. For example, the dog in Fig. 2(a) is nearly covered by blue bounding boxes, implying that features related to the dog are in the same cluster. In Fig. 2(b), the target object is clearly divided into multiple clusters. Furthermore, we can perceive that option of cluster number $k = 10$ is better than cluster number $k = 15$, which might explain why the result of choosing 10 clusters is higher than that of choosing 15 clusters in Table 1.

(a) Cluster $k = 10$ (b) Cluster $k = 15$

Fig. 2. Cluster visualization. (a) and (b) represent clusters of image contents in dog category. Bounding boxes with different colour indicate different clusters. (Color figure online)

Features Embedding. In this visualization, we sample 5 categories from the three datasets respectively, and each category contains 30 examples. The total 150 images of each dataset are input into Spatial Attention Network, and obtain 150 attention features. We reduce dimension of the features into two-dimensional points via t-SNE [13], and plot them in a 2D figure. The visualized result can be seen in Fig. 3. Note that embeddings in CUB show promising with large inter-class variance and small intra-class variance. Although embeddings in *mini*ImageNet and *mini*DogsNet have no absolutely obvious boundaries between disparate categories, it makes sense that most of features in the same category gather together and keep a certain distance with features in disjoint categories.

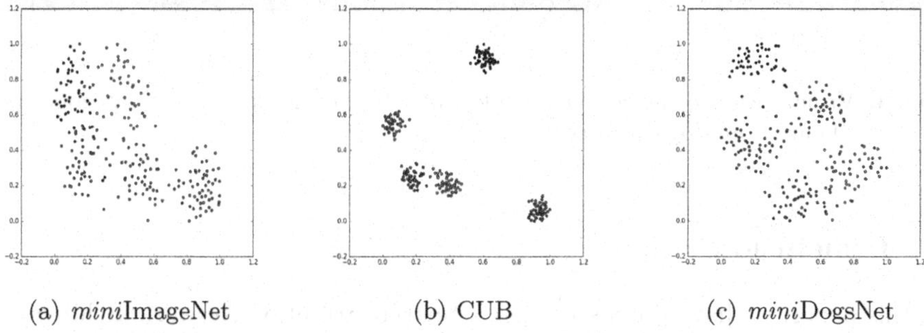

(a) *mini*ImageNet (b) CUB (c) *mini*DogsNet

Fig. 3. 2D embedding figure. (a), (b), and (c) represent embeddings in *mini*ImageNet, CUB and *mini*DogsNet respectively. Points with the same color come from identical category.

Attention Module. We visualize attention module in feature maps to see whether Spatial Attention Network works as our hypothesis. According to Sect. 3.2, attention module generates attention weights $\{\alpha_1, \alpha_2, \cdots, \alpha_k\}$. For feature map with size of $W \times W \times C$, we can produce a mask of $W \times H$ which exhibits weights of corresponding feature map cells. Following [28], the mask is resized to 224×224 (input image's shape) and covered on input image. Figure 4 demonstrates this visualization from bird and dog category. Heat maps indicate that attention module endeavors to capture the key region related to target objects in images. From 4(d), (e) and (f), we can see that our model tackles the issues of distinguishing targets from multi-object images and occlusion of other objects.

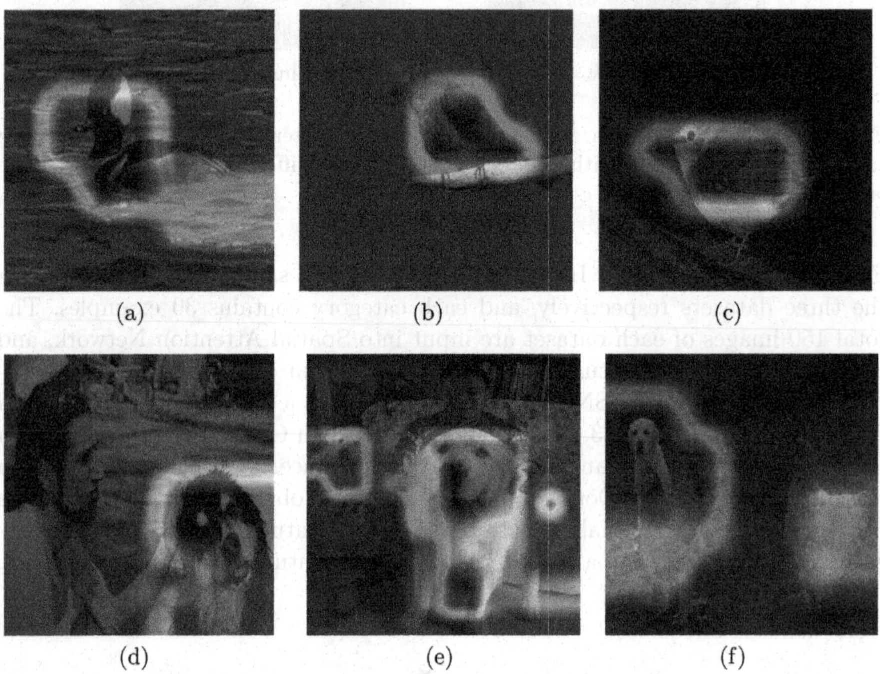

Fig. 4. Visualization of attention module. (a), (b), (c) are from bird category, and (d), (e), (f) are from dog category

5 Conclusion

In this paper, we have proposed a novel Spatial Attention Network architecture for few-shot learning. Spatial Attention Network applies attention module on feature map to generate discriminative features. We evaluate our approach on *mini*ImageNet, Caltech-UCSD Birds and *mini*DogsNet datasets, and Spatial Attention Network has achieved promising performance on these datasets in comparison with previous state-of-the-art models. We visualize clusters of image contents, features embedding and attention module to figure out what Spatial Attention Network learns, and observe that in the new embedding space, features in identical category are grouped together and the model tries to focus on salient image area with target objects.

Acknowledgements. This paper is supported by the National Key Research and Development Program of China (Grant No. 2018YFB1003405) and the National Natural Science Foundation of China (Grant No. 61732018).

References

1. Pytorch. https://github.com/pytorch/pytorch
2. Deng, J., Dong, W., Socher, R., Li, L.J., Li, K., Fei-Fei, L.: ImageNet: a large-scale hierarchical image database. In: 2009 IEEE Conference on Computer Vision and Pattern Recognition. IEEE, June 2009. https://doi.org/10.1109/cvprw.2009.5206848
3. Finn, C., Abbeel, P., Levine, S.: Model-agnostic meta-learning for fast adaptation of deep networks. arXiv preprint arXiv:1703.03400 (2017)
4. Fu, J., Zheng, H., Mei, T.: Look closer to see better: recurrent attention convolutional neural network for fine-grained image recognition. In: 2017 IEEE Conference on Computer Vision and Pattern Recognition (CVPR), p. 3. IEEE, July 2017. https://doi.org/10.1109/cvpr.2017.476
5. Hara, K., Liu, M.Y., Tuzel, O., Farahmand, A.m.: Attentional network for visual object detection. arXiv preprint arXiv:1702.01478 (2017)
6. He, K., Zhang, X., Ren, S., Sun, J.: Deep residual learning for image recognition. In: 2016 IEEE Conference on Computer Vision and Pattern Recognition (CVPR), pp. 770–778. IEEE, June 2016. https://doi.org/10.1109/cvpr.2016.90
7. Hilliard, N., Phillips, L., Howland, S., Yankov, A., Corley, C.D., Hodas, N.O.: Few-shot learning with metric-agnostic conditional embeddings. arXiv preprint arXiv:1802.04376 (2018)
8. Ji, Z., Fu, Y., Guo, J., Pang, Y., Zhang, Z.M., et al.: Stacked semantics-guided attention model for fine-grained zero-shot learning. In: Advances in Neural Information Processing Systems, pp. 5998–6007 (2018)
9. Koch, G., Zemel, R., Salakhutdinov, R.: Siamese neural networks for one-shot image recognition. In: ICML Deep Learning Workshop, vol. 2 (2015)
10. Krizhevsky, A., Sutskever, I., Hinton, G.E.: ImageNet classification with deep convolutional neural networks. In: Advances in Neural Information Processing Systems, pp. 1097–1105 (2012)
11. Li, Z., Zhou, F., Chen, F., Li, H.: Meta-SGD: learning to learn quickly for few shot learning. arXiv preprint arXiv:1707.09835 (2017)
12. Luo, W., Li, Y., Urtasun, R., Zemel, R.: Understanding the effective receptive field in deep convolutional neural networks. In: Advances in Neural Information Processing Systems, pp. 4898–4906 (2016)
13. Maaten, L.v.d., Hinton, G.J.: Visualizing data using T-SNE. Mach. Learn. Res. **9**, 2579–2605 (2008)
14. Mathe, S., Pirinen, A., Sminchisescu, C.: Reinforcement learning for visual object detection. In: 2016 IEEE Conference on Computer Vision and Pattern Recognition (CVPR), pp. 2894–2902. IEEE, June 2016. https://doi.org/10.1109/cvpr.2016.316
15. Ravi, S., Larochelle, H.: Optimization as a model for few-shot learning. In: International Conference on Learning Representations (2017)
16. Rippel, O., Paluri, M., Dollar, P., Bourdev, L.: Metric learning with adaptive density discrimination. arXiv preprint arXiv:1511.05939 (2015)
17. Schwartz, E., et al.: Delta-encoder: an effective sample synthesis method for few-shot object recognition. In: Advances in Neural Information Processing Systems, pp. 2850–2860 (2018)

18. Simonyan, K., Zisserman, A.: Very deep convolutional networks for large-scale image recognition. arXiv preprint arXiv:1409.1556 (2014)
19. Snell, J., Swersky, K., Zemel, R.: Prototypical networks for few-shot learning. In: Advances in Neural Information Processing Systems, pp. 4077–4087 (2017)
20. Srivastava, N., Hinton, G., Krizhevsky, A., Sutskever, I., Salakhutdinov, R.: Dropout: a simple way to prevent neural networks from overfitting. J. Mach. Learn. Res. **15**(1), 1929–1958 (2014)
21. Sung, F., Yang, Y., Zhang, L., Xiang, T., Torr, P.H., Hospedales, T.M.: Learning to compare: relation network for few-shot learning. In: 2018 IEEE/CVF Conference on Computer Vision and Pattern Recognition, pp. 1199–1208. IEEE, June 2018. https://doi.org/10.1109/cvpr.2018.00131
22. Vinyals, O., Blundell, C., Lillicrap, T., Wierstra, D., et al.: Matching networks for one shot learning. In: Advances in Neural Information Processing Systems, pp. 3630–3638 (2016)
23. Xiao, T., Xu, Y., Yang, K., Zhang, J., Peng, Y., Zhang, Z.: The application of two-level attention models in deep convolutional neural network for fine-grained image classification. In: 2015 IEEE Conference on Computer Vision and Pattern Recognition (CVPR), pp. 842–850. IEEE, June 2015. https://doi.org/10.1109/cvpr.2015.7298685
24. Xu, K., et al.: Show, attend and tell: neural image caption generation with visual attention. In: International Conference on Machine Learning, pp. 2048–2057 (2015)
25. Yosinski, J., Clune, J., Bengio, Y., Lipson, H.: How transferable are features in deep neural networks? In: Advances in Neural Information Processing Systems, pp. 3320–3328 (2014)
26. You, Q., Jin, H., Wang, Z., Fang, C., Luo, J.: Image captioning with semantic attention. In: 2016 IEEE Conference on Computer Vision and Pattern Recognition (CVPR), pp. 4651–4659. IEEE, June 2016. https://doi.org/10.1109/cvpr.2016.503
27. Zheng, H., Fu, J., Mei, T., Luo, J.: Learning multi-attention convolutional neural network for fine-grained image recognition. In: 2017 IEEE International Conference on Computer Vision (ICCV). IEEE, October 2017. https://doi.org/10.1109/iccv.2017.557
28. Zhou, B., Khosla, A., Lapedriza, A., Oliva, A., Torralba, A.: Learning deep features for discriminative localization. In: 2016 IEEE Conference on Computer Vision and Pattern Recognition (CVPR), pp. 2921–2929. IEEE, June 2016. https://doi.org/10.1109/cvpr.2016.319

Routine Modeling with Time Series Metric Learning

Paul Compagnon[1,2(✉)], Grégoire Lefebvre[1], Stefan Duffner[2], and Christophe Garcia[2]

[1] Orange Labs, Grenoble, France
{paul.compagnon,gregoire.lefebvre}@orange.com
[2] LIRIS, UMR 5205 CNRS INSA-Lyon, Lyon, France
{stefan.duffner,christophe.garcia}@liris.cnrs.fr

Abstract. Traditionally, the automatic recognition of human activities is performed with supervised learning algorithms on limited sets of specific activities. This work proposes to recognize recurrent activity patterns, called routines, instead of precisely defined activities. The modeling of routines is defined as a metric learning problem, and an architecture, called SS2S, based on sequence-to-sequence models is proposed to learn a distance between time series. This approach only relies on inertial data and is thus non intrusive and preserves privacy. Experimental results show that a clustering algorithm provided with the learned distance is able to recover daily routines.

Keywords: Metric learning · Sequence-to-sequence model · Activity recognition · Time series · Inertial data

1 Introduction

Human Activity Recognition (HAR) is a key part of several intelligent systems interacting with humans: smart home services [10], actigraphy and telemedecine, sport applications [3], etc. It is particularly useful for developing eHealth services and monitoring a person in its everyday life. It has been so far mainly performed in supervised contexts with data annotated by experts or with the help of video recordings [8]. Not only is this approach time consuming, but it also restricts the number of activities that can be recognized. It is associated with scripted datasets where subjects are asked to perform sequences of predefined tasks. This approach is thus unrealistic and difficult to set up for real environments where people do a vast variety of specific activities everyday and can diverge from a pre-established behavior in many different ways (e.g., falls, accidents, contingencies of life, etc.). Besides, most people present some kind of habitual behavior, called *routines* in this paper: the time they go to sleep, morning ritual before going to work, meal times, etc. Results from behavioral psychology show that habits are hard and long to form but also hard to break when well installed [20]. From a data-driven perspective, Gonzalez et al. [14] observed the high regularity of human trajectories thanks to localization data and show that "humans follow

I. V. Tetko et al. (Eds.): ICANN 2019, LNCS 11728, pp. 579–592, 2019.
https://doi.org/10.1007/978-3-030-30484-3_47

simple reproducible patterns". Routines produce distinguishable patterns in the data which, if not identifiable semantically, could be retrieved over time and so produce a relevant signature of the daily life of a person. In this paper, we advocate for the modeling of such routines instead of activity recognition, and we propose a machine learning model able to identify routines in the daily life of a person. We want this system to be unintrusive and to respect people's privacy and therefore to rely only on inertial data that can be gathered by a mobile phone or a smart watch. Moreover, routines do not need to be semantically characterized, and the model does not have to use any activity labels. The daily routines of a person may present characteristics of almost-periodic functions, periodic similarity, regarding a certain metric which we propose to learn. To do so, we adapted the siamese neural network architecture proposed by Bromley et al. [7] to learn a distance from pairs of sequences and propose experiments to evaluate the quality of the learned metric on the problem of routine modeling. The contributions of this paper are threefold:

1. a formulation of routine modeling as a metric learning problem by defining routines as almost-periodic functions,
2. an architecture to jointly learn a representation and a metric for time series using siamese sequence-to-sequence models and an improvement of the loss functions to minimize,
3. results showing that the proposed architecture is effectively able to recover human routines from inertial data without using any activity labels.

The remainder of the paper is organized as follows. Section 2 is dedicated to routine modeling definition. Section 3 gives an overview of time series metrics. The proposed approach to recognize routines is presented in Sect. 4 and Sect. 5 presents experimental protocols and results. Finally, conclusions and perspectives are drawn in the last section.

2 Routine Modeling

A routine can be seen as a recurrent behavior of an individual's daily life. For example, a person roughly does the same thing in the same order when waking up or going to work. These sequences of activities should produce distinguishable patterns in the data and can thus be used to monitor the life of an individual without knowing what he or she is doing exactly. The purpose of this work is to design an intelligent system which is able to recognize routines. To tackle routines with machine learning, we propose a starting principle similar to the one used in natural language processing: *similar words appear in similar contexts.* The context surrounding a word designates the previous and following words of the sentence, for example. The context of a routine corresponds here to the moment of the day or the week, etc. it generally happens.

Principle 1. *Similar routines occur at similar moments, almost periodically.*

From this principle, we seek now to propose a mathematical formulation of routines which would include the notions of periodicity and similarity. The almost periodic functions defined by Bohr [6] show similar properties:

Definition 1. *Let $f : \mathbb{R} \rightarrow \mathbb{C}$ be a continuous function. f is an almost-periodic function with respect to the uniform norm if $\forall \epsilon > 0$, $\exists T > 0$ called an ϵ-almost period of f such as:*

$$sup\ |f(t+T) - f(t)| \leqslant \epsilon. \tag{1}$$

Obviously, the practical issue of routine modeling presents several divergences from this canonical definition: data are discrete time series and the periodicity of activities cannot be evaluated point-wise. Nevertheless, it is possible to adapt it to our problem. Let $S : \mathbb{N} \rightarrow \mathbb{R}^n$ be an ordered discrete sequence of vectors of dimension n. If the frequency of S is sufficiently high, it is possible to get a continuous approximation of it, by interpolation for example. We now consider a function f_S of the following form with a fixed interval length l:

$$\begin{aligned} f_S :\ & \mathbb{R}_+ \rightarrow \mathbb{R}^{n \times l} \\ & t \mapsto [S(t) : S(t+l)[, \end{aligned} \tag{2}$$

where $[S(t) : S(t+l)]$ is the set of vectors between $S(t)$ and $S(t+l)$ sampled at a certain frequency from the continuous approximation. l is typically one or several hours: a sufficiently long period of time to absorb the little changes from one day to another (e.g., waking up a little earlier or later, etc.). The objective is to define almost-periodicity with respect to a distance d between sequences, such that $\forall \epsilon > 0$, $\exists T > 0$:

$$d(f_S(t), f_S(t+T)) \leqslant \epsilon. \tag{3}$$

The parameter T can be a day, a week or a sufficiently long period of time to observe repetitions of behavior. The metric d must be sufficiently flexible to handle the high variability of activities which can be similar but somewhat different in their execution while exhibiting a similar pattern. We therefore postulate that d may be learned for a specific user from its data and we will now show that f_S respects the condition established in Eq. (3) with respect to d. To learn d if pairs of similar and dissimilar sequences are known, a Recurrent Neural Network (RNN) encoder parametrized by W, called G_W, can encode the sequences into vector representations and the contrastive loss [15] can be used to learn the metric from pairs of sequence encodings:

$$L(W, Y_1, Y_2, y) = (1-y)\frac{1}{2}d(Y_1, Y_2)^2 + y\frac{1}{2}\max(0, m - d(Y_1, Y_2))^2, \tag{4}$$

where y is equal to zero or one depending if the sequences are respectively similar or not, Y_1 and Y_2 are the last output of the RNN for both sequences and $m > 0$ a margin that defines the minimal distance between dissimilar samples. Several justifications arise for the use of a margin in metric learning. It is necessary to prevent flat energy surface, according to energy-based learning theory [21], a situation where the energy is low for every input/output associations, not only those in the training set. It also insures that metric learning models are robust to noise [29]. As the learning process aims to minimize the distances between similar sequences which are, by definition, shifted by a period T, we get, for a fixed $T > 0$ and $\forall t \in \mathbb{R}_+$:

$$d(G_W(f_S(t)), G_W(f_S(t+T))) \leqslant m. \quad (5)$$

The margin m can be chosen as close to zero as possible and thus Eq. (5) identifies itself with Eq. (3). In practice, this optimization is only possible up to some point, depending on the model and the data. This argumentation suggests the interest of modeling routines with metric learning as, in this case, the main property of almost-periodic functions is fulfilled.

3 Related Work

The traditional approach to compute distances between sequences (or time series, or trajectories) is to perform Dynamic Time Warping (DTW) [25] which was introduced in 1978. Since then, several improvements of the algorithm have been published, notably a fast version by Salvador et al. [26]. DTW is considered one of the best metric to use for sequence classification [31] combined with k-nearest neighbors. Recently, Abid et al. [1] proposed a neural network architecture to learn the parameters of a warping distance accordingly to the euclidean distances in a projection space. However, DTW, as other shaped-based distances [11], is only able to retrieve local similarities when time series have a relatively small length and are just shifted or not well aligned.

Similar routines could present different data profiles which would necessitate a more complex and global notion of similarity. This justifies the extraction of high-level features to produce a vector representation of the structure and the semantics of the data [22]. Traditional metrics can be used to compare vector representations: Euclidean, cosine or Mahalanobis. These vectors can be build with features extracted by various methods such as discrete Fourier and Wavelet transforms, signal processing, singular value decomposition or Hidden Markov Models (HMM) [2]. HMM belong to a category of approaches which suppose the existence of an underlying model which has produced the data; other examples include AutoRegressive-Moving-Average (ARMA) or multivariate extensions (VARIMA), Markov chains, etc. In this case, similarity can be assess by comparing model parameters. More theoretical approaches based on the study of the spectral properties of these models have also been proposed in [18,23]. The problem with these approaches is that it is difficult to select relevant features and/or to chose an accurate model and parameters for a given task. It would be better if an appropriate representation of the data could automatically be extracted accordingly to the problem, by a Neural Network (NN) for example.

Besides, Bromley et al. [7] proposed a Siamese Neural Network (SNN) architecture to learn a metric. They have since then been used for many applications

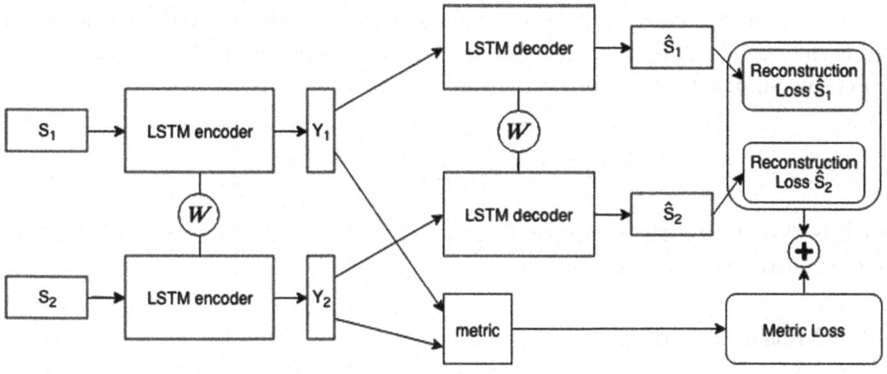

Fig. 1. Proposed SS2S architecture.

with feedforward or convolutionnal NN such as person reidentification [32], gesture recognition [4], object tracking [5], etc. RNN and particularly Long-Short Term Memory (LSTM) NN [16] are well-adapted to work with long sequential data as they are able to deal with long-term dependencies. Müller et al. [24] used a siamese recurrent architecture to learn sentence similarity by encoding sequence of word vectors previously extracted belonging to the same sentence.

In the following section, we propose a novel Siamese Sequence to Sequence (SS2S) neural network architecture to learn to model routines without label supervision. The model effectively combines automatic feature extraction and a similarity metric by jointly learning a robust projection of time series in a metric space. This approach is able to deal with long sequences by using LSTM networks and do not necessitate to choose a model to fit or features to extract.

4 Siamese Sequence to Sequence Model

4.1 Feature Extraction Approach

The time series data obtained from inertial sensors may be very noisy and certainly vary for the same general activity (e.g., cooking). Robust feature representations of time series should therefore be learned before learning a metric. We thus propose (Fig. 1) to map each sequence to a vector using a Sequence to Sequence model [1,9,27]. The sequence is given as input to the first LSTM network (the encoder) to produce an output sequence, the last output vector is considered as the learned representation. This representation is then given to the second LSTM (the decoder) which tries to reconstruct the input sequence. Typically, an autoencoder is trained to reconstruct the original sequence with the Mean Squared Error (MSE):

$$\mathrm{MSE}(S,\hat{S}) = \frac{1}{l}\sum_{t=0}^{l-1}(S(t)-\hat{S}(t))^2, \qquad (6)$$

where S is the sequence and $\hat{S}$ the output sequence produced by the autoencoder from the vector. Similarly, we propose a new Reconstruction Loss (RL) based on cosine similarity, the Cosine Reconstruction Loss (CRL):

$$\mathrm{CRL}(S, \hat{S}) = l - \sum_{t=0}^{l-1} \cos(S(t), \hat{S}(t)). \tag{7}$$

CRL is close to 0 if the cosine similarity between each pair of vectors is close to one when the vectors are collinear.

4.2 Metric Learning

Our architecture is a siamese network [7], that is to say it is constituted of two subnetworks sharing the same parameters W (see Fig. 1). It takes pairs of similar or dissimilar sequences as input constituted with what is called *equivalence constraints*. The objective of our architecture is therefore to learn a metric which makes close similar elements and separates the dissimilar ones in the projection space. Three metric forms can generally be used: Euclidean, cosine or Mahalanobis [12,15,32]. The first two are not parametric and only a projection is learned. Learning a Mahalanobis-like metric implies not only learning the projection but also the matrix which will be used to compute the metric. One different Metric Loss (MeL) is proposed to learn each metric form. Y_1 and Y_2 are the representations learned by the autoencoder from the inputs of the siamese network. The first is the contrastive loss [15] (see Eq. (4)) to learn an euclidean distance. The second is a cosine loss to learn a cosine distance:

$$L(W, Y_1, Y_2, y) = \begin{cases} 1 - \cos(Y_1, Y_2), & \text{if } y = 1 \\ \max(0, \cos(Y_1, Y_2) - m), & \text{if } y = -1. \end{cases} \tag{8}$$

Finally, Mahalanobis metric learning can be performed with the KISSME algorithm [19] which can be integrated into a NN [12]. This algorithm aims to maximize the dissimilarity log-likelihood of dissimilar pairs and conversely for similar pairs. The model learns a mapping under the form of a matrix W and an associated metric matrix M of the dimension of the projection space. W is integrated into the network as a linear layer (just after the recurrent encoding layers in SS2S) trained with backpropagation while M is learned in a closed-form manner and updated after a fix number of epochs with the following formula:

$$M = \mathrm{Proj}((W^T \Sigma_S W)^{-1} - (W^T \Sigma_D W)^{-1}). \tag{9}$$

Σ_S and Σ_D are the covariance matrices of similar and dissimilar elements in the projection space and Proj is the projection onto the positive semi definite cone. We propose a modified version of the KISSME loss proposed in [12] which we found was easier to train based on the contrastive loss (Eq. (4)):

$$\begin{aligned} L(W, Y_1, Y_2, y) =& (1 - y)\frac{1}{2}(Y_1 - Y_2)M(Y_1 - Y_2)^T \\ &+ y\frac{1}{2}\max(0, m - (Y_1 - Y_2)M(Y_1 - Y_2)^T). \end{aligned} \tag{10}$$

4.3 Training Process

Two training processes can be considered for this architecture. Train the autoencoder and then "freeze" the network parameters to learn the metric if it is parametric. Or, add the metric loss to the reconstruction loss and learn jointly both tasks. In this case, several difficulties could appear. Both losses must have similar magnitudes to have similar influences on the training process. The interaction between the two must also be considered. Both tasks could have eventually divergent or not completely compatible objectives. Indeed, we proposed the CRL with the *a priori* that it should better interact with the learning of a cosine metric than MSE due to the similar form between the two. This leads to our first hypothesis (H1):

Hypothesis 1. *Learning a cosine distance along a representation with CRL gives better results than with MSE.*

Despite the possible issues, we hope that learning both tasks jointly should lead to the learning of more appropriate representations and thus to better results. This leads to our second hypothesis (H2):

Hypothesis 2. *Jointly learning a metric and a representation with a sequence to sequence model gives better results than learning both separately.*

5 Experiments

5.1 Experimental Setup

Dataset Presentation. Long-term unscripted data from wearable sensors are difficult to gather. The only dataset we found that could fit our requirements has been obtained by Weiss et al. [30] and is called Long Term Movement Monitoring dataset (LTMM)[1]. This dataset contains recordings of 71 elderly people which have worn an accelerometer and a gyroscope during three days with no instructions. This dataset contains no labels. Figure 2a presents two days of data coming from one axis of the accelerometer: similar profiles can be observed at similar moment. Figure 2b presents the autocorrelation of the accelerometer signal: the maximum of 0.4 is reached for a phase of 24 h. These figures show the interest of this dataset as the data show periodic nature while presenting major visual differences. That said, the definition of periodicity that our algorithm is made to achieve is stronger as it is based on a metric between extracted feature vectors, not just correlations of signal measurements.

To constitute our dataset, we selected in the original dataset a user who did not remove the sensor during the three days to avoid missing values. We set up a data augmentation process to artificially increase the quantity of data while preserving its characteristic structure. The dataset is sampled at 100 Hz and thus, to multiply the number of days by ten, each vector measurement at the

[1] https://www.physionet.org/physiobank/database/ltmm.

same index modulo 10 will be affected to a new day (the order is respected). This new dataset has a sampling rate of 10 Hz which means that one hour of data is a sequence of size 36000, we consider only non overlapping sequences. Thus, to make the computation more tractable, polyphase filtering is applied to resample each sequence of one hour to a size of 100. Finally, equivalence constraints need to be defined in order to make similar and dissimilar pairs: two sequences of one hour, not from the same day but recorded at the same time are considered similar, all other combinations are considered dissimilar. This approach does not therefore require semantic labels.

Model Parameters and Training Details. We describe here the hyperparameters used to train the models. The autoencoders are constituted of one layer of 100 LSTM neurons for the encoder and the decoder. For the KISSME version, the encodings are then projected into a 50-dimensional space, and the distance matrix, which thus has also dimension 50, was updated with the closed-form every 30 epochs. These parameters were determined after preliminary tests where deeper architectures and higher dimensional spaces were tested. Models are trained with 20 similar pairs for each time slot and the same total number of dissimilar pairs for a total of 960 training pairs coming from 12 different days of data. The training was stopped based on the loss computed on the validation set which contains three days of data i.e., 72 sequences. The testing set is composed of 15 days or 360 sequences. The data in the training set were standardized to have a mean of 0 and a variance of 1, the same parameters were applied on the testing set. A learning rate of 0.001 was used and divided by 10 if the loss did not decrease anymore during 10 epochs. A batch size of 50, a margin of 1 for the contrastive loss and of 0.5 for the cosine loss were chosen. We also observed that changing to zero 30% of the values of the training sequences sliglty improved the results as suggested in [28].

5.2 Experimental Results and Discussion

Since the only available labels are time indications and to keep minimal supervision, the evaluation metrics rely on clustering. We report average values on 20 tests for 4 clustering evaluation metrics. *Completeness* assesses if sequences produced at the same hour are in the same clusters. *Silhouette* describes the cluster shapes, if they are dense and well-separated. *Normalized Mutual Information* (NMI) is a classical metric for clustering and measures how two clustering assigments concur, the second being the time slots. *Adjusted Mutual Information* (AMI) is the adjusted against chance version of NMI. A spectral clustering into 5 clusters is performed with the goal not to find the precise number of clusters maximizing the metrics but to choose a number which will make appear coherent and interpretable routines of the day, namely sleep moments, meals and other daily activities performed every day. Finally, to make our distances usable by the spectral clustering, they are converted to kernel functions. The following transformation was applied to the Euclidean, Mahalanobis and DTW distances: $\exp(-\text{dist}\cdot\gamma)$ where γ is the inverse of the length of an encoding vector

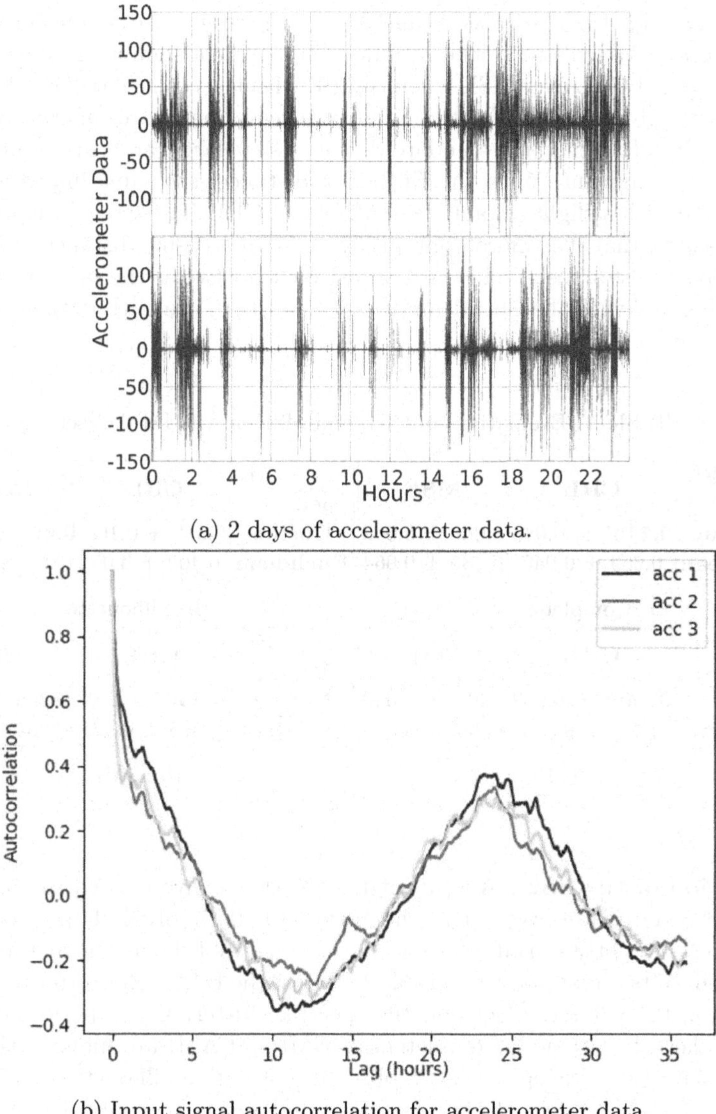

(a) 2 days of accelerometer data.

(b) Input signal autocorrelation for accelerometer data.

Fig. 2. LTMM dataset used to evaluate routine modeling procedure.

(respectively number of features time length of sequence for DTW). 1 was added to the cosine similarity so it becomes a kernel.

Evaluation of Cosine Reconstruction Loss. The performance of the CRL on LTMM is first evaluated. An experiment was performed by jointly training models for Euclidean or cosine distances with CRL or MSE. The results are reported in Table 1. An asterisk means the average results are significantly higher according to a Welch's test. The results demonstrate a significant improvement of the proposed CRL over MSE when trained with the cosine similarity for Completeness, NMI and AMI. For the Silhouette score, better results are obtained with the MSE. However, the standard deviations are large, and this improvement is thus not significant. With the Euclidean distance, the same improvement is not realized with a slight advantage of MSE over CRL. These results confirm our hypothesis H1 that it is more appropriate to learn a cosine distance with CRL. They also suggest a positive interaction between the two as the same effect could not be observed with the Euclidean distance. We then use CRL in the remaining of the paper.

Table 1. Evaluations of CRL and MSE on LTMM dataset.

MeL \ RL	**CRL**	**MSE**
Cosine	**0.714*** ± 0.048	0.666 ± 0.066
Euclidean	0.609 ± 0.042	0.635 ± 0.064

(a) Completeness

MeL \ RL	**CRL**	**MSE**
Cosine	0.618 ± 0.105	**0.667** ± 0.144
Euclidean	0.402 ± 0.05	0.408 ± 0.042

(b) Silhouette

MeL \ RL	**CRL**	**MSE**
Cosine	**0.449*** ± 0.032	0.397 ± 0.040
Euclidean	0.419 ± 0.033	0.434 ± 0.047

(c) NMI

MeL \ RL	**CRL**	**MSE**
Cosine	**0.253*** ± 0.03	0.205 ± 0.033
Euclidean	0.255 ± 0.027	0.264 ± 0.038

(d) AMI

Evaluation of the SS2S Architecture. Next, we investigated the benefit of the SS2S architecture over DTW and Siamese LSTM (SLSTM) [24] as well as the interest of jointly learning the encoder-decoder and the metric on the LTMM dataset. Results are presented in Table 2. To test the DTW, the better radius was selected on the validation set and the spectral clustering was performed using DTW as kernel. Although Completeness, NMI and AMI are higher than every SS2S architectures except one, we observe a negative silhouette value which indicates a poor quality of the clustering and seems to confirm than indeed shaped based distances are not suitable for this type of data. Concerning the encoding architecture, SS2S gives overall better results than SLSTM and the best results are achieved by using the disjoint version of KISSME with a completeness of 0.983 and an NMI of 0.619. These results are not surprising as KISSME uses a parametric distance which can therefore be more adapted to the data. For the silhouette score, cosine distances performed best, i.e., they learned more compact and well-defined clusters. We also note that disjoint versions of the architectures performed better than the joint versions, thus invalidating our hypothesis H2.

To investigate the reasons of this difference which could be due to the autoencoder not being learned properly, Table 3 reports average best Reconstruction Errors on Validation set (REV). The lowest errors are systematically achieved when the encoder is learned alone before the metric therefore supporting the hypothesis that learning the metric prevents the autoencoder from being trained at its full potential. It explains why the joint learning does not perform best. For the CRL, results are closer than for MSE suggesting why this reconstruction loss is easier to learn jointly.

Finally, Fig. 3 shows clustering representations for two approaches: DTW and disjoint KISSME. The clusterings reflect the sequences of one hour that were found similar across the days on the testing set. If these sequences are at the same hour or cover the same time slots, we can argue it is a recurrent activity (or succession of activities) and therefore a routine. The disjoint KISSME version exhibits more coherent discrimination of routines, which, according to the 4 evaluation metrics reported was predictable. Several misclassified situations seem to appear for DTW which is coherent with the negative silhouette score. High regularities can be observed, and it is actually possible to make interpretations: yellow probably corresponds to sleeping moments and nights, and purple to activities during the day. Other clusters seem to correspond to activities at the evening or during meal time. Consequently, the SS2S architecture is able to learn a metric which cluster and produce a modeling of the daily routines of the person without labels. In this example, the clusters are coarse, the granularity of this analysis could be improved simply by working with sequences of half an hour or even shorter and produce more clusters.

Table 2. Evaluations on LTMM dataset of the SS2S architecture (x means non applicable).

Metric	Model	Joint	Completeness	Silhouette	NMI	AMI
DTW [26]	x	x	0.804	−0.93	0.528	0.32
Euclidean	SLSTM	x	0.616 ± 0.032	0.427 ± 0.053	0.414 ± 0.022	0.246 ± 0.019
Cosine	SLSTM	x	0.617 ± 0.06	0.572 ± 0.143	0.372 ± 0.052	0.192 ± 0.046
Euclidean	SS2S	no	0.674 ± 0.04	0.528 ± 0.07	0.458 ± 0.03	0.28 ± 0.027
Euclidean	SS2S	yes	0.635 ± 0.064	0.408 ± 0.042	0.434 ± 0.047	0.264 ± 0.038
Cosine	SS2S	no	0.71 ± 0.05	**0.756*** ± 0.089	0.467 ± 0.028	0.275 ± 0.024
Cosine	SS2S	yes	0.714 ± 0.048	0.618 ± 0.105	0.449 ± 0.032	0.253 ± 0.03
KISSME	SS2S	no	**0.983*** ± 0.016	0.439 ± 0.077	**0.619*** ± 0.035	**0.363*** ± 0.046
KISSME	SS2S	yes	0.667 ± 0.021	0.316 ± 0.039	0.446 ± 0.012	0.266 ± 0.012

Table 3. Average reconstruction errors on the validation set of LTMM.

Metric	REV
Euclidean	0.707 ± 0.112
KISSME	0.736 ± 0.099
Disjoint	**0.55*** ± 0.083

(a) MSE

Metric	REV
Cosine	0.339 ± 0.036
Disjoint	**0.298*** ± 0.03

(b) CRL

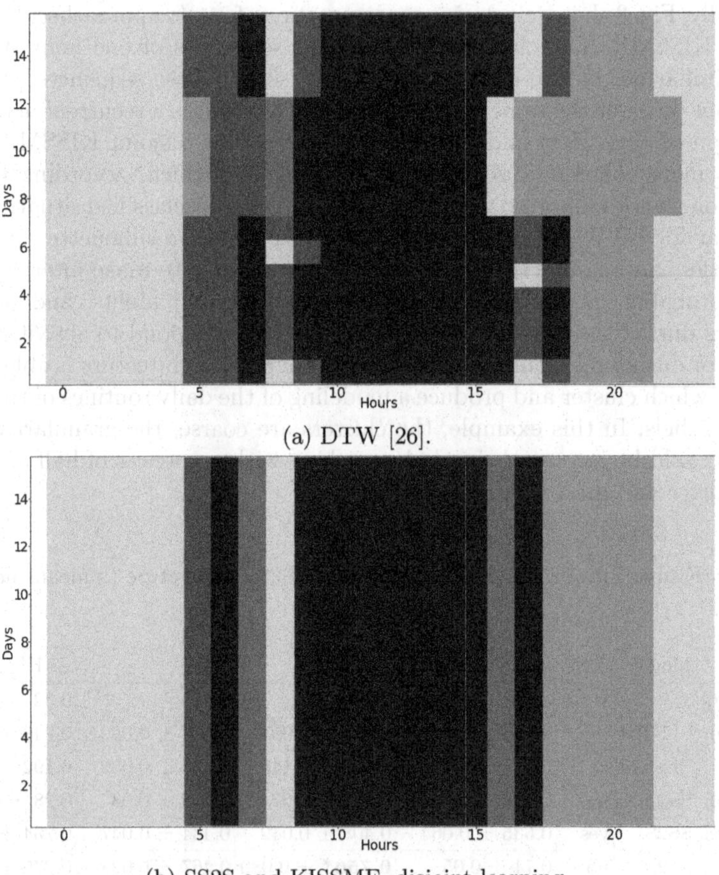

(a) DTW [26].

(b) SS2S and KISSME, disjoint learning.

Fig. 3. Examples of clustering obtained with our model on LTMM.

6 Conclusions and Perspectives

We presented a metric learning model to cluster routines in the daily behavior of individuals. By defining routines as almost-periodic functions, we have been able to study them in a metric learning framework. We thus proposed an approach which combines metric learning and representation learning of sequences. Our proposed architecture relies on no labels and is learned only from time slots. A new reconstruction loss was also proposed to be learned jointly with a cosine metric and it showed better results than MSE in this case. Our SS2S architecture with KISSME and disjoint learning process achieved stimulating results with 0.983 of completeness and 0.619 of NMI. A visual evaluation analysis allows to interpret the recurrent behaviors discovered by the architecture. However, these results invalidate in this case our second hypothesis that combining metric learning and sequence to sequence learning would give better results.

In the future, we will investigate more deeply joint learning of representations and metrics. Several architecture improvements could also be made, for examples: work with triplets instead of pairs, replace the LSTM with a convolutionnal neural network [13] or an echo states network [17]. This last approach works quite differently from a normal neural network and would require subsequent modifications of the architecture. Finally, we will study in further details the link between almost-periodic functions and metric learning.

References

1. Abid, A., Zou, J.: Autowarp: learning a warping distance from unlabeled time series using sequence autoencoders. arXiv preprint arXiv:1810.10107 (2018)
2. Aghabozorgi, S., Shirkhorshidi, A.S., Wah, T.Y.: Time-series clustering-a decade review. Inf. Syst. **53**, 16–38 (2015)
3. Avci, A., Bosch, S., Marin-Perianu, M., Marin-Perianu, R., Havinga, P.: Activity recognition using inertial sensing for healthcare, wellbeing and sports applications: a survey. In: ARCS, pp. 1–10. VDE (2010)
4. Berlemont, S., Lefebvre, G., Duffner, S., Garcia, C.: Class-balanced siamese neural networks. Neurocomputing **273**, 47–56 (2018)
5. Bertinetto, L., Valmadre, J., Henriques, J.F., Vedaldi, A., Torr, P.H.S.: Fully-convolutional siamese networks for object tracking. In: Hua, G., Jégou, H. (eds.) ECCV 2016. LNCS, vol. 9914, pp. 850–865. Springer, Cham (2016). https://doi.org/10.1007/978-3-319-48881-3_56
6. Bohr, H.: Zur theorie der fastperiodischen funktionen. Acta Mathematica **46**(1–2), 101–214 (1925)
7. Bromley, J., Guyon, I., LeCun, Y., Säckinger, E., Shah, R.: Signature verification using a "siamese" time delay neural network. In: NIPS, pp. 737–744 (1994)
8. Chatzaki, C., Pediaditis, M., Vavoulas, G., Tsiknakis, M.: Human Daily Activity and Fall Recognition Using a Smartphone's Acceleration Sensor. In: Röcker, C., O'Donoghue, J., Ziefle, M., Helfert, M., Molloy, W. (eds.) ICT4AWE 2016. CCIS, vol. 736, pp. 100–118. Springer, Cham (2017). https://doi.org/10.1007/978-3-319-62704-5_7
9. Cho, K., et al.: Learning phrase representations using rnn encoder-decoder for statistical machine translation. arXiv preprint arXiv:1406.1078 (2014)
10. Cumin, J., Lefebvre, G., Ramparany, F., Crowley, J.L.: Human activity recognition using place-based decision fusion in smart homes. In: Brézillon, P., Turner, R., Penco, C. (eds.) CONTEXT 2017. LNCS (LNAI), vol. 10257, pp. 137–150. Springer, Cham (2017). https://doi.org/10.1007/978-3-319-57837-8_11
11. Esling, P., Agon, C.: Time-series data mining. ACM CSUR **45**(1), 12 (2012)

12. Faraki, M., Harandi, M.T., Porikli, F.: Large-scale metric learning: a voyage from shallow to deep. IEEE TNNLS **29**(9), 4339–4346 (2018)
13. Gehring, J., Auli, M., Grangier, D., Yarats, D., Dauphin, Y.N.: Convolutional sequence to sequence learning. In: ICML, pp. 1243–1252 (2017)
14. Gonzalez, M.C., Hidalgo, C.A., Barabasi, A.L.: Understanding individual human mobility patterns. Nature **453**(7196), 779 (2008)
15. Hadsell, R., Chopra, S., LeCun, Y.: Dimensionality reduction by learning an invariant mapping. In: CVPR, vol. 2, pp. 1735–1742. IEEE (2006)
16. Hochreiter, S., Schmidhuber, J.: Long short-term memory. Neural comput. **9**(8), 1735–1780 (1997)
17. Jaeger, H.: The "echo state" approach to analysing and training recurrent neural networks-with an erratum note. Bonn, Germany: German National Research Center for Information Technology GMD Technical report 148(34), 13 (2001)
18. Kalpakis, K., Gada, D., Puttagunta, V.: Distance measures for effective clustering of arima time-series. In: IEEE ICDM, pp. 273–280. IEEE (2001)
19. Koestinger, M., Hirzer, M., Wohlhart, P., Roth, P.M., Bischof, H.: Large scale metric learning from equivalence constraints. In: CVPR, pp. 2288–2295. IEEE (2012)
20. Lally, P., Van Jaarsveld, C.H., Potts, H.W., Wardle, J.: How are habits formed: modelling habit formation in the real world. Eur. J. Soc. Psychol. **40**(6), 998–1009 (2010)
21. LeCun, Y., Chopra, S., Hadsell, R., Ranzato, M., Huang, F.: A tutorial on energy-based learning. Predicting structured data 1, (2006)
22. Lin, J., Li, Y.: Finding structural similarity in time series data using bag-of-patterns representation. In: Winslett, M. (ed.) SSDBM 2009. LNCS, vol. 5566, pp. 461–477. Springer, Heidelberg (2009). https://doi.org/10.1007/978-3-642-02279-1_33
23. Martin, R.J.: A metric for ARMA processes. IEEE Trans. Signal Process. **48**(4), 1164–1170 (2000)
24. Müller, J., Thyagarajan, A.: Siamese recurrent architectures for learning sentence similarity. In: AAAI, pp. 2786–2792 (2016)
25. Sakoe, H., Chiba, S.: Dynamic programming algorithm optimization for spoken word recognition. IEEE Trans. Acoust. Speech Signal Process. **26**(1), 43–49 (1978)
26. Salvador, S., Chan, P.: Toward accurate dynamic time warping in linear time and space. Intell. Data Anal. **11**(5), 561–580 (2007)
27. Sutskever, I., Vinyals, O., Le, Q.V.: Sequence to sequence learning with neural networks. In: NIPS, pp. 3104–3112 (2014)
28. Vincent, P., Larochelle, H., Bengio, Y., Manzagol, P.A.: Extracting and composing robust features with denoising autoencoders. In: Proceedings of the 25th international conference on Machine learning, pp. 1096–1103. ACM (2008)
29. Weinberger, K.Q., Saul, L.K.: Distance metric learning for large margin nearest neighbor classification. JMLR **10**(Feb), 207–244 (2009)
30. Weiss, A., et al.: Does the evaluation of gait quality during daily life provide insight into fall risk? A novel approach using 3-day accelerometer recordings. Neurorehabilitation Neural Repair **27**(8), 742–752 (2013)
31. Xi, X., Keogh, E., Shelton, C., Wei, L., Ratanamahatana, C.A.: Fast time series classification using numerosity reduction. In: Proceedings of the 23rd international conference on Machine learning, pp. 1033–1040. ACM (2006)
32. Yi, D., Lei, Z., Liao, S., Li, S.Z.: Deep metric learning for person re-identification. In: ICPR, pp. 34–39. IEEE (2014)

Domain Knowledge Incorporation

Leveraging Domain Knowledge for Reinforcement Learning Using MMC Architectures

Rajkumar Ramamurthy[1,2(✉)], Christian Bauckhage[1,2], Rafet Sifa[1,2], Jannis Schücker[1,2], and Stefan Wrobel[1,2]

[1] Fraunhofer Center for Machine Learning, Sankt Augustin, Germany
[2] Fraunhofer IAIS, Sankt Augustin, Germany
{rajkumar.ramamurthy,christian.bauckhage,rafet.sifa, jannis.schuecker,stefan.wrobel}@iais.fraunhofer.de

Abstract. Despite the success of reinforcement learning methods in various simulated robotic applications, end-to-end training suffers from extensive training times due to high sample complexity and does not scale well to realistic systems. In this work, we speed up reinforcement learning by incorporating domain knowledge into policy learning. We revisit an architecture based on the mean of multiple computations (MMC) principle known from computational biology and adapt it to solve a "reacher task". We approximate the policy using a simple MMC network, experimentally compare this idea to end-to-end deep learning architectures, and show that our approach reduces the number of interactions required to approximate a suitable policy by a factor of ten.

1 Introduction

Recent progress in training deep neural networks has facilitated the use of deep reinforcement learning (RL) at large scales. Even in complex domains, RL agents can now learn diverse behaviours ranging from playing games [14,22] over navigating complex environments [13,28] to controlling robots [7,20]. Nevertheless, RL faces two main challenges inherent to the learning approach which is purely based on reward signals.

On the one hand, agents often learn sub-optimal behavior because of the nature of reward signals, which are usually sparse and available only when agents are in a goal state. On the other hand, the training process suffers from very high sample complexity. While even simple tasks already require millions of interactions, the problem becomes more severe for high dimensional control tasks.

Another drawback of modern RL systems is the lack of interpretability regarding their decisions. Deep reinforcement learning uses function approximators such as deep neural networks to learn policy functions that map states to actions. Although effective, the resulting networks are largely black-boxes which, for mainly legal reasons, can not be applied in safety critical systems such as autonomous vehicles where decisions must be transparent. Accordingly, recently there has been a increased interest in interpretable deep reinforcement learning and human-readable policies [11,27].

I. V. Tetko et al. (Eds.): ICANN 2019, LNCS 11728, pp. 595–607, 2019.
https://doi.org/10.1007/978-3-030-30484-3_48

Here, we address the problem of high sample complexity as well as the black-box nature of RL systems. By injecting expert knowledge into the models, we intend to improve transparency and to build more reliable systems. In particular, we inform the architecture of policy networks with domain knowledge to create transparent, modular, and data-efficient policy networks.

We demonstrate our approach in the context of a reacher task where the agent (a 2D multi joint arm) has to reach an unknown target based on feedback and rewards. We first revisit a model based on the *mean of multiple computations* (MMC) principle [24]. It has previously been successfully applied to biological system modeling, e.g. for analyzing walking behaviors of six-legged insects [4]. An MMC Net has several attractive properties. First, it is a simple recurrent neural network that can produce geometrically correct solution by predicting a trajectory to reach a target. Second, it can easily be extended to other tasks, e.g. a 3D 6-DoF arm, with little domain knowledge. Third, it has two components: a linear part which can be optimized numerically based on rewards and a known off-the-shelf non-linear component. This way, it is inherently modular and enables easy transfer of learned policies.

Our main contributions are: (i) we introduce the idea of MMCs to build modular policy networks using expert knowledge (ii) we extend MMC nets by adapting recurrent connections through reward signals and use it to solve the reacher task (iii) we experimentally compare the performance and sample complexity of MMC nets against end-to-end policy networks.

2 Related Work

Earlier work on injecting prior knowledge into RL focused extensively on designing reward signals by considering multiple sub-goals and intermediate rewards based on the relative progress made [6,12]. More recent work [3,9] considers hand-designed behavioural characteristics (BCs) to incorporate a novelty objective into the existing reward objective. This improves exploration in situations where no explicit reward signals are available to the agents.

Another approach to use domain expertise is to learn from expert demonstrations through inverse reinforcement learning [8,25,29]. Approaches that involve human interaction [10,16], rely on attaining positive and negative feedback about policies from human trainers to learn desired optimal behavior.

Prior work on building modular policy networks focused on transfer learning by sharing layers of networks across different tasks [2,5]. Interesting work in autonomous systems [15] uses networks which are decomposed into modules for perception and controllers and has proven to be deployable to other vehicles and environmental conditions with ease.

Differing from these approaches, we here focus on designing policy architectures using domain knowledge. In particular we focus on modular networks with hand-designed components rather than learning them in an end-to-end fashion. Importantly, by designing components as MMC networks, we derive a simple method which learns from a reduced number of interactions.

3 Preliminaries

Markov Decision Processes: We consider a standard reinforcement learning setting where an agent interacts with an environment. At time t, the agent receives an observation $\boldsymbol{o}_t$ about the environment state $\boldsymbol{s}_t$, performs an action $\boldsymbol{a}_t$, and receives a reward r_t. Typically, the environment is stochastic and formulated as a Markov Decision Process (MDP) defined by a tuple: $\langle \boldsymbol{S}, \boldsymbol{A}, \boldsymbol{T}, \boldsymbol{R_a} \rangle$ where $\boldsymbol{S}$ is a set of states, $\boldsymbol{A}$ is a set of actions, $\boldsymbol{R_a}$ is the reward function, and $\boldsymbol{T}$ is the transition probability. Upon an action $\boldsymbol{a}_t$, the environment moves to a new state $\boldsymbol{s}_{t+1}$ according to the transition function $\boldsymbol{T}(\boldsymbol{s}_{t+1}, \boldsymbol{s}_t, \boldsymbol{a}_t)$ and responds with a scalar reward $r_t = \boldsymbol{R_a}(\boldsymbol{s}_{t+1}, \boldsymbol{s}_t, a_t)$. The agent's behavior is characterized by a policy function $\pi(\boldsymbol{s}_t, \boldsymbol{a}_t)$ which maps each state-action pair $(\boldsymbol{s}_t, \boldsymbol{a}_t)$ to the probability of selecting the action in the particular state. In RL, the goal of the agent is to maximize the return discounted by $\lambda \in (0, 1)$ over a period of time T given as

$$G_T = \sum_{t=1}^{T} \lambda^{t-1} r_t. \tag{1}$$

Policy Networks: For high-dimensional state and action spaces, it is not feasible to tabulate the probabilities for each state-action pair. Therefore, the policy π is often represented as a deep neural network $\pi_{\boldsymbol{\theta}}$ with weights $\boldsymbol{\theta}$. The goal is to determine optimal weights $\boldsymbol{\theta}^*$ that maximize the expected cumulative reward

$$\boldsymbol{\theta}^* = \underset{\boldsymbol{\theta}}{argmax}\, \mathbb{E}_{\pi_{\boldsymbol{\theta}}} \big[G_T\big]. \tag{2}$$

Optimization is typically achieved via stochastic gradient ascent where the gradient $\nabla_{\boldsymbol{\theta}} \mathbb{E}_{\pi_{\boldsymbol{\theta}}} \big[G_T\big]$ is obtained using sampled sequences $(\boldsymbol{s}_t, \boldsymbol{a}_t, r_t, \boldsymbol{s}_{t+1} \ldots)$ of interactions with the environment and can be computed via various policy gradient methods [17,19,21].

Reacher Task: To test our methods, we consider a reacher task where a planar three-segmented robotic arm with end effector has to reach a target position. The target is generated randomly in every episode and its position is unknown to the agent. The observation available to the agent consists of joint angles and a feedback signal. The actions are desired joint angles in the trajectory. And the reward is given as the negative norm of the distance of end effector to the target. This setup is similar to the simulation available on OpenAI Gym [1] and DeepMind's control suite [26] but varies slightly w.r.t. observations and actions.

4 Background

Linear MMC Networks: Consider a simple manipulator (a robotic arm) with three joints operating in a 2D space as shown in Fig. 1. Orientation and length of the three segments of the arm are denoted as vectors $\boldsymbol{L}_1$, $\boldsymbol{L}_2$ and $\boldsymbol{L}_3$ in a Cartesian coordinate system with the origin located at the shoulder joint.

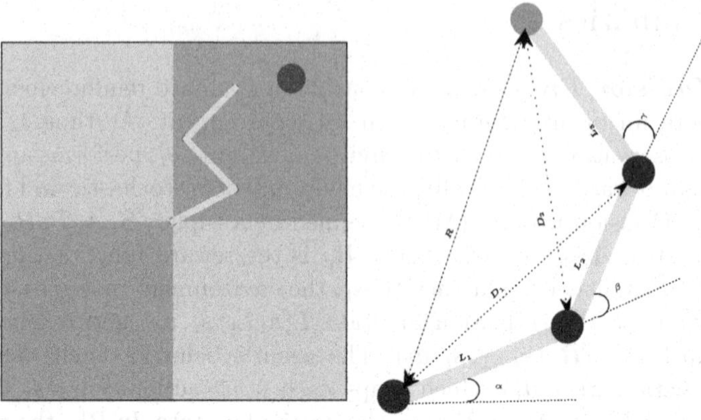

Fig. 1. Reacher environment: (a) A simple three-segmented robot arm with a randomized target. (b) A robotic arm consisting of three segments denoted as $\boldsymbol{L_1}$, $\boldsymbol{L_2}$ and $\boldsymbol{L_3}$. The relative angles at the joints are denoted as α, β, and γ. The vector pointing to the end-effector (in green) is described as $\boldsymbol{R}$. (Color figure online)

Two additional vectors $\boldsymbol{D}_1$, $\boldsymbol{D}_2$ connect the shoulder to the second joint and the first joint to the end effector respectively; a vector $\boldsymbol{R}$ connects shoulder and end effector. This setting provides the following over-determined system of equations

$$\begin{aligned} \boldsymbol{L}_1 + \boldsymbol{L}_2 + \boldsymbol{L}_3 - \boldsymbol{R} &= 0 \\ \boldsymbol{L}_2 + \boldsymbol{R} - \boldsymbol{D}_2 - \boldsymbol{D}_1 &= 0 \\ \boldsymbol{L}_1 - \boldsymbol{L}_3 + \boldsymbol{D}_2 - \boldsymbol{D}_1 &= 0 \\ \boldsymbol{L}_1 + \boldsymbol{L}_2 - \boldsymbol{D}_1 &= 0 \\ \boldsymbol{L}_2 + \boldsymbol{L}_3 - \boldsymbol{D}_2 &= 0 \\ \boldsymbol{L}_3 - \boldsymbol{R} + \boldsymbol{D}_1 &= 0 \\ \boldsymbol{L}_1 - \boldsymbol{R} + \boldsymbol{D}_2 &= 0 \end{aligned} \tag{3}$$

In (3) each vector appears exactly four times and according to the MMC principle, we can write every vector as a mean of the corresponding entries in the four equations. For instance, $\boldsymbol{L}_1$ can be computed as

$$\boldsymbol{L}_1 = \frac{1}{4}(-2\boldsymbol{L}_2 + 2\boldsymbol{R} - 2\boldsymbol{D}_2 + 2\boldsymbol{D}_1) \tag{4}$$

Given a desired target position $\boldsymbol{R}$, this setting is an instance of inverse kinematics in which the goal is to solve for the values $\boldsymbol{L}_{1,2,3}$ in an iterative manner. Thus, the mean values are fed back as input to the system for the next iteration until the system relaxes to the desired position. Note that $\boldsymbol{R}$ is kept constant throughout and its mean value is suppressed during the feedback. Furthermore, self-excitations are introduced via damping factors d_1, d_2, d_3, with the goal

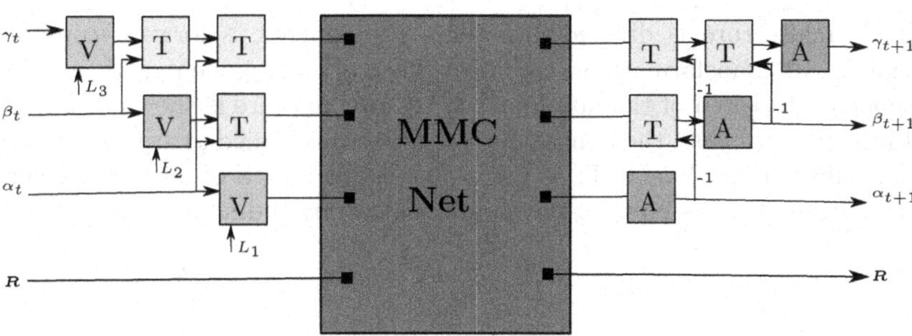

Fig. 2. A sketch of MMC architecture described in this paper; it consists of components for MMC Net sandwiched by forward and inverse transformations.

to suppress oscillations. In summary, the system represents a simple form of a recurrent neural network whose dynamics can be written as

$$\begin{aligned}
\boldsymbol{L}_1(t+1) &= \frac{1}{4+d_1}[d_1\boldsymbol{L}_1(t) - 2\boldsymbol{L}_2(t) + 2\boldsymbol{R} - 2\boldsymbol{D}_2(t) + 2\boldsymbol{D}_1(t)] \\
\boldsymbol{L}_2(t+1) &= \frac{1}{4+d_2}[-2\boldsymbol{L}_1(t) + d_2\boldsymbol{L}_2 - 2\boldsymbol{L}_3(t) + 2\boldsymbol{D}_2(t) + 2\boldsymbol{D}_1(t)] \\
\boldsymbol{L}_3(t+1) &= \frac{1}{4+d_3}[-2\boldsymbol{L}_2(t) + d_3\boldsymbol{L}_3 + 2\boldsymbol{R} + 2\boldsymbol{D}_2(t) - 2\boldsymbol{D}_1(t)]
\end{aligned}$$

The coefficients of this system of equations can be collected in a matrix $\boldsymbol{\theta}$ (scaling factors are ignored for readability)

$$\boldsymbol{\theta} = \begin{bmatrix} d_1 & -2 & 0 & 2 & -2 & 2 \\ -2 & d_2 & -2 & 0 & 2 & 2 \\ 0 & -2 & d_3 & 2 & 2 & -2 \end{bmatrix} \tag{5}$$

which will later be subject to a reinforcement learning policy.

During the relaxation the lengths of the arm vectors may change, which is, of course, undesirable. Rather the system should find a suitable joint configurations to reach the target while leaving the arm lengths constant. This can be achieved via a non-linear model.

Non-linear MMC Networks: In order to keep the lengths of the three arm segments fixed, we follow [24] and describe the arm segments in terms of their lengths L_1, L_2 and L_3 and orientations α, β, γ. At time t, α_t, β_t, γ_t are given as input to the system and the outputs are the predicted orientations α_{t+1}, β_{t+1}, γ_{t+1} that will serve as the input for the next iteration.

The architecture is divided into three components, a forward component for non-linear transformations, an MMC network component and an inverse component. A sketch of the non-linear MMC architecture is shown in Fig. 2.

In the forward pass, the joint angles are first transformed to arm vectors using the transformations **V** and **T**. **V** takes a constant length of an arm segment L and a joint angle α as inputs to compute the corresponding arm vector

$$\boldsymbol{L} = L \begin{bmatrix} \cos\alpha \\ \sin\alpha \end{bmatrix} \tag{6}$$

The transformation **T** takes an arm vector $\boldsymbol{L}$ and an angle α as input and applies a corresponding rotation

$$\boldsymbol{L}' = \begin{bmatrix} L'_x \\ L'_y \end{bmatrix} = \begin{bmatrix} \cos\alpha & -\sin\alpha \\ \sin\alpha & \cos\alpha \end{bmatrix} \begin{bmatrix} L_x \\ L_y \end{bmatrix} \tag{7}$$

The transformations are applied in sequence; for instance, γ_t is transformed by (**V**, **T**, **T**), where the latter two transformations are necessary because the joint angles are all relative to their own axis [Fig. 1].

The output of the forward pass are the arm vectors $\boldsymbol{L}_1(t)$, $\boldsymbol{L}_2(t)$, $\boldsymbol{L}_3(t)$ which are then fed to the linear MMC Net to compute the predicted arm vectors for the next time step, $\boldsymbol{L}_1(t+1)$, $\boldsymbol{L}_2(t+1)$, $\boldsymbol{L}_3(t+1)$.

Finally, in the inverse component, these vectors are converted back to the corresponding arm orientations α_{t+1}, β_{t+1}, γ_{t+1} using the inverse of **T** and **A**, which is the inverse of **V** and computes the arm orientation given an arm vector

$$\alpha = \arctan(L_y, L_x) \tag{8}$$

5 Learning a Modular Policy Network

So far we discussed the planning of a trajectory towards a target position using MMC networks. However, in an RL setting, the agent does not have access target positions directly. For instance, in the reacher task, the agent instead receives a feedback vector which is usually the distance between the end-effector and the target denoted as $\boldsymbol{R}_t$. Thus, it can be treated as a proxy for the actual target position. In this case, too, the coefficients of the MMC Net have to be solved but instead of solving by hand, they can now be trained based on reward signals. To this end, we define the policy π as a MMC policy network $\pi_{\boldsymbol{\theta}}$ with weights $\boldsymbol{\theta}$ which can be then adapted by a policy learning method.

5.1 Approach for Solving Reacher Tasks

The main idea is to decompose our MMC policy network π_θ into linear and non-linear components and to adapt only the linear component while non-linear components are used off-the-shelf. At time t, observation o_t is processed as

1. **Forward Component**: This part of the network converts the joint angles contained in the given observation $\boldsymbol{o}_t = (\alpha_t, \beta_t, \gamma_t, \boldsymbol{R}_t)$ into input vectors $\boldsymbol{L}_1(t)$, $\boldsymbol{L}_2(t)$ and $\boldsymbol{L}_3(t)$ via transformations $\mathbf{V}$ and $\mathbf{T}$.
2. **MMC Component**: This is a linear MMC net with weights $\boldsymbol{\theta}$ which are adapted by a learning method through interaction with the environment. This component then acts as a planning module which predicts the next point in the trajectory $\boldsymbol{L}_1(t+1)$, $\boldsymbol{L}_2(t+1)$ and $\boldsymbol{L}_3(t+1)$.
3. **Inverse Component**: This complements the forward component. Outputs of the MMC net, such as the predicted arm vectors $\boldsymbol{L}_1(t+1)$, $\boldsymbol{L}_2(t+1)$ and $\boldsymbol{L}_3(t+1)$, will be converted back to joint angles α_{t+1}, β_{t+1}, γ_{t+1} resulting in an action vector $\boldsymbol{a}_t$

Using such a modular system, forward- and inverse components can be shared between similar tasks or can be engineered using domain knowledge to solve different tasks. Only the MMC net needs to be trained for the given task. Most importantly, by designing the inputs that are passed to MMC net, the task can be solved efficiently.

5.2 Learning Method

Our goal is to find the optimal value for coefficients $\boldsymbol{\theta}$ of MMC net such that the expected cumulative reward is maximized $\boldsymbol{\theta}^* = \text{argmax}_{\boldsymbol{\theta}} J(\boldsymbol{\theta})$ where $J(\boldsymbol{\theta}) = \mathbb{E}_{\pi_\theta}\big[G_T\big]$. To train $\boldsymbol{\theta}$ of the MMC net, we use a stochastic approximation, namely Simultaneous Perturbation Stochastic Approximation (SPSA). SPSA [23] offers a simple approach to iteratively update $\boldsymbol{\theta}$ by using gradient estimates

$$\boldsymbol{\theta}_{k+1} = \boldsymbol{\theta}_k + a_k\, \hat{\boldsymbol{g}}_k(\boldsymbol{\theta}_k) \tag{9}$$

where $\hat{\boldsymbol{g}}_k(\boldsymbol{\theta}_k)$ is an estimator of the gradient at $\boldsymbol{\theta}_k$ and a_k is the learning rate in iteration k. To estimate the gradient, two perturbations are generated, namely $(\boldsymbol{\theta}_k + c_k\, \boldsymbol{\delta}_k)$ and $(\boldsymbol{\theta}_k - c_k\, \boldsymbol{\delta}_k)$ where $\boldsymbol{\delta}_k$ is a perturbation vector and c_k is a scaling parameter. The objective function at $J(\boldsymbol{\theta}_k + c_k, \boldsymbol{\delta}_k)$ and $J(\boldsymbol{\theta}_k - c_k\, \boldsymbol{\delta}_k)$ is measured by rolling out an episode with MMC network with weights $(\boldsymbol{\theta}_k + c_k\, \boldsymbol{\delta}_k)$ and $(\boldsymbol{\theta}_k - c_k\, \boldsymbol{\delta}_k)$ respectively. Then, the gradient is estimated using a two-sided gradient approximation

$$\hat{\boldsymbol{g}}_k(\boldsymbol{\theta}_k) = \frac{J(\boldsymbol{\theta}_k + c_k\, \boldsymbol{\delta}_k) - J(\boldsymbol{\theta}_k - c_k\, \boldsymbol{\delta}_k)}{2\, c_k\, \boldsymbol{\delta}_k}. \tag{10}$$

For the convergence of the algorithm, the learning rate a_k must satisfy Robbins-Monro conditions [18], namely $a_k > 0$ and $\sum_{k=1}^{\infty} a_k = \infty$, therefore a typical choice in practice is $a_k = \frac{a}{(A+k)^\eta}$ where $a, \eta, A > 0$. Similarly, the scaling factor c_k must satisfy $\sum_{k=1}^{\infty} \left(\frac{a_k}{c_k}\right)^2 < \infty$ so that a good choice would be $c_k = \frac{c}{k^\tau}$ where $c, \tau > 0$. And, finally, each element of the perturbation vector $\boldsymbol{\delta}_k$ is sampled from a uniform distribution over the set $\{-1, +1\}$.

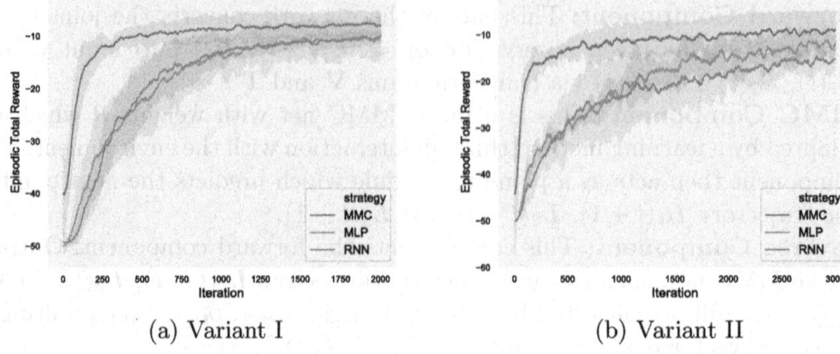

(a) Variant I (b) Variant II

Fig. 3. Learning curves: Evolution of episodic total reward in learning of Reacher task with two variants; (a) Variant I: in which target position as given in the observation and (b) Variant II: in which target position is not directly available, but as a feedback signal in the observation. As observed, MMC networks outperform end-end approaches in both variants.

6 Results and Discussion

In this section, we demonstrate the performance of the proposed MMC policy network using a simulation environment as shown in Fig. 1. In particular, we focus on performance metrics such as episodic total reward and sample complexity. Furthermore, we consider **Variant I**, where the agent observes the target position directly, and **Variant II**, where the agent receives a feedback signal based on the difference between end effector position and target position. We evaluate our MMC policy network against end-end policy networks on learning a deterministic policy which predicts joint angles. Since angular velocities are not included in the observation, we also consider a recurrent neural network as a baseline treating it as a partially observable task.

In each experiment, the length of an episode is limited to 30 time steps. Therefore, the goal is not just to reach fast but also to maintain the end effector around the target. Our MMC net is a linear model consisting of 8 input neurons and 6 output neurons. Our baselines are (i) a fully connected multi-layer perceptrons (MLP) with 3 hidden layers consisting of 30 neurons with tanh activation, (ii) a recurrent neural network (RNN) of gated recurrent units (GRU) with 3 hidden layers consisting of 30 neurons. All networks are trained using SPSA parameters $a = 0.01, A = 10, \eta = 0.1, c = 0.01, \tau = 0.1$. Gradients are smoothed via RMSprop with decay 0.9. Finally, for stable learning, K pairs of perturbations are evaluated to compute average gradients; K is tuned to the size of the network (100 for the baseline models and 50 for the MMC net).

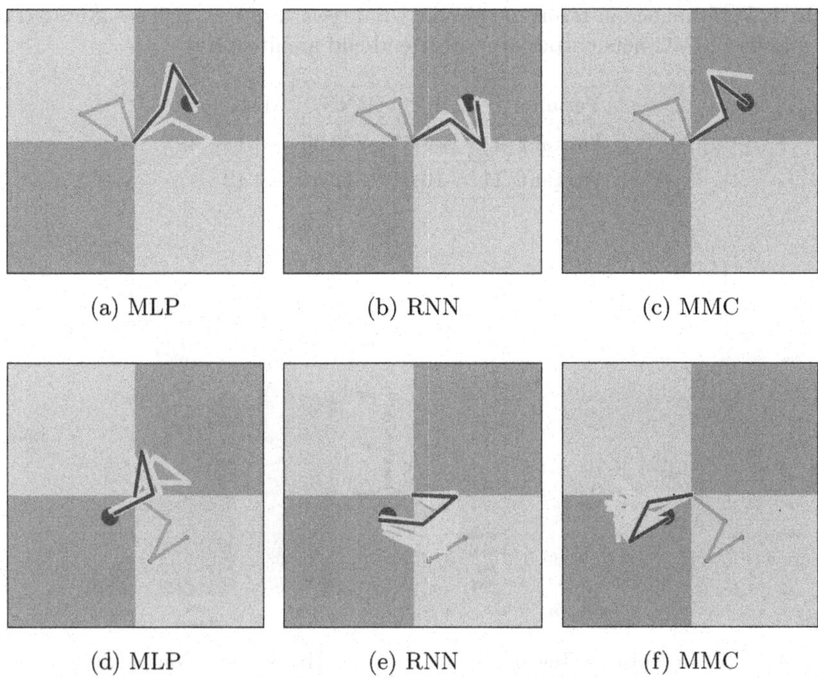

(a) MLP (b) RNN (c) MMC

(d) MLP (e) RNN (f) MMC

Fig. 4. Agent behaviors: Initial and final arm positions are shown in orange and red respectively; (a), (d) trajectories toward the target with MLP agent; (b), (e) with RNN agent; (c), (f) with MMC agent. MMC agents quickly approach the target and maintain their position around the target throughout an episode. (Color figure online)

6.1 Learning Performance

In order to evaluate the performance of the MMC network quantitatively, we consider the learning of an optimal policy using MMC networks and compare them to baseline techniques. Figure 3 shows the evolution of episodic total reward (averaged over different random seeds) in the learning process (the higher the better) for both variants of the task. These results suggest that the MMC policy network is able to learn optimal behaviors in only a few iterations. MMC networks also perform similarly well in both variants of the task which shows the robustness of the proposed modular architecture. On the other hand, the end-to-end approaches seem to have more difficulties when learning a suitable policy for variant II than in the case of variant I. Finally, we compare the performance of the best policies of each network in 100 episodes and summarize their average performance in Table 1.

In order to compare the behavior of agents, we ran the task with two random seeds with final trained best policies from each network and plotted their behaviors observed throughout the episode in Fig. 4. Figure 4(a), (d) show the

Table 1. Performance in terms of episodic total reward of best policies averaged over 100 episodes; MMC nets outperform other end-end architectures

Variants	MLP	RNN	MMC
`Variant I`	−7.37	−9.06	−3.18
`Variant II`	−10.01	−12.64	−4.12

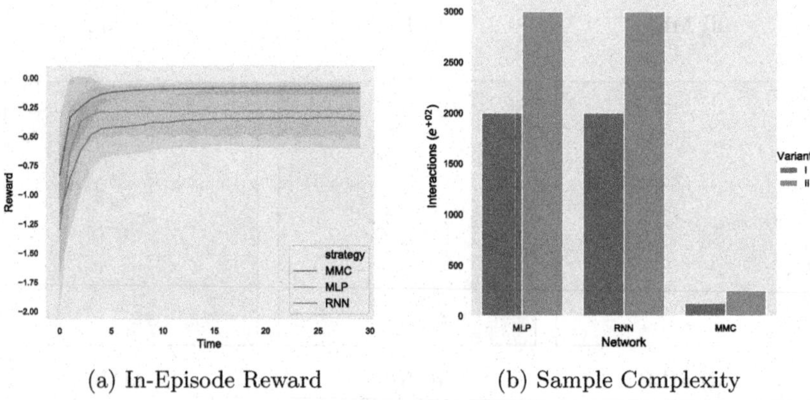

(a) In-Episode Reward (b) Sample Complexity

Fig. 5. (a) **In-Episode Reward**: Evolution of reward averaged over 100 runs; MMC networks quickly relax to high reward gaining trajectories as soon as an episode starts. (b) **Sample Complexity**: A summary of total interactions with environment to learn an optimal policy with different networks and variants of Reacher task; MMC networks are 10 times sample-efficient than end-end approaches

behavior of agents whose policies were learned using multi-layer perceptrons; (b), (e) reflect policies learned by gated recurrent units, and, finally (c) and (f) were obtained from MMC policy networks. These examples suggest that agents trained with the MMC policy network quickly approach the target thus gaining high rewards whereas the other methods slowly adapt to the feedback signal. Figure 5(a) captures the similar behavior in terms of reward obtained at each step in an episode. By averaging over 100 runs, we observe that MMC networks are able to stabilize themselves to high reward positions from very early in the episode (approx $t = 2$) when compared to end-to-end approaches.

6.2 Sample Complexity

To evaluate the sample complexity of policy learning with MMC networks, we consider the number of interactions with the environment required for achieving the best performance of the baseline models. To this end, we consider the learning curves in Fig. 3. For variant I, the baseline models required 2000 iterations to reach their best performance whereas a similar performance was achieved by

MMC within only about 250 iterations. While training the baseline networks, gradient updates in each iteration are computed after evaluating 100 pairs of perturbations. Similarly, with our MMC policy network, an update is performed after evaluating 50 pairs of perturbations. Therefore, a total of 200.000 interactions is required for the baselines. However, the MMC approach required only $250 \times 50 = 12.500$ interactions with the data. This shows that our MMC network is 16 times more data-efficient than the end-to-end approaches. A similar analysis for variant II shows a 12 fold speed up for the MMC networks. These results are summarized in Fig. 5(b).

7 Conclusion

We presented a novel way of using MMC architectures for reinforcement learning. The proposed approach allows experts to inject domain knowledge into policy networks by designing and building task specific modular components. In our experiments, we showed that the proposed policy network learns better policies for variants of the "reacher" task in a more sample-efficient manner than several baseline techniques and attains over 10× speed up compared to competing architectures. The resulting modular structure has the advantage that the non-linear part is known in terms of explicit transformations which, in practical applications, is often an advantage over black box end-to-end systems composed of neural networks. Therefore, the injection of domain knowledge not only reduces the sample complexity but is also an important step towards more explainable systems.

MMC networks can be extended in several ways. First, forward and inverse components for other continuous control tasks such as a bi-pedal walking, hopping, etc. [26] can be engineered using expert domain knowledge. Second, the inherent recurrent nature of the approach and the capability to predict the next states in a trajectory towards the target enables unrolling trajectories over time. This unrolling can then be used for the planning of extended actions, i.e., actions that are performed over extended periods of time. Thus, systems which learn hierarchical policies can also be developed. Third, the architecture itself is biologically inspired. By evolving just the MMC component, we can create systems that can learn to imagine and choose actions effectively based on imagined trajectories. In future work, we intend to solve similar robotic tasks with reinforcement learning and MMC architectures by incorporating domain knowledge in particular pertaining to bi-pedal walking.

References

1. Brockman, G., et al.: OpenAI Gym. arXiv:1606.01540 (2016)
2. Clavera, I., Held, D., Abbeel, P.: Policy transfer via modularity and reward guiding. In: Proceedings Intelligent Robots and Systems (2017)
3. Conti, E., Madhavan, V., Such, F.P., Lehman, J., Stanley, K.O., Clune, J.: Improving exploration in evolution strategies for deep reinforcement learning via a population of novelty-seeking agents. arXiv preprint arXiv:1712.06560 (2017)

4. Cruse, H., Kindermann, T., Schumm, M., Dean, J., Schmitz, J.: Walknet-a-biologically inspired network to control six-legged walking. Neural Networks **11**(7–8), 1435–1447 (1998)
5. Devin, C., Gupta, A., Darrell, T., Abbeel, P., Levine, S.: Learning modular neural network policies for multi-task and multi-robot transfer. In: Proceedings International Conference on Robotics and Automation (2017)
6. Dorigo, M., Colombetti, M.: Robot shaping: developing autonomous agents through learning. Artif. Intell. **71**(2), 321–370 (1994)
7. Gu, S., Holly, E., Lillicrap, T., Levine, S.: Deep reinforcement learning for robotic manipulation with asynchronous off-policy updates. In: Proceedings International Conference on Robotics and Automation (2017)
8. Ho, J., Ermon, S.: Generative adversarial imitation learning. In: Proceedings Neural Information Processing Systems (2016)
9. Lehman, J., Stanley, K.O.: Evolving a diversity of virtual creatures through novelty search and local competition. In: Proceedings International Conference on Genetic and Evolutionary Computation (2011)
10. Loftin, R., et al.: Learning behaviors via human-delivered discrete feedback: modeling implicit feedback strategies to speed up learning. Auton. Agent. Multi-Agent Syst. **30**(1), 30–59 (2016)
11. Maes, F., Fonteneau, R., Wehenkel, L., Ernst, D.: Policy search in a space of simple closed-form formulas: towards interpretability of reinforcement learning. In: Ganascia, J.-G., Lenca, P., Petit, J.-M. (eds.) DS 2012. LNCS (LNAI), vol. 7569, pp. 37–51. Springer, Heidelberg (2012). https://doi.org/10.1007/978-3-642-33492-4_6
12. Mataric, M.J.: Reward Functions for Accelerated Learning. In: Machine Learning Proceedings 1994 (1994)
13. Mirowski, P., et al.: Learning to navigate in complex environments. arXiv preprint arXiv:1611.03673 (2016)
14. Mnih, V., et al.: Human-level control through deep reinforcement learning. Nature **518**(7540), 529 (2015)
15. Müller, M., Dosovitskiy, A., Ghanem, B., Koltun, V.: Driving policy transfer via modularity and abstraction. arXiv preprint arXiv:1804.09364 (2018)
16. Peng, B., MacGlashan, J., Loftin, R., Littman, M.L., Roberts, D.L., Taylor, M.E.: A need for speed: adapting agent action speed to improve task learning from non-expert humans. In: Proceedings of the 2016 International Conference on Autonomous Agents & Multiagent Systems (2016)
17. Ramamurthy, R., Bauckhage, C., Sifa, R., Wrobel, S.: Policy learning using SPSA. In: Kůrková, V., Manolopoulos, Y., Hammer, B., Iliadis, L., Maglogiannis, I. (eds.) ICANN 2018. LNCS, vol. 11141, pp. 3–12. Springer, Cham (2018). https://doi.org/10.1007/978-3-030-01424-7_1
18. Robbins, H., Monro, S.: A stochastic approximation method. Annals of Mathematical Statistics **22**(3), 400–407 (1951)
19. Salimans, T., Ho, J., Chen, X., Sutskever, I.: Evolution strategies as a scalable alternative to reinforcement learning. arXiv:1703.03864 (2017)
20. Schulman, J., Levine, S., Abbeel, P., Jordan, M., Moritz, P.: Trust Region Policy Optimization. In: Proceedings International Conference on Machine Learning (2015)
21. Silver, D., Lever, G., Heess, N., Degris, T., Wierstra, D., Riedmiller, M.: Deterministic policy gradient algorithms. In: Proceedings International Conference on Machine Learning (2014)

22. Silver, D., et al.: Mastering the game of go without human knowledge. Nature **550**(7676), 354 (2017)
23. Spall, J.C.: Multivariate stochastic approximation using a simultaneous perturbation gradient approximation. IEEE Trans. Autom. Control **37**(3), 332–341 (1992)
24. Steinkühler, U., Cruse, H.: A holistic model for an internal representation to control the movement of a manipulator with redundant degrees of freedom. Biol. Cybern. **79**(6), 457–466 (1998)
25. Suay, H.B., Brys, T., Taylor, M.E., Chernova, S.: Learning from demonstration for shaping through inverse reinforcement learning. In: Proceedings of the 2016 International Conference on Autonomous Agents & Multiagent Systems (2016)
26. Tassa, Y., et al.: DeepMind Control Suite. arXiv preprint arXiv:1801.00690 (2018)
27. Verma, A., Murali, V., Singh, R., Kohli, P., Chaudhuri, S.: Programmatically interpretable reinforcement learning. arXiv preprint arXiv:1804.02477 (2018)
28. Zhu, Y., et al.: Target-driven visual navigation in indoor scenes using deep reinforcement learning. In: Proceedings International Conference on Robotics and Automation (2017)
29. Zhu, Y., et al.: Reinforcement and imitation learning for diverse visuomotor skills. arXiv preprint arXiv:1802.09564 (2018)

Conditions for Unnecessary Logical Constraints in Kernel Machines

Francesco Giannini(✉) and Marco Maggini

Department of Information Engineering and Mathematical Sciences, University of Siena, via Roma 56, Siena, Italy
{fgiannini,maggini}@diism.unisi.it

Abstract. A main property of support vector machines consists in the fact that only a small portion of the training data is significant to determine the maximum margin separating hyperplane in the feature space, the so called *support vectors*. In a similar way, in the general scheme of learning from constraints, where possibly several constraints are considered, some of them may turn out to be unnecessary with respect to the learning optimization, even if they are active for a given optimal solution. In this paper we extend the definition of support vector to *support constraint* and we provide some criteria to determine which constraints can be removed from the learning problem still yielding the same optimal solutions. In particular, we discuss the case of logical constraints expressed by Łukasiewicz logic, where both inferential and algebraic arguments can be considered. Some theoretical results that characterize the concept of *unnecessary constraint* are proved and explained by means of examples.

Keywords: Support vectors · First–order logic · Kernel machines

1 Introduction

Support vector machines (SVMs) are a class of kernel methods originally conceived by Vapnik and Chervonenkis [3]. One of the main advantages of this approach is the capacity to create nonlinear classifiers by applying the kernel trick to maximum–margin hyperplanes [1,3]. This property derives from the implicit definition of a (possibly infinite) high–dimensional feature representation of data determined by the chosen kernel. In the supervised case, the learning strategy consists in the optimization of an objective function, given by a regularization term, subject to a set of constraints that enforce the membership of the example points to the positive or negative class, as specified by the provided targets. The satisfaction of these constraints can be obtained also by the minimization of a hinge loss function that does not penalize output values "beyond" the target. As a consequence, the solution of the optimization problem will depend only on a subset of the given training data, namely those that contribute to the definition of the maximum–margin hyperplane separating the two classes in the feature space. In fact, if we approach the problem in the framework of constrained optimization, these points will correspond to the *active* constraints in

I. V. Tetko et al. (Eds.): ICANN 2019, LNCS 11728, pp. 608–620, 2019.
https://doi.org/10.1007/978-3-030-30484-3_49

the Lagrangian formulation. This means that we can split the training examples into two categories, the *support vectors*, that completely determine the optimal solution of the problem, and the *straw vectors*. By solving the Lagrangian dual of the optimization problem, the support vectors are those supervised examples corresponding to constraints whose Lagrangian multiplier is not null. In this paper we extend this paradigm to a class of semi–supervised learning problems where logical constraints are enforced on the available samples.

Learning from constraints has been proposed in the framework of kernel machines as an approach to combine prior knowledge and learning from examples [9]. In particular, some techniques to exploit knowledge expressed in a description logic language [4] and by means of first-order logic (FOL) rules have been proposed in the literature [5,15]. In general, these techniques assume a multi–task learning paradigm where the functions to be learnt are subject to a set of logical constraints, which provide an expressive and formally well–defined representation for abstract knowledge. For instance, logical formulas may be translated into continuous functions by means of t-norms theory [6]. This mapping allows the definition of an optimization problem that integrates supervised examples and the enforcement of logical constraints on a set of available groundings. In general, the resulting optimization problem is not guaranteed to be convex as in the original SVM framework due to contribution of the constraints. However, it turns out to be convex when considering formulas expressed with a fragment of the Łukasiewicz logic [7]. In this case, the problem can be formulated as quadratic optimization since the constraints are convex piece-wise linear functions. Other related methods to embed logical rules into learning schemes have been considered, such as [18,19], where a framework called Logic Tensor Networks has been proposed, and [13], where logic rules are combined with neural network learning.

The notion of *support constraints* has been proposed in [10,11] to provide an extension of the concept of support vector when dealing with learning from constraints. The idea is based on the definition of entailment relations among constraints and the possibility of constraint checking on the data distribution. In this paper, we provide a formal definition of *unnecessary constraints* that refines the concept of support constraint and we provide some theoretical results characterizing the presence of such constraints. These results are illustrated by examples that show in practice how the conditions are verified. The main idea is that unnecessary constraints can be removed from a learning problem without modifying the set of optimal solutions. Similarly, with the specific goal to define algorithms accelerating the search for solutions in optimization problems, it is worth to mention the works in the Constraint Reduction (CR) field. In particular, in [14] it is shown how to reduce the computational burden in a convex optimization problem by considering at each iteration the subset of the constraints that contains only the most critical (or necessary) ones. In this sense, our approach allows us to determine theoretically which are the unnecessary constraints as well as to enlighten their logical relations with the other constraints.

The paper is organized as follows. In Sect. 2 we introduce the notation and the problem formulation. Then, Sect. 3 analyzes the structure of the optimal solutions, providing the conditions to determine the presence of unnecessary constraints. The formal definition of *unnecessary constraint* and the related theorems are reported in Sect. 3.2. In Sect. 4 we show how the proposed method is applied by means of some examples and finally, some conclusions and future directions are discussed in Sect. 5.

2 Learning from Constraints in Kernel Machines

We consider a multi–task learning problem with $\mathbf{P} = \{p_j : \mathbb{R}^{n_j} \to \mathbb{R} : j \leq J\}$ denoting a set of $J > 0$ functions to be learned. We assume that each p_j belongs to a *Reproducing Kernel Hilbert Space* (RKHS) [16] $\mathcal{H}_j$ and it is expressed as

$$p_j(x) = \omega_j \cdot \phi_j(x) + b_j,$$

where ϕ_j is a function that maps the input space into a feature space (possibly having infinite dimensions), such that $k_j(x, y) = \phi_j(x)^T \cdot \phi_j(y)$, where $k_j \in \mathcal{H}_j$ is the j-th kernel function. The notation is quite general to take into account the fact that predicates (f.i. unary or binary) can be defined on different domains and approximated by different kernel functions[1].

We assume a semi-supervised scheme in which each p_j is trained on two datasets, $\mathscr{L}_j$ containing the supervised examples and $\mathscr{U}_j$ containing the unsupervised ones, while all the available input samples for p_j are collected in $\mathscr{S}_j$, as follows

$$\begin{aligned}
&\mathscr{L}_j = \{(x_l, y_l) : l \leq l_j, x_l \in \mathbb{R}^{n_j}, y_l \in \{-1, +1\}\},\\
&\mathscr{U}_j = \{x_u : u \leq u_j, x_u \in \mathbb{R}^{n_j}\},\\
&\mathscr{S}_j = \{x_s : s \leq s_j\} = \{x_l : (x_l, y_l) \in \mathscr{L}_j\} \cup \mathscr{U}_j, \quad S = \textstyle\sum_{j=1}^{J} s_j \ .
\end{aligned}$$

In the following, whenever we write $p_j(x_s)$, we assume $x_s \in \mathscr{S}_j$. Functions in $\mathbf{P}$ are assumed to be predicates subject to some prior knowledge expressed by a set of *First–Order Logic* (FOL) formulas φ_h with $h \leq H$ in a knowledge base KB, and evaluated on the available samples for each predicate.

2.1 Constraints

The learning problem is formulated to require the satisfaction of three classes of constraints, defined as follows.

- *Consistency* constraints derive from the need to limit the values of predicates into $[0, 1]$, in order to be consistent with the logical operators:

$$0 \leq p_j(x_s) \leq 1, \qquad x_s \in \mathscr{S}_j, j \leq J \ .$$

- *Pointwise* constraints derive from the supervisions by requiring the output of the functions to be 1 for target $y_l = 1$ and 0 for $y_l = -1$:

$$y_l(2p_j(x_l) - 1) \geq 1, \qquad (x_l, y_l) \in \mathscr{L}_j, j \leq J \ .$$

[1] Predicates sharing the same domain may be approximated in the same RKHS by using the same kernel function.

Table 1. Logic connectives and their algebraic semantics for the Łukasiewicz logic. From left to right: *negation, strong conjunction (t-norm), weak conjunction, weak disjunction, strong disjunction (t-conorm), implication (residuum).*

$\neg x$	$x \otimes y$	$x \wedge y$	$x \vee y$	$x \oplus y$	$x \Rightarrow y$
$1-x$	$\max\{0, x+y-1\}$	$\min\{x,y\}$	$\max\{x,y\}$	$\min\{1, x+y\}$	$\min\{1, 1-x+y\}$

- *Logical* constraints are obtained by mapping each formula φ_h in KB into a continuous real-valued function f_h according to the operations of a certain t-norm fuzzy logic[2] (see Table 1 for the Łukasiewicz fuzzy logic) and then forcing their satisfaction by

$$1 - f_h(\boldsymbol{p}) \leq 0, \qquad h \leq H,$$

where for any $j \leq J$, $\boldsymbol{p}_j = [p_j(x_1), \ldots, p_j(x_{s_j})] \in [0,1]^{s_j}$ is the vector of the evaluations (groundings) of the j-th predicate on the samples in $\mathscr{S}_j$ and $\boldsymbol{p} = [\boldsymbol{p}_1, \ldots \boldsymbol{p}_J] \in [0,1]^S$ is the concatenation of the groundings of all the predicates.

2.2 Optimization Problem

Given the previously defined constraints, the learning problem can be formulated as *primal* optimization as,

Problem 1.

$$\min_{\omega_j} \frac{1}{2}\sum_{j=1}^{J} ||\omega_j||^2 \qquad \text{subject to:}$$

$$\begin{array}{ll} 0 \leq p_j(x_s) \leq 1, & \text{for } x_s \in \mathscr{S}_j,\ j \leq J \\ y_l(2p_j(x_l) - 1) \geq 1, & \text{for } (x_l, y_l) \in \mathscr{L}_j,\ j \leq J \\ 1 - f_h(\boldsymbol{p}) \leq 0, & \text{for } h \leq H \end{array}$$

This problem was shown to be solvable by quadratic optimization provided the formulas in KB belong to the convex Łukasiewicz fragment (i.e. formulas exploiting only the operators $(\wedge, \oplus)$ in Table 1 [8]) and, in the following, we keep this assumption. This yields the functional constraints to be both convex and piecewise linear functions, hence they can be expressed as the max of a set of I_h affine functions[3] (see Theorem 2.49 in [17])

$$1 - f_h(\boldsymbol{p}) = \max_{i \leq I_h}(M_{h,i} \cdot \boldsymbol{p} + q_{h,i}) \tag{1}$$

where $M_{h,i} = [m^{h,i}_{1,1}, \ldots, m^{h,i}_{1,s_1}, \ldots, m^{h,i}_{J,s_J}] \in \mathbb{R}^S$ is a vector defining the i-th linear piece depending on the structure of the h-th formula, and $q_{h,i} \in \mathbb{R}$. Basically

[2] See e.g. [12] for more details on fuzzy logics.

[3] The number of linear pieces I_h depends on both the formula and the number of groundings used in that formula.

any $m^{h,i}_{j,s}$ weighs the contribution of the s-th sample in $\mathscr{S}_j$ for the j-th predicate in the i-th linear piece deriving from the Łukasiewicz formula of the h-th logic constraint. The matrix M, obtained concatenating all the $M_{h,i}$ by row, may have several null elements, as shown in the examples reported in the following.

Example 1. Let p_1, p_2 be a unary and a binary predicate, respectively, evaluated on $\mathscr{S}_1 = \{x_1, x_2\}$ and $\mathscr{S}_2 = \{(x_1,x_1),(x_1,x_2),(x_2,x_1),(x_2,x_2)\} = \mathscr{S}_1 \times \mathscr{S}_1$ so that $\boldsymbol{p}_1 = [p_1(x_1), p_1(x_2)]$, $\boldsymbol{p}_2 = [p_2(x_1,x_1), p_2(x_1,x_2), p_2(x_2,x_1), p_2(x_2,x_2)]$ denote their grounding vectors. Given the formula $\varphi = \forall x \forall y\, (p_1(x) \wedge p_1(y)) \Rightarrow p_2(x,y)$, according to the convex Łukasiewicz operators, its corresponding functional constraint $1 - f_\varphi$ can be rewritten as the max of a set of affine functions, i.e. $\max_{x,y}\{0,\, p_1(x) + p_1(y) - p_2(x,y) - 1\}$, that can be made explicit with respect to the grounding vectors of p_1 and p_2 by:

$$\max\{0,\, 2p_1(x_1) - p_2(x_1,x_1) - 1,\, p_1(x_1) + p_1(x_2) - p_2(x_1,x_2) - 1,$$
$$p_1(x_1) + p_1(x_2) - p_2(x_2,x_1) - 1,\, 2p_1(x_2) - p_2(x_2,x_2) - 1\}.$$

In this case $I_h = 5$, and, for instance, $M_{\varphi,2} = [2, 0, -1, 0, 0, 0]$ and $q_{h,1} = -1$.

According to Eq. (1), any logical constraint $1 - f_h(\boldsymbol{p}) \le 0$ for $h \le H$ can be replaced by I_h linear constraints $M_{h,i} \cdot \boldsymbol{p} + q_{h,i} \le 0$, yielding *Problem* 1 to be reformulated as quadratic programming. Hence, assuming to satisfy the associated KKT–conditions and that the feasible set of solutions is not empty, for any $j \le J$ the optimal solution obtained by differentiating the Lagrangian function of *Problem* 1 (see [8]) is computed as:

$$p_j^*(x) = 2\sum_{l=1}^{l_j} \lambda^*_{jl} y_l k_j(x_l, x) - \sum_{h=1}^{H}\sum_{i=1}^{I_h} \lambda^*_{h_i} \cdot \sum_{s=1}^{s_j} m^{h,i}_{j,s} \cdot k_j(x_s, x)$$
$$+ \sum_{s=1}^{s_j} (\eta^*_{j_s} - \bar{\eta}^*_{j_s}) k_j(x_s, x) + b^*_j. \qquad (2)$$

Each solution can be written as an expansion of the j-th kernel k_j with respect to the three different types of constraints on the corresponding sample points. As in classical SVMs, we may study the constraints whose optimal Lagrange multipliers $\lambda^*_{j,l}, \lambda^*_{h,i}, \eta^*_{j,s}, \bar{\eta}^*_{j,s}$ are not null, namely the *support (active) constraints.*

3 Unnecessary Constraints

The optimal solution of *Problem* 1 is determined only by the support constraints. The problem is convex if the Gram matrix of the chosen kernel is positive-semidefinite and strictly convex if it is positive-definite. The solution is guaranteed to be unique only in this second case [2]. For both cases, different multiplier vectors λ, η may yield an optimal solution for the Lagrangian function associated to the problem, e.g. see *Example* 3.

In this study, we are interested in constraints that are *not necessary* for the optimization, even if they may turn out to be active for a certain solution. The main results of this paper establish some criteria to discover unnecessary constraints and their relationship with the underling consequence relation among formulas in Łukasiewicz logic.

3.1 About Multipliers for Logical Constraints

By construction, pointwise and consistency constraints are both related to a single sample x for a given predicate. This means that the contribution of the active constraints of this type in any point is weighted by a specific multiplier, as expressed by the first and third summations in Eq. (2). On the opposite, each logical constraint involves in general more predicates eventually evaluated on different points (each Lagrange multiplier in the second summation of Eq. (2) is associated to a set of samples). Hence we may wonder if it exists a vector of Lagrange multipliers yielding the same contribution to the solution for each point, for which as much as possible multipliers are null.

For simplicity, Eq. (2) can be rewritten more compactly by grouping the terms with respect to any sample x_s as

$$p_j^*(x) = \sum_{s=1}^{s_j} \left(\alpha_{j,s}^{*(P)} + \alpha_{j,s}^{*(L)} + \alpha_{j,s}^{*(C)} \right) k_j(x_s, x) = \sum_{s=1}^{s_j} \alpha_{j,s}^* k_j(x_s, x) \tag{3}$$

where $\alpha_j^{*(P)}(\lambda_{j,l}^*), \alpha_j^{*(L)}(\lambda_{h,i}^*), \alpha_j^{*(C)}(\eta_{j,s}^*, \bar{\eta}_{j,s}^*)$ denote the vectors of optimal coefficients (depending on optimal Lagrange multipliers) of the kernel expansion for pointwise, logical and consistency constraints respectively. In particular, the term for the logical constraints is defined as

$$\alpha_{j,s}^{*(L)} = \sum_{h=1}^{H} \sum_{i=1}^{I_h} \lambda_{h,i}^* m_{j,s}^{h,i} . \tag{4}$$

Since (4) corresponds to the overall contribution of the logical constraints to the j-th optimal solution in its s-th point, we are interested in the case where we obtain the same term with different values for the multipliers $\lambda_{h,i}^*$. In particular, we would like to verify if there exists $\bar{h} \leq H$ such that for every $j \leq J$ and for every $s \leq s_j$, it is possible to compute $\bar{\lambda}_{h,i}$ such that

$$\alpha_{j,s}^{*(L)} = \sum_{\substack{h=1 \\ h \neq \bar{h}}}^{H} \sum_{i=1}^{I_h} \bar{\lambda}_{h,i} m_{j,s}^{h,i} . \tag{5}$$

This condition yields the same solution to the original problem but without any direct dependence on the $\bar{h}$-th constraint. This case can be determined as defined in the following *Problem* 2, where a matrix formulation is considered, and then by looking for a solution (if there exist) with null components for the $\bar{h}$-th constraint.

Problem 2. Given an optimal solution α^* for *Problem* 1, find $\lambda \in \mathbb{R}^N$ such that

$$M \cdot \lambda = \alpha^*,$$

where $N = \sum_{h=1}^{H} I_h$ and $M = [M_{1,1}, \ldots, M_{h,I_h}] \in \mathbb{R}^{S \times N}$.

Let $v_1, \ldots, v_n$ be an orthonormal base of the space generated by $Ker(M) = \{\lambda : M \cdot \lambda = 0\}$, such that any solution can be expressed as

$$\lambda = \lambda^* + \sum_{i=1}^{n} t_i v_i ,$$

for some $t_i \in \mathbb{R}$. We have the following cases:

(i) if $dim(Ker(M)) = 0$ then the system allows the unique solution λ^*;
(ii) if $dim(Ker(M)) \neq 0$ then there exist infinite solutions.

In the first case, the only constraints whose multipliers give null contribution to the optimal solution are the original straw constraints. Whereas in the second case, we look for a solution $\bar{\lambda}$ (if there exists) where $\bar{\lambda}_{\bar{h},i} = 0$ for any $i \leq I_{\bar{h}}$ for some $\bar{h} \leq H$. Indeed in such a case, we can replace λ^* with $\bar{\lambda}$ by transferring the contribution of the $\bar{h}$-th constraint to the other constraints still obtaining the same optimal solution for the predicates. This is carried out by solving the linear system with $I_{\bar{h}}$ equations $\bar{\lambda}_{\bar{h},i} = 0$ and n variables $t_1, \ldots, t_n$.

Remark 1. In the following, we will say that a vector $(\lambda_{h,i})_{h \leq H, i \leq I_h}$ is a solution of *Problem* 2 with respect to $\bar{h}$, if it is a solution and $\lambda_{\bar{h},i} = 0$ for every $i \leq I_{\bar{h}}$.

3.2 Unnecessary Hard–Constraints

Roughly speaking, we say that a given constraint is *unnecessary* for a certain optimization problem if its enforcement does not affect the solution of the problem. The main idea is that if we consider two problems (defined on the same sample sets and with the same loss), one with and one without the considered constraint, both have the same optimal solutions. The relation between logical inference and deducible constraints arises naturally in this frame, indeed logical deductive systems involve truth-preserving inference. In addition, logical constraints are quite general to include both pointwise and consistency constraints. A supervision (x_l, y_l) for a predicate p can be expressed by $1 \rightarrow p(x_l)$ if $y_l = 1$ and by $p(x_l) \rightarrow 0$ if $y_l = -1$, while the consistency constraints by $(0 \rightarrow p(x_l)) \wedge (p(x_l) \rightarrow 1)$. We note that in this uniform view, *Problem* 2 applies to all the constraints.

Definition 1. *Let us consider the learnable functions in* **P** *evaluated on a sample* $\mathscr{S}$ *and* $KB = \{\varphi_1, \ldots, \varphi_H\}$. *We say that* $\varphi_{\bar{h}} \in KB$ *is* unnecessary *for* **HP** *if the optimal solutions of problems* **HP** *and* $\overline{\textbf{HP}}$ *coincide, where*

$$(\textbf{HP}) \ \min_{\alpha} Loss(\alpha), \ \ with \ 1 - f_h(\mathbf{p}) \leq 0, \ \ for \ h \leq H ,$$

$$(\overline{\textbf{HP}}) \ \min_{\alpha} Loss(\alpha), \ \ with \ 1 - f_h(\mathbf{p}) \leq 0, \ \ for \ h \leq H, h \neq \bar{h}$$

$Loss(\alpha) = \sum_{j \leq J} \alpha_j' K_j \alpha_j$ *and* $K_j = (k_j(x_i, x_k))_{i,k \leq s_j}$ *is the Gram matrix of* k_j.

If $\mathcal{F}$ and $\overline{\mathcal{F}}$ are the feasible sets of **HP** and $\overline{\textbf{HP}}$ respectively, we have $\mathcal{F} \subseteq \overline{\mathcal{F}}$, however in general they are not the same set.

Since all the considered constraints correspond to logical formulas, we can also exploit some consequence relation among formulas in Łukasiewicz logic. In the following, we will write $\Gamma \models \phi$, where $\Gamma \cup \{\phi\}$ is a set of propositional formulas, to express the true-preserving logical consequence in **Ł**, stating that ϕ has to be evaluated as true for any assignation satisfying all the formulas in Γ.

Proposition 1. *If* $\{\varphi_h : h \leq H,\, h \neq \bar{h}\} \models \varphi_{\bar{h}}$ *then* $\varphi_{\bar{h}}$ *is unnecessary for* **HP**.

Proof. By hypothesis, any solution satisfying the constraints of $\overline{\textbf{HP}}$ satisfies the constraints of **HP** as well, namely we have $\mathcal{F} = \overline{\mathcal{F}}$. The conclusion easily follows since the two problems have the same loss function with the same feasible set.

One advantage of this approach is providing some criteria to determine the constraints that are not necessary for a learning problem. Indeed, in presence of a large amount of logical rules, *Proposition* 1 guarantees we can remove all the deducible constraints simplifying the optimization still getting the same solutions.

The vice versa of *Proposition* 1 is not achievable, since the logical consequence has to hold for every assignation. The notion of unnecessary constraint is local to a given dataset, indeed the available sample is limited and fixed in general. However, if a constraint is unnecessary then the optimal solutions with or without it coincide and we have that such constraint is satisfied whenever the other ones are satisfied by any optimal assignations. Such consequence among constraints, taking into account only the assignations leading to best solutions on a given dataset, provides an equivalence with the notion of unnecessary constraint. It is interesting to notice that a slightly different version of this consequence has already been considered in [10].

3.3 Towards an Algebraic Characterization

In Sec. 3.1 we introduced a criterion to discover if a given constraint $\varphi_{\bar{h}}$ can be deactivated solving *Problem* 2. The method consists in finding a vector of Lagrange multipliers with null components corresponding to $\varphi_{\bar{h}}$. We are now interested in discovering the relation between this criterion and the notion of unnecessary constraint. Some results are stated by the following propositions.

Proposition 2. *If* $\varphi_{\bar{h}}$ *is unnecessary for* **HP** *then for any optimal solution of this problem there exists a KKT-solution* $\bar{\lambda}$ *of* Problem 2 *with respect to* $\bar{h}$.

Proof. If $\varphi_{\bar{h}}$ is unnecessary then **HP** and $\overline{\textbf{HP}}$ have the same optimal solutions. Let us consider one of them, lets say α^*, where $\alpha^* = \alpha(\lambda^*_{h,i}) = \alpha(\hat{\lambda}^*_{h,i})$ for the two problems with respect to some multipliers vectors $(\lambda^*_{h,i})_{h \leq H,\, i \leq I_h}$ and $(\hat{\lambda}^*_{h,i})_{h \leq H,\, h \neq \hat{h},\, i \leq I_h}$. Since the two vectors of multipliers yield the same optimal solution, then we can define for every $h \leq H, i \leq I_h$ a solution still satisfying the KKT-conditions (also called a KKT-solution) $\bar{\lambda}$ of *Problem* 2 as:

$$\bar{\lambda}_{h,i} = \begin{cases} \hat{\lambda}^*_{h,i} & \text{for } h \neq \bar{h} \\ 0 & \text{otherwise}\,. \end{cases}$$

This has to be thought of as a necessary condition to discover which logical constraints can be removed from **HP** still preserving its optimal solutions. However, the other way round does hold in case either **HP** or $\overline{\mathbf{HP}}$ has a unique solution α^*, but in general we can only prove a weaker result.

Proposition 3. *If there exists a KKT-solution* $\bar{\lambda}$ *of* Problem 2 *with respect to* $\bar{h}$ *(for a certain optimal solution* $\bar{\alpha}^* = \alpha(\bar{\lambda})$ *of* **HP***), then the set of optimal solutions of* **HP** *is included in the set of optimal solutions of* $\overline{\mathbf{HP}}$.

Proof. Given any optimal solution α^* of **HP**, since the problem is (at least) convex, we have $Loss(\alpha^*) = Loss(\bar{\alpha}^*)$. At this point, we note that $\bar{\alpha}^*$ is also feasible for $\overline{\mathbf{HP}}$ and that the restriction of $\bar{\lambda}$ on components $h \neq \bar{h}$ is a vector of Lagrange multipliers for $\overline{\mathbf{HP}}$ satisfying the KKT-conditions. The convexity of the problem guarantees that the KKT-conditions are sufficient as well. This means that $\bar{\alpha}^*$ is also an optimal solution for $\overline{\mathbf{HP}}$, hence its loss value is a global minimum and the same holds for α^*.

In this case we can not conclude that any optimal solution of $\overline{\mathbf{HP}}$ is an optimal solution for **HP** because in general this solution could be not feasible for this problem. However as we pointed out above, we have the following result.

Corollary 1. *If either* **HP** *or equivalently* $\overline{\mathbf{HP}}$ *has a unique solution then the premise of* **Proposition** 3 *is also sufficient.*

Proof. The solution is unique if the Gram matrix K, that is the same in both the problems, is positive-definite. Hence, requiring the uniqueness of the solution for the two problems is equivalent and the claim is trivial from **Proposition** 3.

4 Some Examples

Here we illustrate, by means of some cases solved in MATLAB with the interior-point-convex algorithm, how the method works and we discuss the results to clarify what described so far. In particular, we exploit the *transitive law* as an example to enlighten how the presented theoretical results apply.

Example 2. We are given the predicates p_1, p_2, p_3 subject to $\forall x\, p_1(x) \rightarrow p_2(x)$, $\forall x\, p_2(x) \rightarrow p_3(x)$, $\forall x\, p_1(x) \rightarrow p_3(x)$. Given a common evaluation dataset $\mathscr{S}$, the logical formulas can be translated into the following linear constraints

$$\max_{x\in\mathscr{S}}\{0, p_1(x) - p_2(x)\},\ \max_{x\in\mathscr{S}}\{0, p_2(x) - p_3(x)\},\ \max_{x\in\mathscr{S}}\{0, p_1(x) - p_3(x)\}$$

and yield the following terms for the Lagrangian associated to *Problem* 1,

$$\lambda_{1,1}(p_1(x_1) - p_2(x_1)), \ldots, \lambda_{3,s}(p_1(x_s) - p_3(x_s)) .$$

At first we solve the optimization problem where, to avoid trivial solutions, we provide few supervisions for the predicates and we exploit a polynomial kernel. To keep things clear, we consider only two points defined in $\mathbb{R}^2$,

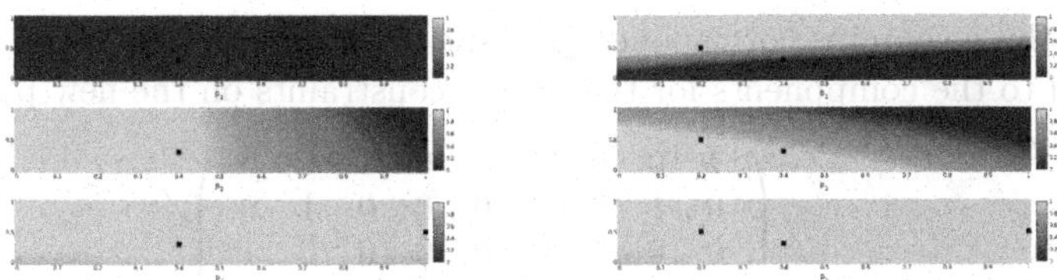

Fig. 1. From left to right we report the evaluation of the learnt functions p_1, p_2, p_3 in the example space for *Example* 2 and *Example* 3, respectively. Filled squares correspond to the provided sample points.

$\mathscr{S} = \{(1, 0.5), (0.4, 0.3)\}$. Hence, given the solution $\alpha(\lambda^*)$ (uniqueness holds) of *Problem* 1 (see Fig. 1), where $\lambda^* = (0.5549, 0, 0, 0.5706, 0, 0)$, we have

$$M_2 = \begin{pmatrix} 1 & 0 & 0 & 0 & 1 & 0 \\ 0 & 1 & 0 & 0 & 0 & 1 \\ -1 & 0 & 1 & 0 & 0 & 0 \\ 0 & -1 & 0 & 1 & 0 & 0 \\ 0 & 0 & -1 & 0 & -1 & 0 \\ 0 & 0 & 0 & -1 & 0 & -1 \end{pmatrix}, \ \alpha = M_2 \cdot \lambda^* = \begin{pmatrix} \lambda^*_{1,1} + \lambda^*_{3,1} \\ \lambda^*_{1,2} + \lambda^*_{3,2} \\ -\lambda^*_{1,1} + \lambda^*_{2,1} \\ -\lambda^*_{1,2} + \lambda^*_{2,2} \\ -\lambda^*_{2,1} - \lambda^*_{3,1} \\ -\lambda^*_{2,2} - \lambda^*_{3,2} \end{pmatrix} = \begin{pmatrix} 0.5549 \\ 0 \\ -0.5549 \\ 0.5706 \\ 0 \\ -0.5706 \end{pmatrix}.$$

In this case all the solutions of *Problem* 2 are given for any $t_1, t_2 \in \mathbb{R}$ by

$$\lambda = \lambda^* + t_1 \cdot \begin{pmatrix} -1 \\ 0 \\ -1 \\ 0 \\ 1 \\ 0 \end{pmatrix} + t_2 \cdot \begin{pmatrix} 0 \\ -1 \\ 0 \\ -1 \\ 0 \\ 1 \end{pmatrix} = \begin{pmatrix} \lambda^*_{1,1} - t_1 \\ \lambda^*_{1,2} - t_2 \\ \lambda^*_{2,1} - t_1 \\ \lambda^*_{2,2} - t_2 \\ \lambda^*_{3,1} + t_1 \\ \lambda^*_{3,2} + t_2 \end{pmatrix} = \begin{pmatrix} 0.5549 - t_1 \\ -t_2 \\ -t_1 \\ 0.5706 - t_2 \\ t_1 \\ t_2 \end{pmatrix},$$

where the pair of vectors $v_1 = (-1, 0, -1, 0, 1, 0)'$, $v_2 = (0, -1, 0, -1, 0, 1)'$ is a base for $Ker(M_2)$. From this, we get that the only way to obtain the same α nullifying the contribution of the third constraint is taking $t_1 = t_2 = 0$, namely taking $\lambda = \lambda^*$. It is worth to notice that we can also decide to nullify the contribution of the first or of the second constraint taking $t_1 = 0.5549, t_2 = 0$ or $t_1 = 0, t_2 = 0.5706$. In these cases we get $\lambda^*_1 = (0, 0, -0.5549, 0.5706, 0.5549, 0)'$, $\lambda^*_2 = (0.5549, -0.5706, 0, 0, 0, 0.5706)'$, but the third one is a support constraint.

Although it is easy to see that the third constraint is deducible from the other ones, *Problem* 1 may give a different perspective in terms of support constraints.

Example 3. Given the same problem as *Example* 2 with the additional point $(0.2, 0.5)$ in $\mathscr{S}$, we get $\lambda^* = (0.3520, 0.3453, 0, 1.1529, 0, 0.5631, 0.4202, 0, 0)$, hence the third constraint turns out to be initially supporting. However we may wonder if there is another solution of *Problem* 2 where the components of the third constraint are null. The matrix M_3 is obtained from M_2 by adding three rows and three columns corresponding to the additional grounding of the predicates and to the components for the logical constraints on the new point.

$$M_3 = \begin{pmatrix} 1 & 0 & 0 & 0 & 0 & 0 & 1 & 0 & 0 \\ 0 & 1 & 0 & 0 & 0 & 0 & 0 & 1 & 0 \\ 0 & 0 & 1 & 0 & 0 & 0 & 0 & 0 & 1 \\ -1 & 0 & 0 & 1 & 0 & 0 & 0 & 0 & 0 \\ 0 & -1 & 0 & 0 & 1 & 0 & 0 & 0 & 0 \\ 0 & 0 & -1 & 0 & 0 & 1 & 0 & 0 & 0 \\ 0 & 0 & 0 & -1 & 0 & 0 & -1 & 0 & 0 \\ 0 & 0 & 0 & 0 & -1 & 0 & 0 & -1 & 0 \\ 0 & 0 & 0 & 0 & 0 & -1 & 0 & 0 & -1 \end{pmatrix}$$

In this case, the dimension of $Ker(M_3)$ is increased exactly by one, as the number of affine components of any involved logical constraint. This means, we can try to find a $\bar{\lambda}^*$ in which a certain constraint has null values. For instance, the vector $\bar{\lambda}^*= (0.7722, 0.3453, 0, 1.5731,\ 0, 0.5631, 0, 0, 0)$ is a solution of *Problem* 2 with respect to the third constraint. However, as in *Example* 2, it is the only KKT-solution allowing us to remove the contribution of a constraint.

4.1 From Support to Necessary Constraints

Combining pointwise and consistency constraints brings any optimal solution to be evaluated exactly to 0 or 1 on any supervised sample and all the corresponding Lagrange multipliers to be different from zero, namely they will turn out to be support constraints. However, they could be unnecessary constraints for the problem and we could actually remove them from the optimization.

Example 4. We consider the same problem as *Example* 2 where $\mathscr{S} = \{(0.4, 0.3)\}$ is labelled as negative for p_1 and positive for both p_2 and p_3. We express the pointwise and the consistency constraints in logical form. All the constraints are obtained requiring the following linear functions to be less or equal to zero:

$$\begin{array}{ccc} \text{(logical)} & \text{(pointwise)} & \text{(consistency)} \\ & & \\ p_1(x_1) - p_2(x_1), & p_1(x_1), & -p_1(x_1), p_1(x_1) - 1, \\ p_2(x_1) - p_3(x_1), & 1 - p_2(x_1), & -p_2(x_1), p_2(x_1) - 1, \\ p_1(x_1) - p_3(x_1), & 1 - p_3(x_1), & -p_3(x_1), p_3(x_1) - 1. \end{array}$$

Exploiting the complementary slackness and the condition for the Lagrange multipliers given by *Problem* 2, we can provide several combinations of values for the multipliers yielding the same solution. The Gram matrix K is positive-definite ($K = 1.25$) and the solution $\alpha^* = (0, 0.8, 0.8)$ provided by a linear kernel is unique. For this simple example we have only two possible KKT-solutions of *Problem* 2 minimizing the number of necessary constraints, they are $\bar{\lambda} = (0, 0, 0, 0, 0, 0, 0, 0, 0, 0.8, 0, 0.8)'$ and $\hat{\lambda} = (0, 0.8, 0, 0, 0, 0, 0, 0, 0, 0, 0, 1.6)'$.

This may be easily shown since the complementarity slackness force $\lambda_1 = \lambda_3 = \lambda_8 = \lambda_9 = \lambda_{11} = 0$ and multiplying by M the remaining multipliers, they have to satisfy:

$$\begin{cases} \lambda_4 - \lambda_7 = 0 \\ \lambda_2 - \lambda_5 + \lambda_{10} = 0.8 \\ -\lambda_2 - \lambda_6 + \lambda_{12} = 0.8. \end{cases}$$

Since **HP** has a unique solution, from **Corollary** 1, we have two different minimal optimization problems. One with only $p_2(x_1) - 1 \leq 0$ and $p_3(x_1) - 1 \leq 0$ as necessary constraints and the other with only $p_2(x_1) - p_3(x_1) \leq 0$ and $p_3(x_1) - 1 \leq 0$ once again.

5 Conclusions

In general, in learning from constraints, several constraints are combined into an optimization scheme and often it is quite difficult to identify the contribution of each of them. In particular, some constraints could turn out to be not necessary for finding a solution. In this paper, we propose a formal definition of unnecessary constraint as well as a method to determine which are the unnecessary constraints for a learning process in a multi-task problem. The necessity of a certain constraint is related to the notion of consequences among the other constraints that are enforced at the same time. This is a reason why we suppose to deal with logical constraints that are quite general to include both pointwise and consistency constraints. The logical consequence among formulas is a sufficient condition to conclude that a constraint, corresponding to a certain formula, is unnecessary. However, we also provide an algebraic necessary condition that turns out to be sufficient in case the Gram matrices associated to the kernel functions are positive-definite.

References

1. Boser, B.E., Guyon, I.M., Vapnik, V.N.: A training algorithm for optimal margin classifiers. In: Proceedings of the Fifth Annual Workshop on Computational Learning Theory, pp. 144–152. ACM (1992)
2. Boyd, S., Vandenberghe, L.: Convex Optimization. Cambridge University Press, Cambridge (2004)
3. Cortes, C., Vapnik, V.: Support-vector networks. Mach. Learn. **20**(3), 273–297 (1995). https://doi.org/10.1023/A:1022627411411
4. Cumby, C.M., Roth, D.: On kernel methods for relational learning. In: Proceedings of the 20th International Conference on Machine Learning (ICML 2003), pp. 107–114 (2003)
5. Diligenti, M., Gori, M., Maggini, M., Rigutini, L.: Bridging logic and kernel machines. Mach. Learn. **86**(1), 57–88 (2012)
6. Diligenti, M., Gori, M., Saccà, C.: Semantic-based regularization for learning and inference. Artif. Intell. **244**, 143–165 (2015)

7. Giannini, F., Diligenti, M., Gori, M., Maggini, M.: Learning Łukasiewicz logic fragments by quadratic programming. In: Ceci, M., Hollmén, J., Todorovski, L., Vens, C., Džeroski, S. (eds.) ECML PKDD 2017. LNCS (LNAI), vol. 10534, pp. 410–426. Springer, Cham (2017). https://doi.org/10.1007/978-3-319-71249-9_25
8. Giannini, F., Diligenti, M., Gori, M., Maggini, M.: On a convex logic fragment for learning and reasoning. IEEE Trans. Fuzzy Syst. **27**(7), 1407–1416 (2018)
9. Gnecco, G., Gori, M., Melacci, S., Sanguineti, M.: Foundations of support constraint machines. Neural computation **27**(2), 388–480 (2015)
10. Gori, M., Melacci, S.: Support constraint machines. In: Lu, B.-L., Zhang, L., Kwok, J. (eds.) ICONIP 2011. LNCS, vol. 7062, pp. 28–37. Springer, Heidelberg (2011). https://doi.org/10.1007/978-3-642-24955-6_4
11. Gori, M., Melacci, S.: Constraint verification with kernel machines. IEEE Trans. Neural Networks Learn. Syst. **24**(5), 825–831 (2013)
12. Hájek, P.: Metamathematics of Fuzzy Logic. Trends in Logic, vol. 4, 1st edn. Springer, Dordrecht (1998). https://doi.org/10.1007/978-94-011-5300-3
13. Hu, Z., Ma, X., Liu, Z., Hovy, E., Xing, E.: Harnessing deep neural networks with logic rules. arXiv preprint arXiv:1603.06318 (2016)
14. Jung, J.H., O'Leary, D.P., Tits, A.L.: Adaptive constraint reduction for convex quadratic programming. Comput. Optim. Appl. **51**(1), 125–157 (2012)
15. Muggleton, S., Lodhi, H., Amini, A., Sternberg, M.J.E.: Support vector inductive logic programming. In: Hoffmann, A., Motoda, H., Scheffer, T. (eds.) DS 2005. LNCS (LNAI), vol. 3735, pp. 163–175. Springer, Heidelberg (2005). https://doi.org/10.1007/11563983_15
16. Paulsen, V.I., Raghupathi, M.: An Introduction to the Theory of Reproducing Kernel Hilbert spaces, vol. 152. Cambridge University Press, Cambridge (2016)
17. Rockafellar, R.T., Wets, R.J.B.: Variational analysis. Grundlehren der mathematischen Wissenschaften, vol. 317, 1st edn. Springer, Heidelberg (2009)
18. Serafini, L., Garcez, A.d.: Logic tensor networks: deep learning and logical reasoning from data and knowledge. arXiv preprint arXiv:1606.04422 (2016)
19. Serafini, L., d'Avila Garcez, A.S.: Learning and reasoning with logic tensor networks. In: Adorni, G., Cagnoni, S., Gori, M., Maratea, M. (eds.) AI*IA 2016. LNCS (LNAI), vol. 10037, pp. 334–348. Springer, Cham (2016). https://doi.org/10.1007/978-3-319-49130-1_25

HiSeqGAN: Hierarchical Sequence Synthesis and Prediction

Yun-Chieh Tien, Chen-Min Hsu, and Fang Yu(✉)

National Chengchi University, Taipei, Taiwan
{106356004,107356019,yuf}@nccu.edu.tw
http://soslab.nccu.edu.tw

Abstract. High-dimensional data sequences constantly appear in practice. State-of-the-art models such as recurrent neural networks suffer prediction accuracy from complex relations among values of attributes. Adopting unsupervised clustering that clusters data based on their attribute value similarity results data in lower dimensions that can be structured in a hierarchical relation. It is essential to consider these data relations to improve the performance of training models. In this work, we propose a new approach to synthesize and predict sequences of data that are structured in a hierarchy. Specifically, we adopt a new hierarchical data encoding and seamlessly modify loss functions of SeqGAN as our training model to synthesize data sequences. In practice, we first use the hierarchical clustering algorithm, GHSOM, to cluster our training data. By relabelling a sample with the cluster that it falls to, we are able to use the GHSOM map to identify the hierarchical relation of samples. We then converse the clusters to the coordinate vectors with our hierarchical data encoding algorithm and replace the loss function with maximizing cosine similarity in the SeqGAN model to synthesize cluster sequences. Using the synthesized sequences, we are able to achieve better performance on high-dimension data training and prediction compared to the state-of-the-art models.

Keywords: Hierarchical sequence · Sequence synthesis · SeqGAN · GHSOM · Cosine similarity

1 Introduction

With the progress and the fast development of technology, artificial intelligence forecasting techniques have been receiving much attention in recent years. Deep learning is one of the advanced machine learning technique which is highly used in artificial intelligence. It relies on sophisticated mathematical and statistical computations for solving complicated real-world problems. Since AlphaGo [3], an application of deep neural network, gained victory with a Chinese Go master, there have been a lot of applications of deep learning in our lives such as automatic classification of emails [2,29], chatbot [26] and image recognition [30]. Among all the deep learning algorithms, three most commonly used models are

I. V. Tetko et al. (Eds.): ICANN 2019, LNCS 11728, pp. 621–638, 2019.
https://doi.org/10.1007/978-3-030-30484-3_50

convolutional neural network (CNN) [17], recurrent neural network (RNN) [35] and generative adversarial network (GAN) [11].

CNN is a model which is most commonly applied to analyze visual imagery. It is built by the visual cortex of the human brain and consists of convolutional layers and pooling layer. The former applies a convolution operation to the input and pass the result to the next layer. And then the convolution emulates the response of an individual neuron to visual stimuli. The latter combines the outputs of neuron clusters at one layer into a single neuron in the next layer. Through the structure, CNN can optimize the correlation between pattern recognition and adjacent data, which shows excellent performance on recognition especially in the data type of image [30] and sound [1].

Sequence modeling has been one of the most complicated tasks in real-world problems. When it comes to sequence modeling, noise, the length of time and pattern variabilities always hamper the progress. RNN is a model that heavily used in sequence modeling. It is different from the general feedforward neural network since the neurons in the RNN have a temporary internal memory that remembers the previous output state, and then the neuron can calculate different output values based on the previous state. Also because RNN can remember the feature of a previous output state, this model can handle input data of different lengths, which has a good performance in applications such as automatic translation [31] and speech recognition [12].

However, RNN encounters vanishing gradient problem and exploding gradient problem in the practice training. These problems lead the stochastic gradient descent method to produce volatile results, and this situation also affects the performance of analyzing longer sequence data. In order to solve these problem encountered by RNN, long-short-term memory (LSTM) is proposed by Hochreiter et al. [15]. In the neurons of LSTM, three gates for input, forget, and output is added to this model. After inputting the data, it determines the opening and closing of each gate according to the respective weight calculation results. According to Gers et al. [10], when training data are longer sequences, the forget gate can reset the neuron state to zero or reduce the value of the neuron state slowly, thereby effectively avoiding the problem of over-amplification of the neuron.

GAN proposed by Goodfellow et al. [11] has shown excellent performance for data generation. It is an unsupervised learning method in deep learning that learns through two neural networks, generator and discriminator. The generator samples the data randomly as input from the latent pace and is similar to a forger who tries to mimic the real-world data in training, while the discriminator is a policeman who tries to distinguish the fake data generated by the generator. Through iterative training on generator and discriminator, both the generator and the discriminator advance.

Nevertheless, GAN has limitations on training discrete sequences. The first reason is that the generator usually needs an LSTM model, so when the generator passes data to the discriminator, it gets a sequence of discrete values, which makes the gradient update challenging to handle. The second reason is that the discriminator can only accept a complete sentence. The generation process is a sequential decision process, and it is crucial to balance its current score and future score. The sequence generative adversarial nets (SeqGAN) [39] adopts reinforcement learning and policy gradient to solve this problem. It is the first work that extends GAN to generate sequences of discrete tokens.

However, for high-dimensional data sequences, we have observed that SeqGAN suffers from complex computations on relations of attributes. It is challenging to model and draw data samples from high dimensional distributions. We can learn the parameters of conditional probability distributions that map intermediate, latent variables from simpler distributions to more complex ones [4]. Some researches also use the learned intermediate representations on retrieval and classification [22,25,28,33]. Myszkowski et al. [23] use hierarchical clustering to build a hierarchy of documents which gives them a useful advantage in navigation of document search on visual content.

In this work, we propose a two phase analysis. We first adopt growing hierarchical self-organizing maps (GHSOM) as the unsupervised clustering means to construct high-dimensional data into hierarchical clusters. Samples that fall into the same cluster have relatively similar attribute values. This enables us to use clusters, instead of the high-dimension values, to represent the input data, and turn the problem of synthesizing high-dimensional data sequences into the problem of synthesizing hierarchical data sequences. In the second phase of our analysis, we propose HiSeqGAN that adopts the SeqGAN model to synthesize sequences that have their data in a hierarchical relation. To this aim, we propose a novel coordinate encoding to represent clusters in a hierarchical relation. We modify the reward function in HiSeqGAN on maximizing sequence cosine similarity to integrate the hierarchical relations of clusters into SeqGAN. Compared to loss function on mean square errors, considering the hierarchical relations improves the quality of data that we have generated. In our experiments, we showed that the synthesized sequences can be used as new input data to train a better RNN model. Furthermore, we synthesize sequences that have lengths longer than the training set, and show how to use them to predict the future movement of sequences that are similar to the prefix of synthesized sequences. Finally, we discuss how to predict actual attribute values from the predicted cluster. We are able to achieve better accuracy compared to the state-of-the-art model.

2 Related Work

Many researchers show interest in the generative aspects of CNN recently to figure out what the model learn and how to improve the model. Dai et al. [5] have constructed a generative model for the CNN and have proposed a method of visualization which can directly draw synthetic samples for any given node in a trained CNN by the Hamiltonian Monte Carlo (HMC) algorithm. Xie et al. [38] used the Gaussian distribution which is used initially in convolutional neural networks as an example to simulate the way of probability distribution in the process of CNN. Moreover, they used auto-encoder which is commonly used in unsupervised learning and Langevin dynamics algorithm to learn reconstructed pictures. Also, they found a generative random field model has the potential to learn from big unlabeled data. After that, they proposed a CoopNets [37] which can train a bottom-up descriptor network and a top-down generator network simultaneously. Both the descriptor and the generator are involved in Langevin sampling and are in the form of alternating back-propagation.

Recently, GAN has shown excellent performance especially in the field of computer visions. However, Dai et al. [6] explained the doubts about semi-supervised learning with GAN. In their research, they improved the drawbacks of feature matching GAN and presented a semi-supervised learning framework. Also, Salimans et al. [28] focused on semi-supervised learning and the generation of images in their research. Moreover, they proposed an evaluation metric for comparing the quality of these models. Radford et al. [25] proposed a deep convolutional generative adversarial networks (DCGAN) and demonstrated its efficacy through image data, which proved that unsupervised learning has excellent and stable results. Besides, it is an essential issue for models to produce high-resolution images. Denton et al. [8] proposed the LAPGAN model with a Laplacian pyramid framework to create a pyramid structure, which uses a generation network at each level of the pyramid to produce a higher resolution image.

Besides, many research proposed a variant based on the original architecture. Ho et al. [14] have implemented the imitation learning of deep reinforcement learning in a given environment. They combined this method with GAN, and it can ultimately be implemented in robots and self-driving vehicles. Luc et al. [20] applied the GAN model to semantic segmentation for the first time. They add a discriminator to the semantic segmentation model and finally proved that this method could improve the consistency of high-order potentials in their experiments. Liu et al. [19] proposed coupled generative adversarial networks (CoGAN) which enforced a weight sharing constraint on learning a joint distribution of multi-domain images. Finally, they applied this model to several learning tasks, including color and depth images, and face images with different attributes. All of the tasks show successful results by learning the joint distribution without any tuple of corresponding images. Besides, Zhu et al. [40] proposed a cycle-consistent adversarial network (CycleGAN) in conjunction with the concept of cycle consistency. They presented a method that can learn to capture the unique characteristics of one images collection and to translate these characteristics into the other image collection.

Besides, Tulyakov et al. [32], Saito, Matsumoto et al. [27] and Vondrick et al. [34] have researched for recent video generative models based on GAN. Nevertheless, GAN does not infer the latent noise vectors while VAE needs to design an inference model for the sequence of noise vectors, which is a non-trivial task due to the complex dependency structure. Xie et al. [36] proposed a learning dynamic generator model, using alternating back-propagation through time to learn realistic models for dynamic textures and action patterns. It does not require an extra model such as a discriminator in GAN or an inference model in VAE.

3 Hierarchical Data Construction and Representation

The first phase of our analysis is to cluster high-dimensional data into a hierarchical relation. In this way, we are able to reduce the data dimension. Similar to symbolic dynamics, we seek for a partition of the state space that describes the trajectories of points to represent the dynamics in a simple way. However, it is hard to extract the best partition associated to Markov process [13]. In this paper, we propose hierarchical clustering to achieve unsupervised partition, where number of partitions is dynamically determined based on sample variations. Particularly, we adopt growing hierarchical self-organizing map (GHSOM) algorithm [9] to cluster our data first, and then investigate hierarchical data sequence model training in the second phase. One can predict actual attribute values from samples that fall into the predicted cluster as we show in the experiments.

3.1 Growing Hierarchical Self-Organizing Map (GHSOM)

Unsupervised clustering is one common way to reduce data dimensions. GHSOM [9] is a self-organizing map that grows hierarchically based on data distribution. It expands self-organization maps in a hierarchy according to the variance between and within clusters. When the horizontal and vertical expansion thresholds are set, the algorithm continuously grows the map and checks whether variations between the clusters and within the clusters meet the set requirement. Unlike K-means [21] or SOM [16] where number of clusters is given in advance, using GHSOMs, given tolerances on variations of between and within clusters, samples are separated and clustered iteratively on the fly until the given tolerances are satisfied.

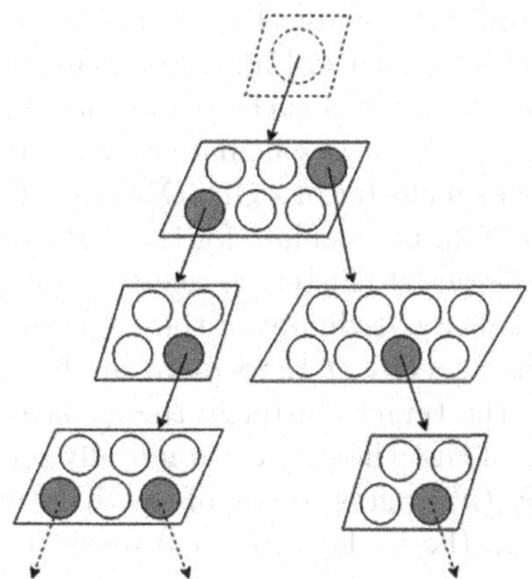

Fig. 1. A GHSOM structure

3.2 Hierarchical Data Encoding

The GHSOM map results data in clusters of a tree-like structure. We use decimal encoding [18] to label the clusters. Each digit in the decimal number corresponds to a cluster of a layer. We append zero at the end of the decimal number as a padding symbol to indicate clusters that have no child clusters in the next layer. As shown in Fig. 2, labels 230, 164 and 475 represent some clusters in a three layer map, and the 230 refers to a cluster that does not has any of its child clusters in the third layer.

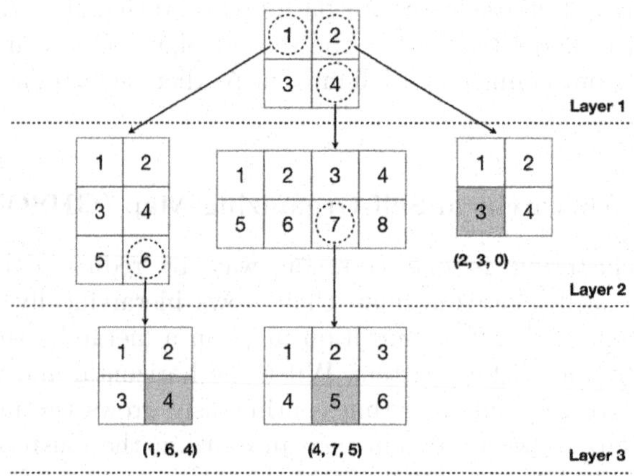

Fig. 2. Decimal number labelling on clusters of a GHSOM map

After using the decimal number to label clusters, we converse each number to the two-dimensional coordinate vector. The idea is to squeeze all the clusters in one square layer by layer as shown in Fig. 3. Each label can then be encoded as the coordinate of the center point of each square that represents to the cluster.

Equations (1) to (4) show how we calculate coordinates of the center point of each square that represents a cluster in a GHSOM map. P_x (P_y) is the coordinate of x-axis (y-axis) that we aim to calculate for the center point of the square that represents the label of the target cluster; m refers to the number of the GHSOM layers; P_i^x (P_i^y) refers to the coordinate in the i_{th} layer and B_i^x (B_i^y) refers to the unit width of x-axis (y-axis) of the square in the i_{th} layer, where x_i (y_i) refers to the position of the target cluster in the i_{th} layer. Both B_0^x and B_0^y are set to 1, i.e., the square of the whole space is initially set to 1, where its central point is set (0.5, 0.5). n_i^x (n_i^y) refers to size of the SOM map, i.e., the number of x-axis (y-axis) clusters, in the i_{th} layer; r_x (r_y) refers to the offset as the width of x-axis (y-axis) of the last square (the last layer of the cluster). The coordinate of x-axis P_x (of y-axis P_y), can be calculated using the following formulas.

$$P_x = r_x + \sum_{i=1}^{m} P_i^x; \quad P_y = r_y + \sum_{i=1}^{m} P_i^y, \tag{1}$$

Cluster	Point	Cluster	Point	Cluster	Point	Cluster	Point	Cluster	Point
110	$(\frac{1}{8}, \frac{11}{12})$	162	$(\frac{7}{16}, \frac{5}{8})$	240	$(\frac{7}{8}, \frac{5}{8})$	450	$(\frac{9}{16}, \frac{1}{8})$	475	$(\frac{13}{16}, \frac{1}{16})$
120	$(\frac{3}{8}, \frac{11}{12})$	163	$(\frac{5}{16}, \frac{13}{24})$	300	$(\frac{1}{4}, \frac{1}{4})$	460	$(\frac{11}{16}, \frac{1}{8})$	476	$(\frac{41}{48}, \frac{1}{16})$
130	$(\frac{1}{8}, \frac{3}{4})$	164	$(\frac{7}{16}, \frac{13}{24})$	410	$(\frac{9}{16}, \frac{3}{8})$	471	$(\frac{37}{48}, \frac{3}{16})$	480	$(\frac{15}{16}, \frac{1}{8})$
140	$(\frac{3}{8}, \frac{3}{4})$	210	$(\frac{5}{8}, \frac{7}{8})$	420	$(\frac{11}{16}, \frac{3}{8})$	472	$(\frac{13}{16}, \frac{3}{16})$		
150	$(\frac{1}{8}, \frac{7}{12})$	220	$(\frac{7}{8}, \frac{7}{8}$	430	$(\frac{13}{16}, \frac{3}{8})$	473	$(\frac{41}{48}, \frac{3}{16})$		
161	$(\frac{5}{16}, \frac{5}{8})$	230	$(\frac{5}{8}, \frac{5}{8})$	440	$(\frac{15}{16}, \frac{3}{8})$	474	$(\frac{37}{48}, \frac{1}{16})$		

Fig. 3. Coordinate encoding of clusters with decimal labels

where

$$B_i^x = B_{i-1}^x \times \frac{1}{n_i^x}; \quad B_i^y = B_{i-1}^y \times \frac{1}{n_i^y} \quad (B_0^x = 1 \quad and \quad B_0^y = 1) \tag{2}$$

$$P_i^x = B_i^x \times x_i; \quad P_i^y = B_i^y \times y_i \tag{3}$$

$$r_x = B_m^x \times \frac{1}{2}; \quad r_y = B_m^y \times \frac{1}{2} \tag{4}$$

4 Hierarchical Data Synthesis with SeqGAN

In the second phase of our analysis, we propose HiSeqGAN as our primary training model on hierarchical data sequence synthesis. HiSeqGAN adopts the sequence generation framework of SeqGAN [39] but with its optimization function on maximizing sequence similarity based on cosine similarity of coordinates to take the hierarchical relations among data into account.

4.1 HiSeqGAN

Figure 4 shows the structure of HiSeqGAN, similar to the proposed framework in [39]. The generator used in the sequence generation is an RNN model with LSTM cells, while the discriminator is a CNN model. First, HiSeqGAN uses the real-world data and the native samples generated by the generator (fake samples) to train the discriminator, so that the discriminator can distinguish real-world data from fake samples. Then, the reward is passed back to the intermediate state-action steps by using the Monte Carlo search. Second, the generator updates by reinforcement learning (RL). To be more specific, the generator is treated as an RL agent; the state refers to the currently produced tokens; the action refers to the next token to be generated. In a stochastic parameterized policy, the actions are drawn from a distribution that parameterizes the policy and the objective of the policy is to generate a sequence from the start state in such a way that maximizes the expected end reward.

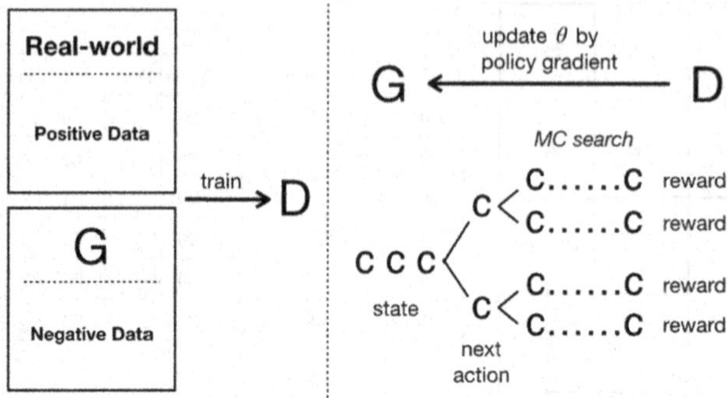

Fig. 4. The HiSeqGAN framework

4.2 Sequence Similarity

As defined in Sect. 3, we represent the cluster in a GHSOM map as the coordinates of the center point of its square. To evaluate the prediction on clusters between two labels, we propose three-dimensional cosine similarity on their coordinates. The reason that we extend two-dimensional to three-dimensional is to prevent the distortion of the original point on the same plane. As shown in Fig. 5, the 2D cosine similarity of point A and point B is larger than point A and point C at two-dimensional coordinate while the variance between point A and point C is smaller since they have the same first layer in the hierarchical cluster. To increase the accuracy of our generated points, we add a dimension to separate the points and the origin of the coordinate at the different planes. That is to say, point A, point B and point C are transformed into $(\frac{3}{8}, \frac{3}{4}, 1)$, $(\frac{5}{8}, \frac{7}{8}, 1)$ and $(\frac{7}{16}, \frac{13}{24}, 1)$ respectively while O is $(0, 0, 0)$. Then, the cosine similarity of point A and point C is larger than point A and point B at a three-dimensional coordinate, which means the variance between point A and point C is also smaller.

Given the synthesized sequence as $Y_{1:t} = (y_1, \ldots, y_t)$ and $Y^c_{1:t} = (y^c_1, \ldots, y^c_t)$ as raw sequence of clusters. We define the metric of sequence similarity as Eq. (5), where $\vec{p}_i$ and $\vec{p}^{\,c}_i$ are the three-dimensional vectors, which refer to the coordinate transformation of y_i and y^c_i respectively.

$$\texttt{SequenceSimilarity}(Y_{1:t}, Y^c_{1:t}) = \sum_{i=1}^{t} \frac{\vec{p}_i \cdot \vec{p}^{\,c}_i}{\left\|\vec{p}_i\right\| \left\|\vec{p}^{\,c}_i\right\|} \tag{5}$$

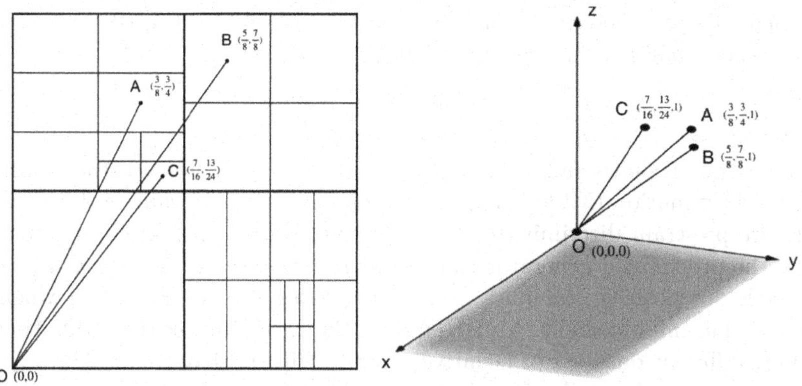

Fig. 5. Clusters with 2D coordinates and 3D coordinates

4.3 Sequence Synthesis

Following SeqGAN, our generator model is updated by employing a policy gradient and Monte Carlo search, where the final reward signal is provided by the discriminator based on Eq. (5) and is passed back to the intermediate action value. Given a dataset, train a generative model G_θ of parameter θ to produce a sequence $Y_{1:T} = (y_1, \ldots, y_t)$, and train a discriminative model D_ϕ of the parameter ϕ to distinguish real or fake data for improving the generator. Then, we use an N time Monte Carlo search with a roll-out policy G_β to sample the unknown last $T - t$ tokens. Equation (6) shows how we use the roll-out policy to get a batch of output samples.

$$Q_{D_\phi}^{G_\theta}(s = Y_{1:t-1}, a = y_t) = \begin{cases} \frac{1}{N}\sum_{n=1}^{N} D_\phi\left(Y_{1:T}^n\right), \left(Y_{1:T}^n\right) \in MC^{G_\beta}\left(Y_{1:t}; N\right), & \text{for } t < T \\ D_\phi\left(Y_{1:t}\right), & \text{for } t = T \end{cases} \tag{6}$$

To keep a good pace with the generator, the discriminator shall re-train as long as the generator generates more realistic sequences.

$$\min_\phi -\mathbb{E}_{Y\sim_p}\left[\log D_\phi\left(Y\right)\right] - \mathbb{E}_{Y\sim G_\theta}\left[\log\left(1 - D_\phi\left(Y\right)\right)\right] \tag{7}$$

After a new discriminator model has been obtained, we update the generator for optimizing a parameterized policy to maximize the long-term reward. Following, the objective function can be derived as Eq. (8)

$$\nabla_\theta J(\theta) = \sum_{t=1}^{T} \mathbb{E}_{Y_{1:t-1}\sim G_\theta}\left[\sum_{y_t \in \mathcal{Y}} \nabla_\theta G_\theta(y_t|Y_{1:t-1}) \cdot Q_{D_\phi}^{G_\theta}(Y_{1:t-1}, y_t)\right] \tag{8}$$

Then, the parameters of generator can be updated by Eq. (9). α_h refers to the corresponding learning rate at i^{th} step.

$$\theta \leftarrow \theta + \alpha_h \nabla_\theta J(\theta) \tag{9}$$

Algorithm 1 shows full details of our model. Firstly, we use the maximum likelihood estimation (MLE) to pre-train generator on the training dataset. Secondly, we pre-train discriminator by maximizing the cosine similarity, the output of the pre-trained generator can be our negative samples whereas the given dataset is our positive examples. Next, we re-train our discriminator when the generator has improvement. Also, to reduce the variability of the estimation, we combine different datasets of negative samples with positive ones [24].

Algorithm 1. Sequence Synthesis Algorithm

```
Initialize Gθ, Dφ with random parameter θ, φ
Pre-train Gθ via MLE
Assign parameter θ to the roll-out policy
Pre-train Dφ by Eq. (5)
repeat
  for g-steps do
    Generate a sequence
    for t in 1:T do
      Compute Q by Eq. (6)
    end for
    Update θ by Eq. (9)
  end for
  for d-steps do
    Train Dφ by Eq. (7)
  end for
  Update the parameter of roll-out policy
until model converges
```

4.4 Sequence Prediction

In order to predict next tokens of training sequences, we use the trained generator G_θ to generate sequences that have more periods, and the extended tokens are used as our prediction on sequences that have similar prefix.

Formally speaking, given the length of sequences of our training data, denoted as t, to predict the next t' periods of the sequence, we synthesize sequence $Y = (y_1, \ldots, y_t, y_{t+1}, \ldots, y_{t+t'})$.

Given a set of synthesized sequences S, and a real item sequence Y^{item} that has its length t, Eq. (10) defines the way to find a synthesized sequence $Y_{1:t+t'} \in S$ that has its prefix $Y_{1:t}$ most similar to the item sequence Y^{item}. Then, we use the postfix $Y_{t+1:t+t'} = (y_{t+1}, \ldots, y_{t+t'})$ to predict the future movement.

$$\max_{Y \in S} \texttt{SequenceSimilarity}(Y_{1:t}, Y^{item}) \tag{10}$$

5 Experiments

In this section, we evaluate our approach against supply chain management data from real worlds. All the experiment data are collected from real transactions of the company W, one of the world's largest semiconductor component distributor in the Asia Pacific area. With more than 30 branches and over 60 international electronics component suppliers, company W plays a key role as a supply chain buffer for a franchise partner, including Intel, Philips, Texas Instruments, Hynix, Vishay and Omni Vision. Our goal is to predict at the item level the values of essential attributes on demand and inventory.

5.1 Data Settings

The raw data of transactions contain more than eighty thousand weekly transaction records over thousands of semiconductor component items and customers. Each item-customer pair has records up to 96 weeks. (Weeks that have no demands have no transaction records). For each record, we label it with nominal attributes including item, customer and date (on week), and use numerical attributes including all the predefined indicators of demand and inventory in supply chain management as the sample attributes of that record. Each item-week record consists of 8 demand and inventory attributes as shown in Table 1.

5.2 From Hi-Dimension Data to Hierarchical Data

We first apply GHSOM to cluster samples based on these numerical attributes. (All the values are normalized with max and min, i.e., n(d) = d-min/max-min.) Figure 6 shows the partition result, a GHSOM map (in decimal encoding) that consists of three layers with 70 clusters. Based on the GHSOM map, one can label each item-week 8-dimension record with its corresponding cluster. We generate 5712 cluster sequences from raw transaction records, where each cluster sequence refers to an item-customer trajectory movement on demand and inventory attributes. We denote this set as $Data_{raw}$.

Table 1. Numerical attributes

Indicators	Name	Description
Inventory	Actual AWU	Average weekly usage (i.e., actual demand) in the past
	FCST M	Managers forecast of monthly demand for the future
Demand	BL <= 9WKs	In-transit inventory to be delivered by upstream supplier within 9 weeks
	Backlog (BL)	Total in-transit inventory (to be delivered)
	DC-OH	On-hand (OH) inventory in the distribution center (DC)
	Hub-OH	On-hand (OH) inventory in warehouse nearby downstream customer production plant
	TTL OH	In stock quantities
	Available	Company backlog

5.3 Sequence Synthesis

In our first experiment, we use $Data_{raw}$ and the GHSOM map to train our HiSeqGAN model and synthesize another 2500 cluster sequences (denoted as the set $Data_{syn}$). To evaluate the quality of our synthesized sequences, we use RNN as the training model that uses the cluster sequence of week 1 to 95 to predict the cluster in week 96. We first train the RNN model [18] with $Data_{raw}$, the prediction accuracy rate (on average over 5712 item-customer pairs) is 82% on the first layer, 61% on the second layer and 45% on the third layer. That is to say, for an item has its week 96 cluster in 164, the prediction as 1xx (first-layer accurate) is 82%, 16x (second-layer accurate) is 61%, and 164 (third-layer accurate) is 45%. Under the same setting of the RNN, but using both $Data_{raw}$ and $Data_{syn}$ as training inputs, we can improve the precision to 85% on the first layer, 72% on the second layer and 52% on the third layer. The performance is shown in Table 2. The result shows our first contribution that we can synthesize additional training inputs for the state of the art models and improve their performance.

Table 2. Layer Accuracy of *Exp.*1

Dataset	Layer Accuracy		
	l^1	l^1, l^2	l^1, l^2, l^3
$Data_{raw}$	0.82	0.61	0.45
$Data_{HiSeqGAN}$	0.85	0.72	0.52

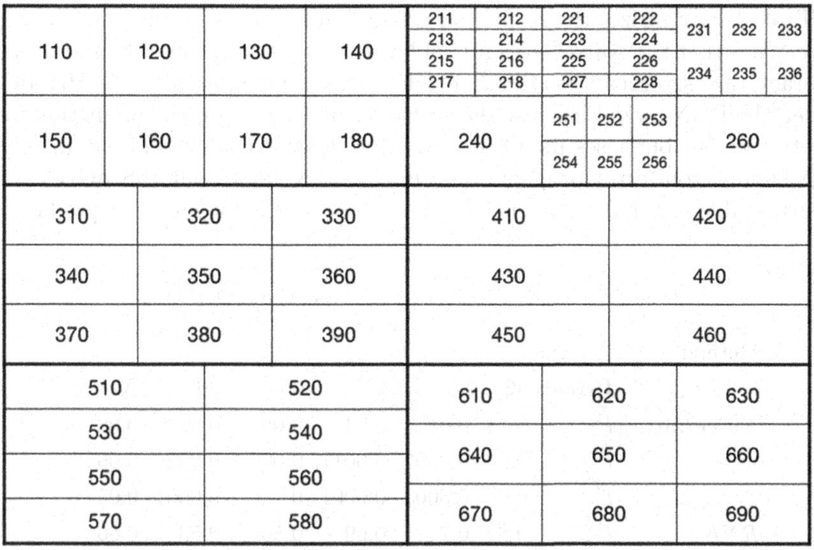

110 120 130 140 211 212 221 222 213 214 223 224 215 216 225 226 217 218 227 228 231 232 233 234 235 236

150 160 170 180 240 251 252 253 254 255 256 260

310 320 330 410 420

340 350 360 430 440

370 380 390 450 460

510 520 530 540 550 560 570 580 610 620 630 640 650 660 670 680 690

Fig. 6. GHSOM clustering result

5.4 Sequence Prediction

We conduct experiments on sequence prediction in the second experiment and compare the prediction accuracy against (1) the Naive Bayes method, and (2) the RNN model. The setting is to use week 1–95 to predict week 92–96. The Naive Bayes method [7] is the learning algorithm based on a conditional probabilistic model, which counts observed sequences for prediction. The RNN has the same setting as the previous experiment but this time it has to use its prediction to predict next periods. For both NaiveBayes and RNN models, we use $Data_{raw}$ with week 1 to 91 for training, and for each item, predict its week 92 cluster, and then with week 2 to 92, to predict week 93, and so on so forth until the prediction on week 96. For our HiSeqGAN model, we use $Data_{raw}$ with week 1 to 91 to synthesize 3840 sequences with week 1 to 96 (denoted as the set S). Then for each item ($Y^{i}tem$), we use Eq. (10) to find a synthesized sequence Y that has its prefix best match to Y^{item}, and then use the postfix (clusters on week 92 to 96) of the selected synthesized sequence for prediction.

Table 3 summarizes the results on prediction accuracy on different layers. As one can see that the NaiveBayes model has the worst accuracy rate and drops its accuracy rate significantly after multiple periods. Compared to the HiSeqGAN model, the RNN model has a slight better accuracy rate on the prediction in the first two weeks, but loses its advantage after the third week. This confirms that RNN suffers from error propagation. On the other hand, our HiSeqGAN model is more stable and has better performance on average for long run prediction.

Table 3. Layer accuracy on multi-periods prediction

Method	Accuracy						
	Period	92	93	94	95	96	Average
NaiveBayes	l^1	0.28	0.01	0.04	0.06	0.01	0.08
	l^2	0.27	0.0007	0.0017	0.0007	0.0026	0.06
	l^3	0.26	0.0003	0.0001	0	0.0001	0.05
RNN	l^1	0.82	0.71	0.69	0.55	0.53	0.66
	l^2	0.61	0.58	0.51	0.42	0.43	0.51
	l^3	0.46	0.47	0.43	0.42	0.38	0.43
HiSeqGAN	l^1	0.79	0.74	0.74	0.68	0.63	0.72
	l^2	0.62	0.59	0.57	0.54	0.49	0.56
	l^3	0.54	0.51	0.49	0.48	0.43	0.49

5.5 From Cluster Prediction to Actual Value Prediction

Finally, we discuss how we use the predicted cluster to estimate attribute values. This is done by computing the distribution of attribute values with samples that fall into the cluster. For instance, consider that we are interested in the attribute value of AWU (demand on the item). Figure 7 shows the five period prediction on the AWU value of item *itemA*. The points are the actual value of *itemA* in the 92nd to 96th weeks and the boxplots refer to the statistics on AWU values of samples that fall into our predicted clusters.

5.6 Discussion

Note that predicted values have their variation depending on the layer accuracy. The variations are smaller when the accurate layer of the predicted cluster is higher. Since clusters in 1xx contain more samples than clusters in 16x, the second layer accuracy can have better prediction on actual values than the first layer accuracy. We can get most precise estimation when we have the third layer accuracy.

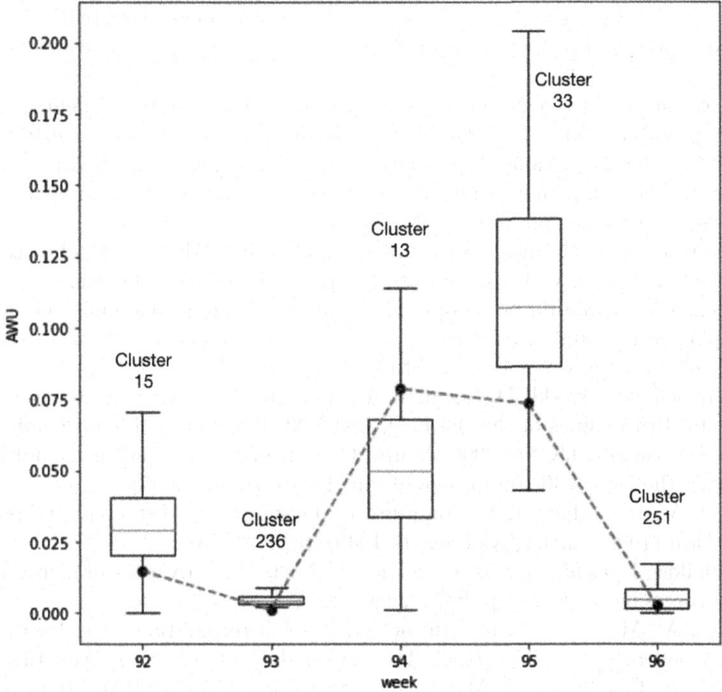

Fig. 7. A sampled item for prediction on the AWU value of five periods

6 Conclusion

We present a GAN-like model for synthesizing and predicting sequences of structured data effectively. By using coordinate and cosine similarity to express hierarchical data and loss functions, we are able to adopt SeqGAN to generate more realistic and representative sequences of structured data. In our experiments, we show that the synthesized sequences can be used in two folds: (1) as input data to improve the training process of the state-of-the-art models, and (2) as the prediction of sequences that match the prefix and achieve higher accuracy compared to the state-of-the-art models.

References

1. Abdel-Hamid, O., Mohamed, A.R., Jiang, H., Deng, L., Penn, G., Yu, D.: Convolutional neural networks for speech recognition. IEEE/ACM Trans. Audio Speech Lang. Process. **22**(10), 1533–1545 (2014)
2. Awad, W., ELseuofi, S.: Machine learning methods for e-mail classification. Int. J. Comput. Appl. **16**(1), 39–45 (2011). https://doi.org/10.5120/1974-2646
3. Churchland, P.S., Sejnowski, T.J., Poggio, T.A.: The Computational Brain. MIT press, Cambridge (2016). https://doi.org/10.7551/mitpress/9780262533393.001.0001

4. Creswell, A., Bharath, A.A.: Denoising adversarial autoencoders. IEEE Trans. Neural Networks Learn. Syst. **99**, 1–17 (2018). https://doi.org/10.1049/iet-cvi.2018.5243
5. Dai, J., Lu, Y., Wu, Y.N.: Generative modeling of convolutional neural networks. arXiv preprint arXiv:1412.6296 (2014). https://doi.org/10.4310/sii.2016.v9.n4.a8
6. Dai, Z., Yang, Z., Yang, F., Cohen, W.W., Salakhutdinov, R.R.: Good semi-supervised learning that requires a bad gan. In: Advances in Neural Information Processing Systems, pp. 6510–6520 (2017)
7. Demšar, J., et al.: Orange: data mining toolbox in python. J. Mach. Learn. Res. **14**, 2349–2353 (2013). http://jmlr.org/papers/v14/demsar13a.html
8. Denton, E.L., Chintala, S., Fergus, R., et al.: Deep generative image models using a Laplacian pyramid of adversarial networks. In: Advances in Neural Information Processing Systems, pp. 1486–1494 (2015)
9. Dittenbach, M., Merkl, D., Rauber, A.: The growing hierarchical self-organizing map. In: Proceedings of the IEEE-INNS-ENNS International Joint Conference on Neural Networks, IJCNN 2000, Neural Computing: New Challenges and Perspectives for the New Millennium, vol. 6, pp. 15–19. IEEE (2000)
10. Gers, F.A., Schmidhuber, J., Cummins, F.: Learning to forget: continual prediction with lstm (1999). https://doi.org/10.1049/cp:19991218
11. Goodfellow, I., et al.: Generative adversarial nets. In: Advances in neural information processing systems, pp. 2672–2680 (2014)
12. Graves, A., Mohamed, A.R., Hinton, G.: Speech recognition with deep recurrent neural networks. In: 2013 IEEE International Conference on Acoustics, Speech and Signal Processing (ICASSP), pp. 6645–6649. IEEE (2013). https://doi.org/10.1109/icassp.2013.6638947
13. Hadriche, A., Jmail, N., Elleuch, R.: Different methods of partitioning the phase space of a dynamic system. Int. J. Comput. Appl. **93**, 1–5 (2014). https://doi.org/10.5120/16288-5931
14. Ho, J., Ermon, S.: Generative adversarial imitation learning. In: Advances in Neural Information Processing Systems, pp. 4565–4573 (2016)
15. Hochreiter, S., Schmidhuber, J.: Long short-term memory. Neural Comput. **9**(8), 1735–1780 (1997)
16. Kohonen, T.: Neurocomputing: Foundations of research. chap. Self-organized Formation of Topologically Correct Feature Maps, pp. 509–521. MIT Press, Cambridge, (1988). https://doi.org/10.1016/0893-6080(89)90025-7, http://dl.acm.org/citation.cfm?id=65669.104428
17. LeCun, Y., Bengio, Y., et al.: Convolutional networks for images, speech, and time series. In: The Handbook of Brain Theory and Neural Networks, vol. 3361, no. 10 (1995)
18. Lin, T.Y., Chuang, H.H.C., Yu, F.: Tracking supply chain process variability with unsupervised cluster traversal. In: 2018 IEEE 16th International Conference on Dependable, Autonomic and Secure Computing, 16th International Conference on Pervasive Intelligence and Computing, 4th International Conference on Big Data Intelligence and Computing and Cyber Science and Technology Congress (DASC/PiCom/DataCom/CyberSciTech), pp. 966–973. IEEE (2018). https://doi.org/10.1109/dasc/picom/datacom/cyberscitec.2018.000-2
19. Liu, M.Y., Tuzel, O.: Coupled generative adversarial networks. In: Advances in neural information processing systems, pp. 469–477 (2016)
20. Luc, P., Couprie, C., Chintala, S., Verbeek, J.: Semantic segmentation using adversarial networks. arXiv preprint arXiv:1611.08408 (2016)

21. Macqueen, J.: Some methods for classification and analysis of multivariate observations. In: In the 5th Berkeley Symposium on Mathematical Statistics and Probability, pp. 281–297 (1967)
22. Makhzani, A., Shlens, J., Jaitly, N., Goodfellow, I., Frey, B.: Adversarial autoencoders. arXiv preprint arXiv:1511.05644 (2015)
23. Myszkowski, P.B., Buczek, B.: Growing hierarchical self-organizing map for searching documents using visual content. In: 2011 Federated Conference on Computer Science and Information Systems (FedCSIS), pp. 77–81. IEEE (2011)
24. Quinlan, J.R., et al.: Bagging, boosting, and c4. 5. In: AAAI/IAAI, vol. 1, pp. 725–730 (1996)
25. Radford, A., Metz, L., Chintala, S.: Unsupervised representation learning with deep convolutional generative adversarial networks. arXiv preprint arXiv:1511.06434 (2015)
26. Rauch-Hindin, W.B.: Artificial Intelligence in Business, Science, and Industry: Fundamentals. Prentice-Hall, Upper Saddle River (1986)
27. Saito, M., Matsumoto, E., Saito, S.: Temporal generative adversarial nets with singular value clipping. In: Proceedings of the IEEE International Conference on Computer Vision, pp. 2830–2839 (2017). https://doi.org/10.1109/iccv.2017.308
28. Salimans, T., Goodfellow, I., Zaremba, W., Cheung, V., Radford, A., Chen, X.: Improved techniques for training gans. In: Advances in Neural Information Processing Systems, pp. 2234–2242 (2016)
29. Sebastiani, F.: Machine learning in automated text categorization. ACM Comput. Surv. (CSUR) **34**(1), 1–47 (2002). https://doi.org/10.1145/505282.505283
30. Simonyan, K., Zisserman, A.: Very deep convolutional networks for large-scale image recognition. arXiv preprint arXiv:1409.1556 (2014)
31. Sutskever, I., Vinyals, O., Le, Q.V.: Sequence to sequence learning with neural networks. In: Advances in neural information processing systems, pp. 3104–3112 (2014)
32. Tulyakov, S., Liu, M.Y., Yang, X., Kautz, J.: Mocogan: decomposing motion and content for video generation. In: Proceedings of the IEEE conference on computer vision and pattern recognition, pp. 1526–1535 (2018). https://doi.org/10.1109/cvpr.2018.00165
33. Vincent, P., Larochelle, H., Bengio, Y., Manzagol, P.A.: Extracting and composing robust features with denoising autoencoders. In: Proceedings of the 25th international conference on Machine learning, pp. 1096–1103. ACM (2008). https://doi.org/10.1145/1390156.1390294
34. Vondrick, C., Pirsiavash, H., Torralba, A.: Generating videos with scene dynamics. In: Advances In Neural Information Processing Systems, pp. 613–621 (2016)
35. Williams, R.J., Zipser, D.: A learning algorithm for continually running fully recurrent neural networks. Neural Comput. **1**(2), 270–280 (1989). https://doi.org/10.1162/neco.1989.1.2.270
36. Xie, J., Gao, R., Zheng, Z., Zhu, S.C., Wu, Y.N.: Learning dynamic generator model by alternating back-propagation through time. arXiv preprint arXiv:1812.10587 (2018)
37. Xie, J., Lu, Y., Gao, R., Zhu, S.C., Wu, Y.N.: Cooperative training of descriptor and generator networks. arXiv preprint arXiv:1609.09408 (2016). https://doi.org/10.1109/tpami.2018.2879081
38. Xie, J., Lu, Y., Zhu, S.C., Wu, Y.: A theory of generative convnet. In: International Conference on Machine Learning, pp. 2635–2644 (2016)

39. Yu, L., Zhang, W., Wang, J., Yu, Y.: Seqgan: sequence generative adversarial nets with policy gradient. In: AAAI, pp. 2852–2858 (2017)
40. Zhu, J.Y., Park, T., Isola, P., Efros, A.A.: Unpaired image-to-image translation using cycle-consistent adversarial networks. arXiv preprint (2017). https://doi.org/10.1109/iccv.2017.244

DeepEX: Bridging the Gap Between Knowledge and Data Driven Techniques for Time Series Forecasting

Muhammad Ali Chattha[1,2,3(✉)], Shoaib Ahmed Siddiqui[2,3], Mohsin Munir[1,2], Muhammad Imran Malik[3,4], Ludger van Elst[2], Andreas Dengel[1,2], and Sheraz Ahmed[2(✉)]

[1] TU Kaiserslautern, Kaiserslautern, Germany
[2] German Research Center for Artificial Intelligence (DFKI) GmbH, Kaiserslautern, Germany
{muhammad_ali.chattha,sheraz.ahmed}@dfki.de
[3] School of Electrical Engineering and Computer Science (SEECS), National University of Sciences and Technology (NUST), Islamabad, Pakistan
[4] Deep Learning Laboratory, National Center of Artificial Intelligence, Islamabad, Pakistan

Abstract. Artificial Intelligence (AI) can roughly be categorized into two streams, knowledge driven and data driven both of which have their own advantages. Incorporating knowledge into Deep Neural Networks (DNN), that are purely data driven, can potentially improve the overall performance of the system. This paper presents such a fusion scheme, DeepEX, that combines these seemingly parallel streams of AI, for multi-step time-series forecasting problems. DeepEX achieves this in a way that merges best of both worlds along with a reduction in the amount of data required to train these models. This direction has been explored in the past for single step forecasting by opting for a residual learning scheme. We analyze the shortcomings of this simple residual learning scheme and enable DeepEX to not only avoid these shortcomings but also scale to multi-step prediction problems. DeepEX is tested on two commonly used time series forecasting datasets, CIF2016 and NN5, where it achieves competitive results even when trained on a reduced set of training examples. Incorporating external knowledge to reduce network's reliance on large amount of accurately labeled data will prove to be extremely effective in training of neural networks for real-world applications where the dataset sizes are small and labeling is expensive.

Keywords: Deep Neural Networks · Knowledge incorporation · Time-Series · Residual learning

1 Introduction

Recent advances in computational hardware have made it possible to achieve state-of-the-art performance in various domains, by utilizing DNNs, ranging from image

Code available at https://www.github.com/MAchattha4/DeepEX.

I. V. Tetko et al. (Eds.): ICANN 2019, LNCS 11728, pp. 639–651, 2019.
https://doi.org/10.1007/978-3-030-30484-3_51

classification [21], playing board games [15], natural language processing [6] to speech recognition [8]. As a result, there is heightened interest, both academically and industrially, in DNNs with deep learning being listed at the top of Gartner hype cycle for emerging technologies [5]. This increased interest coupled with advances in hardware has paved the way for the development of more sophisticated DNN algorithms, which may contain millions of parameters to train and optimize. Version of NASNet-A [21] model, for example, with highest accuracy on ImageNet dataset contains around 88.9M parameters. Optimizing such a huge number of parameters is a challenge itself and requires equivalently bigger training dataset that allows the model to extract enough features to train its parameters. As a result, these models perform exceptionally well in domains where ample data is available but in data scarce domains, these model suffer as they can easily overfit. This is even more so true for time-series domain, where scantiness of data is further compounded by the fact that time-series often do not have enough features for deep networks to work with. Leveraging information present in the form of knowledge can be particularly useful here. These techniques, especially the statistical ones, have shown considerable success in time-series domain which is evident from results of forecasting competitions, like M3 [11], M4 [12] and NN5 [16], which were dominated by statistical based techniques.

In contrast to DNNs, humans tend to rely on their knowledge while solving problems. This knowledge is acquired not only from problem specific examples but also from other sources, like education and experiences [10]. However, the very notion of "knowledge" is tricky to explain and equivalently difficult to collect and store in a form that is understandable or transferable to a computing program. Knowledge-Based Systems (KBS) aims to store such knowledge expressed in the form of logic rules or some other declarative language which can then be used to find solution to complex problems [19]. Similarly, there are statistical methods that are based on strong logical reasoning, like Auto-Regressive Integrated Moving Average (ARIMA), that do perform exceptionally well in their respective domains and are used by many experts to aid them in decision-making process. Hence, it is undeniable that knowledge about the problem is equally important for its solution. Nevertheless, exceptional performance of DNNs also prove that apart from knowledge, the raw data itself contains many hidden features which are useful in solving problems. In a nutshell, both of these streams i.e knowledge driven and data driven, have their own strengths and advantages. A natural step forward is to bridge the gap between these two streams to improve the overall performance of the system.

In fact, complementing DNNs with expert knowledge or some form of extra knowledge has been actively researched upon [3,9,20]. Most of the work in the literature, although improves performance of the DNNs but adds extra dependency on the network on quality of expert information used [9,17]. The focus of this work is to combine knowledge driven and data driven streams in a way that retains advantages of both while suppressing their individual disadvantages. Specifically, we aim to reduce the dependency of DNNs on the data by leveraging information contained in the knowledge stream. Finding state-of-the-art knowledge-based system or DNN model is not the focus here, but instead, the goal is to devise a knowledge incorporation scheme that bridges the gap between data and knowledge driven approaches and combines their strengths. Chattha et al. [4] recently introduced Knowledge Integrated Neural Network (KINN), a residual framework that combined information contained in the knowledge stream with the data stream in order to reduce the dependence of DNN on large amount of accurately labeled data. However, KINN [4] failed to produce acceptable results on benchmark time-series datasets. KINN particularly suffered when dealing with time-series that encapsulated significant trend variation. This resulted in poor performance on more sophisticated time-series datasets. In this paper, we present DeepEX, that not only addresses the shortcomings of KINN [4], but also strengthens the network allowing information in the two streams to complement each other. We tested DeepEX on the CIF2016 and NN5 time-series forecasting benchmark datasets to signify its performance. In particular, following are the contributions of DeepEX:

- We introduce a novel approach to combine knowledge and data driven systems in an end-to-end learning framework
- We introduce new regularization on the activity of the network that helps the network in identifying strengths and weakness of both domains and decide optimal combination of both
- Introduction of a new network to capture the trend in order to decompose the problem into sub-problems which can be effectively solved
- Scale DeepEX to multi-step ahead prediction which is significantly difficult for the current generation of expert knowledge incorporation techniques

The rest of the paper is structured as follows. We will first briefly cover the previous literature in the direction of expert knowledge incorporation in Sect. 2. Then we will describe the proposed method in detail in Sect. 3. We will present the results from the various experiments, and discuss the findings in Sect. 3.5. Finally, we conclude the paper with concluding remarks in Sect. 3.6.

2 Related Work

Integrating domain knowledge or any sort of extra information to boost DNN's performance has been actively researched upon. Ghazvininejad et al. [7] presented a knowledge-grounded conversation model based on neural networks. In addition to utilizing data containing the conversation history, they also conditioned the output of their sequence-to-sequence (seq2seq) model on external details within the context of conversation. The resulting conversation model was able to produce more accurate responses that were labeled as more informative and appropriate by human judges. Although such schemes encouraged knowledge incorporation to improve the performance of the system, however, it made the system more dependent on both the external contextual information data.

Knowledge-based Artificial Neural Networks (KBANN) were proposed by Towell et al. [17]. They utilized propositional rules for knowledge representation which were structured in a hierarchical manner. The neural network was designed to have a one-to-one correspondence with the elements of the rule set. The rule set directly defined the number of neurons along with their corresponding weights. Additional neurons were also introduced to learn features not specified in the rule set. Tran et al. [18] followed a similar approach where the network defined a logic rule set. Such techniques directly incorporates the information contained in the knowledge stream into the neural network. However, as a result of this direct incorporation, the network is confined to a structure that strictly complies to the hierarchical structure defined in the rule set. Additionally, this also abolishes the flexibility to be able to use different network architectures.

Venugopalan et al. [20] also proposed a neural network based video descriptor model that leveraged knowledge from both a neural language model as well as semantics obtained from a large text corpus in a LSTM based architecture. The results demonstrated significant improvements in grammar while also improving the overall descriptive quality. They introduced two fusion techniques, namely Late fusion and Deep fusion where they concatenated the hidden states from both video to text network and language LSTM network, fusing the information contained in both of the domains. The system is strongly dependent on the quality of the expert which in turn is dependent of large amount of data.

Buda et al. [3] used statistical forecasting models to aid neural network in producing forecasting results for an anomaly detection problem. They utilized multiple statistical forecasting models in conjunction with deep learning model. Predictions made by all of these individual models were combined into one framework. The predicted values from all models were compared with the ground-truth and value giving the lowest Root Mean Square Error (RMSE) score was selected as the final prediction. They refer this approach as single-step merge. Another voting based approach was also proposed where RMSE score is used to select a single model for all of the predictions. The system treats the predictions form the individual models separately, hence, it not able to leverage the advantages from both streams simultaneously. Munir et al. [13] also used statistical methods to enhance performance of the neural network in anomaly detection problem. Here auto-ARIMA was employed to forecast future values of the time series. These predictions were then integrated into neural network by using a residual scheme. The resulting model, FuseAD, achieves better performance compared to individual networks when used separately.

Hu et al. [9] again leveraged expert knowledge in the form of first order logic rules. Iterative knowledge distillation technique is used to transfer knowledge to network parameters. The expert network acts as a teacher network to the student network, the DNN. DNN tries to follow the teacher network by mimicking its predictions. Both the student and the teacher networks are updated at each iteration step. The goal is to find the best teacher network that fits the prediction of the rule set while also staying close to prediction made by the student network. KL-divergence between the probability distribution of the predictions made by the teacher network and the output distribution of predictions made by the student network is used to minimize the difference between the two distributions. The proposed framework achieved state-of-the-art performance for the evaluated classification tasks. However, the framework strongly relied on the expert network and as the student network is trying to emulate predictions made by the teacher network.

Chattha et al. [4] proposed a residual learning scheme, called as KINN, where they incorporated expert knowledge in the form of prediction in the network by adding it to the network's output. Although the approach is highly promising, it couldn't be scaled for multi-step predictions. The first limitation is its inability to control the network's correction factor. The network makes useless corrections even in cases where it is not necessary. The second limitation is its inability to cope up with trend present in the sequence. This proves to be an impediment in the production of convincing results for complex time-series data. DeepEX addresses both these limitations.

3 DeepEX: The Proposed Method

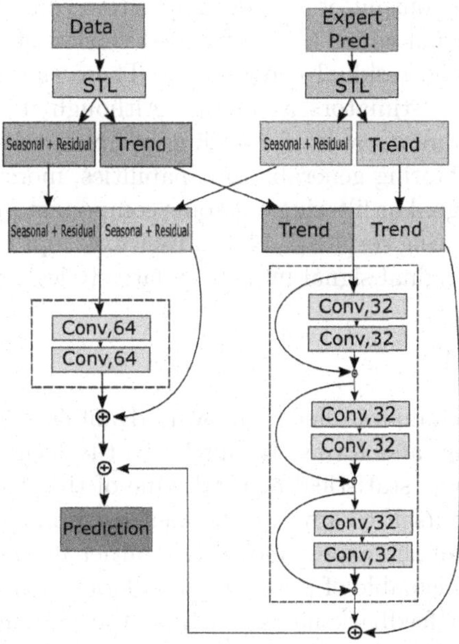

Fig. 1. Overview of DeepEX architecture

Fig. 1 shows the overall architecture of the DeepEX framework. There are several different components in DeepEX each targeted to cater for specific task.

The first component is the expert module which contains information about expert opinion. The second component is the STL decomposition module which decomposes the input signal into its constituent parts. Finally, there are two CNN models, where one model is dedicated to handle the trend part while the other one handles the remaining signal.

The data and the expert model output is log normalized before feeding it to the STL decomposition layer. Log normalization has two major advantages: (i) re-scaling values and (ii) transformation of the multiplicative relation between the STL components to an additive one, which makes it easier to decouple the decomposed components. We will now describe each of these components in detail.

3.1 STL Decomposition

The Seasonal and Trend decomposition using Loess (STL) is a well-known time-series decomposition method which splits a time-series into three components namely (i) trend, (ii) seasonality, and the (iii) residual. In DeepEX, input data and output of the expert model are both fed into the STL decomposition module and trend from each of the signals is extracted from the rest of the signal. Residual and seasonal components are added together since only the trend is of relevance to us. Hence, output of STL decomposition contains two signals, trend and the rest of the signal which is a de-trended version of the input comprising of the seasonal and the residual components. These signals are then given to their respective CNN estimators as inputs. Although it is a common notion that neural networks are capable of modeling complex structures in data owing to their strong self adapting generalizing capabilities, more recent studies argue decomposing input signal or filtering out some component prior to modelling can produce better forecasting results [1,14,16]. Hence, we opt for a similar approach and decompose the original signal into two relatively less complex components.

3.2 Expert Model

Knowledge driven techniques offer their own advantages. Knowledge, however, can take many shapes and forms. It can be in the form of a human expert, logic rules or even some statistical method. One of the strengths of DeepEX is that it does not limit itself to any specific knowledge model as it is not dependent on architecture of the expert model but rather its predictions. Therefore, any knowledge model capable of producing predictions can be used. The expert model can be human feedback integrated into the system or a KBS or some other technique. For this particular paper, we used the 4Theta method[1] as our expert network. 4Theta is based on theta model that decomposes the original signal into theta lines, where theta lines are derived by modifying the local curvature of the time-series through the coefficient θ. This θ is then applied to the

[1] https://github.com/M4Competition/M4-methods/blob/master/005%20-%20vangspiliot/Method-Description-4Theta.pdf.

second differences of the data. 4Theta is an improvement to the Theta model, enabling it to handle complex time-series more efficiently which is evident from its performance M4 benchmark dataset [12].

3.3 CNN Models

DeepEX has two different CNN models aimed to estimate trend and de-trended signal which are obtained after STL decomposition. Although the focus of this work was to develop a knowledge incorporation technique and not the individual DNN or knowledge models but considerable effort has been invested in estimating hyperparameters of DNN. It was particularly observed that simple CNN model struggled the most in modeling the trend component of the signal, hence, model responsible for the estimation of trend is relatively complex compared to the seasonal and residual signal estimator. The trend estimation network comprises of three residual blocks, each containing two convolutional layers with 32 filters each. The other CNN model comprises of two convolution layers with each layer each having 64 filters. It is important to mention that although we have chosen convolutional neural network as our DNN, because CNNs are generally easier to optimize, DeepEX is flexible enough to work with any other DNN architecture.

3.4 Knowledge Incorporation Scheme

Expert predictions are incorporated in the form of a residual scheme, where expert predictions are added to the output of the DNN model and are also used for conditioning the DNN. This conditioning is achieved by sequentially stacking the expert predictions ($x_t^{tr'}$) to the input from the data. The proposed residual scheme changes the underlying mapping learned by the network and instead of learning the complete input to output projection, the network only learns the modification factor needed in the input to give the desired output. In a way it can be said that the DeepEX framework estimates efficacy of expert model and makes corrections to it by using information from the data. As we have used a statistical method (Sect. 3.2) as our expert model, some portion of the data (25% of the training set) is used to estimate parameters of 4Theta model. The resulting expert model is then used for making predictions on remaining portion of the dataset, by employing a rolling window approach where forecast for the next horizon is obtained by using all of the previous data. Hence, DeepEX is trained on 75% of the training data, which is the only portion of the dataset where expert predictions are available, since we do not have any expert predictions on 25% of the data on which 4Theta is trained. It should be noted that the test set was never used in either estimating parameters of the 4Theta model or in training DeepEX. Validation set was obtained by $\max(0.2 * |X|, H)$ where $|X|$ denotes the cardinality of the training set, while H denotes the horizon.

The input signal and expert predictions both are decomposed using STL (Sect. 3.1). Trend from both, the expert predictions and the data is fed into

CNN responsible for trend estimation. This optimization problem for the trend estimating CNN ($\Phi : \mathbb{R}^h \mapsto \mathbb{R}^h$) can be represented as:

$$[\hat{x}_t^{tr}, \hat{x}_{t+1}^{tr}, \ldots, \hat{x}_{t+h-1}^{tr}] = \Phi([x_{t-1}^{tr}, x_{t-2}^{tr}, \ldots, x_{t-w}^{tr}; x_t^{tr'}, x_{t+1}^{tr'}, \ldots, x_{t+h-1}^{tr'}]; \mathcal{W}) + [x_t^{tr'}, x_{t+1}^{tr'}, \ldots, x_{t+h-1}^{tr'}] \quad (1)$$

where $x_t^{tr'}$ represents the decomposed trend values predicted by the expert model, x_{t-1}^{tr} represents the decomposed trend values of the original input and $\hat{x}_t^{tr}$ output trend values by the network. As the network is just producing an offset, i.e the required change in the input signal to produce the desired output, instead of finding the complete input to output mapping it makes the optimization problem significantly easier to tackle. Expert predictions are incorporated in a similar fashion as in case of other CNN model. Finally, the overall output of the system is the sum of the output of the two CNNs, which can be represented as:

$$[\hat{x}_t, \hat{x}_{t+1}, \ldots, \hat{x}_{t+h-1}] = [\hat{x}_t^{tr}, \hat{x}_{t+1}^{tr}, \ldots, \hat{x}_{t+h-1}^{tr}] + [\hat{x}_t^{sr}, \hat{x}_{t+1}^{rr}, \ldots, \hat{x}_{t+h-1}^{rr}] \quad (2)$$

where $\hat{x}_t^{sr}$ represents the output from the trend network, $\hat{x}_t^{rr}$ represents the output of the seasonality and residual network, and $\hat{x}_t$ represents the output of the overall system. Both of the CNN models are optimized separately. A regularization term β is also added on top of the network activations in order to hinder the network from making unnecessary modifications. Therefore, The optimization problem for the CNN can be represented as:

$$\begin{aligned} \mathcal{W}^* = \arg\min_{\mathcal{W}} \| [x_t^{tr}, x_{t+1}^{tr}, .., x_{t+h-1}^{tr}] - \\ (\Phi([x_{t-1}^{tr}, x_{t-2}^{tr}, \ldots, x_{t-w}^{tr}; x_t^{tr'}, x_{t+1}^{tr'}, \ldots, x_{t+h-1}^{tr'}]; \mathcal{W}) + [x_t^{tr'}, x_{t+1}^{tr'}, \ldots, x_{t+h-1}^{tr'}]) \|_2 \\ + \beta \| \Phi([x_{t-1}^{tr}, x_{t-2}^{tr}, \ldots, x_{t-w}^{tr}; x_t^{tr'}, x_{t+1}^{tr'}, \ldots, x_{t+h-1}^{tr'}]; \mathcal{W}) \|_2 \quad (3) \end{aligned}$$

where β is a hyperparameter which controls the activity of the network. This formulation is used for both of the CNN models and the value of β is obtained via validation.

3.5 Results and Discussion

CIF2016 and NN5 forecasting benchmark datasets were chosen to evaluate the performance of DeepEX. Figure 2 shows the performance of DeepEX on a randomly selected time-series from the NN5 dataset. It is evident from the Fig. 2b that DeepEX does a better job at following the trend of the time-series compared to the expert network, which struggled in correctly modeling the magnitude of the peaks. KINN [4] also closely followed the expert model. Similar pattern can be observed from Fig. 2a where DeepEX was able to capture minor variations in seasonal and residual components, especially in cases of minimas, as compared to the other models. DeepEX had a Symmetric Mean Absolute Percentage Error (SMAPE) score of 15.04 on this particular time-series whereas the SMAPE score of the expert model was 22.40, highlighting the efficacy of DeepEX in modeling the sequence. This dominance of DeepEX was found to be consistent on the entire dataset.

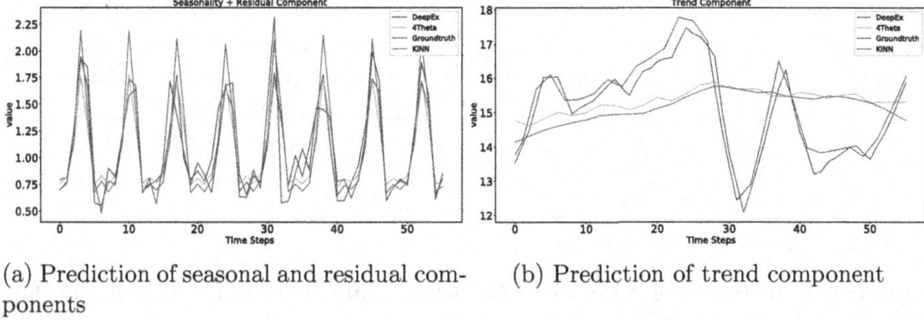

(a) Prediction of seasonal and residual components

(b) Prediction of trend component

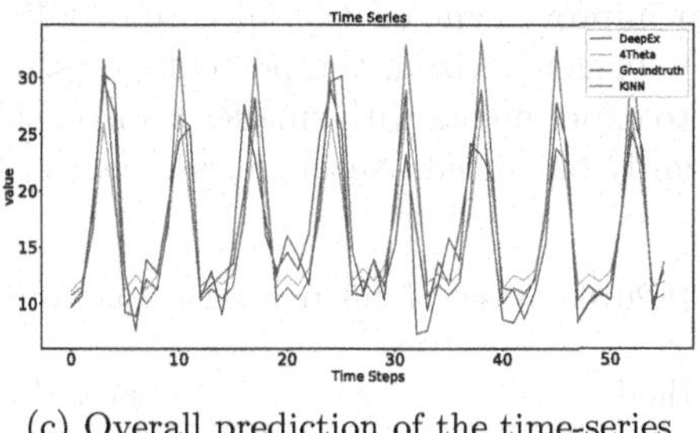

(c) Overall prediction of the time-series

Fig. 2. Prediction of DeepEX and other networks on a randomly selected time-series from the NN5 dataset with a horizon 1

We performed a series of experiments in order to validate the effectiveness of DeepEX's knowledge incorporation scheme in helping DNN to reduce its dependence on data, along with its ability to scale to multi-step ahead prediction. As mentioned previously, for the first set of experiments, only 75% of the training data was utilized to train parameters of the DNNs. For NN5 dataset, the performance was evaluated for a horizon of 1, 3, 8 and 56. While for CIF2016, the performance was evaluated for a horizon of 1, 3 and 6/12. In the next set of experiments, training data was further reduced to 50% while the horizons were kept same. When the size of the dataset was reduced to half, many time-series in CIF2016 became so small that even having a horizon of one in the validation set was not possible. Hence, in this particular experimental setting, CIF2016 dataset was not evaluated for a horizon of 6/12.

Table 1 shows the results of the aforementioned experiments. In almost all of the experiments, DeepEX achieved lower SMAPE score compared to the other techniques. Even in data scarce scenarios, DeepEX showed an improvement of

Table 1. SMAPE scores for the different models

Dataset Percentage	Horizon	Dataset					
		CIF2016			NN5		
		4Theta	KINN [4]	DeepEX	4Theta	KINN [4]	DeepEX
75%	1	9.2	99.2	**7.5**	20.1	24.4	**17.2**
	3	10.1	117	**9.4**	20.6	27.2	**18.2**
	6/12/8	13	96	**12.8**	20.6	29.3	**19.8**
	56	–	–	–	21.5	65	**21.4**
50%	1	30.4	99	**18.9**	35.3	39.5	**19.0**
	3	32.3	105	**22.5**	35.1	44.8	**21.3**
	6/12/8	–	–	–	34.9	46.8	**28.1**
	56	–	–	–	34.0	93	**32.8**

almost 46% in terms of SMAPE score when trained on only 50% of the data from the NN5 dataset with a horizon of 1. Similarly, for the same experimental setting, it showed an improvement of 38% in case of CIF2016 dataset. It was also observed that for bigger horizon, the percentage gain in terms of SMAPE was lower compared to experiments with smaller horizon since the complexity of the task was significantly enhanced. Nevertheless, even in these cases, DeepEX

Table 2. Results of CIF2016 dataset of different techniques ordered by mean SMAPE

Method	Mean SMAPE
LSTM.Cluster	10.53
LSTMs and ETS	10.83
ETS	11.87
MLP	12.13
REST	12.45
ES	12.73
DeepEX(trained on 75% data)	**12.80**
FRBE	12.90
HEM	13.04
Avg	13.05
BaggedETS	13.13
LSTM	13.33
Fuzzy c-regression	13.73
PB-GRNN	14.50
PB-RF	14.50
ARIMA	14.56
Theta	14.76

still outperformed other techniques. KINN [4] particularly struggled on these datasets as could not handle time series with trend component.

We compared DeepEX with the top performing techniques for both of these competitions i.e NN5 and CIF2016. Table 2 shows the comparison of results on CIF2016 dataset. DeepEX trained with 75% of the training data outperformed most of the other techniques, including BaggesETS [2], ARIMA and Theta methods, which were considered as benchmarks, in the competition and achieved comparative performance with that of the top performing models.

Table 3 shows the results obtained on the NN5 dataset including both DeepEX and other state-of-the-art models. Similar to the case of CIF2016,

Table 3. Results of NN5 dataset of different techniques ordered by Mean SMAPE

Name	Mean SMAPE
Wildi	19.9
Andrawis	20.4
Vogel	20.5
D'yakonov	20.6
Noncheva	21.1
DeepEX(trained on 75% data)	**21.4**
LSTM.Cluster	21.6
Rauch	21.7
Luna	21.8
Lagoo	21.9
Wichard	22.1
Gao	22.3
LSTM.All	23.4
Puma-Villanueva	23.7
Autobox(Reilly)	24.1
Lewicke	24.5
Brentnall	24.8
Dang	25.3
Pasero	25.3
Adeodato	25.3
undisclosed	26.8
undisclosed	27.3
Tung	28.1
Naive Seasonal	28.8
DeepEx(trained on 50% data)	**32.8**
undisclosed	33.1

DeepEX trained on 75% of the data outperformed most of the techniques and is even slightly better then *LSTM.Cluster* [1] which was the best performing model for the CIF2016 dataset. This demonstrates the robustness of DeepEX and its ability to work on a different datasets.

3.6 Conclusion

We have presented a new knowledge incorporating residual framework that combines best of both knowledge as well as data driven approaches. In particular the aim of this work was to use information contained in the knowledge stream to reduce the dependence of DNNs on large amount of data without compromising the performance. Results obtained by DeepEX show that DeepEX not only alleviates data dependence but also significantly boosts the performance of the network. DeepEX trained on only 75% of the data ranked at 6th place overall in the NN5 competition and 7th in the CIF2016 competition. This is achieved by separating the forecasting model into two different components where the first one captures the trend while the second one captures the rest of the signal. Finally, these two outputs are added to the prediction made by the expert. Regularization term is also added that controls the activation of the DNN model which inhibits the neural network from making unnecessary modifications. High rank achieved by DeepEX on different datasets belonging to different domains demonstrates that the model indeed generalizes well by leveraging a combination of the two streams.

This is only a step in the direction of merging knowledge and data driven techniques. There is still a large room for improvement, particularly in cases where forecasting horizon is large.

References

1. Bandara, K., Bergmeir, C., Smyl, S.: Forecasting across time series databases using recurrent neural networks on groups of similar series: a clustering approach. arXiv preprint arXiv:1710.03222 (2017)
2. Bergmeir, C., Hyndman, R.J., Benítez, J.M.: Bagging exponential smoothing methods using STL decomposition and box-cox transformation. Int. J. Forecast. **32**(2), 303–312 (2016)
3. Buda, T.S., Caglayan, B., Assem, H.: DeepAD: a generic framework based on deep learning for time series anomaly detection. In: Phung, D., Tseng, V.S., Webb, G.I., Ho, B., Ganji, M., Rashidi, L. (eds.) PAKDD 2018. LNCS (LNAI), vol. 10937, pp. 577–588. Springer, Cham (2018). https://doi.org/10.1007/978-3-319-93034-3_46
4. Chattha, M.A., Siddiqui, S.A., Malik, M.I., van Elst, L., Dengel, A., Ahmed, S.: Kinn. arXiv preprint arXiv:1902.05653 (2019)
5. Columbus, L.: Gartner's hype cycle for emerging technologies, 2017 adds 5g and deep learning for first time. Forbes/Tech/# CuttingEdge (2017)
6. Conneau, A., Kiela, D., Schwenk, H., Barrault, L., Bordes, A.: Supervised learning of universal sentence representations from natural language inference data. arXiv preprint arXiv:1705.02364 (2017)

7. Ghazvininejad, M., et al.: A knowledge-grounded neural conversation model. In: AAAI (2018)
8. Hinton, G., et al.: Deep neural networks for acoustic modeling in speech recognition: the shared views of four research groups. IEEE Signal Process. Mag. **29**(6), 82–97 (2012)
9. Hu, Z., Ma, X., Liu, Z., Hovy, E., Xing, E.: Harnessing deep neural networks with logic rules. arXiv preprint arXiv:1603.06318 (2016)
10. Lake, B.M., Salakhutdinov, R., Tenenbaum, J.B.: Human-level concept learning through probabilistic program induction. Science **350**(6266), 1332–1338 (2015)
11. Makridakis, S., Hibon, M.: The M3-Competition: results, conclusions and implications. Int. J. Forecast. **16**(4), 451–476 (2000)
12. Makridakis, S., Spiliotis, E., Assimakopoulos, V.: The M4 Competition: results, findings, conclusion and way forward. Int. J. Forecast. **34**(4), 802–808 (2018)
13. Munir, M., Siddiqui, S.A., Chattha, M.A., Dengel, A., Ahmed, S.: FuseAD: unsupervised anomaly detection in streaming sensors data by fusing statistical and deep learning models. Sensors **19**(11), 2451 (2019)
14. Nelson, M., Hill, T., Remus, W., O'Connor, M.: Time series forecasting using neural networks: should the data be deseasonalized first? Journal of forecasting **18**(5), 359–367 (1999)
15. Silver, D., et al.: Mastering the game of go without human knowledge. Nature **550**(7676), 354 (2017)
16. Taieb, S.B., Bontempi, G., Atiya, A.F., Sorjamaa, A.: A review and comparison of strategies for multi-step ahead time series forecasting based on the NN5 forecasting competition. Expert Syst. Appl. **39**(8), 7067–7083 (2012)
17. Towell, G.G., Shavlik, J.W.: Knowledge-based artificial neural networks. Artif. Intell. **70**(1–2), 119–165 (1994)
18. Tran, S.N., Garcez, A.S.D.: Deep logic networks: inserting and extracting knowledge from deep belief networks. IEEE Trans. Neural Networks Learn. Syst. **29**(2), 246–258 (2018)
19. Ullman, J.D.: Principles of Database and Knowledge-base Systems, vol. 1. Computer Science Press Incorporated, Rockville (1988)
20. Venugopalan, S., Hendricks, L.A., Mooney, R., Saenko, K.: Improving lstm-based video description with linguistic knowledge mined from text. arXiv preprint arXiv:1604.01729 (2016)
21. Zoph, B., Vasudevan, V., Shlens, J., Le, Q.V.: Learning transferable architectures for scalable image recognition. In: (CVPR), June 2018

Domain Adaptation Approaches

Transferable Adversarial Cycle Alignment for Domain Adaption

Yingcan Wei(✉)

The University of Hong Kong, Pok Fu Lam, Hong Kong
ycwei@connect.hku.hk

Abstract. Domain adaption is definitely critical for success in bridging source and target domains that data distribution shifts exist in domain or task. The state-of-the-art of the adversarial feature learning model named Bidirectional Generative Adversarial Networks (BiGAN), forces generative models to align with an arbitrarily complex distribution in a latent space. However, BiGAN only matches single data distribution without exploiting multi-domain structure, which means the learned latent representation could not transfer to related target domains. Recent research has proved that GANs combined with Cycle Consistent Constraints are effective at image translation. Therefore, we propose a novel framework named Transferable Bidirectional Generative Adversarial Networks combining with Cycle-Consistent Constraints (Cycle-TBiGAN) be applied in cross-domain translation, which aims at learning an alignment latent feature representation and achieving a mapping function between domains. Our framework is suitable for a wide variety of domain adaption scenarios. We show the surprising results in the task of image translation without prior ground-truth knowledge. Extensive experiments are presented on several public datasets. Quantitative comparisons demonstrate the superiority of our approach against previous methods.

Keywords: Domain adaption · Cycle constraints · Transferable alignment · GAN · Image translation

1 Introduction

Domain adaptation is an actively researched topic in many areas of Artificial Intelligence. Earlier approaches of domain adaptation focused on building the feature representations [1]. This was accomplished by exploring the inner structure of unlabeled data, such as Self-taught Learning [13, 16], Traditional methods, including Feature Reweighting and Selection [7, 9, 10, 20, 21], Adversarial Alignment [2, 5], Regularization Methods [6, 14], Matrix Completion and Mapping [22, 23, 25], Kernel Methods [3, 15]. The underlying idea behind these methods is to minimize a specific objective that reduces domain discrepancy or to learn a public feature mapping that aligns distribution between domains.

Generative Adversarial Networks (GANs) was first proposed by Goodfellow et al. [11]. When GANs are applied in domain adaption, existing domain divergence forces GAN's training easily to suffer from model collapse and become barbaric. For image domain adaption, cycle constraint [24] provides an assumption that a mapping between

I. V. Tetko et al. (Eds.): ICANN 2019, LNCS 11728, pp. 655–672, 2019.
https://doi.org/10.1007/978-3-030-30484-3_52

domains should be reversible. Donahue et al. [8] independently proposed an unsupervised feature learning method, Bidirectional GAN, an approach contains an encoder which maps data to a latent representation space and learns to invert the generator's operation.

Based on Transferable BiGAN, we proposed a novel framework that integrating the Adversarial Feature Learning with Cycle Consistent Constraints, namely **Cycle-TBiGAN**. The Cycle-TBiGAN is different from previous approaches as the following advantages: (1). TBiGAN aims to learn a distribution alignment space from domains thus we can transfer this space to any supervised task. (2). Cycle-TBiGAN is two-way and ensures the one-to-one relationship between domains.

2 Related Work

2.1 Structural Risk Minimization

Domain adaptation is a challenging field since the target domain almost has no labeled sample with respect to the source domain follows different distributions. Many methods aim to bound the target error by source error plus a discrepancy metric between the source and target distributions [4], which is theoretically supported by domain adaptation learning bounds. SRM theory aims to minimize the distribution discrepancy for mismatched features so that the model achieves adaption by reducing even removing the domain discrepancy. Based on the SRM principle [18], domain adaption model needs to learn an unbiased and invariant feature space so that the structural target model risk of $\hat{R}_{x_t}(f)$ is minimized as [4]:

$$\hat{R}_{x_t}(f) \leq \hat{R}_{x_s}(f) + \frac{1}{2} D_f(x_s, x_t) + \lambda \tag{1}$$

As (1) shows, the target risk $\hat{R}_{x_t}(f)$ is the upper-bounded by summation of pre-trained source model risk $\hat{R}_{x_s}(f)$, a constant λ (an expected complexity of target hypothesis VC-dimensionality space) and $D_f(\cdot)$ (a divergence measurement between source distribution p and target distribution q). Only minimizing the risk of source model or estimating the optimal error λ is not enough to extract the invariant feature space because the cross-domain distribution discrepancy can't be estimated. In order to measure the difference between the data distributions, the feature-based methods learn a mapping function that projects the data from the original domain to a latent code space where the distribution divergence could be bounded with a distance measurement.

2.2 Adversarial Feature Learning

The Generative Adversarial Networks (GAN) has an ability to learn a function or a distribution that generates the latent code or feature from an arbitrarily noise simple distribution. Therefore, we could use the generator to predict the latent representation for more complex data distribution based on the prerequisite that model has already learned a semantically related feature space from different distributions. Aim at transferring the invariant and relevant semantic information to any target domain.

Most of the existing methods only focus on one-way generation or extraction, which means only generate the latent code from original data without inverse operation. Interpolations in the latent space of the generator produce smooth and plausible semantic variations, and meaningful directions in this space correspond to particular semantic attributes along which the data distribution varies. Donahue et al. [8] put forward an intuitive question: can GAN be applied in unsupervised learning with sufficient latent features for any arbitrary data distribution?

Therefore, we proposed a Transferable Bidirectional Generative Adversarial Networks - **TBiGAN**, which is a significant improvement for existing Bidirectional Generative Adversarial Networks (BiGAN) framework and endued with a Transferable ability. The above generic adversarial learning framework can also be extended to tackle multiple target domains directly.

2.3 Cycle Consistency

A number of recently proposed cycle-consistent adversarial learning methods have achieved remarkable success in addressing cross-domain image generation problem, as a new Cycle Consistency GAN framework, called CycleGAN [24], it highlights superiority in image-to-image translation problem.

More recently, variant forms of cycle consistency have been applied in structured data transformation. Some scholars regard cycle consistency loss as a transitivity measurement for supervised Deep Neural Networks. CycleGAN provides an effective adversarial learning inference by cycle-consistency estimation and invertible mapping between two domains, which could effectively solve the visual domain adaption problem, like image generation. Combining the cycle consistency loss with the original adversarial objective loss in domain adaption could obtain a complete learning objective for unpaired image-to-image translation problem.

3 Method

Existing methods aim to learn an alignment representation space to implement the image translation. There are still several fundamental challenging problems: (1). How to ensure the distribution discrepancy keep measurement consistency between low-dimensional latent space and high-dimensional original space; (2). How to transfer an alignment latent representation space to target domain; (3). How to alleviate GAN highly unstable and model collapse issues during training; (4). How to obtain an integrated framework to solve the above issues simultaneously; Next, we will introduce the optimization work for the proposed framework correspond to these problems in detail.

3.1 Adversarial Feature Learning - Transferable Bidirectional GAN

Adversarial Feature Learning: BiGANs [8] has been trained to extract the latent code given a source domain space with effective semantic representation. However, how to successfully apply this framework in unsupervised domain adaption, the goal is to train a model that could learn a cross-domain invariant feature representation space.

We need to extend BiGANs to target domain by (1). Forcing the shared Encoder to be domain-invariant; (2). Training separately generators that contain the domain-specific properties. Moreover, transfer the source semantic information to the target domain in order to obtain an invariant latent feature space.

Definition 1. *Let $p_{x_s}(X_S)$ presents the probability distribution of a source domain for $X_S \in \Omega_{X_S}$ and $p_{x_t}(X_T)$ be the probability distribution of target domain for $X_T \in \Omega_{X_T}$.*

Let $p_{z_s}(Z_S)$ be the distribution of latent code of source feature representation for $Z_S \in \Omega_{Z_S}$ and $p_{z_t}(Z_T)$ be the distribution of latent code of target feature representation for $Z_T \in \Omega_{Z_T}$.

The goal of Encoder $\mathbf{E}$ is capturing data distribution with encoding result for Z that $Z \in \Omega_{Z_S} \cup \Omega_{Z_T}$.

The goal of source Generator $\mathbf{G_S}$ is reconstructing the source data X_S given the latent code Z_S.

The goal of target Generator $\mathbf{G_T}$ is reconstructing the target data X_T given the latent code Z_T.

Based on the Definition 1, we need to train a shared Encoder that extracts latent codes from both domains so as to obtain a feature representation space without domain discrepancy. Furthermore, the shared encoder should learn a cross-domain semantic justice. However, two generators should be situated out of the crossing-domain, which means training such two generators will focus on domain private semantic justice. As a result, two generators should have the ability to reconstruct the corresponding original domain data.

Assumption 1. *Transferable BiGAN (TBiGAN) instead of modeling the data probability distribution as a generative model for a fixed latent distribution $p_z(Z)$ where $Z \in \Omega_{Z_S} \cup \Omega_{Z_T}$. This generation process is bidirectional, is represented as a deterministic feed-forward networks:*

$G_S : \Omega_{Z_S} \rightarrow \Omega_{X_S}$ *with* $p_{G_S}(X_S|Z_S) = \delta(X - G_S(Z_S))$, $p_{G_S}(X_S) = E_{z \sim p_{z_s}}[p_{G_S}(X_S|Z_S)]$

$G_T : \Omega_{Z_T} \rightarrow \Omega_{X_T}$ *with* $p_{G_T}(X_T|Z_T) = \delta(X - G_T(Z_T))$, $p_{G_T}(X_T) = E_{z \sim p_{z_t}}[p_{G_T}(X_T|Z_T)]$

The objective is to train source and target generators such that $p_{G_S}(X) = p_{x_s}(X_S)$ and $p_{G_T}(X) = p_{x_t}(X_T)$.

$G_S : \Omega_{Z_T} \rightarrow \Omega_{X_S}$ *with* $p_{G_S}(X_{T \rightarrow S}|Z_T) = \delta(X - G_S(Z_T))$, $p_{G_S}(X_{T \rightarrow S}) = E_{z \sim p_{z_t}}[p_{G_S}(X_{T \rightarrow S}|Z_T)]$

$G_T : \Omega_{Z_S} \rightarrow \Omega_{X_T}$ *with* $p_{G_T}(X_{S \rightarrow T}|Z_S) = \delta(X - G_T(Z_S))$, $p_{G_T}(X_{S \rightarrow T}) = E_{z \sim p_{z_s}}[p_{G_T}(X_{S \rightarrow T}|Z_S)]$

At the same time, minimize the distribution divergence between $p_{x_s}(X_S)$ with $p_{G_T}(X_{S \rightarrow T})$, $p_{x_t}(X_T)$ with $p_{G_S}(X_{T \rightarrow S})$

From Fig. 1, Discriminator $D1$ needs distinguish the $(Z_S, G_S(Z_S))$ versus (Z_S, X_S) and $(Z_T, G_T(Z_T))$ versus (Z_T, X_T) pairs, which means the latent code Z could be considered as conditional information for $D1$ while the Generators $G \in \{G_S, G_T\}$ could learn how to generate the real-like data given latent code.

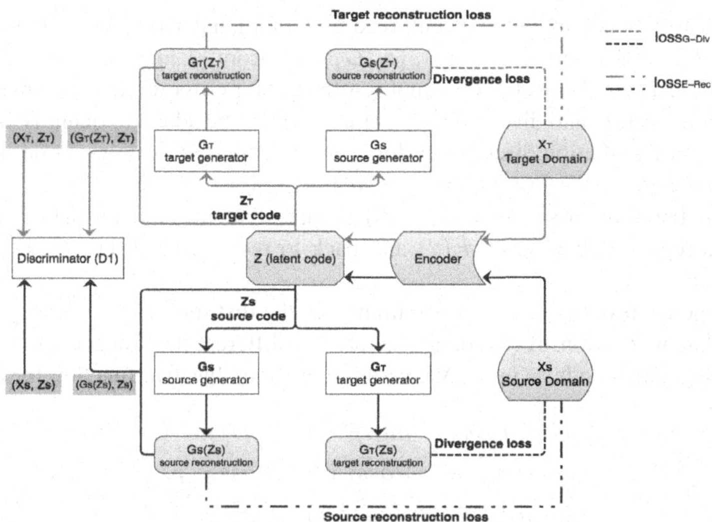

Fig. 1. Transferable Bidirectional Generative Adversarial Networks. Thence, given two Generators for the specific domain (G_S for source domain and G_t for target domain), which could generate the real-like instances based on the latent representation space Z. The objective of adversarial learning is to learn an invariant feature representation from both domains. Blue lines for source domain and red lines for target domain. (Color figure online)

Domain Divergence Alignment: In order to obtain an alignment feature representation space, we need an optimal discriminator decouple the domain generators from encoder, where the discriminator allows us to define the objective and demonstrate that it could reduce the divergence between the joint probability distributions $P_{E \bigcup X}$ and $P_{G \bigcup Z}$. Additionally, in order to "confuse" an expected discriminator, a deterministic encoder and generators should implement inverse operation each other [19].

Given a Bidirectional discriminator with the input pair denotes as (x, z), which should satisfy both adversarial and alignment objective. The objective of generators $G \in \{G_S, G_T\}$ and encoder E provided an optimal discriminator $max_{D1}V(E, G, D1)$ [8] can be rewritten as a autoencoder loss function. Formally, define the objective function for Discriminator $D1$ as:

$$\begin{aligned} min_{G,E}max_{D1}V(E, G, D1) = E_{x \sim p_x(x)}[logD1(x, E(x))] \\ + E_{z \sim p_z(z)}[1 - logD1(G(z), z)] \end{aligned} \tag{2}$$

$$\begin{aligned} min_{D1}loss_{D1} &= max_{D1}V(E, G, D1) \\ &= loss_{D1-E} + loss_{D1-G} \end{aligned} \tag{3}$$

where $loss_{D1-E}$, $loss_{D1-G}$ defined as:

$$loss_{D1-E} = L_b\Big(D1(x, E(x)), 1\Big) \tag{4}$$

$$loss_{D1-G} = L_b\Big(D1(z, G(z)), 0\Big) \tag{5}$$

where $L_b(\cdot)$ is a binary cross-entropy loss.

The distributional alignment is enforced by training a discriminator $D1$ to discriminate $(z_s, G_S(z_s))$ from $(E(x_s), x_s)$, $(z_t, G_T(z_t))$ from $(E(x_t), x_t)$ pairs. Only standard GAN adversarial constraint was not insufficient for cross-domain alignment. Additional reconstruction and divergence constraints should be added to quantify the reconstruction and distribution discrepancy loss. In this case, two-way inversion mappings are presented as $z = E(G(z))$ and $x = G(E(x))$.

Reconstruction loss ($loss_{E-Rec}$) (8) ensures that the domain data x mapping to feature representation space $E(x)$ and back to reconstructed data $G(E(x))$ keep unchanged.

Divergence loss ($loss_{G-Div}$) (9) minimizes the distribution discrepancy between original data with reconstructed data generated by different domain generator that uses original data latent code as input. We could define the objective function for E and G as:

$$\begin{aligned} min_E loss_E &= min_E V(E, G, D1) \\ &= (loss_{D1-E} + loss_{E-Rec}) \end{aligned} \tag{6}$$

$$\begin{aligned} min_G loss_G &= min_G V(E, G, D1) \\ &= (loss_{D1-G} + loss_{G-Div}) \end{aligned} \tag{7}$$

where $loss_{E-Rec}$ and $loss_{G-Div}$ defined as:

$$loss_{E-Rec} = \left\{ \begin{array}{l} L_1\Big(x_s, G_S\big(E(x_s)\big)\Big) \\ L_1\Big(x_t, G_T\big(E(x_t)\big)\Big) \end{array} \right. \tag{8}$$

$$loss_{G-Div} = \left\{ \begin{array}{l} L_d\Big(x_s, G_T\big(E(x_s)\big)\Big) \\ L_d\Big(x_t, G_S\big(E(x_t)\big)\Big) \end{array} \right. \tag{9}$$

where $L_1(\cdot)$ is a L_1 loss and $L_d(\cdot)$ denotes a "divergence loss" measurement, which is based on domain distribution measurements, such as Maximum Mean Discrepancy (MMD), Wasserstein Metric and etc.

3.2 Image Translation Cross Domain - Cycle TBiGAN

Image-to-image translation is a task of image processing whereby the goal of translation is to learn the mapping between different image domains with aligned pairs. To enforce simple binary-directional and forward-backward consistency became a fundamental solution for image translation task in recent years.

Previous methods were proposed for the image translation objective without prior ground-truth knowledge in the form of correspondences [12]. Most existing models aim to use similar minds to guarantee that the generative domain is indistinguishable from the original domain. However, these methods more or less suffer from known training instability and model collapse issues. Additionally, in order to obtain a one-to-one mapping, most methods rely on "cycle" relationships between domains.

We introduce a method: Cycle-Consistent Constraints combine with the TBiGAN framework, name as **Cycle-TBiGAN**, which takes advantage of the invariant feature representation space learned from TBiGAN. Cycle-TBiGAN relies heavily on pre-trained generators from source and target domains. Furthermore, the most important pre-trained Encoder could align both domains in the latent code space while jointly optimizing a cross-domain mapping function.

Cross-Domain Translation Alignment: Suppose we have obtained the generators and encoder in the previous Sect. 3.1. Specifically, Generator G_S, target Generator G_T and Encoder E, all of these components are depicted in Definition 1 and learned from TBiGAN framework. The objective of the task aims to match every source image X_S against with an analogous target fake image X_{T-fake} derived from the target domain but preserves the unique style or properties of the original target image. The same operation for a target image X_T matches a source fake image X_{S-fake}.

Definition 2. *The objective is jointly to learn a mapping function $G_c(\cdot)$, which maps the latent code of source domain Z_S and target domain Z_T to the synthesized latent code Z_{syn}, denotes as $Z_{syn} = G_c(Z_S, Z_T)$.*
Based on source Generator (G_S), we could generate a source-fake image $X_{S-fake} = G_S(Z_{syn})$ corresponding to every target input image X_T. Mathematical expression as:
$X_T \rightarrow X_{S-fake} = G_S\Big(G_c\big(E(X_S), E(X_T)\big)\Big)$
Based on target Generator (G_T), we could generate a target-fake image $X_{T-fake} = G_T(Z_{syn})$ corresponding to every source input image X_S. Mathematical expression as:
$X_S \rightarrow X_{T-fake} = G_T\Big(G_c\big(E(X_S), E(X_T)\big)\Big)$

The distribution alignment is required by training another discriminator $D2$ to distinguish mapped fake images X_{S-fake} from original source images $X_S \in \Omega_{X_S}$, where the distribution of X_S is denoted by $p_{x_s}(X_S)$, $p_{G_S(Z_{syn})}(X_{S-fake})$ denotes the distribution of X_{S-fake} instances be mapped by $G_S(Z_{syn})$. At the same time, $G_c(\cdot)$ is optimized so that the discriminator will not have an ability to discriminate between the $p_{x_s}(X_S)$ and $p_{G_S(Z_{syn})}(X_{S-fake})$. As a result, the loss functions of Discriminator $D2$ and mapping function G_c are:

$$min_{D2} loss_{D2} = L_b\Big(D2\big(G_S(Z_{syn})\big), 0\Big) + L_b\big(D2(X_S), 1\big) \tag{10}$$

$$min_{G_C} loss_{G_C} = L_b\Big(D2\big(G_S(Z_{syn})\big), 1\Big) \tag{11}$$

Where $L_b(\cdot)$ is a binary cross-entropy loss, $loss_{D2}$ and $loss_{G_C}$ are trained iteratively.

Cycle Consistent Constraints: Mode collapse appears when the generator drops into parameters setting in which always generates the same value [17]. Reflected in image translation problem that the generator produces a single mode with fixed images in respect to target domain, while the gradient of the GAN model will go towards several fixed directions with similar points. But the original data space is complex high-dimensional and it is almost impossible to ensure adaptive learning direction during the

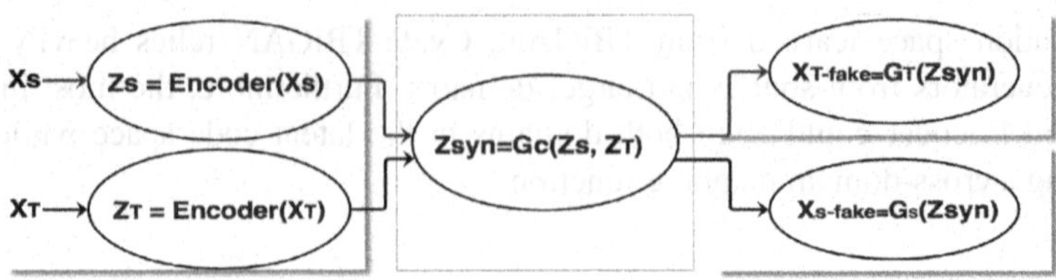

Fig. 2. A mapping function G_c could be regarded as a generative model trained under standard GAN. For each source or target latent code there is a synthetic code $Z_{syn} = G_c(Z_S, Z_T)$ exists, which could be used to reconstruct the domain fake images X_{S-fake} or X_{T-fake} given corresponding domain Generators G.

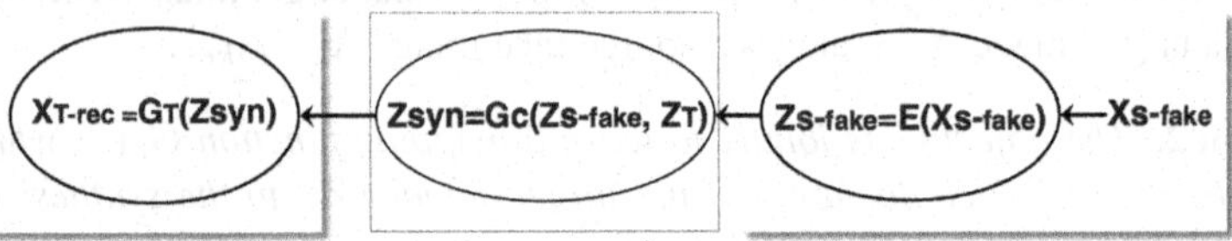

Fig. 3. Cycle-Consistent Constraints map source-fake image X_{S-fake} back to reconstruction target domain image X_{T-rec}.

training. But the latent space is low-dimensional and controllable for learning adaptive direction as expected. For the problem that GAN is not invertible to map the data back to the original space thus could be solved by Cycle-Consistent Constraints effectively.

Therefore, we propose a method to constrain the model and enforce no such mode collapse issue appears during training. Figures 2 and 3 show two-sided approaches implement cycle reversible mapping from X_T to X_{S-fake} and then reconstructs X_{S-fake} back to X_{T-rec}.

Cycle Consistent Reconstruction ($loss_{cyc}$) provides a matching between every target sample X_T with a reconstruction target domain image X_{T-rec}, it could be defined as:

$$X_{T-rec} = G_T\Big(G_C\big(E(X_{S-fake}), E(X_T)\big)\Big) \tag{12}$$

From the Fig. 4, the complete Cycle Consistent loss is given by:

$$min\ loss_{cyc} = L_p(X_T,\ X_{T-rec}) \tag{13}$$

Where $L_p(\cdot)$ is a "perceptual loss", which is based on image representation measurements, such as Laplacian pyramid by VGG, L_1 or L_2 loss. Finally, we summarize the objective of Adversarial Featuring Learning with Cycle Consistent Constraints for image translation is:

$$min_{D2} loss_{D2} = L_b\Big(D2(G_S(Z_{syn})), 0\Big) + L_b\big(D2(X_S), 1\big) \tag{14}$$

$$min_{G_C}\ loss_{G_C} = L_b\Big(D2\big(G_S(Z_{syn})\big), 1\Big) + loss_{cyc} \tag{15}$$

Where $L_b(\cdot)$ is a binary cross-entropy loss, $loss_{cyc}$ is defined in (13).

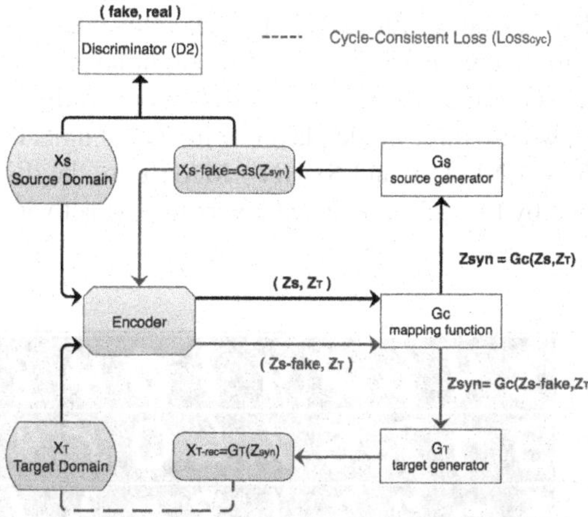

Fig. 4. The framework of Cycle-TBiGAN. The black line shows cross-domain translation flow and the red line shows the Cycle-Consistent Constraints measurement flow. (Color figure online)

4 Experiment

We demonstrate the performance of Cycle-TBiGAN against two benchmarks with 4 public exact datasets (including MNIST, MNIST_m, USPS, SVHN). (1). Attempt to verify whether TBiGAN can learn an invariant latent code space between domains. (2). A task of learning a mapping function between the different distributions of domain images so as to verify whether Cycle-TBiGAN can implement cross-domain translation.

- TBiGAN: We work with a quantitative evaluation for the quality of reconstruction images and the stability of the model training. Compared with TBiGAN, original GAN [11], Bidirectional GAN (BiGAN) [8] and Cycle-GAN [24] are trained under the same datasets. The Cycle-GAN learns pairwise translation functions between pairs of datasets (rather than mapping through a central latent space). We obtain BiGAN through objective loss defined in [8]. TBiGAN needs to achieve the Discriminator, Encoder, and Generators separately by (3), (6) and (7).
- Cycle-TBiGAN: Implement the translation from source domain images to target domain images. The source generator, target generator (G_S, G_T) and shared encoder (E) are obtained from TBiGAN. The discriminator $(D2)$ and generator (G_c) of Cycle-TBiGAN are trained by (14) and (15). The Non-Adversarial Mapping model [12] and Cycle-GAN [24] are used for comparison.

4.1 Transferable Bidirectional Generative Adversarial Networks (TBiGAN)

Implementation Detail. All the network architectures are repetition by two blocks, full connected block and convolutional (deconvolutional) block, each defined by a Batch Normalization layer and a Dropout layer followed by a Convolutional layer with

RELU or Leak_RELU activation function. The generator consists of the Deconvolution layers with a sigmoid unit and full connected output layers. In particular, MNIST, USPS, MNIST_m datasets, all components consist of simple fully connected layers. For MNIST→MNIST_m, we use three hidden layers with ReLU units throughout the architectures. For MNIST→ MNIST_m and SVHN→MNIST_m, the discriminator has five hidden layers followed by two full-connected layers that be activated by sigmoid units.

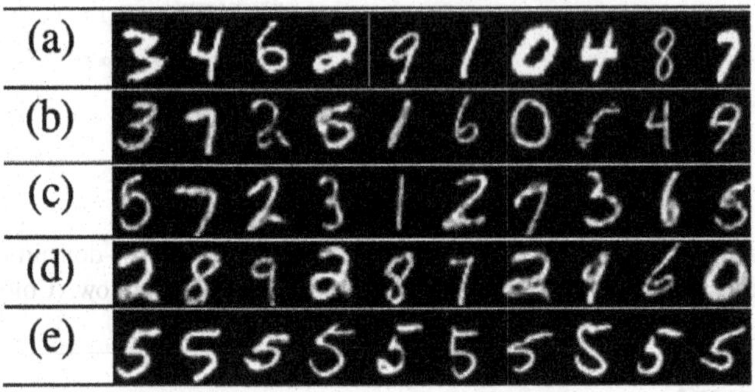

Fig. 5. Example results for MNIST are reconstructed by the different frameworks' Generator at the different training epochs. (a) TBiGAN (40 epochs). (b) GAN (300 epochs). (c) BiGAN (400 epochs). (d) Cycle-GAN (200 epochs). (e) Real MNIST.

Experiment Result. Evaluating the TBiGAN on adversarial feature learning task while comparing with original GAN, BiGAN and Cycle-GAN benchmarks. From Fig. 5, TBiGAN only needs 40 training epochs that have almost the same reconstruction result corresponds to 400 epochs of BiGAN and 200 epochs of Cycle-GAN. From Fig. 6, we could easily find TBiGAN has obtained expected reconstruction result at the number of 50 epoch compared with other algorithms that have the same network architecture at the same epoch. Figure 7 presents that TBiGAN initialized by source pre-trained model (G_S) even could reduce the loss reconstruction error of the target model (G_T) from $e-3$ to $e-4$ and converge to optimal value faster.

From the reconstruction results, it is easy to find that the source Generator and Encoder are actually pre-trained models for the target domain. In other words, we obtain a domain invariant feature space and transfer it to the target domain effectively. For the same random noise input, the output generated by TBiGAN has better performance than BiGAN and Cycle-GAN.

A quantitative comparison of images reconstruction quality from representative datasets is presented in Table 1. We can easily find that the TBiGAN demonstrates higher accuracies, especially for SVHN dataset with more complex context noise.

Fig. 6. Example results for MNIST_m that reconstructed by the different frameworks' Generator at same training epoch (50 epochs). (a) TBiGAN. (b)GAN. (c) BiGAN. (d) Cycle-GAN. (e) Real MNIST_m.

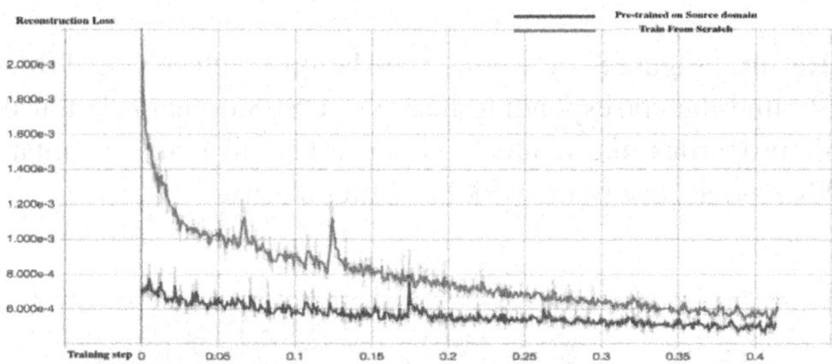

Fig. 7. Reconstruction loss of MNIST_m: Target Generator model learned from scratch (orange) against initialized by pre-trained source domain model (blue) (Color figure online)

4.2 Cycle-Consistent Cross-Domain Translation

Implementation Detail. Our task is to find for every target domain image x_t, a synthetic source domain latent code Z_{syn} when mapped to the source domain $X_{S-fake} = G_S(Z_{syn})$. The task is therefore twofold: (i) for each target image, we need to find the latent code Z_{syn} which will synthesize the source fake X_{S-fake} image, and (ii) the mapping function $G_c(\cdot)$ needs to be learned.

The Generator $G_c(\cdot)$ is actually a translator that maps the latent code space of target domain Z_T and source domain Z_S to a synthesized code space Z_{syn}. Let us assume that every target image latent code z_{t_i} there exists a corresponding source image code z_{s_j}. Let $\omega_{i,j}$ be the proposed match matrix or weight coefficient between z_{s_j} and z_{t_i}, i.e., every z_{t_i} matches a mixture of related latent code subset z_{s_j} in source latent code space, using weights $\omega_{i,:}$, and similarly for z_{s_j} for a weighing using $\omega_{:,j}$ of the subset from target latent code space. Ideally, we would like a binary matrix with $\omega_{i,j} = 1$ for the proposed match and 0 for the rest. This task is formally written as:

$$Z_{syn} = G_c(Z_S, Z_T) = \sum_{z_{t_i}, z_{s_j}} \omega_{i,j} \cdot L_m(z_{t_i}, z_{s_j}) \tag{16}$$

Table 1. Reconstruction images measured by digit classification accuracy (%). Pre-trained classifier from the original target domain (accuracies around 99.5% on real MNIST and 95.0% on real SVHN).

Dataset	MNIST	SVHN
GAN	81.5 ± 0.8	52.6 ± 0.8
Cycle-GAN	89.5 ± 0.2	57.5 ± 0.2
BiGAN	88.6 ± 0.4	48.3 ± 0.4
TBiGAN	$\mathbf{90.5} \pm 0.4$	$\mathbf{68.3} \pm 0.3$

Where the $L_m(\cdot)$ is a "similarity measurement", which is used to find a subset of z_{s_j} that similar to target image latent code z_{t_i}, like clustering and etc. The optimization is continuous on G_c and coefficient $\omega_{i,j}$.

Experiment Result. Figure 8 shows the translation result, Cycle-TBiGAN not only can successfully find the corresponding image in USPS domains but also preserve the domain-specific properties like written style in respect to USPS. Compare with NAM and Cycle-GAN models, our framework has better clarity.

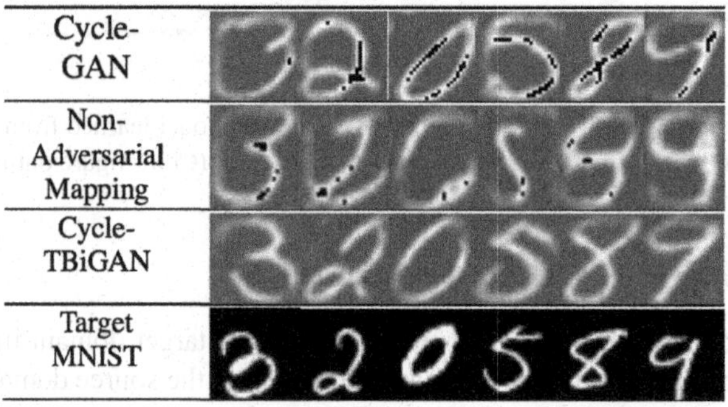

Cycle-GAN	
Non-Adversarial Mapping	
Cycle-TBiGAN	
Target MNIST	

Fig. 8. Translation results from target MNIST (bottom row) to source USPS (top three rows)

Since the USPS has a relatively simple image structure, which means the domain shifts or distribution discrepancy between MNIST and USPS datasets is well learned by TBiGAN. From Fig. 9, we can easily observe our method presents a precise matching in a more complicated cross-domain from SVHN to MNIST_m. Therefore, cycle Consistent mapping outperforms NAM and Cycle-GAN.

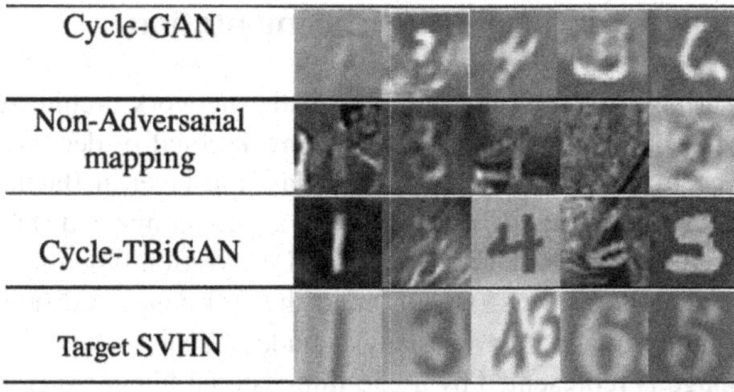

Fig. 9. Translation results from target SVHN (bottom row) to source MNIST_m (top three rows)

Comparing the translation results of MNIST → USPS and SVHN → MNIST_m, the latter of invariant feature space contains more complex domain structure whereby captures more generic information from domains. As SVHN contains too much noise and confusion context, it requires more training time to avoid model collapse and keep training stable. We perform using the median residuals (average pixel difference median) to measure the quality of translated images in Table 2. Cycle-TBiGAN significantly has better performance than Non-Adversarial Mapping.

Table 2. Image-to-image median pixel difference from linear comparison (lower is better)

Dataset	MNIST → USP	SVNH → MNIST_m
Cycle-GAN	0.077 ± 0.05	0.105 ± 0.05
Non-Adversarial	0.089 ± 0.02	0.153 ± 0.02
Cycle-TBiGAN	**0.053** ± 0.01	**0.087** ± 0.02

5 Conclusion

In this paper, we proposed a novel method (Cycle-TBiGAN) that integrating the Transferable Bi-GAN with Cycle Consistent Constraints by learning a mapping function for image translation task, specifically aimed to reduce even remove the distribution discrepancy between domains and relieved the training instability and model collapse issues. Combine with domain alignment objective to transfer the invariant feature representation to a target domain.

A Supplement for Experiment Implementation

As we have described in Sects. 4.1 and 4.2, all the network architectures are repetition by two blocks, full connected block and convolutional or deconvolutional block, each defined by a fully connected layer at the last top layer, a Batch Normalization layer (BN), and a Dropout layer(P), followed by a fully connected (FC) layer or Convolutional layer (CON) with RELU or Leak_RELU activation functions. The Generator consists of Deconvolution layers (DCON) and the full connected output layers with sigmoid hidden units. Image preprocessing includes linear scaling all image sizes to 28×28, each image is represented by a 256-dimensional feature vector in feature representation space, which encodes the pixel information of the image.

In this section, we will give a detailed introduction about the specific design used to generate the result presented for Transferable Bidirectional Generative Adversarial Networks (TBiGAN) and Cycle-Consistent TBiGAN. A detailed description of architectures and hyperparameters (learning rate, batch sizes, etc.) is displayed in the following sections. We provide a basic necessary understanding of our experiments.

A.1 Transferable Bidirectional Generative Adversarial Networks (TBiGAN)

We apply TBiGAN to a task that aims at learning an invariant feature representation from the different domain distributions. We attempt to verify whether TBiGAN can learn a latent code space between domains by the objective we define in (3), (6) and (7).

For MNIST→USPS, MNIST→MNIST_m in Table 3, the generative model networks only contain several fully connected layers, the discriminator and Encoder both have the same structure with the generator. Since MNIST and USPS have similar domain distributions, a relatively simple network structure is proposed.

Table 3. Network architectures of TBiGAN for MNIST→USPS, MNIST→MNIST_m experiments

Layer	Encoder, Generator and Discriminator
1	FC-(1024), BN, PReLU
2	FC-(1024), BN, PReLU
3	FC-(784=28 * 28), Sigmoid

For MNIST→MNIST_m in Table 4, we define a different network like conv-pool-conv-pool-fc-softmax. The Discriminator contains three conv-pool layers followed by two fully connected layers (depends on the different image preprocessing methods) activated by sigmoid units. In particular the Encoder for MNIST_m domain only has two hidden layers activated by ReLU units. A fully connected layer still be used as the last output layer.

Since SVHN has its own domain-specific properties, a single image contains several adjacent digits. The architectures of network need more convolutional layers to capture the domain information. Therefore, the discriminator has five conv-pool layers followed by last two full-connected layers activated with a sigmoid unit. The specific details of the Generator and Encoder are shown in Table 5.

A.2 Cycle-Consistent Crossing Domain Translation

The fundamental network architectures of Cycle-TBiGAN are similar to TBiGAN. We assume that necessary components such as generators (G_S, G_T) and encoder (E) corresponding to specific domain have been obtained from TBiGAN. The Generator $G_c(\cdot)$ is actually a translator that maps the latent code space of target domain Z_T and source domain Z_S to a synthesized code space Z_{syn}, which means the invariant feature representation space is regarded as input for $G_c(\cdot)$. A specific network description of mapping function $G_c(\cdot)$ is showed in Table 6.

As defined in (16), the $L_m(\cdot)$ is a "similarity measurement", which is used to find a subset of z_{s_j} that similar to target image latent code z_{t_i}. Since the training of Cycle-TBiGAN is high computational cost and it should be relaxed, we use the K-Nearest-Neighbor (KNN) algorithm to find a subset of $z_{s_{1\dots k}}$ with size k from source latent code space. In other words, the latent subset should be similar to z_{t_i}. Therefore, the relaxed (16) could be presented as:

$$Z_{syn} = G_c(Z_S, Z_T) = \sum_{z_{t_i}} \omega_{i,j} \cdot KNN_k(z_{t_i}, z_{s_j}) \tag{17}$$

The relaxed objective could be optimized using SGD.

Table 4. Network architectures of TBiGAN for MNIST→MNIST_m

Layer	Encoder
1	CON-(N32,K5x5,S1), POOL-(MAX,2)
2	CON-(N48,K5x5,S1), POOL-(MAX,2)
3	FC-(N1024), BN, PReLU
4	FC-(N256), None
Layer	**Discriminator**
1	CON-(N32,K5x5,S1), POOL-(MAX,2)
2	CON-(N48,K3x3,S1), Latent Feature
3	CON-(N48,K5x5,S1), POOL-(MAX,2)
	CONCAT(Image, Latent Feature)
4	FC-(N1024), BN, PReLU
5	FC-(N1), None
Layer	**Generator**
1	FC-(N7x7x48), BN, Normal(0, 0.05)
2	DECONV-(N48,K5x5,S2), PLeakRELU
3	DECONV-(N32,K5x5,S2), PLeakRELU
4	FC-(N1024), BN, PReLU
5	FC-(N784 = 28x28), Sigmoid

Table 5. Network architectures of TBiGAN for SVHN→ MNIST_m

Layer	Encoder
1	CON-(N32,K5x5,S1), POOL-(MAX,2)
2	CON-(N64,K5x5,S1), POOL-(MAX,2)
3	CON-(N128,K5x5,S1), POOL-(MAX,2)
4	FC-(N1024), BN, PReLU
5	FC-(N256), None
Layer	**Discriminator**
1	CON-(N64,K3x3,S1), POOL-(MAX,2)
2	CON-(N128,K3x3,S1), Latent Feature
3	CON-(N128,K3x3,S1), POOL-(MAX,2) CONCAT(Image, Latent Feature)
4	CON-(N256,K3x3,S1), POOL-(MAX,2)
5	CON-(N128,K3x3,S1), POOL-(MAX,3)
6	FC-(N1024), BN, PLeakRELU
7	FC-(1), None
Layer	**Generator**
1	DECONV-(N512,K4x4,S2), PLeakRELU
2	DECONV-(N126,K4x4,S2), PLeakRELU
3	DECONV-(N128,K4x4,S2), PLeakRELU
4	DECONV-(N64,K4x4,S2), PLeakRELU
5	DECONV-(N3,K4x4,S2), PLeakRELU
6	FC-(N784 = 28 * 28), Sigmoid

Table 6. Network architectures of Cycle-TBiGAN for MNIST→USPS, SVHN→MNIST_m image translation

Layer	Discriminator
1	CON-(N64,K3x3,S1), POOL-(MAX,2)
2	CON-(N128,K3x3,S1), Latent Feature
3	CON-(N128,K3x3,S1), POOL-(MAX,2) CONCAT(Image, Latent Feature)
4	CON-(N256,K3x3,S1), POOL-(MAX,2)
5	CON-(N128,K3x3,S1), POOL-(MAX,3)
6	FC-(N1024), BN, PLeakRELU
7	FC-(N1), None

References

1. Bengio, Y., Courville, A.C., Vincent, P.: Representation learning: a review and new perspectives. IEEE Trans. Pattern Anal. Mach. Intell. **35**, 1798–1828 (2013). https://doi.org/10.1109/TPAMI.2013.50
2. Beutel, A., Chen, J., Zhao, Z., Hsin Chi, E.H.: Data decisions and theoretical implications when adversarially learning fair representations. CoRR abs/1707.00075 (2017). https://arxiv.org/abs/1707.00075
3. Cao, B., Pan, S.J., Zhang, Y., Yeung, D.Y., Yang, Q.: Adaptive transfer learning. In: AAAI (2010). https://www.ntu.edu.sg/home/sinnopan/publications/[AAAI10]Adaptive%20Transfer%20Learning.pdf
4. Cao, Y., Long, M., Wang, J.: Unsupervised domain adaptation with distribution matching machines (2018). https://aaai.org/ocs/index.php/AAAI/AAAI18/paper/view/17187
5. Cao, Z., Long, M., Huang, C., Wang, J.: Transfer adversarial hashing for hamming space retrieval. In: AAAI (2018). https://www.aaai.org/ocs/index.php/AAAI/AAAI18/paper/viewPaper/17256
6. Che, T., Li, Y., Jacob, A.P., Bengio, Y., Li, W.: Mode regularized generative adversarial networks. CoRR abs/1612.02136 (2016). https://arxiv.org/abs/1612.02136
7. Dai, W., Yang, Q., Xue, G., Yu, Y.: Boosting for transfer learning. In: AAAI 2010 Proceedings of the Twenty-Fourth AAAI Conference on Artificial Intelligence, vol. 8, pp. 193–200 (2007). https://doi.org/10.1145/1273496.1273521
8. Donahue, J., Krähenbühl, P., Darrell, T.: Adversarial feature learning. ArXiv abs/1605.09782 (2016). https://arxiv.org/abs/1605.09782
9. Eric Eaton, M.d.: Selective transfer between learning tasks using task-based boosting. In: Proceedings of the Twenty-Fifth AAAI Conference on Artificial Intelligence, pp. 337–342 (2011). https://dl.acm.org/citation.cfm?id=2900476
10. Gao, J., Fan, W., Jiang, J., Han, J.: Knowledge transfer via multiple model local structure mapping. In: ACM SIGKDD International Conference on Knowledge Discovery and Data Mining, pp. 283–291 (2008). https://doi.org/10.1145/1401890.1401928
11. Goodfellow, I., et al.: Generative adversarial nets. In: Ghahramani, Z., Welling, M., Cortes, C., Lawrence, N.D., Weinberger, K.Q. (eds.) Advances in Neural Information Processing Systems, vol. 27, pp. 2672–2680. Curran Associates, Inc. (2014). http://papers.nips.cc/paper/5423-generative-adversarial-nets.pdf
12. Hoshen, Y., Wolf, L.: Nam: Non-adversarial unsupervised domain mapping (2018). https://doi.org/10.1007/978-3-030-01264-9_27
13. Huayan Wang, Q.Y.: Transfer learning by structural analogy. In: AAAI 2011 Proceedings of the Twenty-Fifth AAAI Conference on Artificial Intelligence, vol. 6, 513–518 (2011). https://dl.acm.org/citation.cfm?id=2900505
14. Long, M., Wang, J., Ding, G., Shen, D., Yang, Q.: Transfer learning with graph co-regularization. IEEE Trans. Knowl. Data Eng. **26**, 1805–1818 (2012). https://doi.org/10.1109/TKDE.2013.97
15. Long, M., Wang, J., Sun, J.G., Yu, P.S.: Domain invariant transfer kernel learning. IEEE Trans. Knowl. Data Eng. **27**, 1519–1532 (2015). https://doi.org/10.1109/TKDE.2014.2373376
16. Raina, R., Battle, A., Lee, H., Packer,B., Ng, A.: Self-taught learning: transfer learning from unlabeled data. In: Proceedings of the 24th International Conference on Machine Learning, vol. 8, no. 227, pp. 759–766 (2007). https://doi.org/10.1145/1273496.1273592
17. Tran, N.T., Bui, T.A., Cheung, N.M.: Dist-gan: An improved gan using distance constraints. In: ECCV (2018). https://doi.org/10.1007/978-3-030-01264-9_23

18. Vapnik, V.: An overview of statistical learning theory. IEEE Trans. Neural Networks **10**(5), 988–999 (1999). https://doi.org/10.1109/72.788640
19. Volpi, R., Morerio, P., Savarese, S., Murino, V.: Adversarial feature augmentation for unsupervised domain adaptation, pp. 5495–5504 (2017). https://doi.org/10.1109/cvpr.2018.00576
20. Pan, W., Xiang, E.W., Liu, N.N., Yang, Q.: Transfer learning in collaborative filtering for sparsity reduction. In: Proceedings of the Twenty-Fourth AAAI Conference on Artificial Intelligence, pp. 230–235 (2010). https://dl.acm.org/citation.cfm?id=2898644
21. Pan, W., Xiang, E.W., Yang, Q.: Transfer learning in collaborative filtering with uncertain ratings. In: AAAI 2012 Proceedings of the Twenty-Sixth AAAI Conference on Artificial Intelligence, pp. 662–668 (2012). https://dl.acm.org/citation.cfm?id=2900823
22. Xu, Y., et al.: A unified framework for metric transfer learning. IEEE Trans. Knowl. Data Eng. **29**, 1158–1171 (2017). https://doi.org/10.1109/TKDE.2017.2669193
23. Zhou, J.T., Pan, S.J., Tsang, I.W., Ho, S.S.: Transfer learning for cross-language text categorization through active correspondences construction. In: AAAI, pp. 2400–2406 (2016). https://dl.acm.org/citation.cfm?id=3016234
24. Zhu, J.Y., Park, T., Isola, P., Efros, A.A.: Unpaired image-to-image translation using cycle-consistent adversarial networks. In: 2017 IEEE International Conference on Computer Vision (ICCV), pp. 2242–2251 (2017). https://doi.org/10.1109/ICCV.2017.244
25. Zhu, Y., et al.: Heterogeneous transfer learning for image classification. In: AAAI 2011 Proceedings of the Twenty-Fifth AAAI Conference on Artificial Intelligence, pp. 1304–1309 (2011). https://dl.acm.org/citation.cfm?id=2900630

Evaluation of Domain Adaptation Approaches for Robust Classification of Heterogeneous Biological Data Sets

Michael Schneider[1,2P], Lichao Wang[1(✉)], and Carsten Marr[1(✉)]

[1] Institute of Computational Biology, Helmholtz Zentrum München, German Research Center for Environmental Health, 85764 Neuherberg, Germany
lichaowang@gmail.com, carsten.marr@helmholtz-muenchen.de
[2] Cancer Research UK Cambridge Institute, Cambridge, UK

Abstract. Most machine learning algorithms require that training data are identically distributed to ensure effective learning. In biological studies, however, even small variations in the experimental setup can lead to substantial deviations. Domain adaptation offers tools to deal with this problem. It is particularly useful for cases where only a small amount of training data is available in the domain of interest, while a large amount of training data is available in a different, but relevant domain.

We investigated to what extent domain adaptation was able to improve prediction accuracy for complex biological data. To that end, we used simulated data and time-lapse movies of differentiating blood stem cells in different cell cycle stages from multiple experiments and compared three commonly used domain adaptation approaches. *EasyAdapt*, a simple technique of structured pooling of related data sets, was able to improve accuracy when classifying the simulated data and cell cycle stages from microscopic images. Meanwhile, the technique proved robust to the potential negative impact on the classification accuracy that is common in other techniques that build models with heterogeneous data. Despite its implementation simplicity, *EasyAdapt* consistently produced more accurate predictions compared to conventional techniques.

Domain adaptation is therefore able to substantially reduce the amount of work required to create a large amount of annotated training data in the domain of interest necessary whenever the domain changes even a little, which is common not only in biological experiments, but universally exists in almost all data collection routines.

Keywords: Transfer learning · Domain adaptation · EasyAdapt · Batch effect

I. V. Tetko et al. (Eds.): ICANN 2019, LNCS 11728, pp. 673–686, 2019.
https://doi.org/10.1007/978-3-030-30484-3_53

1 Introduction

Over the last decade, machine learning, especially supervised learning, has become increasingly important in biological and medical research. Example applications range from protein structure prediction [1,2] and the identification of new disease subgroups from gene expression data [3,4], to the identification of cell connectivity [5] and the prediction of phenotypes from time-lapse [6] data and high throughput imaging [7]. With improving capabilities of data collection and growing computational resources, machine learning will be playing an even more important role in understanding of underlying biological processes.

One of the most well-known limitations of supervised learning, however, is the need for a large amount of annotated data. In biological and medical research, this requirement is often difficult to meet, as it necessitates expert knowledge and intensive manual work. With an increase in high-throughput data it becomes more and more unrealistic to annotate all observations. An appealing alternative is to combine already-annotated data from one or multiple sources in order to build a model for a new problem for which there is only little annotated data.

Another limitation of classic supervised learning techniques is the poor performance in dealing with data from multiple sources. A typical problem in biological research are batch effects. Batch effects describe qualitative changes in measurements because of experimental changes that are unrelated to the biological feature under investigation [8]. Typically, differences in the experimental setup, the use of different protocols, reagents or different machine settings can all lead to such effects. Conventional machine learning techniques are less effective in data with batch effects, due to differences in underlying distributions. Even in the case of an experiment being designed to be a replicate, the classifier trained with data from one experiment often tends to have lower predictive accuracy when applied to data from another replicate [9]. While it is possible to build a new model using only data from one experiment, this would mean wasting expert knowledge and involve labor-intensive annotation for each separate experiment. Consequently, it is desirable to have a model that can achieve a high performance with limited additional annotation work.

Domain adaptation describes the case where at least a part of the data used to train a model follows a different distribution from the data on which the model is finally applied [10]. It is closely related to the notion of transfer learning and mutlitask learning [10–12]. We follow Pan and Yang [11] and consider transfer learning as the more general term, with domain adaptation being one special form of transfer learning. Domain adaptation can be applied where a large number of annotated data are available in one or more domains that are not of direct interest (the source domain), while only a limited amount of annotated data is available in the domain of interest (the target domain) (Fig. 1). The idea of domain adaptation is to transfer the knowledge from the source to improve the learning in the target domain. Technically, it can be understood that the pre-trained decision boundary only requires some 'minor' tuning from a smaller amount of data to be applied to the new domain. Domain adaptation techniques have originally been developed to address text classification problems [13–15].

Domains in this context correspond to different types, styles or topics, e.g., a model trained with news articles can be adapted to classify a corpus containing fiction texts [14]. However, the concept is very broad and can be applied to any variable that is likely to lead to differences in the data distribution, e.g. different machines, protocols or reagents. Here, we consider domains representing different replicates of a biological experiment, where each replicate can be seen as a different domain.

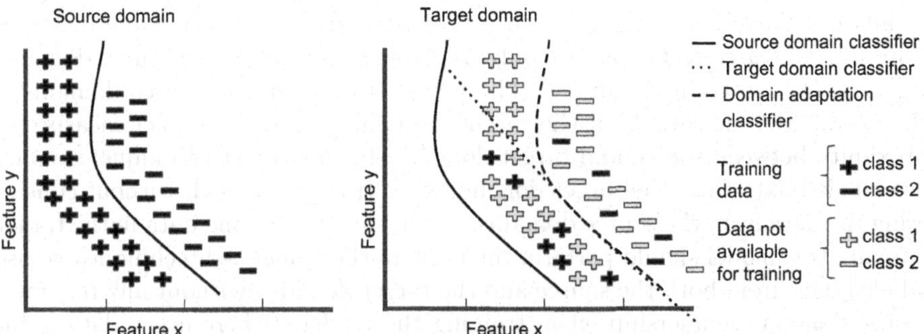

Fig. 1. Illustration of a domain adaptation classifier in the target domain that leverages knowledge from a related, but different problem in the source domain. A direct application of the source domain (left) classifier (solid line) would lead to a poor classification in the target domain (right). On the other hand, using only data available in the target domain to train a target domain classifier (dotted line) would also lead to poor performance, as the available data is not sufficient to fully learn the decision boundary. Transferring the knowledge from the source to the target domain using domain adaptation leads to an enhanced classification performance.

2 Methodology

2.1 Definitions

We define a domain D as a feature space X with the marginal probability distribution $P(X)$ and a label space Y. A function $f(\cdot)$ maps x_i to y_i, where $x_i \in X$ and $y_i \in Y$. We consider problems with an arbitrary number of source domains $D_{s_1}, \ldots, D_{s_m} (m \geq 1)$ and a single target domain D_t. For a multi-class classification problem, we convert to a set of binary classification problems in a one-vs-all manner, i.e. by training a single classifier per class, with the observations of that class as the positive examples and all other observations as negative examples. The aim of domain adaptation is to use the knowledge from the source domains and limited labeling information from the target domain to effectively learn the objective predictive function $f(\cdot)$ for the target domain.

2.2 Learning Techniques

We compare a particular domain adaptation algorithm, the *EasyAdapt* technique [16], with four more conventional techniques of building classifiers. We refer to these as the '*Source*', '*Target*', '*Combined*' and '*Domain*' techniques. In this study, all domains share the same feature space X. In general, the techniques require a common feature subspace across domains. The details of these techniques are outlined below and illustrated in Fig. 2. For all techniques, we assume that the number of observations in the source domains is sufficiently large to estimate a model that will generalize to unseen data from the same distribution. In the *Source* technique, we only use labeled data from the source domains $D_{s_1}, \ldots, D_{s_m}$ to train the model. The model trained on the source domains is then evaluated on data from the target domain, giving an indirect measure of proximity between source and target domains. In the *Target* technique, we only use labeled data from the target domain D_t to train the model, without considering the data from the source domains. Given enough training data in the target domain, this model should perform the best. In the *Combined* technique, we use labeled data from both the source and the target domains without any reference to the domain membership when training the models (where every data point is weighted equally). This is arguably one of the most common approaches in practice [17–19], where a typical scenario consists of a relatively large amount of labeled data from the source domains and a limited amount of data from the target domain. In the *Domain* technique, we slightly adapt the *Combined* approach. An additional set of binary variables encoding the domain membership, in the form of one-hot-encoding, is added to the existing feature set [20]. It is expected to enable the estimated function to have a different offset for each domain, while making use of all the other predictors from all domains to define the shape of the function in common. The *EasyAdapt* domain adaptation technique [16,21], uses a simple transformation to create a representation for the general data structure common to source and target domains and a separate representation for each domain. The transformations $\Phi^{s_1}, \Phi^{s_2}, \ldots, \Phi^{s_m}, \Phi^t : \mathbf{X} \mapsto \check{\mathbf{X}}$ between the features spaces of the different domains have the following form:

$$\begin{aligned}
\Phi^{s1}(\mathbf{X}_{D_{s1}}) &= \langle \mathbf{X}_{D_{s1}}, \mathbf{X}_{D_{s1}}, \mathbf{0}_{D_{s2}}, \ldots, \mathbf{0}_{D_{sm}}, \mathbf{0}_{D_t} \rangle \\
\Phi^{s2}(\mathbf{X}_{D_{s2}}) &= \langle \mathbf{X}_{D_{s2}}, \mathbf{0}_{D_{s1}}, \mathbf{X}_{D_{s2}}, \ldots, \mathbf{0}_{D_{sm}}, \mathbf{0}_{D_t} \rangle \\
&\vdots \\
\Phi^{t}(\mathbf{X}_{D_t}) &= \langle \mathbf{X}_{D_t}, \mathbf{0}_{D_{s1}}, \mathbf{0}_{D_{s2}}, \ldots, \mathbf{0}_{D_{sm}}, \mathbf{X}_{D_t} \rangle
\end{aligned}$$

$\mathbf{0}_{D_d}$ denotes a matrix of dimensions corresponding to the dimensions of domain d filled with zeros. *EasyAdapt* can be applied to an arbitrary number m of source domains $D_{s_1}, \ldots, D_{s_m}$ and a single target domain D_t (see Fig. 2 for a visualization and a comparison with other techniques). Features only available in the target domain could also be incorporated by setting the relevant entries for the other domains to 0. The technique is simple and flexible and can be used with any supervised classifier. However, it is recommended that the number of features per domain is not too large, because the feature space increases to $\mathbb{R}^{(m+2)p}$ dimensions with p being the dimension of the shared feature space.

$$\underset{Source}{\begin{bmatrix} y_{s_1} & x_{s_1} \\ y_{s_2} & x_{s_2} \\ y_{s_3} & x_{s_3} \\ \vdots & \vdots \end{bmatrix}} \quad \underset{Target}{\begin{bmatrix} y_t & x_t \end{bmatrix}} \quad \underset{Combined}{\begin{bmatrix} y_{s_1} & x_{s_1} \\ y_{s_2} & x_{s_2} \\ y_{s_3} & x_{s_3} \\ \vdots & \vdots \\ y_t & x_t \end{bmatrix}} \quad \underset{Domain}{\begin{bmatrix} y_{s_1} & x_{s_1} & \underline{1} & \underline{0} & \underline{0} & \cdots & \underline{0} \\ y_{s_2} & x_{s_2} & \underline{0} & \underline{1} & \underline{0} & \cdots & \underline{0} \\ y_{s_3} & x_{s_3} & \underline{0} & \underline{0} & \underline{1} & \cdots & \underline{0} \\ \vdots & \vdots & \vdots & \vdots & \vdots & \ddots & \underline{0} \\ y_t & x_t & \underline{0} & \underline{0} & \underline{0} & \underline{0} & \underline{1} \end{bmatrix}} \quad \underset{EasyAdapt}{\begin{bmatrix} y_{s_1} & x_{s_1} & x_{s_1} & \underline{\underline{0}} & \underline{\underline{0}} & \cdots & \underline{\underline{0}} \\ y_{s_2} & x_{s_2} & \underline{\underline{0}} & x_{s_2} & \underline{\underline{0}} & \cdots & \underline{\underline{0}} \\ y_{s_3} & x_{s_3} & \underline{\underline{0}} & \underline{\underline{0}} & x_{s_3} & \cdots & \underline{\underline{0}} \\ \vdots & \vdots & \vdots & \vdots & \vdots & \ddots & \underline{\underline{0}} \\ y_t & x_t & \underline{\underline{0}} & \underline{\underline{0}} & \underline{\underline{0}} & \underline{\underline{0}} & x_t \end{bmatrix}}$$

Fig. 2. Schematic overview over the different learning techniques. We denote the feature matrices with x_{s_1} to x_{s_m} for the m source domains and with x_t for the target domain. Label vectors are denoted by y_{s_i} and y_t, respectively. Single underlined zeros and ones are column vectors, while double underline indicates matrices of dimensions matching the dimensions of x_i. The *Domain* technique is adding an additional feature encoding the domain membership in the form of a one-hot encoding, where the kth domain is encoded via a 1 at position k. The *EasyAdapt* technique creates both a unified representation of the data across all domains (analogously to the *Combined* technique) and a separate representation for each domain (diagonal entries).

3 Results

3.1 Simulation Study

In order to visualize how the different techniques work and to test their performance, we created a two dimensional artificial data set with one source domain and one target domain (each with 200 data points), where the ground truth is known (see Fig. 3A). The data was created as follows: In the source domain, we simulate the positive class by sampling 200 data points uniformly around a central point with coordinates $(1.0, 0.0)$. The distance from the centre is sampled from a uniform distribution with mean 0.5 and a range between 0.1 and 0.9. The radial angle is uniformly distributed between 0 and 360°. For the negative class, 200 data points are sampled uniformly around the same central point, but the distance from the centre is sampled from a uniform distribution with mean 0.9 and a range between 0.5 and 1.3. Again, the radial angle is uniformly distributed between 0 and 360°. In order to create the data for the target domain, we translate both classes in the source domain by $y' = y - 0.60$, where y is the horizontal coordinate in the source domain while y' is the horizontal coordinate in the target domain. 15% of the data in the target domain was used for training. The remainder of data in the target domain was used for performance evaluation. Support Vector Machine (SVM) [22,23] with a radial basis function (RBF) kernel was chosen as the basic classifier for all the five learning techniques described in the previous section. Parameters were selected using a grid search with 5-fold cross-validation. From both the contour lines (Fig. 3B–F) and the ROC curves

(Fig. 3G) it is evident that the *EasyAdapt* technique captured the distribution of the target domain most accurately (AUC = 0.91), by leveraging information from both the source domain and the limited amount of training data from the target domain in building the classifier. Figure 3B illustrates that due to the limited amount of training data in the target domain, the *Target* technique (AUC = 0.86) learned a decision boundary that was much more complicated than the underlying distribution. The *Source* technique (AUC = 0.55, Fig. 3C) directly applied the decision boundary learned from the source to the target domain, leading to an evident discrepancy with respect to the target domain distribution. The *Combined* technique (AUC = 0.64, Fig. 3D), shifts towards the target domain when building the model. Due to the comparatively large number of source domain data, however, the model is strongly biased towards the source distribution. The *Domain* technique (AUC = 0.89, Fig. 3E) learned a model that describes the target domain quite well, especially in regions close to the centre. In regions that were farther away, however, the contour lines were clearly distracted by source domain information. Compared with these four techniques, the *EasyAdapt* technique (Fig. 3F) learned a model that described the target distribution the best, by successfully integrating the information from the two domains.

3.2 Imaging Data Set

For a realistic evaluation case, we applied the techniques to a biological data set [25] consisting of 2888 cells with 186 cell texture and shape features from time lapse microscopy experiments, where 8 different cell cycle stages have been manually annotated. The data comes from three experiments, with 1468, 726, and 694 cells, respectively. It is important to note that the experiments differ regarding the microscope objectives and the magnification factor (10x for experiments 1 and 3, and 20x for experiment 2) used, and were conducted by different lab technicians [25]. The different techniques were trained and tested in a one-vs-all manner on the 8 cell cycle stages (where each stage is treated as a separate class). We always picked two experiments to represent the source domains and the remaining experiment as the target domain. We tested all three possible combinations of two source domains and one target domain. All data from the source domains together with the data from the target train set were centered and scaled to unit variance. Subsequently, we applied a principal component analysis (PCA) to the data, (i) keeping only factors explaining 98% of variance (reducing the number of features to roughly 20–30), and (ii) keeping only the 16 highest loaded principal components. We used 4-fold cross-validation and a grid search to select parameters and subsequently evaluated performance on a test set in the target domain. The procedure was repeated 50 times for different target training set sizes of 100, 120, 150, 200, 250, 300, and 400 samples in order to obtain robust estimates for variable performance, especially when using small training set sizes. Independent of the amount of data available in the target domain, we used a fixed-sized test set with 240 samples for performance evaluation, which was randomly chosen for every iteration and for every new

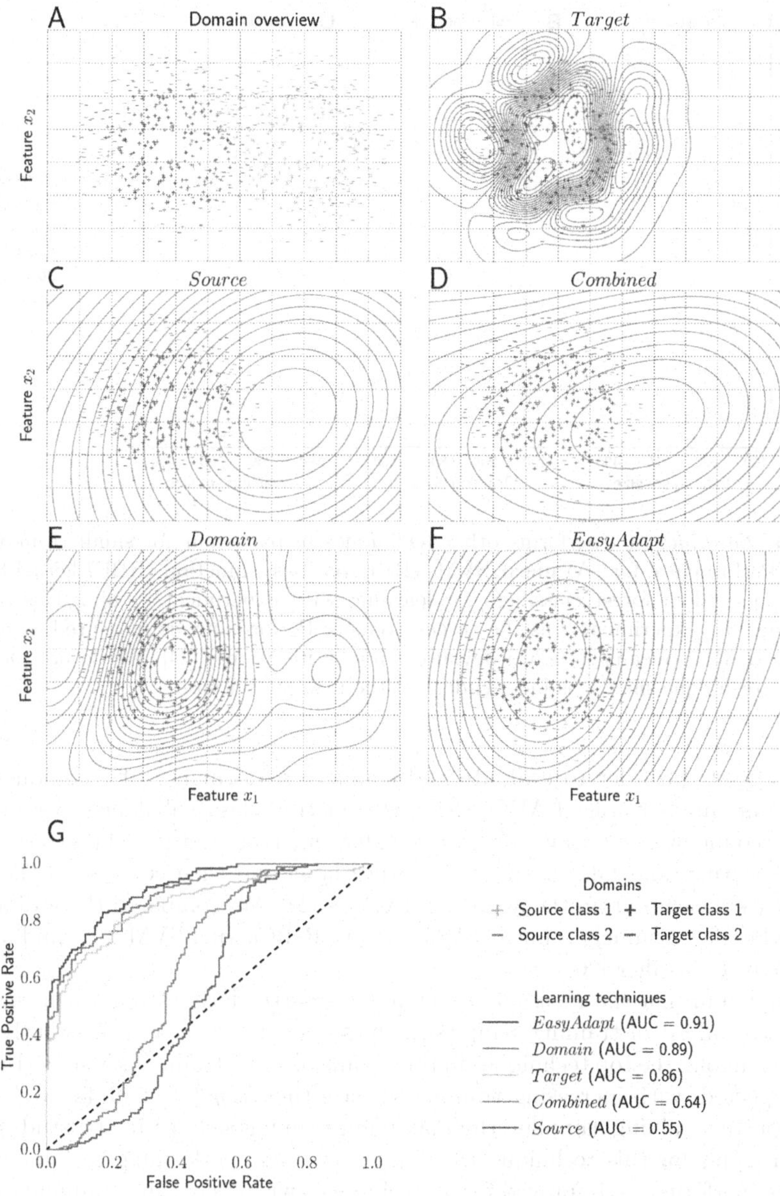

Fig. 3. Simulated data: with limited training data and sufficient domain similarity, *EasyAdapt* has the best classification performance on the target domain. (A) Distribution of the two classes in the source (light blue and orange symbols, right) and target domain (blue and red symbols, left). The target domain was divided into a training set and a test set. The target training set consisted of 15% randomly sampled data from the target domain. Classifiers were trained using RBF kernel SVM. (B-F) Classifiers created using *Target* (B), *Source* (C), *Combined* (D), *Domain* (E) and *EasyAdapt* (F). Contour lines represent different thresholds of the decision boundary of the corresponding classifier. (G) ROC curves for the different techniques. (Color figure online)

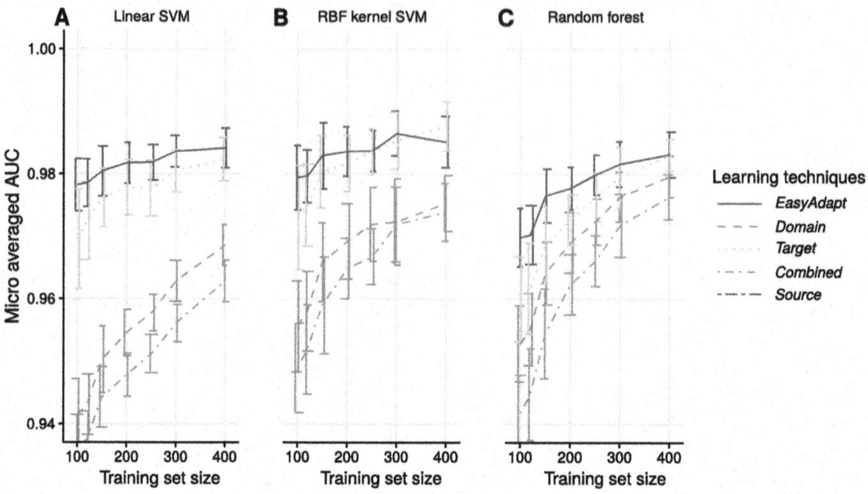

Fig. 4. *EasyAdapt* outperforms other techniques in particular for small training set sizes. Performance for (A) linear SVM, (B) radial basis function (RBF) kernel SVM, and (C) random forest classifiers for learning with experiments 1 and 3 as source domains and experiment 2 as the target domain. Performance is measured as micro-averaged AUC (mean±standard deviation, n = 50 iterations) [24]. We do not plot the *Source* technique since it is independent of the training set size.

training set. In order to evaluate and compare performance of techniques, we chose the micro-averaged AUC. Using this metric, class imbalances were taken into account by computing cumulative values for true positives, false negatives, true negatives and false positives for every label and then computing the performance measure from the aggregated values [24]. We compared three different base classifiers, namely a linear SVM [23], an RBF kernel SVM [22], and a random forest classifier [26].

We found that the *EasyAdapt* technique is particularly robust when working with a small set of training samples in the target domain and consistently performed among the top techniques in the regime of small training set sizes (Fig. 4). As expected, with increasing training set size the *Target* technique catches up and for 400 training samples (the maximum training set size in the study), the performance for this technique was among the best performing techniques. In general performance improved for all techniques with increasing training set size with exception of the *Source* technique, which was not trained with any of the target domain data. Results from all experiments are summarised in Table 1, showing the performances of the five learning techniques across three different base classifiers, two different feature selection methods and three different target domains (each combination of a base classifier, a feature selection method and a target domain is referred to as a 'setting' below).

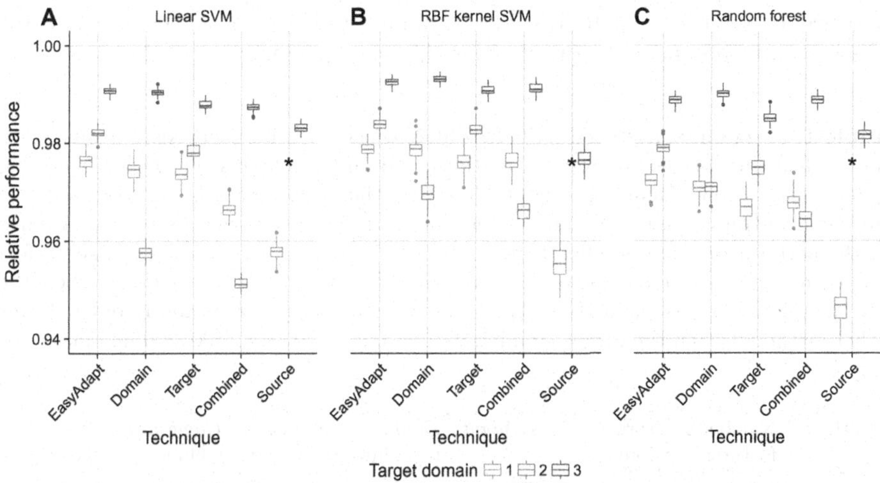

Fig. 5. Relative performance, measured as area under the curve for each of the 50 iterations that were used to generate the average performance lines in 4. Each data point shows performance over the range of training set sizes (100–400) for one iteration of the target domain; each box plot comprises data from 50 iterations. Performance is shown for (A) linear SVM, (B) radial basis function (RBF) kernel SVM, and (C) random forest classifiers.

To assess performance of the different techniques across training set sizes (Fig. 4), we measured the area under the curve for each of the 50 iterations for a given setting. This renders an aggregated performance for each train/test split across the range of training set sizes we used and gives us an estimate of performance for small to medium training set sizes. In contrast to the micro-averaged AUC across different training set sizes, this measure takes into account the fact that we tested more smaller training set sizes (in the range of 100–200 samples) and is a more conservative measure than simple averaging in our case. This is achieved by weighting performance according to train set size sampling frequency. Additionally, we normalized performance, so that a perfect classifier would achieve an relative performance of 1, corresponding to an AUC of 1 for all training set sizes in the range from 100 to 400 samples. Figure 5 shows the distribution of this performance measure for different techniques, classifiers and transfer directions. Across all settings, the *EasyAdapt* technique consistently showed superior performance over other techniques: Among 18 different settings, *EasyAdapt* ranked 15 times the best or tied for the best and 3 times as the second best. This not only demonstrates the effectiveness of knowledge transfer of *EasyAdapt*, but also shows its generality with respect to base classifiers and feature selection methods under different transfer situations. The second best technique was the *Domain* technique, with 8 times the best or tied for the best and 3 times in the second place. This indicated that in many cases the membership feature used by the *Domain* technique was also able to leverage some knowledge from related domains. The technique with the lowest performance was the *Source* technique, which ranked last in every setting.

Table 1. Mean micro-averaged AUC for different classification methods, learning techniques, feature sets (see text for explanation), and target domains. The best performing technique in a row is marked in bold. Note that the performance is averaged over the full range of training set sizes and that one value in the table corresponds to an average of the performance across different training set sizes. Thus, while the average performance for the *Target* technique appears relatively high, it is much lower when the target training size is small. *EasyAdapt*, on the other hand, consistently outperforms other methods, when the target training data size is small (e.g., 100–200 instances, see Fig. 4).

Method	Number of features	Target domain	*EasyAdapt*	*Domain* technique	*Target* technique	*Combined* technique	*Source* technique
linear SVM	16	1	**0.972**	0.970	0.971	0.959	0.952
		2	**0.978**	0.949	0.976	0.941	0.803
		3	**0.987**	**0.987**	0.986	0.983	0.981
	98%	1	**0.976**	0.974	0.974	0.966	0.958
		2	**0.982**	0.958	0.978	0.951	0.800
		3	**0.991**	0.990	0.988	0.987	0.983
RBF kernel SVM	16	1	**0.976**	**0.976**	0.974	0.973	0.956
		2	**0.982**	0.967	**0.982**	0.963	0.512
		3	0.991	**0.992**	0.990	0.990	0.985
	98%	1	**0.979**	**0.979**	0.976	0.967	0.955
		2	**0.984**	0.970	0.983	0.966	0.531
		3	**0.993**	**0.993**	0.991	0.991	0.977
Random forest	16	1	**0.970**	**0.970**	0.967	0.965	0.943
		2	**0.980**	0.976	0.977	0.970	0.693
		3	0.988	**0.989**	0.986	0.986	0.979
	98%	1	**0.972**	0.971	0.967	0.968	0.950
		2	**0.979**	0.971	0.975	0.965	0.696
		3	0.989	**0.990**	0.985	0.989	0.982

In practice, it is hard to predict whether pooling of data will actually improve prediction performance or lead to negative transfer, i.e. learning in the target domain might be negatively affected by the use of additional information, if domains are too different [11,27]. An example for such negative transfer is the case of experiment 2 as the target domain. Here, both the *Combined* and *Domain* techniques performed considerably worse compared to the *Target* technique (see Table 1). This can probably be explained by stronger differences in distributions between experiments 1 and 3 on the one hand, and experiment 2 on the other, as experiment 2 used a different magnification. This difference can also be seen from the extremely poor performance of the *Source* technique for experiment 2 as the target domain. It is worth noting that the negative transfer that affected the

Combined and *Domain* techniques with experiment 2 as target domain appears stable across different training set sizes (Fig. 4). Importantly, we do not observe such negative transfer in the case of the *EasyAdapt* technique. Performance of *EasyAdapt* was comparable or even slightly better than the *Target* technique when looking at experiment 2 as the target domain.

4 Discussion

In the present study, we investigated whether accounting for experimental variation in biological data using a domain adaptation techniques can help improve prediction performance and reduce the need for labeled data. We show that indeed, given only limited training data, the *EasyAdapt* domain adaptation technique boosts prediction performance both in a simulation study and a data set of imaged single cells [25] and leads to more robust predictions in the presence of experimental variation.

Recently, there have been a number of approaches that try to improve generalization of deep neural network performance across multiple domains. This is important, as neural networks have been known to generalize relatively poorly [28]. Often, the approach is to learn transferable representations that both identify the factors driving variation within the data and match feature distributions across domains [29,30]. Recent work has used models that are able to adapt to different domain very quickly by using an efficient parametrization of deep neural networks and adapter residual modules [31,32]. There is also interesting work combining generative adversarial networks with domain adaptation [33–35]. It is worth noting that the approach described in this work is orthogonal to these models, and can be used with any type of supervised machine learning algorithm, including but not limited to deep neural networks.

Applications of domain adaptation techniques in biological research have so far been mostly restricted to genomic sequence analysis [36,37]. Widmer et al. [38,39] used a more general multi-task learning framework in conjunction with regularization based supervised learning methods, such as SVM and logistic regression for splice-site and binding site prediction and to transfer model parameters learned on 2D images to 3D images in order to enhance learning. In contrast to [39], we do not learn domain specific differences explicitly. In practice, this information is also often hard to quantify. Here, we rather focus on the effect of training set size and the pooling of heterogeneous data without quantitative knowledge about the relationship between domains. We compare performance of the *EasyAdapt* technique across three different machine learning algorithms. Furthermore, we consider a range of common ways of combining information from different domains, e.g. via explicit encoding of domain membership, a procedure that is often used in practice. We demonstrate that the *EasyAdapt* technique is relatively robust to negative effects of data pooling.

Our results have implications for dealing with biological batch effects in machine learning tasks and for improving learning in settings with limited training data, if additional source data is available. The *EasyAdapt* technique allows the reuse of existing data sets as source data and avoids cost-intensive manual labelling of training data. Results confirm the problem that is one major motivation of this work: a model trained using data from one biological experiment is likely to have much inferior performance when applied to a different experiment, despite the experiments sharing similar experimental setups. Importantly, the *EasyAdapt* technique is general in that it does not change the machine learning method used and can therefore be applied to a wide set of problems. Because the feature space grows linearly in the number of domains, the approach is not applicable in cases with very large feature spaces or a large number of domains.

In general, classification accuracy in the transfer learning setting will be an increasing function of both the number of training samples available and the homogeneity and level of relatedness of the training samples to the test set. Given a limited set of training samples and reasonable relatedness between training and test set, transfer learning can help to improve classification accuracy. However, in the case when the relatedness between training and test set is insufficient to enable transfer, there is potential for negative impact when adding additional data from a different domain (known as negative transfer). *EasyAdapt* strikes a balance between improving performance in cases when additional information is available and robustness to experimental variations. Compared with classic techniques such as the *Domain* and *Combined* techniques, the *EasyAdapt* technique is less affected by negative transfer and for small to medium training set sizes it can improve learning in the target domain.

The technique is limited by the necessity to identify domains, i.e. it is necessary to have domain knowledge about potential differences in experimental conditions and fundamental differences in feature distributions that define domains. Furthermore, it requires that the domains have a shared feature subspace and are distinct [16]. Both requirements are typically fulfilled in biological data. Further research will be necessary to develop empirical measures of domain relationships that help to identify cases where the use of domain adaptation in machine learning can be particularly helpful.

References

1. Golkov, V., et al.: Protein contact prediction from amino acid co-evolution using convolutional networks for graph-valued images. In: Advances in Neural Information Processing Systems, pp. 4222–4230 (2016)
2. Rost, B., Sander, C.: Combining evolutionary information and neural networks to predict protein secondary structure. Proteins Struct. Funct. Bioinform. **19**(1), 55–72 (1994). https://doi.org/10.1002/prot.340190108
3. Xiong, H.Y., et al.: The human splicing code reveals new insights into the genetic determinants of disease. Science **347**(6218), 1254806 (2015). https://doi.org/10.1126/science.1254806
4. Alizadeh, A.A., et al.: Distinct types of diffuse large B-cell lymphoma identified by gene expression profiling. Nature **403**(6769), 503–511 (2000). https://doi.org/10.1038/35000501

5. Helmstaedter, M., Briggman, K.L., Turaga, S.C., Jain, V., Seung, H.S., Denk, W.: Connectomic reconstruction of the inner plexiform layer in the mouse retina. Nature **500**(7461), 168–174 (2013). https://doi.org/10.1038/nature12346
6. Buggenthin, F., et al.: Prospective identification of hematopoietic lineage choice by deep learning. Nat. Methods **14**(4), 403 (2017). https://doi.org/10.1038/nmeth.4182
7. Blasi, T., et al.: Label-free cell cycle analysis for high-throughput imaging flow cytometry. Nat. Commun. **7**, 10256 (2016). https://doi.org/10.1038/ncomms10256
8. Leek, J.T., et al.: Tackling the widespread and critical impact of batch effects in high-throughput data. Nat. Rev. Genet. **11**(10), 733 (2010). https://doi.org/10.1038/nrg2825
9. Bernau, C., et al.: Cross-study validation for the assessment of prediction algorithms. Bioinformatics **30**(12), i105–i112 (2014). https://doi.org/10.1093/bioinformatics/btu279
10. Patricia, N., Caputo, B.: Learning to learn, from transfer learning to domain adaptation: a unifying perspective. In: Proceedings of the IEEE Conference on Computer Vision and Pattern Recognition, pp. 1442–1449 (2014)
11. Pan, S.J., Yang, Q.: A survey on transfer learning. IEEE Trans. Knowl. Data Eng. **22**(10), 1345–1359 (2010)
12. Patel, V.M., Gopalan, R., Li, R., Chellappa, R.: Visual domain adaptation: a survey of recent advances. IEEE Signal Process. Magaz. **32**(3), 53–69 (2015). https://doi.org/10.1109/MSP.2014.2347059
13. Hwa, R.: Supervised grammar induction using training data with limited constituent information. In: Proceedings of the 37th Annual Meeting of the Association for Computational Linguistics on Computational Linguistics, pp. 73–79. Association for Computational Linguistics, Stroudsburg (1999). https://doi.org/10.3115/1034678.1034699
14. Gildea, D.: Corpus variation and parser performance. In: Proceedings of the 2001 Conference on Empirical Methods in Natural Language Processing, pp. 167–202 (2001)
15. Daume III, H., Marcu, D.: Domain adaptation for statistical classifiers. J. Artif. Intell. Res. **26**, 101–126 (2006)
16. Daumé III, H.: Frustratingly easy domain adaptation. In: ACL, p. 256 (2007)
17. Laing, E.E., Möller-Levet, C.S., Poh, N., Santhi, N., Archer, S.N., Dijk, D.J.: Blood transcriptome based biomarkers for human circadian phase. eLife **6**, e20214 (2017). https://doi.org/10.7554/eLife.20214
18. Chen, L., et al.: Identification of breast cancer patients based on human signaling network motifs. Sci. Rep. **3** (2013). https://doi.org/10.1038/srep03368
19. Wang, X., El Naqa, I.M.: Prediction of both conserved and nonconserved microRNA targets in animals. Bioinformatics **24**(3), 325–332 (2008). https://doi.org/10.1093/bioinformatics/btm595
20. Hsu, C.W., Chang, C.C., Lin, C.J., et al.: A practical guide to support vector classification (2003)
21. Daumé, III, H., Kumar, A., Saha, A.: Frustratingly easy semi-supervised domain adaptation. In: Proceedings of the 2010 Workshop on Domain Adaptation for Natural Language Processing, pp. 53–59. Association for Computational Linguistics (2010)
22. Cortes, C., Vapnik, V.: Support-vector networks. Mach. Learn. **20**(3), 273–297 (1995). https://doi.org/10.1007/BF00994018

23. Boser, B.E., Guyon, I.M., Vapnik, V.N.: A training algorithm for optimal margin classifiers. In: Proceedings of the Fifth Annual Workshop on Computational Learning Theory, pp. 144–152. ACM (1992)
24. Sokolova, M., Lapalme, G.: A systematic analysis of performance measures for classification tasks. Inf. Process. Manage. **45**(4), 427–437 (2009). https://doi.org/10.1016/j.ipm.2009.03.002
25. Held, M., et al.: Cell cognition: time-resolved phenotype annotation in high-throughput live cell imaging. Nat. Methods **7**(9), 747–754 (2010). https://doi.org/10.1038/nmeth.1486
26. Breiman, L.: Random forests. Mach. Learn. **45**(1), 5–32 (2001). https://doi.org/10.1023/A:1010933404324
27. Rosenstein, M.T., Marx, Z., Kaelbling, L.P., Dietterich, T.G.: To transfer or not to transfer. In: NIPS 2005 Workshop on Transfer Learning, vol. 898, pp. 1–4 (2005)
28. Yosinski, J., Clune, J., Bengio, Y., Lipson, H.: How transferable are features in deep neural networks? In: Advances in Neural Information Processing Systems, pp. 3320–3328 (2014)
29. Ganin, Y., et al.: Domain-adversarial training of neural networks. In: Csurka, G. (ed.) Domain Adaptation in Computer Vision Applications. ACVPR, pp. 189–209. Springer, Cham (2017). https://doi.org/10.1007/978-3-319-58347-1_10
30. Long, M., Zhu, H., Wang, J., Jordan, M.I.: Deep transfer learning with joint adaptation networks. In: Proceedings of the 34th International Conference on Machine Learning, vol. 70, pp. 2208–2217 (2017)
31. Rebuffi, S.A., Bilen, H., Vedaldi, A.: Learning multiple visual domains with residual adapters. In: Advances in Neural Information Processing Systems, vol. 30, pp. 506–516 (2017)
32. Rebuffi, S.A., Bilen, H., Vedaldi, A.: Efficient parametrization of multi-domain deep neural networks. In: Proceedings of the IEEE Conference on Computer Vision and Pattern Recognition, pp. 8119–8127 (2018)
33. Tzeng, E., Hoffman, J., Darrell, T., Saenko, K.: Simultaneous deep transfer across domains and tasks. In: Proceedings of the IEEE International Conference on Computer Vision, pp. 4068–4076 (2015)
34. Tzeng, E., Hoffman, J., Saenko, K., Darrell, T.: Adversarial discriminative domain adaptation. In: Proceedings of the IEEE Conference on Computer Vision and Pattern Recognition, pp. 7167–7176 (2017)
35. Long, M., Cao, Z., Wang, J., Jordan, M.I.: Conditional adversarial domain adaptation. In: Advances in Neural Information Processing Systems, vol. 31, pp. 1640–1650 (2018)
36. Jacob, L., Vert, J.P.: Efficient peptide-MHC-I binding prediction for alleles with few known binders. Bioinformatics **24**(3), 358–366 (2007). https://doi.org/10.1093/bioinformatics/btm611
37. Schweikert, G., Rätsch, G., Widmer, C., Schölkopf, B.: An empirical analysis of domain adaptation algorithms for genomic sequence analysis. In: Advances in Neural Information Processing Systems, pp. 1433–1440 (2009)
38. Widmer, C., Rätsch, G.: Multitask learning in computational biology. In: Proceedings of ICML Workshop on Unsupervised and Transfer Learning, pp. 207–216 (2012)
39. Widmer, C., Kloft, M., Lou, X., Rätsch, G.: Regularization-based multitask learning with applications to genome biology and biological imaging. KI-Künstliche Intelligenz **28**(1), 29–33 (2014)

Named Entity Recognition for Chinese Social Media with Domain Adversarial Training and Language Modeling

Yong Xu[1], Qi Lu[2], and Muhua Zhu[3(✉)]

[1] Fudan University, Shanghai 200433, China
[2] Meituan, Beijing 100000, China
[3] Alibaba Group, Hangzhou 311121, Zhejiang, China
muhua.zmh@alibaba-inc.com

Abstract. Recent years have seen a surge of interest in natural language processing (NLP) for social media because the massive unstructured data from social media provide valuable information. However, natural language processing in this domain often suffers from the lack of large scale labeled data used for building models. In this paper, we focus specifically on the task of named entity recognition (NER) for Chinese social media. We propose a neural network model for domain adaptation which builds on domain-adversarial training and language modeling. The model is capable of learning from multiple sources of training data: labeled in-domain data, labeled out-of-domain data, as well as (large-scale) unlabeled in-domain data. To demonstrate the effectiveness of our approach, we experiment on an enlarged Chinese social media corpus. Results show that the approach outperforms baselines significantly.

Keywords: Named entity recognition · Language model · Domain-adversarial training

1 Introduction

Named entity recognition (NER) is one of the most important natural language processing (NLP) tasks. Many NLP tasks such as relation extraction [3], entity linking [22], and question answering [18] take NER as a preceding processing step. Their performance highly depends on how accurate named entities can be recognized. In brief, the task of NER is defined to be identifying names in formal or informal texts and then assigning appropriate semantic categories [5,15,25].

Most state-of-the-art NER systems are built with supervised learning on the base of large-scale human-labeled corpora. For domains in which NER has been extensively studied, for example the newswire domain, large-scale labeled datasets are readily available. However, for domains like social media, there is a lack of such corpora. One example is NER for Chinese social media, where a dataset of 1,897 posts from the Chinese microblogging service *Sina Weibo* is

I. V. Tetko et al. (Eds.): ICANN 2019, LNCS 11728, pp. 687–699, 2019.
https://doi.org/10.1007/978-3-030-30484-3_54

[陈雄/PER]围脖：请解释[北京/LOC]电工[老李/PER]
微博二传手瘦驼tuodi1968

Chenxiong Weibo: please explain Beijing electrician
laoli Weibo passer Thin Camel toudi1968

Fig. 1. An example of Weibo posts annotated with named entities (highlighted in blue); the text contains nonstandard orthography, ungrammaticality, and noises like user IDs and nicknames (highlighted in red). (Color figure online)

constructed and used for supervised learning and evaluation [20,21]. A corpus of such a size is less than enough for supervised learning of NER models. Lack of large-scale labeled data renders NER for social media a challenging task.

Another factor hindering NER for social media is attributed to informality of social media texts. Figure 1 presents an example of Sina Weibo posts with named entity annotations. We can see that the text is ungrammatical and contains nonstandard orthography and noises that would disturb recognition of entities. Moreover, social media texts tend to contain entity mentions which seldom appear in formal texts. For this reason, NER systems trained on formal texts, for example newswire corpora, often see a dramatic performance drop when they are applied to processing informal texts.

In such a situation, a widely accepted idea is to resort to domain adaptation approaches that can learn from multiple datasets of diverse domains, including labeled out-of-domain data, labeled in-domain data and unlabeled in-domain data. In this direction, He and Sun [10] propose a unified framework that utilizes domain similarities to adjust learning rates for data from different domains. In this paper we instead examine the problem of NER domain adaptation from the perspective of domain discrimination [2,7]. We propose a neural network model whose major building block is conditional random fields based on character-level bidirectional long short-term memory (Bi-LSTM) CRF [12]. In addition, the model defines an auxiliary objective function through a network called *domain adversarial training* which could learn common representations between domains. Moreover, language models can learn general representations from unlabeled in-domain data, so we define a second auxiliary objective function through a network of Bi-LSTM language model. To demonstrate the effectiveness of our approach, we focus on the task of NER for Chinese social media and conduct domain adaptation experiments from the newswire domain to the social media domain. To make experimental results more reliable, we also expand the corpus released by Peng and Dredze [20] to the double size and use the new corpus in our experiments. The final results show that our approach improves over the baselines significantly. This paper makes the following contributions.

- We propose a novel neural model for domain adaptation of NER whose building blocks are domain adversarial training and language modeling. Experiments on Chinese social media data show the effectiveness of the model.

- To experiment with a bigger Chinese NER corpus in social media, we expand a previously released dataset and render the new corpus publicly available for research in this direction.[1]

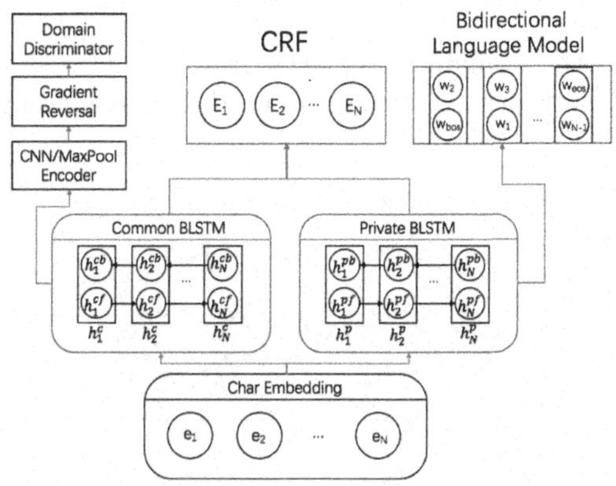

Fig. 2. Architecture of our neural network model for NER domain adaptation.

2 Approach

2.1 Overview of the Adaptation Model

Figure 2 depicts the architecture of the proposed model. The model is an integration of several neural networks. The lowermost position is a layer of character embeddings. Although richer representations like concatenation of character embeddings and word-level embeddings have been proven beneficial to overall NER accuracy [21], we stick to character embedding in this paper in order to focus on the discussion of domain adaptation model. On the top of embedding layer, there are two bidirectional recurrent neural networks (RNNs) [1] which adopt long short-term memory (LSTM) units [11]. The BiLSTM on the left is used as common representations between domains and the one on the right one is used to learn private representations. LSTM is a sophisticated implementation of RNNs which can capture long-distance information in the input sentence. Bidirectional LSTM is an extension of LSTM to capture information from both directions [8].

On the basis of the two BiLSTM representation, we implement a CRF network for the purpose of recognizing named entities. In addition, two auxiliary objective function are defined by (1) the domain adversarial training network which builds on the common BiLSTM only, and (2) the language modeling network which builds on the private BiLSTM only.[2] The domain adversarial network

[1] Data will be made available upon acceptance.

[2] A previous work on cross-lingual learning [13] builds language models on both common and private BiLSTM, but our preliminary experiments show that language modeling on private BiLSMT can achieve better performance.

is where domain adaptation takes effect. Finally, the overall objective function of the NER model is defined to be the weighted sum of the objectives of the component networks:

$$Loss = L_{CRF} + \lambda_1 L_{DA} + \lambda_2 L_{LM}$$

Here, **DA** refers to the domain adversarial training network and **LM** refers to the language model network. λ_1 and λ_2 are used to weight component objectives.

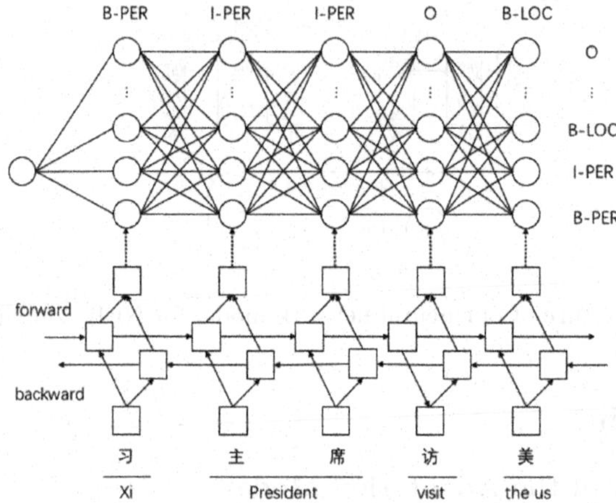

Fig. 3. Illustration of bidirectional LSTM-CRF.

2.2 BiLSTM CRF for NER

In this paper, the task of NER is formalized as a sequence labeling problem where each character is assigned to one of the following labels: *B-TYPE*, *I-TYPE*, and *O*. Here the label *B-TYPE* refers to the case that the current character is at the leading position of an entity of the specified type; the label *I-TYPE* means that the current character is inside an entity of the specified type but does not appear at the beginning; the label *O* tells that the current character is not inside any entity. So the sequence labeling problem is to seek an optimal label sequence Y given an input sentence X.

BiLSTM-CRFs [12] are well-suited for sequence labeling. BiLSTM-CRF can be regarded as a combination of bidirectional LSTM and CRF, as shown in Fig. 3. In CRF [16], the probability of output sequence Y given input sequence X of length m could be formalized as:

$$p(Y|X) = \frac{\Psi(Y|X)}{\sum_{Y\prime \in \zeta^n} \Psi(Y\prime|X)}$$

Here, $\Psi(Y|X)$ is the potential function, and we only consider interactions between two adjacent labels:

$$\Psi(Y|X) = \prod_{i=2}^{n} \psi(X, i, y_{i-1}, y_i)$$

$$\psi(X, i, y\prime, y) = exp(s(X, i)_y + b_{y\prime y})$$

where $b_{y\prime y}$ are trainable parameters representing transition scores between labels $(y\prime, y)$. $s(X, i)$ assigns a score for each plausible label on the i-th character:

$$s(X, i) = W_s^T h_i + b_s$$

where h_i is the hidden state of Bi-LSTM at position i. In our model, h_i refers to the concatenation of the hidden states of common BiLSTM and private BiLSTM at the same position, that is, $h_i = [h_i^{common}, h_i^{private}]$.

2.3 Domain-Adversarial Training

We encourage the outputs of the common BiLSTM to be domain-agnostic by using domain-adversarial training [2, 7]. The first layer of the domain-adversarial training network is a convolutional neural network (CNN), which is implemented in the same way as a CNN for text classification [14]. The CNN encoder consists of three convolutional filters whose sizes are 3, 4, and 5, respectively. For each filter, we pass the hidden state sequence of BiLSTM as the input to the filter and then apply max-pooling to obtain a single vector as the output of the filter. The output of a filter is then fed to a non-linear activation function *tanh* to get a transformed vector. Then, the vectors from the three filters are concatenated and forwarded to the domain discriminator through the gradient reversal layer. The discriminator is implemented as a fully-connected neural network with a single hidden layer, whose activation function is Leaky ReLU [17].

Note the necessity of the gradient reversal layer. Since the gradient reversal layer is below the domain discriminator, the gradients minimizing domain classification errors are passed back with opposed sign to the sentence encoder, which adversarially encourages the sentence encoder to be domain-agnostic. The loss function of the domain classifier is formulated as:

$$L_{DA} = -\sum_{i=1}^{S} d_i log(\hat{d}_i)$$

where $\hat{d}_i$ is the output of the domain discriminator and d_i is the corresponding domain category.

2.4 Bidirectional LSTM Language Model

Rei [23] show the effectiveness of bidirectional language models as an auxiliary objective for sequence labeling. The objective of language models is designed to predict the next word in the sequence based on the previous hidden representation. So the prediction are two directional: (1) in the forward-moving direction, predict the word w_{i+1} give the hidden representation $\overrightarrow{h_i}$, and (2) in the backward-moving direction, predict the next word w_{i-1} given the hidden representation $\overrightarrow{h_i}$. We first map hidden representations into a new space.

$$\overrightarrow{m_i} = tanh(\overrightarrow{W_m}\ \overrightarrow{h_i})$$

$$\overleftarrow{m_i} = tahn(\overleftarrow{W_m}\ \overleftarrow{h_i})$$

where $\overrightarrow{W_m}$ and $\overleftarrow{W_m}$ are parameters to be learned. These representation are then passed to a softmax layer to predict the next word.

$$p(w_{i+1}|\overrightarrow{m_i}) = softmax(\overrightarrow{W_q}\ \overrightarrow{m_i})$$

$$p(w_{i-1}|\overleftarrow{m_i}) = softmax(\overleftarrow{W_q}\ \overleftarrow{m_i})$$

The negative log-likelihood of a sequence is thus defined to be the sum of the probability that a next word is predicted.

$$\overrightarrow{E} = -\sum_{i=1}^{T-1} p(w_{i+1}|\overrightarrow{m_i})$$

$$\overleftarrow{E} = -\sum_{i=2}^{T} p(w_{i-1}|\overleftarrow{m_i})$$

The final loss of bidirectional language models is simply defined to the negation of the sum of $\overrightarrow{E}$ and $\overleftarrow{E}$, that is, $L_{LM} = -(\overrightarrow{E} + \overleftarrow{E})$.

2.5 Training Strategies

We still need to decide strategies for model training. One consideration is what data should be used for the three component objectives. For BiLSTM-CRF, labeled in-domain and out-of-domain data are used together to optimize its objective. Regarding the objective of domain adversarial training which is actually a binary classification problem, we assign labeled in-domain data to the positive class and labeled out-of-domain data to the negative class. Note that reversion of class assignment does not change the essence of the training problem. Finally, language models are trained on unlabeled in-domain data which are generally larger in size than labeled in-domain and out-of-domain data.

Another noteworthy issue is that gradients from language models are bigger than the gradients from the other two components. So we choose not to optimize all the objectives at the same rate. Instead, we first train language models on unlabeled data with a relatively big learning rate. This stage acts as "warm up" for model training. Then we learn the three objectives alternatively with a smaller learning rate.

3 Experiments

To demonstrate the effectiveness of our approach, we conducted experiments for domain adaptation of NER from the newswire domain to the social media domain. We focus specifically on NER for Chinese texts.

3.1 Datasets

We utilized the MSR corpus of the sixth SIGHAN Workshop on Chinese language processing as the labeled out-of-domain corpus. For the labeled in-domain data, we reused the Chinese NER corpus released by Peng and Dredze [20]. The corpus contains 1,890 Weibo posts annotated with both named and nominal entities of four types: **person** (**PER**), **location** (**LOC**), **organization** (**ORG**), and **geo-political entities** (**GPE**). Because the MSR corpus only annotates named entities of three types: **PER**, **LOC**, and **ORG**, we thus omitted the annotations of nominal entities in the Weibo NER corpus and changed named entities of the type **GPE** to the type of **ORG**. This way, we ensure that labeled in-domain and out-of-domain data contain named entities only and the named entities belong to the same set of entity types.

In addition, taking into consideration the fact that the Weibo NER corpus is small in size, we chose not to split the corpus into training, development, and test set, as previous works do [10,20]. Instead, we used the corpus as in-domain data only for system development and performance evaluation. In order to obtain labeled in-domain training data, we additionally annotated 2,000 Weibo posts with named entities of the three types mentioned above. Regarding unlabeled in-domain data for training language models, we collected 1M Weibo posts. The statistics of all the above mentioned datasets are presented in Table 1.

3.2 Baseline Systems

We built three baseline systems for performance comparison. The baseline system named **BiLSTM-CRF-OOD** is a BiLSTM-CRF model trained on labeled

Table 1. Statistics of the out-of-domain and in-domain data. * We regard each Weibo post as a sentence.

Data partitions	#Sent*	#Char	#Entity
MSR Train	46,364	2,169,879	74,703
MSR Test	4,365	172,601	6,181
Weibo Train	2,000	119,714	8,092
Weibo Dev	890	52,719	698
Weibo Test	1,000	50,336	744
Weibo Unlabeled	1,000,000 Weibo posts		

Table 2. Results of the baseline systems and our models on the in-domain test set. †Here the symbol ∗ refers to **Bi-LSTM CRF**.

Systems†	Precision	Recall	F1
∗-OOD	30.3	34.1	32.1
∗-ID	46.5	37.6	41.6
∗-Merge	47.4	42.3	44.7
∗+DA	50.0	41.4	45.3
∗+DA+LM	55.9	46.2	50.6

out-of-domain training data (MSR training data); the baseline system named **BiLSTM-CRF-ID** is a BiLSTM-CRF model trained on labeled in-domain training data (Weibo training data); the baseline called **BiLSTM-CRF-Merge** is a BiLSTM-CRF model trained on the combination of labeled out-of-domain and in-domain training data. Combining labeled data from multiple-source domains is a simple but strong baseline approach to domain adaptation.

3.3 Settings

We pre-trained character embeddings using word2vec [19] on a dataset of 5M Weibo posts. The resulting character embeddings were used to initialize all the models that we experimented in the paper. The dimension of character embedding was set to 100. We used one layer of bidirectional LSTM and the hidden vector dimension was set to 200. Our models are trained using stochastic gradient descent with $L2$ regularizer. When training language models for "warm up", the learning rate was set to 0.1; when we come to the stage of training the component objectives jointly, the learning rate was set to 0.01. Finally, we did not tune λ_1 and λ_2 for weighting objective functions and set them to 1.

3.4 Main Results

Table 2 shows the results of the baseline systems and our models on the Weibo test set, in terms of NER precision, recall, and F1 scores. **BiLSTM-CRF+DA** denotes the model which consists of BiLSTM-CRF and domain adversarial training. **BiLSTM-CRF+DA+LM** refers to the model with domain adversarial training and language models being combined with BiLSTM-CRF. For the experiments here, we sampled 40,000 sentences from the MSR training set and used the sample as labeled out-of-domain training data; the whole set of Weibo training data (2,000 Weibo posts) was used as labeled in-domain training data.

By comparing the results of the three baselines we can get two observations: (1) The CRF model trained on labeled out-of-domain data (BiLSTM-CRF-OOD) dramatically lags behind the model trained on labeled in-domain data (BiLSTM-CRF-ID), though the size (the number of sentences) of out-of-domain training data is about 20 times the size (the number of posts) of in-domain training data, and (2) Merging the labeled out-of-domain and in-domain training data (BiLSTM-CRF-Merge) can build a better model than using labeled in-domain data only. These two observations suggest that labeled out-of-domain data helps improve performance in the target domain, though it is not a good idea to train a model solely on labeled out-of-domain data. By comparing the baseline systems and our models, we can see that BiLSTM-CRF+DA outperforms BiLSTM-CRF-Merge by 0.6% F1 score, which implies that domain-adversarial training is better at capturing cross-domain information than simply merging training data from multiple domains. Finally, adding language models as an auxiliary objective can achieve an absolute improvement of 5.3% over BiLSTM-CRF-DA, which demonstrates the effectiveness of language models on learning general-domain representations.

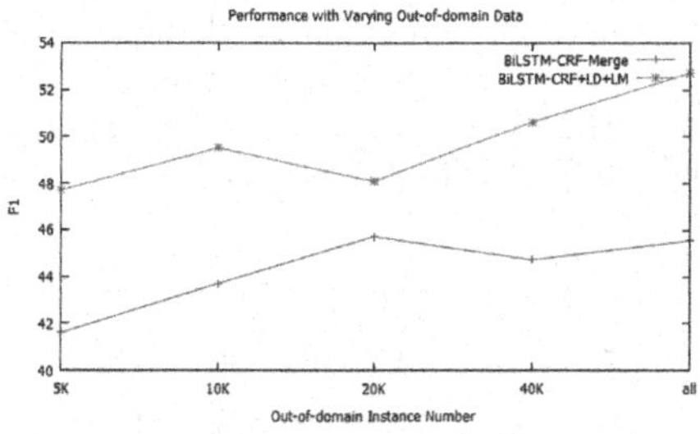

Fig. 4. Varying sizes of labeled out-of-domain training data.

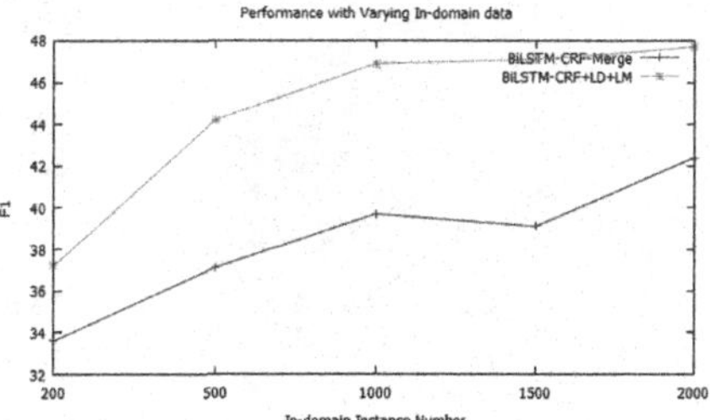

Fig. 5. Varying sizes of labeled in-domain training data.

We also examined how the sizes of labeled in-domain and out-of-domain training data affected the performance of our model. To this end, we conducted two comparison experiments. One experiment varies the size of labeled out-of-domain training data while fixing the in-domain training data to 2,000 Weibo posts. The results are depicted in Fig. 4 where we compare two models: BiLSTM-CRF-Merge and BiLSTM-CRF+DA+LM. Another experiment varies the size of labeled in-domain training data while fixing the size of labeled out-of-domain training data to 5,000 sentences. Here, we set the size of labeled out-of-domain training data to 5,000 for the purpose of training efficiency. The results are depicted in Fig. 5 where we also compare BiLSTM-CRF-Merge and BiLSTM-CRF+DA+LM. In the experiments we always used the 1M unlabeled Weibo posts to train language models in BiLSTM-CRF+DA+LM.

From the results in Fig. 4, we can see that increase of labeled out-of-domain training data continues to benefit BiLSTM-CRF+DA+LM, although there is an exception when 20,000 labeled out-of-domain data were used. For BiLSTM-CRF-Merge, however, the performance starts to level off when the size of labeled out-of-domain data reaches 20,000. This observation suggests that BiLSTM-CRF+DA+LM makes better use of labeled out-of-domain data than BiLSTM-CRF-Merge does. From the results in Fig. 5 we can see that increase of labeled in-domain training data improves the performance of BiLSTM-CRF-Merge and BiLSTM-CRF+DA+LM. A more interesting observation is that the accuracy of BiLSTM-CRF+DA+LM with 500 labeled in-domain training data is higher than the accuracy achieved by BiLSTM-CRF-Merge with 2,000 labeled in-domain training data. This observation implies that learning from unlabeled data through language models can help to reduce the demands for labeled in-domain data.

3.5 Analysis

Although our approach outperforms the baselines, the performance on social media data still lags behind the state of the art on formal texts (for example, the state-of-the-art performance of NER on the MSR corpus is 92.81%). We need conduct analysis to find out where the errors come from. For this purpose, we

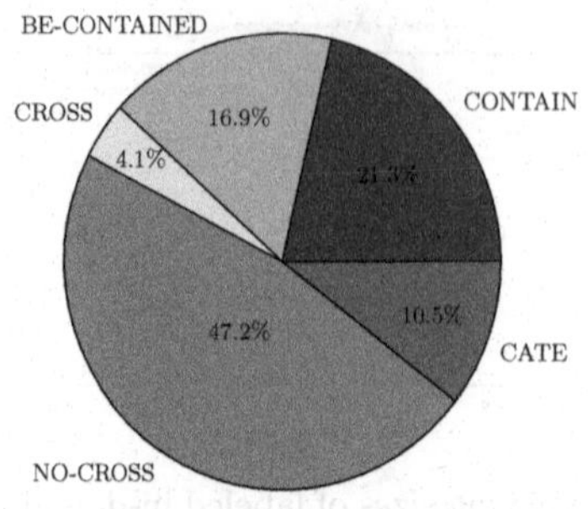

Fig. 6. Error types and theirs distribution by BiLSTM-CRF-Merge on the Weibo test.

Table 3. Effect of our models changing the numbers of errors of each error type: CONTAIN(CO), BE-CONTAIN(BC), CROSS(CR), NO-CROSS(NC), CATEGORY(CA).

System	CO	BC	CR	NC	CA	All
Base	73	58	14	162	36	343
+DA	62	51	11	136	37	297
+DA+LM	70	36	7	129	31	273

follow the methodology used in He and Sun [10] and conducted error analysis on the main results (Table 2) from the following metrics.

Error Types: He and Sun [10] group errors into five categories: **CONTAIN** (some gold entity contains the predicted one), **BE-CONTAINED** (some gold entity is contained in the predicted one), **SPLIT** (there are gaps in the predictions), **CROSS** (some gold entity cross the predicted one), and **NO-CROSS** (there are no common words between a gold entity and the prediction one). He and Sun [10] find that there are no wrong predictions belonging to **SPLIT** error type. This is also the case with our experiments. So we omitted this type and add a new type **CATEGORY** which means a gold entity and the predicted one span the same character subsequence but have different entity types. Figure 6 shows the distribution of the five error types produced by the baseline BiLSTM-CRF-Merge on the Weibo test set. From the figure we can see that NO-CROSS is the most frequent error type, although its percentage is not so high as the percentage of this error type reported in He and Sun [10] (47.2% vs. 83.55%). We also examined how BiLSTM-CRF+DA and BiLSTM-CRF+DA+LM changed the number of each error type compared to the baseline BiLSTM-CRF-Merge. The comparison is shown in Table 3. From the table we can see that adding domain adversarial training and language models help to reduce errors of all the types, especially **BE-CONTAIN**, **CROSS**, and **NO-CROSS**.

Entity Length: We counted correct and wrong predictions in different entity lengths when BiLSTM-CRF, BiLSTM-CRF+DA, and BiLSTM-CRF+DA+LM were evaluated on the Weibo test set. The results are depicted in Fig. 7 where x coordinates 0, 1, 2 denote the ranges of [1,4], [5,8], [9,12], respectively. The ranges refers to entity lengths measured in the number of characters contained in entities. From the figure we can see that using domain-adversarial training and language models manages to improve prediction precision, just as we expect. In addition, we can infer from the results that domain-adversarial training and language models tend to predict relatively short entities because the ratio of entities whose lengths are bigger than 5 is reduced.

4 Related Work

English NER has been extensively studied [5,15,25]. Moreover, the performance gap of NER in English social media and formal domains has been narrowed [4]. NER For Chinese social media is still relatively new and remains very challenging due to the lack of enough manually annotated texts. Peng and Dredze [20] annotate occurrences of names (NAM) and nominal phrase (NOM) in 1,890 Weibo posts with four types: person (PER), organization (ORG), geo-political entities (GPE), and locations (LOC). On the curated dataset, Peng and Dredze [20] explore several types of embeddings and study a joint training model for embedding and NER. Peng and Dredze [21] continue in this direction to examine how word segmentation representation improved NER.

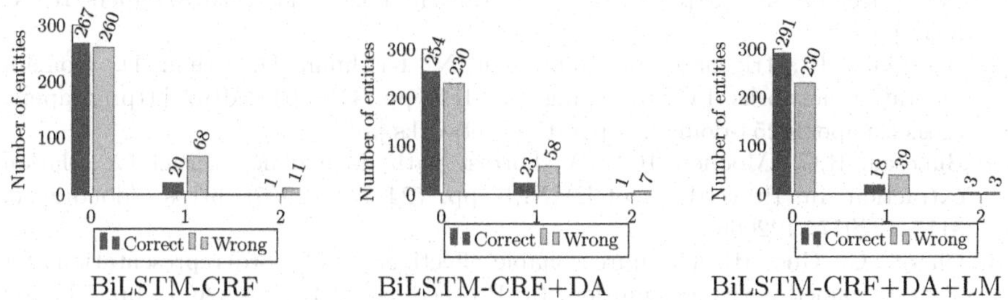

Fig. 7. Correct and wrong prediction numbers in different entity lengths with BiLSTM-CRF, BiLSTM-CRF+DA, and BiLSTM-CRF+DA+LM. The x coordinates 0, 1, 2 refer to the length ranges of [1,4], [5,8], and [9,12], respectively.

Previous works on domain adaptation can be grouped into two categories. One relies on computation of domain similarities. Shimodaira [24] use covariant to assign weights to out-of-domain instances. He and Sun [10] utilize the similarities between domains as weights to adjust learning rates. Another category is to learn common representations between domains. Hal [6] construct common and private feature space by simply copying feature vectors to different positions. Recent years have seen interest in learning common representations using adversarial training. Ganin et al. [7] propose a deep neural architecture to incorporate in-domain unlabeled data and labeled out-of-domain data. The idea is to learn domain-specific and domain-invariant features separately. However, the proposed model is designed specifically for classification tasks. Zhang et al. [26] apply adversarial networks to sentiment analysis. The most related work is Gui et al. [9] that is designed for cross-lingual POS tagging. Our model is similar to the model there with the difference that we only apply language models to learning private BiLSTM instead of both common and private BiLSTM. Preliminary experiments show that the simple change affects the performance a lot.

5 Conclusion

We proposed a novel neural network model for domain adaptation of named entity recognition in Chinese social media. The model builds its capability on domain adversarial training and language modeling. Thus the model can learn from labeled out-of-domain data, labeled in-domain data, and unlabeled in-domain data. We experimented the model with a new Chinese social medial corpus by considering the MSR corpus as out-of-domain data. Results showed that the proposed approach could improve over the baselines significantly.

References

1. Boden, M.: A guide to recurrent neural networks and back-propagation. The Dallas Project (2002). http://axon.cs.byu.edu/~martinez/classes/678/Papers/RNN_Intro.pdf
2. Bousmalis, K., Trigeorgis, G., Silberman, N., Krishnan, D., Erhan, D.: Domain separation networks. In: Proceedings of NIPS, pp. 343–351 (2016). http://papers.nips.cc/paper/6254-domain-separation-networks.pdf
3. Bunescu, R.C., Mooney, R.J.: A shortest path dependency kernel for relation extraction. In: Proceedings of EMNLP, pp. 724–731 (2005). https://doi.org/10.3115/1220575.1220666
4. Cherry, C., Guo, H.: The unreasonable effectiveness of word representations for Twitter named entity recognition. In: Proceedings of HLT-NAACL, pp. 735–745 (2015). https://doi.org/10.3115/v1/N15-1075
5. Collins, M., Singer, Y.: Unsupervised models for named entity classification. In: Proceedings of EMNLP, pp. 100–110 (1999). https://doi.org/10.3115/1072228.1072316
6. Daumé III, H.: Frustrating easy domain adaptation. In: Proceedings of ACL, pp. 256–263 (2007). https://www.aclweb.org/anthology/P07-1033
7. Ganin, Y., et al.: Domain-adversarial training of neural networks. In: Csurka, G. (ed.) Domain Adaptation in Computer Vision Applications. ACVPR, pp. 189–209. Springer, Cham (2017). https://doi.org/10.1007/978-3-319-58347-1_10
8. Graves, A., Mohamed, A.r., Hinton, G.: Speech recognition with deep recurrent neural networks. In: arXiv preprint arXiv:1303.5778 (2013). https://doi.org/10.1109/ICASSP.2013.6638947
9. Gui, T., Zhang, Q., Huang, H., Peng, M., Huang, X.: Part-of-speech tagging for Twitter with adversarial neural networks. In: Proceedings of EMNLP (2017). https://doi.org/10.18653/v1/D17-1256
10. He, H., Sun, X.: A unified model for cross-domain and semi-supervised named entity recognition in Chinese social media. In: Proceedings of AAAI (2017). https://www.aaai.org/ocs/index.php/AAAI/AAAI17/paper/download/14484/14201
11. Hochreiter, S., Schmidhuber, J.: Long short-term memory (2005). https://doi.org/10.1162/neco.1997.9.8.1735
12. Huang, Z., Xu, W., Kai, Y.: Bidirectional LSTM-CRF models for sequence tagging. arXiv preprint arXiv:1508.01991 (2015)
13. Kim, M.K., Kim, Y.B., Sarikaya, R., Lussier, E.F.: Cross-lingual transfer learning for POS tagging without cross-lingual resources. In: Proceedings of EMNLP (2017). https://doi.org/10.18653/v1/D17-1302

14. Kim, Y.: Convolutional neural networks for sentence classification. In: Proceedings of EMNLP, pp. 1746–1751 (2014). https://doi.org/10.3115/v1/D14-1181
15. Klein, D., Smarr, J., Nguyen, H., Manning, C.D.: Named entity recognition with character-level models. In: Proceedings of CoNLL (2003). https://doi.org/10.3115/1119176.1119204
16. Lafferty, J.D., McCallum, A., Pereira, F.C.: Conditional random fields: probabilistic models for segmenting and labeling sequence data. In: Proceedings of ICML (2001). https://dl.acm.org/citation.cfm?id=655813
17. Maas, A.L., Hannun, A.Y., Ng, A.Y.: Rectifier nonlinearities improve neural network acoustic models. In: Proceedings of ICML (2013). http://robotics.stanford.edu/~amaas/papers/relu_hybrid_icml2013_final.pdf
18. Martin, J.H., Jurafsky, D.: Speech and Language Processing. Prentice Hall (2008). https://web.stanford.edu/~jurafsky/slp3/ed3book.pdf
19. Mikolov, T., Sutskever, I., Chen, K., Corrado, G., Dean, J.: Distributed representations of words and phrases and their compositionality. In: Proceedings of NIPS, pp. 735–745 (2013). https://dl.acm.org/citation.cfm?id=2999959
20. Peng, N., Dredze, M.: Named entity recognition for Chinese social media with jointly trained embeddings. In: Proceedings of EMNLP, pp. 548–554 (2015). https://doi.org/10.18653/v1/D15-1064
21. Peng, N., Dredze, M.: Improving named entity recognition for Chinese social media with word segmentation representation learning. In: Proceedings of ACL, pp. 149–155 (2016). https://doi.org/10.18653/v1/P16-2025
22. Ratinov, L., Roth, D., Downey, D., Anderson, M.: Local and global algorithms for disambiguation to Wikipedia. In: Proceedings of ACL, pp. 1375–1384 (2011). https://www.aclweb.org/anthology/P11-1138
23. Rei, M.: Semi-supervised multitask learning for sequence labeling. In: Proceedings of ACL, pp. 2121–2130 (2017). https://doi.org/10.18653/v1/P17-1194
24. Shimodaira, H.: Improving predictive inference under covariate shift by weighting the log-likelihood (2000). https://doi.org/10.1016/S0378-3758(00)00115-4
25. Sun, X., Matsuzaki, T., Okanohara, D., Tsujii, J.: Latent variable perceptron algorithm for structured classification. In: Proceedings of IJCAI, pp. 1236–1234 (2009). http://ijcai.org/Proceedings/09/Papers/208.pdf
26. Zhang, Y., Barzilay, R., Jaakkola, T.: Aspect-augmented adversarial networks for domain adaptation. arXiv preprint arXiv:1701.00188 (2017). https://doi.org/10.1162/tacl_a_00077

Deep Domain Knowledge Distillation for Person Re-identification

Junjie Yan(✉)

Fudan University, Shanghai, China
jjyan17@fudan.edu.cn

Abstract. Learning generic and robust representations with data from multiple domains is a big challenge in Person ReID. In this paper, we propose an end-to-end framework called Deep Domain Knowledge Distillation (D^2KD) for leaning more generic and robust features with Convolutional Neural Networks (CNNs). Domain-specific knowledge learned by the auxiliary network is transferred to the domain-free subnetwork and guides the optimization of the feature extractor. While person identity information is transferred to the auxiliary network to further accurately identify domain classes. In the test period, just with a single base model as the feature extractor, we improve the Rank-1 and mAP by a clear margin. Experiments on Market-1501, CUHK03 and DukeMTMC-reID demonstrate the effectiveness of our method.

Keywords: Person re-identification · Domain · Knowledge distillation

1 Introduction

Person Re-identification is a cross-camera retrieval task, which aims at retrieving images of a specific pedestrian in a large dataset when given a specific query. The key challenge in this task is the large appearance and background variations, caused by changes in human body poses and camera views as shown in Fig. 1.

Recent years, deep convolutional neural networks have led to a series of breakthroughs for image classification [5,9] and these architectures can be easily transferred into other computer vision tasks. CNNs are also successfully employed in Person ReID with significant performance. For example, several works [3,17,25] employ deep classification model to learn feature representations of images.

In addressing the challenge of camera variations, a previous body of literature chooses to learn stable feature representations that have invariant properties under different cameras. Some networks [21,25] are trained with a pairwise verification loss, which measures the similarity between two images. However, these methods have to be used in a cross-image representation mode. During test time, the query image has to pair with each image in the gallery dataset and passes through the forward network, which is time inefficient and intolerant for large-scale real-world applications. Methods such as [6] directly optimize the distance

I. V. Tetko et al. (Eds.): ICANN 2019, LNCS 11728, pp. 700–713, 2019.
https://doi.org/10.1007/978-3-030-30484-3_55

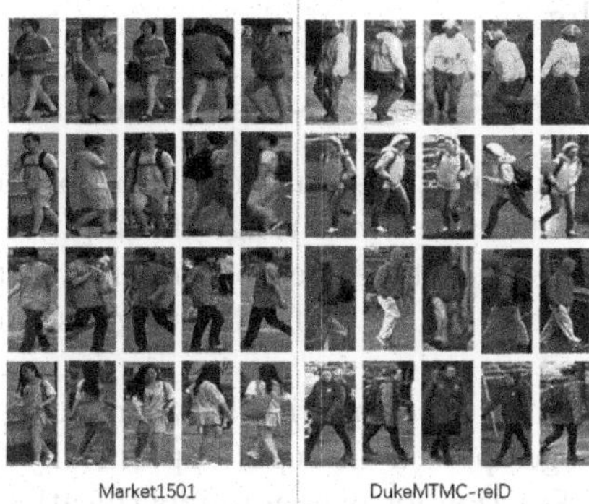

Fig. 1. Example of images from two person re-identification datasets [23,27]. In both datasets, samples in each line have the same identity but are observed from different cameras. Our goal is to extract generic feature representations for each specific identity.

of the images in embedding space and easy to employ in real task, but it does not take advantage of person identity label and waste abundant domain information.

Upon above discussions, this paper focuses on finding the robust feature representations for each person identity among different domains. Based on TriNet [6], we propose a Deep Domain Knowledge Distillation (D^2KD) method for further obtaining more robust features, by taking full advantage of pedestrian labels and wasted abundant domain information.

Inspired by [7], we are trying to find a higher soft bound for the feature extractor to optimize. Based on a traditional end-to-end classification model, we further apply dynamic label smoothing regularization on the training data via knowledge distillation [7], whose typical application is to transfer knowledge from a teacher network to a student network.

We propose an end-to-end framework named Deep Domain Knowledge Distillation which contains two subnetworks, one for extracting domain-free information and the other for domain-specific information. In the training period, we exchange the information between the two networks to generate more discriminative features. While at test time, only the domain-free part is used for further evaluation.

Our experiments improve the Rank-1 and mAP on image based dataset Market-1501, CUHK03 and DukeMTMC-reID by a clear margin.

The main contributions of this paper are summarized as follows:

- We propose an end-to-end framework that helps to learn higher quality camera-invariant property.
- We make full use of domain-specific information and obtain a theoretically higher bound for the classifier to optimize and demonstrate the effectiveness through the experiments.
- In the test period, domain-specific network only plays an auxiliary role. That is to say, there is no additional parameter but a pure base model like ResNet-50.

2 Related Works

2.1 Deep Learning for Person Re-identification

Recent years, feature representations learned by Convolutional Neural Networks have shown great effectiveness in a wide range of computer vision tasks including Person Re-identification. And these methods mainly focus on two categories: learning robust metrics [1,19,21,25] and extracting discriminative features [3,6, 16,17,24].

Some methods focus on the similarity between instances. In [1], a pair of cropped pedestrian images passed through a specifically designed CNN with a binary verification loss function for person re-identification. In [21], to formulate the similarity between pairs, images were partitioned into three horizontal parts respectively and calculated the cosine similarity through a siamese CNN [2] model.

Another strategy is directly learning discriminative embeddings which makes full use of the ReID labels. [24] proposed the ID-discriminative embedding (IDE) to train the ReID model in an image classification manner based on imagenet pretrained model. [17] simply partitioned image into several horizontal parts and gave each part a pedestrian identity label supervision individually which helps learn stable part features. And [3] extracted features from multiple sizes to enhance the stability of features.

2.2 Knowledge Distillation

Knowledge distillation [7] is an effective and widely used technique to transfer knowledge from a teacher to a student network. The typical application is to transfer from a cumbersome network to a small network, making the model memory-efficient and fast execution.

3 The Proposed D^2KD Method

In this section, we firstly provide necessary background and notion for person Re-identification. Then we introduce our network architecture in detail and give an insight into our Deep Domain Knowledge Distillation (D^2KD) method.

The overall framework is illustrated in Fig. 2. Our pipeline consists of two subnetworks, one focus on extracting domain-free features and another mainly learns domain-specific features and plays an auxiliary role during the training period. Besides, a Deep Domain Knowledge Distillation (D^2KD) module is implemented to exchange information between two subnetworks.

3.1 Problem Formulation

Suppose the training set contains n labeled images from C persons, we denote the training set as $T = \{x_i, y_i\}_{i=1}^{n}$, where x_i is the i-th image and y_i is a C-dimentional one hot vector which indicates the label of x_i.

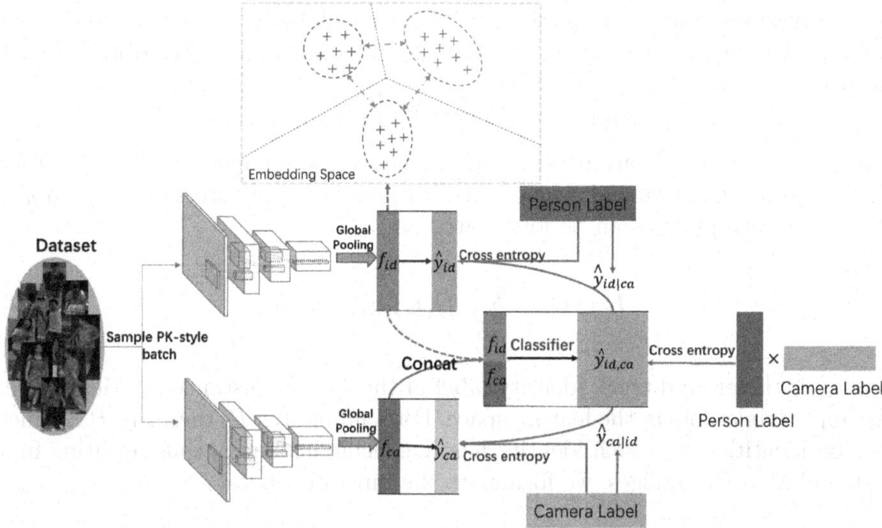

Fig. 2. Structure of our D^2KD framework. The input image passes through the two distinct backbone networks and obtains two 2048-dimentional feature vectors f_{id} and f_{ca} respectively. A following fully-connected layer is added to both feature vectors for the classification task. After that we concatenate f_{id} and f_{ca} together and force the classifier to learn a joint distribution $p(id, ca|x)$. Conditional probabilities $p(id|ca, x)$ and $p(ca|id, x)$ are then used as the supervision of two subnetworks. By the way, we take full advantage of triplet loss and apply it in the feature space to learn stable domain-free features. The dash line means we ignore the gradient from the output in this way at training time.

Based on the training set T, Person Re-identification is to learn a function $f_\theta(x) : \mathbb{R}^F \rightarrow \mathbb{R}^D$ which maps semantically similar points $\mathbb{R}^F$ from data manifold to be closer in the embedding space $\mathbb{R}^D$, where $D \ll F$.

When given a query person image x_q, ReID targets to return images which contain identical person in x_q from a gallery set G. Formally, for a specific query instance x_q, we rank the images in G by the distance $\mathcal{D}(f_\theta(x_q), f_\theta(x_g))$ in an ascending order, where x_g means image sampled from G, $\mathcal{D}(.,.)$ is some kind of distance function like Euclidean distance. Larger distance $\mathcal{D}(.,.)$ is equivalent to lower similarity.

3.2 Domain-Free Network

We formulate the domain-free subnetwork as $f_{id}(x) : \mathbb{R}^F \rightarrow \mathbb{R}^D$ and use the ResNet-50 [5] architecture with parameters pretrained on imagenet. Given an image x with identical person label, we can obtain a D-dimentional features $f_{id}(x)$ by feeding the image to the network.

Suppose there are C pedestrian labels in the dataset, we obtain pedestrian label probability by passing $f_{id}(x)$ through a single fully connected layer. That is to say:

$$\hat{y}_{id}(x) = softmax(W_{id}^T f_{id}(x) + b_{id}) \tag{1}$$

where W_{id} is a $D \times C$ parameter matrix and b_{id} is a C-dimentional bias. In order to learn discriminative and domain-free features, we apply cross entropy on $\hat{y}_{id}$. The cross entropy loss can be formulated as:

$$L_{id} = -\frac{1}{n}\sum_{i=1}^{n} y_{id}^T(x_i)log(\hat{y}_{id}(x_i)) \tag{2}$$

$y_{id}(x_i)$ is the ground truth identity label of the specific instance x_i. Meanwhile, we apply triplet loss in the feature space. For a minibatch B, there are P distinct person identities, and each identity has K specific instances, thus resulting in a batch of $B = PK$ images, we formulate the function as:

$$L_{tri\_batch}(\theta; B) = \sum_{a=1}^{B=PK} [m + \max_{\substack{p=1...B \\ y_p=y_a}} \mathcal{D}(f_a, f_p) - \min_{\substack{n=1...B \\ y_n \neq y_a}} \mathcal{D}(f_a, f_n)]_+ \tag{3}$$

That is to say in a minibatch, for an anchor point x_a, we optimize its distance from a positive data point x_p to be lower than a negative data point x_n by at least a margin m in the embedding space.

The triplet loss directly optimizes the distance among instances in feature space. However, only applying the triplet loss does not make use of domain-specific information, resulting in the decrease of the classification ability.

3.3 Domain-Specific Network

Similar to domain-free network, we use another auxiliary ResNet-50 network to learn domain-specific features. We formulate the network as $f_{ca}(x) : \mathbb{R}^F \to \mathbb{R}^D$, and the domain(camera) classification probability can be formulated as:

$$\hat{y}_{ca}(x) = softmax(W_{ca}^T f_{ca}(x) + b_{ca}) \tag{4}$$

where W_{ca}^T is a $D \times M$ matrix and M is the number of domains(cameras), b_{ca} is a M-dimentional bias. And the cross entropy loss can also be applied as:

$$L_{ca} = -\frac{1}{n}\sum_{i=1}^{n} y_{ca}^T(x_i)log(\hat{y}_{ca}(x_i)) \tag{5}$$

where $y_{ca}(x_i)$ is ground truth camera label for x_i in the dataset.

3.4 Distillation Module

In order to make the embeddings more discriminative while applying triplet loss at the same time, we propose Deep Domain Knowledge Distillation (D^2KD) method which aims at finding a higher soft bound for the identity classifier to optimize. By smoothing label in a dynamic manner, our method improves the classification accuracy bound while taking advantage of triplet loss at the same time.

Given an input image x, We concatenate the features $f_{id}(x)$ and $f_{ca}(x)$ together and denote $\phi(x) = [f_{id}(x), f_{ca}(x)]$ which contains person identity and domain information at the same time. We detach the gradient from $\phi(x)$ to $f_{id}(x)$.

Since $\phi(x)$ contains both person identity information and domain specific information, we choose to pass it through a simple classifier (here we use fc-relu-fc-softmax layers), and resize the outputs to a $C \times M$ matrix which represents the joint distribution $P(id, ca|x)$. And the cross entropy loss function for the joint distribution is given by:

$$\begin{aligned} L_{joint}(x) &= -\frac{1}{n}\sum_{i=1}^{n}\sum_{j=1}^{C}\sum_{k=1}^{M} y_{j,k}(x_i)log(p(j,k|x_i)) \\ &= -\frac{1}{n}\sum_{i=1}^{n}\sum_{j=1}^{C}\sum_{k=1}^{M} y_{j,k}(x_i)log(\hat{y}_{j,k}(x_i)) \end{aligned} \tag{6}$$

where $y_{j,k}(x)$ is the ground truth one-hot label for the joint distribution $p(id, ca|x)$, and $y_{j,k}(x) = 1$ when the image instance x belongs to the i-th person identity and j-th domain(camera), otherwise $y_{j,k}(x) = 0$. $\hat{y}_{j,k}(x)$ is a element of the output probability matrix in the j-th row and k-th column $(0 \le j < C, 0 \le k < M)$.

Apparently, from the bayes perspective, the posteriori $P(id|ca, x)$ should be a soft target to the prior $\hat{y}_{id}(x) = P(id|x)$, and similarly $P(ca|id, x)$ is a soft higher bound to $\hat{y}_{ca}(x) = P(ca|x)$, this greatly correspond to the knowledge distillation condition. It seems quite simple that the conditional probability can be computed like:

$$\begin{aligned} P(id|ca = k, x) &= \frac{[\hat{y}_{1,k}(x), \hat{y}_{2,k}(x), \ldots, \hat{y}_{C,k}(x)]}{\sum_{j=1}^{C} \hat{y}_{j,k}(x)} \\ P(ca|id = j, x) &= \frac{[\hat{y}_{j,1}(x), \hat{y}_{j,2}(x), \ldots, \hat{y}_{j,M}(x)]}{\sum_{k=1}^{C} \hat{y}_{j,k}(x)} \end{aligned} \tag{7}$$

Upon the conditional probability $P(id|ca, x)$ and $P(ca|id, x)$, we apply the pedestrian identity and the camera label as the supervision for the conditional probability, the loss function can be written as:

$$L_{cond} = -\frac{1}{n}\sum_{i=1}^{n} y_{id}^{T}(x_i)log(P(id|ca = y_{ca}(x_i), x_i)) - \frac{1}{n}\sum_{i=1}^{n} y_{ca}^{T}(x_i)log(P(ca|id = y_{id}(x_i), x_i)) \tag{8}$$

After exchanging information between two subnetworks, we hope to distillate useful knowledge from the joint distribution. The distillation loss can be formulated as:

$$L_{KD} = \frac{1}{n}\sum_{i=1}^{n}[H(\hat{y}_{id}(x_i), P(id|ca = y_{ca}(x_i), x_i)) + H(\hat{y}_{ca}(x_i), P(ca|id = y_{id}(x_i), x_i))] \tag{9}$$

where $\hat{y}_{id}$ and $\hat{y}_{ca}$ is the probability produced by the two subnetworks respectively. $H(.,.)$ is the binary cross entropy loss function as follows:

$$H(P, Q) = -\sum_{i=1}^{\mathcal{C}}[q_i log(p_i) + (1 - q_i)log(1 - p_i)] \tag{10}$$

Our total loss function is:

$$L_{total} = L_{xent} + \lambda_1 L_{tri} + \lambda_2 L_{KD} \tag{11}$$

where $L_{xent} = L_{id} + L_{ca} + L_{joint} + L_{cond}$ is the total cross entropy loss for classification. λ_1 and λ_2 are loss tradeoffs.

By exchanging the information between two subnetworks, our D^2KD method take the predicted probability $P(id|x, ca)$ as a soft target for the base feature extractor and $P(ca|x, id)$ a supervision for the auxiliary network to obtain higher quality domain- specific features. With the collaboration of two subnetworks, our method can learn more generic and robust features.

3.5 Test Strategy

At test time, we only apply the domain-specific network to extract feature vectors from images. That is to say, the domain specific features just play an auxiliary role in the training period and were not used in the test phase. The network architecture is shown in Fig. 3, images are fed into the domain-free network and obtain a D-dimentional feature representation.

Our D^2KD method offers a soft target for the domain-free network and erases domain information by applying the triplet loss at the same time, making the backbone network generate more discriminative features.

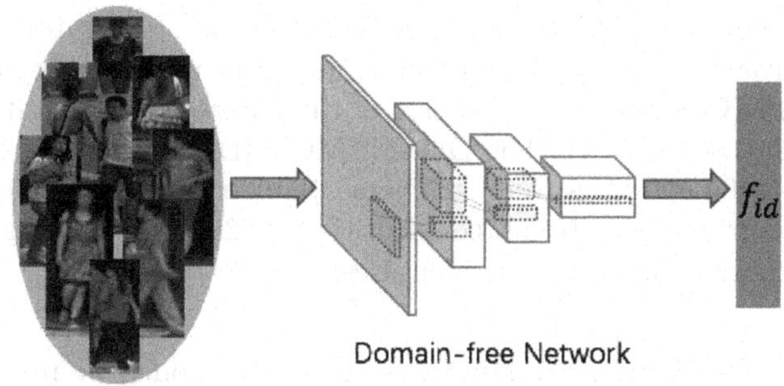

Fig. 3. Test network for our D^2KD method. Only the domain-free subnetwork is used to extract features for further evaluation.

4 Experiment

4.1 Datasets and Settings

Datasets. We conduct experiments mainly on three large scale image-based person re-identification benchmark datasets that contain multiple positive samples for each query in the gallery: including Market-1501 [23], CUHK03 [11] and DukeMTMC-reID [27]. The overview of these datasets is in Table 1.

Market-1501 [23] is the most famous large image-based ReID benchmark dataset. It contains 1,501 identities and 32,668 labeled bounding boxes captured from 6 different view points. The bounding boxes are detected using Deformable Part Model (DPM) [4]. The dataset is split into two parts: the training set contains 12,936 bounding boxes of 751 identities, the rest 19,732 images with 750 identities are included in the test set. In the test period, 3,368 images with 750 identities are used for the query to identify the correct identities on the gallery set. We use the single-query (SQ) evaluation for this dataset.

Table 1. Statistics on three person re-id datasets.

Datasets	Cams	IDs	Identity split		Person bounding box split		
			Training	Test	Training	Gallery	Query
Market-1501 [23]	6	1,501	751	750	12,936	19,732	3,368
CUHK03 [11]	2	1,467	767	700	7,368	5,328	1,400
DukeMTMC-reID [27]	8	1,404	702	702	16,522	17,661	2,228

CUHK03 [11] is constructed by both manual labeling and auto-detection (DPM) [4]. It contains 14,096 images of 1,467 identities and each identity is captured from 2 cameras in the CUHK campus. Each identity has an average of 4.8 images in each camera. The dataset is split into the training set and the test set. The training set contains 7,368 images with 767 identities and the test

set contains the rest 6,728 images with 700 identities. In the test period 1400 queries are given to identity corresponding identities in the gallery dataset.

DukeMTMC-reID [27] is a subset of the DukeMTMC website in the format of Market-1501 dataset. The DukeMTMC-reID dataset has 34,611 images belonging to 1,404 identities from 8 cameras. Similar to Market-1501, it consists of 16,522 training images from 702 identities, 2,228 query images and 17,661 gallery images from the other 702 identities.

Backbone CNN Model for ReID. To train our model, we resize all images of size $H \times W$ to $1\frac{1}{8}(H \times W)$, of which we take random cropping and random horizontal flipping and get $H \times W$ cropped images. Specifically, we keep the aspect ratio $H \times W$ of all the images to 256×128.

We performed all our experiments using the Pytorch [14] framework. We use the Imagenet pretrained ResNet-50 [5] model from Pytorch official repository for both subnetworks and replace the last 1000-dimensional classification layer with a new fully connected layer on both two networks, with output dimensions equal to the count of identities and camera classes respectively.

The network generates $D = 2048$ dimentional feature vector for each image. In the test period, the D-dimentional Pool-5 feature vector are used for further evaluation and we apply the Euclidean distance to compute the similarity between pairs.

We use the Adam optimizer [8] with the default hyper-parameter ($\epsilon = 10^{-3}, \beta_1 = 0.9, \beta_2 = 0.999$) for all experiments. The distillation temperature T is set to be a constant 1 all over the experiments. The loss tradeoffs λ_1 and λ_2 are set to a constant 1 during all the experiments.

Data Sampling and Batch Generation. In each training epoch, we shuffle all the images in the training set together and map the images with their identities. Then for each specific identity, we sample K different instances. After that, we rerank the dataset with random permutation of person identities. This preprocess is quite convenient when we apply triplet loss in the following training schedule.

Since the triplet loss in Eq. 3 requires slightly different mini-batches. At each iteration, we sequentially sample PK images from the training preprocessed dataset. Under above sampling settings, we train our model on quite a different dataset at every epoch.

Evaluation Metrics. In the test period, for each instance sequentially sampled from the query dataset, we rank the images from the gallery dataset by the distance to the specific instance for further evaluation.

We employ two evaluation metrics to evaluate the performance. The first one is the Cumulated Matching Characteristics (CMC) and the other one is the mean average precision (mAP) while considering ReID as an object retrieval problem, as describe in [23].

Table 2. Comparison of several methods on Market-1501. Rank-1, Rank-5 and mAP are shown. We use ResNet-50 as backbone. '-': No reported result available

Methods	Rank-1	Rank-5	mAP
BoW + KISSME [23]	44.4	63.9	20.8
LOMO + Null Space [22]	55.43	-	29.87
Gated siamese CNN [18]	65.88	-	39.55
CAN [13]	60.3	-	35.9
ResNet 50(I+V) [25]	79.51	90.91	59.87
Latent Parts(Fusion) [10]	80.31	-	57.53
IDE(R)(Re-ranked) [28]	74.85	-	59.87
MultiScale [3]	88.9	-	73.1
TriNet [6]	84.92	94.21	69.14
TriNet [6] (Re-ranked)	86.67	93.38	81.07
AACN [20]	85.90	-	66.87
AACN [20] (Re-ranked)	88.69	-	82.96
PSE [15]	87.7	-	69.0
PSE [15] (Re-ranked)	90.2	-	83.5
D^2KD	**91.09**	97.03	**76.76**
D^2KD(Re-ranked)	**92.73**	96.11	**88.93**

4.2 Performance Evaluation

Evaluation on Market1501. We compare the ReID performance of several existing methods against the proposed D^2KD method on the Market-1501 benchmark. Every epoch we sample $K = 8$ images from each person identity as the training dataset and set the batch size equal to 128. So each iteration contains $P = 128/K = 16$ different identities. By taking above sampling strategy, we are able to make our training dataset spread more uniformly and this can be quite helpful. Since all bounding boxes were given by auto-detection, this dataset represents a more scalable deployment scenario than other datasets with manually labelled bounding boxes.

Table 2 shows the superiority of our D^2KD model over all the competitions. The left column lists several methods these years, Rank-1, Rank-5 and mAP of these methods are given at the same time. Without any additional parameters, our model's performance is substantially better. Our method outperforms TriNet [6] by a clear margin, improving Rank-1 by 6.17% and mAP by 7.62 %. And after re-ranking [28], the difference changes to 6.06% and 7.86%, which means re-ranking methods still can significantly enhance our model's performance. This indicates the robustness of features generated by our method by transferring domain-specific knowledge to guide the optimization of the domain-free feature extractor.

Table 3. Comparison of several methods on CUHK03. Rank-1 accuracy (%) and mAP (%) are shown. We apply the new evaluation protocal on the CUHK03 proposed in [28]. We use ResNet-50 as backbone.

Methods	CUHK03		DukeMTMC-reID	
	Rank-1	mAP	Rank-1	mAP
BoW + KISSME [23]	6.4	6.4	25.1	12.2
LOMO + XQDA [12]	12.8	11.5	30.8	17.0
IDE [24]	21.3	19.7	65.2	45.0
PAN [26]	36.3	34.0	71.6	51.5
MultiScale [3]	40.7	37.0	79.2	60.6
SVDNet [16]	41.5	37.2	76.7	56.8
TriNet [6]	50.5	46.5	72.4	53.5
D^2KD	**60.9**	**56.3**	**80.5**	**64.1**

Evaluation on CUHK03 and DukeMTMC-reID. We also evaluate the ReId performance of our method compared to several existing methods on CUHK03 and DukeMTMC-reID. Unlike Market-1501, CUHK03 provides both manually labeled and auto detected bounding boxes of the same identity. We only apply our experiments on the detected bounding box since it's enough to test our model's ability. In DukeMTMC-reID the person bounding boxes of images are manually cropped in a labour-intensive manner.

Table 3 shows the competition between our model and others. From the statistics we can see that our model outperforms other methods by a clear margin. This further validates that our model can maintain more information via applying a knowledge distillation strategy.

4.3 Further Evaluation and Discussion

Experiments on all three above mentioned benchmark datasets show that our method is superior to several state-of-the-art methods these years.

D^2KD Improve the Baseline Performance. In order to further prove the effectiveness of our methods. We compare our D^2KD method with two baselines. Both based on TriNet and choose ResNet-50 as the backbone network, one is optimized with only the triplet loss, while another is optimized with both the triplet loss and the classification loss. Figure 4 illustrates the CMC curve for both above mentioned baselines and our D^2KD methods. Rank-1 to Rank-20 accuracy is shown in the Fig. 4.

D^2KD Outperforms Traditional Label Smoothing. Label smoothing (LS) is a method which assigns less confidence on the ground-truth label and assigns small weights to the other classes.

Formally, in the classification task, we assume $y(x)$ is the ground truth one-hot label for instance x. We assign $y_i(x) = 1$ when x belongs to the i-th person

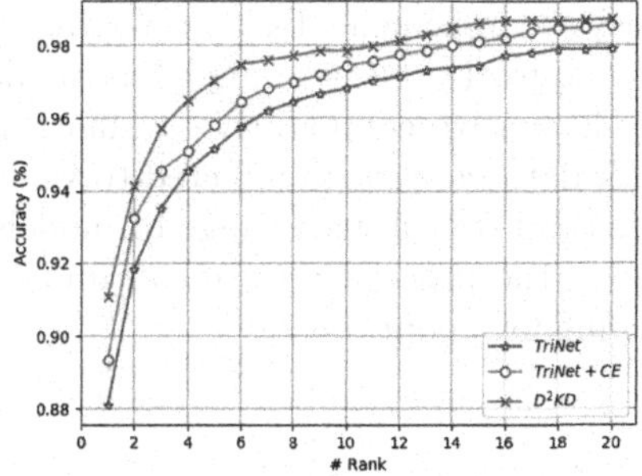

Fig. 4. CMC curve for pure TriNet, TriNet with classification loss and our D^2KD method. All the three methods output a 2048-dimentional feature vector for evaluation. We use ResNet-50 as backbone and single-query setting. The tag "TriNet" means pure ResNet-50 trained with triplet loss. "TriNet+CE" is the baseline when we apply a classification loss on TriNet.

identity otherwise $y_i(x) = 0$. In label smoothing, $y_i(x) = 1 - \epsilon$ for ground-truth label and otherwise $y_i(x) = \epsilon/(C-1)$, where C is total class number, ϵ is usually set to 0.1.

Table 4. Comparison of our D^2KD method to label smoothing (LS)

Methods	Rank-1
TriNet	88.0
TriNet + CE	89.3
TriNet + LS	89.8
D^2KD	91.1

The results are shown in Table 4. Compared to label smoothing (LS), our D^2KD method smooths the label in a dynamic manner. Our method outperforms traditional label smoothing.

From the results, we have the following observations: (1) TriNet with cross entropy loss can achieve higher performance. We can infer that applying the classification task can help to generate more discriminative features. (2) Our Deep Domain Knowledge Distillation (D^2KD) method outperforms both two baselines and label smoothing (LS). This indicates that our D^2KD method which smooths the label in a dynamic manner can lead to a better performance in the person re-identification task.

5 Conclusion

In this paper, we propose a method named Deep Domain Knowledge Distillation (D^2KD) by learning to provide a higher soft bound for the subnetwork to optimize and it is easy to implement. By transferring domain-specific knowledge to the domain-free network, the base model is capable of extracting more discriminative features. Extensive comparative evaluations on three person re-identification benchmark datasets were conducted to validate the advantages of the proposed D^2KD method over a wide range of models on three benchmark datasets. We hope that in the future work we can find a more satisfied higher soft bound for the base model to optimize.

References

1. Ahmed, E., Jones, M., Marks, T.K.: An improved deep learning architecture for person re-identification. In: Proceedings of the IEEE Conference on Computer Vision and Pattern Recognition, pp. 3908–3916 (2015). https://doi.org/10.1109/CVPR.2015.7299016
2. Bromley, J., Guyon, I., LeCun, Y., Säckinger, E., Shah, R.: Signature verification using a "siamese" time delay neural network. In: Advances in Neural Information Processing Systems, pp. 737–744 (1994)
3. Chen, Y., Zhu, X., Gong, S., et al.: Person re-identification by deep learning multi-scale representations (2018). https://doi.org/10.1109/ICCVW.2017.304
4. Felzenszwalb, P.F., Girshick, R.B., McAllester, D., Ramanan, D.: Object detection with discriminatively trained part-based models. IEEE Trans. Pattern Anal. Mach. Intell. **32**(9), 1627–1645 (2010)
5. He, K., Zhang, X., Ren, S., Sun, J.: Deep residual learning for image recognition. In: Proceedings of the IEEE Conference on Computer Vision and Pattern Recognition, pp. 770–778 (2016). https://doi.org/10.1109/CVPR.2016.90
6. Hermans, A., Beyer, L., Leibe, B.: In defense of the triplet loss for person re-identification. arXiv preprint: arXiv:1703.07737 (2017)
7. Hinton, G., Vinyals, O., Dean, J.: Distilling the knowledge in a neural network. arXiv preprint: arXiv:1503.02531 (2015)
8. Kingma, D.P., Ba, J.: Adam: a method for stochastic optimization. arXiv preprint: arXiv:1412.6980 (2014)
9. Krizhevsky, A., Sutskever, I., Hinton, G.E.: ImageNet classification with deep convolutional neural networks. In: Advances in Neural Information Processing Systems, pp. 1097–1105 (2012). https://doi.org/10.1145/3065386
10. Li, D., Chen, X., Zhang, Z., Huang, K.: Learning deep context-aware features over body and latent parts for person re-identification. In: Proceedings of the IEEE Conference on Computer Vision and Pattern Recognition, pp. 384–393 (2017)
11. Li, W., Zhao, R., Xiao, T., Wang, X.: DeepReID: deep filter pairing neural network for person re-identification. In: Proceedings of the IEEE Conference on Computer Vision and Pattern Recognition, pp. 152–159 (2014). https://doi.org/10.1109/CVPR.2014.27
12. Liao, S., Hu, Y., Zhu, X., Li, S.Z.: Person re-identification by local maximal occurrence representation and metric learning. In: Proceedings of the IEEE Conference on Computer Vision and Pattern Recognition, pp. 2197–2206 (2015). https://doi.org/10.1109/CVPR.2015.7298832
13. Liu, H., Feng, J., Qi, M., Jiang, J., Yan, S.: End-to-end comparative attention networks for person re-identification. IEEE Trans. Image Process. **26**(7), 3492–3506 (2017). https://doi.org/10.1109/TIP.2017.2700762. ISSN: 1057-7149
14. Paszke, A., et al.: Automatic differentiation in PyTorch (2017)

15. Sarfraz, M.S., Schumann, A., Eberle, A., Stiefelhagen, R.: A pose-sensitive embedding for person re-identification with expanded cross neighborhood re-ranking. arXiv preprint: arXiv:1711.10378 (2017). https://doi.org/10.1109/CVPR.2018.00051
16. Sun, Y., Zheng, L., Deng, W., Wang, S.: Svdnet for pedestrian retrieval. arXiv preprint **1**(6) (2017). https://doi.org/10.1109/ICCV.2017.410
17. Sun, Y., Zheng, L., Yang, Y., Tian, Q., Wang, S.: Beyond part models: person retrieval with refined part pooling. arXiv preprint: arXiv:1711.09349 (2017)
18. Varior, R.R., Haloi, M., Wang, G.: Gated Siamese convolutional neural network architecture for human re-identification. In: Leibe, B., Matas, J., Sebe, N., Welling, M. (eds.) ECCV 2016, Part VIII. LNCS, vol. 9912, pp. 791–808. Springer, Cham (2016). https://doi.org/10.1007/978-3-319-46484-8_48
19. Varior, R.R., Shuai, B., Lu, J., Xu, D., Wang, G.: A Siamese long short-term memory architecture for human re-identification. In: Leibe, B., Matas, J., Sebe, N., Welling, M. (eds.) ECCV 2016, Part VII. LNCS, vol. 9911, pp. 135–153. Springer, Cham (2016). https://doi.org/10.1007/978-3-319-46478-7_9
20. Xu, J., Zhao, R., Zhu, F., Wang, H., Ouyang, W.: Attention-aware compositional network for person re-identification. arXiv preprint: arXiv:1805.03344 (2018). https://doi.org/10.1109/CVPR.2018.00226
21. Yi, D., Lei, Z., Liao, S., Li, S.Z.: Deep metric learning for person re-identification. In: 2014 22nd International Conference on Pattern Recognition (ICPR), pp. 34–39. IEEE (2014)
22. Zhang, L., Xiang, T., Gong, S.: Learning a discriminative null space for person re-identification. In: Proceedings of the IEEE Conference on Computer Vision and Pattern Recognition, pp. 1239–1248 (2016). https://doi.org/10.1109/CVPR.2016.139
23. Zheng, L., Shen, L., Tian, L., Wang, S., Wang, J., Tian, Q.: Scalable person re-identification: a benchmark. In: Proceedings of the IEEE International Conference on Computer Vision, pp. 1116–1124 (2015). https://doi.org/10.1109/ICCV.2015.133
24. Zheng, L., Yang, Y., Hauptmann, A.G.: Person re-identification: past, present and future. arXiv preprint: arXiv:1610.02984 (2016)
25. Zheng, Z., Zheng, L., Yang, Y.: A discriminatively learned CNN embedding for person reidentification. ACM Trans. Multimed. Comput. Commun. Appl. (TOMM) **14**(1), 13 (2017). https://doi.org/10.1145/3159171. ISSN: 1551-6857
26. Zheng, Z., Zheng, L., Yang, Y.: Pedestrian alignment network for large-scale person re-identification. arXiv preprint: arXiv:1707.00408. https://doi.org/10.1109/TCSVT.2018.2873599 (2017). ISSN: 1051-8215
27. Zheng, Z., Zheng, L., Yang, Y.: Unlabeled samples generated by GAN improve the person re-dentification baseline in vitro. https://doi.org/10.1109/ICCV.2017.405. arXiv preprint: arXiv:1701.07717 (2017)
28. Zhong, Z., Zheng, L., Cao, D., Li, S.: Re-ranking person re-identification with k-reciprocal encoding. In: 2017 IEEE Conference on Computer Vision and Pattern Recognition (CVPR), pp. 3652–3661. IEEE (2017). https://doi.org/10.1109/CVPR.2017.389

A Study on Catastrophic Forgetting in Deep LSTM Networks

Monika Schak(✉) and Alexander Gepperth

University of Applied Sciences Fulda, 36037 Fulda, Germany
{monika.schak,alexander.gepperth}@cs.hs-fulda.de

Abstract. We present a systematic study of Catastrophic Forgetting (CF), i.e., the abrupt loss of previously acquired knowledge, when retraining deep recurrent LSTM networks with new samples. CF has recently received renewed attention in the case of feed-forward DNNs, and this article is the first work that aims to rigorously establish whether deep LSTM networks are afflicted by CF as well, and to what degree. In order to test this fully, training is conducted using a wide variety of high-dimensional image-based sequence classification tasks derived from established visual classification benchmarks (MNIST, Devanagari, FashionMNIST and EMNIST). We find that the CF effect occurs universally, without exception, for deep LSTM-based sequence classifiers, regardless of the construction and provenance of sequences. This leads us to conclude that LSTMs, just like DNNs, are fully affected by CF, and that further research work needs to be conducted in order to determine how to avoid this effect (which is not a goal of this study).

Keywords: LSTM · Catastrophic Forgetting

1 Introduction

This article is in the context of deep recurrent neural networks (more specifically: deep Long Short-Term Memory (LSTM) networks [12]) applied to the classification of sequences. Sequence classification presents many challenges, such as their variable length and the fact that their elements are often presented one after the other (see [36] for a more in-depth review of this topic). Typical applications of sequence classifiers are hand gesture recognition [7], human activity recognition [33] and natural language processing [22]. Prominent recent methods for sequence classification are Recurrent Neural Networks (RNNs), and in particular LSTM networks and their deep "extensions", see [11] and references therein. These classification architectures are based on a similar concept as prior work on echo state networks or reservoir computing [13], where the dynamical state of a recurrent system (reservoir, LSTM layer) represents the current and previously presented sequence elements, and a linear read-out mechanism is added "on top" of that to infer the sequence class. LSTM networks are attractive for this purpose since they are trained by gradient descent, so the "reservoir" can be adapted to the sequences it should represent.

I. V. Tetko et al. (Eds.): ICANN 2019, LNCS 11728, pp. 714–728, 2019.
https://doi.org/10.1007/978-3-030-30484-3_56

Especially in situations where sequence classifiers need to be retrained *in situ*, typically based on user interaction (e.g., learning a new hand gesture by demonstration), the question of incremental or continual learning becomes relevant: what happens to knowledge of previously trained sequences when a new sequence class is presented to a deep LSTM sequence classifier? In addition, sequence elements in common applications, like hand gesture or human activity recognition, are typically images (or depth images) and thus quite high-dimensional and hard to classify in their own right. So a study on Catastrophic Forgetting in deep LSTM networks should be sure to address this case in particular.

1.1 Related Work

The Catastrophic Forgetting Effect. Catastrophic forgetting in feed-forward neural networks was first observed in [24] and subsequently studied in, e.g., [6]. Recent studies in the context of Deep Neural Networks (DNNs) are described below. Essentially, CF is observed when a neural network is first trained on a dataset D_1 and subsequently re-trained on a disjunct dataset D_2. Very counter-intuitively, the typical outcome of such an experimental scheme is that all that was learned from D_1 is forgotten virtually immediately, within one or two mini-batch steps. We consider exactly such a scenario in this article, a minor difference being that samples from D_1 and D_2 are image sequences, which is why LSTM classifiers are used.

Catastrophic Forgetting in Deep Neural Networks. The field of incremental learning is broad, e.g., [25] and [8]. Recent systematic comparisons between different DNN approaches to avoid CF are performed in, e.g., [17,29] or [26]. Principal recent approaches to avoid CF include ensemble methods [5,28], dual-memory systems [9,16,27,30] and regularization approaches. Whereas [10] suggest Dropout for alleviating CF, the Elastic Weight Consolidation (EWC) method [19] proposes to add a term to the energy function that protects weights that are important for the previous sub-task(s). Importance is determined by approximating the Fisher information matrix of the DNN. A related approach is pursued by the Incremental Moment Matching technique (IMM) (see [21]), where weights from DNNs trained on current and past sub-tasks are "merged" using the Fisher information matrix. Other regularization-oriented approaches are proposed in [2,32] and [18] which focus on enforcing sparsity of neural activities by lateral interactions within a layer.

Catastrophic Forgetting in (Deep) LSTM Networks. Although there is little to no previous work on measuring Catastrophic Forgetting in LSTM networks, it seems to be a tentative consensus that LSTM might subject to CF, but we found no scientific work documenting this systematically for complex, high-dimensional sequence classification problems. A simpler recurrent sequence classification model is tested for CF in [4] with the result that this model (without modifications) exhibits strong CF. This article uses short image sequences derived from MNIST as a basis for its investigation, and individual sequence elements are further reduced in dimensionality by Principal Component Analysis

(PCA). A modified form of LSTM based on the EWC method [19] is presented in [22], but CF behavior is not systematically analyzed as the objective of the article is the incremental training of conversational agents. A dual-memory approach to incremental LSTM is presented in [14] for the purpose of land cover prediction in high-dimensional images, again without documenting the CF effect systematically.

Table 1. Overview of each dataset's detailed properties. Image dimensions are given as width × height × channels. Concerning data imbalance, the largest percentual difference in sample count between any two classes is given for training and test data, a value of 0 indicating a perfectly balanced dataset.

Dataset	Properties				
	Image size	Number of elements		Class balance (%)	
		Train	Test	Train	Test
Devanagari	32 × 32 × 1	18.000	2.000	0.3	2.7
EMNIST	28 × 28 × 1	345.035	57.918	2.0	2.0
FashionMNIST	28 × 28 × 1	60.000	10.000	0	0
MNIST	28 × 28 × 1	55.000	10.000	2.2	2.4

1.2 Goals and Contributions of the Article

We aim at determining unambiguously whether LSTM and deep LSTM-based sequence classifiers are prone to the Catastrophic Forgetting effect or not when retrained with samples from one or more additional sequence classes, especially for the case where sequence elements are high-dimensional images that require deep networks in order to be solved satisfactorily. We do not impose application constraints on memory consumption or execution time when performing incremental learning experiments as it is done in [26] since LSTM training is memory-consuming in any case. However, we ensure realism w.r.t. causality, meaning that the number and nature of additional classes are not known beforehand (i.e., in order to select a good topology for deep LSTM), which is in accordance with [26].

Regardless of the actual outcome (CF, no CF or CF in some cases), such an investigation is important because it provides solid justification for further work on avoiding the CF effect in deep LSTM classifiers, or else why CF can be ignored in applications of such architectures.

We wish to make it clear that this study does not propose methods to get rid of Catastrophic Forgetting (which has proven difficult for DNNs): for the time being, we just aim at clearly showing that this effect is an universally occurring one for LSTM networks.

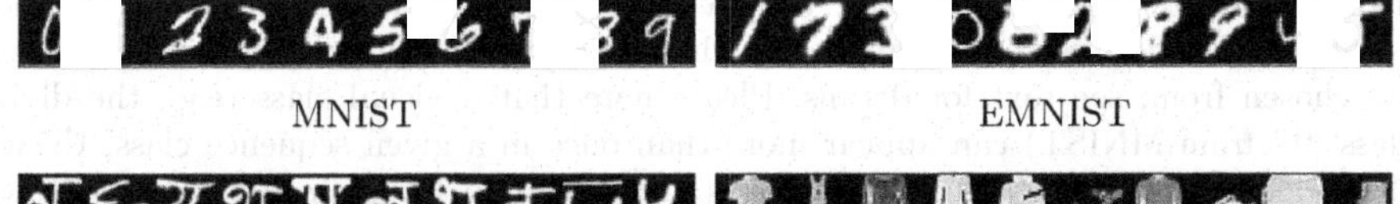

Fig. 1. Visualization of one sample per class from the four visual classification benchmarks used in this article.

2 Methods

The experimental paradigm is based on the notion of an incremental sequence classification task (ISCT), which is, simply put, a sequence classification problem divided into two disjunct parts. The first part is used for the initial training of a deep LSTM network, whereas the second part is used for subsequent retraining. While training on the second part of the ISCT, accuracy on the union of test sets from both parts is monitored to detect Catastrophic Forgetting.

2.1 Visual Benchmarks for Constructing Sequence Classification Tasks

We construct incremental sequence classification tasks based on images taken from the following visual classification benchmarks (see Table 1 for details about the benchmarks and Fig. 1 for a visual impression).

MNIST [20] is the common benchmark for computer vision systems and classification problems. It consists of gray scale images of handwritten digits (0–9).

EMNIST [3] is an extended version of MNIST with additional classes of handwritten letters. There are different variations of this dataset: we extract the ten best-represented classes from the *By_Class* variation containing 62 classes.

Devanagari [1] contains gray-scale images of Devanagari handwritten letters. From the 46 character classes (1.700 images per class) we extract ten random classes.

FashionMNIST [35] consists of images of clothes in ten classes and is structured like the MNIST dataset. We use this dataset for our investigations because it is a "more challenging classification task than the simple MNIST digits data [35]".

2.2 Incremental Sequence Classification Tasks

Construction of Sequence Classes. We construct a common pool of ten ($k = 0, \ldots, 9$) sequence classes characterized by vectors $\boldsymbol{s}^k \in \mathbb{R}^{N_k}$, whose length

Table 2. All ten sequence classes, with sequence class k being characterized by the vector $\boldsymbol{s}_k$ that defines the visual classes where individual sequence elements (frames) are chosen from, see text for details. Please note that a visual class (e.g., the digit class "1" from MNIST) can appear more than once in a given sequence class. Using these definitions, the ten sequence classes are generated for each of the four visual benchmarks.

Seq. class	Seq. def $\boldsymbol{s}^k$	Seq. class	Seq. def $\boldsymbol{s}^k$
0	44671365876	1	1373561961
2	35445909328241	3	9314487292918
4	3675082469	5	45406816421282
6	7534519793178	7	02890
8	69959	9	21024269755

N_k is randomly varied between 5 and 15, and whose integer entries s_i^k are randomly chosen from the range $[0, 9]$. Each sample from a sequence class k thus has N_k elements (frames) $\boldsymbol{e}_i, i = 0, \ldots, N_k - 1$, each being a (flattened) image randomly taken from class s_i^k of one of the four visual benchmarks (see Sect. 2.1). An overview of the constructed sequence classes is given in Table 2, and Fig. 2 gives a visual impression of actual sequence samples. The chosen sequence construction strategy assumes the presence of ten visual classes in each benchmark: where more than ten classes are available, we keep the ten best-represented ones (EMNIST), or we keep ten random ones if all classes are equally well represented (Devanagari).

Construction of Incremental Sequence Classification Tasks. From the pool of ten sequence classes, we construct four incremental sequence classification tasks (ISCT) for measuring Catastrophic Forgetting. Two of them (denoted 5-5a and 5-5b) use a subset of five sequence classes for initial training and five sequence classes for retraining, whereas the two others (denoted 5-1a and 5-1b) use five sequence classes for initial training and one sequence class for retraining. Each ISCT contains training and test sets that are constructed from an 80/20 partition of available sequence samples. Table 3 gives an overview of the ISCTs used for measuring Catastrophic Forgetting in this article.

Table 3. Incremental sequence classification tasks (ISCTs) used for measuring Catastrophic Forgetting. Shown are the sequence classes (see Table 2) used for initial training and retraining of deep LSTM models. Each ISCT is constructed for all the benchmarks: MNIST, FashionMNIST, EMNIST and Devanagari.

ISCT	Initial	Retrain
5-5a	0,4,5,6,9	1,2,3,7,8
5-5b	0,1,2,3,4	5,6,7,8,9
5-1a	0,4,5,6,9	8
5-1b	0,1,2,3,4	9

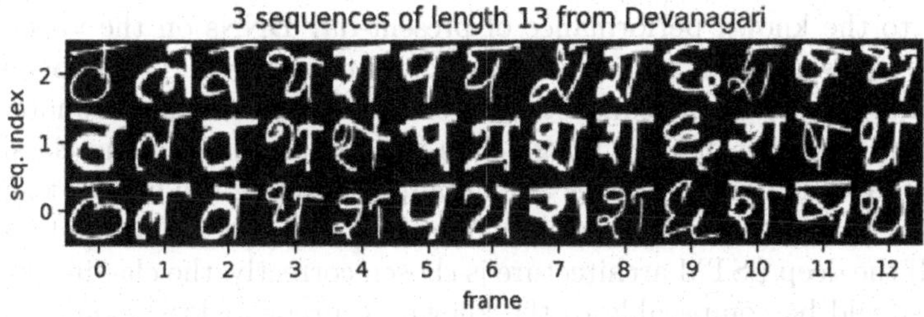

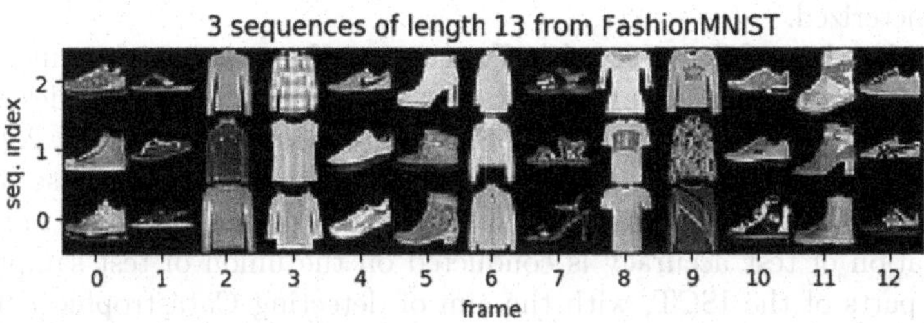

Fig. 2. Visualization of 3 samples (sequences), taken from an exemplary sequence class with 13 elements (frames) shown for Devanagari (top) and FashionMNIST (bottom).

2.3 Deep LSTM Models

We use a standard deep LSTM architecture with linear softmax readout layer and cross-entropy loss function as outlined in [12]. Number and size of hidden layers, which are all set to have the same number of LSTM cells, will be varied in the experiments and are denoted (L, S). The LSTM model equations for computing activations $\boldsymbol{h}_t$ of a single LSTM layer read as follows:

$$\begin{aligned}
\boldsymbol{i}_t &= \sigma\left(W_{xi}\boldsymbol{x}_t + W_{hi}\boldsymbol{h}_{t-1} + W_{ci}\boldsymbol{c}_{t-1} + \boldsymbol{b}_i\right) \\
\boldsymbol{f}_t &= \sigma\left(W_{xf}\boldsymbol{x}_t + W_{hf}\boldsymbol{h}_{t-1} + W_{cf}\boldsymbol{c}_{t-1} + \boldsymbol{b}_f\right) \\
\boldsymbol{c}_t &= \boldsymbol{f}_t\boldsymbol{c}_{t-1} + \boldsymbol{i}_t \tanh\left(W_{xc}\boldsymbol{x}_t + W_{hc}\boldsymbol{h}_{t-1} + \boldsymbol{b}_c\right) \\
\boldsymbol{o}_t &= \sigma\left(W_{xo}\boldsymbol{x}_t + W_{ho}\boldsymbol{h}_{t-1} + W_{co}\boldsymbol{c}_t + \boldsymbol{b}_o\right) \\
\boldsymbol{h}_t &= \boldsymbol{o}_t \tanh(\boldsymbol{c}_t)
\end{aligned} \tag{1}$$

3 Experiments

For our experiments we use the TensorFlow (v1.11) implementation of a Recurrent Neural Network with multiple LSTM cells under Python (v3.6). We always use the Adam optimizer included in TensorFlow for performing gradient descent. We distinguish two principal experimental objectives:

- **Consistency of deep LSTM models** In this step, we verify that our architecture is working correctly on the given classification problems by comparing them to the known performance of present-day DNNs on the visual benchmarks we use. For all visual benchmarks we train deep LSTM models on ten sequence classes, each sequence class containing one element randomly chosen from a single, distinct image class in the benchmark. The classification of such one-element sequences amounts to classifying the images themselves, with recurrency being effectively switched off since the sequences have length one. If the deep LSTM architecture is chosen correctly, the classification accuracy should be comparable to the known accuracy of DNNs on a particular benchmark, thus establishing that our deep LSTMs are correctly used and parameterized.

- **Investigation of Catastrophic Forgetting** Here, we introduce incremental learning to our architecture: we train deep LSTM networks as described in Sect. 2.3 on the incremental sequence classification tasks (see Sect. 2.2) in two steps as outlined in Table 3: first on an initial set of sequence classes followed by retraining on a different set of sequence classes. During retraining, an evaluation of test accuracy is conducted on the union of test samples from both parts of the ISCT, with the aim of detecting Catastrophic Forgetting after the onset of retraining.

3.1 Consistency

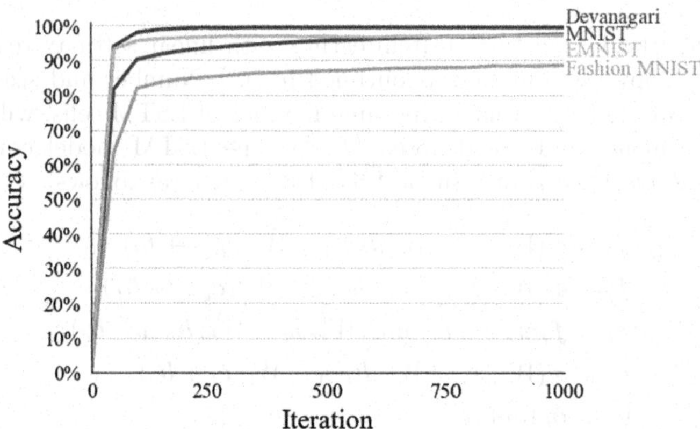

Fig. 3. Consistency test results

We vary the number of hidden layers and their size $(L, S) \in \{(1, 100), (1, 200), (1, 500), (3, 800), (5, 200)\}$ and use a fixed learning rate of $\epsilon = 0.0001$, a fixed batch size of $b = 1.000$ and a fixed number of iterations $I = 1.000$. To make sure the results are significant and consistent we repeat every experiment five times and calculate the average loss and accuracy. Table 4 shows the results for this preliminary experiment. As can be seen, our networks achieve accuracies that are generally comparable to those one would obtain when using simple DNN architectures. This makes it very plausible that our deep LSTMs are correctly parameterized and excludes gross errors in the deep LSTM setup. Figure 3 shows the best result for each benchmark (in percent).

Table 4. Results of the consistency tests: Averaged accuracy over five experiments.

(L, S)	$(1, 100)$	$(1, 200)$	$(1, 500)$	$(3, 800)$	$(5, 200)$
MNIST	94.6	95.7	96.8	97.4	95.2
EMNIST	87.1	88.8	91.0	97.1	95.2
Devanagari	87.9	93.3	97.1	99.4	98.4
Fashion MNIST	86.7	87.7	88.5	88.4	85.8

3.2 Investigation of Catastrophic Forgetting

To test whether deep LSTM networks are prone to Catastrophic Forgetting when retraining an already trained one with new sequences we perform initial training and retraining using the generated ISCTs (see Fig. 2 and Sect. 2.2). To exclude that results are due to a particular choice of topology we vary the number and size of hidden layers $(L, S) \in \{(1, 100), (1, 200), (1, 500), (3, 800), (5, 200)\}$ and use

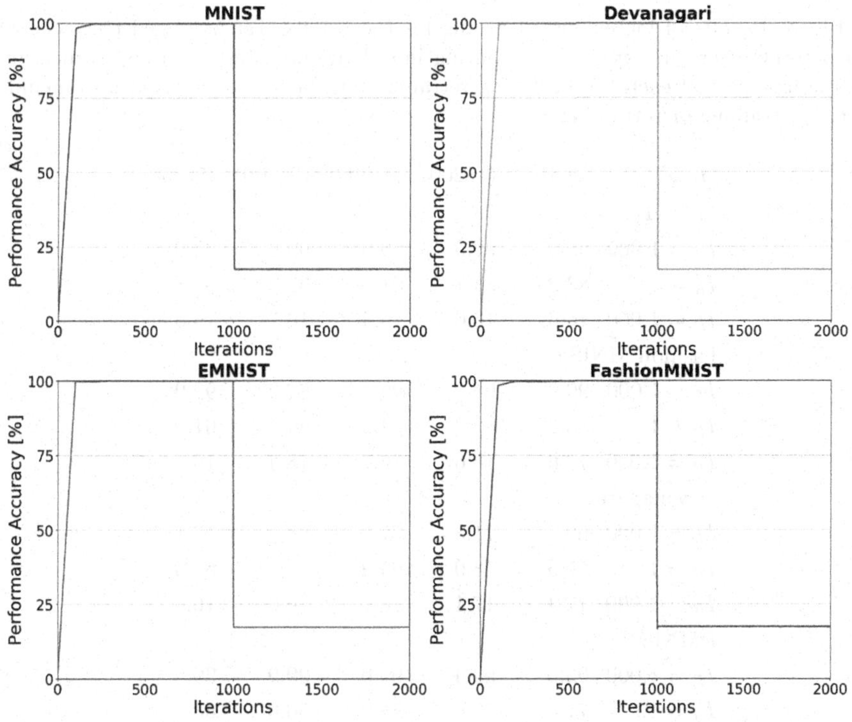

Fig. 4. Results of incremental learning for the 5-1 ISCTs.

a fixed learning rate $\epsilon = 0.0001$, a fixed batch size $b = 1.000$ and a fixed number of iterations for initial training and retraining $I_T = I_R = 1.000$. To make sure the results are significant we repeat every experiment five times and calculate the average classification accuracy. To ensure the results are not influenced by our choice of sequence classes for initial training and retraining we additionally average results over the 5-5a/5-5b and 5-1a/5-1b experiments. In total, we run 400 different incremental learning experiments:

- 5 different topologies: $(L, S) \in \{(1, 100), (1, 200), (1, 500), (3, 800), (5, 200)\}$
- 4 different ISCTs (5-5a, 5-5b, 5-1a, 5-1b) from 4 visual benchmarks
- 10 repetitions for each ISCT

Table 5 shows the averaged accuracy for the 5-1 ISCTs for all tested architectures at the end of initial training and during retraining ($I_T = 1000, t < I_R, t \in \{1, 1000\}$). The best achieved results for those experiments are shown in Fig. 4. As can be seen, the first part of the experiments where we perform initial training shows similar results to the ones achieved in our consistency tests (which is unsurprising). In the majority of cases, the results on five-element sequences are even better than those we obtain on single-element sequences in the consistency tests. As soon as we retrain the network with additional sequence classes the accuracy decreases drastically and almost instantaneously to 60–80% after one

Table 5. Results of incremental learning for the 5-1 ISCTs: Averaged test accuracy (in percent) over ten experiments. During initial training, test accuracy is measured on the first part of each ISCT, during retraining on the six sequence classes included in either training or retraining.

(L, S)	$(1, 100)$	$(1, 200)$	$(1, 500)$	$(3, 800)$	$(5, 200)$
MNIST					
$I_T = 1.000$	99.9	99.9	99.9	99.9	99.9
$I_R = 1$	83.2	83.1	81.9	67.2	68.8
$I_R = 1.000$	16.6	16.6	16.4	16.7	16.8
Fashion MNIST					
$I_T = 1.000$	99.9	99.9	99.9	99.9	99.9
$I_R = 1$	83.2	82.8	74.3	64.1	61.9
$I_R = 1.000$	16.6	16.6	16.7	18.4	16.8
Devanagari					
$I_T = 1.000$	69.7	71.3	77.7	98.9	97.1
$I_R = 1$	57.9	58.9	64.9	59.4	57.4
$I_R = 1.000$	17.4	17.1	16.7	16.0	16.6
EMNIST					
$I_T = 1.000$	93.0	93.4	95.0	99.9	99.9
$I_R = 1$	77.5	77.6	78.9	56.6	68.4
$I_R = 1.000$	17.6	16.7	16.5	16.8	16.8

Table 6. Results of incremental learning for the 5-5 ISCTs: averaged test accuracy (in percent) over ten experiments. During initial training, test accuracy is measured on the first part of each ISCT, during retraining on all ten sequence classes.

(L, S)	$(1, 100)$	$(1, 200)$	$(1, 500)$	$(3, 800)$	$(5, 200)$
MNIST					
$I_T = 1.000$	99.9	99.9	99.9	99.9	99.9
$I_R = 1$	50.1	49.8	48.3	32.1	20.2
$I_R = 1.000$	55.3	55.0	55.1	54.8	54.9
Fashion MNIST					
$I_T = 1.000$	99.9	99.9	99.9	99.9	99.9
$I_R = 1$	49.9	49.2	44.6	32.2	19.9
$I_R = 1.000$	55.0	55.1	54.9	55.3	55.0
Devanagari					
$I_T = 1.000$	70.1	71.0	78.3	98.8	96.7
$I_R = 1$	34.9	36.3	38.6	39.1	25.7
$I_R = 1.000$	46.1	46.2	49.2	55.5	53.9
EMNIST					
$I_T = 1.000$	92.9	93.4	95.4	99.9	99.9
$I_R = 1$	46.5	46.8	47.6	37.7	24.1
$I_R = 1.000$	54.4	54.1	54.1	55.0	54.9

iteration and then to about 17% during the next few iterations, where it remains. This is indeed the result one would expect for a classifier that has learned about one sequence class and has totally forgotten about the other five it has learned before.

Similarly, Table 6 shows the averaged accuracy for the 5-5 ISCTs for all tested architectures at the end of initial training and during retraining ($I_T = 1000, t < I_R, t \in \{1, 1000\}$). The best results for this part of our study are shown in Fig. 4. During the first couple iterations of retraining the network, the accuracy drops to between 20% and 50% (depending on the architecture). It then increases to about 50–55% during the next 25 iterations and remains there until we stop the tests after 1.000 iterations. Again, this is the accuracy one would expect if half of the ten sequence classes has been well learned during retraining, but the other half has been completely forgotten.

4 Discussion and Conclusions

Principal Outcomes. We find that sequence classifiers based on deep LSTM networks are heavily afflicted by Catastrophic Forgetting for complex, high-dimensional incremental sequence classification tasks. Within only a few mini-batch iterations, almost all knowledge about previously trained data is lost and the network is able to perform an accurate classification only on the newly trained sequences. The LSTM topology has no influence at all on this effect, to the extent we were able to test this, which is different from feed-forward DNNs where topology has a small influence without however in any way eliminating the problem [26]. It is relatively intuitive why this should be the case, since recurrent networks are conceivably more sensitive to even small changes in weights due to retraining, since each change is amplified by recurrent connections. Also in slight contrast to feed-forward DNNs, it does not make a difference whether a single or many classes are added during re-training, although the effect is slim at best even for DNNs, see [26].

Significance of Results. We find this to be a very important result about LSTM sequence classifiers: Catastrophic Forgetting is a universally occurring effect. So it is not possible to add new knowledge to a trained LSTM classifier in a naive way without losing all previously acquired knowledge. While forgetting in such a scenario is not unreasonable to expect simply due to limited network resources, it should be gradual so that re-training can be stopped whenever the onset of forgetting is detected. This "graceful decay" behavior is however not what is observed in our experiments and once forgetting is detected it is already too late to stop re-training.

Justification of Using LSTMs. We employ deep LSTM classifiers in this article because the problems treated here are inherently high-dimensional and, above all, sequential. The most important property of sequences, for the purpose of this article, is that the different sequence classes do not have to be of the same length, i.e., samples from different sequence classes may very well contain a different number of frames. This, together with the high-dimensional nature of the images, effectively excludes strategies that concatenate all images in a given sequence and present the result to a feed-forward DNN. First of all, memory usage would be excessive. More importantly, a sequence could only be classified once its end was reached: but to determine that, its class would have to be known. Of course, a fixed upper limit on sequence length could be imposed, but this would incur even higher memory requirements. For all these reasons, we believe that the use of deep LSTMs is the only feasible choice for the problems presented here, which are typical representatives for, e.g., video classification tasks.

Datasets Used for this Study. The datasets, that is, the incremental sequence classification tasks (ISCTs) used in this study consist of image sequences and are thus related to videos. The reason for not using datasets containing real videos is that we wish to treat problems which, when not treating sequential learning problems, can be solved to a high degree of precision so that the forgetting effect is pronounced enough to be observed. Thus, while it might be argued that we used artificial data that are really too simple to give meaningful results, we point out that if CF occurs even for relatively simple problems like these, it is sure to occur for more complex problems as well (as it is the case for DNNs, see, e.g., [26]).

Context and Next Steps. This study deliberately does not propose a solution to the problem because we believe the existence of the problem needs to be rigorously established first. It is conceivable that EWC or IMM-like mechanisms [19,21] may alleviate Catastrophic Forgetting for deep LSTM networks, and approaches based on generative replay [15,30,34] presumably generalize to sequence classification although the generation of sequences as opposed to single images may prove challenging. Approaches based on the so-called "distillation loss" regularization [23,31] will be looked into as well, mostly because they should be pretty straightforward to implement for LSTM networks. We hope, by presenting these results, to encourage researchers to investigate continual training methods not only for DNNs, but for LSTM sequence classifiers as well.

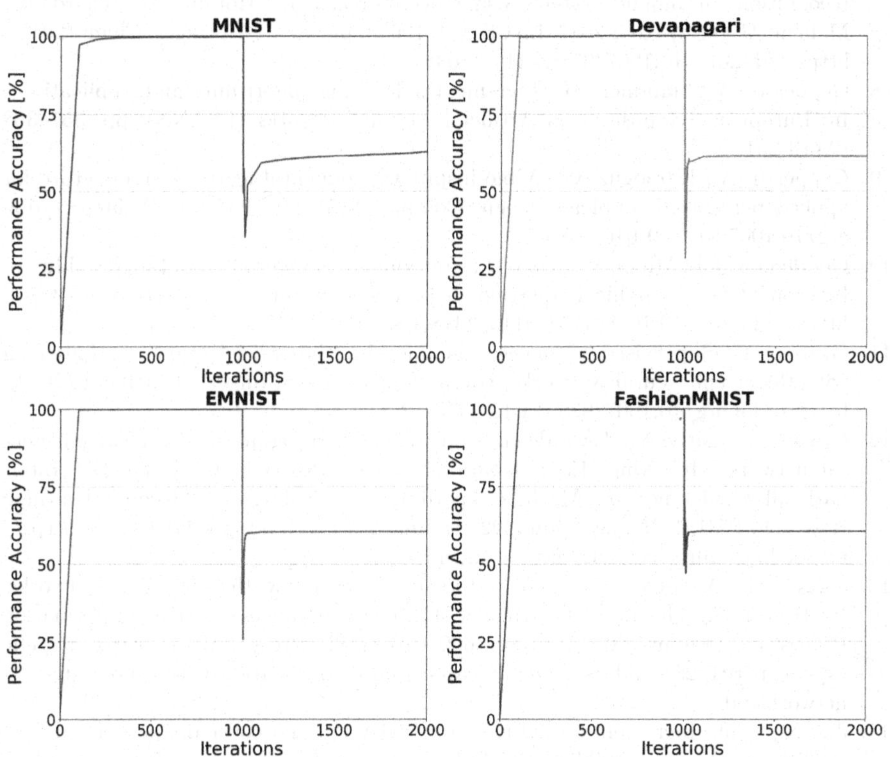

Fig. 5. Results of incremental learning for the 5-5 ISCTs.

References

1. Acharya, S.: Deep Learning Based Large Scale Handwritten Devanagari Character Recognition (2015). https://doi.org/10.31979/etd.3yh5-xs5s
2. Aljundi, R., Rohrbach, M., Tuytelaars, T.: Selfless Sequential Learning (2018)

3. Cohen, G., Afshar, S., Tapson, J., Van Schaik, A.: EMNIST: extending MNIST to handwritten letters. In: Proceedings of the International Joint Conference on Neural Networks 2017-May, pp. 2921–2926 (2017). https://doi.org/10.1109/IJCNN.2017.7966217
4. Coop, R., Arel, I.: Mitigation of catastrophic forgetting in recurrent neural networks using a fixed expansion layer. In: The 2013 International Joint Conference on Neural Networks (IJCNN), pp. 1–7, August 2013. https://doi.org/10.1109/IJCNN.2013.6707047
5. Fernando, C., et al.: PathNet: Evolution Channels Gradient Descent in Super Neural Networks (2017)
6. French, R.: Catastrophic forgetting in connectionist networks. Trends Cogn. Sci. **3**(4), 128–135 (1999). https://doi.org/10.1016/S1364-6613(99)01294-2
7. Sarkar, A., Gepperth, A., Handmann, U., Kopinski, T.: Dynamic hand gesture recognition for mobile systems using deep LSTM. In: Horain, P., Achard, C., Mallem, M. (eds.) IHCI 2017. LNCS, vol. 10688, pp. 19–31. Springer, Cham (2017). https://doi.org/10.1007/978-3-319-72038-8_3
8. Gepperth, A., Hammer, B.: Incremental learning algorithms and applications. In: European Symposium on Artificial Neural Networks (ESANN), pp. 357–368 (April 2016)
9. Gepperth, A., Karaoguz, C.: A bio-inspired incremental learning architecture for applied perceptual problems. Cogn. Comput. **8**(5), 924–934 (2016). https://doi.org/10.1007/s12559-016-9389-5
10. Goodfellow, I.J., Mirza, M., Xiao, D., Courville, A., Bengio, Y.: An Empirical Investigation of Catastrophic Forgetting in Gradient-Based Neural Networks (2013). https://doi.org/10.1088/1751-8113/44/8/085201
11. Graves, A.: Supervised sequence labelling. In: Supervised Sequence Labelling with Recurrent Neural Networks, vol. 385, pp. 5–13. Springer, Heidelberg (2012). https://doi.org/10.1007/978-3-642-24797-2_2
12. Graves, A., Jaitly, N.: Towards end-to-end speech recognition with recurrent neural networks. In: Xing, E.P., Jebara, T. (eds.) Proceedings of the 31st International Conference on Machine Learning. Proceedings of Machine Learning Research, PMLR, Bejing, China, 22–24 June 2014, vol. 32, pp. 1764–1772. http://proceedings.mlr.press/v32/graves14.html
13. Jaeger, H.: Adaptive nonlinear system identification with echo state networks. In: Becker, S., Thrun, S., Obermayer, K. (eds.) Advances in Neural Information Processing Systems, vol. 15. pp. 609–616. MIT Press (2003). http://papers.nips.cc/paper/2318-adaptive-nonlinear-system-identification-with-echo-state-networks.pdf
14. Jia, X., et al.: Incremental dual-memory LSTM in land cover prediction. In: Proceedings of the 23rd ACM SIGKDD International Conference on Knowledge Discovery and Data Mining, KDD 2017, pp. 867–876. ACM, New York (2017). https://doi.org/10.1145/3097983.3098112, https://doi.org/10.1145/3097983.3098112
15. Kamra, N., Gupta, U., Liu, Y.: Deep generative dual memory network for continual learning. arXiv preprint arXiv:1710.10368 (2017). http://arxiv.org/abs/1710.10368
16. Kemker, R., Kanan, C.: FearNet: Brain-Inspired Model for Incremental Learning, pp. 1–16 (2017)
17. Kemker, R., McClure, M., Abitino, A., Hayes, T., Kanan, C.: Measuring Catastrophic Forgetting in Neural Networks (2017). https://doi.org/10.1073/pnas.1611835114

18. Kim, H.-E., Kim, S., Lee, J.: Keep and learn: continual learning by constraining the latent space for knowledge preservation in neural networks. In: Frangi, A.F., Schnabel, J.A., Davatzikos, C., Alberola-López, C., Fichtinger, G. (eds.) MICCAI 2018. LNCS, vol. 11070, pp. 520–528. Springer, Cham (2018). https://doi.org/10.1007/978-3-030-00928-1_59
19. Kirkpatrick, J., et al.: Overcoming catastrophic forgetting in neural networks (2016). https://doi.org/10.1073/pnas.1611835114, http://arxiv.org/abs/1612.00796
20. LeCun, Y., Bottou, L., Bengio, Y., Haffner, P.: Gradient-Based Learning Apllied to Document Recognition (1998). https://doi.org/10.1109/5.726791
21. Lee, S.W., Kim, J.H., Jun, J., Ha, J.W., Zhang, B.T.: Overcoming Catastrophic Forgetting by Incremental Moment Matching, pp. 4652–4662 (2017). http://papers.nips.cc/paper/7051-overcoming-catastrophic-forgetting-by-incremental-moment-matching.pdf
22. Lee, S.: Toward continual learning for conversational agents. CoRR abs/1712.09943 (2017). http://arxiv.org/abs/1712.09943
23. Li, Z., Hoiem, D.: Learning without forgetting. IEEE Trans. Pattern Anal. Mach. Intell. **40**(12), 2935–2947 (2018). https://doi.org/10.1109/TPAMI.2017.2773081
24. McCloskey, M., Cohen, N.J.: Catastrophic interference in connectionist networks: the sequential learning problem. Psychol. Learn. Motiv. **24**, 109–165 (1989). https://doi.org/10.1016/S0079-7421(08)60536-8. http://www.sciencedirect.com/science/article/pii/S0079742108605368
25. Parisi, G.I., Kemker, R., Part, J.L., Kanan, C., Wermter, S.: Continual Lifelong Learning with Neural Networks: A Review, pp. 1–29 (2018). https://doi.org/10.1016/j.neunet.2019.01.012
26. Pfülb, B., Gepperth, A.: A comprehensive, application-oriented study of catastrophic forgetting in DNNs, vol. abs/1905.08101 (2019). http://arxiv.org/abs/1905.08101
27. Rebuffi, S.a., Kolesnikov, A., Sperl, G., Lampert, C.H.: iCaRL : Incremental Classifier and Representation Learning, pp. 2001–2010 (2017). https://doi.org/10.1109/CVPR.2017.587
28. Ren, B., Wang, H., Li, J., Gao, H.: Life-long learning based on dynamic combination model. Appl. Soft Comput. J. **56**, 398–404 (2017). https://doi.org/10.1016/j.asoc.2017.03.005
29. Serrà, J., Surís, D., Miron, M., Karatzoglou, A.: Overcoming catastrophic forgetting with hard attention to the task. arXiv preprint arXiv:1801.01423 (2018)
30. Shin, H., Lee, J.K., Kim, J., Kim, J.: Continual Learning with Deep Generative Replay (NIPS) (2017)
31. Shmelkov, K., Schmid, C., Alahari, K.: Incremental learning of object detectors without catastrophic forgetting. In: Proceedings of the IEEE International Conference on Computer Vision, pp. 3400–3409 (2017). https://doi.org/10.1109/ICCV.2017.368
32. Srivastava, R.K., Masci, J., Kazerounian, S., Gomez, F., Schmidhuber, J.: Compete to Compute, pp. 2310–2318 (2013). http://papers.nips.cc/paper/5059-compete-to-compute.pdf
33. Wang, J., Chen, Y., Hao, S., Peng, X., Hu, L.: Deep learning for sensor-based activity recognition: a survey. Pattern Recogn. Lett. (2018). https://doi.org/10.1016/j.patrec.2018.02.010, http://www.sciencedirect.com/science/article/pii/S016786551830045X

34. Wu, C., Herranz, L., Liu, X., Wang, Y., van de Weijer, J., Raducanu, B.: Memory replay GANs: learning to generate images from new categories without forgetting. arXiv preprint arXiv:1809.02058 (2018). http://dl.acm.org/citation.cfm?id=3327345.3327496
35. Xiao, H., Rasul, K., Vollgraf, R.: Fashion-MNIST: a novel image dataset for benchmarking machine learning algorithms. CoRR abs/1708.07747 (2017). http://arxiv.org/abs/1708.07747
36. Xing, Z., Pei, J., Keogh, E.: A brief survey on sequence classification. ACM SIGKDD Explor. Newsl. **12**(1), 40–48 (2010). https://doi.org/10.1145/1882471.1882478

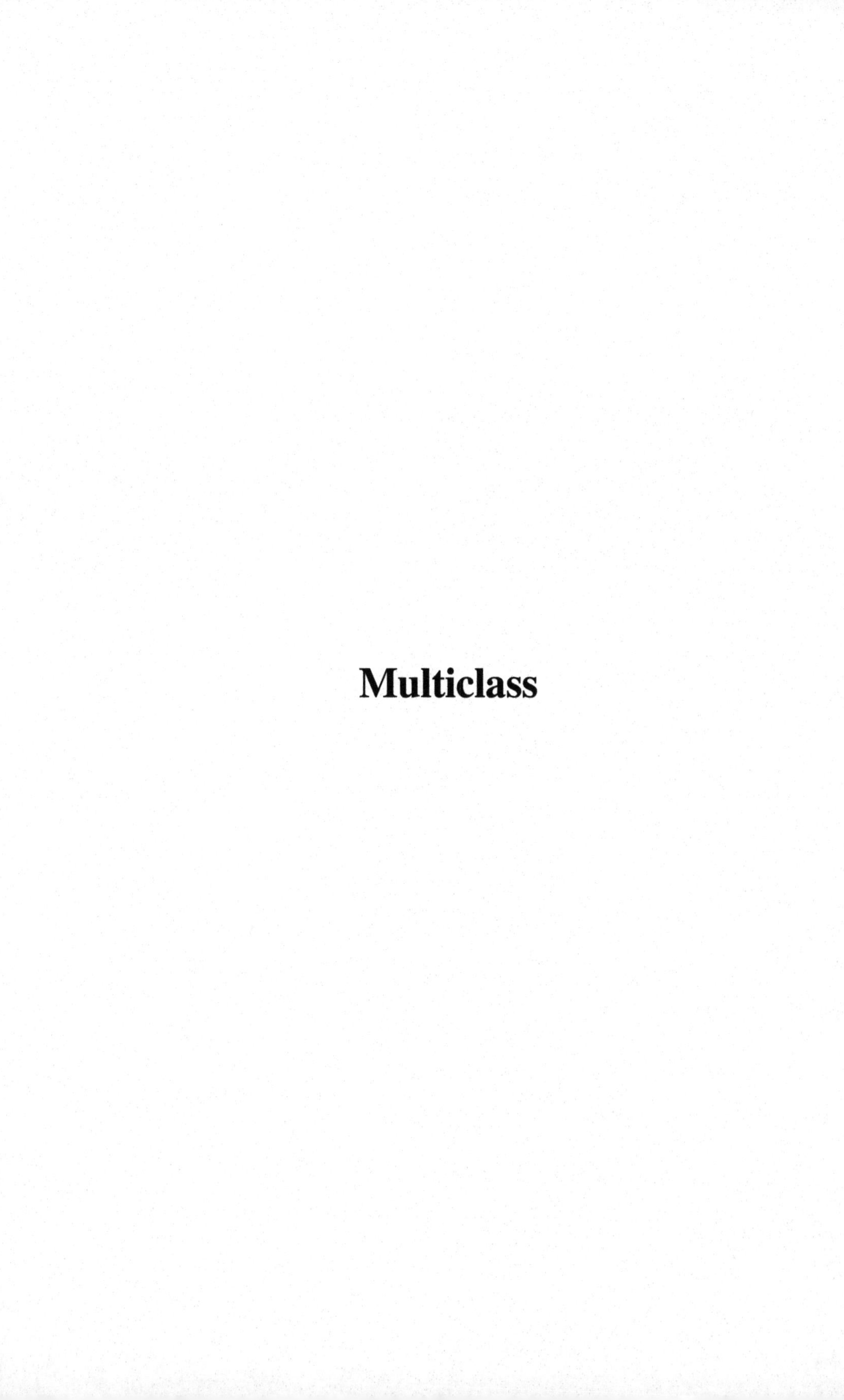

Multiclass

A Label-Specific Attention-Based Network with Regularized Loss for Multi-label Classification

Xiangyang Luo, Xiangying Ran, Wei Sun, Yunlai Xu, and Chongjun Wang(✉)

National Key Laboratory for Novel Software Technology, Nanjing University, Nanjing 210023, China
lxypaul2016@gmail.com, lebronran@gmail.com, weisun_@outlook.com, yunlaixu@gmail.com, chjwang@nju.edu.cn

Abstract. In a multi-label text classification task, different parts of a document do not contribute equally to predicting labels. Most existing approaches failed to consider this problem. Several methods have been proposed to take this problem into account. However, they just utilized hidden representations of neural networks as input of attention mechanism, not combining with label information. In this work, we propose an improved attention-based neural network model for multi-label text classification, which can obtain the weights of attention mechanism by computing the similarity between each label and each word of documents. This model adds the label information into text representations which can select the most informative words accurately for predicting labels. Besides, compared with single-label classification, the labels of multi-label classification may have some correlations such as co-occurrence or conditional probability relationship. So we also propose a special regularization term for this model, which can help to exploit label correlations by using label co-occurrence matrix. Experimental results on AAPD and RCV1-V2 datasets demonstrate that the proposed model yields a significant performance gain compared to many state-of-the-art approaches.

Keywords: Multi-label classification · Attention-based Network · Label correlations

1 Introduction

Multi-label classification (MLC) is one of the most important tasks in natural language processing. Different from single-label classification, it aims to assign multiple labels to an instance. Besides, the output label space can have more multiple combinations. Therefore, it is a more difficult and challenging task.

Binary Relevance (BR) [1] is one of the simplest methods, which decomposes the MLC task into multiple single-label classification problems. However, it ignores the correlations between labels. Other methods take the issue of resolving the correlations between labels into consideration, such as Classifier Chains

I. V. Tetko et al. (Eds.): ICANN 2019, LNCS 11728, pp. 731–742, 2019.
https://doi.org/10.1007/978-3-030-30484-3_57

(CC) [2], Ranking Support Vector Machine (Rank-SVM) [3], Calibrated Label Ranking(CLR) [4], and so on. But the calculation becomes more complicated when the number of labels increases.

Recently, deep learning methods have achieved good results in MLC tasks. Kurata et al. [5] proposed to utilize the Convolutional Neural Network (CNN) for multi-label classification. Chen et al. [6] used CNN and Recurrent Neural Network (RNN) to capture the semantic information of texts. However, they either neglected the fact that different words do not contribute equally when predicting labels or ignored the correlations between labels.

In this paper, we propose a Label-specific Attention-based Network (LSABN) for multi-label text classification. We verify the hypothesis that better document representations can be obtained by incorporating the relationship between texts and labels into the attention mechanism. Our model utilizes attention mechanism with Bidirectional Long Short-Term Memory Network (Bi-LSTM) to capture the most important semantic information in a document. Unlike other attention mechanisms which only utilize hidden representations of neural networks to build attention weights, we use the similarity between each label and each word of documents to construct attention weights. Experimental results on AAPD and RCV1-V2 datasets demonstrate that our model performs better than most of the existing methods in the literature.

Our main contributions can be listed as follows:

(1) We propose a Label-specific Attention-based Network (LSABN) model which can utilize label information to assign different attention weights to words in a document.
(2) We propose a special regularization term by making use of label co-occurrence matrix to capture the correlations between labels.
(3) Experimental results demonstrate that our proposed model can achieve significant improvement on two widely used datasets.

The remainder of the paper is structured as follows. In Sect. 2, we review related work about multi-label classification. Section 3 presents our LSABN model in details. In Sect. 4, we describe the experiments and make analysis and discussions. Finally Sect. 5 concludes this paper.

2 Related Work

The traditional MLC methods can be classified into two main types: problem transformation methods and algorithm adaptation methods.

Problem transformation methods are the most direct ways to deal with multi-label classification. They transform a multi-label classification problem into single-label problems, such as several binary problems, multi-class problems or label ranking problems. Binary Relevance (BR) [1] decomposes the MLC task into independent binary classification problems. But Unfortunately, it ignores the correlations between labels. Classifier Chains (CC) [2] transforms the MLC task into a chain of binary classification problems which considers the correlations. Label Powerset (LP) [7] transforms a multi-label learning problem into a multi-class (single-label) classification problem.

Algorithm adaptation methods extend existing single-label classification algorithms to deal with multi-label classification. Multi-Label k-Nearest-Neighbor-hood(MLKNN) [8] is a lazy approach which utilizes maximum a posteriori (MAP) to determine the label set for prediction. Ranking Support Vector Machine (Rank-SVM) [3] adapts maximum margin strategy to deal with multi-label data and minimizes the empirical ranking loss. Collective Multi-Label Classifier (CML) [9] adapts maximum entropy principle to deal with multi-label data where correlations among labels are encoded as constraints.

Recently, neural network (NN) approaches have achieved surprising results in MLC tasks. Zhang et al. [10] proposed the BP-MLL model, which is adapted from a 3-layer forward neural network, to take dependencies between labels into account by utilizing a pairwise ranking loss function. Nam et al. [11] replaced the ranking loss with a neural network using cross-entropy loss. Kurata et al. [5] utilized word embeddings based on CNN to capture label correlations. Chen et al. [6] proposed to combine CNN with RNN to model high-order label correlations. Lin et al. [12] proposed a new model for extracting an interpretable sentence embedding by introducing self-attention. Different from [12], our model use the similarity between each label and each word of documents to construct attention weights.

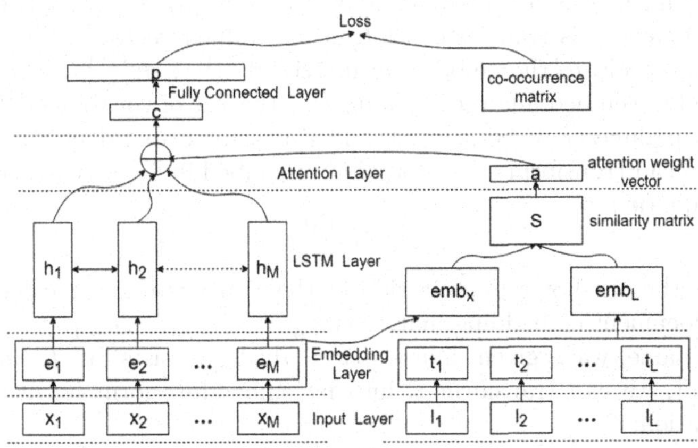

Fig. 1. Label-specific attention-based network with regularized loss

3 Model

In this section, we propose our LSABN model in details. As shown in Fig. 1, our model contains five components:

(1) Input layer: input a document to this model;
(2) Embedding layer: map each word in this document and descriptions of labels into a low dimension vector;
(3) Bi-LSTM layer: utilize Bi-LSTM to get high level features from step (2);
(4) Label-specific attention layer: construct a weight vector, and merge word-level features into a document-level feature vector by multiplying the weight vector;
(5) Output layer: the document-level feature vector is finally used for multi-label classification.

These components will be presented in details in the following.

3.1 Multi-label Classification

Before going into the details of our model, we first introduce some notations and describe the MLC task. Suppose $\mathcal{L} = \{l_1, l_2, ..., l_L\}$ is a finite domain of L possible labels. Formally, Multi-label classification may be defined as follows: Given the dataset $D = \{(X_k, Y_k) \,|k = 1, 2, ..., N\}$ where N is the number of examples in D, the task is to assign a subset Y_k containing n labels in the label space $\mathcal{L}$ to X_k.

3.2 Word Embeddings and Label Embeddings

Given a document which consists of M words $X = \{x_1, x_2, ..., x_M\}$, every word x_i in this document is transformed into a real-valued vector e_i. For each word in X, we first look up the embedding matrix $W^{d|V|} \in \mathbb{R}^{d \times |V|}$, where d is the dimension of the embedding vector, and $|V|$ is the size of vocabulary. The matrix $W^{d|V|}$ is a parameter to be learned, and d is a hyper-parameter to be chosen by user. We can transform a word x_i into an embedding vector e_i by using the following equation:

$$e_i = W^{d|V|} p_i \tag{1}$$

where p_i is the one-hot representation of the i-th word. After calculation, we can get a document embedding matrix $emb_X = \{e_1, e_2, ..., e_M\}$.

In the same way, given label space which consists of L labels $\mathcal{L} = \{l_1, l_2, ..., l_L\}$, we can transform $\mathcal{L}$ into its embedding form by using the following equation:

$$t_i = W^{d|V|} v_i \tag{2}$$

where v_i is the one-hot representation of the i-th label. After calculation, we can get an embedding matrix $emb_{\mathcal{L}} = \{t_1, t_2, ..., t_L\}$. The words out of the vocabulary are randomly initialized. If the description of the label uses more than one word, we just use the average of the word embeddings.

3.3 Bidirectional Network

LSTM units are firstly proposed by Hochreiter et al. [13], which can overcome gradient vanishing problem. The main idea of LSTM is to introduce an adaptive gating mechanism, which decides the degree to which LSTM units keep the previous state and memorize the extracted features of the current data input.

We use a bidirectional LSTM used in [14] to read the input document X from both directions and compute the hidden states for each word,

$$\overrightarrow{h_i} = \overrightarrow{LSTM}\left(e_i, \overrightarrow{h_{i-1}}\right) \tag{3}$$

$$\overleftarrow{h_i} = \overleftarrow{LSTM}\left(e_i, \overleftarrow{h_{i+1}}\right) \tag{4}$$

We obtain the final hidden representation of the i-th word by concatenating the hidden states from both directions, $h_i = \left[\overrightarrow{h_i}, \overleftarrow{h_i}\right]$, which ensures that the i-th word can have the information near it. H is a matrix consisting of output vectors $[h_1, h_2, ..., h_M]$ that the BiLSTM layer produced, where M is the document length. The hidden unit number for each unidirectional LSTM is u, so H has the size M-by-$2u$.

3.4 Label-Specific Attention Mechanism

In this section, we propose the label-specific attention mechanism. Firstly, we calculate the cosine similarity matrix S between emb_X and $emb_{\mathcal{L}}$. We can obtain the element of matrix S by using the following equation:

$$s\left(t_i, e_j\right) = \cos\left(t_i, e_j\right) \tag{5}$$

where cos is the cosine similarity given by $\cos(a, b) = \frac{a \cdot b}{|a||b|}$. The element $s\left(t_i, e_j\right)$ is the similarity between i-th label and j-th word. All the elements form the similarity matrix $S = [s_{ij}]_{L \times M}$. We can transform embedding matrix emb_X and $emb_{\mathcal{L}}$ into unit matrix so that matrix S can be calculated as following:

$$S = {emb_{\mathcal{L}}}^T emb_X \tag{6}$$

The element $s\left(t_i, e_j\right)$ in cosine similarity matrix S means the importance of the j-th word to predicting i-th label. So what we need to do is transforming the matrix S into a weight vector z with size M. Then we use nonlinear activation functions to achieve approximation of complex functions:

$$z = w_2 \tanh\left(W_1 S\right) \tag{7}$$

Here W_1 is a weight matrix with a shape of q-by-L. And w_2 is a vector of parameters with size q, where q is a hyperparameter we can set arbitrarily. Since H is sized M-by-$2u$, the attention weight vector z will have a size M. The element z_t in the attention weight vector z means the importance of the t-th word to the prediction of labels. Then we can get a normalized importance weight vector α for the document through a softmax function:

$$\alpha = softmax(z) \tag{8}$$

where the t-th element of α is calculated as: $\alpha_t = \frac{exp_{z_t}}{\sum_t exp_{z_t}}$.

The representation c of the document is formed by a weighted sum of these output vectors:

$$c = \sum_t \alpha_t h_t \tag{9}$$

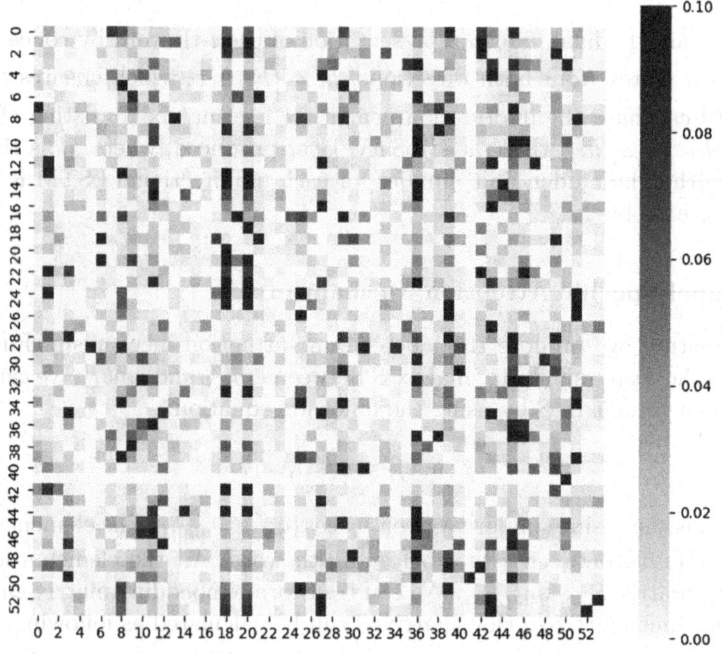

Fig. 2. The co-occurrence frequency of the labels on the AAPD dataset

3.5 Regularized Loss

The document vector c is a high level representation of the document and we can use the feature vector to obtain label scores by fully connected layer:

$$p = softmax(cW_c + b_c) \tag{10}$$

where W_c is a weight matrix with a shape of $2u$-by-L, and b_c is a vector of parameters with size L. So p is a label score vector with size L.

Our model can be trained in a supervised manner by minimizing the following Binary Cross Entropy (BCE) loss function:

$$L = \sum_{i}^{L} \left(y_i \log p_i + (1 - y_i) \left(1 - \log p_i \right) \right) + \lambda ||\theta||^2 \quad (11)$$

Here, y is the vector representation of the ground truth (for instance $y = (1, 0, 0, 1, 0)$), and p is the estimated probability for each instance by softmax (the subscript i represents the i-th element of the vector). λ is the weight for L_2-regularization, and θ denotes the set of all parameters. In this paper, we combine dropout with L_2 regularization to alleviate overfitting.

Inspired by the idea that the co-occurrence relationship between labels may have a significant impact on the prediction of labels, we further proposed to incorporate the label correlations into the BCE loss.

As shown in Fig. 2, we found that if the co-occurrence frequency between i-th label and j-th label is high we can think that these two labels are more likely to appear together. On this basis, the union loss function is defined as:

$$L = \sum_{i}^{L} \left(y_i \log p_i + (1 - y_i) \left(1 - \log p_i \right) \right) + \lambda_1 \sum_{i,j}^{L} m_{i,j} ||t_i - t_j||^2 + \lambda_2 ||\theta||^2 \quad (12)$$

Here, $m_{i,j}$ is the co-occurrence frequency between i-th label and j-th label. The behind motivation is that if the two labels are highly correlated, we hope the two label embeddings remain similar.

4 Experiments

4.1 Datasets

In this paper, we evaluate our model on two datasets.

Arxiv Academic Paper Dataset (AAPD): This dataset is provided by Yang et al. [15]. They collected the abstract and the corresponding subjects of 55840 papers in the computer science field from the arxiv website. An academic paper may have multiple subjects and there are 54 subjects in total. The target is to predict corresponding subjects of an academic paper according to the content of the abstract.

Reuters Corpus Volume I (RCV1-V2): This dataset is provided by Glewis et al. [16]. It consists of over 800000 manually categorized newswire stories made available by Reuters Ltd for research purposes. Multiple topics can be assigned to each newswire story and there are 103 topics in total.

We divide each dataset into training, validation and test sets as [15]. The statistics of the two datasets are shown in Table 1. Total Samples, Label Sets denote the total number of samples and labels, respectively. Words/Sample is the average number of words per sample and Labels/Sample is the average number of labels per sample.

Table 1. Summary of datasets

Dataset	Total Samples	Label Sets	Words/Sample	Labels/Sample
AAPD	55840	54	163.42	2.41
RCV1-V2	804414	103	123.94	3.24

4.2 Evaluation Metrics

We use four evaluation metrics which is widely used in multi-label learning in this paper, i.e., hamming loss [17], micro-precision, micro-recall, micro-F1 score [18]. For hamming loss, a lower value indicates a better performance. For the last three metrics, the higher the metric value is, the better the performance is.

4.3 Experimental Details

For both of the datasets, the dimension of word embedding vectors is set as 300 and the size of hidden layer is set as 200. We extract the vocabulary from the training sets. For the AAPD dataset, the size of the vocabulary is 32872 and out-of-vocabulary (OOV) words are randomly initialized. Each document is truncated at the length of 250.

For the RCV1-V2 dataset, the size of the vocabulary is 49128 and OOV words are randomly initialized. Each document is truncated at the length of 500.

All weight matrices and bias are randomly initialized by a uniform distribution $U(-0.1, 0.1)$. TensorFlow is used to implement our neural network model. In model training, learning rate is set as 0.001, L_2-norm regularization is set as 1e-4, the parameter λ_1 are set as 0.1 and 0.025 on two datasets, respectively. We use the stochastic gradient descent (SGD) algorithm and Adam update rule with shuffled mini-batch for parameter optimization.

4.4 Experimental Results

We compare our proposed methods with Binary Relevance (BR) [1], Classifier Chains (CC) [2], Label Powerset (LP) [7], CNN [19], CNN-RNN [6], SGM and SGM+GE [15]. The compared algorithms are shown as follows:

- **BR** decomposes the MLC task into some independent binary classification problems which does not take label correlations into consideration.
- **CC** transforms the MLC task into a chain of binary classification problems which considers the label correlations.
- **LP** transforms the MLC task into a multi-class (single-label) classification problem.
- **CNN** uses a simple CNN with one layer of convolution to extract sentence feature.
- **CNN − RNN** utilizes an ensemble application of convolutional and recurrent neural networks that is capable of efficiently representing textual features.

- **SGM** uses a sequence generation model with a novel decoder structure to solve the MLC task.
- **SGM + GE** is derived on the basis of SGM. To alleviate exposure bias, it optimizes combination of the original embedding and the weighted average embedding by using transform gate.

Table 2 compares our LSABN model with other baseline methods of multi-label classification on the AAPD dataset. Table 3 compares our LSABN model with other baseline methods of multi-label classification on the RCV1-V2 dataset.

Table 2. Experimental results in comparison with all baseline methods on the AAPD dataset. '↓' means that the smaller the value is, the better the performance is. '↑' is the opposite. Boldface highlights the best performance.

Models	Hamming loss(↓)	Precision(↑)	Recall(↑)	Micro F1-score(↑)
BR	0.0316	0.644	0.648	0.646
CC	0.0306	0.657	0.651	0.654
LP	0.0312	0.662	0.608	0.634
CNN	0.0256	**0.849**	0.545	0.664
CNN-RNN	0.0278	0.718	0.618	0.664
SGM	0.0251	0.746	0.659	0.699
SGM+GE	0.0245	0.748	0.675	0.710
LSABN	**0.0229**	0.766	**0.698**	**0.729**

Table 3. Experimental results in comparison with all baseline methods on the RCV1-V2 dataset. '↓' means that the smaller the value is, the better the performance is. '↑' is the opposite. Boldface highlights the best performance.

Models	Hamming loss(↓)	Precision(↑)	Recall(↑)	Micro F1-score(↑)
BR	0.0086	0.904	0.816	0.858
CC	0.0087	0.887	0.828	0.857
LP	0.0087	0.896	0.824	0.858
CNN	0.0089	**0.922**	0.798	0.855
CNN-RNN	0.0085	0.889	0.825	0.856
SGM	0.0081	0.887	0.850	0.869
SGM+GE	0.0075	0.897	0.860	0.878
LSABN	**0.0068**	0.892	**0.887**	**0.889**

From Tables 2 and 3, the fact is that the differences between LSABN and the compared models are statistically significant. On the AAPD dataset, we can

Table 4. The performance of LSABN and two reduced versions of LSABN on the AAPD dataset. '↓' means that the smaller the value is, the better the performance is. '↑' is the opposite. Boldface highlights the best performance.

Models	Hamming loss(↓)	Precision(↑)	Recall(↑)	Micro F1-score(↑)
LSABN	**0.0229**	**0.766**	**0.698**	**0.729**
LSABN-S-Att	0.0241	0.745	0.696	0.719
LSABN-No-RLoss	0.0236	0.753	0.696	0.724

Table 5. The performance of LSABN and two reduced versions of LSABN on the RCV1-V2 dataset. '↓' means that the smaller the value is, the better the performance is. '↑' is the opposite. Boldface highlights the best performance.

Models	Hamming loss(↓)	Precision(↑)	Recall(↑)	Micro F1-score(↑)
LSABN	**0.0068**	0.892	**0.887**	**0.889**
LSABN-S-Att	0.0073	**0.902**	0.856	0.879
LSABN-No-RLoss	0.0071	0.891	0.880	0.885

find that the LP model is the worst, and CNN and CNN-RNN model perform better than tradition models, such as BR, CC, LP. Among all the baseline methods, SGM+GE performs the best. However, our model improves the SGM+GE method with an significant improvement in all four evaluation metrics, i.e., 1.6% reduction in hamming loss, 1.8% increase in precision, 2.3% increase in recall and 1.9% increase in micro F1-score. On the RCV1-V2 dataset, the difference is smaller than above. But compare to SGM+GE model, we still can get 0.8% reduction in hamming loss, 0.5% increase in precision, 2.7% increase in recall and 1.1% increase in micro F1-score.

In short, it can be observed that our LSABN model performs consistently the best on almost all evaluation measures. The improvements are significant on the two datasets.

4.5 Ablation Study

In order to verify the effectiveness of our model and find out if every part of our model has contribution, we design the following two models:

(1) LSABN-S-Att model is a simplified version of LSABN, where we remove the attention and just use the hidden state vector to produce attention vector.
(2) LSABN-No-RLoss just utilizes the BCE loss function, which has not incorporated the label correlations.

Table 4 shows the performances of all these models on the AAPD dataset. Table 5 shows the performances of all these models on the RCV1-V2 dataset.

From the Tables 4 and 5, we can see that the LSABN-S-Att model performs much worse than LSABN. The results verify that the LSABN model may capture more important words than the self attention model. Experimental results on the LSABN-No-RLoss model prove that utilizing the co-occurrence matrix leads to performance improvement for multi-label text classification. In summary, label-specific attention mechanism contributes more than label relations in our model.

5 Conclusion

In this paper, we propose a Label-specific Attention-based Network (LSABN) for multi-label classification. Unlike existing multi-label learning neural networks, our model considers the fact that different words in a document do not contribute equally to predicting labels. In addition, we add the label information into text representations which can better select the most informative words for predicting labels. Furthermore, the label co-occurrence prior is also utilized to capture the correlations between labels. The experimental results on AAPD and RCV1-V2 datasets show that our model yields a significant performance gain compared to both traditional multi-label classification methods and the representative neural network models.

Acknowledgments. This paper is supported by the National Key Research and Development Program of China (Grant No. 2018YFB1403400), the National Natural Science Foundation of China (Grant No. 61876080), the Collaborative Innovation Center of Novel Software Technology and Industrialization at Nanjing University.

References

1. Boutell, M.R., Luo, J., Shen, X., Brown, C.M.: Learning multi-label scene classification. Pattern Recogn. **37**(9), 1757–1771 (2004)
2. Read, J., Pfahringer, B., Holmes, G., Frank, E.: Classifier chains for multi-label classification. Mach. Learn. **85**(3), 333 (2011)
3. Elisseeff, A., Weston, J.: A kernel method for multi-labelled classification. In: Advances in Neural Information Processing Systems, pp. 681–687 (2002)
4. Fürnkranz, J., Hüllermeier, E., Mencía, E.L., Brinker, K.: Multilabel classification via calibrated label ranking. Mach. Learn. **73**(2), 133–153 (2008)
5. Kurata, G., Xiang, B., Zhou, B.: Improved neural network-based multi-label classification with better initialization leveraging label co-occurrence. In: Proceedings of the 2016 Conference of the North American Chapter of the Association for Computational Linguistics: Human Language Technologies, pp. 521–526 (2016)
6. Chen, G., Ye, D., Xing, Z., Chen, J., Cambria, E.: Ensemble application of convolutional and recurrent neural networks for multi-label text categorization. In: 2017 International Joint Conference on Neural Networks (IJCNN), pp. 2377–2383. IEEE (2017)
7. Tsoumakas, G., Katakis, I.: Multi-label classification: an overview. Int. J. Data Warehouse. Min. (IJDWM) **3**(3), 1–13 (2007)
8. Zhang, M.-L., Zhou, Z.-H.: ML-KNN: a lazy learning approach to multi-label learning. Pattern Recogn. **40**(7), 2038–2048 (2007)
9. Ghamrawi, N., McCallum, A.: Collective multi-label classification. In: Proceedings of the 14th ACM International Conference on Information and Knowledge Management, pp. 195–200. ACM (2005)

10. Zhang, M.-L., Zhou, Z.-H.: Multilabel neural networks with applications to functional genomics and text categorization. IEEE Trans. Knowl. Data Eng. **18**(10), 1338–1351 (2006)
11. Nam, J., Kim, J., Loza Mencía, E., Gurevych, I., Fürnkranz, J.: Large-scale multi-label text classification — revisiting neural networks. In: Calders, T., Esposito, F., Hüllermeier, E., Meo, R. (eds.) ECML PKDD 2014. LNCS (LNAI), vol. 8725, pp. 437–452. Springer, Heidelberg (2014). https://doi.org/10.1007/978-3-662-44851-9_28
12. Lin, Z., et al.: A structured self-attentive sentence embedding. CoRR, abs/1703.03130 (2017)
13. Hochreiter, S., Schmidhuber, J.: Long short-term memory. Neural Comput. **9**(8), 1735–1780 (1997)
14. Zhou, P., et al.: Attention-based bidirectional long short-term memory networks for relation classification. In: Proceedings of the 54th Annual Meeting of the Association for Computational Linguistics (Volume 2: Short Papers), vol. 2, pp. 207–212 (2016)
15. Yang, P., Sun, X., Li, W., Ma, S., Wu, W., Wang, H.: SGM: sequence generation model for multi-label classification. In: Proceedings of the 27th International Conference on Computational Linguistics, pp. 3915–3926 (2018)
16. Glewis, Y.Y.R.T.G., David, D., Li, F.: A new benchmark collection for text categorization research. J. Mach. Learn. Res. (2004)
17. Schapire, R.E., Singer, Y.: Improved boosting algorithms using confidence-rated predictions. Mach. Learn. **37**(3), 297–336 (1999)
18. Manning, C., Raghavan, P., Schütze, H.: Introduction to information retrieval. Nat. Lang. Eng. **16**(1), 100–103 (2010)
19. Kim, Y.: Convolutional neural networks for sentence classification. In: Proceedings of the 2014 Conference on Empirical Methods in Natural Language Processing (EMNLP), pp. 1746–1751 (2014)

An Empirical Study of Multi-domain and Multi-task Learning in Chinese Named Entity Recognition

Yun Hu[1,2(✉)], Mingxue Liao[2], Pin Lv[2], and Changwen Zheng[2]

[1] University of Chinese Academy of Sciences, Beijing, China
[2] Institute of Software, Chinese Academy of Sciences, Beijing, China
{huyun2016,mingxue,lvpin,changwen}@iscas.ac.cn

Abstract. Named entity recognition (NER) often suffers from lack of annotation data. Multi-domain and multi-task learning solve this problem in some degree. However, previous multi-domain and multi-task learning are often studied in English. In the other part, multi-domain and multi-task learning are often researched independently. In this manuscript, we first summarize the previous works of multi-domain and multi-task learning in NER. Then, we introduce the multi-domain and multi-task learning in Chinese NER. Finally, we explore the universal models between multi-domain and multi-task learning. Experiments show that the universal models can be used in Chinese NER and outperform the baseline model.

Keywords: Chinese named entity recognition · Multi-domain learning · Multi-task learning

1 Introduction

Name entity recognition is a fundamental Natural Language Processing task. The NER system labels each word in sentences with predefined types, such as Person (PER), Location (LOC), Organization (ORG) and so on. The results of NER can be used in many downstream NLP tasks, such as question answering [27] and relation extraction [1]. The neural network methods [4,10] are used to realize the NER system recently. Large annotated data is required in neural network methods. However, the annotated data is usually scarce.

In order to improve the performance of NER system in low resource, multi-domain and multi-task methods are often used [2,7,18,26]. Multi-domain learning tries to transfer information from the source domain to the target domain [7]. Multi-task learning tries to transfer information from the source task to the target task [2].

There existing some challenges in previous works. First, most of the previous models only test in English. Can the models work well in Chinese NER? For example, the tasks are part-of-speech (POS) tagging and named entity recognition in English

The work is supported by both National scientific and Technological Innovation Zero (No. 17-H863-01-ZT-005-005-01) and State's Key Project of Research and Development Plan (No. 2016QY03D0505).

I. V. Tetko et al. (Eds.): ICANN 2019, LNCS 11728, pp. 743–754, 2019.
https://doi.org/10.1007/978-3-030-30484-3_58

multi-task learning [4], however, the tasks are Chinese Word Segmentation (CWS) and named entity recognition in Chinese multi-task learning [17]. Second, previous works often consider the multi-domain methods and multi-task methods separately. For example, Cao et al. only consider the multi-task learning [2]. Can the multi-task models be directly used in multi-domain, vice versa?

In this manuscript, we do an empirical study in Chinese NER. First, we summarize the previous multi-domain and multi-task models according to the model architecture. The neural network methods are considered in this manuscript. Second, we suppose that the multi-domain and multi-task learning methods are independent of languages. We use Chinese social media domain as the target domain and Chinese news domain as the source domain. The Chinese NER task is the target task and CWS task is the source task. These domains and tasks are similar and the information can be transferred. Third, we suppose that the methods used in multi-domain and multi-task are similar. The methods come from transfer learning. The methods used in multi-domain can be directly used in multi-task, vice versa. In other words, the model architecture is not required to be changed when the model is used in multi-domain or in multi-task, and only the data is required to be changed. Three types of universal model architectures are demonstrated: SHA (share model), FEAT (feature used model) and ADV (adversarial network model). Experiments show that the universal models are useful in Chinese NER and outperform the baseline model.

Specifically, we make contributions as follows:

- We summarize the previous multi-domain and multi-task models in NER.
- We explore the performance of the multi-domain and multi-task methods in Chinese NER task.
- We demonstrate three types of universal model architectures in multi-domain and multi-task learning.

2 Overview

2.1 Previous Summaries of NER

The existing surveys mainly focus on summarizing the methods used in named entity recognition, including supervised, semi-supervised, and unsupervised methods [14,20]. Yadav et al. provided recent advances in NER from deep learning models [25]. The transfer learning surveys mainly focus on general methods in multi-domain and multi-task learning [15]. Tan et al. presented a survey of deep transfer learning [21]. Compared with the previous summaries of NER, we focus on multi-domain and multi-task learning in Chinese NER.

2.2 Domains and Tasks in Multi-domain and Multi-task NER

Previous works show that multi-domain and multi-task learning improve the performance of English NER [4,12]. In multi-domain and multi-task learning, the target domains and tasks are often similar to the source domains and tasks. In English, the target domain is often twitter domain and the source domain is news domain. The target task is NER and the source task is chunk or POS. In this manuscript, the source domain is Chinese news domain, and the target domain is Chinese weibo domain. The source task is CWS, and the target task is NER. An example is shown in Fig. 1. We suppose that Chinese weibo NER is similar to Chinese news NER. The weibo NER and news NER are the same task and use different domain data. Some tokens and labels are the same in two domains. For example, the "洛阳机场" is labeled as "LOC" in both news and weibo domains. We suppose that CWS task is similar to the NER. The CWS and NER all belong to sequence labeling task. CWS tries to find the word boundary. For example, "洛阳机场" is an independent word. NER tries to find the word boundary and types. For example, "洛阳机场" is seen as an independent word and the entity type of "洛阳机场" is "LOC".

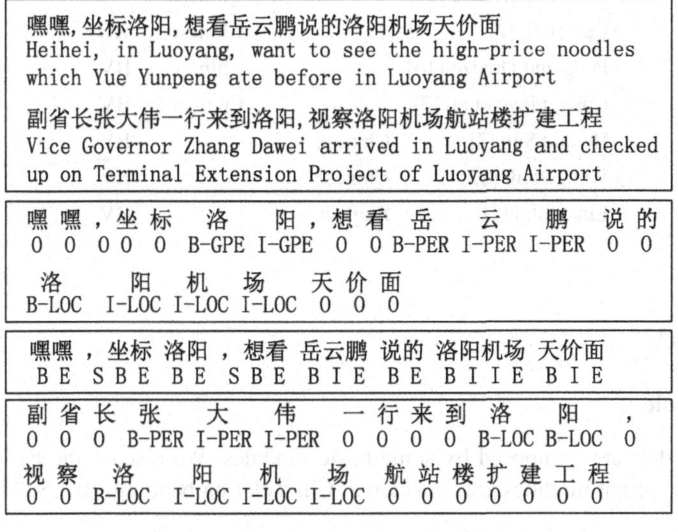

Fig. 1. The first block is the Chinese-English translation pair for understanding. The second block is from weibo NER. The third block is from weibo CWS. The fourth block is from news NER.

2.3 Methods in Multi-domain and Multi-task NER

A list of neural multi-domain and multi-task learning models are shown in Table 1. The multi-domain and multi-task models are divided into four types: SHA, FEAT, ADV and BV (variant of base model). The SHA model is prevalent in previous works [4,8,18, 26]. The multi-task learning of English named entity recognition was first proposed by Collobert et al. using neural network model [4]. Lee et al. trained the model using the source data and retrained the model using the target data [8]. Yang et al. explored the transferring module in multi-domain and multi-task separately [26]. Peng and Dredze used domain projection and specific task Conditional Random Fields (CRF) combining the multi-domain and multi-task [18]. The FEAT model was first proposed by [17] used for multi-task in NER. Cao et al. used the adversarial network to integrate the task-shared word boundary information into Chinese NER task [2]. The BV models are variant of base model. The BV models can not be directly used between multi-domain and multi-task.

Table 1. A summary of the multi-domain and multi-task learning.

	Multi-domain	Multi-task	Model
Yang et al. [26]	English	English	SHA
Peng and Dredze [18]	Chinese	Chinese	SHA
Lee et al. [8]	English	–	SHA
Collobert et al. [4]	–	English	SHA
Peng and Dredze [17]	–	Chinese	FEAT
Cao et al. [2]	–	Chinese	ADV
Peng and Dredze [16]	–	Chinese	BV
Changpinyo et al. [3]	–	English	BV
He and Sun [7]	Chinese	–	BV
Wang et al. [22]	Chinese	–	BV
Lin et al. [12]	English	–	BV

3 Model

3.1 Module

All the models are composed by some basic modules. We discuss the basic modules first. Four types of modules are considered: Character embedding, Bi-LSTM, CRF and Classifier.

Character Embedding. Character embedding is the first step of neural network models in Chinese NER. Character embedding is similar to the word embedding in English. For example, "洛" is a character and is mapped to a low dimension vector in Character embedding layer. Pre-trained character embedding is often used to utilize the information from the large unannotated data. For a sequence of character $c = \{x_1, x_2, ..., x_n\}$, we obtain $x = \{e_{x_1}, e_{x_2}, ..., e_{x_n}\}$ though looking up pre-trained character embedding.

Bi-LSTM. Bi-LSTM is used to extract the features from the sentence. The Bi-LSTM concatenates the forward LSTM output and backward LSTM output as the final output and can capture the information of a character from right context and left context [6].

A common LSTM unit is composed of a cell, an input gate, an output gate and a forget gate. The implementations of LSTM are as follows:

$$i_t = \sigma(W_i h_{t-1} + U_i e_{x_t} + b_i) \tag{1}$$
$$f_t = \sigma(W_f h_{t-1} + U_f e_{x_t} + b_f) \tag{2}$$
$$\tilde{c_t} = tanh(W_c h_{t-1} + U_c e_{x_t} + b_c) \tag{3}$$
$$c_t = f_t \odot c_{t-1} + i_t \odot \tilde{c_t} \tag{4}$$
$$o_t = \sigma(W_o h_{t-1} + U_o e_{x_t} + b_o) \tag{5}$$
$$h_t = o_t \odot tanh(c_t) \tag{6}$$

where e_{x_t} is the input vector at time t, h_t is the output of LSTM model, σ is the element-wise sigmoid function, and $\odot$ is the element-wise product.

CRF. The CRF is used to predict the label sequence $y = \{y_1, y_2, ..., y_n\}$. The CRF uses the feature extracted by the Bi-LSTM and considers the neighborhood information in a sequence to make prediction. We define the source s of the sentence when X is used as the input sequence list and y is used as the output NER tag list:

$$s(X, y) = \sum_{i=0}^{n} A_{y_i, y_{i+1}} + \sum_{i=1}^{n} P_{h_i, y_i} \tag{7}$$

where $A_{y_i, y_{i+1}}$ describes the cost from tag y_i transferring to y_{i+1}, and P represents the probability from h_i predicting the tag y_i. The probability of tag sequences can be represented as:

$$P(y|X) = \frac{e^{s(X,Y)}}{\sum_{\tilde{y} \in Y_{all}} e^{s(X,\tilde{y})}} \tag{8}$$

where $\tilde{y}$ is the possible NER tags and Y_{all} is all the possible NER tags. When the model is trained, we maximize the log-probability of the correct sequence:

$$logP(y|X) = s(X, y) - log(\sum_{\tilde{y}} e^{s(X,\tilde{y})}) \tag{9}$$

When the model is tested, we can obtain the best NER tag sequence y^* by:

$$y^* = \underset{\tilde{y} \in Y_{all}}{\text{argmax}}\, s(X, \tilde{y}) \tag{10}$$

Classifier. For the multi-domain models, the classifier discriminates the sentence from news domain or weibo domain. For the multi-task models, the classifier discriminates the sentence from NER or CWS. The classifier contains maxpooling and softmax.

$$h = Maxpooling(H) \tag{11}$$
$$D(h, \theta_d) = softmax(W_d h + b_d) \tag{12}$$

where H is the feature representation of the sentences and θ_d is the parameters in softmax, including W_d and b_d.

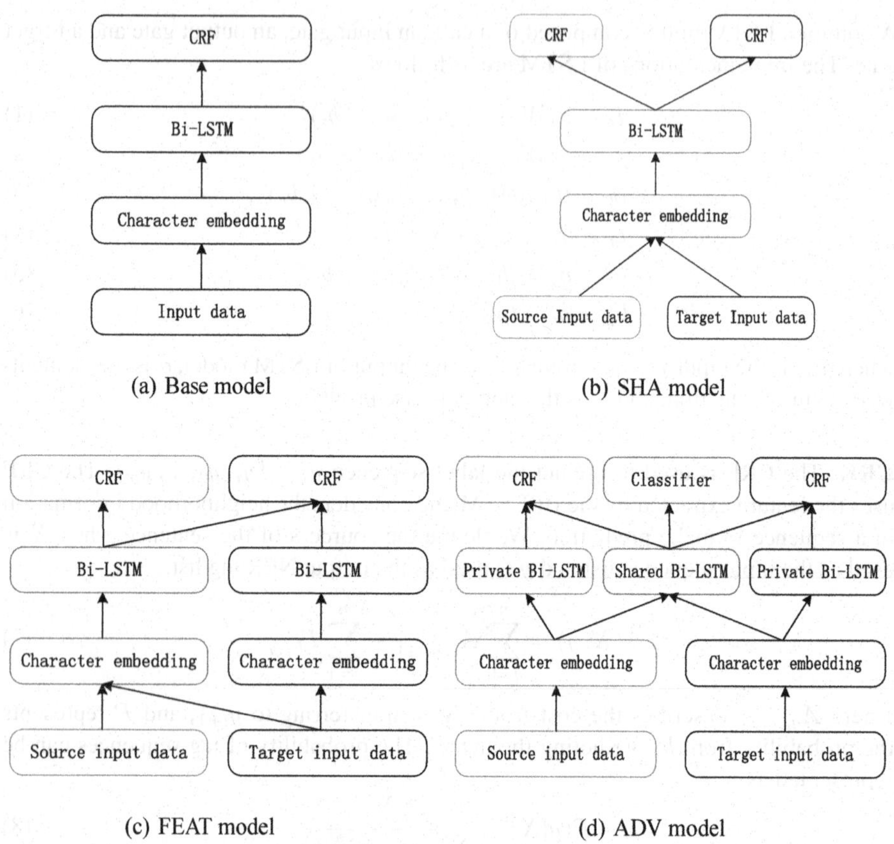

(a) Base model

(b) SHA model

(c) FEAT model

(d) ADV model

Fig. 2. Four types of architectures in multi-domain and multi-task learning. The blue block is source part, the black block is target part, and the red block is the share part. (Color figure online)

3.2 Base Model

We use LSTM-CRF model as the base model which is widely used for a single domain and task NER [5, 10]. The architecture of the model is shown in Fig. 2(a). The model contains three parts. The character embedding part is used to utilize the word level features from the large unannotated data. The Bi-LSTM is used to extract the sentence level features. The features are fed into CRF to predict the sequence labels. Compared with the multi-domain and multi-task model, the LSTM-CRF model is a single task and domain model, which only uses weibo NER dataset as input.

3.3 Multi-domain and Multi-task Model

Multi-domain and multi-task methods are shown to improve the single task and domain NER performance. However, most of the models only focus on English NER.

In the other part, most of the models are only used in one specific situation: in multi-domain learning or in multi-task learning. In this manuscript, we do an empirical study in 3 types of Chinese named entity recognition models: SHA, FEAT and ADV. For the specificity of the BV model, we will do the experiments in the future. In the multi-domain and multi-task model, the models use two types of data as inputs. For the multi-domain model, the weibo NER dataset and news NER dataset are used. For the multi-task model, the weibo NER dataset and weibo CWS dataset are used.

SHA. The SHA model shares the feature extractor between different tasks or domains [4,8,18,26]. The feature extractor trained by source data can contain useful information for target task or domain. The architecture of the SHA model is shown in Fig. 2(b). The character embedding layer and the Bi-LSTM layer are shared. Different domains or tasks have specific CRFs. With different training methods, the SHA model can be divided into three different sub-models.

SHA-INIT. The training method is divided into two steps. First, the model uses the source data as the input to train the model until convergence. In the second step, target data is fed as the input of the model to continually train until convergence. Two steps use different CRFs. The parameters in character embedding layer and the Bi-LSTM layer are all updated in two steps.

SHA-CRF. The training method is the same as SHA-INIT except for the second step. In the second step, the parameters of character embedding and Bi-LSTM layer are frozen and we only update the parameters in CRF layer.

SHA-MUL. The model trains the source data and target data simultaneously. In one epoch, source data and target data are fed to the model alternatively. A hyper-parameter α can be used to control the size between source data and target data.

FEAT. The FEAT model supposes that the features extracted by the source part can be used as auxiliary information for the target part [17]. The architecture of the model is shown in Fig. 2(c). The target part uses the intermedia results of the source part. The Bi-LSTM output of the target part is concatenated with the output of the source part before being fed into CRF layer. Three different training methods lead to three sub-models.

FEAT-INIT. The model first uses the source data to train a base model. Then, the source part of the model is initialized by the pre-trained model. Finally, the target data is used to train the model. All parameters are updated in the model.

FEAT-CRF. The training method is the same as FEAT-INIT except for the final parameters updating step. In the FEAT-CRF model, the source part is initialized by the pre-trained model and then the parameters are frozen. The model only updates the target part parameters.

FEAT-MUL. The source part and the target part are trained alternatively. When the source data is used as input, the parameters in the source part are updated. When the target data is used as input, the parameters in the source part and target part are updated.

ADV. The ADV model uses the private feature extractor extracts the private information, and uses the shared feature extractor extract the shared information [2]. The architecture of the model is shown in Fig. 2(d). The model uses private character embedding,

Bi-LSTM and CRF to capture the different information between source domain and target domain, and uses shared Bi-LSTM to capture the common information between source domain and target domain. Character embedding tries to capture the word level representation. Bi-LSTM tries to extract the sentence level feature representation of the words. The classifier tries to guarantee that specific features of tasks do not exist in shared space. The source data and target data are fed to the model alternatively.

BV. The BV models are the models that can not find the universal models in multi-domain and multi-task learning [3,7,12,22]. For example, Wang et al. required the source domain and the target domain has the same label sets [22]. However, different tasks have different label sets. Lin et al. used a domain adaptation layer to reduce the disparity between different pre-trained character embeddings [12]. However, pre-trained embeddings are the same in different tasks.

4 Experiments and Results

4.1 Datasets

The Chinese weibo NER corpus is from [16]. The Chinese news NER corpus is from Sighan NER [11]. The Chinese weibo word segmentation corpus is from [19]. The sentence numbers of the different corpora are shown in Table 2.

Table 2. The details of the corpora.

	#Train	#Dev	#Test
Weibo NER	1350	270	270
News NER	16814	1868	4636
Weibo CWS	38086	3834	16673

4.2 Parameters Setting

The character embedding is initialized by pre-trained character embedding. The news embedding is pre-trained on Chinese Wikipedia data using word2vec [13]. The weibo embedding is pretrained on Chinese social media data using word2vec. The embedding dimension is 100. The LSTM dimension in both source and target part are 100. The optimization method we used is adam [9].

4.3 Results

The overview results of Chinese weibo NER are shown in Table 3. The results show that the multi-domain and multi-task learning can be used in Chinese named entity recognition. The FEAT and ADV models can always outperform the baseline model. The SHA-CRF model obtains the worst F1 score which is far worse than the baseline model. The reason may be that the CRF is hard to process the features extracted by a source feature extractor. Meanwhile, the experiments show that multi-domain and multi-task learning can use the universal models. The same model architecture can directly be used in both multi-domain and multi-task learning.

Table 3. The overview results of multi-domain and multi-task learning in Chinese weibo NER. P represents precision, R represents recall, and F represents F1 score.

	Multi-domain			Multi-task		
	P	R	F	P	R	F
Base	56.07	44.50	49.62	56.07	44.50	49.62
SHA-INIT	58.06	41.28	48.25	62.00	42.66	50.54
SHA-CRF	65.52	17.43	27.53	69.49	18.81	29.61
SHA-MUL	61.64	46.39	52.94	60.65	48.45	53.87
FEAT-INIT	53.55	49.11	51.23	62.93	44.13	51.88
FEAT-CRF	59.64	45.41	51.56	62.24	46.77	53.41
FEAT-MUL	59.86	45.36	51.61	61.39	50.00	55.11
ADV	57.06	52.06	54.45	60.92	47.42	53.33

In Table 4, we make a survey in the performance of previous works in Chinese weibo NER. Compared with previous performances, the three types of models achieve competitive results.

Table 4. The performance of previous Chinese weibo NER models.

	P	R	F	Model
Peng and Dredze [17]	66.67	47.22	55.28	FEAT
Cao et al. [2]	59.51	50.00	54.34	ADV
Peng and Dredze [16]	74.78	39.81	51.96	BV
He and Sun [7]	52.94	51.18	52.05	BV

To show the generalization of the models in Chinese NER, the Ontonote NER dataset is also tested [23]. The broadcast news domain is used as the source domain, and the web text domain is used as the target domain. The Chinese weibo word segmentation is used as the source task, and the Chinese Ontonote web text named entity recognition is used as the target task. The broadcast news data contains 10083 sentences, and the web text contains 8405 sentences. In Table 5, the results show that the universal models can be used in different datasets.

5 Discussion

Experiments show that the multi-domain and multi-task learning can improve the performance of Chinese NER. More works can be done in the future.

Table 5. The overview results of multi-domain and multi-task learning in Ontonote dataset.

	Multi-domain			Multi-task		
	P	R	F	P	R	F
Base	48.23	44.60	46.34	48.23	44.60	46.34
SHA-INIT	48.39	43.45	45.79	47.84	44.26	45.98
SHA-CRF	36.34	25.17	29.74	30.31	19.43	23.68
SHA-MUL	59.78	55.24	57.42	62.93	44.85	52.37
FEAT-INIT	52.79	49.49	51.09	51.56	47.70	49.55
FEAT-CRF	51.90	51.15	51.52	52.45	47.75	49.99
FEAT-MUL	53.32	58.37	55.73	57.24	45.52	50.71
ADV	55.40	55.60	55.50	50.56	50.47	50.51

First, Chinese specific features can be considered in multi-domain and multi-task learning. In this manuscript, we only use the Chinese models which is similar to the English models. Some Chinese specific features are shown very helpful in Chinese NER, such as radical feature [5], glyph representation of Chinese character [24]. We will explore these features in multi-domain and multi-task learning.

Second, the BV model can be universal model through small changes. For example, some models require the same labels in source and target domain. The requirement can extend to that the source and target domain labels are related. The model architecture required small changes in the future.

Third, the multi-domain and multi-task have high similarity. Two works can be combined together. For example, Peng and Dredze used domain projection and specific task CRF combining the multi-domain and multi-task [18]. However, the Peng and Dredze only processed the situation that the domains have the same label sets. In the future, more general models could be considered.

6 Conclusion

In this manuscript, we focus on utilizing Chinese news domain information and Chinese word segmentation information to improve the performance of Chinese weibo named entity recognition by multi-domain and multi-task learning. Three types of universal model architectures are explored. Experiments show that the universal models outperform the baseline model.

References

1. Bunescu, R., Mooney, R.: A shortest path dependency kernel for relation extraction. In: Proceedings of Human Language Technology Conference and Conference on Empirical Methods in Natural Language Processing (2005). http://aclweb.org/anthology/H05-1091
2. Cao, P., Chen, Y., Liu, K., Zhao, J., Liu, S.: Adversarial transfer learning for Chinese named entity recognition with self-attention mechanism. In: Proceedings of the 2018 Conference on Empirical Methods in Natural Language Processing, pp. 182–192. Association for Computational Linguistics (2018). http://aclweb.org/anthology/D18-1017
3. Changpinyo, S., Hu, H., Sha, F.: Multi-task learning for sequence tagging: an empirical study. In: Proceedings of the 27th International Conference on Computational Linguistics, pp. 2965–2977. Association for Computational Linguistics (2018). http://aclweb.org/anthology/C18-1251
4. Collobert, R., Weston, J., Bottou, L., Karlen, M., Kavukcuoglu, K., Kuksa, P.: Natural language processing (almost) from scratch. J. Mach. Learn. Res. **12**(Aug), 2493–2537 (2011). http://dl.acm.org/citation.cfm?id=2078186
5. Dong, C., Zhang, J., Zong, C., Hattori, M., Di, H.: Character-based LSTM-CRF with radical-level features for chinese named entity recognition. In: Lin, C.-Y., Xue, N., Zhao, D., Huang, X., Feng, Y. (eds.) ICCPOL/NLPCC -2016. LNCS (LNAI), vol. 10102, pp. 239–250. Springer, Cham (2016). https://doi.org/10.1007/978-3-319-50496-4_20
6. Graves, A., Schmidhuber, J.: Framewise phoneme classification with bidirectional LSTM networks. In: 2005 IEEE International Joint Conference on Neural Networks, IJCNN 2005, Proceedings, vol. 4, pp. 2047–2052 (2005). https://doi.org/10.1016/j.neunet.2005.06.042
7. He, H., Sun, X.: A unified model for cross-domain and semi-supervised named entity recognition in Chinese social media. In: AAAI, pp. 3216–3222 (2017). http://aaai.org/ocs/index.php/AAAI/AAAI17/paper/view/14484
8. Ji, Y.L., Dernoncourt, F., Szolovits, P.: Transfer learning for named-entity recognition with neural networks (2017). http://www.lrec-conf.org/proceedings/lrec2018/summaries/878.html
9. Kingma, D.P., Ba, J.: Adam: a method for stochastic optimization. Comput. Sci. (2014). http://arxiv.org/abs/1412.6980
10. Lample, G., Ballesteros, M., Subramanian, S., Kawakami, K., Dyer, C.: Neural architectures for named entity recognition. In: Proceedings of the 2016 Conference of the North American Chapter of the Association for Computational Linguistics: Human Language Technologies, pp. 260–270. Association for Computational Linguistics (2016). https://doi.org/10.18653/v1/N16-1030
11. Levow, G.A.: The third international Chinese language processing bakeoff: word segmentation and named entity recognition. In: Proceedings of the Fifth SIGHAN Workshop on Chinese Language Processing, pp. 108–117. Association for Computational Linguistics (2006). http://www.aclweb.org/anthology/W06-0115
12. Lin, B.Y., Lu, W.: Neural adaptation layers for cross-domain named entity recognition. In: Proceedings of the 2018 Conference on Empirical Methods in Natural Language Processing, pp. 2012–2022. Association for Computational Linguistics (2018). http://aclweb.org/anthology/D18-1226
13. Mikolov, T., Sutskever, I., Chen, K., Corrado, G.S., Dean, J.: Distributed representations of words and phrases and their compositionality. In: Advances in Neural Information Processing Systems, pp. 3111–3119 (2013)
14. Nadeau, D., Sekine, S.: A survey of named entity recognition and classification. Lingvisticae Investigationes **30**(1), 3–26 (2007)

15. Pan, S.J., Yang, Q.: A survey on transfer learning. IEEE Trans. Knowl. Data Eng. **22**(10), 1345–1359 (2010)
16. Peng, N., Dredze, M.: Named entity recognition for Chinese social media with jointly trained embeddings. In: Proceedings of the 2015 Conference on Empirical Methods in Natural Language Processing, pp. 548–554. Association for Computational Linguistics (2015). http://www.aclweb.org/anthology/D15-1064, https://doi.org/10.18653/v1/D15-1064
17. Peng, N., Dredze, M.: Improving named entity recognition for Chinese social media with word segmentation representation learning. In: Proceedings of the 54th Annual Meeting of the Association for Computational Linguistics (Volume 2: Short Papers), pp. 149–155. Association for Computational Linguistics (2016). http://www.aclweb.org/anthology/P16-2025, https://doi.org/10.18653/v1/P16-2025
18. Peng, N., Dredze, M.: Multi-task domain adaptation for sequence tagging. In: Proceedings of the 2nd Workshop on Representation Learning for NLP, pp. 91–100. Association for Computational Linguistics (2017). http://aclweb.org/anthology/W17-2612
19. Qian, P., Qiu, X., Huang, X.: A new psychometric-inspired evaluation metric for Chinese word segmentation. In: Proceedings of the 54th Annual Meeting of the Association for Computational Linguistics (Volume 1: Long Papers), pp. 2185–2194. Association for Computational Linguistics (2016). http://www.aclweb.org/anthology/P16-1206, https://doi.org/10.18653/v1/P16-1206
20. Sharnagat, R.: Named entity recognition: a literature survey. Center For Indian Language Technology (2014)
21. Tan, C., Sun, F., Tao, K., Zhang, W., Chao, Y., Liu, C.: A survey on deep transfer learning, pp. 270–279 (2018). https://doi.org/10.1007/978-3-030-01424-7_27
22. Wang, Z., et al.: Label-aware double transfer learning for cross-specialty medical named entity recognition. In: Proceedings of the 2018 Conference of the North American Chapter of the Association for Computational Linguistics: Human Language Technologies, Volume 1 (Long Papers), pp. 1–15. Association for Computational Linguistics (2018). http://aclweb.org/anthology/N18-1001
23. Weischedel, R., et al.: Ontonotes release 5.0 ldc2013t19. Linguistic Data Consortium, Philadelphia (2013)
24. Wu, W., et al.: Glyce: Glyph-vectors for Chinese character representations. arXiv preprint arXiv:1901.10125 (2019)
25. Yadav, V., Bethard, S.: A survey on recent advances in named entity recognition from deep learning models. In: Proceedings of the 27th International Conference on Computational Linguistics, pp. 2145–2158. Association for Computational Linguistics (2018). http://aclweb.org/anthology/C18-1182
26. Yang, Z., Salakhutdinov, R., Cohen, W.W.: Transfer learning for sequence tagging with hierarchical recurrent networks (2017). https://openreview.net/forum?id=ByxpMd9lx
27. Yao, X., Van Durme, B.: Information extraction over structured data: Question answering with freebase. In: Proceedings of the 52nd Annual Meeting of the Association for Computational Linguistics (Volume 1: Long Papers), pp. 956–966. Association for Computational Linguistics (2014). https://doi.org/10.3115/v1/P14-1090

Filter Method Ensemble with Neural Networks

Anuran Chakraborty[1], Rajonya De[1], Agneet Chatterjee[1], Friedhelm Schwenker[2](✉), and Ram Sarkar[1]

[1] Jadavpur University, Kolkata, India
[2] Institute of Neural Information Processing, University of Ulm, Ulm, Germany
friedhelm.schwenker@uni-ulm.de

Abstract. The main concept behind designing a multiple classifier system is to combine a number of classifiers such that the resulting system succeeds to topple the individual classifiers by pooling together the decisions of all classifiers. Uniting relatively simple pattern recognition models with limited performance is commonly found in the literature. It performs better when each learner be trained well, but different learners have different working principles which adds diversity in the ensemble. In this paper, we first select three optimal subsets of features using three different filter methods namely Mutual Information (MI), Chi-square, and Anova F-Test. Then with the selected features we build three learning models using Multi-layer Perceptron (MLP) based classifier. Class membership values provided by these three classifiers for each sample are concatenated which is then fed to next MLP based classifier. Experimentation performed on five UCI Machine Learning Repository, namely Arrhythmia, Ionosphere, Hill-Valley, Waveform, Horse Colic shows the effectiveness of the proposed ensemble model.

Keywords: Ensemble · Neural networks · Feature selection

1 Introduction

An ensemble of classifiers combines individual decisions from base classifiers using unweighted or weighted procedures. The notion behind using ensembles is such that they prove to be more accurate in comparison to when individual classifiers are used on their own. It has been well-established in literature that an ensemble is more accurate when it is diverse is nature. This diversity is required to be maintained to ensure that the member classifiers do not make correlated errors, i.e. they do not make the same errors on the same dataset. This ensures that when these methods are combined, they, by some means of combination, provide the correct results. If diversity does not prevail, then an ensemble might even function worse than a single classifier. Dietterich [1] goes onto explain the statistical, computational and representational advantages of an ensemble. The first advantage is observed when the hypothesis space is too extensive to explore the limited training data. As a result, many hypotheses may give the same results on the training data. If a single such hypothesis is chosen, then the learner runs the risk of being misguided. A simple average voting reduces the chances of choosing an incorrect classification. The computational superiority is attained as starting the

I. V. Tetko et al. (Eds.): ICANN 2019, LNCS 11728, pp. 755–765, 2019.
https://doi.org/10.1007/978-3-030-30484-3_59

search from several different points, for finding the true unknown hypothesis, increases the chance of finding one and reduces the probability of the learner getting stuck at a local optimum. In many learning cases, the true hypothesis function cannot be represented in the search space. By using ensembles, the search space representation is expanded which gives the learning a better chance at approximation of the true hypothesis. The process of combining these individual classifier's decisions also plays an important part, as this phase decides the weightage given to each classifier. The weighted procedure might be static in nature, for example the usage of majority voting [2] or it might be dynamic as to use a meta-classifier [3] to choose which base learners are added to the ensemble at each stage. Kittler [4] explains the importance of using different training sets for the base classifiers. The different sets allow each classifier to interpret the data in its own way, therefore allowing the efficient exploration of the search space which would otherwise be not possible. Due to its robust nature, ensemble techniques have thereby been used in various domains such as financial decision applications [5], power demand prediction [6], bioinformatics [7] environmental sciences [8] and image processing [9].

Hereby, we propose a two-level neural network ensemble method, where which makes use of standard feature selection techniques, to ensure the best training samples for classification, at every step, followed by a Multi-Layer Perceptron ensemble, each of which are fitted by a unique training set sampled of the same dataset. This training process generates a matrix of class membership degrees per every MLP, which are then concatenated and used as an input to another MLP, which outputs the class label of the validation set. The method firstly, is robust in nature, because we only train the most optimized set of feature sets at every step and secondly, is shown to generate high classification accuracies, on a range of datasets, which vary in their number of classes as well as their feature lengths.

2 Preliminaries

In this section the feature selection methods used in the proposed method are described in brief.

2.1 Chi-square

The chi-square [10] statistics give a quantitative measure of the amount of dependence between a particular feature and the target class, and can be compared with chi-square distribution to judge the extremeness. If the feature assumes continuous values, it is discretized into intervals. The frequency of a class (may be due to the split) is then compared against the expected frequency. If we have a c – class problem and the range of values for the concerned feature has been split into I intervals, then the chi-square statistic is given by,

$$\chi^2 = \sum_{i=1}^{c}\sum_{j=1}^{I}\frac{\left(N_{ij} - E_{ij}\right)^2}{E_{ij}} \quad (1)$$

Here, N_{ij} represents the number of instances of class C_i in the interval j and E_{ij} is the expected number of samples, which is computed as $E_i = num * p_i$, where p_i is the probability of occurrence of event i and num is the total number of events. Higher the value of chi-square, higher is the level of dependence.

2.2 Mutual Information

Mutual information [11] between two random variables X and Y quantifies the reduction in uncertainty of the outcome of one random variable (X) upon knowing the outcome of the other random variable (Y), by determining how similar the joint distribution $p(X, Y)$ is to the products of the factored marginal distribution $p(X) * p(Y)$. It is intricately linked to the concept of entropy of a random variable.

2.3 Anova F-Test

The Analysis of Variance (ANOVA) and the F-Test is used to determine the variation present in a sample. The observed variance gives a measure of the well-spread nature of a particular component (or feature) of a dataset. ANOVA uses Sum of Squared Errors (SSE), Treatment sum of squares (SST) and Total Sum of Squares (TotalSS), to calculate the variance exhibited by a feature:

$$TotalSS = SSE + SST \tag{2}$$

$$Variance = SST/TotalSS \tag{3}$$

The SSE in ANOVA indicates the proportion of variance explained by the feature to the total variance in the data. The features that explain the largest proportion of the variance are retained as more informative entities.

The methods have been selected such that each function on different principles and are thus able to select different kind of features which capture different aspects of the dataset.

3 Proposed Method

We use a two-stage MLP architecture. Following gives a step-by-step overview of the model employed.

1. The entire dataset is divided into three disjoint sets of samples – a train set, a validation set and a test set. The train set is used for training the MLP1, MLP2 and MLP3 in the first stage. The validation set is used to train the MLP4 in the second stage. Finally, the test set is used to evaluate the performance of the whole ensemble. Figure 1 shows a flowchart depicting the overall training process.

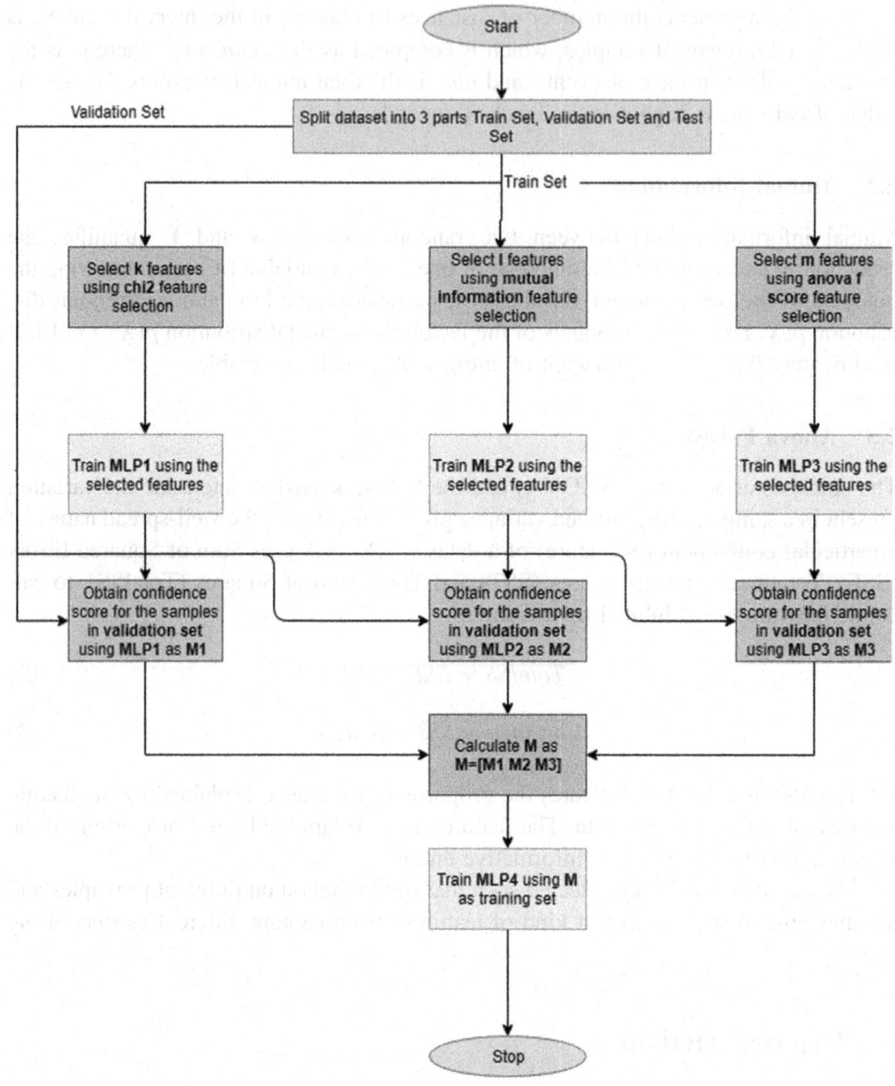

Fig. 1. Flowchart showing overview of the training process

3.1 Stage 1 (Use Train Set)

2. Three optimum feature sets were selected independently using the three feature selection techniques described in Section. In order to find the optimum number of features, we started by selecting a few of the top ranked features for each filter method and evaluating the performance of the corresponding MLP, thereby repeating the process by increasing the number of features each time. When there was no significant improvement in performance by increasing the size of feature set, the iterations were stopped and the current feature length was used to proceed.
3. The selected feature sets were used to train the corresponding MLPs separately.

3.2 Stage 2 (Use Validation Set)

4. The specified features were picked up for each sample and these were provided as input to the respective MLPs. For a given sample, the output probability of each class was normalized to give the Class Membership Degree for each class. M1, M2, M3 are the vector of Class Membership Degrees output by MLP1, MLP2, MLP3 respectively for the sample.
5. M1, M2, M3 were concatenated to give $\boldsymbol{M} = [M1 \quad M2 \quad M3]$
6. Treating M for each sample as input, MLP4 is trained with the encoded class label as target output.

3.3 Testing Phase (Use Test Set)

7. Perform Step 4 and Step 5 for each sample.
8. Provide M as input to MLP4. The corresponding output denotes the predicted class label.
9. Compare the predicted class label for each sample with the ground truth value to compute final accuracy of model.

Thus, an intelligent ensemble has been devised for different feature selection techniques using a neural network in the second stage that tries to capture as much complementary information as possible from the different methods and removes manual mathematical formulation.

4 Results, Analysis and Discussion

This section gives a brief description of the datasets used for the experiments and a comparative study of results of the proposed method with other existing methods on these datasets.

4.1 Datasets Used

The experiments have been carried out on 5 different datasets from UCI Machine Learning Repository, namely Arrhythmia, Ionosphere, Hill-Valley, Waveform, Horse Colic. Given below is a brief description of each dataset and Table A gives a summary of all of the datasets. Note that experiments have been performed on datasets of greatly varying sizes as well as number of features and classes, in order to prove the versatility and robustness of the model.

(1) **Arrhythmia** [12] – This dataset was designed to demarcate between the presence and absence of cardiac arrythmia. In this, the first class denotes a normal heart-beat, the next 14 denote various cases of arrythmia while the 16th class is the class assigned in case of misclassification in the other 15th. It is a popular dataset used in outlier analysis. Some features used in the dataset are height, weight, QRS duration, heart beat etc.

(2) **Ionosphere** [13] – This dataset is used for binary classification, which was originally used to train a neural network to distinguish between bad and good radar returns from the ionosphere. The feature set represents 17 pairs of discrete values of the real and imaginary part of the Autocorrelation function.
(3) **Hill-Valley** [14] – Two class classification is performed on this dataset which was originally used to classify a set of points which either generated a hill or a valley. The feature set denotes 100 points on the y-axis, which when plotted sequentially would either lead to a bump (hill) or a plunge (valley) on the plane.
(4) **Waveform** [15] – The waveform dataset is a 3-class problem identifying 3 waveforms, with each sampled at 21 intervals. Each class is a random convex combination of 2 of the 3 base classes. The dataset consists of 40 attributes, of which the latter 19 attributes are all noise, with a mean of 0 and variance of 1.
(5) **Horse Colic** [16] – Dataset used to predict the life and death of a horse based on its past medical conditions. The data types range from continuous to discrete in nature. Some features which are continuous are pulse and respiratory rate, while discrete features include mucous membrane color and capillary refill time. Table 1 gives a summary of the datasets used.

Table 1. Summary of the datasets

Name of dataset	No. of samples	No. of classes	No. of features
Arrhythmia	452	16	279
Ionosphere	351	2	34
Hill-Valley	606	2	101
Waveform	5000	3	40
Horse Colic	368	2	27

4.2 Results and Analysis

The experiments have been performed separately on each dataset five times, and the mean accuracy has been noted. For the proposed method, the entire dataset has been split into a separate train set, validation set, and test set, each one disjoint of the other. The split has been made in the ratio of 0.3:0.3:0.4 respectively. In order to compare the performance of the proposed method with other traditional ensemble paradigms like the sum rule, product rule, weighted sum rule, experiments have also been performed using these paradigms, keeping all parameters same as that of the proposed method. For the other methods, each dataset has been split into an independent train and test set in the ratio of 0.6:0.4. Initially, the features were ranked according to the order of importance for each filter method. In order to find the optimum number of features, we started by selecting a few of the top ranked features for each filter method and evaluating the performance of the corresponding Neural Network, thereby repeating the process by increasing the number of features each time. When there was no significant improvement in performance by increasing the size of feature set, the iterations were stopped and the current feature length was used to proceed. In this way, the redundant features were removed and the feature length was also reduced for training without much degradation in performance. Table 2 shows the accuracy obtained by each individual Neural Network and also the optimum number of features selected by each filter method. It also shows the accuracy obtained by the proposed ensemble.

Table 2. Accuracy of the proposed method at different stages

Name of dataset	Number of features selected			Average accuracy (%)			
	Chi2	ANOVA F-Test	Mutual-info-classif	MLP1	MLP2	MLP3	Proposed ensemble
Arrhythmia	20	10	30	60.52	52.31	54.50	**63.30**
Ionosphere	20	20	20	89.86	91.55	91.55	**94.36**
Hill-Valley	50	50	50	51.11	55.31	51.60	**60.74**
Waveform	20	20	20	86.38	**87.08**	87.16	86.83
Horse Colic	6	6	6	85.41	88.10	87.30	**88.65**

It is to be noted that the accuracy of the proposed ensemble is greater than the accuracy of the individual neural networks in most of the cases.

In order to optimize performance, each filter method tries to select the set of features which it considers most relevant for the classification at hand. Each uses its own metric for selection and thus the features selected by each method is completely independent of the other. For example, for the ionosphere dataset, out of the 20 features selected by the methods: chi2 and mutual-info-classif, 13 of them are common while the 7 others are distinct for each method. Thus, one method may overlook some of the important features which can be captured by the other methods. In this way, we can capture some of the complementary information provided by each. The second stage neural network takes into account the decisions of each of the networks of the first stage and arrives at a consensus. This results in noticeable increase in the classification performance. Sometimes, as for the horse-colic dataset where 4 of the 6 features selected by the two methods: chi2 and mutual-info-classif are same, each of the methods may separately be able to capture most of the information. In such cases, the performance of the ensemble is not drastically better than the individual classifiers. However, as the votes of all the classifiers are considered, the ensemble still gives a better performance.

Table 3 gives the statistical measures of the experiment and Fig. 2 gives the stability graph of for the different datasets.

Table 3. Statistical measures of the experiments performed

Name of dataset	Accuracy (%)		
	Max	Average	Standard deviation
Arrythmia	68.13	63.30	4.29
Ionosphere	97.18	94.36	3.58
Hill Valley	67.08	60.74	3.87
Waveform	88.00	86.83	1.03
Horse Colic	90.12	88.65	2.05

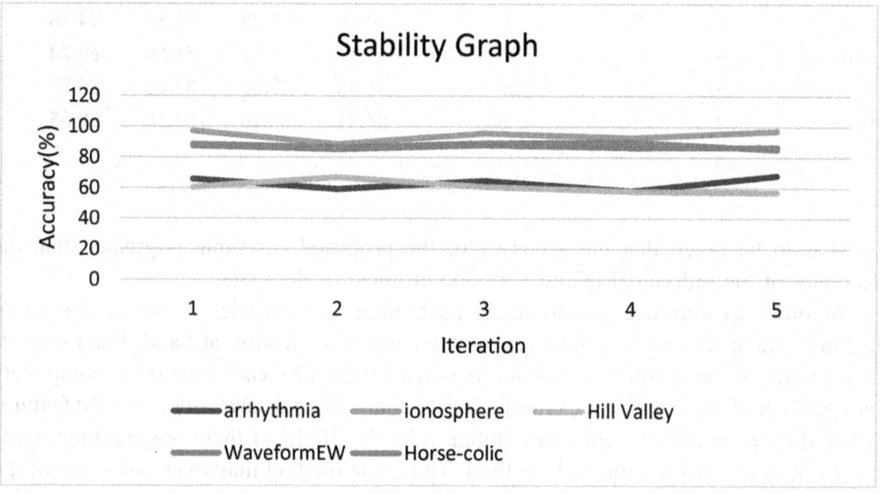

Fig. 2. Stability graph of the experiment on various datasets

Table 4 provides a comparison of the performance of the proposed ensemble with other traditional ensemble paradigms such as sum rule [17], product rule [17], weighted sum rule [18].

Table 4. Comparison of the results of the proposed method with traditional ensemble techniques

Name of dataset	Accuracy (%)			
	Sum rule	Product rule	Weighted sum rule	Proposed ensemble
Arrhythmia	55.16	53.84	55.16	63.30
Ionosphere	91.83	91.83	91.83	94.36
Hill-Valley	55.14	55.06	55.39	60.74
Waveform	87.20	86.83	87.2	86.83
Horse Colic	88.91	88.91	88.91	88.65

The proposed method outperforms the traditional methods in 3 out of the 5 cases. Thus, it can be said that the proposed ensemble is more robust than all of the others. The traditional ensemble methods such as sum rule, product rule assign equal importance to the decisions of each classifier regardless of its individual performance. For the arrhythmia dataset, one neural network (61.54% accuracy) clearly outperforms the other two (48.35% and 56.04% accuracies). However, equal weightage is assigned to each of their results. Such phenomena significantly degrade the performance of the ensemble. The weighted sum rule does take the individual accuracies into account but there may be other important indicators of performance which it overlooks. Table 5 provides a comparison of our method against state-of-the art ensemble techniques such as boosting [19].

Table 5. Comparison of the results of the proposed method with state-of-the-art ensemble techniques.

Name of dataset	Accuracy (%)			
	Ada boost	Stochastic gradient boosting	XG boost	Proposed ensemble
Arrhythmia	60.22	**70.71**	70.165	63.30
Ionosphere	**95.03**	90.78	89.36	94.36
Hill-Valley	58.35	59.58	58.73	**60.74**
Waveform	78.35	82.45	81.85	**86.83**
Horse Colic	81.75	82.43	85.135	**88.65**

As discernible from the above table, our proposed method achieves a better accuracy in comparison to most of the state-of-the art ensemble techniques. Due to its consistent superior performance, it is clear that the ensemble neural network learns to spot many dependencies which may not have been possible by manual tuning. An individual classifier may perform poorly in a particular region of the feature space. The ensemble network notices this pattern during its training and thus, assigns less importance to it in such cases. We suspect that some of the neurons activate for even more complex phenomena than we are able to find by intuition, such as spotting high entropy for a classifier to indicate low classification confidence and consequently, low importance. Overall, not only does the ensemble network remove the hassle of manual tuning of the weights, it also provides a better performance than the traditional models.

All the training was performed on a machine with Intel Core i5-7200U CPU @ 2.5 GHz $\times$ 4 with 4 GB of RAM. As feature selection is performed on the dataset the dimensionality is reduced and hence the number of nodes in the layers of the MLPs used in the first stage of training are also reduced thus reducing the computational cost and the time taken to train the MLPs. For the Ionosphere dataset, MLP1 takes 1.75 s, MLP2 takes 1.85 s, MLP3 takes 2.11 s, while the MLP4 (second stage) took 3.53 s. Though in total 4 MLPs have been trained, the 3 MLPs in the first stage are trained independently and hence can be parallelized. Thus effectively, the equivalent time taken in the first stage is the time taken to train 1 MLP. Total equivalent time for the two stages is the time taken to train two MLPs. Hence, for the first stage, the time taken was 2.13 s (about the maximum of the first three) and the total turnaround time was 5.66 s (= 2.13 + 5.13). For the horse-colic dataset, the total time was 5.63 s.

5 Conclusion

In this paper, an ensemble of classification models has been proposed following a two-stage approach. In the first stage we have used three filter methods for feature ranking – MI, Chi-square and ANOVA F-Test. These three optimized feature subsets are used to train three MLP classifiers. Outcomes of three such learning models are concatenated and fed to the next MLP classifier. The proposed ensemble model has been evaluated on five datasets taken from UCI Machine learning data repository and it has been observed that the proposed model outperforms some conventionally used ensemble approaches.

Limitations with future scope:

- Only one classifier - MLP has been used; so, in future other popularly used and standard classifiers can be applied.
- More real-life datasets can be used for experimentation so the robustness of the proposed approach can be established.
- Information fusion at the initial stage can be thought of – i.e. we can make a consensus among the features selected by the three filter methods. Even more varied filter methods can be applied.

References

1. Dietterich, T.G.: Ensemble methods in machine learning. In: Kittler, J., Roli, F. (eds.) MCS 2000. LNCS, vol. 1857, pp. 1–15. Springer, Heidelberg (2000). https://doi.org/10.1007/3-540-45014-9_1
2. Hansen, L.K., Salamon, P.: Neural network ensembles. IEEE Trans. Pattern Anal. Mach. Intell. **12**, 993–1001 (1990). https://doi.org/10.1109/34.58871
3. Cruz, R.M.O., Sabourin, R., Cavalcanti, G.D.C., Ing Ren, T.: META-DES: a dynamic ensemble selection framework using meta-learning. Pattern Recogn. **48**, 1925–1935 (2015). https://doi.org/10.1016/j.patcog.2014.12.003
4. Kittler, J., Hatef, M., Duin, R.P.W., Matas, J.: On combining classifiers. IEEE Trans. Pattern Anal. Mach. Intell. **20**, 226–239 (1998). https://doi.org/10.1109/34.667881
5. West, D., Dellana, S., Qian, J.: Neural network ensemble strategies for financial decision applications. Comput. Oper. Res. **32**, 2543–2559 (2005). https://doi.org/10.1016/j.cor.2004.03.017
6. Ai, S., Chakravorty, A., Rong, C.: Household power demand prediction using evolutionary ensemble neural network pool with multiple network structures. Sensors **19**, 721 (2019). https://doi.org/10.3390/s19030721
7. Zhang, L., Yu, G., Xia, D., Wang, J.: Protein–protein interactions prediction based on ensemble deep neural networks. Neurocomputing **324**, 10–19 (2019). https://doi.org/10.1016/j.neucom.2018.02.097

8. Feng, X., Fu, T.M., Cao, H., Tian, H., Fan, Q., Chen, X.: Neural network predictions of pollutant emissions from open burning of crop residues: application to air quality forecasts in southern China. Atmos. Environ. **204**, 22–31 (2019). https://doi.org/10.1016/j.atmosenv.2019.02.002
9. Wang, R., Li, W., Zhang, L.: Blur image identification with ensemble convolution neural networks. Sig. Process. **155**, 73–82 (2019). https://doi.org/10.1016/j.sigpro.2018.09.027
10. Jin, X., Xu, A., Bie, R., Guo, P.: Machine learning techniques and chi-square feature selection for cancer classification using SAGE gene expression profiles. In: Li, J., Yang, Q., Tan, A.-H. (eds.) BioDM 2006. LNCS, vol. 3916, pp. 106–115. Springer, Heidelberg (2006). https://doi.org/10.1007/11691730_11
11. Uğuz, H.: A two-stage feature selection method for text categorization by using information gain, principal component analysis and genetic algorithm. Knowl. Based Syst. **24**, 1024–1032 (2011). https://doi.org/10.1016/j.knosys.2011.04.014
12. Guvenir, H.A., Acar, B., Demiroz, G., Cekin, A.: A supervised machine learning algorithm for arrhythmia analysis. Comput. Cardiol. **1997**, 433–436 (1997). https://doi.org/10.1109/CIC.1997.647926
13. Sigillito, V.G., Wing, S.P., Hutton, L.V., Baker, K.B.: Classification of radar returns from the ionosphere using neural networks. In: Johns Hopkins APL Technical Digest (Applied Physics Laboratory), pp. 262–266 (1989)
14. The University of Waikato: WEKA: Waikato Environment for Knowledge Analysis. In: Proceedings of the New Zealand Computer Science Research Students Conference, pp. 57–64 (2014)
15. Breiman, L.: Classification and Regression Trees. Routledge, New York (1984). https://doi.org/10.1201/9781315139470
16. Greensmith, J.: New frontiers for an artificial immune system. Master's Thesis in Digital Media (2003)
17. Alexandre, L.A., Campilho, A.C., Kamel, M.: On combining classifiers using sum and product rules. Pattern Recogn. Lett. **22**, 1283–1289 (2001). https://doi.org/10.1016/S0167-8655(01)00073-3
18. Jimenez, D.: Dynamically weighted ensemble neural networks for classification. In: 1998 IEEE International Joint Conference on Neural Networks Proceedings. IEEE World Congress on Computational Intelligence (Cat. No. 98CH36227), vol. 1, pp. 753–756 (1998). https://doi.org/10.1109/IJCNN.1998.682375
19. Chen, T., Guestrin, C.: XGBoost: a scalable tree boosting system. In: Proceedings of the 22nd ACM SIGKDD International Conference on Knowledge Discovery and Data Mining, pp. 785–794. ACM, New York, NY, USA (2016). https://doi.org/10.1145/2939672.2939785

Dynamic Centroid Insertion and Adjustment for Data Sets with Multiple Imbalanced Classes

Evandro J. R. Silva(✉) and Cleber Zanchettin

Centro de Informática, Universidade Federal de Pernambuco, Recife, Brazil
{ejrs,cz}@cin.ufpe.br

Abstract. The imbalance problem is receiving an increasing attention in the literature. Studies on binary cases are recurrent but limited when considering the multiple classes approach. Solutions to imbalance domains may be divided into two groups, data level approaches, and algorithmic approaches. The first approach is more common and focuses on changing the training data aiming to balance the data set, oversampling the smallest classes, undersampling the biggest ones or using a combination of both. Instance reduction is another approach to the problem. It tries to find the best-reduced set of instances that represent the original training set. In this work, we propose a new Prototype Generation method called DCIA. It dynamically inserts new prototypes for each class and then adjusts their positions with a search algorithm. The set of generated prototypes may be used to train any classifier. Experiments showed its potentiality by enabling an 1NN classifier to perform sometimes as well or even better than some ensemble classifiers created for different multiclass imbalanced domains.

Keywords: Prototype Generation · Imbalanced domains · Multiclass

1 Introduction

Machine learning algorithms usually assumed that in the training data the number of observations for each class is equal or at least quite similar. In the last decade the impact of data imbalance to the machine learning algorithms came to attention [8] due to some inference problems, like performance reduction, misleading metrics, border overlapping, small disjuncts, rare classes and data set shift [6,10,11,16,19,21]. These problems are well studied in the case of binary data sets [5,26], when only two classes are present (in which one is the majority (or negative) class and the other is the minority (or positive) class). Considering multiple classes the learning process may be harder and literature solutions proposed for the binary case may not be directly applicable or may achieve a lower performance than expected [5]. A multiclass problem may also require a different focus, i.e., there will not be a single minority class to be focused and the method needs to focus on all classes simultaneously.

I. V. Tetko et al. (Eds.): ICANN 2019, LNCS 11728, pp. 766–778, 2019.
https://doi.org/10.1007/978-3-030-30484-3_60

There are two main approaches to the imbalance domain, the data level solutions and the algorithmic level solutions [6]. The first approach tries to preprocess the data by oversampling the minority classes or undersampling the majority ones [11]. On the other hand, the second approach tries to adapt classifiers and learning models to deal with the imbalance problem. Classifiers can be modified to become *ad hoc* or be trained with cost-sensitive learning techniques [8].

For the first approach the goal usually is to balance the number of samples in each class, growing the smaller ones, reducing the biggest ones, or using hybrid techniques to resize all classes. However, there is an alternative that still receives little attention, the use of instance reduction methods. These methods aim to find the best-reduced set that represents the original training data set [12]. Reduction methods can be divided into Prototype Selection (PS) and Prototype Generation (PG) [12]. PS methods try to select a subset of the original training set while PG methods build a new set of instances which can be completely different from the original training set.

In [14] authors suggest that resampling a training set followed by simple PS techniques increases the performance of the used classifiers. In [25] a Fuzzy Rough Imbalanced Prototype Selection (FRIPS) is used to improve SMOTE and the performance of the 1NN classifier. On the other hand, an Adaptive Self-Generating Prototype (ASGP) is proposed as a PG method to handle imbalanced classes [17]. Its improvement called Evolutionary Adaptive Self-Generating Prototypes (EASGP) is proposed in [18]. In [12] the authors proposed IPADE-ID, a position adjustment PG method to deal with imbalanced datasets. Their results suggest that Instance Reduction algorithms are suitable options for imbalance domains.

However, all of these algorithms deal only with binary data sets. For the best of our knowledge, a centroid-based PG method called VDBC [22] is the only algorithm that investigates Instance Reduction on the imbalanced multiclass scenario. After investigations, we verify that VDBC did not perform as well as some *ad hoc* algorithms but had potentialities as a new approach to the problem.

Some authors suggest that among the PG methods, position adjustment is more likely to stand out [12,24]. Exploring this characteristic may result in performance improvement for the VDBC algorithm. In this work, we explore this assumption proposing a Dynamic Centroid Insertion and Adjustment (DCIA) algorithm for multiclass imbalanced domains. The proposed algorithm is based on IPADE-ID concepts and dynamically inserts centroids in the problem space and adjust their positions using some search algorithm. As the search algorithm, we also propose a new approach named Simple Gravity Search Algorithm (SGSA).

We evaluate DCIA by comparing its performance to VDBC and some different state-of-the-art algorithms. Nominally AdaBoost.NC [26], which combines AdaBoost with negative correlation learning; AdaC2.M1 [23], which is an extension of the cost-sensitive AdaC2 to multiclass case; AMCS [27], which is an adaptive junction of several methods of feature selection, resampling and ensemble learning; and DECOC [3], a combination of Diversified OVO (DOVO) and an improved ECOC (imECOC).

DCIA is a simple data level solution that gives a transformed training set to the 1NN classifier, which is one of the simplest classifiers found in the literature. On the other hand, the related state-of-the-art algorithms are, at different levels, complex ensemble methods. It is not expected that 1NN using DCIA performs better than ensemble solutions. Therefore the objective of this work is to analyze how close the performance of the 1NN classifier can get to the ensemble methods just after processing and improving the training data.

The rest of the paper is organized as follows. In Sect. 2 the proposed algorithms are presented. Section 3 describes the experimental analyses. Conclusions and future works are shown in Sect. 4.

2 Dynamic Centroid Insertion and Adjustment: DCIA

DCIA is a Prototype Generation algorithm for multiclass imbalanced domains. The generated prototypes are also adjusted in space to allow classifiers to get better performance. The method may be divided into two phases, i.e., a preprocessing phase and then a three steps phase.

In the preprocessing phase, data normalization and an attribute selection occur. Data normalization attempts to give all attributes an equal weight. It transforms the data to fall within a smaller or common range, e.g., [0, 1]. Normalization is particularly useful for classification algorithms including those based on distance measurements such as *kNN* [9]. Furthermore, experimentally we observed that DCIA gets better performance with normalized data.

Feature, or attribute selection is recently gaining some interest from researchers as a way to address the imbalanced class problem [15]. Within feature selection, there are three further sub-approaches: filter, wrapper and hybrid (also known as embedded). The second and third approaches were proposed to produce a more targeted feature subset [15]. The wrapper approach aims to find a subset that gives a better performance. If one uses a metric proper to imbalance domains this approach might select a subset of attributes that will improve the generalization of all classes.

The data normalization is carried out with $z - score$:

$$A'_i = \frac{A_i - \bar{A}}{\sigma_A} \tag{1}$$

where A is an attribute, A_i is the value of the attribute A in the instance i, A'_i is the new value of A_i, $\bar{A}$ is the arithmetic mean of all values of A, and σ_A is the respective standard deviation. Test set instances can be normalized following the training instances mean and standard deviation. This is possible due to the assumption that test samples have similar characteristics of training samples. At the same time, this is necessary to keep test samples unknown.

The attribute selection is executed with a wrapper approach [15]. In this approach, the best subset of attributes is selected through a search process and validated by classifying data with the selected subset [13]. The search algorithm used is the Competitive Swarm Optimizer (CSO) [4] as suggested in [7]. The validation of the best set is accomplished with the 1NN classifier and AUCarea metric, which is more sensitive to lower AUC values obtained by pairs of classes [27].

The second phase is based on IPADE-ID concepts, hence the three steps: initialization, adjustment of centroids and addition of prototypes. In the first step, one centroid is selected for each class. The adjustment, or optimization step, is carried out with SGSA. The third step consists of extracting a random instance of each class from the training set and insert it into the best solution so far. The main differences between IPADE-ID and DCIA are the following:

1. DCIA begins with a preprocess phase consisting of data normalization and attribute selection to reduce the space dimensionality;
2. IPADE-ID treats each prototype as an individual population while DCIA treats as individual a set of prototypes;
3. IPADE-ID is initialized with one centroid of each class, and DCIA begins with several sets of prototypes, including the set with one centroid of each class;
4. The former tries to insert new prototypes for classes marked as optimizable; this attempt occurs with more adjustment for each new prototype being inserted. DCIA selects an instance of each class randomly and tries to insert it into the best prototype set without further adjustment. In case of success, all other sets are updated.

In the following subsections, we present the three steps of DCIA in detail. Furthermore, Algorithm 1 shows the pseudo-code of DCIA.

2.1 Initialization

The selection of a good initial set is important as it guides the search towards promissory solutions and the prototypes that are selected in this stage are maintained or modified into the final generated training set [12]. At the same time, it could be a good practice to allow a wide search area since the beginning.

As the number of prototypes may increase, all individuals start with one prototype per class. The first created individual holds each class centroid (lines 11 and 12). All other solutions are filled with one random instance from each class (lines 13 and 14).

2.2 Adjustment

Each solution is a set of centroids which are used to classify the data with the 1-NN algorithm. Therefore, each solution has its performance calculated over the training instances.

The search algorithm is used to adjust the position of centroids aiming the maximization of the AUCarea metric. The adjustment step is performed with SGSA, which is a simplification of the Gravity Search Algorithm (GSA) [20].

Algorithm 1. DCIA Pseudo-code

```
Inputs: Training set, S as the pool of solutions, N as the size of population, C as number of
    classes, I as number of iterations.

Preprocess
Normalize data;
for iter = 1 to I do
    Execute CSO to select the best subset of attributes;
end for

Initialization
for n = 1 to N do
    if n == 1 then
        For each class, find it's respective centroid;
    else
        Select a random instance from the class as centroid;
    end if
end for

Adjustment and Addition of Prototypes
for i = 1 to Stop Criterion do
    Execute the search algorithm to adjust the centroids of each solution S_i;

    Create S' as a copy of the solution set S;
    Select the best solution of S';
    for c = 1 to C do
        Select a random instance and add it to the solution;
        Verify the performance of the current solution with the training set;
        if current performance > existent performance then
            Select a random instance for all other solutions;
            Override S with S';
        end if
    end for
end for
```

Gravity Search Algorithm. The GSA [20] is a recent swarm based search technique, which has a flexible and well-balanced mechanism to enhance exploration and exploitation abilities. It has been inspired by Newtonian laws of gravity and motion. In this algorithm, mass interactions are simulated and objects move through a search space under the influence of gravitation [20].

All objects attract each other by a gravity force, and this force causes the movement of all objects globally toward objects with heavier masses, which correspond to good solutions of the problem.

Each object has its fitness value and mass influenced by a gravitational force, which is the sum of its gravitational interaction with all other objects. From this force, the resulting acceleration is used to calculate the current object's velocity. Finally, the object's new position is calculated with the sum of its current position and velocity. More details may be consulted in [20].

Simple Gravity Search Algorithm. SGSA is a new approach proposed in this paper. Its main idea is to simplify GSA without loss of performance. The modifications are detailed below.

Instead of all objects influencing each other from the beginning, in SGSA only the best solution influences all others. The first consequence is the reduction of parameters and calculations. In SGSA there is no more force, acceleration, and velocity, but only what we call the *pull*:

$$pull_i = best(t)/dist^2 \tag{2}$$

where $best(t)$ is the best solution at the iteration t and $dist^2$ is the squared distance between current object and $best(t)$. At each iteration, all solutions move, except the best one. The distance they move depends on how good is the best solution and how close they are from each other.

However, in SGSA the best solution does not stay idle. It performs *micro* movements in the space, exploiting its vicinity for improvements. For each dimension in each centroid, it is randomly decided if a small movement may occur. In the positive case, it is randomly decided if the value of the current dimension is increased or decreased. At the end of the movement, if the exploiter solution improves the performance, it replaces the best solution. The entire cycle is repeated until it reaches a stop criterion.

Comparisons between GSA and SGSA were carried out with statistical analysis. The conclusion is that SGSA is indeed similar to GSA in terms of performance.

2.3 Addition of New Prototypes

DCIA starts with one centroid per class as prototypes. These initial prototypes go through an adjustment process resulting in an improved set of prototypes. However, some classes may need more prototypes for a better representation of their distribution. In DCIA the addition of new prototypes is performed as follows.

Create a solution set S' and copy S. Select the best solution S'_{best}. For each class select a random instance from the training set, insert it into S'_{best} and classify the training set. If S'_{best} performance is better than S_{best}, insert a random instance of the same class in every other solution of S' and override S.

After the final override, the solution set S has an improved best solution with new prototypes. All other solutions have also the same amount of prototypes for each class. The execution of DCIA continues with adjustment and addition process until a stop criterion is reached.

3 Experiments and Analysis of Results

In this work we use seventeen data sets with multiple imbalanced classes from KEEL [1] and UCI [2] repositories. They are presented in Table 1, in which the columns refer respectively to the name of the data set, the number of instances, the number of features, the number of classes and the Multiclass Imbalance Ratio (MIR) [22]. Missing values were replaced with the arithmetic mean from other instances of the same class.

3.1 Comparisons

We compare DCIA with other related algorithms found in the literature. Results of VDBC [22] were obtained after running the online available source code[1]. The metric used is the MAUC.

Results of AdaBoost.NC [26], AdaC2.M1 [23] and DECOC [3] were obtained after running the codes provided by DECOC authors [3][2]. The results of AMCS [27] were also obtained by running a source code provided online[3]. No modifications were performed in the codes, and the results are expressed in terms of the AUCarea metric.

We use 5-fold cross-validation before all algorithms. However, not all data sets could be tested in all algorithms, due to time shortage and mainly because of some inherent limitations of the algorithms. Table 2 shows which data sets were tested in each classifier. In the second column, *Several* refers to VDBC, AdaBoost.NC and AdaC2.M1 algorithms.

Table 1. Summary of the used data sets

Name	#Inst.	#Feat.	#Cls.	MIR
Balance Scale	625	4	3	2.6985
Contraceptive	1473	9	3	0.2159
Gene	3190	60	3	0.4134
Glass	214	9	6	5.0133
Horse	366	14	3	1.2592
Landsat	2000	36	6	0.7463
Lymphography	148	18	4	24.8133
Nursery	12960	8	5	1300.8
Page Blocks	5473	10	5	59.5996
Penbased	1100	16	10	0.0162
Post Operative	90	8	3	13.7188
Satimage	6435	36	6	0.9564
Shuttle	58000	9	7	1676.8
Thyroid	7200	21	3	18.3396
Wine	178	13	3	0.0774
Yeast	1484	8	10	44.7543
Zoo	101	16	7	4.9225

The values of parameters used in DCIA during feature selection with CSO were the same as suggested in [7]. During the second and third steps of DCIA the

[1] https://github.com/EvandroJRSilva/VDBC.
[2] https://github.com/chongshengzhang/Multi_Imbalance.
[3] https://github.com/liyijing024/AMCS.

Table 2. Data sets tested in each classifier.

Dataset/Classifier	Several	AMCS	DECOC
Balance Scale	•	•	•
Contraceptive	•	•	•
Gene	•		•
Glass	•		•
Horse	•		•
Landsat		•	
Lymphography		•	
Nursery	•		
Page Blocks	•	•	•
Penbased		•	
Post Operative	•		
Satimage	•		•
Shuttle	•		
Thyroid	•		•
Wine	•	•	•
Yeast	•	•	
Zoo	•	•	

size of the population is equal to 50, the stop criterion is 50 iterations, and the distance of exploitation is $rand/100$, in which $rand$ is a random number between 0 and 1. TWe defined these values empirically. Both adjustment and insertion of new prototypes are validated with MAUC metric and 1NN classifier. It was also found that using AUCarea in this part of the algorithm may be harmful.

Statistical analyses were carried out with *t-student* and Wilcoxon's *ranksum* for parametric and non-parametric tests respectively.

Figure 1 shows a comparison between VDBC and DCIA. The performance of each algorithm for each data set is shown as a small circle, which marks the obtained mean value. Each circle is followed by bars, which represent the standard deviation. As VDBC's base classifier is also 1NN the comparison demonstrate that DCIA is able to generate a better set of prototypes than its competitor, allowing the classifier to achieve better performance in almost all data sets. The performance was statistically equivalent in data sets with a high number of classes and a low number of instances, i.e., *Glass* and *Zoo*. It was also equivalent in *Horse* data set due to the high value of DCIA standard deviation, which was caused by an outlier. Besides, only in *Satimage* data set VDBC performed statistically better with a small advantage.

Performance comparisons among DCIA and state-of-the-art algorithms are shown in Fig. 2. The diagonal line represents DCIA's performance. For each data set, if another algorithm performs better than DCIA, its marker is placed

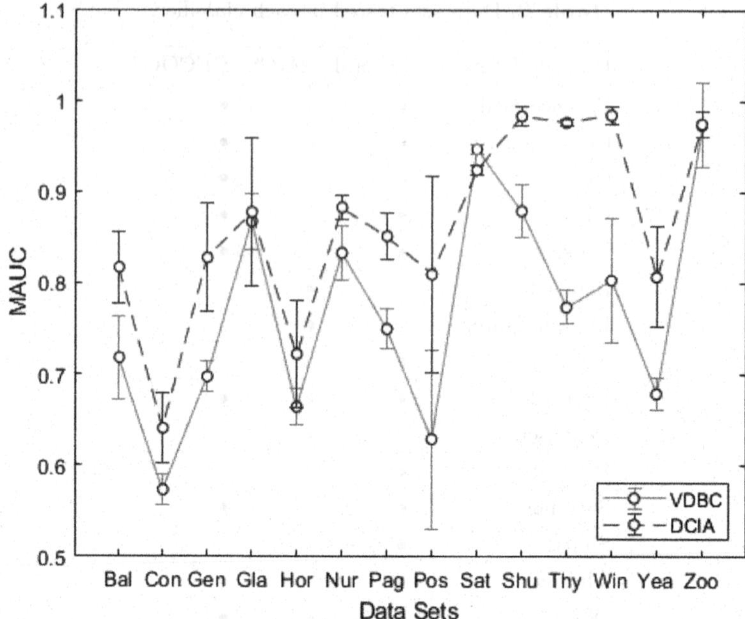

Fig. 1. Comparison of performance results between DCIA and VDBC.

above the diagonal line. Otherwise, the marker is set in the line for equivalent performance or under the line when the performance is worst.

Statistical analyses show that DCIA's performance is equivalent to or better than AdaBoost.NC's in seven data sets, i.e., half the time. When compared to AdaC2.M1, DCIA is equivalent or better in 9 out of 14 data sets. AMCS has better performance, and DCIA is equivalent or better only in 3 out of 9 data sets. Finally, DCIA is equivalent to DECOC in 8 out of 9 data sets, yet it was never statistically better.

It is interesting to notice that a simple Prototype Generation algorithm allows the 1NN classifier to be sometimes better than ensemble classifiers, and several times perform equivalently. In a few data sets, DCIA was also able to reach AMCS, probably the most complex algorithm among its pairs which has better performances overall.

It also should be noticed that these ensembles were built specifically for the multiclass imbalance problem. That is the reason it was not expected for DCIA to outperform any of the algorithmic level competitors. However, it could be observed that a data level approach, which can be seen as a third approach besides oversampling and undersampling, is able to help a very simple classifier to increase its performance.

Despite being a simple algorithm, DCIA has a relatively high computational cost. The wrapper attribute selection is usually computationally expensive [7]. The same training set is classified several times for each different set of attributes,

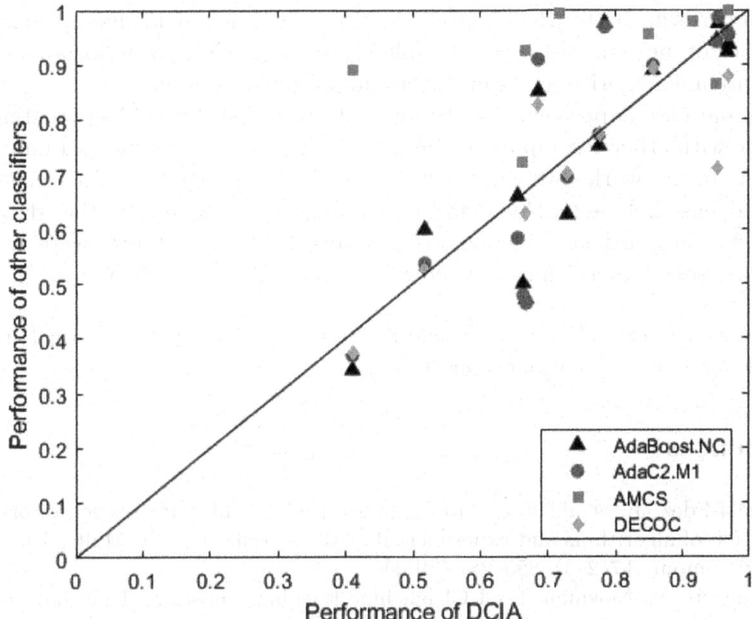

Fig. 2. Summary comparison among DCIA and AdaBoost.NC, AdaC2.M1, AMCS and DECOC.

i.e., the pool of solutions. The cost increases with more instances and more features. In this work, we implemented a solution proposed by [7], i.e., use memory to keep track of visited solutions avoiding the reclassification of training data with a specific attribute subset.

The adjustment and prototype addition steps are also costly. Several sets of prototypes move in problem space; then the training set is classified with all solutions. For each class, each attempt to add a new prototype requires a new classification. As the validation is made with the 1NN classifier, each instance classification is made with some distance calculations. The cost increases as the number of prototypes increases and as high is the number of instances. In summary, small to medium size data sets do not take long to be classified. However, large to huge data sets require some time to be classified.

4 Conclusion

In this paper we have presented DCIA, a new approach to deal with the problem of classification with multiple imbalanced classes. The proposal modifies the training set with a PG technique and a search algorithm. In this work, it was used the SGSA, a modification to the recent GSA algorithm.

The experimental study focused on comparing DCIA with its direct competitor VDBC and some state-of-the-art classifiers. We observed that the proposed method performs better than VDBC. At the same time, an adequately generated set of prototypes enables a very simple classifier as 1NN to perform as well as some ensemble algorithms on multiclass imbalanced domains.

As a data level approach, the Prototype Generation showed its potentiality to compete with other resampling techniques, such as oversampling and undersampling. As future works, we will verify how DCIA may influence other classifiers, including ensemble algorithms, and how it can be compared to other data level approaches in multiclass imbalanced domains. It is also interesting to research how other search algorithms beyond SGSA may influence DCIA.

Acknowledgment. The authors would like to thank CNPq and FACEPE (Brazilian research agencies) for financial support.

References

1. Alcalá-Fdez, J., et al.: Keel data-mining software tool: data set repository, integration of algorithms and experimental analysis framework. J. Mult. Valued Log. Soft Comput. **17**(2–3), 255–287 (2011)
2. Asuncion, A., Newman, D.: UCI machine learning repository. University of California, Irvine, School of Information and Computer Sciences (2007). http://www.ics.uci.edu/~mlearn/MLRepository.html
3. Bi, J., Zhang, C.: An empirical comparison on state-of-the-art multi-class imbalance learning algorithms and a new diversified ensemble learning scheme. Knowl. Based Syst. **158**, 81–93 (2018). https://doi.org/10.1016/j.knosys.2018.05.037
4. Cheng, R., Jin, Y.: A competitive swarm optimizer for large scale optimization. IEEE Trans. Cybern. **45**(2), 191–204 (2015). https://doi.org/10.1109/TCYB.2014.2322602
5. Fernández, A., López, V., Galar, M., del Jesus, M.J., Herrera, F.: Analysing the classification of imbalanced data-sets with multiple classes: binarization techniques and ad-hoc approaches. Knowl. Based Syst. **42**, 97–110 (2013). https://doi.org/10.1016/j.knosys.2013.01.018
6. García, V., Sánchez, J.S., Mollineda, R.A.: On the effectiveness of preprocessing methods when dealing with different levels of class imbalance. Knowl. Based Syst. **25**(1), 13–21 (2012). https://doi.org/10.1016/j.knosys.2011.06.013
7. Gu, S., Cheng, R., Jin, Y.: Feature selection for high-dimensional classification using a competitive swarm optimizer. Soft Comput. **22**(3), 811–822 (2018). https://doi.org/10.1007/s00500-016-2385-6
8. Haixiang, G., Yijing, L., Shang, J., Mingyun, G., Yuanyue, H., Bing, G.: Learning from class-imbalanced data: review of methods and applications. Expert Syst. Appl. **73**, 220–239 (2017). https://doi.org/10.1016/j.eswa.2016.12.035
9. Han, J., Kamber, M., Pei, J.: Data Mining Concepts and Techniques, 3rd edn. Morgan Kaufmann Publishers, Waltham (2012)
10. Japkowicz, N., Stephen, S.: The class imbalance problem: a systematic study. Intell. Data Anal. **6**(5), 429–449 (2002). https://doi.org/10.3233/IDA-2002-6504
11. López, V., Fernández, A., García, S., Palade, V., Herrera, F.: An insight into classification with imbalanced data: empirical results and current trends on using data intrinsic characteristics. Inf. Sci. **250**, 113–141 (2013). https://doi.org/10.1016/j.ins.2013.07.007

12. López, V., Triguero, I., Carmona, C.J., García, S., Herrera, F.: Addressing imbalanced classification with instance generation techniques: IPADE-ID. Neurocomputing **126**, 15–28 (2014). https://doi.org/10.1016/j.neucom.2013.01.050
13. Mafarja, M., Mirjalili, S.: Whale optimization approaches for wrapper feature selection. Appl. Soft Comput. **62**, 441–453 (2018). https://doi.org/10.1016/j.asoc.2017.11.006
14. Millán-Giraldo, M., García, V., Sánchez, J.S.: Prototype selection in imbalanced data for dissimilarity representation - a preliminary study. In: Proceedings of the 1st International Conference on Pattern Recognition Applications and Methods, ICPRAM, vol. 1, pp. 242–247 (2012). https://doi.org/10.5220/0003795502420247
15. Moayedikia, A., Ong, K., Boo, Y.L., Yeoh, W.G.S., Jensen, R.: Feature selection for high dimensional imbalanced class data using harmony search. Eng. Appl. Artif. Intell. **57**, 38–49 (2017). https://doi.org/10.1016/j.engappai.2016.10.008
16. Napierala, K., Stefanowski, J.: BRACID: a comprehensive approach to learning rules from imbalanced data. J. Intell. Inf. Syst. **39**(2), 335–373 (2012). https://doi.org/10.1007/s10844-011-0193-0
17. Oliveira, D.V.R., Magalhaes, G.R., Cavalcanti, G.D.C., Ren, T.I.: Improved self-generating prototypes algorithm for imbalanced datasets. In: 2012 IEEE 24th International Conference on Tools with Artificial Intelligence, pp. 904–909. IEEE Computer Society (2012). https://doi.org/10.1109/ICTAI.2012.126
18. Oliveira, D.V.R., Cavalcanti, G.D.C., Ren, T.I., Silva, R.M.A.: Evolutionary adaptive self-generating prototypes for imbalanced datasets. In: 2015 International Joint Conference on Neural Networks, IJCNN 2015, Killarney, Ireland, 12–17 July 2015, pp. 1–8. IEEE (2015). https://doi.org/10.1109/IJCNN.2015.7280702
19. Prati, R.C., Batista, G.E.A.P.A., Monard, M.C.: Class imbalances *versus* class overlapping: an analysis of a learning system behavior. In: Monroy, R., Arroyo-Figueroa, G., Sucar, L.E., Sossa, H. (eds.) MICAI 2004. LNCS (LNAI), vol. 2972, pp. 312–321. Springer, Heidelberg (2004). https://doi.org/10.1007/978-3-540-24694-7_32
20. Rashedi, E., Nezamabadi-pour, H., Saryazdi, S.: GSA: a gravitational search algorithm. Inf. Sci. **179**, 2232–2248 (2009). https://doi.org/10.1016/j.ins.2009.03.004
21. Silva, E.J.R., Zanchettin, C.: On the existence of a threshold in class imbalance problems. In: IEEE International Conference on Systems, Man, and Cybernetics, Hong Kong, pp. 2714–2719 (2015). https://doi.org/10.1109/SMC.2015.474
22. Silva, E.J.R., Zanchettin, C.: A voronoi diagram based classifier for multiclass imbalanced data sets. In: 2016 5th Brazilian Conference on Intelligent Systems (BRACIS), pp. 109–114 (2016). https://doi.org/10.1109/BRACIS.2016.030
23. Sun, Y., Kamel, M.S., Wang, Y.: Boosting for learning multiple classes with imbalanced class distribution. In: ICDM, pp. 592–602. IEEE Computer Society (2006). https://doi.org/10.1109/ICDM.2006.29
24. Triguero, I., Derrac, J., García, S., Herrera, F.: A taxonomy and experimental study on prototype generation for nearest neighbor classification. IEEE Trans. Syst. Man Cybern. Part C **42**(1), 86–100 (2012). https://doi.org/10.1109/TSMCC.2010.2103939
25. Verbiest, N., Ramentol, E., Cornelis, C., Herrera, F.: Improving SMOTE with fuzzy rough prototype selection to detect noise in imbalanced classification data. In: Pavón, J., Duque-Méndez, N.D., Fuentes-Fernández, R. (eds.) IBERAMIA 2012. LNCS (LNAI), vol. 7637, pp. 169–178. Springer, Heidelberg (2012). https://doi.org/10.1007/978-3-642-34654-5_18

26. Wang, S., Yao, X.: Multiclass imbalance problems: analysis and potential solutions. IEEE Trans. Syst. Man Cybern. Part B **42**(4), 1119–1130 (2012). https://doi.org/10.1109/TSMCB.2012.2187280
27. Yijing, L., Haixiang, G., Xiao, L., Yanan, L., Jinling, L.: Adapted ensemble classification algorithm based on multiple classifier system and feature selection for classifying multi-class imbalanced data. Knowl. Based Syst. **94**, 88–104 (2016). https://doi.org/10.1016/j.knosys.2015.11.013

Increasing the Generalisaton Capacity of Conditional VAEs

Alexej Klushyn(✉), Nutan Chen, Botond Cseke, Justin Bayer, and Patrick van der Smagt

Machine Learning Research Lab, Volkswagen Group, Munich, Germany
alexej.klushyn@argmax.ai

Abstract. We address the problem of one-to-many mappings in supervised learning, where a single instance has many different solutions of possibly equal cost. The framework of conditional variational autoencoders describes a class of methods to tackle such structured-prediction tasks by means of latent variables. We propose to incentivise informative latent representations for increasing the generalisation capacity of conditional variational autoencoders. To this end, we modify the latent variable model by defining the likelihood as a function of the latent variable only and introduce an expressive multimodal prior to enable the model for capturing semantically meaningful features of the data. To validate our approach, we train our model on the Cornell Robot Grasping dataset, and modified versions of MNIST and Fashion-MNIST obtaining results that show a significantly higher generalisation capability.

Keywords: Structured prediction · Latent variable models · Conditional variational autoencoders · Empirical bayes

1 Introduction

The problem of approximating conditional probability distributions $p(\mathbf{y} \mid \mathbf{x})$ is a central point in the field of supervised learning. Although, learning a complex many-to-one mapping is straightforward if a sufficient amount of data is available [7,13], most methods fail when it comes to structured-prediction problems, where a distribution with multiple modes (one-to-many mapping) has to be modelled [16].

Conditional variational autoencoders (CVAEs) [14] are a class of latent variable models for approximating one-to-many functions. They define a lower bound on the intractable marginal likelihood by introducing a variational posterior distribution. The learned generative model and the corresponding (approximate) posterior distribution of the latent variables provide a decoder/encoder pair that captures semantically meaningful features of the data. In this paper we address the issue of learning informative encodings/latent representations with the goal of increasing the generalisation capacity of CVAEs.

I. V. Tetko et al. (Eds.): ICANN 2019, LNCS 11728, pp. 779–791, 2019.
https://doi.org/10.1007/978-3-030-30484-3_61

In contrast to variational autoencoders (VAEs) [6,12], the decoder of CVAEs is a function of the latent variable *and* the condition $\mathbf{x}$. Thus, the model is not incentivised to learn an informative latent representation. To tackle this problem, we propose to apply a VAE-like decoder that depends only on the latent variable. This modification requires that the model is capable of learning a rich encoding. We follow the line of argument in [4]—where the expressiveness of the generative model is increased by introducing a flexible prior—and show that a *multimodal* prior substantially improves optimisation.

Building on that, we propose to apply a learnable mixture distribution as prior. We show that the classical mixture of Gaussians prior suffers from focusing on outliers during optimisation causing a badly trained generative model. Instead of learning the means and variances of the respective mixture components directly, we address this issue by introducing a Gaussian mixture prior, inspired by [17], that is parameterised through both the encoder and the decoder, and evaluated at learned pseudo latent variables.

2 Methods

2.1 Preliminaries: Conditional VAEs

In structured prediction problems each condition $\mathbf{x}$ can be related to several targets $\mathbf{y}$ (one-to-many mapping), which results in a multimodal conditional distribution $p_\theta(\mathbf{y}\,|\,\mathbf{x})$. Conditional-latent-variable models (CLVM), defined by

$$p_\theta(\mathbf{y}\,|\,\mathbf{x}) = \int p_\theta(\mathbf{y}\,|\,\mathbf{x},\mathbf{z})\,p_\theta(\mathbf{z}\,|\,\mathbf{x})\,\mathrm{d}\mathbf{z}, \tag{1}$$

are capable of modelling multimodality by means of latent variables $\mathbf{z}$. However, in most cases the integral in Eq. (1) is intractable. Amortised variational inference [6,12] allows to address this issue by approximating $p_\theta(\mathbf{y}\,|\,\mathbf{x})$ through maximising the evidence lower bound (ELBO):

$$\log p_\theta(\mathbf{y}\,|\,\mathbf{x}) \geq \mathbb{E}_{q_\phi(\mathbf{z}|\mathbf{x},\mathbf{y})}\left[\log \frac{p_\theta(\mathbf{y}\,|\,\mathbf{x},\mathbf{z})\,p_\theta(\mathbf{z}\,|\,\mathbf{x})}{q_\phi(\mathbf{z}\,|\,\mathbf{x},\mathbf{y})}\right] =: \mathcal{L}_{\mathrm{ELBO}}(\theta,\phi), \tag{2}$$

where the parameters of the approximate posterior $q_\phi(\mathbf{z}\,|\,\mathbf{x},\mathbf{y})$, the likelihood $p_\theta(\mathbf{y}\,|\,\mathbf{x},\mathbf{z})$, and the prior $p_\theta(\mathbf{z}\,|\,\mathbf{x})$ are defined as neural-network functions of the conditioning variables. This model is known as conditional variational autoencoder (CVAE) [14]. Consequently, we will refer to the neural networks representing $q_\phi(\mathbf{z}\,|\,\mathbf{x},\mathbf{y})$ and $p_\theta(\mathbf{y}\,|\,\mathbf{x},\mathbf{z})$ as encoder and decoder, respectively.

2.2 Incentivising Informative Latent Representations

In the CVAE, the likelihood is conditioned on $\mathbf{z}$ *and* $\mathbf{x}$. Therefore, the model is not incentivised to learn an informative latent representation. Rather, latent variables can be viewed as an assistance for enabling multimodality in $p_\theta(\mathbf{y}\,|\,\mathbf{x})$.

For being able to fully exploit the generalisation capacity of CVAEs, we argue that an informative latent representation is necessary. Thus, $\mathbf{z}$ determines $\mathbf{y}$ completely, i.e. the mutual information $\mathrm{I}(\mathbf{x}\,;\,\mathbf{y}\,|\,\mathbf{z}) = 0$. Following this line of argument, we obtain $\mathbf{x} \perp \mathbf{y}\,|\,\mathbf{z}$, and thus $p_\theta(\mathbf{y}\,|\,\mathbf{x},\mathbf{z}) = p_\theta(\mathbf{y}\,|\,\mathbf{z})$, leading to the following CLVM:

$$p_\theta(\mathbf{y}\,|\,\mathbf{x}) = \int p_\theta(\mathbf{y}\,|\,\mathbf{z})\, p_\theta(\mathbf{z}\,|\,\mathbf{x})\, \mathrm{d}\mathbf{z}. \tag{3}$$

This modification enforces the model to learn a richer latent representation because all the information given by the training data has to be encoded.

However, the model must also be capable of learning such a complex latent representation. In case of CVAEs, the prior $p_\theta(\mathbf{z}\,|\,\mathbf{x})$ is usually defined as a Gaussian distribution, leading to limited flexibility of the model, and hence to a worse generalisation, as addressed in [4] and shown in Sects. 4.2 and 4.3. We build on the line of argumentation in [4], where the above limitation is tackled by introducing an expressive prior. The KL-divergence $\mathbb{KL}\left(q_\phi(\mathbf{z}\,|\,\mathbf{x},\mathbf{y})\|\; p_\theta(\mathbf{z}\,|\,\mathbf{x})\right)$ in Eq. 2 can be viewed as a regulariser to avoid over-fitting. Therefore, a flexible prior allows for learning a more complex latent representation and leads automatically to a more expressive generative model $p_\theta(\mathbf{y}\,|\,\mathbf{z})\, p_\theta(\mathbf{z}\,|\,\mathbf{x})$.

2.3 Modelling Low-Density Regions

In the previous section, we discussed the need of expressive priors in our setting. Next, we will specify an important property the prior has to posses. In most models within the VAE/CVAE framework, the prior is defined as a *unimodal* distribution. This leads to a significant shortcoming illustrated by the following structured-prediction task: generating grasping poses (targets) for a certain object (condition). Imagine a generated grasping pose is located in the middle of a plate instead of on the edge. Hence, generating targets between modes of $p_\theta(\mathbf{y}\,|\,\mathbf{x})$ might be an exclusion criterion.

To understand the cause, let us assume a dataset consisting of only a single condition with different targets. Thus, $q_\phi(\mathbf{z}\,|\,\mathbf{x},\mathbf{y}) = q_\phi(\mathbf{z}\,|\,\mathbf{y})$, $p_\theta(\mathbf{y}\,|\,\mathbf{x}) = p_\theta(\mathbf{y})$, and $p_\theta(\mathbf{z}\,|\,\mathbf{x}) = p_\theta(\mathbf{z})$ (note that this is equivalent to a vanilla VAE). We want to represent $p_\theta(\mathbf{y})$ by transforming $p_\theta(\mathbf{z})$ through a bijective function $g(\cdot)$, i.e. $\mathbf{y} = g(\mathbf{z})$. By applying the change of variables, we derive:

$$p_\theta(g(\mathbf{z})) = \frac{1}{\sqrt{\det(\mathbf{J}^T\,\mathbf{J})}}\, p_\theta(\mathbf{z}), \quad \text{with} \quad \mathbf{J} = \frac{\partial g(\mathbf{z})}{\partial \mathbf{z}}.$$

In this context, we define the magnification factor $\mathrm{MF} := \sqrt{\det(\mathbf{J}^T\,\mathbf{J})}$ [2]. Setting $p_\theta(g(\mathbf{z})) = 0$ requires either $p_\theta(\mathbf{z}) = 0$ or $\mathrm{MF} \to \infty$. Thus, zero-density regions can only be represented at $\mathbf{y}$ if either the original density is zero or the MF becomes infinitely large (see Sect. 4.1 for visualisation). For example, when using a Gaussian distribution as prior, near-zero density regions occur only at its tails. If $g(\cdot)$ is the likelihood neural network and we assume it to be continuous, zero-density regions can only be obtained in tails. For zero densities elsewhere, infinitely large MF-values are required. Thus, the derivative of $g(\cdot)$ becomes infinitely large: $\mathbf{J} \to \infty$, leading to a badly-conditioned optimisation problem. The above line of argument applies equally to datasets with multiple conditions.

2.4 Expressive Priors for Conditional VAEs

A natural approach to address the difficulties introduced in Sects. 2.2 and 2.3 is a flexible multimodal prior. This could be realised by a conditional mixture of Gaussians (CMoG) prior $p_\theta(\mathbf{z} \mid \mathbf{x}) = \frac{1}{K}\sum_{k=1}^{K} \mathcal{N}\big(\mu_k(\mathbf{x}), \mathrm{diag}(\sigma_k^2(\mathbf{x}))\big)$, where K is the number of mixture components. As in case of the vanilla CVAE, the parameters of the prior $\{\mu_k(\mathbf{x}), \mathrm{diag}(\sigma_k^2(\mathbf{x}))\}_{k=1}^{K} \in \mathbb{R}^{N_\mathbf{z}}$ are represented by a neural network. Unfortunately, this approach performs badly, especially in high dimensional latent spaces (see Sect. 4.2).

We suspect this mainly due to the following reason: the prior is optimised through minimising $\mathbb{KL}\big(q_\phi(\mathbf{z} \mid \mathbf{x}, \mathbf{y}) \| \, p_\theta(\mathbf{z} \mid \mathbf{x})\big)$ (see Eq. 2). The optimal Bayes prior is the aggregated posterior $p^*(\mathbf{z} \mid \mathbf{x}) = \mathbb{E}_{\mathbf{y} \sim \hat{p}(\mathbf{x},\mathbf{y})}\, q_\phi(\mathbf{z} \mid \mathbf{x}, \mathbf{y})$—representing the manifold of the encoded data. Since the parameters of each mixture component of the CMoG prior are learned independently, it is not possible to avoid that mixture components leave the manifold of the encoded data by focusing on outliers (see Sect. 4.2 for experimental support). This leads to a badly trained generative model. Thus, the problem is that the prior is not incentivised to stay on the manifold of the encoded data.

Instead of learning the mean and variance of each mixture component of the prior directly, we tackle the above issue by introducing a parameterisation through both the encoder and the decoder. This approach is inspired by the VampPrior [17] (VAE framework), which is parameterised through the encoder. When extending it to the CVAE framework, we obtain the conditional VampPrior $p(\mathbf{z} \mid \mathbf{x}) = \frac{1}{K}\sum_{k=1}^{K} q_\phi(\mathbf{z} \mid \mathbf{x}, \tilde{\mathbf{y}}_k)$, which is evaluated at learned pseudo targets $\{\tilde{\mathbf{y}}_k\}_{k=1}^{K} \in \mathbb{R}^{N_\mathbf{y}}$. However, pseudo latent variables $\tilde{\mathbf{z}}$ would require less parameters and thus are less complex to optimise for representing the manifold of the encoded data. Evaluating the conditional VampPrior at decoded $\tilde{\mathbf{z}}$ would make use of this advantage (see Sect. 4.2 for experimental support). Below, we introduce the conditional decoder-based Vamp (CDV) prior:

$$p_\pi(\mathbf{z} \mid \mathbf{x}) = \frac{1}{K}\sum_{k=1}^{K} q_\phi\big(\mathbf{z} \mid \mathbf{x}, \mu_\theta(\tilde{\mathbf{z}}_k(\mathbf{x}))\big), \tag{4}$$

where $\mu_\theta(\cdot)$ is the mean of the likelihood and $\{\tilde{\mathbf{z}}_k(\mathbf{x})\}_{k=1}^{K} \in \mathbb{R}^{N_\mathbf{z}}$ are defined as functions of the condition and approximated by a single neural network $f_\psi(\mathbf{x})$, which is trained through backpropagation. Thus, the parameters of the prior are $\pi = \{\psi, \theta, \phi\}$. As an additional feature, this approach requires less parameters than the CMoG prior, since only the pseudo latent variables ($\in \mathbb{R}^{N_\mathbf{z}}$)) have to be learned instead of the means and variances (each $\in \mathbb{R}^{N_\mathbf{z}}$) of the CMoG prior.

The CLVM in Eq. 3 was introduced to incentivise a more informative latent representation for achieving a higher generalisation capacity. This step demands a flexible multimodal prior that allows the model for capturing semantically meaningful features of the data. The CDV prior meets these requirements and, in contrast to a classical Gaussian mixture prior, it facilitates a well trained generative model.

3 Related Work

Learning informative latent representations in VAEs is an ongoing field of research [1,5,15]. The connection between informative latent representations and a flexible prior was pointed out in [4] and motivated through Bits-Back Coding. Several additional works improved VAEs by learning more complex priors [10,17]. The reason for increasing the expressiveness of the prior is a lower KL-divergence—and thus a better trained decoder, leading to more qualitative samples of the generative model. Based on that, it can be derived that the optimal Bayes prior is the aggregated posterior [17]. The VampPrior [17] approximates the aggregated posterior by a uniform mixture of approximate posteriors, evaluated at learned pseudo inputs in the observable space.

In contrast to the (conditional) VampPrior, the CDV prior is parameterised through both the encoder and the decoder, and evaluated at learned pseudo latent variables. Since the latent space has in general a lower dimension than the observable space, pseudo latent variables need less parameters and are easier to optimise for approximating the aggregated posterior.

Several applications based on the concept of CVAEs were published: they can be used for filling pixels given a partial image [14], for image inpainting conditioned on visual attributes (e.g., colour and gender) [21], or for predicting events by conditioning the distribution of possible movements on a scene [19]. As in [14], we use CVAEs to complete images—with the aim of obtaining a widest possible variety of generations, thus a classical one-to-many mapping. However, with an additional difficulty: it is learned from a dataset of one-to-one mappings to validate the generalisation capacity of the models.

Another important field where CVAEs are applied is robot grasping: earlier work has focused on detecting robust grasping poses [9,11], while recent work is often based on structured prediction with the idea of learning multimodal conditional probability distributions for generating grasping poses [18]. In [9,11], classifiers are applied to detect whether a grasping pose is robust. A problem here is that suitable grasping poses need to be proposed by hand. In our approach, CVAEs are used to generate grasping poses for unknown objects. Afterwards, similar to [9], a discriminator is applied to validate them.

4 Experiments

We conduct five experiments to compare the introduced models: first, we visualise on a simplified task the difficulty of unimodal priors. Building on that, we demonstrate on a synthetic toy dataset that CMoG- and CDV-CVAEs are capable of modelling near-zero-density regions. Second, we show on a modified version of MNIST and Fashion-MNIST that the variety of generated samples is significantly larger when combining the CVAE with the CMoG or CDV prior. Finally, we compare the CVAE with the CDV-CVAE on real world data, the Cornell Robot Grasping dataset.

To train our models we applied a linear annealing scheme [3] for the first epoch. This is especially important for the CDV-CVAE because it is sensitive to over-regularisation by the KL-term in the initial optimisation phase.

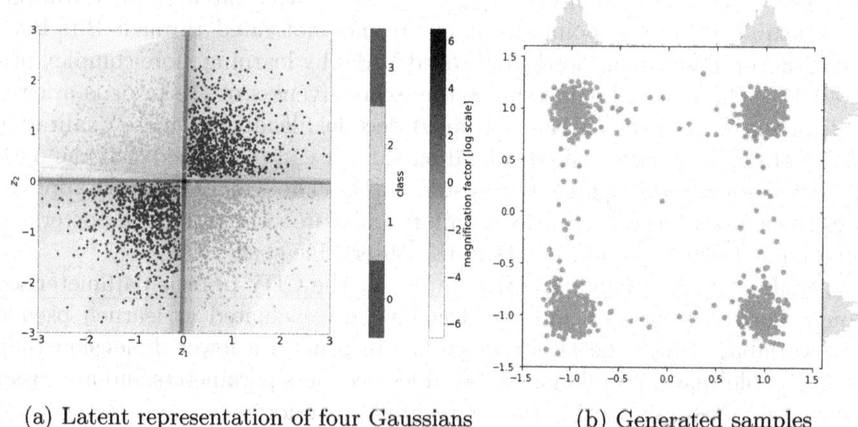

(a) Latent representation of four Gaussians (b) Generated samples

Fig. 1. Effect of unimodal priors on the performance of VAEs/CVAEs. For illustration, we use a dataset of four Gaussian distributions arranged in a square. Latent representation (a): the colours encode the four different Gaussians. The greyscale indicates the gradients of the decoder, which are required to map from a unimodal to a multimodal distribution. 1,000 generated samples (b): we also obtain samples between modes, since the decoder is a continuous function approximated by a neural network. (see Sect. 4.1)

4.1 Modelling Low-Density Regions

Visualisation of the Problem. To reduce complexity, we trained a vanilla VAE with a Gaussian prior on a simple toy dataset consisting of four Gaussian distributions. This toy dataset can be interpreted as a simplified structured-prediction task with only one condition and four targets.

Figure 1a shows the two-dimensional latent space, which depicts the aggregated posterior of the model. Each of the four Gaussians is encoded by a different colour. To map from a unimodal to a multimodal distribution, the decoder has to model large gradients, as discussed in Sect. 2.3. The magnification factor is visualised by the greyscale in Fig. 1a, which represents the Jacobian of the decoder. The support of the aggregated posterior is noticeably smaller than the support of the prior. Since the decoder is a continuous function, a gap at the boundaries of different classes in the latent space (as shown in Fig. 1a) represents the distance between the modes in the observable space. The size of the gap depends on the gradients that our model is able to achieve: the higher the gradient, the smaller the gap in the latent space.

When sampling from the generative model, we first sample from the prior. If the sample comes from a region which is not supported by the aggregated posterior, the decoded sample will end up between two modes, as demonstrated in Fig. 1b.

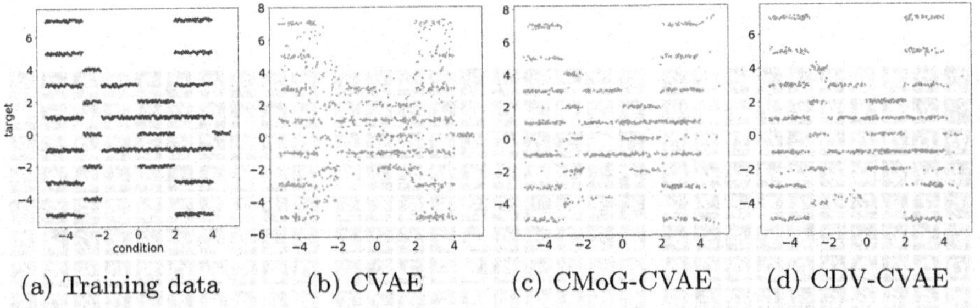

(a) Training data (b) CVAE (c) CMoG-CVAE (d) CDV-CVAE

Fig. 2. Synthetic toy dataset (a) of one-dimensional one-to-many mappings. The horizontal axis represents the conditions, the vertical axis the targets. Generated samples (b–d): a near-zero-density between different modes is only achieved through multimodal priors, as shown in (c) and (d). (see Sect. 4.1)

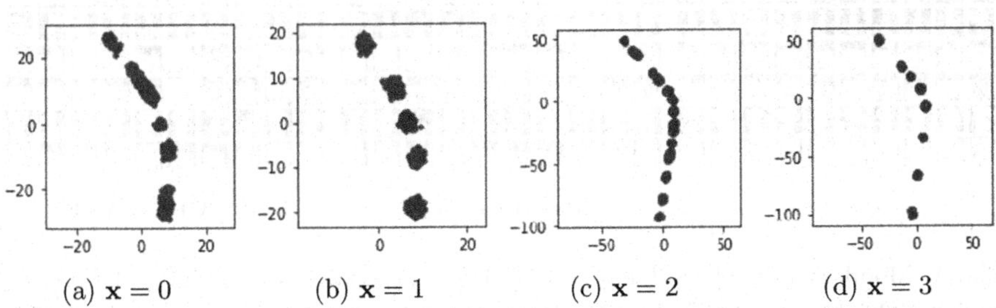

(a) $\mathbf{x} = 0$ (b) $\mathbf{x} = 1$ (c) $\mathbf{x} = 2$ (d) $\mathbf{x} = 3$

Fig. 3. Samples from the CDV prior depending on the condition $\mathbf{x}$ (trained on the synthetic toy dataset Fig. 2a). The number of modes of the prior and of the likelihood distribution are similar (see Fig. 2d). If the number of targets changes, the prior modes merge, as shown in (a) and (c). (see Sect. 4.1)

Synthetic Toy Dataset. In this experiment we reused a synthetic toy dataset [16] for validating models for structured-prediction tasks. It consists of one-dimensional one-to-many mappings (see Fig. 2a): the horizontal-axis represents the conditions and the vertical-axis the targets. Even though the dataset is simple, the abrupt changes of the number and location of the targets are quite challenging to model.

For all three models, we used latent spaces with two dimensions. CMoG-CVAE ($\mathcal{L}_{\text{ELBO}} = -0.586$) and CDV-CVAE ($\mathcal{L}_{\text{ELBO}} = -0.518$) outperformed the original CVAE ($\mathcal{L}_{\text{ELBO}} = -1.12$) as shown in Fig. 2. Multimodal priors facilitate the modelling of near-zero-density regions between different modes (Fig. 2c, d), as discussed in Sect. 2.3. Figure 3 shows how the CDV prior distribution changes with the condition $\mathbf{x}$.

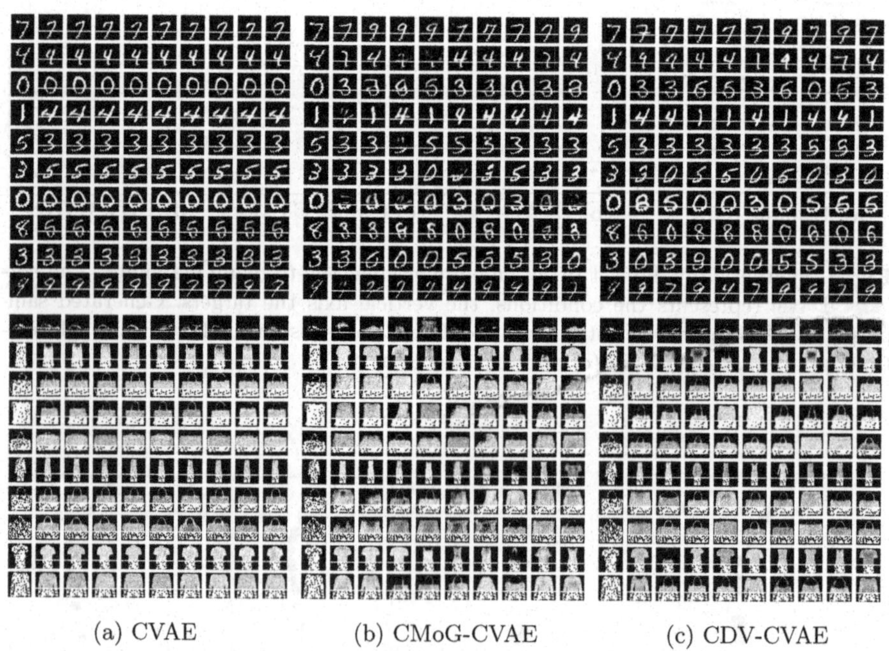

(a) CVAE (b) CMoG-CVAE (c) CDV-CVAE

Fig. 4. Modified MNIST and Fashion-MNIST: the goal is to validate whether the models can generalise and learn a one-to-many from a dataset of one-to-one mappings. The respective first column shows images of the test set, consisting of a condition (lower third) and a target (upper two-thirds). The remaining nine columns show generations conditioned on the lower third of the first image (marked by the white line). The variety of generated targets in (b) and (c) is significantly larger than in (a). However, in case of the CMoG prior (b) we obtained a high amount of poor generations. (see Sect. 4.2)

4.2 Verifying the Generalisation Capacity

We created a modified version of MNIST [8] and Fashion-MNIST [20] to evaluate the generalisation capacity of the different models. For this purpose, we split binarised MNIST/Fashion-MNIST images into two parts: a conditional part, the lower third (last 28 × 10 pixels) of the image—and a target part, the upper two-thirds (first 28 × 18 pixels). The dataset has therefore only one target per condition. The goal is to investigate whether the models are able to define a set of new targets for each condition of the test set. In other words, whether they can learn a one-to-many from a one-to-one mapping.

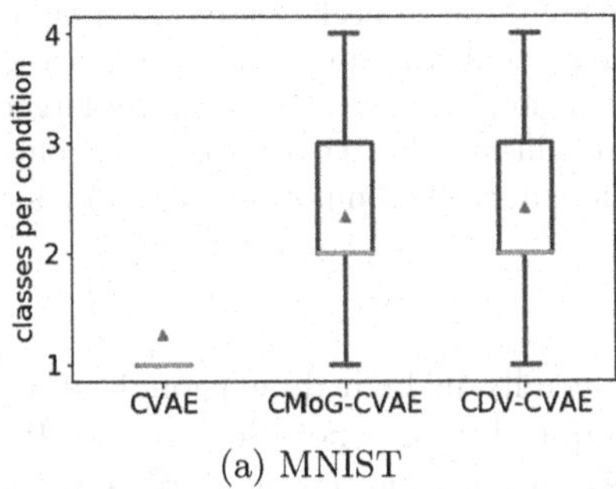

(a) MNIST

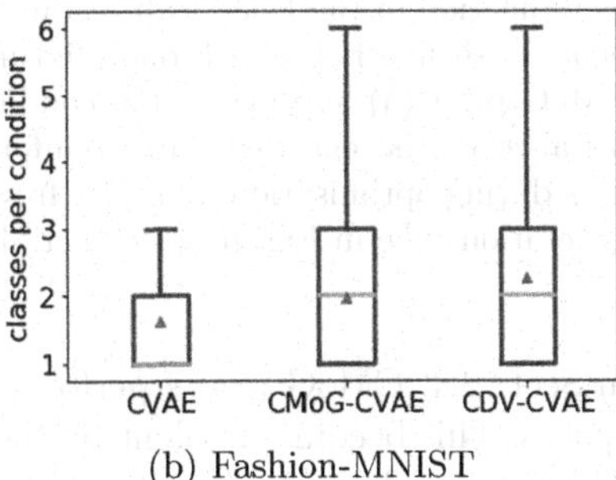

(b) Fashion-MNIST

Fig. 5. Variety of generated targets: for each condition in the test dataset, 10 targets were generated. A classifier was used to determine the number of different classes per condition. The box plots in (a) and (b) show that CMoG- and CDV-CVAEs generate targets with a larger variety for both datasets. (see Sect. 4.2)

In all three models, we used a 32-dimensional latent space. CMoG-CVAEs (Fig. 4b) and CDV-CVAEs (Fig. 4c) were able to represent a multimodal likelihood distribution, in contrast to vanilla CVAEs (Fig. 4a). This is shown by the significantly larger variety of generated targets per condition.

To measure the variety of the generated targets, we trained a classifier on MNIST/Fashion-MNIST and sampled 10 targets for each condition of the test set. Afterwards, we used the classifier to determine how many different classes were generated per condition. Figure 5 shows the results for the different models and datasets. Note that we only took sampled targets into account, which could be clearly assigned to a class—especially to avoid treating poor generations as additional classes. In case of both datasets, CMoG- and CDV-CVAEs learned to generate several classes per condition, and thus a one-to-many from a one-to-one mapping. Additionally, CMoG- and CDV-CVAEs achieved a larger variety of generations within the same class (see Fig. 4).

Based on the above results, we can deduce that CMoG- and CDV-CVAEs have a higher generalisation capacity. The larger variety of the generations is due to the structure of the priors: since they are mixtures of K distributions, each target is represented by one or more mixture components. However, as discussed

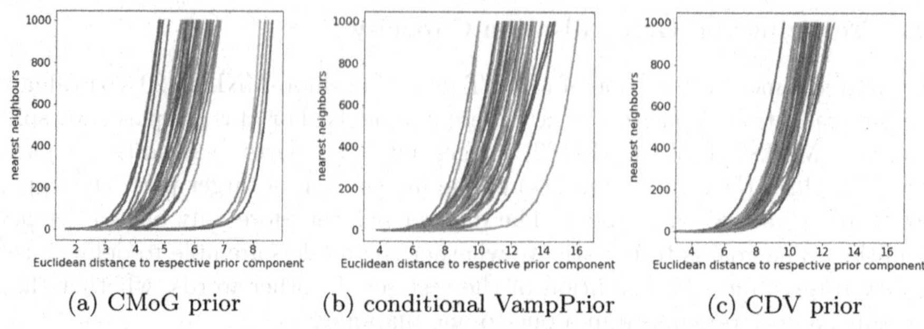

(a) CMoG prior (b) conditional VampPrior (c) CDV prior

Fig. 6. The plots show the number of nearest neighbours (encoded MNIST data points) as a function of the Euclidean distance to the mean of the respective mixture component. Each line belongs to one mixture component. Four mixture components of the CMoG prior (a) and one of the conditional VampPrior (b) have a significantly larger distance to the encoded data, reinforcing the conclusion that they focused on outliers during optimisation. Samples from one of these mixture components lead to poor generations like in Fig. 4b. (see Sect. 4.2)

in Sect. 2.4, CMoG priors perform badly, especially in high dimensional latent spaces. This becomes evident by the high amount of poor generations in Fig. 4b. To verify our hypothesis—that the poor generations are caused by mixture components of the CMoG prior that focused on outliers during optimisation—we encoded our training data (MNIST) and measured the Euclidean distance to the respective mean of each prior component. Figure 6 shows the number of nearest neighbours (encoded data points) as a function of the Euclidean distance in the latent space. Each line represents one of the 32 mixture components. In contrast to the CDV prior (Fig. 6c), four mixture components of the CMoG prior (Fig. 6a) have a significantly larger distance to the encoded data. This reinforces the conclusion that these mixture components focused on outliers during the optimisation process. We obtain poor generations like in Fig. 4b if a generated target is based on one of these four components, because $p_\theta(\mathbf{x} \mid \mathbf{z})$ is only optimised (see Eq. 2) to decode samples that lie on the manifold of the encoded training data.

Additionally, we show that the CDV prior outperforms the conditional VampPrior (Fig. 6b), where one mixture component has a significantly larger distance to the encoded data. As discussed in Sect. 2.4, we suspect this due to the higher dimension of the pseudo targets $\tilde{\mathbf{y}}$, making them more complex to optimise than pseudo latent variables $\tilde{\mathbf{z}}$.

4.3 Generating Grasping Poses

In this experiment we want to assess the generalisation capabilities of CVAE and CDV-CVAE on a real-world dataset. To this end, we use the Cornell Robot Grasping dataset, which consists of 885 conditions (250 × 250 pixels greyscale images of objects) and 5,110 targets (proposed grasping poses) [9]. The latent

(a) Test objects with proposed grasping poses

(b) CVAE

(c) CDV-CVAE

Fig. 7. Cornell Robot Grasping dataset: (a) objects (conditions) with proposed grasping poses (targets) defined by the test dataset. The CDV-CVAE (c) generates more realistic grasping poses for unknown objects than the original CVAE (a). 29% of the grasping poses generated by the CDV-CVAE were above a discrimination score of 0.99, whereas the CVAE reached 22%. (see Sect. 4.3)

spaces of both models are 16-dimensional. For training, we resized the conditions to 64×64 pixels. Furthermore, we adapted the way how the grasping poses are represented: the rectangles (original representation) were redefined by a centre, a short and long axis, and a rotation angle.

Figure 7a shows a selection of objects and proposed grasping poses defined by the test dataset. Figures 7b and c depict grasping poses generated by the CVAE and CDV-CVAE, respectively. As discussed in Sects. 4.1 and 4.2, CDV-CVAEs have a higher capability of modelling one-to-many mappings and enable a larger variety of generated targets.

To verify whether the CDV-CVAE has actually learned to generate more realistic grasping poses for unknown objects, we apply a similar approach as proposed in [9]. It is based on a discriminator for validating proposed grasping poses. For this purpose, we trained the discriminator in equal parts with samples from joint and marginal empirical distribution $(\mathbf{x}, \mathbf{y}) \sim \hat{p}(\mathbf{x}, \mathbf{y})$ and $(\mathbf{x}, \mathbf{y}) \sim \hat{p}(\mathbf{x})\,\hat{p}(\mathbf{y})$, respectively. Subsequently, we generated 10 grasping poses for each condition in the test set and filtered out those with a discrimination score below 0.99. As a result, 29% of the grasping poses generated by the CDV-CVAE were above this threshold, whereas the CVAE reached 22%. This allows the conclusion that the CDV-CVAE is a useful extension to the CVAE framework.

5 Conclusion

In this paper, we have introduced a modified conditional latent variable model to incentivise informative latent representations. To enable the model for capturing semantically meaningful features of the data, we have proposed an expressive multimodal prior that facilitates, in contrast to a classical Gaussian mixture prior, a well trained generative model.

We have shown that our approach increases the generalisation capacity of CVAEs on a modified version of MNIST and Fashion-MNIST by achieving a significantly larger variety of generated targets—and on the Cornell Robot Grasping dataset by generating more realistic grasping poses. Additionally, we have demonstrated that a straightforward application of CVAEs to structured-prediction problems suffers from a difficulty to represent multimodal distributions and that our approach overcomes this limitation.

References

1. Alemi, A.A., Poole, B., Fischer, I., Dillon, J.V., Saurous, R.A., Murphy, K.: Fixing a broken ELBO. In: ICML (2018)
2. Bishop, C.M., Svens' en, M., Williams, C.K.I.: Magnification factors for the SOM and GTM algorithms. In: Proceedings Workshop on Self-Organizing Maps (1997)
3. Bowman, S.R., Vilnis, L., Vinyals, O., Dai, A.M., Jozefowicz, R., Bengio, S.: Generating sentences from a continuous space. In: CoNLL (2016)
4. Chen, X., et al.: Variational Lossy Autoencoder. CoRR (2016)
5. Higgins, I., et al.: beta-VAE: Learning basic visual concepts with a constrained variational framework. In: ICLR (2017)
6. Kingma, D.P., Welling, M.: Auto-encoding variational Bayes. CoRR (2013)
7. Krizhevsky, A., Sutskever, I., Hinton, G.E.: Imagenet classification with deep convolutional neural networks. In: NeurIPS (2012)
8. LeCun, Y., Bottou, L., Bengio, Y., Haffner, P., et al.: Gradient-based learning applied to document recognition. In: Proceedings of the IEEE (1998)
9. Lenz, I., Lee, H., Saxena, A.: Deep learning for detecting robotic grasps. Int. J. Robot. Res. (2015)
10. Nalisnick, E., Smyth, P.: Stick-breaking variational autoencoders. In: ICLR (2017)
11. Pinto, L., Gupta, A.: Supersizing self-supervision: learning to grasp from 50k tries and 700 robot hours. In: ICRA (2016)
12. Rezende, D.J., Mohamed, S., Wierstra, D.: Stochastic backpropagation and approximate inference in deep generative models. In: ICML (2014)
13. Simonyan, K., Zisserman, A.: Very deep convolutional networks for large-scale image recognition. In: ICLR (2015)
14. Sohn, K., Lee, H., Yan, X.: Learning structured output representation using deep conditional generative models. In: NeurIPS (2015)
15. Sønderby, C.K., Raiko, T., Maaløe, L., Sønderby, S.K., Winther, O.: Ladder variational autoencoders. In: NeurIPS (2016)

16. Tang, Y., Salakhutdinov, R.R.: Learning Stochastic Feedforward Neural Networks. In: NeurIPS (2013)
17. Tomczak, J., Welling, M.: VAE with a VampPrior. In: AISTATS (2018)
18. Veres, M., Moussa, M., Taylor, G.W.: Modeling grasp motor imagery through deep conditional generative models. IEEE Robot. Autom. Lett. **2**, 757–764 (2017)
19. Walker, J., Doersch, C., Gupta, A., Hebert, M.: An uncertain future: forecasting from static images using variational autoencoders. In: Leibe, B., Matas, J., Sebe, N., Welling, M. (eds.) ECCV 2016. LNCS, vol. 9911, pp. 835–851. Springer, Cham (2016). https://doi.org/10.1007/978-3-319-46478-7_51
20. Xiao, H., Rasul, K., Vollgraf, R.: Fashion-MNIST: a novel image dataset for benchmarking machine learning algorithms. arXiv:1708.07747 (2017)
21. Yan, X., Yang, J., Sohn, K., Lee, H.: Attribute2Image: conditional image generation from visual attributes. In: Leibe, B., Matas, J., Sebe, N., Welling, M. (eds.) ECCV 2016. LNCS, vol. 9908, pp. 776–791. Springer, Cham (2016). https://doi.org/10.1007/978-3-319-46493-0_47

Playing the Large Margin Preference Game

Mirko Polato[1(✉)], Guglielmo Faggioli[1], Ivano Lauriola[1,2], and Fabio Aiolli[1]

[1] Department of Mathematics, University of Padova, Padua, Italy
{mpolato,gfaggiol,aiolli}@math.unipd.it
[2] Fondazione Bruno Kessler, Trento, Italy
lauriola@phd.unipd.it

Abstract. We propose a large margin preference learning model based on game theory to solve the label ranking problem. Specifically, we show the proposed formulation is able to perform multiclass classification by solving a single convex optimization problem. Generally, such formulation, although theoretically well-founded, requires to learn a large number of parameters. To reduce the computational complexity, we propose a strategy based on the solution of smaller subproblems, that can be further optimized by exploiting techniques borrowed from multi-armed bandits literature. Finally, we show how the proposed framework exhibits state-of-the-art results on many benchmark datasets.

Keywords: Game theory · SVM · Large margin · Kernel method · Large scale

1 Introduction

For many years, Support Vector Machine (SVM) has been one of the most studied and heavily used Machine Learning (ML) method. Besides its state-of-the-art performance in many learning tasks, its success is mainly due to its theoretical foundation. SVM roots in statistical learning theory [20] and follows the principle of structural risk minimization to control the generalization ability of a learning machine. It belongs to the family of large margin models and its elegant formulation makes it suitable for connections with other theoretical fields, e.g., its strong relation with game theory (GT). For instance, it is well known that hard margin SVM can be cast into a two-players zero-sum game [1]. GT has also been related to other ML techniques, including, boosting [8] and linear regression [13]. More recently, similar connections have been made between Preference Learning (PL) and GT [16].

Starting from this last finding, we present a theoretically well-founded preference learning framework inspired by game theory for multi-class classification problems. Specifically, we define a (generalized) linear PL model in which the large margin problem is cast into a two-players zero-sum game. The proposed

I. V. Tetko et al. (Eds.): ICANN 2019, LNCS 11728, pp. 792–804, 2019.
https://doi.org/10.1007/978-3-030-30484-3_62

framework is general enough to be easily used with kernels in order to handle non-linear problems. We show how this model can be trained by solving a simple convex optimization problem. However, akin other kernel methods, like SVM, it could not be suited for large scale problems. To this regard we also propose a technique inspired by multi-armed bandits to speed up the learning process.

The remainder of the paper is structured as follows: Sect. 2 introduces all the necessary background. Sections 3 and 4 describe the main contributions of the paper. Finally, Sects. 5 and 6 show the experimental assessment and discuss possible future research directions.

2 Background

2.1 Preference Learning

Preference learning (PL) is a sub-task in machine learning in which the input data consists of preference relations. In PL problems, the goal is to construct a preference model able to predict preferences for previously unseen items. The typical assumption is that preferences are in agreement with some utility function g_θ. The task then becomes to find the parameters θ of the utility function g.

Label ranking is one of the main PL tasks [10]: given a set of input patterns $\mathbf{x}_i \in \mathcal{X}$, $i \in [1, \ldots, n]$, and a finite set of labels $\mathcal{Y} \equiv \{y_1, y_2, \ldots, y_m\}$ the goal is to learn the utility function $g_\theta : \mathcal{X} \times \mathcal{Y} \to \mathbb{R}$ which assigns a fitness score for each instance-label pair $(\mathbf{x}, y)$. Label ranking represents a generalization of a classification task, since, given an instance $\mathbf{x}$, g_θ implicitly defines a total order over $\mathcal{Y}$. In the label ranking context, the training set consists of pairwise preferences $y_i \succ_\mathbf{x} y_j$, $i \neq j$, i.e., for the pattern $\mathbf{x}$, y_i is preferred to y_j. In the special case of classification, in which $\mathbf{x}$ is associated to a unique label y_i, the preferences' set is

$$\{y_i \succ_\mathbf{x} y_j \mid 1 \leq j \neq i \leq m\}.$$

In this work we focus on (generalized) linear preference models [2,19] on some feature space $\mathcal{F}$ induced by an embedding function ϕ, i.e., $g_\mathbf{w}(\phi(\mathbf{x}), y) = \mathbf{w}^\intercal \psi(\phi(\mathbf{x}), y)$, where $\mathbf{w}$ is the parameters vector, ψ is a joint representation of instance-label pairs, and $\phi : \mathcal{X} \to \mathbb{R}^d$ is the embedding function.

Since the preferences are ranked according to the utility function, given a preference $y_i \succ_\mathbf{x} y_j$ then $g_\mathbf{w}(\phi(\mathbf{x}), y_i) > g_\mathbf{w}(\phi(\mathbf{x}), y_j)$ should hold, and thus

$$\mathbf{w}^\intercal \psi(\phi(\mathbf{x}), y_i) > \mathbf{w}^\intercal \psi(\phi(\mathbf{x}), y_j) \Rightarrow \mathbf{w}^\intercal (\psi(\phi(\mathbf{x}), y_i) - \psi(\phi(\mathbf{x}), y_j)) > 0,$$

which can be interpreted as the *margin* (or *confidence*) of the preference.

The instance-label joint representation used in this work is based on the Kesler's construction for multi-class classification [6,11,15]. Kesler's construction is a very powerful tool for extending learning algorithms for binary classifiers to the multi-class setting. The Kesler's construction allows, by using an appropriate instances' representation, to solve multi-class problems using a single linear function instead of decomposing them into many binary sub-problems. The construction can be formalized as in the following.

Given an instance (possibly embedded in a feature space) $\phi(\mathbf{x})$ with label y, we define the instance-label representation $\psi : \mathbb{R}^d \times \mathcal{Y} \to \mathbb{R}^{d \cdot m}$ as $\psi(\phi(\mathbf{x}), y) = \mathbf{e}_y^m \otimes \phi(\mathbf{x})$, where the symbol $\otimes$ indicates the Kronecker product and $\mathbf{e}_y^m$ is the y-*th* canonical basis of $\mathbb{R}^m$:

$$\psi(\phi(\mathbf{x}), y) = \mathbf{e}_y^m \otimes \phi(\mathbf{x}) = (\underset{\substack{\uparrow\\1}}{\mathbf{0}}\,;\underset{\substack{\uparrow\\2}}{\mathbf{0}}\,;\ldots;\underset{\substack{\uparrow\\y}}{\phi(\mathbf{x})}\,;\mathbf{0};\ldots;\underset{\substack{\uparrow\\m}}{\mathbf{0}}\,) \in \mathbb{R}^{d \cdot m},$$

where $\mathbf{0}$ are d-dimensional zero vectors. Therefore, given a preference $y_i \succ_{\mathbf{x}} y_j$ we construct its corresponding embedding $\mathbf{z} \in \mathbb{R}^{d \cdot m}$ as

$$\begin{aligned}\mathbf{z} &= \psi(\phi(\mathbf{x}), y_i) - \psi(\phi(\mathbf{x}), y_j) = (\mathbf{e}_{y_i}^m - \mathbf{e}_{y_j}^m) \otimes \phi(\mathbf{x}) \\ &= (\mathbf{0};\ldots;\underset{\substack{\uparrow\\y_i}}{\phi(\mathbf{x})}\,;\mathbf{0};\ldots;\underset{\substack{\uparrow\\y_j}}{-\phi(\mathbf{x})}\,;\mathbf{0};\ldots;\mathbf{0}) \in \mathbb{R}^{d \cdot m}.\end{aligned}$$

At prediction time, given a new instance $\mathbf{x}_{\text{new}}$, labels are ranked according to the score $g_{\mathbf{w}}(\phi(\mathbf{x}_{\text{new}}), y)$, $\forall y \in \mathcal{Y}$. In case of classification, the predicted label for $\mathbf{x}_{\text{new}}$ is $\hat{y} = \arg\max_{y \in \mathcal{Y}} g_{\mathbf{w}}(\phi(\mathbf{x}_{\text{new}}), y)$.

2.2 Game Theory

Game theory is the science of strategic reasoning that studies the behaviour of rational game players who are trying to maximize their utility. Specifically, in this paper, we focus on finite two-players zero-sum games. The strategic form of a two-players zero-sum game is defined by a triplet (P, Q, M), where P and Q are finite non-empty set of strategies for player P and Q, respectively, and $M : P \times Q \to \mathbb{R}$ is a function that associates a value $M(i, j)$ to each pair of strategies (i, j) s.t. $i \in P$, and $j \in Q$. $M(i, j)$ represents the payoff of Q and the loss of P. Since P and Q are finite sets, M can be represented as a matrix $\mathbf{M} \in \mathbb{R}^{|P| \times |Q|}$, called payoff matrix (or game matrix), such that $\mathbf{M}_{ij} = M(i, j)$, where $|P|$ and $|Q|$ are the number of available strategies for P and Q, respectively. Each matrix entry $\mathbf{M}_{i,j}$ represents the loss of P, or equivalently the payoff of Q, when the strategies i and j are played by the players. The game takes place in rounds in which the two players play simultaneously: the row player (P) picks a row $p \in P$, and the column player (Q) picks a column $q \in Q$ of $\mathbf{M}$. The goal of the player P is to define a strategy that minimizes its expected loss V. Conversely, the player Q aims at finding a strategy that maximizes its payoff. Players strategies are typically represented as stochastic vectors $\mathbf{p} \in \mathscr{S}_P$ and $\mathbf{q} \in \mathscr{S}_Q$, respectively, where $\mathscr{S}_P = \{\mathbf{p} \in \mathbb{R}_+^{|P|} \mid \|\mathbf{p}\|_1 = 1\}$ and $\mathscr{S}_Q = \{\mathbf{q} \in \mathbb{R}_+^{|Q|} \mid \|\mathbf{q}\|_1 = 1\}$. It is well known [14] that the best pair of optimal strategies $(\mathbf{p}^*, \mathbf{q}^*)$, i.e., the saddle-point (or Nash equilibrium) of $\mathbf{M}$, can be computed by

$$V^* = \mathbf{p}^{*\intercal}\mathbf{M}\mathbf{q}^* = \min_{\mathbf{p}} \max_{\mathbf{q}} \mathbf{p}^\intercal \mathbf{M}\mathbf{q} = \max_{\mathbf{q}} \min_{\mathbf{p}} \mathbf{p}^\intercal \mathbf{M}\mathbf{q},$$

where V^* is the value of the game.

3 Maximal Margin PL as a Two-Players Zero-Sum Game

In Sect. 2.1 we have introduced the concept of margin of a preference. Akin classical classification scenarios [17], also in PL contexts large margins correspond to good generalization capability of the ranker [1].

As mentioned previously, we consider a hypothesis space $\mathcal{H}$ composed by linear functions, i.e., $\mathcal{H} \equiv \{\mathbf{z} \mapsto \mathbf{w}^\intercal\mathbf{z} \mid \mathbf{w}, \mathbf{z} \in \mathbb{R}^{d \cdot m}\}, \|\mathbf{w}\|_2 = 1\}$. Given a hypothesis $\mathbf{w}$, we say that $\mathbf{w}$ satisfies a preference $\mathbf{z}$ if its margin is strictly positive, that is, iff $\rho_\mathbf{w}(\mathbf{z}) = \mathbf{w}^\intercal\mathbf{z} > 0$. We consider classification tasks, hence we assume to have a set of training preferences of the form $\mathcal{T} \equiv \{(y_+ \succ_\mathbf{x} y_-)\}$ ($|\mathcal{T}| = n(m-1)$) which can be easily transformed to their corresponding vectorial representation as previously described. According to the maximum margin principle, we aim to select $\mathbf{w}$ such that it maximizes the minimum margin over the training preferences. Following the line of [1,16], we cast the margin maximization problem into a two-players zero-sum game. Specifically, let $Q \equiv \mathcal{H}$, and let $P \equiv \mathcal{T}$ be the set of strategies for the player Q and P, respectively. The game takes place in rounds, where Q selects an hypothesis $\mathbf{w} \in \mathcal{H}$ and P selects a preference $\mathbf{z}$ from $\mathcal{T}$. Q wants to maximize its payoff, which is the margin achieved by $\mathbf{w}$ on $\mathbf{z}$. Conversely, P aims to minimize its loss by defining a mixed strategy over the set of training preferences, which can be seen as a probability distribution $\mathbf{p} \in \mathscr{S}_P$ over the preferences. The value of this game, i.e., the expected margin, is computed by solving

$$V^* = \min_{\mathbf{p}} \max_{\|\mathbf{w}\|_2=1} \mathbb{E}_\mathbf{p}[\rho_\mathbf{w}(\mathbf{z})] = \min_{\mathbf{p}} \max_{\|\mathbf{w}\|_2=1} \sum_{i=1}^{|P|} p_i \rho_\mathbf{w}(\mathbf{z}_i) \tag{1}$$

$$= \min_{\mathbf{p}} \max_{\|\mathbf{w}\|_2=1} \sum_{i=1}^{|P|} p_i \mathbf{w}^\intercal \mathbf{z}_i = \min_{\mathbf{p}} \max_{\|\mathbf{w}\|_2=1} \mathbf{w}^\intercal \left(\sum_{i=1}^{|P|} p_i \mathbf{z}_i \right). \tag{2}$$

It is well known that the unitary norm maximizer of Eq. (2) is

$$\mathbf{w} \propto \sum_{i=1}^{|P|} p_i \mathbf{z}_i = \mathbf{Z}^\intercal \mathbf{p},$$

where $\mathbf{Z} \in \mathbb{R}^{|P| \times (d \cdot m)}$ is the matrix with the preference embeddings arranged in the rows, and hence we can rewrite Eq. (2) as

$$V^* = \min_{\mathbf{p}} \sum_{i=1}^{|P|} p_i \sum_{j=1}^{|P|} p_j \mathbf{z}_i^\intercal \mathbf{z}_j = \min_{\mathbf{p}} \mathbf{p}^\intercal \mathbf{K}_\mathbf{z} \mathbf{p}, \tag{3}$$

where $\mathbf{K}_\mathbf{z} \in \mathbb{R}^{|P| \times |P|}$ is a kernel matrix between preferences, that is $\mathbf{K}_\mathbf{z}[i,j] = \mathbf{z}_i^\intercal \mathbf{z}_j$. Given the Kesler's construction described in Sect. 2.1, then $\mathbf{K}_\mathbf{z}$ can be computed as:

$$\mathbf{K}_\mathbf{z}[i,j] = (\mathbf{0}, \ldots, \underset{\substack{\uparrow \\ y_i^+}}{\phi(\mathbf{x}_i)}; \ldots; \underset{\substack{\uparrow \\ y_i^-}}{-\phi(\mathbf{x}_i)}; \ldots; \mathbf{0})^\intercal (\mathbf{0}; \ldots; \underset{\substack{\uparrow \\ y_j^+}}{\phi(\mathbf{x}_j)}; \ldots; \underset{\substack{\uparrow \\ y_j^-}}{-\phi(\mathbf{x}_j)}; \ldots; \mathbf{0})$$

$$= ([\![y_i^+ = y_j^+]\!] + [\![y_i^- = y_j^-]\!] - [\![y_i^+ = y_j^-]\!] - [\![y_i^- = y_j^+]\!])\kappa(\mathbf{x}_i, \mathbf{x}_j),$$

where $\kappa(\mathbf{x}_i, \mathbf{x}_j) = \phi(\mathbf{x}_i)^\intercal\phi(\mathbf{x}_j)$ is the kernel function induced by ϕ, and $[\![\cdot]\!]$ is the indicator function. Equation (3) shows that it is possible to learn the maximal margin hypothesis in the preference space by solving a quadratic optimization problem. This formulation allows to solve a multi-class classification problem without the need of decomposing it in multiple binary classification problems. However, when the number of preferences is huge, computing (3) on the whole kernel matrix $\mathbf{K_z}$ can be prohibitive. For this reason in the next section we provide a technique for efficiently approximating the value of the game, and thus learning the model.

4 Approximating the Value of the PL Game

There is a large body of research in the game theory community which deals with the problem of approximating the value of the game for huge game matrices [3–5, 7, 9]. However, such techniques assume the availability of the whole game matrix which is not always feasible in our context. More recently [16], an incremental approach for solving large game matrices w.r.t. the number of columns has been proposed in which only a budget of columns are considered at each iteration. Unfortunately, limiting the number of columns only could not be enough when the number of preferences is huge. For this reason, we propose a method that approximates the value of the game (as well as the strategies of the players) by combining the solutions of many sub-games that consider only squared sub-matrices of the whole game matrix $\mathbf{K_z}$.

Specifically, let T be the number of sub-games we want to solve, and let $\boldsymbol{\Pi}_t \in \{0,1\}^{|P|\times s}$ be the selection matrix used to select rows/columns from $\mathbf{K}_z$ for the t-th game. Thus, each sub-game matrix $\mathbf{K}_t \in \mathbb{R}^{s\times s}$ ($s \ll |P|$) can be obtained as $\mathbf{K}_t = \boldsymbol{\Pi}_t^\intercal \mathbf{K_z} \boldsymbol{\Pi}_t$. Let $\hat{\mathbf{p}}_t$ be the optimal strategy for the t-th sub-game, then we can project back the solution by computing $\mathbf{p}_t = \boldsymbol{\Pi}_t \hat{\mathbf{p}}_t$.

Once all $\mathbf{p}_t$ have been computed, we aim to combine these sub-strategies in order to get a strategy for the whole game. The best convex combination of the $\mathbf{p}_t$'s can be achieved by solving the following convex optimization problem

$$\boldsymbol{\alpha}^* = \min_{\boldsymbol{\alpha}\in\mathscr{S}^T} \boldsymbol{\alpha}^\intercal \left(\mathbf{P}^\intercal \mathbf{K_z} \mathbf{P}\right) \boldsymbol{\alpha} = \min_{\boldsymbol{\alpha}\in\mathscr{S}^T} \boldsymbol{\alpha}^\intercal \mathbf{G} \boldsymbol{\alpha}, \tag{4}$$

where $\mathbf{P} \in \mathbb{R}^{T\times|P|}$ is the matrix where the strategies ($\mathbf{p}_t$) of the sub-games are arranged in the rows, and $\mathbf{G} = \mathbf{P}^\intercal \mathbf{K_z} \mathbf{P} \in \mathbb{R}^{T\times T}$. Clearly, the value of the game $\widetilde{V} = \boldsymbol{\alpha}^* \mathbf{G} \boldsymbol{\alpha}^*$ is an approximation of V^* and specifically $V^* \leq \widetilde{V}$.

From the formulation given in (4) it seems that it is still necessary to compute the whole kernel matrix $\mathbf{K_z}$. However, it can be observed that since $\mathbf{P}$ is built upon the best strategies of the sub-games, in each row at most s entries are non zero. Hence, computing $\mathbf{G}$ can be highly optimized, e.g., by computing each row individually. Nevertheless, when the number of preferences is particularly large computing $\mathbf{G}$ remains computationally expensive. Anyhow, it is possible to get a reasonable approximation avoiding to solve the optimization problem by fixing $\boldsymbol{\alpha}^*$ to the uniform distribution, which corresponds to computing the average over $\mathbf{p}_t$.

4.1 Sub-game Selection Strategy

Even though $\widetilde{V}$ is the best we can achieve from the combination of the partial strategies $\mathbf{p}_t$, the sub-game selection plays a key role to get good value of the game with the proposed method.

A naïve way of computing the sub-game matrix is by randomly drawing rows/columns from the uniform distribution. This strategy has the advantage of being highly parallelizable, since each sub-game can be solved independently.

Borrowing from the reinforcement learning literature, we propose a generalization of the strategy presented above in which samples are randomly drawn from a distribution that depends on the solution of the previous sub-games. The main idea is to iteratively adjust the distribution according to how much the previously selected preferences (i.e., strategies) contributed to the mixed-strategy (i.e., their weight in the hypothesis). Specifically, let $\mathbf{d}_t \in \mathscr{S}^{|P|}$ be probability distributions over all the training preferences at iteration t, and let $\mathbf{d}_1 = \mathbf{1}\frac{1}{|P|}$ be the uniform distribution over all preferences. At iteration $t+1$ a new random sample of preferences is drawn according to $\mathbf{d}_{t+1}$ which is defined as

$$\mathbf{d}_{t+1} = (1-\lambda)\mathbf{d}_t + \lambda\mathbf{p}_t$$

where $0 \leq \lambda \leq 1$, and $\mathbf{p}_t$ is the solution of the t-th game as in Sect. 4. Essentially, λ defines how much the previous strategies influence the sampling distribution for the next games. $\lambda = 0$ means that the previous games have no influence in the next sampling. Conversely, $\lambda = 1$ indicates that all random samples will be drawn according to $\mathbf{p}_1$ (i.e., the solution of the first sub-game). In other words λ is a trade-off between exploration ($\lambda \to 0$) and exploitation ($\lambda \to 1$), with a similar effect of ϵ in the ϵ-greedy algorithm [18] for the multi-armed bandit problem.

Finally, the ranker hypothesis is computed as a combination over all $\mathbf{p}_t$, that is

$$\mathbf{w} \propto \left[\sum_{t=1}^{T} \alpha_t \mathbf{p}_t\right]^{\mathsf{T}} \mathbf{Z},$$

where $\boldsymbol{\alpha}$ can be optimized as in Eq. (4), or fixed, for example, to the uniform distribution. Algorithm 1, dubbed LMPG (Large Margin Preference Game), provides the pseudo-code of the method just described. In the following we will indicate with LMPG* the algorithm when $s = |P|$, LMPG-α when $\boldsymbol{\alpha}$ is optimized according to (4), and with LMPG when $\boldsymbol{\alpha}$ is fixed to the uniform distribution.

5 Experiments

In this section all the performed experiments are described.

The proposed techniques have been evaluated on five different publicly available datasets:

Algorithm 1: LMPG: Large Margin Preference Game

Input:
P: set of training preferences
s : sample size
λ: exploration-exploitation trade-off hyper-parameter
T: number of iterations
Output:
$\widetilde{\mathbf{w}}$: preference ranking model

$\mathbf{d}_1 \leftarrow \mathbf{1}\frac{1}{|P|}$
for $t \leftarrow 1$ **to** T **do**
  $Q \leftarrow$ random sampling (w/o replacement) over P of s preferences according to $\mathbf{d}_t$
  $\mathbf{K}_t \leftarrow$ kernel matrix s.t. $\mathbf{K}_t[i,j] = \mathbf{z}_i^\intercal \mathbf{z}_j, \forall \mathbf{z}_i, \mathbf{z}_j \in Q$
  $\mathbf{p}_t \leftarrow \min_{\mathbf{p}} \mathbf{p}^\intercal \mathbf{K}_t \mathbf{p}$
  $\mathbf{d}_{t+1} \leftarrow (1-\lambda)\mathbf{d}_t + \lambda \mathbf{p}_t$
end
computing $\boldsymbol{\alpha}$ (e.g., by means of (4))
$\overline{\mathbf{p}} \leftarrow \sum_{t=1}^{T} \alpha_t \mathbf{p}_t$
$\widetilde{\mathbf{w}} \leftarrow \sum_{i=1}^{|P|} \overline{p}_i \mathbf{z}_i, \mathbf{z}_i \in P$
return $\widetilde{\mathbf{w}}$

`tic-tac-toe` is a dataset containing 958 ending positions of the game tic-tac-toe, and the task is to classify whether the $\times$ is the winner;

`breast-cancer` is the well known Breast Cancer Wisconsin Diagnostic Dataset, where the task is to classify a tumor as malignant or benign. For more details about the dataset please refer to [12];

`mnist-49` `mnist` is a (well known) dataset of handwritten digits. We extracted from it a single classification task which consists in classifying the digit 4 against the digit 9;

`segment` This dataset is an image segmentation database. 7 outdoor images are possible instances and images have been randomly selected. The images were hand-segmented to create a classification for every pixel. Each instance is a 3×3 region;

`w8a` Dataset used for fast training of support vector machines using sequential minimal optimization;

`vehicle` The dataset was originally used to distinguish 3D objects within a 2D image using a feature extractor on 2D silhouettes of objects. Four classes of vehicles were used for the experiment: a double decker bus, Cheverolet van, Saab 9000 and an Opel Manta 400.

Table 1. Datasets information: number of classes, training set and test set size, and number of features. In parenthesis the corresponding number of preferences. When not indicated the number of preferences is equal to the number of examples.

Dataset	# Classes	Training set size	Test set size	# Features
`tic-tac-toe`	2	766	192	27
`breast-cancer`	2	545	137	90
`mnist-49`	2	11025	2757	779
`segment`	7	1848 (11088)	462	19
`w8a`	2	39799	9950	300
`vehicle`	4	677 (2031)	169	18

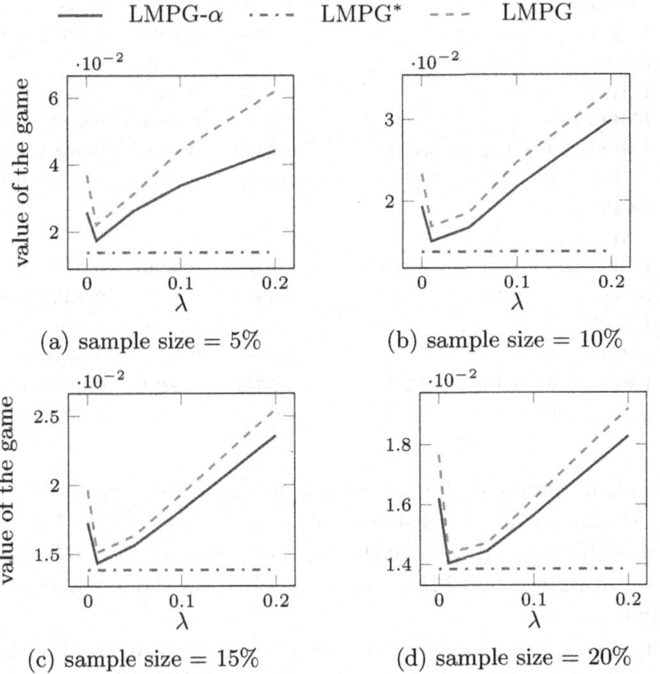

Fig. 1. Value of the game on the `breast-cancer` dataset varying both the sample size and λ. (Color figure online)

Table 1 summarizes the information of the selected datasets. Note that, since `segment` is a multiclass dataset, the number of preferences correspond to the number of examples, multiplied the number of classes (minus 1), for a total of 11088 preferences.

All experiments concerning the LMPG method have been carried out using the same procedure. We set $T = 500$, λ have been tested in the set of values $\{0, 0.01, 0.02, 0.1, 0.2\}$ and we considered as sample size 5%, 10%, 15% and 20% of the whole number of preferences.

Table 2. Performance of all proposed methods against SVM with polynomial kernel. For each dataset the best results are highlighted in **boldface**. Missing values (–) indicate the computation did not end in a reasonable amount of time.

	Method	Hyper-parameters	Accuracy	Precision	Recall	F1
breast	LMPG*		0.9635	0.9625	0.9585	0.9605
	LMPG-α		0.9635	0.9625	0.9585	0.9605
	LMPG	$\lambda = 0.1$, $s = 0.05\|P\|$	**0.9708**	**0.9685**	**0.9685**	**0.9685**
	SVM	C = 1, d = 2	**0.9708**	**0.9685**	**0.9685**	**0.9685**
t-t-t	LMPG*		**1.0000**	**1.0000**	**1.0000**	**1.0000**
	LMPG-α		**1.0000**	**1.0000**	**1.0000**	**1.0000**
	LMPG	$\lambda = 0.01$, $s = 0.2\|P\|$	**1.0000**	**1.0000**	**1.0000**	**1.0000**
	SVM	C =10, d = 5	**1.0000**	**1.0000**	**1.0000**	**1.0000**
mnist-49	LMPG*		0.9935	0.9935	0.9935	0.9935
	LMPG-α		0.9935	0.9935	0.9935	0.9935
	LMPG	$\lambda = 0.01$, $s = 0.2\|P\|$	**0.9938**	**0.9938**	**0.9938**	**0.9938**
	SVM	C = 10^3, d = 4	0.9935	0.9935	0.9935	0.9935
segment	LMPG*		0.9524	0.9561	0.9569	0.9560
	LMPG-α		0.9545	0.9600	0.9586	0.9587
	LMPG	$\lambda = 0.1$, $s = 0.15\|P\|$	**0.9654**	**0.9692**	**0.9682**	**0.9684**
	SVM	C = 10, d = 2	0.9632	0.9670	0.9670	0.9665
w8a	LMPG*		–	–	–	–
	LMPG-α		–	–	–	–
	LMPG	$\lambda = 0.01$, $s = 0.2\|P\|$	0.9853	**0.9340**	0.7947	0.8502
	SVM	C = 10, d = 2	**0.9861**	0.9147	**0.8308**	**0.8677**
vehicle	LMPG*		0.8471	0.8294	0.8289	0.8290
	LMPG-α		0.7706	0.7738	0.7686	0.7651
	LMPG	$\lambda = 0.01$, $s = 0.2\|P\|$	**0.8647**	**0.8486**	**0.8518**	**0.8501**
	SVM	C = 10, d = 2	0.8095	0.7662	0.7662	0.7652

The plots presented in Figs. 1 and 2 describe how the value of the game changes according to the dimension of the sample size, and λ. The baseline (red line) describes the optimal value of the game obtained by LMPG*, the continuous curve is the value given by LMPG$-\alpha$, while the dashed one is the value obtained using LMPG.

Both figures exhibit the same pattern: the game values produced using $\lambda = 0$ are significantly worse than the one achieved by LMPG*. The best value for λ to obtain small values of the game seems to be 0.01. It is possible to observe that, with sufficient sample size and a small $\lambda > 0$, the approximated value obtained thanks to sampling and without the optimization of α is close enough to the optimal value and thus is able to perform well also in classification tasks. These findings reflect what was supposed theoretically in previous sections, especially about the values' magnitude ordering.

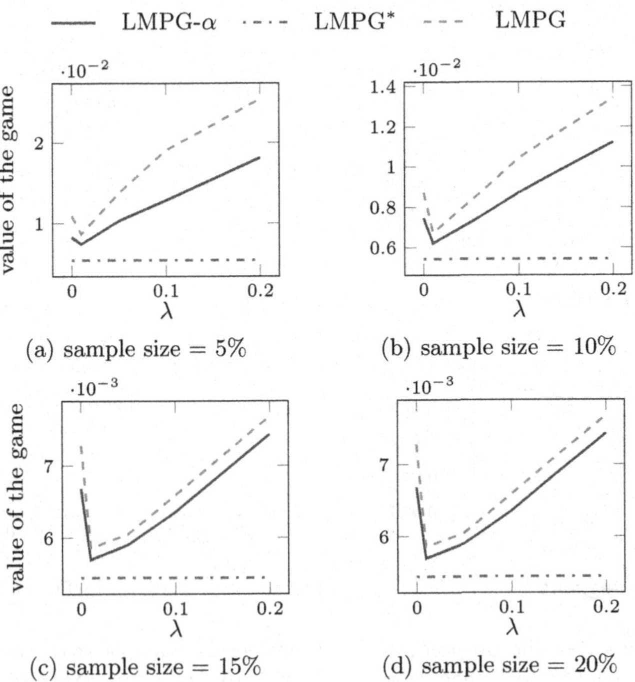

Fig. 2. Value of the game on the `tic-tac-toe` dataset varying both the sample size and λ. (Color figure online)

Figure 3 presents the accuracy results obtained by our algorithms using different sample sizes and λ. These charts show a pattern that follows the previous findings: generally speaking, a small λ produces the best results and again the sample size seems to be relevant to obtain good results, although in `segment` best results are obtained using the sample size equal to the 15% of the dataset.

The proposed strategies have been compared to soft SVM. SVMs have been validated using 5-fold validation: C has been validated in the set $\{1, 10, 10^2, 10^3\}$ and the degree of the homogeneous polynomial kernel in the range [1,5]. For our methods we used the best performing kernel (during validation) for SVM. Table 2 shows the comparison of the proposed technique with the λ and sample size that produce the best results against validated SVM. It is possible to observe that the proposed strategy performs better or as good as SVM in 4 out of 5 datasets (`tic-tac-toe`, `mnist-49`, `segment` and `breast-cancer`). The ranker produced by averaging over different strategies performs almost always (except on `tic-tac-toe`) better than the hypothesis obtained considering the optimal strategy distribution. This phenomenon can be explained by the fact that the optimal distribution corresponds to solving a hard margin problem, while the averaged one might represent a more soft solution. Note that this can be correlated with the low values for C obtained when validating SVM.

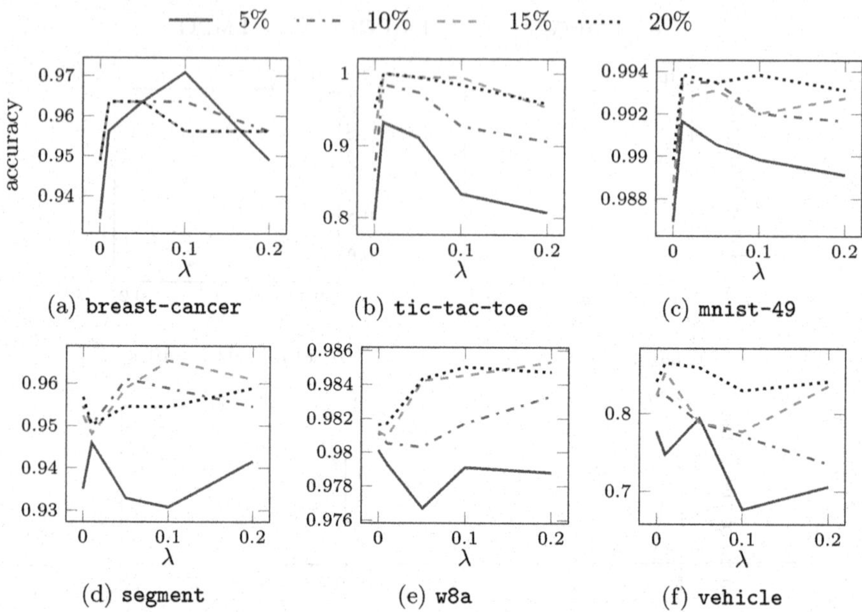

Fig. 3. Accuracy of the proposed method varying the sample size (curves) and the value of λ (x axis) on (a) `breast-cancer`, (b) `tic-tac-toe`, (c) `mnist-49`, (d) `segment`, (e) `w8a`, and (f) `vehicle`.

6 Conclusions

We proposed a principled game theoretical framework used for the multi-class classification task. We presented the mathematical formulation of a preference learning model able to solve the multi-class classification task as a single optimization problem. To reduce the complexity of the problem, we presented optimization strategies that exploit typical properties of reinforcement learning and solves reduced-size subproblems. In the experimental section, the proposed framework has exhibited state-of-the-art results. Among the future research paths we plan to explore, we aim to study the efficiency of the proposed algorithms. As already pointed out, using uniform sampling leads to a highly parallelizable version of the algorithm, yet results are not as good as those obtained by using adaptive sampling for preferences selection. One aspect of the theoretical framework that needs to be further developed is the study of theoretical bounds limiting the differences in the value of the games when using different approaches. Empirical results suggest that these bounds can be strict provided mild assumptions, thus our technique can be easily applied to other domains.

References

1. Aiolli, F., Da San Martino, G., Sperduti, A.: A kernel method for the optimization of the margin distribution. In: Kůrková, V., Neruda, R., Koutník, J. (eds.) ICANN 2008. LNCS, vol. 5163, pp. 305–314. Springer, Heidelberg (2008). https://doi.org/10.1007/978-3-540-87536-9_32
2. Aiolli, F., Sperduti, A.: A preference optimization based unifying framework for supervised learning problems. In: Fürnkranz, J., Hüllermeier, E. (eds.) Preference Learning, pp. 19–42. Springer, Heidelberg (2010). https://doi.org/10.1007/978-3-642-14125-6_2
3. Bopardikar, S.D., Borri, A., Hespanha, J.P., Prandini, M., Benedetto, M.D.D.: Randomized sampling for large zero-sum games. In: 49th IEEE Conference on Decision and Control (CDC), pp. 7675–7680 (2010). https://doi.org/10.1109/CDC.2010.5717870
4. Bopardikar, S.D., Langbort, C.: Incremental approximate saddle-point computation in zero-sum matrix games. In: 53rd IEEE Conference on Decision and Control, pp. 1936–1941 (2014). https://doi.org/10.1109/CDC.2014.7039681
5. Brown, G.W.: Iterative solutions of games by fictitious play. In: Activity Analysis of Production and Allocation, pp. 374–376 (1951)
6. Duda, R.O., Hart, P.E.: Pattern Classification and Scene Analysis. Willey, Hoboken (1973)
7. Freund, Y., Schapire, R.E.: Game theory, on-line prediction and boosting. In: COLT, pp. 325–332 (1996). https://doi.org/10.1145/238061.238163
8. Freund, Y., Schapire, R.E.: A decision-theoretic generalization of on-line learning and an application to boosting. J. Comput. Syst. Sci. **55**(1), 119–139 (1997)
9. Freund, Y., Schapire, R.E.: Adaptive game playing using multiplicative weights. Games Econ. Behav. **29**(1–2), 79–103 (1999). https://doi.org/10.1006/jcss.1997.1504
10. Fürnkranz, J., Hüllermeier, E.: Preference Learning, 1st edn. Springer, Heidelberg (2010). https://doi.org/10.1007/978-3-642-14125-6
11. Har-Peled, S., Roth, D., Zimak, D.: Constraint classification: a new approach to multiclass classification. In: Cesa-Bianchi, N., Numao, M., Reischuk, R. (eds.) ALT 2002. LNCS (LNAI), vol. 2533, pp. 365–379. Springer, Heidelberg (2002). https://doi.org/10.1007/3-540-36169-3_29
12. Hayashi, Y., Nakano, S.: Use of a recursive-rule extraction algorithm with j48graft to achieve highly accurate and concise rule extraction from a large breast cancer dataset. Inform. Med. Unlocked **1**, 9–16 (2015). https://doi.org/10.1016/j.imu.2015.12.002
13. Ioannidis, S., Loiseau, P.: Linear regression as a non-cooperative game. In: Chen, Y., Immorlica, N. (eds.) WINE 2013. LNCS, vol. 8289, pp. 277–290. Springer, Heidelberg (2013). https://doi.org/10.1007/978-3-642-45046-4_23
14. von Neumann, J.: Zur theorie der gesellschaftsspiele. Mathematische Annalen **100**, 295–320 (1928)
15. Nilsson, N.J.: Learning machines: foundations of trainable pattern-classifying systems (1965)
16. Polato, M., Aiolli, F.: A game-theoretic framework for interpretable preference and feature learning. In: Kůrková, V., Manolopoulos, Y., Hammer, B., Iliadis, L., Maglogiannis, I. (eds.) ICANN 2018. LNCS, vol. 11139, pp. 659–668. Springer, Cham (2018). https://doi.org/10.1007/978-3-030-01418-6_65

17. Schapire, R.E., Freund, Y., Barlett, P., Lee, W.S.: Boosting the margin: a new explanation for the effectiveness of voting methods. In: Proceedings of the Fourteenth International Conference on Machine Learning, ICML 1997, pp. 322–330 (1997)
18. Sutton, R.S., Barto, A.G.: Introduction to Reinforcement Learning, 1st edn. MIT Press, Cambridge (1998)
19. Tsochantaridis, I., Hofmann, T., Joachims, T., Altun, Y.: Support vector machine learning for interdependent and structured output spaces. In: Proceedings of the Twenty-first International Conference on Machine Learning, ICML 2004, 104 p. ACM (2004). https://doi.org/10.1145/1015330.1015341
20. Vapnik, V.N.: The Nature of Statistical Learning Theory. Springer, New York (1995). https://doi.org/10.1007/978-1-4757-2440-0

Author Index

Printed in the United States
By Bookmasters